The **Themes**
and **Writers**
Series

G. Robert Carlsen

General Editor

INSIGHTS *Themes in Literature*

ENCOUNTERS *Themes in Literature*

AMERICAN LITERATURE *Themes and Writers*

WESTERN LITERATURE *Themes and Writers*

G. Robert Carlsen, professor of English and Education at the University of Iowa, has taught English in the public schools of Minnesota and at the universities of Minnesota, Colorado, Texas, Hawaii, and Iowa. He has served as consultant in curriculum revision to the Texas State Department of Education and was book review editor of young people's books for the *English Journal.* In 1962, Dr. Carlsen was the president of the National Council of Teachers of English. He has written extensively for professional journals and is co-author of the Brown-Carlsen *Test of Listening Comprehension* and of *Social Understanding Through Literature,* published in 1953 by the National Council of Social Studies.

Ruth Christoffer Carlsen is co-author with Dr. Carlsen of several anthologies for young readers. She has also written successful juvenile books. Her research was of particular value in the development of the anthology materials.

Edgar H. Schuster has taught in both urban and suburban high schools in the Philadelphia area. He has written articles for many professional journals, including *Educational Leadership* and *The English Journal.* Mr. Schuster, who is currently a member of the faculty of Beaver College, is the author of *Grammar, Usage, and Style,* a high-school language text.

Richard M. Ludwig is Associate Professor of English at Princeton University. Dr. Ludwig has also taught at Harvard University, where he was awarded the Doctor of Philosophy degree in 1950. A member of the Modern Language Association, Dr. Ludwig is a recognized authority on American and English literature. In addition to numerous scholarly articles, he is a co-author of *Major American Writers* and other college and high-school texts. He is a co-editor of *Literary History of the United States* and has recently published the collected letters of the British novelist Ford Madox Ford.

Anthony Tovatt is professor of English at Burris Laboratory School of Ball State University. Dr. Tovatt has been the Director of an extended research study on the teaching of composition under the Program for English of the United States Office of Education. Since 1955 he has been a column editor of the *English Journal.* His articles have been published in many professional journals and his poetry has appeared in magazines and newspapers.

Patricia O. Tovatt, former teacher of English at Storer Junior High School, Muncie, Indiana, assisted her husband in the development of this anthology.

Richard S. Alm, professor of English Education and Director of the Reading Clinic at the University of Hawaii, has taught in the public schools of Minnesota and Washington and at the universities of Minnesota, Colorado, Wisconsin, California at Berkeley, as well as at the Teachers College, Columbia University. Dr. Alm is the Editor of the *English Journal* and of the 1964 edition of *Books for You.*

Donald W. Lee, professor of English at the University of Houston, Texas, contributed the vocabulary study program for the *Themes and Writers* Series. Dr. Lee is a lexicographer of note who served on the staff of G. & C. Merriam Co. during the preparation of the *Webster's Third International Dictionary.* Dr. Lee has taught at Duke University, Penn State, the U.S. Naval Academy, and the universities of Pittsburgh and of Connecticut.

Jeannette Morgan, formerly instructor of English at the University of Houston, assisted Dr. Lee in the preparation of the vocabulary materials for this series.

The Last Scalp

AMERICAN LITERATURE

Themes and Writers

G. Robert Carlsen
Professor of English and Education
University of Iowa

Richard M. Ludwig
Associate Professor of English
Princeton University

Edgar H. Schuster
Instructor of English
Beaver College

Anthony Tovatt
Professor of English, Burris Laboratory School
Ball State University

Richard S. Alm
Professor of English Education
University of Hawaii

Ruth Christoffer Carlsen
Professional Writer
Iowa City, Iowa

The *Themes and Writers* Series

Webster Division, McGraw-Hill Book Company

St. Louis, New York, San Francisco, Dallas

The Militia Muster

PREFACE

Literature transmits the loves and hates, the hopes and fears, the ambitions and frustrations, the failures and the triumphs, the questions, problems, experiences, and answers of man confronting life. Literature records man's struggle to come to know life and the world. In recording this struggle, certain themes, certain ideas, emerge and persist in literature. To know man's voice, and hence to find his own, the reader must come to grips with the universal problems and concerns of man as revealed in the themes that have absorbed writers from Homer to Hemingway.

The reader, faced with a conglomeration of works loosely strung together because they pretend to show some kind of historical evolution or because they accidentally share a common genre, can hardly be expected to get excited about literature, much less to reach significant insights about literature, life, and the world. No worthy writer ever wrote merely to demonstrate a particular genre or to fill a gap in the literary history of his time. Writers write because they have someting to say about themselves and about the human condition. The sooner readers discover the themes which give literature its meaning and value, the sooner they become enthusiastic about literature, because they have discovered its power to reveal life and the world. They will see that all human experience is their own.

Recent insights in the psychology of learning have shown that learning is better and more enduring when persons discover fundamental principles and truths for themselves. Since one of the great joys of literature is discovery, this text is organized in a way that allows the reader to explore significant themes in American literature. A score of themes emerged from the editors' study of the whole body of enduring American literature. From these we selected the six which most vividly reveal the intellectual and emotional life of America. The first theme, ENDLESS FRONTIERS, expresses one of the basic forces in our heritage. Note that we do not call this set of writings "The Pioneer and Westward Movements," for the latter states a topic, a fact of history, not the inner meaning, the concept of the westering spirit which cannot be confined to a particular group of Americans or to a particular time. Rather, the concept of "endless frontiers" is something that reflects the spirit inside man himself. The final theme, SEARCH FOR VALUES, defines the twentieth-century writer's struggle to answer for each of us the troubling questions, "Why was I born? Why am I living?" In between are explorations of other concepts that shape American literature and our being: THE INNER STRUGGLE, the role of conscience and the psyche; COMIC IMAGINATION, humorists' thrusts at our absurdities, ironies, and foibles; STRUGGLE FOR JUSTICE, the ancient cry for justice evolving in America; THE INDEPENDENT SPIRIT, the diversity of character and the personal challenge to excellence.

The editors have carefully devised the structure of individual themes to promote the progressive discovery of meaning. Each contains a balanced variety of prose, fiction and nonfiction, poetry, and drama (in three of the six themes) through which the theme can be traced and compared from one work to another. This organization emphasizes the specific personal elements in both the fundamental attitude of the writer and in the external form of expression he chose.

In the previous books in the *Themes and Writers* Series the study of a major work followed each theme. In this book the study of two major writers follows each theme. Our choice and placement of major writers is not an inflexible decision. The sum total of a writer's work, in most cases, transcends a single theme, yet the works of writers like Willa Cather, Robert Frost, Emily Dickinson, and Nathaniel Hawthorne, for example, show greater continuity with one theme than another. While allowing that a major writer may have several thematic concerns, it will be clear to the imaginative reader that the major writers, as placed, serve as superb codas to the themes they follow.

Each theme is further illuminated by the paintings or sculptures that portray different and more graphic insights into the particularly human concern that is the subject of each theme. The galleries that accompany the themes are the unique product of the cooperative efforts of art historians and teachers of literature. Through these galleries the teaching of literature is broadened into the teaching of the humanities as the exploration of theme is enhanced by the vision of major artists of the Western world.

The editorial study notes that accompany the selections for each theme are divided into four sections. First, there is a commentary that raises considerations about the selection and its relationship to the theme. Second, there is a body of implications—questions and propositions that lead students to explore the relationship of the ideas in the selection to the theme as a whole and to their own lives in particular. Third, each theme concentrates on two or three major literary concerns or techniques and progressively examines them through the entire theme. This makes for a more effective study by tracing and comparing specific techniques as they are employed by different major

John Adams

writers. Fourth, there are organized units of vocabulary study at wide intervals throughout each theme. In this book they focus on the use of context clues, semantic diction, especially synonyms and antonyms, and dialects.

This text places the emphasis where it should be in the study of literature—on the work as a literary experience and work of art revealing the timeless values and basic concerns of American man. Matters of history, of cultural growth, of genre and literary techniques grow out of the works themselves as the reader discovers his own needs to understand them.

This anthology invites the student to approach American literature through close reading of poetry and fiction, drama and the essay, through which and in which enduring themes are discovered and grow progressively more meaningful as they are traced and compared from work to work. If the method succeeds, the end of the course will be the beginning of new discoveries.

THE EDITORS

*In Search
of the Land
of Milk and Honey*

ENDLESS FRONTIERS

THE INNER STRUGGLE

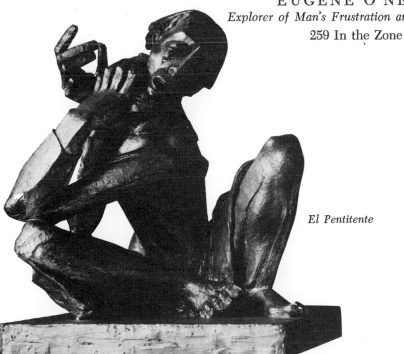

El Pentitente

THE
COMIC
IMAGINATION

Home

Struggle: From the History of the American People

THE STRUGGLE FOR JUSTICE

Amelia Earhart

INDEPENDENT SPIRIT

A Portrait of Albert Einstein

THE SEARCH FOR VALUES

ENDLESS
FRONTIERS

ON THE ROAD
Thomas P. Otter
Nelson Gallery, Atkins Museum,
Kansas City, Missouri

When the first settlers from the Old World began to push inland from the East Coast, America must indeed have seemed endless. The westering spirit that encouraged men to explore seemingly "endless" frontiers inevitably engendered such traits and values in the American character as independence, a deep-rooted optimism, physical stamina and courage, a profound belief in equality, and a pride in democracy and in democratic institutions. The pioneers who explored the American frontier

1

had to be independent and optimistic and courageous or they would never have survived their battles with man and nature in the vast wilderness. Moreover, they saw that such distinctions as ancestry, wealth, and rank mattered little, if at all, in one's ability to succeed in the difficult frontier life. Such experiences encouraged in them the conviction that men were in most respects equal. And if men were equal, then democracy would be the only form of government to which they could pledge allegiance.

Most of the writers whose works you will read in ENDLESS FRONTIERS are not themselves frontiersmen. They are modern writers looking back on events and movements in the American past. They seek to vivify that past, but some of them seek more: They are interested in discovering how the experiences of our forefathers have shaped our national character; they are interested in how the past has affected the present and in how it may affect the future.

Today the geographical frontiers of America are closed, but there are still other kinds of frontiers that remain to be explored —frontiers in space and in human relations, to offer but two examples. But the important question is the one that Grandfather poses in the following story: Is westering a hunger any more? And particularly, is it a hunger of the people as a whole? Ultimately, it will be for you to define the westering urge and to decide on the basis of your reading and experience whether it and traits and values like independence, courage, and equality are still vital aspects of American society.

"The Leader of the People" by John Steinbeck,
the winner of the Nobel Prize in Literature in 1962,
serves as a somewhat ironic opening for the theme ENDLESS FRONTIERS.
As you read this story, which focuses upon three generations
of the same family, try to determine what the grandfather means
by "westering." Also consider whether you agree or disagree
with the ideas he expresses on the theme of endless frontiers.

The Leader of the People

JOHN STEINBECK

On Saturday afternoon Billy Buck, the ranch-hand, raked together the last of the old year's haystack and pitched small forkfuls over the wire fence to a few mildly interested cattle. High in the air small clouds like puffs of cannon smoke were driven eastward by the March wind. The wind could be heard whishing in the brush on the ridge crests, but no breath of it penetrated down into the ranch-cup.[1]

The little boy, Jody, emerged from the house eating a thick piece of buttered bread. He saw Billy working on the last of the haystack. Jody tramped down scuffling his shoes in a way he had been told was destructive to good shoe-leather. A flock of white pigeons flew out of the black cypress tree as Jody passed, and circled the tree and landed again. A half-grown tortoiseshell cat[2] leaped from the bunkhouse[3] porch, galloped on stiff legs across the road, whirled and galloped back again. Jody picked up a stone to help the game along, but he was too late, for the cat was under the porch before the stone could be discharged. He threw the stone into the cypress tree and started the white pigeons on another whirling flight.

Arriving at the used-up haystack, the boy leaned against the barbed wire fence. "Will that be all of it, do you think?" he asked.

The middle-aged ranch-hand stopped his careful raking and stuck his fork into the ground. He took off his black hat and smoothed down his hair. "Nothing left of it that isn't soggy from ground moisture," he said. He replaced his hat and rubbed his dry leathery hands together.

"Ought to be plenty mice," Jody suggested.

"Lousy with them," said Billy. "Just crawling with mice."

"Well, maybe, when you get all through, I could call the dogs and hunt the mice."

"Sure, I guess you could," said Billy Buck. He lifted a forkful of the damp ground-hay and threw it into the air. Instantly three mice leaped out and burrowed frantically under the hay again.

Jody sighed with satisfaction. Those plump, sleek, arrogant mice were doomed. For eight months they had lived and multiplied in the haystack. They had been immune from cats, from traps, from poison and from Jody. They had grown smug in their security, overbearing and fat. Now the time of disaster had come; they would not survive another day.

Billy looked up at the top of the hills that surrounded the ranch. "Maybe you better ask your father before you do it," he suggested.

---

1. **ranch-cup,** low area in the land.
2. **tortoiseshell cat,** cat with patches of yellow and brown.
3. **bunkhouse,** sleeping quarters for ranch hands.

From *The Red Pony* by John Steinbeck. Copyright 1938 by John Steinbeck. Reprinted by permission of The Viking Press, Inc.

"Well, where is he? I'll ask him now."

"He rode up to the ridge ranch[4] after dinner. He'll be back pretty soon."

Jody slumped against the fence post. "I don't think he'd care."

As Billy went back to his work he said ominously, "You'd better ask him anyway. You know how he is."

Jody did know. His father, Carl Tiflin, insisted upon giving permission for anything that was done on the ranch, whether it was important or not. Jody sagged farther against the post until he was sitting on the ground. He looked up at the little puffs of wind-driven cloud. "Is it like to rain, Billy?"

"It might. The wind's good for it, but not strong enough."

"Well, I hope it don't rain until after I kill those damn mice." He looked over his shoulder to see whether Billy had noticed the mature profanity. Billy worked on without comment.

Jody turned back and looked at the side-hill where the road from the outside world came down. The hill was washed with lean March sunshine. Silver thistles, blue lupins[5] and a few poppies bloomed among the sagebushes. Halfway up the hill Jody could see Doubletree Mutt, the black dog, digging in a squirrel hole. He paddled for a while and then paused to kick bursts of dirt out between his hind legs, and he dug with an earnestness which belied the knowledge he must have had that no dog had ever caught a squirrel by digging in a hole.

Suddenly, while Jody watched, the black dog stiffened, and backed out of the hole and looked up the hill toward the cleft in the ridge where the road came through. Jody looked up too. For a moment Carl Tiflin on horseback stood out against the pale sky and then he moved down the road toward the house. He carried something white in his hand.

The boy started to his feet. "He's got a letter," Jody cried. He trotted away toward the ranch house, for the letter would probably be read aloud and he wanted to be there. He reached the house before his father did, and ran in. He heard Carl dismount from his creaking sad-dle and slap the horse on the side to send it to the barn where Billy would unsaddle it and turn it out.

Jody ran into the kitchen. "We got a letter!" he cried.

His mother looked up from a pan of beans. "Who has?"

"Father has. I saw it in his hand."

Carl strode into the kitchen then, and Jody's mother asked, "Who's the letter from, Carl?"

He frowned quickly. "How did you know there was a letter?"

She nodded her head in the boy's direction. "Big-Britches Jody told me."

Jody was embarrassed.

His father looked down at him contemptuously. "He *is* getting to be a Big-Britches," Carl said. "He's minding everybody's business but his own. Got his big nose into everything."

Mrs. Tiflin relented a little. "Well, he hasn't enough to keep him busy. Who's the letter from?"

Carl still frowned on Jody. "I'll keep him busy if he isn't careful." He held out a sealed letter. "I guess it's from your father."

Mrs. Tiflin took a hairpin from her head and slit open the flap. Her lips pursed judiciously. Jody saw her eyes snap back and forth over the lines. "He says," she translated, "he says he's going to drive out Saturday to stay for a little while. Why, this is Saturday. The letter must have been delayed." She looked at the postmark. "This was mailed day before yesterday. It should have been here yesterday." She looked up questioningly at her husband, and then her face darkened angrily. "Now what have you got that look on you for? He doesn't come often."

Carl turned his eyes away from her anger. He could be stern with her most of the time, but when occasionally her temper arose, he could not combat it.

---

4. **ridge ranch,** building on hills between two valleys used when checking cattle grazing in the mountains.
5. **blue lupins**\ˈlū·pənz\ also spelled **lupine**\ˈlū·pən\ a wild plant of pale blue, common in the sandy soil of both eastern and western United States.

"What's the matter with you?" she demanded again.

In his explanation there was a tone of apology Jody himself might have used. "It's just that he talks," Carl said lamely. "Just talks."

"Well, what of it? You talk yourself."

"Sure I do. But your father only talks about one thing."

"Indians!" Jody broke in excitedly. "Indians and crossing the plains!"

Carl turned fiercely on him. "You get out, Mr. Big-Britches! Go on, now! Get out!"

Jody went miserably out the back door and closed the screen with elaborate quietness. Under the kitchen window his shamed, downcast eyes fell upon a curiously shaped stone, a stone of such fascination that he squatted down and picked it up and turned it over in his hands.

The voices came clearly to him through the open kitchen window. "Jody's right," he heard his father say. "Just Indians and crossing the plains. I've heard that story about how the horses got driven off about a thousand times. He just goes on and on, and he never changes a word in the things he tells."

When Mrs. Tiflin answered her tone was so changed that Jody, outside the window, looked up from his study of the stone. Her voice had become soft and explanatory. Jody knew how her face would have changed to match the tone. She said quietly, "Look at it this way, Carl. That was the big thing in my father's life. He led a wagon train clear across the plains to the coast, and when it was finished, his life was done. It was a big thing to do, but it didn't last long enough. Look!" she continued, "it's as though he was born to do that, and after he finished it, there wasn't anything more for him to do but think about it and talk about it. If there'd been any farther west to go, he'd have gone. He's told me so himself. But at last there was the ocean. He lives right by the ocean where he had to stop."

She had caught Carl, caught him and entangled him in her soft tone.

"I've seen him," he agreed quietly. "He goes down and stares off west over the ocean." His voice sharpened a little. "And then he goes up to the Horseshoe Club in Pacific Grove,[6] and he tells people how the Indians drove off the horses."

She tried to catch him again. "Well, it's everything to him. You might be patient with him and pretend to listen."

Carl turned impatiently away. "Well, if it gets too bad, I can always go down to the bunkhouse and sit with Billy," he said irritably. He walked through the house and slammed the front door after him.

Jody ran to his chores. He dumped the grain to the chickens without chasing any of them. He gathered the eggs from the nests. He trotted into the house with the wood and interlaced it so carefully in the wood-box that two armloads seemed to fill it to overflowing.

His mother had finished the beans by now. She stirred up the fire and brushed off the stove-top with a turkey wing. Jody peered cautiously at her to see whether any rancor toward him remained. "Is he coming today?" Jody asked.

"That's what his letter said."

"Maybe I better walk up the road to meet him."

Mrs. Tiflin clanged the stove-lid shut. "That would be nice," she said. "He'd probably like to be met."

"I guess I'll just do it then."

Outside, Jody whistled shrilly to the dogs. "Come on up the hill," he commanded. The two dogs waved their tails and ran ahead. Along the roadside the sage had tender new tips. Jody tore off some pieces and rubbed them on his hands until the air was filled with the sharp wild smell. With a rush the dogs leaped from the road and yapped into the brush after a rabbit. That was the last Jody saw of them, for when they failed to catch the rabbit, they went back home.

Jody plodded on up the hill toward the ridge top. When he reached the little cleft where the road came through, the afternoon wind struck

---

6. **Pacific Grove,** a residential and resort city at the south end of Monterey Bay, California.

him and blew up his hair and ruffled his shirt. He looked down on the little hills and ridges below and then out at the huge green Salinas Valley. He could see the white town of Salinas[7] far out in the flat and the flash of its windows under the waning sun. Directly below him, in an oak tree, a crow congress had convened. The tree was black with crows all cawing at once. Then Jody's eyes followed the wagon road down from the ridge where he stood, and lost it behind a hill, and picked it up again on the other side. On that distant stretch he saw a cart slowly pulled by a bay horse. It disappeared behind the hill. Jody sat down on the ground and watched the place where the cart would reappear again. The wind sang on the hilltops and the puff-ball clouds hurried eastward.

Then the cart came into sight and stopped. A man dressed in black dismounted from the seat and walked to the horse's head. Although it was so far away, Jody knew he had unhooked the check-rein, for the horse's head dropped forward. The horse moved on, and the man walked slowly up the hill beside it. Jody gave a glad cry and ran down the road toward them. The squirrels bumped along off the road, and a road-runner[8] flirted its tail and raced over the edge of the hill and sailed out like a glider.

Jody tried to leap into the middle of his shadow at every step. A stone rolled under his foot and he went down. Around a little bend he raced, and there, a short distance ahead, were his grandfather and the cart. The boy dropped from his unseemly running and approached at a dignified walk.

The horse plodded stumble-footedly up the hill and the old man walked beside it. In the lowering sun their giant shadows flickered darkly behind them. The grandfather was dressed in a black broadcloth suit and he wore kid congress gaiters[9] and a black tie on a short, hard collar. He carried his black slouch hat in his hand. His white beard was cropped close and his white eyebrows overhung his eyes like mustaches. The blue eyes were sternly merry. About the whole face and figure there was a granite dignity, so that every motion seemed an impossible thing. Once at rest, it seemed the old man would be stone, would never move again. His steps were slow and certain. Once made, no step could ever be retraced; once headed in a direction, the path would never bend nor the pace increase nor slow.

When Jody appeared around the bend, Grandfather waved his hat slowly in welcome, and he called, "Why, Jody! Come down to meet me, have you?"

Jody sidled near and turned and matched his step to the old man's step and stiffened his body and dragged his heels a little. "Yes, sir," he said. "We got your letter only today."

"Should have been here yesterday," said Grandfather. "It certainly should. How are all the folks?"

"They're fine, sir." He hesitated and then suggested shyly, "Would you like to come on a mouse hunt tomorrow, sir?"

"Mouse hunt, Jody?" Grandfather chuckled. "Have the people of this generation come down to hunting mice? They aren't very strong, the new people, but I hardly thought mice would be game for them."

"No, sir. It's just play. The haystack's gone. I'm going to drive out the mice to the dogs. And you can watch, or even beat the hay a little."

The stern, merry eyes turned down on him. "I see. You don't eat them then. You haven't come to that yet."

Jody explained. "The dogs eat them, sir. It wouldn't be much like hunting Indians, I guess."

"No, not much—but then later, when the troops were hunting Indians and shooting children and burning teepees, it wasn't much different from your mouse hunt."

They topped the rise and started down into the ranch-cup, and they lost the sun from their

<hr />

7. **Salinas**\sə ᐧlē·nəs\ city in Monterey County, west California; birthplace of Steinbeck.
8. **road-runner,** a long-tailed bird that resembles the cuckoo and is noted for running at great speeds.
9. **congress gaiters**\ᐧkŏn·grəs ᐧgā·tərz\ ankle-high shoes with elastic inserts in the upper portion to provide for expansion; formerly popular with members of Congress.

shoulders. "You've grown," Grandfather said. "Nearly an inch, I should say."

"More," Jody boasted. "Where they mark me on the door, I'm up more than an inch since Thanksgiving even."

Grandfather's rich throaty voice said, "Maybe you're getting too much water and turning to pith and stalk. Wait until you head out, and then we'll see."

Jody looked quickly into the old man's face to see whether his feelings should be hurt, but there was no will to injure, no punishing nor putting-in-your-place light in the keen blue eyes. "We might kill a pig," Jody suggested.

"Oh, no! I couldn't let you do that. You're just humoring me. It isn't the time and you know it."

"You know Riley, the big boar, sir?"

"Yes. I remember Riley well."

"Well, Riley ate a hole into that same haystack, and it fell down on him and smothered him."

"Pigs do that when they can," said Grandfather.

"Riley was a nice pig, for a boar, sir. I rode him sometimes, and he didn't mind."

A door slammed at the house below them, and they saw Jody's mother standing on the porch waving her apron in welcome. And they saw Carl Tiflin walking up from the barn to be at the house for the arrival.

The sun had disappeared from the hills by now. The blue smoke from the house chimney hung in flat layers in the purpling ranch-cup. The puff-ball clouds, dropped by the falling wind, hung listlessly in the sky.

Billy Buck came out of the bunkhouse and flung a wash basin of soapy water on the ground. He had been shaving in mid-week, for Billy held Grandfather in reverence, and Grandfather said that Billy was one of the few men of the new generation who had not gone soft. Although Billy was in middle age, Grandfather considered him a boy. Now Billy was hurrying toward the house too.

When Jody and Grandfather arrived, the three were waiting for them in front of the yard gate.

Carl said, "Hello, sir. We've been looking for you."

Mrs. Tiflin kissed Grandfather on the side of his beard, and stood still while his big hand patted her shoulder. Billy shook hands solemnly, grinning under his straw mustache. "I'll put up your horse," said Billy, and he led the rig away.

Grandfather watched him go, and then, turning back to the group, he said as he had said a hundred times before, "There's a good boy. I knew his father, old Mule-tail Buck. I never knew why they called him Mule-tail except he packed mules."

Mrs. Tiflin turned and led the way into the house. "How long are you going to stay, Father? Your letter didn't say."

"Well, I don't know. I thought I'd stay about two weeks. But I never stay as long as I think I'm going to."

In a short while they were sitting at the white oilcloth table eating their supper. The lamp with the tin reflector hung over the table. Outside the dining-room windows the big moths battered softly against the glass.

Grandfather cut his steak into tiny pieces and chewed slowly. "I'm hungry," he said. "Driving out here got my appetite up. It's like when we were crossing. We all got so hungry every night we could hardly wait to let the meat get done. I could eat about five pounds of buffalo meat every night."

"It's moving around does it," said Billy. "My father was a government packer.[10] I helped him when I was a kid. Just the two of us could about clean up a deer's ham."

"I knew your father, Billy," said Grandfather. "A fine man he was. They called him Mule-tail Buck. I don't know why except he packed mules."

"That was it," Billy agreed. "He packed mules."

Grandfather put down his knife and fork and looked around the table. "I remember one time

---

10. **government packer,** official chosen to supervise packing of marketable items, as beef, pork, tobacco.

On the right, one group is headed north to Oregon; on the left, another group heads west to California.

we ran out of meat—" His voice dropped to a curious low sing-song, dropped into a tonal groove the story had worn for itself. "There was no buffalo, no antelope, not even rabbits. The hunters couldn't even shoot a coyote. That was the time for the leader to be on the watch. I was the leader, and I kept my eyes open. Know why? Well, just the minute the people began to get hungry they'd start slaughtering the team oxen. Do you believe that? I've heard of parties that just ate up their draft cattle.[11] Started from the middle and worked towards the ends. Finally they'd eat the lead pair,[12] and then the wheelers.[13] The leader of a party had to keep them from doing that."

In some manner a big moth got into the room and circled the hanging kerosene lamp. Billy got up and tried to clap it between his hands. Carl struck with a cupped palm and caught the moth and broke it. He walked to the window and dropped it out.

"As I was saying," Grandfather began again, but Carl interrupted him. "You'd better eat

---

11. **draft cattle,** cattle suitable for drawing heavy loads.
12. **lead pair,** oxen fastened to vehicle in front of all others in the same team.
13. **wheelers,** oxen harnessed nearest the wheels.

some more meat. All the rest of us are ready for our pudding."

Jody saw a flash of anger in his mother's eyes. Grandfather picked up his knife and fork. "I'm pretty hungry, all right," he said. "I'll tell you about that later."

When supper was over, when the family and Billy Buck sat in front of the fireplace in the other room, Jody anxiously watched Grandfather. He saw the signs he knew. The bearded head leaned forward; the eyes lost their sternness and looked wonderingly into the fire; the big lean fingers laced themselves on the black knees.

"I wonder," he began, "I just wonder whether I ever told you how those thieving Piutes[14] drove off thirty-five of our horses."

"I think you did," Carl interrupted. "Wasn't it just before you went up into the Tahoe[15] country?"

Grandfather turned quickly toward his son-in-law. "That's right. I guess I must have told you that story."

"Lots of times," Carl said cruelly, and he avoided his wife's eyes. But he felt the angry eyes on him, and he said, "'Course I'd like to hear it again."

Grandfather looked back at the fire. His fingers unlaced and laced again. Jody knew how he felt, how his insides were collapsed and empty. Hadn't Jody been called a Big-Britches that very afternoon? He arose to heroism and opened himself to the term Big-Britches again. "Tell about Indians," he said softly.

Grandfather's eyes grew stern again. "Boys always want to hear about Indians. It was a job for men, but boys want to hear about it. Well, let's see. Did I ever tell you how I wanted each wagon to carry a long iron plate?"

Everyone but Jody remained silent. Jody said, "No. You didn't."

"Well, when the Indians attacked, we always put the wagons in a circle and fought from between the wheels. I thought that if every wagon carried a long plate with rifle holes, the men could stand the plates on the outside of the wheels when the wagons were in the circle and

they would be protected. It would save lives and that would make up for the extra weight of the iron. But of course the party wouldn't do it. No party had done it before and they couldn't see why they should go to the expense. They lived to regret it, too."

Jody looked at his mother, and knew from her expression that she was not listening at all. Carl picked at a callus on his thumb and Billy Buck watched a spider crawling up the wall.

Grandfather's tone dropped into its narrative groove again. Jody knew in advance exactly what words would fall. The story droned on, speeded up for the attack, grew sad over the wounds, struck a dirge at the burials on the great plains. Jody sat quietly watching Grandfather. The stern blue eyes were detached. He looked as though he were not very interested in the story himself.

When it was finished, when the pause had been politely respected as the frontier of the story, Billy Buck stood up and stretched and hitched his trousers. "I guess I'll turn in," he said. Then he faced Grandfather. "I've got an old powder horn and a cap and ball pistol down to the bunkhouse. Did I ever show them to you?"

Grandfather nodded slowly. "Yes, I think you did, Billy. Reminds me of a pistol I had when I was leading the people across." Billy stood politely until the little story was done, and then he said, "Good night," and went out of the house.

Carl Tiflin tried to turn the conversation then. "How's the country between here and Monterey?[16] I've heard it's pretty dry."

"It is dry," said Grandfather. "There's not a drop of water in the Laguna Seca.[17] But it's a long pull from '87. The whole country was

---

14. **Piutes**\ˈpai·ūt\ variation of Paiute\ˈpai·ūt\ Indian people of Western Utah, northwestern Arizona, southeastern Nevada, and southeastern California.
15. **Tahoe**\ˈta ˈhō\ country, area around California-Nevada boundary.
16. **Monterey,** city in west California, south end of Monterey Bay.
17. **Laguna Seca**\la ˈgū·nə ˈsē·kə\ meaning "dry lake."

powder then, and in '61 I believe all the coyotes starved to death. We had fifteen inches of rain this year."

"Yes, but it all came too early. We could do with some now." Carl's eye fell on Jody. "Hadn't you better be getting to bed?"

Jody stood up obediently. "Can I kill the mice in the old haystack, sir?"

"Mice? Oh! Sure, kill them all off. Billy said there isn't any good hay left."

Jody exchanged a secret and satisfying look with Grandfather. "I'll kill every one tomorrow," he promised.

Jody lay in his bed and thought of the impossible world of Indians and buffaloes, a world that had ceased to be forever. He wished he could have been living in the heroic time, but he knew he was not of heroic timber. No one living now, save possibly Billy Buck, was worthy to do the things that had been done. A race of giants had lived then, fearless men, men of a staunchness unknown in this day. Jody thought of the wide plains and of the wagons moving across like centipedes. He thought of Grandfather on a huge white horse, marshaling the people. Across his mind marched the great phantoms, and they marched off the earth and they were gone.

He came back to the ranch for a moment, then. He heard the dull rushing sound that space and silence make. He heard one of the dogs, out in the doghouse, scratching a flea and bumping his elbow against the floor with every stroke. Then the wind arose again and the black cypress groaned and Jody went to sleep.

He was up half an hour before the triangle[18] sounded for breakfast. His mother was rattling the stove to make the flames roar when Jody went through the kitchen. "You're up early," she said. "Where are you going?"

"Out to get a good stick. We're going to kill the mice today."

"Who is 'we'?"

"Why, Grandfather and I."

"So you've got him in it. You always like to have some one in with you in case there's blame to share."

"I'll be right back," said Jody. "I just want to have a good stick ready for after breakfast."

He closed the screen door after him and went out into the cool blue morning. The birds were noisy in the dawn and the ranch cats came down from the hill like blunt snakes. They had been hunting gophers in the dark, and although the four cats were full of gopher meat, they sat in a semi-circle at the back door and mewed piteously for milk. Doubletree Mutt and Smasher moved sniffing along the edge of the brush, performing the duty with rigid ceremony, but when Jody whistled, their heads jerked up and their tails waved. They plunged down to him, wriggling their skins and yawning. Jody patted their heads seriously, and moved on to the weathered scrap pile. He selected an old broom handle and a short piece of inch-square scrap wood. From his pocket he took a shoelace and tied the ends of the sticks loosely together to make a flail.[19] He whistled his new weapon through the air and struck the ground experimentally, while the dogs leaped aside and whined with apprehension.

Jody turned and started down past the house toward the old haystack ground to look over the field of slaughter, but Billy Buck, sitting patiently on the back steps, called to him, "You better come back. It's only a couple of minutes till breakfast."

Jody changed his course and moved toward the house. He leaned his flail against the steps. "That's to drive the mice out," he said. "I'll bet they're fat. I'll bet they don't know what's going to happen to them today."

"No, nor you either," Billy remarked philosophically, "nor me, nor anyone."

Jody was staggered by this thought. He knew it was true. His imagination twitched away from the mouse hunt. Then his mother came out on the back porch and struck the triangle, and all thoughts fell in a heap.

---

18. **triangle,** a steel rod bent into the shape of a triangle, sounded by striking with a metal rod; used for calling ranch hands to eat.
19. **flail**\flāl\ an instrument for threshing grain.

Grandfather hadn't appeared at the table when they sat down. Billy nodded at his empty chair. "He's all right? He isn't sick?"

"He takes a long time to dress," said Mrs. Tiflin. "He combs his whiskers and rubs up his shoes and brushes his clothes."

Carl scattered sugar on his mush. "A man that's led a wagon train across the plains has got to be pretty careful how he dresses."

Mrs. Tiflin turned on him. "Don't do that, Carl! Please don't!" There was more of threat than of request in her tone. And the threat irritated Carl.

"Well, how many times do I have to listen to the story of the iron plates, and the thirty-five horses? That time's done. Why can't he forget it, now it's done?" He grew angrier while he talked, and his voice rose. "Why does he have to tell them over and over? He came across the plains. All right! Now it's finished. Nobody wants to hear about it over and over."

The door into the kitchen closed softly. The four at the table sat frozen. Carl laid his mush spoon[20] on the table and touched his chin with his fingers.

Then the kitchen door opened and Grandfather walked in. His mouth smiled tightly and his eyes were squinted. "Good morning," he said, and he sat down and looked at his mush dish.

Carl could not leave it there. "Did—did you hear what I said?"

Grandfather jerked a little nod.

"I don't know what got into me, sir. I didn't mean it. I was just being funny."

Jody glanced in shame at his mother, and he saw that she was looking at Carl, and that she wasn't breathing. It was an awful thing that he was doing. He was tearing himself to pieces to talk like that. It was a terrible thing to him to retract a word, but to retract it in shame was infinitely worse.

Grandfather looked sidewise. "I'm trying to get right side up," he said gently. "I'm not being mad. I don't mind what you said, but it might be true, and I would mind that."

"It isn't true," said Carl. "I'm not feeling well this morning. I'm sorry I said it."

"Don't be sorry, Carl. An old man doesn't see things sometimes. Maybe you're right. The crossing is finished. Maybe it should be forgotten, now it's done."

Carl got up from the table. "I've had enough to eat. I'm going to work. Take your time, Billy!" He walked quickly out of the dining-room. Billy gulped the rest of his food and followed soon after. But Jody could not leave his chair.

"Won't you tell any more stories?" Jody asked.

"Why, sure I'll tell them, but only when—I'm sure people want to hear them."

"I like to hear them, sir."

"Oh! Of course you do, but you're a little boy. It was a job for men, but only little boys like to hear about it."

Jody got up from his place. "I'll wait outside for you, sir. I've got a good stick for those mice."

He waited by the gate until the old man came out on the porch. "Let's go down and kill the mice now," Jody called.

"I think I'll just sit in the sun, Jody. You go kill the mice."

"You can use my stick if you like."

"No, I'll just sit here a while."

Jody turned disconsolately away, and walked down toward the old haystack. He tried to whip up his enthusiasm with thoughts of the fat juicy mice. He beat the ground with his flail. The dogs coaxed and whined about him, but he could not go. Back at the house he could see Grandfather sitting on the porch, looking small and thin and black.

Jody gave up and went to sit on the steps at the old man's feet.

"Back already? Did you kill the mice?"

"No, sir. I'll kill them some other day."

The morning flies buzzed close to the ground and the ants dashed about in front of the steps.

---

20. **mush spoon,** a utensil for eating mush, a porridge of thick consistency made from cornmeal.

The heavy smell of sage slipped down the hill. The porch boards grew warm in the sunshine.

Jody hardly knew when Grandfather started to talk. "I shouldn't stay here, feeling the way I do." He examined his strong old hands. "I feel as though the crossing wasn't worth doing." His eyes moved up the side-hill and stopped on a motionless hawk perched on a dead limb. "I tell those old stories, but they're not what I want to tell. I only know how I want people to feel when I tell them.

"It wasn't Indians that were important, nor adventures, nor even getting out here. It was a whole bunch of people made into one big crawling beast. And I was the head. It was westering and westering. Every man wanted something for himself, but the big beast that was all of them wanted only westering. I was the leader, but if I hadn't been there, someone else would have been the head. The thing had to have a head.

"Under the little bushes the shadows were black at white noonday. When we saw the mountains at last, we cried—all of us. But it wasn't getting here that mattered, it was movement and westering.

"We carried life out here and set it down the way those ants carry eggs. And I was the leader. The westering was as big as God, and the slow steps that made the movement piled up and piled up until the continent was crossed.

"Then we came down to the sea, and it was done." He stopped and wiped his eyes until the rims were red. "That's what I should be telling instead of stories."

When Jody spoke, Grandfather started and looked down at him. "Maybe I could lead the people some day," Jody said.

The old man smiled. "There's no place to go. There's the ocean to stop you. There's a line of old men along the shore hating the ocean because it stopped them."

"In boats I might, sir."

"No place to go, Jody. Every place is taken. But that's not the worst—no, not the worst. Westering has died out of the people. Westering isn't a hunger any more. It's all done. Your

father is right. It is finished." He laced his fingers on his knee and looked at them.

Jody felt very sad. "If you'd like a glass of lemonade I could make it for you."

Grandfather was about to refuse, and then he saw Jody's face. "That would be nice," he said. "Yes, it would be nice to drink a lemonade."

Jody ran into the kitchen where his mother was wiping the last of the breakfast dishes. "Can I have a lemon to make a lemonade for Grandfather?"

His mother mimicked—"And another lemon to make a lemonade for you."

"No, ma'am. I don't want one."

"Jody! You're sick!" Then she stopped suddenly. "Take a lemon out of the cooler," she said softly. "Here, I'll reach the squeezer down to you."

1
WHAT'S IN A TITLE?

In fiction, particularly, titles are often of great importance; they give the reader cues on what to look for in the pages that follow. Sometimes a title tells the reader that the work of fiction is going to center on a certain character or a certain action; at other times a title may give the reader some indication of the author's theme.

On the basis of the title, "The Leader of the People," what aspect of his story does Steinbeck wish to emphasize? What relationship would you say exists between leaders and endless frontiers? In particular, is some sort of leader necessary for the exploration of frontiers, or can such explorations be made without individual leadership? What qualities did a leader need in Grandfather's day? How many of these same qualities are needed today?

II
IMPLICATIONS

Any work of fiction or nonfiction has several purposes. Sometimes—particularly in fiction—its main purpose may be to give pleasure, to entertain; at other times it may be to stimulate thinking or to move individuals to action. Whatever the main purpose of a piece of writing, however, it is almost certain that it will both give pleasure, of one sort or another, *and* stimulate thought. After most of the selections in this anthology, an "Implications" section will invite you to do some thinking about the selections you have read. Whether you take up the various propositions in a class debate or in a written essay, the main point should always be the quality of your thinking.

The object of these activities is not to provide an outlet for the expression of prejudices. If you really think about the selections you read and the implications you are asked to consider, you should at the very least find your favorite ideas modified. For even if you agree with the point of view expressed by the author, it is unlikely that you will think precisely as he does.

Consider each of the following statements in the light of Steinbeck's story, your own experience, and your understanding of the theme, ENDLESS FRONTIERS, and be prepared to state and defend your own point of view.

1. Generations view events from different perspectives, and this often leads to antagonism between generations.

2. Viewed through the rosy glow of retrospection, events of the past are surrounded by romance.

3. It is foolish to spend billions of dollars trying to land a man on the moon. What will we accomplish by it?

4. Every man is potentially a leader. All he needs are the right circumstances to bring out the leadership qualities he possesses.

5. The "westering" spirit is dead and no new worthy spirit has yet taken its place.

III
TECHNIQUES

The Greek word for art is *technikos*, a word from which we get our word *technique*. (Our word *art* comes from the Latin, *ars*.) Technique is as important in literature as it is in music, painting, and sculpturing. It is largely the writer's mastery of his medium—words, sentences, paragraphs, rhythms, etc.—that distinguishes a good writer from an amateur. The knowledge of a writer's technique is important to the reader as well, for such knowledge

adds greatly to one's appreciation and enjoyment of literature.

In this section of the anthology the techniques by which writers create *setting* and *character* will be emphasized. In subsequent themes other aspects of technique will be taken up. In addition, throughout the anthology these sections will focus more or less constant attention upon the matter of how authors develop their themes.

Setting

In the broadest sense, setting includes the elements of *place, time,* and *atmosphere*. The relative importance of each of these elements depends upon the writer's purpose and upon the type of writing he is doing. In historical fiction, for example, we usually expect an author to give us a solid feeling of both place and time. In mystery or "ghost" stories it is important for a writer to create an appropriate atmosphere or mood. On the other hand, setting may be a minor consideration or not a consideration at all in certain types of essays.

In "The Leader of the People," the place setting is a farm in the Salinas Valley of California. Steinbeck makes the reader aware of this setting in various ways. The haystack, for example, which stands as a kind of shorthand symbol of farm life, is mentioned throughout the story. Steinbeck also continually reminds his reader that the story is taking place in the far West, "right by the ocean," at the edge of the frontier.

Specific details are particularly helpful in realizing a locality. Such details as pitchforks, black cypress trees, silver thistles, blue lupins, road-runners, and the Laguna Seca give the reader a sense of really being on a farm in the West, even though he may have only a fuzzy notion of what these things look like.

The time setting is less specifically realized than the place setting. We are never told that the story occurs in such and such a year. But we are still kept quite conscious of a special aspect of time—we know that the story takes place two generations after the frontier has been reached. And this, of course, is what matters to the theme of Steinbeck's story, not the specific year in which the action occurs.

Atmosphere is usually more difficult to describe than place and time. But Steinbeck, like most good short-story writers, subtly begins to build the atmosphere through specific details early in the story. At the end of the first paragraph we read, "The wind could be heard whishing in the brush on the ridge crests, but no breath of it penetrated down into the ranch-cup." A moment later we find Billy *looking up* at the top of the hills, and shortly after Jody *looks up* at "the little puffs of wind-driven cloud." Thereafter, Steinbeck reminds us several times that the ranch is located in a *cup* in the hills. It seems clear from these and many other details that Steinbeck is trying to create the impression that the ranch is a settled, even a sterile, place protected from the outside world, a place where the westering spirit is hardly likely to grow.

The atmosphere associated with the ranch is in direct contrast with the spirit of Grandfather and with Jody's hunger for frontiers to explore. Steinbeck points up this contrast by having Jody leave the "ranch-cup" just as he is about to meet the old man for the first time in the story. At that point we find Jody standing on a hill where the wind that blows over the ranch strikes him, blows his hair and ruffles his shirt. Wind—a natural symbol for creativity, change, and the westering urge—does not touch Carl, but when Grandfather arrives, we read, "The wind sang on the hilltops and the puff-balls of clouds hurried eastward."

Details like these are not accidental. Whether or not the reader consciously takes note of them is perhaps not of great importance; but they are there, doing their work of creating an atmosphere, a mood that the author hopes the reader will *feel*.

To appreciate the techniques a writer uses to create atmosphere, it would be worthwhile for you to reread this story. As you do, make a list of the various phrases and sentences which help to communicate the feeling that the Tiflin ranch is "sealed off," removed from outside influences and thus from the westering spirit which endlessly sought new frontiers to explore.

Characterization

The writer of fiction or of nonfiction has at his disposal a number of ways to reveal the character of the persons about whom he is writing. Perhaps the most important means is through what the character himself does and says. This is an especially good way of developing characters because it allows the reader himself to make his own estimate of the real or fictitious persons he meets. In addition to this method, an author may describe a character directly in expository passages. He may also reveal him through what other characters say about him and how they react to him. Finally, he may make comparisons between one character and another or others.

The reader learns about Grandfather, the central figure in "The Leader of the People" (1) from what Grandfather says and does: "I tell these old stories, but they're not what I want to tell. I only know how I want people to feel when I tell them"; (2) from the author's description: "The blue eyes were sternly merry. About the whole face and figure there was a granite dignity, so that every motion seemed an impossible thing"; (3) from what others say: "Well, how many times do I have to listen to the story of the iron plates, and the thirty-five horses? That time's done. Why can't he forget it, now it's done?"; and (4) from the implicit comparison between Grandfather and Carl, which runs throughout the story.

When an author wants to impress a character on the reader's mind, he often repeats a detail or a series of related details about that character. Grandfather, for example, is described as possessing "granite dignity"; the adjective "stern" is used several times to describe him; and of course he dresses sternly, with "granite dignity," all in black.

Steinbeck's characters in this story are obviously of greater importance than the plot. There is a climax in the story—Grandfather's overhearing his son-in-law's insulting remarks—but it is hardly more than a brief episode in a series. The characters, however, loom large in importance. By what methods does Steinbeck reveal the character of Jody, of his mother, his father, and of the ranch-hand, Billy? Can you find any particular repetition of adjectives or phrases used to describe any of these characters?

More than a hundred years after Columbus's voyage,
the spirit of westering touched increasing numbers of men in Europe.
What kind of men came to the New World, and why did they risk
its uncertainties rather than remain in the land of their birth?
In the following excerpt from "Western Star," a long narrative poem,
Stephen Vincent Benét must have been troubled by the same questions.
He must have asked, "What was it like on the voyage and at the landing
of the men sent by the London Company to Virginia in the early 1600's?"

Western Star

STEPHEN VINCENT BENÉT

There was a wind over England, and it blew.
(Have you heard the news of Virginia?)
A west wind blowing, the wind of a western star,
To gather men's lives like pollen and cast them forth,
Blowing in hedge and highway and seaport town,   5
Whirling dead leaf and living, but always blowing,
A salt wind, a sea wind, a wind from the world's end,
From the coasts that have new, wild names, from the huge unknown. . . .

Gather them up, the bright and drowning stars,
And with them gather, too,   10
The clay, the iron, and the knotted rope,
The disinherited, the dispossessed,
The hinds[1] of the midland, eaten by the squire's sheep,
The outcast yeoman, driven to tramp the roads,
The sturdy beggars, roving from town to town,   15
Workless, hopeless, harried by law and State,
The men who lived on nettles[2] in Merry England,
The men of the blackened years
When dog's meat was a dainty in Lincolnshire,
(Have you heard the news from Virginia?)   20
The poor, the restless, the striving, the broken knights,
The cast-off soldiers, bitter as their own scars,
The younger sons without office or hope of land,

"Western Star" by Stephen Vincent Benét. Published by Holt, Rinehart & Winston, Inc. Copyright, 1943, by Rosemary Carr Benét. Reprinted by permission of Brandt & Brandt.

1. **hinds,** hired farm laborers.
2. **nettles,** herbs with minute hairs that sting.

Glover and cooper, mercer and cordwainer,[3]
("Have you heard the news from Virginia? Have you heard?   25
Wat swears he'll go, for the gold lies heaped on the ground
And Ralph, the hatter, is ready as any man.
I keep my shop but my shop doth not keep me.
Shall I give such chances the go-by and walk the roads?
I am no hind to scratch in the earth for bread.   30
Nay, a stocking-weaver I, and of good repute
Though lately dogged by mischances. They'll need such men.
Have you heard the news from Virginia?")
Gather the waifs of the London parishes,
The half-starved boys, the sparrows of London streets,   35
The ones we caught before they could cut a purse,
And bind them out and send them across the sea.
("They will live or die but at least we are rid of them.
We'll pick the likeliest ones. Boy, what's your name?
Good lad. You sail in *The Fortune*. The fool looks mazed.   40
Well, give him a wash and see he is fitted out.
We'll settle his master later.")
                                        Oh, spread the news,
The news of golden Virginia across the sea,
And let it sink in the hearts of the strange, plain men   45
Already at odds with government and church,
The men who read their Bibles late in the night,
Dissenter and nonconformist and Puritan,
Let it go to Scrooby[4] and stop at the pesthouse[5] there,

---

3. **cooper**\ˈkū·pər\ maker of wooden casks; **mercer**, dealer in textile fabrics; **cordwainer**
\kɔr ˈdwā·nər\ shoemaker.
4. **Scrooby**\ˈskrū·bĭ\ The Separatists, those who advocated withdrawal from the Church
of England, formed a group in Scrooby, England; then the group fled to Holland in
1608, to America on the *Mayflower* in 1620.
5. **pesthouse**, a public hospital for patients suffering from plague or infectious diseases.

Let it go to the little meeting at Austerfield.   50
(We must worship God as we choose. We must worship God
Though King and law and bishop stand in the way.
It is far, in the North, and they will not touch us here,
Yet I hear they mean to harry the sheep of God
And His elect[6] must be steadfast. I hear a sound   55
Like the first, faint roll of thunder, but it is far.
It is very far away.
Have you heard the news of Virginia?
                                        Friend, I have heard
The burning news of the elections of God,   60
The comfortable word, the clear promise sealed,
My heart is shaken with grace to my heart's root.
I have prayed and wrestled and drunk at the living fount
And God walks with me, guiding me with His hand.
What matter your little news and your tinsel world?)   65

Have you heard the news of Virginia? Have you heard
The news, the news of Virginia? . . .

There were a hundred and forty-four, all told,
In the three small ships.[7] You can read the names, if you like,
In various spellings. They are English names,   70
William Tankard, Jeremy Alicock,
Jonas Profit, the sailor, James Read, the blacksmith,
Love, the tailor, and Nicholas Scot, the drum.
One laborer is put down with a mere "Ould Edward",
Although, no doubt, they knew his name at the time,   75
But, looking back and remembering, it is hard
To recollect every name. . . .

—It is so they perish, the cast grains of corn,
The blown, chance pollen, lost in the wilderness—
And we have done well to remember so many names,   80
Crofts and Tavin and Johnson, Clovell and Dixon,
And even the four boys, come with the gentlemen,
In a voyage somewhat topheavy with gentlemen,
As John Smith[8] found.
                           A hundred and forty-four   85
Men, on a five months' voyage to settle Mars.
And a hundred and five men landed on the strange shore. . . .

———————

6. **elect,** belief that certain persons are favored, chosen by God for salvation.
7. **three small ships,** *Sarah Constant* under Captain Christopher Newport who was given complete command of the group; the *Goodspeed* under Bartholomew Gosnold; the *Discovery* under John Ratcliffe.
8. **John Smith** became head of government in September, 1608.

17

And yet, a good voyage,
And others would fare worse in other ships,
Bad water, crowded quarters, stinking beef,   90
And, at the end, the hurricane and death.
Though this voyage carried a locked Pandora's box,[9]
Sure to make trouble, sealed orders from the Company,
Naming a council of seven to rule the colony
But not to be opened till they reached their goal.   95
It was the way of the East India Company[10]
But it worked badly here—on a four months' voyage,
With fifty-five gentlemen scattered in three ships
And each one thinking himself as good as the rest.
There were plots and gossiping, wranglings and suspicions,   100
"Have you heard what So-and-so planneth? Nay, bend closer.
My fellow heard him roaring in the great cabin,
Swears, when he's of the Council,[11] he'll have thy head.
But we'll pull him down from his perch."
                                        The idle, human   105
Gossip of hot-blooded, quarrelsome men,
Cooped up together too long through the itching weeks
When you get to hate a man for the way he walks
Or snores at night or dips his hand in the dish,
But, most of all, because you keep seeing him   110
And cannot help but see him, day after day,
And yet, working harm, for when land rose out of the West,
The council-to-be was already badly jangled
And Smith, accused of mutiny, under arrest.[12]

And so, at dawn, on the twenty-sixth day of April,   115
Just over four months from London,
They sailed between Cape Henry[13] and Cape Charles[14]
And saw the broad Chesapeake,[15] and the wished-for shore.
We shall not see it as they, for no men shall
Till the end and the ruin have come upon America,   120

----

9. **Pandora's box** contained all human ills. Pandora, in Greek mythology, was the first woman sent to earth, as punishment of man. She opened the lid of the box, allowing all the ills to escape, leaving only hope at the bottom of the box.
10. **East India Company** (1600–1858), chartered by English Parliament for trade with the Eastern Hemisphere.
11. **Council,** Council of Seven established by the Virginia Company to govern the colony.
12. **John Smith,** elected as president of the colony, became unpopular and was somewhat of a dictator. He was charged with inciting the Indians, starving the company, and planning to marry Pocahontas and make himself king.
13. **Cape Henry,** named for King James's elder son.
14. **Cape Charles,** named for the King's younger son, later Charles I.
15. **Chesapeake\ˈchĕ·sə·pēk** inlet of the Atlantic Ocean with its lower section in Virginia and upper in Maryland.

The murmuring green forest, the huge god,
Smiling, cruel, lying at ease in the sun,
And neither smiling nor cruel, but uncaring,
The vastness where no road ran but the Indian trail
And the little clearings of man were small in the forest, 125
The little dirt of man soon washed away,
The riches of man white shells and opossum skins,
The scalp of a foe, the ritual of the clan,
Squash-vine and pumpkin-seed and the deer's sinew
And the yellow, life-giving corn. 130
We shall not see the birds in their multitudes,
The thundercloud of pigeons, blotting the sun,
The fish that had never struck at an iron hook,
The beaver, breeding faster than men could kill,
The green god, with the leaves at his fingertips 135
And a wreath of oak and maple twining his brows,
Smiling, cruel, majestic and uncaring,
As he lies beside bright waters under the sun,
Whose blood is the Spring sap and the running streams,
Whose witchery is the fever of the marsh, 140
Whose bounty is sun and shadow and life and death,
The huge, wild god with the deerhorns and the green leaf.
We shall not see their Americas as they saw them
And this was what they saw.
Now we must follow them, into the wood. 145

They landed and explored.
It was the first flood of Virginia Spring,
White with new dogwood, smelling of wild strawberries,
Warm and soft-voiced, cornflower-skied and kind.
And they were ravished with it, after the sea, 150
And half-forgot their toils, half-forgot the gold,
As they went poking and prying a little way
In childish wonderment.
A handful of men in hot, heavy, English gear,
With clumsy muskets, sweating but light at heart, 155
Staring about them, dubiously but ravished,
As a flying-squirrel leapt from a swaying branch
And a gray opossum squeaked and scuttled away.
Oh, the fair meadows, the goodly trees and tall,
The fresh streams running in silver through the woods! 160
'Twas a land, a land!

I
"A FIVE MONTHS' VOYAGE TO SETTLE MARS"

In the fragment of a line quoted above Benét makes an implicit comparison—a *metaphor,* to use the technical term—between the voyage sponsored by the London Company and a comparable undertaking today. As with any good metaphor, the comparison is not between two things that are totally similar—that is, the voyage to Virginia does not compare in *every* respect with a trip to Mars today—but it is rich in suggestive power. Those who settled first in the New World knew almost as little about the land to which they journeyed as we today know about Mars. Also, the voyage was dangerous in the extreme. As the reader learns in the poem, thirty-nine men never touched the "strange shore." (Sixty-six others died by autumn.) Finally, note how effectively and briefly the metaphor makes this particular event take on meaning for modern man. Is this Benét's purpose in choosing the past as the subject for a contemporary poem?

II
IMPLICATIONS

Based upon your reading of Benét's poem, what truth do you find in the following statements?

1. Virginia's first settlers were malcontents, criminals, and religious fanatics.

2. The lure of adventure in the new, wild "huge unknown" was the principal motive for coming to America.

3. Many men felt that death in America was better than life in England.

4. New environments help men rise above petty jealousies and quarrels.

5. America has squandered her natural resources and destroyed the original beauty of the land.

III
TECHNIQUES

Since "Western Star" is a *narrative* poem, a poem that tells a story, you might assume that Benét shares the concerns of any storyteller. In much narrative poetry—and in some lyrical poetry as well—the author *is* concerned with place and time setting and with characterization.

Setting

In the excerpt you have read, find the places where Benét gives you a firm sense of locality and some specific indications of time. What specific details about the ships help explain some of the antagonisms bred during the voyage? What specific details does Benét give to point up the hatreds that existed among the men?

Characterization

Although Benét does not focus on the character of any specific individual, he does provide some details that characterize briefly some individuals and the men as a group. What specific details help you to understand the kinds of persons who sailed to the New World and the reasons why they came?

Metaphor

Of Stephen Vincent Benét's work the critic Christopher Morley once said, "He has raked the campfire embers of the American story and found them still live coal." Through his metaphor Morley implies that Benét had the power of dramatically intensifying American history. Metaphor is one of the resources used by writers to achieve intensity.

Unless a reader understands the implications of metaphorical language, he can hardly hope to appreciate literature. Study the following metaphors and be prepared to say what the implied comparisons are. For example, in ". . . a five months' voyage to settle Mars," Benét compares a voyage to settle Mars and a voyage to settle Virginia.

1. —It is so they perish, *the cast grains of corn* (line 78)

2. The murmuring green forest, *the huge god* (line 121)

3. The *thundercloud* of pigeons, blotting the sun (line 132)

4. The green god, with the leaves at *his fingertips* (line 135)

5. It was the first flood of Virginia Spring, . . . Warm and *soft-voiced,* . . . (lines 147–149)

Now consider whether each metaphor makes for a more vivid effect than would a nonmetaphorical passage. You can determine this by replacing Benét's metaphors with direct language. For example, compare the effect of the metaphor, ". . . a five months' voyage to settle *Mars,*" with the nonmetaphorical passage, ". . . a five months' voyage to settle *Virginia.*"

As Americans moved West they found two aspects of nature
unlike anything they had known in Europe: the vast forests of towering trees
and the broad, empty, hilly seas of grass we call prairies.
Both of these natural phenomena emphasized the smallness of man
and the difficulty of the pioneer's task. It was probably for these reasons
that they excited the imaginations of writers. Among the writers impressed
by the grandeur of the prairies was William Cullen Bryant,
who is often considered America's first great poet. Bryant composed
the following lyric poem after his visit to the Midwest
early in the nineteenth century.

The Prairies

WILLIAM CULLEN BRYANT

These are the Gardens of the Desert, these
The unshorn fields, boundless and beautiful,
For which the speech of England has no name—
The Prairies. I behold them for the first,
And my heart swells, while the dilated sight   5
Takes in the encircling vastness. Lo! they stretch
In airy undulations, far away,
As if the Ocean, in his gentlest swell,
Stood still, with all his rounded billows fixed,
And motionless forever.—Motionless?—   10
No—they are all unchained again. The clouds
Sweep over with their shadows, and, beneath,
The surface rolls and fluctuates to the eye;
Dark hollows seem to glide along and chase
The sunny ridges. Breezes of the South!   15
Who toss the golden and the flame-like flowers,
And pass the prairie-hawk that, poised on high,
Flaps his broad wings, yet moves not—ye have played
Among the palms of Mexico and vines
Of Texas, and have crisped the limpid brooks   20
That from the fountains of Sonora[1] glide
Into the calm Pacific—have ye fanned
A nobler or a lovelier scene than this?
Man hath no part in all this glorious work:
The hand that built the firmament hath heaved   25

---

1. **Sonora**\sō ⁴nō•rə\ a state in northwest Mexico.

And smoothed these verdant[2] swells, and sown their slopes
With herbage, planted them with island groves,
And hedged them round with forests. Fitting floor
For this magnificent temple of the sky—
With flowers whose glory and whose multitude   30
Rival the constellations! The great heavens
Seem to stoop down upon the scene in love,—
A nearer vault, and of a tenderer blue,
Than that which bends above our eastern hills.

    As o'er the verdant waste I guide my steed,   35
Among the high rank grass that sweeps his sides
The hollow beating of his footstep seems
A sacrilegious sound. I think of those
Upon whose rest he tramples. Are they here—
The dead of other days?—and did the dust   40
Of these fair solitudes once stir with life
And burn with passion? Let the mighty mounds
That overlook the rivers, or that rise
In the dim forest crowded with old oaks,
Answer. A race, that long has passed away,   45
Built them;—a disciplined and populous race
Heaped, with long toil, the earth, while yet the Greek
Was hewing the Pentelicus[3] to forms
Of symmetry, and rearing on its rock
The glittering Parthenon.[4] These ample fields   50
Nourished their harvests, here their herds were fed,
When haply by their stalls the bison lowed,
And bowed his manèd shoulder to the yoke.
All day this desert murmured with their toils,
Till twilight blushed, and lovers walked, and wooed   55
In a forgotten language, and old tunes,
From instruments of unremembered form,
Gave the soft winds a voice. The red man came—
The roaming hunter tribes, warlike and fierce,
And the mound-builders vanished from the earth.   60
The solitude of centuries untold
Has settled where they dwelt. The prairie-wolf
Hunts in their meadows, and his fresh-dug den
Yawns by my path. The gopher mines the ground
Where stood their swarming cities. All is gone;   65

---

2. **verdant**\vər·dənt\ green, covered with growing vegetation.
3. **Pentelicus**\pĕn ▴tĕ·lĭ·kəs\ (Greek: Pentelikon\pĕn ▴tĕ·lĭ·kon\) a mountain famous for its marble, located northwest of Athens, Greece.
4. **Parthenon**\▴par·thə·nŏn\ temple of Athena on the Acropolis at Athens; one of the finest examples of Doric architecture.

All—save the piles of earth that hold their bones,
The platforms where they worshipped unknown gods,
The barriers which they builded from the soil
To keep the foe at bay—till o'er the walls
The wild beleaguerers broke, and, one by one,   70
The strongholds of the plain were forced, and heaped
With corpses. The brown vultures of the wood
Flocked to those vast uncovered sepulchres,
And sat unscared and silent at their feast.
Haply some solitary fugitive,   75
Lurking in marsh and forest, till the sense
Of desolation and of fear became
Bitterer than death, yielded himself to die.
Man's better nature triumphed then. Kind words
Welcomed and soothed him; the rude conquerors   80
Seated the captive with their chiefs; he chose
A bride among their maidens, and at length
Seemed to forget—yet ne'er forgot—the wife
Of his first love, and her sweet little ones,
Butchered, amid their shrieks, with all his race.   85

   Thus change the forms of being. Thus arise
Races of living things, glorious in strength,
And perish, as the quickening breath of God
Fills them, or is withdrawn. The red man, too—
Has left the blooming wilds he ranged so long,   90
And, nearer to the Rocky Mountains, sought
A wilder hunting-ground. The beaver builds
No longer by these streams, but far away,
On waters whose blue surface ne'er gave back
The white man's face—among Missouri's springs,   95
And pools whose issues swell the Oregon,
He rears his little Venice.[5] In these plains
The bison feeds no more. Twice twenty leagues
Beyond remotest smoke of hunter's camp,
Roams the majestic brute, in herds that shake   100
The earth with thundering steps—yet here I meet
His ancient footprints stamped beside the pool.

   Still this great solitude is quick with life.
Myriads of insects, gaudy as the flowers
They flutter over, gentle quadrupeds,[6]   105
And birds, that scarce have learned the fear of man,

5. **Venice,** a seaport in Italy consisting of many small islands separated by small canals crossed by approximately 380 bridges.
6. **quadrupeds**\ˈkwɔd ˈrū·pədz\ animals having four feet.

And here, the sliding reptiles of the ground,
Startlingly beautiful. The graceful deer
Bounds to the wood at my approach. The bee,   110
A more adventurous colonist than man,
With whom he came across the eastern deep,
Fills the savannas[7] with his murmurings,
And hides his sweets, as in the golden age,
Within the hollow oak. I listen long
To his domestic hum, and think I hear   115
The sound of that advancing multitude
Which soon shall fill these deserts. From the ground
Comes up the laugh of children, the soft voice
Of maidens, and the sweet and solemn hymn
Of Sabbath worshippers. The low of herds   120
Blends with the rustling of the heavy grain
Over the dark-brown furrows. All at once
A fresher wind sweeps by, and breaks my dream,
And I am in the wilderness alone.

---

7. **savannas**\sə ˄văn•əz\ open, level regions containing scattered shrubs
and subjected to heavy rains followed by dry periods.

I
THE FRONTIER VIEWED ROMANTICALLY

"The Prairies" is not a very realistic poem. For one thing, Bryant exaggerates and personifies often, notably when he imagines the heavens stooping to the prairies "in love." For another, the author ignores the dangers and hardships of frontier life. For example, he calls attention to "reptiles" that are "startlingly beautiful" but says nothing about "snakes" that are "full of deadly poison."

Poems—like "The Prairies"—in which the individual, personal point of view and experience is stressed and in which imagination prevails over the factual and even sometimes over the rational, are often called *romantic*.

II
IMPLICATIONS

Discuss "The Prairies" in terms of the following questions.

1. What specific details in the poem prove it to be *subjective* ("personal") rather than *objective*?

Would you say that "Western Star" is more or less subjective than "The Prairies"?

2. What qualities of the prairie frontier as revealed in the poem would tend to inspire the westering spirit in man?

III
TECHNIQUES

Setting

We have defined *setting* broadly as the elements of place, time, and atmosphere. Atmosphere may be defined as the *mood* of a literary work or as its *emotional aura*. One of the ways a writer creates an atmosphere is by his *tone*, that is, by his *attitude toward his subject and toward his readers*.

Which of the following adjectives—you may choose more than one—designates Bryant's tone in "The Prairies"?

playful	dignified	sonorous
ironic	informal	fawning
sweet	brassy	jovial
condescending	intimate	sarcastic

Beyond the prairies, pioneers such as the men and women
of the Stevens Party faced the imposing natural barriers of mountains,
deserts, and canyons. As you read the following historical sketch,
ask yourself who the "smart ones" were and whether the author
uses his title satirically or seriously. Also ask yourself what qualities
it took to get through such barriers as the Rockies and the Sierras.

The Smart Ones Got Through

GEORGE R. STEWART

The difference between "an historical event" and "a dramatic event" is well illustrated by the stories of the Stevens Party and the Donner Party. The former is historically important, and the pioneers who composed it brought the first wagons to California and discovered the pass across the Sierra Nevada that serves still as the chief route for railroad, highway, telephone, and airlines. The Donner Party, however, is of negligible importance historically, but the story has been told and retold, published and republished, because of its dramatic details of starvation, cannibalism, murder, heroism, and disaster. Against every American who knows of the one, a thousand must know of the other. As a kind of final irony, the pass discovered by the Stevens Party has come to be known as Donner Pass.[1]

Yet actually the two parties had much in common. They were groups of Middle Westerners, native and foreign-born, migrating to California. Both included women and children, and traveled overland in ox-drawn covered wagons. Over much of the way they followed the same route. Both were overtaken by winter, and faced their chief difficulties because of snow. Some of the Donner Party spent the winter in a cabin built by three members of the Stevens Party. One individual, Caleb Greenwood, actually figures in both stories.

The difference in the significance, however, springs from two differences in actuality. First, the Stevens Party set out in 1844, two years before the Donner Party; they were the trail breakers. Second, the Stevens Party was efficiently run, used good sense, had fairly good luck—in a word, was so successful that it got through without the loss of a single life. The Donner Party, roughly speaking, was just the opposite, and the upshot was that the casualty list piled up to 42, almost half of the total roster and nearly equaling the whole number of persons in the Stevens Party. The latter, incidentally, arrived in California more numerous by two than at the start because of babies born on the road.

The contrast between the parties is shown even in the nature of the sources of material available on them. No one bothered to record much about the nondramatic Stevens Party, and we should have scarcely any details if it had not been for Moses Schallenberger, a lad of seventeen at the time of the actual events, who forty years later dictated to his schoolmarm daughter his memories of the journey. On the other hand, the story of the Donner Party is possibly the

"The Smart Ones Got Through" appeared in *American Heritage* magazine. Reprinted by permission of American Heritage Publishing Company, Inc.

1. **Donner Pass,** pass in the Sierra Nevada mountains; today the site of a weather bureau observatory and crossed by a highway.

Council Bluffs Ferry and Cottonwood trees.

best documented incident of any in the early history of the West. Its dramatic quality was such that everyone and his brother rushed in to tell what he knew about it or thought he knew about it, either at first- or second-hand, and publishers took it all.

Of course, this is still the everyday tale. Drive efficiently about your business, and no one ever hears of you. Scatter broken glass and blood over the highway, and a picture of the twisted wreck makes the front page . . .

The Donner Party—to summarize briefly—was formed from family groups of other emigrant parties in July, 1846, and set out by themselves from Little Sandy Creek, in what is now Wyoming, to reach California by the so-called Hastings Route. They lost much time, found the gateway to California blocked by snow, built cabins to winter it out, and ran short of food. Soon they were snowed in deeply, and began to die of starvation. A few escaped across

the mountains on improvised snowshoes. Others were saved by the heroic work of rescue parties from the settlements in California. As the result of hardships the morale of the party degenerated to the point of inhumanity, cannibalism, and possibly murder. Of 89 people—men, women, and children—involved with the misfortunes of the party, 47 survived, and 42 perished.

The Stevens Party left Council Bluffs[2] on May 18, 1844. Before doing so, they performed what may well have been the act that contributed most to their final success—they elected Elisha[3] Stevens to be their captain.

He was an unusual enough sort of fellow, that Stevens—about forty years old with a big hawk nose and a peaked head; strange-acting, too. He seemed friendly enough, but he was solitary, having his own wagon but neither chick nor child. Born in South Carolina, raised in Georgia, he had trapped in the Rockies for some years, then spent a while in Louisiana, and now finally he was off for California, though no one knows why.

How such a man came to be elected captain is more than can be easily figured out. How did he get more votes than big-talking Dr. John Townsend, the only member of the party with professional status and of some education? Or more than Martin Murphy, Jr., who could muster kinsmen and fellow Irishmen numerous enough to make up a majority of votes? Perhaps Stevens was a compromise candidate between the native American and the Irish contingents that split the party and might well have brought quarrels and disaster. He had good experience behind him, indeed. And perhaps there was something about him that marked him for the natural leader of men that he apparently was. His election seems to me one of those events giving rise to the exclamation, "It makes you believe in democracy!"

2. **Council Bluffs,** southwest Iowa, on the Missouri River opposite Omaha, Nebraska; center for emigrants bound for California.
3. **Elisha**\ē ▲lai·sha\.

Yes, he took the wagons through. If there were justice in history, his name would stand on the pass he found and conquered, and not merely on a little creek that runs into San Francisco Bay.

So they pushed off from the Missouri River that spring day, numbering 26 men, eight women, and about seventeen children. During the first part of the journey they traveled in company with a larger party bound for Oregon. The swollen Elkhorn River[4] blocked the way, but they emptied the wagons, ferried everything across in a waterproofed wagon bed, swam the cattle, and kept ahead. They chased buffalo, saw their first wild Indians at Fort Laramie.[5] At Independence Rock they halted a week to rest the oxen, "make meat" by hunting buffalo, and allow Helen Independence Miller to be born. They were the first to take wagons across the Green River Desert by what was later known as Sublette's (or Greenwood's) cutoff. On the cutoff they suffered from thirst, had their cattle stampede (but got them back), were scared by a Sioux[6] war party (but had no real trouble). All this, of course, is mere routine for a covered wagon journey, nothing to make copy of.

At Fort Hall they separated from the Oregon party. At Raft River, eleven wagons in the line, they left the Oregon Trail, and headed south and west, following the wheel tracks of an emigrant party that Joe Walker, the famous mountain man, had tried to take to California the year before. Whether the people in the Stevens Party knew of his failure—the people got through, but the wagons were abandoned—is only one of the many details we do not know. Uneventfully and monotonously they followed his trail all the way to Humboldt Sink,[7] a matter of 500 miles. Then, after careful scouting and on the advice of an intelligent Paiute[8] chief, whom they called Truckee, they decided to quit following Walker and strike west.

From that point they were on their own, making history by breaking trail for the forty-niners, the Central Pacific, and U.S. 40. They made it across the Forty-Mile Desert with less trouble

than might have been expected, considering that they were the first. Even so, the crossing took 48 hours, and the oxen were thirst-crazed by the time they approached the cottonwoods marking the line of a stream. The men of the party, with their usual good sense, unyoked the oxen some distance from the stream to prevent them from scenting water while still attached to the wagons and stampeding toward it. Thankful to their guide, the emigrants named the stream the Truckee, and prudently camped two days among its cottonwoods for rest and recuperation.

They knew no route, except to follow the river. The canyon got tighter and tighter until in places they merely took their wagons upstream like river boats. The oxen began to give out, hoofs softening because of being in the water so much. Now it came November, and a foot of snow fell. The oxen would have starved except for some tall rushes growing along the water.

Finally they came to where the river forked. Which way to go? They held "a consultation," which must have been close to a council of desperation. It was past the middle of November—snow two feet deep now, high mountain crags in view ahead, oxen footsore and gaunt, food low, womenfolks getting scared. But they were good men and staunch. They must have been—or we would have had the Donner story two years earlier.

Yes, there must have been some good men, and we know the names, if not much else about them. Old Caleb Greenwood the trapper was there, and he would have been heard with respect, though personally I do not cast him for the hero's part, as some do. Neither do I have much confidence in "Doc" Townsend, though

---

4. **Elkhorn River,** river in northeast Nebraska that flows into the Platte River.
5. **Fort Laramie,** in southeastern Wyoming.
6. **Sioux**\sū\ Indian tribe that lived on the northern plains of the United States.
7. **Humboldt Sink,** lake in western Nevada.
8. **Paiute**\ˈpaɪ·ūt\ Shoshonean tribe living in western Utah, northwestern Arizona, southeastern Nevada, and southeastern California.

The Murphy Party in the Sierras, 1844.
In the foreground is represented
the Indian guide, "Old Truckee," pointing
out the trail to Martin Murphy.
Donner Lake in the distance.

his name is sometimes used to identify the whole party; he was full of wild ideas. But "Young" Martin Murphy, Irish as his name, was probably a good man, and so, I think, was Dennis Martin, Irish too. Then there was Hitchcock, whose Christian name has been lost because everyone has referred to him just as "Old Man" Hitchcock; he should have been valuable in the council, having been a mountain man in his day. But the one on whom I put my money is Stevens himself, who had taken them all the way, so far, without losing a man.

He or some other, or all of them together, worked out the plan, and it came out in the end as what we would call today a calculated risk, with a certain hedging of the bets. Leave five wagons below the pass at what is now called Donner Lake,[9] and three young men with them, volunteers, to build a cabin and guard the wagons and goods through the winter. Take six wagons ahead over the pass, and

with them the main body including all the mothers and children. Up the other fork of the river, send a party of two women and four men, all young, well-mounted and well-armed, prepared to travel light and fast and live off the country. Unencumbered they can certainly make it through somewhere; when they get to Sutter's Fort,[10] they can have help sent back, if necessary.

So Captain Stevens and the main body took the six wagons ahead to the west, and with a heave and a ho, in spite of sheer granite ledges and ever-deepening snow, they hoisted those wagons up the pass, which is really not a pass so much as the face of a mountain. Even today, when you view those granite slopes, close to precipices, and imagine taking wagons up through the snow, it seems incredible.

Beyond the pass, some days' journey, they got snowed in, but by that time they were over

---

9. **Donner Lake,** few miles northwest of Lake Tahoe, boundary of California and Nevada.
10. **Sutter's Fort,** built by John Augustus Sutter who came to California in 1838; while building a mill, he discovered gold.

the worst. On Yuba River[11] they built a cabin to winter it out, and Elizabeth Yuba Murphy was born there. Eventually all of them, including E. Y. M., together with the wagons, got safely through to Sutter's.

As for the light-cavalry unit that took the other fork, they went up the stream, were the first white people of record to stand on the shore of Lake Tahoe, then turned west across the mountains. They suffered hardship, but got through.

That brings everybody in except the three young men who were with the wagons at the lake. They had built themselves a cabin, and were just settling down to enjoy a pleasant winter of hunting in the woods when snow started falling. Before long, the cabin was up to the eaves, all game had disappeared, no man could walk. The three were left with two starving cows that they slaughtered, but they themselves were soon close to starving. They decided to get out of there fast, and so manufactured themselves crude snowshoes of the hickory strips that held up the canvases on the covered wagons.

One morning they set out—each with ten pounds of dried beef, rifle and ammunition, and two blankets. The snow was light and powdery, ten feet deep. The improvised snowshoes were heavy and clumsy, and exhausting to use. By evening the three had reached the summit of the pass, but young Moses Schallenberger, a mere gawky lad of seventeen, was sick and exhausted.

In the morning he realized that he could not make it through. Rather than impede his companions, he said good-by and turned back—with no expectation but death. The two others went on, and reached Sutter's Fort.

All in now but Moses Schallenberger! He had barely managed to make it back, collapsing at the very cabin and having to drag himself over the doorsill. He felt a little better the next day, forced himself to go out hunting on his snowshoes, saw nothing except fox tracks. Back at the cabin, "discouraged and sick at heart," he

happened to notice some traps that Captain Stevens had left behind.

Next day he set traps, and during the night caught a coyote. He tried eating it, but found the flesh revolting, no matter how cooked. Still, he managed to live on that meat for three days, and then found two foxes in the traps. To his delight, the fox meat was delicious. This was about the middle of December. From then on, he managed to trap foxes and coyotes. He lived on the former, and hung the latter up to freeze, always fearing that he would have to eat another one, but keeping them as a reserve.

Alone in the snow-buried cabin, through the dim days and long nights of midwinter, week after week, assailed by fierce storms, often despairing of his life, he suffered from deep depression. As he put it later, "My life was more miserable than I can describe," but he never lost the will to live. Fortunately he found some books that "Doc" Townsend had been taking to California, and reading became his solace. The two works that he later mentioned as having pored over were the poems of Byron, and (God save the Mark!) the letters of Lord Chesterfield.[12]

Thus the boy lived on, despondent but resolute, eating his foxes and hanging up his coyotes until he had a line of eleven of them. The weeks dragged along until it was the end of February, and still the snow was deep and the mountain winter showed no sign of breaking. Then, one evening a little before sunset, he was standing near the cabin, and suddenly saw someone approaching. At first he imagined it to be an Indian, but then he recognized his old comrade Dennis Martin!

Martin had traveled a long road since he went over the pass with the main body, in the middle of November. He had been picked up in the swirl of a California revolution[13] and

11. **Yuba River** \ˈyü·bə\ river in central California that flows into the Sacramento River.
12. **Letters of Lord Chesterfield** (1694–1773), written to his son and containing witty advice to a young gentleman about manners and behavior.
13. **California revolution,** possibly a reference to the attempts of Californians to gain independence from Mexico, 1844–1848.

marched south almost to Los Angeles. Returning, he had heard of Schallenberger's being left behind, and had come across the pass on snowshoes to see if he were still alive to be rescued.

Martin had lived for some years in Canada, and was an expert on snowshoes. He made a good pair for Schallenberger, and taught him their use. Thus aided, the lad made it over the pass without great difficulty. The last one was through!

The men of the party even went back the next summer, and brought out the wagons that had been left east of the pass. The only loss was their contents, taken by wandering Indians, except for the firearms, which the Indians considered bad medicine . . .

If we return to the story that offers natural comparison with that of the Stevens Party, we must admit that the historical significance of the Donner Party is negligible. The road that the Donners cut through the Wasatch Mountains was useful to the Mormons when they settled by Great Salt Lake, but they would have got through without it. The Donners served as a kind of horrible example to later emigrants, and so may have helped to prevent other such covered wagon disasters. That is about all that can be totaled up.

There is, of course, no use arguing. The Donner Party has what it takes for a good story, even a dog—everything, you might say, except young love. So, when I drive past the massive bronze statue of the Donner Memorial and up over the pass, I think of these folk who endured and struggled, and died or lived, to produce what may be called the story of stories of the American frontier.

But as I drive over the pass, fighting the summer traffic of U.S. 40 or the winter blizzard, I also like to remember those earlier ones, to think of hawk-nosed Elisha Stevens; of Caleb Greenwood and "Old Man" Hitchcock; or gawky Moses Schallenberger, letting his comrades go on and facing death; of Mrs. Townsend, Moses' sister, riding her Indian pony with the horseback party; of Martin Murphy

and fantastic "Doc" Townsend; of Dennis Martin who knew about snowshoes.

These are the ones who discovered the pass and took the wagons over, who kept out of emergencies or had the wit and strength to overcome them, who did not make a good story by getting into trouble, but made history by keeping out of trouble.

––––––––––––––––––

I
THE QUALITIES
THAT MAKE TRAILBLAZERS

In 1840 there were more than 45 inhabitants per square mile in the state of Connecticut, but almost everywhere west of the Mississippi there were fewer than 6 inhabitants per square mile. Even in 1850—after gold had been discovered—California, a state thirty times larger than Connecticut, had a population of only 92,000 while the population of Connecticut was more than 370,000. It is obvious that many persons preferred not to move westward, at least not until the paths to the West were well-worn.

What were some of the important qualities of the men and women of the Stevens Party? What qualities did they possess before they left home? What qualities did they develop because of the conditions under which they traveled?

II
IMPLICATIONS

Each of the following statements is at least partly true. Rewrite each statement, adding or deleting a word or phrase in such a way that it more accurately expresses your own opinion. In some cases you may want to add a sentence or more to the original statement.

1. Those who remained in the East in the 1840's were less courageous than those who went West.

2. History-making events are made by those who keep out of trouble.

3. The men and women of the Stevens Party were not romantic heroes, but just average persons like "you and me."

4. In a democratic group a man has to be popular in order to get elected to a position of leadership.

5. "Historical events" and "dramatic events" are typically poles apart.

III
TECHNIQUES

George Stewart's "The Smart Ones Got Through" is probably best classified as an *essay;* it is nonfictional and its author's main intention is to communicate an idea. Stewart, however, knows that a reader's attention may best be gained and held when ideas are absorbed in events and people. Partly because of this, his essay has a large narrative element.

Setting

Stewart wrote his essay for *American Heritage* magazine. He could therefore assume that his audience knew something about and was interested in the American past. For this reason his use of place names—Elkhorn River, Sublette's cutoff, Fort Hall, Humboldt Sink, and so forth—is a legitimate method of creating setting. Writers of fiction also use place names to establish setting, but they rarely rely on them as heavily as Stewart has in his essay. How do you account for this difference?

How important is the setting to the action? to the development and revelation of character?

Characterization

An important difference between Stewart's methods of characterization and those typically used by short-story writers is that Stewart never lets his characters speak directly to the reader. What difference did this make in your enjoyment of his essay? Could he have legitimately used this method of characterization? Why, or why not?

IV
WORDS

A. Words gather meaning from the context, and the context determines which meaning of a word is intended. Information given in the sentence or paragraph often provides clues to the meaning of an unfamiliar word. Context clues may be appositives, examples, or references to familiar objects and ideas. Using the contexts of the following sentences, phrases, or clauses, try to determine what the italicized words mean.

1. Jody peered cautiously at her to see whether any *rancor* toward him remained.

2. The story *droned* on, speeded up for the attack, grew sad over the wounds, struck a dirge at the burials. . . .

3. . . . to retract it [a word] in shame was *infinitely* worse.

4. . . . when dog's meat was a *dainty* in Lincolnshire. . . .

5. . . . *compromise* candidate between the native American and the Irish *contingents* that split the party. . . .

6. Fortunately he found some books . . . and reading became his *solace.*

B. The dictionary lists *silent* and *secretive* as synonyms for *taciturn. Taciturn, silent,* and *secretive* share a common meaning, or denotation, and yet they do not mean exactly the same thing. The word *silent* implies the absence of an utterance; *taciturn* suggests a temperamental unwillingness to talk; and *secretive* implies cautious speech. Give two synonyms for each of the italicized words in the following phrases. What common meaning do they share? How do they differ?

(1) have been *immune* from cats; (2) have grown *smug* in their security; (3) looked at them *contemptuously;* (4) Jody *sidled* near; (5) prudently *camped* two days.

C. The English language is word-rich, and many of these words represent the same idea but cannot always be used interchangeably. Consider these words: *eminent, excellent, first-class, crack, cool; fatigued, exhausted, spent, all in, dog-tired, bushed.* The words *eminent* and *fatigued* are more appropriate in a formal or semiformal situation than *crack* or *bushed* which are acceptable in a casual conversation.

Words fall into certain levels of usage determined by the oral or written situation. Decide which of the following words would be more appropriate in a formal conversation or serious writing: *puny—debilitated; precipitation—rainfall; stupefy—flabbergast; ubiquitous—everywhere; laceration—cut.*

With the cry of "Gold!" at Sutter's Mill in California
in 1848, men of adventure all over the world went off to "Californy"
with their wash-pans on their knees. Sailors jumped ship in San Francisco;
pioneers who were headed elsewhere made sudden changes of direction;
and within six months nearly every resident of the Far West
became a gold miner. Read carefully the long descriptive passage
at the beginning of this story, noting how London's tone reveals
where his sympathies lie in the conflict between man and nature.

All Gold Canyon

JACK LONDON

It was the green heart of the canyon, where the walls swerved back from the rigid plan and relieved their harshness of line by making a little sheltered nook and filling it to the brim with sweetness and roundness and softness. Here all things rested. Even the narrow stream ceased its turbulent downrush long enough to form a quiet pool. Knee-deep in the water, with drooping head and half-shut eyes, drowsed a red-coated, many-antlered buck.

On one side, beginning at the very lip of the pool, was a tiny meadow, a cool, resilient surface of green that extended to the base of the frowning wall. Beyond the pool a gentle slope of earth ran up and up to meet the opposing wall. Fine grass covered the slope—grass that was spangled with flowers, with here and there patches of color, orange and purple and golden. Below, the canyon was shut in. There was no view. The walls leaned together abruptly and the canyon ended in a chaos of rocks, moss-covered and hidden by a green screen of vines and creepers and boughs of trees. Up the canyon rose far hills and peaks, the big foothills, pine-covered and remote. And far beyond, like clouds upon the border of the sky, towered minarets of white, where the Sierra's eternal snows flashed austerely the blazes of the sun.

There was no dust in the canyon. The leaves and flowers were clean and virginal. The grass was young velvet. Over the pool three cottonwoods sent their snowy fluffs fluttering down the quiet air. On the slope the blossoms of the wine-wooded manzanita[1] filled the air with springtime odors, while the leaves, wise with experience, were already beginning their vertical twist against the coming aridity of summer. In the open spaces on the slope, beyond the farthest shadow-reach of the manzanita, poised the mariposa lilies,[2] like so many flights of jeweled moths suddenly arrested and on the verge of trembling into flight again. Here and there that woods harlequin,[3] the madroña,[4] permitting itself to be caught in the act of changing its pea-green trunk to madder red, breathed its fragrance into the air from great clusters of waxen bells. Creamy white were these bells, shaped like lilies of the valley, with

---

1. **manzanita**\\'man·zə ▲nē·da\ a variety of several evergreen shrubs of the western United States.
2. **mariposa lilies**\ma·rə·▲pō·sə\ plants of the lily family whose flowers of white, red, yellow, or violet are somewhat turban, or tulip, shaped.
3. **harlequin**\\▲har·lə 'kwĭn\ a comic character dressed in multicolored tights, usually carrying a wooden wand or sword.
4. **madroña**\ma ▲drō·nya\ an evergreen tree or shrub with smooth bark, large shiny leaves, and edible red berries.

Reprinted by permission of Mr. Irving Shepard.

the sweetness of perfume that is of the spring-time.

There was not a sigh of wind. The air was drowsy with its weight of perfume. It was a sweetness that would have been cloying had the air been heavy and humid. But the air was sharp and thin. It was as starlight transmuted into atmosphere, shot through and warmed by sunshine, and flower-drenched with sweetness.

An occasional butterfly drifted in and out through the patches of light and shade. And from all about rose the low and sleepy hum of mountain bees—feasting sybarites[5] that jostled one another good-naturedly at the board, nor found time for rough discourtesy. So quietly did the little stream drip and ripple its way through the canyon that it spoke only in faint and occasional gurgles. The voice of the stream was as a drowsy whisper, ever interrupted by dozings and silences, ever lifted again in the awakenings.

The motion of all things was a drifting in the heart of the canyon. Sunshine and butterflies drifted in and out among the trees. The hum of the bees and the whisper of the stream were a drifting of sound. And the drifting sound and drifting color seemed to weave together in the making of a delicate and intangible fabric which was the spirit of the place. It was a spirit of peace that was not of death, but of smooth-pulsing life, of quietude that was not silence, of movement that was not action, of repose that was quick with existence without being violent with struggle and travail. The spirit of the place was the spirit of the peace of the living, somnolent with the easement and content of prosperity, and undisturbed by rumors of far wars.

The red-coated, many-antlered buck acknowledged the lordship of the spirit of the place and dozed knee-deep in the cool, shaded pool. There seemed no flies to vex him and he was languid with rest. Sometimes his ears moved when the stream awoke and whispered; but they moved lazily, with foreknowledge that it was merely the stream grown garrulous at discovery that it had slept.

The "well-dressed" miner in 1857.

But there came a time when the buck's ears lifted and tensed with swift eagerness for sound. His head was turned down the canyon. His sensitive, quivering nostrils scented the air. His eyes could not pierce the green screen through which the stream rippled away, but to his ears came the voice of a man. It was a steady, monotonous, singsong voice. Once the buck heard the harsh clash of metal upon rock. At the sound he snorted with a sudden start that jerked him through the air from water to meadow, and his feet sank into the young velvet, while he pricked his ears and again scented

---

5. **sybarites**\ˈsibə ˈrīts\ inhabitants of the ancient city of Sybaris, a city noted for its love of luxury and pleasure.

the air. Then he stole across the tiny meadow, pausing once and again to listen, and faded away out of the canyon like a wraith,[6] soft-footed and without sound.

The clash of steel-shod soles against the rocks began to be heard, and the man's voice grew louder. It was raised in a sort of chant and became distinct with nearness, so that the words could be heard:

"Tu'n around an' tu'n yo' face
Untoe them sweet hills of grace.
*   (D' pow'rs of sin yo' am scornin'!)*
Look about an' look aroun',
Fling yo' sin pack on d' groun'.
*   (Yo' will meet wid d' Lord in d' mornin'!)"*

A sound of scrambling accompanied the song, and the spirit of the place fled away on the heels of the red-coated buck. The green screen was burst asunder, and a man peered out at the meadow and the pool and the sloping sidehill. He was a deliberate sort of man. He took in the scene with one embracing glance, then ran his eyes over the details to verify the general impression. Then, and not until then, did he open his mouth in vivid and solemn approval:

"Smoke of life an' snakes of purgatory! Will you just look at that! Wood an' water an' grass an' a sidehill! A pocket hunter's[7] delight an' a cayuse's[8] paradise! Cool green for tired eyes! Pink pills for pale people ain't in it. A secret pasture for prospectors and a resting place for tired burros by damn!"

He was a sandy-complexioned man in whose face geniality and humor seemed the salient characteristics. It was a mobile face, quick-changing to inward mood and thought. Thinking was in him a visible process. Ideas chased across his face like windflaws across the surface of a lake. His hair, sparse and unkempt of growth, was as indeterminate and colorless as his complexion. It would seem that all the color of his frame had gone into his eyes, for they were startlingly blue. Also they were laughing and merry eyes, within them much of the naïveté and wonder of the child; and yet, in an unassertive way, they contained much of calm self-reliance and strength of purpose founded upon self-experience and experience of the world.

From out the screen of vines and creepers he flung ahead of him a miner's pick and shovel and gold pan. Then he crawled out himself into the open. He was clad in faded overalls and black cotton shirt, with hobnailed brogans[9] on his feet, and on his head a hat whose shapelessness and stains advertised the rough usage of wind and rain and sun and camp smoke. He stood erect, seeing wide-eyed the secrecy of the scene and sensuously inhaling the warm, sweet breath of the canyon garden through nostrils that dilated and quivered with delight. His eyes narrowed to laughing slits of blue, his face wreathed itself in joy, and his mouth curled in a smile as he cried aloud:

"Jumping dandelions and happy hollyhocks, but that smells good to me! Talk about your attar o' roses[10] an' cologne factories! They ain't in it!"

He had the habit of soliloquy. His quick-changing facial expressions might tell every thought and mood, but the tongue, perforce, ran hard after, repeating, like a second Boswell.[11]

The man lay down on the lip of the pool and drank long and deep of its water. "Tastes good to me," he murmured, lifting his head and gazing across the pool at the sidehill, while he wiped his mouth with the back of his hand. The sidehill attracted his attention. Still lying on his stomach, he studied the hill formation long and

6. **wraith\rāth** a ghost, figure of living person supposedly seen just before or after death.
7. **pocket-hunter,** someone who hunts a small cavity containing gold.
8. **cayuse\'kai ᴬūs** a native range horse, an Indian pony.
9. **hobnailed brogans,** coarse shoes of untanned leather with broad-headed nails on the soles to prevent wear or slipping.
10. **attar o' roses,** a fragrant oil made from the petals of roses.
11. **James Boswell** (1740–1795), famed biographer of Samuel Johnson who took meticulous notes of Johnson's conversations.

carefully. It was a practiced eye that traveled up the slope to the crumbling canyon wall and back and down again to the edge of the pool. He scrambled to his feet and favored the side-hill with a second survey.

"Looks good to me," he concluded, picking up his pick and shovel and gold pan.

He crossed the stream below the pool, stepping agilely from stone to stone. Where the sidehill touched the water he dug up a shovelful of dirt and put it into the gold pan. He squatted down, holding the pan in his two hands, and partly immersing it in the stream. Then he imparted to the pan a deft circular motion that sent the water sluicing in and out through the dirt and gravel. The larger and the lighter particles worked to the surface, and these, by a skillful dipping movement of the pan, he spilled out and over the edge. Occasionally, to expedite matters, he rested the pan and with his fingers raked out the large pebbles and pieces of rock.

The contents of the pan diminished rapidly until only fine dirt and the smallest bits of gravel remained. At this stage he began to work very deliberately and carefully. It was fine washing, and he washed fine and finer, with a keen scrutiny and delicate and fastidious touch. At last the pan seemed empty of everything but water; but with a quick semicircular flirt[12] that sent the water flying over the shallow rim into the stream he disclosed a layer of black sand on the bottom of the pan. So thin was this layer that it was like a streak of paint. He examined it closely. In the midst of it was a tiny golden speck. He dribbled a little water in over the depressed edge of the pan. With a quick flirt he sent the water sluicing across the bottom, turning the grains of black sand over and over. A second tiny golden speck rewarded his effort.

The washing had now become very fine— fine beyond all need of ordinary placer mining.[13] He worked the black sand, a small portion at a time, up the shallow rim of the pan. Each small portion he examined sharply, so that his eyes saw every grain of it before he allowed it to slide over the edge and away. Jeal-

ously, bit by bit, he let the black sand slip away. A golden speck, no larger than a pin point, appeared on the rim, and by his manipulation of the water it returned to the bottom of the pan. And in such fashion another speck was disclosed, and another. Great was his care of them. Like a shepherd he herded his flock of golden specks so that not one should be lost. At last, of the pan of dirt nothing remained but his golden herd. He counted it, and then, after all his labor, sent it flying out of the pan with one final swirl of water.

But his blue eyes were shining with desire as he rose to his feet. "Seven," he muttered aloud, asserting the sum of the specks for which he had toiled so hard and which he had so wantonly thrown away. "Seven," he repeated, with the emphasis of one trying to impress a number on his memory.

He stood still a long while, surveying the hillside. In his eyes was a curiosity, now-aroused and burning. There was an exultance about his bearing and a keenness like that of a hunting animal catching the fresh scent of game.

He moved down the stream a few steps and took a second panful of dirt.

Again came the careful washing, the jealous herding of the golden specks, and the wantonness with which he sent them flying into the stream when he had counted their number.

"Five," he muttered, and repeated, "five."

He could not forbear another survey of the hill before filling the pan farther down the stream. His golden herds diminished. "Four, three, two, two, one," were his memory tabulations as he moved down the stream. When but one speck of gold rewarded his washing he stopped and built a fire of dry twigs. Into this he thrust the gold pan and burned it till it was blue-black. He held up the pan and examined it critically. Then he nodded approbation. Against such a color background he could defy the tiniest yellow speck to elude him.

---

12. **flirt,** a rapid, jerky movement.
13. **placer** **plă·sĕr**\\ **mining,** the process of extracting gold by washing away sand and gravel.

This old print shows the many different methods used to mine gold in California.

Still moving down the stream, he panned again. A single speck was his reward. A third pan contained no gold at all. Not satisfied with this, he panned three times again, taking his shovels of dirt within a foot of one another. Each pan proved empty of gold, and the fact, instead of discouraging him, seemed to give him satisfaction. His elation increased with each barren washing, until he arose, exclaiming jubilantly:

"If it ain't the real thing, may God knock off my head with sour apples! "

Returning to where he had started operations, he began to pan up the stream. At first his golden herds increased—increased prodigiously. "Fourteen, eighteen, twenty-one, twenty-six," ran his memory tabulations. Just above the pool he struck his richest pan—thirty-five colors.

"Almost enough to save," he remarked regretfully as he allowed the water to sweep them away.

The sun climbed to the top of the sky. The man worked on. Pan by pan he went up the stream, the tally of results steadily decreasing.

"It's just booful, the way it peters out," he exulted when a shovelful of dirt contained no more than a single speck of gold.

And when no specks at all were found in several pans he straightened up and favored the hillside with a confident glance.

"Aha! Mr. Pocket!" he cried out as though to an auditor hidden somewhere above him beneath the surface of the slope. "Aha! Mr. Pocket! I'm a-comin', I'm a-comin', an' I'm shorely gwine to get yer! You heah me, Mr. Pocket? I'm gwine to get yer as shore as punkins ain't cauliflowers!"

He turned and flung a measuring glance at the sun poised above him in the azure of the cloudless sky. Then he went down the canyon, following the line of shovel holes he had made in filling the pans. He crossed the stream below the pool and disappeared through the green screen. There was little opportunity for the spirit of the place to return with its quietude and repose, for the man's voice, raised in rag-time song, still dominated the canyon with possession.

After a time, with a greater clashing of steel-shod feet on rock, he returned. The green screen was tremendously agitated. It surged back and forth in the throes of a struggle. There was a loud grating and clanging of metal. The man's voice leaped to a higher pitch and was sharp with imperativeness. A large body plunged and panted. There was a snapping and ripping and rending, and amid a shower of falling leaves a horse burst through the screen. On its back was a pack, and from this trailed broken vines and torn creepers. The animal gazed with astonished eyes at the scene into which it had been precipitated, then dropped its head to the grass and began contentedly to graze. A second horse scrambled into view, slipping once on the mossy rocks and regaining equilibrium when its hoofs sank into the yielding surface of the meadow. It was riderless, though on its back was a high-horned Mexican saddle, scarred and discolored by long usage.

The man brought up the rear. He threw off pack and saddle, with an eye to camp location, and gave the animals their freedom to graze. He unpacked his food and got out frying pan and coffeepot. He gathered an armful of dry wood, and with a few stones made a place for his fire.

"My," he said, "but I've got an appetite! I could scoff iron filings an' horseshoe nails an' thank you kindly, ma'am, for a second helpin'."

He straightened up, and while he reached for matches in the pocket of his overalls his eyes traveled across the pool to the sidehill. His fingers had clutched the matchbox, but they relaxed their hold and the hand came out empty. The man wavered perceptibly. He looked at his preparations for cooking and he looked at the hill.

"Guess I'll take another whack at her," he concluded, starting to cross the stream.

"They ain't no sense in it, I know," he mumbled apologetically. "But keepin' grub back an hour ain't goin' to hurt none, I reckon."

A few feet back from his first line of test pans he started a second line. The sun dropped down the western sky, the shadows lengthened, but the man worked on. He began a third line of test pans. He was crosscutting the hillside, line by line, as he ascended. The center of each line produced the richest pans, while the ends came where no colors showed in the pan. And as he ascended the hillside the lines grew perceptibly shorter. The regularity with which their length diminished served to indicate that somewhere up the slope the last line would be so short as to have scarcely length at all, and that beyond could come only a point. The design was growing into an inverted V. The converging sides of this V marked the boundaries of the gold-bearing dirt.

The apex of the V was evidently the man's goal. Often he ran his eye along the converging sides and on up the hill, trying to divine the apex, the point where the gold-bearing dirt must cease. Here resided "Mr. Pocket"—for so the man familiarly addressed the imaginary point above him on the slope, crying out:

"Come down, out o' that, Mr. Pocket. Be right smart an' agreeable, an' come down!"

"All right," he would add later, in a voice resigned to determination. "All right, Mr. Pocket. It's plain to me I got to come right up an' snatch you out bald-headed. An' I'll do it! I'll do it!" he would threaten still later.

Each pan he carried down to the water to wash, and as he went higher up the hill the pans grew richer, until he began to save the gold in an empty baking-powder can which he carried carelessly in his lap pocket. So engrossed was he in his toil that he did not notice the long twilight of oncoming night. It was not until he tried vainly to see the gold colors in the bottom of the pan that he realized the passage of time. He straightened up abruptly. An expression of whimsical wonderment and awe overspread his face as he drawled:

"Gosh darn my buttons, if I didn't plumb forget dinner!"

He stumbled across the stream in the darkness and lighted his long-delayed fire. Flapjacks and bacon and warmed-over beans constituted his supper. Then he smoked a pipe by the smoldering coals, listening to the night noises and watching the moonlight stream through the canyon. After that he unrolled his bed, took off his heavy shoes, and pulled the blankets up to his chin. His face showed white in the moonlight, like the face of a corpse. But it was a corpse that knew its resurrection, for the man rose suddenly on one elbow and gazed across at his hillside.

"Good night, Mr. Pocket," he called sleepily. "Good night."

He slept through the early gray of morning until the direct rays of the sun smote his closed eyelids, when he awoke with a start and looked about him until he had established the continuity of his existence and identified his present self with the days previously lived.

To dress, he had merely to buckle on his shoes. He glanced at his fireplace and at his hillside, wavered, but fought down the temptation and started the fire.

"Keep yer shirt on, Bill; keep yer shirt on," he admonished himself. "What's the good of rushin'? No use in gettin' all het up an' sweaty. Mr. Pocket'll wait for you. He ain't a runnin' away before you can get yer breakfast. Now what you want, Bill, is something fresh in yer bill o' fare. So it's up to you to go an' get it."

He cut a short pole at the water's edge and drew from one of his pockets a bit of line and a draggled fly that had once been a royal coachman.

"Mebbe they'll bite in the early morning," he muttered as he made his first cast into the pool. And a moment later he was gleefully crying: "What'd I tell you, eh? What'd I tell you?"

He had no reel nor any inclination to waste time, and by main strength, and swiftly, he drew out of the water a flashing ten-inch trout. Three more, caught in rapid succession, furnished his breakfast. When he came to the steppingstones on his way to his hillside, he was struck by a sudden thought, and paused.

"I'd just better take a hike downstream a ways," he said. "There's no tellin' what cuss may be snoopin' around."

But he crossed over on the stones, and with a "I really oughter take that hike" the need of the precaution passed out of his mind and he fell to work.

At nightfall he straightened up. The small of his back was stiff from stooping toil, and as he put his hand behind him to soothe the protesting muscles he said:

"Now what d'ye think of that, by damn? I clean forgot my dinner again! If I don't watch out I'll sure be degeneratin' into a two-meal-a-day crank."

"Pockets is the damnedest things I ever see for makin' a man absentminded," he communed that night as he crawled into his blankets. Nor did he forget to call up the hillside, "Good night, Mr. Pocket! Good night!"

Rising with the sun, and snatching a hasty breakfast, he was early at work. A fever seemed to be growing in him, nor did the increasing richness of the test pans allay this fever. There was a flush in his cheek other than that made by the heat of the sun, and he was oblivious to fatigue and the passage of time. When he filled a pan with dirt he ran down the hill to wash it; nor could he forbear running up the hill again, panting and stumbling profanely, to refill the pan.

He was now a hundred yards from the water, and the inverted V was assuming definite proportions. The width of the pay dirt steadily decreased, and the man extended in his mind's eye the sides of the V to their meeting place far up the hill. This was his goal, the apex of the V, and he panned many times to locate it.

"Just about two yards above the manzanita bush an' a yard to the right," he finally concluded.

Then the temptation seized him. "As plain as the nose on your face," he said as he abandoned his laborious crosscutting and climbed to the indicated apex. He filled a pan and carried it down the hill to wash. It contained no trace of gold. He dug deep, and he dug shallow, filling and washing a dozen pans, and was unrewarded even by the tiniest golden speck. He was enraged at having yielded to the temptation, and cursed himself blasphemously and pridelessly. Then he went down the hill and took up the crosscutting.

"Slow an' certain, Bill; slow an' certain," he crooned. "Short cuts to fortune ain't in your line, an' it's about time you know it. Get wise, Bill; get wise. Slow an' certain's the only hand you can play; so go to it, an' keep to it, too."

As the crosscuts decreased, showing that the sides of the V were converging, the depth of the V increased. The gold trace was dipping into the hill. It was only at thirty inches beneath the surface that he could get colors in his pan. The dirt he found at twenty-five inches from the surface, and at thirty-five inches, yielded barren pans. At the base of the V, by the water's edge, he had found the gold colors at the grass roots. The higher he went up the hill, the deeper the gold dipped. To dig a hole three feet deep in order to get one test pan was a task of no mean magnitude; while between the man and the apex intervened an untold number of such holes to be dug. "An' there's no tellin' how much deeper it'll pitch,"[14] he sighed in a moment's pause, while his fingers soothed his aching back.

Feverish with desire, with aching back and stiffening muscles, with pick and shovel gouging and mauling the soft brown earth, the man toiled up the hill. Before him was the smooth slope, spangled with flowers and made sweet with their breath. Behind him was devastation. It looked like some terrible eruption breaking out on the smooth skin of the hill. His slow progress was like that of a slug, befouling beauty with a monstrous trail.

Though the dipping gold trace increased the man's work, he found consolation in the increasing richness of the pans. Twenty cents, thirty cents, fifty cents, sixty cents, were the values of the gold found in the pans, and at nightfall he washed his banner pan, which gave him a dollar's worth of gold dust from a shovelful of dirt.

"I'll just bet it's my luck to have some inquisitive cuss come buttin' in here on my pasture," he mumbled sleepily that night as he pulled the blankets up to his chin.

Suddenly he sat upright. "Bill!" he called sharply. "Now listen to me, Bill; d'ye hear! It's up to you, tomorrow mornin', to mosey round an' see what you can see. Understand? Tomorrow morning, an' don't you forget it!"

He yawned and glanced across at his sidehill. "Good night, Mr. Pocket," he called.

In the morning he stole a march on the sun, for he had finished breakfast when its first rays caught him, and he was climbing the wall of the canyon where it crumbled away and gave footing. From the outlook at the top he found himself in the midst of loneliness. As far as he could see, chain after chain of mountains heaved themselves into his vision. To the east his eyes, leaping the miles between range and range and between many ranges, brought up at last against the white-peaked Sierras—the main crest, where the backbone of the Western world reared itself against the sky. To the north and south he could see more distinctly the cross systems that broke through the main trend of the sea of mountains. To the west the ranges fell away, one behind the other, diminishing and fading into the gentle foothills that, in turn, descended into the great valley which he could not see.

And in all that mighty sweep of earth he saw no sign of man nor of the handiwork of man—save only the torn bosom of the hillside at his feet. The man looked long and carefully. Once, far down his own canyon, he thought he saw in the air a faint hint of smoke. He looked again and decided that it was the purple haze of the hills made dark by a convolution of the canyon wall at its back.

"Hey, you, Mr. Pocket!" he called down into the canyon. "Stand out from under! I'm a-comin', Mr. Pocket! I'm a-comin'!"

The heavy brogans on the man's feet made him appear clumsy-footed, but he swung down

---

14. **pitch**, refers to the downward slant of a vein.

from the giddy height as lightly and airily as a mountain goat. A rock, turning under his foot on the edge of the precipice, did not disconcert him. He seemed to know the precise time required for the turn to culminate in disaster, and in the meantime he utilized the false footing itself for the momentary earth contact necessary to carry him on into safety. Where the earth sloped so steeply that it was impossible to stand for a second upright, the man did not hesitate. His foot pressed the impossible surface for but a fraction of the fatal second and gave him the bound that carried him onward. Again, where even the fraction of a second's footing was out of the question, he would swing his body past by a moment's handgrip on a jutting knob of rock, a crevice, or a precariously rooted shrub. At last, with a wild leap and yell, he exchanged the face of the wall for an earth slide and finished the descent in the midst of several tons of sliding earth and gravel.

His first pan of the morning washed out over two dollars in coarse gold. It was from the center of the V. To either side the diminution in the values of the pans was swift. His lines of crosscutting holes were growing very short. The converging sides of the inverted V were only a few yards apart. Their meeting point was only a few yards above him. But the pay streak was dipping deeper and deeper into the earth. By early afternoon he was sinking the test holes five feet before the pans could show the gold trace.

For that matter the gold trace had become something more than a trace; it was a placer mine in itself, and the man resolved to come back after he had found the pocket and work over the ground. But the increasing richness of the pans began to worry him. By late afternoon the worth of the pans had grown to three and four dollars. The man scratched his head perplexedly and looked a few feet up the hill at the manzanita bush that marked approximately the apex of the V. He nodded his head and said oracularly:

"It's one o' two things, Bill; one o' two things. Either Mr. Pocket's spilled himself all out an'

down the hill, or else Mr. Pocket's that damned rich you maybe won't be able to carry him all away with you. And that'd be hell, wouldn't it, now?" He chuckled at contemplation of so pleasant a dilemma.

Nightfall found him by the edge of the stream, his eyes wrestling with the gathering darkness over the washing of a five-dollar pan.

"Wisht I had an electric light to go on working," he said.

He found sleep difficult that night. Many times he composed himself and closed his eyes for slumber to overtake him; but his blood pounded with too strong desire, and as many times his eyes opened and he murmured wearily, "Wisht it was sunup."

Sleep came to him in the end, but his eyes were open with the first paling of the stars, and the gray of dawn caught him with breakfast finished and climbing the hillside in the direction of the secret abiding place of Mr. Pocket.

The first crosscut the man made, there was space for only three holes, so narrow had become the pay streak and so close was he to the fountainhead of the golden stream he had been following for four days.

"Be ca'm, Bill; be ca'm," he admonished himself as he broke ground for the final hole where the sides of the V had at last come together in a point.

"I've got the almighty cinch on you, Mr. Pocket, an' you can't lose me," he said many times as he sank the hole deeper and deeper.

Four feet, five feet, six feet, he dug his way down into the earth. The digging grew harder. His pick grated on broken rock. He examined the rock. "Rotten quartz," was his conclusion as, with the shovel, he cleared the bottom of the hole of loose dirt. He attacked the crumbling quartz with the pick, bursting the disintegrating rock asunder with every stroke.

He thrust his shovel into the loose mass. His eye caught a gleam of yellow. He dropped the shovel and squatted suddenly on his heels. As a farmer rubs the clinging earth from fresh-dug potatoes, so the man, a piece of rotten quartz held in both hands, rubbed the dirt away.

"Sufferin' Sardanopolis!"[15] he cried. "Lumps an' chunks of it! Lumps an' chunks of it!"

It was only half rock he held in his hand. The other half was virgin gold. He dropped it into his pan and examined another piece. Little yellow was to be seen, but with his strong fingers he crumbled the rotten quartz away till both hands were filled with glowing yellow. He rubbed the dirt away from fragment after fragment, tossing them into the gold pan. It was a treasure hole. So much had the quartz rotted away that there was less of it than there was of gold. Now and again he found a piece to which no rock clung—a piece that was all gold. A chunk, where the pick had laid open the heart of the gold, glittered like a handful of yellow jewels, and he cocked his head at it and slowly turned it around and over to observe the rich play of the light upon it.

"Talk about yer Too Much Gold diggin's!" the man snorted contemptuously. "Why, this diggin'd make it look like thirty cents. This diggin' is all gold. An' right here an' now I name this yere canyon 'All Gold Canyon,' b' gosh!"

Still squatting on his heels, he continued examining the fragments and tossing them into the pan. Suddenly there came to him a premonition of danger. It seemed a shadow had fallen upon him. But there was no shadow. His heart had given a great jump up into his throat and was choking him. Then his blood slowly chilled and he felt the sweat of his shirt cold against his flesh.

He did not spring up nor look around. He did not move. He was considering the nature of the premonition he had received, trying to locate the source of the mysterious force that had warned him, striving to sense the imperative presence of the unseen thing that threatened him. There is an aura of things hostile, made manifest by messengers too refined for the senses to know; and this aura he felt, but knew not how he felt it. His was the feeling as when a cloud passes over the sun. It seemed that between him and life had passed something dark and smothering and menacing; a

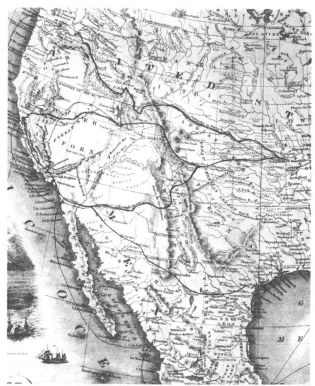

Map of Western United States, 1849, showing land and sea routes to the west coast.

gloom, as it were, that swallowed up life and made for death—his death.

Every force of his being impelled him to spring up and confront the unseen danger, but his soul dominated the panic, and he remained squatting on his heels, in his hands a chunk of gold. He did not dare to look around, but he knew by now that there was something behind him and above him. He made believe to be interested in the gold in his hand. He examined it critically, turned it over and over, and rubbed the dirt from it. And all the time he knew that something behind him was looking at the gold over his shoulder.

Still feigning interest in the chunk of gold in his hand, he listened intently and he heard the

---

15. **Sardanopolis**\ˈsar·də·nǎ ˈpŏ·ləs\ probably a reference to Sardanapalus, a weak, corrupt ruler of Assyria (*c.* 822 B.C.) who supposedly burned himself, his queen, and his treasures when threatened with capture.

breathing of the thing behind him. His eyes searched the ground in front of him for a weapon, but they saw only the uprooted gold, worthless to him now in his extremity. There was his pick, a handy weapon on occasion; but this was not such an occasion. The man realized his predicament. He was in a narrow hole that was seven feet deep. His head did not come to the surface of the ground. He was in a trap.

He remained squatting on his heels. He was quite cool and collected; but his mind, considering every factor, showed him only his helplessness. He continued rubbing the dirt from the quartz fragments and throwing the gold into the pan. There was nothing else for him to do. Yet he knew that he would have to rise up, sooner or later, and face the danger that breathed at his back. The minutes passed, and with the passage of each minute he knew that by so much he was nearer the time when he must stand up or else—and his wet shirt went cold against his flesh again at the thought—or else he might receive death as he stooped there over his treasure.

Still he squatted on his heels, rubbing dirt from gold and debating in just what manner he should rise up. He might rise up with a rush and claw his way out of the hole to meet whatever threatened on the even footing aboveground. Or he might rise up slowly and carelessly, and feign casually to discover the thing that breathed at his back. His instinct and every fighting fiber of his body favored the mad, clawing rush to the surface. His intellect, and the craft thereof, favored the slow and cautious meeting with the thing that menaced and which he could not see. And while he debated, a loud, crashing noise burst on his ear. At the same instant he received a stunning blow on the left side of the back, and from the point of impact felt a rush of flame through his flesh. He sprang up in the air, but halfway to his feet collapsed. His body crumpled in like a leaf withered in sudden heat, and he came down, his chest across his pan of gold, his face in the dirt and rock, his legs tangled and twisted because of the restricted space at the bottom of

the hole. His legs twitched convulsively several times. His body was shaken as with a mighty ague. There was a slow expansion of the lungs, accompanied by a deep sigh. Then the air was slowly, very slowly, exhaled, and his body as slowly flattened itself down into inertness.

Above, revolver in hand, a man was peering down over the edge of the hole. He peered for a long time at the prone and motionless body beneath him. After a while the stranger sat down on the edge of the hole so that he could see into it, and rested the revolver on his knee. Reaching his hand into a pocket, he drew out a wisp of brown paper. Into this he dropped a few crumbs of tobacco. The combination became a cigarette, brown and squat, with the ends turned in. Not once did he take his eyes from the body at the bottom of the hole. He lighted the cigarette and drew its smoke into his lungs with a caressing intake of the breath. He smoked slowly. Once the cigarette went out and he relighted it. And all the while he studied the body beneath him.

In the end he tossed the cigarette stub away and rose to his feet. He moved to the edge of the hole. Spanning it, a hand resting on each edge, and with the revolver still in the right hand, he muscled his body down into the hole. While his feet were yet a yard from the bottom he released his hands and dropped down.

At the instant his feet struck bottom he saw the pocket miner's arm leap out, and his own legs knew a swift, jerking grip that overthrew him. In the nature of the jump his revolver hand was above his head. Swiftly as the grip had flashed about his legs, just as swiftly he brought the revolver down. He was still in the air, his fall in process of completion, when he pulled the trigger. The explosion was deafening in the confined space. The smoke filled the hole so that he could see nothing. He struck the bottom on his back, and like a cat's the pocket miner's body was on top of him. Even as the miner's body passed on top, the stranger crooked in his right arm to fire; and even in that instant the miner, with a quick thrust of elbow, struck his wrist. The muzzle was thrown up and the bullet thudded into the dirt of the side of the hole.

The next instant the stranger felt the miner's hand grip his wrist. The struggle was now for the revolver. Each man strove to turn it against the other's body. The smoke in the hole was clearing. The stranger, lying on his back, was beginning to see dimly. But suddenly he was blinded by a handful of dirt deliberately flung into his eyes by his antagonist. In that moment of shock his grip on the revolver was broken. In the next moment he felt a smashing darkness descend upon his brain, and in the midst of the darkness even the darkness ceased.

But the pocket miner fired again and again, until the revolver was empty. Then he tossed it from him and, breathing heavily, sat down on the dead man's legs.

The miner was sobbing and struggling for breath. "Measly skunk!" he panted; "a-campin' on my trail an' lettin' me do the work, an' then shootin' me in the back!"

He was half crying from anger and exhaustion. He peered at the face of the dead man. It was sprinkled with loose dirt and gravel, and it was difficult to distinguish the features.

"Never laid eyes on him before," the miner concluded his scrutiny. "Just a common an' ordinary thief, damn him! An' he shot me in the back! He shot me in the back!"

He opened his shirt and felt himself, front and back, on his left side.

"Went clean through, and no harm done!" he cried jubilantly. "I'll bet he aimed all right, all right; but he drew the gun over when he pulled the trigger—the cuss! But I fixed 'm! Oh, I fixed 'm!"

His fingers were investigating the bullet hole in his side, and a shade of regret passed over his face. "It's goin' to be stiffer'n hell," he said. "An' it's up to me to get mended an' get out o' here."

He crawled out of the hole and went down the hill to his camp. Half an hour later he returned, leading his pack horse. His open shirt disclosed the rude bandages with which he had dressed his wound. He was slow and awkward with his left-hand movements, but that did not prevent his using the arm.

The bight of the pack rope under the dead man's shoulders enabled him to heave the body out of the hole. Then he set to work gathering up his gold. He worked steadily for several hours, pausing often to rest his stiffening shoulder and to exclaim:

"He shot me in the back, the measly skunk! He shot me in the back!"

When his treasure was quite cleaned up and wrapped securely into a number of blanket-covered parcels, he made an estimate of its value.

"Four hundred pounds or I'm a Hottentot,"[16] he concluded. "Say two hundred in quartz an' dirt—that leaves two hundred pounds of gold. Bill! Wake up! Two hundred pounds of gold! Forty thousand dollars! An' it's yourn—all yourn!"

He scratched his head delightedly and his fingers blundered into an unfamiliar groove. They quested along it for several inches. It was a crease through his scalp where the second bullet had plowed.

He walked angrily over to the dead man.

"You would, would you?" he bullied. "You would, eh? Well, I fixed you good an' plenty, an' I'll give you decent burial, too. That's more'n you'd have done for me."

He dragged the body to the edge of the hole and toppled it in. It struck the bottom with a dull crash, on its side, the face twisted up to the light. The miner peered down at it.

"An' you shot me in the back!" he said accusingly.

With pick and shovel he filled the hole. Then he loaded the gold on his horse. It was too great a load for the animal, and when he had gained his camp he transferred part of it to his saddle horse. Even so, he was compelled to abandon a portion of his outfit—pick and shovel and gold pan, extra food and cooking utensils, and divers odds and ends.

----

16. **Hottentot** \ˈhŏt·ən ˈtŏt\ a member of the Negroid race living in South Africa.

The sun was at the zenith when the man forced the horses at the screen of vines and creepers. To climb the huge boulders the animals were compelled to uprear and struggle blindly through the tangled mass of vegetation. Once the saddle horse fell heavily and the man removed the pack to get the animal on its feet. After it started on its way again the man thrust his head out from among the leaves and peered up at the hillside.

"The measly skunk!" he said, and disappeared.

There was a ripping and tearing of vines and boughs. The trees surged back and forth, marking the passage of the animals through the midst of them. There was a clashing of steel-shod hoofs on stone, and now and again an oath or a sharp cry of command. Then the voice of the man was raised in song:

"Tu'n around an' tu'n yo' face
Untoe them sweet hills of grace.
  (D' pow'rs of sin yo' am scornin'!)
Look about an' look aroun',
Fling yo' sin pack on d' groun'.
  (Yo' will meet wid d' Lord in d' mornin'!)"

The song grew faint and fainter, and through the silence crept back the spirit of the place. The stream once more drowsed and whispered; the hum of the mountain bees rose sleepily. Down through the perfume-weighted air fluttered the snowy fluffs of the cottonwoods. The butterflies drifted in and out among the trees, and over all blazed the quiet sunshine. Only remained the hoofmarks in the meadow and the torn hillside to mark the boisterous trail of the life that had broken the peace of the place and passed on.

I

MAN VS. NATURE, MAN VS. MAN

There are two distinct conflicts in "All Gold Canyon." The one involves the miner and the stranger. The second is between man and nature. How do you know which side the author takes in each conflict? How does London try to sway the reader to his side?

A short-story writer strives for *unity* by trying to create *a single effect,* and therefore his story usually has only one major conflict. Yet "All Gold Canyon" has two conflicts. If in your opinion the story creates a single effect, either one conflict is distinctly minor or some larger consideration gives the story unity by subordinating both conflicts. Assuming that the story does have unity—and therefore is artistically successful and satisfying—what accounts for its unity?

II

IMPLICATIONS

The exploration of frontiers does not involve honor, glory, and romance only. In "All Gold Canyon" London shows negative factors such as greed, murder, and the destruction of nature. What positive qualities of the "westering spirit" does the miner display? What bad qualities does he have? Are they necessarily part of the "westering spirit"?

III

TECHNIQUES

Setting

Jack London shows in "All Gold Canyon" a deep concern for the relationships between man and nature (including animal nature). For him, setting was not merely a matter of establishing a background against which characters could move, but rather an essential element of theme.

Notice how carefully London describes the locality at the beginning of the story and how he communicates its atmosphere of sweetness and tranquillity. Pick out some of the details that create this atmosphere, and then contrast them with the details given when the miner appears with a "harsh clash of metal upon rock." Note particularly the similarity of the description at the beginning and the end of the story, especially the last two paragraphs. What accounts for the similarities?

Tone

It is also of great importance that the reader grasp London's tone; if he does not, he may miss the whole point of the story. Point out some of the words and phrases that show that London regards the miner as an intruder, an alien force. How might he feel about a person who settled on the prairies and built a farm?

Conrad Richter, the author of the following selection,
is a contemporary writer, well-known for both his short stories
and his novels. In the following short story he portrays
two teen-agers—Nancy Belle, sixteen, and her brother Rife, fifteen.
If they seem more mature than teen-agers of today, ask yourself
to what extent the frontier life they led might account
for such greater maturity.

Early Marriage

CONRAD RICHTER

For two days the leathery face of Asa Putman had been a document in cipher to anyone who could read the code. Since Saturday but one traveler had passed his solitary post, a speck of adobe and picket corrals lost on the vast, sandy stretch of the Santa Ana plain. Far as the eye could see from his doorway, the rutted El Paso trail, unfenced, gutterless, innocent of grading, gravel, culverts, or telephone poles, imprinted only by iron tires, the hoofs of horses and oxen, sheep and cattle, and the paw of the loping lobo wolf,[1] lay with dust unraised.

Ordinarily, there were freighters with cracking whips and trailers rumbling on behind. Army trains to and from the forts set up their tents for the night beyond the springs. The private coaches of Santa Fe and Colorado merchants, of cattle kings and Government officials, stopped long enough for the Putman children to admire the ladies, the magnificent woodwork, and the luxurious cushions inside. Trail herds of gaunt red steers bawled for the water in the earthen tank, and pairs and companies of horsemen rode up and down.

But since Saturday not even a solitary buckboard[2] from the far settlements in the Cedar country had called for supplies or letters. Only

a girl from the Blue Mesa had ridden in for her and her neighbors' mail. She had eaten dinner with the Putmans, refused to stay overnight and started her long ride home.

A stranger from the East would have spoken about the stillness, the deadly waiting, and asked uneasily why Uncle Gideon hadn't come as promised. But in the Putman household it was not mentioned.

Asa deliberately busied himself about the post, filling the bin beneath the counter with navy beans and green coffee, leafing through the packet of letters in the drawer, and making a long rite out of feeding the occupants of the picket corrals—four horses of which were fresh for the next stage.

Rife, just turned fifteen, carried water and gathered cow chips[3] in an old hide dragged by a rope to his saddle horn. Ignacita,[4] the Mexican housekeeper, spat sharply on her heavy irons in the torrid kitchen and kept glancing over her shoulder and out of the open door and windows.

And Nancy Belle, going on seventeen, packed and repacked the high, iron-bound trunk that

---

1. **lobo wolf**, a large, broad-headed, gray timber wolf found in western United States.
2. **buckboard**, a horse-drawn vehicle with flooring of sturdy planks laid directly on the axles.
3. **cow chips**, cow dung, dried and used as fuel.
4. **Ignacita**\ĕg·nä ᵃsē·ta\.

her father had bought for her at Santa Fe and sang softly to herself in the way that women sang fifty and sixty years ago.

Saturday she was being married at Gunstock, two hundred miles away—five days' journey in a wagon, four in a saddle or buckboard.

For six months she had thought of little else. The almanac fell apart at June as naturally as her mother's Bible did at the Twenty-third Psalm. So often had she run her finger down the page that anyone might tell from the worn line of type the very day she and Stephen Dewee would be man and wife. The Dewees lived four hundred miles west across the territory in the Beaverhead[5] country. She and Stephen were taking a mountain ranch near his people, and for the wedding they had compromised on Gunstock, nearly equidistant from both families and convenient to friends scattered up and down the Rio Grande.

She had lighted a candle in the dusk, when a figure appeared reluctantly in her doorway. Asa Putman had never been at ease in his daughter's bedroom. A tall, rawhide man in an unbuttoned, sagging vest, he was visibly embarrassed by any furnishings that suggested refinement. Invariably he kept his hat on in the house. He had it on now, a flat top and a flat brim, not so much like the Western hats you see now. Nancy Belle knew that her mother's people had never forgiven him for bringing his young wife and their two small children to this lonely post, at the mercy of outlaws and the worse Apaches.

Tonight she could see that something bothered him. He gave her a sidewise glance, so sharp and characteristic.

"I don't expect, Nancy Belle, you could put off your weddin'?"

The girl stood quietly gazing at him with a face like the tintype of her mother. But under her sedate gray dress, with tight waist and full skirts to the instep, she had frozen. She looked much older than her years. Her air of gentlefolk and her wide-apart gray eyes came from her mother. But the chin, tipped up with resolute fearlessness, was her father's.

"No, papa!" Her two clear words held all the steady insistence of the desert.

"I figured how you'd feel," he nodded, avoiding her eyes. "I just wanted to put it up to you. I'd 'a' covered the *jornada*[6] on foot to be on time at my own weddin', but I didn't have to count on Gideon to hold me up."

"Are you telling me, papa, that you can't go to Gunstock tomorrow?" Her voice remained quiet, but a coldness had seized her. Of all the people she had visualized at her wedding, the one next to Stephen she could least spare was the tall, grave figure of her father.

"I reckon I kind of can't, Nancy Belle," he said soberly. "Rife could tend to the stage all right and do the feedin'. But they's men come to this post no boy can handle." He shifted his position. "I figured once on closin' up the post till I got back. But the stage is comin' and the mail. And the freighters count on me for feed and grub. Then I got to protect my own property and the mail and freight for the Cedar country that's in the storage room."

"I know," Nancy Belle said steadily. "I can get to Gunstock all right."

Far back in her father's assaying eyes, she fancied she saw a glint of pride.

"You're pretty nigh a woman now, Nancy Belle. And Rife's a good slice of a man. It's a straight trail to the Rio Grande, once you turn at the old post. Both you and Rife's been over it before. Of course, I'd like to be at the weddin', but the boy can tell me about it." He went to the window. "Rife!" he called.

Nancy Belle's brother came in presently. A slight boy, with his father's blue eyes, he seldom made a fuss over anything, even when he shot a stray duck on the tank or when they braked down the last cedar hill into Santa Fe with all the open doors of the plaza shops in sight. And when his father told him now, he showed neither enthusiasm nor regret—merely straightened.

---

5. **Beaverhead,** Catron County, eastern New Mexico on the Gila River.
6. **jornada**\hɔr ˈna·da\ a journey over a long, waterless stretch of desert country.

"Sure. I can take you, Nancy Belle," he said.

Something pulled under his sister's tight basque.[7] She remembered the long miles they would have in the wagon, the camps at lonely places, the ugly shadow ever hovering over the outposts of this frontier country, and the blight that, since Saturday, seemed to have fallen on the trail. Her eyes swam. Now, at the last minute, she yielded.

"If you'll let me ride, papa, I'll wait another day for Uncle Gideon," she promised.

Her father's eyes moved to the ruffled red calico curtains at the shadeless windows.

"I don't hardly count on Gideon comin' any more, Nancy Belle. Besides, it's too long in the saddle to Gunstock—especially for a girl to get married. You'd be plumb wore out, and you wouldn't have your trunk. You couldn't get dressed for your weddin'."

He turned thoughtfully and went out, Rife close behind. Nancy Belle could hear her father's tones, slow and grave, coming from near one of the picket corrals.

It was too far to catch the words; but when they came in, she saw that her brother's features looked a little pale under the tan.

"You better get some sleep, Nancy Belle," her father said. "You and Rife are startin' before daylight. If Gideon comes, I'll ride after."

They had scarcely gone from the room when Ignacita came in from the kitchen, her black eyes glittering over a pile of freshly starched white in her arms.

"Nancy Belle, *chinita!*"[8] she whispered, plucking at the girl's sleeve. "You don't say to your *papacito*[9] I talk to you! I have promise I don't scare you. But I can't see you go so far in the wildness alone, *pobrecita!*[10] Sometimes people go safe from one place to the other, oh, *si!* But sometimes, *chinita,* they don't come back! You have not the oldness like Ignacita. Ay, I tell you these old eyes have see men and women quartered from a tree like sheep or maybe tied over a stove like I don't have the words to say to you."

Nancy Belle did not answer except to lay, one by one, the ironed pieces in her trunk—a bride's muslin underwear trimmed with red and blue feather stitching; long petticoats stiffly flounced with ruffles, and nightgowns long in the sleeve and high in the neck, with ruffles at wrist and throat. The Mexican woman went on hoarsely. The girl folded away her winter's cashmere dress, buttoned up the front and with a white fichu.[11] She unwrapped and wrapped again in crumpled white tissue the red slippers the old gentleman on the stage had sent her as a wedding present from Philadelphia.

When Ignacita had left, she opened her keepsake box covered with colored shells. The mirror on the inside lid turned back a face as calm as the little golden clouds that hung of an evening over the east to catch the desert sunset. But after she had undressed and put on her nightdress, for a long time she was aware of the soft pound of her heart faintly swaying the bed on its rawhide springs.

At the first sound of Ignacita's hand on the kitchen stove, Nancy Belle sprang out of bed. She dressed on the brown pool of burro skin, the only carpet on her adobe floor. Through the west window she could see the morning star burning like a brilliant candle. It hung, she told herself, over Gunstock and the Beaverhead, where Stephen, at this moment, in their new log ranch house, lay thinking about her.

They ate in the kitchen by lamplight. She had never been so conscious of every detail—the great white cups and saucers, the familiar steel knives, the homy smell of the scorched paper lamp-shade, the unreadable eyes of her father, Rife, and Ignacita.

Asa Putman himself carried out the trunk. There was already hay in the wagon, a gunny sack of oats, food in a canned-tomato box and utensils in another, a water-keg, bed roll tied in a wagon sheet, an ax, a bridle, and her own

---

7. **basque**\băsk\ a tight-fitting pullover blouse, usually of knitted cotton with a round ribbed collar and horizontal stripes.
8. **chinita**\chē ˄nē·ta\ dear.
9. **papacito**\'pa·pa ˄sē·tō\ little father, "daddy."
10. **pobrecita**\'pō·brĕ ˄sē·ta\ "You poor thing."
11. **fichu**\˄fē 'shū\ a woman's scarf in triangular shape, draped over the shoulders and fastened in the front.

side-saddle, made to order over a man's tree.[12] Her eyes caught the gleam of a rifle leaning up against the seat in the lantern-light. Tethered to the rear of the wagon stood her saddle mare, Fancy, with pricked-up ears. She was going along to their new ranch home. Nancy Belle felt that she was still among intimate things, but outside the little circle of light lay darkness and the unknown.

When she said good-by to her father, he kissed her—something he had not done for years.

"You haven't changed your mind, Nancy Belle?" he asked.

She climbed quickly up over the wheel to the spring seat of the wagon before he might see that she was crying. Rife swung up like a monkey on the other side and pushed the rifle into the crevice behind the seat cushion. The lines tautened and the wagon lurched.

"*Dios* go with you safe to your husband, Nancy Belle!" she heard Ignacita cry after her.

The morning star had set. They moved into a world of silent blackness. Nancy Belle could not see how the horses remained on the trail. When she looked back, the only light in all these square miles of black, unfriendly earth was the yellow window of her father's post.

It was almost a vision, golden and far away, like all beautiful things. She didn't trust herself to look again.

Two hours later the wagon was a lonely speck of boat rocking in an illimitable sage-green sea beneath the sun. The canvas wagon sheet fastened over the bows was a kind of sail, and eastward the sandy water did not stop rolling till it washed up at the foot of the faintly blue ramparts of the distant Espiritu Range.

Just before they turned west on the cross trail to the Rio Grande, a heavy wagon with a yoke of oxen in front and a cow behind toiled round the crumbling adobe walls of the old, abandoned post house. A bearded man and a thin woman with a white face sat on the seat. She held a baby in her arms, and three black-eyed children peered from under the wagon sheet.

The bearded man saluted and stopped his willing team. Rife did likewise. The woman spoke first. Her tongue was swift and slightly acid.

"You better turn around and follow us if you want to save your hair!" she called. "Yesterday a sheep-herder told us he saw—"

A sharp word from the bearded man caused her to relapse into sullen silence. He asked Rife where he might be going, then climbed down to the trail and said he wanted to talk to him a little. The boy followed reluctantly behind his wagon. Nancy Belle could hear the bearded man's tones coming slow and grave like her father's, while the woman made silent and horribly expressive lip language.

Rife came back, walking stiffly. The bearded man climbed up beside the woman.

"They got to go on," he told her in a low tone, then saluted with his whip. "Good luck, boy! And you, miss!"

Rife raised his whip in stiff acknowledgment. The wagons creaked apart. Nancy Belle saw in front of her the trail to the Rio Grande, little more than a pair of wheel tracks, that lost itself on the lonely plain. Rife seemed relieved that she did not ask what the bearded man had said. But it was enough for her not to be able to forget the woman's fearful signs and mouthings and the horror in the curious eyes of the staring children.

Sister and brother talked very little. Nancy Belle saw her brother's eyes keep sweeping the country, scanning the horizons. Bunches of bear grass[13] that might have been feathers pinioned his blue gaze, and clumps of cane cactus that seemed to hold pointing gun barrels. At arroyos[14] thick with chamiso[15] and Apache plume she could see his feet tighten on the footboard. Once he pulled out the rifle, but

12. **tree,** saddletree, the frame of a saddle. A **side-saddle** was a woman's saddle made so both feet were on the same side of the horse.
13. **bear grass,** a plant of the lily family with grasslike leaves and white flowers.
14. **arroyos**\ə ˈrɔi·yōz\ dry gullies.
15. **chamiso**\cha ˈmē·so\ shrub that forms a dense thicket.

it was only a herd of antelopes moving across the desert page.

They camped for the night when the sun was still high. Nancy Belle asked no questions as the boy drove far off the trail into a grassy *cañada*.[16] She sang softly to herself as she fried the salt side bacon and put the black coffee-pot to boil.

Rife hobbled Anton Chico and the Bar X horse and staked out Fancy close to the wagon.

She pretended not to notice when, before dark, he poured earth on the fire till not a spark or wisp of smoke remained. Out of one eye she watched him climb the side of the *cañada* and stand long minutes sweeping the country from the ridge, a slight, tense figure against the sullen glow of the sunset.

"It's all right," he said when he came down. "You can go to bed."

"What's all right?" she asked him.

"The horses," he said, turning away, and Nancy Belle felt a stab of pain that so soon this boy must bear a man's responsibilities and tell a man's lies.

She prayed silently on her blankets spread on the hay in the wagon box, and lay down with her head on the side-saddle, her unread Testament in her hand. She heard Rife unroll his camp bed on the ground beneath the wagon. It was all very strange and hushed without her father. Just to feel the Testament in her hand helped to calm her and to remember the day at the post when she had first met Stephen.

Her father had never let her come in contact with the men of the trail. Always, at the first sign of dust cloud on the horizon, he would tell both children to heap up the chip-box, fill the water-buckets and carry saddles and bridles into the house. But this day Asa Putman and Rife had gone to Fort Sumner.[17] And to Nancy Belle, Uncle Gideon could seldom say no.

It had been a very hot day. She had been sitting in the shade of the earthen bank of the tank, moving her bare feet in the cool water, watching the ripples in the hot south wind. The leaves of the cottonwoods clashed overhead, and she heard nothing until she looked up, and

there was a young man on a blue-gray horse with dust clinging to his hat brim and mustache. His eyes were direct as an eagle's. Firm lines modeled his lean face. But what she noticed most at the time was the little bow tie on his dark shirt.

Instantly she had tucked her bare, wet legs under her red dress. Her face burned with shame, but the young stranger talked to her about her father coolly, as if she, a girl of fifteen, had not been caught barefooted. Then he did what in her mind was a noble thing. When Uncle Gideon came out, he magnificently turned his back for her to run into the house and pull on shoes and stockings.

She thought of Stephen constantly next day and the next. She had grown a little used to the journey without her father now—the still, uncertain nights under the wagon sheet, sitting, lying, listening, waiting; the less uncertain days with the sun on the endless spaces; her never-quiet perch on the high spring seat under the slanted bow; the bumps, creaks, and lumberings of the wagon; the sand sifting softly over the red, turning wheels; all afternoon the sun in their faces; ahead the far haze and heat waves in which were still lost Gunstock and the Rio Grande. Almost she had forgotten the bearded man with the oxen and the curious, detached horror in the eyes of his children.

Since morning of the third day their progress had been slower. The trail seemed level, except for the heavy breathing of the horses. But when Nancy Belle glanced back she could see the steady grade they had been climbing. Abruptly, in mid-afternoon, she found that the long, blue Espiritu Range had disappeared, vanished behind a high pine-clad hill which was its southernmost beginning. It was like the lizard that swallowed itself, a very real lizard. At this moment they were climbing over the lizard's tail.

"Cedars!" Rife said briefly, pointing with the whip to dark sprawling growths ahead.

---

16. **cañada**\ka ᵃnya•da\ a small canyon, glen.
17. **Fort Sumner**, military post established in New Mexico, 1862, at Bosque Redondo on the Pecos River; named for Col. Edwin V. Sumner, U.S. Army.

"You breathe deep up here!" Nancy Belle drank in the light air.

Rife took a sniff, but his blue eyes never ceased to scan the high, black-thatched hill under whose frowning cliff they must pass.

"Soon we can see the Gunstock Mountains," Nancy Belle said.

"And Martin Cross's cabin," Rife nodded. "It's the last water to the Rio Grande."

"He's a nice old man," Nancy Belle ventured casually. "It would be nice to camp by his cabin tonight and talk."

The boy inclined his head. After a few moments he started to whistle softly. At the first cedar Nancy Belle leaped off the moving wagon and climbed back with an evergreen branch. The twig, crushed in her hand, smelled like some store in Santa Fe.

They gained the summit. A breeze was sweeping here from the southwest, and the horses freshened. But Rife had suddenly stopped whistling and Nancy Belle's sprig of cedar lay on her lap. The frowning cliff of the pine-clad hill was still there. But Martin Cross's cabin had turned to a desolate mound of ashes. As they stared, a gust of wind sent wisps of smoke scurrying from the mound, and a red eye opened to watch them from the embers. Nancy Belle felt an uncontrollable twitching in the hair roots at the base of her scalp.

Where Martin Cross's eastbound wheel tracks met the trail, Rife reluctantly halted the horses and wet his air-dried lips.

"The water keg's dry, and the horses. If papa was here, he'd drive over."

"I'm the oldest." Nancy Belle found her voice steady. "I'll ride over. There might be something we can do."

The boy rose quickly. His eyes seemed to remember something his father had said.

"You can drive the wagon over if I wave."

He had thrown her the lines and slipped back through the canvas-covered tunnel of wagon box, picking up Fancy's bridle and the rifle. Barebacked he rode toward the smoldering ashes at the foot of that frowning hill. The chestnut mare's tail and mane streamed like something gold in the wind.

When she looked back to the trail, her eyes were pinioned by a light object in the wheel track ahead of the Bar X horse. It was a long gray feather. Instantly she told herself that it had come from some wild turkey Martin Cross had shot, and yet never had air anywhere become so suddenly horrible and choking as in this canyon.

Rife did not signal her to drive over. She saw him come riding back at full speed. The mare was snorting. As he stopped her at the wagon, her chestnut head kept turning back toward what had once been a cabin. Rife slipped the lead rope about her neck and climbed into the seat with the rifle in his hands.

"The water—you wouldn't want it!" he said thickly. His cheeks, she noticed, were the color of *yeso*.[18]

"Rife"—Nancy Belle touched his arm when she had driven down the canyon—"what did you see at the cabin?"

The boy sat deaf and rigid beside her, eyes staring straight ahead. She saw that his young hands were still tortured around the barrel of his rifle.

Far down on the pitch-dark mesa she stopped the horses in the trail and listened. There were no stars, not a sound but the flapping of the wagon sheet in the wind and the clank of coffee-pot and water-bucket under the wagon. Half standing on the footboard, she guided the team off the trail in the intense blackness. Her swift hands helped the trembling boy stake out the mare and hobble the team. They did not light a lantern. Rife declined to eat. Nancy Belle chewed a few dry mouthfuls.

The wind came drawing out of the blackness with a great draft. It hissed through the grass, sucked and tore at the wagon sheet, and whistled through the spokes and brake rigging. Rife did not take his bed roll under the wagon

---

18. **yeso**\ˈyä·sō\ gypsum, found in sedimentary rocks and used on the walls of pioneer houses as a plaster and whitewash.

tonight. He drew the ends of the wagon sheet together and lay down in the wagon box near his sister. For a long time they were silent. When she heard his heavy breathing, she lifted the rifle from his chest.

The storm grew. Sand began pelting against the canvas and sifted into the wagon box. An invisible cloud of choking dust found its way into eyes, mouth, ears, and lungs. Nancy Belle laid down the rifle a moment to pull a blanket over the face of the boy. He tossed and muttered pitifully, but he slept on.

Magically the rain, when it came, stopped the sand and dust. The girl drank in the clean-washed air. At daylight she slipped out to the ground. The mesa, stretching away in the early light, touched here and there with feathers of mist, would have been beautiful except for a sharp new loneliness. The horses were gone!

At her exclamation, Rife appeared from the wagon box. His shame at having slept through the night was quickly overshadowed by their misfortune.

Together they found where Fancy's stake had been pulled out and dragged. Yards farther on they could tell by Anton Chico's tracks that his hobbles had parted.

Nancy Belle made her brother come back to the wagon and stuff his pockets with cold biscuits and antelope jerky.[19] She said she would have a hot breakfast ready when he returned. The horses, perhaps, were just down in some draw where they had drifted with the wind.

When he had gone with the rifle, she filled the coffee-pot from a clearing water-hole in the nearest arroyo. She fried potatoes and onions in the long-handled skillet. And when he did not come, she set fresh biscuits in the Dutch oven. Each biscuit held a square of salt side bacon in its top, and as it baked, the fat oozed down and incased it in a kind of glazed tastiness.

At noon she thought she heard a shot. Nowhere could she see him on the endless sweep of mesa. By late afternoon she was still alone. She read her Testament and wondered how many women over the world had read it in hours like this. Sitting in the shadow of the wagon, facing the direction in which he had gone, she looked up every few minutes. But all her eyes could find were cloud shadows racing across the lonely face of the mesa. All she could hear were the desolate cries from the unseen lark sparrows.

Darkness, stillness settled down on the empty land. She climbed back into the wagon and sat on the chuck-box, hands rigid on her knees. Again and again she convinced herself that the horses could not have been driven off or she would have seen the drivers' tracks. When wild, sharp barks shattered the stillness and set wires jerking in her limbs, she talked to herself steadily, but a little meaninglessly, of the post —on and on as the darkness was filled with the ringing and counter-ringing of shrill, cracked yappings—not long tones like a dog's, but incredibly short syllables rising, rising in a mad eternal scale and discord.

"I wish papa had given me two of the chairs," she repeated. "Mamma said they were post oak from Texas. She said they had got white from scrubbing. I liked the laced rawhide seats with the hair left on. It made them soft to sit on. The seats in the parlor were black. And the ones in the kitchen were red. But I liked the brockle[20] one in my room best."

The insane din around the wagon had become terrific. There were only two or three of the animals, Nancy Belle guessed, but they threw their voices and echoes together to make a score.

"When I was little I liked to go in the storage room," her voice went on, scarcely intelligible to her own ears. "It was dark and cool, and smelled of burlap and kerosene and whisky, and sweetish with brown sugar. I can see the fat sacks of green coffee. And the round tins of kerosene had boards on the side. The flour-sacks were printed: 'Rough and Ready' in red

---

19. **antelope jerky,** antelope meat that has been cut into long slices and dried in the sun.
20. **brockle**\brŏk•əl\ striped or spotted with black and white.

letters. Mamma once used to make our underwear out of the sacking. I can smell the salt side bacon in the gunny sacks."

She could tell from the sounds that one of the animals was running insanely back and forth near the wagon tongue. She had never noticed before that they yelped both when breathing in and out. Suddenly came silence. It warned her. Instinctively she felt for the ax.

"Nancy Belle!" a boy's far, anxious voice called from the darkness.

She hallooed and leaned out over the tailboard. Three shadowy forms were coming across the mesa in the starlight. Never had horses looked so good.

"Were you scared?" Rife greeted. "Anything bother you?"

"Nothing," Nancy Belle said. "Just coyotes."

"I had to give Fancy her head after it got dark." He slid wearily to the ground. "She brought us straight back to the wagon."

Nancy Belle had wanted to put her arms around her brother. Now she hugged the mare instead. Rife ate fresh biscuits and a tin plate of cold potatoes. He drank several tin cups of coffee. Nancy Belle had slipped the oats-laden gunny-sack *morrals*[21] over the horses' heads.

"I had to walk halfway to the mountain," Rife said.

"Just help hitch up; then you can sleep all night," she promised.

It rained again heavily toward midnight. Flashes of lightning lit the drenched plain. For minutes at a time, quivering fingers of blue phosphorescence stood on the ears of the toiling horses. At dawn Nancy Belle still held the reins as the mud-splashed wagon crawled through a world bathed in early purple splendor.

Four days they had been crossing a hundred and seventy miles of desolate plain. Now the end waited in sight. To the west lay a land broken and tumbled by a mighty hand. Hill shouldered hill and range peered over range, all indescribably violet except where peaks tipped by the unseen sun were far-off flaming towers of copper.

It was a new land, her promised land, Stephen's land, Nancy Belle told herself, where nobody burned cow chips, but snapping cedar and pine, where cold water ran in the wooded canyons, and the eye, weary of one flat circle the horizon round, had endless geometric designs to refresh the retina.

She sang softly as the wagon lumbered to the edge of a long, shallow valley, brown and uninhabited, running north and south, and desolate except for a winding ribbon that was white with sky and narrowly bordered with green.

"Rife!" Nancy Belle cried. "The Rio Grande!"

An hour afterwards they pulled out of the sun into the shade of the long cottonwood *bosque*.[22] Nancy Belle wasn't singing now. Where she remembered wide sandbars glistening with sky and tracked by waterfowl, a chocolate-red flood rolled. Where had been the island, tops of tule[23] and scrub willow swung to and fro with the current.

Anton Chico and the Bar X horse stopped of their own accord in the trail, ears pricked forward at the swirling brown wash. While Rife turned the three horses loose to graze, Nancy Belle silently fried bacon and made coffee. When she had washed skillet and tin dishes in the river, the boy had wired the wagon box to the brake rigging. Now he was tying securely one end of his rope to the center of the coupling pole under the wagon. The other end she knew he would fasten to the inadequate upper horn of the side-saddle.

"I wouldn't mind the river if I just had my own saddle," he mourned.

They hitched up the team silently. Rife cinched the side-saddle on Fancy and straddled it, the single stirrup useless to a man. Nancy Belle climbed into the wagon and picked up the lines. The other bank looked as far away as the Espiritu Range from the post. She wanted to say something to her brother—some last

---

21. **morrals**\mə ˈrălz\ feed bags for horses.
22. **bosque**\bŏs·kā\ a dense growth of trees.
23. **tule**\ˈtu·lē\ a large grasslike plant growing in clumps on overflowed marshes.

word, in case they didn't make it. But all she did was cluck her tongue to the horses.

Gingerly, one slow foot at a time, the team moved down the trail into the water.

"Give 'em their heads!" Rife called from the right rear.

Nancy Belle held a rein in each hand. The red channel water came to the wagon tongue, covered it, reached the horses' bellies. The team wanted to stop. Nancy Belle swung her whip, a stick tipped with a long rawhide lash. The wagon went on. The collars of both horses kept dipping, but never entirely out of sight. Still barely wading, the slow team reached the firmer footing of the island.

Two-thirds of the river still rolled in front of the wagon. The west bank did not seem to have grown much closer, but the east bank behind them had moved far away. The team had to be whipped into the violent current. The water churned white through the wagon wheels. Suddenly both horses appeared to stumble and drop out of sight. Their heads came up wildly, spray blowing from their nostrils. The muddy water hid their legs, but by their bobbing motions Nancy Belle knew that they were swimming.

"Keep 'em pointed up the river!" Rife shouted.

Already she felt the wagon floating. It swung downstream with the current; then Rife's rope from Fancy's saddle snubbed it. The team was snorting with every breath. The Bar X horse swam high in the water, his withers and part of his back out of the chocolate current. But all she could see of Anton Chico were his nose and ears.

Down between her ankles she saw water in the wagon box. She thought of the hemstitched sheets at the bottom of her trunk, the towels and pillowcases crocheted with shell lace. Her blue velvet corduroy dress was probably wet already, and all the cunning print aprons with dust caps to match. River water couldn't hurt the little yellow creamer, sugar bowl, and covered butter dish that had been her mother's. And the gingham dresses could be washed.

What worried her were her wedding dress and the keepsake box, especially the tintypes,[24] one of which was Rife in a child's suit edged with black braid, his brand-new hat on his knee.

An older Rife was shouting something behind her now. She couldn't catch the words. Then she found what it was. The neck and withers of Anton Chico raised suddenly out of the water and both horses were scrambling up the steep bank below the ford. Only quick work with the lines saved the wagon from turning over. Safe and blowing on the high bank, the dripping horses shook themselves like puppies.

Nancy Belle couldn't go on until she had opened the trunk and appraised the damage. Rife unsaddled Fancy and drove on with the refreshed team. Behind his slight back in the wagon box, the girl changed to her blue velvet corduroy, which was hardly wet at all. Then she combed her hair and rolled into a cranny of her trunk the old felt hat that had been too large for her father.

A half-dozen riders met the wagon some miles down the Gunstock Canyon. All of them, Nancy Belle noticed, carried guns. Stephen wore a new white shirt and a gray hat with curled brim she had not seen before. He stood in his stirrups and swung her down in front of him on the saddle, where he kissed her. She had never felt his lips press into such a straight line.

"Papa couldn't come," she said. "So Rife brought me."

She felt Stephen's rigid arm around her.

"We just got in from the Beaverhead ourselves."

"He means they never get any news out in the Beaverhead or he'd 'a' come further east to meet you!" Uncle Billy Williams put in. He had a lovable, squeaky voice. "The Apaches been breakin' loose again. Funny you didn't hear anything over in your country."

---

24. **tintype**, a positive photograph made on a thin, sensitized iron or tin plate and having a darkened, usually enameled, surface.

Nancy Belle gave him an inscrutable look with her gray eyes. Uncle Billy pulled out his bandanna and blew his nose.

"They got my old friend Judge Hower and his wife and kid in a buggy on the Upper Espiritu. The man that found what they did to 'em, they say, cried like a baby."

"That's all right, Uncle Billy," Stephen said in a gentle voice.

Nancy Belle glanced at Rife. Her brother's face looked gray, the eyes staring as when he had ridden in the late afternoon sunlight from the smoking ashes of Martin Cross's cabin.

Nearly fifty people, gathered in the big parlor upstairs at the hotel, greeted Nancy Belle. An old man whose young black eyes twinkled out of a bearded face said he was glad to see that she had her "hair on straight." Rife stopped with the trunk before driving to the livery, and Stephen's mother showed Nancy Belle to a room to dress.

The guests stopped talking when she came into the parlor in her white wedding dress. Her basque came to a point in the front and back. It fitted like a glove. The silk underskirt came to her instep, and the ruffled overskirt to her knees. She had parted her hair from side to side and brushed the bangs down on her forehead. She felt very light-headed. The wagon still seemed to be jerking under her.

She glimpsed Rife gazing at her, a rapt expression in his reticent blue eyes. She was glad to see that he had brushed his hair. The brass swinging lamp had been lighted and the dark woodwork of the parlor festooned with evergreen branches. White streamers from the wall met in a papier-mâché bell in one corner. She noticed two children peering eagerly from the dark hall.

Stephen came to her, very straight in a long coat and stand-up collar with a black tie. He led her up beneath the papier-mâché bell. In a sibilant, church-like whisper, the Gunstock preacher made sure of her full name. Then he coughed and began the ceremony. He had a deep voice, but Nancy Belle didn't hear all of the service. Her mind kept going back to a tall,

grave man in a lonely adobe post on the wide Santa Ana plain. And after she had said: "I do," her lips moved, but she was not praying for Stephen, her husband.

I
READING BETWEEN THE LINES

The phrase, "reading between the lines," means reading to understand what the writer implies as opposed to what he states directly. In "Early Marriage" you never meet an Apache, nor do you get any specific description of what they did to captured white men; nevertheless, by paying attention to the details Richter gives, you can imagine what would have happened to Nancy Belle and Rife if they had been caught.

Writers often purposely force one to read between the lines, for this technique gets the reader *inside* the story. For example, when you have to imagine for yourself what the Apaches might do, you are in the same position as Nancy Belle, who also has never seen one of their victims. Like her, you have to form your judgment from such details as "the horror in the curious eyes of staring children" and the "deaf and rigid" Rife, whose eyes stared "straight ahead" after he saw Martin Cross. All this helps you to *identify* with Nancy Belle; you share her experiences in a much more intimate way than you would if you saw her from the outside only.

II
IMPLICATIONS

Discuss the implications of the following statements.

1. Asa Putman and/or Stephen should never have let Nancy Belle travel so far to the wedding; she should have been married in her own home.

2. Rife at 15 was much too young to bear the responsibilities his father placed on him. It is inconceivable that a 15-year-old boy would have the sensitivity to shield his older sister from things that terrified him and that he would be willing to go on in the face of the difficulties he met.

3. A willingness to let an individual make his own decisions is characteristic of the frontier spirit.

4. In times of crisis, it helps to concentrate on the commonplace details of life.

5. Courage was so common among the men and women of the frontier that it was taken for granted.

III
TECHNIQUE

Setting

Today, a journey of two hundred miles is a matter of minutes by air, a few hours by automobile, but to Nancy Belle and Rife the journey meant five days by wagon or four days by saddle or buckboard. Picture this scene: Two hours away from the Putman cabin: ". . . The wagon was a lonely speck of boat rocking in an illimitable sage-green sea beneath the sun." Be prepared to point up other details that help the reader to appreciate more fully the conditions of the bride's journey.

In "Early Marriage" Richter creates an atmosphere of suspense, beginning almost in the first words of the story. Trace the specific details through which the author builds this atmosphere.

Characterization

By which of the following techniques does Richter develop character?

1. character action?

2. character's own speech?

3. other characters' remarks?

4. expository passages?

5. comparisons with others?

IV
WORDS

A. Context clues may be modifiers; signal words, such as *however, in other words, or;* examples; appositives; or definitions. How does the context help you get the meaning of the following italicized words?

1. . . . a tiny meadow, a cool, *resilient* surface of green. . . .

2. It was a sweetness that would have been *cloying* had the air been heavy. . . .

3. . . . delicate and *intangible* fabric which was the spirit of the place.

4. He was *languid* with rest.

5. . . . an *aura* of things hostile, made *manifest* by messengers too refined for the senses to know. . . .

6. . . . her eyes were *pinioned* by a light object in the wheel track ahead of the Bar X horse.

B. Synonyms are words that share a common meaning. *Remember* and *recall* are synonymous. "I *remember* the incident" and "I *recall* the incident" express the same general idea. *Naiveté* and *simplicity* are synonyms and can be used interchangeably in the expression "the naiveté and wonder of the child." Yet the two words are not always interchangeable. Can you think of a context in which only *simplicity* seems appropriate? Find a synonym for each of the following italicized words, and then analyze the similarities and differences, if any, between the pair.

(1) delicate and *fastidious* touch; (2) *gaunt* red steers; (3) *reticent* blue eyes; (4) *precariously* rooted shrub; (5) *somnolent* with the easement; (6) *geniality* and humor seemed *salient* characteristics.

Although the physical frontiers of the United States
have been closed for generations, the persistence of "westerns"
in the movies, television, and popular magazines testifies to the fact
that Americans everywhere are still fascinated by the West and its history.
How do you explain this special appeal of the West?

The West Is Our Great Adventure of the Spirit

A. B. GUTHRIE, JR.

Americans east and west are a sunset people. From the Atlantic seaboard, over the Appalachians, through the wooded valleys, past the flatlands, on to the high plains, the Rockies and the Pacific, there goes our course, and somewhere along the western way lies heart's desire.

Millions of us have made the trip in fact and, settled, keep making it, in association with travelers before our time and through episodes and over trails outside our experience. Others, not so lucky as to have made the actual journey, travel altogether by way of illusion, on page or screen becoming one with Lewis and Clark, with buckskinned beaver hunters, with homeseekers on the Oregon Trail, with Wild Bill Hickok and Calamity Jane, with the panners of gold at the grass roots and the cowmen to whom grass was gold, with the men good and bad of Dodge City and Tombstone. It doesn't matter for our purposes that true characters have been altered often and real situations falsified or that some presentations are downright silly and others endlessly repetitious. Somehow they still are the West.

The direction was pointed a long time ago by one whose words roll down the centuries.

That was Cabeza de Vaca, sixteenth-century Spanish adventurer. In his search for the golden Seven Cities he had endured much, and now, as before, he was lost, this time near the present dividing line between Texas and New Mexico, but still he could say of that summer of 1535, " . . . We ever held it certain that going toward the sunset we must find what we desired."

Some 300 years went by before another man so well expressed the sentiment. From his little vantage point in New England, Henry David Thoreau[1] wrote, "When I go out of the house for a walk, uncertain as yet whither I will bend my steps, and submit myself to my instinct to decide for me, I find, strange and whimsical as it may seem, that I finally and inevitably settle southwest. . . . The future lies that way to me, and the earth seems more unexhausted and richer on that side. . . . Eastward I go only by force; but westward I go free."

Though he was a native and lifelong resident of the Atlantic coast, Walt Whitman [see page 477], too, felt the pull of sun. "These States," he said, "tend inland and toward the Western sea, and I will also."

---

1. **Henry David Thoreau** witnessed the beginning of urbanization in America and in his Journal and his masterpiece *Walden,* he complained about the conversion of the "country into the town." (See page 600.)

From "How the West Relives a Lively Past" by A. B. Guthrie, Jr. Copyright © Time, Inc. Reprinted by permission of Brandt & Brandt.

The feeling is in a majority of us still. It helps to account for our fascination with American history, since all parts of our country inland from the Atlantic shore once were west and we chose with Thoreau—as if the choice were hard!—to "walk toward Oregon, and not toward Europe." It helps particularly to account for our fascination with the present West and its history.

This fascination reveals itself in a multitude of ways. . . .

We are captivated by sheer adventure, by the rediscovery of adventure, by the hard simplicities of loneliness, privation, danger, the elemental contests of man versus nature and man versus man.

We are caught up in admiration for the men who went before, as courageous and hardy as we wish to be and never can or shall be.

We are atavistic,[2] in rebellion against the conventions and limitations and order and tameness of what we call civilization. Give us the good old raw days! The South has always taken pride in gracious living. Almost from the start the North has had its gods of culture, government, shipping and finance. Both sections celebrate aspects of civilization. But more important in our whole thinking and inclination is the old and uncivilized West, the West of rugged individuality, of lawlessness, hardship, license, dispute and resolution by revolver and rifle, the West whether in legend or fact that opposes propriety.

We watch motion picture and TV Westerns because they give us the simple choices of good and bad and don't tax our minds.

We like the West because it underscores our ancient and vestigial dislike of things European, like wiggery on the bench and the anti-democracy of caste.

These reasons apply east and west, though eastern critics keep asking why actual Westerners buy the myth of the West when they know better. Why do they read and write formula Western fiction, which takes a germ of fact and by artificial insemination[3] procreates a whole colony? Why do they go to Western movies? Why do they sit hypnotized when the gunman of legend comes on the TV screen? Why do they affect big hats, jeans or frontier pants and cowboy boots when most of them never bridle a horse, can't harness a team and live by virtue of commerce in oil or insurance or underwear?

Because the "becauses" are common to all of us. Because the state of knowing better never has been fatal to fantasy. That a time never quite was, that a represented thing never happened, that hero and "heavy"[4] in actual life weren't that way, all these detractions grow niggling against gallop and gunshot. And except for the plainly functional, all styles of dress are affectations anyway, made popular by custom, designers, whim or whatever. Think of the Homburg[5] or Ivy League suits, or the vaunted variations of old Congress gaiters.[6] (It can be thrown in here that the cowboy boot with its high heel, though fashioned for the foot in the stirrup, is in fact a great comfort to the foot on the throttle.)

The foregoing explanations are all true but do not constitute the whole truth. Other and deeper ones hit closer home.

The greatest value in the West, if not the first reason for our fascination with its history, actual and exaggerated, is the specialty of space. Though the great open spaces is a term turned comic, its appeal abides. While thronging the earth with his offspring, man still hankers for room for himself, room, as the late Joseph Kinsey Howard of Montana put it, to swing his elbows and his mind. He not only

---

2. **atavistic**\ˈăt·ə ˈvĭs·tĭk\ marked by a resemblance to an ancestor more remote than the parents.

3. **artificial insemination** here means a gradual implanting of an idea or knowledge artificially, without actual experience.

4. **heavy**, villain or antagonist.

5. **Homburg**\ˈhŏm·bərg\ a man's hat made of felt with a stiff brim turned up slightly at the sides and a high tapered crown dented from front to back.

6. **Congress gaiters**\ˈkŏn·grəs ˈgā·tərz\ ankle-high shoes with elastic inserts in the sides of the upper portion to provide for expansion.

On the Trail with a Guide, Frederic Remington.
". . . We ever held it certain that going toward the sunset we must find what we desired."

hankers for it; he insists on having it, whether in fact or vicariously.

Early in our national experience that compulsion was recognized. Writing in 1786, Thomas Jefferson expressed the belief that a density of ten persons to the square mile was about the limit of endurance. "Wherever we reach that," he wrote, "the inhabitants become uneasy as too much compressed, and go off in great numbers to search for vacant country." His opinion is kinder and truer than the postulation that misfits and neurotics populated the West, which served the happy function of a safety valve for the pressures of social and economic conflict in the East.

Space, then.

By Jeffersonian standards a sizable portion of the old West still qualifies, if not as vacant, then as generally agreeable. Consider the

Rocky Mountain states. Colorado with its great and growing city of Denver numbers only about thirteen people to the square mile. A hundred and fifty years and more after Jefferson, the states of Utah, Idaho, Arizona, New Mexico, Montana, Wyoming and Nevada are well under his limit. Today he might revise his maximum and include border and Pacific states —Texas, Kansas, Nebraska, Oregon and Washington—which count far fewer than forty people to the mile. (California, with the population of its crowded cities spread by average into still-existent space, would have to be excluded.)

Massachusetts, by contrast with her Western sisters, can count 596.2 noses per unit, New York 309.3.

The West, the thinly peopled West, thus satisfies a basic desire, in actuality or image, as does the larger West of history and fiction. A man still has room to gallop a horse, unequipped with rear-vision mirror. He can look across the miles without being reminded that the continent is infested with his kind.

Space breeds its own type of man, and here again is a reason for the general leaning. The true Westerner is not necessarily better or worse than the product of congestion, but he is very likely to be different. He is commonly freer and friendlier. He hasn't learned to be suspicious. He appraises a man for his worth, not his wealth and for sure not his ancestry. Weather and work and the demands on himself alone have shaped him, and chance has taught him to take fortune as it unfolds. Ordinarily he has a stout sense of humor. He can dismiss an adversity with a shrug or a wisecrack.

Perhaps above all, he is democratic. In him lingers the old liberalizing effect of free land. No class system could develop where acres were to be had for the asking, and the lines that exist today are few and faint. In all probability the penniless Westerner wouldn't know what you meant by "proletarian." Broke, he's still as good as the next man.

These attitudes, these ways will pass and are passing now, but while they endure we can think, all of us, that life can be different and good and refreshing, and when they are gone, we shall keep digging them up for page and screen and festival, and somehow we shall feel renewed.

The West is our youth, the youth of our nation and, by translation, the youth of us all. Beyond the beckoning vestige, it is a harking back to simpler and more vigorous and buoyant —yes, and more violent—days. Its history, like our green years, is right there, or just was. We can almost catch it by the coattails. The fragrance of its leaving lingers in the still unsettled dust of departure. We reach for it, for the stout heart and muscles of yesterday, for the great and exciting pastures of innocence, for the young simplicities of right and wrong, for the vanished opportunities to do our stuff.

It doesn't matter too much that our hands come back empty. They were close, so close that for a moment we hunted furs with the mountain men and caught the firelight playing in the eyes of Indian girls. Or we traveled the Oregon Trail with old Joel Palmer[7] and fought the muscled waters of the Snake. Or we panned the gleaming gold from the placer mines of California, Colorado, Idaho. Or we helped string up Henry Plummer, the murderous sheriff of the Montana gold camps, or walked with Doc Holliday to the fight at the O.K. Corral. Or we stood stout with Captain Benteen against the circling Sioux after Custer had fallen.

We were young for that moment, and the land was young, and the old westering was fresh in our blood. And maybe, despite the immediate toil and excitement, we thought *America, America,* from the pygmy beginnings of Jamestown and Plymouth across the unimagined miles to the bar and balm of the Pacific. Farms are chopped out along the way. Cabins rise. Ferries start up. Here's a fort or a cross-trail tavern, germ of a city to be. Out of the woods, then, to the new land, to the strange and bare land, to the Great American Desert, where undreamed-of herdsmen and tillers and armed contestants soon will add to knowledge and legend. On toward the still brief-storied mountains, on toward Oregon, California, maybe Washington, and the hell with Indians, Mexicans, British, the hell with weather and windfall and river and range. Men drop out along the way to try their luck here and there, but wheels roll on, hoofs plod, and other men won't turn or tarry.

Furs. Fish. Small crops. Lumber. Gold in the mountains. Fat grass on the plains, fertile soil in the desert. Ranches. Irrigation. Dryland farms. Cities and towns. Industries. Today.

It all happened almost under our eyes. Two long lifetimes span much of it. Seeing it again on the screens of our minds, we think how happy is that hard phrase, Manifest Destiny.[8] And we know that, more than journey's end, it

7. **Joel Palmer** (1810–1881), pioneer and author of *Journal of Travel over the Rocky Mountains,* a day-by-day account of his journey along the Oregon Trail.
8. **Manifest Destiny,** a belief in the inevitable expansion of a people to the geographical limits.

is the journey itself that enchants us. The fresh and free years. The years of youth.

If there is a prime reason less than mystic for our enduring attachment to the West of fact and story, it can now perhaps be capsuled. The West freed and frees us. It emphasized and emphasizes us as individuals—this is an elsewhere and nowadays world which at its freest and best still dwarfs individuality by congestion and restricts high adventure to a Sunday afternoon picnic. The West still makes the blood sing as it used to sing when hearts were stout and vistas inviting and the limit of hope in each of us was the far-western sea.

The West is an adventure of the spirit.

Each passing generation of actual inhabitants loses the West, and each succeeding one rediscovers it. For mountain men like Jim Bridger and Tom Fitzpatrick the end came when beaver thinned out and Londoners ruined the market, to boot, by quitting fur hats in favor of them newfangled silk ones. It came for the hide-hunter when he had killed all the buffalo and put himself out of business. In Montana a bunch of them named a place Belly Ups. It came for the placer miner when the placers played out. With the wolves gone, the West was gone for the wolfer. The cowpuncher rode high, wide and handsome, but not for long after some fool invented barbed wire. Fences, internal combustion and the increasing number of pilgrims finished the good life for Charlie Russell, the famous western painter, himself once a pilgrim. His later years were years of lament. Owen Wister married the West, only to divorce it when it turned false. Today's aging homesteaders, destroyers of one West, pine for their own good old days.

Out of informed imagination, sympathy and perhaps a touch of the same personal sentiment, Walter Prescott Webb, the Texas historian, speaks eloquently in his study, *The Great Frontier:*

"The period of fusion is about over, the loom is about full, the tapestry of an epoch is almost finished. . . . The imagination cannot play any more with the mystery and uncertainty of a half-known world, for there is no such thing. The map is finished, the roads are surveyed, and all the paths to that kind of adventure are plainly marked and tended. . . . The end of an age is always touched with sadness for those who lived it and those who love it. . . . The people are going to miss the frontier more than words can express. For four centuries they heard its call, listened to its promises, and bet their lives and fortunes on its outcome. It calls no more, and regardless of how they bend their ears for its faint whisper they cannot hear the suggestion of a promise."

Admit the broad position but take some exception. All is not lost. They come season after season, the new finders of the West: tourists, dude-ranch guests, members of the military, chain-company transplantees, traveling men who have not been this way before. After New York or Chicago or St. Louis here is virgin land, here is the real thing, the unpossessed and pristine property. They look with wonder and delight, many of them do, feeling within themselves the cozy excitement of discovery. This foot may be the first that trod here. These lungs breathe air no others ever breathed. *Space is mine. I am filled. I flow with it, and so at last am free.*

An astonishing number of these new discoverers stay in the West. An astonishing number return whenever they can. An astonishing number hate the necessity of leaving. But were they all to settle, the last vestige of the West would vanish.

I have made the trip west many times, and never with a lessening of old elation. Once, flying, I went instantly from Courthouse Rock to Chimney Rock, a whole day's journey on the trail to Oregon, but I could see them underneath me there in present-day Nebraska, the laden wagons, the patient oxen, the striving men, the anxious and long-suffering women, all wheeling out our history. The pistons pounded and the props tore air, but above the din came "Gee" and "Haw."

By car I approach or reach or pass the 98th meridian, the rough dividing line between woodland and plain. I come to Tulsa or Topeka or Fargo or Fort Worth or Sioux Falls, and I can smell home. Even eastward along the Mississippi, at Dubuque or Davenport or Burlington or St. Louis or Minneapolis, its scent blows in the wind. When I attain the Missouri, if my route lies that way, I'm in full chase. From here all ways lie west. The Black Hills. The Little Bighorn. The Sweetwater and the Wind River range. The Colorado Rockies and the mountain parks where wintered mountain men. Virginia City and the Comstock Lode. Taos and old Santa Fe. The Grand Canyon. Between me and them the fields of truth and story. And always beyond, the golden shore.

In these directions, any of them, the roads will straighten and traffic thin. The land will shine, the long and young yet memoried land of wish, and distance will expand my chest. Here, now, looking westward, I've got the whole world in my hand, and going toward the sunset I shall find what I desire.

I
A WRITER'S VIEW OF THE WEST

In an essay a writer tries to argue persuasively for his own point of view. A good reader, therefore, always reads an essay critically, noting especially what evidence the author offers for his viewpoint while at the same time considering what contrary evidence might be offered in opposition to his viewpoint. You should expect an essayist to be *biased*—to favor his own point of view. On the other hand, he should not be prejudiced—make hasty judgments with little or no knowledge to back them up. Would you say that Guthrie is biased in favor of the West? Is his opinion prejudiced?

Guthrie gives two essential reasons why Americans are fascinated by the West: (1) "the specialty of space," and (2) the type of man that space breeds, a type that Guthrie implies we would all like to resemble.

1. What does the author mean by "the specialty of space"? In what specific ways do persons who live in "crowded States" show that the open spaces still appeal to them?

2. Make a list of the values and characteristics possessed by the man that "space breeds," according to Guthrie. How do these compare with your own values and characteristics?

II
IMPLICATIONS

Below are five pairs of contradictory statements. On the basis of your reading of Guthrie's essay and your own experience, decide which statement in each pair you agree with. Discuss your position with those who hold the opposite view.

1a. The West is vastly different from other sections of the United States.

b. The West is no different from any other section of the country, except that it is younger.

2a. Americans are more fascinated by the American West than by any other section of the world.

b. The desire of Americans to visit Europe shows that they are not a "sunset people," as Guthrie maintains.

3a. Most Americans would like to live in the "wide open spaces."

b. Statistics prove that Americans like to live in crowded areas; for many decades now our urban population has increased by a much greater percentage than our rural population.

4a. Individuality is dwarfed by congested places.

b. People who live in small towns and in open spaces are much less individualistic than those who live in large cities.

5a. The ways of thinking of the frontiersmen have been more influential in shaping American values than have the ways of thinking of any other group.

b. The men who founded our democracy were not frontiersmen, and they have been more influential in shaping American values than have any other group of Americans.

The name Ford is perhaps better known by more people than any other name
in American history. But what has Henry Ford to do with "endless frontiers"
of the kind you have been reading about? Was he animated by something
of the same spirit that animated the people in "Early Marriage"?
In the following biographical sketch the historian,
Allan Nevins, probes the many-sided character of this famous American.

Henry Ford

ALLAN NEVINS

One of the most remarkable facts about Henry Ford is that his fame and the Ford legend were born almost simultaneously, and born full-grown. Both came late in life, when he was fifty. The industrialist, we may say without exaggeration, was little known until he suddenly became a world celebrity. He was tossed into international eminence on January 5, 1914, when the Ford Motor Company startled the globe with its "Five Dollar Day."[1]

Until then, Henry Ford had touched the national consciousness but occasionally and glancingly. He had founded the Ford Motor Company in 1903, when already forty; after some years of uncertain struggle, he had produced a model, distinguished from previous Models B, N, and S by the letter T, which precisely filled a ravenous national want; he had erected at Highland Park, just outside Detroit, one of the best-planned and most efficient factories in the world. He and a group of tireless, gifted associates were bringing to birth that magic implement of global change termed mass production; still little understood (for most people ignorantly equate it with quantity production, which is merely one of its half-dozen chief components), and then not understood at all. Ford was, of course, known in the Detroit area as an astonishingly successful manufac-turer, and in the automotive world as the dauntless leader of the battle against the Selden[2] patent monopoly. But elsewhere until 1914 the name Ford connoted a brand, not a man.

Henry Ford's sudden fame did not burst and fade; it remained fixed in the skies as a brightening star. Seekers for facts on the mind and character of the man before 1914 find that the materials are scanty, that most of them pertain to his activities as a racer and in the shop, and that when pieced together they furnish no real portrait. But after 1914, what a change! The spate of articles, books, interviews, and reminiscences becomes ever more torrential. "The Ford and Charlie Chaplin," remarked Will Rogers, "are the best known objects in the world." As the renown grew, unfortunately, so did the confusing legend. As one parodist of the Ford Motor Company slogan put it, "Watch the Ford myths go by!"

Lord Northcliffe[3] extolled Henry Ford to the British public as symbol and exemplar of American energy, confidence and resourcefulness. In

1. **Five Dollar Day,** the day Henry Ford raised wages from $2.25 to $5.00.
2. **Selden, George Baldwin,** granted first American patent for gasoline-driven car. Ford refused to pay royalties and finally gained decision that his motor was fundamentally different.
3. **Lord Northcliffe,** Viscount; Alfred Charles William Harmsworth, family of British publishers and politicians.

"Henry Ford" appeared in *American Heritage* magazine. Reprinted by permission of American Heritage Publishing Company, Inc.

Paris Charles M. Schwab,[4] invited to a dinner by Baron Rothschild,[5] electrified the table by describing Ford's achievements. For a time in 1923–24 Ford's quasi-autobiography, translated as *Mein Leben und Werke,*[6] was one of the two best-selling books in Germany. From Sweden to Turkey a new word, *Fordismus,* epitomized the new mass production engineering, the new low-price economy of abundance, and the new efficiency speed-up. Throughout Latin America Ford's personality was regarded as summing up the quintessential American traits and gifts. As for Russia, painfully aware of her industrial backwardness, Henry Ford was a figure about whom *moujiks*[7] and mechanics wove wistful dreams. *Fordizatsia* or Fordization was one of the terms of power in the new era. A visit from Ford, wrote Maurice Hindus,[8] would have called out Russian admirers in hordes.

In the United States, too, the Ford of fact and the Ford of myth were for a time indistinguishably blended. "While I do not accept all of Mr. Ford's industrial philosophy," wrote John A. Ryan, Director of the National Catholic Welfare Council, after reading *My Life and Work,* "I realize more strongly than ever that he has made the greatest contribution toward a solution of more than one of our industrial problems that has yet been made by any captain of industry." The public devoured books about him by Allan Benson, William L. Stidger, Rose Franklin Lane, Charles Merz, Ralph Graves, Dean Marquis and others. Technologists and manufacturers studied the classic work on Ford machines and Ford methods by Arnold and Faurote, an able primer of mass production requirements.

The fifteen years 1914–29 saw Henry Ford at apogee. The American masses took him to their hearts; every clerk and farmer had his own image of the man. But which lines in that image were false, and which true? The task of gaining a true portrait was not simplified by writers who tried to establish an artificial pattern, for of all human beings the complicated, disorganized Ford least responds to that effort.

Nor was it simplified by the fact that Henry Ford discovered himself about the time the world did, and announced his discovery by pronunciamentos from on high and essays in self portraiture which wove oriental embroideries about the real man.

At once the most impressive and most disturbing fact about Henry Ford is the extent to which he held up a mirror to the modern American character. In his technological talents, his feats as organizer, his individualistic economics, his social blindness, his frequent brilliant insights, his broad veins of ignorance, prejudice and suspicion, he at first glance seems unique; a man fascinating in his intricacy even to those who most detest some of his traits. Assuredly, we say, nobody else ever existed like Henry Ford. Nothing in industrial history is more inspiring than the triumphs of his early days at the Piquette and Highland Park plants. Nothing in the same history is more depressing than some of the pages he wrote later, pages that would approach high tragedy but for their stupidity and harshness. We seek for threads to explain his labyrinthine complications, and we suddenly realize that in strength and weakness, pioneering thrust and reactionary conservatism, generosity and selfishness, he came near typifying the America of his time.

What made him a tremendous American force was his clear perception of four or five fundamental facts: that the American people not only wanted but needed cars in millions; that a single durable inexpensive model could meet that demand; that new technological elements (precise standardization of parts, the multiplication and perfection of machine tools,

4. **Charles M. Schwab**\shwŏb\ American industrialist; president of Carnegie Steel Co., U.S. Steel Corp., Bethlehem Steel Corp.
5. **Baron Rothschild**\rŏth·chaild\ member of the famous family of financiers; first of Jewish faith to be admitted to the House of Lords, English Parliament.
6. **Mein Leben und Werke**\main lĕ·bĕn ʊnd vĕr·kə\ *My Life and Work.*
7. **moujiks**\mū ᴧzhēkz\, also muzhiks\mū ᴧzhēkz\ Russian peasants in the time of the Czars.
8. **Maurice Hindus**\ᴧhĭn·dəs\ a Russian-born writer who came to the United States in 1905.

separation of the job into minutely specialized functions, quantity manufacture, continuous motion, Taylor time studies), when woven together to create mass production, could furnish the millions of cheap vehicles; that steady price reduction meant steady marked expansion ("Every time I lower the price a dollar we gain a thousand new buyers"); and that high wages meant high buying power.

All this was as obvious, when demonstrated, as Columbus' art of standing the egg on end. Until demonstrated it was so far from patent that the ablest manufacturers scoffed, and Ford had to battle his principal partner and the current trend to prove it. A special kind of genius lies in seeing what everybody says is obvious— once somebody thinks of it; and Ford, in relation to his time, had that genius. It changed the world.

Next to this insight, Henry Ford's most striking gift was unquestionably his peculiar engineering talent. In mechanics, he combined much of da Vinci's creative quality with much of James Watt's practical acumen. As a few rare men are born with the power of instantaneously performing intricate mathematical computations, Ford had the power of divining almost any mechanism at a glance. He *read* engines. Indeed, his associate, W. J. Cameron, says that the great engine collections he made in his museum and at Greenfield Village were his historical library. "They were living things to him, those machines. He could almost diagnose the arrangement by touching it. There was a peculiar sympathy between him and a machine." That gift had been with him when as a boy he took apart and reassembled every watch he could reach, and spent a Sunday afternoon, his father away, in disassembling and restoring much of a steam engine.

This flair generated a passion which explains another of his traits, his remarkable power of hard, sustained work. The relaxed air which the mature Henry Ford wore in public, together with his well-advertised recreations in square dancing, collecting Americana, and making excursions with Edison, Firestone and Burroughs,

concealed from some observers the fact that from boyhood to old age (he was seventy in 1933) he led a singularly laborious, concentrated life. In his prime his frequent periods of intense industry would have exhausted a less resilient man. At Highland Park and River Rouge his responsibilities were always enormous. But his engineering passion made one important part of them—the responsibility for steady mechanical experiment—almost a refreshment.

Day-to-day study of his activities gives us the picture of a man in whose quick brain exploded a steady succession of technological ideas. A helical type of spring band to use in planetary transmission for holding the drum; a new element in the carburetor; a bolder mode of casting the engine block—always some novel ingenuity had to be tried. That side of his mind never rested. "He was up at Harbor Beach one time," writes E. G. Liebold, "where he had a summer cottage, and he was coming home with Edsel. Suddenly he said: 'I've got the idea. We're going to put a worm drive on the tractor.'" That idea solved the theretofore vexatious problem of power transmission to the rear axle —or so he hoped; and he drove his tractor factory ahead with enhanced zest.

In experimentation, pioneering, the quest for fruitful mechanical innovations, Henry Ford at his apogee was happiest. Anything was worth trying. In 1914–15 he became interested in making a better electric car than any on the market, and reports spread that he and Edison were collaborating. If the idea proved good (which it did not) he thought of forming a separate company. A later scheme called for the use of plastics in building cars; in fact, a plastic-body car *was* built. This experiment was connected with Ford's intense interest in promoting soy bean culture, for he realized that American agriculture needed new crops and that American industry suffered from a growing shortage of vegetable oils.

Now and then some incident suggested how far back in Ford's career his experimental passion reached. He once turned his attention to a slide-valve engine on which Knight, of Willys-

Knight, held some patents. Reflecting that he might wish some time to build such an engine, Ford decided to protect himself by recovering an old slide-valve that, as a humble mechanic, he put in a Westinghouse steam engine. He actually recalled that the engine had been No. 345 and had been shipped to McKean County, Pa. A searcher found the battered engine; found an old bill of sale which proved that it *was* No. 345; and found the name-plate, which was being used on a stove-grate. Brought to Dearborn, the engine was triumphantly restored to the condition in which Ford had known it.

His technological genius was one aspect of a mind peculiar for its intuitive nature. Ford hit upon truths (and errors) by divination, not ratiocination. His aides credited him with what Dean Marquis called a "supernormal perceptive faculty" and W. J. Cameron "some gadgets in his head that the rest of us didn't have." Marquis termed him "a dreamer," adding that he had a different view from other men of what was possible and impossible. "I suppose the reason is that men who dream walk by faith, and faith laughs at mountains." As Ford himself told Fred L. Black, he worked partly by hunches. Even his understanding of his lieutenants was largely intuitive.

Obviously, if intuition moved some mountains, it collided disastrously with certain more massive ranges. Reliance on intuition was one reason why Ford was so amazingly unpredictable; men never knew which of a half-dozen Fords they were going to meet. It was also one reason for the crippling isolation of his mind, for a brain that cannot be reasoned with is a brain that cannot be penetrated. Down to 1914 Ford was open to the counsel of men who had a right to insist on being heard: his partners Alex Malcomson and John S. Gray, his indispensable business manager James Couzens, the brilliant designer Harold Wills, and others. Later, with the amazing expansion of the business, the rise of employees to six figures, his achievement of autocratic power by the ousting of all his partners, and increasing age, Henry Ford placed

himself beyond advice. His mental isolation "is about as perfect as he can make it," wrote Marquis as early as 1923. Charles E. Sorensen, who ought to know, believes that Ford had only two lifelong friends: Sorensen himself, and the strong head of his British company, Percival L. D. Perry.

Henry Ford

His complex, inconsistent, intuitive mind has naturally lent itself to a Jekyll and Hyde concept of two (or more) Fords dwelling in the same body; but we may repeat that these efforts at pattern-making are delusive. One clue, however, does explain much in the Dearborn wizard. The dreamer, the man of intuitive mind, is usually an artist; and many puzzling vagaries, many contradictions, even many repugnant acts in Ford become comprehensible if we view him as essentially a man of artistic temperament. His detachment, his arch, wry humor, his constant self-projection into the spotlight (though all his intimates call him essentially modest), his ability to lift himself above those business minutiae which absorbed most industrialists, his readiness to do some terrible things with as little seeming consciousness of their quality as Byron or Swift showed in *their* misdeeds, all suggest an artistic bent. The Model T was homely awkwardness itself but it had artistic elements. Highland Park was the most artistic factory, in architecture, shining cleanliness, and harmonic arrangement, built in America in its day. The painter Charles Sheeler caught the beauty of the River Rouge plant. And what of the aesthetic element in the old dances, old folksongs, old buildings, and old machines Ford loved so well?

Above all, he had the artist's desire to remake the world after his own pattern. His gospel of abundant work, high wages, and low prices; his plans for decentralizing industry to combine it with rural life and rural virtues; his enthusiastic forays into "better" agriculture, "better" education, "better" recreation; his warm promotion from 1914–20 of the welfare work of his "sociological department"—what else were these but the artist's effort to impose his own vision on life? He would remold American society and the American economy to fit his vision, himself the potter at the whirling wheel.

If there was a Jekyll and Hyde element in the man, it lay in the complex enmity between Ford the artist and Ford the untutored countryman whose parents had been Michigan pioneers, and whose own formal education was limited to a few years in a very common school. This conflict twisted the whole skein of his character. An artist needs a cultivated background: Henry Ford's background was that of Anglo-Irish tenant farmers, and of Springwells Township lately wrested from the forest. Though from his homely early environment he drew many advantages, its limitations always fettered him.

He always remained a countryman in his plain way of living, for despite Keith Sward's statements, it *was* plain. When his fortune first grew, he said plaintively that the chief difference in his way of life was that "Mrs. Ford no longer does the cooking"—and he preferred her cookery. He refused a butler, for he wanted no man behind his chair at dinner "while I am taking the potatoes' jackets off." His puritanic condemnation of smoking, drinking and marital irregularities conformed to the principles described in Thorstein Veblen's essay *The Country Town*. He rejected the eminent Delancey Nicoll as attorney in the Sapiro case because, when the New York lawyer came to Dearborn, Ford saw him chain-smoking cigarettes. "I'm for Mr. Coolidge if he will enforce the Prohibition laws," he said in 1923. He was a countryman also in his devotion to work as a virtue in itself. His cure for nearly all ills was more work.

True to the frontiersman's instinct, he consistently preferred trial and error to precise planning. Contemptuous of elaborate record-keeping, he once shocked Perry by making a bonfire of forms used to keep track of spare parts. Hostile to meticulous organization, he ran even the huge Highland Park plant without formal titles or administrative grades. He long derided careful cost accounting. In this, thinks one surviving executive, H. L. Moekle, he was right. Success in the automotive industry at first depended not on computation of costs to the third decimal point in Rockefeller's fashion, but on courageous innovations in design and engineering and on the acceptability of models and prices to the public. Ford stayed in the field of bold experiment—cost accounting might have hampered him. He of course stuck to Model T too long, but meanwhile he was experimenting with tractors, a tri-motored airplane, a weekly journal, a railroad, and a dozen other matters.

He had also the frontiersman's intense hatred of monopoly and special privilege. To be sure, he long enjoyed a practical monopoly of the low-priced car, but he could say that he achieved it without favor and without warring on any competitor. His dislike of patents, his earnest counsel to George Holley to take out no patent on his carburetor, his course in throwing open to public view and general use Ford machines and methods, his determined battle against George Selden, all harmonized with the frontier attitude. He extended the principle beyond automotive patents. His early broadcasting station WWI carried on research, worked out (so associates say) the first directional airplane controls, and gained a patent—which he shared with all. Once his purchaser, Fred Diehl, was offered spark plugs free for River Rouge production if the supplier were allowed to sell all replacements to dealers. "Mr. Ford himself turned that down," reports a lieutenant. "He said he didn't want anything from anybody for nothing." A true countryman's speech; for a scheme that would have meant monopoly supply was abhorrent to Henry Ford.

Much more might be said on the pleasanter inheritances from the rural environment—on his rather appealing inarticulateness which kept him from making public speeches (the longest ever recorded was 28 words): on his dislike of class lines, which was one of several reasons for his aversion from Grosse Pointe[9] society; on the rugged comradeship with fellow workers which he showed in his early career, but unhappily lost; on his warm love of nature, and the feeling for wild life which made him build shelters for rabbits, grow corn for crows, and keep warm water available all winter in the hope of retaining migratory songbirds in the North. One of the most important parts of his countryman's heritage was his stubborn originality of thought—when he did think. Neither from books nor men did he take ideas secondhand; he hammered them out for himself, usually on walks in field and woods. Often they were immature. Just sometimes, between intuition and lonely thinking, he seized a concept which startled men with its novel glint of truth.

Meanwhile, what penalties his early environment, and his invincible ignorance in many areas, laid upon him! Like other untutored men, he had a deep suspicion of the uncomprehended, a strong inclination to prejudice, and a susceptibility to bad counsel. Some thought his antagonism to Wall Street traceable to a memory of Populist[10] speeches, others to his anxieties in the depression of 1921; but surely three-fourths of it was simple distrust of what he did not understand. It is significant that his suspiciousness, hardly visible in his first years

of success, grew marked when he came under fire. "Ford has the idea that he is persecuted," a writer in the *Forum* accurately stated in 1919. He thought that some journals had begun to "hound" him when he announced the $5 day, and others when he battled for peace and the League.

"A good part of the American press, not all, is not free," he told reporters. It lay, he thought, under various controls, it was warped by sensationalism. "They misquoted me, distorted what I said, made up lies." The gibing, malicious attitude of part of the press toward the Peace Ship,[11] the aspersions on his motives in lifting wages from $2.25 to $5, the mean attacks on Edsel as an alleged draftdodger, and the storm of ridicule accompanying the Chicago *Tribune* trial and the senatorial campaign, were indeed outrageous. Since Ford was a sensitive man, they had a perceptible effect in hardening his temper and converting his early idealism into cynicism. Had he possessed more education, poise, and perspective, he would not only have avoided some of the occasions for ridicule; he would have met ridicule with a heavier armor.

Out of his sense of needing an agency for defense and for stating his ideas came the Dearborn[12] Independent. Out of his ignorance, sensitiveness, and suspiciousness came the lamentable anti-Semitic campaign of that weekly, for which he apologized only after vast harm had been done. In this unhappy crusade he had collaborators. The shrewd F. G. Pipp, who resigned as editor rather than share in it, made a brutally frank statement to Cameron: "You are furnishing the brains, Ford the money, and E. G. Liebold the prejudices." Cameron and Liebold furnished some of the methods, too, but as Liebold says, "As long as Mr. Ford wanted it

9. **Grosse Pointe,** residential city in southeast Michigan on Lake St. Clair, 8 miles east of Detroit.
10. **Populist,** political party advocating increase in currency, free coinage of silver, public control of railroads, income tax, limited ownership of property.
11. **Peace Ship,** the label given the ship Ford chartered and sailed to Christiania, Norway, 1915, in a personal gesture to end the war.
12. **Dearborn,** site of Ford's manufacturing plant.

done, it was done." His was the responsibility. That he had no deep-seated race prejudices, but really believed in a fictitious bogy called the International Jew, does not palliate his offense. We can only say that this, like the short-sighted harshness which he showed toward labor organizations, was the abortion of an uninformed mind and uncultivated spirit.

Some aspects of the man, defying any efforts to fix a pattern, remain—as in such other contradictory personages as Edwin M. Stanton or Woodrow Wilson—quite inexplicable. Highly diffident in some ways, he had an irrepressible desire to be oracular about topics of which he knew nothing. Kindly in most personal relations, he nevertheless countenanced such cruel treatment of subordinates as the smashing of their desks in token of discharge. At times he indulged a good humored liking for horseplay—"he was a proper Puck,"[13] as Lord Perry expressed it; at other times he was sternly unapproachable. Sharply practical, he yet cherished some curious superstitions. A churchgoing Episcopalian, he leaned strongly to an unorthodox belief in metempsychosis.[14] There was always something in him of an urchin, a wry, cross-grained, brilliant adolescent; and like an energetic urchin, he was so kinetic that only a motion picture could have caught his multifarious activities and swiftly changing moods.

Yet in this fascinating personality, with its bright lights, dark shadows, and intermediate *chiaroscuro*[15] traits, we come back always to the image of the artist. John Reed, interviewing him in 1916, thought he looked like an artist, with "thin, long, sure hands, incessantly moving"; "the mouth and nose of a simple-minded saint"; "a lofty forehead"; "the lower part of his face extraordinarily serene and naïve, the upper part immensely alive and keen." His swiftness, his agility, his intense interest in everything he observed, contributed to the impression of an artistic temperament. Much that is otherwise puzzling becomes comprehensible if we think of him as an artist, struggling, despite many limitations and handicaps, to remake his world a little nearer to the heart's desire. He wanted

to abolish war ("a habit, and a filthy habit," he said) from his world, and hence the great gesture of the Peace Ship. He wanted to exclude drink, class divisions, idleness and disorder. He wanted to get rid of money as anything but a part of the mechanism of production: "part of the assembly line," or "the connecting rod."

Perhaps his poignant failure lay in his relationship to his son, to whom he gave both intense devotion and total incomprehension. Edsel was a man of the finest qualities of character and mind, upright, idealistic, public-spirited, and hard-working. He was highly philanthropic. In the factory he got on well with other executives, many of whom felt a warm affection for him. In the world at large, as old associates testify, he had a broader vision than his father. Some of Henry Ford's acts, such as the anti-Jewish campaign, grieved Edsel greatly, though he was too loyal to speak out publicly. Yet the father, while justly proud of him, committed a fundamental error in their relationship. "He tried to make Edsel in his own image," says Mr. Sorensen. In the process he did incidental injustice to some men like Clarence W. Avery who, coming close to Edsel, aroused his jealousy. Of course he failed in his effort, with anguish to both himself and the son. But the attempt was again, in part, an expression of the artist's desire to make the world over to suit his own vision.

As the years pass and as we gain perspective, the absurd blunders and shabby misdeeds in Henry Ford's record will arouse less interest. His social primitivism will seem more a part of the general ignorance and gullibility of our adolescent American civilization. His great achievement, in the direct line of Watt and

---

13. **Puck**, a character from English folklore, either a mischievous elf or goblin, as in Shakespeare's *A Midsummer Night's Dream*.
14. **metempsychosis**\mə ˈtɛm·sə ˌkō·səs\ belief that after death the soul passes to another body, human or animal; transmigration of the soul.
15. **chiaroscuro**\kē ˈɔr·ə ˌskyūr·ō\ variety of dissimilar qualities thought of in terms of black and white, light and shade.

Stephenson, Eli Whitney and Cyrus McCormick, yet in some ways transcending theirs, will loom up as the really significant fact of his career. By his labors in bringing mass production to birth, by his gospel of high production, low prices, and large consumption, he became the key figure in a far-reaching revolution. This fumbling artist actually did remold the world according to his vision. Talking with Edsel one day, he said of his great company: "Well, we'll build this as well as we know how, and if we don't use it, somebody will use it. Anything that is good enough will be used." Of few of the industrial path-hewers of his time can it be said that they produced so much that is permanently and profitably usable.

I
HENRY FORD—THE CHARACTER OF AN INDUSTRIAL PIONEER

Along with certain other men of his time, Henry Ford has been called an industrial pioneer. Do you think the term "pioneer" or "frontiersman" is an appropriate label for a man like Ford? In what important ways did he resemble a pioneer? What were the "frontiers" that he "explored"?

II
IMPLICATIONS

A good biographer not only makes generalizations about his subject, he also cites specific details to prove his points. Cite some of the specific details that Professor Nevins used as a basis for the generalizations he made about Henry Ford.

1. What happened in 1914 to change Ford's name from the name of a brand to the name of a man?

2. How was Ford himself responsible for some of the myths that grew up about him?

3. What is gained by viewing Ford as an artist? How specifically did he resemble one? According to Nevins, in what important way did Ford differ from an artist?

4. How would more education have helped Ford?

III
TECHNIQUES
Characterization

As a biographer, Professor Nevins' concern with the character of his subject is understandably different from the concern of a novelist or a short-story writer. We expect writers of fiction to *select* certain facets of their characters' personalities for emphasis and to neglect others. From a biographer, however, we commonly expect a more objective and fully rounded portrait. Remembering that Nevins was writing only a short sketch and not a full-scale biography, do you think that he created an objective and fully rounded portrait of his subject?

IV
WORDS

A. Using the context as a clue, what do the following italicized words mean? Use a dictionary to check your answers.

1. Poverty-stricken, unspeakably *forlorn,* the caravan creaked along, advancing at a snail's pace. . . .

2. . . . he kept his eyes *resolutely* fixed on the scene ahead.

3. But more important in our whole thinking and *inclination* is the old and uncivilized West, the West . . . of lawlessness, hardship, *license,* dispute and resolution by revolver and rifle, the West . . . that opposes *propriety.*

4. . . . Ford's personality was regarded as summing up the *quintessential* American traits and gifts.

5. . . . seek for threads to explain his *labyrinthine* complications. . . .

6. . . . irrepressible desire to be *oracular* about topics of which he knew nothing.

7. Only a motion picture could have caught his *multifarious* activities. . . .

B. Below are pairs of synonyms. What common meaning does each pair share? How do they differ?

1. vestige—trace; ravenous—greedy; acumen—insight.

2. resilient—flexible; ingenuity—cleverness; ingenuous—simple.

3. repugnant — disagreeable; countenanced — faced; poignant—piercing.

Gallery | ENDLESS FRONTIERS

Endlessly the frontiers of the human experience stretch out beyond men's reach. Repeatedly, men find that each goal grasped opens a new horizon, the new frontier waiting for the daring and the courageous.

This gallery of paintings traces briefly the progress of the American frontier which surged from the familiar European culture of the coastal cities through thousands of miles of wilderness with such expanding power that in its path rose the wealthiest society the world has yet known—vast cities, new technologies, a wide-based culture, and a view of new frontiers that opens on the universe itself. Though widely different in subject matter, the tension and excitement of this rich theme explodes out of all of the paintings. Depicting the American frontier has been a frontier of its own.

DANIEL BOONE ESCORTING A BAND OF PIONEERS INTO THE WESTERN COUNTRY
George Caleb Bingham

The renowned frontiersman, Daniel Boone, not only blazed the Wilderness Road over the Cumberland Mountains from Tennessee to Kentucky, but also spent many years leading settlers to new territory. After building Fort Boonesboro near the end of the Wilderness Road, Boone brought his courageous wife Rebecca and their daughter Jemima to the new settlement. This view of Boone leading settlers may record that entrance of the first white women into the Kentucky frontier.

Though he was only nine years old when Boone died, the careful observations with which the famous portrait painter Bingham filled his sketchbooks provided the treasure trove from which he created the many realistic paintings which were his monument to the Westward Movement.

IN SEARCH OF THE LAND
OF MILK AND HONEY
Harvey Dunn

Farther west and nearly one hundred years later, dauntless Americans continued to search for the "Land of Milk and Honey," the fair country where they could carve out a new and abundant life. A tribute to the pioneers, this painting hangs in the Library of DeSmet, South Dakota.

Once the land had been found, the frontier became the working of it, a frontier worthily met by the enduring spirit of the resourceful homesteaders.
The Kansas-bred painter Curry pioneered his own frontier in an American regional style of painting.

HOMESTEADERS
John Steuart Curry

APPROACHING
BUFFALO—
BATISTE BEYOND
AND I
George Catlin

The sheer physical presence of endless frontiers is felt
in Catlin's painting of his guide and himself approaching a winding herd
of buffalo. This self-taught artist of the last century lived
among many different tribes of Indians, recording a way of life
that was already disappearing—yielding to the advance of homesteads and
railroads, "talking wires" and the miner's shovel.

SONG OF THE TALKING WIRE
Henry Farny

Despite the still lonely prairie,
the frontier was ending
for the Indian trying to decode
with his hunter's ear the strange
new song from the "Talking
Wires." Throughout man's
history, a young people pushing
along their new frontiers
have spelled the end
of the ancient cultures
in their path.
Farny's painting
pictures the problem
with touching clarity.

Linking the frontier with small towns and Eastern cities, America's first train travels west in 1864 on Union Pacific rails. This popular Currier and Ives print was copied from a painting the successful printmakers had commissioned on a subject dear to the hearts of Americans.

ACROSS THE CONTINENT
Currier and Ives

A devoted painter of the American scene, Burchfield has given us a strong watercolor statement about the early industrial frontier. From BLACK IRON can you imagine how he felt? In a sense his meaning may be basically the same as that of the SONG OF THE TALKING WIRE. What dies along this frontier?

BLACK IRON
Charles Burchfield

73

The sea as well as
the land is a frontier,
one challenged
by hardy Americans,
especially around the
middle of the last century.
As the WHALEMAN suggests
there are men who prefer
the excitement of its
endless dangers to the
victories to be won on land.
Again, the secondary
theme within a theme:
one man's frontier
can spell death
to those
who were before him.

WHALEMAN
Ben Stahl

A frontier is reached, and stretching out
beyond is the almost limitless expanse
of electric power to be explored and mastered.
Notice the detailed and amusing portraits
included in this painting of a historic moment
in the laboratory of Thomas Edison.

EDISON AND HIS WORKERS IN THE PROCESS OF TESTING
THE FIRST PRACTICAL INCANDESCENT LAMP
Dean Cornwell

Thomas Price's laboratory was
in San Francisco. He was
California State Mineralogist
and Chemist. The scientific frontier
is exacting but endlessly fascinating
in its myriad implications for man's life.

THE LABORATORY
OF THOMAS PRICE
Henry Alexander

Centered on the soaring cables of a suspension bridge, this painting by Joseph Stella speaks of the frontiers of the modern city.

THE BRIDGE
Joseph Stella
Collection of the
Newark Museum

On December 17, 1903, at the end of the same year in which Henry Ford founded the Ford Motor Company, yet another frontier was opened. As you read of the Wright brothers in the following selection, consider their likeness to pioneers such as Columbus and Henry Ford. "The Campers at Kitty Hawk" is an excerpt from *The Big Money* (1936), the last of the three novels in John Dos Passos' famous trilogy, *U.S.A.* You will find that Dos Passos' style in this excerpt is rather impressionistic and poetic; note how this helps him to achieve a more dramatic effect.

The Campers at Kitty Hawk

JOHN DOS PASSOS

On December seventeenth, nineteen hundred and three, Bishop Wright of the United Brethren onetime editor of the *Religious Telescope* received in his frame house on Hawthorn Street in Dayton, Ohio, a telegram from his boys Wilbur and Orville who'd gotten it into their heads to spend their vacations in a little camp out on the dunes of the North Carolina coast tinkering with a homemade glider they'd knocked together themselves. The telegram read:

SUCCESS FOUR FLIGHTS THURSDAY MORNING ALL AGAINST TWENTYONE MILE WIND STARTED FROM LEVEL WITH ENGINEPOWER ALONE AVERAGE SPEED THROUGH AIR THIRTYONE MILES LONGEST FIFTY-SEVEN SECONDS INFORM PRESS HOME CHRISTMAS

The figures were a little wrong because the telegraph operator misread Orville's hasty penciled scrawl
but the fact remains
that a couple of young bicycle mechanics from Dayton, Ohio
had designed constructed and flown
for the first time ever a practical airplane.

From *U.S.A.* by John Dos Passos. Published by Houghton Mifflin Company; copyright by John Dos Passos. Reprinted by permission of John Dos Passos.

After running the motor a few minutes to heat it up I released the wire that held the machine to the track and the machine started forward into the wind. Wilbur ran at the side of the machine holding the wing to balance it on the track. Unlike the start on the 14th made in a calm the machine facing a 27 mile wind started very slowly. . . . Wilbur was able to stay with it until it lifted from the track after a forty-foot run. One of the lifesaving men snapped the camera for us taking a picture just as it reached the end of the track and the machine had risen to a height of about two feet. . . . The course of the flight up and down was extremely erratic, partly due to the irregularities of the air, partly to lack of experience in handling this machine. A sudden dart when a little over a hundred and twenty feet from the point at which it rose in the air ended the flight. . . . This flight lasted only 12 seconds but it was nevertheless the first in the history of the world in which a machine carrying a man had raised itself by its own power into the air in full flight, had sailed forward without reduction of speed and had finally landed at a point as high as that from which it started.

A little later in the day the machine was caught in a gust of wind and turned over and smashed, almost killing the coastguardsman who tried to hold it down;

> it was too bad
> but the Wright brothers were too happy to care
> they'd proved that the damn thing flew.

When these points had been definitely established we at once packed our goods and returned home knowing that the age of the flying machine had come at last.

They were home for Christmas in Dayton, Ohio, where they'd been born in the seventies of a family who had been settled west of the Alleghenies since eighteen fourteen, in Dayton, Ohio, where they'd been to grammarschool and highschool and joined their father's church and played baseball and hockey and worked out on the parallel bars and the flying swing and sold newspapers and built themselves a printingpress out of odds and ends from the junkheap and flown kites and tinkered with mechanical contraptions and gone around town as boys doing odd jobs to turn an honest penny.

The folks claimed it was the bishop's bringing home a helicopter, a fiftycent mechanical toy made of two fans worked by elastic bands that was supposed to hover in the air, that had got his two youngest boys hipped on the subject of flight.

so that they stayed home instead of marrying the way the other boys did, and puttered all day about the house picking up a living with jobprinting,

> bicyclerepair work,
> sitting up late nights reading books on aerodynamics.

Still they were sincere churchmembers, their bicycle business was prosperous, a man could rely on their word. They were popular in Dayton.

In those days flyingmachines were the big laugh of all the crackerbarrel philosophers. Langley's[1] and Chanute's[2] unsuccessful experiments had been jeered down with an I-told-you-so that rang from coast to coast. The Wrights' big problem was to find a place secluded enough to carry on their experiments without being the horsclaugh of the countryside. Then they had no money to spend;

they were practical mechanics; when they needed anything they built it themselves.

They hit on Kitty Hawk,

on the great dunes and sandy banks that stretch south towards Hatteras[3] seaward of Albemarle Sound,[4]

> a vast stretch of seabeach
> empty except for a coastguard station, a few fishermen's shacks and the swarms of mosquitoes and the ticks and chiggers in the crabgrass behind the dunes
> and overhead the gulls and swooping terns, in the evening fishhawks and cranes flapping across the saltmarshes, occasionally eagles
> that the Wright brothers followed soaring with their eyes
> as Leonardo[5] watched them centuries before
> straining his sharp eyes to apprehend
> the laws of flight.

Four miles across the loose sand from the scattering of shacks, the Wright brothers built themselves a camp and a shed for their gliders. It was a long way to pack their groceries, their tools, anything they happened to need; in summer it was hot as blazes, the mosquitoes were hell;

> but they were alone there
> and they'd figured out that the loose sand was as soft as anything they could find to fall in.

There with a glider made of two planes and a tail in which they lay flat on their bellies and controlled the warp of the planes by shimmy-

---

1. **Langley,** Samuel Pierpont (1834–1902), his heavier-than-air machine achieved flight, but his machine designed to carry a person failed.
2. **Chanute\\shə ⁕nūt** Octave (1832–1910), designed a biplane glider that exhibited some stability in flight.
3. **Hatteras,** cape off North Carolina.
4. **Albemarle \\⁕ăl·bĕ 'marl\\ Sound,** narrow strip of water about 60 miles long from the Atlantic Ocean extending into North Carolina.
5. **Leonardo,** Leonardo da Vinci\\də ⁕vĭn·chē\\ early sixteenth-century painter, sculptor, architect, engineer, scientist; left behind sketches of a man in flight.

ing their hips, taking off again and again all day from a big dune named Kill Devil Hill,
   they learned to fly.

   Once they'd managed to hover for a few seconds and soar ever so slightly on a rising aircurrent they decided the time had come to put a motor in their biplane.

   Back in the shop in Dayton, Ohio, they built an airtunnel, which is their first great contribution to the science of flying, and tried out model planes in it.
   They couldn't interest any builders of gasoline engines so they had to build their own motor.
   It worked; after that Christmas of nineteen three the Wright brothers weren't doing it for fun any more; they gave up their bicycle business, got the use of a big old cowpasture belonging to the local banker for practice flights, spent all the time when they weren't working on their machine in promotion, worrying about patents, infringements, spies, trying to interest government officials, to make sense out of the smooth involved heartbreaking remarks of lawyers.
   In two years they had a plane that would cover twentyfour miles at a stretch round and round the cowpasture.
   People on the interurban car used to crane their necks out of the windows when they passed along the edge of the field, startled by the clattering pop pop of the old Wright motor and the sight of the white biplane like a pair of ironingboards one on top of the other chugging along a good fifty feet in the air. The cows soon got used to it.

   As the flights got longer
   the Wright brothers got backers,
   engaged in lawsuits,
   lay in their beds at night sleepless with the whine of phantom millions, worse than the mosquitoes at Kitty Hawk.

   In nineteen seven they went to Paris,
   allowed themselves to be togged out in dress suits and silk hats,

   learned to tip waiters
   talked with government experts, got used to gold braid and postponements and vandyke beards[6] and the outspread palms of politicos. For amusement
   they played diabolo in the Tuileries gardens.[7]

   They gave publicized flights at Fort Myers, where they had their first fatal crackup, St. Petersburg, Paris, Berlin; at Pau they were all the rage,
   such an attraction that the hotelkeeper wouldn't charge them for their room.
   Alfonso of Spain shook hands with them and was photographed sitting in the machine,
   King Edward watched a flight,
   the Crown Prince insisted on being taken up,
   the rain of medals began.

   They were congratulated by the Czar
   and the King of Italy and the amateurs of sport, and the society climbers and the papal titles,
   and decorated by a society for universal peace.

   Aeronautics became the sport of the day.
   The Wrights don't seem to have been very much impressed by the upholstery and the braid and the gold medals and the parades of plush horses,
   they remained practical mechanics
   and insisted on doing all their own work themselves,
   even to filling the gasolinetank.

   In nineteen eleven they were back on the dunes
   at Kitty Hawk with a new glider.
   Orville stayed up in the air for nine and a half minutes, which remained a long time the record for motorless flight.
   The same year Wilbur died of typhoidfever in Dayton.

---

6. **Vandyke**\văn ᴧdaɪk\ **beards,** a trim, pointed beard.
7. **Tuileries**\ᴧtwē·lə 'rēz\ **gardens,** gardens of a former royal palace in Paris and now a public park near the Louvre\ᴧlūv, ᴧlū·vrə\.

In the rush of new names: Farman, Blériot, Curtiss, Ferber, Esnault-Peltrie, Delagrange;[8]

in the snorting impact of bombs and the whine and rattle of shrapnel and the sudden stutter of machineguns after the motor's been shut off overhead,

and we flatten into the mud

and make ourselves small cowering in the corners of ruined walls,

the Wright brothers passed out of the headlines

but not even headlines or the bitter smear of newsprint or the choke of smokescreen and gas or chatter of brokers on the stockmarket or barking of phantom millions or oratory of brasshats laying wreaths on new monuments

can blur the memory

of the chilly December day

two shivering bicycle mechanics from Dayton, Ohio,

first felt their homemade contraption

whittled out of hickory sticks,

gummed together with Arnstein's[9] bicycle cement,

stretched with muslin they'd sewn on their sister's sewingmachine in their own backyard on Hawthorn Street in Dayton, Ohio,

soar into the air

above the dunes and the wide beach

at Kitty Hawk.

I
AGAINST THE GRAIN

The Wright brothers chose Kitty Hawk to carry on their experiments because in a less secluded place they would have been "the horselaugh of the countryside." In his day, Columbus had to sail against the admonition that "Man should not

---

8. All pioneer aviators.
9. **Arnstein,** Karl, associated with Goodyear Tire and Rubber Co., vice-president Goodyear-Zeppelin.

tempt the Almighty by seeking unknown depths of ocean." Still other pioneers had to face persecution because of their attempts to open new frontiers. What is there in human nature or in society that has made many men so ready to scoff at and even destroy those who have attempted to explore the unknown? Do you think that such attitudes are less prevalent today?

II
IMPLICATIONS

Discuss the meanings and the implications of each of the following quotations.

1. . . . a couple of young bicycle mechanics from Dayton, Ohio

had designed constructed and flown
for the first time ever a practical airplane.

2. . . . after that Christmas of nineteen three the Wright brothers weren't doing it for fun any more. . . .

3. They [the Wright brothers] were . . . decorated by a society for universal peace.

4. Aeronautics became the sport of the day.

5. The Wrights don't seem to have been very much impressed by the upholstery and the braid and the gold medals and the parades of plush horses,

they remained practical mechanics. . . .

III
TECHNIQUES

Tone

The tone of a prose writer is revealed largely through his word choice and his selection of details. Dos Passos, for instance, shows how he feels toward the skeptics who opposed attempts at flight by referring to them as "crackerbarrel philosophers." How would you describe his attitude toward the Wright brothers? Be prepared to cite some details or some word choices that reveal his attitude.

Toward the end of the selection the author expresses his attitude toward the uses to which the airplane has been put. How is this attitude revealed? Does he blame the Wright brothers themselves because the machine they invented has been used for destructive purposes? How can you tell that he does or does not?

We have been a restless, imaginative people;
our image of America has always been an image of the future. We have never
long remained satisfied with past accomplishments; we have ever sought
new frontiers to conquer, new dreams to realize. But today,
Archibald MacLeish asks, are we at a resting place? Have we fallen back
on the past? Will we find the courage to imagine a new, dynamic America,
an America that will once again look to the future?

The Unimagined America

ARCHIBALD MacLEISH

It is a strange and curious picture of Americans. If ever a people had behind them a tradition of great purposes, tremendous dreams, the people of America have that tradition. There is not one of us, there is not a child in this Republic, who does not know the story. The whole history of our continent is a history of the imagination. Men imagined land beyond the sea and found it. Men imagined the forests, the great plains, the rivers, the mountains—and found these plains, these mountains. No force of terror, no pressure of population, drove our ancestors across this continent. They came, as the great explorers crossed the Atlantic, because of the imagination of their minds—because they imagined a better, a more beautiful, a freer, happier world; because they were men not only of courage, not only of strength and hardiness, but of warm and vivid desire; because they desired; because they had the power to desire.

And what was true of the continent was true of the Republic we created. Because our forefathers were able to conceive a freeman's government, they were able to create it. Because those who lived before us in this nation were able to imagine a new thing, a thing unheard of in the world before, a thing the skeptical

and tired men who did not trust in dreams had not been able to imagine, they erected on this continent the first free nation—the first society in which mankind was to be free at last.

The courage of the Declaration of Independence is a far greater courage than the bravery of those who risked their necks to sign it. The courage of the Declaration of Independence is the courage of the act of the imagination. Jefferson's document is not a call to revolution only. Jefferson's document is an image of a life, a plan of life, a dream—indeed a dream. And yet there were men as careful of their own respect, as hard-headed, as practical, as eager to be thought so, as any now in public life, who signed that Declaration for the world to look at.

The *truth* is that the tradition of imagination is behind us as behind no people in the history of the world. But our right to live as we imagine men should live is not a right drawn from tradition only. There are nations of the earth in which the act of the imagination would be an act *in* the imagination only—an action of escape. But not with us.

We have, and we know we have, the abundant means to bring our boldest dreams to pass —to create for ourselves whatever world we have the courage to desire. We have the metal and the men to take this country down, if we please to take it down, and to build it again as

Reprinted by permission of the Beacon Press, © 1943 by Archibald MacLeish.

we please to build it. We have the tools and the skill and the intelligence to take our cities apart and to put them together, to lead our roads and rivers where we please to lead them, to build our houses where we want our houses, to brighten the air, to clean the wind, to live as men in this Republic, free men, should be living. We have the power and the courage and the resources of good-will and decency and common understanding—a long experience of decency and common understanding—to enable us to live, not in this continent alone but in the world, as citizens in common of the world, with many others.

We have the power and the courage and the resources of experience to create a nation such as men have never seen. And, more than that, we have the moment of creation in our hands. Our forefathers, when they came to the New England valleys or the Appalachian meadows, girdled the trees and dragged the roots into fences and built themselves shelters and, so roughly sheltered, farmed the land for their necessities. Then, later, when there were means to do it, when there was time, when the occasion offered, they burned the tangled roots and rebuilt their fences and their houses—but rebuilt them with a difference: rebuilt them as villages, as neighborhoods; rebuilt them with those lovely streets, those schools, those churches which still speak of their conception of the world they wanted. When the means offered, when the time offered, men created, on the clearings of the early useful farms, the towns that made New England and the Alleghenies.

Now is the time for the re-creation, the rebuilding, not of the villages and towns but of a nation. Now is the time to consider that the trees are down, that the land has been broken, that the means are available and the continent itself must be rebuilt. Our necessities have been accomplished as men have always accomplished their necessities—with wastefulness, with ugliness, with cruelty, as well as with the food of harvests. Our necessities have been accomplished with the roots of the broken trees

along the fences, the rough shelters, the lonely lives. Now is the time to build the continent itself—to take down and to rebuild; and not the houses and the cities only, but the life itself, raising upon the ready land the brotherhood that can employ it and delight in it and use it as a people such as ours should use it.

We stand at the moment of the building of great lives. . . . But to seize the moment and the means we must agree, as men in those New England valleys were agreed, upon the world we mean to bring about. We must agree upon the image of that world. . . .

When we speak of our ideal conception of ourselves, we speak still in terms of the agricultural and sparsely settled nation Thomas Jefferson and his contemporaries had in mind. The ideal landscape of America which Jefferson painted hangs unaltered in the American imagination—a clean, small landscape with its isolated figures, its pleasant barns, its self-reliant rooftrees, its horizons clear of the smoke and the fumes of cities, its air still, its frontiers protected by month-wide oceans, year-wide wildernesses. No later hand has touched it, except Lincoln's maybe, deepening the shadow, widening the sky, broadening the acreage of the name of freedom, giving the parts a wholeness that in brighter, sharper light they lacked. For fifty years and longer it has been a landscape of a world that no man living could expect to see except behind him, a landscape no Americans could bring to being, a dream—but of the past, and not the future.

And yet we keep this image in our minds. This, and not the world beyond us, is the world we turn to: the lost, nostalgic image of a world that was the future to a generation dead a hundred years. No other image has been made to take its place. No one has dreamed a new American dream of the new America—the industrial nation of the huge machines, the limitless earth, the vast and skillful population, the mountains of copper and iron, the mile-long plants, the delicate laboratories, the tremendous dams. No one has imagined this America—what its life should be; what life it should lead with its great wealth and the tools in its hands and the men to employ them.

The plants and the factories and their products have been celebrated often enough—perhaps too often. The statistics have been added up. The camera has held its mirror to the great machines. But the central question we have never asked. What are they *for,* these plants and products, these statistics? *What are they for in terms of a nation of men*—in Jefferson's terms? What is the ideal landscape of this new America? What are we trying to become, to bring about? What is our dream of ourselves as a great people? What would we be if we could: what would our lives be? And how will we use this skill, this wealth, this power to create those lives?

What is demanded of us in this time of change, what our whole history and our present need demand of us, is that we find the answers to these questions—that we consider what we wish this new America to be. For what we wish to be we can become.

And if we cannot wish—we shall become that also.

There are men, it is true, who believe there are no answers. There are men, and among the wisest of our time, who do not believe that an image of this new America can be conceived—who do not believe in a world of plenty; do not believe in it with their hearts whatever their senses tell them; do not believe that the lives of men can be good lives in the industrialized society which alone makes plenty possible. . . .

Is the fault with the machines or with ourselves? Is it because we have automobiles to ride in, because we can purchase certain commodities easily, because our presses can turn out tons of printed paper in a day, that our fiber is soft, our will feeble, our suggestibility infantile? Or is it because we do not use these things as we should use them—because we have not made them serve our moral purpose as a people, but only contribute to our private comfort as their owners?

Is the whole question indeed not a question of ourselves instead of our devices? Is it not for us to *say* how these devices, these inventions, should be used? Does their use not rest upon the purpose of their use? And does the purpose not depend upon our power to conceive the purpose—our power as a people to conceive the purpose of the tools we use; our power as a people to conceive and to imagine?

A hundred and fifty years ago de Crèvecoeur[1] asked a famous question which has echoes now: "What then is the American, this new man?" But what then *is* he? What then is he now? A man incapable of the act of the imagination or a man to whom it is native and natural? A man to dare the dream of plenty with all its risks and dangers, or a man to hold to the old nostalgic landscape with the simple virtues safely forced upon him by the necessary self-denial?

. . . A man who has the hardihood or the courage to believe that the machines which have enslaved his fathers will make his children free—free as no human beings in the world have yet known freedom; free of the twisting miseries and hungers; free to become themselves? Or a man to reject the hope of that enfranchised freedom and to seek his independence in the ancient narrow circle of his old dependence on himself?

Which of these two men is the American? We should have said a while ago we knew. We should have said the American character was self-evident: A restless man. A great builder and maker and shaper, a man delighting in size and height and dimensions: the world's tallest; the town's biggest. A man never satisfied—never—with anything: his house or the town where his grandfather settled or his father's profession or even his own, for that matter. An inveterate voyager and changer and finder. A man naturally hopeful; a believing man, believing that things progress, that things get forwarder. A skillful man with contraptions of one kind and another—machines, engines, various devices: familiar with all of them. A man of

---

1. **de Crèvecoeur**\krĕv·kər\ born in France, became a naturalized United States citizen. Famous for his "Letters from an American Farmer."

certain unquestioned convictions—of a strong, natural attachment to certain ideas and to certain ideals. But first of all and foremost of all a restless man and a believing man, a builder and changer of things and of nations.

We should have said, a generation back, there was no possible doubt or question of the will and power of this nation to propose the kind of future for itself which would employ the means of plenty for a human purpose. We should have said the principal characteristic of the American people was a confidence in the future and themselves—confidence that the future was the thing they'd make it. I cannot think, for myself, we have so changed that we do not believe this now. I cannot believe we are so changed that we'll let ourselves go with the drag and the current of history—that we'll let the future happen to us as the future happens to chips on a river or sheep in a blizzard; that we'll let the peace make us; not us the peace. I cannot believe we have so changed that we do not believe in ourselves and the future.

And yet we have not done what must be done if we believe the future is the thing we'll make it. We have not named that future.

And the time is short.

It is many years since Matthew Arnold saw his generation standing between two worlds, one dead, the other waiting to be born.[2] Our time is still the time between these worlds; and the wars we suffer, the disasters, the uneasiness, are natural to the time we live in like the continuing and violent storms that drive the days between the seasons. We shall not have peace in truth, peace for our lives, peace for the purposes of our lives, until the world we wait for has been born. But it will not be born until we recognize it, until we shape it with our expectation and our hope. The new worlds do not bring themselves to being. Men's minds, when they are ready for them, find them. The labor and the longing must be ours.

They must be ours as men and also—and this is the truth our generation in this country must accept—as Americans. For the future is Amer-

ica's to make. It is not our future, as a few Americans have asked us to believe, to master or exploit. It is not an American future for some vast imperial enterprise, some huge dominion of the earth or sky. And yet it is our future. It is ours to shape. It is ours to shape, not because we have many planes or great numbers of ships or rich industrial resources but for a different reason: because we have the power as a people to conceive so great a future as mankind must now conceive—because we have behind us a tradition of imagination in the people.

But because we have the power we have also a responsibility to use the power. While there still is time.

I

TRACING THE LINE
OF AN ARGUMENT

Although "The Unimagined America" is a passionate, poetic essay, there is a clear line of reasoning running through it. Let us attempt to trace MacLeish's argument point by point.

The first question MacLeish asks is, "What is an American?" He answers the question historically, pointing out that our ancestors were imaginative people who looked constantly to the future. Is this a definition the critical reader can accept?

MacLeish then asserts that contemporary Americans have forsaken the tradition of the imagination and have turned from the future to the past. What evidence does he offer for this assertion? Is it true, in your opinion? What evidence can you offer for your belief?

The author next claims that it is imperative that we recover the tradition of the imagination. *Why* does he feel that this is necessary? Do you agree that it is? What is wrong with clinging to an image of America of the past?

---

2. From Matthew Arnold's poem "Stanzas from the Grande Chartreuse." "Wandering between two worlds, one dead, \The other powerless to be born . . ."

Finally, MacLeish says that Americans must agree upon and build a new image of America. He does not give a fully rounded description of his image, but he notes a few details in various places. What are some of these details? Assuming that you agree with him up to this point, explain why you would include or exclude the same details in your image of the future America.

II
IMPLICATIONS

Thoughtfully consider each of the following statements. Decide whether, on the whole, you would classify the statement as true or false. Be prepared to defend your opinion.

1. If the United States were to become part of a world federation, we would lose all sense of identity as Americans.

2. Americans have not used their material wealth to serve their moral purposes as a people.

3. Most persons settle into a routine of life and do not like to have that routine disturbed.

4. The fact that a man is practical means that he probably is not imaginative.

5. A single individual is helpless to do anything to change the future of his country.

6. A principal quality of Americans is confidence in the future and in themselves.

7. The high standard of living in America has left us free to become ourselves and we have proved to be a passive people.

8. Today the people of America have a strong sense of identity and a clear sense of purpose.

III
WORDS

A. The English language is a mixture of words from many languages. The word *cool* goes back to the Old English period; *composed* was borrowed from Latin; *calm* was borrowed from Old Italian through Middle French. The history of our language explains in part its richness of words which share a common meaning. Look up the origins of the synonyms listed below.

1. maudlin, intoxicated, disguised, fuddled

2. apprehend, seize, catch

3. genial, cheery

4. multifarious, diverse

5. intrinsic, inherent, ingrained

6. conjecture (v.), guess, fancy

7. agitate, fret, startle

8. incredible, unbelievable

B. Formal English is used more in writing than in speaking. The vocabulary of formal English consists of words used infrequently in speech, such as *quintessence, inveterate, ominous, precursor.* It avoids contractions and uses more complex sentence constructions. Analyze the list of synonyms in Exercise A. Which seem more appropriate to formal English, to general use, to informal speaking?

FINAL REFLECTIONS

Endless Frontiers

In the foregoing literature you have seen how the westering urge brought men from Europe to America, and from the Atlantic Coast over Eastern ridges, through the prairies, over the Rockies and Sierras, down into the valleys of California. When the land was fully explored, men like Henry Ford and Orville and Wilbur Wright opened new frontiers; and American writers like A. B. Guthrie, Jr., and Archibald MacLeish challenged Americans to consider and explore frontiers of the mind and of the spirit.

The writers you have studied have shown that the westering urge is made up of a number of character traits and values. On the basis of these selections, make up a list of the essential traits and values of the frontiersman. Be prepared to cite the selections in which they are illustrated.

Which traits and values on your list are essential qualities of Americans today? Which are not? If Americans have lost some qualities, how did it happen?

Finally, consider the frontiers of the future. What are some of the specific conquests that might be made in the next century? How are Americans preparing to make them? What preparations should Americans make?

IMPLICATIONS

Answer each of the questions below in terms of your reading and your own experience. Support your opinions with specific illustrations from the selections you have read.

1. Is it true—as Grandfather said in "The Leader of the People"—that "Westering isn't a hunger any more"? Is "westering" in the sense in which he meant it a good term to describe the hunger that motivated such Americans as Ford and the Wright brothers? Or were they motivated by something else?

2. The American philosopher George Santayana wrote a sonnet in which he said, "Columbus found a world, and had no chart,/Save one that faith deciphered in the skies." The poem continues by pointing out that knowledge is not enough, that man needs faith if he is going to achieve the highest goals. What part did faith play in the exploration of American frontiers? What part does it play in present-day American life?

3. By contrast with Rife and Nancy Belle, many teen-agers of today have a wealth of material possessions. How has this affected the American teen-ager, if at all? Specifically, is he less likely to possess the frontiering qualities of the teen-agers in Conrad Richter's story?

4. Americans today are among the most economically secure and "well-off" people on the earth. How might this fact affect their pioneering spirit? Does a pioneer risk security often? For what reasons might an average person, or even an above-average person, risk losing his security?

5. In addition to Bryant's "The Prairies," several other selections in this unit could be described as "romantic." Which are they? Why, or why not, is the spirit of romance an important one for the American character of the past and of the future?

TECHNIQUES

Setting

The time and place setting in which events occur may be of no significance, of relatively minor importance, or of major importance. From the titles below, select two or more in which setting is of very little importance and two or more in which it is of major importance. Discuss *why* setting is

as important or as unimportant as it is in each selection.

1. "The Leader of the People"
2. "Western Star"
3. "The Prairies"
4. "The Smart Ones Got Through"
5. "All Gold Canyon"
6. "Early Marriage"
7. "The West Is Our Great Adventure of the Spirit"
8. "Henry Ford"
9. "The Campers at Kitty Hawk"
10. "The Unimagined America"

Tone

From the titles above (except for "The Prairies") choose the selection you liked best and the selection you liked least. In each case state the writer's attitude toward his subject and toward his readers. Then determine how much of a factor his attitude (tone) was in influencing your reaction to his work.

Characterization

In a brief poem or an essay a writer usually reveals aspects of his own character; in a biography he reveals the character of real persons other than himself; and in narrative poems, short stories, and other works of fiction he reveals the character of imaginary persons. In short, characterization is one of the most important aspects of most literary work.

Choose five selections above in which you feel the author was particularly successful in creating character. Be prepared to discuss how the author created his character or characters and why you liked them particularly.

BIOGRAPHICAL NOTES

John Steinbeck

The sixth American to win the Nobel Prize in Literature (1962), John Steinbeck (1902–   ) was born and grew up in California. He turned from his college studies in marine biology to writing. His first novel to catch the attention of both critics and the public was *Tortilla Flat,* published in 1935. Other novels about his native Monterey are *Cannery Row* and *Sweet Thursday.* His social documentaries were to draw even greater attention; *In Dubious Battle* is the story of a strike of migratory workers in California; *Grapes of Wrath* is the powerful and moving story of the dust-bowl victims who moved to Califonia. This novel won the Pulitzer Prize in 1940. Other widely read works include three of his novels—*Of Mice and Men, The Pearl,* and *East of Eden*—and "The Red Pony," a sensitive, carefully wrought short story. A recent book is *Travels with Charley,* the story of his journey over the United States with his dog.

Stephen Vincent Benét

Stephen Vincent Benét (1898–1943), son of an army officer, lived in many parts of the country and, as he grew older, developed a deep interest in America's past. His first writings were ballads, such as "William Sycamore," combining American folklore and humor. He then turned to the writing of epic poems, notably the Pulitzer-prize-winning *John Brown's Body,* the story of men and women in both the North and South during the Civil War, and *Western Star,* in which he captured the flavor, excitement, and color of a robust young country. Benét also wrote five novels, two one-act operas, and many short stories.

William Cullen Bryant

William Cullen Bryant (1794–1878), born in Massachusetts, had his first verses, satirizing President Jefferson, published at the age of thirteen. One of his most famous poems, "Thanatopsis," concerned with nature and death, was written at seventeen. In his long life, Bryant achieved fame as critic, editor, biographer, and civic leader. His catholic interests and activities, ranging from his study of nature and the American landscape to his fight for freedom of speech and the abolition of slavery, were reflected in his writings. His poetry was acclaimed in England and America, but his literary reputation is not as great today as during his own lifetime.

George R. Stewart

George R. Stewart (1895–   ), long a professor of English at the University of California at Berkeley, has written on a wide range of scholarly subjects as well as several popular novels and historical accounts. His most famous novels are *Storm,* the story of a storm moving across the country, and *Fire,* the story of a raging forest fire. In *Ordeal by Hunger* he recreated the tragic story of the Donner party crossing the Sierras. In *Names on the Land,* Stewart presented a fascinating as well as a scholarly historical account of place-naming in the United States.

Conrad Richter

Conrad Richter (1890–   ) grew up in Pennsylvania and became a newspaper reporter and writer of children's stories. He moved to New Mexico in 1928 and immersed himself in the history and lore of the Southwest. In the 1940's he published his trilogy of pioneer stories, *The Trees, The Fields,* and *The Town* (Pulitzer Prize, 1951). Other widely read works are a novel, *The Light in the Forest,* and a collection of short stories, *Early Americana.*

Jack London

Sailor, oyster pirate, Alaskan gold hunter, hobo, war correspondent, adventurer, and writer, Jack London (1876–1916) was born in San Francisco. He grew up in poverty, educated by his reading in the public library and by experiences along the Oakland waterfront. When he sold several stories to the *Overland Monthly,* he settled down seriously to a writing career. His most successful works were several short stories and two novels, the dog stories *Call of the Wild* and *White Fang.* His major themes were the survival of the fittest and reversion to savagery. He wrote three autobiographical novels: *The Road, Martin Eden,* and *John Barleycorn.* He became the champion of social revolution in the early years of his century and wrote several volumes of political propaganda.

A. B. Guthrie, Jr.

Born in 1901 in Indiana, A. B. Guthrie, Jr., grew up and was educated in Montana. He moved to Lexington, Kentucky, to become a news reporter and eventually editor of the *Lexington Leader.* In 1944 Guthrie had a Nieman Fellowship at Harvard and there began the writing that led him to resign from his editorship. His first novel, *The Big Sky,* published in 1947, a story of frontier life between 1830 and 1843, became a best-seller. *The Way West,* published three years later and a Pulitzer

Prize winner, is the story of pioneers on the trail from Missouri to Oregon in 1846.

Allan Nevins

American historian Allan Nevins (1890–   ) is most famous for four biographies: two Pulitzer Prize winners: *Grover Cleveland: A Study in Courage* and *Hamilton Fish: The Inner History of the Grant Administration;* and those of two major industrialists, *Study in Power: John D. Rockefeller, Industrialist and Philanthropist* and—with Frank Ernest Hill—*Ford: the Times, the Man, the Company.* Nevins, born in Illinois, was graduated from the University of Illinois. A succession of newspaper jobs preceded his years of teaching, first at Cornell University and then from 1931 to 1958 at Columbia University. In 1958 he went to Huntington Library in San Marino, California, as a senior research fellow.

John Dos Passos

The reputation of John Dos Passos (1896–   ) as a novelist was established with the publication of *Manhattan Transfer* (1925) and the trilogy, *U.S.A.,* which included *The 42nd Parallel, 1919,* and *The Big Money. U.S.A* presents, with headlines, popular songs, newsreels, vignettes, and biographical sketches, the gradual disintegration of American civilization during the first three decades of this century. Chicago-born, Dos Passos was graduated from Harvard in 1916. His study of architecture in Spain was interrupted by service with the French Ambulance Service, the Red Cross, and later the U.S. Medical Corps in World War I. Dos Passos has been an influence on a number of twentieth-century writers, but his own later works, using the same kind of kaleidoscopic style, have failed to equal the impact and significance of *U.S.A.*

Archibald MacLeish

Archibald MacLeish, who was born in Glencoe, Illinois, in 1892, was educated at Yale and at Harvard Law School. After serving with the American Army in France during World War I, he returned to Boston to practice law. Soon, however, he gave up his practice to devote full time to traveling and to writing. Among his travels was retracing the route of Cortez through Mexico, which led to his writing *Conquistador.* Caught up in the country's mood of social protest in the thirties, he wrote *Frescoes for Mr. Rockefeller's City* and *America Was Promises.* Twice winner of the Pulitzer Prize for poetry, versatile MacLeish also wrote prose, a ballet, and radio and stage plays. From 1939–1944 he was Librarian of Congress. In 1949 he returned to Harvard as a professor of rhetoric and oratory.

WASHINGTON IRVING

1783-1859

What James Fenimore Cooper did for the early American novel and William Cullen Bryant for poetry, Irving did for belles lettres—*witty, entertaining essays and tales that incorporated history, biography, legend, and a fertile imagination. It is not surprising that Washington Irving's sketches and short stories inspired Hawthorne and Poe and many of their contemporaries. He set high standards.*

In 1820, Sydney Smith, an English clergyman, asked in the pages of the *Edinburgh Review:* "In the four quarters of the globe, who reads an American book? or goes to an American play? or looks at an American picture or statue?" He did not have to wait long for his answer. Washington Irving was our first genuine man of letters, and the English who had delighted in looking down on the uncultured American colonies were happy to welcome him to the company of Byron and Coleridge and Scott. America to be sure had produced political writers, competent historians, and even poets in the years before the Revolution; but our stylists, masters of polished prose, were few in number. That Irving came to a literary career through a side door, as it were, makes his life and his achievements all the more fascinating.

Born in New York City, the youngest of eleven children, he began reading for the law at the age of sixteen, but his heart was not in his studies. "I was always fond of visiting new scenes and observing strange characters and manners," he later recalled. "Even when a mere child I began my traveling, and made many tours of discovery into foreign parts and unknown regions of my native city, to the frequent alarm of my parents." Travel continued to entice him, first to the Hudson Valley and Canada, then to France, Italy, and Holland where he spent two years as a literary vagabond, reading whatever he pleased and endlessly observing the customs and especially the theater of Europe.

When he became a lawyer at the age of twenty-three, his family expected him to settle down. Irving preferred the literary to the legal world. He and his brother William published the *Salmagundi* papers, satirical essays and poems written to ridicule local theater, politics, and fashions. The next year, 1809, he began *A History of New York,* signing it Diedrich Knickerbocker. It was one of America's first pieces of comic literature, a burlesque of serious history that dared to satirize the persons and policies of John Adams, Madison, and Jefferson as well as the old Dutch administrator and symbol of the old aristocracy Peter Stuyvesant, "the Headstrong." One of Irving's favorite character studies in this history is still a delight today: the "golden reign of Wouter Van Twiller," governor of New Amsterdam. A "model of majesty and lordly grandeur," he was "exactly five feet six inches in height, and six feet five inches in circumference," and when he stood erect "he had not a little the appearance of a beer barrel on skids."

As Diedrich Knickerbocker, Irving established an enviable reputation. New York feted the young, witty lawyer, but again he was restless and by no means convinced that he could sustain a literary career. He worked for a while in the family hardware business, then served as a staff colonel during the War of 1812, finally sailed for Europe in 1815, little realizing that he would remain abroad for seventeen years. For business reasons he lived chiefly in England; but when the family business failed he realized that he would have to support himself by other means, and literary work seemed the most attractive. Always a collector of tales, a keen observer, and an amateur artist, he naturally drifted into writing familiar essays and sketches. Under the pseudonym Geoffrey Crayon, Gent., they were published serially in the United States in 1819–1820. When he gathered them into a volume called *The Sketch Book* for publication in England in 1820, he was greeted with a reception such as no American author had ever received from the British public. Lord Byron declared that "Crayon is very good"; Sir Walter Scott and Thomas Moore, personal friends by now, gave him public acclaim. American literary critics were as quick to recognize his considerable achievement.

As a visitor to England, Irving had filled his journals with anecdotes, quotations, notes of his travels, and details of English life taken from close observation. *The Sketch Book* is a graceful reworking of these notes. Most of the thirty-six pieces recount the pleasures of the English countryside, typical village life, and landmarks no visitor should miss. With much genial humor, he describes Westminster Abbey, Stratford-on-Avon, the Boar's Head Tavern, an English Christmas, and more. Six of the chapters treat American subjects; not surprisingly they were the ones to achieve lasting fame, especially "Rip Van Winkle" and "The Legend of Sleepy Hollow."

Irving wrote these American narratives as though he were recounting well-known legends of colonial Dutch-American life in the lower Hudson Valley. We know now that he borrowed the tales from German folklore and simply blended the two cultures, creating the first American short stories. It is possible that not even Irving was aware of how widely his *Sketch Book* would be publicized in the next decades or how carefully he had caught the mood of romantic melancholy so popular with both English and American readers. "The truth presses home upon us as we advance in life," he wrote in his notebook, "that everything around us is transient and uncertain. . . . When I look back for a few short years, what changes of all kind have taken place, what wrecks of time and

Sunnyside, Irving residence near Tarrytown, New York.

fortune are strewn around me." In these tales and essays of time past, Irving had found his talent, and he knew it.

Bracebridge Hall followed in 1822. Like so many sequels, it hardly measures up to the charms of his first success. This collection of sketches begins in England, then moves across the channel to France and Spain for its settings; but only "Dolph Heyliger" and "The Storm-Ship" are remembered. Irving's interest in tales of the supernatural continued to grow, however, and he crossed the Rhine to visit Dresden and Vienna, to explore "the rich mine of German literature." *Tales of a Traveller* (1824) resulted, a highly uneven collection but notable for "The Devil and Tom Walker,"

a short story far superior to the Gothic romances—tales filled with magic, mystery, and medieval trappings—that make up most of the volume.

During the next eight years before his return to the United States, Irving made two diplomatic journeys to Spain, living for a time in the Alhambra as attaché to the American envoy; and he served in London as secretary to the American legation. These were highly productive years in terms of his reputation abroad and of newly published volumes. A huge life of Christopher Columbus appeared in 1828; *The Conquest of Granada,* a mixture of romance and history, in 1829. Both works were the result of prodigious research, but there is no doubt that *The Alhambra* (1832) struck the familiar chord and more clearly reflects Irving's genuine talents. His American public called it the "Spanish Sketch Book." They welcomed his return to the leisurely narrative, the intimate legends of barbaric Spain, the sights and sounds of an opulent era of history. In describing this Moorish palace at Granada, one of the architectural wonders of Western Europe, his purpose, he said, was "to depict its half Spanish, half Oriental character, . . . to revive the traces of grace and beauty fast fading from its walls." Irving was never happier than when he was recreating a historical personage. Here he dotes on frail Boabdil, the last Moorish king to possess the Alhambra, known to his subjects as El Rey Chico, "King Do-Nothing." He is only one of the many delights of this collection.

The United States seemed strange to Irving when he returned in 1832, and some of his American critics were quick to suggest that his long stay abroad had "Europeanized" him. Irving set out to prove the charge exaggerated. After a journey to the West, he set down his impressions in *A Tour on the Prairies* (1835). Compared with H. L. Ellsworth's account of the same trip, Irving's impressions are more quaint than accurate, more idealized than realistic. But his Eastern readers were accustomed to this aspect of his art. They were willing to accept the picturesque, even the sentimental, because Irving could hold their attention with intimate, vibrant description. What is more, they had never seen a savage Indian or a buffalo hunt. By now the professional writer, Irving sensed a market. He never again equaled the quality of his *Sketch Book* prose, but he supplied his public with what they wanted. *Astoria* (1836) is a history of John Jacob Astor's fur trade in the Northwest, written from original materials in a New York library, not from notes of personal expeditions. *The Adventures of Captain Bonneville* (1837) recounts life in the Rocky Mountains, but it too was done under Astor's patronage.

Perhaps if Irving had not achieved such acclaim as a young man, his later years would not strike us as anticlimactic. In 1836, he moved into Sunnyside, his home near Tarrytown, New York, and for the next two decades he played the country squire, the successful writer pursued by politicians and public alike. He turned down nominations for Congress and for mayor of New York; he refused President Van Buren's invitation to be Secretary of the Navy. He agreed, however, to spend four years in Spain as United States Minister, but he longed to return to Sunnyside and his nieces and this time he came home without a copiously filled notebook from which to create new work. His last volumes are rather plodding biographies of the eighteenth-century writer Oliver Goldsmith and of Mahomet and a monumental five-volume biography of George Washington, completed just before his death on the eve of the Civil War. A glimmer of the lively young Irving remains in *Wolfert's Roost and Miscellanies* (1855), a volume of sketches he published under several pseudonyms in the *Knickerbocker Magazine,* a New York journal established in his honor. The splendid urbanity of style is still there, the pleasant variety of subject (Spanish legends, colonial American history, frontier explorations), and above all Irving's stamp: personal observations couched in homely, memorable details.

For these superlative familiar essays American letters will always be in Irving's debt. For too long the colonies and the young nation had been fed on political tracts, harsh sermons, propaganda, and factual histories. What James Fenimore Cooper did for the early American novel and William Cullen Bryant for poetry, Irving did for *belles lettres*—witty, entertaining essays that incorporated history, biography, legend, and a fertile imagination. These three American writers earned international reputations at a time when American letters were in their infancy, acquainting European audiences with American regional life and establishing a respect for literary artists in a young country only beginning to discover its cultural heritage. It is not surprising that Washington Irving's sketches and short stories inspired Hawthorne and Poe and many of their contemporaries. He set high standards.

Four years after the success
of *The Sketch Book*, Irving collected
32 stories and essays, written chiefly
from notes gathered during a tour
of Germany, and published them as *Tales
of a Traveller* (1824). Though not
as well received as his earlier work,
they continued to demonstrate his mastery
of the anecdotal style—relaxed, graceful
reminiscences mixed with genial humor
and credible incident. Although the first three
sections of the book have European backgrounds,
the last section, "The Money Diggers," is set
in New York and New England and contains
five tales "found among the papers
of the late Diedrich Knickerbocker." The best
by far is this tale of the miserly Tom Walker
and his encounter with "the black woodsman."
Here again Irving blends European legend
with American folklore.

The Devil and Tom Walker

A few miles from Boston in Massachusetts, there is a deep inlet, winding several miles into the interior of the country from Charles Bay, and terminating in a thickly-wooded swamp or morass. On one side of this inlet is a beautiful dark grove; on the opposite side the land rises abruptly from the water's edge into a high ridge, on which grow a few scattered oaks of great age and immense size. Under one of these gigantic trees, according to old stories, there was a great amount of treasure buried by Kidd[1] the pirate. The inlet allowed a facility to bring the money in a boat secretly and at night to the very foot of the hill; the elevation of the place permitted a good lookout to be kept that no one

was at hand; while the remarkable trees formed good landmarks by which the place might easily be found again. The old stories add, moreover, that the devil presided at the hiding of the money, and took it under his guardianship; but this, it is well known, he always does with buried treasure, particularly when it has been ill-gotten. Be that as it may, Kidd never returned to recover his wealth; being shortly after seized at Boston, sent out to England, and there hanged for a pirate.

About the year 1727, just at the time that earthquakes were prevalent in New England, and shook many tall sinners down upon their knees, there lived near this place a meagre, miserly fellow, of the name of Tom Walker. He had a wife as miserly as himself: they were so miserly that they even conspired to cheat each other. Whatever the woman could lay hands on, she hid away; a hen could not cackle but she was on the alert to secure the new-laid egg. Her husband was continually prying about to detect her secret hoards, and many and fierce were the conflicts that took place about what ought to have been common property. They lived in a forlorn-looking house that stood alone, and had an air of starvation. A few straggling savin-trees, emblems of sterility, grew near it; no smoke ever curled from its chimney; no traveller stopped at its door. A miserable horse, whose ribs were as articulate as the bars of a gridiron, stalked about a field, where a thin carpet of moss, scarcely covering the ragged beds of pudding-stone, tantalized and balked his hunger; and sometimes he would lean his head over the fence, look piteously at the passer-by, and seem to petition deliverance from this land of famine.

The house and its inmates had altogether a bad name. Tom's wife was a tall termagant, fierce of temper, loud of tongue, and strong of arm. Her voice was often heard in wordy warfare with her husband; and his face sometimes

---

1. **William Kidd** (1645?–1701), known as Captain Kidd, tried and convicted for murder and piracy; hanged in London, 1701.

showed signs that their conflicts were not confined to words. No one ventured, however, to interfere between them. The lonely wayfarer shrunk within himself at the horrid clamor and clapper-clawing; eyed the den of discord askance; and hurried on his way, rejoicing, if a bachelor, in his celibacy.

One day that Tom Walker had been to a distant part of the neighborhood, he took what he considered a short cut homeward, through the swamp. Like most short cuts, it was an ill-chosen route. The swamp was thickly grown with great gloomy pines and hemlocks, some of them ninety feet high, which made it dark at noonday, and a retreat for all the owls of the neighborhood. It was full of pits and quagmires,[2] partly covered with weeds and mosses, where the green surface often betrayed the traveller into a gulf of black, smothering mud: there were also dark and stagnant pools, the abodes of the tadpole, the bullfrog, and the water-snake; where the trunks of pines and hemlocks lay half-drowned, half-rotting, looking like alligators sleeping in the mire.

Tom had long been picking his way cautiously through this treacherous forest; stepping from tuft to tuft of rushes and roots, which afforded precarious footholds among deep sloughs; or pacing carefully, like a cat, along the prostrate trunks of trees; startled now and then by the sudden screaming of the bittern, or the quacking of a wild duck rising on the wing from some solitary pool. At length he arrived at a firm piece of ground, which ran out like a peninsula into the deep bosom of the swamp. It had been one of the strongholds of the Indians during their wars with the first colonists. Here they had thrown up a kind of fort, which they had looked upon as almost impregnable, and had used as a place of refuge for their squaws and children. Nothing remained of the old Indian fort but a few embankments, gradually sinking to the level of the surrounding earth, and already overgrown in part by oaks and other forest trees, the foliage of which formed a contrast to the dark pines and hemlocks of the swamp.

It was late in the dusk of evening when Tom Walker reached the old fort, and he paused there awhile to rest himself. Any one but he would have felt unwilling to linger in this lonely, melancholy place, for the common people had a bad opinion of it, from the stories handed down from the time of the Indian wars; when it was asserted that the savages held incantations here, and made sacrifices to the evil spirit.

Tom Walker, however, was not a man to be troubled with any fears of the kind. He reposed himself for some time on the trunk of a fallen hemlock, listening to the boding cry of the tree-toad, and delving with his walking-staff into a mound of black mould at his feet. As he turned up the soil unconsciously, his staff struck against something hard. He raked it out of the vegetable mould, and lo! a cloven skull, with an Indian tomahawk buried deep in it, lay before him. The rust on the weapon showed the time that had elapsed since this deathblow had been given. It was a dreary memento of the fierce struggle that had taken place in this last foothold of the Indian warriors.

"Humph!" said Tom Walker, as he gave it a kick to shake the dirt from it.

"Let that skull alone!" said a gruff voice. Tom lifted up his eyes, and beheld a great black man seated directly opposite him, on the stump of a tree. He was exceedingly surprised, having neither heard nor seen any one approach; and he was still more perplexed on observing, as well as the gathering gloom would permit, that the stranger was neither negro nor Indian. It is true he was dressed in a rude half-Indian garb, and had a red belt or sash swathed round his body; but his face was neither black nor copper-color, but swarthy and dingy, and begrimed with soot, as if he had been accustomed to toil among fires and forges. He had a shock of coarse black hair, that stood out from his head in all directions, and bore an axe on his shoulder.

---

2. **quagmires**\ˈkwăg 'mairz\ soft, wet, miry land that gives way under foot.

He scowled for a moment at Tom with a pair of great red eyes.

"What are you doing on my grounds?" said the black man, with a hoarse growling voice.

"Your grounds!" said Tom, with a sneer, "no more your grounds than mine; they belong to Deacon Peabody."

"Deacon Peabody be d——d," said the stranger, "as I flatter myself he will be, if he does not look more to his own sins and less to those of his neighbors. Look yonder, and see how Deacon Peabody is faring."

Tom looked in the direction that the stranger pointed, and beheld one of the great trees, fair and flourishing without, but rotten at the core, and saw that it had been nearly hewn through, so that the first high wind was likely to blow it down. On the bark of the tree was scored the name of Deacon Peabody, an eminent man, who had waxed wealthy by driving shrewd bargains with the Indians. He now looked around, and found most of the tall trees marked with the name of some great man of the colony, and all more or less scored by the axe. The one on which he had been seated, and which had evidently just been hewn down, bore the name of Crowninshield; and he recollected a mighty rich man of that name, who made a vulgar display of wealth, which it was whispered he had acquired by buccaneering.

"He's just ready for burning!" said the black man, with a growl of triumph. "You see I am likely to have a good stock of firewood for winter."

"But what right have you," said Tom, "to cut down Deacon Peabody's timber?"

"The right of a prior claim," said the other. "This woodland belonged to me long before one of your white-faced race put foot upon the soil."

"And pray, who are you, if I may be so bold?" said Tom.

"Oh, I go by various names. I am the wild huntsman in some countries; the black miner in others. In this neighborhood I am known by the name of the black woodsman. I am he to whom the red men consecrated this spot, and in honor of whom they now and then roasted a white man, by way of sweet-smelling sacrifice. Since the red men have been exterminated by you white savages, I amuse myself by presiding at the persecutions of Quakers and Anabaptists;[3] I am the great patron and prompter of slave-dealers, and the grand-master of the Salem witches."

"The upshot of all which is, that, if I mistake not," said Tom, sturdily, "you are he commonly called Old Scratch."

"The same, at your service!" replied the black man, with a half civil nod.

Such was the opening of this interview, according to the old story; though it has almost too familiar an air to be credited. One would think that to meet with such a singular personage, in this wild, lonely place, would have shaken any man's nerves; but Tom was a hard-minded fellow, not easily daunted, and he had lived so long with a termagant wife, that he did not even fear the devil.

It is said that after this commencement they had a long and earnest conversation together, as Tom returned homeward. The black man told him of great sums of money buried by Kidd the pirate, under the oak trees on the high ridge, not far from the morass. All these were under his command, and protected by his power, so that none could find them but such as propitiated his favor. These he offered to place within Tom Walker's reach, having conceived an especial kindess for him; but they were to be had only on certain conditions. What these conditions were may be easily surmised, though Tom never disclosed them publicly. They must have been very hard, for he required time to think of them, and he was not a man to stick at trifles when money was in view. When they had reached the edge of the swamp, the stranger paused. "What proof have I that all you have been telling me is true?" said Tom. "There's my signature," said the black man, pressing his

---

3. **Anabaptists,** religious sect, originating in Zurich, advocated return to primitive Christianity, denied necessity of infant baptism, and opposed union of church and state.

finger on Tom's forehead. So saying, he turned off among the thickets of the swamp, and seemed, as Tom said, to go down, down, down, into the earth, until nothing but his head and shoulders could be seen, and so on, until he totally disappeared.

When Tom reached home, he found the black print of a finger burnt, as it were, into his forehead, which nothing could obliterate.

The first news his wife had to tell him was the sudden death of Absalom Crowninshield, the rich buccaneer. It was announced in the papers, with the usual flourish, that "A great man had fallen in Israel."

Tom recollected the tree which his black friend had just hewn down, and which was ready for burning. "Let the freebooter roast," said Tom, "who cares!" He now felt convinced that all he had heard and seen was no illusion.

He was not prone to let his wife into his confidence; but as this was an uneasy secret, he willingly shared it with her. All her avarice was awakened at the mention of hidden gold, and she urged her husband to comply with the black man's terms, and secure what would make them wealthy for life. However Tom might have felt disposed to sell himself to the Devil, he was determined not to do so to oblige his wife; so he flatly refused, out of the mere spirit of contradiction. Many and bitter were the quarrels they had on the subject; but the more she talked, the more resolute was Tom not to be damned to please her.

At length she determined to drive the bargain on her own account, and if she succeeded, to keep all the gain to herself. Being of the same fearless temper as her husband, she set off for the old Indian fort towards the close of a summer's day. She was many hours absent. When she came back, she was reserved and sullen in her replies. She spoke something of a black man, whom she had met about twilight hewing at the root of a tall tree. He was sulky, however, and would not come to terms: she was to go again with a propitiatory offering, but what it was she forebore to say.

The next evening she set off again for the swamp, with her apron heavily laden. Tom waited and waited for her, but in vain; midnight came, but she did not make her appearance: morning, noon, night returned, but still she did not come. Tom now grew uneasy for her safety, especially as he found she had carried off in her apron the silver tea-pot and spoons, and every portable article of value. Another night elapsed, another morning came; but no wife. In a word, she was never heard of more.

What was her real fate nobody knows, in consequence of so many pretending to know. It is one of those facts which have become confounded by a variety of historians. Some asserted that she lost her way among the tangled mazes of the swamp, and sank into some pit or slough; others, more uncharitable, hinted that she had eloped with the household booty, and made off to some other province; while others surmised that the tempter had decoyed her into a dismal quagmire, on the top of which her hat was found lying. In confirmation of this, it was said a great black man, with an axe on his shoulder, was seen late that very evening coming out of the swamp, carrying a bundle tied in a check apron, with an air of surly triumph.

The most current and probable story, however, observes, that Tom Walker grew so anxious about the fate of his wife and his property, that he set out at length to seek them both at the Indian fort. During a long summer's afternoon he searched about the gloomy place, but no wife was to be seen. He called her name repeatedly, but she was nowhere to be heard. The bittern alone responded to his voice, as he flew screaming by: or the bull-frog croaked dolefully from a neighboring pool. At length, it is said, just in the brown hour of twilight, when the owls began to hoot, and the bats to flit about, his attention was attracted by the clamor of carrion crows hovering about a cypress-tree. He looked up, and beheld a bundle tied in a check apron, and hanging in the branches of the tree, with a great vulture perched hard by, as if keeping watch upon it. He leaped with joy;

The Devil and Tom Walker, John Quidor.
Inspired by Irving's tale, Quidor gives his
impression of Tom Walker's first meeting with
"Old Scratch."

for he recognized his wife's apron, and supposed it to contain the household valuables.

"Let us get hold of the property," said he, consolingly to himself, "and we will endeavor to do without the woman."

As he scrambled up the tree, the vulture spread its wide wings, and sailed off, screaming, into the deep shadows of the forest. Tom seized the checked apron, but, woeful sight! found nothing but a heart and liver tied up in it!

Such, according to this most authentic old story, was all that was to be found of Tom's wife. She had probably attempted to deal with the black man as she had been accustomed to deal with her husband; but though a female scold is generally considered a match for the devil, yet in this instance she appears to have had the worse of it. She must have died game, however; for it is said Tom noticed many prints of cloven feet deeply stamped about the tree, and found handfuls of hair, that looked as if they had been plucked from the coarse black shock of the woodman. Tom knew his wife's prowess by experience. He shrugged his shoulders, as he looked at the signs of a fierce clapper-clawing. "Egad," said he to himself, "Old Scratch must have had a tough time of it!"

Tom consoled himself for the loss of his property, with the loss of his wife, for he was a man of fortitude. He even felt something like gratitude towards the black woodman, who, he considered, had done him a kindness. He sought, therefore, to cultivate a further acquaintance with him, but for some time without success; the old blacklegs played shy, for whatever people may think, he is not always to be had for calling for: he knows how to play his cards when pretty sure of his game.

At length, it is said, when delay had whetted Tom's eagerness to the quick, and prepared him to agree to anything rather than not gain the promised treasure, he met the black man one evening in his usual woodman's dress, with his axe on his shoulder, sauntering along the swamp, and humming a tune. He affected to receive Tom's advances with great indifference, made brief replies, and went on humming his tune.

By degrees, however, Tom brought him to business, and they began to haggle about the terms on which the former was to have the pirate's treasure. There was one condition which need not be mentioned, being generally understood in all cases where the devil grants favors; but there were others about which, though of less importance, he was inflexibly obstinate. He insisted that the money found through his means should be employed in his service. He proposed, therefore, that Tom should employ it in the black traffic; that is to say, that he should fit out a slave-ship. This, however, Tom resolutely refused: he was bad enough in all conscience; but the devil himself could not tempt him to turn slave-trader.

Finding Tom so squeamish on this point, he did not insist upon it, but proposed, instead, that he should turn usurer; the devil being extremely anxious for the increase of usurers, looking upon them as his peculiar people.

To this no objections were made, for it was just to Tom's taste.

"You shall open a broker's shop in Boston next month," said the black man.

"I'll do it to-morrow, if you wish," said Tom Walker.

"You shall lend money at two per cent a month."

"Egad, I'll charge four!" replied Tom Walker.

"You shall extort bonds, foreclose mortgages, drive the merchants to bankruptcy"——

"I'll drive them to the d——," cried Tom Walker.

"You are the usurer for my money!" said black-legs with delight. "When will you want the rhino?"[4]

"This very night."

"Done!" said the devil.

"Done!" said Tom Walker.—So they shook hands and struck a bargain.

A few days' time saw Tom Walker seated behind his desk in a counting-house in Boston.

His reputation for a ready-moneyed man, who would lend money out for a good consideration, soon spread abroad. Everybody remembers the time of Governor Belcher, when money was particularly scarce. It was a time of paper credit. The country had been deluged with government bills, the famous Land Bank had been established; there had been a rage for speculating; the people had run mad with schemes for new settlements; for building cities in the wilderness; land-jobbers went about with maps of grants, and townships, and Eldorados,[5] lying nobody knew where, but which everybody was ready to purchase. In a word, the great speculating fever which breaks out every now and then in the country, had raged to an alarming degree, and everybody was dreaming of making sudden fortunes from nothing. As usual the fever had subsided; the dream had gone off, and the imaginary fortunes with it; the patients were left in doleful plight, and the whole country resounded with the consequent cry of "hard times."

At this propitious time of public distress did Tom Walker set up as usurer in Boston. His door was soon thronged by customers. The needy and adventurous; the gambling speculator; the dreaming land-jobber; the thriftless

---

4. **rhino,** money, cash (origin of the word unknown).
5. **Eldorado,** the fabulously rich city sixteenth-century Spanish explorers vainly sought for in South America.

tradesman; the merchant with cracked credit; in short, everyone driven to raise money by desperate means and desperate sacrifices, hurried to Tom Walker.

Thus Tom was the universal friend of the needy, and acted like a "friend in need"; that is to say, he always exacted good pay and good security. In proportion to the distress of the applicant was the highness of his terms. He accumulated bonds and mortgages; gradually squeezed his customers closer and closer: and sent them at length, dry as a sponge, from his door.

In this way he made money hand over hand; became a rich and mighty man, and exalted his cocked hat upon 'Change. He built himself, as usual, a vast house, out of ostentation; but left the greater part of it unfinished and unfurnished, out of parsimony. He even set up a carriage in the fulness of his vainglory, though he nearly starved the horses which drew it; and as the ungreased wheels groaned and screeched on the axle-trees, you would have thought you heard the souls of the poor debtors he was squeezing.

As Tom waxed old, however, he grew thoughtful. Having secured the good things of this world, he began to feel anxious about those of the next. He thought with regret on the bargain he had made with his black friend, and set his wits to work to cheat him out of the conditions. He became, therefore, all of a sudden, a violent church-goer. He prayed loudly and strenuously, as if heaven were to be taken by force of lungs. Indeed, one might always tell when he had sinned most during the week, by the clamor of his Sunday devotion. The quiet Christians who had been modestly and steadfastly travelling Zionward,[6] were struck with self-reproach at seeing themselves so suddenly outstripped in their career by this new-made convert. Tom was as rigid in religious as in money matters; he was a stern supervisor and censurer of his neighbors, and seemed to think every sin entered up to their account became a credit on his own side of the page. He even talked of the expediency of reviving the persecution of Quakers and Anabaptists. In a word, Tom's zeal became as notorious as his riches.

Still, in spite of all this strenuous attention to forms, Tom had a lurking dread that the devil, after all, would have his due. That he might not be taken unawares, therefore, it is said he always carried a small Bible in his coat-pocket. He had also a great folio Bible on his counting-house desk, and would frequently be found reading it when people called on business; on such occasions he would lay his green spectacles in the book, to mark the place, while he turned round to drive some usurious bargain.

Some say that Tom grew a little crack-brained in his old days, and that, fancying his end approaching, he had his horse new shod, saddled and bridled, and buried with his feet uppermost; because he supposed that at the last day the world would be turned upside down; in which case he should find his horse standing ready for mounting, and he was determined at the worst to give his old friend a run for it. This, however, is probably a mere old wives' fable. If he really did take such a precaution, it was totally superfluous; at least so says the authentic old legend; which closes his story in the following manner.

One hot summer afternoon in the dogdays, just as a terrible black thunder-gust was coming up, Tom sat in his counting-house, in his white linen cap and India silk morning-gown. He was on the point of foreclosing a mortgage, by which he would complete the ruin of an unlucky land-speculator for whom he had professed the greatest friendship. The poor land-jobber begged him to grant a few months' indulgence. Tom had grown testy and irritated, and refused another day.

"My family will be ruined, and brought upon the parish," said the land-jobber.

"Charity begins at home," replied Tom; "I must take care of myself in these hard times."

"You have made so much money out of me," said the speculator.

6. **Zionward**\ˈzaɪ·ən·wərd\ heavenward. Zion is identified with Jerusalem, considered the earthly home of God by the Israelites and early Christians.

Tom lost his patience and his piety. "The devil take me," said he, "if I have made a farthing!"

Just then there were three loud knocks at the street-door. He stepped out to see who was there. A black man was holding a black horse, which neighed and stamped with impatience.

"Tom, you're come for," said the black fellow, gruffly. Tom shrank back, but too late. He had left his little Bible at the bottom of his coat-pocket, and his big Bible on the desk buried under the mortgage he was about to foreclose: never was sinner taken more unawares. The black man whisked him like a child into the saddle, gave the horse the lash, and away he galloped, with Tom on his back, in the midst of the thunder-storm. The clerks stuck their pens behind their ears, and stared after him from the windows. Away went Tom Walker, dashing down the streets; his white cap bobbing up and down; his morning-gown fluttering in the wind, and his steed striking fire out of the pavement at every bound. When the clerks turned to look for the black man, he had disappeared.

Tom Walker never returned to foreclose the mortgage. A countryman, who lived on the border of the swamp, reported that in the height of the thunder-gust he had heard a great clattering of hoofs and a howling along the road, and running to the window caught sight of a figure, such as I have described, on a horse that galloped like mad across the fields, over the hills, and down into the black hemlock swamp towards the old Indian fort; and that shortly after a thunder-bolt falling in that direction seemed to set the whole forest in a blaze.

The good people of Boston shook their heads and shrugged their shoulders, but had been so much accustomed to witches and goblins, and tricks of the devil, in all kinds of shapes, from the first settlement of the colony, that they were not so much horror-struck as might have been expected. Trustees were appointed to take charge of Tom's effects. There was nothing, however, to administer. On searching his coffers, all his bonds and mortgages were found

reduced to cinders. In place of gold and silver, his iron chest was filled with chips and shavings; two skeletons lay in his stable instead of his half-starved horses, and the very next day his great house took fire and was burnt to the ground.

Such was the end of Tom Walker and his ill-gotten wealth. Let all griping money-brokers lay this story to heart. The truth of it is not to be doubted. The very hole under the oak-trees, whence he dug Kidd's money, is to be seen to this day; and the neighboring swamp and old Indian fort are often haunted in stormy nights by a figure on horseback, in morning-gown and white cap, which is doubtless the troubled spirit of the usurer. In fact, the story has resolved itself into a proverb, and is the origin of that popular saying, so prevalent throughout New England, of "The Devil and Tom Walker."

I

AN AMERICAN FABLE

A fable is a brief story told to point a moral. Its subject matter deals with supernatural and unusual incidents often originating in folklore. The Faust theme—the legend of men bargaining with the devil for their souls—originating from a medieval fable, has for centuries inspired much European literature, always deadly serious—even harrowing. Although Irving's tale is more leisurely than most fables, it still has a fablelike flavor—frequent references to popular local legend, the extraordinary meetings with "Old Scratch" as well as Tom's and his wife's remarkable exits from life, criticism of men and institutions, and the explicit pointing of a moral in the closing paragraph. But unlike its European ancestors, the story does not take itself seriously, for Irving won't let it. He lingers too long and fondly over rich descriptions, chuckles too genially over old folk figures and situations—shrewish wives, pretentious aristocrats, misers, marriage—and keeps the reader too emotionally distant from the characters for the reader to take the proceedings seriously. In short, for

Irving the old fable is not so much an occasion to point a moral as to tell a good story.

IMPLICATIONS

A. Explain what Irving is criticizing in the following statements. Is his tone solemn, playful, bitter?

1. The lonely wayfarer shrunk within himself at the horrid clamor and clapper-clawing; eyed the den of discord askance; and hurried on his way, rejoicing, if a bachelor, in his celibacy.

2. . . . Tom was the universal friend of the needy, and acted like a "friend in need"; that is to say, he always exacted good pay and good security.

3. Tom was as rigid in religious as in money matters; he was a stern supervisor and censurer of his neighbors, and seemed to think every sin entered up to their account became a credit on his own side of the page.

B. Below are opposed statements about this story. Select the statement that best expresses your own opinion.

a. The theme of Irving's story is universal; it could therefore be placed in any geographical setting.

b. The idea of a man selling his soul to the devil is essentially a European theme, and Irving should have used a European setting for his story.

III

TECHNIQUES

Setting

Much of the charm of this story can be attributed to Irving's careful creation of an atmosphere foreboding mystery and evil. What specific sights, colors, sounds, and feelings contribute to this atmosphere: (1) in the swamp, (2) at the old Indian fort, (3) when Tom finds his wife's remains?

Characterization

(1) Look back to the second paragraph. How do the house, the farm, and the horse help to show the Walkers' chief character trait? (2) What new traits of each are revealed throughout the remainder of the story? (3) What details of the black woodsman's physical appearance suggest his inner nature?

In 1835, Irving published a collection of autobiographical pieces called *A Tour on the Prairies,* based on his visit three years earlier to the Indian territories on the frontier, what is now the state of Oklahoma. He visited the Pawnee, Osage, and Creek tribes, taking notes on frontier customs, living conditions, and local legends. The following excerpt describes a camp on the Arkansas River.

The Camp of the Wild Horse

We had encamped in a good neighborhood for game, as the reports of rifles in various directions speedily gave notice. One of our hunters soon returned with the meat of a doe, tied up in the skin, and slung across his shoulders. Another brought a fat buck across his horse. Two other deer were brought in, and a number of turkeys. All the game was thrown down in front of the Captain's fire, to be portioned out among the various messes. The spits and camp-kettles were soon in full employ, and throughout the evening there was a scene of hunters' feasting and profusion.

We had been disappointed this day in our hopes of meeting with buffalo, but the sight of the wild horse had been a great novelty, and gave a turn to the conversation of the camp for the evening. There were several anecdotes told of a famous gray horse, which has ranged the prairies of this neighborhood for six or seven years, setting at naught every attempt of the hunters to capture him. They say he can pace

Chapter 20 of *A Tour on the Prairies,* 1835.

and rack (or amble) faster than the fleetest horses can run. Equally marvellous accounts were given of a black horse on the Brassos, who grazed the prairies on that river's banks in the Texas. For years he outstripped all pursuit. His fame spread far and wide; offers were made for him to the amount of a thousand dollars; the boldest and most hard-riding hunters tried incessantly to make prize of him, but in vain. At length he fell a victim to his gallantry, being decoyed under a tree by a tame mare, and a noose dropped over his head by a boy perched among the branches.

The capture of the wild horse is one of the most favorite achievements of the prairie tribes; and, indeed, it is from this source that the Indian hunters chiefly supply themselves. The wild horses which range those vast grassy plains, extending from the Arkansas to the Spanish settlements, are of various forms and colors, betraying their various descents. Some resemble the common English stock, and are probably descended from horses which have escaped from our border settlements. Others are of a low but strong make, and are supposed to be of the Andalusian breed,[1] brought out by the Spanish discoverers.

Some fanciful speculatists have seen in them descendants of the Arab stock, brought into Spain from Africa, and thence transferred to this country; and have pleased themselves with the idea that their sires may have been of the pure coursers of the desert, that once bore Mahomet[2] and his warlike disciples across the sandy plains of Arabia.

The habits of the Arab seem to have come with the steed. The introduction of the horse on the boundless prairies of the Far West changed the whole mode of living of their inhabitants. It gave them that facility of rapid motion, and of sudden and distant change of place, so dear to the roving propensities of man. Instead of lurking in the depths of gloomy forests, and patiently threading the mazes of a tangled wilderness on foot, like his brethren of the north, the Indian of the West is a rover of the plain; he leads a brighter and more sun-shiny life; almost always on horseback, on vast flowery prairies and under cloudless skies.

I was lying by the Captain's fire, late in the evening, listening to stories about those coursers of the prairies, and weaving speculations of my own, when there was a clamor of voices and a loud cheering at the other end of the camp; and word was passed that Beatte, the half-breed, had brought in a wild horse.

In an instant every fire was deserted; the whole camp crowded to see the Indian and his prize. It was a colt about two years old, well grown, finely limbed, with bright prominent eyes, and a spirited yet gentle demeanor. He gazed about him with an air of mingled stupefaction and surprise, at the men, the horses, and the camp-fires; while the Indian stood before him with folded arms, having hold of the other end of the cord which noosed his captive, and gazing on him with a most imperturbable aspect. Beatte, as I have before observed, has a greenish olive complexion, with a strongly marked countenance, not unlike the bronze casts of Napoleon; and as he stood before his captive horse, with folded arms and fixed aspect, he looked more like a statue than a man.

If the horse, however, manifested the least restiveness, Beatte would immediately worry him with the lariat, jerking him first on one side, then on the other, so as almost to throw him on the ground; when he had thus rendered him passive, he would resume his statue-like attitude and gaze at him in silence.

The whole scene was singularly wild; the tall grove, partially illumined by the flashing fires of the camp, the horses tethered here and there among the trees, the carcasses of deer hanging around, and, in the midst of all, the wild huntsman and his wild horse, with an admiring throng of rangers almost as wild.

In the eagerness of their excitement, several of the young rangers sought to get the horse

---

1. **Andalusian breed**\ˈan·də ᵃlū·zhən\ named for an old province of Southern Spain.
2. **Mahomet**\mə ᵃhŏm·ĭt\ Mohammed, Arabian founder of Islam whose revelations are found in the *Koran*.

by purchase or barter, and even offered extravagant terms; but Beatte declined all their offers. "You give great price now," said he; "tomorrow you be sorry, and take back, and say d—d Indian!"

The young men importuned him with questions about the mode in which he took the horse, but his answers were dry and laconic; he evidently retained some pique at having been undervalued and sneered at by them; and at the same time looked down upon them with contempt as greenhorns little versed in the noble science of woodcraft.

Afterwards, however, when he was seated by our fire, I readily drew from him an account of his exploit; for, though taciturn among strangers, and little prone to boast of his actions, yet his taciturnity, like that of all Indians, had its times of relaxation.

He informed me, that on leaving the camp, he had returned to the place where we had lost sight of the wild horse. Soon getting upon its track, he followed it to the banks of the river. Here, the prints being more distinct in the sand, he perceived that one of the hoofs was broken and defective, so he gave up the pursuit.

As he was returning to the camp, he came upon a gang of six horses, which immediately made for the river. He pursued them across the stream, left his rifle on the river-bank, and putting his horse to full speed, soon came up with the fugitives. He attempted to noose one of them, but the lariat hitched on one of his ears, and he shook it off. The horses dashed up a hill, he followed hard at their heels, when, of a sudden, he saw their tails whisking in the air, and they plunging down a precipice. It was too late to stop. He shut his eyes, held in his breath, and went over with them—neck or nothing. The descent was between twenty and thirty feet, but they all came down safe upon a sandy bottom.

He now succeeded in throwing his noose round a fine young horse. As he galloped alongside of him, the two horses passed each side of a sapling, and the end of the lariat was jerked out of his hand. He regained it, but an intervening tree obliged him again to let it go. Having once more caught it, and coming to a more open country, he was enabled to play the young horse with the line until he gradually checked and subdued him, so as to lead him to the place where he had left his rifle.

He had another formidable difficulty in getting him across the river, where both horses stuck for a time in the mire, and Beatte was nearly unseated from his saddle by the force of the current and the struggles of his captive. After much toil and trouble, however, he got across the stream, and brought his prize safe into camp.

For the remainder of the evening the camp remained in a high state of excitement; nothing was talked of but the capture of wild horses; every youngster of the troop was for this harum-scarum kind of chase; every one promised himself to return from the campaign in triumph, bestriding one of these wild coursers of the prairies. Beatte had suddenly risen to great importance; he was the prime hunter, the hero of the day. Offers were made him by the best-mounted rangers, to let him ride their horses in the chase, provided he would give them a share of the spoil. Beatte bore his honors in silence, and closed with none of the offers. Our stammering, chattering, gasconading little Frenchman, however, made up for his taciturnity by vaunting as much upon the subject as if it were he that had caught the horse. Indeed he held forth so learnedly in the matter, and boasted so much of the many horses he had taken, that he began to be considered an oracle; and some of the youngsters were inclined to doubt whether he were not superior even to the taciturn Beatte.

The excitement kept the camp awake later than usual. The hum of voices, interrupted by occasional peals of laughter, was heard from the groups around the various fires, and the night was considerably advanced before all had sunk to sleep.

With the morning dawn the excitement revived, and Beatte and his wild horse were again the gaze and talk of the camp. The captive had been tied all night to a tree among the other horses. He was again led forth by Beatte, by a long halter or lariat, and, on his manifesting the least restiveness, was, as before, jerked and worried into passive submission. He appeared to be gentle and docile by nature, and had a beautifully mild expression of the eye. In his strange and forlorn situation, the poor animal seemed to seek protection and companionship in the very horse which had aided to capture him.

Seeing him thus gentle and tractable, Beatte, just as we were about to march, strapped a light pack upon his back, by way of giving him the first lesson in servitude. The native pride and independence of the animal took fire at this indignity. He reared, and plunged, and kicked, and tried in every way to get rid of the degrading burden. The Indian was too potent for him. At every paroxysm[3] he renewed the discipline of the halter, until the poor animal, driven to despair, threw himself prostrate on the ground, and lay motionless, as if acknowledging himself vanquished. A stage hero, representing the despair of a captive prince, could not have played his part more dramatically. There was absolutely a moral grandeur in it.

The imperturbable Beatte folded his arms, and stood for a time, looking down in silence upon his captive; until seeing him perfectly subdued, he nodded his head slowly, screwed his mouth into a sardonic smile of triumph, and, with a jerk of the halter, ordered him to rise. He obeyed, and from that time forward offered no resistance. During that day he bore his pack patiently, and was led by the halter; but in two days he followed voluntarily at large among the supernumerary horses of the troop.

I could not but look with compassion upon this fine young animal, whose whole course of existence had been so suddenly reversed. From being a denizen of these vast pastures, ranging at will from plain to plain and mead to mead, cropping of every herb and flower, and drinking of every stream, he was suddenly reduced to perpetual and painful servitude, to pass his life under the harness and the curb, amid, perhaps, the din and dust and drudgery of cities. The transition in his lot was such as sometimes takes place in human affairs, and in the fortunes of towering individuals:—one day, a prince of the prairies—the next day, a packhorse!

I
A WILD AND NOBLE WEST

Carefully omitting the harsher aspects of camp life—stifling dust, overpowering smells of animals and crusty men, rough and often vulgar language—Irving delights his Eastern reader with vivid glimpses of noble savage and beast set against the expected, classic background of flashing camp fires, rustic feasts, and story telling before the tent. Although some may object to his avoidance of realism, Irving still captures and preserves those beautiful and dramatic flashes of color and nobility that are lost on cruder souls.

II
IMPLICATIONS

What do the following quotations reveal either about Irving, the prairies, or life in general?

1. There was absolutely a moral grandeur in it [the wild horse's fall].

2. The transition in his lot was such as sometimes takes place in human affairs, and in the fortunes of towering individuals:—one day, a prince of the prairies—the next day, a packhorse!

III
TECHNIQUES

Setting

Irving is very sparing with details about the camp, but those he chooses are quite picturesque. What specific details does he cite? Why would these broad strokes be particularly effective for readers who have never seen such a camp?

---

3. **paroxysm**\\ˈpă•rĕk ˈsĭz•əm\\ a sudden outburst of action or emotion, usually occurring at intervals.

During the last years of his life,
Irving devoted most of his energy to lengthy
biographies, but *Wolfert's Roost
and Miscellanies* (1855) is an attempt
to strike the same vein he tapped in *The Sketch
Book:* the familiar essay and simple tale.
"A Creole Village" is one of the 19 sketches
in this collection. It recalls a visit
Irving made by steamboat to a tiny Louisiana
village and the people he met there.

The Creole Village

A SKETCH
FROM A STEAMBOAT

In travelling about our motley country, I am often reminded of Ariosto's[1] account of the moon, in which the good paladin[2] Astolpho[3] found everything garnered up that had been lost on earth. So I am apt to imagine that many things lost in the Old World are treasured up in the New; having been handed down from generation to generation, since the early days of the colonies. A European antiquary, therefore, curious in his researches after the ancient and almost obliterated customs and usages of his country, would do well to put himself upon the track of some early band of emigrants, follow them across the Atlantic, and rummage among their descendants on our shores.

In the phraseology of New England might be found many an old English provincial phrase, long since obsolete in the parent country; with some quaint relics of the Roundheads; while Virginia cherishes peculiarities characteristic of the days of Elizabeth and Sir Walter Raleigh.

In the same way, the sturdy yeomanry of New Jersey and Pennsylvania keep up many usages fading away in ancient Germany; while many an honest, broad-bottomed custom, nearly extinct in venerable Holland, may be found flourishing in pristine vigor and luxuriance in Dutch villages, on the banks of the Mohawk and the Hudson.

In no part of our country, however, are the customs and peculiarities imported from the old world by the earlier settlers kept up with more fidelity than in the little, poverty-stricken villages of Spanish and French origin, which border the rivers of ancient Louisiana. Their population is generally made up of the descendants of those nations, married and interwoven together, and occasionally crossed with a slight dash of the Indian. The French character, however, floats on top, as, from its buoyant qualities, it is sure to do, whenever it forms a particle, however small, of an intermixture.

In these serene and dilapidated villages, art and nature stand still, and the world forgets to turn round. The revolutions that distract other parts of this mutable planet, reach not here, or pass over without leaving any trace. The fortunate inhabitants have none of that public spirit which extends its cares beyond its horizon, and imports trouble and perplexity from all quarters in newspapers. In fact, newspapers are almost unknown in these villages; and, as French is the current language, the inhabitants have little community of opinion with their republican neighbors. They retain, therefore, their old habits of passive obedience to the decrees of government, as though they still lived under the absolute sway of colonial commandants, instead of being part and parcel of

---

1. **Ariosto**\'ă·rĭ ᵃŏs·tō\ Italian poet (1474–1533) author of *Orlando Furioso*.
2. **paladin**\ᵃpă·lə·dĭn\ a knight or heroic champion; originally one of the twelve peers of Charlemagne's court.
3. **Astolpho**\'ăs ᵃtŏl·fō\ in medieval romances, one of Charlemagne's twelve paladins. In *Orlando Furioso*, he makes a trip to the moon to bring back Orlando's wits.

From *Wolfert's Roost and Miscellanies*, 1855.

the sovereign people, and having a voice in public legislation.

A few aged men, who have grown gray on their hereditary acres, and are of the good old colonial stock, exert a patriarchal sway in all matters of public and private import; their opinions are considered oracular, and their word is law.

The inhabitants, moreover, have none of that eagerness for gain, and rage for improvement, which keep our people continually on the move, and our country towns incessantly in a state of transition. There the magic phrases, "town lots," "water privileges," "railroads," and other comprehensive and soul-stirring words from the speculator's vocabulary, are never heard. The residents dwell in the houses built by their forefathers, without thinking of enlarging or modernizing them, or pulling them down and turning them into granite stores. The trees under which they have been born, and have played in infancy, flourish undisturbed; though, by cutting them down, they might open new streets, and put money in their pockets. In a word, the almighty dollar, that great object of universal devotion throughout our land, seems to have no genuine devotees in these peculiar villages; and unless some of its missionaries penetrate there, and erect banking-houses and other pious shrines, there is no knowing how long the inhabitants may remain in their present state of contented poverty.

In descending one of our great western rivers in a steamboat, I met with two worthies from one of these villages, who had been on a distant excursion, the longest they had ever made, as they seldom ventured far from home. One was the great man, or Grand Seigneur[4] of the village; not that he enjoyed any legal privileges or power there, everything of the kind having been done away when the province was ceded by France to the United States. His sway over his neighbors was merely one of custom and convention, out of deference to his family. Beside, he was worth full fifty thousand dollars, an amount almost equal, in the imagi-

nations of the villagers, to the treasures of King Solomon.[5]

This very substantial old gentleman, though of the fourth or fifth generation in this country, retained the true Gallic[6] feature and deportment, and reminded me of one of those provincial potentates that are to be met with in the remote parts of France. He was of a large frame, a ginger-bread complexion, strong features, eyes that stood out like glass knobs, and a prominent nose, which he frequently regaled from a gold snuff-box, and occasionally blew with a colored handkerchief, until it sounded like a trumpet.

He was attended by an old negro, as black as ebony, with a huge mouth, in a continual grin; evidently a privileged and favorite servant, who had grown up and grown old with him. He was dressed in creole style, with white jacket and trousers, a stiff shirt-collar, that threatened to cut off his ears, a bright Madras[7] handkerchief tied round his head, and large gold ear-rings. He was the politest negro I met with in a western tour, and that is saying a great deal, for, excepting the Indians, the negroes are the most gentlemanlike personages to be met with in those parts. It is true they differ from the Indians in being a little extra polite and complimentary. He was also one of the merriest; and here, too, the negroes, however we may deplore their unhappy condition, have the advantage of their masters. The whites are, in general, too free and prosperous to be merry. The cares of maintaining their rights and liberties, adding to their wealth, and making presidents, engross all their thoughts and dry up all the moisture of their souls. If you hear a broad, hearty, devil-may-care laugh, be assured it is a negro's.

4. **Grand Seigneur**\sēn ˄yər\ title of respect, like Sir; formerly meant a feudal lord.
5. **King Solomon,** son of David and Bathsheba; king of Israel, tenth century B.C.
6. **Gallic**\˄găl·ĭk\ reference to ancient Gaul or modern France.
7. **Madras**\˄măd·rəs\ handkerchief, a large brightly colored kerchief, usually striped or checkered.

Beside this African domestic, the seigneur of the village had another no less cherished and privileged attendant. This was a huge dog, of the mastiff breed, with a deep, hanging mouth, and a look of surly gravity. He walked about the cabin with the air of a dog perfectly at home, and who had paid for his passage. At dinner-time he took his seat beside his master, giving him a glance now and then out of a corner of his eye, which bespoke perfect confidence that he would not be forgotten. Nor was he. Every now and then a huge morsel would be thrown to him, peradventure the half-picked leg of a fowl, which he would receive with a snap like the springing of a steel trap,—one gulp, and all was down; and a glance of the eye told his master that he was ready for another consignment.

The other village worthy, travelling in company with the seigneur, was of a totally different stamp. Small, thin, and weazen-faced, as Frenchmen are apt to be represented in caricature, with a bright, squirrel-like eye, and a gold ring in his ear. His dress was flimsy, and sat loosely on his frame, and he had altogether the look of one with but little coin in his pocket. Yet, though one of the poorest, I was assured he was one of the merriest and most popular personages in his native village.

Compère[8] Martin, as he was commonly called, was the factotum of the place,—sportsman, schoolmaster, and land-surveyor. He could sing, dance, and, above all, play on the fiddle, an invaluable accomplishment in an old French creole village, for the inhabitants have a hereditary love for balls and *fêtes*. If they work but little, they dance a great deal; and a fiddle is the joy of their heart.

What had sent Compère Martin travelling with the Grand Seigneur I could not learn. He evidently looked up to him with great deference, and was assiduous in rendering him petty attentions; from which I concluded that he lived at home upon the crumbs which fell from his table. He was gayest when out of his sight, and had his song and his joke when forward among the deck passengers; but, alto-

gether, Compère Martin was out of his element on board of a steamboat. He was quite another being, I am told, when at home in his own village.

Like his opulent fellow-traveller, he too had his canine follower and retainer,—and one suited to his different fortunes,—one of the civilest, most unoffending little dogs in the world. Unlike the lordly mastiff, he seemed to think he had no right on board of the steamboat; if you did but look hard at him, he would throw himself upon his back, and lift up his legs, as if imploring mercy.

At table he took his seat a little distance from his master; not with the bluff, confident air of the mastiff, but quietly and diffidently; his head on one side, with one ear dubiously slouched, the other hopefully cocked up; his under-teeth projecting beyond his black nose, and his eye wistfully following each morsel that went into his master's mouth.

If Compère Martin now and then should venture to abstract a morsel from his plate, to give to his humble companion, it was edifying to see with what diffidence the exemplary little animal would take hold of it, with the very tip of his teeth, as if he would almost rather not, or was fearful of taking too great a liberty. And then with what decorum would he eat it! How many efforts would he make in swallowing it, as if it stuck in his throat; with what daintiness would he lick his lips; and then with what an air of thankfulness would he resume his seat, with his teeth once more projecting beyond his nose, and an eye of humble expectation fixed upon his master.

It was late in the afternoon when the steamboat stopped at the village which was the residence of these worthies. It stood on the high bank of the river, and bore traces of having been a frontier trading-post. There were the remains of stockades that once protected it from the Indians, and the houses were in the ancient Spanish and French colonial taste, the

---

8. **Compère**\ˈkɔm·pār\ godfather.

place having been successively under the domination of both those nations prior to the cession of Louisiana to the United States.

The arrival of the seigneur of fifty thousand dollars, and his humble companion, Compère Martin, had evidently been looked forward to as an event in the village. Numbers of men, women, and children, white, yellow, and black, were collected on the river bank; most of them clad in old-fashioned French garments, and their heads decorated with colored handkerchiefs or white nightcaps. The moment the steamboat came within sight and hearing, there was a waving of handkerchiefs, and a screaming and bawling of salutations and felicitations, that baffle all description.

The old gentleman of fifty thousand dollars was received by a train of relatives, and friends, and children, and grandchildren, whom he kissed on each cheek, and who formed a procession in his rear, with a legion of domestics, of all ages, following him to a large, old-fashioned French house, that domineered over the village.

His black *valet de chambre,*[9] in white jacket and trousers, and gold ear-rings, was met on the shore by a boon, though rustic companion, a tall negro fellow, with a long good-humored face, and the profile of a horse, which stood out from beneath a narrow-rimmed straw hat, stuck on the back of his head. The explosions of laughter of these two varlets on meeting and exchanging compliments, were enough to electrify the country round.

The most hearty reception, however, was that given to Compère Martin. Everybody, young and old, hailed him before he got to land. Everybody had a joke for Compère Martin, and Compère Martin had a joke for everybody. Even his little dog appeared to partake of his popularity, and to be caressed by every hand. Indeed, he was quite a different animal the moment he touched the land. Here he was at home; here he was of consequence. He barked, he leaped, he frisked about his old friends, and then would skim round the place in a wide circle, as if mad.

I traced Compère Martin and his little dog to their home. It was an old ruinous Spanish house, of large dimensions, with verandas overshadowed by ancient elms. The house had probably been the residence, in old times, of the Spanish commandant. In one wing of this crazy, but aristocratical abode, was nestled the family of my fellow-traveller; for poor devils are apt to be magnificently clad and lodged, in the cast-off clothes and abandoned palaces of the great and wealthy.

The arrival of Compère Martin was welcomed by a legion of women, children, and mongrel curs; and, as poverty and gayety generally go hand-in-hand among the French and their descendants, the crazy mansion soon resounded with loud gossip and light-hearted laughter.

As the steamboat paused a short time at the village, I took occasion to stroll about the place. Most of the houses were in the French taste, with casements and rickety verandas, but most of them in flimsy and ruinous condition. All the wagons, ploughs, and other utensils about the place were of ancient and inconvenient Gallic construction, such as had been brought from France in the primitive days of the colony. The very looks of the people reminded me of the villages of France.

From one of the houses came the hum of a spinningwheel, accompanied by a scrap of an old French *chanson,*[10] which I have heard many a time among the peasantry of Languedoc,[11] doubtless a traditional song, brought over by the first French emigrants, and handed down from generation to generation.

Half a dozen young lasses emerged from the adjacent dwellings, reminding me, by their light step and gay costume, of scenes in ancient France, where taste in dress comes natural to

---

9. **valet de chambre**\va‧lā də ‧shɔm‧bər\ a gentlemen's personal manservant.
10. **chanson**\‧shan‧sōn\ song.
11. **Languedoc**\laŋ‧dōk\ a region and former province of southern France, between the Pyrenees and Loire \lwar\ River.

every class of females. The trim bodice and colored petticoat, and little apron, with its pockets to receive the hands when in an attitude for conversation; the colored kerchief wound tastefully round the head, with a coquettish knot perking above one ear; and the neat slipper and tight-drawn stocking, with its braid of narrow ribbon embracing the ankle where it peeps from its mysterious curtain. It is from this ambush that Cupid sends his most inciting arrows.

While I was musing upon the recollections thus accidentally summoned up, I heard the sound of a fiddle from the mansion of Compère Martin, the signal, no doubt, for a joyous gathering. I was disposed to turn my steps thither, and witness the festivities of one of the very few villages I had met with in my wide tour that was yet poor enough to be merry; but the bell of the steamboat summoned me to reëmbark.

As we swept away from the shore, I cast back a wistful eye upon the moss-grown roofs and ancient elms of the village, and prayed that the inhabitants might long retain their happy ignorance, their absence of all enterprise and improvement, their respect for the fiddle, and their contempt for the almighty dollar. I fear, however, my prayer is doomed to be of no avail. In a little while the steamboat whirled me to an American town, just springing into bustling and prosperous existence.

The surrounding forest had been laid out in town lots; frames of wooden buildings were rising from among stumps and burnt trees. The place already boasted a court-house, a jail, and two banks, all built of pine boards, on the model of Grecian temples. There were rival hotels, rival churches, and rival newspapers; together with the usual number of judges and generals and governors; not to speak of doctors by the dozen, and lawyers by the score.

The place, I was told, was in an astonishing career of improvement, with a canal and two railroads in embryo. Lots doubled in price every week; everybody was speculating in land; everybody was rich; and everybody was growing richer. The community, however, was torn to pieces by new doctrines in religion and in political economy; there were camp-meetings, and agrarian meetings; and an election was at hand, which, it was expected, would throw the whole country into a paroxysm.

Alas! with such an enterprising neighbor, what is to become of the poor little creole village!

I
THE WISTFUL EYE

Some writers see their function as one of preserving the treasures of the past, especially those which their own times are in danger of heedlessly destroying. That Irving regards the Creole Village as such a treasure is clear, for he sees it as one of those rare Old World gems somehow miraculously preserved in the New. And although he yearns to live in such a world, he knows his wish can never be fulfilled. Yet before the village dies his art may preserve something still. His sharp eye for a moment fixes for us the "transient and uncertain" world, snatching something priceless from the "wrecks of time and fortune" that "are strewn around."

II
IMPLICATIONS

Irving sees many advantages to living in the Creole Village. Explain those suggested in the statements below. In your opinion would they be considered desirable today?

1. The fortunate inhabitants have none of that public spirit which extends its cares beyond its horizon, and imports trouble and perplexity from all quarters in newspapers.

2. The inhabitants, moreover, have none of that eagerness for gain, and rage for improvement, which keep our people continually on the move, and our country towns incessantly in a state of transition.

3. . . . the almighty dollar, that great object of universal devotion throughout our land, seems to have no genuine devotees in these peculiar villages; . . . .

4. I was disposed to turn my steps thither, and witness the festivities of one of the very few vil-

lages I had met with . . . that was yet poor enough to be merry.

III
TECHNIQUES

Setting

Part of the charm of the village is conveyed through the physical properties of the village. Contrast the appearance of the Creole village with the American town. What spirit or atmosphere does the Creole village have which the American town lacks?

Characterization

The reader's impression of the village also depends upon his acquaintance with the inhabitants, here largely represented by the old gentleman and Compère Martin, and their dogs. What impression of each is conveyed through build, dress, actions, and reception by the village?

IV
WORDS

A. Using what you know about context clues, determine the meaning of the italicized words. Which clue or clues helped you work out the meaning?

1. A miserable horse, whose ribs were as *articulate* as the bars of a gridiron. . . .

2. . . . hurried on his way, rejoicing, if a bachelor, in his *celibacy*.

3. . . . pacing carefully, like a cat, along the *prostrate* trunks of trees. . . .

4. . . . a kind of fort, which they had looked upon as almost *impregnable*, and had used as a place of refuge. . . .

5. All her *avarice* was awakened at the mention of hidden gold. . . .

6. . . . evidently retained some *pique* at having been undervalued and sneered at. . . .

7. . . . screwed his mouth into a *sardonic* smile of triumph. . . .

8. . . . shuffled out from the group and advanced with a certain *deference*. . . .

9. . . . there was not that *repose* we expect to find in the faces of the dead.

10. . . . with features swollen and blurred by *dissipation*. . . .

B. 1. No two synonyms have exactly the same meaning. To know the precise distinctions among synonyms adds force and exactness to one's speaking and writing. Explain the differences between these pairs of synonyms:

a. *swarthy* and *dingy; reserved* and *sullen; ugliness* and *sordidness.*

b. *fearfully* and *apprehensively; dry* and *laconic; dun* and *dust; salutations* and *felicitations.*

2. Find synonyms for *propensities, demeanor, deference, assiduous, edifying, diffidence.*

WILLA CATHER

1873-1947

Willa Cather poured out her feelings about the rugged settlers of the West, their codes of behavior and their love for the earth. All of her major work comes out of her youthful impressions of the West, her wide reading in histories of its development, and frequent revisits to her relatives and her favorite towns. What she sought was the spiritual truths that are illuminated by a discriminating choice of fact and detail.

When Willa Cather began writing she had little intention of becoming a spokesman for the Middle West. Born in the Virginia hills around Winchester, Virginia, she was nine years old before her father moved the family to a ranch near Red Cloud, Nebraska, and then to the little frontier village itself. Here she began her schooling, having been tutored previously by her grandmother. The young girl's love for foreign languages was evident at once. She spoke French and German with her neighbors and read the classics with "Uncle Billy" Ducker, a local amateur scholar. But she loved just as much the explorations with her brothers, Roscoe and Douglass, of the Republican River country south of Red Cloud and the high plains region—"The Divide"—where she revisited the Swedish, German, and Bohemian friends of her first days in Nebraska.

After a year at a preparatory school in Lincoln, Willa Cather entered the University of Nebraska thinking she wanted to study medicine and classics. After helping to found a college paper, she spent more and more of her time on English compositions and journalism, particularly dramatic criticism for the *Nebraska State Journal* at one dollar a column. The experience was fruitful. Her first job after graduation was editorial work on *The Home Monthly* in Pittsburgh and then dramatic criticism for the Pittsburgh *Daily Leader*, her hardest years financially and emotionally. In order to have more time to write the poetry and stories she was selling occasionally to New York magazines, she spent five years, 1901–1906, teaching Latin and English in Pittsburgh high schools. A volume of verse, *April Twilights,* appeared in 1903, and in 1905 the critics praised her first collection of short stories, *The Troll Garden,* especially "Paul's Case" and "The Sculptor's Funeral." The next year she made the break from apprenticeship to professional status with an appointment as associate and then managing editor of *McClure's Magazine* in New York City.

Working for S. S. McClure was something like living in a whirlwind, but Willa Cather thrived on it. She spent almost a year in Boston on a special assignment and part of another traveling in New England and to London. In a Boston drawing room she first met Sarah Orne Jewett, then widely known as the author of the splendid Maine sketches *The Country of the Pointed Firs.* Miss Jewett urged her to give over her whole life to fiction, no matter what the cost. "It is impossible for you to work so hard," she wrote, "and yet have your gifts mature as they should. . . . To work in silence and with all one's heart, that is the writer's lot; he is the only artist who must be solitary, and yet needs the widest outlook upon the world." After six years as an editor, Willa Cather took Miss Jewett's advice and left the McClure offices. She had published "The Enchanted Bluff" in *Harper's Magazine,* a short story in which for the first time she used the Southwest as a locale, and *Alexander's Bridge,* her first novel. She was ready to risk her future on her pen.

A visit to her brother in Winslow, Arizona, early in 1912, introduced her to the ancient cliff-dwellings of nearby canyons. On the way back to New York, she spent two months renewing her memories of the sights and sounds of Red Cloud. Though she continued to live in Greenwich Village, she was fully aware that nothing inspired her as much as the windy plains of Nebraska and the deserts of the Southwest. *Alexander's Bridge* had been a contrived novel, a "studio picture," as she later called it. Now she was ready to pour out her feelings about the rugged settlers of the West, their codes of behavior and their love for the earth. Except for *Shadows on the Rock* (1931; set in colonial Quebec) and *Sapphira and the Slave Girl* (1940; set in Virginia), all of Willa Cather's major work comes out of her youthful impressions of the West, her wide reading in histories of its development, and frequent revisits to her relatives and her favorite towns. In no sense was she exploiting her material, as might be said of some nineteenth-century humorists, nor did she feel compelled to paint the dismal, pessimistic portraits our naturalist novelists were painting. That was sensationalism, she said, and what she sought was the spiritual

Willa Cather's childhood home described in The Song of the Lark, *"Old Mrs. Harris," and "The Best Years."*

Red Cloud, Nebraska, 1885. Town of
Willa Cather's childhood.

truths that are illuminated by a discriminating choice of fact and detail. Her characters are ordinary men and women; her plots are not in the least melodramatic or artificially heightened; and her style, though always concise, is steady and quiet rather than dazzling.

O Pioneers! (1913), the first of three novels concerned with the Nebraska frontier, begins: "One January day, thirty years ago, the little town of Hanover, anchored on a windy Nebraska tableland, was trying not to be blown away. A mist of fine snowflakes was curling and eddying about the cluster of low drab buildings huddled on the gray prairie, under a gray sky. The dwelling-houses were set about haphazard on the tough prairie sod; some of them looked as if they had been moved in overnight, and others as if they were straying off by themselves, headed straight for the open plain. None of them had any appearance of permanence, and the howling wind blew under them as well as over them." The reader knows at once that he is in good hands because the novelist, with a shrewd eye for descriptive details, writes as though she were reliving, not just imagining, winter on *tough* sod in *drab* buildings under a *gray* sky. There is a sureness of touch in Willa Cather's style; she merely tells us how it really

was. In the same relaxed way she builds her plot around Alexandra Bergson, the first of many strong-willed heroines, unfolding her life after her father's untimely death. She makes of this novel not so much a hymn to the pioneer virtues—perseverance, courage, hard work—as a history of what one girl with vision could do with the stubborn land. "*O Pioneers!* interested me tremendously," she recalled later, "because it had to do with a kind of country I loved, because it was about old neighbors, once very dear, whom I had almost forgotten in the hurry and excitement of growing up and finding out what the world was like and trying to get on in it."

She recalled her old neighbors even more vividly when she plotted her third novel of the Nebraska frontier, *My Ántonia* (1918). In the Miners' house, next door to the Cathers in Red Cloud, had lived a young Bohemian hired girl, Annie Sadílek, an industrious and lively newcomer to Nebraska. Willa Cather turned her into Ántonia Shimerda, and though her life in Black Hawk is described by young Jim Burden, a native of the town, she is still the focus of the novel. It is a disarmingly simple story, a welding of earthy characters with the stubborn land. Again the young girl has to shoulder the family's burden after the father's suicide, but here we come to know the valiant heroine far better than Willa Cather's earlier heroines. When she moves to town we share her fears and frustrations at adjusting to "city" ways and being a "hired girl"; we sympathize with her in her unhappy love affairs; and we sense the relief she feels when she returns to till the land with Cusak, her husband, and their swarming brood of healthy children. *My Ántonia* has always been, for good reasons, one of Willa Cather's most popular novels. It has vitality and honesty in its telling. Its central character is no Earth Goddess, no epic heroine, but an adolescent who grows up in a land that demands perseverance and offers in return, at least in Ántonia's case, the joy of self-discovery.

After the first World War, Willa Cather published two collections of short stories and eight more novels. They are not all, understandably, of equal quality but all bear her particular mark. The war left her more disillusioned than she wished to admit; and as a growing materialism evidenced itself in America in the 1920's, she lost some of the glow of the optimism of her earlier work. In its place appeared a concern with moral failures. *A Lost Lady* (1923) is an unforgettable portrait of the young wife of a railroad engineer who succumbs to the town upstart, Ivy Peters. *My Mortal Enemy* (1926) is a depressing study of a marriage in slow collapse and the degeneration of the heroine. *Lucy Gayheart* (1935) chronicles the life of a Nebraska girl in Chicago who falls in love with a singer much older than she and who comes to grief after he dies in a boating accident.

With *Death Comes for the Archbishop* (1927), however, Willa Cather achieved lasting fame. It is her most ambitious work, a re-creation of history rather than a study of the contemporary Midwest. The lure of Arizona and New Mexico had increased in the years after the war and, though not a Catholic, she became enthralled with the history of the Church in the Southwest and of two eminent French missionary clerics, Archbishop Lamy and Bishop Machebeuf who became Archbishop Latour and Father Vaillant of the novel. The title is unfortunate; there are no murders in the book and the death of Latour is hardly the climax of the story. But climaxes never bothered Willa Cather. From the opening sentence—"One afternoon in the autumn of 1851 a solitary horseman, followed by a pack-mule, was pushing through an arid stretch of country somewhere in central New Mexico"—to the burial of the Archbishop in the great Santa Fé cathedral, the story proceeds with assurance and inevitability. There may be emotional scenes which a more ruthless narrator would have cut from the book, but no reader questions her religious devotion; her love for the brilliant landscape; her knowledge of Indian customs, corrupt Spanish priests, and the simple folk virtues of this last frontier. *Death Comes for the Archbishop* and *My Ántonia*, two quite different novels, must be experienced, not merely described, if one is to understand what Willa Cather meant by pioneer vision and courage.

The Troll Garden (1905)
was Willa Cather's first book in prose.
It is composed of three stories about artists
and their audiences, three stories
about artistic temperaments in conflict
with prairie town citizens, and a long,
widely popular story set in Pittsburgh, called
"Paul's Case." In "The Sculptor's Funeral,"
Miss Cather tells the story of Harvey Merrick,
a sculptor of rare ability, and his return
to Sand City, Kansas, where he was
neither understood nor appreciated. Sand City
resembles Red Cloud and the hostility
of its inhabitants is not unlike
the hostility Miss Cather met
in her own career.

The Sculptor's Funeral

A group of the townspeople stood on the station siding of a little Kansas town, awaiting the coming of the night train, which was already twenty minutes overdue. The snow had fallen thick over everything; in the pale starlight the line of bluffs across the wide, white meadows south of the town made soft, smoke-coloured curves against the clear sky. The men on the siding stood first on one foot and then on the other, their hands thrust deep into their trousers pockets, their overcoats open, their shoulders screwed up with the cold; and they glanced from time to time toward the southeast, where the railroad track wound along the river shore. They conversed in low tones and moved about restlessly, seeming uncertain as to what was expected of them. There was but one of the company who looked as if he knew exactly why he was there, and he kept con-

spicuously apart; walking to the far end of the platform, returning to the station door, then pacing up the track again, his chin sunk in the high collar of his overcoat, his burly shoulders drooping forward, his gait heavy and dogged. Presently he was approached by a tall, spare, grizzled man clad in a faded Grand Army suit, who shuffled out from the group and advanced with a certain deference, craning his neck forward until his back made the angle of a jackknife three-quarters open.

"I reckon she's a-goin' to be pretty late agin tonight, Jim," he remarked in a squeaky falsetto. "S'pose it's the snow?"

"I don't know," responded the other man with a shade of annoyance, speaking from out an astonishing cataract of red beard that grew fiercely and thickly in all directions.

The spare man shifted the quill toothpick he was chewing to the other side of his mouth. "It ain't likely that anybody from the East will come with the corpse, I s'pose," he went on reflectively.

"I don't know," responded the other, more curtly than before.

"It's too bad he didn't belong to some lodge or other. I like an order funeral myself. They seem more appropriate for people of some reputation," the spare man continued, with an ingratiating concession in his shrill voice, as he carefully placed his toothpick in his vest pocket. He always carried the flag at the G. A. R.[1] funerals in the town.

The heavy man turned on his heel, without replying, and walked up the siding. The spare man rejoined the uneasy group. "Jim's ez full ez a tick, ez ushel," he commented commiseratingly.

Just then a distant whistle sounded, and there was a shuffling of feet on the platform. A number of lanky boys, of all ages, appeared as suddenly and slimily as eels wakened by the crack of thunder; some came from the waiting-room, where they had been warming them-

---

1. **G.A.R.** (Grand Army of the Republic), men who served with the Union Army during the Civil War.

selves by the red stove, or half asleep on the slat benches; others uncoiled themselves from baggage trucks or slid out of express wagons. Two clambered down from the driver's seat of a hearse that stood backed up against the siding. They straightened their stooping shoulders and lifted their heads, and a flash of momentary animation kindled their dull eyes at that cold, vibrant scream, the worldwide call for men. It stirred them like the note of a trumpet; just as it had often stirred the man who was coming home tonight, in his boyhood.

The night express shot, red as a rocket, from out the eastward marsh lands and wound along the river shore under the long lines of shivering poplars that sentinelled the meadows, the escaping steam hanging in grey masses against the pale sky and blotting out the Milky Way. In a moment the red glare from the headlight streamed up the snow-covered track before the siding and glittered on the wet, black rails. The burly man with the dishevelled red beard walked swiftly up the platform toward the approaching train, uncovering his head as he went. The group of men behind him hesitated, glanced questioningly at one another, and awkwardly followed his example. The train stopped, and the crowd shuffled up to the express car just as the door was thrown open, the man in the G. A. R. suit thrusting his head forward with curiosity. The express messenger appeared in the doorway, accompanied by a young man in a long ulster[2] and travelling cap.

"Are Mr. Merrick's friends here?" inquired the young man.

The group on the platform swayed uneasily. Philip Phelps, the banker, responded with dignity: "We have come to take charge of the body. Mr. Merrick's father is very feeble and can't be about."

"Send the agent out here," growled the express messenger, "and tell the operator to lend a hand."

The coffin was got out of its rough-box and down on the snowy platform. The townspeople drew back enough to make room for it and then formed a close semicircle about it, looking curi-

ously at the palm leaf which lay across the black cover. No one said anything. The baggage man stood by his truck, waiting to get at the trunks. The engine panted heavily, and the fireman dodged in and out among the wheels with his yellow torch and long oil-can, snapping the spindle boxes. The young Bostonian, one of the dead sculptor's pupils who had come with the body, looked about him helplessly. He turned to the banker, the only one of that black, uneasy, stoop-shouldered group who seemed enough of an individual to be addressed.

"None of Mr. Merrick's brothers are here?" he asked uncertainly.

The man with the red beard for the first time stepped up and joined the others. "No, they have not come yet; the family is scattered. The body will be taken directly to the house." He stooped and took hold of one of the handles of the coffin.

"Take the long hill road up, Thompson, it will be easier on the horses," called the liveryman as the undertaker snapped the door of the hearse and prepared to mount to the driver's seat.

Laird, the red-bearded lawyer, turned again to the stranger: "We didn't know whether there would be any one with him or not," he explained. "It's a long walk, so you'd better go up in the hack."[3] He pointed to a single battered conveyance, but the young man replied stiffly: "Thank you, but I think I will go up with the hearse. If you don't object," turning to the undertaker, "I'll ride with you."

They clambered up over the wheels and drove off in the starlight up the long, white hill toward the town. The lamps in the still village were shining from under the low, snow-burdened roofs; and beyond, on every side, the plains reached out into emptiness, peaceful and wide as the soft sky itself, and wrapped in a tangible, white silence.

---

2. **ulster**\ˈəls·tər\ a long, loose overcoat, of Irish origin.
3. **hack**, vernacular for taxicab.

When the hearse backed up to a wooden sidewalk before a naked, weather-beaten frame house, the same composite, ill-defined group that had stood upon the station siding was huddled about the gate. The front yard was an icy swamp, and a couple of warped planks, extending from the sidewalk to the door, made a sort of rickety footbridge. The gate hung on one hinge, and was opened wide with difficulty. Steavens, the young stranger, noticed that something black was tied to the knob of the front door.

The grating sound made by the casket, as it was drawn from the hearse, was answered by a scream from the house; the front door was wrenched open, and a tall, corpulent woman rushed out bareheaded into the snow and flung herself upon the coffin, shrieking: "My boy, my boy! And this is how you've come home to me!"

As Steavens turned away and closed his eyes with a shudder of unutterable repulsion, another woman, also tall, but flat and angular, dressed entirely in black, darted out of the house and caught Mrs. Merrick by the shoulders, crying sharply: "Come, come, mother; you mustn't go on like this!" Her tone changed to one of obsequious solemnity as she turned to the banker: "The parlour is ready, Mr. Phelps."

The bearers carried the coffin along the narrow boards, while the undertaker ran ahead with the coffin-rests. They bore it into a large, unheated room that smelled of dampness and disuse and furniture polish, and set it down under a hanging lamp ornamented with jingling glass prisms and before a "Rogers group" of John Alden and Priscilla, wreathed with smilax.[4] Henry Steavens stared about him with the sickening conviction that there had been a mistake, and that he had somehow arrived at the wrong destination. He looked at the clover-green Brussels, the fat plush upholstery, among the hand-painted china placques and panels and vases, for some mark of identification,—for something that might once conceivably have belonged to Harvey Merrick. It was not until he recognized his friend in the crayon portrait of a little boy in kilts and curls, hanging above

the piano, that he felt willing to let any of these people approach the coffin.

"Take the lid off, Mr. Thompson; let me see my boy's face," wailed the elder woman between her sobs. This time Steavens looked fearfully, almost beseechingly into her face, red and swollen under its masses of strong, black, shiny hair. He flushed, dropped his eyes, and then, almost incredulously, looked again. There was a kind of power about her face—a kind of brutal handsomeness, even; but it was scarred and furrowed by violence, and so coloured and coarsened by fiercer passions that grief seemed never to have laid a gentle finger there. The long nose was distended and knobbed at the end, and there were deep lines on either side of it; her heavy, black brows almost met across her forehead, her teeth were large and square, and set far apart—teeth that could tear. She filled the room; the men were obliterated, seemed tossed about like twigs in an angry water, and even Steavens felt himself being drawn into the whirlpool.

The daughter—the tall, raw-boned woman in crêpe, with a mourning comb in her hair which curiously lengthened her long face—sat stiffly upon the sofa, her hands, conspicuous for their large knuckles, folded in her lap, her mouth and eyes drawn down, solemnly awaiting the opening of the coffin. Near the door stood a mulatto woman, evidently a servant in the house, with a timid bearing and an emaciated face pitifully sad and gentle. She was weeping silently, the corner of her calico apron lifted to her eyes, occasionally suppressing a long, quivering sob. Steavens walked over and stood beside her.

Feeble steps were heard on the stairs, and an old man, tall and frail, odorous of pipe smoke, with shaggy, unkept grey hair and a dingy beard, tobacco stained about the mouth, entered uncertainly. He went slowly up to the coffin and stood rolling a blue cotton handkerchief between his hands, seeming so pained

---

4. **smilax**\ˆsmai·lăks\ woody vine, usually prickly, with bright-green leaves.

and embarrassed by his wife's orgy of grief that he had no consciousness of anything else.

"There, there, Annie, dear, don't take on so," he quavered timidly, putting out a shaking hand and awkwardly patting her elbow. She turned and sank upon his shoulder with such violence that he tottered a little. He did not even glance toward the coffin, but continued to look at her with a dull, frightened, appealing expression, as a spaniel looks at the whip. His sunken cheeks slowly reddened and burned with miserable shame. When his wife rushed from the room, her daughter strode after her with set lips. The servant stole up to the coffin, bent over it for a moment, and then slipped away to the kitchen, leaving Steavens, the lawyer, and the father to themselves. The old man stood looking down at his dead son's face. The sculptor's splendid head seemed even more noble in its rigid stillness than in life. The dark hair had crept down upon the wide forehead; the face seemed strangely long, but in it there was not that repose we expect to find in the faces of the dead. The brows were so drawn that there were two deep lines above the beaked nose, and the chin was thrust forward defiantly. It was as though the strain of life had been so sharp and bitter that death could not at once relax the tension and smooth the countenance into perfect peace—as though he were still guarding something precious, which might even yet be wrested from him.

The old man's lips were working under his stained beard. He turned to the lawyer with timid deference: "Phelps and the rest are comin' back to set up with Harve, ain't they?" he asked. "Thank 'ee, Jim, thank 'ee." He brushed the hair back gently from his son's forehead. "He was a good boy, Jim; always a good boy. He was ez gentle ez a child and the kindest of 'em all—only we didn't none of us ever onderstand him." The tears trickled slowly down his beard and dropped upon the sculptor's coat.

"Martin, Martin! Oh, Martin! come here," his wife wailed from the top of the stairs. The old man started timorously: "Yes, Annie, I'm com-ing." He turned away, hesitated, stood for a moment in miserable indecision; then reached back and patted the dead man's hair softly, and stumbled from the room.

"Poor old man, I didn't think he had any tears left. Seems as if his eyes would have gone dry long ago. At his age nothing cuts very deep," remarked the lawyer.

Something in his tone made Steavens glance up. While the mother had been in the room, the young man had scarcely seen any one else; but now, from the moment he first glanced into Jim Laird's florid face and blood-shot eyes, he knew that he had found what he had been heartsick at not finding before—the feeling, the understanding, that must exist in some one, even here.

The man was red as his beard, with features swollen and blurred by dissipation, and a hot, blazing blue eye. His face was strained—that of a man who is controlling himself with difficulty—and he kept plucking at his beard with a sort of fierce resentment. Steavens, sitting by the window, watched him turn down the glaring lamp, still its jangling pendants with an angry gesture, and then stand with his hands locked behind him, staring down into the master's face. He could not help wondering what link there had been between the porcelain vessel and so sooty a lump of potter's clay.

From the kitchen an uproar was sounding; when the dining-room door opened, the import of it was clear. The mother was abusing the maid for having forgotten to make the dressing for the chicken salad which had been prepared for the watchers. Steavens had never heard anything in the least like it; it was injured, emotional, dramatic abuse, unique and masterly in its excruciating cruelty, as violent and unrestrained as had been her grief of twenty minutes before. With a shudder of disgust the lawyer went into the dining-room and closed the door into the kitchen.

"Poor Roxy's getting it now," he remarked when he came back. "The Merricks took her out of the poor-house years ago; and if her loyalty would let her, I guess the poor old thing could tell tales that would curdle your blood. She's the mulatto woman who was standing in here a while ago, with her apron to her eyes. The old woman is a fury; there never was anybody like her. She made Harvey's life a hell for him when he lived at home; he was so sick ashamed of it. I never could see how he kept himself sweet."

"He was wonderful," said Steavens slowly, "wonderful; but until tonight I have never known how wonderful."

"That is the eternal wonder of it, anyway; that it can come even from such a dung heap as this," the lawyer cried, with a sweeping gesture which seemed to indicate much more than the four walls within which they stood.

"I think I'll see whether I can get a little air. The room is so close I am beginning to feel rather faint," murmured Steavens, struggling with one of the windows. The sash was stuck, however, and would not yield, so he sat down dejectedly and began pulling at his collar. The lawyer came over, loosened the sash with one blow of his red fist and sent the window up a few inches. Steavens thanked him, but the nausea which had been gradually climbing into his throat for the last half hour left him with but one desire—a desperate feeling that he must get away from this place with what was left of Harvey Merrick. Oh, he comprehended well enough now the quiet bitterness of the smile that he had seen so often on his master's lips!

Once when Merrick returned from a visit home, he brought with him a singularly feeling and suggestive bas-relief[5] of a thin, faded old woman, sitting and sewing something pinned to her knee; while a full-lipped, full-blooded little urchin, his trousers held up by a single gallows, stood beside her, impatiently twitching her gown to call her attention to a butterfly he had caught. Steavens, impressed by the tender and delicate modelling of the thin, tired face, had asked him if it were his mother. He remembered the dull flush that had burned up in the sculptor's face.

The lawyer was sitting in a rocking-chair beside the coffin, his head thrown back and his eyes closed. Steavens looked at him earnestly, puzzled at the line of the chin, and wondering why a man should conceal a feature of such distinction under that disfiguring shock of beard. Suddenly, as though he felt the young sculptor's keen glance, Jim Laird opened his eyes.

"Was he always a good deal of an oyster?" he asked abruptly. "He was terribly shy as a boy."

"Yes, he was an oyster, since you put it so," rejoined Steavens. "Although he could be very fond of people, he always gave one the impression of being detached. He disliked violent emotion; he was reflective, and rather distrustful of himself—except, of course, as regarded his work. He was sure enough there. He distrusted men pretty thoroughly and women even more, yet somehow without believing ill of them. He was determined, indeed, to believe the best; but he seemed afraid to investigate."

"A burnt dog dreads the fire," said the lawyer grimly, and closed his eyes.

Steavens went on and on, reconstructing that whole miserable boyhood. All this raw, biting ugliness had been the portion of the man whose mind was to become an exhaustless gallery of beautiful impressions—so sensitive that the mere shadow of a poplar leaf flickering against a sunny wall would be etched and held there for ever. Surely, if ever a man had the magic word in his finger tips, it was Merrick. Whatever he touched, he revealed its holiest secret; liberated it from enchantment and restored it to its pristine loveliness. Upon whatever he had come in contact with, he had left a beautiful record of the experience—a sort of ethereal signature; a scent, a sound, a colour that was his own.

Steavens understood now the real tragedy of his master's life; neither love nor wine, as many had conjectured; but a blow which had fallen earlier and cut deeper than anything else could have done—a shame not his, and yet so un-

---

5. **bas-relief**\\⁁ba·rĭ⁁lēf, ⁁băs-\\ piece of sculpture in which the figure stands out only slightly from the background.

escapably his, to hide in his heart from his very boyhood. And without—the frontier warfare; the yearning of a boy, cast ashore upon a desert of newness and ugliness and sordidness, for all that is chastened and old, and noble with traditions.

At eleven o'clock the tall, flat woman in black announced that the watchers were arriving, and asked them to "step into the dining-room." As Steavens rose, the lawyer said dryly: "You go on—it'll be a good experience for you. I'm not equal to that crowd tonight; I've had twenty years of them."

As Steavens closed the door after him he glanced back at the lawyer, sitting by the coffin in the dim light, with his chin resting on his hand.

The same misty group that had stood before the door of the express car shuffled into the dining-room. In the light of the kerosene lamp they separated and became individuals. The minister, a pale, feeble-looking man with white hair and blond chin-whiskers, took his seat beside a small side table and placed his Bible upon it. The Grand Army man sat down behind the stove and tilted his chair back comfortably against the wall, fishing his quill toothpick from his waistcoat pocket. The two bankers, Phelps and Elder, sat off in a corner behind the dinner-table, where they could finish their discussion of the new usury law and its effect on chattel security loans. The real estate agent, an old man with a smiling, hypocritical face, soon joined them. The coal and lumber dealer and the cattle shipper sat on opposite sides of the hard coal-burner, their feet on the nickel-work. Steavens took a book from his pocket and began to read. The talk around him ranged through various topics of local interest while the house was quieting down. When it was clear that the members of the family were in bed, the Grand Army man hitched his shoulders and, untangling his long legs, caught his heels on the rounds of his chair.

"S'pose there'll be a will, Phelps?" he queried in his weak falsetto.

The banker laughed disagreeably, and began trimming his nails with a pearl-handled pocket-knife.

"There'll scarcely be any need for one, will there?" he queried in his turn.

The restless Grand Army man shifted his position again, getting his knees still nearer his chin. "Why, the old man says Harve's done right well lately," he chirped.

The other banker spoke up. "I reckon he means by that Harve ain't asked him to mortgage any more farms lately, so as he could go on with his education."

"Seems like my mind don't reach back to a time when Harve wasn't bein' edycated," tittered the Grand Army man.

There was a general chuckle. The minister took out his handkerchief and blew his nose sonorously. Banker Phelps closed his knife with a snap. "It's too bad the old man's sons didn't turn out better," he remarked with reflective authority. "They never hung together. He spent money enough on Harve to stock a dozen cattle-farms, and he might as well have poured it into Sand Creek. If Harve had stayed at home and helped nurse what little they had, and gone into stock on the old man's bottom farm, they might all have been well fixed. But the old man had to trust everything to tenants and was cheated right and left."

"Harve never could have handled stock none," interposed the cattleman. "He hadn't it in him to be sharp. Do you remember when he bought Sander's mules for eight-year olds, when everybody in town knew that Sander's father-in-law give 'em to his wife for a wedding present eighteen years before, an' they was full-grown mules then?"

The company laughed discreetly, and the Grand Army man rubbed his knees with a spasm of childish delight.

"Harve never was much account for anything practical, and he shore was never fond of work," began the coal and lumber dealer. "I mind the last time he was home; the day he left, when the old man was out to the barn helpin' his hand hitch up to take Harve to the train, and Cal Moots was patchin' up the fence; Harve, he come out on the step and sings out, in his lady-like voice: 'Cal Moots, Cal Moots! please come cord my trunk.'"

"That's Harve for you," approved the Grand Army man. "I kin hear him howlin' yet, when he was a big feller in long pants and his mother used to whale him with a rawhide in the barn for lettin' the cows git foundered in the cornfield when he was drivin' 'em home from pasture. He killed a cow of mine that-a-way onct— a pure Jersey and the best milker I had, an' the ole man had to put up for her. Harve, he was watchin' the sun set acrost the marshes when the anamile got away."

"Where the old man made his mistake was in sending the boy East to school," said Phelps, stroking his goatee and speaking in a deliberate, judicial tone. "There was where he got his head full of nonsense. What Harve needed, of all people, was a course in some first-class Kansas City business college."

The letters were swimming before Steaven's eyes. Was it possible that these men did not understand, that the palm on the coffin meant nothing to them? The very name of their town would have remained for ever buried in the postal guide had it not been now and again mentioned in the world in connection with Harvey Merrick's. He remembered what his master had said to him on the day of his death, after the congestion of both lungs had shut off any probability of recovery, and the sculptor had asked his pupil to send his body home. "It's not a pleasant place to be lying while the world is moving and doing and bettering," he had said with a feeble smile, "but it rather seems as though we ought to go back to the place we came from, in the end. The townspeople will come in for a look at me; and after they have had their say, I shan't have much to fear from the judgment of God!"

The cattleman took up the comment. "Forty's young for a Merrick to cash in; they usually hang on pretty well. Probably he helped it along with whisky."

"His mother's people were not long lived, and Harvey never had a robust constitution," said the minister mildly. He would have liked to say more. He had been the boy's Sunday-school teacher, and had been fond of him; but he felt that he was not in a position to speak. His own sons had turned out badly, and it was not a year since one of them had made his last trip home in the express car, shot in a gambling-house in the Black Hills.

"Nevertheless, there is no disputin' that Harve frequently looked upon the wine when it was red, also variegated, and it shore made an oncommon fool of him," moralized the cattleman.

Just then the door leading into the parlour rattled loudly and every one started involuntarily, looking relieved when only Jim Laird came out. The Grand Army man ducked his head when he saw the spark in his blue, bloodshot eye. They were all afraid of Jim; he was a drunkard, but he could twist the law to suit his client's needs as no other man in all western Kansas could do, and there were many who tried. The lawyer closed the door behind him, leaned back against it and folded his arms, cocking his head a little to one side. When he assumed this attitude in the court-room, ears were always pricked up, as it usually foretold a flood of withering sarcasm.

"I've been with you gentlemen before," he began in a dry, even tone, "when you've sat by the coffins of boys born and raised in this town; and, if I remember rightly, you were never any too well satisfied when you checked them up. What's the matter, anyhow? Why is it that reputable young men are as scarce as millionaires in Sand City? It might almost seem to a stranger that there was some way something the matter with your progressive town. Why did Ruben Sayer, the brightest young lawyer you ever turned out, after he had come home from the university as straight as a die, take to drinking and forge a check and shoot himself? Why did Bill Merrit's son die of the shakes in a saloon in Omaha? Why was Mr. Thomas's son, here, shot in a gambling-house? Why did young Adams burn his mill to beat the insurance companies and go to the pen?"

The lawyer paused and unfolded his arms, laying one clenched fist quietly on the table. "I'll tell you why. Because you drummed nothing but money and knavery into their ears from the time they wore knickerbockers; because you carped away at them as you've been carping here tonight, holding our friends Phelps and Elder up to them for their models, as our grandfathers held up George Washington and John Adams. But the boys were young, and raw at the business you put them to, and how could they match coppers with such artists as Phelps and Elder? You wanted them to be successful rascals; they were only unsuccessful ones—that's all the difference. There was only one boy ever raised in this borderland between ruffianism and civilization who didn't come to grief, and you hated Harvey Merrick more for winning out than you hated all the other boys who got under the wheels. Lord, Lord, how you did hate him! Phelps, here, is fond of saying that he could buy and sell us all out any time he's a mind to; but he knew Harve wouldn't have given a tinker's damn for his bank and all his cattle-farms put together; and a lack of appreciation, that way, goes hard with Phelps.

"Old Nimrod thinks Harve drank too much; and this from such as Nimrod and me!

"Brother Elder says Harve was too free with the old man's money—fell short in filial consideration, maybe. Well, we can all remember the very tone in which brother Elder swore his own father was a liar, in the county court; and we all know that the old man came out of that partnership with his son as bare as a sheared lamb. But maybe I'm getting personal, and I'd better be driving ahead at what I want to say."

The lawyer paused a moment, squared his heavy shoulders, and went on: "Harvey Merrick and I went to school together, back East. We were dead in earnest, and we wanted you all to be proud of us some day. We meant to be great men. Even I, and I haven't lost my sense of humour, gentlemen, I meant to be a great man. I came back here to practise, and I found

you didn't in the least want me to be a great man. You wanted me to be a shrewd lawyer— oh, yes! Our veteran here wanted me to get him an increase of pension, because he had dyspepsia;[6] Phelps wanted a new county survey that would put the widow Wilson's little bottom farm inside his south line; Elder wanted to lend money at 5 per cent a month, and get it collected; and Stark here wanted to wheedle old women up in Vermont into investing their annuities in real-estate mortgages that are not worth the paper they are written on. Oh, you needed me hard enough, and you'll go on needing me!

"Well, I came back here and became the damned shyster you wanted me to be. You pretend to have some sort of respect for me; and yet you'll stand up and throw mud at Harvey Merrick, whose soul you couldn't dirty and whose hands you couldn't tie. Oh, you're a discriminating lot of Christians! There have been times when the sight of Harvey's name in some Eastern paper has made me hang my head like a whipped dog; and, again, times when I liked to think of him off there in the world, away from all this hog-wallow, climbing the big, clean up-grade he'd set for himself.

"And we? Now that we've fought and lied and sweated and stolen, and hated as only the disappointed strugglers in a bitter, dead little Western town know how to do, what have we got to show for it? Harvey Merrick wouldn't have given one sunset over your marshes for all you've got put together, and you know it. It's not for me to say why, in the inscrutable wisdom of God, a genius should ever have been called from this place of hatred and bitter waters; but I want this Boston man to know that the drivel he's been hearing here tonight is the only tribute any truly great man could have from such a lot of sick, side-tracked, burnt-dog, land-poor sharks as the here-present financiers of Sand City—upon which town may God have mercy!"

---

6. **dyspepsia**\dĭs ˈpĕp·shə\ indigestion.

The lawyer thrust out his hand to Steavens as he passed him, caught up his overcoat in the hall, and had left the house before the Grand Army man had had time to lift his ducked head and crane his long neck about at his fellows.

Next day Jim Laird was drunk and unable to attend the funeral services. Steavens called twice at his office, but was compelled to start East without seeing him. He had a presentiment that he would hear from him again, and left his address on the lawyer's table; but if Laird found it, he never acknowledged it. The thing in him that Harvey Merrick had loved must have gone under ground with Harvey Merrick's coffin; for it never spoke again, and Jim got the cold he died of driving across the Colorado mountains to defend one of Phelps's sons who had got into trouble out there by cutting government timber.

I
FRONTIER WARFARE

In the popular imagination, warfare in a Western town means two tall Texans squared off in a dusty street in front of the local saloon. In this story, however, Miss Cather portrays a conflict, perhaps less violent, but far more serious in its implications for society. In this borderland "between ruffianism and civilization" where the rawness and bitterness of primitive struggle for physical survival sometimes fosters soul-crushing materialism, how, she asks, can the sensitive, refined, civilizing spirit find root, grow, and flourish. It is the latter, the creative mind filled with "an exhaustive gallery of beautiful impressions," that lifts life above the savage. Yet the conflict between the civilizing and the savage spirits is a warfare never wholly resolved; each age—indeed, each individual—must make the choice anew.

II
IMPLICATIONS

A. What does each of the following quotations reveal about the speaker, the person spoken about, or both?

1. Mrs. Merrick: "My boy, my boy! And this is how you've come home to me!"

2. Mr. Merrick: "He was a good boy, Jim; always a good boy. He was ez gentle ez a child and the kindest of 'em all—only we didn't none of us ever onderstand him."

3. Steavens: "He was wonderful . . . ; but until tonight I have never known how wonderful."

4. Banker Phelps: "It's too bad the old man's sons didn't turn out better. . . . He spent money enough on Harve to stock a dozen cattle-farms, and he might as well have poured it into Sand Creek."

5. The coal and lumber dealer: "Harve never was much account for anything practical, and he shore was never fond of work."

6. Jim Laird: "Harvey Merrick wouldn't have given one sunset over your marshes for all you've got put together, and you know it."

B. On the basis of this story and your own experience, discuss the following propositions:

1. Beauty and art have no place in the business world.

2. A great man is great precisely because he overcomes great obstacles.

3. People usually find fault with those ideas and individuals they don't understand.

4. A prophet is never honored in his own town.

III
TECHNIQUES

Setting

The mood of this story is somber. Much of this feeling is created by the setting. What specific details in the opening paragraph generate this feeling? How would the mood have been different if the story had opened at noon on a bright day early in May?

Characterization

Miss Cather contrasts one set of characters with another in order to highlight the central conflict of the story. Which set of characters represents the values of Sand City; and which the values of Harvey Merrick? Are there any characters which fall into both groups?

In 1932, Willa Cather collected
three more stories based on her years
in Red Cloud and published them in a volume
called *Obscure Destinies*. "Neighbour Rosicky"
is drawn from the Cather family, but the hero
is a blending of Miss Cather's father
with the husband of a childhood friend.
This simply-told story was written early
in 1928, during the months in which Charles
Cather was dying from angina.
Having recently returned from a visit
with her father, Miss Cather was filled
with memories of the family home
in Red Cloud and the hidden strength
in these people who lived close to the land.
She finished the story a few months
after her father's death.

Neighbour Rosicky

I

When Doctor Burleigh told neighbour Rosicky he had a bad heart, Rosicky protested.

"So? No, I guess my heart was always pretty good. I got a little asthma, maybe. Just a awful short breath when I was pitchin' hay last summer, dat's all."

"Well now, Rosicky, if you know more about it than I do, what did you come to me for? It's your heart that makes you short of breath, I tell you. You're sixty-five years old, and you've always worked hard, and your heart's tired. You've got to be careful from now on, and you can't do heavy work any more. You've got five boys at home to do it for you."

The old farmer looked up at the Doctor with

a gleam of amusement in his queer triangular-shaped eyes. His eyes were large and lively, but the lids were caught up in the middle in a curious way, so that they formed a triangle. He did not look like a sick man. His brown face was creased but not wrinkled, he had a ruddy colour in his smooth-shaven cheeks and in his lips, under his long brown moustache. His hair was thin and ragged around his ears, but very little grey. His forehead, naturally high and crossed by deep parallel lines, now ran all the way up to his pointed crown. Rosicky's face had the habit of looking interested,—suggested a contented disposition and a reflective quality that was gay rather than grave. This gave him a certain detachment, the easy manner of an onlooker and observer.

"Well, I guess you ain't got no pills fur a bad heart, Doctor Ed. I guess the only thing is fur me to git me a new one."

Doctor Burleigh swung round in his desk-chair and frowned at the old farmer. "I think if I were you I'd take a little care of the old one, Rosicky."

Rosicky shrugged. "Maybe I don't know how. I expect you mean fur me not to drink my coffee no more."

"I wouldn't, in your place. But you'll do as you choose about that. I've never yet been able to separate a Bohemian from his coffee or his pipe. I've quit trying. But the sure thing is you've got to cut out farm work. You can feed the stock and do chores about the barn, but you can't do anything in the fields that makes you short of breath."

"How about shelling corn?"

"Of course not!"

Rosicky considered with puckered brows.

"I can't make my heart go no longer'n it wants to, can I, Doctor Ed?"

"I think it's good for five or six years yet, maybe more, if you'll take the strain off it. Sit around the house and help Mary. If I had a good wife like yours, I'd want to stay around the house."

His patient chuckled. "It ain't no place fur a man. I don't like no old man hanging round the kitchen too much. An' my wife, she's a awful hard worker her own self."

"That's it; you can help her a little. My Lord, Rosicky, you are one of the few men I know who has a family he can get some comfort out of; happy dispositions, never quarrel among themselves, and they treat you right. I want to see you live a few years and enjoy them."

"Oh, they're good kids, all right," Rosicky assented.

The Doctor wrote him a prescription and asked him how his oldest son, Rudolph, who had married in the spring, was getting on. Rudolph had struck out for himself, on rented land. "And how's Polly? I was afraid Mary mightn't like an American daughter-in-law, but it seems to be working out all right."

"Yes, she's a fine girl. Dat widder woman bring her daughters up very nice. Polly got lots of spunk, an' she got some style, too. Da's nice, for young folks to have some style." Rosicky inclined his head gallantly. His voice and his twinkly smile were an affectionate compliment to his daughter-in-law.

"It looks like a storm, and you'd better be getting home before it comes. In town in the car?" Doctor Burleigh rose.

"No, I'm in de wagon. When you got five boys, you ain't got much chance to ride round in de Ford. I ain't much for cars, noway."

"Well, it's a good road out to your place; but I don't want you bumping around in a wagon much. And never again on a hay-rake, remember!"

Rosicky placed the Doctor's fee delicately behind the desk-telephone, looking the other way, as if this were an absent-minded gesture. He put on his plush cap and his corduroy jacket with a sheepskin collar, and went out.

The Doctor picked up his stethoscope and frowned at it as if he were seriously annoyed with the instrument. He wished it had been telling tales about some other man's heart, some old man who didn't look the Doctor in the eye so knowingly, or hold out such a warm brown hand when he said good-bye. Doctor Burleigh had been a poor boy in the country before he

went away to medical school; he had known Rosicky almost ever since he could remember, and he had a deep affection for Mrs. Rosicky.

Only last winter he had had such a good breakfast at Rosicky's, and that when he needed it. He had been out all night on a long, hard confinement case at Tom Marshall's,—a big rich farm where there was plenty of stock and plenty of feed and a great deal of expensive farm machinery of the newest model, and no comfort whatever. The woman had too many children and too much work, and she was no manager. When the baby was born at last, and handed over to the assisting neighbour woman, and the mother was properly attended to, Burleigh refused any breakfast in that slovenly house, and drove his buggy—the snow was too deep for a car—eight miles to Anton Rosicky's place. He didn't know another farm-house where a man could get such a warm welcome, and such good strong coffee with rich cream. No wonder the old chap didn't want to give up his coffee!

He had driven in just when the boys had come back from the barn and were washing up for breakfast. The long table, covered with a bright oilcloth, was set out with dishes waiting for them, and the warm kitchen was full of the smell of coffee and hot biscuit and sausage. Five big handsome boys, running from twenty to twelve, all with what Burleigh called natural good manners,—they hadn't a bit of the painful self-consciousness he himself had to struggle with when he was a lad. One ran to put his horse away, another helped him off with his fur coat and hung it up, and Josephine, the youngest child and the only daughter, quickly set another place under her mother's direction.

With Mary, to feed creatures was the natural expression of affection,—her chickens, the calves, her big hungry boys. It was a rare pleasure to feed a young man whom she seldom saw and of whom she was as proud as if he belonged to her. Some country housekeepers would have stopped to spread a white cloth over the oil-cloth, to change the thick cups and plates for their best china, and the wooden-handled knives for plated ones. But not Mary.

"You must take us as you find us, Doctor Ed. I'd be glad to put out my good things for you if you was expected, but I'm glad to get you any way at all."

He knew she was glad,—she threw back her head and spoke out as if she were announcing him to the whole prairie. Rosicky hadn't said anything at all; he merely smiled his twinkling smile, put some more coal on the fire, and went into his own room to pour the Doctor a little drink in a medicine glass. When they were all seated, he watched his wife's face from his end of the table and spoke to her in Czech. Then, with the instinct of politeness which seldom failed him, he turned to the Doctor and said slyly: "I was just tellin' her not to ask you no questions about Mrs. Marshall till you eat some breakfast. My wife, she's terrible fur to ask questions."

The boys laughed, and so did Mary. She watched the Doctor devour her biscuit and sausage, too much excited to eat anything herself. She drank her coffee and sat taking in everything about her visitor. She had known him when he was a poor country boy, and was boastfully proud of his success, always saying: "What do people go to Omaha for, to see a doctor, when we got the best one in the State right here?" If Mary liked people at all, she felt physical pleasure in the sight of them, personal exultation in any good fortune that came to them. Burleigh didn't know many women like that, but he knew she was like that.

When his hunger was satisfied, he did, of course, have to tell them about Mrs. Marshall, and he noticed what a friendly interest the boys took in the matter.

Rudolph, the oldest one (he was still living at home then), said: "The last time I was over there, she was lifting them big heavy milkcans, and I knew she oughtn't to be doing it."

"Yes, Rudolph told me about that when he come home, and I said it wasn't right," Mary put in warmly. "It was all right for me to do them things up to the last, for I was terrible strong, but that woman's weakly. And do you think she'll be able to nurse it, Ed?" She sometimes forgot to give him the title she was so proud of. "And to think of your being up all night and then not able to get a decent breakfast! I don't know what's the matter with such people."

"Why, Mother," said one of the boys, "if Doctor Ed had got breakfast there, we wouldn't have him here. So you ought to be glad."

"He knows I'm glad to have him, John, any time. But I'm sorry for that poor woman, how bad she'll feel the Doctor had to go away in the cold without his breakfast."

"I wish I'd been in practice when these were getting born." The doctor looked down the row of close-clipped heads. "I missed some good breakfasts by not being."

The boys began to laugh at their mother because she flushed so red, but she stood her ground and threw up her head. "I don't care, you wouldn't have got away from this house without breakfast. No doctor ever did. I'd have had something ready fixed that Anton could warm up for you."

The boys laughed harder than ever, and exclaimed at her: "I'll bet you would!" "She would, that!"

"Father, did you get breakfast for the doctor when we were born?"

"Yes, and he used to bring me my breakfast, too, mighty nice. I was always awful hungry!" Mary admitted with a guilty laugh.

While the boys were getting the Doctor's horse, he went to the window to examine the house plants. "What do you do to your geraniums to keep them blooming all winter, Mary? I never pass this house that from the road I don't see your windows full of flowers."

She snapped off a dark red one, and a ruffled new green leaf, and put them in his buttonhole. "There, that looks better. You look too solemn for a young man, Ed. Why don't you git married? I'm worried about you. Settin' at breakfast, I looked at you real hard, and I seen you've got some grey hairs already."

"Oh, yes! They're coming. Maybe they'd come faster if I married."

"Don't talk so. You'll ruin your health eating at the hotel. I could send your wife a nice loaf of nut bread, if you only had one. I don't like to see a young man getting grey. I'll tell you something, Ed; you make some strong black tea and keep it handy in a bowl, and every morning just brush it into your hair, an' it'll keep the grey from showin' much. That's the way I do!"

Sometimes the Doctor heard the gossipers in the drug-store wondering why Rosicky didn't get on faster. He was industrious, and so were his boys, but they were rather free and easy, weren't pushers, and they didn't always show good judgment. They were comfortable, they were out of debt, but they didn't get much ahead. Maybe, Doctor Burleigh reflected, people as generous and warm-hearted and affectionate as the Rosickys never got ahead much; maybe you couldn't enjoy your life and put it into the bank, too.

II

When Rosicky left Doctor Burleigh's office he went into the farm-implement store to light his pipe and put on his glasses and read over the list Mary had given him. Then he went into the general merchandise place next door and stood about until the pretty girl with the plucked eyebrows, who always waited on him, was free. Those eyebrows, two thin India-ink strokes, amused him, because he remembered how they used to be. Rosicky always prolonged his shopping by a little joking; the girl knew the old fellow admired her, and she liked to chaff with him.

"Seems to me about every other week you buy ticking, Mr. Rosicky, and always the best quality," she remarked as she measured off the heavy bolt with red stripes.

"You see, my wife is always makin' goose-fedder pillows, an' de thin stuff don't hold in dem little down-fedders."

"You must have lots of pillows at your house."

"Sure. She makes quilts of dem, too. We sleeps easy. Now she's makin' a fedder quilt for my son's wife. You know Polly, that married my Rudolph. How much my bill, Miss Pearl?"

"Eight eighty-five."

"Chust make it nine, and put in some candy fur de women."

"As usual. I never did see a man buy so much candy for his wife. First thing you know, she'll be getting too fat."

"I'd like dat. I ain't much fur all dem slim women like what de style is now."

"That's one for me, I suppose, Mr. Bohunk!" Pearl sniffed and elevated her India-ink strokes.

When Rosicky went out to his wagon, it was beginning to snow,—the first snow of the season, and he was glad to see it. He rattled out of town and along the highway through a wonderfully rich stretch of country, the finest farms in the county. He admired this High Prairie, as it was called, and always liked to drive through it. His own place lay in a rougher territory, where there was some clay in the soil and it was not so productive. When he bought his land, he hadn't the money to buy on High Prairie; so he told his boys, when they grumbled, that if their land hadn't some clay in it, they wouldn't own it at all. All the same, he enjoyed looking at these fine farms, as he enjoyed looking at a prize bull.

After he had gone eight miles, he came to the graveyard, which lay just at the edge of his own hay-land. There he stopped his horses and sat still on his wagon seat, looking about at the snowfall. Over yonder on the hill he could see his own house, crouching low, with the clump of orchard behind and the windmill before, and all down the gentle hill-slope the rows of pale gold cornstalks stood out against the white field. The snow was falling over the cornfield and the pasture and the hay-land, steadily, with very little wind,—a nice dry snow. The grave-yard had only a light wire fence about it and was all overgrown with long red grass. The fine snow, settling into this red grass and upon the few little evergreens and the headstones, looked very pretty.

It was a nice graveyard, Rosicky reflected, sort of snug and homelike, not cramped or mournful,—a big sweep all round it. A man could lie down in the long grass and see the complete arch of the sky over him, hear the wagons go by; in summer the mowing-machine rattled right up to the wire fence. And it was so near home. Over there across the cornstalks his own roof and windmill looked so good to him that he promised himself to mind the Doctor and take care of himself. He was awful fond of his place, he admitted. He wasn't anxious to leave it. And it was a comfort to think that he would never have to go farther than the edge of his own hayfield. The snow, falling over his barnyard and the graveyard, seemed to draw things together like. And they were all old neighbours in the graveyard, most of them friends; there was nothing to feel awkward or embarrassed about. Embarrassment was the most disagreeable feeling Rosicky knew. He didn't often have it,—only with certain people whom he didn't understand at all.

Well, it was a nice snowstorm; a fine sight to see the snow falling so quietly and graciously over so much open country. On his cap and shoulders, on the horses' back and manes, light, delicate, mysterious it fell; and with it a dry cool fragrance was released into the air. It meant rest for vegetation and men and beasts, for the ground itself; a season of long nights for sleep, leisurely breakfasts, peace by the fire. This and much more went through Rosicky's mind, but he merely told himself that winter was coming, clucked to his horses, and drove on.

When he reached home, John, the youngest boy, ran out to put away his team for him, and he met Mary coming up from the outside cellar with her apron full of carrots. They went into the house together. On the table, covered with oilcloth figured with clusters of blue grapes, a place was set, and he smelled hot coffee-cake of some kind. Anton never lunched in town; he thought that extravagant, and anyhow he didn't like the food. So Mary always had something ready for him when he got home.

After he was settled in his chair, stirring his coffee in a big cup, Mary took out of the oven a pan of *kolache*[1] stuffed with apricots, examined them anxiously to see whether they had got too dry, put them beside his plate, and then sat down opposite him.

Rosicky asked her in Czech if she wasn't going to have any coffee.

She replied in English, as being somehow the right language for transacting business: "Now what did Doctor Ed say, Anton? You tell me just what."

"He said I was to tell you some compliments, but I forgot 'em." Rosicky's eyes twinkled.

"About you, I mean. What did he say about your asthma?"

"He says I an't got no asthma." Rosicky took one of the little rolls in his broad brown fingers. The thickened nail of his right thumb told the story of his past.

"Well, what is the matter? And don't try to put me off."

"He don't say nothing much, only I'm a little older, and my heart ain't so good like it used to be."

Mary started and brushed her hair back from her temples with both hands as if she were a little out of her mind. From the way she glared, she might have been in a rage with him.

"He says there's something the matter with your heart? Doctor Ed says so?"

"Now don't yell at me like I was a hog in de garden, Mary. You know I always did like to hear a woman talk soft. He didn't say anything de matter wid my heart, only it ain't so young like it used to be, an' he tell me not to pitch hay or run de corn-sheller."

Mary wanted to jump up, but she sat still. She admired the way he never under any circumstances raised his voice or spoke roughly. He was city-bred, and she was country-bred; she often said she wanted her boys to have their papa's nice ways.

---

1. kolache\\ᵃkō 'lach\ a sweet bun filled with jam or fruit pulp.

"You never have no pain there, do you? It's your breathing and your stomach that's been wrong. I wouldn't believe nobody but Doctor Ed about it. I guess I'll go see him myself. Didn't he give you no advice?"

"Chust to take it easy like, an' stay round de house dis winter. I guess you got some carpenter work for me to do. I kin make some new shelves for you, and I want dis long time to build a closet in de boys' room and make dem two little fellers keep dere clo'es hung up."

Rosicky drank his coffee from time to time, while he considered. His moustache was of the soft long variety and came down over his mouth like the teeth of a buggy-rake over a bundle of hay. Each time he put down his cup, he ran his blue handkerchief over his lips. When he took a drink of water, he managed very neatly with the back of his hand.

Mary sat watching him intently, trying to find any change in his face. It is hard to see anyone who has become like your own body to you. Yes, his hair had got thin, and his high forehead had deep lines running from left to right. But his neck, always clean shaved except in the busiest seasons, was not loose or baggy. It was burned a dark reddish brown, and there were deep creases in it, but it looked firm and full of blood. His cheeks had a good colour. On either side of his mouth there was a half-moon down the length of his cheek, not wrinkles, but two lines that had come there from his habitual expression. He was shorter and broader than when she married him; his back had grown broad and curved, a good deal like the shell of an old turtle, and his arms and legs were short.

He was fifteen years older than Mary, but she had hardly ever thought about it before. He was her man, and the kind of man she liked. She was rough, and he was gentle,—city-bred, as she always said. They had been shipmates on a rough voyage and had stood by each other in trying times. Life had gone well with them because, at bottom, they had the same ideas about life. They agreed, without discussion, as to what was most important and what was secondary. They didn't often exchange opinions,

even in Czech,—it was as if they had thought the same thought together. A good deal had to be sacrificed and thrown overboard in a hard life like theirs, and they had never disagreed as to the things that could go. It had been a hard life, and a soft life, too. There wasn't anything brutal in the short, broad-backed man with the three-cornered eyes and the forehead that went on to the top of his skull. He was a city man, a gentle man, and though he had married a rough farm girl, he had never touched her without gentleness.

They had been at one accord not to hurry through life, not to be always skimping and saving. They saw their neighbours buy more land and feed more stock than they did, without discontent. Once when the creamery agent came to the Rosickys to persuade them to sell him their cream, he told them how much money the Fasslers, their nearest neighbours, had made on their cream last year.

"Yes," said Mary, "and look at them Fassler children! Pale, pinched little things, they look like skimmed milk. I'd rather put some colour into my children's faces than put money into the bank."

The agent shrugged and turned to Anton.

"I guess we'll do like she says," said Rosicky.

III

Mary very soon got into town to see Doctor Ed, and then she had a talk with her boys and set a guard over Rosicky. Even John, the youngest, had his father on his mind. If Rosicky went to throw hay down from the loft, one of the boys ran up the ladder and took the fork from him. He sometimes complained that though he was getting to be an old man, he wasn't an old woman yet.

That winter he stayed in the house in the afternoons and carpentered, or sat in the chair between the window full of plants and the wooden bench where the two pails of drinking-water stood. This spot was called "Father's corner," though it was not a corner at all. He had a shelf there, where he kept his Bohemian papers and his pipes and tobacco, and his shears and needles and thread and tailor's thimble. Having been a tailor in his youth, he couldn't bear to see a woman patching at his clothes, or at the boys'. He liked tailoring, and always patched all the overalls and jackets and work shirts. Occasionally he made over a pair of pants one of the older boys had outgrown, for the little fellow.

While he sewed, he let his mind run back over his life. He had a good deal to remember, really; life in three countries. The only part of his youth he didn't like to remember was the two years he had spent in London, in Cheapside, working for a German tailor who was wretchedly poor. Those days, when he was nearly always hungry, when his clothes were dropping off him for dirt, and the sound of a strange language kept him in continual bewilderment, had left a sore spot in his mind that wouldn't bear touching.

He was twenty when he landed at Castle Garden in New York, and he had a protector who got him work in a tailor shop in Vesey Street, down near the Washington Market. He looked upon that part of his life as very happy. He became a good workman, he was industrious, and his wages were increased from time to time. He minded his own business and envied nobody's good fortune. He went to night school and learned to read English. He often did overtime work and was well paid for it, but somehow he never saved anything. He couldn't refuse a loan to a friend, and he was self-indulgent. He liked a good dinner, and a little went for beer, a little for tobacco; a good deal went to the girls. He often stood through an opera on Saturday nights; he could get standing-room for a dollar. Those were the great days of opera in New York, and it gave a fellow something to think about for the rest of the week. Rosicky had a quick ear, and a childish love of all the stage splendour; the scenery, the costumes, the ballet. He usually went with a chum, and after the performance they had beer and maybe some oysters somewhere. It was a fine life; for the first five years or so it satisfied him

completely. He was never hungry or cold or dirty, and everything amused him: a fire, a dog fight, a parade, a storm, a ferry ride. He thought New York the finest, richest, friendliest city in the world.

Moreover, he had what he called a happy home life. Very near the tailor shop was a small furniture-factory, where an old Austrian, Loeffler, employed a few skilled men and made unusual furniture, most of it to order, for the rich German housewives up-town. The top floor of Loeffler's five-storey factory was a loft, where he kept his choice lumber and stored the odd pieces of furniture left on his hands. One of the young workmen he employed was a Czech, and he and Rosicky became fast friends. They persuaded Loeffler to let them have a sleeping-room in one corner of the loft. They bought good beds and bedding and had their pick of the furniture kept up there. The loft was low-pitched, but light and airy, full of windows, and good-smelling by reason of the fine lumber put up there to season. Old Loeffler used to go down to the docks and buy wood from South America and the East from the sea captains. The young men were as foolish about their house as a bridal pair. Zichec, the young cabinet-maker, devised every sort of convenience, and Rosicky kept their clothes in order. At night and on Sundays, when the quiver of machinery underneath was still, it was the quietest place in the world, and on summer nights all the sea winds blew in. Zichec often practised on his flute in the evening. They were both fond of music and went to the opera together. Rosicky thought he wanted to live like that for ever.

But as the years passed, all alike, he began to get a little restless. When spring came round, he would begin to feel fretted, and he got to drinking. He was likely to drink too much of a Saturday night. On Sunday he was languid and heavy, getting over his spree. On Monday he plunged into work again. So he never had time to figure out what ailed him, though he knew something did. When the grass turned green in Park Place, and the lilac hedge at the back of Trinity churchyard put out its blossoms, he was tormented by a longing to run away. That was why he drank too much; to get a temporary illusion of freedom and wide horizons.

Rosicky, the old Rosicky, could remember as if it were yesterday the day when the young Rosicky found out what was the matter with him. It was on a Fourth of July afternoon, and he was sitting in Park Place in the sun. The lower part of New York was empty. Wall Street, Liberty Street, Broadway, all empty. So much stone and asphalt with nothing going on, so many empty windows. The emptiness was intense, like the stillness in a great factory when the machinery stops and the belts and bands cease running. It was too great a change, it took all the strength out of one. Those blank buildings, without the stream of life pouring through them, were like empty jails. It struck young Rosicky that this was the trouble with big cities; they built you in from the earth itself, cemented you away from any contact with the ground. You lived in an unnatural world, like the fish in an aquarium, who were probably much more comfortable than they ever were in the sea.

On that very day he began to think seriously about the articles he had read in the Bohemian papers, describing prosperous Czech farming communities in the West. He believed he would like to go out there as a farm hand; it was hardly possible that he could ever have land of his own. His people had always been workmen; his father and grandfather had worked in shops. His mother's parents had lived in the country, but they rented their farm and had a hard time to get along. Nobody in his family had ever owned any land,—that belonged to a different station of life altogether. Anton's mother died when he was little, and he was sent into the country to her parents. He stayed with them until he was twelve, and formed those ties with the earth and the farm animals and growing things which are never made at all unless they are made early. After his grandfather died, he went back to live with his father and stepmother, but she was very

hard on him, and his father helped him to get passage to London.

After that Fourth of July day in Park Place, the desire to return to the country never left him. To work on another man's farm would be all he asked; to see the sun rise and set and to plant things and watch them grow. He was a very simple man. He was like a tree that has not many roots, but one tap-root that goes down deep. He subscribed for a Bohemian paper printed in Chicago, then for one printed in Omaha. His mind got farther and farther west. He began to save a little money to buy his liberty. When he was thirty-five, there was a great meeting in New York of Bohemian athletic societies, and Rosicky left the tailor shop and went home with the Omaha delegates to try his fortune in another part of the world.

IV

Perhaps the fact that his own youth was well over before he began to have a family was one reason why Rosicky was so fond of his boys. He had almost a grandfather's indulgence for them. He had never had to worry about any of them—except, just now, a little about Rudolph.

On Saturday night the boys always piled into the Ford, took little Josephine, and went to town to the moving-picture show. One Saturday morning they were talking at the breakfast table about starting early that evening, so that they would have an hour or so to see the Christmas things in the stores before the show began. Rosicky looked down the table.

"I hope you boys ain't disappointed, but I want you to let me have de car tonight. Maybe some of you can go in with de neighbours."

Their faces fell. They worked hard all week, and they were still like children. A new jack-knife or a box of candy pleased the older ones as much as the little fellow.

"If you and Mother are going to town," Frank said, "maybe you could take a couple of us along with you, anyway."

"No, I want to take de car down to Rudolph's, and let him an' Polly go in to de show.

She don't git into town enough, an' I'm afraid she's gettin' lonesome, an' he can't afford no car yet."

That settled it. The boys were a good deal dashed. Their father took another piece of apple-cake and went on: "Maybe next Saturday night de two little fellers can go along wid dem."

"Oh, is Rudolph going to have the car every Saturday night?"

Rosicky did not reply at once; then he began to speak seriously: "Listen, boys; Polly ain't lookin' so good. I don't like to see nobody lookin' sad. It comes hard fur a town girl to be a farmer's wife. I don't want no trouble to start in Rudolph's family. When it starts, it ain't so easy to stop. An American girl don't git used to our ways all at once. I like to tell Polly she and Rudolph can have the car every Saturday night till after New Year's, if it's all right with you boys."

"Sure it's all right, Papa," Mary cut in. "And it's good you thought about that. Town girls is used to more than country girls. I lay awake nights, scared she'll make Rudolph discontented with the farm."

The boys put as good a face on it as they could. They surely looked forward to their Saturday nights in town. That evening Rosicky drove the car the half-mile down to Rudolph's new, bare little house.

Polly was in a short-sleeved gingham dress, clearing away the supper dishes. She was a trim, slim little thing, with blue eyes and shingled yellow hair, and her eyebrows were reduced to a mere brush-stroke, like Miss Pearl's.

"Good evening, Mr. Rosicky. Rudolph's at the barn, I guess." She never called him father, or Mary mother. She was sensitive about having married a foreigner. She never in the world would have done it if Rudolph hadn't been such a handsome, persuasive fellow and such a gallant lover. He had graduated in her class in the high school in town, and their friendship began in the ninth grade.

Rosicky went in, though he wasn't exactly asked. "My boys ain't goin' to town tonight, an'

I brought de car over fur you two to go in to de picture show."

Polly, carrying dishes to the sink, looked over her shoulder at him. "Thank you. But I'm late with my work tonight, and pretty tired. Maybe Rudolph would like to go in with you."

"Oh, I don't go to de shows! I'm too old-fashioned. You won't feel so tired after you ride in de air a ways. It's a nice clear night, an' it ain't cold. You go an' fix yourself up, Polly, an' I'll wash de dishes an' leave everything nice fur you."

Polly blushed and tossed her bob. "I couldn't let you do that, Mr. Rosicky. I wouldn't think of it."

Rosicky said nothing. He found a bib apron on a nail behind the kitchen door. He slipped it over his head and then took Polly by her two elbows and pushed her gently toward the door of her own room. "I washed up de kitchen many times for my wife, when de babies was sick or somethin'. You go an' make yourself look nice. I like you to look prettier'n any of dem town girls when you go in. De young folks must have some fun, an' I'm goin' to look out fur you, Polly."

That kind, reassuring grip on her elbows, the old man's funny bright eyes, made Polly want to drop her head on his shoulder for a second. She restrained herself, but she lingered in his grasp at the door of her room, murmuring tearfully: "You always lived in the city when you were young, didn't you? Don't you ever get lonesome out here?"

As she turned round to him, her hand fell naturally into his, and he stood holding it and smiling into her face with his peculiar, knowing, indulgent smile without a shadow of reproach in it. "Dem big cities is all right fur de rich, but dey is terrible hard fur de poor."

"I don't know. Sometimes I think I'd like to take a chance. You lived in New York, didn't you?"

"An' London. Da's bigger still. I learned my trade dere. Here's Rudolph comin', you better hurry."

"Will you tell me about London some time?"

"Maybe. Only I ain't no talker, Polly. Run an' dress yourself up."

The bedroom door closed behind her, and Rudolph came in from the outside, looking anxious. He had seen the car and was sorry any of his family should come just then. Supper hadn't been a very pleasant occasion. Halting in the doorway, he saw his father in a kitchen apron, carrying dishes to the sink. He flushed crimson and something flashed in his eye. Rosicky held up a warning finger.

"I brought de car over fur you an' Polly to go to de picture show, an' I made her let me finish here so you won't be late. You go put on a clean shirt, quick!"

"But don't the boys want the car, Father?"

"Not tonight dey don't." Rosicky fumbled under his apron and found his pants pocket. He took out a silver dollar and said in a hurried whisper: "You go an' buy dat girl some ice cream an' candy tonight, like you was courtin'. She's awful good friends wid me."

Rudolph was very short of cash, but he took the money as if it hurt him. There had been a crop failure all over the county. He had more than once been sorry he'd married this year.

In a few minutes the young people came out, looking clean and a little stiff. Rosicky hurried them off, and then he took his own time with the dishes. He scoured the pots and pans and put away the milk and swept the kitchen. He put some coal in the stove and shut off the draughts, so the place would be warm for them when they got home late at night. Then he sat down and had a pipe and listened to the clock tick.

Generally speaking, marrying an American girl was certainly a risk. A Czech should marry a Czech. It was lucky that Polly was the daughter of a poor widow woman; Rudolph was proud, and if she had a prosperous family to throw up at him, they could never make it go. Polly was one of four sisters, and they all worked; one was book-keeper in the bank, one taught music, and Polly and her younger sister had been clerks, like Miss Pearl. All four of them were musical, had pretty voices, and sang in the Methodist choir, which the eldest sister directed.

Polly missed the sociability of a store position. She missed the choir, and the company of her sisters. She didn't dislike housework, but she disliked so much of it. Rosicky was a little anxious about this pair. He was afraid Polly would grow so discontented that Rudy would quit the farm and take a factory job in Omaha. He had worked for a winter up there, two years ago, to get money to marry on. He had done very well, and they would always take him back at the stockyards. But to Rosicky that meant the end of everything for his son. To be a landless man was to be a wage-earner, a slave, all your life; to have nothing, to be nothing.

Rosicky thought he would come over and do a little carpentering for Polly after the New Year. He guessed she needed jollying. Rudolph was a serious sort of chap, serious in love and serious about his work.

Rosicky shook out his pipe and walked home across the fields. Ahead of him the lamplight shone from his kitchen windows. Suppose he were still in a tailor shop on Vesey Street, with a bunch of pale, narrow-chested sons working on machines, all coming home tired and sullen to eat supper in a kitchen that was a parlour also; with another crowded, angry family quarrelling just across the dumb-waiter shaft, and squeaking pulleys at the windows where dirty washings hung on dirty lines above a court full of old brooms and mops and ash-cans. . . .

He stopped by the windmill to look up at the frosty winter stars and draw a long breath before he went inside. That kitchen with the shining windows was dear to him; but the sleeping fields and bright stars and the noble darkness were dearer still.

V

On the day before Christmas the weather set in very cold; no snow, but a bitter, biting wind that whistled and sang over the flat land and lashed one's face like fine wires. There was baking going on in the Rosicky kitchen all day, and Rosicky sat inside, making over a coat that Albert had outgrown into an overcoat for John. Mary had a big red geranium in bloom for Christmas, and a row of Jerusalem cherry trees, full of berries. It was the first year she had ever grown these; Doctor Ed brought her the seeds from Omaha when he went to some medical convention. They reminded Rosicky of plants he had seen in England; and all afternoon, as he stitched, he sat thinking about those two years in London, which his mind usually shrank from even after all this while.

He was a lad of eighteen when he dropped down into London, with no money and no connexions except the address of a cousin who was supposed to be working at confectioner's. When he went to the pastry shop, however, he found that the cousin had gone to America. Anton tramped the streets for several days, sleeping in doorways and on the Embankment, until he was in utter despair. He knew no English, and the sound of the strange language all about him confused him. By chance he met a poor German tailor who had learned his trade in Vienna, and could speak a little Czech. This tailor, Lifschnitz, kept a repair shop in a Cheapside basement, underneath a cobbler. He didn't much need an apprentice, but he was sorry for the boy and took him in for no wages but his keep and what he could pick up. The pickings were supposed to be coppers given you when you took work home to a customer. But most of the customers called for their clothes themselves, and the coppers that came Anton's way were very few. He had, however, a place to sleep. The tailor's family lived upstairs in three rooms; a kitchen, a bedroom, where Lifschnitz and his wife and five children slept, and a living-room. Two corners of this living-room were curtained off for lodgers; in one Rosicky slept on an old horsehair sofa, with a feather quilt to wrap himself in. The other corner was rented to a wretched, dirty boy, who was studying the violin. He actually practised there. Rosicky was dirty, too. There was no way to be anything else. Mrs. Lifschnitz got the water she cooked and washed with from a pump in a brick court, four flights down. There were bugs in the place, and multitudes of fleas, though the poor woman did the best she could. Rosicky knew she often went empty to give another potato or a spoonful of dripping to the two hungry, sad-eyed boys who lodged with her. He used to think he would never get out of there, never get a clean shirt to his back again. What would he do, he wondered, when his clothes actually dropped to pieces and the worn cloth wouldn't hold patches any longer?

It was still early when the old farmer put aside his sewing and his recollections. The sky had been a dark grey all day, with not a gleam of sun, and the light failed at four o'clock. He went to shave and change his shirt while the turkey was roasting. Rudolph and Polly were coming over for supper.

After supper they sat round in the kitchen, and the younger boys were saying how sorry they were it hadn't snowed. Everybody was sorry. They wanted a deep snow that would lie long and keep the wheat warm, and leave the ground soaked when it melted.

"Yes, sir!" Rudolph broke out fiercely; "if we have another dry year like last year, there's going to be hard times in this country."

Rosicky filled his pipe. "You boys don't know what hard times is. You don't owe nobody, you got plenty to eat an' keep warm, an' plenty water to keep clean. When you got them, you can't have it very hard."

Rudolph frowned, opened and shut his big right hand, and dropped it clenched upon his knee. "I've got to have a good deal more than that, Father, or I'll quit this farming gamble. I can always make good wages railroading, or at the packing house, and be sure of my money."

"Maybe so," his father answered dryly.

Mary, who had just come in from the pantry and was wiping her hands on the roller towel, thought Rudy and his father were getting too serious. She brought her darning-basket and sat down in the middle of the group.

"I ain't much afraid of hard times, Rudy," she said heartily. "We've had a plenty, but we've always come through. Your father wouldn't never take nothing very hard, not even hard times. I got a mind to tell you a story on him. Maybe you boys can't hardly remember the year we had that terrible hot wind, that burned everything up on the Fourth of July? All the corn an' the gardens. An' that was in the days when we didn't have alfalfa yet,—I guess it wasn't invented.

"Well, that very day your father was out cultivatin' corn, and I was here in the kitchen makin' plum preserves. We had bushels of plums that year. I noticed it was terrible hot, but it's always hot in the kitchen when you're preservin', an' I was too busy with my plums to mind. Anton come in from the field about three o'clock, an' I asked him what was the matter.

"'Nothin',' he says, 'but it's pretty hot, an' I think I won't work no more today.' He stood round for a few minutes, an' then he says: 'Ain't you near through? I want you should git up a nice supper for us tonight. It's Fourth of July.'

"I told him to git along, that I was right in the middle of preservin', but the plums would taste good on hot biscuit. 'I'm goin' to have fried chicken, too,' he says, and he went off an' killed a couple. You three oldest boys was little fellers, playin' round outside, real hot an' sweaty, an' your father took you to the horse tank down by the windmill an' took off your clothes an' put you in. Them two box-elder trees was little then, but they made shade over the tank. Then he took off all his own clothes, an' got in with you. While he was playin' in the water with you, the Methodist preacher drove into our place to say how all the neighbours was goin' to meet at the schoolhouse that night, to pray for rain. He drove right to the windmill, of course, and there was your father and you three with no clothes on. I was in the kitchen door, an' I had to laugh, for the preacher acted like he ain't never seen a naked man before. He surely was embarrassed, an'

your father couldn't git to his clothes; they was all hangin' up on the windmill to let the sweat dry out of 'em. So he laid in the tank where he was, an' put one of you boys on top of him to cover him up a little, an' talked to the preacher.

"When you got through playin' in the water, he put clean clothes on you and a clean shirt on himself, an' by that time I'd begun to get supper. He says: 'It's too hot in here to eat comfortable. Let's have a picnic in the orchard. We'll eat our supper behind the mulberry hedge, under them linden trees.'

"So he carried our supper down, an' a bottle of my wild-grape wine, an' everything tasted good, I can tell you. The wind got cooler as the sun was goin' down, and it turned out pleasant, only I noticed how the leaves was curled up on the linden trees. That made me think, an' I asked your father if that hot wind all day hadn't been terrible hard on the gardens an' the corn.

"'Corn,' he says, 'there ain't no corn.'

"'What you talkin' about?' I said. 'Ain't we got forty acres?'

"'We ain't got an ear,' he says, 'nor nobody else ain't got none. All the corn in this country was cooked by three o'clock today, like you'd roasted it in an oven.'

"'You mean you won't get no crop at all?' I asked him. I couldn't believe it, after he'd worked so hard.

"'No crop this year,' he says. 'That's why we're havin' a picnic. We might as well enjoy what we got.'

"An' that's how your father behaved, when all the neighbours was so discouraged they couldn't look you in the face. An' we enjoyed ourselves that year, poor as we was, an' our neighbours wasn't a bit better off for bein' miserable. Some of 'em grieved till they got poor digestions and couldn't relish what they did have.

The younger boys said they thought their father had the best of it. But Rudolph was thinking that, all the same, the neighbours had managed to get ahead more, in the fifteen years since that time. There must be something wrong about his father's way of doing things. He wished he knew what was going on in the back of Polly's mind. He knew she liked his father, but he knew, too, that she was afraid of something. When his mother sent over coffee-cake or prune tarts or a loaf of fresh bread, Polly seemed to regard them with a certain suspicion. When she observed to him that his brothers had nice manners, her tone implied that it was remarkable they should have. With his mother she was stiff and on her guard. Mary's hearty frankness and gusts of good humour irritated her. Polly was afraid of being unusual or conspicuous in any way, of being "ordinary," as she said!

When Mary had finished her story, Rosicky laid aside his pipe.

"You boys like me to tell you about some of dem hard times I been through in London?" Warmly encouraged, he sat rubbing his forehead along the deep creases. It was bothersome to tell a long story in English (he nearly always talked to the boys in Czech), but he wanted Polly to hear this one.

"Well, you know about dat tailor shop I worked in in London? I had one Christmas dere I ain't never forgot. Times was awful bad before Christmas; de boss ain't got much work, an' have it awful hard to pay his rent. It ain't so much fun, bein' poor in a big city like London, I'll say! All de windows is full of good t'ings to eat, an' all de pushcarts in de streets is full, an' you smell 'em all de time, an' you ain't got no money,—not a damn bit. I din't mind de cold so much, though I didn't have no overcoat, chust a short jacket I'd outgrowed so it wouldn't meet on me, an' my hands was chapped raw. But I always had a good appetite, like you all know, an' de sight of dem pork pies in de windows was awful fur me!

"Day before Christmas was terrible foggy dat year, an' dat fog gits into your bones and makes you all damp like. Mrs. Lifschnitz didn't give us nothin' but a little bread an' drippin' for supper, because she was savin' to try for to give us a good dinner on Christmas Day. After

supper de boss say I can go an' enjoy myself, so I went into de streets to listen to de Christmas singers. Dey sing old songs an' make very nice music, an' I run round after dem a good ways, till I got awful hungry. I t'ink maybe if I go home, I can sleep till morning an' forgit my belly.

"I went into my corner real quiet, and roll up in my fedder quilt. But I ain't got my head down, till I smell somet'ing good. Seem like it git stronger an' stronger, an' I can't git to sleep noway. I can't understand dat smell. Dere was a gas light in a hall across de court, dat always shine in at my window a little. I got up an' look round. I got a little wooden box in my corner fur a stool, 'cause I ain't got no chair. I picks up dat box, and under it dere is a roast goose on a platter! I can't believe my eyes. I carry it to de window where de light comes in, an' touch it and smell it to find out, an' den I taste it to be sure. I say, I will eat chust one little bite of dat goose, so I can go to sleep, and tomorrow I won't eat none at all. But I tell you, boys, when I stop, one half of dat goose was gone!"

The narrator bowed his head, and the boys shouted. But little Josephine slipped behind his chair and kissed him on the neck beneath his ear.

"Poor little Papa, I don't want him to be hungry!"

"Da's long ago, child. I ain't never been hungry since I had your mudder to cook fur me."

"Go on and tell us the rest, please," said Polly.

"Well, when I come to realize what I done, of course, I felt terrible. I felt better in de stomach, but very bad in de heart. I set on my bed wid dat platter on my knees, an' it all come to me; how hard dat poor woman save to buy dat goose, and how she got some neighbour to cook it dat got more fire, an' how she put it in my corner to keep it away from dem hungry children. Dey was an old carpet hung up to shut my corner off, an' de children wasn't allowed to go in dere. An' I know she put it in my corner because she trust me more'n she did de violin boy. I can't stand it to face her after I spoil de Christmas. So I put on my shoes and go out into de city. I tell myself I better throw myself in de river; but I guess I ain't dat kind of a boy.

"It was after twelve o'clock, an' terrible cold, an' I start out to walk about London all night. I walk along de river awhile, but dey was lots of drunks all along; men, and women too. I chust move along to keep away from de police. I git onto de Strand, an' den over to New Oxford Street, where dere was a big German restaurant on de ground floor, wid big windows all fixed up fine, an' I could see de people havin' parties inside. While I was lookin' in, two men and two ladies come out, laughin' and talkin' and feelin' happy about all dey been eatin' an' drinkin', and dey was speakin' Czech, —not like de Austrians, but like de home folks talk it.

"I guess I went crazy, an' I done what I ain't never done before nor since. I went right up to dem gay people an' begun to beg dem: 'Fellow-countrymen, for God's sake give me money enough to buy a goose!'

"Dey laugh, of course, but de ladies speak awful kind to me, an' dey take me back into de restaurant and give me hot coffee and cakes, an' make me tell all about how I happened to come to London, an' what I was doin' dere. Dey take my name and where I work down on paper, an' both of dem ladies give me ten shillings.

"De big market at Covent Garden ain't very far away, an' by dat time it was open. I go dere an' buy a big goose an' some pork pies, an' potatoes and onions, an' cakes an' oranges fur de children,—all I could carry! When I git home, everybody is still asleep. I pile all I bought on de kitchen table, an' go in an' lay down on my bed, an' I ain't waken up till I hear dat woman scream when she come out into her kitchen. My goodness, but she was surprise! She laugh an' cry at de same time, an' hug me and waken all de children. She ain't stop fur no breakfast; she git de Christmas dinner ready dat morning, and we all sit down an' eat all we can hold. I ain't never seen dat violin boy have all he can hold before."

"Two three days after dat, de two men come to hunt me up, an' dey ask my boss, and he give me a good report an' tell dem I was a steady boy all right. One of dem Bohemians was very smart an' run a Bohemian newspaper in New York, an' de odder was a rich man, in de importing business, an' dey been travelling togedder. Dey told me how t'ings was easier in New York, an' offered to pay my passage when dey was goin' home soon on a boat. My boss say to me: 'You go. You ain't got no chance here, an' I like to see you git ahead, fur you always been a good boy to my woman, and fur dat fine Christmas dinner you give us all.' An' da's how I got to New York."

That night when Rudolph and Polly, arm in arm, were running home across the fields with the bitter wind at their backs, his heart leaped for joy when she said she thought they might have his family come over for supper on New Year's Eve. "Let's get up a nice supper, and not let your mother help at all; make her be company for once."

"That would be lovely of you, Polly," he said humbly. He was a very simple, modest boy, and he, too, felt vaguely that Polly and her sisters were more experienced and worldly than his people.

VI

The winter turned out badly for farmers. It was bitterly cold, and after the first light snows before Christmas there was no snow at all,— and no rain. March was as bitter as February. On those days when the wind fairly punished the country, Rosicky sat by his window. In the fall he and the boys had put in a big wheat planting, and now the seed had frozen in the ground. All that land would have to be ploughed up and planted over again, planted in corn. It had happened before, but he was younger then, and he never worried about what had to be. He was sure of himself and of Mary; he knew they could bear what they had to bear, that they would always pull through somehow. But he was not so sure about the young ones, and he felt troubled because Rudolph and Polly were having such a hard start.

Sitting beside his flowering window while the panes rattled and the wind blew in under the door, Rosicky gave himself to reflection as he had not done since those Sundays in the loft of the furniture-factory in New York, long ago. Then he was trying to find what he wanted in life for himself; now he was trying to find what he wanted for his boys, and why it was he so hungered to feel sure they would be here, working this very land, after he was gone.

They would have to work hard on the farm, and probably they would never do much more than make a living. But if he could think of them as staying here on the land, he wouldn't have to fear any great unkindness for them. Hardships, certainly; it was a hardship to have the wheat freeze in the ground when seed was so high; and to have to sell your stock because you had no feed. But there would be other years when everything came along right, and you caught up. And what you had was your own. You didn't have to choose between bosses and strikers, and go wrong either way. You didn't have to do with dishonest and cruel people. They were the only things in his experience he had found terrifying and horrible; the look in the eyes of a dishonest and crafty man, of a scheming and rapacious woman.

In the country, if you had a mean neighbour, you could keep off his land and make him keep off yours. But in the city, all the foulness and misery and brutality of your neighbours was part of your life. The worst things he had come upon in his journey through the world were human,—depraved and poisonous specimens of man. To this day he could recall certain terrible faces in the London streets. There were mean people everywhere, to be sure, even in their own country town here. But they weren't tempered, hardened, sharpened, like the treacherous people in cities who live by grinding or cheating or poisoning their fellow-men. He had helped to bury two of his fellow-workmen in the tailoring trade, and he was distrustful of the organized industries that see one

out of the world in big cities. Here, if you were sick, you had Doctor Ed to look after you; and if you died, fat Mr. Haycock, the kindest man in the world, buried you.

It seemed to Rosicky that for good, honest boys like his, the worst they could do on the farm was better than the best they would be likely to do in the city. If he'd had a mean boy, now, one who was crooked and sharp and tried to put anything over on his brothers, then town would be the place for him. But he had no such boy. As for Rudolph, the discontented one, he would give the shirt off his back to anyone who touched his heart. What Rosicky really hoped for his boys was that they could get through the world without ever knowing much about the cruelty of human beings. "Their mother and me ain't prepared them for that," he sometimes said to himself.

These thoughts brought him back to a grateful consideration of his own case. What an escape he had had, to be sure! He, too, in his time, had had to take money for repair work from the hand of a hungry child who let it go so wistfully; because it was money due his boss. And now, in all these years, he had never had to take a cent from anyone in bitter need,—never had to look at the face of a woman become like a wolf's from struggle and famine. When he thought of these things, Rosicky would put on his cap and jacket and slip down to the barn and give his work-horses a little extra oats, letting them eat it out of his hand in their slobbery fashion. It was his way of expressing what he felt, and made him chuckle with pleasure.

The spring came warm, with blue skies,— but dry, dry as a bone. The boys began ploughing up the wheat-fields to plant them over in corn. Rosicky would stand at the fence corner and watch them, and the earth was so dry it blew up in clouds of brown dust that hid the horses and the sulky plough and the driver. It was a bad outlook.

The big alfalfa-field that lay between the home place and Rudolph's came up green, but Rosicky was worried because during that open windy winter a great many Russian thistle plants had blown in there and lodged. He kept asking the boys to rake them out; he was afraid their seed would root and "take the alfalfa." Rudolph said that was nonsense. The boys were working so hard planting corn, their father felt he couldn't insist about the thistles, but he set great store by that big alfalfa field. It was a feed you could depend on,—and there was some deeper reason, vague, but strong. The peculiar green of that clover woke early memories in old Rosicky, went back to something in his childhood in the old world. When he was a little boy, he had played in fields of that strong blue-green colour.

One morning, when Rudolph had gone to town in the car, leaving a work-team idle in his barn, Rosicky went over to his son's place, put the horses to the buggy-rake, and set about quietly raking up those thistles. He behaved with guilty caution, and rather enjoyed stealing a march on Doctor Ed, who was just then taking his first vacation in seven years of practice and was attending a clinic in Chicago. Rosicky got the thistles raked up, but did not stop to burn them. That would take some time, and his breath was pretty short, so he thought he had better get the horses back to the barn.

He got them into the barn and to their stalls, but the pain had come on so sharp in his chest that he didn't try to take the harness off. He started for the house, bending lower with every step. The cramp in his chest was shutting him up like a jack-knife. When he reached the windmill, he swayed and caught at the ladder. He saw Polly coming down the hill, running with the swiftness of a slim greyhound. In a flash she had her shoulder under his armpit.

"Lean on me, Father, hard! Don't be afraid. We can get to the house all right."

Somehow they did, though Rosicky became blind with pain; he could keep on his legs, but he couldn't steer his course. The next thing he was conscious of was lying on Polly's bed, and Polly bending over him wringing out bath towels in hot water and putting them on his chest. She stopped only to throw coal into the stove, and she kept the tea-kettle and the black pot going. She put these hot applications on him for nearly an hour, she told him afterwards, and all that time he was drawn up stiff and blue, with the sweat pouring off him.

As the pain gradually loosed its grip, the stiffness went out of his jaws, the black circles round his eyes disappeared, and a little of his natural colour came back. When his daughter-in-law buttoned his shirt over his chest at last, he sighed.

"Da's fine, de way I feel now, Polly. It was a awful bad spell, an' I was so sorry it all come on you like it did."

Polly was flushed and excited. "Is the pain really gone? Can I leave you long enough to telephone over to your place?"

Rosicky's eyelids fluttered. "Don't telephone, Polly. It ain't no use to scare my wife. It's nice and quiet here, an' if I ain't too much trouble to you, just let me lay still till I feel like myself. I ain't got no pain now. It's nice here."

Polly bent over him and wiped the moisture from his face. "Oh, I'm so glad it's over!" she broke out impulsively. "It just broke my heart to see you suffer so, Father."

Rosicky motioned her to sit down on the chair where the tea-kettle had been, and looked up at her with that lively affectionate gleam in his eyes. "You was awful good to me, I won't never forget dat. I hate it to be sick on you like dis. Down at de barn I say to myself, dat young girl ain't had much experience in sickness, I don't want to scare her, an' maybe she's got a baby comin' or somet'ing."

Polly took his hand. He was looking at her so intently and affectionately and confidingly; his eyes seemed to caress her face, to regard it with pleasure. She frowned with her funny streaks of eyebrows, and then smiled back at him.

"I guess maybe there is something of that kind going to happen. But I haven't told anyone yet, not my mother or Rudolph. You'll be the first to know."

His hand pressed hers. She noticed that it was warm again. The twinkle in his yellow-brown eyes seemed to come nearer.

"I like mighty well to see dat little child,

Polly," was all he said. Then he closed his eyes and lay half-smiling. But Polly sat still thinking hard. She had a sudden feeling that nobody in the world, not her mother, not Rudolph, or anyone, really loved her as much as old Rosicky did. It perplexed her. She sat frowning and trying to puzzle it out. It was as if Rosicky had a special gift for loving people, something that was like an ear for music or an eye for colour. It was quiet, unobtrusive; it was merely there. You saw it in his eyes,—perhaps that was why they were merry. You felt it in his hands, too. After he dropped off to sleep, she sat holding his warm, broad, flexible brown hand. She had never seen another in the least like it. She wondered if it wasn't a kind of gypsy hand, it was so alive and quick and light in its communications,—very strange in a farmer. Nearly all the farmers she knew had huge lumps of fists, like mauls, or they were knotty and bony and uncomfortable-looking, with stiff fingers. But Rosicky's was like quicksilver, flexible, muscular, about the colour of a pale cigar, with deep, deep creases across the palm. It wasn't nervous, it wasn't a stupid lump; it was a warm brown human hand, with some cleverness in it, a great deal of generosity, and something else which Polly could only call "gypsy-like,"—something nimble and lively and sure, in the way that animals are.

Polly remembered that hour long afterwards; it had been like an awakening to her. It seemed to her that she had never learned so much about life from anything as from old Rosicky's hand. It brought her to herself; it communicated some direct and untranslatable message.

When she heard Rudolph coming in the car, she ran out to meet him.

"Oh, Rudy, your father's been awful sick! He raked up those thistles he's been worrying about, and afterwards he could hardly get to the house. He suffered so I was afraid he was going to die."

Rudolph jumped to the ground. "Where is he now?"

"On the bed. He's asleep. I was terribly scared, because, you know, I'm so fond of your father." She slipped her arm through his and they went into the house. That afternoon they took Rosicky home and put him to bed, though he protested that he was quite well again.

The next morning he got up and dressed and sat down to breakfast with his family. He told Mary that his coffee tasted better than usual to him, and he warned the boys not to bear any tales to Doctor Ed when he got home. After breakfast he sat down by his window to do some patching and asked Mary to thread several needles for him before she went to feed her chickens,—her eyes were better than his, and her hands steadier. He lit his pipe and took up John's overalls. Mary had been watching him anxiously all morning, and as she went out of the door with her bucket of scraps, she saw that he was smiling. He was thinking, indeed, about Polly, and how he might never have known what a tender heart she had if he hadn't got sick over there. Girls nowadays didn't wear their heart on their sleeve. But now he knew Polly would make a fine woman after the foolishness wore off. Either a woman had that sweetness at her heart or she hadn't. You couldn't always tell by the look of them; but if they had that, everything came out right in the end.

After he had taken a few stitches, the cramp began in his chest, like yesterday. He put his pipe cautiously down on the window-sill and bent over to ease the pull. No use,—he had better try to get to his bed if he could. He rose and groped his way across the familiar floor, which was rising and falling like the deck of a ship. At the door he fell. When Mary came in, she found him lying there, and the moment she touched him she knew that he was gone.

Doctor Ed was away when Rosicky died, and for the first few weeks after he got home he was hard driven. Every day he said to himself that he must get out to see that family that had lost their father. One soft, warm moonlight night in early summer he started for the farm. His mind was on other things, and not until his road ran by the graveyard did he realize that Rosicky wasn't over there on the hill where the red lamplight shone, but here, in the moonlight. He stopped his car, shut off the engine, and sat there for a while.

A sudden hush had fallen on his soul. Everything here seemed strangely moving and significant, though signifying what, he did not know. Close by the wire fence stood Rosicky's mowing-machine, where one of the boys had been cutting hay that afternoon; his own work-horses had been going up and down there. The new-cut hay perfumed all the night air. The moonlight silvered the long, billowy grass that grew over the graves and hid the fence; the few little evergreens stood out black in it, like shadows in a pool. The sky was very blue and soft, the stars rather faint because the moon was full.

For the first time it struck Doctor Ed that this was really a beautiful graveyard. He thought of city cemeteries; acres of shrubbery and heavy stone, so arranged and lonely and unlike anything in the living world. Cities of the dead, indeed; cities of the forgotten, of the "put away." But this was open and free, this little square of long grass which the wind forever stirred. Nothing but the sky overhead, and the many-coloured fields running on until they met that sky. The horses worked here in summer; the neighbours passed on their way to town; and over yonder, in the cornfield, Rosick's own cattle would be eating fodder as winter came on. Nothing could be more undeathlike than this place; nothing could be more right for a man who had helped to do the work of great cities and had always longed for the open country and had got to it at last. Rosicky's life seemed to him complete and beautiful.

I
THE GOOD HEART

Although the story of Anton Rosicky opens ironically with the news that he has a "bad" heart, the reader soon comes to realize that his physical affliction in no way impairs his "special gift for lov-

ing people"—his good heart. Contrary to Harvey Merrick who fled the prairies to find truth, culture, and freedom, Rosicky, after searching long, sought the prairies because they were open and free. Here, close to nature, his Old World sensitivity and gentleness find their fullest expressions in the simple folk virtues of this last frontier. If Anton Rosicky's sincerity, compassion, and charity differ from the savagery of Sand City, it is not only because his life in the cities helps him appreciate the cleanness and beauty of the countryside but especially because he comes to it and life with the "good heart"—eager to love, to give of himself.

II
IMPLICATIONS

In your opinion, how true are the following statements from the story:

1. Maybe, Doctor Burleigh reflected, people as generous and warm-hearted and affectionate as the Rosickys never got ahead much; maybe you couldn't enjoy your life and put it into the bank, too.

2. To be a landless man was to be a wage-earner, a slave, all your life; to have nothing, to be nothing.

3. Rosicky: "No crop this year. . . . We might as well enjoy what we got."

III
TECHNIQUES

Setting

Through the flashbacks which relate Rosicky's past life in London and in New York, Miss Cather emphasizes the peace and beauty of his life on the farm. What specific details help you see his life in these two cities? What atmosphere pervades each? In what ways does the life and atmosphere of the farm differ from that of the cities?

Characterization

Miss Cather creates a well-rounded character and wins the reader's esteem for him by placing him in various roles which show off his qualities and virtues. She shows Rosicky as patient, shopper, immigrant, tenant, tailor's apprentice, farmer, husband, father-in-law, father, and neighbor. What traits of Rosicky's character does Miss Cather reveal in each role?

THE INNER STRUGGLE

From the shrewd Yankee trader and the wealthy Southern aristocrat through the "captains of industry" to the modern "organization man," Americans have frequently been characterized as men concerned with material things, with "getting

In marble of heroic size, Barnard treats a timeless conflict. Which is which and who is winning?

STRUGGLE OF TWO NATURES IN MAN, *George Gray Barnard*

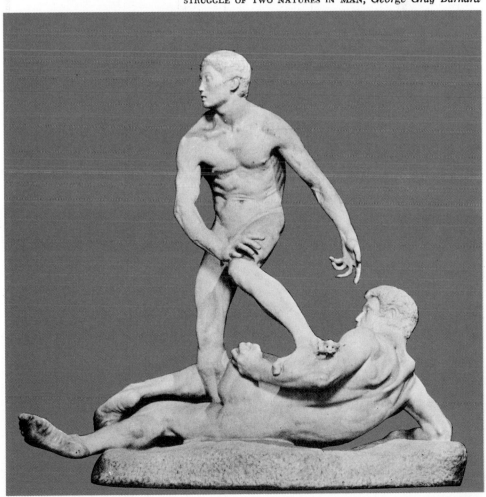

and spending." These material involvements—some have said—have made us a people overconcerned with "show," with the outer rather than with the inner world.

America does have a high standard of living, a standard that probably could not have been achieved unless we had put great value on material things. On the other hand, there is much in American life to prove that we have had and have now an intense concern with the inner as well as with the outer reality.

Even a very brief study of major American writers would reveal this quite clearly. Writers like Edgar Allan Poe, Nathaniel Hawthorne, Herman Melville, Henry James, and William Faulkner have become internationally famous for their explorations of the moral, spiritual, and psychological nature of the inner man. They—and others—have written of the struggles of man with his own nature, with his conscience; they have been intensely concerned with the causes and consequences of man's choices.

More than a century ago, Alexis de Tocqueville, the famous French critic of American culture, predicted that American writers would focus on "man himself, taken aloof from his age and his country and standing in the presence of nature and God, with his passions, his doubts, his rare propensities and inconceivable wretchedness."

THE INNER STRUGGLE does focus on "man himself," on the drama of decision and on the role conscience plays in this drama. Unlike the individuals in THE INDEPENDENT SPIRIT (page 517 ff.), the characters in these selections are for the most part ordinary people, but we meet them at critical moments in their lives. Because they are ordinary people it is easy to identify with them and thus to share in their trials of conscience. As we share their tests and decisions, we gain a deeper insight into the inner nature of man, into the inner nature of ourselves.

In its simplest form, the inner struggle
involves an evil side of human nature on the one hand and a good side,
usually represented as the voice of conscience, on the other.
In modern times, psychologists have told us a good deal
about both of these forces, but long before the advent of modern psychology,
Edgar Allan Poe showed, in his *Tales of the Grotesque and Arabesque*,
that he had a deep knowledge of the inner man, especially of the darker side
of human nature. "William Wilson," one of the first stories
in that collection, illustrates how the evil forces within one man
came to prevail completely over his conscience.

William Wilson

EDGAR ALLAN POE

What say of it? what say CONSCIENCE grim,
That spectre in my path?
　　　　—*Chamberlain's Pharronida.*

Let me call myself, for the present, William Wilson. The fair page now lying before me need not be sullied[1] with my real appellation.[2] This has been already too much an object for the scorn—for the horror—for the detestation of my race. To the uttermost regions of the globe have not the indignant winds bruited[3] its unparalleled infamy? Oh, outcast of all outcasts most abandoned!—to the earth art thou not for ever dead? to its honors, to its flowers, to its golden aspirations?—and a cloud, dense, dismal, and limitless, does it not hang eternally between thy hopes and heaven?

I would not, if I could, here or to-day, embody a record of my later years of unspeakable misery and unpardonable crime. This epoch—these later years—took unto themselves a sudden elevation in turpitude,[4] whose origin alone it is my present purpose to assign. Men usually grow base by degrees. From me, in an instant, all virtue dropped bodily as a mantle. From comparatively trivial wickedness I passed, with the stride of a giant, into more than the enormities of an Elah-Gabalus.[5] What chance—what one event brought this evil thing to pass, bear with me while I relate. Death approaches; and the shadow which foreruns him has thrown a softening influence over my spirit. I long, in passing through the dim valley, for the sympathy—I had nearly said for the pity—of my fellow men. I would fain[6] have them believe that I have been, in some measure, the slave of circumstances beyond human control. I would wish them to seek out for me, in the details I am about to give, some little oasis of *fatality*[7] amid a wilderness of error. I would have them allow—what they cannot refrain from allowing—that, although temptation may have erewhile existed as great, man was never *thus,* at least, tempted before—certainly, never *thus* fell. And is it therefore that he has never thus suffered? Have I not indeed been living in a dream? And am I not now dying a victim to the horror and the mystery of the wildest of all sublunary[8] visions?

---

1. **sullied**\ˈsəl·lēd\ soiled, stained.
2. **appellation**\ăp 'ə ˈlā·shən\ name by which a person is called.
3. **bruited**\ˈbrūt·əd\ spread news of.
4. **turpitude**\ˈtər·pə 'tūd\ disgusting wickedness, baseness.
5. **Elah-Gabalus**\ˈē·lä gə ˈba·ləs\ also Elagabălus, a profligate Roman emperor.
6. **fain**\fān\ poetic word meaning eagerly, gladly.
7. **oasis of fatality,** some agent of fate, some reasonable explanation.
8. **sublunary**\ˈsŭb·lū·nĕ·rē\ earthly.

I am the descendant of a race whose imaginative and easily excitable temperament has at all times rendered them remarkable; and, in my earliest infancy, I gave evidence of having fully inherited the family character. As I advanced in years it was more strongly developed; becoming, for many reasons, a cause of serious disquietude to my friends, and of positive injury to myself. I grew self-willed, addicted to the wildest caprices,[9] and a prey to the most ungovernable passions. Weak-minded, and beset with constitutional infirmities akin to my own, my parents could do but little to check the evil propensities[10] which distinguished me. Some feeble and ill-directed efforts resulted in complete failure on their part, and, of course, in total triumph on mine. Thenceforward my voice was a household law; and at an age when few children have abandoned their leading-strings, I was left to the guidance of my own will, and became, in all but name, the master of my own actions.

My earliest recollections of a school-life are connected with a large, rambling, Elizabethan house, in a misty-looking village of England, where were a vast number of gigantic and gnarled trees, and where all the houses were excessively ancient. In truth, it was a dream-like and spirit-soothing place, that venerable old town. At this moment, in fancy, I feel the refreshing chilliness of its deeply-shadowed avenues, inhale the fragrance of its thousand shrubberies, and thrill anew with undefinable delight, at the deep hollow note of the church-bell, breaking, each hour, with sullen and sudden roar, upon the stillness of the dusky atmosphere in which the fretted Gothic[11] steeple lay imbedded and asleep.

It gives me, perhaps, as much of pleasure as I can now in any manner experience, to dwell upon minute recollections of the school and its concerns. Steeped in misery as I am—misery, alas! only too real—I shall be pardoned for seeking relief, however slight and temporary, in the weakness of a few rambling details. These, moreover, utterly trivial, and even ridiculous in themselves, assume, to my fancy,

adventitious[12] importance, as connected with a period and a locality when and where I recognize the first ambiguous monitions[13] of the destiny which afterward so fully overshadowed me. Let me then remember.

The house, I have said, was old and irregular. The grounds were extensive, and a high and solid brick wall, topped with a bed of mortar and broken glass, encompassed the whole. This prison-like rampart formed the limit of our domain; beyond it we saw but thrice a week—once every Saturday afternoon, when, attended by two ushers, we were permitted to take brief walks in a body through some of the neighboring fields—and twice during Sunday, when we were paraded in the same formal manner to the morning and evening service in the one church of the village. Of this church the principal of our school was pastor. With how deep a spirit of wonder and perplexity was I wont to regard him from our remote pew in the gallery, as, with step solemn and slow, he ascended the pulpit! This reverend man, with countenance so demurely benign, with robes so glossy and so clerically flowing, with wig so minutely powdered, so rigid and so vast,—could this be he who, of late, with sour visage, and in snuffy habiliments,[14] administered, ferule[15] in hand, the Draconian Laws[16] of the academy? Oh, gigantic paradox, too utterly monstrous for solution!

---

9. **caprices**\kə ▲prēs•əz\ sudden, impulsive changes of mind, seemingly unmotivated.
10. **propensities**\prə ▲pĕn•sə•tēz\ inclinations or tendencies.
11. **Gothic**, style of architecture developed after 1140 in western Europe and characterized by pointed arches, ribbed vaulting, buttresses extending into space, enclosed walls, wholly or partially stained windows.
12. **adventitious**\▲ăd•vĕn ▲tĭsh•əs\ added from the outside but lacking an innate connection.
13. **monitions**\mə ▲nĭsh•ənz\ warnings; signals to exercise caution.
14. **habiliments**\hə ▲bĭ•lə•mənts\ wearing apparel suitable for occasion, occupation.
15. **ferule**\▲fĕ•rəl\ a rod or switch used to punish school children.
16. **Draconian Laws**\'dra ▲kō•nē•ən\ Severe code of laws; named for Athenian lawyer Draco, 621 B.C.

At an angle of the ponderous wall frowned a more ponderous gate. It was riveted and studded with iron bolts, and surmounted with jagged iron spikes. What impressions of deep awe did it inspire! It was never opened save for the three periodical egressions and ingressions already mentioned; then, in every creak of its mighty hinges, we found a plentitude of mystery—a world of matter for solemn remark, or for more solemn meditation.

The extensive enclosure was irregular in form, having many capacious recesses. Of these, three or four of the largest constituted the playground. It was level, and covered with fine hard gravel. I well remember it had no trees, nor benches, nor any thing similar within it. Of course it was in the rear of the house. In front lay a small parterre,[17] planted with box and other shrubs, but through this sacred division we passed only upon rare occasions indeed—such as a first advent to school or final departure thence, or perhaps, when a parent or friend having called for us, we joyfully took our way home for the Christmas or Midsummer holidays.

But the house!—how quaint an old building was this!—to me how veritable a palace of enchantment! There was really no end to its windings—to its incomprehensible subdivisions. It was difficult, at any given time, to say with certainty upon which of its two stories one happened to be. From each room to every other there were sure to be found three or four steps either in ascent or descent. Then the lateral branches were innumerable—inconceivable—and so returning in upon themselves, that our most exact ideas in regard to the whole mansion were not very far different from those with which we pondered upon infinity. During the five years of my residence here, I was never able to ascertain with precision, in what remote locality lay the little sleeping apartment assigned to myself and some eighteen or twenty other scholars.

The school-room was the largest in the house —I could not help thinking, in the world. It was very long, narrow, and dismally low, with pointed Gothic windows and a ceiling of oak. In a remote and terror-inspiring angle was a square enclosure of eight or ten feet, comprising the *sanctum,* "during hours," of our principal, the Reverend Dr. Bransby. It was a solid structure, with massy door, sooner than open which in the absence of the "Dominie," we would all have willingly perished by the *peine forte et dure.*[18] In other angles were two other similar boxes, far less reverenced, indeed, but still greatly matters of awe. One of these was the pulpit of the "classical" usher, one of the "English and mathematical." Interspersed about the room, crossing and recrossing in endless irregularity, were innumerable benches and desks, black, ancient, and time-worn, piled desperately with much bethumbed books, and so beseamed with initial letters, names at full length, grotesque figures, and other multiplied efforts of the knife, as to have entirely lost what little of original form might have been their portion in days long departed. A huge bucket with water stood at one extremity of the room, and a clock of stupendous dimensions at the other.

Encompassed by the massy walls of this venerable academy, I passed, yet not in tedium or disgust, the years of the third lustrum[19] of my life. The teeming brain of childhood requires no external world of incident to occupy or amuse it; and the apparently dismal monotony of a school was replete with more intense excitement than my riper youth has derived from luxury, or my full manhood from crime. Yet I must believe that my first mental development had in it much of the uncommon—even much of the *outré.*[20] Upon mankind at large the events of very early existence rarely leave in mature age any definite impression. All is gray shadow—a weak and irregular remembrance

---

17. **parterre**\par ▲tĕr\ an ornamental garden in which the flower beds and shrubs form a pattern.
18. **peine forte et dure**\pĕn fɔr tĕ dūr\ literally, strong and severe punishment; a form of torture by crushing the chest with weights or stones.
19. **lustrum**\▲ləs·trəm\ a five-year period.
20. **outré**\'ū ▲trā\ eccentric.

—an indistinct regathering of feeble pleasures and phantasmagoric[21] pains. With me this is not so. In childhood I must have felt with the energy of a man what I now find stamped upon memory in lines as vivid, as deep, and as durable as the *exergues*[22] of the Carthaginian medals.[23]

Yet in fact—in the fact of the world's view—how little was there to remember! The morning's awakening, the nightly summons to bed; the connings, the recitations; the periodical half-holidays, and perambulations;[24] the playground, with its broils, its pastimes, its intrigues;—these, by a mental sorcery long forgotten, were made to involve a wilderness of sensation, a world of rich incident, an universe of varied emotion, of excitement, the most passionate and spirit-stirring. *"Oh, le bon temps, que ce siècle de fer!"*[25]

In truth, the ardor, the enthusiasm, and the imperiousness of my disposition, soon rendered me a marked character among my schoolmates, and by slow, but natural gradations, gave me an ascendancy over all not greatly older than myself;—over all with a single exception. This exception was found in the person of a scholar, who, although no relation, bore the same Christian and surname as myself;—a circumstance, in fact, little remarkable; for notwithstanding a noble descent, mine was one of those every-day appellations which seem, by prescriptive right, to have been, time out of mind, the common property of the mob. In this narrative I have therefore designated myself as William Wilson, —a fictitious title not very dissimilar to the real. My namesake alone, of those who in school phraseology constituted "our set," presumed to compete with me in the studies of the class—in the sports and broils of the playground—to refuse implicit belief in my assertions, and submission to my will—indeed, to interfere with my arbitrary dictation in any respect whatsoever. If there is on earth a supreme and unqualified despotism, it is the despotism of a master-mind in boyhood over the less energetic spirits of its companions.

Wilson's rebellion was to me a source of the greatest embarrassment; the more so as, in spite of the bravado with which in public I made a point of treating him and his pretensions, I secretly felt that I feared him, and could not help thinking the equality which he maintained so easily with myself, a proof of his true superiority; since not to be overcome cost me a perpetual struggle. Yet this superiority—even this equality—was in truth acknowledged by no one but myself; our associates, by some unaccountable blindness, seemed not even to suspect it. Indeed, his competition, his resistance, and especially his impertinent and dogged interference with my purposes, were not more pointed than private. He appeared to be destitute alike of the ambition which urged, and of the passionate energy of mind which enabled me to excel. In his rivalry he might have been supposed actuated solely by a whimsical desire to thwart, astonish, or mortify myself; although there were times when I could not help observing, with a feeling made up of wonder, abasement, and pique,[26] that he mingled with his injuries, his insults, or his contradictions, a certain most inappropriate, and assuredly most unwelcome *affectionateness* of manner. I could only conceive this singular behavior to arise from a consummate self-conceit assuming the vulgar airs of patronage and protection.

Perhaps it was this latter trait in Wilson's conduct, conjoined with our identity of name, and the mere accident of our having entered the school upon the same day, which set afloat the notion that we were brothers, among the senior classes in the academy. These do not usually inquire with much strictness into the

---

21. **phantasmagoric**\făn 'tăz·mə ▲gor·ĭk\ rapidly changing things, seen or imagined as in a dream.
22. **exergue**\▲ĕk 'sərg\ space on medal between rim and design, often containing the date.
23. **Carthaginian medals**, medals manufactured by natives of Carthage, an ancient city and State in Northern Africa destroyed by the Romans during Punic War (146 B.C.).
24. **perambulations**\pĕr ▲ăm·byū·lā·shənz\walks about, strolls.
25. **le bon temps, que ce siècle der fer**\ lə bon tan kə sə sĭ·ĕ·kl də fĕr\ the good times in this period of strength.
26. **pique**\pēk\ resentfulness, displeasure.

affairs of their juniors. I have before said, or should have said, that Wilson was not, in a most remote degree, connected with my family. But assuredly if we *had* been brothers we must have been twins; for, after leaving Dr. Bransby's, I casually learned that my namesake was born on the nineteenth of January, 1813—and this is a somewhat remarkable coincidence; for the day is precisely that of my own nativity.

It may seem strange that in spite of the continual anxiety occasioned me by the rivalry of Wilson, and his intolerable spirit of contradiction, I could not bring myself to hate him altogether. We had, to be sure, nearly every day a quarrel in which, yielding me publicly the palm of victory, he, in some manner, contrived to make me feel that it was he who had deserved it; yet a sense of pride on my part, and a veritable dignity on his own, kept us always upon what are called "speaking terms," while there were many points of strong congeniality in our tempers, operating to awake in me a sentiment which our position alone, perhaps, prevented from ripening into friendship. It is difficult, indeed, to define, or even to describe, my real feelings toward him. They formed a motley and heterogeneous admixture;—some petulant animosity,[27] which was not yet hatred, some esteem, more respect, much fear, with a world of uneasy curiosity. To the moralist it will be necessary to say, in addition, that Wilson and myself were the most inseparable of companions.

It was no doubt the anomalous state of affairs existing between us, which turned all my attacks upon him, (and there were many, either open or covert) into the channel of banter or practical joke (giving pain while assuming the aspect of mere fun) rather than into a more serious and determined hostility. But my endeavors on this head were by no means uniformly successful, even when my plans were the most wittily concocted; for my namesake had much about him, in character, of that unassuming and quiet austerity which, while enjoying the poignancy of its own jokes, has no heel of Achilles[28] in itself, and absolutely refuses to be laughed at. I could find, indeed, but one vulnerable point, and that, lying in a personal peculiarity, arising, perhaps, from constitutional disease, would have been spared by any antagonist less at his wit's end than myself;—my rival had a weakness in the faucial[29] or guttural organs, which precluded him from raising his voice at any time *above a very low whisper.* Of this defect I did not fail to take what poor advantage lay in my power.

Wilson's retaliations in kind were many; and there was one form of his practical wit that disturbed me beyond measure. How his sagacity first discovered at all that so petty a thing would vex me, is a question I never could solve; but having discovered, he habitually practised the annoyance. I had always felt aversion to my uncourtly patronymic,[30] and its very common, if not plebeian prænomen.[31] The words were venom in my ears; and when, upon the day of my arrival, a second William Wilson came also to the academy, I felt angry with him for bearing the name, and doubly disgusted with the name because a stranger bore it, who would be the cause of its twofold repetition, who would be constantly in my presence, and whose concerns, in the ordinary routine of the school business, must inevitably, on account of the detestable coincidence, be often confounded with my own.

The feeling of vexation thus engendered grew stronger with every circumstance tending to show resemblance, moral or physical, between my rival and myself. I had not then discovered the remarkable fact that we were of the same age; but I saw that we were of the

---

27. **petulant animosity**\ˈpĕch·ŭ·lənt ˈăn·ə ˈmŏ·sə·tē\ peevish or bad-tempered hostility.
28. **heel of Achilles**, Achilles' mother, Thetis, attempting to protect him from all wounds, dipped him into the River Styx\stĭks\; the water covered all except the heel by which she held him; he died from a wound to his one vulnerable spot, his heel.
29. **faucial**\ˈfɔ·shəl\ passage from the back of the mouth into the pharynx.
30. **patronymic**\ˈpăt·rə ˈnĭ·mĭk\ name showing descent from a father or ancestor.
31. **plebeian prænomen**\plĭ ˈbē·ən prē ˈnō 'mĕn\ common first name.

same height, and I perceived that we were even singularly alike in general contour of person and outline of feature. I was galled, too, by the rumor touching a relationship, which had grown current in the upper forms. In a word, nothing could more seriously disturb me, (although I scrupulously concealed such disturbance,) than any illusion to a similarity of mind, person, or condition existing between us. But, in truth, I had no reason to believe that (with the exception of the matter of relationship, and in the case of Wilson himself,) this similarity had ever been made a subject of comment, or even observed at all by our schoolfellows. That *he* observed it in all its bearings, and as fixedly as I, was apparent; but that he could discover in such circumstances so fruitful a field of annoyance, can only be attributed, as I said before, to his more than ordinary penetration.

His cue, which was to perfect an imitation of myself, lay both in words and in actions; and most admirably did he play his part. My dress it was an easy matter to copy; my gait and general manner were without difficulty, appropriated; in spite of his constitutional defect, even my voice did not escape him. My louder tones were, of course, unattempted, but then the key, —it was identical; *and his singular whisper, it grew the very echo of my own.*

How greatly this most exquisite portraiture harassed me (for it could not justly be termed a caricature), I will not now venture to describe. I had but one consolation—in the fact that the imitation, apparently, was noticed by myself alone, and that I had to endure only the knowing and strangely sarcastic smiles of my namesake himself. Satisfied with having produced in my bosom the intended effect, he seemed to chuckle in secret over the sting he had inflicted, and was characteristically disregardful of the public applause which the success of his witty endeavors might have so easily elicited. That the school, indeed, did not feel his design, perceive its accomplishment, and participate in his sneer, was, for many anxious months, a riddle I could not resolve. Perhaps

the *gradation* of his copy rendered it not readily perceptible; or, more possibly, I owed my security to the masterly air of the copyist, who, disdaining the letter (which in a painting is all the obtuse[32] can see), gave but the full spirit of his original for my individual contemplation and chagrin.[33]

I have already more than once spoken of the disgusting air of patronage which he assumed toward me, and of his frequent officious interference with my will. This interference often took the ungracious character of advice; advice not openly given, but hinted or insinuated. I received it with a repugnance which gained strength as I grew in years. Yet, at this distant day, let me do him the simple justice to acknowledge that I can recall no occasion when the suggestions of my rival were on the side of those errors or follies so usual to his immature age and seeming inexperience; that his moral sense, at least, if not his general talents and worldly wisdom, was far keener than my own; and that I might, to-day, have been a better and thus a happier man, had I less frequently rejected the counsels embodied in those meaning whispers which I then but too cordially hated and too bitterly despised.

As it was I at length grew restive in the extreme under his distasteful supervision, and daily resented more and more openly, what I considered his intolerable arrogance. I have said that, in the first years of our connection as schoolmates, my feelings in regard to him might have been easily ripened into friendship; but, in the latter months of my residence at the academy, although the intrusion of his ordinary manner had, beyond doubt, in some measure, abated, my sentiments, in nearly similar proportion, partook very much of positive hatred. Upon one occasion he saw this, I think, and afterward avoided, or made a show of avoiding me.

---

32. **obtuse**\ŏb ˈtūs\ slow to understand, insensitive.
33. **chagrin**\shə ˈgrĭn\ embarrassment, disappointment.

It was about the same period, if I remember aright, that, in an altercation of violence with him, in which he was more than usually thrown off his guard, and spoke and acted with an openness of demeanor rather foreign to his nature, I discovered, or fancied I discovered, in his accent, in his air, and general appearance, a something which first startled, and then deeply interested me, by bringing to mind dim visions of my earliest infancy—wild, confused, and thronging memories of a time when memory herself was yet unborn. I cannot better describe the sensation which oppressed me, than by saying that I could with difficulty shake off the belief of my having been acquainted with the being who stood before me, at some epoch very long ago—some point of the past even infinitely remote. The delusion, however, faded rapidly as it came; and I mention it at all but to define the day of the last conversation I there held with my singular namesake.

The huge old house, with its countless subdivisions, had several large chambers communicating with each other, where slept the greater number of the students. There were, however (as must necessarily happen in a building so awkwardly planned), many little nooks or recesses, the odds and ends of the structure; and these the economic ingenuity of Dr. Bransby had also fitted up as dormitories, although, being the merest closets, they were capable of accommodating but a single individual. One of these small apartments was occupied by Wilson.

One night, about the close of my fifth year at the school, and immediately after the altercation just mentioned, finding every one wrapped in sleep, I arose from bed, and, lamp in hand, stole through a wilderness of narrow passages, from my own bedroom to that of my rival. I had long been plotting one of those ill-natured pieces of practical wit at his expense in which I had hitherto been so uniformly unsuccessful. It was my intention, now, to put my scheme in operation, and I resolved to make him feel the whole extent of the malice with which I was imbued. Having reached his closet, I noise-lessly entered, leaving the lamp, with a shade over it, on the outside. I advanced a step and listened to the sound of his tranquil breathing. Assured of his being asleep, I returned, took the light, and with it again approached the bed. Close curtains were around it, which, in the prosecution of my plan, I slowly and quietly withdrew, when the bright rays fell vividly upon the sleeper, and my eyes at the same moment, upon his countenance. I looked;—and a numbness, an iciness of feeling instantly pervaded my frame. My breast heaved, my knees tottered, my whole spirit became possessed with an abjectness yet intolerable horror. Gasping for breath, I lowered the lamp in still nearer proximity to the face. Were these—*these* the lineaments[34] of William Wilson? I saw, indeed, that they were his, but I shook as if with a fit of the ague, in fancying they were not. What *was* there about them to confound me in this manner? I gazed;—while my brain reeled with a multitude of incoherent thoughts. Not thus he appeared—assuredly not *thus*—in the vivacity of his waking hours. The same name! the same contour of person! the same day of arrival at the academy! And then his dogged and meaningless imitation of my gait, my voice, my habits, and my manner! Was it, in truth, within the bounds of human possibility, that *what I now saw* was the result, merely, of the habitual practice of this sarcastic imitation? Awestricken, and with a creeping shudder, I extinguished the lamp, passed silently from the chamber, and left, at once, the halls of that old academy, never to enter them again.

After a lapse of some months, spent at home in mere idleness, I found myself a student at Eton.[35] The brief interval had been sufficient to enfeeble my remembrance of the events at Dr. Bransby's, or at least to effect a material change in the nature of the feelings with which I remembered them. The truth—the tragedy—of the drama was no more. I could now find room

---

34. **lineament**\lĭ ⁴nĭ·ə·mənt\ outline of the features of the face.
35. **Eton,** a private preparatory school in England.

to doubt the evidence of my senses; and seldom called up the subject at all but with wonder at the extent of human credulity, and a smile at the vivid force of the imagination which I hereditarily possessed. Neither was this species of skepticism likely to be diminished by the character of the life I led at Eton. The vortex[36] of thoughtless folly into which I there so immediately and so recklessly plunged, washed away all but the froth of my past hours, ingulfed at once every solid or serious impression, and left to memory only the veriest levities[37] of a former existence.

I do not wish, however, to trace the course of my miserable profligacy[38] here—a profligacy which set at defiance the laws, while it eluded the vigilance of the institution. Three years of folly, passed without profit, had but given me rooted habits of vice, and added, in a somewhat unusual degree, to my bodily stature, when, after a week of soulless dissipation, I invited a small party of the most dissolute students to a secret carousal in my chambers. We met at a late hour of the night; for our debaucheries were to be faithfully protracted until morning. The wine flowed freely, and there were not wanting other and perhaps more dangerous seductions; so that the gray dawn had already faintly appeared in the east while our delirious extravagance was at its height. Madly flushed with cards and intoxication, I was in the act of insisting upon a toast of more than wonted profanity, when my attention was suddenly diverted by the violent, although partial, unclosing of the door of the apartment, and by the eager voice of a servant from without. He said that some person, apparently in great haste, demanded to speak with me in the hall.

Wildly excited with wine, the unexpected interruption rather delighted than surprised me. I staggered forward at once, and a few steps brought me to the vestibule[39] of the building. In this low and small room there hung no lamp; and now no light at all was admitted, save that of the exceedingly feeble dawn which made its way through the semi-circular window. As I put my foot over the threshold, I became aware

of the figure of a youth about my own height, and habited in a white kerseymere morning frock,[40] cut in the novel fashion of the one I myself wore at the moment. This the faint light enabled me to perceive; but the features of his face I could not distinguish. Upon my entering, he strode hurriedly up to me, and, seizing me by the arm with a gesture of petulant impatience, whispered the words "William Wilson" in my ear.

I grew perfectly sober in an instant.

There was that in the manner of the stranger, and in the tremulous shake of his uplifted finger, as he held it between my eyes and the light, which filled me with unqualified amazement; but it was not this which had so violently moved me. It was the pregnancy of solemn admonition in the singular, low, hissing utterance; and, above all, it was the character, the tone, *the key*, of those few, simple, and familiar, yet *whispered* syllables, which came with a thousand thronging memories of by-gone days, and struck upon my soul with the shock of a galvanic battery. Ere I could recover the use of my senses he was gone.

Although this event failed not of a vivid effect upon my disordered imagination, yet was it evanescent[41] as vivid. For some weeks, indeed, I busied myself in earnest enquiry, or was wrapped in a cloud of morbid speculation. I did not pretend to disguise from my perception the identity of the singular individual who thus perseveringly interfered with my affairs, and harassed me with his insinuated counsel. But who and what was this Wilson?—and whence came he?—and what were his purposes? Upon neither of these points could I be satisfied—

---

36. **vortex**\ˈvȯr·tĕks\ activity that resembles a whirling mass.
37. **veriest levities,** barest, most unbecoming flippancy, lack of seriousness.
38. **profligacy**\ˈprȯf·lə·gə·sē\ abandonment to vice.
39. **vestibule**\ˈvĕs·tə ˈbyūl\ a small entrance hall within a building.
40. **kerseymere**\kʊr ˈzē·mĭr\ **morning frock,** long coat of a fine, twilled woolen cloth.
41. **evanescent**\ˈĕ·və ˈnĕ·sənt\ fading from sight, vague.

merely ascertaining, in regard to him, that a sudden accident in his family had caused his removal from Dr. Bransby's academy on the afternoon of the day in which I myself had eloped. But in a brief period I ceased to think upon the subject, my attention being all absorbed in a contemplated departure for Oxford. Thither I soon went, the uncalculating vanity of my parents furnishing me with an outfit and annual establishment, which would enable me to indulge at will in the luxury already so dear to my heart—to vie in profuseness of expenditure with the haughtiest heirs of the wealthiest earldoms in Great Britain.

Excited by such appliances to vice, my constitutional temperament broke forth with redoubled ardor, and I spurned even the common restraints of decency in the mad infatuation of my revels. But it were absurd to pause in the detail of my extravagance. Let it suffice, that among spendthrifts I out-Heroded Herod,[42] and that, giving name to a multitude of novel follies, I added no brief appendix to the long catalogue of vices then usual in the most dissolute university of Europe.

It could hardly be credited, however, that I had, even here, so utterly fallen from the gentlemanly estate, as to seek acquaintance with the vilest arts of the gambler by profession, and, having become an adept in his despicable science, to practice it habitually as a means of increasing my already enormous income at the expense of the weak-minded among my fellow-collegians. Such, nevertheless, was the fact. And the very enormity of this offence against all manly and honorable sentiment proved, beyond doubt, the main if not the sole reason of the impunity with which it was committed. Who, indeed, among my most abandoned associates, would not rather have disputed the clearest evidence of his senses, than have suspected of such courses, the gay, the frank, the generous William Wilson—the noblest and most liberal commoner at Oxford—him whose follies (said his parasites) were but the follies of youth and unbridled fancy—whose errors

but inimitable whim—whose darkest vice but a careless and dashing extravagance?

I had been now two years successfully busied in this way, when there came to the university a young *parvenu* nobleman,[43] Glendenning—rich, said report, as Herodes Atticus[44]—his riches, too, as easily acquired. I soon found him of weak intellect, and, of course, marked him as a fitting subject for my skill. I frequently engaged him in play, and contrived, with the gambler's usual art, to let him win considerable sums, the more effectually to entangle him in my snares. At length, my schemes being ripe, I met him (with the full intention that this meeting should be final and decisive) at the chambers of a fellow-commoner (Mr. Preston), equally intimate with both, but who, to do him justice, entertained not even a remote suspicion of my design. To give to this a better coloring, I had contrived to have assembled a party of some eight or ten, and was solicitously careful that the introduction of cards should appear accidental, and originate in the proposal of my contemplated dupe himself. To be brief upon a vile topic, none of the low finesse[45] was omitted, so customary upon similar occasions, that it is a just matter for wonder how any are still found so besotted[46] as to fall its victim.

We had protracted our sitting far into the night, and I had at length effected the manœuvre of getting Glendenning as my sole antagonist. The game, too, was my favorite *écarté*.[47] The rest of the company, interested in the extent of our play, had abandoned their own cards, and were standing around us as

---

42. **Herod,** probably a reference to Herod the Great, King of Judea (37–34 B.C.), who spent much building temples and adorning his cities, especially Jerusalem.
43. **parvenu\\ˈpar·və·nū\ nobleman,** a man who has suddenly acquired riches.
44. **Herodes Atticus\\hĭ ˈrō·dēz ˈă·tĭ·kəs** Greek teacher, rhetorician, c.101–c.177; spent a fortune adorning Athens and other Greek cities.
45. **finesse\\fĭ ˈnĕs** ability to handle difficult situations skillfully, artfully.
46. **besotted\\bē ˈsŏt·ĭd** foolish; confused, as with alcohol.
47. **écarté\\ā·kŏr ˈtā** a card game for two persons played with thirty-two cards (sevens up through aces).

spectators. The *parvenu*, who had been induced by my artifices in the early part of the evening, to drink deeply, now shuffled, dealt, or played, with a wild nervousness of manner for which his intoxication, I thought, might partially, but could not altogether account. In a very short period he had become my debtor to a large amount, when, having taken a long draught of port, he did precisely what I had been coolly anticipating—he proposed to double our already extravagant stakes. With a well-feigned show of reluctance, and not until after my repeated refusal had seduced him into some angry words which gave a color of *pique* to my compliance, did I finally comply. The result, of course, did but prove how entirely the prey was in my toils: in less than an hour he had quadrupled his debt. For some time his countenance had been losing the florid tinge lent it by the wine; but now, to my astonishment, I perceived that it had grown to a pallor truly fearful. I say, to my astonishment. Glendenning had been represented to my eager inquiries as immeasurably wealthy; and the sums which he had as yet lost, although in themselves vast, could not, I supposed, very seriously annoy, much less so violently affect him. That he was overcome by the wine just swallowed, was the idea which most readily presented itself; and, rather with a view to the preservation of my own character in the eyes of my associates, than from any less interested motive, I was about to insist, peremptorily, upon a discontinuance of the play, when some expressions at my elbow from among the company, and an ejaculation evincing utter despair on the part of Glendenning, gave me to understand that I had effected his total ruin under circumstances which, rendering him an object for the pity of all, should have protected him from the ill offices even of a fiend.

What now might have been my conduct it is difficult to say. The pitiable condition of my dupe had thrown an air of embarrassed gloom over all; and, for some moments, a profound silence was maintained, during which I could not help feeling my cheeks tingle with the many burning glances of scorn or reproach cast upon me by the less abandoned of the party. I will even own that an intolerable weight of anxiety was for a brief instant lifted from my bosom by the sudden and extraordinary interruption which ensued. The wide, heavy folding doors of the apartment were all at once thrown open, to their full extent, with a vigorous and rushing impetuosity that extinguished, as if by magic, every candle in the room. Their light, in dying, enabled us just to perceive that a stranger had entered, about my own height, and closely muffled in a cloak. The darkness, however, was now total; and we could only *feel* that he was standing in our midst. Before any one of us could recover from the extreme astonishment into which this rudeness had thrown all, we heard the voice of the intruder.

"Gentlemen," he said, in a low, distinct, and never-to-be-forgotten *whisper* which thrilled to the very marrow of my bones, "Gentlemen, I make an apology for this behavior, because in thus behaving, I am fulfilling a duty. You are, beyond doubt, uninformed of the true character of the person who has to-night won at *écarté* a large sum of money from Lord Glendenning. I will therefore put you upon an expeditious and decisive plan of obtaining this very necessary information. Please to examine, at your leisure, the inner linings of the cuff of his left sleeve, and the several little packages which may be found in the somewhat capacious pockets of his embroidered morning wrapper."

While he spoke, so profound was the stillness that one might have heard a pin drop upon the floor. In ceasing, he departed at once and as abruptly as he had entered. Can I—shall I describe my sensations? Must I say that I felt all the horrors of the damned? Most assuredly I had little time for reflection. Many hands roughly seized me upon the spot, and lights were immediately reproduced. A search ensued. In the lining of my sleeve were found all the court cards essential in *écarté,* and in the pockets of my wrapper, a number of packs, fac-similes of those used at our sittings, with the single exception that mine were of the species called, technically, *arrondées*;[48] the honors[49] being slightly convex at the ends, the lower cards slightly convex at the sides. In this disposition, the dupe who cuts, as customary, at the length of the pack, will invariably find that he cuts his antagonist an honor; while the gambler, cutting at the breadth, will, as certainly, cut nothing for his victim which may count in the records of the game.

Any burst of indignation upon this discovery would have affected me less than the silent contempt, or the sarcastic composure, with which it was received.

"Mr. Wilson," said our host, stooping to remove from beneath his feet an exceedingly luxurious cloak of rare furs, "Mr. Wilson, this is your property." (The weather was cold; and, upon quitting my own room, I had thrown a cloak over my dressing wrapper, putting it off upon reaching the scene of play.) "I presume it is supererogatory[50] to seek here (eyeing the folds of the garment with a bitter smile) for any farther evidence of your skill. Indeed, we have had enough. You will see the necessity, I hope, of quitting Oxford—at all events, of quitting instantly my chambers."

Abased, humbled to the dust as I then was, it is probable that I should have resented this galling language by immediate personal violence, had not my whole attention been at the moment arrested by a fact of the most startling character. The cloak which I had worn was of a rare description of fur; how rare, how extravagantly costly, I shall not venture to say. Its fashion, too, was of my own fantastic invention; for I was fastidious to an absurd degree of coxcombry,[51] in matters of this frivolous nature. When, therefore, Mr. Preston reached me that which he had picked up upon the floor, and near the folding-doors of the apartment, it was with an astonishment nearly bordering upon terror, that I perceived my own already hanging on my arm, (where I had no doubt unwittingly placed it,) and that the one presented me was but its exact counterpart in

every, in even the minutest possible particular. The singular being who had so disastrously exposed me, had been muffled, I remembered, in a cloak; and none had been worn at all by any of the members of our party, with the exception of myself. Retaining some presence of mind, I took the one offered me by Preston; placed it, unnoticed, over my own; left the apartment with a resolute scowl of defiance; and, next morning ere dawn of day, commenced a hurried journey from Oxford to the continent, in a perfect agony of horror and of shame.

I fled in vain. My evil destiny pursued me as if in exultation, and proved, indeed, that the exercise of its mysterious dominion had as yet only begun. Scarcely had I set foot in Paris, ere I had fresh evidence of the detestable interest

48. **arrondées**\a 'rȯn ▲dā\ cards marked, sides rounded, slightly curved outwardly.
49. **honors**, ace, king, queen, jack.
50. **supererogatory**\'sü·pĕ·rĭ ▲rŏ·gə·tō·rē\ unnecessary.
51. **coxcombry**\▲kŏks 'kōm·rē\ vanity, foolish conceit.

taken by this Wilson in my concerns. Years flew, while I experienced no relief. Villain!—at Rome, with how untimely, yet with how spectral an officiousness, stepped he in between me and my ambition! at Vienna, too—at Berlin—and at Moscow! Where, in truth, had I *not* bitter cause to curse him within my heart? From his inscrutable tyranny did I at length flee, panic-stricken, as from a pestilence; and to the very ends of the earth *I fled in vain.*

And again, and again, in secret communion with my own spirit, would I demand the questions "Who is he?—whence came he?—and what are his objects?" But no answer was there found. And now I scrutinized, with a minute scrutiny, the forms, and the methods, and the leading traits of his impertinent supervision. But even here there was very little upon which to base a conjecture. It was noticeable, indeed, that, in no one of the multiplied instances in which he had of late crossed my path, had he so crossed it except to frustrate those schemes, or to disturb those actions, which, if fully carried out, might have resulted in bitter mischief. Poor justification this, in truth, for an authority so imperiously assumed! Poor indemnity for natural rights of self-agency so pertinaciously,[52] so insultingly denied!

I had also been forced to notice that my tormentor, for a very long period of time, (while scrupulously and with miraculous dexterity maintaining his whim of an identity of apparel with myself) had so contrived it, in the execution of his varied interference with my will, that I saw not, at any moment, the features of his face. Be Wilson what he might, *this,* at least, was but the veriest of affectation, or of folly. Could he, for an instant, have supposed that, in my admonisher at Eton—in the destroyer of my honor at Oxford,—in him who thwarted my ambition at Rome, my revenge at Paris, my passionate love at Naples, or what he falsely termed my avarice in Egypt,—that in this, my arch-enemy and evil genius, I could fail to recognize the William Wilson of my school-boy days,—the name-sake, the companion, the rival,—the hated and dreaded rival at Dr.

Bransby's? Impossible!—But let me hasten to the last eventful scene of the drama.

Thus far I had succumbed supinely to this imperious domination. The sentiment of deep awe with which I habitually regarded the elevated character, the majestic wisdom, the apparent omnipresence and omnipotence of Wilson, added to a feeling of even terror, with which certain other traits in his nature and assumptions inspired me, had operated, hitherto, to impress me with an idea of my own utter weakness and helplessness, and to suggest an implicit, although bitterly reluctant submission to his arbitrary will. But, of late days, I had given myself up entirely to wine; and its maddening influence upon my hereditary temper rendered me more and more impatient of control. I began to murmur,—to hesitate,—to resist. And was it only fancy which induced me to believe that, with the increase of my own firmness, that of my tormentor underwent a proportional diminution? Be this as it may, I now began to feel the inspiration of a burning hope, and at length nurtured in my secret thoughts a stern and desperate resolution that I would submit no longer to be enslaved.

It was at Rome, during the Carnival of 18—, that I attended a masquerade in the palazzo[53] of the Neapolitan Duke Di Broglio. I had indulged more freely than usual in the excesses of the wine-table; and now the suffocating atmosphere of the crowded rooms irritated me beyond endurance. The difficulty, too, of forcing my way through the mazes of the company contributed not a little to the ruffling of my temper; for I was anxiously seeking (let me not say with what unworthy motive) the young, the gay, the beautiful wife of the aged and doting Di Broglio. With a too unscrupulous confidence she had previously communicated to me the secret of the costume in which she would be habited, and now, having caught a glimpse of her person, I was hurrying to make my way

---

52. **pertinaciously**\'pur·tə ᴀnā·shəs·lē\ holding firmly to some belief.
53. **palazzo**\pə ᴀlät 'zō\ a large, imposing residence.

into her presence. At this moment I felt a light hand placed upon my shoulder, and that ever-remembered, low, damnable *whisper* within my ear.

In an absolute frenzy of wrath, I turned at once upon him who had thus interrupted me, and seized him violently by the collar. He was attired, as I had expected, in a costume altogether similar to my own; wearing a Spanish cloak of blue velvet, begirt about the waist with a crimson belt sustaining a rapier. A mask of black silk entirely covered his face.

"Scoundrel!" I said, in a voice husky with rage, while every syllable I uttered seemed as new fuel to my fury; "scoundrel! impostor! accursed villain! you shall not—you *shall not* dog me unto death! Follow me, or I stab you where you stand!"—and I broke my way from the ball-room into a small ante-chamber adjoining, dragging him unresistingly with me as I went.

Upon entering, I thrust him furiously from me. He staggered against the wall, while I closed the door with an oath, and commanded him to draw. He hesitated but for an instant; then, with a slight sigh, drew in silence, and put himself upon his defence.

The contest was brief indeed. I was frantic with every species of wild excitement, and felt within my single arm the energy and power of a multitude. In a few seconds I forced him by sheer strength against the wainscoting,[54] and thus, getting him at mercy, plunged my sword, with brute ferocity, repeatedly through and through his bosom.

At that instant some person tried the latch of the door. I hastened to prevent an intrusion, and then immediately returned to my dying antagonist. But what human language can adequately portray *that* astonishment, *that* horror which possessed me at the spectacle then presented to view? The brief moment in which I averted my eyes had been sufficient to produce, apparently, a material change in the arrangements at the upper or farther end of the room. A large mirror,—so at first it seemed to me in my confusion—now stood where none had been perceptible before; and as I stepped up to it in extremity of terror, mine own image, but with features all pale and dabbled in blood, advanced to meet me with a feeble and tottering gait.

Thus it appeared, I say, but was not. It was my antagonist—it was Wilson, who then stood before me in the agonies of his dissolution. His mask and cloak lay, where he had thrown them, upon the floor. Not a thread in all his raiment—not a line in all the marked and singular lineaments of his face which was not, even in the most absolute identity, *mine own!*

It was Wilson; but he spoke no longer in a whisper, and I could have fancied that I myself was speaking while he said:

"You have conquered, and I yield. Yet henceforward art thou also dead—dead to the World, to Heaven, and to Hope! In me didst thou exist—and, in my death, see by this image, which is thine own, how utterly thou hast murdered thyself."

I
"THAT SPECTRE IN MY PATH"

Poe opens his story with a quotation referring to conscience as "That spectre in my path," and he treats that inner force throughout the story as if it were a distinct person totally detached from the person of his hero. In this way Poe emphasizes the fact that people do ordinarily think of their consciences as a force separate from their egos. If it is a spectre in *my* path, it is not *me*. Yet at the same time conscience is very closely related to the ego, and Poe shows this by having Wilson and his "double" look and dress exactly alike. Ultimately he attempts here to examine the nature of human conscience and its relation to the human ego.

II
IMPLICATIONS

Each of the following is a quotation from the story in which William Wilson speaks of his

---

54. **wainscoting**\ˈwān·skə·tĭŋ\ paneling of wood or other material laid on like wood.

"double." Discuss how each shows some aspect of conscience and its relationship to the rest of the personality. In what respects is Wilson's conscience like everyone's conscience and in which respects is it different?

1. . . . there were times when I could not help observing . . . that he mingled with his injuries, his insults, or his contradictions, a certain . . . *affectionateness* of manner.

2. He appeared to be destitute alike of the ambition which urged and of the passionate energy of mind which enabled me to excel.

3. It is difficult . . . to describe my real feelings toward him. They formed a motley and heterogeneous admixture;—some petulant animosity, which was not yet hatred, some esteem, more respect, much fear, with a world of uneasy curiosity.

4. . . . my rival had a weakness in the faucial or guttural organs, which precluded him from raising his voice at any time *above a very low whisper.*

5. . . . I can recall no occasion when the suggestions of my rival were on the side of those errors or follies so usual to his immature age and seeming inexperience; . . . his moral sense . . . was far keener than my own.

6. From his inscrutable tyranny did I at length flee, panic-stricken, as from a pestilence; and to the very ends of the earth *I fled in vain.*

7. It was noticeable, indeed, that, in no one of the multiplied instances in which he had of late crossed my path, had he so crossed it except to frustrate those schemes, or to disturb those actions, which, if fully carried out, might have resulted in bitter mischief.

III
TECHNIQUES

Conflict

Short stories have a *plot*. The simplest definition of the term "plot" is *action*. Now a narrative of everything that happened to one from the time he arose to the time he went to bed would surely involve some action, but chances are that it would not be the same sort of action that a short story has. The fact is that the action in a short story is centered about a *conflict,* a struggle between two opposed forces.

Because the plot of a short story is based upon conflict, it is best to define "plot" not simply as action, but rather as *structured* or *patterned* action. Clearly, if the person writing the narrative of a day in his life had lived a typical day, his account would lack two of the important elements of a plot: a main conflict and a single point at which it reaches its climax.

A short story may have a number of conflicts; but if the story is to have unity, there must be one main conflict to which the others are subordinated.

Consider Poe's story. The main conflict is certainly the one between William Wilson and his "double," but there is also a minor conflict in the story between Wilson and Glendenning, the Oxford student. Here there is no question of which is the major conflict, because the first extends over the entire length of the story while the second is relatively brief; also, the first absorbs the second.

Climax

Short stories also contain a *central climax,* the moment or episode in which the action reaches its peak. This moment or episode also leads to or brings on the final resolution of the conflict. The main conflict can usually be located if you know the central climax, and vice versa.

The moment in this story in which the action reaches its peak is the moment when Wilson kills his "double." Or you might call it the episode in which the fight takes place. Note that this moment or episode then brings on the final resolution.

Moment of Illumination

The climax of a story is related to its plot; the moment of illumination is related to its meaning or theme. It may be defined as the moment in which the full meaning of the story becomes clear. This moment may come at the climax, but it often occurs after the climax. In "William Wilson," for example, the moment of illumination occurs at the end of the story when we learn that it is his own conscience that Wilson has killed.

IV
WORDS

A few archaic words still occur in certain phrases, such as "much ado," "albeit," "methinks," "in good stead," "yesteryear." Do you find any other examples in "William Wilson"?

In early America the Puritans were intensely concerned
with the struggle between good and evil fought within the heart of man. They believed
that human nature was essentially evil and that man could, therefore,
be saved only through God's grace and mercy, not through his own deeds.
Since God was not likely to save a "sinner," however, the Puritans developed
and subscribed to a strict moral code and became men of strong conscience.
Following the dictates of this strong conscience was no easy matter,
especially as they became involved in profit-making business enterprises. But good
and evil were strongly and clearly distinguished for them, and there was thus
no question about what was the right thing to do—the only question was
whether or not one had the courage to follow the proper path.

You Can't Do That

JOHN P. MARQUAND

Since the year 1806 a cloak of red-and-yellow feathers has hung in the hallway of the March house on the Ridge, with a helmet made from the same plumage suspended above it. These two articles have always held the same position on the wall, except for such times as they have been put away in camphor to protect them from the moths. The cloak was brought there by John March and indicates very accurately the first venture of the March ships in the fur-and-sandalwood[1] trade with China. It was hung there by John March when he returned as supercargo[2] on the brig *Polly*, Moses March, owner, and Elihu Griggs, master. A single glance at that cloak in the shady, spacious hallway of that square Federalist house is startling to anyone who is even remotely familiar with the curiosities of the South Seas.

It hangs there, an alien object, and yet, through association, somehow strangely suitable to a house like the old March house in a New England seaport town. Granted that its presence there is known to many scholars, familiarity cannot avert a shock of surprise at a

sight of that vivid garment, for it is one of the most beautiful objects ever conceived by the mind or executed by the hand of man. It is strange, too, to realize that if that cloak and the helmet above it were sold today, their price would probably equal the March profits in their precarious trade of another century. It is a long, fine cloak—and the Marches have always been careful of everything they have laid their hands on—one of the best of the hundred-and-some-odd feather garments which are known to be extant today, and there will never be another made. The o-o[3] which supplied those yellow feathers, only one beneath each wing, a shy bird which once fluttered through the crimson-blossomed ohia and the tree-fern forests of the Hawaiian mountains, is virtually extinct, and the bird that wore the red plumage is in hardly a better case. He is vanishing from the face of this earth like the genial race whose ancestors collected and attached those feathers

---

1. **sandalwood,** yellowish wood used for ornamental carving and cabinet work.
2. **supercargo,** an officer or person on a merchant ship who manages commercial concerns of the voyage.
3. **o-o**\ō·ō\colorful Hawaiian bird whose plumage was used to make feather cloaks.

to their delicate base of fiber netting in a manner so admired by Captain Cook.[4] Granted that the labor which went into the making of that garment is beyond all accurate calculation, the result was worth it. The reds and yellows are nearly as vivid as when the coat was new. They glisten there in the hallway, jewel-like, with a depth of luster and lacy velvet texture that is more vital than inanimate. On an evening when the lights are lit, John March's cloak glows like flame and there is an element of awe in its splendor.

This is not odd, for it was intended to indicate greatness. The red lozenge pattern[5] upon the yellow marks it as belonging not alone to one of the *alii*[6] but to a Hawaiian chief of a royal lineage that was very near to kingship. Its size and the amount of yellow is a sufficient indication of its former owner's greatness. If the shadow of a commoner were to touch the shadow of the man who wore it, that commoner would suffer death, for the man who wore it was sublimated in the complicated feudal ritual of his islands into a being more than human. The feather *kahili*[7] was carried behind him; an attendant bore his calabash[8] of koa[9] wood to preserve his spittle, his nail parings, and his fallen hair, so that they might not fall into the hands of enemies whose kahunas, or witch doctors, might use them in fatal incantations. When the man who wore that cloak walked abroad, the populace assumed a prone position on pain of death. Some trace of the majesty of its first owner's presence still seems to linger about that feather cloak, incongruously, in a New England town.

The cloak was owned by the chieftain Kualai, as his name is spelled, probably incorrectly, in the March letter books and the log of the brig *Polly*, since there were no missionaries then to bring order to the Hawaiian phonetics—no missionaries, no mosquitoes, no red ants to kill the kou trees, no colds, and no disease. Kualai ruled his share of the Kona coast[10] on what is now known as the Big Island, under the protection of the great king Kamehameha[11] in the days when John March was young. In Kualai's youth he had been one of the king's best warriors; in the war exercises he could evade six spears thrown at him simultaneously from varying directions; and he could trace his descent from one of the gods who had sailed with his attendants from the south.

Kualai gave his cloak and helmet to young John March when the *Polly* anchored in a bay on the Kona coast to exchange Yankee notions for sandalwood before proceeding to Canton.[12] There is no doubt that John March valued the gift, for it is mentioned in his will. The clause reads:

"Item, the Feather Cloak that was given me by my friend Kualai on my first voyage to the Sandwich Islands,[13] and the feather hat that goes with it, I leave to my daughter, Polly March, and I ask her to guard it carefully."

John March sailed other seas before he died and brought back other curious things, but there is every reason why the cloak should have had a value to him which was more than intrinsic; and his descendants have never sold that cloak because of the reason why it was given him, a reason that is closely connected with honor and integrity. John March was a shrewd trader, but he was an honest man.

In the New England harbor town which was the home port for the March ships, a voyage around the world was not an unusual matter when John March was young. As long as John

---

4. **Captain Cook** (1728–1779), English mariner and explorer; visited Hawaii where he was killed in an argument over a stolen boat.
5. **lozenge pattern**\ˈlŏz·ənj\ diamond-shaped pattern.
6. **alii**\a ˈlē ˈē\ a Polynesian chief or king.
7. **kahili**\kä ˈhē·lē\ a long pole used as a ceremonial emblem of authority in Hawaii.
8. **calabash**\ˈkă·lə·băsh\ a utensil, such as a dipper, bowl.
9. **koa**\ˈkō·ə\ fine-grained red wood.
10. **Kona coast**\ˈkō·nä\ district of northern Hawaii.
11. **Kamehameha**\ka ˈmä·ha ˈmä·ha\king 1795–1819, who controlled Northern Hawaii, conquered the other islands, united them, and organized the government; he visited Captain Cook's ships.
12. **Canton**\kăn ˈtŏn\, officially **Kwangdiou**\ˈkwɔŋ ˈjō\ important city and seaport of South China.
13. **Sandwich Islands**, Hawaiian islands named Sandwich Islands by Captain Cook, 1778.

March could remember, his town had been a port of travelers, although a part of it was cast in the narrow mold of puritanical tradition. When John March was young, no music was allowed in the white church with the rooster on its spire where merchants and clerks and shipwrights and returned mariners listened for three hours each Sunday to discourses on original sin. Not even the note of a pipe was allowed, to indicate the pitch for the singing of the psalms, because such a concession was considered an encouragement to the idolatrous errors of papacy. Yet in such surroundings of a Sunday one could see from the square box of the March pew a distinctly cosmopolitan congregation, for the world across the seas was closer to the town in those days than it has ever been since. Nearly every man and boy and most of the women in the pews and the Reverend Thomas himself, who thundered forth his nasal sermon while the sands ran from his hourglass on the pulpit, knew their geography as well as they knew the intricacies of their catechism. They could talk familiarly of the Baltic ports and of St. Eustatius[14] and St. Kitts.[15] There were plenty who knew the ivory factories and the slave pens on the Grain Coast[16] and the anchorages along Fernando Po.[17] There were plenty who had seen the sand upon the lead from soundings off Madagascar.[18] The weather off Cape Horn was common talk. A restless, burning energy that made the town a lively place, except on Saturday nights and Sunday, had driven others to the factories at Canton. The townspeople were familiar with nearly every world port where money could be gained, for the town lived from shipping. One had to go, of necessity, a long way to make money then, what with European wars and privateers and orders in council and blockades. It was a time for gambling with lives and ships, a time of huge losses and huge gains, and no one could judge which until the ships came in.

It seemed hardly more than a piece of everyday business to John March when his father called him into the square parlor of the March house on the Ridge. It was an evening in April; a bright, fresh fire was burning in the parlor, and the candles were lighted on the mahogany table in the center of the room. Moses March and a man whom John March had never seen before were seated somewhat stiffly by the table with a punch bowl between them. When John March saw the punch, he knew that they were discussing important business, for his father, particularly in his later years, was abstemious with liquor. Moses March had not changed much since John March could remember him. His brown hair, done in a queue,[19] was heavily streaked with gray, and the shrewd lines around his eyes and mouth were deeper and more pronounced. There was an added stoop to his lanky shoulders, but his eyes were as bright as ever and his voice was vibrant, without any quaver of age.

"John," said Moses March, nodding at his guest, "this here is Captain Griggs from Boston. Captain Griggs, he's been sailing for the Perkinses in the fur trade."

In many ways it seemed to John March that Captain Griggs was a younger replica of his father. The captain had the same bony facial contours and the same slouch to his shoulders. When he spoke he had the same flat voice, but his eyes were different—more mobile and less steady. The captain raised a hand before his tight-lipped mouth and coughed, then he rose from his chair with a creaking of his joints, a tall, somber man who might have been a deacon in a church. His eyes met John's and looked away toward some invisible object on the floor, then darted back and looked away again.

---

14. **St. Eustatius**\\'sänt·ū ᵃstā·shĭ·us\\ small island in West Indies.
15. **St. Kitts** or **Saint Christopher,** island of east West Indies. Discovered by Columbus 1493.
16. **Grain Coast,** section of coast of Upper Guinea, West Africa.
17. **Fernando Po,** Spanish island off the west coast of Africa.
18. **Madagascar**\\ᵃmă·də 'găs·kĕr\\ island in the Indian Ocean off east coast of South Africa.
19. **queue**\\kyū\\plait of hair worn hanging from the back of the head.

"Pleased to meet you," he said. . . . "I compliment you, Mr. March; he's handy looking, that's a fact."

"He's kind of peaked," said Moses March, "but John here's almighty quick at figures."

There was a silence. Captain Griggs ladled himself a fresh tumbler of punch, drank it at a gulp, and said, "He needs to be. It pays to be sharp, don't it, Mr. March?"

Moses March smiled in faint embarrassment. He had never been able to acquire a manner with his captains, nor to stop undue familiarity.

"Yes," he said, "I guess so . . . John, Captain Griggs is taking out the *Polly*. You're sailing with him, supercargo."

John March looked at Captain Griggs again. The captain was staring intently at a lemon peel in the bottom of his glass. The news was entirely unexpected.

"Where to, Father?" he asked.

"Where you haven't been, Son," said Moses March, "but you've heard the talk, I guess. Up along the Northwest Coast for sea otter, trading with the savages, then to these new islands you've heard Enoch Mayo talk about, to put aboard sandalwood, then the whole cargo sold at Canton for tea. The *Polly*, she's sailing the end of the month. You'll start in working over the cargo tomorrow. Your mother, she'll get your things packed."

John March nodded without speaking, and he showed no emotion. It was not the first time that his father had surprised him, because it was one of his father's maxims never to talk about what he proposed to do until he was ready. His father was always reaching for something new; his mind was always working. Probably he had been pondering over the matter all winter, and now, as though he were speaking about arrangements for hauling firewood, he was making plans to send one of his vessels where a March ship had never gone before.

It was strange to think that while he sat there, a homely, uncouth man, his mind could reach around the world and back. His life had never seemed so plain or matter-of-fact. The

order of the March house, each piece of furniture exactly in its place, had never seemed so perfect as when he spoke of that voyage. That literal order of the letter books and the columns in the ledger were all a part of the business. There was no expression of doubt, because they all knew by then that a ship could go wherever there was water.

Captain Griggs ladled himself another tumbler of punch and blew his nose on a long blue handkerchief which seemed to have imparted some of its own color to his nose. Not having been asked to sit down, John March stood examining his new captain, comparing him with other seafaring men whom he had met. The captain was evidently a heavy and competent drinker and no doubt a capable master, but behind his lantern jaws and his high, narrow forehead there were hidden convolutions of character beyond John March's grasp. He only knew that by the time the voyage ended he would know the captain like a book. At the present time all John March could do was to stand staring at the pictures of his own imagination, striving to conjure up the sights which he and Captain Griggs would see. Captain Griggs was staring at him moodily across the brim of his glass.

"He'll do. He'll fill out," he said. "He'll be aft with the mate and me, of course. Does he know navigation, sir?"

"Yes," said Moses March; "he ain't a fool, but I hadn't aimed to make him a sailor. He'll handle this business ashore when I get through."

Captain Griggs nodded in a melancholy way. "I hope he ain't squeamish," he said. "He'll see some rough sights, like as not. We have a saying on the coast: 'You hang your conscience on the Horn.'"

"Yes," said Moses March, "I've heard it, but you, Captain, I'd like for you to keep your conscience on your ship."

"God bless you, sir," Captain Griggs said quickly, "no owner's ever complained of me. I'm always in my owner's interest. It's just dealing with these here savages, I mean. They've killed crews on the coast and they're murdering thieves on the islands." He rose stiffly. "You'll be satisfied, Mr. March. You'll be pleased as punch with me. There ain't no tricks in the trade that I don't know thereabouts. Four four-pounders and a bow chaser will be enough, and the grapeshot and plenty of small arms, and thanking you. I'll pick my own mate, and now I'll be under way, and I'll wish you a very good evening, and you, mister." He nodded to John March.

When the captain was gone, Moses March called to John March again.

"John," he said, "set down. You've been to the Baltic; you've been to the Indies; and I'd proposed keeping you ashore, but I want for you to learn this trade when it's still new." Moses March paused and rubbed his jaw. "I hear tell there's money in it, and we're going where there's money."

"Yes sir," said John March.

"It seems," his father continued, staring at the fire, "as how these savages put aboard furs, and these other savages put aboard sandal-wood, for nothing more than notions and novelties in trading goods. Well, I got 'em for you; you and Griggs can get the rest. He'll try hard. He has his money and more than the usual prerequisites."

"Yes sir," said John March.

"And sandalwood and furs are worth a mint of money in Canton."

"Yes sir," said John March.

"You know about it, do you?"

"Yes sir," said John March; "I've heard 'em talking."

His father smiled. "That's right," he said, "listen to 'em talk, but keep your own mouth shut. Have you anything to say?"

John March thought a moment. He had a number of things to say, but he kept them to himself. "No," he said. "I can obey orders, I guess. You know what you're doing, I guess, Father."

Moses March stroked his chin slowly, and then he asked a sudden question: "How did you like Griggs?"

"He looks too sharp to me," John March said, "but I guess we'll get along."

"Yes," said Moses March, "he's sharp, but maybe that's all right. But mind you watch him, John. I'm sharp, but I guess I'm honest. Mind you watch him."

Even when he was three thousand miles away from town and farther than that by water, something of the town was always with him. The *Polly* was a part of the town because she had been built in the yards by the river, a good tight brig of two hundred and fifty tons. The crew was a part of the town, because most of the men before the mast had been born within its limits. The sense of the nearness of things he knew gave John March a certain peace when everything else was strange. The emptiness of the Pacific coast, the incredible size of its fir trees, the frowning menace of its mountains, would have oppressed him if it had not been for that sense of home. As it was, everyone stood together and behaved, in order to keep reputations intact when they got home.

John March was used to work. He was satisfactory to Captain Griggs, and he was treated well because he was the owner's son. Once they began bartering for furs off the Northwest Coast, there was no doubt that the captain knew his business, and John March admired in silence the way the captain worked. Martin Sprague, the mate, knew his business, too, in caring for the ship. The men were armed; there was a sharp lookout day and night. The four-pounders[20] were loaded with grapeshot,[21] and the matches were kept burning. Only a definite number of the painted dugout canoes of the Indians were allowed alongside, and only a certain number of savages were permitted on deck to trade. There were very few ships off the coast that year, so that the selection of pelts was particularly fine. Sea-otter pelts came aboard in great quantity in exchange for powder, shot, nails, muskets, beads, and blankets.

---

20. **fourpounders,** cannons.
21. **grapeshot,** a cluster of small iron balls fired to disperse the enemy.

It was a pretty sight to see the captain read faces and weigh the desire to sell. He seemed to have an intuitive sense of when to bargain and when to buy immediately.

"If there's any trade goods left after the islands," he said, "we'll stand back here again and use 'em up. It's a pity to see this fine fur wasting here. I wish we had six ships."

John March could feel the excitement as small goods turned suddenly into a valuable cargo. It was better than any figuring in the countinghouse to see the fur pelts come aboard and to estimate their probable value in a Chinese port.

"Yes, sir," said Captain Griggs, "it seems a pity to haul off and leave this. We ought to buy the villages out and to the devil with the islands and the wood."

They were in the cabin at the time, the captain and Sprague, the mate, a heavy muscular man, and John March, a thin blond boy.

"Mr. Sprague," said the captain, "pass the rum. What do you think, mister? Shall we do all the trading here and simply water at the islands?"

Martin Sprague rubbed the palm of his left hand over the knuckles of his right. "I never seen trading so easy," he said. "Yes sir, I think I should."

Then John March spoke up; it was the first time on the voyage that he'd made a positive statement. "We can't," he said.

Captain Griggs set down his glass and scowled. "Young man," he said, "I'm surprised at you. You ought to know better. You do know better. You've behaved yourself fine up till now, my boy. You've done your duty, and more, and I shall be pleased to report favorably to your father if you continue, but there's two things for you to get inside your head. The first is, you were sent here to learn to trade. You don't know this business, and don't you forget it. The second is, I'm captain, and this brig goes where I tell it. I'm sorry to be obliged to tell you straight."

John March did not shift his position at the table. He knew that he was young and that he was green. He had interrupted solely from a conscientious sense inherited from his race. It had come over him that he was a representative of the March family and of the March cargo. Now that the eyes of the older men were upon him, he found himself stammering, because he was shy in those days, but his hesitation only made him the more determined to speak out.

"Captain," he said, "I understand what you say. This is your ship, of course, but you are under owner's orders, just as I am. A portion of these trade goods was allotted for furs and the rest for sandalwood. The owner's orders are to stop and trade at the Sandwich Islands. There may be more profit here, but we are to establish relations there. We may send out another ship."

Captain Griggs leaned half across the table. "Young man," he inquired, "are you insinuating I'm not looking after owner's interests? Because if you are, I will not tolerate it. I'm thinking of my owner all the time, and a sight better than you are, maybe. We'll make for the islands tomorrow, and there's an end to that, but if there's any trade goods left when we're through there, why, then, with your kind permission, we'll come back here. I hope that satisfies you."

"Yes," said John March, "it does, and I ask your pardon, Captain."

Mr. Sprague rose. "I must be up with the watch," he said, "if you'll excuse me, sir. . . . Will you come with me, Mr. March?"

It was a fine night on deck, clear, with bright stars and a faint, quivering circle of the northern lights. The night was cool, without a breath of wind. The ship, with her own small lights, was like an insignificant fragment of a distant world anchored there in space. The mate took out his pipe and tinderbox.[22] There was a flash of spark as he expertly hit the flint against the steel, and then the tinder glowed.

"Johnny March," he said, "I've kind of got to like you. Now you listen to what I say. This kind of spark's all right, but not the kind that you were striking in the cabin. You leave the

---

22. **tinderbox,** a metal box containing inflammable material (tinder), flint, and steel for starting a fire.

old man be. He's as good a master as there is, and he's honest with the owners, and that's all we have to care for. I've sailed with Griggs before. I don't need to tell you that a master's king aboard his ship, and you know it makes 'em queer. I've never seen a skipper yet who liked to be crossed. You better leave him be."

"Yes sir," said John March.

"And listen, Johnny," the mate said, "the islands are a fine place. You'll like the islands. The islands are like heaven, pretty near. The captain will take you ashore, of course, to make the bargain. You'll see plenty of funny sights, but keep your mouth shut, Johnny, except to say 'Yes sir' to the captain. We've got a long way yet to go."

"Yes sir," said John March.

"That's right," said Sprague, "that's right. I like a tight-lipped boy."

It was said in the forecastle of the *Polly*, just as it was said aft, that Johnny March was taciturn. As a supercargo he had no fixed duties in working the ship, and few knew much about him except that he was March's son. They only saw him as a thin, brown-faced, gray-eyed boy with yellow hair who made no trouble or complaint. They did not know the impression which strange sights made upon him, because he was studiously silent on that voyage to the islands, hardly ever venturing a remark, only answering courteously when addressed. No one on the *Polly* knew—and perhaps it was just as well—that his thoughts were poetic, because there was no room for poetry on a Yankee trading brig.

The evening before they sighted land, he had a sense of the land's nearness. The banks of clouds off the port bow as the sun went down were pink and gold, and were more like land clouds than sea clouds. The *Polly* was moving in the steady breath of the trades, and the setting sun struck the bellying sails forward, making their colors soft and golden. The only sounds were the creaking of wood, the straining of ropes, and the splash of waves on the bow. He had seen many evenings like that one,

but subtly this was different. There was a mystery in the warmth of the air, an intangible unreality in the cloud banks. Captain Griggs came and stood beside him, smelling strongly of rum.

"Mr. Sprague," he said, "you've got everything locked up, I hope. Tomorrow we'll be overrun by black thieves and their women. Clew[23] up the courses and continue under topsails. Set a watch up in the crosstree and keep an eye out for breakers. We must not get in too close tonight. . . . And, Mr. March—"

"Yes sir," said John.

"You and I will go ashore."

"Yes sir," said Johnny March, and then he cleared his throat: "How will we speak to them, sir?"

"You'll soon learn, boy," said Captain Griggs. "You've got a lot to learn. These islands have kings, or chiefs, and the chiefs will have someone who can speak trading English. The sandalwood is up in the mountains. It will be the property of the king, or chief. We will agree to purchase so many piculs,[24] and he'll send his people to cut it. The chief will come aboard to see our goods, and we will make a bargain for the cargo, payable when the wood is safe aboard, you understand. There's no need to make our crew work when the chief will make his people load it. The islanders are handy men on ships. We'll go to see the chief, and we'll make the chief a present. Break out that clock that strikes the hour, and two cutlasses. That will be enough, and maybe"—Captain Griggs paused and hesitated—"three yards of bright print calico; he ought to like it—paper's all they dress in."

"Yes sir," said Johnny March. "Did you say that they dressed in paper?"

The hard lines of the captain's face wrinkled into an indulgent smile.

"Young man," he said, "it's a fact they dress in paper, when they dress at all, which isn't

---

23. **clew**\klū\ haul a sail up to mast by a system of ropes attached to corners.
24. **piculs**\pĭ▲kŭlz\ measure of weight used in China and Southeast Asia; unit equal to approximately 133 pounds.

often. The women, they pound it out of the bark of a tree. They have nothing else on the islands, or almost nothing. Time was when they'd sell a pig for three tenpenny nails. Will you come below for a glass of rum?"

"No, thank you, sir," said Johnny March. "I'll stay on deck—that is, if you don't mind."

The sun had dipped out of sight behind a bank of clouds, and then suddenly the light was gone. Without a prelude of dusk, the dark came over them like a warm black garment. It seemed only a second before that the sky had been red and gold. Then, in another second, the sky was a void of darkness, filled with the trade wind and with stars. He stood for a while listening to the wind singing through the ropes, and then he went below. It was still dark when John March was awakened by a long-drawn-out call and by Mr. Sprague's voice shouting, "Where away?" and he knew that they had come in sight of land. Once he was up on deck, the topsails were slatting sleepily, and off the starboard bow there was a glow in the sky like fire.

"We've hit it to a second, sir," the mate was saying to Captain Griggs. "Yonder's the volcano; we're in the lee of the mountains."

Captain Griggs was a shadow in the starlight. It was too dark to see his face, but his voice was satisfied. "A pretty piece of navigating," he said, "if I do say so, mister. There'll be an inshore breeze by dawn, and then we'll make the bay." He sniffed the air. "We can't be far from land," he said, "but there's no use heaving lead. It shelves off here as deep as hell. There'll be an inshore breeze with dawn."

"Is that a light yonder, sir?" asked Johnny March.

Near the horizon there was a twinkling, glimmering point.

"Your eyesight's good," the captain said. "Yes, that will be a fire. We're close to land."

The dawn came as suddenly as the dark, in a swift rush of light, as though a hand had snatched away a veil, and John March saw the land. It was a solemn sight to see land which seemed to have risen out of nowhere. Off the

bows of the *Polly* was a mountain, black and green, that rose in a gradual slope up into snow and clouds. The coast was dark from volcanic rock which made ugly black gashes between green forests. Close to the water's edge there was a fringe of palms and beeches between black lava headlands. The sea was smooth and calm and streaked with violet; the air was as soft as the air of spring at home and was subtly laden with the smells of land. All the colors were soft in a faint, early-morning haze. The black rocks merged into reds and purples. The greens of the upland forest blended subtly from shades of silver to emerald, and Captain Griggs was right—a soft breeze was filling the sails, moving the *Polly* gently along the coast.

"That's where the sandalwood comes from," Mr. Sprague was saying, "up yonder in the mountains. The coast hereabouts is the favorite place of the kings. Do you see the stone walls and the yellow thatch of the houses of the villages? The chiefs own straight from the tops of the mountains to the sea. How do you like it, son?"

The question made John March tongue-tied. "I think it's very handsome, sir," he said, "a very pleasant island."

The *Polly* was moving under topsails into a small bay. It opened out before them, a smooth amphitheater of water, surrounded by high cliffs. "Yonder's where the kings are buried," the mate said. "They scrape the flesh off their bones and tie them up in paper cloth and put them there in caves with their canoes."

At the head of the bay John March could see a beach fringed with tall palm trees, the leaves of which moved idly in the breeze, and he could see the thatch of houses beneath them. There was a dark crowd of people on the beach, pushing canoes into the water, log dugouts, balanced by an outrigger and manned by naked paddlers. Captain Griggs was wearing clean linen and a black broadcloth coat, although the day was hot.

"Mister," he said, "we'll anchor. Let go falls and clew up lower topsails and order the stern boat cleared."

By the time the anchor struck the water, the *Polly* was surrounded by canoes and the water was full of swimmers who were pulling themselves up the anchor chain, smiling and laughing; men and women as beautiful as statues, their straight dark hair glistening with the water. Captain Griggs stared at his visitors sourly from the quarterdeck.

"They've got the minds of children," he said. "The chief's man should be here. Look at those shameless hussies, will you? There's no decency on these islands. They don't care for decency; no, they don't care."

As Captain Griggs finished speaking, a native pushed his way through the crowd at the waist and walked aft; evidently a man of importance, because the crowd gave way respectfully. He wore a pair of sailor's castoff trousers, and his skin was lighter than the others'. His voice rose above the babel of strange words in English.

"Mr. Captain," he called out, "I am Kualai's man."

"Who's he?" asked Captain Griggs. "The chief?"

The other nodded, bobbing his head up and down, still smiling. "Yes," he said, "yes, yes. And he sends me because I speak English good. I've been a sailor on a Boston boat. I speak English very good. Kualai sends me to say *aloha*. He is glad to see you. He asks you will you trade for wood?"

"Yes," said Captain Griggs, "we're here for wood. What's your name?"

"Moku," said the native. "Billy Adams Moku. Kualai ask what name."

The captain nodded condescendingly. "Captain Griggs," he said, "brig *Polly*. Moses March, owner. We're carrying very fine calicoes, ironware, tinware, lead and copper, and even a few muskets. Has your chief got wood?" Moku nodded. "The wood is coming down. Kualai, he will see you." He pointed to a laden canoe. "Kualai sends you food."

Captain Griggs looked at the canoe carefully as it drew alongside. "Very good," he said. "When will he see me?"

"Now," said Moku. "He waits on the shore."

"Mister," the captain called, "have the stern boat lowered. Mr. March and I will go ashore, and, Mr. March, give that man a pocketknife and bring along the presents."

The dark sand of the beach at the head of the bay seemed insecure under John March's feet, since he had been so long on the water. In the sunshine like a warm June day at home, every sight and sound was new. The crowd of natives standing on the beach drew back from them shyly and smiled, but their tongues kept chattering busily; commenting, probably, on the way these strangers looked. The chief's man walked first, then Captain Griggs, nonchalant and cool, and then John March behind him. They walked along a path beneath a grove of coconut palms and beneath large broad-leafed trees such as he had never seen. They were threading their way through a settlement of houses made of dried grass, past small gardens enclosed between walls of black volcanic rock. His memory of that day always brought back living green against dark rock, and dark smiling faces and red hibiscus flowers. In his memory of the place a soft breeze was always blowing and there was always a strange dry rattle from the leaves of the coconut palms. There was a group of larger houses not far back from the beach which evidently belonged to men of importance. Natives were busying themselves about a fire in a pit; women and children were staring from open doorways. There was an open pavilion near the center of this group of buildings, and the chief's man led them toward it. Seated in a Cantonese armchair under the pavilion was one of the largest men that John March had ever seen. He was middle-aged, and so corpulent that the chair seemed to creak beneath his weight. A single look at his face was enough to indicate that he was the ruler, Kualai, of whom the man had spoken. The face was set in benign lines that could only have come upon it through suave and complete authority. It was all that was necessary to indicate his rank, but he also had the exterior show of office. He was wearing a yellow-and-red cloak of feathers, dazzlingly bright, which fell below his waist, and an attendant stood behind him holding a large stick which bore a tuft of colored feathers on the end. Moku stopped dead still at the entrance of the pavilion, and the great man rose from his chair and stepped slowly forward, gracefully, in spite of his heavy paunch. It was plain that he had seen other white men and knew something of their manners, because he smiled graciously and held out his right hand. At the same time he spoke melodiously in a language that was all vowels, so that his words sounded like rippling water.

"What's he saying?" asked Captain Griggs.

"Kualai," Moku translated, "he say he's, oh, very glad to see you."

"Well, I guess we're glad to see him too," said Captain Griggs as he shook hands. Then John March saw that Kualai was looking at him.

"He wants to know," said Moku, "who is the other man?"

"Tell him he's the son of the man who owns the vessel," said Captain Griggs.

"He wants to know," said Moku, "is he a chief's son?"

"Tell him yes," said Captain Griggs.

"He would like," said Moku, "to feel his hair. He would like to know if it is real."

"Take off your hat," said Captain Griggs, "and let him feel your hair. Don't be afraid of him. He won't hurt you."

"All right," said Johnny March. He felt very much like a child as he walked toward Kualai, for the man, now that he was standing, must have been close to seven feet in height. His skin was glistening with coconut oil. He was stretching out his arm. He touched Johnny March's hair gently and then he pulled it softly. Johnny March looked at him and smiled, and Kualai smiled back.

"Break out the presents," said Captain Griggs, "bow to him and put 'em on the ground."

Kualai's face lighted up at the sight of the clock when John March held it toward him. It was evident that he had never seen such a mechanism—a battered ship's chronometer

whose useful days were over. He touched it gingerly and imitated its sound.

"Tick-tick," he said, and John March nodded and repeated after him, "Tick-tick." That interchange of words always seemed to him ridiculous, but somehow there was an exchange of thought with the words that made them friends.

"He asks you to stay and eat," said Moku. "He will come on the ship tomorrow and see the goods, and he asks the young man to stay with him until the trade is over, to sleep inside his house."

Captain Griggs muttered something beneath his breath, and then he said, "March, you'd better stay."

"Yes, sir," said John March, "I'd be very glad to stay." He turned to Moku. "Tell him I'll be glad."

Then Moku spoke again: "Kualai says he will trade with the young man."

"All right," said Captain Griggs, "as long as I'm there too. And tell him"—Captain Griggs's eyes shifted toward the bay and back—"you tell him I want the wood measured on the beach and put aboard by his people. Tell him my men are tired." And then he drew a bottle of rum from his pocket and added plaintively: "Ain't we had enough of this? Let's everybody have a drink, and bring on the dancing girls." Some half perceptible change in Captain Griggs's voice made John March turn to watch him. The captain's face was bleak and impassive, but his eyes were shifting from point to point, from the chief to John March, then away to the matting on the ground, then to the houses of the settlement. John March knew him well enough by then to know that the captain was turning over in his mind some thought which he wished entirely to conceal.

"Ah," he said suddenly, "here comes some wood," and he nodded toward a path which led upward to the mountains.

A dozen men and women were staggering down the path in single file, each bearing a burden of long sticks, and John March knew from hearsay that these were the chief's people who had been sent to the upland forests where the sandalwood grew. The chief called out an order, which Moku ran to obey, and a few moments later a pile of the sandalwood lay on the matting before his chair, a heap of sticks which varied in size from a few inches to a foot in diameter. The bark had been stripped off, leaving a heavy wood of deep yellow which verged on orange. Captain Griggs ripped out his clasp knife, whittled at the sticks, and sniffed the shavings.

"It ain't bad," he said; "in fact, it's prime."

He was right that the wood was fine, since sandalwood was plentiful in the islands then, when the trade was new, and John March did not suspect that he would live to see the time when hardly a stick would be left standing on the entire island group. Captain Griggs stood there, staring at the pile of wood, apparently lost in thought.

"Tell him we'll pay him well for it," he said, and his voice was soft and almost kindly, "once he lands it on the deck."

But all the while John March was sure that Captain Griggs was concealing some other thought.

It took nearly two weeks to collect the wood and measure it, a space of time which moved in a peculiar series of days and nights, but it was strange to John March how soon the life there grew familiar. Though he could hardly understand a word which was spoken, though nearly every sight and sound in those two weeks was new, he became aware immediately of certain human values. Kualai, in his way, was a cultivated man of gentle breeding, who had developed his own taste for the arts, and qualities of understanding which were the same on that isolated island as they were elsewhere. He would sit for hours of an evening watching interpretive dances and listening to his minstrels sing of the exploits of his ancestors. He had a good eye for patterns in the tapa cloth, and a nice skill in various games of chance, which he played daily with his choice companions, but, above all, he had a sense of hospitality. He lost no occasion to make John

March feel politely that he was a welcome guest. He took him fishing in his war canoe; he took him to the caves and the lava rocks; he took him to watch the young men perform feats of strength; he was even careful that John March's privacy should not be disturbed unduly. When he came aboard the *Polly*, he kept John March beside him. He was greatly pleased with the calico and nails and lead and copper in the trading cargo, but he went through the intricacies of the bargain in a detached way, like a gentleman. In those days trading was easy on the islands, before the chiefs were glutted with material possessions.

"He say he want you to be happy," Moku said the last time Kualai came aboard; "he want you to come again."

"Tell him we're happy," said Captain Griggs. "He understands when all the wood's aboard that we'll give out the goods."

Moku nodded. "He understands," he said; "he knows you're good men."

Captain Griggs coughed slightly. "I shall want Mr. March back with me," he said, "tomorrow morning. . . . Mr. March, you come here; I want to speak with you in the cabin."

It occurred to John March, when they were in the cabin, that it was the first time since they had been on the islands that he and Captain Griggs had been alone. Captain Griggs rubbed his long hands together and poured himself a glass of rum.

"Young man," he said, "you've done fine. You've kept that old heathen happy, and that's all we needed—to keep him happy—and now we're all finished shipshape. We'll get the wood stowed tonight"—Captain Griggs smiled happily—"and tomorrow they can come and take off their goods, but I want you aboard first, understand?"

"Yes, sir," said John March, "but there's one thing I don't see. I don't see why you haven't put the goods ashore before this, sir."

Captain Griggs poured himself a second tumbler of rum.

"Young man," he said, "when you take a few more voyages you'll understand you can't trust

167

natives. How do you know we'd get the wood if we put the goods ashore?"

"Because Kualai's honest," John March said.

Captain Griggs looked thoughtfully at the ceiling. "Maybe," he said, "and maybe not. Anyways, we've got the wood. You come aboard tomorrow." And Captain Griggs smiled genially, but even when he smiled, John March had a suspicion that something had been left unsaid, that there was some thought in the captain's mind of which he had not spoken.

Mr. Sprague came up to get him the next morning, carrying a bundle of small presents and perspiring in the heat of the early sun.

"Say good-by to the chief," he said. "The captain's orders are to leave right now. You're to stay aboard until we sail. The quarter boat's waiting at the beach."

John March was sorry, now that it was time to go. He walked to Kualai and held out his hand. "Thank you very much," he said, and the interpreter, Moku, gave him back the chief's answer:

"He say for you to come back soon."

The canoes were gathering about the *Polly* already, by the time he reached the beach. He and Mr. Sprague sat in the stern sheets of the quarter boat while two men rowed, helped by a light breeze offshore.

It was only when they were halfway out that John March was aware of something disturbing.

"Look," he said; "they're setting the lower topsails!"

"Yes," said Mr. Sprague shortly, "so they are. We've got a fair breeze, haven't we?"

"But it'll take a good six hours to put off those goods," said Johnny March.

Mr. Sprague put a heavy hand on his knee and smiled. "Don't you worry, boy," he said. "Captain Griggs will see about those goods."

They were beside the companion ladder by that time, and even John March was puzzled, but nothing more. He was not aware of Captain Griggs's idea until he was on the poop, then he saw the tarpaulins were off the guns

and that men were beside them with matches, and then he saw that the decks were clear and that the sandalwood and the trade goods were all back in the hold. Captain Griggs grinned at him.

"Safe and sound," he said. "You've done very well, Mr. March; your father will be very pleased, I think. . . . Mister, you can man the capstan[25] now."

John March found himself stammering: "But what about the goods, Captain? We haven't put the goods ashore."

"No, boy," said Captain Griggs, "we ain't going to. What's the use when we've got the wood aboard? Those goods are going to go for skins."

Even then John March did not entirely understand him. "But you can't do that," he said. "We owe the chief the goods."

"Listen, boy," said Captain Griggs, "this ain't like home. They're plenty of other chiefs, and plenty of other islands. Let 'em come and get the goods, and I'll blow 'em out of water. There ain't no law out here. Now you be quiet, boy."

For a moment John March found it impossible to speak. Now that the whole matter was completely clear, he knew that he should have suspected long ago what must have been in the back of the captain's mind. Captain Griggs proposed sheer robbery, but he would not have called it that. He would have called it a clever piece of business in a place where there was no law.

"You see," Captain Griggs was saying, "it isn't as though they were white people, Mr. March. More fools they, that's all."

Then John March found his voice. "Captain," he said, "this is a March ship. You don't leave until you've set those goods on shore. We don't do things that way, Captain. You can't—"

Captain Griggs turned toward him quickly.

"That'll be enough from you," he said. "Who says I can't? I'm trying to make a profit on this

---

25. capstan\ˈkăp·stən\ large, spool-shaped cylinder with levers used mainly for hauling in cables and anchor.

voyage. I can, and I will, and I'm taking full responsibility. If you don't like it, get below."

John March's tongue felt dry and parched as he tried to speak. Even in that short while a hundred things were happening. The fore-and-aft staysails and the lower topsail were set by then, and the call came from forward, "Hawser[26] short!" A glance toward the beach was enough to show him that the islanders were aware of the captain's trick. Men were running toward the water. He could hear the beating of a drum. Men in canoes were gesticulating and shouting. Men with spears and clubs and slings were hurrying to the beach.

"Break out anchor, mister," shouted Captain Griggs, "and stand by them guns! Forward there, pass out the small arms! By God, we'll show 'em!"

"Captain," said John March suddenly. He knew there was only one thing to do as he spoke. "If you go, you'll leave me here. I'm going back ashore."

Captain Griggs looked at him and laughed. "They'll kill you back ashore," he said. "Look at 'em on the beach."

John March spoke with difficulty. "You and I are different sorts of men," he said. "You can either set those goods ashore or I'm going."

"May I inquire," said Captain Griggs, "how're you going to go? Keep your mouth shut, boy!"

In the haste of getting under way, the quarter boat was still drifting alongside, and the captain must have perceived John March's intention from his glance.

He made a lunge at John March, but John March broke away, and then he went on the bulwarks.

"Get ahold of that fool!" shouted Captain Griggs. "Lay ahold of him!"

Two of the crew ran toward him, and he jumped, crashing into the quarter boat. "Get in there after him!" Captain Griggs was shouting. "Don't let him go!"

And then John March cut the painter[27] and the quarter boat was drifting from the side.

"You fool!" shouted Captain Griggs. "You hear my orders! Come back here or they'll kill you, March!"

Once the boat was drifting from the side, John March was amazed at himself. His anger and his lack of fear amazed him. He was standing amidships in the quarter boat, shouting back at Captain Griggs.

"I'd rather be killed ashore," he shouted, "than stay aboard with you!" Then he picked up the oars and began to row ashore, slowly, because the boat was heavy for a single man to handle.

"You hear me?" Captain Griggs was shouting. "Stay there and that will be the end of you."

John March saw that the anchor was aweigh and the *Polly* was standing slowly out to the open sea. His back was to the beach as he pulled toward it, but he heard the shouting and the beating of the drums. It must have been his anger at Captain Griggs that did not make him afraid, or an assurance within himself that he was right and Captain Griggs was wrong. A glance astern of the quarter boat as he strained at the oars showed him the *Polly* standing out to sea, but he did not look over his shoulder toward the beach. He did not look until the bottom of the quarter boat grated on the sand, then he shipped his oars carefully and stepped ashore. He found himself surrounded by shouting men who waved their spears and their fists in his face, but somehow they were not so real to him as the reality which lay inside himself. He only realized later that a single gesture of fear might have meant his death, but then he was so involved in his own preoccupation and with the single desire which was in him that he walked calmly enough across the beach toward the palm trees and the thatched houses; the crowd in front of him gave way as he walked, and then followed on his heels. He was taking the path to Kualai's house, and the shouting around him died away as he drew near it.

---

26. **hawser** \ˈhɔ·zĕr\ small cable by which ship is anchored.
27. **painter**, rope attached to bow of ship for securing the boat or towing.

Then he saw Kualai walking toward him in the feather cloak which he had worn the first day they had met, carrying a light throwing spear in his right hand. Kualai was shouting something to him—obviously a question which he could not understand—and Moku was standing near him.

"Tell Kualai," said John March, "that I come from honest people. Tell him that I have come here to stay until he is paid for his wood." He saw Kualai listening intently to his answer, and then Kualai raised his right arm and drove his spear into the earth.

"He says you are his son," Moku said. "He asks you: Will you please to shake his hand?"

The reaction from what he had done came over him when Kualai grasped his hand. He knew the harsh and accurate consequences of his action then, as the smells and sounds of that Polynesian village came over him like a wave. Captain Griggs had left him, and every vestige of home was gone. He was a stranger among savages, and he might be there forever, for anything he knew, yet even then he knew that he had done the only proper thing. Suddenly he found that he was homesick, because the chief was kind.

"Ask him if I can be alone," he said. "Tell him I want to be alone."

He was given a house of his own that night, next to where the chief slept. He was given a pile of woven mats for his bed and a piece of tapa cloth[28] to cover him. He was given baked pig and sweet potatoes and the gray paste made from the taro root, called poi, for his evening meal, and mullet from Kualai's fish pond. He was as comfortable as he could have hoped to be that night. For a moment, when he was awakened early the next morning, he thought he was at home, until he saw the rafters and the thatch above him. Moku was standing near him in his ragged sailor breeches, and Kualai himself was bending his head, just entering the door.

"Wake up!" Moku was saying. "The ship is back!"

John March sat up on his bed of mats and rubbed his arms across his face. Although he spoke to Moku, his eyes were on Kualai.

"The ship?" he asked. "What ship?"

"Your ship," said Moku. "She come back, and now the captain, he unloads the goods."

John March stood up. He had no great capacity for showing emotion.

"Ask Kualai if he is satisfied," he said.

Moku nodded. "He says, 'Yes, very much,'" he said, and Kualai nodded back. "He asks for you to stay a long time—always."

"Thank him, please," said John March, "but tell him it's my ship. Tell him I must go to see that the goods are right."

"Kualai," Moku answered, "says he will go with you to the beach."

Mr. Sprague had landed in the longboat by the time they had reached the shore, and the beach was already covered with bolts of calico and small goods and ironware and lead and copper. Mr. Sprague nodded to John March formally as though nothing had happened. "The captain sends his compliments," he said, "and asks you to come aboard, so that he can resume the voyage." And Sprague grinned and added, "It's lucky for you, John March, that you're the owner's son."

John March looked at the goods upon the shore. "You can thank the captain for me for coming back," he answered. "You can tell him that I hope we both can forget what has happened, but the complete consignment is not landed yet. I'll stay here until the list is checked."

"You're an accurate man," said Sprague.

John March nodded. "I've been taught to be," he said, and he stayed there on the beach until every item was verified. Then he turned to Kualai and his interpreter.

"Tell the chief," he said, "that I believe that everything is right. Ask his pardon for the delay, but tell him our house will make any mistakes correct. Thank him, and tell him that I am going."

---

28. tapa\ˈta·pə\ **cloth,** coarse cloth made from pounded bark of plants.

Moku spoke quickly in the musical language of the islands while Kualai stood, looking first at John March and then at the ship that brought him. After Kualai had listened, he stood silently for a moment. Then he smiled and spoke swiftly. He raised a hand and took off his feather helmet, and one of his men very carefully removed his feather cloak from his shoulders.

"He says there will always be wood for you," said Moku. "He asks you to take his coat."

I

A SYMBOLIC FRAME

For the most part short-story writers introduce their main conflict quite early, often in the first or second paragraph. Marquand, however, holds back his main conflict while he describes and tells the story of the cloak that hung in the March house. The reader who wants action may grow impatient at this delay; but if he reflects, he will realize that the cloak must be important for the story. The cloak raises a tension, or problem, and a careful and curious reader will want to learn what its symbolic function is, what it "stands for."

Indeed, Marquand has used a "frame" for his story, since it both begins and ends with reference to the cloak. If the story has unity, however, the cloak should not merely be a device to raise the reader's curiosity, but an integral part of the story. Try to determine what the cloak symbolizes and how it relates to John March's inner struggle.

II

IMPLICATIONS

Discuss each of the following propositions.

1. Good and evil are purely relative matters, and one can argue that there was really nothing basically evil in Captain Griggs's decision to follow his owner's instructions and make as large a profit as he could.

2. The only difference between the evil William Wilson and Captain Griggs is that Griggs represents evil that is not easily recognized.

3. John March's inner struggle was intense because there were many pressures on him and the consequences of his jumping ship were full of danger.

4. It was easy for John March to decide what was right because he had "a conscientious sense inherited from his race." For persons who have not inherited a strong moral code, however, questions of right and wrong are more difficult to resolve.

5. In these days of the large corporation, the "organization man," and decision by committee, integrity is of little importance to individuals in business because they do not feel personally responsible for the decisions that are made.

III

TECHNIQUES

Conflict

An interesting way of approaching the study of some fiction—particularly of longer fiction—is to locate in the story the opposing "poles" of the action and give them general names. In this story, for example, the poles might be identified as "dishonesty" or "shrewdness" on the one hand, and "honesty" or "integrity" on the other. The various phenomena of the story—the characters, actions, details of setting, and so on—can then be grouped under one pole or the other. In this way the reader can gain a clearer picture of the total pattern. Try to organize some of the details in this story around the suggested poles and see if this helps you to understand the story better.

Climax

There are at least two related, but distinct, conflicts in this story: the external conflict between John March and Griggs, and the internal conflict of March. Each of these reaches a climax at the same time, but the external conflict is not fully resolved until much later in the story, when we learn of the ultimate resolution of the March-Griggs conflict. How did this stretching out of the resolution affect your enjoyment of the story?

Moment of Illumination

The full meaning of this story does not become apparent until the final moment when the island chief gives his cloak to John March. This is the moment of illumination. Note how it ties the end of the story to the beginning and helps the reader see better the full symbolic significance of the cloak.

In 1862–63, the famous Confederate general John Hunt Morgan led a number of daring raids behind the Union lines in West Virginia, Indiana, and Ohio. The following selection tells of the effect of one of these raids on a Quaker family whose land and lives are threatened. As you may know, Quakers believe that war is contrary to the letter and spirit of the Gospel; they are religiously committed to nonviolence. Though the conflict here touches all members of the Birdwell family, the chief focus is on Josh, the eighteen-year-old son. In the foregoing stories there was a rather sharp line between moral right and wrong. In Josh's case, however, the difference between good and evil is more cloudy and his decision, therefore, is more difficult to make. "The Battle of Finney's Ford" is one of the episodes in Jessamyn West's *The Friendly Persuasion*, a collection of tales centering on the Birdwell family.

The Battle of Finney's Ford

JESSAMYN WEST

Except for the name of Morgan the morning of the eleventh opened up like any other in July: clear, with promise of heat to come. Overhead arched the great cloudless sky of summer, tranquil above the reports, the rumors, the whisperings, the fears. And above the true evidence. The evidence brought in by the eye witnesses; by the boy who had hid himself and horse in the thicket while Morgan's outriders[1] galloped past; by the girl who had waded along the branch and was not seen; the stories of the burnings, the shootings, the looting.

The mind knew Morgan's name had altered the day, yet the untutored eye could find no difference, either in it or the horizon which framed it. Eliza, standing in the doorway of the summer kitchen, breakfast bell in hand, searched every crevice of the landscape, but in so far as she could see there was no shred of alteration in it. The cows, milked early, stood in the shade along the banks of the south branch; heat waves already rippled above the

well-tasseled corn; the windmill turned round three or four times with considerable speed, then stopped, as if forever.

Eliza lifted her breakfast bell to ring, then let arm and soundless bell drop to her side. She felt a profound reluctance to disturb in any way the morning quiet. She had a conviction unreasoning, but deep, that the sound of her bell might be all that was needed to shatter tranquillity, call up from out of the wood lot, or across the river side, John Morgan himself.

Jess looked down at his wife. "Thee want me to ring it?" he asked.

"No," Eliza said. "I'll ring it. The boys need to be called up for their breakfasts." But she did not raise her arm nor sound the bell. "All's so quiet," she said. "It gives me the feeling I'd oughtn't disturb it. As if ringing the bell might be the beginning . . . as if hearing it, John Mor-

---

1. **Morgan's outriders**, John Hunt Morgan (1825–1864). American Confederate cavalry commander famed for raids in Kentucky, Ohio, Indiana, and Tennessee; killed near Greenville, Tennessee (September 4, 1864).

gan might ride up and say, 'Has thee[2] any horses . . . any silver . . . any blankets?' "

"He don't ask, from what I hear," Jess said. "He takes."

"Ride up and take," Eliza said, as if digesting the fact. "Well, that's a happen-chance. Flood or fire could do the same. One bolt of lightning's enough if it's the Lord's will. Talking's not my concern. It's what the boys would do."

"The boys?" Jess asked.

"Joshua," his wife answered.

Jess nodded.

"If hearing the name alone's enough . . ." Eliza began, "if the very sound of it's strong enough . . ."

"Yes," Jess said, nodding again.

Morgan's name had been heard in the southern counties before July, but it was in July that it began to be heard above everything else: above the rustle of the growing corn, the clack of mills, the plop of the big bass in the deep pools. Women churning stopped their dashers to listen, children stayed away from the wood lots, men worked quietly behind their horses, foregoing all talk lest their words muffle the approach of Morgan's scouts.

But it was the young men who listened most intently, the skin tightening across their cheek bones. Not with apprehension or fear so much as with wonder. What would they do? If the hoofbeats along the wood's trace were made by John Morgan's men? If the press-gang said, "Unhitch your horses, bub, bring out your hams and bacon, show us where the old man keeps his silver." Would they unhitch, the young men wondered . . . hand over Prince and Dolly, walk up through the fine dust of the field-path, lay the meat and silver on the outstretched hands? Would they? The young men did not know. They had no way of knowing.

Since childhood they had dreamed of resistance, but the foes they had resisted were mythical: the vanished Indian, the unseen highwayman, the long-gone river pirate, figures who fled easily, whose bullets ricocheted from resolute hearts. Morgan's men were not mythical,

they did not flee, their bullets pierced even the most steadfast hearts. The young men at dusk on the river road, where the banks were shoulder high and fox-grapes, thick as curtains, hung between the shadowy trees, did not look back, nor hasten. But they listened. And wondered. And hearing nothing, were not reassured. Silence also was ominous.

Eliza once again lifted the breakfast bell. "Thee think I should ring it?" she asked.

"Ring it," Jess told her. "I got no mind to meet John Morgan on an empty stomach."

Breakfast was almost over when Joshua came in. He noted with astonishment the nearly empty gravy bowl, the meat platter with its single egg, the plates crusted with jam and biscuit crumbs. It was a wonder to him that people had been able on such a morning to sit down to the table, put gravy onto biscuits, spear slices of ham and then opening and shutting their mouths, chew such things with relish. Such eating, such self-concern, seemed, when their neighbors were dying, calloused and unspiritual.

It was not only that these men were their neighbors nor that their deaths were in a sense for them, since they had died defending beliefs Joshua and his family held dear: it was the whole matter of death to which Joshua was not yet reconciled. Nor was he reconciled to the apathy of his elders in the face of death, their indifference and mild acceptance. They said Amen and God's will be done. This he could have borne, had he been convinced that they really suffered, that God's name and the Amen had not come easy. Old people, and for Joshua all who were somewhat advanced beyond his own eighteen years were old, did suffer when they lost a member of their own households. This, Joshua was ready to admit.

But Josh sorrowed over death as an abstract fact: he resented it for unknown men and women. He went without meals because of an

---

2. **thee**, older objective form of personal pronoun still used by Quakers, often in subject position.

item in The Banner *News* about a woman dead in a millpond in another county; because of a man dragged to death behind his team. He made himself forego all one fall—in so far as he was able—any sight of the frosty, autumnal constellations in which he delighted because of a conversation of his mother's which he had overheard. After a long sickness stretching through more than a year (his mother had told a visitor) a young woman, whose name was Lydia, had said, "I know I must die, but I wish I could live long enough to see Orion[3] outside my window once more." This girl (unknown to him) named Lydia had died, his mother said, in early August, long before Orion had come near her window. All that fall Joshua had kept his eyes off the evening sky, saying stubbornly, "I won't take anything she can't have. I won't look since she can't."

For the most part Josh kept these feelings to himself, for when they burst out, as they occasionally did, what his mother and father had to say about them angered him.

"Thee should rejoice, son," Eliza had once said when he had spoken sorrowfully of the death of a young boy who had gone through the ice and drowned. "Thee should rejoice. Young Quincy's in heaven, spared all this world's misery."

"Quincy didn't think this world was a miserable place," Joshua, who had known the boy, said.

"He'll find heaven a better place, Josh," his mother had insisted.

"He's cheated," Josh had flashed out. "He's cheated."

"Thee's not to question the Lord, Joshua," his mother said.

Ordinarily he was able to hear his father speak about death with more tolerance than his mother. His father was not so sure as his mother. Joshua saw that possibilities his mother had never laid an eye on opened their long avenues of chance to his father's sight. But his father had a kind of calm, a tolerant pliability which sometimes set Joshua's teeth on edge. Old people, Josh thought, get so eroded by time

and events that they are as slippery as a handful of wettened stones at a branch bottom. Rolling and tumbling against each other, slippery as soap, not a single rough, jagged spot left with which to hold on—or resist, or strike out.

"Thee'll find a lot of things worse than death, Josh," his father had said to him one day—more as if reading his mind than answering anything Josh had spoken.

Joshua had answered his father sharply. "Death was a curse, wasn't it? A curse put on man for his disobedience?"

"Well, yes," Jess had said. "In a way thee can . . ."

But Joshua had not waited for qualifications. "What's worse than the Lord's curse? If the Lord put a curse on thee, thee'd be wrong to find anything worse, wouldn't thee?"

This logic seemed inescapable to Joshua, but his father, with his usual suppleness, escaped it. "The Lord's curses," he said mildly, "can usually be borne. There are some few man devises for himself that bite deeper."

Joshua never spoke of these things to his brother, Laban, but Labe once asked him, incuriously, Josh thought, and in his usual sleepy way, "Is thee afraid to die, Josh?"

Josh had not known what to answer. He was opposed to dying . . . was he afraid of it? He didn't know. He remembered being frightened, years ago, by sounds at night which he couldn't account for, being so frightened that the thumping of his heart had stirred the bed covers like a hand. Then he had been able to calm himself by thinking: What's the worst that can happen to me? Nothing but this: the burglar will creep nearer and nearer, finally give me one hard clunk on the head and I'll be killed. This had always calmed him, had seemed so insignificant a thing that he would cease listening and fearing and sleep.

That was imagined death, though, and imagined danger; the sounds he heard, perhaps mice

---

3. **Orion** \ə ˈrai·ən\ constellation of seven stars located east of Taurus.

in back of the studding or nails snapping in a heavy frost. If the death were real death—the sounds of danger real sounds? The click of the breech-lock in the musket before firing, a man's sucked-in breath as he pressed the trigger? He didn't know.

"I don't know, Labe," he said. But like the other young men he wondered.

Now Josh stood with hands tightly clenched over the rounded top of the chair in which his brother, Little Jess, sat. He knew, in his self-conscious way, that his family was looking at him, and he made a strong effort to control his feelings. He was particularly aware of Labe's calm, cool gaze, and he supposed that Labe, in what he thought of as Labe's belittling way, was enumerating his own physical shortcomings (Labe who was muscular, smooth-jointed, supple): Built like a beanpole, black hair like a wig, high, burning cheekbones, a lopsided mouth that trembles when he's in earnest.

"What kept thee, son?" his father asked.

"I went over to Whiteys'," Josh said.

"Sit, sit, Josh," his mother bade, bustling up from her place. "I'll cook thee fresh eggs."

"I couldn't swallow an egg," said Josh.

"What do they hear at the Whiteys'?" asked his father.

"Morgan's heading this way—he's following the railroad up from Vienna.[4] He's making for Vernon.[5] He'll be there today or tomorrow."

"Vernon," said his mother. She put the two eggs she had in her hand back in the egg crock. Vernon was home. Josh had as well've said the Maple Grove Nursery. Or the south forty.[6]

"How they know so much over at Whiteys'?" his father asked. "Morgan didn't cross the Ohio till evening of fourth day. Morgan's lost out there in the woods . . . got guerrillas trained to stay out of sight. Yet people'll sit at their breakfast tables and say just where John Morgan is. Tell you whether he's shaved yet this morning . . . and where he'll be this time tomorrow."

Josh felt, many times, like a stone beneath the cold waves of his father's detached unconcern. As if in spite of all he knew, and burningly

believed, he would in time be worn down, effaced by all that ceaseless, quiet questioning.

"People at breakfast tables . . ." he began angrily, then stopped. "Ben Whitey was in Harrison County[7] when Morgan crossed over. He's been riding ahead of him for three days."

"Did thee talk to Ben?" asked his father.

"Yes."

"What did he say?"

This shift of approach, this willingness to learn, cutting from beneath his feet ground for reasonable anger, angered Josh anew.

"Nothing about whether Morgan'd shaved yet, or not, this morning."

"Son," said his father, "sit thyself down and tell us. Get up, Little Jess. Give thy brother thy chair."

Little Jess went around the table to Eliza's chair and hung over his mother's shoulder, awaiting Josh's word. Josh himself, without intending to do so, sat suddenly in the chair that was pushed out for him—and also without conscious intent, began to chew hurriedly on a cold biscuit. His mother made a gesture toward passing him butter and jam, but Jess shook his head and said, "Well, Josh?"

Josh spoke rapidly, his voice a little muffled by dry biscuit crumbs. "Ben Whitey passed a dozen of Morgan's outriders last night camped down this side of Blocher. Not more'n twenty miles from Vernon. They're following the railroad. They'll raid Vernon."

"Raid Vernon," said his mother. "What does that mean?" It was a word whose meaning on the page of any book she knew perfectly well. But, "Raid Vernon"—the town where she sold her eggs, the church town, the county fair town, with its whitewashed brick houses, its quiet, dusty streets, its snowball bushes dangling their white blossoms over the unpainted picket fences—what did that mean? "Raid Vernon," she said once again as if the words themselves

---

4. **Vienna,** Scott County, southeast Indiana.
5. **Vernon,** southeast Indiana.
6. **south forty,** forty-acre plot of land.
7. **Harrison County,** southwest corner of Ohio.

might somehow suddenly focus, as a stereopticon glass[8] did when given just the proper shove, to show a landscape, lifelike in its dimensions, distances—and ruin.

Josh knew what the word meant. Ben Whitey had told him. "Raid means," he said, "burn, kill, take what you want."

"Are Morgan's men killing people?" Eliza asked.

For a second the world his mother saw flickered before Josh's eyes: a world of such loving companionableness that the word war had no other meaning for her than murder; where deliberate killing was unthinkable as though in her own household son should turn on son; but it flickered for a second only, then disappeared, leaving him angry again.

"Doesn't thee know there's a war?" Josh asked with intensity. "Doesn't thee know what a war is?"

"Thy mother knows there's a war, Josh," his father reminded him, "but she don't know what a war is. Let alone what a war in Vernon'd be like. She's more used to think of caring for people than killing them."

"John Morgan thinks of killing them," Josh said. "He shot a boy through the legs who didn't run fast enough. He shot an old man in the back. I don't know how many's dead in Harrison County. Ben Whitey said he could smell the smoke of Morgan's burnings the whole way up. He said he didn't think there was a mill left standing in Harrison County. He said the country's scoured of horses—and anything else in any house a trooper wanted and could carry across his saddle-bow."[9]

Eliza leaned across the table. "The earth," she said, "and the fullness thereof, is the Lord's. What's Morgan's men but a ruckus of boys with their pants in their boots? Trying to get something they've never had a taste of before? We've got more'n we need here. High time we're called on to share it with someone. If John Morgan's men came here," Eliza said—and Josh saw his mother's eyes turn toward the door of the summer kitchen as if she saw there a dusty, slouch-hatted trooper, "I'd offer them

the best I had on hand. No man's my enemy," she said.

Josh stood up, crumbling in one hand the biscuit he had been quickly munching. "Some men are my enemies," he said. "Any man's my enemy who kills innocent men and makes slaves. They're my mortal enemies."

Josh felt his sister Mattie's hand, long-fingered—and cold for so warm a morning—touch, then feel its way into his clenched fist, and he gave way to its insistent downward pressure and sat again. "I will share with my friends," he said. "If thee gives all thee's got to a thief, thy friends will have to go hungry—there's not enough to go around. What's good about that?" he asked.

No one answered his question, but Jess said evenly, "Tales like these are always a part of war times."

Tales were lies. Josh picked up a case-knife and tried to ease off some of his feelings in clenching it. "Ben Whitey don't lie . . . some he saw with his own eyes . . . some was told him. He saw the fires . . . he heard the people whose horses were stolen. He saw an outrider with a bird-cage and bird looped to his saddle. They said he'd been carrying that bird all the way from Maukport."

Josh was interrupted by his mother. She had started up, taken two steps toward the kitchen window where Ebony, the starling, hung in his cage. There, after the two steps, she stopped, stood stock still in her tracks, as if just then aware of what she'd been doing. "This is thy chance," Josh told himself, "to keep thy mouth shut, not shove a contradiction down thy own mother's throat." But he could not do it. He wrapped his hand round the cutting edge of the case-knife, but there was not enough pain in its blunt edge to divert him.

"I thought thee said," Josh told his mother, his mouth trembling with scorn for himself,

---

8. **stereopticon glass,** apparatus for transparent slides, especially one using double pictures each with a separate lens producing dissolving views and an effect of depth.
9. **saddle-bow,** the arch in front of a saddle.

"that this was our chance to share? Thee's got a good chance now to share Ebony. Thee's had that bird a long time and every single man riding with Morgan's never had him once in his life time."

Eliza turned back facing the table and her family. Josh gazed at his mother's neat, dark head, saw her black eyes move for a moment toward the head of the table where his father sat, then turn resolutely toward himself. "I was thinking he might be mistreated," she said. "I've grown over-fond of the particular."

"Mistreated," Josh shouted, ignoring her admission. "Thee can worry about a bird's being mistreated while men are being shot. Thee'd try to save it and not turn thy hand to help the men. No man's thy enemy . . . unless he tries to take thy bird. Every man's enemy is my enemy. I'd do as much any day for a man as a bird."

Jess and Labe both started at once to speak, but Eliza held up her hand, as if she were in meeting. "I was wrong, Joshua," she said. "I'd give Ebony to any man who'd care for him."

"Care for him," Josh again shouted. "Thee was right the first time. Thee think that bird Ben Whitey saw's alive now? Its neck's been wrung long ago. If it was a big bird it's been boiled and eat. Ebony'd end up in no time on a forked stick over a fire."

Joshua leaned across the table toward his mother, gesturing with the case-knife, making Ebony the whole issue of war and peace, of life and death; talking to Eliza, but for his whole family . . . for Labe . . . to hear and contradict. "Thee has responsibilities. Thee can't just take birds and make them tame. Slit their tongues and fatten them so's they can't fly. Then let anybody grab them. And cook them. Thee don't have any right to be good and generous to such a price. A price thee don't pay. Old Ebony's got to pay that price. And that old man. And the boy shot in the legs. And the Harrison County Militia. And the Vernon Militia. I'd rather die," Josh said.

There was a long silence about the breakfast table. Eliza reseated herself. Little Jess looked from face to face with nervousness. He was em-

barrassed when grown-ups showed emotion. He thought it did not suit their faces. He saw it break the smooth surface of authority and knowledgeability with which they were accustomed to front him. And without that where were they? And where was he? Lost, not a thing to fall back on, floundering from notion to notion.

Mattie gazed at Ebony, jauntily cracking sunflower seeds in his wooden cage. She saw there both her mother's bird, who was first of all God's bird, and now was no man's bird, but belonged to all, and she saw Joshua's bird, the defenseless pet who would be plucked like a chicken and eaten unless they were willing to fight and die for him. And because she oscillated between the two ways of seeing Ebony, she suffered: when she was generous and peaceful, as was her mother, she thought herself a coward, and when she was, like Joshua, ready to fight (she supposed) she felt herself a renegade, an outcast from faith and scriptures.

Only Labe sat quietly at the table, his calm face touched neither by sorrow nor eagerness. One way only opened before him, and except that he believed this to be a matter between his mother and brother, and presently his father, he would have spoken, and said better words, he thought, for loving all men than his mother had said. And he would have gotten that bird from out the center of the conversation, where its feathers, its litter, its long periods of sulky quiet muffled and strangled the thing they should be really speaking of.

In the long silence . . . while there was no talk, sounds of great clarity filled the room. All, except Little Jess, harkened to them as if they were omens; as if each, properly apprehended, might carry some kind of a revelation: the slow grating start of the windmill easing into rhythmic clicking as the wind freshened; two distant notes as old Bess the bell-cow reached forward toward uncropped grass; the prolonged, sweet morning trill of a warbler, who, uncaged and undesired either by raiders or raided, flew, singing, near the windows, then flipped out of sight.

Jess, from his place at the head of the table, looked down toward his eldest son. He bent upon him a face of so much love and regard— and good humor, too, as if behind this talk of war there were still a few reasons to laugh— that Josh thought he might be unable to bear his father's gaze, would have to lay his arms across the table and bury his face in them, and so hidden, say, "Yes, pa," or "No, pa," to whatever his father had to say. But as his father continued to gaze, quizzically and lovingly, Josh knew that he had left behind him forever the happy time of freedom from decision and sat very straight, back teeth clamped together, lips trembling, waiting his father's word.

"Thee knows, Josh," his father said, "dying's only half of it. Any of us here, I hope"—and Jess included Little Jess and Mattie in the nod of his head—"is ready to die for what he believes. If it's asked of us and can be turned to good account. I'm not for dying, willy-nilly, thee understands," Jess said, his big nose wrinkling at the bridge. "It's an awful final thing, and more often and not nobody's much discommoded by it, except thyself, but there are times when it's the only answer a man can give to certain questions. Then I'm for it. But thee's not been asked such a question, now, Josh. Thee can go out on the pike, and if thee can find John Morgan, die there in front of him by his own hand if thee can manage it, and nothing'll be decided. He'll move right on, take Ebony, if he's a mind to, though I give John Morgan credit for being a smarter man than that and thee'll be back there on the pike just as dead and just as forgotten as if thee'd tied a stone round thy neck and jumped off Clifty Falls. No, Josh, dying won't turn the trick. What thee'll be asked to do now—is kill."

The word hung in the air. A fly circled the table, loudly and slowly, and still the sound of the word was there . . . louder than the ugly humming. It hung in the air like an open wound. Kill. In the Quaker household the word was bare and stark. Bare as in Cain and Abel's time with none of the panoply of wars and regiments and campaigns to clothe it. Kill. Kill a man. Kill thy brother. Josh regarded the word. He explored it, his hand tightening again about the knife.

"I know that," he said. "I am ready to fight." But that wouldn't do. He could not pretend that he was ready for the necessary act so long as he flinched away—from even the word. "I will kill these men if I have to."

"No, Josh," Eliza said.

Josh was glad to be relieved of the need of facing his father and regarding death abstractly. He turned to his mother. "Yes," he said. "I will. I'm going to meet Ben Whitey at eight. Soon as he's had two hours' rest. The Governor's made a proclamation. Every man's to join the Home Guard and help defend his town. We're going right down to Vernon and join. Morgan'll be there any time. I'd ought to've gone a week ago."

"Joshua, Joshua," cried his mother. "Thee knows what thee's turning thy back on? On thy church. On thy God. Thy great-grandfather came here with William Penn[10] to establish ways of peace. And he did," Eliza declared passionately. "With savage Indians. Men of blood. Now thee proves thyself to be worse than the Indians. They kept the peace."

Josh felt better. The picture of himself as bloodier than a savage Indian was so fantastic it hid for the time such savagery and bloodthirstiness as he did possess—and hid too, what Josh felt to be, perhaps even worse, his lack of these qualities. "The Indians," he said, "weren't dealing with John Morgan."

Jess spoke. First that bird, now William Penn and the Indians. The human mind could move, if it moved at all, only from symbol to symbol and these so chosen that sharp and even final issues were padded enough to make them more tolerable. "Josh," he said, "those who take the sword shall perish by it."

---

10. **William Penn,** founder of the colony of Pennsylvania.

They were back to dying: only a nicer word. "I am ready to perish," said Josh.

But Jess wouldn't let them stay there. "'Thou shalt not kill,'" said Jess.

There it was. "But He said, 'Render unto Caesar the things that are Caesar's,'" Josh said desperately. "I live here—in Jennings County. My town is Vernon. The Governor said to defend it. My body is my country's."

"Thy soul, son, is God's."

"God won't want it," Josh said, "if I don't do what I think's my duty." He was standing again, half crying, a horrible way for a man to be starting to war. "Thee can live with God now, maybe. I can't. I don't want to die . . . and I don't even know if I could kill anyone if I tried. But I got to try," he said, "as long as people around me have to. I'm no better'n they are. I can't be separated from them."

He left the table and ran toward the kitchen stairway. "I'm going," he said. "I'm meeting Ben Whitey at eight."

As he went up the stairs he heard his father say, "No, Eliza, no."

In his room Josh said, "Packing to go to war," but it didn't mean much. He scarcely believed it; though the pain that started at the bottom of his throat and seemed to run the whole length of his chest told him this was no ordinary departure. There wasn't much packing to do. Extra socks, Ben Whitey said. Spare handkerchiefs—good in case of a wound. Stout shoes—he had them on. A heavy coat—no telling how long they'd be in the field; they might have to chase Morgan the length of the state. Musket—his musket was always oiled, cleaned, ready; shot—he didn't know whether he had enough or not. He didn't know how many . . . He didn't know how good he'd be at . . . Knife—yes. Cup —he'd get that downstairs, and the tin plate. Two blankets to roll round all the stuff, saddle old Snorty—Morgan'd have to be a pretty slow runner if old Snorty was ever to catch up with him.

He was finished. Getting ready for war was a short horse[11] and soon curried, it seemed. There was nothing to do now but go. He'd keep that a short horse, too, but it'd be a horse of a different color. Josh marveled at himself. Cracking jokes, for that was what it was even though there was no one to hear. Ten minutes ago he'd been crying, his mouth full of death, duty and the scriptures and here he was, dry-eyed, a pain in his chest, to be sure, but somewhat outside the whole matter, far enough apart, anyway, to say it was like this or that. It was very peculiar—but the pain itself lay like a bar between him and what had gone before. There was the pain, wide, heavy, real, and he needn't, indeed he couldn't, cross over it to explore its causes.

He looked about the room—his and Labe's— neat, orderly, the bedcovers tossed back to air, the way his mother had taught them, clothes on pegs, chest drawers closed. He felt as if he wanted to say a prayer of some kind . . . God, take care of this room, or something like that, but he thought perhaps he'd better not. He wasn't sure God was with him in this move, in spite of what he had said downstairs, and there was no use involving Him in something He wouldn't approve. He'd picked up his bed-roll to go when Mattie came in. He would rather have seen almost anyone else.

As far as Josh could tell Mattie acted parts from morning to night: very delicate and fainty at one hour like she's too fine-haired to live on a farm, the next loud and yelling as if she had Comanche blood and a quarter section wasn't big enough to give her scope. She'd help him with a piece of work, doing more than her share, one time—the next sit half a day on a tree-stump, breathing, Josh supposed, but giving no sign of it.

"Oh, Joshua," said Mattie.

Josh held onto his bed-roll. Mattie'd been crying and Josh wasn't sure who he was seeing: sister Mattie or actress Mattie. A little of both, maybe, but when she threw her arms around his neck he thought he knew which one was clasping him most warmly.

---

11. **short horse,** quarter horse bred for short legs.

"Oh, Joshua," said Mattie again.

"I've got to go, Matt," Josh said. "I'm late now."

Mattie took her arms down. "Josh," she said, "I want thee to take this." She had a little New Testament in her hand and she reached up and slipped it gently into Josh's shirt pocket. "There," she said. "Over thy heart it will guard thee from all harm." Then in her natural voice she added, "I read about two soldiers who'd've been shot through the heart except for their Bibles." Then sister Mattie was hidden away again, lost behind inclined head and folded hands.

Josh couldn't help laughing, so long and loud he was surprised.

"What's so funny?" Mattie asked. "Thee setting up to be an atheist?"

"No," Josh said, "I ain't. I'll take it, and read it, too, maybe." He put the little book in his hip pocket.

"Thee going to sit on it?" Mattie asked.

Josh shouldered his bed-roll again and went to the door. "It's the one sure foundation," he said.

"Why, Josh Birdwell," said Mattie. She had come upstairs expecting a pious and tearful farewell, and here was Josh laughing and joking, and not very reverently, either. Outside the door Josh turned back to reassure his sister. "Thee don't sit on thy hip pockets," he said. "Thee sits between them."

Mattie said feebly, "Good-bye, Josh."

The rest of the good-byes, Josh figured, had been said, in as far as they could be said, downstairs about the breakfast table. He went quietly out the front door and to the barn without seeing anyone. Not until he had saddled and tied his bed-roll to the saddle and led old Snorty out into the sunny barnyard did he see his mother and Little Jess standing at the bottom of the lane waiting for him. Seeing them, he was glad they were there.

Eliza's face was very serious but she wasn't crying. She held up a package to Josh. "Here's food, Josh. You'll have to eat. I didn't know what was best. This's mostly meat and cold biscuits."

Thinking of food Josh remembered the forgotten tin cup and plate.

"Run fetch them, Little Jess," Eliza said. "Be lively," she called after him. "Josh mustn't be late."

Josh let old Snorty's reins hang and laid his arms about his mother's shoulders, hugging her tight.

"Good-bye, Joshua," his mother said, and then not a word about his coming home safe, only, "I hope thee doesn't have to kill anyone." Joshua shut his eyes for a minute. "If thee has to die that's thy own business and thee won't anyway unless it's the Lord's will—but, oh, son," Eliza said, "I hope thee don't have to kill."

Josh opened his eyes and smiled. That was just the right thing to say . . . the words he would've chosen for her. He patted his mother's shoulder. Sticking by her principles and not getting over-fond of the particular—even when it was her own son. Josh bent and kissed her.

He could not have borne it if she had broken down, put his safety first.

"Good-bye," Josh said. "Don't thee worry. I'll be shaking too hard to hit or get hit." He kissed his mother and got into the saddle. Eliza made a gesture toward him of love and farewell and walked resolutely back up the lane.

Little Jess trotted along the pike beside Josh for a way. Before turning homewards he held onto the stirrup for a minute and whispered fiercely up to his brother, "Thee shoot one for me, Josh." Josh then, looking down into Little Jess' drawn face and lips thinned with whispering, saw that no man acted to himself.

Josh was to meet Ben Whitey at the Milford cut-off, but even now, riding alone, he supposed he was a soldier and he tried to carry himself, through the warm morning and down the dusty road, like a Home Guardsman: scanning the horizon for signs of smoke or dust, keeping an eye out for single horsemen. There was no telling; if outriders of Morgan's were only twenty miles away last night, they could easily be in this neighborhood now.

In spite of his conviction that his intentions made him a militiaman, sworn to hunt down and stop or kill John Morgan, Josh would fall into looking at the farmland with a country man's eyes: sizing up a field of wheat unaccountably left standing, or noting how the apples were shaping up in an orchard. To offset this he stopped and loaded his gun. If he were to meet or sight a raider it would be his duty to shoot. He tried to think how it would be to come upon a man, emerging from the woods, say, or around a sharp turn, not speak, not pause to pass the time of day, but instantly with raised musket fire and hope to blow the stranger's head off. The idea made Josh sweat. My God, Josh thought or prayed—he didn't know which—I hope it's no boy nor old man. I hope it's some hard, old slave-driving bugger. Thinking of this hard old slave-driving bugger Josh remembered that he might be a man handy with firearms himself, and he settled deeper into the saddle and listened more intently.

The pain he had felt in his chest after breakfast was gone: in its place he now had in his middle a curious, dry, empty, swollen feeling. As if he carried something inside him, hollow, but beyond his size and growing bigger.

Ben Whitey was waiting for him at the Milford cut-off, impatient, fuming. "You're half an hour late," he yelled.

"I know it," Josh said. "We'll make up for it now," but they were only fairly started when Ben, looking back down the pike, said, "Looks like Labe on Rome Beauty. He joining too?"

"No," Josh said, "he's got convictions the other way."

"Well, you forgot something then," Ben Whitey said, "and your ma's sending it you." He rode on while Josh turned back to meet Labe.

Labe came up at a long trot, the only kind Rome Beauty had, dismounted and said, "Get on. Father said for thee to take Rome."

Josh sat atop old Snorty, unmoving, unbelieving.

"Get down," said Labe. "If thee's going to fight Morgan, fight him. Don't set there like a bump on a log."

"Father's against my going," said Josh.

"He's against it, but that didn't stop thee. Now get on. He says as far as he knows, Rome's no Quaker. From all he can tell thee and Rome think about alike. Get on."

Josh got off Snorty, transferred his bed-roll to Rome's saddle and stood in the dusty road beside his brother. He was taller than Labe but Labe's shoulders and stance made him feel small.

"Tell father," he began, but Labe interrupted him.

"Father said to tell thee most killing's caused by fear. . . . Rome's being under thee ought to help a little. He don't send thee Rome because his mind's changed about anything."

"Labe," Josh asked, "thee don't think about going?"

"No," said Labe, "I don't."

"I got to," said Josh. "Otherwise I'd always think maybe it was because . . ."

"Get on," said Labe, giving him no time to finish.

Astride the big red horse Josh rode after Ben Whitey, but before he overtook him he finished his sentence. "I am afraid," he said.

"You got a fine mount now," Ben Whitey told him when he drew alongside. "If you can just keep his nose headed the right direction you ought to make out."

"Never thee fear," Josh began . . . but he shut his mouth at that point. "Thee don't know," he told himself.

They rode into Vernon together; a roan, and a claybank, two rawboned farm boys: Ben Whitey, a born fighter, and Josh who was trying to do his duty. They entered Vernon and saw it the way a man who thinks he has been dreaming wakes and sees the landscape of his dream lying all about him, the disaster real, hard and unmelting as sunlight—and dreaming the only means of escape. Deep in the country, on the farms they had believed—and not believed. To come here with loaded guns had been an act of faith and now their faith was justified. Morgan was true; he existed; he was killing and looting; he would be here at any hour. There were tens of mouths to tell them.

The town blazed under the July sun; it throbbed with the heat of the season—and the heat of fear and excitement and wonder and resolution. At first Josh thought it was alive as he had seen it for an August fair or Fourth of July celebration. And there was something of a holiday spirit in the plunging, headlong activity. As if fifty years of seeing the Muscatatuck[12] rise and fall, the crops ripen and be harvested, the summer rains harden and whiten into winter's snow and hail, were enough for Vernon, as if tired now of this placid punkin-butter existence, they would turn to something with sharper flavor.

That was the surface: the movement, the shouts, the numbers of horses in the street, the vehicles, the laughter even. That was what Josh saw when he saw everything at once and heard everything at once. A medley in which all the sounds, blending, were a holiday roar; all the sights, the excess movements of celebration when steps reach higher and higher into the air, bows go lower and lower toward earth and smiles strain at the limitations of a single face.

When he saw the sights, one by one, there was no holiday in them. There were spring wagons full of women, children and bedding headed for back country farms and supposedly greater safety.

"No sense in that," Ben Whitey said. "That way a couple of outriders can pick up the best any household has to offer without being put to the bother of ripping up the feather ticks and taking the insides out of clocks."

But in spite of what Ben Whitey thought, they were there: spring wagons, democrats, gigs, buckboards, all filled with women, children and valuables, and headed for back country and the hills. There were men throwing shovelfuls of earth out of deep holes, preparing to bury silver, money, keepsakes: whatever they and their wives cherished and thought a raider might fancy. There were boys barricading doors, boarding up windows, reinforcing bolts. There was a man who had turned his house into a store and was now busy ripping down his sign and trying to make his store look like a house again. There was an old fellow atop the gable of his house, peering off to the south through a long spy-glass. The voices, too, when Josh listened were not celebrating anything; they rasped; they started even, then broke; a man began yelling, looked around, ended whispering.

"Let's get out of this," Ben Whitey said. "Let's find the Home Guard."

They pulled up beside a one-legged man calmly taking his ease on a street corner.

"Where's Morgan?" yelled Ben Whitey.

"Don't know for sure. Reports are thicker'n toads after a rain, but he's near. Hear tell the old boy slept in Lexington last night."

---

12. **Muscatatuck**\ˈməs·kə ˈtă·tək\ river in southeast Indiana; flows into East fork of White River.

"We're here to join the Home Guard," said Ben.

"'Bout a week late," said the one-legged man, sucking on a cold pipe.

"We know that," Ben told him, "but we come up as fast as we could. We're here now. We got prime horses and we'll give good accounts of ourselves. Where's the commander?"

"Not sittin' on his pratt recruiting."

Ben Whitey put his heel in his horse's flank. "Come on back," yelled the one-legged man. More quietly he said, "You johnnies rile me, through. Every drumstick of a boy comes in here from back country, brasher'n a parched pea, and ready to spit in old Johnnie Morgan's eye. It'll take more spit'n you got, bub, or I miss my guess. Morgan's clear grit, ginger to the backbone and no more fear in him than a rifle."

"Which side you on?" Ben asked.

"Our side. I'm for whipping Morgan but you ain't gonna do it by . . ."

"Save thy breath to cool thy broth," Josh said. "Where's the Home Guard?"

"Well, God kiss me," said the peg-legger. He took his pipe from his mouth and elevated his weather-beaten chops as if awaiting the salutation. "A Quaker sure's the Lord made Moses. What's thee planning to do, sonny? Pray for the boys?"

"Come on," said Ben and the two rode on down the street.

"How we going to get any place with men like that?" Josh asked.

"They ain't all like that," said Ben.

From across a picket fence an old man beckoned to them. "Want to mix in it?" he asked.

"That's what we're here for. Where's the Home Guard?"

"Everywhere," said the old man. He picked up the end of his long beard and used it to point with. "Spread thin, but mostly to the south. Morgan could circle us—but reports are he's hitting us solid from the south. Coming up the railroad from Vienna. They got companies posted at every ford, road and bridge south of town."

"Where you figger we could do the most good?"

"The bridge below the Forks. I been thinking about this for two days. I figger John Morgan being the man he is will come straight in, cross the bridge and bust into town from there. If you want to get in some telling licks that's the place I'd head for."

"That's the place we want," Ben said.

The Muscatatuck where it is bridged below the forks flows between banks of considerable height. Here the Home Guard Commander had massed as many men as could be spared from the other approaches to Vernon. Of these, the majority and among them the men Colonel Williams considered most steady and level headed were stationed on the west bank of the stream ready to fall upon the raiders should the smaller force which was holding the approaches to the bridge be overpowered. The Colonel hoped to stop by show of force, if possible, if not, by force itself any thrust the raiders might make before they reached the bridge. Failing this the guard on the west bank would have a fine chance to pick off the men as they debouched[13] from the bridge and headed toward town.

That was the plan. The captain in command of the river could use as many men as he could get and when Ben and Josh showed up, well mounted, he sent them at once to join the company beyond the bridge.

"They're headed this way," the captain told them. "Some of them," he said, pointing, "are sitting right there on top of that hill. Them, we fooled. Our men marched across the cliff road and then out of sight of Morgan—if he's there —a half dozen times over. Musta looked like quite an army to him. But there's likely others and they may be here soon. If we don't stop them nothing will. Once they're past us, it will be Maukport[14] and Salem and Lexington all

---

13. **debouched**\dē ˄bau̇chd\ marched out into open ground.
14. **Maukport**, also **Mauckport**, southern Indiana near Kentucky border; Salem and Lexington, Kentucky.

over again. Keep your guns handy. Dismount and rest your horses, but stay by them and keep them quiet. I'm glad you're here. I need you."

Overhead the July sun had weight as well as heat. It lay across Josh's shoulders like a burning timber. Though Ben was on one side of him, and big Gum Anson, a beefy farmer, was on the other, still Josh felt bereft of shelter, unshielded and alone—a naked target.

For a long time he scanned the road before him with rigid and unrelaxing vigilance. There was not much to be seen: the dusty road, the lush growth of summer, dock, volunteer oats, some daisies, a small field of shoulder high corn, and beyond these a thicket and the road curving out of sight around it. Above earth and river and the river's rank growth were the heat waves, the massive clouds of noon skies, the burning sun. Josh, who felt as if the whole duty of seeing and apprising rested with him, inspected every leaf and shadow. When a sudden movement of air fluttered the leaves of the elders up the road and rasped through the corn he lifted his gun, then put it down shamefacedly. He would feel the sweat trickle down the sides of his chest, then drop to his middle and soak in around his belt.

"Have some cherries," said Gum. "You can't keep that up all afternoon." He held out a big bag. The cherries were cool and firm and Josh took a handful.

"When Nance brought these out this morning," Gum said, "I'd've thrown 'em down except to please her. Goin' off to fight Morgan with a bag of cherries tied to my saddle like a doggone picnicker." He munched away and spat pits. "Looks like they might be the handiest article I brought."

"Wait'll Morgan gets here, Gum," somebody yelled. "It's gonna take more'n cherry-stones to stop that old shite-poke."

"I got more'n cherry-stones," Gum called back and the men around him laughed.

Josh shifted in his saddle and looked about. He was amazed at the sound of laughter, amazed that men waiting to kill or be killed should laugh and joke. He scanned the faces of those who were laughing: old fellows, middle-aged farmers, boys younger than himself. Sweating, chewing tobacco, some lolling in their saddles. Most, dismounted. Some in uniform, others not. Mounted on farm plugs. Mounted on fast animals he had seen at county fairs. Every kind of fire arm. One man with a bayonet even. The sight of that lifted Josh up in his saddle again. Did the raiders carry bayonets? His sweating which he had not noticed for a while had started up once more.

"Have some more cherries?" asked Gum.

Josh took another handful. "Thanks," he said. "I was awful dry. And hungry, too. I can't remember when I had anything to eat last."

"Go kinda slow on them cherries, then. They don't set too good on'n empty stomach."

"They're setting good on mine," Josh said, chewing and spitting, but keeping his eyes uproad.

"Take it easy," advised Gum. "You'll be petered out before Johnnie gets here. They's scouts up ahead. They'll let us know if anything's twitchin'."

Josh felt a fool not to have thought of that before rearing up till his backbone was petrified, and staring till his eyes popped, acting like he was scout, trooper, captain, everything; the other men were relaxed, guns dangling or laid across their bed-rolls; some smoking; a man behind him was having a nip of something that didn't smell like switchel.[15]

"Old Morgan'll never come this way," one bearded farmer was saying. "That boy's shiftier than a creased buck. He ain't never goin' to fight his way in the front door when the back door's open."

"Back door ain't so all-fired wide open's you might think."

"Open or shut—what's it to Morgan? With five thousand men you go in where it pleasures you and don't wait for the welcome mat to be put out."

---

15. **switchel**\\ˈswich·əl\\ drink made of molasses or honey, maple syrup, water, and sometimes rum.

"Five thousand," somebody yelled. "What the hell we doing here? Why ain't we making a good hickory[16] for Indianapolis?"

"Indianapolis, boy? You better stay clear of there. Morton's waitin' for you there with a writ."

"Five thousand or ten thousand," said a quiet voice, "I'm going to stay right here. I'm going to give Morgan the butt-end of my mind if nothing else before he busts over that bridge and into my store."

"Me too. Only I'm goin' to talk with lead. My folks live down in Harrison County."

"Did you hear about old man Yardell?"

"Ya—shot in the back."

"Not doin' a thing—just come to his door to see what the ruckus was about."

"Did you hear about 'em down at Versailles? Had the cannon loaded, ready to let go smack dab in the middle of the rebs."

"What happened?"

"Cannoneer dropped his coal and before they could get another the rebs took the gun."

"Oughta court-martial the feller who done that."

"'Fore the afternoon's over, Grogan, you'll likely change your tune as to that."

The afternoon wore on. To the funky[17] smell of the river and of lush river growth was added that of sweating men and horses. Josh eased Rome's girth and hoisted his blankets so a little air could flow under them. Back in the saddle he felt light-headed and detached. Gum had been right about the cherries; they weren't setting right. He felt kind of sick but happy. He'd got here, he was all right, he was where he belonged. By twisting about he could see a curve of the Muscatatuck where it flowed in shallow ripples across a sandbar, then darkened as the channel deepened near the bridge. It was three or four o'clock. The sun went through the water and onto the sandbar, then flashed, pulsing with the movement of the water in his temples. He could see the silvery glint of the little minnows, like bullets; a dragon-fly ran its darning needle in-and-out—in-and-out of the flowing water. It was July . . . a summer afternoon . . . the cool water . . . the hot sun . . . the darting . . . the silver bullets.

Josh's neck stiffened, his head snapped up, his hand closed round the stock of his gun. A horseman was pounding up the road.

"It's one of our scouts," said Ben Whitey.

The rider, a little fellow in uniform on a lathered black, pulled up beside the captain. Josh couldn't hear what he was saying, but after a minute the captain turned and told them, his voice quiet but with an edge to it that let them know that this was it, the time had come.

"Boys," he said, "they're closing in. They're up the road a couple of miles. Less of 'em than we figured. I expect them to charge. There's just two things to remember: first, stand steady. Second, don't fire till I give the word." He stood in his stirrups and pounded the words home. "Don't fire till I give the word. If you fire before you can make your shots good, it's all over. They'll ride you down. Hold it. Your guns carry just as far as theirs, and you're better shots. Those men've been in the saddle for weeks now, and it's telling on them. Shoot low so's if you miss a man you get a horse. But don't miss."

The scout went on past them at a gallop and Josh could hear the black's hooves ring on the bridge planking, then quiet as he hit the dust of the road on the west bank where the men in hiding were waiting the news. The captain himself wheeled round to await the attack with his men.

Josh reached for his gun. Waves of something, he didn't know what, were hitting his chest. It's like riding through the woods and being hit by branches that leave thee in the saddle, but so belabored thy chest aches, he thought. Other waves, or perhaps the same ones, pounded against his ears, broke in deafening crashes as if he were deep under water, buffeted by currents that could break bones, could rip a man out of his flesh and let him run,

---

16. **making a good hickory,** travel at a rapid pace.
17. **funky,** strong offensive smell.

liquid, away. Then, in the midst of the pain and crashing, Josh thought, it's thy heart beating. Nothing but thy heart.

Gum said, "Fix those lines, boy." And again, "Get those reins fixed. If your horse jerks his head he'll spoil your aim."

Josh saw that Gum was right. He got his hand out of the reins and rubbed it along Rome's neck. "Good boy," he said. "Good old Rome. Thee'll be all right." He knew he was encouraging himself. Rome didn't need cheering —he stood solid as a meeting house, only his big head moving up and down a little.

They were all waiting. Ben Whitey was cussing, a long line of words as if he was dreaming, or singing, in a kind of funny way. But they were mostly quiet—listening. Something came down, or perhaps it came up, out of the earth itself, something very thin and fine, like a spun web, and held them all together. Josh could feel it. Anybody could break away from it, if he liked, but while they headed the same way, waited the same thing, it held them. You could lean against it like steel. Josh felt its support . . . the waves beat against him, but he leaned against that fabric and it held him.

It held him until he heard the first sounds: a rebel yell from up the road, beyond the elder thicket—then another. Josh never knew a man could make a sound like that. It was a screech such as an animal might make—only it was in a man's voice, a voice that could say "Farewell" or "Rain tomorrow" . . . and that made it worse. It sounded crazy . . . it sounded as if the tongue that gave it could lap blood. It broke the web that held them together, it left Josh alone.

He could hear far away the thud of hooves and the waves that had beat against his ears before began now to say words: Rome's fast, Rome's mighty fast. Run for it, run for it. The minute they turn the curve, run for it.

He looked around, he picked out the likely path. "Sure wish I had a cherry-stone to suck on," said Gum Anson. "Sure am parched."

Gum's words drowned out the others. The hoof beats came nearer. What's the worst can happen to thee? Josh asked himself. Get a bul-

let in thy gizzard. Get killed. Nothing else. . . . It was all right. He settled down to wait.

"Hold it, hold it," the captain was calling. "Wait for the word. Hold it. Hold it."

From around the bend, very slowly, came a single man, carrying a white flag. A few paces behind him were perhaps twenty or thirty other mounted men.

"It's a trick, it's a trick," the Home Guardsmen were yelling. "Watch it, captain. It's funny business."

"Don't shoot," shouted the colonel who had ridden up. "Don't fire on a white flag. But watch 'em. Keep 'em covered."

He rode forward a couple of paces. "Are you surrendering?" he called.

The man with the white flag called back, "No. No surrender. We want to parley."

"Come on in," said the colonel. "You," he yelled. "You with the white flag. The rest of you stay back."

"Trying to get up inside our range and ride us down," said Gum.

The flag-bearer came up alongside the Home Guard colonel and saluted.

"Keep your guns on those men," the colonel called back, then lowered his own. Josh couldn't hear his words, but could see that the raider was talking fast and earnestly.

"Could be your brother," said Gum.

It was so. The rebel doing the talking was tow haired and young, a gaunt brown-faced boy, very broad shouldered and supple in the saddle. Josh's gun, which had been leveled on him, wavered, but he brought it to bear, once again.

The Guardsmen were getting restless. "Tell him to make up his mind. Surrender and talk— or shut his mouth and fight."

"What's he doin'? Preachin'?"

"Lectioneering for Jeff Davis."

"Shut him up, colonel. Shut him up."

"We'll make him talk outa the other corner of his mouth."

"You the one shot old man Yardell?"

The colonel turned his back on the raiders and rode up to his own men. "Don't take your guns off them," he told them. "He says we're surrounded. He says they've cut in back of us —that they've got five thousand men circled around Vernon and it's suicide to resist. He says every bridge and ford can be rushed. He says surrender and save bloodshed. He says if we surrender nobody'll be harmed. Provisions and fresh mounts taken only. What do you say?"

The storekeeper who had wanted to give Morgan the butt-end of his mind rose now in his stirrups and delivered a piece of it. "He's lying. Men don't start talking until they're past fighting."

"If he had five thousand men they'd be in Vernon now. Blood shed, so long's it's your blood, ain't nothin' to a reb."

"Horses and provisions, eh? Who appointed us quartermaster corps to the Confederate Army?"

Ben Whitey gave the final answer. He yelled. His yell wasn't practiced like the rebel screech; it hadn't the long falsetto[18] midnight quaver which could raise the hackles and slide between the bones like cold steel, but it was very strong and it lifted toward the end with a raw, unsheathed resonance of its own. It seemed what they had waited for—it seemed the only answer to give. It drained away the uncertainty, the distrust, the fear of the long wait. Above the quiet river it rose in great volume and flowed in a roiled and mounting current across the summer fields. Josh's musket quivered with the violence of his own shouting.

The colonel regarded his men quizzically, then shrugged his shoulders as if to say to the raiders, What can I do with such fire-eaters? and rode back to the rebel leader. There was another conference shorter than the first one, after which the raiders turned, cantered back down the road up which they had just ridden.

"They give us two hours," the colonel said, "to get our women and children out of town. After which, they attack."

At eight that evening they were still waiting, drawn up, ready. The new moon had set and the night was very dark and warm, filled with soft summer stars which seemed to escape from set star shapes and let light shimmer fluidly— and it almost seemed, moistly—across the sky. Some time later the captain with a militiaman came up to the group Josh was in.

"Count off here," he said. "I'm sending twenty of you men to Finney's Ford. The rebs could come through there as well as here if they know the crick.[19] There's a company there now —but no use having any if you don't have enough." He turned to the militiaman. "Let some of your men sleep," he said, "but keep a heavy guard posted."

Josh rode with the twenty men slowly and quietly through the night, back across the bridge and to a bank above the river where any party attempting to use the ford could be fired on while in the water. He rode among strangers. Gum and Ben Whitey had been left behind, and he thought, as he had been thinking all day, Now it begins.

In the darkness the company at the ford seemed very large; the men dismounted, speaking in muffled voices, their horses tethered and resting behind them.

"The crick takes a turn here," the new men were told. "Twenty feet down to the bottom here, so keep your eyes peeled. I'm going to let you men have a couple of hours' sleep, then you can relieve some of us. Get out of your saddles and get some rest—but don't rest so hard you can't hear a raider crossin' that branch."

Josh dismounted and felt his way along the bank in the layered darkness. He felt rather than saw the stream below him, smelled it, really, he believed, though he could hear the occasional lap of a little eddy against a stone, and see here and there a prick of light reflected from a star. He ate cold biscuit with dried beef, gave Rome a biscuit, then stretched out on his blankets, somewhat withdrawn from the main body of the militia and near the bank of the

<hr />

18. **falsetto**\fol ˄sĕ·dō\ artifically produced voice that falls short of full voice.
19. **crick**\krĭk\ dialect for creek.

stream. Rome stood behind him snuffing at the scent of the strange men and horses about him, mouthing the already cropped-over grass in search of a neglected tuft.

War, Josh thought, seemed a hard thing to come at. The dying and killing he had declared himself ready for at the breakfast table, and which he had imagined he would meet face to face as soon as he'd gotten out onto the road, seemed always to lurk around another corner. He had fortified himself for so many encounters with either or both that there were now almost no breastworks he could fling up, or armaments he could assemble. His supply of anticipation was about used up. War appeared to consist not of the dramatic and immediate sacrifice, either of his body in dying, or his spirit in killing, as he had foreseen it at the breakfast table, but of an infinite series of waitings and postponements.

This is it, he had said, and it was only Ben Whitey waiting at the cut-off. This is it, and it was Vernon as much like Fourth of July as war. This surely is it, he had said, and it was the wind in the elder clump. This, this: a man with a white flag. And now in the dark night to defend the vulnerable ford—and this was not it either, but simply lying at ease on his blankets, his cherry-addled stomach settled with good beef and biscuit, Rome munching by his side and the Milky Way banding the sky familiarly. Except for the gun under his hand it could be any summer night, lying outside for a time to cool off before bed time. And if John Morgan himself, lantern in hand, should bend over him, prod him with his toe and say, "This is it, bub," he didn't know whether he'd believe him or not. Maybe John Morgan was waiting and hunting, too, no more an authority on *its* arrival than he. Getting ready for war might be a short horse and soon curried, but war itself was a horse liable to stretch, so far as he could see, from July to eternity . . . head at Maple Grove and hocks[20] in Beulah Land.

Josh closed his eyes to sleep; but beneath his lids there flowed not only the remembered sights of the day, the faces, attitudes, gestures he had seen and noted, but the multitudinous sights that there had been in daylight no time to name, or space within the crowded mind to delineate. Now in darkness, behind shut lids, they lived again. He saw the L-shaped rip in the pants of the raider who had carried the white flag, and beneath the rip, the long, improperly healed wound which reddened the man's calf from knee to ankle. He saw now, what he had missed then, the downward motion of the raider's hand toward his gun when Ben Whitey's yell lunged unexpectedly toward him. He saw now, trying to sleep, the controlled drop of a spider, delicately spinning, from the spire of an unblooming head of goldenrod to the yellowed grass beneath it. He heard Gum Anson's answer to someone who asked him, "What you doing here, Gum?" "I'm a farmer," said Gum, "and you can't farm unless you keep the varmints down." He heard another voice—the storekeeper's, he thought—say, "I'm a man of peace—but there ain't any peace when your neighbors are being killed. And if it's a question of good blood, or bad, on my hands, by God, I choose bad."

At last he slept—and continued to see and hear . . . a raider was trying to take Ebony . . . he had ridden his horse inside the summer kitchen, and overturned the table, trampled the crockery and was snatching at Ebony, who above the sounds of confusion was screaming, "Wake up, wake up."

Josh woke up. He found himself in the center of a great, bubbling cauldron of noise: men shouting, screaming advice, cursing; horses neighing; and in the creek below the splash and clatter of men and animals crossing the ford. There was a spattering of shots. Someone was calling over and over, "Mount, mount, mount."

Josh stepped cautiously, felt for Rome in the dark, said his name, doubled his hands hoping to feel them close upon horse flesh, harkened

---

20. **hocks,** hind limb of a horse, corresponding to ankle of a man.

to the billowing roll of sound. Then suddenly the sound fanned out, burst inside his head, roared against the bones of his skull and breaking through bone and tissue, trickled out by way of mouth and nose; it fluttered a few last times against his ear drums, then left him in quiet.

It was daylight before he was sure what had happened: he had gone over the cliff, through the branches of a willow which grew almost parallel with the stream, and now lay within hand's reach of the creek itself. At first he had tried to call out, but the sound of his own voice had detonated like gun fire inside his head and he was afraid that his skull, which he reckoned was broken, might fall apart with the effort. He was half-conscious, and wholly sick, but between bouts of retching he thought: This is it. I've come to it at last. This is war. It's falling over a cliff, cracking thy skull and puking.

It was just after sunup when Labe found him. He had about given up when he heard sounds from beneath the willow.

"Josh," he cried, "thee's alive, thee's all right."

"No, I'm not," said Josh morosely.

"Oh, Josh," Labe said again, and knelt beside him, "thee's all right."

"I wish thee'd stop saying that," Josh told him. "It makes me feel sicker. I'm not all right. My head's split, I think."

Labe looked at it. "It does kind of look that way," he said, "but if thee's not died yet I reckon thee's not going to."

Josh moaned.

"Why didn't thee call out—get some help?" Labe asked.

"At first," Josh said, "because I didn't know anything. Then when I did, if I even opened my mouth to whisper, my whole head like to fell off. Then I got so's I could talk—but if I did, I puked. I still do," he said, and did. "I wish thee'd go away," he told Labe finally, "and leave me alone. I was beginning to get a little easy." He lay back for a while, then painfully lifted himself on one elbow. "Did we get Morgan?"

"They didn't come this way."

"Didn't come this way?" asked Josh. "I heard them. They crossed the crick last night."

"That wasn't Morgan," Labe said. "That was some cotton-headed farmers over'n the south bank who took a freak to drive their stock across so's the rebs wouldn't get 'em."

"I thought it was Morgan," Josh said. "I was fooled."

"Thee had plenty of company," Labe said. "They's all fooled."

"Where's Morgan now?"

"Dupont, they say. He gave Vernon the go-by."

Josh lay back again. "We stood them off," he said proudly. "We kept Morgan out of Vernon."

There was nothing Labe could say to that. Presently he asked, "If I get some help does thee think thee could move, Josh? They're worried about thee at home."

"How'd thee come to find me?" Josh asked.

"Rome came home without thee."

"I'd just as lief[21] stay here," Josh said bitterly. "Go to war and fall off a cliff."

"Thee needn't let that fash[22] you," Labe said. "More did than didn't."

With the help of Guardsmen who were still lingering about the ford, discussing the night's events, Labe got Josh, unwilling and protesting, up the bank and into Rome's saddle. Labe rode behind and let Josh lean against him, and thus supported Josh was able to travel.

"Am I bleeding?" Josh asked weakly after they'd covered a mile or so. A thin trickle of blood was coming across his shoulder and down his shirt front.

"No," Labe said, "that's me."

"Thee?" asked Josh, for whom the events of the past twenty-four hours were still uncertain. "Thee wasn't fighting, was thee?"

"Well, I was a little," Labe admitted.

"In the Guard?" Josh asked.

"No," Labe said, "just kind of privately."

"Why?"

---

21. lief\lēv\ gladly, willingly.
22. fash\făsh\trouble or bother.

"Well," said Labe, "when I's hunting thee a man sung a song."

"I wouldn't fight anybody about any song," Josh said.

Labe didn't say anything.

"I purely hate fighting," Josh said. "Don't thee, Labe?"

"Not so much," Labe answered.

"I hate it," Josh said. "That's why I got to."

"And I got not to," Labe said, "because I like it."

Josh wanted to be with them, so they carried the sofa out of the sitting-room into the summer kitchen, and he lay on it, a cool wet towel wrapped round his head. He felt as if his skull had been peeled away and his brain left so exposed that even the changed cadence of a voice could strike it like a blow. He pushed the towel a little way off his eyes. Labe was in a chair, head back, wet cloth across his nose, and broken hand in a bucket of hot water. They were both awaiting a doctor if one could be found who was not busy. His mother was changing cloths and minding breakfast, stepping very light so's not to jar his head. His father was at the table where he'd been the morning before. There was a mingling of looks on his face.

"Well," Jess said, "I never had a First Day morning[23] like this before and never hope to again. Though I reckon everybody's done what had to be done. Josh anyway. I'm not so sure about Labe."

Labe lifted the cloth which covered mouth as well as nose. "Mine was kind of an accident," he admitted.

Jess turned toward his eldest son. Their eyes met and Jess nodded. "Well," he said again, "no reason why we can't eat, is there, Eliza? Have a sup of hot coffee and some biscuit and gravy?"

Josh groaned.

"I can't chew," Labe muttered.

Jess seemed to be feeling better and better. "I ain't been doing any fighting," he said, "in the militia or on the side. I got a good appetite. If you boys don't mind, and thy mother'll set it

forth, I'll have a bite. So far's I can remember there wasn't much eating done here yesterday. Eliza," he asked, "won't thee sit and eat?"

"Thee go ahead, Jess," Eliza said. "I'm busy with the boys just now."

"Mattie?"

"No," Mattie said delicately, ". . . all this blood and broken bones . . ."

"Little Jess?"

"Thee don't need to wait for me," said Little Jess.

"Well, then," Jess said heartily, "let us eat. But before we eat let's return thanks. This is First Day morning and we've much to be thankful for."

Josh listened to his father's words . . . they were a part of his happiness. When he had first come to, found himself lying at the edge of the crick, he had thought he would hate coming home, admit he'd been hurt, not by gun or saber, but by falling over a bank onto his head. Now it didn't matter. Yesterday morning and his talk of dying and killing seemed almost a life-time away . . . the past twenty-four hours a prolonged campaign from which he had emerged, a veteran, with mind much cleared as to what mattered and what did not.

Next time . . . he wouldn't talk so big . . . about fighting . . . and dying. But that didn't matter either, now. What mattered was that he had stood there . . . he had been afraid, but he had stood at the bridge. He had thought of running . . . but he hadn't done it . . . he had stood in the front line, not knowing but that Morgan himself might bear down upon them . . . he had stood at the crick's edge in the darkness and confusion and had been hunting gun and horse when he had fallen.

And there were the things he had learned . . . that talk beforehand is no good . . . that in darkness on a twenty-foot cliff it is best not to hurry . . . that death, when you moved toward it, seemed to retreat . . . that it was only when you turned your back on it . . . and ran . . . that it pursued.

---

23. **First Day morning,** Sunday.

With these thoughts the words of his father's grace mingled very well. . . . "Eternal Father . . . blessed Son . . . life everlasting. . . ."

He had thought his father was still praying, his tone was still so prayerful. But the words had changed. Josh once more cautiously pushed the towel away from his eyes. Jess was looking about the sunlit kitchen now, inspecting his family. "All here," he said, "right side up and forked end down." But then, maybe he was still praying, for he said next, "Amen, amen." Either way it was all right with Josh.

I
THE CLASH OF HUMAN NEEDS

Psychologists who have studied the human infant tell us that the basic needs of human beings are very few. So long as the infant has food and rest and love, it will survive and grow. It seems, however, that human needs become more complex as one grows older. In this selection, for example, Josh faces a conflict between his need for the love and affection of his parents and his need to prove his manhood, which might be called a need for self-respect. Also complicating the matter are the family's religious convictions. Offhand, we might suppose that the need for love, being more primitive, would prove stronger than the need for self-respect, but this does not turn out to be the case. Judging from your own experience, would you say that it is generally true that persons of Josh's age have a greater need for self-respect than for the affection of those they love?

II
IMPLICATIONS

Below are a series of propositions about questions raised by this selection. Decide whether each statement is true or false as it stands; for those you consider false or partly true, rephrase the statement to reflect your own belief.

1. When one's country is at war, it requires more courage to resist joining an army than it takes to join it.

2. It is impossible for an individual to predict how he will behave when facing an unusual situation.

3. In time of war a true Christian will not kill, even if it means giving up his own life.

4. One cannot escape guilt in war—those who do not fight and kill are as guilty as those who do, for the man who doesn't fight has on his hands the blood of those who died because he refused to.

5. The major difference between Josh and Labe is that Labe is three years younger than his brother.

6. Since most individuals believe that it is wrong to kill fellow human beings and since most nations have required their citizens to kill their brethren, we must assume that the moral codes of nations are essentially different from the moral codes of individuals.

III
TECHNIQUES

Conflict

Even if one concentrates upon a single character in a story, he is likely to find that individual facing a number of different conflicts. In Josh's case, for example, there is a conflict between him and his parents over the issue of whether or not he should go to battle and kill. This is the most obvious conflict, but it is complicated and intensified by Josh's inner conflict, centering upon his need to prove his manhood. Finally, there is the larger issue of whether or not Morgan's Raiders will succeed in taking Vernon, and Josh is involved in that conflict, too.

Which of these conflicts interested you most? Which did the author intend to be the main conflict, and how do you know this?

Climax

The central climax of this story occurs when Josh wakes up, finds himself in the middle of the rush of men and horses, and then falls off the cliff. Did this climax disappoint you? If so, was it because you thought another climax was coming?

Moment of Illumination

Where is the moment of illumination in this story? How does it help you grasp the theme of the story? Is it ever possible for a reader to criticize an author for not telling the sort of story the reader expects?

ULYSSES GRANT
Harold Von Schmidt

One way of picturing
the inner struggle is
to portray an individual
whose familiar life story
brings this conflict
immediately to mind.
Ulysses Grant is such a person
and this pensive
wartime study
is full of his solitary debate.

TORMENTED MAN
Leonard Baskin
*1956, Ink, Collection
of the Whitney Museum
of American Art, New York,
Gift of Living Arts Foundation Fund*

Gallery

THE INNER STRUGGLE

The contradictions within a human being
challenge the writer to heights of poetry and drama,
but by its very nature the resulting
inner struggles would seem outside the province
of painters and sculptors. This gallery,
however, proves the fascination the theme
has held for artists and suggests the success
they have had in visualizing the conflict
inside the minds and hearts of men.

The intense, symbol-laden styles
of much modern painting
lend themselves especially well to portraying
the TORMENTED MAN. Distorted
and in obvious pain the man is pictured
below the Harpies of Grecian legend—
these dreadful hags have been an enduring symbol
of the conflicts springing
from conscience and tradition.

Meditating sadly
with her hand raised
to ward off
a self-inflicted blow,
THE TRAGIC MUSE
presents a general
statement of the theme.

THE TRAGIC MUSE
Alexander Brooks
Collection of the Newark Museum

EL PENITENTE
Lu Duble

The penitent writhes in guilt and remorse,
his struggle unmistakable
in this terracotta sculpture
by Lu Duble.
    And at the other end of the continuum,
the wood carving of THE OBSESSED
shows man immobilized, bound,
and rigid with his response
to the battle within him.

THE OBSESSED
Jane Wasey

Superficially
an individual conflict
is the wooden carving
entitled MINORITY MAN
NO. 1. Yet, while
the isolated individual
must struggle within
himself for the strength
to carry on, he
looks without
for comfort and aid.

MINORITY MAN
NO. 1
Ed. Wilson

In the ancient days before David became king of Israel,
King Saul had to face a dubious battle. The conflict
and the apprehension were too much for him so that he sought out a
sorcerer (who was forbidden to practice by Saul's own edicts)
and had the ghost of Samuel raised to give him counsel.
As the picture suggests, the foretelling was tragic: Saul's own end was near.
In the eighteenth century when Benjamin West painted,
he could count on wide familiarity
with the Biblical story he pictured.

SAUL AND THE WITCH OF ENDOR
Benjamin West
Wadsworth Atheneum, Hartford, Connecticut

Josh Birdwell's decision was a difficult one to make,
but at least, in the end, he felt morally justified that he had made
a good one. What does one do, however, when he is in a situation
in which he must make a choice between two alternatives, *both* of which
may be wrong morally? This is the question raised in the following story
of a terrible moment of decision in the life of a Civil War soldier.

A Horseman in the Sky

AMBROSE BIERCE

I

One sunny afternoon in the autumn of the year 1861 a soldier lay in a clump of laurel by the side of a road in western Virginia. He lay at full length upon his stomach, his feet resting upon the toes, his head upon the left forearm. His extended right hand loosely grasped his rifle. But for the somewhat methodical disposition of his limbs and a slight rhythmic movement of the cartridge-box at the back of his belt he might have been thought to be dead. He was asleep at his post of duty. But if detected he would be dead shortly afterward, death being the just and legal penalty of his crime.

The clump of laurel in which the criminal lay was in the angle of a road which after ascending southward a steep acclivity to that point turned sharply to the west, running along the summit for perhaps one hundred yards. There it turned southward again and went zigzagging downward through the forest. At the salient of that second angle was a large flat rock, jutting out northward, overlooking the deep valley from which the road ascended. The rock capped a high cliff; a stone dropped from its outer edge would have fallen sheer downward one thousand feet to the tops of the pines. The angle where the soldier lay was on another spur of the same cliff. Had he been awake he would have commanded a view, not only of the short arm of the road and the jutting rock, but of the entire profile of the cliff below it. It might well have made him giddy to look.

The country was wooded everywhere except at the bottom of the valley to the northward, where there was a small natural meadow, through which flowed a stream scarcely visible from the valley's rim. This open ground looked hardly larger than an ordinary door-yard, but was really several acres in extent. Its green was more vivid than that of the inclosing forest. Away beyond it rose a line of giant cliffs similar to those upon which we are supposed to stand in our survey of the savage scene, and through which the road had somehow made its climb to the summit. The configuration of the valley, indeed, was such that from this point of observation it seemed entirely shut in, and one could but have wondered how the road which found a way out of it had found a way into it, and whence came and whither went the waters of the stream that parted the meadow more than a thousand feet below.

No country is so wild and difficult but men will make it a theatre of war; concealed in the forest at the bottom of that military rat-trap, in which half a hundred men in possession of the exits might have starved an army to submission, lay five regiments of Federal infantry. They had marched all the previous day and night and were resting. At nightfall they would take to the road again, climb to the place where their unfaithful sentinel now slept, and descending the other slope of the ridge fall upon a camp of the enemy at about midnight. Their hope was to surprise it, for the road led to the rear of it. In case of failure, their position would be perilous in the extreme; and fail they surely would should accident or vigilance apprise the enemy of the movement.

II

The sleeping sentinel in the clump of laurel was a young Virginian named Carter Druse. He was the son of wealthy parents, an only child, and had known such ease and cultivation and high living as wealth and taste were able to command in the mountain country of western Virginia. His home was but a few miles from where he now lay. One morning he had risen from the breakfast-table and said, quietly but gravely: "Father, a Union regiment has arrived at Grafton.[1] I am going to join it."

The father lifted his leonine head, looked at the son a moment in silence, and replied: "Well, go, sir, and whatever may occur do what you conceive to be your duty. Virginia, to which you are a traitor, must get on without you. Should we both live to the end of the war, we will speak further of the matter. Your mother, as the physician has informed you, is in a most critical condition; at the best she cannot be with us longer than a few weeks, but that time is precious. It would be better not to disturb her."

So Carter Druse, bowing reverently to his father, who returned the salute with a stately courtesy that masked a breaking heart, left the home of his childhood to go soldiering. By conscience and courage, by deeds of devotion and daring, he soon commended himself to his fellows and his officers; and it was to these qualities and to some knowledge of the country that he owed his selection for his present perilous duty at the extreme outpost. Nevertheless, fatigue had been stronger than resolution and he had fallen asleep. What good or bad angel came in a dream to rouse him from his state of crime, who shall say? Without a movement,

without a sound, in the profound silence and the languor of the late afternoon, some invisible messenger of fate touched with unsealing finger the eyes of his consciousness—whispered into the ear of his spirit the mysterious awakening word which no human lips ever have spoken, no human memory ever has recalled. He quietly raised his forehead from his arm and looked between the masking stems of the laurels, instinctively closing his right hand about the stock of his rifle.

His first feeling was a keen artistic delight. On a colossal pedestal, the cliff,—motionless at the extreme edge of the capping rock and sharply outlined against the sky,—was an equestrian statue of impressive dignity. The figure of the man sat the figure of the horse, straight and soldierly, but with the repose of a Grecian god carved in the marble which limits the suggestion of activity. The gray costume harmonized with its aërial background; the metal of accoutrement[2] and caparison[3] was softened and subdued by the shadow; the animal's skin had no points of high light. A carbine strikingly foreshortened lay across the pommel of the saddle, kept in place by the right hand grasping it at the "grip"; the left hand, holding the bridle rein, was invisible. In silhouette against the sky the profile of the horse was cut with the sharpness of a cameo; it looked across the heights of air to the confronting cliffs beyond. The face of the rider, turned slightly away, showed only an outline of temple and beard; he was looking downward to the bottom of the valley. Magnified by its lift against the sky and by the soldier's testifying sense of the formidableness of a near enemy the group appeared of heroic, almost colossal, size.

For an instant Druse had a strange, half-defined feeling that he had slept to the end of the war and was looking upon a noble work of art

---

1. **Grafton,** county seat of Taylor County, northwest Virginia, on Tygart River.
2. **accoutrement**\ə ᵃkü·tĕr·mənt\ soldiers' equipment except clothes and weapons.
3. **caparison**\kə ᵃpă·rə·sən\ covering of the horse.

"Young Soldier," Winslow Homer

body slightly backward from the verge; the man remained immobile as before. Broad awake and keenly alive to the significance of the situation, Druse now brought the butt of his rifle against his cheek by cautiously pushing the barrel forward through the bushes, cocked the piece, and glancing through the sights covered a vital spot of the horseman's breast. A touch upon the trigger and all would have been well with Carter Druse. At that instant the horseman turned his head and looked in the direction of his concealed foeman—seemed to look into his very face, into his eyes, into his brave, compassionate heart.

Is it then so terrible to kill an enemy in war —an enemy who has surprised a secret vital to the safety of one's self and comrades—an enemy more formidable for his knowledge than all his army for its numbers? Carter Druse grew pale; he shook in every limb, turned faint, and saw the statuesque group before him as black figures, rising, falling, moving unsteadily in arcs of circles in a fiery sky. His hand fell away from his weapon, his head slowly dropped until his face rested on the leaves in which he lay. This courageous gentleman and hardy soldier was near swooning from intensity of emotion.

It was not for long; in another moment his face was raised from earth, his hands resumed their places on the rifle, his forefinger sought the trigger; mind, heart, and eyes were clear, conscience and reason sound. He could not hope to capture that enemy; to alarm him would but send him dashing to his camp with his fatal news. The duty of the soldier was plain: the man must be shot dead from ambush —without warning, without a moment's spiritual preparation, with never so much as an unspoken prayer, he must be sent to his account. But no—there is a hope; he may have discovered nothing—perhaps he is but admiring the sublimity of the landscape. If permitted, he may turn and ride carelessly away in the direction whence he came. Surely it will be possible to judge at the instant of his withdrawing whether he knows. It may well be that his fixity of attention—Druse turned his head and looked

reared upon that eminence to commemorate the deeds of an heroic past of which he had been an inglorious part. The feeling was dispelled by a slight movement of the group: the horse, without moving its feet, had drawn its through the deeps of air downward, as from the surface to the bottom of a translucent sea. He saw creeping across the green meadow a sinuous line of figures of men and horses— some foolish commander was permitting the soldiers of his escort to water their beasts in the open, in plain view from a dozen summits!

Druse withdrew his eyes from the valley and fixed them again upon the group of man and horse in the sky, and again it was through the sights of his rifle. But this time his aim was at the horse. In his memory, as if they were a divine mandate, rang the words of his father at their parting: "Whatever may occur, do what you conceive to be your duty." He was calm now. His teeth were firmly but not rigidly closed; his nerves were as tranquil as a sleeping babe's—not a tremor affected any muscle of his body; his breathing, until suspended in the act of taking aim, was regular and slow. Duty had conquered; the spirit had said to the body: "Peace, be still." He fired.

III

An officer of the Federal force, who in a spirit of adventure or in quest of knowledge had left the hidden *bivouac* in the valley, and with aimless feet had made his way to the lower edge of a small open space near the foot of the cliff, was considering what he had to gain by pushing his exploration further. At a distance of a quarter-mile before him, but apparently at a stone's throw, rose from its fringe of pines the gigantic face of rock, towering to so great a height above him that it made him giddy to look up to where its edge cut a sharp, rugged line against the sky. It presented a clean, vertical profile against a background of blue sky to a point half the way down, and of distant hills, hardly less blue, thence to the tops of the trees at its base. Lifting his eyes to the dizzy altitude of its summit the officer saw an aston-

ishing sight—a man on horseback riding down into the valley through the air!

Straight upright sat the rider, in military fashion, with a firm seat in the saddle, a strong clutch upon the rein to hold his charger from too impetuous a plunge. From his bare head his long hair streamed upward, waving like a plume. His hands were concealed in the cloud of the horse's lifted mane. The animal's body was as level as if every hoofstroke encountered the resistant earth. Its motions were those of a wild gallop, but even as the officer looked they ceased, with all the legs thrown sharply forward as in the act of alighting from a leap. But this was a flight!

Filled with amazement and terror by this apparition of a horseman in the sky—half believing himself the chosen scribe of some new Apocalypse,[4] the officer was overcome by the intensity of his emotions; his legs failed him and he fell. Almost at the same instant he heard a crashing sound in the trees—a sound that died without an echo—and all was still.

The officer rose to his feet, trembling. The familiar sensation of an abraded shin[5] recalled his dazed faculties. Pulling himself together he ran rapidly obliquely away from the cliff to a point distant from its foot; thereabout he expected to find his man; and thereabout he naturally failed. In the fleeting instant of his vision his imagination had been so wrought upon by the apparent grace and ease and intention of the marvelous performance that it did not occur to him that the line of march of aërial cavalry is directly downward, and that he could find the objects of his search at the very foot of the cliff. A half-hour later he returned to camp.

This officer was a wise man; he knew better than to tell an incredible truth. He said nothing of what he had seen. But when the commander asked him if in his scout he had learned anything of advantage to ·the expedition he answered:

---

4. **Apocalypse**\ə ▲pŏ·kə ˈlĭps\ Book of Revelation.
5. **abraded**\ə ▲brād·əd\ **shin**, scraped shin.

"Yes, sir; there is no road leading down into this valley from the southward."

The commander, knowing better, smiled.

IV

After firing his shot, Private Carter Druse reloaded his rifle and resumed his watch. Ten minutes had hardly passed when a Federal sergeant crept cautiously to him on hands and knees. Druse neither turned his head nor looked at him, but lay without motion or sign of recognition.

"Did you fire?" the sergeant whispered.

"Yes."

"At what?"

"A horse. It was standing on yonder rock— pretty far out. You see it is no longer there. It went over the cliff."

The man's face was white, but he showed no other sign of emotion. Having answered, he turned away his eyes and said no more. The sergeant did not understand.

"See here, Druse," he said, after a moment's silence, "it's no use making a mystery. I order you to report. Was there anybody on the horse?"

"Yes."

"Well?"

"My father."

The sergeant rose to his feet and walked away. "Good God!" he said.

I
A CONFLICT OF LOYALTIES

Like Josh Birdwell, Carter Druse decides that he is obliged to join an army. This decision thrusts upon him a whole new set of responsibilities: A soldier must obey his commander; he must destroy the enemy; he has a duty to protect his comrades

in arms. These duties seem clear enough, but the army code does not say how one's military obligations affect his other responsibilities—his duties to God, or to his parents. Thus Carter Druse is forced into a situation in which either decision he may make seems morally wrong. How can you justify the choice he finally makes?

II
IMPLICATIONS

Consider the following statements and discuss those that you feel best reflect *the author's basic attitude and meaning* in this story. Justify your choice by citing details from the story.

1. A man's duty to his country is more important than his feelings for his family.

2. The good of the individual must be sacrificed for the good of the many.

3. The desire for personal survival is stronger than the instinct toward family love.

4. In moments of crisis the average man may rise to noble heights.

5. Carter Druse arrived at his decision by logical thought rather than by instinctive action.

6. War is a horrible institution.

III
TECHNIQUES

Conflict

It is often argued that the best conflicts are those in which both sides are evenly balanced; this increases suspense, for the reader cannot be sure which side will prevail. In this story the young man has to weigh the safety of himself and his regiments against the life of his father. Would you say that this is an evenly balanced conflict? How would the story be changed if the man on the horse had not been his father?

Two things help young Druse to make up his mind: (1) The fact that he could shoot the horse, and (2) his father's advice about duty. Why did Bierce bring in these details? To answer this question consider what your reaction might have been if these factors had not been brought in.

Climax and Moment of Illumination

As tense as the climax of this story is, you will probably agree that it would have been even more exciting if Bierce had revealed beforehand that

Carter was aiming at his father. Why, therefore, do you think he chose to withhold this information and use it as his moment of illumination?

IV
WORDS

A. Everyone who reads or listens confronts unfamiliar words. One way to figure out the meaning of a word is through the use of context clues. Using context clues, determine, if possible, enough meaning of the italicized words to make sense of each phrase or clause.

1. . . . for the man who wore it (the cloak) was *sublimated* in the complicated feudal ritual.

2. . . . one of the largest men . . . middle aged and so *corpulent* that the chair seemed to creak beneath his weight.

3. He supposed that Labe, in what he thought of as Labe's belittling way, was *enumerating* his own physical short comings.

4. She *oscillated* between the two ways of seeing Ebony.

5. Josh felt *bereft* of shelter, unshielded, alone.

6. The whole duty of seeing and *apprising* rested with him.

7. . . . road which, after ascending, southward, a steep *acclivity* to that point, turned sharply to the west.

8. . . . in the profound silence and the *languor* of the late afternoon . . .

9. . . . through the deeps of air downward, as from the surface to the bottom of a *translucent* sea . . .

10. In his memory, as if they were a divine *mandate*, rang the words of his father . . .

11. His nerves were as *tranquil* as a sleeping babe's.

12. . . . a strong clutch upon the rein to hold his charge from too *impetuous* a plunge . . .

B. 1. Find synonyms for the words below. Use each word in a sentence and decide if its synonym is able to replace it.

oscillated, tranquil, genial, abraded, intrinsic, taciturn, ominous, multitudinous.

2. Synonyms differ in expressing size, degree, specificity, and judgment. The word *enormous* suggests something that exceeds measurement in size as well as degree; *elephantine* carries a metaphorical suggestion of the elephant; *huge* suggests bulk, whereas *vast* suggests space or extent. The words *censure, condemn,* and *denounce* vary in degree: *censure* suggests fault-finding by some authority, such as a judge or government official; *condemn* adds the severity of a final decision by authority; *denounce* adds the notion of public condemnation. Explain the differences among these sets.

(a) flash, sparkle, scintillate; (b) moral, ethical, virtuous, righteous; (c) follower, partisan, satellite; (d) escalate, intensify, aggravate; (e) plot, intrigue, conspiracy.

C. 1. Look up the word *fash*. What is its origin? Look up *creek*. Does your dictionary label these words *dialect*, words peculiar to a particular region? Dialects show differences in pronunciation, in vocabulary, and in grammar. In "The Battle of Finney's Ford," the hero is a Quaker. In America, the Quakers formed not only a cultural community bound by like customs, but also a speech community which retained many elements of their own language. Look for examples of Quaker speech in "The Battle of Finney's Ford."

2. Dialects do not connote lack of education or social standing. In different localities different words are found for common objects. For example, which of the following do you use?

a. bag, sack, poke

b. earthworm, angleworm, fishworm

c. pop, soda, tonic, sodapop

d. string beans, green beans, snap beans

e. dog irons, fire irons, handirons

f. pancakes, hot cakes, fritters, flannel cakes, batter cakes, flapjacks

It takes great courage to sacrifice one's personal happiness
and security for the sake of some unpopular ideal or cause, especially
when the issue is not a matter of deciding between an obvious good
and a clearly recognized evil. Yet if a man does not live up
to his deepest inner convictions, in spite of popular opinion
and political pressures, how much security and happiness
can he really have? As he stared into his open grave—the decision
which would kill his political life—this is the sort of question
that confronted Edmund Ross, a little-known man who served briefly
as Senator from Kansas during the administration of President
Andrew Johnson. This real-life inner struggle is one of the chapters
from the late President Kennedy's Pulitzer Prize-winning book,
Profiles in Courage.

"*I looked down into my open grave...*" Edmund G. Ross

JOHN F. KENNEDY

In a lonely grave, forgotten and unknown, lies "the man who saved a President," and who as a result may well have preserved for ourselves and posterity constitutional government in the United States—the man who performed in 1868 what one historian has called "the most heroic act in American history, incomparably more difficult than any deed of valor upon the field of battle"—but a United States Senator whose name no one recalls: Edmund G. Ross of Kansas.

The impeachment of President Andrew Johnson, the event in which the obscure Ross was to play such a dramatic role, was the sensational climax to the bitter struggle between the President, determined to carry out Abraham Lincoln's policies of reconciliation with the defeated South, and the more radical Republican leaders in Congress, who sought to administer the downtrodden Southern states as conquered provinces which had forfeited their rights under the Constitution. It was, moreover, a struggle between Executive and Legislative authority. Andrew Johnson, the courageous if untactful Tennessean who had been the only Southern Member of Congress to refuse to secede with his state, had committed himself to the policies of the Great Emancipator to whose high station he had 'succeeded only by the course of an assassin's bullet. He knew that Lincoln prior to his death had already clashed with the extremists in Congress, who had opposed his approach to reconstruction in a constitutional and charitable manner and sought to make the Legislative Branch of the government supreme. And his own belligerent temperament soon destroyed any hope that Congress might now join hands in carrying out Lincoln's policies of permitting the South to resume its place in the Union with as little delay and controversy as possible.

By 1866, when Edmund Ross first came to the Senate, the two branches of the government were already at each other's throats, snarling and bristling with anger. Bill after bill was vetoed by the President on the grounds that they were unconstitutional, too harsh in their treatment of the South, an unnecessary prolongation of military rule in peacetime or undue interference with the authority of the Executive Branch. And for the first time in our nation's history, important public measures were passed over a President's veto and became law without his support.

But not all of Andrew Johnson's vetoes were overturned; and the "Radical" Republicans of the Congress promptly realized that one final step was necessary before they could crush their despised foe (and in the heat of political battle their vengeance was turned upon their President far more than their former military enemies of the South). That one remaining step was the assurance of a two-thirds majority in the Senate—for under the Constitution, such a majority was necessary to override a Presidential veto. And more important, such a majority was constitutionally required to accomplish their major ambition, now an ill-kept secret, conviction of the President under an impeachment and his dismissal from office!

The temporary and unstable two-thirds majority which had enabled the Senate Radical Republicans on several occasions to enact legislation over the President's veto was, they knew, insufficiently reliable for an impeachment conviction. To solidify this bloc became the paramount goal of Congress, expressly or impliedly governing its decisions on other issues—particularly the admission of new states, the readmission of Southern states and the determination of senatorial credentials. By extremely dubious methods a pro-Johnson Senator was denied his seat. Over the President's veto Nebraska was admitted to the Union, seating two more anti-administration Senators. Although last minute maneuvers failed to admit Colorado over the President's veto (sparsely populated Colorado had rejected statehood in a referendum), an unexpected tragedy brought false tears and fresh hopes for a new vote, in Kansas.

Senator Jim Lane of Kansas had been a "conservative" Republican sympathetic to Johnson's plans to carry out Lincoln's reconstruction policies. But his frontier state was one of the most "radical" in the Union. When Lane voted to uphold Johnson's veto of the Civil Rights Bill of 1866 and introduced the administration's bill for recognition of the new state government of Arkansas, Kansas had arisen in outraged heat. A mass meeting at Lawrence had vilified the Senator and speedily reported resolutions sharply condemning his position. Humiliated, mentally ailing, broken in health and laboring under charges of financial irregularities, Jim Lane took his own life on July 1, 1866.

With this thorn in their side removed, the Radical Republicans in Washington looked anxiously toward Kansas and the selection of Lane's successor. Their fondest hopes were realized, for the new Senator from Kansas turned out to be Edmund G. Ross, the very man who had introduced the resolutions attacking Lane at Lawrence.

There could be no doubt as to where Ross's sympathies lay, for his entire career was one of determined opposition to the slave states of the South, their practices and their friends. In 1854, when only twenty-eight, he had taken part in the mob rescue of a fugitive slave in Milwaukee. In 1856, he had joined that flood of anti-slavery immigrants to "bleeding" Kansas who intended to keep it a free territory. Disgusted with the Democratic party of his youth, he had left that party, and volunteered in the Kansas Free State Army to drive back a force of proslavery men invading the territory. In 1862, he had given up his newspaper work to enlist in the Union Army, from which he emerged a Major. His leading role in the condemnation of Lane at Lawrence convinced the Radical Republican leaders in Congress that in Edmund G. Ross they had a solid member of that vital two-thirds.

The stage was now set for the final scene—the removal of Johnson. Early in 1867, Congress enacted over the President's veto the Tenure-of-Office Bill which prevented the

President from removing without the consent of the Senate all new officeholders whose appointment required confirmation by that body. At the time nothing more than the cry for more patronage was involved, Cabinet Members having originally been specifically exempt.

Edmund Ross

On August 5, 1867, President Johnson—convinced that the Secretary of War, whom he had inherited from Lincoln, Edwin M. Stanton, was the surreptitious tool of the Radical Republicans and was seeking to become the almighty dictator of the conquered South—asked for his immediate resignation; and Stanton arrogantly fired back the reply that he declined to resign before the next meeting of Congress. Not one to cower before this kind of effrontery, the President one week later suspended Stanton, and appointed in his place the one man whom Stanton did not dare resist, General Grant. On January 13, 1868, an angry Senate notified the President and Grant that it did not concur in the suspension of Stanton, and Grant vacated the office upon Stanton's return. But the situation was intolerable. The Secretary of War was unable to attend Cabinet meetings or associate with his colleagues in the administration; and

on February 21, President Johnson, anxious to obtain a court test of the act he believed obviously unconstitutional, again notified Stanton that he had been summarily removed from the office of Secretary of War.

While Stanton, refusing to yield possession, barricaded himself in his office, public opinion in the nation ran heavily against the President. He had intentionally broken the law and dictatorially thwarted the will of Congress! Although previous resolutions of impeachment had been defeated in the House, both in committee and on the floor, a new resolution was swiftly reported and adopted on February 24 by a tremendous vote. Every single Republican voted in the affirmative, and Thaddeus Stevens of Pennsylvania—the crippled, fanatical personification of the extremes of the Radical Republican movement, master of the House of Representatives, with a mouth like the thin edge of an ax—warned both Houses of the Congress coldly: "Let me see the recreant who would vote to let such a criminal escape. Point me to one who will dare do it and I will show you one who will dare the infamy of posterity."

With the President impeached—in effect, indicted—by the House, the frenzied trial for his conviction or acquittal under the Articles of Impeachment began on March 5 in the Senate, presided over by the Chief Justice. It was a trial to rank with all the great trials in history—Charles I before the High Court of Justice, Louis XVI before the French Convention, and Warren Hastings before the House of Lords.[1] Two great elements of drama were missing: the actual cause for which the President was being tried was not fundamental to the welfare of the nation; and the defendant himself was at all times absent.

---

1. **Charles I,** King of England (1625–1649); beheaded at Whitehall after being condemned by 67 judges to be a tyrant and enemy of England. **Louis XVI,** King of France (1774–1792); tried for treason, found guilty and condemned to guillotine. **Warren Hastings** (1732–1818), English statesman and administrator in India; impeached for corruption (1788) but acquitted (1795).

But every other element of the highest court-room drama was present. To each Senator the Chief Justice administered an oath "to do impartial justice" (including even the hot-headed Radical Senator from Ohio, Benjamin Wade, who as President Pro Tempore of the Senate was next in line for the Presidency). The chief prosecutor for the House was General Benjamin F. Butler, the "butcher of New Orleans," a talented but coarse and demagogic Congressman from Massachusetts. (When he lost his seat in 1874, he was so hated by his own party as well as his opponents that one Republican wired concerning the Democratic sweep, "Butler defeated, everything else lost.") Some one thousand tickets were printed for admission to the Senate galleries during the trial, and every conceivable device was used to obtain one of the four tickets allotted each Senator.

From the fifth of March to the sixteenth of May, the drama continued. Of the eleven Articles of Impeachment adopted by the House, the first eight were based upon the removal of Stanton and the appointment of a new Secretary of War in violation of the Tenure-of-Office Act; the ninth related to Johnson's conversation with a general which was said to induce violations of the Army Appropriations Act; the tenth recited that Johnson had delivered "intemperate, inflammatory and scandalous harangues . . . as well against Congress as the laws of the United States"; and the eleventh was a deliberately obscure conglomeration of all the charges in the preceding articles, which had been designed by Thaddeus Stevens to furnish a common ground for those who favored conviction but were unwilling to identify themselves on basic issues. In opposition to Butler's inflammatory arguments in support of this hastily drawn indictment, Johnson's able and learned counsel replied with considerable effectiveness. They insisted that the Tenure-of-Office Act was null and void as a clear violation of the Constitution; that even if it were valid, it would not apply to Stanton, for the reasons previously mentioned; and that the only way that a judicial test of the law could be obtained

was for Stanton to be dismissed and sue for his rights in the courts.

But as the trial progressed, it became increasingly apparent that the impatient Republicans did not intend to give the President a fair trial on the formal issues upon which the impeachment was drawn, but intended instead to depose him from the White House on any grounds, real or imagined, for refusing to accept their policies. Telling evidence in the President's favor was arbitrarily excluded. Prejudgment on the part of most Senators was brazenly announced. Attempted bribery and other forms of pressure were rampant. The chief interest was not in the trial or the evidence, but in the tallying of votes necessary for conviction.

Twenty-seven states (excluding the unrecognized Southern states) in the Union meant fifty-four members of the Senate, and thirty-six votes were required to constitute the two-thirds majority necessary for conviction. All twelve Democratic votes were obviously lost, and the forty-two Republicans knew that they could afford to lose only six of their own members if Johnson were to be ousted. To their dismay, at a preliminary Republican caucus, six courageous Republicans indicated that the evidence so far introduced was not in their opinion sufficient to convict Johnson under the Articles of Impeachment. "Infamy!" cried the Philadelphia *Press*. The Republic has "been betrayed in the house of its friends!"

But if the remaining thirty-six Republicans would hold, there would be no doubt as to the outcome. All must stand together! But one Republican Senator would not announce his verdict in the preliminary poll—Edmund G. Ross of Kansas. The Radicals were outraged that a Senator from such an anti-Johnson stronghold as Kansas could be doubtful. "It was a very clear case," Senator Sumner of Massachusetts fumed, "especially for a Kansas man. I did not think that a Kansas man could quibble against his country."

From the very time Ross had taken his seat, the Radical leaders had been confident of his vote. His entire background, as already indicated, was one of firm support of their cause. One of his first acts in the Senate had been to read a declaration of his adherence to Radical Republican policy, and he had silently voted for all of their measures. He had made it clear that he was not in sympathy with Andrew Johnson personally or politically; and after the removal of Stanton, he had voted with the majority in adopting a resolution declaring such removal unlawful. His colleague from Kansas, Senator Pomeroy, was one of the most Radical leaders of the anti-Johnson group. The Republicans insisted that Ross's crucial vote was rightfully theirs, and they were determined to get it by whatever means available. As stated by DeWitt in his memorable *Impeachment of Andrew Johnson,* "The full brunt of the struggle turned at last on the one remaining doubtful Senator, Edmund G. Ross."

When the impeachment resolution had passed the House, Senator Ross had casually remarked to Senator Sprague of Rhode Island, "Well, Sprague, the thing is here; and, so far as I am concerned, though a Republican and opposed to Mr. Johnson and his policy, he shall have as fair a trial as an accused man ever had on this earth." Immediately the word spread that "Ross was shaky." "From that hour," he later wrote, "not a day passed that did not bring me, by mail and telegraph and in personal intercourse, appeals to stand fast for impeachment and not a few were the admonitions of condign visitations upon any indication even of lukewarmness."

Throughout the country, and in all walks of life, as indicated by the correspondence of Members of the Senate, the condition of the public mind was not unlike that preceding a great battle. The dominant party of the nation seemed to occupy the position of public prosecutor, and it was scarcely in the mood to brook delay for trial or to hear defense. Washington had become during the trial the central point of the politically dissatisfied and swarmed with representatives of every state of the Union, demanding in a practically united voice the deposition of the President. The footsteps of the anti-impeaching Republicans were dogged from the day's beginning to its end and far into the night, with entreaties, considerations, and threats. The newspapers came daily filled with not a few threats of violence upon their return to their constituents.

Ross and his fellow doubtful Republicans were daily pestered, spied upon and subjected to every form of pressure. Their residences were carefully watched, their social circles suspiciously scrutinized, and their every move and companions secretly marked in special notebooks. They were warned in the party press, harangued by their constituents, and sent dire warnings threatening political ostracism and even assassination. Stanton himself, from his barricaded headquarters in the War Department, worked day and night to bring to bear upon the doubtful Senators all the weight of his impressive military associations. The Philadelphia *Press* reported "a fearful avalanche of telegrams from every section of the country," a great surge of public opinion from the "common people" who had given their money and lives to the country and would not "willingly or unavenged see their great sacrifice made naught."

The New York *Tribune* reported that Edmund Ross in particular was "mercilessly dragged this way and that by both sides, hunted like a fox night and day and badgered by his own colleague, like the bridge at Arcola[2] now trod upon by one Army and now trampled by the other." His background and life were investigated from top to bottom, and his constituents and colleagues pursued him throughout Washington to gain some inkling of his opinion. He was the target of every eye, his name was on every mouth and his intentions were discussed in every newspaper. Although there is evidence that he gave some hint of agreement to each side, and each attempted to

---

2. Arcola\ˈȯr·kō·la\ a village in northern Italy where for three days (November 15–17, 1796) Napoleon fought a critical battle with Austria.

claim him publicly, he actually kept both sides in a state of complete suspense by his judicial silence.

But with no experience in political turmoil, no reputation in the Senate, no independent income and the most radical state in the Union to deal with, Ross was judged to be the most sensitive to criticism and the most certain to be swayed by expert tactics. A committee of Congressmen and Senators sent to Kansas, and to the states of the other doubtful Republicans, this telegram: "Great danger to the peace of the country and the Republican cause if impeachment fails. Send to your Senators public opinion by resolutions, letters, and delegations." A member of the Kansas legislature called upon Ross at the Capitol. A general urged on by Stanton remained at his lodge until four o'clock in the morning determined to see him. His brother received a letter offering $20,000 for revelation of the Senator's intentions. Gruff Ben Butler exclaimed of Ross, "There is a bushel of money! How much does the damned scoundrel want?" The night before the Senate was to take its first vote for the conviction or acquittal of Johnson, Ross received this telegram from home:

Kansas has heard the evidence and demands the conviction of the President.

[*signed*] D. R. ANTHONY AND 1,000 OTHERS

And on that fateful morning of May 16 Ross replied:

To D. R. Anthony and 1,000 Others: I do not recognize your right to demand that I vote either for or against conviction. I have taken an oath to do impartial justice according to the Constitution and laws, and trust that I shall have the courage to vote according to the dictates of my judgment and for the highest good of the country.

[signed]—E. G. Ross

That morning spies traced Ross to his breakfast; and ten minutes before the vote was taken his Kansas colleague warned him in the presence of Thaddeus Stevens that a vote for acquittal would mean trumped up charges and his political death.

But now the fateful hour was at hand. Neither escape, delay nor indecision was possible. As Ross himself later described it: "The galleries were packed. Tickets of admission were at an enormous premium. The House had adjourned and all of its members were in the Senate chamber. Every chair on the Senate floor was filled with a Senator, a Cabinet Officer, a member of the President's counsel or a member of the House." Every Senator was in his seat, the desperately ill Grimes of Iowa being literally carried in.

It had been decided to take the first vote under that broad Eleventh Article of Impeachment, believed to command the widest support. As the Chief Justice announced the voting would begin, he reminded "the citizens and strangers in the galleries that absolute silence and perfect order are required." But already a deathlike stillness enveloped the Senate chamber. A Congressman later recalled that "Some of the members of the House near me grew pale and sick under the burden of suspense"; and Ross noted that there was even "a subsidence of the shuffling of feet, the rustling of silks, the fluttering of fans, and of conversation."

The voting tensely commenced. By the time the Chief Justice reached the name of Edmund Ross twenty-four "guilties" had been pronounced. Ten more were certain and one other practically certain. Only Ross's vote was needed to obtain the thirty-six votes necessary to convict the President. But not a single person in the room knew how this young Kansan would vote. Unable to conceal the suspense and emotion in his voice, the Chief Justice put the question to him: "Mr. Senator Ross, how say you? Is the respondent Andrew Johnson guilty or not guilty of a high misdemeanor as charged in this Article?" Every voice was still; every eye was upon the freshman Senator from Kansas. The hopes and fears, the hatred and bitterness of past decades were centered upon this one man.

As Ross himself later described it, his "powers of hearing and seeing seemed developed in an abnormal degree."

Every individual in that great audience seemed distinctly visible, some with lips apart and bending forward in anxious expectancy, others with hand uplifted as if to ward off an apprehended blow . . . and each peering with an intensity that was almost tragic upon the face of him who was about to cast the fateful vote. . . . Every fan was folded, not a foot moved, not the rustle of a garment, not a whisper was heard. . . . Hope and fear seemed blended in every face, instantaneously alternating, some with revengeful hate . . . others lighted with hope. . . . The Senators in their seats leaned over their desks, many with hand to ear. . . . It was a tremendous responsibility, and it was not strange that he upon whom it had been imposed by a fateful combination of conditions should have sought to avoid it, to put it away from him as one shuns, or tries to fight off, a nightmare. . . . I almost literally looked down into my open grave. Friendships, position, fortune, everything that makes life desirable to an ambitious man were about to be swept away by the breath of my mouth, perhaps forever. It is not strange that my answer was carried waveringly over the air and failed to reach the limits of the audience, or that repetition was called for by distant Senators on the opposite side of the Chamber.

Then came the answer again in a voice that could not be misunderstood—full, final, definite, unhesitating and unmistakable: "Not guilty." The deed was done, the President saved, the trial as good as over and the conviction lost. The remainder of the roll call was unimportant, conviction had failed by the margin of a single vote and a general rumbling filled the chamber until the Chief Justice proclaimed that "on this Article thirty-five Senators having voted guilty and nineteen not guilty, a two-thirds majority not having voted for conviction, the President is, therefore, acquitted under this Article."

A ten-day recess followed, ten turbulent days to change votes on the remaining Articles. An attempt was made to rush through bills to re-admit six Southern states, whose twelve Senators were guaranteed to vote for conviction. But this could not be accomplished in time. Again Ross was the only one uncommitted on the other Articles, the only one whose vote could not be predicted in advance. And again he was subjected to terrible pressure. From "D. R. Anthony and others," he received a wire informing him that "Kansas repudiates you as she does all perjurers and skunks." Every incident in his life was examined and distorted. Professional witnesses were found by Senator Pomeroy to testify before a special House committee that Ross had indicated a willingness to change his vote for a consideration. (Unfortunately this witness was so delighted in his exciting role that he also swore that Senator Pomeroy had made an offer to produce three votes for acquittal for $40,000.) When Ross, in his capacity as a Committee Chairman, took several bills to the President, James G. Blaine remarked: "There goes the rascal to get his pay." (Long afterward Blaine was to admit: "In the exaggerated denunciation caused by the anger and chagrin of the moment, great injustice was done to statesmen of spotless character.")

Again the wild rumors spread that Ross had been won over on the remaining Articles of Impeachment. As the Senate reassembled, he was the only one of the seven "renegade" Republicans to vote with the majority on preliminary procedural matters. But when the second and third Articles of Impeachment were read, and the name of Ross was reached again with the same intense suspense of ten days earlier, again came the calm answer "Not guilty."

Why did Ross, whose dislike for Johnson continued, vote "Not guilty"? His motives appear clearly from his own writings on the subject years later in articles contributed to *Scribner's* and *Forum* magazines:

In a large sense, the independence of the executive office as a coordinate branch of the government was on trial. . . . If . . . the President must step down . . . a disgraced man and a political outcast . . . upon insufficient proofs and from partisan considerations, the office of President would be degraded, cease to be a coordinate branch of the government, and ever after subordinated to the legislative will. It would practically have revolutionized our splendid political fabric into a partisan Congressional autocracy. . . . This government had never faced so insidious a danger . . . control by the worst element of American politics. . . . If Andrew Johnson were acquitted by a nonpartisan vote . . . America would pass the danger point of partisan rule and that intolerance which so often characterizes the sway of great majorities and makes them dangerous.

The "open grave" which Edmund Ross had foreseen was hardly an exaggeration. A Justice of the Kansas Supreme Court telegraphed him that "the rope with which Judas Iscariot hanged himself is lost, but Jim Lane's pistol is at your service." An editorial in a Kansas newspaper screamed:

On Saturday last Edmund G. Ross, United States Senator from Kansas, sold himself, and betrayed his constituents; stultified his own record, basely lied to his friends, shamefully violated his solemn pledge . . . and to the utmost of his poor ability signed the death warrant of his country's liberty. This act was done deliberately, because the traitor, like Benedict Arnold, loved money better than he did principle, friends, honor and his country, all combined. Poor, pitiful, shriveled wretch, with a soul so small that a little pelf[3] would outweigh all things else that dignify or ennoble manhood.

Ross's political career was ended. To the New York *Tribune*, he was nothing but "a miserable poltroon and traitor." The Philadelphia *Press* said that in Ross "littleness" had "simply borne its legitimate fruit," and that he and his fellow recalcitrant Republicans had "plunged from a precipice of fame into the groveling depths of infamy and death." The Philadelphia *Inquirer* said that "They had tried, convicted and sentenced themselves." For them there could be "no allowance, no clemency."

Comparative peace returned to Washington as Stanton relinquished his office and Johnson served out the rest of his term, later—unlike his Republican defenders—to return triumphantly to the Senate as Senator from Tennessee. But no one paid attention when Ross tried unsuc-cessfully to explain his vote, and denounced the falsehoods of Ben Butler's investigating committee, recalling that the General's "well known grovelling instincts and proneness to slime and uncleanness" had led "the public to insult the brute creation by dubbing him 'the beast.'" He clung unhappily to his seat in the Senate until the expiration of his term, frequently referred to as "the traitor Ross," and complaining that his fellow Congressmen, as well as citizens on the street, considered association with him "disreputable and scandalous," and passed him by as if he were "a leper, with averted face and every indication of hatred and disgust."

Neither Ross nor any other Republican who had voted for the acquittal of Johnson was ever re-elected to the Senate, not a one of them retaining the support of their party's organization. When he returned to Kansas in 1871, he and his family suffered social ostracism, physical attack, and near poverty.

Who was Edmund G. Ross? Practically nobody. Not a single public law bears his name, not a single history book includes his picture, not a single list of Senate "greats" mentions his service. His one heroic deed has been all but forgotten. But who might Edmund G. Ross have been? That is the question—for Ross, a man with an excellent command of words, an excellent background for politics and an excellent future in the Senate, might well have outstripped his colleagues in prestige and power throughout a long Senate career. Instead, he chose to throw all of this away for one act of conscience.

But the twisting course of human events eventually upheld the faith he expressed to his wife shortly after the trial: "Millions of men cursing me today will bless me tomorrow for having saved the country from the greatest peril through which it has ever passed, though none but God can ever know the struggle it has cost me." For twenty years later Congress

---

3. **pelf,** money, riches.

repealed the Tenure-of-Office Act, to which every President after Johnson, regardless of party, had objected; and still later the Supreme Court, referring to "the extremes of that episode in our government," held it to be unconstitutional. Ross moved to New Mexico, where in his later years he was to be appointed Territorial Governor. Just prior to his death when he was awarded a special pension by Congress for his service in the Civil War, the press and the country took the opportunity to pay tribute to his fidelity to principle in a trying hour and his courage in saving his government from a devastating reign of terror. They now agreed with Ross's earlier judgment that his vote had "saved the country from . . . a strain that would have wrecked any other form of government." Those Kansas newspapers and political leaders who had bitterly denounced him in earlier years praised Ross for his stand against legislative mob rule: "By the firmness and courage of Senator Ross," it was said, "the country was saved from calamity greater than war, while it consigned him to a political martyrdom, the most cruel in our history. . . . Ross was the victim of a wild flame of intolerance which swept everything before it. He did his duty knowing that it meant his political death. . . . It was a brave thing for Ross to do, but Ross did it. He acted for his conscience and with a lofty patriotism, regardless of what he knew must be the ruinous consequences to himself. He acted right."

peachment would be to vote for the future welfare of the country as a whole. It takes enormous courage to follow "a different drummer" when doing so means one's personal ruin.

II
IMPLICATIONS

On the basis of this selection and of your own experience, discuss the justification or lack of justification for each of the following statements.

1. As President Kennedy points out, Ross would probably have become an exceptional legislator if he had been able to remain in the Senate. It was, therefore, foolish and even morally wrong for him to risk such a brilliant future for the sake of a single vote of principle.

2. Considering everything, Senator Ross would have been a much happier and a more satisfied person if he had voted with the majority of his colleagues.

3. It is morally wrong for Senators to vote according to their consciences when they know that the great majority of their constituents would not approve of such a vote.

4. When a man's conscience demands that he do something that will entail a loss of power, respect, wealth, and friends, he will usually not follow his conscience.

III
TECHNIQUES

Conflict

Although this selection is nonfiction, President Kennedy has so arranged his details that it reads almost like a short story. Especially evident here is the matter of conflict. How does the author manage to dramatize the conflict, especially at the moment of decision?

Climax

Locate the climaxes in this story. Would it have been better if only one climax had been used? If so, why did the author use more than one?

Moment of Illumination

Is there a moment of illumination in this story? If so, what is it? Judging from this and other nonfiction you have read, explain why you think that nonfiction typically has or has not a moment of illumination.

I
"A DIFFERENT DRUMMER"

Henry David Thoreau once wrote, "If a man does not keep pace with his companions, perhaps it is because he hears a different drummer." Senator Ross certainly did not "keep pace with his companions"—his decision was opposed both to the majority in his political party and to the desires of his constituents. He listened instead to his conscience, which told him that to vote against im-

Inner Conflicts in Love

M ost of us, hopefully, will never have to face momentous decisions
of the sort met by Senator Ross or Carter Druse. But there are probably few people
destined to go through life without experiencing the inner turmoil that comes
from disappointments in love. Each of the following poems dramatizes one such struggle.

◊ In "Parting, Without a Sequel,"
John Crowe Ransom renders a moving portrait of a lady
who has formally and "officially" broken with her sweetheart
by letter. As you read the poem, note the contrast
between the lady's emotional state at the end of the poem
and her sureness in the first stanza.
What might have caused this shift?

Parting, Without a Sequel

She has finished and sealed the letter
At last, which he so richly has deserved,
With characters venomous and hatefully curved,
And nothing could be better.

But even as she gave it   5
Saying to the blue-capped functioner of doom,
"Into his hands," she hoped the leering groom
Might somewhere lose and leave it.

Then all the blood
Forsook the face. She was too pale for tears,   10
Observing the ruin of her younger years.
She went and stood

Under her father's vaunting oak
Who kept his peace in wind and sun, and glistened
Stoical in the rain; to whom she listened   15
If he spoke.

And now the agitation of the rain
Rasped his sere[1] leaves, and he talked low and gentle
Reproaching the wan[2] daughter by the lintel;[3]
Ceasing and beginning again.   20

Away went the messenger's bicycle,
His serpent's track went up the hill forever,
And all the time she stood there hot as fever
And cold as any icicle.

JOHN CROWE RANSOM

1. sere\ˈsĭ·ər\ parched, withered.
2. wan\wɔn\ pale, sickly.
3. lintel\ˈlĭn·təl\ crosspiece over a door
supporting the weight of the structure.

◆ Elinor Wylie's sonnet sequence, "Wild Peaches,"
sets forth the inner struggle of a woman of "Puritan" tastes
whose lover evidently doesn't share them. The contrasts
between the rich life on the "Eastern shore"
and the meager fields of New England serve as vividly rendered mirrors
reflecting the differences in the lovers' characters.

Wild Peaches

1

When the world turns completely upside down
You say we'll emigrate to the Eastern Shore
Aboard a river-boat from Baltimore;
We'll live among wild peach trees, miles from town,
You'll wear a coonskin cap, and I a gown   5
Homespun, dyed butternut's dark gold colour.
Lost, like your lotus-eating[1] ancestor,
We'll swim in milk and honey till we drown.

The winter will be short, the summer long,
The autumn amber-hued, sunny and hot,   10
Tasting of cider and of scuppernong;[2]
All seasons sweet, but autumn best of all.
The squirrels in their silver fur will fall
Like falling leaves, like fruit, before your shot.

2

The autumn frosts will lie upon the grass   15
Like bloom on grapes of purple-brown and gold.
The misted early mornings will be cold;
The little puddles will be roofed with glass.
The sun, which burns from copper into brass,
Melts these at noon, and makes the boys unfold   20
Their knitted mufflers; full as they can hold,
Fat pockets dribble chestnuts as they pass.

---

1. **lotus-eating,** in Greek legend, the inhabitants of a land described
in the *Odyssey* ate fruit of the lotus plant and became indolent and
forgetful.
2. **scuppernong**\ˈskə·pər ˈnɔŋ\ a white, aromatic table wine.

Peaches grow wild, and pigs can live in clover;
A barrel of salted herrings lasts a year;
The spring begins before the winter's over.   25
By February you may find the skins
Of garter snakes and water moccasins
Dwindled and harsh, dead-white and cloudy-clear.

3

When April pours the colours of a shell
Upon the hills, when every little creek   30
Is shot with silver from the Chesapeake
In shoals new-minted by the ocean swell,
When strawberries go begging, and the sleek
Blue plums lie open to the blackbird's beak,
We shall live well—we shall live very well.   35

The months between the cherries and the peaches
Are brimming cornucopias[3] which spill
Fruits red and purple, sombre-bloomed and black;
Then, down rich fields and frosty river beaches
We'll trample bright persimmons, while you kill   40
Bronze partridge, speckled quail, and canvasback.[4]

4

Down to the Puritan marrow of my bones
There's something in this richness that I hate.
I love the look, austere, immaculate,
Of landscapes drawn in pearly monotones.   45
There's something in my very blood that owns
Bare hills, cold silver on a sky of slate,
A thread of water, churned to milky spate
Streaming through slanted pastures fenced with stones.

I love those skies, thin blue or snowy gray,   50
Those fields sparse-planted, rendering meagre sheaves;
That spring, briefer than apple-blossom's breath,
Summer, so much too beautiful to stay,
Swift autumn, like a bonfire of leaves,
And sleepy winter, like the sleep of death.   55

ELINOR WYLIE

---

3. **cornucopias**\ˈkɔr·nyə ▲kō·pē·əz\ something that produces an inexhaustible supply of desirable things.
4. **canvasback**, wild duck.

◈ Though born in England,
W. H. Auden has lived in the United States since 1939
and has been an American citizen since 1946. Auden's ballad
is made up of nine stanzas, eight of which contain
two lines spoken by a woman and two in answer spoken by her lover.
Follow closely both the growing fear of the woman
as she describes the approach of the soldiers and the calm,
matter-of-fact replies of the lover as he evasively tries
to quiet her anxiety.

Ballad

O what is that sound which so thrills the ear
  Down in the valley drumming, drumming?
Only the scarlet soldiers, dear,
  The soldiers coming.

O what is that light I see flashing so clear   5
  Over the distance brightly, brightly?
Only the sun on their weapons, dear,
  As they step lightly.

O what are they doing with all that gear;
  What are they doing this morning, this morning?   10
Only the usual maneuvers, dear,
  Or perhaps a warning.

O why have they left the road down there;
  Why are they suddenly wheeling, wheeling?
Perhaps a change in the orders, dear;   15
  Why are you kneeling?

O haven't they stopped for the doctor's care;
  Haven't they reined their horses, their horses?
Why, they are none of them wounded, dear,
  None of these forces.   20

O is it the parson they want, with white hair;
  Is it the parson, is it, is it?
No, they are passing his gateway, dear,
  Without a visit.

O it must be the farmer who lives so near,   25
    It must be the farmer, so cunning, cunning;
They have passed the farm already, dear,
    And now they are running.

O where are you going? stay with me here.
    Were the vows you swore me deceiving, deceiving?   30
No, I promised to love you, my dear,
    But I must be leaving.

O it's broken the lock and splintered the door,
    O it's the gate where they're turning, turning;
Their feet are heavy on the floor   35
    And their eyes are burning.

W. H. AUDEN

THE LYRIC POET
AS A COMMUNICATOR OF FEELING

Though some poems are written largely to communicate ideas and others are written largely to tell stories, the lyric poem is one whose primary concern is the communication of feelings and emotions. This central purpose is apt to have certain side effects. For example, in each of the lyric poems above, you will find that the story elements are very slight. In the Ransom poem, for example, the reader never learns what happened to cause the lady to write the letter. Someone interested in the story element of this poem might well be curious about this omitted detail; he might even reject the poem because it did not satisfy his curiosity. Such a reaction, however, would be inappropriate, for one should always judge a poem in terms of its intended effect. If Ransom had told why the lady wrote the letter, it is probable that the details would have distracted the reader from the woman's intense inner struggle while at the same time detracting from the wholeness of the poem, and, presumably, it was the woman's emotional reaction the author wanted to communicate.

At the same time that one notes an absence of story elements in lyric poetry, he should note that there is no absence of concrete detail. In Auden's poem, for example, we are not told specifically why the soldiers are coming to the house on the hill, but we do get a vivid and concrete impression of them and of their march; we know that they are dressed in scarlet; that they have a band, or at least drummers, with them; that they carry weapons that flash in the sun, and so on. Such concrete details are necessary in order to make the reader feel the emotion the poet wants to communicate. The poet knows that the mature reader is not going to feel an emotion just because the poet tells him to.

Emotions in life come in response to specific and concrete situations—a strange noise heard in the middle of the night causes the heart to beat with fear; the person one loves enters a room and the pulse rises. Through concrete details—weapons flashing, "dead-white and cloudy-clear" snake skins, an oak rasping sere leaves—the poet tries to create a context parallel—yet somehow more intense—to real life that will give rise to the desired emotions in readers.

In the following quotations, what is being described and what feeling does it give you?

1. vaunting oak . . . glistened/Stoical in the rain.

2. His serpent's track went up the hill forever.

3. . . . a gown/Homespun, dyed butternut's dark gold colour.

4. The little puddles will be roofed with glass.

5. . . . the sleek/Blue plums lie open to the blackbird's beak.

6. Bare hills, cold silver on a sky of slate.

7. Their feet are heavy on the floor/And their eyes are burning.

Not all inner struggles involve significant, far-reaching,
dramatic choices between good and evil. More often the quiet plane
of our lives is daily rippled by almost countless little
nonmoral inner struggles. Should I get up five minutes early this morning?
Should I go to the show or to the ball game? Why don't I do my homework
before I watch television? In the following story George Stoyonovich
discovers that such little struggles can grow until suddenly they threaten
to affect one's very being and shape one's whole future.

A Summer's Reading

BERNARD MALAMUD

George Stoyonovich was a neighborhood boy who had quit high school on an impulse when he was sixteen, run out of patience, and though he was ashamed everytime he went looking for a job, when people asked him if he had finished and he had to say no, he never went back to school. This summer was a hard time for jobs and he had none. Having so much time on his hands, George thought of going to summer school, but the kids in his classes would be too young. He also considered registering in a night high school, only he didn't like the idea of the teachers always telling him what to do. He felt they had not respected him. The result was he stayed off the streets and in his room most of the day. He was close to twenty and had needs with the neighborhood girls, but no money to spend, and he couldn't get more than an occasional few cents because his father was poor, and his sister Sophie, who resembled George, a tall bony girl of twenty-three, earned very little and what she had she kept for herself. Their mother was dead, and Sophie had to take care of the house.

Very early in the morning George's father got up to go to work in a fish market. Sophie left about eight for her long ride in the subway to a cafeteria in the Bronx. George had his coffee by himself, then hung around in the house. When the house, a five-room railroad flat above a butcher store, got on his nerves he cleaned it up—mopped the floors with a wet mop and put things away. But most of the time he sat in his room. In the afternoons he listened to the ball game. Otherwise he had a couple of old copies of the *World Almanac* he had bought long ago, and he liked to read in them and also the magazines and newspapers that Sophie brought home, that had been left on the tables in the cafeteria. They were mostly picture magazines about movie stars and sports figures, also usually the *News* and *Mirror*. Sophie herself read whatever fell into her hands, although she sometimes read good books.

She once asked George what he did in his room all day and he said he read a lot too.

"Of what besides what I bring home? Do you ever read any worthwhile books?"

"Some," George answered, although he really didn't. He had tried to read a book or two that Sophie had in the house but found he was in no mood for them. Lately he couldn't stand made-up stories, they got on his nerves. He wished he had some hobby to work at—as a kid he was good in carpentry, but where could he work at it? Sometimes during the day he went for walks, but mostly he did his walking

Reprinted from *The Magic Barrel* by Bernard Malamud, by permission of Farrar, Straus, and Giroux, Inc. Copyright 1956 by Bernard Malamud. First published in *The New Yorker*.

after the hot sun had gone down and it was cooler in the streets.

In the evening after supper George left the house and wandered in the neighborhood. During the sultry days some of the storekeepers and their wives sat in chairs on the thick, broken sidewalks in front of their shops, fanning themselves, and George walked past them and the guys hanging out on the candy store corner. A couple of them he had known his whole life, but nobody recognized each other. He had no place special to go, but generally, saving it till the last, he left the neighborhood and walked for blocks till he came to a darkly lit little park with benches and trees and an iron railing, giving it a feeling of privacy. He sat on a bench here, watching the leafy trees and the flowers blooming on the inside of the railing, thinking of a better life for himself. He thought of the jobs he had had since he had quit school—delivery boy, stock clerk, runner, lately working in a factory—and he was dissatisfied with all of them. He felt he would someday like to have a good job and live in a private house with a porch, on a street with trees. He wanted to have some dough in his pocket to buy things with, and a girl to go with, so as not to be so lonely, especially on Saturday nights. He wanted people to like and respect him. He thought about these things often but mostly when he was alone at night. Around midnight he got up and drifted back to his hot and stony neighborhood.

One time while on his walk George met Mr. Cattanzara coming home very late from work. He wondered if he was drunk but then could tell he wasn't. Mr. Cattanzara, a stocky, bald-headed man who worked in a change booth on an IRT station, lived on the next block after George's, above a shoe repair store. Nights, during the hot weather, he sat on his stoop in an undershirt, reading the *New York Times* in the light of the shoemaker's window. He read it from the first page to the last, then went up to sleep. And all the time he was reading the paper, his wife, a fat woman with a white face, leaned out of the window, gazing into the street, her thick white arms folded under her loose breast, on the window ledge.

Once in a while Mr. Cattanzara came home drunk, but it was a quiet drunk. He never made any trouble, only walked stiffly up the street and slowly climbed the stairs into the hall. Though drunk, he looked the same as always, except for his tight walk, the quietness, and that his eyes were wet. George liked Mr. Cattanzara because he remembered him giving him nickels to buy lemon ice with when he was a squirt. Mr. Cattanzara was a different type than those in the neighborhood. He asked different questions than the others when he met you, and he seemed to know what went on in all the newspapers. He read them, as his fat sick wife watched from the window.

"What are you doing with yourself this summer, George?" Mr. Cattanzara asked. "I see you walkin' around at nights."

George felt embarrassed. "I like to walk."

"What are you doin' in the day now?"

"Nothing much just right now. I'm waiting for a job." Since it shamed him to admit he wasn't working, George said, "I'm staying home—but I'm reading a lot to pick up my education."

Mr. Cattanzara looked interested. He mopped his hot face with a red handkerchief.

"What are you readin'?"

George hesitated, then said, "I got a list of books in the library once, and now I'm gonna read them this summer." He felt strange and a little unhappy saying this, but he wanted Mr. Cattanzara to respect him.

"How many books are there on it?"

"I never counted them. Maybe around a hundred."

Mr. Cattanzara whistled through his teeth.

"I figure if I did that," George went on earnestly, "it would help me in my education. I don't mean the kind they give you in high school. I want to know different things than they learn there, if you know what I mean."

The change maker nodded. "Still and all, one hundred books is a pretty big load for one summer."

"It might take longer."

"After you're finished with some, maybe you and I can shoot the breeze about them?" said Mr. Cattanzara.

"When I'm finished," George answered.

Mr. Cattanzara went home and George continued on his walk. After that, though he had the urge to, George did nothing different from usual. He still took his walks at night, ending up in the little park. But one evening the shoemaker on the next block stopped George to say he was a good boy, and George figured that Mr. Cattanzara had told him all about the books he was reading. From the shoemaker it must have gone down the street, because George saw a couple of people smiling kindly at him, though nobody spoke to him personally. He felt a little better around the neighborhood and liked it more, though not so much he would want to live in it forever. He had never exactly disliked the people in it, yet he had never liked them very much either. It was the fault of the neighborhood. To his surprise, George found out that his father and Sophie knew about his reading too. His father was too shy to say anything about it—he was never much of a talker in his whole life—but Sophie was softer to George, and she showed him in other ways she was proud of him.

As the summer went on George felt in a good mood about things. He cleaned the house every day, as a favor to Sophie, and he enjoyed the ball games more. Sophie gave him a buck a week allowance, and though it still wasn't enough and he had to use it carefully, it was a helluva lot better than just having two bits now and then. What he bought with the money—cigarettes mostly, an occasional beer or movie ticket—he got a big kick out of. Life wasn't so bad if you knew how to appreciate it. Occasionally he bought a paperback book from the news-stand, but he never got around to reading it, though he was glad to have a couple of books in his room. But he read thoroughly Sophie's magazines and newspapers. And at night was the most enjoyable time, because when he passed the storekeepers sitting outside their stores, he could tell they regarded him highly. He walked erect, and though he did not say much to them, or they to him, he could feel approval on all sides. A couple of nights he felt so good that he skipped the park at the end of the evening. He just wandered in the neighborhood, where people had known him from the time he was a kid playing punchball whenever there was a game of it going; he wandered there, then came home and got undressed for bed, feeling fine.

For a few weeks he had talked only once with Mr. Cattanzara, and though the change maker had said nothing more about the books, asked no questions, his silence made George a little uneasy. For a while George didn't pass in front of Mr. Cattanzara's house anymore, until one night, forgetting himself, he approached it from a different direction than he usually did when he did. It was already past midnight. The street, except for one or two people, was deserted, and George was surprised when he saw Mr. Cattanzara still reading his newspaper by the light of the street lamp overhead. His impulse was to stop at the stoop and talk to him. He wasn't sure what he wanted to say, though he felt the words would come when he began to talk; but the more he thought about it, the more the idea scared him, and he decided he'd better not. He even considered beating it home by another street, but he was too near Mr. Cattanzara, and the change maker might see him as he ran, and get annoyed. So George unobtrusively crossed the street, trying to make it seem as if he had to look in a store window on the other side, which he did, and then went on, uncomfortable at what he was doing. He feared Mr. Cattanzara would glance up from his paper and call him a dirty rat for walking on the other side of the street, but all he did was sit there, sweating through his undershirt, his bald head shining in the dim light as he read his *Times*, and upstairs his fat wife leaned out of the window, seeming to read the paper along with him. George thought she would spy him and yell out to Mr. Cattanzara, but she never moved her eyes off her husband.

George made up his mind to stay away from the change maker until he had got some of his softback books read, but when he started them and saw they were mostly story books, he lost his interest and didn't bother to finish them. He lost his interest in reading other things too. Sophie's magazines and newspapers went unread. She saw them piling up on a chair in his room and asked why he was no longer looking at them, and George told her it was because of all the other reading he had to do. Sophie said she had guessed that was it. So for most of the day, George had the radio on, turning to music when he was sick of the human voice. He kept the house fairly neat, and Sophie said nothing on the days when he neglected it. She was still kind and gave him his extra buck, though things weren't so good for him as they had been before.

But they were good enough, considering. Also his night walks invariably picked him up, no matter how bad the day was. Then one night George saw Mr. Cattanzara coming down the street toward him. George was about to turn and run but he recognized from Mr. Cattanzara's walk that he was drunk, and if so, probably he would not even bother to notice him. So George kept on walking straight ahead until he came abreast of Mr. Cattanzara and though he felt wound up enough to pop into the sky, he was not surprised when Mr. Cattanzara passed him without a word, walking slowly, his face and body stiff. George drew a breath in relief at his narrow escape, when he heard his name called, and there stood Mr. Cattanzara at his elbow, smelling like the inside of a beer barrel. His eyes were sad as he gazed at George, and George felt so intensely uncomfortable he was tempted to shove the drunk aside and continue on his walk.

But he couldn't act that way to him, and, besides, Mr. Cattanzara took a nickel out of his pants pocket and handed it to him.

"Go buy yourself a lemon ice, Georgie."

"It's not that time anymore, Mr. Cattanzara," George said, "I am a big guy now."

"No, you ain't," said Mr. Cattanzara, to which George made no reply he could think of.

"How are all your books comin' along now?" Mr. Cattanzara asked. Though he tried to stand steady, he swayed a little.

"Fine, I guess," said George, feeling the red crawling up his face.

"You ain't sure?" The change maker smiled slyly, a way George had never seen him smile.

"Sure I'm sure. They're fine."

Though his head swayed in little arcs, Mr. Cattanzara's eyes were steady. He had small blue eyes which could hurt if you looked at them too long.

"George," he said, "name me one book on that list that you read this summer, and I will drink to your health."

"I don't want anybody drinking to me."

"Name me one so I can ask you a question on it. Who can tell, if it's a good book maybe I might wanna read it myself."

George knew he looked passable on the outside, but inside he was crumbling apart.

Unable to reply, he shut his eyes, but when—years later—he opened them, he saw that Mr. Cattanzara had, out of pity, gone away, but in his ears he still heard the words he had said when he left: "George, don't do what I did."

The next night he was afraid to leave his room, and though Sophie argued with him he wouldn't open the door.

"What are you doing in there?" she asked.

"Nothing."

"Aren't you reading?"

"No."

She was silent a minute, then asked, "Where do you keep the books you read? I never see any in your room outside of a few cheap trashy ones."

He wouldn't tell her.

"In that case you're not worth a buck of my hard-earned money. Why should I break my back for you? Go on out, you bum, and get a job."

He stayed in his room for almost a week, except to sneak into the kitchen when nobody was home. Sophie railed at him, then begged him to come out, and his old father wept, but George wouldn't budge, though the weather was terrible and his small room stifling. He found it very hard to breathe, each breath was like drawing a flame into his lungs.

One night, unable to stand the heat anymore, he burst into the street at one A.M., a shadow of himself. He hoped to sneak to the park without being seen, but there were people all over the block, wilted and listless, waiting for a breeze. George lowered his eyes and walked, in disgrace, away from them, but before long he discovered they were still friendly to him. He figured Mr. Cattanzara hadn't told on him. Maybe when he woke up out of his drunk the next morning, he had forgotten all about meeting George. George felt his confidence slowly come back to him.

That same night a man on a street corner asked him if it was true that he had finished reading so many books, and George admitted he had. The man said it was a wonderful thing for a boy his age to read so much.

"Yeah," George said, but he felt relieved. He hoped nobody would mention the books anymore, and when, after a couple of days, he accidentally met Mr. Cattanzara again, *he* didn't, though George had the idea he was the one who had started the rumor that he had finished all the books.

One evening in the fall, George ran out of his house to the library, where he hadn't been in years. There were books all over the place, wherever he looked, and though he was struggling to control an inward trembling, he easily counted off a hundred, then sat down at a table to read.

I
DUTY TO ONESELF

On the surface, George's inner struggle differs from those in most of our earlier stories in that no important moral issue seems to be involved in his case. Yet he suffers a great deal because of his indecision. One of the important questions for the reader to ask is how much of this suffering comes from a sense of guilt—guilt which arises from George's failure to meet the moral obligation to develop himself as fully as he can. To what extent do you think Mr. Cattanzara had this obligation in mind when he said to George, "Don't do what I did"?

II
IMPLICATIONS

Examine the following assumptions and discuss them in the light of this selection and of your own experience.

1. The chief factor standing in the way of George's self-realization is his unwholesome environment.

2. The chief factor causing George to move toward self-realization is his need for love and respect.

3. If George had managed to get a job, his conscience would have stopped bothering him.

4. In order to succeed in life men need to have models of success to stimulate them.

5. To develop oneself fully, one must have an education.

6. Before one can have any real success in life, he must accept as his duty the principle that a man is obliged to strive for excellence.

III
TECHNIQUES

Conflict

What are the forces that move George in a positive direction and what are those that influence him negatively? What forces *within* George might be listed on the one side and on the other? Do the inner or the outer forces seem to be the more powerful? Does the conflict seem to be evenly or unevenly balanced?

Climax

A turning point and minor climax occur when George tells Mr. Cattanzara that he is reading good books. After this, George's fortunes definitely improve in the sense that his neighbors and family gain greater respect for him. At the same time, however, the reader is well aware that this moment is not the true climax of the story. How does the reader know this? When does the true climax occur?

IV
WORDS

A. The phrases and clauses below contain modifiers, connectors, appositives, or definitions that act as clues to the meaning of the italicized words. What does each italicized word mean? How does the context help you determine meaning?

1. A mass meeting at Lawrence had *vilified* the Senator and speedily reported resolutions sharply condemning his position.

2. . . . warned in the party press, *harangued* by their constituents. . . .

3. . . . "plunged from a *precipice* of fame into the *groveling* depths of infamy and death."

4. . . . the press and the country took the opportunity to pay tribute to his *fidelity* to principle in a trying hour. . . .

5. . . . what looked like a great grayish bird *flailing* ghostly wings. . . .

6. . . . he held that thought in *abeyance*, carefully . . . he had to pay attention to his driving. . . .

B. 1. The editors of most dictionaries give diction labels that help describe the various levels of usage words suggest. Look up *wan* and *sere*. What diction or usage labels do you find?

2. A term or word used regularly in a certain region is generally labeled *dialect*. Look up *peanuts* and *goobers, tawpie* and *simpleton, bet* and *punt*.

3. A word or sense used by most people in conversation and informal writing is generally marked *colloquial*. Colloquialisms have no particular connection with a certain region, social standing, or education. *Slang* is a label attached to terms used in very informal situations and generally within a small group. Slang may be shortened words, such as *mob, kook, bunk;* newly invented words, such as *snide, to goof;* old words with new meaning, such as *square* (conventional), *eye* (detective); or unusual figures of speech, such as "he *dimed* on me" (he called the police). Look up the italicized words below and note the diction labels given.

(a) put the check on my *cuff;* (b) everyone was there, *even* Tom; (c) he was *ever so polite;* (d) he gives me the *heebie jeebies;* (e) *enthused* about the project; (f) he stopped at the *hostel;* (g) *perchance* our paths shall cross again; (h) a rather *snide* remark; (i) she pointed to the *chesterfield;* (j) he is a *mule* about changing his mind; (k) you better *hump* to it.

FINAL REFLECTIONS
The Inner Struggle

THE FOCUS ON "MAN HIMSELF"

As writers look at man himself they find him a complex being. There is in him a strong animal side, a primitive urge for security and survival. But there is also a moral side, the voice of conscience, which bids him to break neither man's laws nor God's in his attempts to preserve and fulfill himself. In the inner struggles between these forces, as you have seen, man's true worth is tested. If his decisions go against his conscience, he may perhaps suffer no ill effects outwardly, but the inward effects and the loss of self-respect are deeply felt and lasting. No matter how we may define the "self" that stands between man's animal and moral nature, it can never find the highest fulfillment unless man lives by moral principles and practices integrity.

Beyond the individual struggles that you have read about and discussed, there is another and a wider issue: When de Tocqueville predicted that American writers would focus on "man himself," he was especially mindful of the democratic nature of our society. He knew that the welfare of a democracy depended upon the moral strength of its citizens, that in a government of the people the moral fiber of the nation can only be as strong as the moral fiber of the Edmund Rosses and George Stoyonoviches who make it up. Thus, by focusing upon the inner struggle, American writers have frequently served as the living voices of the American conscience.

IMPLICATIONS

Below are seven statements dealing with themes brought up in selections in this unit. After each statement is a list of some of the works you have read. Discuss each statement in the light of *each* of the selections listed.

1. When an individual is faced with the need to make an important decision, the pressures exerted by the members of his family are generally not very important in determining his choice.

"A Horseman in the Sky"

"Parting, Without a Sequel"

"You Can't Do That"

"A Summer's Reading"

"The Battle of Finney's Ford"

2. The need for a sense of integrity, of self-respect, is one of the most powerful impulses influencing human beings.

"The Battle of Finney's Ford"

"You Can't Do That"

"Wild Peaches"

"A Summer's Reading"

"I Looked Down into My Open Grave"

3. Fear freezes individuals and makes them incapable of arriving at intelligent decisions.

"Ballad"

"A Horseman in the Sky"

"I Looked Down into My Open Grave"

4. The depth of affection of one individual for another is best tested and proved in a crisis.

"The Battle of Finney's Ford"

"Ballad"

"A Horseman in the Sky"

"Wild Peaches"

5. Every individual has a powerful need to share with and be understood by others, regardless of his strength or uniqueness.

"Parting, Without a Sequel"

"You Can't Do That"

"William Wilson"

"Wild Peaches"

"I Looked Down into My Open Grave"

6. A man's conscience will direct him to do those things that are socially approved by the society in which he lives. Conscience is essentially a social phenomenon.

"A Summer's Reading"

"William Wilson"

"The Battle of Finney's Ford"

"I Looked Down into My Open Grave"

7. The strength of man's conscience, of his moral side, varies greatly from individual to individual; some men seem to have no conscience at all.

"William Wilson"

"You Can't Do That"

TECHNIQUES

Conflict

Conflicts in literature—as well as conflicts in life—may be broadly divided into external and internal conflicts. Sometimes a conflict may be purely external: a family fighting against a flood, two boxers in a ring, two or more political candidates contesting an election. If we have some stake in the outcome and if there is at least a chance of either side winning, external conflicts may be quite gripping. Detective stories, for example, are good instances of fiction usually based primarily on external conflicts between the pursuer and the pursued.

A great deal of serious literature involves both an external and an internal conflict, and of course there is no reason why an internal conflict can't be just as exciting as an external one. Look over the selections in this unit, and consider the following points in the light of the three or four selections you most enjoyed reading.

1. Describe the external conflict.

2. Describe the internal conflict.

3. Which of the two conflicts held your interest more strongly and why?

4. Which conflict was the more suspenseful?

5. What "extra dimension" (if any) was added by the internal conflict?

Climax

We have defined the climax of a story as the moment when the action reaches its peak, the moment of greatest intensity. Intense moments, both real and fictional, are apt to change people. One of the main outcomes in a fictional crisis, in fact, may be the change in the character of the hero.

Locate the peak of the action in three or four of the selections you have read, and be prepared to discuss the following: (1) Did the climax lead naturally to a change in the fortunes of the main character? (2) Did the climax lead to a change in the character of the hero? Try to describe the change in some detail.

Moment of Illumination

As the point at which the meaning of a story becomes fully clear, the moment of illumination often has rather broad implications; that is, it may not only deal with the final fate of the main character but also with some more general ideas, which can be applied to people in general.

Locate the moment of illumination in two or three of the selections you have read and be prepared to discuss some of their broader implications.

BIOGRAPHICAL NOTES

Edgar Allan Poe

Edgar Allan Poe (1809–1849), one of the most colorful of American writers, was father of the detective story and master of the supernatural tale. Left an orphan at the age of two, he was adopted by the Allans of Richmond, Virginia. He studied abroad for five years and then returned to Virginia, first to study at Richmond Academy and then at the University of Virginia. Withdrawn from school by his foster father for drinking and gambling, he spent a short time in the army before he received an appointment to West Point. The discipline of military life, however, was not to Poe's liking and he was shortly expelled. During this period he was writing poetry and he published two volumes. In 1831 he published a third, *Poems by Edgar Allan Poe,* but it received little notice. Settling in Baltimore, he wrote a prize-winning short story for a newspaper contest: "MS Found in a Bottle." In 1835 he married his young cousin, Virginia Clemm. While editing various magazines, his stories of supernatural horror began appearing, and in 1839 he published *Tales of the Grotesque and Arabesque.* His short story "The Gold Bug" won a newspaper prize in 1843. When his poem "The Raven" appeared in the *Evening Mirror* and then in the *American Review,* his name became known the country over. His verse and short stories continued to appear up until his death in 1849. Poe won considerable fame in Europe, especially in France. His poems and short stories are widely reprinted today, and his works, particularly the writings of horror and mystery, have been a continuing source of radio and television plays and motion pictures.

John P. Marquand

John P. Marquand (1893–   )—though a prolific writer of short stories, essays, and a series of mystery novels about a secret agent, Mr. Moto—is best known for his quietly satiric novels of aristocratic Boston society. Among these novels are *Wickford Point, H. M. Pulham, Esq.,* and *The Late George Apley,* which was awarded the Pulitzer Prize in 1937. His novel *Point of No Return,* which depicts the classic conflict between the values of a static New England society and those of a modern, mobile suburbia, was made into a very successful stage play. Born in Massachusetts, Marquand was educated at Harvard University and later wrote for the Boston *Transcript.*

Jessamyn West

Born in Indiana, Jessamyn West (1907–   ) grew up in California and attended Whittier College. She studied in England and later at the University of California. Stricken with tuberculosis, she was bedridden several years and, during this period, began to keep a journal and to write for publication. Her most famous work, *The Friendly Persuasion,* is an episodic novel about a group of Quakers in Indiana during the Civil War. The story was later the basis of a motion picture. In 1953 *Cress Delahanty* appeared, a series of warm, humorous stories, first published in *The New Yorker,* about an adolescent girl from her twelfth to her eighteenth year.

Ambrose Bierce

Ambrose Bierce (1842–1914?), born in Ohio, fought in the Civil War and then moved west to become a successful journalist in San Francisco. He also lived several years in England and there published three books. In California he was the dominant literary figure in the 1890's, but a series of unhappy personal experiences made him an increasingly bitter man. Primarily a short-story writer, his best collections are *Tales of Soldiers and Civilians* and *Can Such Things Be?* both published in the nineties. In 1913 he went to Mexico to join the civil war there and disappeared.

John F. Kennedy

The 35th President of the United States, John F. Kennedy (1917–1963) was born in Brookline, Massachusetts. A graduate of Harvard University, he wrote a senior honors thesis about England's lack of preparation for war with Germany, published as *Why England Slept*. His father was then U.S. Ambassador to Great Britain. In World War II, Kennedy's role in the dramatic rescue of his PT boat crew won him medals for his leadership and heroism. In 1946 he went to Congress as a Representative from Massachusetts. In 1952 he was elected U.S. Senator. During a long period of hospitalization for back injuries, Kennedy wrote *Profiles in Courage*, a Pulitzer Prize winner in 1957. In 1960, at the age of 43, Kennedy was elected President of the United States, the youngest man to be elected. His assassination in November of 1963 stunned the world. Portions of the four-day television coverage of the tragedy served as the first broadcast of "Profiles in Courage," a television series based upon the book.

John Crowe Ransom

After graduation from Vanderbilt University in Tennessee, John Crowe Ransom (1888–   ) spent three years at Oxford as a Rhodes scholar. In 1914 he returned to teach at Vanderbilt, where he founded *The Fugitive*, a "little magazine" devoted to poetry and criticism. In 1937 he was made Carnegie Professor of Poetry at Kenyon College where, two years later, he established and became editor of the *Kenyon Review*, a quarterly literary journal. Poet, editor, professor, Ransom is also a widely read critic, one of the leaders of the so-called new critics.

Elinor Wylie

Elinor Wylie (1885–1928) spent most of her childhood in Washington, D. C. Her first volume of verse was published anonymously in England in 1912. Upon her return to America she wrote four novels and several collections of poetry: *Nets to Catch the Wind, Black Armour, Trivial Breath,* and *Angels and Earthly Creatures.* When she married William Rose Benét, she joined a family of poets and novelists and a stimulating literary group in New York. After her death in 1928, Benét edited her *Collected Poems* and *Collected Prose.*

W. H. Auden

W. H. Auden (1907–   ), born in England, came to America in 1939 and became a United States citizen in 1946. A prolific writer of poetry and critical essays, he was awarded the Pulitzer Prize for poetry in 1948 for *The Age of Anxiety.* After teaching at the University of Michigan and at Smith College, he became, in 1956, Professor of Poetry at Oxford University.

Bernard Malamud

Born in Brooklyn, Bernard Malamud (1914–   ) grew up there; it is the scene of most of his stories and novels. He began writing in high school, but turned to factory jobs to earn a living during the depression. Educated at the College of the City of New York and Columbia University, Malamud was an English professor at Oregon State College from 1949 to 1961. Since then he has been at Bennington College. He has written three novels, *The Natural, The Assistant,* and *A New Life,* and two volumes of short stories, *The Magic Barrel* and *Idiots First.*

NATHANIEL HAWTHORNE

1804-1864

NATHANIEL HAWTHORNE, *Henry Inman*

Hawthorne began his stories with an idea, then clothed that idea in reality. He was not interested, like Irving, in picturesque descriptions, or, like Poe, in carefully controlled suspense. That is not to say Hawthorne was intent on writing narrative sermons. His poetic imaginations would never allow his tales to become treatises on the Origin of Evil. But they began with the idea of guilt or pride or intolerance and moved from there into complex personal relationships, into the mysteries of the human heart.

New England was in Nathaniel Hawthorne's blood, but rarely has an American writer been so consciously tied to his birthplace and his ancestry and, at the same time, so aware of his aversion to both. Born in Salem, Massachusetts, on Independence Day, 1804, he was descended from wealthy and influential citizens who, in spite of their prominence, left a blot on the family's history which Hawthorne spent a lifetime trying to atone. William Hathorne (Nathaniel changed the spelling), arriving in the American Colonies in 1630, a soldier and eventually a judge, condemned a Quaker woman to be whipped in the streets of Salem for holding to a religion the Puritans strongly opposed. "Grave, bearded, sable-cloaked and steeple-crowned," Hawthorne described him. His son, John, was also a judge; and Hawthorne could not forget that in 1692 this ancestor "made himself so conspicuous in the martyrdom of witches that their blood may be said to have left a stain upon him." Intolerance, cruelty, pride—these sins obsessed the young Hawthorne as he listened to the history of early Salem and his ancestors.

It is true that Bold Daniel Hathorne, his grandfather, belonged to that early Salem. He was a naval captain in the Revolutionary War, of such bravery that he became the hero of a popular ballad. Other ancestors fought Indians, sailed merchant ships, built up considerable fortunes in trade. But Hawthorne grew up in nineteenth-century "joyless" Salem, as he called it, in the "chilliest of social atmospheres," and he loathed it. His own father, a sea captain, died of a fever in Dutch Guiana when Hawthorne was only four, and shortly thereafter his mother was forced to move her three children first into her parents' crowded Salem home, eventually into her brother's house in Raymond, Maine. There is no reason to believe Hawthorne's childhood was abnormally disordered, but certainly the family's impoverishment, his mother's prolonged mourning and fits of seclusion, his own distaste for school, his fragile health—these aspects of his youth, coupled with his sense of inherited guilt, began to shape the young man's mind.

After four years at Bowdoin College, at his uncle's expense, he returned to Salem not to read law or to enter business, as his relatives expected, but to seclude himself in his mother's

Nathaniel Hawthorne's birthplace,
Benjamin Pickman House, Salem, Mass.

house and, quite simply, turn himself into a writer. "I do not want to be a doctor and live by men's diseases," he had written to his mother from Bowdoin, "nor a minister to live by their sins, nor a lawyer and live by their quarrels. So, I don't see that there is anything left for me but to be an author." For the next twelve years he lived physically in "the chamber under the eaves" of his mother's house, seldom going out except at twilight or to make a brief journey to another city; mentally he lived in a world of books. "I had read endlessly all sorts of good and good-for-nothing books," he recalled many years later, "and, in the dearth of other employment, had early begun to scribble sketches and stories most of which I burned." His first novel, *Fanshawe,* was published anonymously at his own expense in 1828. In anger at the lack of sales or at his own immaturity as a writer, he recalled every copy he could find and destroyed them. When a local printer delayed publishing his *Seven Tales of My Native Land,* he withdrew the manuscript and burned it "in a mood half savage, half despairing." Other stories he destroyed before publication because they were "morbid."

A weaker man would have withered under such an apprenticeship. Hawthorne only grew, in self-respect, in determination to succeed on his own terms, in patience with the world "outside." He traveled briefly to New Haven, to Swampscott, to the mountains of Vermont, always keeping a notebook in which he jotted observations of places and people, ideas for stories, phrases which pleased him. He sold tales and sketches to New England magazines; he was even persuaded to edit a Boston magazine for six months. Finally in 1837, at the age of thirty-two, he published his first collection, *Twice-Told Tales.* Longfellow, the most popular poet of the day, gave it a full, almost flattering review. New York magazine editors read it and asked for contributions to their pages. Even Salem recognized its merits. One family in particular, the Nathaniel Peabodys, so wooed the young author that within two years he was engaged to their youngest daughter, Sophia.

The "Old Manse," Concord, Mass.

Supporting a wife, Hawthorne realized, is not a task a recluse can face without qualms. He could never manage it by writing stories, so with as decisive a manner as he entered his apprenticeship he left Salem and his mother's house for a political appointment as measurer of coal and salt in the Boston customhouse. The contrast was a shock. He had hoped to discover what "reality" was like as well as earn a respectable salary, and he gave it a fair try; but after two years he resigned from this "very grievous thraldom." He had been able to write little more than notebook entries, and he found "nothing in the world that [he] thought preferable to [his] old solitude." He thought marriage might be the answer, and in one way it was. He learned to share his life.

With their moving to the Old Manse in rural Concord, Massachusetts, the Hawthornes found a happiness neither expected out of life. "Everybody that comes here," he wrote in 1843, "falls asleep; but for my own part, I feel as if, for the first time in my life, I was awake. I have found a reality, though it looks very much like some of my old dreams." Intellectually he was still content to trust his "dreams," his secret musings, his private thoughts, in spite of conversations with extraordinary neighbors who tried to draw him out of his protective shell. Henry David Thoreau (see pages 596–599) struck him as "ugly as sin, long-nosed, queer mouthed" and yet "a healthy, wholesome man to know." They had long talks together. Emerson (see page 594) was for him "the one great original thinker," but Hawthorne looked upon him as a "poet of deep beauty" rather than a philosopher. They stimulated Hawthorne, they showed him the optimistic side of reality, but he doubted whether either of them had a theory of tragedy, whether they could ever know the dark recesses of the human heart. He produced more than twenty tales during these three years in Concord, sold them to magazines, and then collected them in *Mosses from an Old Manse.* His reputation was growing. Edgar Allan Poe, who knew intimately what made a short story memorable, called Hawthorne "*the* example, *par excellence,* in this country, of the privately admired and publicly unappreciated man of genius."

It took a return to Salem to bring him fame. A Bowdoin classmate, Franklin Pierce, found him a lucrative post as surveyor in the Salem customhouse. After three years of coping with the dullness of the work, he was not distressed

227

to find himself dismissed for political reasons. "Now you can write your book," Sophia told him. In seven months it was finished. In April, 1850, Ticknor and Fields of Boston published *The Scarlet Letter.* Had Hawthorne not written another word than this long tale of Puritan Boston, he would still find a high place in the history of American literature. He called it "positively a hell-fired story, into which I found it almost impossible to throw any cheering light." The contemporary critics, accustomed to Hawthorne's moralizing and his fondness for somber moods, found it unforgettable, perhaps America's first tragedy. Readers of Hester Prynne's story have agreed ever since.

The last fourteen years of Hawthorne's life were such a contrast to his long struggle for recognition that it is almost as though their chronicle belongs to another man. Ambitious with the success of *The Scarlet Letter,* he enlarged his scope with plans for novels and romances. Within a year he had finished the story of the Pyncheon family of Salem and Maule's curse, *The House of the Seven Gables.* "I think it a work more characteristic of my mind," he wrote a friend, "and more proper and natural for me to write." Perhaps it was more proper, if he meant a romance with a happy ending that would charm more readers. But it was hardly characteristic of the best part of Hawthorne's mind and talent. A year later he published *The Blithedale Romance,* a satire of Brook Farm, the co-operative community in West Roxbury where he had lived briefly before his marriage. In spite of a memorable villain, the cold-hearted social reformer, Hollingsworth, the story is static and uninspired. After seven years in Europe (Hawthorne had written a campaign biography for Franklin Pierce who, after his election, rewarded him with the consulship at Liverpool), he tried an even more ambitious novel, *The Marble Faun,* set in contemporary Rome amid the splendors of that alluring city. He took as his theme nothing less than the fall of man, the coming of sin into the world, and tried to illustrate it through two young couples, one of them

a faunlike pagan Roman, called Donatello, and a mysterious American girl, Miriam. But the scope of the novel is too large; too many guidebook details of Rome interfere with our believing the mystery that is supposed to surround these people. Clearly Hawthorne had achieved his most powerful work in his early tales and in his masterpiece, *The Scarlet Letter.*

The moral nature of these early sketches and tales was, for Hawthorne, the reason for their being and the secret of their strength. He began these stories with an idea, then clothed that idea in reality. He was not interested, like Irving, in picturesque description, or, like Poe, in carefully controlled suspense. That is not to say Hawthorne was intent on writing narrative sermons. His poetic imagination would never allow his tales to become treatises on the Origin of Evil. But they began with the idea of guilt or pride or intolerance and moved from there into complex personal relationships, into the mysteries of the human heart.

From his own years of solitude, Hawthorne discovered much about the human heart, and what he discovered left him anxious about man's fate. His tales reflect this anxiety, particularly those in which the pride of intellect is revealed so nakedly as in "Ethan Brand," where the protagonist searches for the Unpardonable Sin only to discover it in himself, or in "Rappaccini's Daughter," where a learned scientist poisons his daughter in a mad experiment which goes beyond nature's limit. When the mind takes precedence over the heart, Hawthorne tells us, only misery, the misery of isolation from our fellowmen, can be the result. In his greatest novel, *The Scarlet Letter,* it is not the adulterers, Hester and the Reverend Dimmesdale, but the evil doctor, the wronged husband, Roger Chillingworth, who is most guilty. "That old man's revenge has been blacker than my sin," Dimmesdale tells Hester. "He has violated, in cold blood, the sanctity of the human heart." Once we are accustomed to the somber colors of Hawthorne's parables, we sense as clearly as he did that through them he speaks for every man.

Hawthorne's first collection
of short stories, *Twice-Told Tales*,
appeared in 1837. It was a volume
of masterpieces, but few critics realized it.
Included among the stories is this fantasy
of Dr. Heidegger and his four aged friends.
Hawthorne had long been interested
in scientific experiments and had doubtless read
in many sources of man's quest for perpetual
youth. The question that intrigued him most
was "What would a person do if he had the
opportunity to regain his youth?"

Dr. Heidegger's Experiment

That very singular man, old Dr. Heidegger, once invited four venerable friends to meet him in his study. There were three white-bearded gentlemen, Mr. Medbourne, Colonel Killigrew, and Mr. Gascoigne,[1] and a withered gentlewoman, whose name was the Widow Wycherly. They were all melancholy old creatures, who had been unfortunate in life, and whose greatest misfortune it was that they were not long ago in their graves. Mr. Medbourne, in the vigor of his age, had been a prosperous merchant, but had lost his all by a frantic speculation, and was now little better than a mendicant. Colonel Killigrew had wasted his best years, and his health and substance, in the pursuit of sinful pleasures, which had given birth to a brood of pains, such as the gout, and divers other torments of soul and body. Mr. Gascoigne was a ruined politician, a man of evil fame, or at least had been so till time had buried him from the knowledge of the present generation, and made him obscure instead of infamous. As for the Widow Wycherly, tradition tells us that she was a great beauty in her day; but, for a long while past, she had lived in deep seclusion, on account of certain scandalous stories which had prejudiced the gentry of the town against her. It is a circumstance worth mentioning that each of these three old gentlemen, Mr. Medbourne, Colonel Killigrew, and Mr. Gascoigne, were early lovers of the Widow Wycherly, and had once been on the point of cutting each other's throats for her sake. And, before proceeding further, I will merely hint that Dr. Heidegger and all his four guests were sometimes thought to be a little besides themselves,—as is not unfrequently the case with old people, when worried either by present troubles or woeful recollections.

"My dear old friends," said Dr. Heidegger, motioning them to be seated, "I am desirous of your assistance in one of those little experiments with which I amuse myself here in my study."

If all stories were true, Dr. Heidegger's study must have been a very curious place. It was a dim, old-fashioned chamber, festooned with cobwebs, and besprinkled with antique dust. Around the walls stood several oaken bookcases, the lower shelves of which were filled with rows of gigantic folios and black-letter quartos,[2] and the upper with little parchment-covered duodecimos.[3] Over the central bookcase was a bronze bust of Hippocrates,[4] with which, according to some authorities, Dr. Heidegger was accustomed to hold consultations in all difficult cases of his practice. In the obscurest corner of the room stood a tall and narrow oaken closet, with its door ajar, within which doubtfully appeared a skeleton. Between two

1. **Mr. Gascoigne**\'găs ▲kɔin\.
2. **quartos**, books of pages approximately 9 x 12 inches in size.
3. **duodecimos**, books consisting of pages approximately 5 x 7½ inches.
4. **Hippocrates**\hĭ ▲pŏk·ra·tēz\ (approx. 460–377 B.C.), Greek physician known as "Father of Medicine" and credited with devising code known today as Hippocratic oath which is administered to men about to enter the medical profession.

of the bookcases hung a looking-glass, presenting its high and dusty plate within a tarnished gilt frame. Among many wonderful stories related of this mirror, it was fabled that the spirits of all the doctor's deceased patients dwelt within its verge, and would stare him in the face whenever he looked thitherward. The opposite side of the chamber was ornamented with the full-length portrait of a young lady, arrayed in the faded magnificence of silk, satin, and brocade, and with a visage as faded as her dress. Above half a century ago, Dr. Heidegger had been on the point of marriage with this young lady; but, being affected with some slight disorder, she had swallowed one of her lover's prescriptions, and died on the bridal evening. The greatest curiosity of the study remains to be mentioned; it was a ponderous folio volume, bound in black leather, with massive silver clasps. There were no letters on the back, and nobody could tell the title of the book. But it was well known to be a book of magic; and once, when a chambermaid had lifted it, merely to brush away the dust, the skeleton had rattled in its closet, the picture of the young lady had stepped one foot upon the floor, and several ghastly faces had peeped forth from the mirror; while the brazen head of Hippocrates frowned, and said,—"Forbear!"

Such was Dr. Heidegger's study. On the summer afternoon of our tale a small round table, as black as ebony, stood in the centre of the room, sustaining a cut-glass vase of beautiful form and elaborate workmanship. The sunshine came through the window, between the heavy festoons[5] of two faded damask[6] curtains, and fell directly across this vase; so that a mild splendor was reflected from it on the ashen visages of the five old people who sat around. Four champagne glasses were also on the table.

"My dear old friends," repeated Dr. Heidegger, "may I reckon on your aid in performing an exceedingly curious experiment?"

Now Dr. Heidegger was a very strange old gentleman, whose eccentricity had become the nucleus for a thousand fantastic stories. Some of these fables, to my shame be it spoken, might possibly be traced back to my own veracious self; and if any passages of the present tale should startle the reader's faith, I must be content to bear the stigma of a fiction monger.

When the doctor's four guests heard him talk of his proposed experiment, they anticipated nothing more wonderful than the murder of a mouse in an air pump, or the examination of a cobweb by the microscope, or some similar nonsense, with which he was constantly in the habit of pestering his intimates. But without waiting for a reply, Dr. Heidegger hobbled across the chamber, and returned with the same ponderous folio, bound in black leather, which common report affirmed to be a book of magic. Undoing the silver clasps, he opened the volume, and took from among its black-letter pages a rose, or what was once a rose, though now the green leaves and crimson petals had assumed one brownish hue, and the ancient flower seemed ready to crumble to dust in the doctor's hands.

"This rose," said Dr. Heidegger, with a sigh, "this same withered and crumbling flower, blossomed five and fifty years ago. It was given me by Sylvia Ward, whose portrait hangs yonder; and I meant to wear it in my bosom at our wedding. Five and fifty years it has been treasured between the leaves of this old volume. Now, would you deem it possible that this rose of half a century could ever bloom again?"

"Nonsense!" said the Widow Wycherly, with a peevish toss of her head. "You might as well ask whether an old woman's wrinkled face could ever bloom again."

"See!" answered Dr. Heidegger.

He uncovered the vase, and threw the faded rose into the water which it contained. At first, it lay lightly on the surface of the fluid, appearing to imbibe none of its moisture. Soon, however, a singular change began to be visible. The crushed and dried petals stirred, and assumed

---

5. **festoons,** ornamental carvings consisting of flowers or leaves linked together and looped between two points.
6. **damask,** a rich, reversible, elaborately patterned fabric.

a deeping tinge of crimson, as if the flower were reviving from a deathlike slumber; the slender stalk and twigs of foliage became green; and there was the rose of half a century, looking as fresh as when Sylvia Ward had first given it to her lover. It was scarcely full blown; for some of its delicate red leaves curled modestly around its moist bosom, within which two or three dewdrops were sparkling.

"That is certainly a very pretty deception," said the doctor's friends; carelessly, however, for they had witnessed greater miracles at a conjurer's show; "pray how was it effected?"

"Did you never hear of the 'Fountain of Youth,'" asked Dr. Heidegger, "which Ponce de Leon, the Spanish adventurer, went in search of two or three centuries ago?"

"But did Ponce de Leon ever find it?" said the Widow Wycherly.

"No," answered Dr. Heidegger, "for he never sought it in the right place. The famous Fountain of Youth, if I am rightly informed, is situated in the southern part of the Floridian peninsula, not far from Lake Macaco. Its source is overshadowed by several gigantic magnolias, which, though numberless centuries old, have been kept as fresh as violets by the virtues of this wonderful water. An acquaintance of mine, knowing my curiosity in such matters, has sent me what you see in the vase."

"Ahem!" said Colonel Killigrew, who believed not a word of the doctor's story; "and what may be the effect of this fluid on the human frame?"

"You shall judge for yourself, my dear colonel," replied Dr. Heidegger; "and all of you, my respected friends, are welcome to so much of this admirable fluid as may restore to you the bloom of youth. For my own part, having had much trouble in growing old, I am in no hurry to grow young again. With your permission, therefore, I will merely watch the progress of the experiment."

While he spoke, Dr. Heidegger had been filling the four champagne glasses with the water of the Fountain of Youth. It was apparently impregnated with an effervescent gas, for little

bubbles were continually ascending from the depths of the glasses, and bursting in silvery spray at the surface. As the liquor diffused a pleasant perfume, the old people doubted not that it possessed cordial[7] and comfortable properties; and though utter sceptics as to its rejuvenescent power, they were inclined to swallow it at once. But Dr. Heidegger besought them to stay a moment.

"Before you drink, my respectable old friends," said he, "it would be well that, with the experience of a lifetime to direct you, you should draw up a few general rules for your guidance, in passing a second time through the perils of youth. Think what a sin and shame it would be, if, with your peculiar advantages, you should not become patterns of virtue and wisdom to all the young people of the age!"

The doctor's four venerable friends made him no answer, except by a feeble and tremulous laugh; so very ridiculous was the idea that, knowing how closely repentance treads behind the steps of error, they should ever go astray again.

"Drink, then," said the doctor, bowing: "I rejoice that I have so well selected the subjects of my experiment."

With palsied hands, they raised the glasses to their lips. The liquor, if it really possessed such virtues as Dr. Heidegger imputed to it, could not have been bestowed on four human beings who needed it more woefully. They looked as if they had never known what youth or pleasure was, but had been the offspring of Nature's dotage, and always the gray, decrepit, sapless, miserable creatures, who now sat stooping round the doctor's table, without life enough in their souls or bodies to be animated even by the prospect of growing young again. They drank off the water, and replaced their glasses on the table.

Assuredly there was an almost immediate improvement in the aspect of the party, not unlike what might have been produced by a glass of generous wine, together with a sudden glow of

---

7. **cordial**\ˈkȯr·jəl\ here, meaning pleasing.

cheerful sunshine brightening over all their visages at once. There was a healthful suffusion on their cheeks, instead of the ashen hue that had made them look so corpse-like. They gazed at one another, and fancied that some magic power had really begun to smooth away the deep and sad inscriptions which Father Time had been so long engraving on their brows. The Widow Wycherly adjusted her cap, for she felt almost like a woman again.

"Give us more of this wondrous water!" cried they, eagerly. "We are younger—but we are still too old! Quick—give us more!"

"Patience, patience!" quoth Dr. Heidegger, who sat watching the experiment with philosophic coolness. "You have been a long time growing old. Surely, you might be content to grow young in half an hour! But the water is at your service."

Again he filled their glasses with the liquor of youth, enough of which still remained in the vase to turn half the old people in the city to the age of their own grandchildren. While the bubbles were yet sparkling on the brim, the doctor's four guests snatched their glasses from the table, and swallowed the contents at a single gulp. Was it delusion? even while the draught was passing down their throats, it seemed to have wrought a change on their whole systems. Their eyes grew clear and bright; a dark shade deepened among their silvery locks, they sat around the table, three gentlemen of middle age, and a woman, hardly beyond her buxom prime.

"My dear widow, you are charming!" cried Colonel Killigrew, whose eyes had been fixed upon her face, while the shadows of age were flitting from it like darkness from the crimson daybreak.

The fair widow knew, of old, that Colonel Killigrew's compliments were not always measured by sober truth; so she started up and ran to the mirror, still dreading that the ugly visage of an old woman would meet her gaze. Meanwhile, the three gentlemen behaved in such a manner as proved that the water of the Fountain of Youth possessed some intoxicating qual-

ities; unless, indeed, their exhilaration of spirits were merely a lightsome dizziness caused by the sudden removal of the weight of years. Mr. Gascoigne's mind seemed to run on political topics, but whether relating to the past, present, or future, could not easily be determined, since the same ideas and phrases have been in vogue these fifty years. Now he rattled forth full-throated sentences about patriotism, national glory, and the people's right; now he muttered some perilous stuff or other, in a sly and doubtful whisper, so cautiously that even his own conscience could scarcely catch the secret; and now, again, he spoke in measured accents, and a deeply deferential tone, as if a royal ear were listening to his well-turned periods. Colonel Killigrew all this time had been trolling forth a jolly bottle song, and ringing his glass in symphony with the chorus, while his eyes wandered toward the buxom figure of the Widow Wycherly. On the other side of the table, Mr. Medbourne was involved in a calculation of dollars and cents, with which was strangely intermingled a project for supplying the East Indies with ice, by harnessing a team of whales to the polar icebergs.

As for the Widow Wycherly, she stood before the mirror curtsying and simpering to her own image, and greeting it as the friend whom she loved better than all the world beside. She thrust her face close to the glass, to see whether some long-remembered wrinkle of crow's foot had indeed vanished. She examined whether the snow had so entirely melted from her hair that the venerable cap could be safely thrown aside. At last, turning briskly away, she came with a sort of dancing step to the table.

"My dear old doctor," cried she, "pray favor me with another glass!"

"Certainly, my dear madam, certainly!" replied the complaisant doctor; "see! I have already filled the glasses."

There, in fact, stood the four glasses, brimful of this wonderful water, the delicate spray of which, as it effervesced from the surface, resembled the tremulous glitter of diamonds. It was now so nearly sunset that the chamber had grown duskier than ever; but a mild and moonlike splendor gleamed from within the vase, and rested alike on the four guests and on the doctor's venerable figure. He sat in a high-backed, elaborately-carved, oaken arm-chair, with a gray dignity of aspect that might have well befitted that very Father Time, whose power had never been disputed, save by this fortunate company. Even while quaffing the third draught of the Fountain of Youth, they were almost awed by the expression of his mysterious visage.

But, the next moment, the exhilarating gush of young life shot through their veins. They were now in the happy prime of youth. Age, with its miserable train of cares and sorrows and diseases, was remembered only as the trouble of a dream, from which they had joyously awoke. The fresh gloss of the soul, so early lost, and without which the world's successive scenes had been but a gallery of faded pictures, again threw its enchantment over all their prospects. They felt like new-created beings in a new-created universe.

"We are young! We are young!" they cried exultingly.

Youth, like the extremity of age, had effaced the strongly-marked characteristics of middle life, and mutually assimilated them all. They were a group of merry youngsters, almost maddened with the exuberant frolicsomeness of their years. The most singular effect of their gayety was an impulse to mock the infirmity and decrepitude of which they had so lately been the victims. They laughed loudly at their old-fashioned attire, the wide-skirted coats and flapped waistcoats of the young men, and the ancient cap and gown of the blooming girl. One limped across the floor like a gouty[8] grandfather; one set a pair of spectacles astride of his nose, and pretended to pore over the black-letter pages of the book of magic; a third seated himself in an arm-chair, and strove to imitate the venerable dignity of Dr. Heidegger. Then all shouted mirthfully, and leaped about the room. The Widow Wycherly—if so fresh a damsel could be called a widow—tripped up

to the doctor's chair, with a mischievous merriment in her rosy face.

"Doctor, you dear old soul," cried she, "get up and dance with me!" And then the four young people laughed louder than ever, to think what a queer figure the poor old doctor would cut.

"Pray excuse me," answered the doctor quietly. "I am old and rheumatic, and my dancing days were over long ago. But either of these gay young gentlemen will be glad of so pretty a partner."

"Dance with me, Clara!" cried Colonel Killigrew.

"No, no, I will be her partner!" shouted Mr. Gascoigne.

"She promised me her hand, fifty years ago!" exclaimed Mr. Medbourne.

They all gathered round her. One caught both her hands in his passionate grasp—another threw his arm about her waist—the third buried his hand among the glossy curls that clustered beneath the widow's cap. Blushing, panting, struggling, chiding, laughing, her warm breath fanning each of their faces by turns, she strove to disengage herself, yet still remained in their triple embrace. Never was there a livelier picture of youthful rivalship, with bewitching beauty for the prize. Yet, by a strange deception, owing to the duskiness of the chamber, and the antique dresses which they still wore, the tall mirror is said to have reflected the figures of the three old, gray, withered grandsires, ridiculously contending for the skinny ugliness of a shrivelled grandam.

But they were young: their burning passions proved them so. Inflamed to madness by the coquetry of the girl-widow, who neither granted nor quite withheld her favors, the three rivals began to interchange threatening glances. Still keeping hold of the fair prize, they grappled fiercely at one another's throats. As they struggled to and fro, the table was overturned, and the vase dashed into a thousand

---

8. **gouty**\gau̇·tē\ having gout, a disease which causes swelling of the joints, especially of the feet and hands.

fragments. The precious Water of Youth flowed in a bright stream across the floor, moistening the wings of a butterfly, which, grown old in the decline of summer, had alighted there to die. The insect fluttered lightly through the chamber, and settled on the snowy head of Dr. Heidegger.

"Come, come, gentlemen!—come, Madam Wycherly," exclaimed the doctor, "I really must protest against this riot."

They stood still and shivered; for it seemed as if gray Time were calling them back from their sunny youth, far down into the chill and darksome vale of years. They looked at old Dr. Heidegger, who sat in his carved arm-chair, holding the rose of half a century, which he had rescued from among the fragments of the shattered vase. At the motion of his hand, the four rioters resumed their seats; the more readily, because their violent exertions had wearied them, youthful though they were.

"My poor Sylvia's rose!" ejaculated Dr. Heidegger, holding it in the light of the sunset clouds; "it appears to be fading again."

And so it was. Even while the party were looking at it, the flower continued to shrivel up, till it became as dry and fragile as when the doctor had first thrown it into the vase. He shook off the few drops of moisture which clung to its petals.

"I love it as well thus as in its dewy freshness," observed he, pressing the withered rose to his withered lips. While he spoke, the butterfly fluttered down from the doctor's snowy head, and fell upon the floor.

His guests shivered again. A strange chillness, whether of the body or spirit they could not tell, was creeping gradually over them all. They gazed at one another, and fancied that each fleeting moment snatched away a charm, and left a deepening furrow where none had been before. Was it an illusion? Had the changes of a lifetime been crowded into so brief a space, and were they now four aged people, sitting with their old friend, Dr. Heidegger?

"Are we grown old again, so soon?" cried they, dolefully.

In truth they had. The Water of Youth possessed merely a virtue more transient than that of wine. The delirium which it created had effervesced away. Yes! they were old again. With a shuddering impulse, that showed her a woman still, the widow clasped her skinny hands before her face, and wished that the coffin lid were over it, since it could be no longer beautiful.

"Yes, friends, ye are old again," said Dr. Heidegger, "and lo! the Water of Youth is all lavished on the ground. Well—I bemoan it not; for if the fountain gushed at my very doorstep, I would not stoop to bathe my lips in it—no, though its delirium were for years instead of moments. Such is the lesson ye have taught me!"

But the doctor's four friends had taught no such lesson to themselves. They resolved forthwith to make a pilgrimage to Florida, and quaff at morning, noon, and night, from the Fountain of Youth.

I
RELIVING THE PAST

If you compare the nonphysical characteristics of Dr. Heidegger's friends before (see p. 231) and after (see p. 233) the experiment, you will see that they have not changed one jot as a result of drinking the Water of Youth. This might suggest that Hawthorne held a rather pessimistic view of the human potential to benefit from experience. It is notable, however, that the four persons chosen for the experiment have all led rather empty lives. Suppose the Doctor had chosen four who had led fuller lives. How—if at all—might the results of the experiment have changed?

II
IMPLICATIONS

Discuss the following statements in terms of this story and of your own experience.

1. One's personality is so fixed by the time he reaches his midteens that nothing short of a miracle is likely to change it.

2. "Repentance treads closely behind the steps of error."

3. The fact that a person would want to relive his life is in itself good evidence that his life has been unsatisfactory.

4. True love or affection does not change with the passage of time.

5. History shows that man has no significant ability to benefit from the mistakes of his past; if he had such ability, he would long ago have learned how to avoid such things as wars and depressions.

III
TECHNIQUES

Conflict and Climax

Accepting Dr. Heidegger as the protagonist, or hero, of this tale, which of the following best describes (describe) the central conflict?

1. The hero vs. another person (or persons).

2. The hero vs. society.

3. The hero vs. nature.

4. The hero vs. forces within himself.

5. The hero vs. fate.

Identify the climax of the conflict or conflicts and discuss both these elements in some detail.

Moment of Illumination

We have defined the moment of illumination as the moment when the meaning of the story becomes fully clear. Is there any particular moment in this story that you would call its moment of illumination? If so, what is it? Also, how would you classify the last sentence of the story?

From his many years of reading, particularly in Cotton Mather's *The Wonders of the Invisible World*, Hawthorne was familiar with the "Witches' Sabbath," a midnight orgy which Puritan Salem dreaded even to talk about. In this famous tale, Goodman Brown (the title means "commoner," as opposed to "mister," a gentleman's title) experiences at first hand so frightful an event that critics have long called this one of Hawthorne's most powerful stories. The moral is timeless, and the evil atmosphere is as ominous as any Hawthorne ever created. It first appeared in 1835 and was later collected in *Mosses from an Old Manse* (1846).

Young Goodman Brown

Young Goodman Brown came forth at sunset into the street at Salem village; but put his head back, after crossing the threshold, to exchange a parting kiss with his young wife. And Faith, as the wife was aptly named, thrust her own pretty head into the street, letting the wind play with the pink ribbons of her cap while she called to Goodman Brown.

"Dearest heart," whispered she, softly and rather sadly, when her lips were close to his ear, "prithee put off your journey until sunrise and sleep in your own bed to-night. A lone woman is troubled with such dreams and such thoughts that she's afeard of herself sometimes. Pray tarry with me this night, dear husband, of all nights in the year."

"My love and my Faith," replied young Goodman Brown, "of all nights in the year, this one night must I tarry away from thee. My journey, as thou callest it, forth and back again, must needs be done 'twixt now and sunrise. What, my sweet, pretty wife, dost thou doubt me already, and we but three months married?"

"Then God bless you!" said Faith, with the pink ribbons; "and may you find all well when you come back."

"Amen!" cried Goodman Brown. "Say thy prayers, dear Faith, and go to bed at dusk, and no harm will come to thee."

So they parted; and the young man pursued his way until, being about to turn the corner by the meetinghouse, he looked back and saw the head of Faith still peeping after him with a melancholy air, in spite of her pink ribbons.

"Poor little Faith!" thought he, for his heart smote him. "What a wretch am I to leave her on such an errand! She talks of dreams, too. Methought[1] as she spoke there was trouble in her face, as if a dream had warned her what work is to be done to-night. But no, no; 't would kill her to think it. Well, she's a blessed angel on earth; and after this one night I'll cling to her skirts and follow her to heaven."

With this excellent resolve for the future, Goodman Brown felt himself justified in making more haste on his present evil purpose. He had taken a dreary road, darkened by all the gloomiest trees of the forest, which barely stood aside to let the narrow path creep through, and closed immediately behind. It was all as lonely as could be; and there is this peculiarity in such a solitude, that the traveller knows not who may be concealed by the innumerable trunks and the thick boughs overhead; so that with lonely footsteps he may yet be passing through an unseen multitude.

"There may be a devilish Indian behind every tree," said Goodman Brown to himself; and he glanced fearfully behind him as he added, "What if the devil himself should be at my very elbow!"

His head being turned back, he passed a crook of the road, and, looking forward again, beheld the figure of a man, in grave and decent attire, seated at the foot of an old tree. He arose at Goodman Brown's approach and walked onward side by side with him.

"You are late, Goodman Brown," said he. "The clock of the Old South[2] was striking as I came through Boston, and that is full fifteen minutes agone."[3]

"Faith kept me back a while," replied the young man, with a tremor in his voice, caused by the sudden appearance of his companion, though not wholly unexpected.

It was now deep dusk in the forest, and deepest in that part of it where these two were journeying. As nearly as could be discerned, the second traveller was about fifty years old, apparently in the same rank of life as Goodman Brown, and bearing a considerable resemblance to him, though perhaps more in expression than features. Still they might have been taken for father and son. And yet, though the elder person was as simply clad as the younger, and as simple in manner too, he had an indescribable air of one who knew the world, and who would not have felt abashed at the governor's dinner table or in King William's[4] court, were it possible that his affairs should call him thither. But the only thing about him that could be fixed upon as remarkable was his staff, which bore the likeness of a great black snake, so curiously wrought that it might almost be seen to twist and wriggle itself like a living serpent. This, of course, must have been an ocular deception, assisted by the uncertain light.

"Come, Goodman Brown," cried his fellow-traveller, "this is a dull pace for the beginning of a journey. Take my staff, if you are so soon weary."

"Friend," said the other, exchanging his slow pace for a full stop, "having kept covenant by meeting thee here, it is my purpose now to return whence I came. I have scruples touching the matter thou wot'st of."

"Sayest thou so?" replied he of the serpent, smiling apart. "Let us walk on, nevertheless,

1. methought, it seems to me.
2. Old South, Old South Church, Boston; secret meeting place of American patriots before the Revolutionary War. The church, however, was not erected until 1729 although the setting of the story seems to be earlier.
3. agone, archaic form of ago.
4. King William III, King of England, 1689–1702.

reasoning as we go; and if I convince thee not thou shalt turn back. We are but a little way in the forest yet."

"Too far! too far!" exclaimed the goodman, unconsciously resuming his walk. "My father never went into the woods on such an errand, nor his father before him. We have been a race of honest men and good Christians since the days of the martyrs; and shall I be the first of the name of Brown that ever took this path and kept"—

"Such company, thou wouldst say," observed the elder person, interpreting his pause. "Well said, Goodman Brown! I have been as well acquainted with your family as with ever a one among the Puritans; and that's no trifle to say. I helped your grandfather, the constable, when he lashed the Quaker woman so smartly through the streets of Salem; and it was I that brought your father a pitch-pine knot, kindled at my own hearth, to set fire to an Indian village, in King Philip's[5] war. They were my good friends, both; and many a pleasant walk have we had along this path, and returned merrily after midnight. I would fain be friends with you for their sake."

"If it be as thou sayest," replied Goodman Brown, "I marvel they never spoke of these matters; or, verily, I marvel not, seeing that the least rumor of the sort would have driven them from New England. We are a people of prayer, and good works to boot, and abide no such wickedness."

"Wickedness or not," said the traveller with the twisted staff, "I have a very general acquaintance here in New England. The deacons of many a church have drunk the communion wine with me; the selectmen of divers towns make me their chairman; and a majority of the Great and General Court are firm supporters of my interest. The governor and I, too — But these are state secrets."

"Can this be so?" cried Goodman Brown, with a stare of amazement at his undisturbed companion. "Howbeit, I have nothing to do with the governor and council; they have their own ways, and are no rule for a simple hus-

bandman[6] like me. But, were I to go on with thee, how should I meet the eye of that good old man, our minister, at Salem village? Oh, his voice would make me tremble both Sabbath day and lecture day."[7]

Thus far the elder traveller had listened with due gravity; but now burst into a fit of irrepressible mirth, shaking himself so violently that his snake-like staff actually seemed to wriggle in sympathy.

"Ha! ha! ha!" shouted he again and again; then composing himself. "Well, go on, Goodman Brown, go on; but, prithee, don't kill me with laughing."

"Well, then, to end the matter at once," said Goodman Brown, considerably nettled, "there is my wife, Faith. It would break her dear little heart; and I'd rather break my own."

"Nay, if that be the case," answered the other, "e'en go thy ways, Goodman Brown. I would not for twenty old women like the one hobbling before us that Faith should come to any harm."

As he spoke he pointed his staff at a female figure on the path, in whom Goodman Brown recognized a very pious and exemplary dame, who had taught him his catechism in youth, and was still his moral and spiritual adviser, jointly with the minister and Deacon Gookin.

"A marvel, truly, that Goody Cloyse[8] should be so far in the wilderness at nightfall," said he. "But with your leave, friend, I shall take a cut through the woods until we have left this Christian woman behind. Being a stranger to you, she might ask whom I was consorting with and whither I was going."

"Be it so," said his fellow-traveller. "Betake you the woods, and let me keep the path."

---

5. **King Philip,** name for Indian Chief, Metacomet (d. 1676), who was last leader of the Indian resistance in Southern New England.
6. **husbandman,** any man of humble station.
7. **lecture day,** day of midweek sermon, usually Thursday.
8. **Goody Cloyse,** contraction of *Goodwife* (cf. *goodman*). Goody Cloyse, Goody Cory, and Martha Carrier were sentenced in 1642 as witches by magistrates of Salem.

Accordingly the young man turned aside, but took care to watch his companion, who advanced softly along the road until he had come within a staff's length of the old dame. She, meanwhile, was making the best of her way, with singular speed for so aged a woman, and mumbling some indistinct words—a prayer, doubtless—as she went. The traveller put forth his staff and touched her withered neck with what seemed the serpent's tail.

"The devil!" screamed the pious old lady.

"Then Goody Cloyse knows her old friend?" observed the traveller, confronting her and leaning on his writhing stick.

"Ah, forsooth, and is it your worship indeed?" cried the good dame. "Yet, truly is it, and in the very image of my old gossip, Goodman Brown, the grandfather of the silly fellow that now is. But—would your worship believe it?—my broomstick hath strangely disappeared, stolen, as I suspect, by that unhanged witch, Goody Cory, and that, too, when I was all anointed with the juice of smallage, and cinquefoil, and wolf's bane"[9]—

"Mingled with fine wheat and the fat of a new-born babe," said the shape of old Goodman Brown.

"Ah, your worship knows the recipe," cried the old lady, cackling aloud. "So, as I was saying, being all ready for the meeting, and no horse to ride on, I made up my mind to foot it; for they tell me there is a nice young man to be taken into communion to-night. But now your good worship will lend me your arm, and we shall be there in a twinkling.

"That can hardly be," answered her friend. "I may not spare you my arm, Goody Cloyse; but here is my staff, if you will."

So saying, he threw it down at her feet, where, perhaps, it assumed life, being one of the rods which its owner had formerly lent to the Egyptian magi.[10] Of this fact, however, Goodman Brown could not take cognizance. He had cast up his eyes in astonishment, and, looking down again, beheld neither Goody Cloyse nor the serpentine staff, but this fellow-traveller alone, who waited for him as calmly as if nothing had happened.

"That old woman taught me my catechism,"[11] said the young man; and there was a world of meaning in this simple comment.

They continued to walk onward, while the elder traveller exhorted his companion to make good speed and persevere in the path, discoursing so aptly that his arguments seemed rather to spring up in the bosom of his auditor than to be suggested by himself. As they went, he plucked a branch of maple to serve for a walking stick, and began to strip it of the twigs and little boughs, which were wet with evening dew. The moment his fingers touched them they became strangely withered and dried up as with a week's sunshine. Thus the pair proceeded, at a good free pace, until suddenly, in a gloomy hollow of the road, Goodman Brown sat himself down on the stump of a tree and refused to go any farther.

"Friend," said he, stubbornly, "my mind is made up. Not another step will I budge on this errand. What if a wretched old woman do choose to go to the devil when I thought she was going to heaven: is that any reason why I should quit my dear Faith and go after her?"

"You will think better of this by and by," said his acquaintance, composedly. "Sit here and rest yourself a while; and when you feel like moving again, there is my staff to help you along."

Without more words, he threw his companion the maple stick, and was as speedily out of sight as if he had vanished into the deepening gloom. The young man sat a few moments by the roadside, applauding himself greatly, and thinking with how clear a conscience he should meet the minister in his morning walk, nor shrink from the eye of good old Deacon Gookin.

---

9. **smallage**\ˈsmȯ·lĭj\ wild celery, credited with magic powers. **cinquefoil**\ˈsĭŋk ˈfȯil\ plant of the rose family. **wolf's bane**, a poisonous plant.
10. **Egyptian magi**, member of the priestly caste believed capable of magical powers.
11. **catechism**\ˈkă·tə·kĭz·əm\ handbook of questions and answers used to teach principles of a religion.

And what calm sleep would be his that very night, which was to have been spent so wickedly, but so purely and sweetly now, in the arms of Faith! Amidst these pleasant and praiseworthy meditations, Goodman Brown heard the tramp of horses along the road, and deemed it advisable to conceal himself within the verge of the forest, conscious of the guilty purpose that had brought him thither, though now so happily turned from it.

On came the hoof tramps and the voices of the riders, two grave old voices, conversing soberly as they drew near. These mingled sounds appeared to pass along the road, within a few yards of the young man's hiding-place; but, owing doubtless to the depth of the gloom at that particular spot, neither the travellers nor their steeds were visible. Though their figures brushed the small boughs by the wayside, it could not be seen that they intercepted, even for a moment, the faint gleam from the strip of bright sky athwart which they must have passed. Goodman Brown alternately crouched and stood on tiptoe, pulling aside the branches and thrusting forth his head as far as he durst without discerning so much as a shadow. It vexed him the more, because he could have sworn, were such a thing possible, that he recognized the voices of the minister and Deacon Gookin, jogging along quietly, as they were wont to do, when bound to some ordination or ecclesiastical council. While yet within hearing, one of the riders stopped to pluck a switch.

"Of the two, reverend sir," said the voice like the deacon's, "I had rather miss an ordination dinner than to-night's meeting. They tell me that some of our community are to be here from Falmouth[12] and beyond, and others from Connecticut and Rhode Island, besides several of the Indian powwows, who, after their fashion, know almost as much deviltry as the best of us. Moreover, there is a goodly young woman to be taken into communion."

"Mighty well, Deacon Gookin!" replied the solemn old tones of the minister. "Spur up, or we shall be late. Nothing can be done, you know, until I get on the ground."

The hoofs clattered again; and the voices, talking so strangely in the empty air, passed on through the forest, where no church had ever been gathered or solitary Christian prayed. Whither, then, could these holy men be journeying so deep into the heathen wilderness? Young Goodman Brown caught hold of a tree for support, being ready to sink down on the ground, faint and overburdened with the heavy sickness of his heart. He looked up to the sky, doubting whether there really was a heaven above him. Yet there was the blue arch, and the stars brightening in it.

"With heaven above and Faith below, I will yet stand firm against the devil!" cried Goodman Brown.

While he still gazed upward into the deep arch of the firmament and had lifted his hands to pray, a cloud, though no wind was stirring, hurried across the zenith and hid the brightening stars. The blue sky was still visible, except directly overhead, where this black mass of cloud was sweeping swiftly northward. Aloft in the air, as if from the depths of the cloud, came a confused and doubtful sound of voices. Once the listener fancied that he could distinguish the accents of towns-people of his own, men and women, both pious and ungodly, many of whom he had met at the communion table, and had seen others rioting at the tavern. The next moment, so indistinct were the sounds, he doubted whether he had heard aught but the murmur of the old forest, whispering without a wind. Then came a stronger swell of those familiar tones, heard daily in the sunshine at Salem village, but never until now from a cloud of night. There was one voice, of a young woman, uttering lamentations, yet with an uncertain sorrow, and entreating for some favor, which, perhaps, it would grieve her to obtain; and all the unseen multitude, both saints and sinners, seemed to encourage her onward.

"Faith!" shouted Goodman Brown, in a voice of agony and desperation; and the echoes of

12. **Falmouth**\ˈfäl·məth\ town in southeast Massachusetts.

the forest mocked him, crying, "Faith! Faith!" as if bewildered wretches were seeking her all through the wilderness.

The cry of grief, rage, and terror was yet piercing the night, when the unhappy husband held his breath for a response. There was a scream, drowned immediately in a louder murmur of voices, fading into far-off laughter, as the dark cloud swept away, leaving the clear and silent sky above Goodman Brown. But something fluttered lightly down through the air and caught on the branch of a tree. The young man seized it, and beheld a pink ribbon.

"My Faith is gone!" cried he, after one stupefied moment. "There is no good on earth; and sin is but a name. Come, devil; for to thee is this world given."

And, maddened with despair, so that he laughed loud and long, did Goodman Brown grasp his staff and set forth again, at such a rate that he seemed to fly along the forest path rather than to walk or run. The road grew wilder and drearier and more faintly traced, and vanished at length, leaving him in the heart of the dark wilderness, still rushing onward with the instinct that guides mortal man to evil. The whole forest was peopled with frightful sounds—the creaking of the trees, the howling of wild beasts, and the yell of Indians; while sometimes the wind tolled like a distant church bell, and sometimes gave a broad roar around the traveller, as if all Nature were laughing him to scorn. But he was himself the chief horror of the scene, and shrank not from its other horrors.

"Ha! ha! ha!" roared Goodman Brown when the wind laughed at him. "Let us hear which will laugh loudest. Think not to frighten me with your deviltry. Come witch, come wizard, come Indian powwow, come devil himself, and here comes Goodman Brown. You may as well fear him as he fear you."

In truth, all through the haunted forest there could be nothing more frightful than the figure of Goodman Brown. On he flew among the black pines, brandishing his staff with frenzied gestures, now giving vent to an inspiration of horrid blasphemy, and now shouting forth such laughter as set all the echoes of the forest laughing like demons around him. The fiend in his own shape is less hideous than when he rages in the breast of man. Thus sped the demoniac on his course, until, quivering among the trees, he saw a red light before him, as when the felled trunks and branches of a clearing have been set on fire, and throw up their lurid blaze against the sky, at the hour of midnight. He paused, in a lull of the tempest that had driven him onward, and heard the swell of what seemed a hymn, rolling solemnly from a distance with the weight of many voices. He knew the tune; it was a familiar one in the choir of the village meetinghouse. The verse died heavily away, and was lengthened by a chorus, not of human voices, but of all the sounds of the benighted wilderness pealing in awful harmony together. Goodman Brown cried out, and his cry was lost to his own ear by its unison with the cry of the desert.

In the interval of silence he stole forward until the light glared full upon his eyes. At one extremity of an open space, hemmed in by the dark wall of the forest, arose a rock, bearing some rude, natural resemblance either to an altar or a pulpit, and surrounded by four blazing pines, their tops aflame, their stems untouched, like candles at an evening meeting. The mass of foliage that had overgrown the summit of the rock was all on fire, blazing high into the night and fitfully illuminating the whole field. Each pendent twig and leafy festoon was in a blaze. As the red light arose and fell, a numerous congregation alternately shone forth, then disappeared in shadow, and again grew, as it were, out of the darkness, peopling the heart of the solitary woods at once.

"A grave and dark-clad company," quoth Goodman Brown.

In truth they were such. Among them, quivering to and fro between gloom and splendor, appeared faces that would be seen next day at the council board of the province, and others which, Sabbath after Sabbath, looked devoutly heavenward, and benignantly over the crowded pews, from the holiest pulpits in the land. Some affirm that the lady of the governor was there. At least there were high dames well known to her, and wives of honored husbands and widows, a great multitude, and ancient maidens, all of excellent repute, and fair young girls, who trembled lest their mothers should espy them. Either the sudden gleams of light flashing over the obscure field bedazzled Goodman Brown, or he recognized a score of the church members of Salem village famous for their especial sanctity. Good old Deacon Gookin had arrived, and waited at the skirts of that venerable saint, his revered pastor. But, irreverently consorting with these grave, reputable, and pious people, these elders of the church, these chaste dames and dewy virgins, there were men of dissolute lives and women of spotted fame, wretches given over to all mean and filthy vice, and suspected even of horrid crimes. It was strange to see that the good shrank not from the wicked, nor were the sinners abashed by the saints. Scattered also among their pale-faced enemies were the Indian priests, or pow-wows, who had often scared their native forest with more hideous incantations than any known to English witchcraft.

"But where is Faith?" thought Goodman Brown; and, as hope came into his heart, he trembled.

Another verse of the hymn arose, a slow and mournful strain, such as the pious love, but joined to words which expressed all that our nature can conceive of sin, and darkly hinted at far more. Unfathomable to mere mortals is the lore of fiends. Verse after verse was sung; and still the chorus of the desert swelled between like the deepest tone of a mighty organ; and with the final peal of that dreadful anthem there came a sound, as if the roaring wind, the rushing streams, the howling beasts, and every other voice of the unconcerted wilderness were mingling and according with the voice of guilty man in homage to the prince of all. The four blazing pines threw up a loftier flame, and obscurely discovered shapes and visages of horror on the smoke wreaths above the impious assembly. At the same moment the fire on the rock shot redly forth and formed a glowing arch above its base, where now appeared a figure. With reverence be it spoken, the figure bore no slight similitude, both in garb and manner, to some grave divine of the New England churches.

"Bring forth the converts!" cried a voice that echoed through the field and rolled into the forest.

At the word, Goodman Brown stepped forth from the shadow of the trees and approached the congregation, with whom he felt a loathful brotherhood by the sympathy of all that was wicked in his heart. He could have well-nigh sworn that the shape of his own dead father beckoned him to advance, looking downward from a smoke wreath, while a woman, with dim features of despair, threw out her hand to warn him back. Was it his mother? But he had no power to retreat one step, nor to resist, even in thought, when the minister and good old Deacon Gookin seized his arms and led him to the blazing rock. Thither came also the slender form of a veiled female, led between Goody Cloyse, that pious teacher of the catechism, and Martha Carrier, who had received the devil's promise to be queen of hell. A rampant hag was she. And there stood the proselytes[13] beneath the canopy of fire.

"Welcome, my children," said the dark figure, "to the communion of your race. Ye have found thus young your nature and your destiny. My children, look behind you!"

They turned; and flashing forth, as it were, in a sheet of flame, the fiend worshippers were seen; the smile of welcome gleamed darkly on every visage.

"There," resumed the sable form, "are all whom ye have reverenced from youth. Ye deemed them holier than yourselves, and shrank from your own sin, contrasting it with their lives of righteousness and prayerful aspirations heavenward. Yet here are they all in

---

13. **proselytes** \ˈprŏ·sə ˈlaits\ persons who have been converted from one religion to another.

my worshipping assembly. This night it shall be granted you to know their secret deeds: how hoary-bearded elders of the church have whispered wanton words to the young maids of their households; how many a woman, eager for widows' weeds, has given her husband a drink at bedtime and let him sleep his last sleep in her bosom; how beardless youths have made haste to inherit their fathers' wealth; and how fair damsels—blush not, sweet ones—have dug little graves in the garden, and bidden me, the sole guest, to an infant's funeral. By the sympathy of your human hearts for sin ye shall scent out all the places—whether in church, bed-chamber, street, field, or forest—where crime has been committed, and shall exult to behold the whole earth one stain of guilt, one mighty blood spot. Far more than this. It shall be yours to penetrate, in every bosom, the deep mystery of sin, the fountain of all wicked arts, and which inexhaustibly supplies more evil impulses than human power—than my power at its utmost—can make manifest in deeds. And now, my children, look upon each other."

They did so; and, by the blaze of the hell-kindled torches, the wretched man beheld his Faith, and the wife her husband, trembling before that unhallowed altar.

"Lo, there ye stand, my children," said the figure, in a deep and solemn tone, almost sad with its despairing awfulness, as if his once angelic nature could yet mourn for our miserable race. "Depending upon one another's hearts, ye had still hoped that virtue were not all a dream. Now are ye undeceived. Evil is the nature of mankind. Evil must be your only happiness. Welcome again, my children, to the communion of your race."

"Welcome," repeated the fiend worshippers, in one cry of despair and triumph.

And there they stood, the only pair, as it seemed, who were yet hesitating on the verge of wickedness in this dark world. A basin was hollowed, naturally, in the rock. Did it contain water, reddened by the lurid light? or was it blood? or, perchance, a liquid flame? Herein did the shape of evil dip his hand and prepare to lay the mark of baptism upon their foreheads, that they might be partakers of the mystery of sin, more conscious of the secret guilt of others, both in deed and thought, than they could now be of their own. The husband cast one look at his pale wife, and Faith at him. What polluted wretches would the next glance show them to each other, shuddering alike at what they disclosed and what they saw.

"Faith! Faith!" cried the husband, "look up to heaven, and resist the wicked one."

Whether Faith obeyed he knew not. Hardly had he spoken when he found himself amid calm night and solitude, listening to a roar of the wind which died heavily away through the forest. He staggered against the rock, and felt it chill and damp; while a hanging twig, that had been all on fire, besprinkled his cheek with the coldest dew.

The next morning young Goodman Brown came slowly into the street of Salem village, staring around him like a bewildered man. The good old minister was taking a walk along the graveyard to get an appetite for breakfast and meditate his sermon, and bestowed a blessing, as he passed, on Goodman Brown. He shrank from the venerable saint as if to avoid an anathema. Old Deacon Gookin was at domestic worship, and the holy words of his prayer were heard through the open window. "What God doth the wizard pray to?" quoth Goodman Brown. Goody Cloyse, that excellent old Christian, stood in the early sunshine at her own lattice, catechizing a little girl who had brought her a pint of morning's milk. Goodman Brown snatched away the child as from the grasp of the fiend himself. Turning the corner by the meetinghouse, he spied the head of Faith, with the pink ribbons, gazing anxiously forth, and bursting into such joy at sight of him that she skipped along the street and almost kissed her husband before the whole village. But Goodman Brown looked sternly and sadly into her face, and passed on without a greeting.

Had Goodman Brown fallen asleep in the forest and only dreamed a wild dream of a witch-meeting?

Be it so if you will; but, alas! it was a dream of evil omen for young Goodman Brown. A stern, a sad, a darkly meditative, a distrustful, if not a desperate man did he become from the night of that fearful dream. On the Sabbath day, when the congregation were singing a holy psalm, he could not listen because an anthem of sin rushed loudly upon his ear and drowned all the blessed strain. When the minister spoke from the pulpit with power and fervid eloquence, and, with his hand on the open Bible, of the sacred truths of our religion, and of saint-like lives and triumphant deaths, and of future bliss or misery unutterable, then did Goodman Brown turn pale, dreading lest the roof thunder down upon the gray blasphemer and his hearers. Often, awaking suddenly at midnight, he shrank from the bosom of Faith; and at morning or eventide, when the family knelt down at prayer, he scowled and muttered to himself, and gazed sternly at his wife, and turned away. And when he had lived long, and was borne to his grave a hoary corpse, followed by Faith, an aged woman, and children and grandchildren, a goodly procession, besides neighbors not a few, they carved no hopeful verse upon his tombstone, for his dying hour was gloom.

I
DREAM OR REALITY?

It would seem very important for the reader to know whether Goodman Brown's experience in the forest was real or imaginary. If the experience was real, then Brown's neighbors, including his own wife and minister, are sinners. On the other hand, if the hero's forest experience was a dream, it may be that his wife and neighbors are not sinners—he may be projecting his own sense of sin onto them.

What evidence can you offer to prove that Goodman Brown's experience in the forest was either real or unreal? If you cannot find enough evidence to justify either of these conclusions, why do you think Hawthorne has left his readers in doubt?

II
IMPLICATIONS

The following statements give interpretations of the story. What are your views on each of them?

1. Hawthorne is less concerned with the causes of the loss of faith in human nature than he is with the effects.

2. The chief theme of "Young Goodman Brown" is not "sin" but "guilt."

3. The moral of this story is that once a man knows evil, his view of the world can never be the same as it was when he was innocent of evil.

III
TECHNIQUE

Conflict and Climax

The most obvious conflict here is that between the hero and the Devil; the struggle has at least two climaxes. The first occurs when Goodman Brown sees Faith's ribbon and exclaims: "My Faith is gone! There is no good on earth; and sin is but a name. Come, devil; for to thee is this world given."

At this point it looks as if the Devil has won the struggle, but then we meet the second climax. It occurs when Goodman Brown and his wife are about to be baptized and he cries out, ". . . Faith! look up to heaven and resist the wicked one."

From the second climax a reader might conclude that the hero was victorious over the Devil. What facts—if any—would seem to confirm this hypothesis, and what facts—if any—would seem to deny it?

The "Device of Multiple-Choice"

The many ambiguities (multiple meanings) of "Young Goodman Brown" might lead a reader to conclude that Hawthorne lost control of his story. This, of course, is always possible in any story, but on the other hand one must not assume that ambiguity in a work of art is necessarily bad. Critics have noted that Hawthorne often purposely suggests two or more possible interpretations for the same action or event. One critic called this "the device of multiple-choice"; another critic has suggested that a good synonym for "ambiguity"—at least in certain works of art—would be "richness." Can you see how this device could lead to richness rather than to confusion of meaning?

In 1844 Hawthorne wrote
in his notebooks: "The search
of an investigator for the Unpardonable Sin;—
he at last finds it in his own heart
and practice." A few months later he elaborated
the same idea in another notebook entry.
In 1850 he first published this memorable story
of a man who suffered the grim fate
of alienation from human society
and was not aware of what was happening
to his soul. Ethan Brand's tale was collected
in *The Snow-Image and Other Tales* (1851)
and has been reprinted many times
since then.

Ethan Brand

A CHAPTER
FROM AN ABORTIVE ROMANCE

Bartram the lime-burner, a rough, heavy-looking man, begrimed with charcoal, sat watching his kiln at nightfall, while his little son played at building houses with the scattered fragments of marble, when, on the hill-side below them, they heard a roar of laughter, not mirthful, but slow, and even solemn, like a wind shaking the boughs of the forest.

"Father, what is that?" asked the little boy, leaving his play, and pressing betwixt his father's knees.

"Oh, some drunken man, I suppose," answered the lime-burner; "some merry fellow from the bar-room in the village, who dared not laugh loud enough within doors lest he should blow the roof of the house off. So here he is, shaking his jolly sides at the foot of Graylock."

"But, father," said the child, more sensitive than the obtuse, middle-aged clown, "he does not laugh like a man that is glad. So the noise frightens me!"

"Don't be a fool, child!" cried his father, gruffly. "You will never make a man, I do believe; there is too much of your mother in you. I have known the rustling of a leaf startle you. Hark! Here comes the merry fellow now. You shall see that there is no harm in him."

Bartram and his little son, while they were talking thus, sat watching the same lime-kiln that had been the scene of Ethan Brand's solitary and meditative life, before he began his search for the Unpardonable Sin. Many years, as we have seen,[1] had now elapsed, since that portentous night when the IDEA was first developed. The kiln, however, on the mountain-side, stood unimpaired, and was in nothing changed since he had thrown his dark thoughts into the intense glow of its furnace, and melted them, as it were, into the one thought that took possession of his life. It was a rude, round, tower-like structure about twenty feet high, heavily built of rough stones, and with a hillock of earth heaped about the larger part of its circumference; so that the blocks and fragments of marble might be drawn by cart-loads, and thrown in at the top. There was an opening at the bottom of the tower, like an oven-mouth, but large enough to admit a man in a stooping posture, and provided with a massive iron door. With the smoke and jets of flame issuing from the chinks and crevices of this door, which seemed to give admittance into the hill-side, it resembled nothing so much as the private entrance to the infernal regions, which the shepherds of the Delectable Mountains[2] were accustomed to show to pilgrims.

There are many such lime-kilns in that tract of country, for the purpose of burning the white marble which composes a large part of the substance of the hills. Some of them, built years

---

1. **as we have seen,** refers to earlier nonexistent chapters of "An Abortive Romance," which, if ever written, do not now exist.
2. **Delectable Mountains,** mountains in Bunyan's *Pilgrims' Progress* from which Christian first sees the Celestial City.

ago, and long deserted, with weeds growing in the vacant round of the interior, which is open to the sky, and grass and wildflowers rooting themselves into the chinks of the stones, look already like relics of antiquity, and may yet be overspread with the lichens of centuries to come. Others, where the lime-burner still feeds his daily and night-long fire, afford points of interest to the wanderer among the hills, who seats himself on a log of wood or a fragment of marble, to hold a chat with the solitary man. It is a lonesome, and, when the character is inclined to thought, may be an intensely thoughtful occupation; as it proved in the case of Ethan Brand, who had mused to such strange purpose, in days gone by, while the fire in this very kiln was burning.

The man who now watched the fire was of a different order, and troubled himself with no thoughts save the very few that were requisite to his business. At frequent intervals, he flung back the clashing weight of the iron door, and, turning his face from the insufferable glare, thrust in huge logs of oak, or stirred the immense brands with a long pole. Within the furnace were seen the curling and riotous flames, and the burning marble, almost molten with the intensity of heat; while without, the reflection of the fire quivered on the dark intricacy of the surrounding forest, and showed in the foreground a bright and ruddy little picture of the hut, the spring beside its door, the athletic and coal-begrimed figure of the lime-burner, and the half-frightened child, shrinking into the protection of his father's shadow. And when, again, the iron door was closed, then reappeared the tender light of the half-full moon, which vainly strove to trace out the indistinct shapes of the neighboring mountains; and, in the upper sky, there was a flitting congregation of clouds, still faintly tinged with the rosy sunset, though thus far down into the valley the sunshine had vanished long and long ago.

The little boy now crept still closer to his father, as footsteps were heard ascending the hill-side, and a human form thrust aside the bushes that clustered beneath the trees.

"Halloo! who is it?" cried the lime-burner, vexed at his son's timidity, yet half infected by it. "Come forward, and show yourself, like a man, or I'll fling this chunk of marble at your head!"

"You offer me a rough welcome," said a gloomy voice, as the unknown man drew nigh. "Yet I neither claim nor desire a kinder one, even at my own fireside."

To obtain a distincter view, Bartram threw open the iron door of the kiln, whence immediately issued a gush of fierce light, that smote full upon the stranger's face and figure. To a careless eye there appeared nothing very remarkable in his aspect, which was that of a man in a coarse, brown, country-made suit of clothes, tall and thin, with the staff and heavy shoes of a wayfarer. As he advanced, he fixed his eyes—which were very bright—intently upon the brightness of the furnace, as if he beheld, or expected to behold, some object worthy of note within it.

"Good evening, stranger," said the lime-burner; "whence come you, so late in the day?"

"I come from my search," answered the wayfarer; "for, at last, it is finished."

"Drunk!—or crazy!" muttered Bartram to himself. "I shall have trouble with the fellow. The sooner I drive him away, the better."

The little boy, all in a tremble, whispered to his father, and begged him to shut the door of the kiln, so that there might not be so much light; for that there was something in the man's face which he was afraid to look at, yet could not look away from. And, indeed, even the lime-burner's dull and torpid sense began to be impressed by an indescribable something in that thin, rugged, thoughtful visage, with the grizzled hair hanging wildly about it, and those deeply sunken eyes, which gleamed like fires within the entrance of a mysterious cavern. But, as he closed the door, the stranger turned towards him, and spoke in a quiet, familiar way, that made Bartram feel as if he were a sane and sensible man, after all.

"Your task draws to an end, I see," said he. "This marble has already been burning three days. A few hours more will convert the stone to lime."

"Why, who are you?" exclaimed the lime-burner. "You seem as well acquainted with my business as I am myself."

"And well I may be," said the stranger; "for I followed the same craft many a long year, and here, too, on this very spot. But you are a new-comer in these parts. Did you never hear of Ethan Brand?"

"The man that went in search of the Unpardonable Sin?" asked Bartram, with a laugh.

"The same," answered the stranger. "He has found what he sought, and therefore he comes back again."

"What! then you are Ethan Brand himself?" cried the lime-burner, in amazement. "I am a newcomer here, as you say, and they call it eighteen years since you left the foot of Gray-lock. But, I can tell you, the good folks still talk about Ethan Brand, in the village yonder, and what a strange errand took him away from his lime-kiln. Well, and so you have found the Unpardonable Sin?"

"Even so!" said the stranger, calmly.

"If the question is a fair one," proceeded Bartram, "where might it be?"

Ethan Brand laid his finger on his own heart. "Here!" replied he.

And then, without mirth in his countenance, but as if moved by an involuntary recognition of the infinite absurdity of seeking throughout the world for what was the closest of all things to himself, and looking into every heart, save his own, for what was hidden in no other breast, he broke into a laugh of scorn. It was the same slow, heavy laugh, that had almost appalled the lime-burner when it heralded the wayfarer's approach.

The solitary mountain-side was made dismal by it. Laughter, when out of place, mistimed, or bursting forth from a disordered state of feeling, may be the most terrible modulation of the human voice. The laughter of one asleep, even if it be a little child,—the madman's laugh,—the wild, screaming laugh of a born idiot,—are sounds that we sometimes tremble to hear, and

would always willingly forget. Poets have imagined no utterance of fiends or hobgoblins so fearfully appropriate as a laugh. And even the obtuse lime-burner felt his nerves shaken, as this strange man looked inward at his own heart, and burst into laughter that rolled away into the night, and was indistinctly reverberated among the hills.

"Joe," said he to his little son, "scamper down to the tavern in the village, and tell the jolly fellows there that Ethan Brand has come back, and that he has found the Unpardonable Sin!"

The boy darted away on his errand, to which Ethan Brand made no objection, nor seemed hardly to notice it. He sat on a log of wood, looking steadfastly at the iron door of the kiln. When the child was out of sight, and his swift and light footsteps ceased to be heard treading first on the fallen leaves and then on the rocky mountain-path, the lime-burner began to regret his departure. He felt that the little fellow's presence had been a barrier between his guest and himself, and that he must now deal, heart to heart, with a man who, on his own confession, had committed the one only crime for which Heaven could afford no mercy. That crime, in its indistinct blackness, seemed to overshadow him. The lime-burner's own sins rose up within him, and made his memory riotous with a throng of evil shapes that asserted their kindred with the Master Sin, whatever it might be, which it was within the scope of man's corrupted nature to conceive and cherish. They were all of one family; they went to and fro between his breast and Ethan Brand's, and carried dark greetings from one to the other.

Then Bartram remembered the stories which had grown traditionary in reference to this strange man, who had come upon him like a shadow of the night, and was making himself at home in his old place, after so long absence that the dead people, dead and buried for years, would have had more right to be at home, in any familiar spot, than he. Ethan Brand, it was said, had conversed with Satan himself in the lurid blaze of this very kiln. The legend had been matter of mirth heretofore, but looked grisly now. According to this tale, before Ethan Brand departed on his search, he had been accustomed to evoke a fiend from the hot furnace of the lime-kiln, night after night, in order to confer with him about the Unpardonable Sin; the man and the fiend each laboring to frame the image of some mode of guilt which could neither be atoned for nor forgiven. And, with the first gleam of light upon the mountain-top, the fiend crept in at the iron door, there to abide the intensest element of fire until again summoned forth to share in the dreadful task of extending man's possible guilt beyond the scope of Heaven's else infinite mercy.

While the lime-burner was struggling with the horror of these thoughts, Ethan Brand rose from the log, and flung open the door of the kiln. The action was in such accordance with the idea in Bartram's mind, that he almost expected to see the Evil One issue forth, red-hot, from the raging furnace.

"Hold! hold!" cried he, with a tremulous attempt to laugh; for he was ashamed of his fears, although they overmastered him. "Don't, for mercy's sake, bring out your Devil now!"

"Man!" sternly replied Ethan Brand, "what need have I of the Devil? I have left him behind me, on my track. It is with such half-way sinners as you that he busies himself. Fear not, because I open the door, I do but act by old custom, and am going to trim your fire, like a lime-burner, as I was once."

He stirred the vast coals, thrust in more wood, and bent forward to gaze into the hollow prison-house of the fire, regardless of the fierce glow that reddened upon his face. The lime-burner sat watching him, and half suspected this strange guest of a purpose, if not to evoke a fiend, at least to plunge bodily into the flames, and thus vanish from the sight of man. Ethan Brand, however, drew quietly back, and closed the door of the kiln.

"I have looked," said he, "into many a human heart that was seven times hotter with sinful passions than yonder furnace is with fire. But I found not there what I sought. No, not the Unpardonable Sin!"

"What is the Unpardonable Sin?" asked the lime-burner; and then he shrank farther from his companion, trembling lest his question should be answered.

"It is a sin that grew within my own breast," replied Ethan Brand, standing erect, with a pride that distinguishes all enthusiasts of his stamp. "A sin that grew nowhere else! The sin of an intellect that triumphed over the sense of brotherhood with man and reverence for God, and sacrificed everything to its own mighty claims! The only sin that deserves a recompense of immortal agony! Freely, were it to do again, would I incur the guilt. Unshrinkingly I accept the retribution!"

"The man's head is turned," muttered the lime-burner to himself. "He may be a sinner like the rest of us,—nothing more likely,—but I'll be sworn, he is a madman too."

Nevertheless, he felt uncomfortable at his situation, alone with Ethan Brand on the wild mountain-side, and was right glad to hear the rough murmur of tongues, and the footsteps of what seemed a pretty numerous party, stumbling over the stones and rustling through the underbrush. Soon appeared the whole lazy regiment that was wont to infest the village tavern, comprehending three or four individuals who had drunk flip beside the bar-room fire through all the winters, and smoked their pipes beneath the stoop through all the summers, since Ethan Brand's departure. Laughing boisterously, and mingling all their voices together in unceremonious talk, they now burst into the moonshine and narrow streaks of firelight that illuminated the open space before the lime-kiln. Bartram set the door ajar again, flooding the spot with light, that the whole company might get a fair view of Ethan Brand, and he of them.

There, among other old acquaintances, was a once ubiquitous man, now almost extinct, but whom we were formerly sure to encounter at the hotel of every thriving village throughout the country. It was the stage-agent. The present specimen of the genus was a wilted and smoke-dried man, wrinkled and red-nosed, in a smartly cut, brown, bobtailed coat, with brass buttons, who, for a length of time unknown, had kept his desk and corner in the bar-room, and was still puffing what seemed to be the same cigar that he had lighted twenty years before. He had great fame as a dry joker, though, perhaps, less on account of any intrinsic humor than from a certain flavor of brandy-toddy and tobacco-smoke, which impregnated all his ideas and expressions, as well as his person. Another well-remembered, though strangely altered, face was that of Lawyer Giles, as people still called him in courtesy; an elderly ragamuffin, in his soiled shirt-sleeves and tow-cloth trousers. This poor fellow had been an attorney, in what he called his better days, a sharp practitioner, and in great vogue among the village litigants; but flip, and sling, and toddy, and cocktails, imbibed at all hours, morning, noon, and night, had caused him to slide from intellectual to various kinds and degrees of bodily labor, till at last, to adopt his own phrase, he slid into a soap-vat. In other words, Giles was now a soap-boiler, in a small way. He had come to be but the fragment of a human being, a part of one foot having been chopped off by an axe, and an entire hand torn away by the devilish grip of a steam-engine. Yet, though the corporeal[3] hand was gone, a spiritual member remained; for, stretching forth the stump, Giles steadfastly averred that he felt an invisible thumb and fingers with as vivid a sensation as before the real ones were amputated. A maimed and miserable wretch he was; but one, nevertheless, whom the world could not trample on, and had no right to scorn, either in this or any previous stage of his misfortunes, since he had still kept up the courage and spirit of a man, asked nothing in charity, and with his one hand—and that the left one—fought a stern battle against want and hostile circumstances.

Among the throng, too, came another personage, who, with certain points of similarity to Lawyer Giles, had many more of difference. It was the village doctor; a man of some fifty years, whom, at an earlier period of his life, we introduced as paying a professional visit to

Ethan Brand during the latter's supposed insanity. He was now a purple-visaged, rude, and brutal, yet half-gentlemanly figure, with something wild, ruined, and desperate in his talk, and in all the details of his gesture and manners. Brandy possessed this man like an evil spirit, and made him as surly and savage as a wild beast, and as miserable as a lost soul; but there was supposed to be in him such wonderful skill, such native gifts of healing, beyond any which medical science could impart, that society caught hold of him, and would not let him sink out of its reach. So, swaying to and fro upon his horse, and grumbling thick accents at the bedside, he visited all the sick-chambers for miles about among the mountain towns, and sometimes raised a dying man, as it were, by miracle, or quite as often, no doubt, sent his patient to a grave that was dug many a year too soon. The doctor had an everlasting pipe in his mouth, and, as somebody said, in allusion to his habit of swearing, it was always alight with hell-fire.

These three worthies pressed forward, and greeted Ethan Brand each after his own fashion, earnestly inviting him to partake of the contents of a certain black bottle, in which, as they averred, he would find something far better worth seeking for than the Unpardonable Sin. No mind, which has wrought itself by intense and solitary meditation into a high state of enthusiasm, can endure the kind of contact with low and vulgar modes of thought and feeling to which Ethan Brand was now subjected. It made him doubt—and, strange to say, it was a painful doubt—whether he had indeed found the Unpardonable Sin, and found it within himself. The whole question on which he had exhausted life, and more than life, looked like a delusion.

"Leave me," he said bitterly, "ye brute beasts, that have made yourselves so, shrivelling up your souls with fiery liquors! I have done with you. Years and years ago, I groped

---

3. **corporeal**\kɔr ˈpō·rĭ·əl\ of the body.

into your hearts and found nothing there for my purpose. Get ye gone!"

"Why, you uncivil scoundrel," cried the fierce doctor, "is that the way you respond to the kindness of your best friends? Then let me tell you the truth. You have no more found the Unpardonable Sin than yonder boy Joe has. You are but a crazy fellow,—I told you so twenty years ago,—neither better nor worse than a crazy fellow, and the fit companion of old Humphrey, here!"

He pointed to an old man, shabbily dressed, with long white hair, thin visage, and unsteady eyes. For some years past this aged person had been wandering about among the hills, inquiring of all travellers whom he met for his daughter. The girl, it seemed, had gone off with a company of circus-performers, and occasionally tidings of her came to the village, and fine stories were told of her glittering appearance as she rode on horseback in the ring, or performed marvellous feats on the tight-rope.

The white-haired father now approached Ethan Brand, and gazed unsteadily into his face.

"They tell me you have been all over the earth," said he, wringing his hands with earnestness. "You must have seen my daughter, for she makes a grand figure in the world, and everybody goes to see her. Did she send any word to her old father, or say when she was coming back?"

Ethan Brand's eye quailed beneath the old man's. That daughter from whom he so earnestly desired a word of greeting, was the Esther of our tale,[4] the very girl whom, with such cold and remorseless purpose, Ethan Brand had made the subject of a psychological experiment, and wasted, absorbed, and perhaps annihilated her soul, in the process.

"Yes," murmured he, turning away from the hoary wanderer, "it is no delusion. There is an Unpardonable Sin!"

While these things were passing, a merry scene was going forward in the area of cheerful light, beside the spring and before the door of the hut. A number of the youth of the village,

young men and girls, had hurried up the hillside, impelled by curiosity to see Ethan Brand, the hero of so many a legend familiar to their childhood. Finding nothing, however, very remarkable in his aspect,—nothing but a sunburnt wayfarer, in plain garb and dusty shoes, who sat looking into the fire as if he fancied pictures among the coals,—these young people speedily grew tired of observing him. As it happened, there was other amusement at hand. An old German Jew travelling with a diorama[5] on his back, was passing down the mountain-road towards the village just as the party turned aside from it, and, in hopes of eking out the profits of the day, the showman had kept them company to the lime-kiln.

"Come, old Dutchman," cried one of the young men, "let us see your pictures, if you can swear they are worth looking at!"

"Oh yes, Captain," answered the Jew,— whether as a matter of courtesy or craft, he styled everybody Captain,—"I shall show you, indeed, some very superb pictures!"

So, placing his box in a proper position, he invited the young men and girls to look through the glass orifices of the machine, and proceeded to exhibit a series of the most outrageous scratchings and daubings, as specimens of the fine arts, that ever an itinerant showman had the face to impose upon his circle of spectators. The pictures were worn out, moreover, tattered, full of cracks and wrinkles, dingy with tobacco-smoke, and otherwise in a most pitiable condition. Some purported to be cities, public edifices, and ruined castles in Europe; others represented Napoleon's battles and Nelson's sea-fights; and in the midst of these would be seen a gigantic brown, hairy hand,—which might have been mistaken for the Hand of Destiny, though, in truth, it was only the showman's,—pointing its forefinger to various scenes of the conflict, while its owner gave historical illustrations. When, with much merriment at its

---

4. **Esther of our tale,** refers to nonexistent earlier chapters. Note the subtitle of this story.
5. **diorama**\\'dī·ə ᐧrä·mə\\ a miniature scenic display using sculptured figures and lifelike details.

abominable deficiency of merit, the exhibition was concluded, the German bade little Joe put his head into the box. Viewed through the magnifying-glasses, the boy's round, rosy visage assumed the strangest imaginable aspect of an immense Titanic child[6] the mouth grinning broadly, and the eyes and every other feature overflowing with fun at the joke. Suddenly, however, that merry face turned pale, and its expression changed to horror, for this easily impressed and excitable child had become sensible that the eye of Ethan Brand was fixed upon him through the glass.

"You make the little man to be afraid, Captain," said the German Jew, turning up the dark and strong outline of his visage from his stooping posture. "But look again, and, by chance, I shall cause you to see somewhat that is very fine, upon my word!"

Ethan Brand gazed into the box for an instant, and then starting back, looked fixedly at the German. What had he seen? Nothing, apparently; for a curious youth, who had peeped in almost at the same moment, beheld only a vacant space of canvas.

"I remember you now," muttered Ethan Brand to the showman.

"Ah, Captain," whispered the Jew of Nuremburg, with a dark smile, "I find it to be a heavy matter in my showbox,—this Unpardonable Sin! By my faith, Captain, it has wearied my shoulders, this long day, to carry it over the mountain."

"Peace," answered Ethan Brand, sternly, "or get thee into the furnace yonder!"

The Jew's exhibition had scarcely concluded, when a great, elderly dog—who seemed to be his own master, as no person in the company laid claim to him—saw fit to render himself the object of public notice. Hitherto, he had shown himself a very quiet, well-disposed old dog, going round from one to another, and, by way of being sociable, offering his rough head to be patted by any kindly hand that would take so much trouble. But now, all of a sudden, this grave and venerable quadruped, of his own mere motion, and without the slight-

est suggestion from anybody else, began to run round after his tail, which, to heighten the absurdity of the proceeding, was a great deal shorter than it should have been. Never was seen such headlong eagerness in pursuit of an object that could not possibly be attained; never was heard such a tremendous outbreak of growling, snarling, barking, and snapping,— as if one end of the ridiculous brute's body were at deadly and most unforgivable enmity with the other. Faster and faster, round about went the cur; and faster and still faster fled the unapproachable brevity of his tail; and louder and fiercer grew his yells of rage and animosity; until, utterly exhausted, and as far from the goal as ever, the foolish old dog ceased his performance as suddenly as he had begun it. The next moment he was as mild, quiet, sensible, and respectable in his deportment, as when he first scraped acquaintance with the company.

As may be supposed, the exhibition was greeted with universal laughter, clapping of hands, and shouts of encore, to which the canine performer responded by wagging all that there was to wag of his tail, but appeared totally unable to repeat his very successful effort to amuse the spectators.

Meanwhile, Ethan Brand had resumed his seat upon the log, and moved, it might be, by a perception of some remote analogy between his own case and that of this self-pursuing cur, he broke into the awful laugh, which, more than any other token, expressed the condition of his inward being. From that moment, the merriment of the party was at an end; they stood aghast, dreading lest the inauspicious sound should be reverberated around the horizon, and that mountain would thunder it to mountain, and so the horror be prolonged upon their ears. Then, whispering one to another that it was late,—that the moon was almost down,—that the August night was growing chill,—they hurried homewards, leaving the lime-burner and little Joe to deal as they

6. **Titanic child,** of great size.

might with their unwelcome guest. Save for these three human beings, the open space on the hill-side was a solitude, set in a vast gloom of forest. Beyond that darksome verge, the fire-light glimmered on the stately trunks and almost black foliage of pines, intermixed with the lighter verdure of sapling oaks, maples, and poplars, while here and there lay the gigantic corpses of dead trees, decaying on the leaf-strewn soil. And it seemed to little Joe—a timorous and imaginative child—that the silent forest was holding its breath until some fearful thing should happen.

Ethan Brand thrust more wood into the fire, and closed the door of the kiln, then looking over his shoulder at the lime-burner and his son, he bade, rather than advised, them to retire to rest.

"For myself, I cannot sleep," said he. "I have matters that it concerns me to meditate upon. I will watch the fire, as I used to do in the old time."

"And call the Devil out of the furnace to keep you company, I suppose," muttered Bartram, who had been making intimate acquaintance with the black bottle above mentioned. "But watch, if you like, and call as many devils as you like! For my part, I shall be all the better for a snooze. Come, Joe!"

As the boy followed his father into the hut, he looked back at the wayfarer, and the tears came into his eyes, for his tender spirit had an intuition of the bleak and terrible loneliness in which this man had enveloped himself.

When they had gone, Ethan Brand sat listening to the crackling of the kindled wood, and looking at the little spirits of fire that issued through the chinks of the door. These trifles, however, once so familiar, had but the slightest hold of his attention, while deep within his mind he was reviewing the gradual but marvellous change that had been wrought upon him by the search to which he had devoted himself. He remembered how the night dew had fallen upon him,—how the dark forest had whispered to him,—how the stars had gleamed upon him,—a simple and loving man, watching his fire in the years gone by, and ever musing as it burned. He remembered with what tenderness, with what love and sympathy for mankind, and what pity for human guilt and woe, he had first begun to contemplate those ideas which afterwards became the inspiration of his life; with what reverence he had then looked into the heart of man, viewing it as a temple originally divine, and, however desecrated, still to be held sacred by a brother; with what awful fear he had deprecated the success of his pursuit, and prayed that the Unpardonable Sin might never be revealed to him. Then ensued that vast intellectual development, which, in its progress, disturbed the counterpoise between his mind and heart. The Idea that possessed his life had operated as a means of education; it had gone on cultivating his powers to the highest point of which they were susceptible; it had raised him from the level of an unlettered laborer to stand on a star-lit eminence, whither the philosophers of the earth, laden with the lore of universities, might vainly strive to clamber after him. So much for the intellect! But where was the heart? That, indeed, had withered,—had contracted,—had hardened,—had perished! It had ceased to partake of the universal throb. He had lost his hold of the magnetic chain of humanity. He was no longer a brother-man, opening the chambers or the dungeons of our common nature by the key of holy sympathy, which gave him a right to share in all its secrets; he was now a cold observer, looking on mankind as the subject of his experiment, and, at length, converting man and woman to be his puppets, and pulling the wires that moved them to such degrees of crime as were demanded for his study.

Thus Ethan Brand became a fiend. He began to be so from the moment that his moral nature had ceased to keep the pace of improvement with his intellect. And now, as his highest effort and inevitable development,—as the bright and gorgeous flower, and rich, delicious fruit of his life's labor,—he had produced the Unpardonable Sin!

"What more have I to seek? what more to achieve?" said Ethan Brand to himself. "My task is done, and well done!"

Starting from the log with a certain alacrity in his gait and ascending the hillock of earth that was raised against the stone circumference of the lime-kiln, he thus reached the top of the structure. It was a space of perhaps ten feet across, from edge to edge, presenting a view of the upper surface of the immense mass of broken marble with which the kiln was heaped. All these innumerable blocks and fragments of marble were red-hot and vividly on fire, sending up great spouts of blue flame, which quivered aloft and danced madly, as within a magic circle, and sank and rose again, with continual and multitudinous activity. As the lonely man bent forward over this terrible body of fire, the blasting heat smote up against his person with a breath that, it might be supposed, would have scorched and shrivelled him up in a moment.

Ethan Brand stood erect, and raised his arms on high. The blue flames played upon his face, and imparted the wild and ghastly light which alone could have suited its expression; it was that of a fiend on the verge of plunging into his gulf of intensest torment.

"O Mother Earth," cried he, "who art no more my Mother, and into whose bosom this frame shall never be resolved! O mankind, whose brotherhood I have cast off, and trampled thy great heart beneath my feet! O stars of heaven, that shone on me of old, as if to light me onward and upward!—farewell all, and forever. Come, deadly element of Fire,—henceforth my familiar friend! Embrace me, as I do thee!"

That night the sound of a fearful peal of laughter rolled heavily through the sleep of the lime-burner and his little son; dim shapes of horror and anguish haunted their dreams, and seemed still present in the rude hovel, when they opened their eyes to the daylight.

"Up, boy, up!" cried the lime-burner, staring about him. "Thank Heaven, the night is gone, at last; and rather than pass such another, I would watch my lime-kiln, wide awake, for a twelvemonth. This Ethan Brand, with his humbug[7] of an Unpardonable Sin, has done me no such mighty favor, in taking my place!"

He issued from the hut, followed by little Joe, who kept fast hold of his father's hand. The early sunshine was already pouring its gold upon the mountaintops, and though the valleys were still in shadow, they smiled cheerfully in the promise of the bright day that was hastening onward. The village, completely shut in by hills, which swelled away gently about it, looked as if it had rested peacefully in the hollow of the great hand of Providence. Every dwelling was distinctly visible; the little spires of the two churches pointed upwards, and caught a fore-glimmering of brightness from the sun-gilt skies upon their gilded weathercocks.[8] The tavern was astir, and the figure of the old, smoke-dried stage-agent, cigar in mouth, was seen beneath the stoop. Old Graylock was glorified with a golden cloud upon his head. Scattered likewise over the breasts of the surrounding mountains, there were heaps of hoary mist, in fantastic shapes, some of them far down into the valley, others high up towards the summits, and still others, of the same family of mist or cloud, hovering in the gold radiance of the upper atmosphere. Stepping from one to another of the clouds that rested on the hills, and thence to the loftier brotherhood that sailed in air, it seemed almost as if a mortal man might thus ascend into the heavenly regions. Earth was so mingled with sky that it was a day-dream to look at it.

To supply that charm of the familiar and homely, which Nature so readily adopts into a scene like this, the stage-coach was rattling down the mountain-road, and the driver sounded his horn, while Echo caught up the notes, and intertwined them into a rich and varied and elaborate harmony, of which the

---

7. **humbug,** something intending to deceive.
8. **weathercocks,** weather vanes in the form of a cock which swing to point the direction of the wind.

original performer could lay claim to little share. The great hills played a concert among themselves, each contributing a strain of airy sweetness.

Little Joe's face brightened at once.

"Dear father," cried he, skipping cheerily to and fro, "that strange man is gone, and the sky and the mountains all seem glad of it!"

"Yes," growled the lime-burner, with an oath, "but he has let the fire go down, and no thanks to him if five hundred bushels of lime are not spoiled. If I catch the fellow hereabouts again, I shall feel like tossing him into the furnace!"

With his long pole in his hand, he ascended to the top of the kiln. After a moment's pause, he called to his son.

"Come up here, Joe!" said he.

So little Joe ran up the hillock, and stood by his father's side. The marble was all burnt into perfect, snow-white lime. But on its surface, in the midst of the circle,—snow-white too, and thoroughly converted into lime,—lay a human skeleton, in the attitude of a person who, after long toil, lies down to long repose. Within the ribs—strange to say—was the shape of a human heart.

"Was the fellow's heart made of marble?" cried Bartram, in some perplexity at this phenomenon. "At any rate, it is burnt into what looks like special good lime, and, taking all the bones together, my kiln is half a bushel the richer for him."

So saying, the rude lime-burner lifted his pole, and, letting it fall upon the skeleton, the relics of Ethan Brand were crumbled into fragments.

I
STORY VS. ESSAY

If one were to make an arbitrary division of this story into the elements of setting, characterization, plot, and theme, he might readily conclude that theme is its dominant element. As a matter of fact, theme dominates so much of Hawthorne's work that one may be tempted to ask why he didn't write essays rather than short stories and novels. Wouldn't an essay on "The Unpardonable Sin" be just as effective as "Ethan Brand"?

It is possible to learn a good deal about the nature of fiction by trying to answer this question. Consider, by way of example, the setting of "Ethan Brand." An essay on "The Unpardonable Sin" would not have a physical setting, and by virtue of this fact alone, it would lose much of the dramatic intensity of the story. The chief item of setting here, the lime-kiln, stands at the center of the stage; indeed, it *is* a kind of stage—a lighted area surrounded by darkness—upon which the story unfolds. The reader may feel himself a member of a theater audience.

The lime-kiln also has symbolic value as an entrance to Hell; it relates to the theme in that it serves as the instrument of Brand's final retribution. It also serves to reinforce the idea that the Unpardonable Sin is in the hero's own breast, for Brand both begins and ends his search at the same point, the kiln.

If the setting had been ineffectively realized or *if* it had been unrelated to the theme, we might have been partially justified in saying that Hawthorne might just as well have written an essay. As it is, however, that conclusion would be hard to support.

II
IMPLICATIONS

Discuss the following questions relating to Hawthorne's characterization.

1. Compare Bartram and his son. Which of the two better understands Ethan Brand?

2. Compare and contrast the characters from the tavern (the stage-agent, Lawyer Giles, and the village doctor). What do they have in common? In what way or ways do they differ from Ethan Brand?

3. What is the function of Old Humphrey, of the German-Jew?

4. How might someone argue that Brand is not a wholly evil and unsympathetic character?

5. Discuss the following statement in the light of this story: "The characters are the tools by which the author realizes his theme."

III
TECHNIQUES

Conflict, Climax,
and Moment of Illumination

Hawthorne calls "Ethan Brand" a chapter from a romance, and in certain respects it is more like the final chapter of a book than a short story. Note, for example, that there is no pronounced physical conflict in the story. There is, however, a strongly marked climax. Locate the climax and decide what conflict it relates to.

The moment of illumination may occur before, at, or after the climax. At which of these points would you say the moment comes in this story? Be prepared to discuss how it serves to illuminate the meaning of the tale.

Foreshadowing

To "foreshadow" is to give a hint beforehand of something that is going to occur later. Foreshadowing is one of Hawthorne's favorite literary devices, and he uses it extensively in this story. Note, for example, how the italicized portions of the following quotations—both of which occur quite early in the story—subtly hint at the final fate of Ethan Brand:

The kiln . . . stood unimpaired . . . *since he* [Brand] *had thrown his dark thoughts into the intense glow of its furnace, and melted them.* . . .

At frequent intervals, he [Bartram] flung back the clashing weight of the iron door, and . . . thrust in huge logs of oak, or *stirred the immense brands with a long pole.* (Compare this quotation with the last sentence of the story.)

Try to find other instances of foreshadowing in the early portions of the story. What is the purpose of this literary device? Does the reader have to be fully conscious of foreshadowing in order for it to affect him?

IV
WORDS

A. Determine from context the meaning of the italicized words.

1. . . . I must be content to bear the *stigma* of a fiction monger.

2. . . . Goodman Brown recognized a very pious and *exemplary* dame. . . .

3. . . . the figure bore no slight *similitude,* both in garb and manner, to some grave divine of the New England churches.

4. . . . burst into laughter that rolled away into the night, and was indistinctly *reverberated* among the hills.

5. "The only sin that deserves a *recompense* of immortal agony!"

6. . . . louder and fiercer grew his yells of rage and *animosity.* . . .

7. . . . he was as mild, quiet, sensible, and respectable in his *deportment,* as when he first scraped acquaintance with the company.

B. 1. A good writer chooses his words carefully. In each of the following phrases, how would Hawthorne's meaning be changed by substituting the suggested synonyms for the italicized word?

a. traced back to my own *veracious* self (genuine, truthful, precise)

b. stigma of a fiction *monger* (dealer, trader, salesman)

c. healthful *suffusion* on their cheeks (fire, inspiration, animation)

d. replied the *complaisant* doctor (obliging, good-natured, amiable)

e. all the unseen *multitude* (army, host, legion)

f. the *lore* of fiends (knowledge, science, learning)

g. *obtuse,* middle aged man (dull, dense, stupid)

2. Find two synonyms for each of the following words. Explain the differences.

rejuvenescent, decrepit, coquetry, fervid, portentous, torpid, lurid, litigants.

EUGENE O'NEILL

1888-1953

The advent of Eugene O'Neill did more to change the face of American drama than anyone could have anticipated when his first play, *Bound East for Cardiff*, opened in 1916. The son of the famous actor, James O'Neill, he was introduced to the theater through the stage door, as it were: touring with his parents, managing his father's company, even acting for a time, but all with little success until he turned his hand to writing one-act plays of the sea. O'Neill had left Princeton in 1907, after one disastrous year, and thereafter spent much of his time on tramp steamers, beachcombing in Buenos Aires, gold-prospecting in Honduras, living at waterfront bars in New York City. If his health had not broken down, he might never have tried playwriting. When he entered a tuberculosis sanatorium in 1912, he was ill and despondent; when he left six months later he had found his vocation.

O'Neill destroyed many of his early plays (he wrote at least ten during his recuperation), but the others he took with him to George Pierce Baker's "47 Workshop" at Harvard in

EUGENE O'NEILL, *William Zorach*

In almost every play he wrote he was trying, with "deep pity and understanding," to probe human nature, to show his audiences the causes for neuroses and frustrations and tragedy. Into his plays he put his deep knowledge of man's nature, and he wrote with as sure a mastery of stagecraft as Hawthorne had of fiction and Emily Dickinson of poetry. The time and setting of his plays are of little import. Their themes of illusions, frustrations, dreams, and death are universal.

1914 where he studied playwriting for a time. It was a short distance from there to Provincetown, Massachusetts. A group of young actors and producers in this Cape Cod resort had turned an abandoned fish house into the Wharf Theatre. George Cram Cook and his wife, Susan Glaspell, were the organizers of the Provincetown Players, as they called themselves, and when they later settled in Greenwich Village, New York, O'Neill moved with them, for the best of reasons. They had not only produced his first play but they also followed it the next year with three one-act companion pieces: *The Moon of the Caribbees,* *The Long Voyage Home,* and *In the Zone.* All four take place on the British tramp steamer *S. S. Glencairn,* and into them O'Neill poured his memories of life at sea. The audience may have been shocked at the frank, often brutal language, but they also recognized the vitality O'Neill was able to bring to his characters. Cook and his Players "represented the spirit of revolt," as O'Neill put it, "against the old worn-out traditions, the commercial theater, the tawdry artificialities of the stage." What is more, they encouraged him to "work out [his] ideas in freedom," the best possible atmosphere for a young artist.

Broadway beckoned in 1920. Although O'Neill won the Pulitzer Prize (the first of three) for *Beyond the Horizon,* his first full-length play, it is a static, conventional tragedy in comparison with *The Emperor Jones* (1920) and *The Hairy Ape* (1921), two experimental plays that left no doubt about O'Neill's power to move his audience. As a tragic hero, Brutus Jones, the giant Negro "emperor" of a West Indian island, is less memorable than Yank, the stupid and profane stoker known to his shipmates as "the hairy ape"; but both characters set Broadway to talking about this daring young playwright. O'Neill had obviously found his subject: psychological revelation; and he was determined to show the world that the stage could handle it as brilliantly as the novel. To underscore Jones's fear, he introduced offstage tom-toms that beat with in-

creasing intensity as the "emperor" loses his way in the jungle, pursued by rebellious natives. To emphasize Yank's rejection by society, he set the last scene in a zoo where, ironically, Yank is crushed to death by the ape he wants to liberate. Of course, man's struggle with his environment is a problem, O'Neill argued, but his struggle with himself is often greater. To express these subjective states, these inner struggles and secret fears, O'Neill became more and more inventive theatrically as his view of the human condition matured.

Between 1924 and 1931, O'Neill produced four major works which established his reputation internationally and eventually earned him the Nobel Prize. All four are built around psychological complications that develop, as the action unfolds, into tragic proportions. *Desire Under the Elms* (1924) is set in 1850 in a New England farmhouse. Ephraim Cabot, aged 75, has taken a new wife, Abbie, aged 35. His youngest son, Eben, shares this farmhouse, and before the last curtain has fallen an illegitimate child is dead, Abbie and Eben are under arrest, and Ephraim is left to face the future alone. In *The Great God Brown* (1926), O'Neill used the same triangle—two men and a woman—but here it is the woman who survives and the men who destroy each other. *Strange Interlude* (1928) is aptly named. The heroine, Nina Leeds, surrounded by men but happy with none of them, eventually loses her son, her husband, and her lover. *Mourning Becomes Electra* (1931), O'Neill's trilogy based on Greek tragedy and the most violent of all his plays, is set in post-Civil War America. We see daughter turn against mother, wife against husband, and ultimately the two children against each other as the family literally destroys itself.

Recounted so baldly, these plays sound unbearably grim. The truths of the human heart are frequently grim, O'Neill reminds us, but the theater can make their revelation memorable, even exalting. "Sure I'll write about happiness," he told one literary critic, "if I can meet up with that luxury, and find it sufficiently dramatic and in harmony with any deep rhythm in life. But happiness is a word. What does it mean? Exaltation: an intensified feeling of the significant worth of man's being and becoming? Well, if it means that—and not a mere smirking contentment with one's lot—I know there is more of it in one real tragedy than in all the happy-ending plays ever written. It's mere present-day judgment to think of tragedy as unhappy. . . . I don't love life because it is pretty. Prettiness is only clothes-deep. I am a truer lover than that. I love it naked. There is beauty to me even in its ugliness."

To these ends he experimented endlessly with technical innovations, hoping to bring all the ingenuity of his stagecraft to the elaboration of his themes. In *Desire Under the Elms*, for example, the fourth wall of the entire Cabot farmhouse is removed in the stage set. Two enormous brooding elms on each side of the house suggest "a sinister maternity in their aspect, a crushing, jealous absorption." The irony of O'Neill's lines is beautifully underscored as we watch simultaneous action in kitchen, parlor, and upstairs bedrooms. In *The Great God Brown*, O'Neill uses masks to suggest the concept of multiple personality, a confusing idea for the audience at first but not after it realizes that the characters remove their masks, particularly Billy Brown and Dion Anthony, when they are alone or with sympathetic persons in order to reveal their true selves. How we disguise our true selves in meaningless words is made clear by a technique O'Neill borrowed from the stream-of-consciousness novel and developed in *Strange Interlude*. In this nine-act play about the neurotic Nina Leeds, the dialogue is interspersed with each actor's thoughts spoken aloud as asides for only the audience to hear as the action freezes on stage. We are admitted, as it were, into the minds of his characters, noting at once the ironic contrast between what one says to a wife or a son and what one is thinking to himself.

Barrett House, 1884, at the corner of Broadway and 43rd. Eugene O'Neill was born here.

Mourning Becomes Electra marked the climax of this phase of O'Neill's career, for here he attempted three plays in one evening, beginning with *Homecoming* at 5 p.m. and following a dinner intermission with *The Hunted* and then *The Haunted*. As in Aeschylus' treatment of the Agamemnon legend, we observe the death of the returning hero and the consequent disintegration of the whole family; but O'Neill, true to his view of life, focuses on psychological pressures, interior motives rather than the fate the gods have in store for man. Lavinia's last speech says it all: "I'm the last Mannon. I've got to punish myself! Living alone here with the dead is a worse act of justice than death or prison! I'll never go out or see anyone! I'll have the shutters nailed closed so no sunlight can ever get in. I'll live alone with the dead, and keep their secrets, and let them hound me, until the curse is paid out and the last Mannon is let die! (*With a strange cruel smile of gloating over the years of self-torture.*) I know they will see to it I live for a long time! It takes the Mannons to punish themselves for being born!"

If O'Neill's health, in 1934, had not once again broken down, we might have seen him turn on occasion to lighter subjects as a relief from perpetual tragedy. *Ah, Wilderness!* (1933), a cheerful, nostalgic comedy, is his only venture in that vein, and when it closed O'Neill went into virtual retirement. He lived in France, Georgia, and California with his third wife, working on a cycle of nine, perhaps eleven, plays which traced the history of one family, the Harfords, from 1755 to 1932. He wanted to call the group *A Tale of Possessors Self-Dispossessed,* a title which with some adjustment might have fit his whole body of forty plays. But he kept only two of the Harford plays, having destroyed the rest in manuscript before he died in 1953. Two other plays, however, broke his long silence and did much to spark an O'Neill revival in his last years. *The Iceman Cometh* opened in New York in 1946. It is set in Harry Hope's saloon and centers on Hickey, an itinerant salesman who once a year visits his friends, New York Bowery bums, to persuade them to give up their illusions and face reality. But as the play closes, and Hickey is arrested (he has murdered his wife rather than endure her constant forgiveness), we see that illusions are all these derelicts have to live with. Take them away (take man's dreams away?), and all support crumbles.

The same theme is worked out more explicitly, and more movingly, in *Long Day's Journey into Night* (1956), one of O'Neill's masterpieces. It is a play so close to his own life and family that he once thought of forbidding production for at least twenty-five years after his death. Fortunately for us, he relented and his wife eventually released it. Recent productions have shown it to be, in spite of its length and repetitions, a brilliant

study of the emotional erosion four members of a family are forced to endure on a summer day in 1912. The Tyrones are the O'Neills, of course—father, mother, elder son Jaimie, and the playwright himself disguised as Edmund—and the last scene, like life itself, offers no resolution at all. In dedicating this play to his wife, O'Neill says that she helped him "to face his dead at last and write this play—write it with deep pity and understanding for *all* the four haunted Tyrones."

As we look back on O'Neill's career, we realize that in almost every play he wrote he was trying, with "deep pity and understanding," to probe human nature, to show his audience the causes for neuroses and frustrations and tragedy. His last plays are such a far cry, in scope and setting, from his early one-act sea plays that we sometimes wonder whether they were written by the same man, though they surely were. When we consider Smitty in the *Glencairn* series with Hickey of *The Iceman* or the Tyrones of *Long Day's Journey*, we see a strong similarity in the tenderness with which O'Neill treats these "homeless" human beings, lonely, life-weary, trapped in their own egos. O'Neill's early plays are slight and sometimes sentimental; but every audience that listened to their flat prose rhythms and their obsession with the ominous, omnipresent sea knew, without being told, that they were in the presence of a man with strong, true theatrical instincts. Once he had left his beachcombing days behind, the stage became his whole world. Into his plays he put his deep knowledge of man's nature, and he wrote with as sure a mastery of stagecraft as Nathaniel Hawthorne had of fiction and Emily Dickinson of the poetic mode. The time and the setting of his plays are of little import. Their themes of illusions, frustrations, dreams, and death are universal.

Of the four *Glencairn* plays,
only *In the Zone* takes place
during the early days of World War I.
The other three are set in peacetime. Smitty,
a young Englishman and a central figure,
is introduced briefly in *Bound East for Cardiff*,
then developed more fully in *The Moon
of the Caribbees*. In the latter play,
the *Glencairn* is at anchor off an island
in the West Indies, and Smitty is seeking
to drown his sorrows in rum. He succeeds only
in making himself more morose, unable to sleep
because of his haunting memories and unable
to enjoy life aboard. *In the Zone* focuses
on a more sensational situation. It is now 1915.
The *Glencairn* is carrying ammunition
through the submarine zone, and the crew
is suspicious of Smitty's peculiar behavior.
They wonder if he could be a German agent.
As hysteria mounts they decide
they must find out.

In the Zone

A PLAY IN ONE ACT

Characters

SMITTY
DAVIS
SWANSON
SCOTTY
IVAN   } Seamen on the British Tramp
PAUL   Steamer Glencairn
JACK
DRISCOLL
COCKY

Scene—The seamen's forecastle.[1] *On the right
above the bunks three or four portholes*

*covered with black cloth can be seen. On
the floor near the doorway is a pail with a
tin dipper. A lantern in the middle of the
floor, turned down very low, throws a dim
light around the place. Five men,* SCOTTY,
IVAN, SWANSON, SMITTY *and* PAUL, *are in
their bunks apparently asleep. It is about
ten minutes of twelve on a night in the fall
of the year 1915.*

SMITTY *turns slowly in his bunk and, leaning
out over the side, looks from one to another
of the men as if to assure himself that they
are asleep. Then he climbs carefully out of
his bunk and stands in the middle of the
forecastle fully dressed, but in his stocking
feet, glancing around him suspiciously. Reassured, he leans down and cautiously pulls
out a suit-case from under the bunks in front
of him.*

Just at this moment DAVIS *appears in the doorway, carrying a large steaming coffee-pot in
his hand. He stops short when he sees* SMITTY.
*A puzzled expression comes over his face,
followed by one of suspicion, and he retreats
farther back in the alleyway, where he can
watch* SMITTY *without being seen.*

*All the latter's movements indicate a fear of
discovery. He takes out a small bunch of
keys and unlocks the suit-case, making a
slight noise as he does so.* SCOTTY *wakes up
and peers at him over the side of the bunk.*
SMITTY *opens the suit-case and takes out a
small black tin box, carefully places this
under his mattress, shoves the suit-case back
under the bunk, climbs into his bunk again,
closes his eyes and begins to snore loudly.*

DAVIS *enters the forecastle, places the coffee-
pot beside the lantern, and goes from one
to the other of the sleepers and shakes them
vigorously, saying to each in a low voice:*
Near eight bells, Scotty. Arise and shine,
Swanson. Eight bells, Ivan. SMITTY *yawns*

1. forecastle\ᵃfōk•səl\ front part of a ship where the
sailors' quarters are located.

loudly with a great pretense of having been dead asleep. All of the rest of the men tumble out of their bunks, stretching and gaping, and commence to pull on their shoes. They go one by one to the cupboard near the open door, take out their cups and spoons, and sit down together on the benches. The coffee-pot is passed around. They munch their biscuits and sip their coffee in dull silence.

DAVIS. [*Suddenly jumping to his feet—nervously.*] Where's that air comin' from? [*All are startled and look at him wonderingly.*]

SWANSON. [*A squat, surly-faced Swede—grumpily.*] What air? I don't feel nothing.

DAVIS. [*Excitedly.*] I kin feel it—a draft. [*He stands on the bench and looks around—suddenly exploding.*] Damn fool square-head! [*He leans over the upper bunk in which PAUL is sleeping and slams the porthole shut.*] I got a good notion to report him. Serve him bloody well right! What's the use o' blindin' the ports when that thickhead goes an' leaves 'em open?

SWANSON. [*Yawning—too sleepy to be aroused by anything—carelessly.*] Dey don't see what little light go out yust one port.

SCOTTY. [*Protestingly.*] Dinna be a loon, Swanson! D'ye no ken the dangerr o' showin' a licht wi' a pack o' submarrines lyin' aboot?

IVAN. [*Shaking his shaggy ox-like head in an emphatic affirmative.*] Dot's right, Scotty. I don' li-ike blow up, no, by devil!

SMITTY. [*His manner slightly contemptuous.*] I don't think there's much danger of meeting any of their submarines, not until we get into the war zone, at any rate.

DAVIS. [*He and SCOTTY look at SMITTY suspiciously—harshly.*] You don't, eh? [*He lowers his voice and speaks slowly.*] Well, we're in the war zone right this minit if you wants to know. [*The effect of this speech is instantaneous. All sit bolt upright on their benches and stare at DAVIS.*]

SMITTY. How do you know, Davis?

DAVIS. [*Angrily.*] 'Cos Drisc heard the First

send the Third below to wake the skipper when we fetched the zone—bout five bells, it was. Now whata y' got to say?

SMITTY. [*Conciliatingly.*] Oh, I wasn't doubting your word, Davis; but you know they're not pasting up bulletins to let the crew know when the zone is reached—especially on ammunition ships like this.

IVAN. [*Decidedly.*] I don't li-ike dees voyage. Next time I ship on windjammer Boston to River Plate, load with wood only so it float, by golly!

SWANSON. [*Fretfully.*] I hope British navy blow 'em to hell, those submarines, py damn!

SCOTTY. [*Looking at SMITTY, who is staring at the doorway in a dream, his chin on his hands. Meaningly.*] It is no the submarrines only we've to fear, I'm thinkin'.

DAVIS. [*Assenting eagerly.*] That's no lie, Scotty.

SWANSON. You mean the mines?

SCOTTY. I wasna thinkin' o' mines eitherr.

DAVIS. There's many a good ship blown up and at the bottom of the sea, what never hit no mine or torpedo.

SCOTTY. Did ye neverr read of the Gerrman spies and the dirrty work they're doin' all the war? [*He and DAVIS both glance at SMITTY, who is deep in thought and is not listening to the conversation.*]

DAVIS. An' the clever way they fool you!

SWANSON. Sure; I read it in paper many time.

DAVIS. Well—[*He is about to speak but hesitates and finishes lamely.*] you got to watch out, that's all I says.

IVAN. [*Drinking the last of his coffee and slamming his fist on the bench explosively.*] I tell you dis rotten coffee give me belly-ache, yes! [*They all look at him in amused disgust.*]

SCOTTY. [*Sardonically.*] Dinna fret about it, Ivan. If we blow up ye'll no be mindin' the pain in your middle. [*JACK enters. He is a young American with a tough, good-natured face. He wears dungarees and a heavy jersey.*]

JACK. Eight bells, fellers.

IVAN. [*Stupidly.*] I don' hear bell ring.

JACK. No, and yuh won't hear any ring, yuh boob—[*Lowering his voice unconsciously.*] now we're in the war zone.

SWANSON. [*Anxiously.*] Is the boats all ready?

JACK. Sure; we can lower 'em in a second.

DAVIS. A lot o' good the boats'll do, with us loaded deep with all kinds o' dynamite and stuff the like o' that! If a torpedo hits this hooker we'll all be in hell b'fore you could wink your eye.

JACK. They ain't goin' to hit us, see? That's my dope. Whose wheel is it?

IVAN. [*Sullenly.*] My wheel. [*He lumbers out.*]

JACK. And whose lookout?

SWANSON. Mine, I tink. [*He follows* IVAN.]

JACK. [*Scornfully.*] A hell of a lot of use keepin' a lookout! We couldn't run away or fight if we wanted to. [*To* SCOTTY *and* SMITTY.] Better look up the bo'sun or the Fourth, you two, and let 'em see you're awake. [SCOTTY *goes to the doorway and turns to wait for* SMITTY, *who is still in the same position, head on hands, seemingly unconscious of everything.* JACK *slaps him roughly on the shoulder and he comes to with a start.*] Aft and report, Duke! What's the matter with yuh—in a dope dream? [SMITTY *goes out after* SCOTTY *without answering.* JACK *looks after him with a frown.*] He's a queer guy. I can't figger him out.

DAVIS. Nor no one else. [*Lowering his voice—meaningly.*] An' he's liable to turn out queerer than any of us think if we ain't careful.

JACK. [*Suspiciously.*] What d'yuh mean? [*They are interrupted by the entrance of* DRISCOLL *and* COCKY.]

COCKY. [*Protestingly.*] Blimey if I don't fink I'll put in this 'ere watch ahtside on deck. [*He and* DRISCOLL *go over and get their cups.*] I down't want to be caught in this 'ole if they 'its us. [*He pours out coffee.*]

DRISCOLL. [*Pouring his.*] Divil a bit ut wud matther where ye arre. Ye'd be blown to smithereens b'fore ye cud say your name. [*He sits down, overturning as he does so the un-*

touched cup of coffee which SMITTY *had forgotten and left on the bench. They all jump nervously as the tin cup hits the floor with a bang.* DRISCOLL *flies into an unreasoning rage.*] Who's the dirty scut left this cup where a man 'ud sit on ut?

DAVIS. It's Smitty's.

DRISCOLL. [*Kicking the cup across the forecastle.*] Does he think he's too much av a bloody gentleman to put his own away loike the rist av us? If he does I'm the bye'll beat that noshun out av his head.

COCKY. Be the airs 'e puts on you'd think 'e was the Prince of Wales. Wot's 'e doin' on a ship, I arsks yer? 'E ain't now good as a sailor, is 'e?—dawdlin' abaht on deck like a chicken wiv 'is 'ead cut orf!

JACK. [*Good-naturedly.*] Aw, the Duke's all right. S'posin' he did ferget his cup—what's the dif? [*He picks up the cup and puts it away—with a grin.*] This war zone stuff's got yer goat, Drisc—and yours too, Cocky—and I ain't cheerin' much fur it myself, neither.

COCKY. [*With a sigh.*] Blimey, it ain't no bleedin' joke, yer first trip, to know as there's a ship full of shells li'ble to go orf in under your bloomin' feet, as you might say, if we gets 'it be a torpedo or mine. [*With sudden savagery.*] Calls theyselves 'uman bein's, too! Blarsted 'Uns!

DRISCOLL. [*Gloomily.*] 'Tis me last trip in the bloody zone, God help me. The divil take their twenty-foive percent bonus—and be drowned like a rat in a trap in the bargain, maybe.

DAVIS. Wouldn't be so bad if she wasn't carryin' ammunition. Them's the kind the subs is layin' for.

DRISCOLL. [*Irritably.*] Fur the love av hivin, don't be talkin' about ut. I'm sick wid thinkin' and jumpin' at iviry bit av a noise. [*There is a pause during which they all stare gloomily at the floor.*]

JACK. Hey, Davis, what was you sayin' about Smitty when they come in?

DAVIS. [*With a great air of mystery.*] I'll tell

you in a minit. I want to wait an' see if he's comin' back. [*Impressively.*] You won't be callin' him all right when you hears what I seen with my own eyes. [*He adds with an air of satisfaction.*] An' you won't be feelin' no safer, neither. [*They all look at him with puzzled glances full of a vague apprehension.*]

DRISCOLL. God blarst ut! [*He fills his pipe and lights it. The others, with an air of remembering something they had forgotten, do the same.* SCOTTY *enters.*]

SCOTTY. [*In awed tones.*] Mon, but it's clear outside the nicht! Like day.

DAVIS. [*In low tones.*] Where's Smitty, Scotty?

SCOTTY. Out on the hatch starin' at the moon like a mon half-daft.

DAVIS. Kin you see him from the doorway?

SCOTTY. [*Goes to doorway and carefully peeks out.*] Aye; he's still there.

DAVIS. Keep your eyes on him for a moment. I've got something I wants to tell the boys and I don't want him walkin' in the middle of it. Give a shout if he starts this way.

SCOTTY. [*With suppressed excitement.*] Aye, I'll watch him. And I've somethin' myself to tell aboot his Lordship.

DRISCOLL. [*Impatiently.*] Out wid ut! You're talkin' more than a pair av auld women wud be standin' in the road, and gittin' no further along.

DAVIS. Listen! You 'member when I went to git the coffee, Jack?

JACK. Sure, I do.

DAVIS. Well, I brings it down here same as usual and got as far as the door there when I sees him.

JACK. Smitty?

DAVIS. Yes, Smitty! He was standin' in the middle of the fo'c's'tle there [*Pointing.*] lookin' around sneakin'-like at Ivan and Swanson and the rest 's if he wants to make certain they're asleep. [*He pauses significantly, looking from one to the other of his listeners.* SCOTTY *is nervously dividing his attention between* SMITTY *on the hatch outside*

and DAVIS' *story, fairly bursting to break in with his own revelations.*]

JACK. [*Impatiently.*] What of it?

DAVIS. Listen! He was standin' right there— [*Pointing again.*] in his stockin' feet—no shoes on, mind, so he wouldn't make no noise!

JACK. [*Spitting disgustedly.*] Aw!

DAVIS. [*Not heeding the interruption.*] I seen right away somethin' on the queer was up so I slides back into the alleyway where I kin see him but he can't see me. After he makes sure they're all asleep he goes in under the bunks there—bein' careful not to raise a noise, mind!—an' takes out his bag there. [*By this time every one,* JACK *included, is listening breathlessly to his story.*] Then he fishes in his pocket an' takes out a bunch o' keys an' kneels down beside the bag an' opens it.

SCOTTY. [*Unable to keep silent longer.*] Mon, didn't I see him do that same thing wi' these two eyes. 'Twas just that moment I woke and spied him.

DAVIS. [*Surprised, and a bit nettled to have to share his story with any one.*] Oh, you seen him, too, eh? [*To the others.*] Then Scotty kin tell you if I'm lyin' or not.

DRISCOLL. An' what did he do whin he'd the bag opened?

DAVIS. He bends down and reaches out his hand sort o' scared-like, like it was somethin' dang'rous he was after, an' feels round in under his duds—hidden in under his duds an' wrapped up in 'em, it was—an' he brings out a black iron box!

COCKY. [*Looking around him with a frightened glance.*] Gawd blimey! [*The others likewise betray their uneasiness, shuffling their feet nervously.*]

DAVIS. Ain't that right, Scotty?

SCOTTY. Right as rain, I'm tellin' ye'!

DAVIS. [*To the others with an air of satisfaction.*] There you are! [*Lowering his voice.*] An' then what d'you suppose he did? Sneaks to his bunk an' slips the black box in under his mattress—in under his mattress, mind!—

JACK. And it's there now?

DAVIS. Course it is! [JACK *starts toward* SMITTY'S *bunk.* DRISCOLL *grabs him by the arm.*]

DRISCOLL. Don't be touchin' ut, Jack!

JACK. Yuh needn't worry. I ain't goin' to touch it [*He pulls up* SMITTY'S *mattress and looks down. The others stare at him, holding their breaths. He turns to them, trying hard to assume a careless tone.*] It's there, aw right.

COCKY. [*Miserably upset.*] I'm gointer 'op it aht on deck. [*He gets up but* DRISCOLL *pulls him down again.* COCKY *protests.*] It fair guvs me the trembles sittin' still in 'ere.

DRISCOLL. [*Scornfully.*] Are ye frightened, ye toad? 'Tis a hell av a thing fur grown men to be shiverin' loike childer at a bit av a black box. [*Scratching his head in uneasy perplexity.*] Still, ut's damn queer, the looks av ut.

DAVIS. [*Sarcastically.*] A bit of a black box, eh? How big d'you think them—[*He hesitates*]—things has to be—big as this fo'c's'tle?

JACK. [*In a voice meant to be reassuring.*] Aw, hell! I'll bet it ain't nothin' but some coin he's saved he's got locked up in there.

DAVIS. [*Scornfully.*] That's likely, ain't it? Then why does he act so s'picious? He's been on ship near two year, ain't he? He knows damn well there ain't no thiefs in this fo'c's'tle, don't he? An' you know 's well 's I do he didn't have no money when he came on board an' he ain't saved none since. Don't you? [JACK *doesn't answer.*] Listen! D'you know what he done after he put that thing in under his mattress?—an' Scotty'll tell you if I ain't speakin' truth. He looks round to see if any one's woke up——

SCOTTY. I clapped my eyes shut when he turned round.

DAVIS. An' then he crawls into his bunk an' shuts his eyes, an' starts in *snorin', pretendin'* he was asleep, mind!

SCOTTY. Aye, I could hear him.

DAVIS. An' when I goes to call him I don't even shake him. I just says, "Eight bells, Smitty," in a'most a whisper-like, an' up he gets yawnin' an' stretchin' to fit to kill hisself 's if he'd been dead asleep.

COCKY. Gawd blimey!

DRISCOLL. [*Shaking his head.*] Ut looks bad, divil a doubt av ut.

DAVIS. [*Excitedly.*] An' now I come to think of it, there's the porthole. How'd it come to git open, tell me that? I know'd well Paul never opened it. Ain't he grumblin' about bein' cold all the time?

SCOTTY. The mon that opened it meant no good to this ship, whoever he was.

JACK. [*Sourly.*] What porthole? What're yuh talkin' about?

DAVIS. [*Pointing over* PAUL'S *bunk.*] There. It was open when I come in. I felt the cold air on my neck an' shut it. It would'a been clear's a lighthouse to any sub that was watchin'—an' we s'posed to have all the ports blinded! Who'd do a dirty trick like that? It wasn't none of us, nor Scotty here, nor Swanson, nor Ivan. Who would it be, then?

COCKY. [*Angrily.*] Must'a been 'is bloody Lordship.

DAVIS. For all's we know he might'a been signallin' with it. They does it like that by winkin' a light. Ain't you read how they gets caught doin' it in London an' on the coast?

COCKY. [*Firmly convinced now.*] An' wots 'e doin' aht alone on the 'atch—keepin' 'isself clear of us like 'e was afraid?

DRISCOLL. Kape your eye on him, Scotty.

SCOTTY. There's no a move oot o' him.

JACK. [*In irritated perplexity.*] But, hell, ain't he an Englishman? What'd he wanta——

DAVIS. English? How d'we know he's English? Cos he talks it? That ain't no proof. Ain't you read in the papers how all them German spies they been catchin' in England has been livin' there for ten, often as not twenty years, an' talks English as good's any one? An' look here, ain't you noticed he don't talk natural? He talks it too damn good, that's what I mean. He don't talk exactly like a toff, does he, Cocky?

COCKY. Not like any toff as I ever met up wiv.

DAVIS. No; an' he don't talk it like us, that's certain. An' he don't look English. An' what d'we know about him when you come to look at it? Nothin'! He ain't ever said where he comes from or why. All we knows is he ships on here in London 'bout a year b'fore the war starts, as an A. B.[2]—stole his papers most lik'ly—when he don't know how to box the compass, hardly. Ain't that queer in itself? An' was he ever open with us like a good shipmate? No; he's always had that sly air about him 's if he was hidin' somethin'.

DRISCOLL. [*Slapping his thigh—angrily.*] Divil take me if I don't think ye have the truth av ut, Davis.

COCKY. [*Scornfully.*] Lettin' on be 'is silly airs, and all, 'e's the son of a blarsted earl or something!

DAVIS. An' the name he calls hisself—Smith! I'd risk a quid[3] of my next pay day that his real name is Schmidt, if the truth was known.

JACK. [*Evidently fighting against his own conviction.*] Aw, say, you guys give me a pain! What'd they want puttin' a spy on this old tub for?

DAVIS. [*Shaking his head sagely.*] They're deep ones, an' there's a lot o' things a sailor'll see in the ports he puts in ought to be useful to 'em. An' if he kin signal to 'em an' they blows us up it's one ship less, ain't it? [*Lowering his voice and indicating* SMITTY'S *bunk.*] Or if he blows us up hisself.

SCOTTY. [*In alarmed tones.*] Hush, mon! Here he comes! [SCOTTY *hurries over to a bench and sits down. A thick silence settles over the forecastle. The men look from one to another with uneasy glances.* SMITTY *enters and sits down beside his bunk. He is seemingly unaware of the dark glances of suspicion directed at him from all sides. He slides his hand back stealthily over his mattress and his fingers move, evidently feeling to make sure the box is still there. The others follow this movement carefully with quick looks out of the corners of their eyes. Their attitudes grow tense as if they were about to spring at him. Satisfied the box is safe,* SMITTY *draws his hand away slowly and utters a sigh of relief.*]

SMITTY. [*In a casual tone which to them sounds sinister.*] It's a good light night for the subs if there's any about. [*For a moment he sits staring in front of him. Finally he seems to sense the hostile atmosphere of the forecastle and looks from one to the other of the men in surprise. All of them avoid his eyes. He sighs with a puzzled expression and gets up and walks out of the doorway. There is silence for a moment after his departure and then a storm of excited talk breaks loose.*]

DAVIS. Did you see him feelin' if it was there?

COCKY. 'E ain't arf a sly one wiv 'is talk of submarines, Gawd blind 'em!

SCOTTY. Did ye see the sneakin' looks he gave us?

DRISCOLL. If ivir I saw black shame on a man's face 'twas on his whin he sat there!

JACK. [*Thoroughly convinced at last.*] He looked bad to me. He's a crook, aw right.

DAVIS. [*Excitedly.*] What'll we do? We gotter do somethin' quick or—— [*He is interrupted by the sound of something hitting against the port side of the forecastle with a dull, heavy thud. The men start to their feet in wild-eyed terror and turn as if they were going to rush for the deck. They stand that way for a strained moment, scarcely breathing and listening intently.*]

JACK. [*With a sickly smile.*] Hell! It's on'y a piece of driftwood or a floatin' log. [*He sits down again.*]

DAVIS. [*Sarcastically.*] Or a mine that didn't go off—that time—or a piece o' wreckage from some ship they've sent to Davy Jones.

COCKY. [*Mopping his brow with a trembling hand.*] Blimey! [*He sinks back weakly on a bench.*]

DRISCOLL. [*Furiously.*] God blarst ut! No man at all cud be puttin' up wid the loike av this— an' I'm not wan to be fearin' anything or any man in the worrld'll stand up to me face to face; but this divil's trickery in the darrk——

---

2. **A.B.**, able-bodied seaman.
3. **quid**\kwĭd\ one pound sterling (about $2.80 today).

[*He starts for* SMITTY's *bunk.*] I'll throw ut out wan av the portholes an' be done wid ut. [*He reaches toward the mattress.*]

SCOTTY. [*Grabbing his arm—wildly.*] Arre ye daft, mon?

DAVIS. Don't monkey with it, Drisc. I knows what to do. Bring the bucket o' water here, Jack, will you? [JACK *gets it and brings it over to* DAVIS.] An' you, Scotty, see if he's back on the hatch.

SCOTTY. [*Cautiously peering out.*] Aye, he's sittin' there the noo.

DAVIS. Sing out if he makes a move. Lift up the mattress, Drisc—careful now! [DRISCOLL *does so with infinite caution.*] Take it out, Jack—careful—don't shake it now, for Christ's sake! Here—put it in the water—easy! There, that's fixed it! [*They all sit down with great sighs of relief.*] The water'll git in and spoil it.

DRISCOLL. [*Slapping* DAVIS *on the back.*] Good wurrk for ye, Davis, ye scut! [*He spits on his hands aggressively.*] An' now what's to be done wid that black-hearted thraitor?

COCKY. [*Belligerently.*] Guv 'im a shove in the marf and 'eave 'im over the side!

DAVIS. An' serve him right!

JACK. Aw, say, give him a chance. Yuh can't prove nothin' till yuh find out what's in there.

DRISCOLL. [*Heatedly.*] Is ut more proof ye'd be needin' afther what we've seen an' heard? Then listen to me—an' ut's Driscoll talkin'—if there's divilmint in that box an' we see plain 'twas his plan to murrdher his own shipmates that have served him fair——[*He raises his fist.*] I'll choke his rotten heartt out wid me own hands, an' over the side wid him, and one man missin' in the mornin'.

DAVIS. An' no one the wiser. He's the balmy kind what commits suicide.

COCKY. They 'angs spies ashore.

JACK. [*Resentfully.*] If he's done what yuh think I'll croak him myself. Is that good enough for yuh?

DRISCOLL. [*Looking down at the box.*] How'll we be openin' this, I wonder?

SCOTTY. [*From the doorway—warningly.*] He's standin' up.

DAVIS. We'll take his keys away from him when he comes in. Quick, Drisc! You an' Jack get beside the door and grab him. [*They get on either side of the door.* DAVIS *snatches a small coil of rope from one of the upper bunks.*] This'll do for me an' Scotty to tie him.

SCOTTY. He's turrnin' this way—he's comin'! [*He moves away from door.*]

DAVIS. Stand by to lend a hand, Cocky.

COCKY. Righto. [*As* SMITTY *enters the forecastle he is seized roughly from both sides and his arms pinned behind him. At first he struggles fiercely, but seeing the uselessness of this, he finally stands calmly and allows* DAVIS *and* SCOTTY *to tie up his arms.*]

SMITTY. [*When they have finished—with cold contempt.*] If this is your idea of a joke I'll have to confess it's a bit too thick for me to enjoy.

COCKY. [*Angrily.*] Shut yer marf, 'ear!

DRISCOLL. [*Roughly.*] Ye'll find ut's no joke, me bucko, b'fore we're done wid you. [*To* SCOTTY.] Kape your eye peeled, Scotty, and sing out if any one's comin'. [SCOTTY *resumes his post at the door.*]

SMITTY. [*With the same icy contempt.*] If you'd be good enough to explain——

DRISCOLL. [*Furiously.*] Explain, is ut? 'Tis you'll do the explainin'—an' damn quick, or we'll know the reason why. [*To* JACK *and* DAVIS.] Bring him here, now. [*They push* SMITTY *over to the bucket.*] Look here, ye murrdherin' swab. D'you see ut? [SMITTY *looks down with an expression of amazement which rapidly changes to one of anguish.*]

DAVIS. [*With a sneer.*] Look at him! S'prised, ain't you? If you wants to try your dirty spyin' tricks on us you've gotter git up earlier in the mornin'.

COCKY. Thorght yer weren't 'arf a fox, didn't yer?

SMITTY. [*Trying to restrain his growing rage.*] What—what do you mean? That's only—How dare—What are you doing with my private belongings?

COCKY. [*Sarcastically.*] Ho yus! Private b'long-ings!

DRISCOLL. [*Shouting.*] What is ut, ye swine? Will you tell us to our faces? What's in ut?

SMITTY. [*Biting his lips—holding himself in check with a great effort.*] Nothing but—— That's my business. You'll please attend to your own.

DRISCOLL. Oho, ut is, is ut? [*Shaking his fist in* SMITTY's *face.*] Talk aisy now if ye know what's best for you. Your business, indade! Then we'll be makin' ut ours, I'm thinkin'. [*To* JACK *and* DAVIS.] Take his keys away from him an' we'll see if there's one'll open ut, maybe. [*They start in searching* SMITTY, *who tries to resist and kicks out at the bucket.* DRISCOLL *leaps forward and helps them push him away.*] Try to kick ut over, wud ye? Did ye see him then? Tryin' to murrdher us all, the scut! Take that pail out av his way, Cocky. [SMITTY *struggles with all of his strength and keeps them busy for a few sec-onds. As* COCKY *grabs the pail* SMITTY *makes a final effort and, lunging forward, kicks again at the bucket but only succeeds in hitting* COCKY *on the shin.* COCKY *immediately sets down the pail with a bang and, clutching his knee in both hands, starts hopping around the forecastle, groaning and swearing.*]

COCKY. Ooow! Gawd strike me pink! Kicked me, 'e did! Bloody, bleedin', rotten Dutch 'og! [*Approaching* SMITTY, *who has given up the fight and is pushed back against the wall near the doorway with* JACK *and* DAVIS *hold-ing him on either side—wrathfully, at the top of his lungs.*] Kick me, will yer? I'll show yer what for, yer bleedin' sneak! [*He draws back his fist.* DRISCOLL *pushes him to one side.*]

DRISCOLL. Shut your mouth! D'you want to wake the whole ship? [COCKY *grumbles and retires to a bench, nursing his sore shin.*]

JACK. [*Taking a small bunch of keys from* SMITTY's *pocket.*] Here yuh are, Drisc.

DRISCOLL. [*Taking them.*] We'll soon be knowin'. [*He takes the pail and sits down, placing it on the floor between his feet.* SMITTY *again*

tries to break loose but he is too tired and is easily held back against the wall.*]

SMITTY. [*Breathing heavily and very pale.*] Cowards!

JACK. [*With a growl.*] Nix on the rough talk, see! That don't git yuh nothin'.

DRISCOLL. [*Looking at the lock on the box in the water and then scrutinizing the keys in his hand.*] This'll be ut, I'm thinkin'. [*He selects one and gingerly reaches his hand in the water.*]

SMITTY. [*His face grown livid—chokingly.*] Don't you open that box, Driscoll. If you do, so help me God, I'll kill you if I have to hang for it.

DRISCOLL. [*Pausing—his hand in the water.*] Whin I open this box I'll not be the wan to be kilt, me sonny bye! I'm no dirty spy.

SMITTY. [*His voice trembling with rage. His eyes are fixed on* DRISCOLL's *hand.*] Spy? What are you talking about? I only put that box there so I could get it quick in case we were torpedoed. Are you all mad? Do you think I'm——[*Chokingly.*] You stupid curs! You cowardly dolts! [DAVIS *claps his hand over* SMITTY's *mouth.*]

DAVIS. That'll be enough from you! [DRISCOLL *takes the dripping box from the water and starts to fit in the key.* SMITTY *springs forward furiously, almost escaping from their grasp, and drags them after him half-way across the forecastle.*]

DRISCOLL. Hold him, ye divils! [*He puts the box back in the water and jumps to their aid.* COCKY *hovers on the outskirts of the battle, mindful of the kick he received.*]

SMITTY. [*Raging.*] Cowards! Damn you! Rot-ten curs! [*He is thrown to the floor and held there.*] Cowards! Cowards!

DRISCOLL. I'll shut your dirty mouth for you. [*He goes to his bunk and pulls out a big wad of waste and comes back to* SMITTY.]

SMITTY. Cowards! Cowards!

DRISCOLL. [*With no gentle hand slaps the waste over* SMITTY's *mouth.*] That'll teach you to be misnamin' a man, ye sneak. Have ye a handkerchief, Jack? [JACK *hands him one and he ties it tightly around* SMITTY'S *head over the waste.*] That'll fix your gab. Stand him up, now, and tie his feet, too, so he'll not be movin'. [*They do so and leave him with his back against the wall near* SCOTTY. *Then they all sit down beside* DRIS-COLL, *who again lifts the box out of the water and sets it carefully on his knees. He picks out the key, then hesitates, looking from one to the other uncertainly.*] We'd best be takin' this to the skipper, d'you think, maybe?

JACK. [*Irritably.*] To hell with the Old Man. This is our game and we c'n play it without no help.

COCKY. Now bleedin' horficers, I says!

DAVIS. They'd only be takin' all the credit and makin' heroes of theyselves.

DRISCOLL. [*Boldly.*] Here goes, thin! [*He slowly turns the key in the lock. The others instinctively turn away. He carefully pushes the cover back on its hinges and looks at what he sees inside with an expression of puzzled astonishment. The others crowd up close. Even* SCOTTY *leaves his post to take a look.*] What is ut, Davis?

DAVIS. [*Mystified.*] Looks funny, don't it? Somethin' square tied up in a rubber bag. Maybe it's dynamite—or somethin'—you can't never tell.

JACK. Aw, it ain't got no works so it ain't no bomb, I'll bet.

DAVIS. [*Dubiously.*] They makes them all kinds, they do.

JACK. Open it up, Drisc.

DAVIS. Careful now! [DRISCOLL *takes a black rubber bag resembling a large tobacco pouch from the box and unties the string which is wound tightly around the top. He opens it and takes out a small packet of letters also tied up with string. He turns these over in his hands and looks at the others question-ingly.*]

JACK. [*With a broad grin.*] On'y letters! [*Slapping* DAVIS *on the back.*] Yuh're a hell of a Sherlock holmes, ain't yuh? Letters from his best girl too, I'll bet. Let's turn the Duke loose, what d'yuh say? [*He starts to get up.*]

DAVIS. [*Fixing him with a withering look.*] Don't be so damn smart, Jack. Letters, you says, 's if there never was no harm in 'em. How d'you s'pose spies gets their orders and sends back what they finds out if it ain't by letters and such things? There's many a letter is worser'n any bomb.

COCKY. Righto! They ain't as innercent as they looks, I'll take me oath, when you read 'em. [*Pointing at* SMITTY.] Not 'is Lordship's let-ters; not be no means!

JACK. [*Sitting down again.*] Well, read 'em and find out. [DRISCOLL *commences untying the packet. There is a muffled groan of rage and protest from* SMITTY.]

DAVIS. [*Triumphantly.*] There! Listen to him! Look at him tryin' to git loose! Ain't that proof enough? He knows well we're findin' him out. Listen to me! Love letters, you says, Jack, 's if they couldn't harm nothin'. Listen! I was readin' in some magazine in New York on'y two weeks back how some German spy in Paris was writin' love letters to some woman spy in Switzerland who sent 'em on to Berlin, Germany. To read 'em you wouldn't s'pect nothin'—just mush and all. [*Impres-sively.*] But they had a way o' doin' it—a damn sneakin' way. They had a piece o' plain paper with pieces cut out of it an' when they put it on top o' the letter they sees on'y the words what tells them what they wants to know. An' the Frenchies gets beat in a fight all on account o' that letter.

COCKY. [*Awed.*] Gawd blimey! They ain't 'arf smart bleeders!

DAVIS. [*Seeing his audience is again all with him.*] An' even if these letters of his do sound all right they may have what they calls a code. You can't never tell. [*To* DRISCOLL, *who has finished untying the packet.*] Read one of 'em Drisc. My eyes is weak.

DRISCOLL. [*Takes the first one out of its envelope and bends down to the lantern with it. He turns up the wick to give him a better light.*] I'm no hand to be readin' but I'll try ut. [*Again there is a muffled groan from* SMITTY *as he strains at his bonds.*]

DAVIS. [*Gloatingly.*] Listen to him! He knows. Go ahead, Drisc!

DRISCOLL. [*His brow furrowed with concentration.*] Ut begins: Dearest Man—— [*His eyes travel down the page.*] An' thin there's a lot av blarney tellin' him how much she misses him now she's gone away to singin' school— an' how she hopes he'll settle down to rale worrk an' not be skylarkin'[4] around now that she's away loike he used to before she met up wid him—and ut ends: "I love you betther than anythin' in the worrld. You know that, don't you, dear? But b'fore I can agree to live out my life wid you, you must prove to me that the black shadow—I won't menshun uts hateful name but you know what I mean— which might wreck both our lives, does not exist for you. You can do that, can't you, dear? Don't you see you must for my sake?" [*He pauses for a moment—then adds gruffly.*] Uts signed: "Edith." [*At the sound of the name* SMITTY, *who has stood tensely with his eyes shut as if he were undergoing torture during the reading, makes a muffled sound like a sob and half turns his face to the wall.*]

JACK. [*Sympathetically.*] Hell! What's the use of readin' that stuff even if——

DAVIS. [*Interrupting him sharply.*] Wait! Where's that letter from, Drisc?

DRISCOLL. There's no address on the top av ut.

DAVIS. [*Meaningly.*] What'd I tell you? Look at the postmark, Drisc,—on the envelope.

DRISCOLL. The name that's written is Sidney Davidson, wan hundred an'——

DAVIS. Never mind that. O' course it's a false name. Look at the postmark.

DRISCOLL. There's a furrin stamp on ut by the looks av ut. The mark's blurred so it's hard to read. [*He spells it out laboriously.*] B-e-r— the nixt is an l, I think—i—an' an n.

DAVIS. [*Excitedly.*] Berlin! What did I tell you? I knew them letters was from Germany.

COCKY. [*Shaking his fist in* SMITTY'S *direction.*] Rotten 'ound! [*The others look at* SMITTY *as if this last fact had utterly condemned him in their eyes.*]

DAVIS. Give me the letter, Drisc. Maybe I kin make somethin' out of it. [DRISCOLL *hands the letter to him.*] You go through the others, Drisc, and sing out if you sees anythin' queer. [*He bends over the first letter as if he were determined to figure out its secret meaning.* JACK, COCKY *and* SCOTTY *look over his shoulder with eager curiosity.* DRISCOLL *takes out some of the other letters, running his eyes quickly down the pages. He looks curiously over at* SMITTY *from time to time, and sighs frequently with a puzzled frown.*]

DAVIS. [*Disappointedly.*] I gotter give it up. It's too deep for me, but we'll turn 'em over to the perlice when we docks at Liverpool to look through. This one I got was written a year before the war started, anyway. Find anythin' in yours, Drisc?

DRISCOLL. They're all the same as the first— lovin' blarney, an' how her singin' is doin', and the great things the Dutch teacher says about her voice, an' how glad she is that her Sidney bye is worrkin' harrd an' makin' a man av himself for her sake. [SMITTY *turns his face completely to the wall.*]

---

4. **skylarkin'**, to play about, interested only in having a good time.

DAVIS. [*Disgustedly.*] If we on'y had the code!

DRISCOLL. [*Taking up the bottom letter.*] Hullo! Here's wan addressed to this ship— s. s. Glencairn, ut says—whin we was in Cape Town sivin months ago—— [*Looking at the postmark.*] Ut's from London.

DAVIS. [*Eagerly.*] Read it! [*There is another choking groan from* SMITTY.]

DRISCOLL. [*Reads slowly—his voice becomes lower and lower as he goes on.*] Ut begins wid simply the name Sidney Davidson—no dearest or sweetheart to this wan. "Ut is only from your chance meetin' wid Harry— whin you were drunk—that I happen to know where to reach you. So you have run away to sea loike the coward you are because you knew I had found out the truth— the truth you have covered over with your mean little lies all the time I was away in Berlin and blindly trusted you. Very well, you have chosen. You have shown that your drunkenness means more to you than any love or faith av mine. I am sorry—for I loved you, Sidney Davidson—but this is the end. I lave you—the mem'ries; an' if ut is any satisfaction to you I lave you the real-i-zation that you have wrecked my loife as you have wrecked your own. My one remainin' hope is that nivir in God's worrld will I ivir see your face again. Goodby. Edith." [*As he finishes there is a deep silence, broken only by* SMITTY'S *muffled sobbing. The men cannot look at each other.* DRISCOLL *holds the rubber bag limply in his hand and some small white object falls out of it and drops noiselessly on the floor. Mechanically* DRISCOLL *leans over and picks it up, and looks at it wonderingly.*]

DAVIS. [*In a dull voice.*] What's that?

DRISCOLL. [*Slowly.*] A bit av a dried-up flower —a rose maybe. [*He drops it into the bag and gathers up the letters and puts them back. He replaces the bag in the box, and locks it and puts it back under* SMITTY'S *mattress. The others follow him with their eyes. He steps softly over to* SMITTY *and cuts the ropes about his arms and ankles with his sheath knife, and unties the handkerchief over the gag.* SMITTY *does not turn around but covers his face with his hands and leans his head against the wall. His shoulders continue to heave spasmodically but he makes no further sound.*]

DRISCOLL. [*Stalks back to the others—there is a moment of silence, in which each man is in agony with the hopelessness of finding a word he can say—then* DRISCOLL *explodes:*] God stiffen us, are we never goin' to turn in fur a wink av sleep? [*They all start as if awakening from a bad dream and gratefully crawl into their bunks, shoes and all, turning their faces to the wall, and pulling their blankets up over their shoulders.* SCOTTY *tiptoes past* SMITTY *out into the darkness . . .* DRISCOLL *turns down the light and crawls into his bunk as*

[*The Curtain Falls*]

I

THE ONE-ACT PLAY

O'Neill, quite naturally, began his career with the short play. He had a wealth of experience to draw on for his subject matter, but he had had a limited exposure to the complexities of dramatic structure. Since he wanted to record realistically the men and the language from his days at sea, he sought the immediate impact of the one-act play where action is simple and dialogue must be concentrated.

In the Zone centers on one question: Is Smitty a spy? The play moves relentlessly toward an answer, and though we suspect from the beginning that Smitty is hiding something, we do not know what it is any more than do the seamen in the forecastle. Yet suspense is not the crux of this play. A one-act play based on uncovering a mystery would either be so slight as to be meaningless or so complex (in trying to establish facts and then to unravel them) as to be confusing. O'Neill settles for character portrayal, a certain tension (war, spies, ammunition), and an understated conclusion. No one wins. No rousing last speeches precede the final curtain. The sensationalism of a bomb going off is replaced, ironically, with an emotional bomb: sobs, tears, shame, silence. By selecting a single track on which to operate and, of course, a single set, O'Neill can concentrate his power in dialogue, heartless accusations, stupid actions, and hopeless gestures. He employs all the rewarding means the stage possesses to hold our attention and to make us feel we know these men.

Stage directions play a large part in the *reader's* enjoyment of a play. Note that O'Neill's are unusually explicit. Granted that plays should be seen first and then read, we are nevertheless happy to have the playwright's assistance in envisioning the scene and deciding how a certain line should be read. You may need practice in reading plays, in learning how to take *all* the parts and to give the lines every ounce of meaning. O'Neill's directions offer real assistance.

II
IMPLICATIONS

Even in this brief play from his early career, Eugene O'Neill illustrates a profound understanding of human psychology. Discuss the following psychological implications in the light of this play.

1. Men believe what they want and need to believe, even when it is at variance with the facts.

2. Within an insecure group, even small instances of individual differences can trigger hysterical reactions.

3. Human emotional reactions depend as much upon outer as upon inner circumstances or conditions.

4. Groups dominated by fear are typically leaderless.

5. The main impulse dominating the sailors is the desire to achieve recognition by exposing a spy.

6. Smitty's basic problem is that he is trapped within his own ego. His isolation is as much responsible for the ensuing action as are the fears of his companions.

7. Men typically face emotional climaxes with silence.

III
TECHNIQUES
Conflict and Climax

O'Neill has no problem in establishing the opposing forces in this play. Smitty is the loner, the stranger; the other eight characters are against him. And in answering the simple question, is he a spy, the playwright has only to invent a gimmick (a device) such as the black box to allow the audience to watch as well as hear the discovery. Show how all the tension is centered on the box. Why is it so important?

But O'Neill must also invent a more meaningful climax than the discovery of a bomb. Consider what reaction you would have had if there *had* been explosives in the box. So Davis and Cocky were right, so Smitty is a spy, so the captain locks him in the brig. Result: conflict but no climax. Would code letters have been any better as resolution? Somewhat, perhaps, if the men could not have been certain of Smitty's guilt and would have had to go on living with Smitty. But then the audience would have felt cheated. By making the eight seamen look foolish and cruel, O'Neill develops in a matter of minutes an emotional impasse, a spiritual climax that can only be met by silence. These talkative men are tongue-tied in the face of genuine emotion.

Moment of Illumination

By giving Smitty nothing but sobs as he stands with his face to the wall, his back to the audience, O'Neill achieves an effective moment of revelation. Ironically, Smitty is not the victor. He loses doubly: his secret and his self-respect. Do you think Edith's simple words, read aloud, would have sufficed to make this point clear? Does the playwright need the dried-up flower to underscore the private world these thoughtless actions have uncovered?

"Illumination" may be too strong a word for what follows the reading of the last letter. Yet silence, joined with effective motion on stage, can suggest illumination. How would you direct the last moments of this play? Consider these problems of staging:

a. The pace of the action.

b. The positioning of the actors.

c. The volume of Smitty's sobs.

d. The pitch of Driscoll's last line. Shall he emphasize "God stiffen us"? How seriously does he mean it?

e. The dimming of the lights.

f. The speed with which the curtain descends.

THE COMIC
IMAGINATION

Suppose at lunch one day at school you accidentally drop your lunch tray. The macaroni and cheese spills all down your legs. The milk splashes all over your shoes. You can react in two different ways. You can be terribly embarrassed, flustered,

Such Queer Fish we are, comments this lithograph of people at the aquarium. As humorists have noted, who is queer at the zoo depends on which side of the barrier is yours.

QUEER FISH, *Mabel Dwight,*
Philadelphia Museum of Art

or even angry. In other words, you can treat it as a major catastrophe: You have ruined your clothes and shoes; you'll have to use the rest of your lunch period getting back in order and won't have time to eat. Or, on the other hand, you can treat the accident as a joke. You see how funny you look with macaroni slithering down your front, with your shoes polka-dotted with milk; you can imagine the stupid expression you must have as you hold the tray limply in hand; you can imagine how unamused your math teacher will be when you give him your excuse for missing class. In which direction does your imagination go as you react to the mishap—toward the serious or toward the comic?

A people and a culture also have similar alternatives. Some things society takes seriously and some humorously. What a people laughs at often reveals a good deal about the fundamental nature of that people. And often it is a country's writers who help a nation see things about itself as ridiculous that have customarily been taken seriously.

Thus, humor serves first of all as a kind of balance to keep people on an even keel. Indeed, especially in the early, hard-pressed days of our country and continuing through the awkward, hectic, and uneven periods of growth in the nineteenth century, the comic imagination helped Americans keep themselves and the world in perspective so that the grim business of living did not become too oppressive. In such stock American figures as the Yankee peddler, the heroic and frolicsome frontiersman, the homespun "crackerbox" philosopher, and the Negro minstrel, Americans found needed comic relief.

But at the same time the comic imagination has frequently done much more than serve merely as a kind of safety valve. It has been an irreverent "balloon pricker" humorously attacking, at one time or another, almost every area of American life. Thus, beneath the "fun" and the laughter, American humor often reveals the foibles and the absurdities of American life. It has exposed and ridiculed our weaknesses, and in so doing has given us a clearer picture of ourselves. And in learning to laugh at ourselves, we have learned a healthier way of living with ourselves and the world.

The famous Canadian humorist, Stephen Leacock, once wrote that the "true humorist . . . must present the vision of a better world, if only of a lost one." We trust that all of the following selections do present the vision of a better world—or make this world a more enjoyable one in which to live.

◆ The traveling salesman is a peculiarly American
occupational figure. Meeting new people constantly, always on the move,
he often lives by his wits. The Yankee trader, the medicine man,
the drummer, and the sales representative are all brothers under the skin;
each has a bagful of stories about his adventures on the road. O. Henry
uses this tradition in the following selection.

Jeff Peters as a Personal Magnet

O. HENRY

Jeff Peters has been engaged in as many schemes for making money as there are recipes for cooking rice in Charleston, S. C.

Best of all I like to hear him tell of his earlier days when he sold liniments and cough cures on street corners, living hand to mouth, heart to heart with the people, throwing heads or tails with fortune for his last coin.

"I struck Fisher Hill, Arkansaw," said he, "in a buckskin suit, moccasins, long hair and a thirty-carat diamond ring that I got from an actor in Texarkana. I don't know what he ever did with the pocket knife I swapped him for it.

"I was Dr. Waugh-hoo, the celebrated Indian medicine man. I carried only one best bet just then, and that was Resurrection Bitters. It was made of life-giving plants and herbs accidently discovered by Ta-qua-la, the beautiful wife of the chief of the Choctaw Nation, while gathering truck to garnish a platter of boiled dog for the annual corn dance.

"Business hadn't been good at the last town, so I only had five dollars. I went to the Fisher Hill druggist and he credited me for half a gross of eight-ounce bottles and corks. I had the labels and ingredients in my valise, left over from the last town. Life began to look rosy again after I got in my hotel room with the water running from the tap, and the Resurrection Bitters lining up on the table by the dozen.

"Fake? No, sir. There was two dollars' worth of fluid extract of cinchona[1] and a dime's worth of aniline[2] in that half-gross of bitters. I've gone through towns years afterwards and had folks ask for 'em again.

"I hired a wagon that night and commenced selling the bitters on Main Street. Fisher Hill was a low, malarial town; and a compound hypothetical pneumo-cardiac anti-scorbutic tonic was just what I diagnosed the crowd as needing.[3] The bitters started off like sweetbreads[4]-on-toast at a vegetarian dinner. I had sold two dozen at fifty cents apiece when I felt somebody pull my coat tail. I knew what that meant; so I climbed down and sneaked a five dollar bill into the hand of a man with a German silver star on his lapel.

"'Constable,' says I, 'it's a fine night.'

"'Have you got a city license,' he asks, 'to sell this illegitimate essence of spooju[5] that you flatter by the name of medicine?'

"'I have not,' says I. 'I didn't know you had a city. If I can find it to-morrow I'll take one out if it's necessary.'

---

1. **cinchona**\sĭn ▲kō·nə\ probably quinine, one of the alkaloid extracts from the bark of the cinchona tree.
2. **aniline**\▲ăn·ə·lən\ colorless, oily liquid.
3. **a low, malarial town,** low elevation, subject to malaria. **pneumo-cardiac**\nū·mə ▲kar·dē·ăk\ affecting lungs and heart. **anti-scorbutic**\skər ▲byū·tĭk\ protection against scurvy.
4. **sweetbreads,** glandular tissue located near throat of young animal, especially a calf.
5. **spooju,** possibly a blend of spoon and juice.

" 'I'll have to close you up till you do,' says the constable.

"I quit selling and went back to the hotel. I was talking to the landlord about it.

" 'Oh, you won't stand no show in Fisher Hill,' says he. 'Dr. Hoskins, the only doctor here, is a brother-in-law of the Mayor, and they won't allow no fake doctor to practice in town.'

" 'I don't practice medicine,' says I, 'I've got a State peddler's license, and I take out a city one wherever they demand it.'

"I went to the Mayor's office the next morning and they told me he hadn't showed up yet. They didn't know when he'd be down. So Doc Waugh-hoo hunches down again in a hotel chair and lights a jimpson-weed[6] regalia, and waits.

"By and by a young man in a blue necktie slips into the chair next to me and asks the time.

" 'Half-past ten,' says I, 'and you are Andy Tucker. I've seen you work. Wasn't it you that put up the Great Cupid Combination package on the Southern States? Let's see, it was a Chilian diamond engagement ring, a wedding ring, a potato masher, a bottle of soothing syrup and Dorothy Vernon—all for fifty cents.'

"Andy was pleased to hear that I remembered him. He was a good street man; and he was more than that—he respected his profession, and he was satisfied with 300 per cent. profit. He had plenty of offers to go into the illegitimate drug and garden seed business; but he was never to be tempted off of the straight path.

"I wanted a partner, so Andy and me agreed to go out together. I told him about the situation in Fisher Hill and how finances was low on account of the local mixture of politics and jalap.[7] Andy had just got in on the train that morning. He was pretty low himself, and was going to canvass the town for a few dollars to build a new battleship by popular subscription at Eureka Springs. So we went out and sat on the porch and talked it over.

"The next morning at eleven o'clock when I was sitting there alone, an Uncle Tom shuffles into the hotel and asked for the doctor to come and see Judge Banks, who, it seems, was the Mayor and a mighty sick man.

" 'I'm no doctor,' says I. 'Why don't you go and get the doctor?'

" 'Boss,' says he, 'Doc Hoskins am done gone twenty miles in de country to see some sick persons. He's de only doctor in de town, and Massa Banks am powerful bad off. He sent me to ax you to please, suh, come.'

" 'As man to man,' says I, 'I'll go and look him over.' So I put a bottle of Resurrection Bitters in my pocket and goes up on the hill to the Mayor's mansion, the finest house in town, with a mansard roof[8] and two cast iron dogs on the lawn.

"This Mayor Banks was in bed all but his whiskers and feet. He was making internal noises that would have had everybody in San Francisco hiking for the parks. A young man was standing by the bed holding a cup of water.

" 'Doc,' says the Mayor, 'I'm awful sick. I'm about to die. Can't you do nothing for me?'

" 'Mr. Mayor,' says I, 'I'm not a regular pre-ordained disciple of S. Q. Lapius. I never took a course in a medical college,' says I. 'I've just come as a fellow man to see if I could be of assistance.'

" 'I'm deeply obliged,' says he. 'Doc Waugh-hoo, this is my nephew, Mr. Biddle. He has tried to alleviate my distress, but without success. Oh, Lordy! Ow-ow-ow!!' he sings out.

"I nods at Mr. Biddle and sets down by the bed and feels the Mayor's pulse. 'Let me see your liver—your tongue, I mean,' says I. Then I turns up the lids of his eyes and looks close at the pupils of 'em.

" 'How long have you been sick?' I asked.

" 'I was taken down—ow-ouch—last night,' says the Mayor. 'Gimme something for it, doc, won't you?'

" 'Mr. Fiddle,' says I, 'raise the window shade a bit, will you?'

---

6. **jimpson-weed**\ˈjĭm·sən\ foul-smelling plant.
7. **jalap**\ˈjă·ləp\ dried root of plant from Mexico used as purgative.
8. **mansard roof**\ˈmăn·sȯrd\ roof having two slopes with the lower slope steeper than upper one.

YANKEE PEDDLER *John Whetton Ehninger*
Collection of the Newark Museum

"'Biddle,' says the young man. 'Do you feel like you could eat some ham and eggs, Uncle James?'

"'Mr. Mayor,' says I, after laying my ear to his right shoulder blade and listening, 'you've got a bad attack of super-inflammation of the right clavicle of the harpsichord!'[9]

"'Good Lord!' says he, with a groan. 'Can't you rub something on it, or set it or anything?'

"I picks up my hat and starts for the door.

"'You ain't going, doc?' says the Mayor with a howl. 'You ain't going away and leave me to die with this—superfluity of the clapboards,[10] are you?'

"'Common humanity, Dr. Whoa-ha,' says Mr. Biddle, 'ought to prevent your deserting a fellow-human in distress.'

"'Dr. Waugh-hoo, when you get through plowing,' says I. And then I walks back to the bed and throws back my long hair.

---

9. **clavicle**\ˈklă·və·kəl\ a bone in man just above the first rib connecting the shoulder blade and breastbone; the collarbone. **harpsichord**\ˈhȯrp·sə ˈkȯrd\ musical instrument, forerunner of piano; tone produced by key which plucks strings.
10. **clapboard,** narrow board that is thicker at one edge and used for covering outer walls.

275

"'Mr. Mayor,' says I, 'there is only one hope for you. Drugs will do you no good. But there is another power higher yet, although drugs are high enough,' says I.

"'And what is that?' says he.

"'Scientific demonstrations,' says I. 'The triumph of mind over sarsaparilla.[11] The belief that there is no pain and sickness except what is produced when we ain't feeling well. Declare yourself in arrears. Demonstrate.'

"'What is this paraphernalia you speak of, doc?' says the Mayor. 'You ain't a Socialist, are you?'

"'I am speaking,' says I, 'of the great doctrine of psychic financiering—of the enlightened school of long-distance, sub-conscientious treatment of fallacies and meningitis[12]—of that wonderful in-door sport known as personal magnetism.'

"'Can you work it, doc?' asks the Mayor.

"'I'm one of the Sole Sanhedrims and Ostensible Hooplas[13] of the Inner Pulpit,' says I. 'The lame talk and the blind rubber whenever I make a pass at 'em. I am a medium, a coloratura[14] hypnotist and a spirituous control. It was only through me at the recent seances at Ann Arbor that the late president of the Vinegar Bitters Company could revisit the earth to communicate with his sister Jane. You see me peddling medicine on the streets,' says I, 'to the poor. I don't practice personal magnetism on them. I do not drag it in the dust,' says I, 'because they haven't got the dust.'

"'Will you treat my case?' asks the Mayor.

"'Listen,' says I. 'I've had a good deal of trouble with medical societies everywhere I've been. I don't practice medicine. But, to save your life, I'll give you the psychic treatment if you'll agree as Mayor not to push the license question.'

"'Of course I will,' says he. 'And now get to work, doc, for them pains are coming on again.'

"'My fee will be $250.00, cure guaranteed in two treatments,' says I.

"'All right,' says the Mayor. 'I'll pay it. I guess my life's worth that much.'

"I sat down by the bed and looked him straight in the eye.

"'Now,' says I, 'get your mind off the disease. You ain't sick. You haven't got a heart or a clavicle or a funny bone or brains or anything. You haven't got any pain. Declare error. Now you feel the pain that you didn't have leaving, don't you?'

"'I do feel some little better, doc,' says the Mayor, 'darned if I don't. Now state a few lies about my not having this swelling in my left side, and I think I could be propped up and have some sausage and buckwheat cakes.'

"I made a few passes with my hands.

"'Now,' says I, 'the inflammation's gone. The right lobe of the perihelion[15] has subsided. You're getting sleepy. You can't hold your eyes open any longer. For the present the disease is checked. Now, you are asleep.'

"The Mayor shut his eyes slowly and began to snore.

"'You observe, Mr. Tiddle,' says I, 'the wonders of modern science.'

"'Biddle,' says he, 'when will you give uncle the rest of the treatment, Dr. Pooh-pooh?'

"'Waugh-hoo,' says I. 'I'll come back at eleven to-morrow. When he wakes up give him eight drops of turpentine and three pounds of steak. Good morning.'

"The next morning I went back on time. 'Well, Mr. Riddle,' says I, when he opened the bedroom door, 'and how is uncle this morning?'

"'He seems much better,' says the young man.

"The Mayor's color and pulse was fine. I gave him another treatment, and he said the last of the pain left him.

---

11. **sarsaparilla**\\'să·spə ▲rĭ·lə\\ a beverage similar to root beer with flavor from birch oil and sassafras.
12. **meningitis**\\'mĕ·nən ▲jĭ·dəs\\ inflammation of membranes around brain and spinal cord.
13. **Sanhedrims**\\▲săn·hĭ·drĭmz\\ the highest court and council of the ancient Jewish nation. **Hooplas**\\▲hū·pləz\\ a gaudy, artificial show.
14. **coloratura**\\'kə·lər·ə ▲tū·rə\\ music which is characterized by runs and trills permitting a singer to display skill.
15. **perihelion**\\'pĕ·rə ▲hē·lĭ·ən\\ point in the path of a celestial body that is nearest the sun.

"'Now,' says I, 'you'd better stay in bed for a day or two, and you'll be all right. It's a good thing I happened to be in Fisher Hill, Mr. Mayor,' says I, 'for all the remedies in the cornucopia[16] that the regular schools of medicine use couldn't have saved you. And now that error has flew and pain proved a perjurer, let's allude to a cheerfuller subject—say the fee of $250. No checks, please, I hate to write my name on the back of a check almost as bad as I do on the front.'

"'I've got the cash here,' says the Mayor, pulling a pocket book from under his pillow.

"He counts out five fifty-dollar notes and holds 'em in his hand.

"'Bring the receipt,' he says to Biddle.

"I signed the receipt and the Mayor handed me the money. I put it in my inside pocket careful.

"'Now do your duty, officer,' says the Mayor, grinning much unlike a sick man.

"Mr. Biddle lays his hand on my arm.

"'You're under arrest, Dr. Waugh-hoo, alias Peters,' says he, 'for practising medicine without authority under the State law.'

"'Who are you?' I asks.

"'I'll tell you who he is,' says Mr. Mayor, sitting up in bed. 'He's a detective employed by the State Medical Society. He's been following you over five counties. He came to me yesterday and we fixed up this scheme to catch you. I guess you won't do any more doctoring around these parts, Mr. Fakir.[17] What was it you said I had, doc?' the Mayor laughs, 'compound—well it wasn't softening of the brain, I guess, anyway.'

"'A detective,' says I.

"'Correct,' says Biddle. 'I'll have to turn you over to the sheriff.'

"'Let's see you do it,' says I, and I grabs Biddle by the throat and half throws him out the window, but he pulls a gun and sticks it under my chin, and I stand still. Then he puts handcuffs on me, and takes the money out of my pocket.

"'I witness,' says he, 'that they're the same bills that you and I marked, Judge Banks. I'll turn them over to the sheriff when we get to his office, and he'll send you a receipt. They'll have to be used as evidence in the case.'

"'All right, Mr. Biddle,' says the Mayor. 'And now, Doc Waugh-hoo,' he goes on, 'why don't you demonstrate? Can't you pull the cork out of your magnetism with your teeth and hocus-pocus them handcuffs off?'

"'Come on, officer,' says I, dignified. 'I may as well make the best of it.' And then I turns to old Banks and rattles my chains.

"'Mr. Mayor,' says I, 'the time will come soon when you'll believe that personal magnetism is a success. And you'll be sure that it succeeded in this case, too.'

"And I guess it did.

"When we got nearly to the gate, I says: 'We might meet somebody now, Andy. I reckon you better take 'em off, and—' Hey? Why, of course it was Andy Tucker. That was his scheme; and that's how we got the capital to go into business together.'"

I

THE MYTH

OF THE YANKEE PEDDLER

One of the oldest and continuously popular characters of the American comic tradition was the so-called Yankee peddler. What he was like in real life is uncertain because his image was so early clouded by myth; the myth-figure, however, is relatively clear. He possessed the following characteristics:

1. He was a solitary person who traveled from place to place.

2. He was ingenious and quick-witted.

3. He was a master of masquerade.

4. He could sell anybody anything.

---

16. **cornucopia**\\'kȯr·nə ▲kō·pē·ə\\ the horn of plenty.
17. **Fakir**\\'fā·kər\\ faker or swindler.

O. Henry has obviously drawn both Jeff Peters and Andy Tucker from the Yankee peddler myth. The details of his portraits—for example, the odd mixture of Christian Science, hypnotism, and spiritualism that make Jeff Peters a "personal magnet"—are "modern"; but his general outlines for the two heroes clearly go all the way back to the late eighteenth or very early nineteenth century. We have here, then, a good example of how a writer draws upon his literary heritage.

Point to specific details which show that Peters and Tucker are drawn from the Yankee peddler myth.

II
IMPLICATIONS

Examine the following statements about Americans. First ask yourself how the statement relates to the story; second ask whether it is true for Americans in general; and third ask whether it is a minor fault or a serious one.

1. Americans are impressed by the use of big words.

2. Americans are overly impressed by scientific terminology.

3. Americans really want to believe in magic; therefore they are susceptible to such things as "cure-alls" and Indian remedies.

4. Americans enjoy seeing an individual "put one over" on authorities.

5. Americans basically respect the sharp dealer.

6. Americans tend to believe that if the buyer is stupid enough to be taken in, it's his hard luck.

III
TECHNIQUES

Comedy

O. Henry's humor in this story springs from a number of sources. From the list below select the techniques that were the source of most fun for you.

1. The mistaking of names. ("Riddle" for "Biddle," etc.)

2. The use of manufactured and misapplied words. ("super-inflammation of the right clavicle of the harpsichord," etc.)

3. Turning the tables. (On Peters, then on Mayor Banks.)

4. The double masquerade of Andy Tucker.

5. Exaggeration. (The exaggerated treatment of spiritualism and hypnotism, for example.)

6. Other factors. (You name them.)

Sympathy and Detachment

In comedy the matter of sympathy and detachment is especially important. In one way or another the author must present his characters in such a way that the reader will sympathize with certain of them and remain detached from others. If a reader misplaces his sympathies, the entire effect of a story may be changed. Consider the Mayor in this story: What would be the effect of the story if a reader sympathized strongly with Mayor Banks?

Because readers' natures vary so widely, it is probably impossible for an author to control completely the responses of all of them. The author can and does assume, however, that the majority of his readers will react similarly to certain situations and characters simply because the readers belong to the same culture. Thus, O. Henry assumed that Americans of his day would naturally sympathize with the sharp dealers against the authority, Mayor Banks. Readers, however, from another culture—Indian, for example—might respond quite differently. An early American Puritan might have responded differently, too. Cultural factors, then, powerfully influence our responses to literature.

Whenever people gather they tell stories: In clubs, on airplanes,
at parties, and around campfires, the sharing of jokes is a common activity.
Occasionally, these stories become more and more elaborate as they pass
from person to person. The most interesting ones are often found
among the uneducated, back-country people. In recent years there has been
a concerted effort to collect and print these tales. One such collector,
J. Frank Dobie, heard the following from an East Texas farmer.

Old Bill

J. FRANK DOBIE

They tell me that Jeb Rider's log cabin is still standing, about a quarter of a mile up the slope from the spring on Elm Creek. Nobody has struck oil in this part of East Texas yet, and so things out of the past live on there. People still talk about the Civil War, though years and years ago they put what was left of Uncle Jeb Rider in the ground, in the little graveyard where wild trumpet vines cover the lane fence with red flowers all through the summer months and into the fall. Old Bill disappeared long before that, but Uncle Jeb's story of Old Bill seems to have a chance to keep on blooming with the trumpet vines. This is the way he told it:

When me and my wife married, it was her idear having the house so fur up the slope from where we got water outa the spring on Ellum Creek. She was skeered of floods. I was nacherly agin having to tote water so fur, but 'fore long I sometimes wished it were further. I could walk down that trail and set on the cypress log there at the spring and kinder get peaceful. She was always badgering me to clear more land and plant more sweet pertaters and hoe the corn cleaner and do things like that, and I jest nacherly kinder like to squirrel roun'[1] with the dogs like I'd always done.

The best dog I ever had was Old Bill. He was out of a bitch Pa brung from Tinnissee; that is, figgering in several ginerations between. I never can remember whether it was July 13 or July 14 he died, the year before the war started. Anyhow, one cloudy day about a month after he died I was going down the trail to the spring uncommon low in the mouth and was about halfway when kinder unconscious-like I heard sumpin behind me. Maybe it was a rustle in the leaves. I didn't pay no 'tention till I heared a low rattle. Then I looked, and I'll be dogged if it wasn't the biggest diamon'back rattlesnake I ever see, right in the trail, not more'n six steps back.

When I stopped and looked, he stopped, too, and raised his head up in a curious way and looked at me without shaking his tail a-tall. It's that tail-shaking that makes a rattlesnake so fearsome, puts the jints in a human's backbone to shaking too. Well, I didn't have a thing with me to hit with, not even a water bucket, and when I glanced round fer a stick there weren't none in reach. I started on down the trail agin to a dead dogwood I could break off. Then I looked back and that diamon'back was coming on, too, keeping a respec'ful distance and looking like he didn't mean no harm.

1. **squirrel roun'**, squirrel hunt.

When I got to the dead dogwood and broke off a stick and drew it back to lamm the snake, he looked more harmless than ever. I can't explain it. There he was keeping a respec'ful distance, and all at once he sorter seemed to me like a dog that wants to foller you and be friends but's afraid to come too clost. Well, I stood there a-holding the stick, and he had his head up a little watching me, and his eyes jest seemed to say he understood.

Then I done clear contrary to nature. I throwed the stick away and started agin on down to the spring. Ever' once in a while I'd turn my head and look back. The rattlesnake was still follering, humble and respec'ful. When I set down on the cypress log, he coiled up in a sliver of weak sunshine and kept looking right straight at me. D'reckly I begun to kinder talk to him. I was still a young man, remember, and a blamed fool about feeling sorry fer myself. And that old snake would nod his head aroun' and look like he felt sorry too.

When I started up to the cabin, he did the same, jest follering like a dog. About halfway up he dropped out, and I didn't see nothing more of him till the next day. I was going down to the spring agin to bring up some water fer Abbie to wash with. Right about the halfway place, he fell in behind me like he'd done the first time, and now his follering seemed jest as nacherl as a dog scratching fleas.

"See here," I says to him after we got settled at the spring, "I'm going to call you Bill. Bill, he was the best coon and possum dog I ever had, and he always understood me. When I wanted to squirrel aroun', he never had no idears about clearing off land or putting poles in the fence to keep the hawgs outer the field or anything like that. Yes, sir, you're Bill to me from now on."

And Bill jest nodded his head and looked grateful out of his eyes and shore would've talked if he could of. It was real soothing to be with him, and when Abbie went to squalling fer me to hurry up and bring on the water he acturly winked.

Well, after that we was together lots at the spring. Whenever I went to the store I'd hear talk about the Aberlitionists[2] up North working to take the darkies away from us Southern folks and make 'em our equals, and more talk about the Black Republicans. When I got back I'd tell Bill about 'em—sometimes afore I told Abbie—and, by hoeky, he'd coil up and look fierce enough to bite a crowbar. Then the war did come. I volunteered fer Captain Abercrombie's company and traded off some corn and a mule fer a good, gentle horse and bought Abbie a new ax and got all ready to go. The evening afore I was to set out, I went down to the spring to kinder ca'm myself and tell Bill good-by.

It looked like he understood all about the Yankees. I told him to look after things around the spring as best he could and I'd be back someday. The next morning after Abbie got my things all packed and I'd told her good-by, I turned by the spring to water my horse.

Well, jest as I was coming out under that leaning ellum over the trail between the house and the spring, I felt sumpin drop acrost my shoulders. It would-a scared me if it hadn't been so nacherl. "So you want to go to war too, do you, Bill?" I says.

"I don't know how the fellers in camps would take to you," I says. "They're all Texians, you know," I says, "and got about as much use fer a rattlesnake as a wildcat has for a lost puppy." You see, I hadn't told a soul about Old Bill—not even Abbie. I jest didn't think anybody would understand. But if Bill was so set on going with me, I decided right then I'd try to convert the heathen.

"If you'll promise," I says to him, "not to bother nobody and stay put where I puts you, I'll take you. I'll explain to the fellers and maybe they'll get the idear." He nods and we rode on.

Some of the fellers seemed to think at first that I was jest an idiot, but they left Bill alone

2. **Aberlitionists** (Abolitionists), persons who favored abolishing slavery.

and he left them alone. I shore didn't have no trouble with anybody trying to steal my blankets, and the way Jim Bowie—that's what I named my horse—and Old Bill got to be fren'ly with each other was a caution. Sometimes Jim Bowie would kinder noze Bill along the back, and many a time when Jim Bowie was a-grazing I've seen Bill crawling out in front of him and scaring off devil horses[3] so Jim Bowie wouldn't accerdently chew 'em up and swaller 'em. You know how a devil horse once it's inside the stumick of an animal can kill it. I fixed up a bag for Old Bill to ride comfortable in and, when we moved, hung it on the horn of my saddle.

Fer months we jest practiced marching and squads-righting and squads-lefting and so on. I'd leave Old Bill on the edge of the parade grounds, and I got to noticing how interested he seemed in our movements. When we'd have a parade, he'd get exciteder than the colonel's horse. The band music was what set him up. "Dixie" was his favorite tune, and he got so he could sorter rattle it. It shore was comical to see him histing his tail to get the high notes.

Finally our training was over. We crossed the Mississippi River and joined Gin'ral Albert Sidney Johnston's forces. Then when Shiloh[4] opened up on that Sunday morning in April we was in it. We fought and we fit all day long, sometimes going forwards and sometimes backwards, sometimes in the brush and sometimes acrost clearings. We didn't know till next day that our gin'ral had been killed. If he had-a lived and if we'd-a had a few more like Old Bill, things would have turned out mighty different.

My rigiment was camped on Owl Creek, jest north of Shiloh Chapel, and jest before we went into battle that morning I took Old Bill over to a commissary waggin and told him to stay there and told the driver to kinder keep him. Late evening found us coming back into a long neck of woods that our colonel told us we'd have to clear of Yankees. They'd worked in between us and Owl Creek. We found 'em all right, but they was the deadest Yankees I ever see. At first we was bellying along on the ground, keeping behind trees and expecting fire. Then when we kept finding more and more dead uns, we figgered some other outfit had beat us to 'em. We got to breathing easy, and then somebody noticed that none of the dead Yanks bore bullet marks. It was all-fired strange, and the trees wasn't none of 'em creased neither.

I decided to make a little closer examination, and I pulled up the britches leg of one Yank. Jest above his shoe top on the outside, where the ankle vein runs, I noticed a pair of little holes about the size of pin points. I found the same marks on the leg of the next Yank, on another, on another, and then, all of a suddent, I knowed Old Bill'd been there. I told the boys. They went to looking at the dead Yankee legs and couldn't he'p being convinced.

We kept going through the neck of woods and counting dead Yankees till we got to Owl Creek, a little below camps. My ricollection is that the count run to 417, but it may have been a few less. Course, too, some few might've been counted twicet. I guess the official report would show, if it didn't get burned up at Richmond.

It wasn't more'n a rifle shot from the near side of the woods to camps. We got in a little before sundown, and there Old Bill was stretched out under the commissary waggin. He looked plumb tuckered out and as gant as a gutted snowbird. Well, the night before one of the boys happened to set a trap fer possum right in camps almost. He went to it as soon as we got in and found a big wood rat caught. He brung it in alive and put it in front of Old Bill. As a rule, Old Bill never et nuthin' hardly, but the way he nailed that rat and then swallered him whole was an eddicati'n in appertite. We all shore was proud of him. After that the boys quit figgering on frying him up fer beefsteak. They took to calling him Diamon' Bill and looked on him as a mascot and about the

---

3. **devil horses,** predatory insects having a slender body, four wings, strong jaws; also dragon-fly, devil's darning needle.
4. **Shiloh,** April 6, 1862; Shiloh is located in Tennessee.

best soldier in the Confederate Army, too. Why, the colonel used to get me to send him out on scout duty. No telling how many Yankees he cleaned out of thickets it was dangerous fer a man to enter. He knowed the difference between Confederate gray and Union blue jest as well as Ab Blocker's old cow dog knowed the difference between a branded critter and a mav'rick.[5]

Well, 'taint no use fer me to tell about all the battles we fought in. At Appermatox I was still alive and so was Diamon' Bill. Jim Bowie wasn't, though, and we rode home on a borrered mule. One day way long in the summer I put Bill down at the spring on Ellum Creek, and afore my saddle blanket was dry I was breaking land, putting up the old fences, hoeing weeds out of the patch Abbie had managed to plant, and doing all sorts of things. The dogs was all dead and there jest wasn't no time fer nothing but work. Lots of days I didn't even think about Old Bill.

Then one day in the spring of '66 while I was going in a hurry down to the spring, I heared something that made my mind whirl back. I wheeled around and saw a big diamon'-back running towards me. Afore I could grab fer a stick, I seen it was Old Bill. I called out to him, "Bill," and he sorter nodded his head the way I'd seen him do a thousand times. But he made a new kind of motion that says he wants me to foller him. He turns off the trail and I follers.

About a hundred yards off he sidled up to another rattler, and looked back at me. "Mrs. Bill?" I says. He nodded, and the two went on. D'reckly we come to a nacherl clearing 'bout the size of our courthouse maybe. Old Bill stopped, raised up like a nacherl-borned commander, and give the derndest rattle a man ever heared. Then he moved on ahead about ten paces and rared up agin. By that time squads and troops and companies and battalions of your rattlesnakes was coming out of the brush on all sides. I'm afeared to say how many they was—hundreds, maybe thousands. They come out in regular formations, squads-

righting and squads-lefting and fronting-into-line like old soldiers. Bill lined 'em up fer dress parade about the middle of the field. Then he sounded one rattle fer a signal and, keeping a perfect front, they begun advancing towards me, all rattles a-going and every dod-gumed one of um a-playing Dixie.

Old Bill knowed what he'd done in the war. The trouble was he was the only rattlesnake in it. He didn't seem to realize the war was over. Here he'd come home and raised this army, and now he was offering it to me. I ricollect how the Confederate boys useter always be quoting Gin'ral Bedford Forrest. He said, you know, that the gin'ral wins who gits there fustest with the mostest men. Well, it was jest too late to be fustest. I tried to explain to Diamon' Bill. And that was the last in a military way I ever seen of him.

I

THE TALL TALE

In the first paragraph Dobie sets the stage for the story of Old Bill. He tells of the section of the country from which the story came and the kind of people that produced it. Then he tells the story as if Jeb Rider himself were telling it. Thus he tries to reproduce the whole feeling of the oral folk tale.

The tall tale is essentially (1) a simple, humorous narrative (2) using realistic details and (3) common speech (4) to relate extravagant happenings (5) centered around a superhuman figure. "Old Bill" centers upon a superreptile rather than a superhuman, but in all other respects it is thoroughly typical of the nineteenth-century tall tale.

II

IMPLICATIONS

If we assume that "Old Bill" is a fairly typical example of American folk stories of the tall-tale

---

5. mav'rick (maverick)\ˈmă·və·rĭk\ an unbranded animal.

variety, what does it show about the attitudes of the ordinary American? How are the following statements related to the story? Also what does each suggest about the psychology of the common American man?

1. A wife often drives a man to the point where he will find even a rattlesnake good company.

2. Humor is a useful way of living with defeat.

3. Men try to avoid work around the home as much as possible.

4. Imagination may be a great comfort when realities are uncomfortable.

5. A life lived in communion with nature and with animals is more peaceful than a life lived in communion with human beings.

III
TECHNIQUES

Comedy

The tall tale obviously depends on exaggeration for its comic effect; in its emphasis on the improbable and the impossible, it has an ancestor in fairy tales involving witches and wizards, giants and Prince Charmings. In fairy tales, however, we know that we're in a land of make-believe where anything can happen. The tall tale, by contrast, is told in a matter-of-fact way that encourages the reader to believe that everything it relates is factual.

It is this ironic contrast between the realistic setting, details, and manner on the one hand and the extravagant happenings on the other that is the source of much of the humor in the tall tale. Note how Dobie draws the reader into his tale with many realistic details at the beginning of his story. Note, also, how he begins with small improbabilities and gradually works up to larger ones. Make a brief catalog of the increasingly improbable incidents.

Sympathy and Detachment

A Southern reader would naturally sympathize with Jeb Rider and Old Bill; probably most Northern readers sympathize with the pair too. Many details combine to make us feel sympathy for Jeb. For example, he has to spend a great deal of time in disagreeable work; he is married to a woman who "badgers" him; he has recently lost his best dog, and he is lonely. Later, of course, Old Bill's killing of about 417 Union soldiers would, under

different circumstances, cause most Northern readers to grow unsympathetic toward Jeb and Bill. Yet, in this story most readers will look upon this "mass murder" with detachment. What are some of the factors that help Northern readers look upon such an event in this way?

IV
WORDS

A. The word *foretell* carries the comprehensive meaning of "to tell something before it happens." How is the synonym *predict* set apart from *foretell* in the dictionary? What other synonyms are listed and explained along with *predict*? Distinguish among the following lists of synonyms. The italicized word in each set is taken from the previous selections. What meaning does it add?

1. pale (adj.)
   wan   livid   *pallid*

2. apparent (adj.)
   illusory   seeming   *ostensible*

3. prevent (v.)
   preclude   obviate   *avert*

4. melancholy (adj.)
   plaintive   lugubrious   *dolorous*

5. funny (adj.)
   comical   risible   *droll*

6. forebearing
   tolerant   clement   *indulgent*

7. ashamed
   mortified   *chagrined*

B. In "Old Bill," Dobie uses various devices to illustrate the East Texas speech of Uncle Jeb. Dialects differ in pronunciation, vocabulary, and grammar. To show the differences in pronunciation, the author writes *fur* for *far*, *fer* for *for*, *idear* for *idea*, *kinder* for *kind of*; in vocabulary, he uses words like *tote, critter, fustest*. Study the selection carefully and make a list of words showing differences in pronunciation. How does the writer suggest these differences? Does he use "eye dialect," the deliberate respelling of words to suggest pronunciation, or does he use some other device? What general comments may you make about Uncle Jeb's pronunciation? Make a list of words showing vocabulary differences. Using the context, define these words. List examples of grammatical differences. For what purpose did the author use dialect? To add reality? To make the story more believable? To add humor?

If you have heard the expression "Humor him," you know that "humor"
may be defined as playing along with or indulging the desires of another;
it consists in adapting oneself to another person's temperament.
This sort of humoring is often found in the family, where a parent, say,
might humor a child in order to avoid conflict. Carried to extremes, however,
it can put the person doing the humoring into all sorts of silly situations.
"Little Bit and the *America*" is the first chapter of *Father, Dear Father,*
one of Ludwig Bemelmans' many successful humorous books.

Little Bit and the *America*

LUDWIG BEMELMANS

Look, what a lovely day we have for sailing," I said, pointing my pen toward the lit-up greenery outside the open window. The birds sang in the trees, and the sun shone on a deck of brightly colored luggage tags which I was filling out. Under "S.S. *America*" I had carefully lettered my name, and I answered the gay question of "Destination?" with "Cherbourg."[1]

I was about to fill out a new tag when I noticed Barbara's silence. She was standing at the window, staring at me. I saw clearly the symptoms of wanting something, symptoms long known to me and always the same. I remembered that the day before she had said something about a dog, but I had been called away before I could talk about it at length.

For the most part, Barbara is a sweet and normal child; when she wants something, she changes. The child is then under great stress. A trembling of the lower lip precedes the filling of the beautiful eyes with tears. I am allowed to see these hopeless eyes for a moment, and then, as a spotlight moves from one place to another, she averts her gaze and slowly turns, folds her arms, and looks into the distance, or if there is no distance, at the wall. The crisis is approaching. She swallows, but her throat is constricted; finally, with the urgency of a stammerer, and with her small hands clenched, she manages to convey a few dry words. The small voice is like a cold trumpet. The last word is a choking sound. There is a long, cold silence.

On the morning of sailing I recognized the first stage of this painful condition that overcomes her from time to time. I could tell it by her eyes, her mouth, the position she stood in, the peculiar angles of her arms and legs. She was twisted in an unhappy pose of indecision. Not that she didn't know precisely what she wanted: she was undecided about how to broach the subject.

After the tears, the gaze into the distance, the silence, Barbara blurted out, "You promised I could have a dog."

I steeled myself and answered, "Yes, when we get back from Europe you can have a dog."

An answer like that is worse than an outright no. The mood of "I wish I was dead" descended on Barbara. She stared coldly out of the window, and then she turned and limply dragged herself down the corridor to her room, where she goes at times of crisis. She closed the door not by slamming it, but with a terrible, slow

---

1. **Cherbourg**\\ˈshär·burg\\ a port city in northwest France.

finality. One can see from the corridor how she lets go of the handle inside—in unspeakably dolorous fashion; slowly the handle rises, and there is the barely audible click of the mechanism. There is then the cutting off of human relations, a falling off of appetite, and nothing in the world of joy or disaster matters.

Ordinarily the comatose state lasts for weeks. In this case, however, Barbara was confronted with a deadline, for the ship was sailing at five that afternoon and it was now eleven in the morning. I usually break down after three or four weeks of resistance. The time limit for this operation was five hours.

She decided at first to continue with standard practice, the manual of which I know as well as I do the alphabet.

From the door at the end of the corridor came the sound of heartbreaking sobs. Normally these sobs last for a good while, and then, the crisis ebbing off, there follows an hour or two of real or simulated sleep, in which she gathers strength for renewed efforts. This time, however, the sobs were discontinued ahead of schedule and were followed by a period of total silence, which I knew was taken up with plotting at the speed of calculating machinery. This took about ten minutes. As the door had closed, so it opened again, and fatefully and slowly, as the condemned walk to their place of execution, the poor child, handkerchief in hand, dragged along the corridor past my room into the kitchen. I never knew until that morning that the pouring of milk into a glass could be a bitter and hopeless thing to watch.

I am as hardened against the heartbreak routine as a coroner is to postmortems. I can be blind to tears and deaf to the most urgent pleading. I said, "Please be reasonable. I promise you that the moment we get back you can have a dog."

I was not prepared for what followed—the new slant, the surprise attack.

She leaned against the kitchen doorjamb and drank the last of the milk. Her mouth was ringed with white. She said in measured and accusing tones, "You read in the papers this morning what they did in Albany."

"I beg your pardon?"

"They passed a law that all institutions like the A.S.P.C.A. are to be forced to turn dogs over to hospitals, for vivisection—and you know what will happen. They'll get her and then they'll cut her open and sew her up again over and over until she's dead."

"What has that got to do with me?"

"It has to do with the dog you promised me."

"What dog?"

"The dog that Frances wants to give me."

Frances is a red-headed girl who goes to school with Barbara.

"I didn't know Frances had a dog."

Barbara raised her eyebrows. "You never listen," she said, and as if talking to an idiot and with weary gestures she recited, "Poppy, I told you all about it a dozen times. Doctor Lincoln, that's Frances's father, is going to Saudi Arabia to work for an oil company, and he had to sign a paper agreeing not to take a dog, because it seems the Arabs don't like dogs. So the dog has to be got rid of. So Doctor Lincoln said to Frances, 'If you don't get rid of her, I will.' Now you know how doctors are—they have no feelings whatever for animals. He'll give her to some hospital for experiments."

I resumed filling out baggage tags. When I hear the word "dog" I see in my mind a reasonably large animal of no particular breed, uncertain in outline, like a Thurber dog,[2] and with a rough, dark coat. This image was hovering about when I asked, "What kind of a dog is it?"

"Her name is Little Bit."

"What?"

"Little BIT—that's her name. She's the dearest, sweetest, snow-white, itsy-bitsy tiny little toy poodle you have ever seen. Can I have her, please?"

I almost let out a shrill bark.

---

2. **Thurber dog,** refers to the caricatures by James Thurber.

"Wait till you see her and all the things she's got—a special little wicker bed with a mattress, and a dish with her picture on it, and around it is written 'Always faithful' in French. You see, Poppy, they got Little Bit in Paris last year, and she's the uniquest, sharpest little dog you've ever seen, and naturally she's house-broken, and Frances says she's not going to give her to anybody but me."

I was playing for time. I would have settled for a Corgi, a Yorkshire, a Weimaraner, even a German boxer or a Mexican hairless, but Little Bit was too much. I knew that Doctor Lincoln lived some thirty miles out of the city, and that it would be impossible to get the dog to New York before the ship sailed.

"Where is the dog now?" I asked with faked interest.

"She'll be here any minute, Poppy. Frances is on the way now—and oh, wait till you see, she has the cutest little boots for rainy weather, and a cashmere sweater, sea green, and several sets of leashes and collars—you won't have to buy a thing."

"All right," I said, "you can have the dog. We'll put it in a good kennel until we return."

The symptoms, well known and always the same, returned again. The lower lip trembled. "Kennel," she said—and there is no actress on stage or screen who could have weighted this word with more reproach and misery.

"Yes, kennel," I said and filled out the baggage tag for my portable typewriter.

"Poppy—" she started, but I got up and said, "Now look, Barbara, the ship leaves in a few hours, and to take a dog aboard you have to get a certificate from a veterinary, and reserve a place for him, and buy a ticket."

To my astonishment, Barbara smiled indulgently. "Well, if that's all that's bothering you—first of all, we're going to France; the French, unlike the English, have no quarantine for dogs, and they don't even ask for a health certificate. Second, you can make all the arrangements for the dog's passage on board ship, after it sails. Third, there is plenty of room in the kennels. I know all this because Frances and I went down to the U. S. Lines and got the information day before yesterday."

I stared into the distance. At such times I feel a great deal for the man who's going to marry Barbara. With all hope failing I said, "But we'll have to get a traveling bag or something to put the dog in."

"She has a lovely little traveling bag with her name lettered on it, 'Little Bit.'"

The name stung like a whip. "All right then." I wrote an extra baggage tag to be attached to the dog's bag.

Barbara wore the smug smile of success. "Wait till you see her," she said and ran out of the room. In a moment she returned with Frances, who, I am sure, had been sitting there waiting all the while. The timing was perfect.

Little Bit had shoebutton eyes and a patent-leather nose and a strawberry-colored collar; she was fluffy from the top of her head to her shoulders and then shorn like a miniature Persian lamb. At the end of a stub of a tail was a puff of fluff, and other puffs on the four legs. She wore a pale blue ribbon, and a bell on the collar. I thought that if she were cut open most probably sawdust would come out.

A real dog moves about a room and sniffs its way into corners. It inspects furniture and people, and makes notes of things. Little Bit stood with cocksparrow stiffness on four legs as static as her stare. She was picked up and brought over to me. I think she knew exactly what I thought of her, for she lifted her tiny lip on the left side of her face over her mouse teeth and sneered. She was put down, and she danced on stilts, with the motion of a mechanical toy, back to Frances.

I was shown the traveling bag, which was like one of the pocketbooks that WAC colonels carry.

"We don't need that tag," said Barbara. "I'll carry her in this. Look." The pocketbook, which had a circular opening with a wire screen on each end for breathing purposes, was opened; Little Bit jumped into it, and it was closed. "You see, she won't be any bother whatever."

The bag was opened again. With a standing jump Little Bit hurdled the handles of the bag and stalked toward me. Tilting her head a little, she stood looking up, and then she again lifted her lip over her small fangs.

"Oh, look, Barbara!" said Frances. "Little Bit likes your father—she's smiling at him."

I had an impulse to sneer back, but I took the baggage tags and began to attach them to the luggage. Then I left the room, for Frances showed signs of crisis; her eyes were filling, and the heartbreak was too much for me. Little Bit was less emotional. She ate a hearty meal from her *Toujours fidèle* dish and inspected the house, tinkling about with the small bell that hung from her collar.

It was time to go to the boat. The luggage was taken to a taxi, and Little Bit hopped into her bag. On the way I thought about the things I had forgotten to take care of, and also about Little Bit. It is said that there are three kinds of books that are always a success: a book about a doctor, a book about Lincoln, and a book about a dog. Well, here was Doctor Lincoln's dog, but it didn't seem to hold the elements of anything except chagrin. I wondered if Lincoln had ever had a dog, or a doctor, or if Lincoln's doctor had had a dog. I wondered if that side of Lincoln, perhaps the last remaining side, had been investigated as yet or was still open.

We arrived with Doctor Lincoln's dog at the customs barrier, and our passports were checked. The baggage was brought aboard. In our cabin we found some friends waiting. Frances and Barbara, with Little Bit looking out of her bag, inspected the ship. The gong sounded, and the deck steward sang out, "All ashore that's going ashore!" The passengers lined up to wave their farewells. The last of those that were going ashore slid down the gangplank. Good-by, good-by—and then the engine bells sounded below, and the tugs moaned and hissed, and the ship backed out into the river.

There are few sights in the world as beautiful as a trip down the Hudson and out to sea, especially at dusk. I was on deck until we passed the Ambrose Lightship, and then I went down to the cabin.

Little Bit was lying on a blotter, on the writing desk, and watching Barbara's hand. Barbara was already writing a letter to Frances, describing the beauty of travel and Little Bit's reactions. "Isn't she the best traveling dog we've ever had, Poppy?"

The cabins aboard the *America* are the only ones I have ever been in that don't seem to be aboard ship. They are large—more like rooms in a country home—a little chintzy[3] in decoration, and over the portholes are curtains. In back of these one suspects screened doors that lead out to a porch and a Connecticut lawn rather than the ocean.

I put my things in place and changed to a comfortable jacket. I said, "I guess I better go up and get this dog business settled."

"It's all attended to, Poppy. I took care of it," said Barbara and continued writing.

"Well, then you'd better take her upstairs to the kennels. It's almost dinnertime."

"She doesn't have to go to the kennels."

"Now, look, Barbara—"

"See for yourself, Poppy. Just ring for the steward, or let me ring for him."

"Yes, sir," said the steward, smiling.

"Is it all right for the dog to stay in the cabin?" I asked. The steward had one of the most honest and kind faces I have ever seen. He didn't fit on a ship either. He was more like a person that works around horses, or a gardener. He had bright eyes and squint lines, a leathery skin, and a good smile.

He closed his eyes and announced, "Dog? I don't see no dog in here, sir." He winked like a burlesque comedian and touched one finger to his head in salute. "My name is Jeff," he said. "If you want anything—" And then he was gone.

"You see?" said Barbara. "And besides, you save fifty dollars, and coming back another fifty, makes a hundred."

---

3. **chintzy**\ˈchĭnt·sē\ refers to a brightly colored cotton cloth, usually glazed; in U.S. informal speech suggests cheapness.

I am sure that Little Bit understood every word of the conversation. She stood up on the blotter and tilted her head, listening to Barbara, who said to her, "You know, Little Bit, you're not supposed to be on this ship at all. You mustn't let anybody see you. Now you hide, while we go down to eat."

There was a knock at the door. Silently Little Bit jumped to the floor and was out of sight.

It was the steward. He brought a little raw meat mixed with string beans on a plate covered with another plate. "Yes, sir," was all he said.

Barbara was asleep when the first rapport between me and Little Bit took place. I was sitting on a couch, reading, when she came into my cabin. By some magic trick, like an elevator going up a building shaft, she rose and seated herself next to me. She kept a hand's width of distance, tilted her head, and then lifted her lip over the left side of her face. I think I smiled back at her in the same fashion. I looked at her with interest for the first time— she was embarrassed. She looked away and then suddenly changed position, stretching her front legs ahead and sitting down flat on her hindlegs. She made several jerky movements but never uttered a sound.

Barbara's sleepy voice came from the other room. "Aren't you glad we have Little Bit with us?"

"Yes," I said, "I am." I thought about the miracles of nature, how this tough little lion in sheep's pelt functioned as she did; with a brain that could be no larger than an olive, she had memory, understanding, tact, courage, and no doubt loyalty, and she was completely self-sufficient. She smiled once more, and I smiled back: the relationship was established. Life went on as steadily as the ship.

On the afternoon of the third day out, as I lay in my deck chair reading, Barbara came running. "Little Bit is gone," she stammered with trembling lower lip.

We went down to the cabin. The steward was on all fours, looking under the beds and furniture. "Somebody musta left the door open," he said, "or it wasn't closed properly and swung open, and I suppose she got lonesome here all by herself and went looking for you. You should have taken her up to the movies with you, Miss."

"She's a smart dog," said Barbara. "Let's go to every spot on board where she might look for us."

So we went to the dining room, to the smoking room, the theater, the swimming pool, up the stairs, down the stairs, up on all the decks and around them, and to a secret little deck we had discovered between second and third class at the back of the ship, where Little Bit was taken for her exercise mornings and evenings and could run about freely while I stood guard.

A liner is as big as a city. She was nowhere.

When we got back the steward said, "I know where she is. You see, anybody finds a dog naturally takes it up to the kennels, and that's where she is. And there she stays for the rest of the trip. Remember, I never saw the dog, I don't know anything about her. The butcher— that's the man in charge of the kennels—he's liable to report me if he finds out I helped hide her. He's mean, especially about money. He figures that each passenger gives him ten bucks for taking care of a dog, and he doesn't want any of us to snatch. There was a Yorkshire stowing away trip before last; he caught him at the gangplank as the dog was leaving the ship—the passenger had put him on a leash. Well, the butcher stopped him from getting off. He held up everything for hours, the man had to pay passage for the dog, and the steward who had helped hide him was fired. Herman Haegeli is his name, and he's as mean as they come. You'll find him on the top deck, near the aft chimney, where it says 'Kennels.'"

At such moments I enjoy the full confidence and affection of my child. Her nervous little hand is in mine, she willingly takes direction, her whole being is devotion, and no trouble is too much. She loved me especially then, because she knows that I am larcenous at heart and willing to go to the greatest lengths to beat a game and especially a meany.

"Now remember," I said, "if you want that dog back we have to be very careful. Let's first go and case the joint."

We climbed up into the scene of white and red ventilators, the sounds of humming wires, and the swish of the water. In yellow and crimson fire, the ball of the sun had half sunk into the sea, precisely at the end of the avenue of foam that the ship had plowed through the ocean. We were alone. We walked up and down, like people taking exercise before dinner, and the sea changed to violet and to indigo and then to that glossy gunmetal hue that it wears on moonless nights. The ship swished along to the even pulse of her machinery.

There was the sign. A yellow light shone from a porthole. I lifted Barbara, and inside, in one of the upper cages, was Little Bit, behind bars. There was no lock on her cage.

No one was inside. The door was fastened by a padlock. We walked back and forth for a while, and then a man came up the stairs, carrying a pail. He wore a gray cap, a towel around his neck, and a white coat such as butchers work in.

"That's our man," I said to Barbara.

Inside the kennels he brought forth a large dish that was like the body of a kettledrum. The dogs were barking.

"Now listen carefully, Barbara. I will go in and start a conversation with Mr. Haegeli. I will try to arrange it so that he turns his back on Little Bit's cage. At that moment, carefully open the door of the cage, grab Little Bit, put her under your coat, and then don't run—stand still, and after a while say, 'Oh, please let's get out of here.' I will then say good evening, and we both will leave very slowly. Remember to act calmly, watch the butcher, but don't expect a signal from me. Decide yourself when it is time to act. It might be when he is in the middle of work, or while he is talking."

"Oh, please, Poppy, let's get out of here," Barbara rehearsed.

I opened the door to the kennel and smiled like a tourist in appreciation of a new discovery. "Oh, that's where the dogs are kept," I said. "Good evening."

Mr. Haegeli looked up and answered with a grunt. He was mixing dog food.

"My, what nice food you're preparing for them. How much do they charge to take a dog across?"

"Fifty dollars," said Mr. Haegeli in a Swiss accent. There are all kinds of Swiss, some with French, some with Italian, and some with German accents. They all talk in a singing fashion. The faces are as varied as the accents. The butcher didn't look like a butcher—a good butcher is fat and rosy. Mr. Haegeli was thin-lipped, thin-nosed, his chin was pointed. In the light he didn't look as mean as I expected; he looked rather fanatic, and frustrated.

"How often do you feed them?"

"They eat twice a day and as good as anybody on board," said Mr. Haegeli. "All except Rolfi there—he belongs to an actor, Mr. Kruger, who crosses twice a year and brings the dog's food along." He pointed to the cage where a large police dog was housed. "Rolfi, he is fed once a day, out of cans." He seemed to resent Rolfi and his master.

"You exercise them?"

"Yes, of course—all except Rolfi. Mr. Kruger comes up in the morning and takes him around with him on the top deck and sits with him there on a bench. He doesn't leave him alone. There is such a thing as making too much fuss over a dog."

I said that I agreed with him.

"He tried to keep him in his cabin—he said he'd pay full fare for Rolfi, like a passenger. He'll come up any minute now to say good night to Rolfi. Some people are crazy about dogs." Mr. Haegeli was putting chopped meat, vegetables, and cereal into the large dish. "There are other people that try to get away with something—they try and smuggle dogs across, like that one there." He pointed at Little Bit. "But we catch them," he said in his Swiss accent. "Oh yes, we catch them. They think they're smart, but they don't get away with it—not with me on board they don't. I have ways of finding out. I track them down." The fires of the fanatic burned in his eyes. "I catch them every time." He sounded as if he turned them over to the guillotine after he caught them. "Ah, here comes Mr. Kruger," he said and opened the door.

Kurt Kruger, the actor, said good evening and introduced himself. He spoke to Mr. Haegeli in German—and Mr. Haegeli turned his back on Little Bit's cage to open Rolfi's. The entire place was immediately deafened with barking from a dozen cages. The breathless moment had arrived. Barbara was approaching the door, but the dog-lover Kruger spotted Little Bit and said, "There's a new one." He spoke to Little Bit, and Little Bit, who had behaved as if she had been carefully rehearsed for her liberation, turned away with tears in her eyes.

Mr. Kruger and his dog disappeared.

Mr. Haegeli wiped his hand on his apron and went back to mixing the dog food. The chances for rescuing Little Bit were getting slim.

"Where do you come from, Mr. Haegeli?"

"Schaffhausen. You know Schaffhausen?"[4]

"Yes, yes," I said in German. "*Wunderbar.*"

"Ja, ja, beautiful city."

"And the waterfall!"

"You know the Haegeli Wurstfabrik there?"

"No, I'm sorry."

"Well, it's one of the biggest sausage factories in Switzerland—liverwurst, salami, cervelat, frankfurters, boned hams—a big concern, belongs to a branch of my family. I'm sort of a wanderer. I like to travel—restless, you know—I can't see myself in Schaffhausen." He looked up. He was mixing food with both hands, his arms rotating.

"I understand."

"Besides, we don't get along, my relatives and I. All they think about is money, small money—I think in large sums. I like a wide horizon. Schaffhausen is not for me."

"How long have you been traveling?"

"Oh, I've been two years on this ship. You see, I'm not really a butcher but an inventor."

"How interesting! What are you working on?"

At last Mr. Haegeli turned his back on the cage in which Little Bit waited. "Well, it's something tremendous. It's, so to say, revolutionary."

"Oh?"

"There's a friend of mine, a Swiss, who is a baker, but you know, like I'm not a real butcher, he is not exactly a baker—I mean, he knows his trade but he has ambition to make something of himself—and together we have created something that we call a frankroll." He waited for the effect.

"What is a frankroll?"

"It's a frankfurter baked inside a roll. We've got everything here to experiment with, the material and the ovens. I make the franks and he makes the rolls. We've tried it out on the passengers. Mr. Kruger, for example, says it's a marvelous idea. I might add that the experimental stage is over. Our product is perfect. Now it is a question of selling the patent, or licensing somebody—you know the way that is done. You make much more that way."

"Have you tried?"

Mr. Haegeli came close, the inventor's excitement in his eyes now. "That is where the hitch comes in. On the last trip I saw the biggest frankfurter people in America—they're in New York. Well, the things you find out! They were very nice. The president received us and looked at the product and tasted it. He liked it, because he called for his son and a man who works close to him. 'I think you've got something there,' said the old man. I think with him we would have had clear sailing, but he had one of these wisenheimers for a son."

As Haegeli talked he forgot completely about the dogs. He gesticulated with hands that were sticky with hash, using them as a boxer does when he talks with his gloves on. Standing close to me, he held them away lest dog food soil my clothes. He stood exactly right, with

---

4. **Schaffhausen**\shaf ˄hau·zĕn\ city in north central Switzerland on Rhine, north of Zurich.

his back turned to the spot where Barbara was slowly reaching to the door of Little Bit's cage. It was all foiled again by the return of Mr. Kruger and Rolfi. Mr. Kruger kissed his dog good night and stood waiting while Rolfi slowly walked into his cage. He said to Rolfi that it was only for two more nights that he had to be here, he wished us a good night also, and after a final good night to his dog he went.

"Where was I?" said the butcher.

"With the frankroll, the old man, and the wise-guy son."

"Right. Well, the son was looking at our product with a mixture of doubt, so he took a bite out of it, and in the middle of it he stopped chewing. 'Mmmm,' he said. 'Not bad, not bad at all. But—' He paused a long time, and then he said, 'What about the mustard, gentlemen?'

"I said, 'All right, what about the mustard?'

"So the wise guy says, 'I'm a customer. I'm buying. I'm at a hot dog stand. I watch the man in the white jacket. He picks up the frankfurter roll that's been sliced and placed face down on the hot plate he picks it up in a sanitary fashion—and he takes the skinless frank with his prong and puts it in the roll and hands it to me. Now, I dip into the mustard pot, or maybe I decide on a little kraut, or maybe I want some condiments or relish. Anyway, I put that on the frank—' He held out his hand.

"So I said, 'What's all that got to do with our frankroll?'

"So Junior says, 'A lot. Let me explain. It's got no appeal. Practical maybe, but to put the mustard on the hot dog the customer would have to slice the frankfurter bun first, and that leads us straight back to the old-fashioned frankfurter and the old-fashioned roll. The frankroll may be practical, but it's got no sizzle to it. No eye appeal, no nose appeal—it's no good.'

"Well, the old man was confused, and he got up and said that he'd like to think about it, and then he said he'd like to show us the factory. Well, you'd never think how important a thing a frankfurter is. There are two schools of

thought about frankfurters, the skin frank and the skinless. These people specialize in skinless ones—because the American housewife prefers them without the skin—but did you know that the skinless come with skins and have to be peeled? This factory is spotless. There is a vast hall, and at long tables sit hundreds of women, and music plays, and they all have in their left hand a frankfurter, and in the right a paring knife, and all day long they remove the skins from the frankfurters—an eight-hour day. And at the end of the room is a first-aid station, because at the speed at which they work there is a great deal of laceration. The man in charge —"

"Oh, please, Poppy, let's get out of here!" Barbara broke in.

"The man in charge explained that in spite of elaborate safety precautions there was a great deal of absenteeism on account of carelessness. They had people who were working on a machine to skin the frankfurters. 'Now if you could invent a frankfurter-skinning device,' said the old man to me, 'you'd be a millionaire overnight.' Well, we're not licked yet. The beauty of working on a ship is that you have everything on board. One of the engineers is working with us on a skinning machine, and I have another outfit lined up for the frankroll."

The light in Mr. Haegeli's eyes faded. He wiped his hand again on his apron, and I shook it, and slowly we walked out on deck and down the first flight of stairs to A deck. I said to Barbara, "Run for your life, for by now he has discovered that Little Bit is gone."

We got to the cabin. Little Bit smiled on both sides of her face, and she bounced from floor to chair to dresser. There was a knock on the door—the thrill of the game of cops and robbers had begun. Little Bit vanished.

Barbara asked innocently, "Who is it?"

It was the steward. "Did you find her?"

Barbara smiled.

"You got her back?"

Barbara nodded.

"Well, for heaven's sake, keep her out of sight. That crazy butcher is capable of anything—and I got a wife and family."

"From now on the dog must not be left," I said to Barbara. "She must go with us wherever we go, to the dining room, on deck, to the lounge, and to the movies. And you can't carry her in that bag—you have to cover her with a scarf or have her inside your coat."

Barbara started going about as if she carried her arm in a sling. The steward averted his eyes whenever he met us, and he didn't bring any more dog food.

Mr. Kruger said, "The kennel man suspects you of having removed the dog from the kennel."

"We did."

"Good," said the actor. "Anything I can do, I will."

"Well, act as if you didn't know anything about it. How is Rolfi?"

"Oh, Rolfi is fine. You know, he's never bitten anybody in his life except that kennel man."

Mr. Kruger offered to get Little Bit off the boat. He had a wicker basket in which he carried some of Rolfi's things, and he would empty that, except for Rolfi's coat, and in that he would carry Little Bit off the *America*, for the butcher would follow us and watch us closely, and if he didn't find the dog before he'd catch us at the customs.

"Isn't he a nice man—Mr. Kruger? People always say such mean things about movie actors," said Barbara.

Camouflaged in a scarf, Little Bit rested on Barbara's lap during meals. On the deck chair she lay motionless between my feet, covered by a steamer rug. She traveled about under Barbara's coat, and she took her exercise on the secret afterdeck, while I watched from above.

After the morning walk, the next day, the steward knocked. He looked worried. "The butcher was here," he said, "and went all over the room. He found the dish with those French words and the dog's picture on it, on the bathroom floor."

"How could we be so careless?" I said, my professional pride hurt.

"And of course he saw the bag with *Little Bit* printed on it. I said I didn't know nothing about any dog."

We doubled our precautions. Little Bit's mouth was down at the edges with worry. I contemplated what to do. After all, there were only two more days, and if the worst happened we could sit upstairs with Little Bit, the way Mr. Kruger sat with Rolfi. I said to Barbara, "Perhaps it would be best to pay the passage and have it over with."

The symptoms were back. "No, you can't do that. Think of the poor steward and his family!"

"Well, we could settle that, I think, with the butcher. I don't like to cheat the line—"

"Well, Poppy, you can send them a check afterward, if that worries you, or drink a few extra bottles of champagne, or buy something in the shop."

Knock on the door.

"Who is it?"

"The purser, sir."

"Please come in."

The door opened. Behind the purser stood Mr. Haegeli.

"Just wanted to look and see if everything is all right. Are you comfortable, sir?"

"Everything is fine."

"By the way, sir, we're looking for a small white dog that's been lost. We wondered if by any chance it's in here."

"Come in and look for yourself."

"That's quite all right, sir. Excuse the intrusion. Good evening." The purser closed the door.

"What a nice man!" said Barbara.

The butcher was excluded from pursuing us in the public rooms of the ship; he couldn't follow us to the movies or the dining room. But he seemed to have spies. "What a lovely scarf you have there, Miss," said the elevator boy, and after that we used the stairs. The butcher came on deck in a fatigue uniform and followed us on the evening promenade around deck, during which Little Bit sat inside my overcoat, held in place by my right hand in a Napoleonic pose. We made four turns around deck. I leaned against the railing once, holding Little Bit in place, so that I could stretch my arms; Barbara was skipping rope, and the maneuver fooled him. He ran downstairs, and we caught him as he emerged from near our cabin—he had made another search. We saw his shadow on the wall near the stairs several times. He seemed to be nearing a nervous breakdown. Mr. Kruger told us that he had sworn we had the dog and meant to find it at any cost. There was one more night to go, and the next day the ship would dock.

At ten Barbara would deliver Little Bit to Mr. Kruger, and we would fill the bag in which she traveled with paper tissue, tobacco, soap, extra toothbrushes, razor blades, dental floss, and other things, which can all be bought in Europe but which for some droll reason one always takes along.

Little Bit was fed from luncheon trays which we ordered for ourselves in the cabin instead of going down to lunch.

The steward was shaking. "I don't know," he said, "when that guy butchers, or when he takes care of the other dogs. He's hanging around here all the time. I hope you get off all right."

On the last afternoon on board I became careless. Some passengers and a bearded ship's officer were watching the last game of the deck-tennis tournament, and others were lying this way and that in their deck chairs, forming a protective barricade. Barbara had checked on the butcher—he was busy aft, airing some of his charges.

I thought it safe to take Little Bit out of my coat and place her on deck, so that we all could relax a bit. She had been there but a moment when I heard a cry. "Ha," it went. It was the "Ha" of accusation and discovery, chagrin and triumph, and it had been issued by Mr. Haegeli, who stood with both arms raised. Fortunately he was not a kangaroo and was therefore unable to jump over the occupied deck chairs. I gathered up Little Bit, and we were safe for a few seconds. By now I knew the

ship's plan as well as the man who designed her. We went down two decks on outside stairs, entered through a serving pantry, climbed one inside service stair, and then nonchalantly walked to the bar. I sat down and rang for the steward. I ordered something to drink. In a little while Barbara, with her lemonade in hand, said, "He's watching us through the third window!"

I swept my eyes over the left side of the room, and his face was pressed against the glass, pale and haunting. He kept watch from the outside, and ran back and forth as we moved around inside.

We went down to dinner. When we came back I got a cigar. He was outside the bar. As I went to the saloon to have coffee he was outside that window.

"Don't give Little Bit any sugar," Barbara said. "He's watching us."

The floor was cleared for dancing, and we got up to walk back to the library. There is a passage between the main saloon and the library off which are various pantries and side rooms, and it has no window. In a corner of it is the shop, and on this last evening people stood there in numbers buying cartons of cigarettes, film, small sailor hats, miniature lifebelts and ship models with "S.S. *America*" written on them. Here I suddenly realized the miraculous solution of our problem. It was in front of me, on a shelf. Among stuffed Mickey Mice, Donald Ducks, and teddy bears of various sizes stood the exact replica of Little Bit—the same button eyes and patent-leather nose, the fluff, the legs like sticks, the pompom at the end of the tail, and the blue ribbon in its hair.

"How much is that dog?" I asked the young lady.

"Two ninety-five."

"I'll take it."

"Shall I wrap it up, sir?"

"No, thanks, I'll take it as is."

"What are we going to do now, Poppy?"

"Now you keep Little Bit hidden, and I'll take the stuffed dog, and we'll go into the library."

There we sat down. I placed the stuffed dog at my side and spoke to it. The butcher was on the far side of the ship, but he almost went through the window. He disappeared and ran around to the other side. I had arranged the toy dog so that it seemed to be asleep at my side, partly covered by Barbara's scarf. I told her to take Little Bit down to the cabin and then come back, and we'd have some fun with the butcher.

When she came back Barbara took the toy dog and fixed its hair and combed the fluff Then I said, "Please give me the dog." We walked the length of the ship on the inside. The butcher was sprinting outside, his face flashing momentarily in the series of windows.

At the front of the ship we went out on deck. I held the dog so that the pompom stuck out in back, and I wiggled it a little, to give it the illusion of life. It took the butcher a while to catch up. He walked fast—we walked faster. He almost ran—we ran. He shouted, "Mister!" I continued running. As we came toward the stern I asked Barbara, "Can you let out a terrible scream?"

"Yes, of course," said Barbara.

"One—two—three—*now*."

She screamed, and I threw the dog in a wide curve out into the sea. The butcher, a few feet away, gripped the railing and looked below, where the small white form was bobbing up and down in the turbulent water. Rapidly it was washed away in the wake of the *America*.

We turned to go back into the saloon.

We left the butcher paralyzed at the stern. He wasn't at the gangplank the next day.

Little Bit landed in France without further incident.

I

ADAPTING TO THE PECULIARITIES
OF OTHERS

Ludwig Bemelmans once complained that he couldn't seem to hate the people he wrote about; this is certainly obvious from the foregoing selection, for even the "meany," Herman Haegeli, ap-

pears as an object of fun rather than the butt of strong criticism. Bemelmans has the ability to see and to convey the people, actions, and situations most people take seriously as comic instead. He seems to have learned how to humor human failings. Here much of his humor comes when Poppy's attempts to adapt to his daughter's peculiarities lead him into situations in which grown men rarely find themselves; the humor grows out of the incongruity between his maturity of years and his childish behavior.

II

IMPLICATIONS

Although Bemelmans' treatment is very light, this episode reveals some of the typical foibles in American family life. Discuss the following statements both in relation to the story and to American culture.

1. Americans are overly fond of pets; in fact, they often think more of them than they do of people.

2. Parents are often more childish than their children.

3. Americans think it is funny to see parents outwitted and outmaneuvered by their children.

4. There is nothing wrong with ignoring regulations if you can get by with it.

III

TECHNIQUES

Sympathy and Detachment

The "superiority theory" is sometimes advanced to explain the pleasure we get out of comedy. Essentially the theory maintains that the reader does not sympathize with the characters, but rather remains detached from them; he takes a position *above* them and enjoys the sense of superiority he feels as a result of seeing comic characters behaving like fools.

What is your own opinion of this theory, especially in connection with "Little Bit and the *America*"? Did you sympathize strongly with any of the characters? Did you reject any of them completely? If you don't agree with the superiority theory with respect to this selection, can you think of any other comedies you have seen or read where the theory does apply?

The "Dummy," or naive person, is a favorite comic figure
in American humor. American entertainers, especially comedy groups
and teams, have long exploited the character who "doesn't know the score."
Red Skelton, for example, has delighted millions of people with a host
of characters who stupidly blunder through outrageous episodes.
Much of the humor of the following selection is in this same tradition.
Because of their own misinformation, poor judgment, and misunderstanding,
Miss Skinner and Miss Kimbrough often find themselves in embarrassing,
and amusing, situations.

Interlude in London

CORNELIA OTIS SKINNER *and* EMILY KIMBROUGH

Once arrived in London, we parted company with Mother and Father. They had served their purposes during my illness. Now I was recovered and "raring" to be independent again. They went their way (I daresay somewhat secretly relieved, if truth were told) to their habitual caravansary, the hotel Victoria in Northumberland Avenue, while Emily and I set forth for the more bohemian atmosphere of "lodgings." Through some colorful flight of fancy we had made arrangements to take over the rooms of a former Bryn Mawr[1] student who had spent the previous winter working for a Ph.D. at the University of London. She was one of those brilliant scholars far too intellectual to be concerned with creature comforts, and after we saw the way she lived we came to the conclusion that we weren't intellectual types after all. She had written us that she was leaving for a "hiking" trip (that fine outdoor term implicit of any number of splendid things in the way of blisters, fish and chips and a brave avoidance of baths). However, she assured us that the landlady was fully cognizant of our arrival, and would be waiting for us with welcome at I forget what number Tavistock Square. As a cheery afterthought she added she hoped we'd be happy in her "digs,"[2] a word which slightly startled us and made us wonder if we were to lodge in some sort of cellar.

The "digs," however, proved to be on the topmost floor of an ancient manse which had been converted into a rooming house along about the beginning of the reign of Edward VII. It was situated in a part of London neither chic nor quaint, an extremely commonplace district somewhere back of the British Museum, and from the glimpses we caught of the other lodgers, it looked as if they'd come straight out of some of the cases. One toiled up four flights of extremely audible stairs and collapsed into our quarters consisting of two dreary, barren rooms which, when the residence had known better days, must have housed the tweenie[3] and the second footman. One contained a bed, a studio couch and a washstand with an assortment of bowls, pitchers and soap dishes which didn't match, being for the most part souvenirs from Brighton and

1. **Bryn Mawr**\ˈbrĭn mɔr\ college for women in southeast Pennsylvania.
2. **digs,** lodgings.
3. **tweenie,** a between maid, servant whose work supplements that of the maid and the cook.

the Exhibition of 1854.[4] We gathered this must be the bedroom and through the process of elimination came to the ingenious conclusion that the other was a sitting room, although it looked more like a semi-denuded storeroom. It contained a desk which had been made out of a grand piano, a couple of Morris chairs fancied up with anti-macassars, a small fireplace with a coal grate and a framed picture of Watts' "Hope," that dejected symbol of anything but.[5] There was also a bookcase containing on the top shelf the Bryn Mawr scholar's text books, which were so erudite we couldn't understand even their titles, and on the lower shelf a brass alcohol lamp and a teapot shaped like a duck or some such whimsey. The landlady had gone off for a holiday up the Thames and we were left to the tender mercies of a cockney slavey. She'd clatter in at seven A.M. to fix the one fire we had all day, then at seven-thirty she'd charge back with a pitcher of hot water, which in London June weather didn't stay hot very long. At eight she'd bring us a tasty breakfast, half an orange for each, fried eggs and leathery bacon, a pot of that witch's brew they call coffee, and some slabs of toast arranged in an open-air rack to insure their being nice and cold. When we petitioned ever so meekly permission to receive these blessings a trifle later in the day, she said, "Carn't, Miss. Mrs. 'Iggins's horders." Some mornings we'd say to hell with Mrs. Higgins and breakfast, and turn over for a couple of hours more sleep; but during such periods of oblivion the water would have become the glacial temperature of the room, and the fire would have gone out. Starting the fire required a knack known only to the slavey, who miraculously got those bits of damp kindling and chunks of igneous rock ignited by spreading out a newspaper across the fireplace and blowing vociferously. We'd try that, too, but the only thing to ignite would be the newspaper and one of us would have to come running with a water pitcher to put out the conflagration, not that a conflagration could have made much headway in that room. This commotion would rouse the slavey, who

would poke her face in the doorway and say severely that Mrs. 'Iggins wouldn't 'arf be put out, which was her simple homespun way of implying that if we persisted in such tricks we'd be the ones who'd be put out.

The bathroom was down two flights of stairs, and that involved some interesting encounters with the other tenants, all of whom seemed to be elderly gentlemen in conservative bathrobes, carrying towels, shaving mugs and copies of the *Daily Mail*. Emily nearly knocked one down the stairs one morning, and to hide her confusion spoke to him in her most friendly Indiana way. But he gave her the disdainful look he must in his younger days have cast at a Piccadilly *fille de joie* and shot for sanctuary through the nearest door.

The first morning in this giddy establishment Emily, who had been holding converse with the slavey, said to me, "There's some queer sort of character who lives in this house."

"Queer?"

"Yes," she said, "that girl just told me. He's apparently some sort of old eccentric, and when you see him you have to tip him."

"Just what did the girl say?" I asked.

"She said, 'You'll have to look out for the geezer, Miss. It's always best to have tuppence handy for the geezer.'"

I felt this to be another of Emily's original flights of fancy, but what it meant didn't dawn on me until I went down for my bath. The water for the tub was heated by one of those little gas-jet arrangements which flicker beneath a small copper boiler. After a time, if you're lucky, a forlorn trickle of hot water dribbles forth, cooling off considerably before it hits the tin tub below. I remembered this

4. **Brighton**\ˈbraɪ·tən\ a seaside resort on English Channel, fifty miles south of London. **Exhibition of 1854,** the idea of holding a great international exposition was Prince Albert's, husband of Queen Victoria.
5. **Morris chairs,** designed by decorating firm founded by William Morris (1834–1896), English poet, artist, architect. **anti-macassars**\mə ˈkă·sərz\ cloth coverings thrown over sofas, chairs, and so forth. **Watts' "Hope,"** George Frederic Watts (1817–1904), English painter and sculptor.

was called a *geyser* and went back upstairs to tell Emily so. She became indignant as she always does when she's misunderstood a thing.

"Then why don't they call it a geyser?" she snapped.

"They do. Only they pronounce it geezer."

"I suppose they call Old Faithful a waterpistol!"

The geezer was a mercenary contraption. There was a slot into which one dropped two coppers to pay for the gas. When twopence worth was consumed the gas went out. We were informed that if this occurred when we were still running the water, we must immediately insert two more coins in the slot. If we didn't, the slavey prophesied, "everythink might blow hup." I well remember one morning when, as I was disporting myself like a dolphin in a couple of inches of tepid water, the gas gave a blue spurt, and with a little dying hiccough went out completely. The room was of that bracing June chill and I hadn't even started soaping myself. I yelled to Emily to bring me some more coins. She didn't have any coppers in her purse, but she came down the stairs two at a time with a sixpence. All this accomplished was merely to drop down the slot and onto the floor without in any way rousing the gas. I recalled the slavey's warning about the thing blowing up unless, like Mammon,[6] you kept it stoked with coins. Odd rumblings were issuing from the little copper boiler. Emily, always active if not always logical in an emergency, cried, "Don't move, darling!" and pushed me back into the chilly water. She dashed downstairs, but couldn't find a living soul. The slavey had vanished, and those elderly gentlemen, the other lodgers, had either gone to business or were hiding behind locked doors. She stepped out onto the street in search of a shop or even a flower vendor who might make change. But Tavistock Square is guiltless of any shops. They haven't a newsstand. Then a bus pulled up beside her, and that seemed to solve the problem. Hatless and coatless, she jumped on the back platform, got change for two and six, rode one block and jumped off murmuring to the be-

wildered conductor, "You see, my friend is up there stark naked with the geezer and I have to hurry back to her," which straightened everything out nicely. By the time she returned I had turned quite blue with cold, but Old Faithful had not yet erupted.

For all that little financial lesson in the Montreal hotel, Emily was still confused by British currency. She'd grown highly incensed not only with it but with me because she couldn't understand it. (It was the only thing I ever heard her admit to not understanding.) It was in vain that I tried to show her the difference between a half-crown[7] and a two shilling piece. She refused to admit they were anything but two versions of fifty cents and persisted in being so stubbornly obtuse about it I finally told her if she'd just bring herself to read what was written on them she'd know. This didn't work out so well either, because she'd keep taxi drivers waiting interminably while she'd scan the reading matter of each and every coin, turning it round and round, sometimes breathing on it and rubbing it clear. When I suggested that people might think her awfully queer she said not at all, they'd merely mistake her for a coin collector. I tried explaining to her that "one florin" meant two shillings but that only made her madder. The day we received a bill made out in guineas, and I told her that there was no such thing as a guinea, it was a pound and one shilling,[8] only the swanker shops charged you in guineas, and you paid in pounds and shillings, but you called it guineas although, as I had said, there really was no such thing, she slapped me.

That was the summer when white fur evening wraps were the rage. One saw them everywhere. They ranged from chic models of dazzling ermine to cheap copies in rabbit. Some of

---

6. **Mammon,** personification of riches, avarice, worldly gain.
7. **half-crown,** silver coin equal to two shillings and sixpence; two shillings equals about 24 to 32 cents and sixpence equals about six cents.
8. **a pound and one shilling,** currently about $2.95.

the cheaper ones weren't too bad, or maybe they were bad, all right, but a few smart women wore them, and to us they spelled enchantment. The only fur coat I'd ever had was made of what the salesgirl had vowed was "mountain lion" but what wore into a substance more like circus lion and a retired one at that, while Emily's was a cutdown squirrel of her mother's. As for evening wraps, the best I could boast was a tasty mandarin jacket, while Emily still clung to the green velvet cloak Grandmother Kimbrough had brought her from the San Francisco Exposition. We felt that if ever the day arrived when we could afford white fur evening wraps we'd believe in fairy godmothers. Then suddenly the day arrived when we found we could. Emily out for a solitary stroll one morning had spied a shop whose window displayed a vision of rabbit splendor marked £6–10s–6d. She had a feeling this was within our humble means, but not being quite certain, she rushed back to our dovecote[9] to ask me what "El six, ten esses and six dees" means. With the then rate of exchange it was about the equivalent of $30. We lost no time, rushed to the shop and without a moment's hesitation bought a couple, one each, and exactly alike. That was the incredible era of shapeless dresses and shapeless wraparound coats with voluminous sleeves and rolled collars. Our models were capes, and as I recall them now they must have been daisybells. Made of snowy rabbit (we were later to discover it was not only white but flying) they were fashioned along the lines of a tent, adorned with a deep yoke and an even deeper object known as a "cape collar." They were perfectly enormous and we could wrap them about us twice with a d'Artagnan[10] flourish which we thought was chic and gave us a worldly air. Not daring to entrust these treasures to a delivery boy, we ourselves lugged them in huge boxes back to our lodgings where we spent a lot of time parading in them before a large and pallid mirror hanging above the washstand.

That evening Mother and Father asked us to dinner. The family, with supreme tact, always made a great point of asking us to dine with them, never letting on that they knew we'd leap at every chance. It was their indulgent way of coöperating with us in that fine independence we talked so much about. When they didn't, we felt forlorn and went to places like Lyons or the A.B.C., where we felt even more forlorn. Some evenings, because it was inexpensive and near our lodgings, we ate at a dreadful temperance hotel. The food was tasteless, the napkins grey and damp as the people, and we'd emerge dyspeptic and full of gloom. We longed to, but never dared, venture into any place as worldly as a restaurant, even a modest Soho[11] café, because we were too shy. This particular evening we were invited to dine at the Trocadero, a dizzy prospect. What better occasion than this, we thought, for the world première of those fur coats? After the novelty of trying them on had abated somewhat, we began to feel a slight uneasiness as to just how we'd break the news of their purchase to Mother. She was apt to grow severe over any undue extravagance, particularly abroad, where, according to her standards, it was all right to spend money on culture, but to squander it on clothes came under the heading of original sin. However, we felt confident that our entrance into the restaurant would forestall any objections. We'd be so breathtakingly beautiful to behold, she'd be rendered speechless. Well, she was.

We dressed with care, arraying ourselves in our best evening dresses. Anything less fine would hardly have been worthy of the occasion. It so happened that we also dressed exactly alike because our best evening get-up were bridesmaid's dresses we had worn at a friend's wedding, and so expensive we hadn't been able to buy any others since. Then, wrapping the great bell-shaped cloaks about us, we set forth from the lodging-house feeling like personifications of Queen Marie of Roumania and Peggy

---

9. **dovecote**\ˈdŭv·kōt\ small house for pigeons.
10. **d'Artagnan,** a Gascon adventurer and hero of Alexandre Dumas' *The Three Musketeers.*
11. **Soho**\sō ˈhō\ a district in London famed for its foreign restaurants.

Hopkins Joyce.[12] We had to walk a block or two before we found a taxi. It was one of those evenings characteristic of the London season, when one goes out to dinner in broad daylight. People stared at us somewhat but we didn't mind. We thought it was because we looked so dazzling. We may have looked dazzling, but we also looked like a pair of igloos out for a stroll. We spied a taxi, hailed it and gave with a good deal of grandeur the address of the Trocadero. As we clambered in I rather received the impression that the driver said, "Right you are, Snowball," but decided I must be mistaken. Fearful of harming our new and spotless purchases by sitting on them, we pulled them out from under us, and held them up gingerly about our midriffs and shoulders. The things rose in the breeze and billowed out, filling all available space. We were pretty well snowed under. The taxi came to a stop before the Trocadero, and laboriously we began working our way out of the fur clouds. Getting out of a taxi is not one of life's nimbler activities under the easiest of conditions, but to get out when weighted down by a white fur pup-tent was a feat indeed. We emerged in jack-knife posture, managed to make the pavement on our feet and not our foreheads, shook ourselves out and paid the cabman, who was grinning broadly in what we never doubted was admiration. Then I caught sight of Father. He was waiting for us outside the restaurant. But for some curious reason he was leaning against the wall, and for an even more curious reason tears were running down his face. He looked to be hysterical. I couldn't imagine what was the matter. Emily, who didn't know him so well, thought that he must be in the throes of some unfathomable mood inherent in a great actor, and that whatever might be causing it, the radiant vision of the two of us would bring him out of it pretty quick. We smiled at him and waved graciously the way we thought Mary Garden[13] might. At this he covered his face with a handkerchief and shook as if he were in the throes of some sort of malarial chill. We looked at one another with blank amazement and Emily hissed,

"What's making him take on so?" It never remotely entered our vaguest suspicions that we might have something to do with it. We approached him shyly and were about to inquire softly if there were anything we might do, when he looked out from behind the handkerchief and we realized his tears were due to wild, uncontrollable laughter.

"Oh, my God!" he managed to choke forth. "How could you get so *many* rabbits!" We couldn't believe our ears. "And what," he went on, "in the name of dear, sweet, gentle heaven was that *can-can mouvement* you were doing in the taxi with your skirts up over your heads?"

I was deeply offended and said *"Father!"* in a crushing tone, but he continued being anything but crushed. He led the way into the restaurant and we followed, still trying to look like Mary Garden, but with an uncomfortable hunch that maybe what we most closely resembled were *Flopsey* and *Mopsey* in *Peter Rabbit*. Mother had seen our entrance and by the time we reached the table she was in a condition of hysteria similar to Father's. We were hurt and quite bewildered. The only consoling thing was the fact that Mother was too weak to become cross over my extravagance, and she did agree that it was a *great deal* of fur for $30.00.

They treated us to champagne that evening, which did a lot to soothe our wounded pride. And as a further aid to reëstablishing our self-confidence, Father ordered some especially old Courvoisier. Emily at the sight of the large brandy glass said, "Mercy! I won't be able to drink that big a glassful!" She could never forget her great-grandmother Curry, who shortly after the Civil War had pulled off a spectacular buggy-ride in record time to open the first prohibition campaign in Ohio. She was relieved but also somewhat disappointed when the wine captain poured out a dab which barely covered

12. **Queen Marie of Roumania,** Marie Alexandra Victoria (1875–1938), who showed great courage when Roumania fell to the Germans. **Peggy Hopkins Joyce,** a movie star.
13. **Mary Garden,** operatic soprano.

the bottom. That dab had its effect, however, for after sipping and sniffing it for a time she said she guessed she'd had enough because the room was starting to go round. Father said that was all right, when it came time for us to go home all she'd have to do would be to go across to Trafalgar Square, sit on one of the lions and wait till Tavistock Square came round.

I
DISTANCE LENDS ENCHANTMENT

It is a common experience to discover that painful happenings often become humorous with the passage of time. Part of the reason for this is that we are able to see the experience more objectively; the emotions that gripped us at the time become only memories. Misses Skinner and Kimbrough are experts at laughing at themselves but most of the laughter comes in retrospect, as they look back on their trip to London. Time and the ability to laugh at themselves have softened the original pain and embarrassment.

Think back through the selection and note those incidents which would be painful experiences for you. In each case how have Misses Skinner and Kimbrough played down the unpleasantness?

II
IMPLICATIONS

Discuss the following statements in the light of your own experience and of the selection.

1. A person thinks of himself in a different light from that in which others see him.

2. Because there are so many differences between our culture and the European, Americans abroad for the first time almost invariably make a humorous spectacle of themselves.

3. People in general tend to laugh at things that are strange to them (like Cockney accents), even though the things themselves aren't the least bit funny to those who are familiar with them.

4. It is common for people to become indignant when they have misunderstood something.

5. One of the greatest foibles of young Americans is that they try to appear sophisticated and

independent when they are in fact innocent and dependent.

6. Most of the girls' troubles and much of the humor stem from the fact that they act impulsively rather than thinking things through.

III
TECHNIQUES
Comedy: Sympathy and Detachment

Cultural conditioning plays an important part in our reaction to the girls. They are Americans in a foreign country. The reader is also American. How does this condition your sympathies? Try to imagine that you are an English student reading this selection. What subtle changes might you experience in your reactions?

IV
WORDS

Determine as much meaning as possible from the context clues. Discuss which clues help and which do not. Be sure to look up *plumb*. How do you think it attracted the idiomatic meaning in the phrase "plumb tuckered out"? Look up *droll*. Did the context mislead you?

1. He looked *plumb* tuckered out and as *gant* as a gutted snowbird.

2. . . . as a spotlight moves from one place to another, she *averts* her gaze and slowly turns.

3. She swallows, but her throat is *constricted*. . . .

4. . . . she was undecided about how to *broach* the subject.

5. He *gesticulated* with hands. . . .

6. . . . I decide on a little kraut, or maybe I want some *condiments* or relish.

7. . . . other things, which can all be bought in Europe but which for some *droll* reason one always takes along.

8. . . . she assured us that the landlady was fully *cognizant* of our arrival. . . .

9. . . . the Bryn Mawr scholar's text books . . . were so *erudite* we couldn't understand even their titles. . . .

10. After the novelty of trying them on had *abated* somewhat, we began to feel a slight uneasiness. . . .

Light Verse

◆ Of all Americans writing light verse full-time,
Ogden Nash is probably the best known. His poems have appeared
in numerous magazines ranging widely in appeal,
from *The New Yorker* and *Saturday Review* to *Good Housekeeping*
and *This Week*. Many of his poems are purely for amusement,
but the following selection has a sharp edge.

The Politician

Behold the politician.
Self-preservation is his ambition.
He thrives in the D. of C.,[1]
Where he was sent by you and me.

Whether elected or appointed   5
He considers himself the Lord's anointed,
And indeed the ointment lingers on him
So thick you can't get your fingers on him.

He has developed a sixth sense
About living at the public expense,   10
Because in private competition
He would encounter malnutrition.

He has many profitable hobbies
Not the least of which is lobbies.
He would not sell his grandmother for a quarter   15
If he suspected the presence of a reporter.

He gains votes ever and anew
By taking money from everybody and giving it to a few,
While explaining that every penny
Was extracted from the few to be given to the many.   20

---

1. **D. of C.**, District of Columbia.

Some politicians are Republican, some Democratic,
And their feud is dramatic,
But except for the name
They are identically the same.

When a politician talks the foolishest,   25
And obstructs everything the mulishest,
And bellows the loudest,
Why his constituents are the proudest.

Wherever decent intelligent people get together
They talk about politicians as about bad weather,   30
But they are always too decent to go into politics themselves
    and too intelligent even to go to the polls,
So I hope the kind of politicians they get will have no
    mercy on their pocketbooks or souls.

OGDEN NASH

Before reading this selection, be sure to read
Robert Frost's "Fire and Ice," on page 728. In "Frostbite,"
Conrad Aiken has a little fun at the expense of a fellow poet,
but Mr. Aiken's reputation as poet and short-story writer
rests on far more serious work. He is widely regarded
as one of America's greatest living authors.

Frostbite

Some say the world will end by Fire
And some by Frost
    By verse of ice, or vice of verser,
    (God only knows which were the worser!)
But, anyway, the world well lost.

CONRAD AIKEN

---

e. e. cummings is another major modern poet
who was not primarily known as a writer of light verse.
He did, however, write some light verse and a large amount
of what might be called "borderline" poetry.
The unorthodox typography of "old age sticks" is characteristic
of his style; see if it offers you any clues
as to the best way to read the poem.

old age sticks

old age sticks
up Keep
Off
signs)&

youth yanks them   5
down(old
age
cries No

Tres)&(pas)
youth laughs   10
(sing
old age

scolds Forbid
den Stop
Must   15
n't Don't

&) youth goes
right on
gr
owing old   20

E. E. CUMMINGS

From *95 Poems*, copyright,
1953, by E. E. Cummings.
Reprinted by permission of
Harcourt, Brace & World, Inc.

◆ Richard Armour has expressed his comic imagination
in both verse and prose, prolifically. To appreciate his poem,
"Accessories to the Fact," perhaps you need only be acquainted
with the female of the species, but you might also profit
by recalling the nursery tale, "The House That Jack Built,"
and the fact that "jack"—with the small "j"—is not only
a playing card and something useful in fixing flats
but is also slang for "money."

Accessories to the Fact

This is the bracelet that went with the ring
That went with the costume-jewelry thing
That went with the purse that went with the gloves
That went with the coat she so dearly loves
That went with the stole of mutation mink[1]   5
That went with the hat that would drive you to drink
That went with the hose that went with the shoes
That went with the buckle she couldn't refuse
That went with the buttons that went with the belt
That went with the cluster of flowers of felt   10
That went with the perfume that went with the blouse
That went with the sweet little suit for my spouse
   That my jack bought.

RICHARD ARMOUR

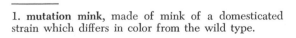

----

1. **mutation mink**, made of mink of a domesticated
strain which differs in color from the wild type.

♦ David McCord has published more than twenty books,
including some verse for children and a well-known anthology
of light verse. He has been highly praised by many of his fellow poets,
notably Louis Untermeyer, who once said of him: "I don't know
any living writer of verse who so lightly combines simplicity
and subtlety, ingenuity and ingenuousness."

Daedalus,[1] Stay Away from My Transom!

The age of flight, the age of flight:
They say it hasn't come yet quite.
The atom somehow got between,
And something else may intervene
Before a man can wear his wings   5
The way he wears his socks and things,
Or jet-propel himself from here
To points beyond the stratosphere.
But still, the experts all agree,
The age of flight is what we'll see;   10
It's what we'll get, it's what we'll be.
    All right, all right:
    If flight means flee—
    That's me.

What is there in this age of flight   15
To make me hug the earth so tight?
The age of flint, the age of stone
Developed from the age of bone,
And in the prehistoric dawn
Our fathers met them axehead on.   20
The age of iron, brass, and tin
And other ages trickled in.
The age of coal, the age of steam
Were mutual, like milk and cream.
The age of coal and steam, alas,   25
Expanded to an age of gas;
And then, as if that wouldn't do,
The age of Edison came through.
So now, with this atomic age,
You think we've turned the final page?   30
Not yet, my friend: the ceiling height
Is coming with the age of flight.

I think about it day and night
    All right, all right,
    For flight means flee   35
    To me.

I do not want a pair of wings
And supersonic underthings.
I do not care to cross the street
Retracting, as I fly, my feet.   40
I do not want O'Malley's[2] gift;
I don't desire that kind of lift.
I do not long for rocket ships
And outer interstellar trips.
I'm glad they have canals on Mars: 45
I'm sorry that the moon has scars.
It's comforting to think that space
May hide the meistermaster[3] race
On some far planet, and contrast
My foolish future with their past.   50
The age of flight is food for thought:
I haven't eaten as I ought.
Out on a limb, this earthbound tree
Just suits me to a Model T—
It's plenty high enough for me   55
    All right, all right.
    And flightless me
    I'll be.

DAVID McCORD

----

1. **Daedalus**\ˈdĕ·də·ləs\ Athenian architect who built
the Cretan Labyrinth; later he escaped from Crete by
use of artificial wings.
2. **O'Malley's gift**, O'Malley, once a famous comic strip
character, was a little man who was invisible to all but
special friends. He had the gift of flight.
3. **meister**\ˈmai·stĕr\ master.

Armored Division

I stopped my walk
Just to watch a hawk.
Then I turned from speed
To an airborne seed,
And I saw for man   5
How it all began.

For a chute of silk
Is the milkweed's milk
And the maple's crop
Is a feathered prop.   10
In the pitcher plant's lap
There's a booby trap.

The sensitive plant
(May it long enchant)
Was the first to use   15
A proximity fuse.
The snapdragon's gun
Is a hair-trigger one.

The black bats fly
In a radar sky,   20
A bee to thistle
Is a guided missile,
And a squid can get
Where it wants by jet.

In the katydid's ode   25
There's a crude Morse code,
And the submerged loon
Has the schnorkel's boon . . .

Ain't Nature the queer
Old engineer?   30

DAVID MCCORD

Phyllis McGinley has been writing first-rate light verse—
with some serious poems mixed in—for better than thirty years.
Though she described herself in one of her poems as "sunk in content,"
we get one of her discontented views in the following poem.

Don't Shake the Bottle, Shake Your Mother-in-Law

When I was young and full of rhymes
  And all my days were salady,[1]
Almost I could enjoy the times
  I caught some current malady.
Then, cheerful, knocked upon my door   5
  The jocular[2] physician,
With tonics and with comfort for
  My innocent condition.
Then friends would fetch me flowers
  And nurses rub my back,   10
And I could talk for hours
  Concerning my attack.
But now, when vapors[3] dog me,
  What solace do I find?
My cronies can't endure me.   15
The doctors scorn to cure me,
And, though I ail, assure me
  It's all a state of mind.

It's psychosomatic,[4] now, psychosomatic.
Whatever you suffer is psychosomatic.   20
Your liver's a-quiver? You're feeling infirm?
Dispose of the notion you harbor a germ.
Angina,
  Arthritis,
    Abdominal pain—   25
They're nothing but symptoms of marital strain.

---

1. **salady,** youthful and inexperienced.
2. **jocular**\ˈjŏk·yū·lər\ humorous, full of fun.
3. **vapors,** depressed spirits.
4. **psychosomatic**\ˈsī·kō·sō ˈmă·tĭk\ physical disorder caused or aggravated by emotional processes.

They're nothing but proof that your love life is minus.
The ego is aching
Instead of the sinus.
So face up and brace up and stifle that sneeze.   30
It's psychosomatic. And ten dollars, please.

There was a time that I recall,
    If one grew pale or thinnish,
The pundits[5] loved to lay it all
    On foods unvitaminish,   35
Or else, dogmatic, would maintain
    Infection somewhere acted.
And when they'd shorn the tonsils twain,
    They pulled the tooth impacted.
But now that orgies dental   40
    Have made a modish halt,
Your ills today are mental
    And likely all your fault.
Now specialists inform you,
    While knitting of their brows,   45
Your pain, though sharp and shooting,
Is caused, beyond disputing,
Because you hate commuting
    Or can't abide your spouse.

It's psychosomatic, now, psychosomatic.   50
You fell down the stairway? It's psychosomatic.
That sprain of the ankle while waxing the floors—
You did it on purpose to get out of chores.
Nephritis,[6]
    Neuritis,[7]   55
        A case of the ague?[8]
You're just giving in to frustrations that plague you.
You long to be coddled, beloved, acclaimed,
So you caught the sniffles.
And aren't you ashamed!   60
And maybe they're right. But I sob through my wheezes,
"They've taken the fun out of having diseases."

PHYLLIS MC GINLEY

---

5. **pundits,** persons of great learning.
6. **Nephritis**\nĕ ᐟfrī·tĭs\ disease of the kidneys.
7. **Neuritis**\nū ᐟrī·tĭs\ inflammation of the nerves.
8. **ague**\ᐟā·gū\fever marked by chills.

In laying bare the foolishness and foibles of the twentieth
century through a comic imagination, Dorothy Parker has few rivals in verse
or in prose. Indeed, she is master of the pithy epigram, as the following
sardonic resume attests.

Résumé

Razors pain you;
Rivers are damp;
Acids stain you;
And drugs cause cramp.
Guns aren't lawful;
Nooses give;
Gas smells awful;
You might as well live.

DOROTHY PARKER

Some light verse is like fencing—one makes a quick thrust
and then withdraws. Brevity is essential in such poems, as you will note
in the following thrust by Countée Cullen.

For a Mouthy Woman

God and the devil still are wrangling
Which should have her, which repel;
God wants no discord in his heaven;
Satan has enough in hell.

COUNTÉE CULLEN

LIGHT VERSE—WHAT IS IT?

"Light verse" is one of those terms that many people know the meaning of and no one can define. Probably the best way to come to understand it is to read a good deal more of the work of poets like Nash, McCord, Armour, and McGinley.

One of the commonest misconceptions about light verse is that writers of light verse have rather simple and friendly intentions. Such intentions do characterize some light verse. But to say that all light verse is simple and friendly is to ignore the serious and critical side of many light poets, including Nash and McGinley. Miss McGinley's poem on psychosomatic illnesses, for example, certainly has a partly serious and critical intention, for all its lightness of tone. And Nash's poem on the politician has a double-edged seriousness: It is directed against both the politician who is irresponsible and, even more so, against his politically irresponsible constituents.

We are not going to find a rigorous definition of light verse, but we can say that such poetry is characterized by *a light or playful manner of expression* and that the poet commonly criticizes some human failing. The criticism itself may be relatively strong, as in "The Politician," or relatively weak, as in "Accessories to the Fact."

II
IMPLICATIONS

Explain what the poet is suggesting about life and the world in the following quotations.

1. . . . they [decent and intelligent people] are always too decent to go into politics themselves and too intelligent even to go to the polls.

2. &) youth goes
   right on
   gr
   owing old

3. . . . this earthbound tree
   Just suits me to a Model T—
   It's plenty high enough for me

4. Ain't Nature the queer
   Old engineer?

5. Whatever you suffer is psychosomatic.

6. This is the bracelet that went with the ring
   . . .
   That my jack bought.

7. You might as well live.

8. God wants no discord in his heaven;
   Satan has enough in hell.

III
TECHNIQUES

Comedy

John Erskine, a well-known writer and educator, once distinguished between humor, wit, and fun. He proposed that a literary work was "funny" if it was the occasion of "harmless laughter" and if it neither called for intelligence nor stimulated sympathy. A work was "witty" if it involved intelligence and had at least a mildly hard edge to it. Finally, he said that a work was "humorous" if it looked sympathetically into common human weaknesses.

Accepting this three-part division of comedy, how would you classify each of the poems in this section? If you can justify doing so, you may place a given poem into more than one category.

In the Comic Style

A good deal of the humorous effect of these poems comes from the use of rhythm and rhyme and word choice in unexpected ways.

1. Find several examples (from one or several poems) of unexpected uses of rhythm and rhyme used to create a humorous effect.

2. Writers of light verse enjoy "playing" with words. Make a brief catalog of the ways in which the foregoing poets play with words.

3. The surprise ending—comparable to the "punch line" in spoken humor—occurs in much light verse. How many such endings do you note in these selections?

In the comic tradition perhaps no subject has been more frequently written about than the so-called battle between the sexes. It is a battle that may occur at any time or place, a war without rules, a struggle in which male logic and female emotion vie for total victory. Max Shulman portrays one such battle comically in the following selection from *The Many Loves of Dobie Gillis*.

Love Is a Fallacy

MAX SHULMAN

Cool was I and logical. Keen, calculating, perspicacious, acute and astute—I was all of these. My brain was as powerful as a dynamo, as precise as a chemist's scales, as penetrating as a scalpel. And—think of it!—I was only eighteen.

It is not often that one so young has such a giant intellect. Take, for example, Petey Bellows, my roommate at the university. Same age, same background, but dumb as an ox. A nice enough fellow, you understand, but nothing upstairs. Emotional type. Unstable. Impressionable. Worst of all, a faddist. Fads, I submit, are the very negation of reason. To be swept up in every new craze that comes along, to surrender yourself to idiocy just because everybody else is doing it—this, to me, is the acme of mindlessness. Not, however, to Petey.

One afternoon I found Petey lying on his bed with an expression of such distress on his face that I immediately diagnosed appendicitis. "Don't move," I said. "Don't take a laxative. I'll get a doctor."

"Raccoon," he mumbled thickly.

"Raccoon?" I said, pausing in my flight.

"I want a raccoon coat," he wailed.

I perceived that his trouble was not physical, but mental. "Why do you want a raccoon coat?"

"I should have known it," he cried, pounding his temples. "I should have known they'd come back when the Charleston came back. Like a fool I spent all my money for textbooks, and now I can't get a raccoon coat."

"Can you mean," I said incredulously, "that people are actually wearing raccoon coats again?"

"All the Big Men on Campus are wearing them. Where've you been?"

"In the library," I said, naming a place not frequented by Big Men on Campus.

He leaped from the bed and paced the room. "I've got to have a raccoon coat," he said passionately. "I've got to!"

"Petey, why? Look at it rationally. Raccoon coats are unsanitary. They shed. They smell bad. They weigh too much. They're unsightly. They——"

"You don't understand," he interrupted impatiently. "It's the thing to do. Don't you want to be in the swim?"

"No," I said truthfully.

"Well, I do," he declared. "I'd give anything for a raccoon coat. Anything!"

My brain, that precision instrument, slipped into high gear. "Anything?" I asked, looking at him narrowly.

"Anything," he affirmed in ringing tones.

I stroked my chin thoughtfully. It so happened that I knew where to get my hands on a raccoon coat. My father had had one in his undergraduate days; it lay now in a trunk in the attic back home. It also happened that Petey had something I wanted. He didn't *have* it exactly, but at least he had first rights on it. I refer to his girl, Polly Espy.

I had long coveted Polly Espy. Let me emphasize that my desire for this young woman was not emotional in nature. She was, to be sure, a girl who excited the emotions, but I was not one to let my heart rule my head. I wanted Polly for a shrewdly calculated, entirely cerebral reason.

I was a freshman in law school. In a few years I would be out in practice. I was well aware of the importance of the right kind of wife in furthering a lawyer's career. The successful lawyers I had observed were, almost without exception, married to beautiful, gracious, intelligent women. With one omission, Polly fitted these specifications perfectly.

Beautiful she was. She was not yet of pin-up proportions, but I felt sure that time would supply the lack. She already had the makings.

Gracious she was. By gracious I mean full of graces. She had an erectness of carriage, an ease of bearing, a poise that clearly indicated the best of breeding. At table her manners were exquisite. I had seen her at the Kozy Kampus Korner eating the specialty of the house—a sandwich that contained scraps of pot roast, gravy, chopped nuts, and a dipper of sauerkraut —without even getting her fingers moist.

Intelligent she was not. In fact, she veered in the opposite direction. But I believed that under my guidance she would smarten up. At any rate, it was worth a try. It is, after all, easier to make a beautiful dumb girl smart than to make an ugly smart girl beautiful.

"Petey," I said, "are you in love with Polly Espy?"

"I think she's a keen kid," he replied, "but I don't know if you'd call it love. Why?"

"Do you," I asked, "have any kind of formal arrangement with her? I mean are you going steady or anything like that?"

"No. We see each other quite a bit, but we both have other dates. Why?"

"Is there," I asked, "any other man for whom she has a particular fondness?"

"Not that I know of. Why?"

I nodded with satisfaction. "In other words, if you were out of the picture, the field would be open. Is that right?"

"I guess so. What are you getting at?"

"Nothing, nothing," I said innocently, and took my suitcase out of the closet.

"Where you going?" asked Petey.

"Home for the week end," I threw a few things into the bag.

"Listen," he said, clutching my arm eagerly, "while you're home, you couldn't get some money from your old man, could you, and lend it to me so I can buy a raccoon coat?"

"I may do better than that," I said with a mysterious wink and closed my bag and left.

"Look," I said to Petey when I got back Monday morning. I threw open the suitcase and revealed the huge, hairy, gamy object that my father had worn in his Stutz Bearcat in 1925.

"Holy Toledo!" said Petey reverently. He plunged his hands into the raccoon coat and then his face. "Holy Toledo!" he repeated fifteen or twenty times.

"Would you like it?" I asked.

"Oh yes!" he cried, clutching the greasy pelt to him. Then a canny look came into his eyes. "What do you want for it?"

"Your girl," I said, mincing no words.

"Polly?" he said in a horrified whisper. "You want Polly?"

"That's right."

He flung the coat from him. "Never," he said stoutly.

I shrugged. "Okay. If you don't want to be in the swim, I guess it's your business."

I sat down in a chair and pretended to read a book, but out of the corner of my eye I kept watching Petey. He was a torn man. First he looked at the coat with the expression of a waif at a bakery window. Then he turned away and set his jaw resolutely. Then he looked back at the coat, with even more longing in his face. Then he turned away, but with not so much resolution this time. Back and forth his head swiveled, desire waxing, resolution waning. Finally he didn't turn away at all; he just stood and stared with mad lust at the coat.

"It isn't as though I was in love with Polly," he said thickly. "Or going steady or anything like that."

"That's right," I murmured.

"What's Polly to me, or me to Polly?"

"Not a thing," said I.

"It's just been a casual kick—just a few laughs, that's all."

"Try on the coat," said I.

He complied. The coat bunched high over his ears and dropped all the way down to his shoe tops. He looked like a mound of dead raccoons. "Fits fine," he said happily.

I rose from my chair. "Is it a deal?" I asked, extending my hand.

He swallowed. "It's a deal," he said and shook my hand.

I had my first date with Polly the following evening. This was in the nature of a survey; I wanted to find out just how much work I had to do to get her mind up to the standard I required. I took her first to dinner. "Gee, that was a delish dinner," she said as we left the restaurant. Then I took her to a movie. "Gee, that was a marvy movie," she said as we left the theater. And then I took her home. "Gee, I had a sensaysh time," she said as she bade me good night.

I went back to my room with a heavy heart. I had gravely underestimated the size of my task. This girl's lack of information was terrifying. Nor would it be enough merely to supply her with information. First she had to be taught to *think*. This loomed as a project of no small dimensions, and at first I was tempted to give her back to Petey. But then I got to thinking about her abundant physical charms and about the way she entered a room and the way she handled a knife and fork, and I decided to make an effort.

I went about it, as in all things, systematically. I gave her a course in logic. It happened that I, as a law student, was taking a course in logic myself, so I had all the facts at my finger tips. "Polly," I said to her when I picked her up on our next date, "tonight we are going over to the Knoll and talk."

"Oo, terrif," she replied. One thing I will say for this girl: you would go far to find another so agreeable.

We went to the Knoll, the campus trysting place, and we sat down under an old oak, and she looked at me expectantly. "What are we going to talk about?" she asked.

"Logic."

She thought this over for a minute and decided she liked it. "Magnif," she said.

"Logic," I said, clearing my throat, "is the science of thinking. Before we can think correctly, we must first learn to recognize the common fallacies of logic. These we will take up tonight."

"Wow-dow!" she cried, clapping her hands delightedly.

I winced, but went bravely on. "First let us examine the fallacy called Dicto Simpliciter."

"By all means," she urged, batting her lashes eagerly.

"Dicto Simpliciter means an argument based on an unqualified generalization. For example: Exercise is good. Therefore everybody should exercise."

"I agree," said Polly earnestly. "I mean exercise is wonderful. I mean it builds the body and everything."

"Polly," I said gently, "the argument is a fallacy. *Exercise is good* is an unqualified generalization. For instance, if you have heart disease, exercise is bad, not good. Many people are ordered by their doctors *not* to exercise. You must *qualify* the generalization. You must say exercise is *usually* good, or exercise is good *for most people*. Otherwise you have committed a Dicto Simpliciter. Do you see?"

"No," she confessed. "But this is marvy. Do more! Do more!"

"It will be better if you stop tugging at my sleeve," I told her, and when she desisted, I continued. "Next we take up a fallacy called Hasty Generalization. Listen carefully: You can't speak French. I can't speak French. Petey

Bellows can't speak French. I must therefore conclude that nobody at the University of Minnesota can speak French."

"Really?" said Polly, amazed. "*Nobody?*"

I hid my exasperation. "Polly, it's a fallacy. The generalization is reached too hastily. There are too few instances to support such a conclusion."

"Know any more fallacies?" she asked breathlessly. "This is more fun than dancing even."

I fought off a wave of despair. I was getting nowhere with this girl, absolutely nowhere. Still, I am nothing if not persistent. I continued. "Next comes Post Hoc.[1] Listen to this: Let's not take Bill on our picnic. Every time we take him out with us, it rains."

"I know somebody just like that," she exclaimed. "A girl back home—Eula Becker, her name is. It never fails. Every single time we take her on a picnic——"

"Polly," I said sharply, "it's a fallacy. Eula Becker doesn't *cause* the rain. She has no connection with the rain. You are guilty of Post Hoc if you blame Eula Becker."

"I'll never do it again," she promised contritely. "Are you mad at me?"

I sighed. "No, Polly, I'm not mad."

"Then tell me some more fallacies."

"All right. Let's try Contradictory Premises."

"Yes, let's," she chirped, blinking her eyes happily.

I frowned, but plunged ahead. "Here's an example of Contradictory Premises: If God can do anything, can He make a stone so heavy that He won't be able to lift it?"

"Of course," she replied promptly.

"But if He can do anything, He can lift the stone," I pointed out.

"Yeah," she said thoughtfully. "Well, then I guess He can't make the stone."

"But He can do anything," I reminded her.

She scratched her pretty, empty head. "I'm all confused," she admitted.

"Of course you are. Because when the premises of an argument contradict each other, there can be no argument. If there is an irresistible force, there can be no immovable object. If

there is an immovable object, there can be no irresistible force. Get it?"

"Tell me some more of this keen stuff," she said eagerly.

I consulted my watch. "I think we'd better call it a night. I'll take you home now, and you go over all the things you've learned. We'll have another session tomorrow night."

I deposited her at the girls' dormitory, where she assured me that she had had a perfectly terrif evening, and I went glumly home to my room. Petey lay snoring in his bed, the raccoon coat huddled like a great hairy beast at his feet. For a moment I considered waking him and telling him that he could have his girl back. It seemed clear that my project was doomed to failure. The girl simply had a logic-proof head.

But then I reconsidered. I had wasted one evening; I might as well waste another. Who knew? Maybe somewhere in the extinct crater of her mind a few embers still smoldered. Maybe somehow I could fan them into flame. Admittedly it was not a prospect fraught with hope, but I decided to give it one more try.

Seated under the oak the next evening I said, "Our first fallacy tonight is called Ad Misericordiam."[2]

She quivered with delight.

"Listen closely," I said. "A man applies for a job. When the boss asks him what his qualifications are, he replies that he has a wife and six children at home, the wife is a helpless cripple, the children have nothing to eat, no clothes to wear, no shoes on their feet, there are no beds in the house, no coal in the cellar, and winter is coming."

A tear rolled down each of Polly's pink cheeks. "Oh, this is awful, awful," she sobbed.

"Yes, it's awful," I agreed, "but it's no argument. The man never answered the boss's question about his qualifications. Instead he appealed to the boss's sympathy. He committed the fallacy of Ad Misericordiam. Do you understand?"

---

1. **Post Hoc,** after this (therefore, on account of this).
2. **Ad Misericordiam**\ăd 'mĭ·sə ⁺rĭ·kɔr·dĭ·əm\ to pity.

"Have you got a handkerchief?" she blubbered.

I handed her a handkerchief and tried to keep from screaming while she wiped her eyes. "Next," I said in a carefully controlled tone, "we will discuss False Analogy. Here is an example: Students should be allowed to look at their textbooks during examinations. After all, surgeons have X rays to guide them during an operation, lawyers have briefs to guide them during a trial, carpenters have blueprints to guide them when they are building a house. Why, then, shouldn't students be allowed to look at their textbooks during an examination?"

"There now," she said enthusiastically, "is the most marvy idea I've heard in years."

"Polly," I said testily, "the argument is all wrong. Doctors, lawyers, and carpenters aren't taking a test to see how much they have learned, but students are. The situations are altogether different, and you can't make an analogy between them."

"I still think it's a good idea," said Polly.

"Nuts," I muttered. Doggedly I pressed on. "Next we'll try Hypothesis Contrary to Fact."

"Sounds yummy," was Polly's reaction.

"Listen: If Madame Curie had not happened to leave a photographic plate in a drawer with a chunk of pitchblende, the world today would not know about radium."

"True, true," said Polly, nodding her head. "Did you see the movie? Oh, it just knocked me out. That Walter Pidgeon is so dreamy. I mean he fractures me."

"If you can forget Mr. Pidgeon for a moment," I said coldly, "I would like to point out that the statement is a fallacy. Maybe Madame Curie would have discovered radium at some later date. Maybe somebody else would have discovered it. Maybe any number of things would have happened. You can't start with a hypothesis that is not true and then draw any supportable conclusions from it."

"They ought to put Walter Pidgeon in more pictures," said Polly. "I hardly ever see him any more."

One more chance, I decided. But just one more. There is a limit to what flesh and blood can bear. "The next fallacy is called Poisoning the Well."

"How cute!" she gurgled.

"Two men are having a debate. The first one gets up and says, 'My opponent is a notorious liar. You can't believe a word that he is going to say.' . . . Now, Polly, think. Think hard. What's wrong?"

I watched her closely as she knit her creamy brow in concentration. Suddenly a glimmer of intelligence—the first I had seen—came into her eyes. "It's not fair," she said with indignation. "It's not a bit fair. What chance has the second man got if the first man calls him a liar before he even begins talking?"

"Right!" I cried exultantly. "One hundred per cent right. It's not fair. The first man has *poisoned the well* before anybody could drink from it. He has hamstrung his opponent before he could even start. . . . Polly, I'm proud of you."

"Pshaw," she murmured, blushing with pleasure.

"You see, my dear, these things aren't so hard. All you have to do is concentrate. Think—examine—evaluate. Come now, let's review everything we have learned."

"Fire away," she said with an airy wave of her hand.

Heartened by the knowledge that Polly was not altogether a cretin, I began a long, patient review of all I had told her. Over and over and over again I cited instances, pointed out flaws, kept hammering away without letup. It was like digging a tunnel. At first everything was work, sweat, and darkness. I had no idea when I would reach the light, or even *if* I would. But I persisted. I pounded and clawed and scraped, and finally I was rewarded. I saw a chink of light. And then the chink got bigger and the sun came pouring in and all was bright.

Five grueling nights this took, but it was worth it. I had made a logician out of Polly; I had taught her to think. My job was done. She was worthy of me at last. She was a fit wife for me, a proper hostess for my many mansions, a suitable mother for my well-heeled children.

It must not be thought that I was without love for this girl. Quite the contrary. Just as Pygmalion[3] loved the perfect woman he had fashioned, so I loved mine. I decided to acquaint her with my feelings at our very next meeting. The time had come to change our relationship from academic to romantic.

"Polly," I said when next we sat beneath our oak, "tonight we will not discuss fallacies."

"Aw, gee," she said, disappointed.

"My dear," I said, favoring her with a smile, "we have now spent five evenings together. We have gotten along splendidly. It is clear that we are well matched."

"Hasty Generalization," said Polly brightly.

"I beg your pardon," said I.

"Hasty Generalization," she repeated. "How can you say that we are well matched on the basis of only five dates?"

I chuckled with amusement. The dear child had learned her lessons well. "My dear," I said, patting her hand in a tolerant manner, "five dates is plenty. After all, you don't have to eat a whole cake to know that it's good."

"False Analogy," said Polly promptly. "I'm not a cake. I'm a girl."

I chuckled with somewhat less amusement. The dear child had learned her lessons perhaps too well. I decided to change tactics. Obviously the best approach was a simple, strong, direct declaration of love. I paused for a moment while my massive brain chose the proper words. Then I began:

"Polly, I love you. You are the whole world to me, and the moon and the stars and the constellations of outer space. Please, my darling, say that you will go steady with me, for if you will not, life will be meaningless. I will languish. I will refuse my meals. I will wander the face of the earth, a shambling, hollow-eyed hulk."

There, I thought, folding my arms, that ought to do it.

"Ad Misericordiam," said Polly.

I ground my teeth. I was not Pygmalion; I was Frankenstein, and my monster had me by the throat. Frantically I fought back the tide of panic surging through me. At all costs I had to keep cool.

"Well, Polly," I said, forcing a smile, "you certainly have learned your fallacies."

"You're darn right," she said with a vigorous nod.

"And who taught them to you, Polly?"

"You did."

"That's right. So you do owe me something, don't you, my dear? If I hadn't come along you never would have learned about fallacies."

"Hypothesis Contrary to Fact," she said instantly.

I dashed perspiration from my brow. "Polly," I croaked, "you mustn't take all these things so literally. I mean this is just classroom stuff. You know that the things you learn in school don't have anything to do with life."

"Dicto Simpliciter," she said, wagging her finger at me playfully.

That did it. I leaped to my feet, bellowing like a bull. "Will you or will you not go steady with me?"

"I will not," she replied.

"Why not?" I demanded.

"Because this afternoon I promised Petey Bellows that I would go steady with him."

I reeled back, overcome with the infamy of it. After he promised, after he made a deal, after he shook my hand! "The rat!" I shrieked, kicking up great chunks of turf. "You can't go with him, Polly. He's a liar. He's a cheat. He's a rat."

"Poisoning the Well," said Polly, "and stop shouting. I think shouting must be a fallacy too."

With an immense effort of will, I modulated my voice. "All right," I said. "You're a logician. Let's look at this thing logically. How could you choose Petey Bellows over me? Look at me— a brilliant student, a tremendous intellectual, a man with an assured future. Look at Petey—a knothead, a jitterbug, a guy who'll never know where his next meal is coming from. Can you

---

3. **Pygmalion**\pĭg ▲mā·lĭ·ən\ in Greek legend, a sculptor who fell in love with his statue of a maiden.

give me one logical reason why you should go steady with Petey Bellows?"

"I certainly can," declared Polly. "He's got a raccoon coat."

I
THE ILLOGICAL LOGICIANS

Early in the episode Dobie brags that he is cool and logical—his brain is a "human dynamo." In his initial attempts to educate and win Polly he demonstrates his emotional control and thorough knowledge of logic. In time, he finally teaches her, or so it seems, that human action should be guided by logic: one must act in accord with conclusions based upon valid reasoning and true premises. Indeed, Polly becomes a master logician herself. Ironically, however, both abandon logic the very first time their emotions are aroused. Dobie the logician tries to win Polly with emotional arguments which Polly the logician turns aside easily, coolly, logically, only to reveal that her basic counterargument is emotional, too—she likes Petey's raccoon coat.

II
IMPLICATIONS

Discuss the following statements in the light of the story and your own experience.

1. People should never allow their emotions to guide them; they should always follow the direction of reason.

2. It is hopeless for people to try to be logical; in the main, people always have been and always will be ruled by their emotions.

3. In general, Americans are suspicious of intellectuals.

4. Americans applaud the "dumb blonde" type who overcomes the brainy schemer.

5. The battle of the sexes usually makes for (interesting, dull) reading.

III
TECHNIQUES

Comedy

We have already noted the tendency of humorists to use the surprise or ironic ending. Shulman's piece is comic partly because of the ironic reversal of the roles of the male and the female—the male becoming emotional and the female growing logical. There is, however, still another ironic twist at the very end of the story. Identify this final "twist" and try to tell how it operates to increase amusement.

Sympathy and Detachment

1. One of the reasons why readers do not sympathize strongly with most characters in many comedies is that the characters are often types rather than individuals. In other words, comic characters tend to be "flat" rather than "round." A test for a flat character is that he may be summed up in a very brief statement; a round character is much more complex. Can you sum up the characters of Dobie, Petey, and Polly in a sentence or less? Would you agree or disagree with the notion that flat characters tend to discourage readers from feeling deep sympathy?

2. The reader is probably prepared for Dobie's failure because his desire to change Polly alienates to a degree the reader's sympathy. The reader wants to see how the retribution comes about. How does the ironic ending swing some sympathy back to Dobie?

THE
COMIC
IMAGINATION

The American culture has been rich in humor
from its beginning. American cartoonists
and comic-strip creators have been a kind
of thermometer indicating our health and vitality.
Our humorists have taken us to task
for shortsighted behavior.
Look at the cartoons and comics of the modern nations;
the creations of their comic imagination
hold many clues to understanding the heart
of a people. What is the point
of the humor? How fully can the nation look
at its ridiculous aspects
and still laugh?

An early American, David Claypool Johnson was born about twenty
years after the United States won independence. Much of his humor
was satirical—comic but not very kindly. THE MILITIA MUSTER
caricaturizes some very unmilitary maneuvers.

THE MILITIA MUSTER   *David Claypool Johnson*

While still a very young man,
another American went to war
and came home a famous cartoonist.
All Americans laughed
at the weary dog-faced infantrymen
Mauldin recorded in the
battlefronts of World War II.
But back home they choked a little
on their laughter. It was
the tired soldiers themselves
who howled loudest as the absurdity
of their situation touched them.
A Pulitzer Prize was given
to Mauldin in 1945 for one cartoon
that is now a classic piece
of American humor.
Irony is one of Bill Mauldin's
greatest resources.

MAULDIN CARTOON
Bill Mauldin

*"Joe, yestiddy ya saved my life an' I swore I'd pay ya back.
Here's my last pair of dry socks."*

*". . . and it's gratifying to note that public co-
operation in the test evacuation of this city was
100%. . . . They had traffic hopelessly snarled
within minutes!"*

GRIN AND BEAR IT
George Maurice Lichtenstein

A cartoonist of the ludicrous situations
on the homefront
is George Maurice Lichtenstein—Lichty.
His characters are utterly nutty
in their straight-faced statements.
His target is society and human nature
in its most pointless inadequacy.

319

PROFESSOR BUTTS INVENTS A TYPEWRITER ERASER
Rube Goldberg

Reuben Lucius Goldberg
had actually been an engineer,
and out of his industrial experience
came the motivation
for his zany inventions.
His observations on things mechanical
convulsed millions of Americans,
even when they were deeply committed
to a mechanically run society.
This strip is "Another nightmare
for the Patent Office, . . . an attempt to
make life easier for the working girl."

The TOONERVILLE FOLKS is the third oldest comic
strip in America. With MUTT AND JEFF
and THE KATZENJAMMER KIDS it ran
for over fifty years, drawn
by its originator, Fontaine Fox. Here is a whole world
of comic individuals that two generations
of Americans came to know and recognize
for their human accuracy.

THE TOONERVILLE TROLLEY *Fontaine Fox*

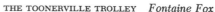

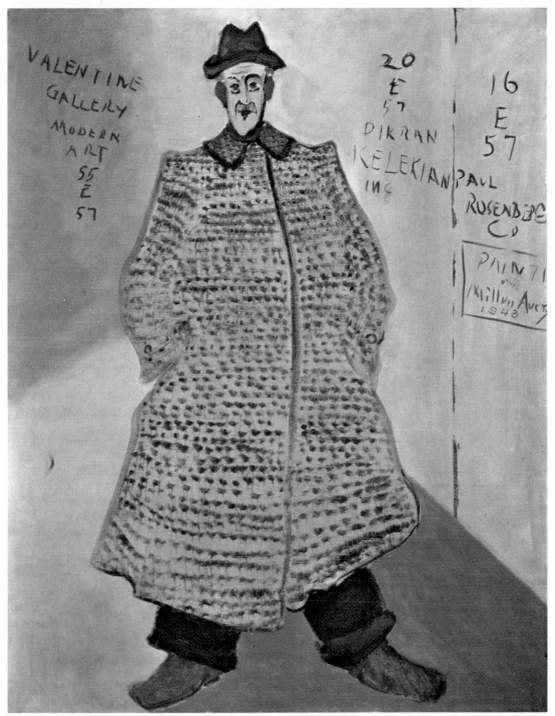

AVERY ON 57TH STREET
Milton Avery

The self-portrait of the painter Milton Avery
displays a biting self-concept.
How many elements of the painting show distortion?
What do you think he is saying about himself?

321

In the same playful vein as AVERY ON 57TH STREET
is Johnson's SOUND ASLEEP AND WIDE AWAKE.
Sheer slapstick on the surface,
it is possible to read this as a social comment
even more cynical
than THE MILITIA MUSTER.

SOUND ASLEEP AND WIDE AWAKE
David Claypool Johnson

SKIPPY
Percy Crosby

For many years SKIPPY was probably
the most popular comic strip in America.
Marked by a scratchily drawn figure, an ample cap set
at a rakish angle, and always in motion,
Skippy conducted a constant warfare
between himself and society.

No collection of humor could be considered complete
without a piece by Thurber. James Thurber, a quiet, gentle
man, created devastating beings. Like many cartoonists,
Thurber repeatedly hit at the overbearing female.

HOME
James Thurber

Society exerts many pressures upon individuals,
and perhaps this is nowhere more apparent than at a social gathering,
such as a dance. In spite of your personal feelings, society expects you
to be pleasant and courteous at all times. What would happen, however,
if others could know not only what you said but also what you really thought?
In "The Waltz," Dorothy Parker, long one of America's most witty commentators
on manners and morals, shows the difference between what one person thought
and what society demanded that she say.

The Waltz

DOROTHY PARKER

W*hy, thank you so much. I'd adore to.*

I don't want to dance with him. I don't want to dance with anybody. And even if I did, it wouldn't be him. He'd be well down among the last ten. I've seen the way he dances; it looks like something you do on Saint Walpurgis[1] Night. Just think, not a quarter of an hour ago, here I was sitting, feeling so sorry for the poor girl he was dancing with. And now *I'm* going to be the poor girl. Well, well. Isn't it a small world?

And a peach of a world, too. A true little corker. Its events are so fascinatingly unpredictable, are not they? Here I was, minding my own business, not doing a stitch of harm to any living soul. And then he comes into my life, all smiles and city manners, to sue me for the favor of one memorable mazurka. Why, he scarcely knows my name, let alone what it stands for. It stands for Despair, Bewilderment, Futility, Degradation, and Premeditated Murder, but little does he wot.[2] I don't wot his name, either; I haven't any idea what it is. Jukes, would be my guess from the look in his eyes. How do you do, Mr. Jukes? And how is that dear little brother of yours, with the two heads?

Ah, now why did he have to come around me, with his low requests? Why can't he let me lead my own life? I ask so little—just to be left alone in my quiet corner of the table, to do my evening brooding over all my sorrows. And he must come, with his bows and his scrapes and his may-I-have-this-ones. And I had to go and tell him that I'd adore to dance with him. I cannot understand why I wasn't struck right down dead. Yes, and being struck dead would look like a day in the country, compared to struggling out a dance with this boy. But what could I do? Everyone else at the table had got up to dance, except him and me. There was I, trapped. Trapped like a trap in a trap.

What can you say, when a man asks you to dance with him? I most certainly will *not* dance with you, I'll see you in hell first. Why, thank you, I'd like to awfully, but I'm having labor pains. Oh, yes, *do* let's dance together—it's so nice to meet a man who isn't a scaredy-cat about catching my beri-beri. No. There was nothing for me to do, but say I'd adore to. Well, we might as well get it over with. All right,

From *The Portable Dorothy Parker*. Originally appeared in *The New Yorker*. Copyright 1933, 1961 by Dorothy Parker. Reprinted by permission of The Viking Press, Inc.

1. **Saint Walpurgis**\sänt·vɔl ⁴pūr·gĭs\ English missionary in Germany during eighth century; the eve of her feast day, April 30, in legend was the night on which the power of demons and witches was at its height.
2. **wot,** know.

Cannonball, let's run out on the field. You won the toss; you can lead.

Why, I think it's more of a waltz, really. Isn't it? We might just listen to the music a second. Shall we? Oh, yes, it's a waltz. Mind? Why, I'm simply thrilled. I'd love to waltz with you.

I'd love to waltz with you. I'd love to waltz with you. I'd love to have my tonsils out, I'd love to be in a midnight fire at sea. Well, it's too late now. We're getting under way. *Oh.* Oh, dear. Oh, dear, dear, dear. Oh, this is even worse than I thought it would be. I suppose that's the one dependable law of life—everything is always worse than you thought it was going to be. Oh, if I had any real grasp of what this dance would be like, I'd have held out for sitting it out. Well, it will probably amount to the same thing in the end. We'll be sitting it out on the floor in a minute, if he keeps this up.

I'm so glad I brought it to his attention that this is a waltz they're playing. Heaven knows what might have happened, if he had thought it was something fast; we'd have blown the sides right out of the building. Why does he always want to be somewhere that he isn't? Why can't we stay in one place just long enough to get acclimated? It's this constant rush, rush, rush, that's the curse of American life. That's the reason that we're all of us so—*Ow!* For God's sake, don't *kick*, you idiot; this is only second down. Oh, my shin. My poor, poor shin, that I've had ever since I was a little girl!

Oh, no, no, no. Goodness, no. It didn't hurt the least little bit. And anyway it was my fault. Really it was. Truly. Well, you're just being sweet, to say that. It really was all my fault.

I wonder what I'd better do—kill him this instant, with my naked hands, or wait and let him drop in his traces. Maybe it's best not to make a scene. I guess I'll just lie low, and watch the pace get him. He can't keep this up indefinitely—he's only flesh and blood. Die he must, and die he shall, for what he did to me. I don't want to be of the over-sensitive type, but you can't tell me that kick was unpremeditated. Freud[3] says there are no accidents. I've led no

cloistered life, I've known dancing partners who have spoiled my slippers and torn my dress; but when it comes to kicking, I am Outraged Womanhood. When you kick me in the shin, *smile.*

Maybe he didn't do it maliciously. Maybe it's just his way of showing his high spirits. I suppose I ought to be glad that one of us is having such a good time. I suppose I ought to think myself lucky if he brings me back alive. Maybe it's captious to demand of a practically strange man that he leave your shins as he found them. After all, the poor boy's doing the best he can. Probably he grew up in the hill country, and never had no larnin'. I bet they had to throw him on his back to get shoes on him.

Yes, it's lovely, isn't it? It's simply lovely. It's the loveliest waltz. Isn't it? Oh, I think it's lovely, too.

Why, I'm getting positively drawn to the Triple Threat here. He's my hero. He has the heart of a lion, and the sinews of a buffalo. Look at him—never a thought of the consequences, never afraid of his face, hurling himself into every scrimmage, eyes shining, cheeks ablaze. And shall it be said that I hung back? No, a thousand times no. What's it to me if I have to spend the next couple of years in a plaster cast? Come on, Butch, right through them! Who wants to live forever?

Oh. Oh, dear. Oh, he's all right, thank goodness. For a while I thought they'd have to carry him off the field. Ah, I couldn't bear to have anything happen to him. I love him. I love him better than anybody in the world. Look at the spirit he gets into a dreary, commonplace waltz; how effete[4] the other dancers seem, beside him. He is youth and vigor and courage, he is strength and gaiety and—*Ow!* Get off my instep, you hulking peasant! What do you think I am, anyway—a gangplank? *Ow!*

No, of course it didn't hurt. Why, it didn't a bit. Honestly. And it was all my fault. You see,

---

3. **Sigmund Freud**,\sĭg·mənd froid\ founder of psychoanalysis.
4. **effete**\ĕ ▲fēt\ worn out, spent.

that little step of yours—well, it's perfectly lovely, but it's just a tiny bit tricky to follow at first. Oh, did you work it up yourself? You really did? Well, aren't you amazing! Oh, now I think I've got it. Oh, I think it's lovely. I was watching you do it when you were dancing before. It's awfully effective when you look at it.

It's awfully effective when you look at it. I bet I'm awfully effective when you look at me. My hair is hanging along my cheeks, my skirt is swaddling about me, I can feel the cold damp of my brow. I must look like something out of "The Fall of the House of Usher."[5] This sort of thing takes a fearful toll of a woman my age. And he worked up his little step himself, he with his degenerate cunning. And it was just a tiny bit tricky at first, but now I think I've got it. Two stumbles, slip, and a twenty-yard dash; yes. I've got it. I've got several other things, too, including a split shin and a bitter heart. I hate this creature I'm chained to. I hated him the moment I saw his leering, bestial face. And here I've been locked in his noxious embrace for the thirty-five years this waltz has lasted. Is that orchestra never going to stop playing? Or must this obscene travesty of a dance go on until hell burns out?

Oh, they're going to play another encore. Oh, goody. Oh, that's lovely. Tired? I should say I'm not tired. I'd like to go on like this forever.

I should say I'm not tired. I'm dead, that's all I am. Dead, and in what a cause! And the music is never going to stop playing, and we're going on like this, Double-Time Charlie and I, throughout eternity. I suppose I won't care any more, after the first hundred thousand years. I suppose nothing will matter then, not heat nor pain nor broken heart nor cruel, aching weariness. Well. It can't come too soon for me.

I wonder why I didn't tell him I was tired. I wonder why I didn't suggest going back to the table. I could have said let's just listen to the music. Yes, and if he would, that would be the first bit of attention he has given it all evening. George Jean Nathan[6] said that the lovely rhythms of the waltz should be listened to in stillness and not be accompanied by strange gyrations of the human body. I think that's what he said. I think it was George Jean Nathan. Anyhow, whatever he said and whoever he was and whatever he's doing now, he's better off than I am. That's safe. Anybody who isn't waltzing with this Mrs. O'Leary's cow[7] I've got here is having a good time.

Still if we were back at the table, I'd probably have to talk to him. Look at him—what could you say to a thing like that! Did you go to the circus this year, what's your favorite kind of ice cream, how do you spell cat? I guess I'm as well off here. As well off as if I were in a cement mixer in full action.

I'm past all feeling now. The only way I can tell when he steps on me is that I can hear the splintering of bones. And all the events of my life are passing before my eyes. There was the time I was in a hurricane in the West Indies, there was the day I got my head cut open in the taxi smash, there was the night the drunken lady threw a bronze ash-tray at her own true love and got me instead, there was that summer that the sailboat kept capsizing. Ah, what an easy, peaceful time was mine, until I fell in with Swifty, here. I didn't know what trouble was, before I got drawn into this *danse macabre.*[8] I think my mind is beginning to wander. It almost seems to me as if the orchestra were stopping. It couldn't be, of course; it could never, never be. And yet in my ears there is a silence like the sound of angel voices. . . .

Oh, they've stopped, the mean things. They're not going to play any more. Oh, darn. Oh, do you think they would? Do you really think so, if you gave them twenty dollars? Oh, that would be lovely. And look, do tell them to play this same thing. I'd simply adore to go on waltzing.

---

5. **The Fall of the House of Usher,** macabre short story by Edgar Allan Poe.
6. **George Jean Nathan** (1882–1958), American editor, author, dramatic critic.
7. **Mrs. O'Leary's cow,** the cow that kicked over the kerosene lamp that set fire to Chicago.
8. **danse macabre**\dans mə ˈka·brə\ dance of death.

I
EVALUATING AN INTERPRETATION

The following statement is an attempt by a critic to look into the deeper implications of the selection you have just read. Study the interpretation carefully, and discuss your own impressions of this interpretation.

"Any reader who has ever hidden his true thoughts behind the mask of false words (and who hasn't?) and who also enjoys seeing himself in a superior position (and who doesn't?) will find himself identifying with the girl in this sketch. He will read 'The Waltz' with great relish thoroughly enjoying Mrs. Parker's witty thrusts and thoroughly unprepared for what she has in store for him. What she has in store, of course, is the final revelation of her 'heroine' as a dependent, lonely, and frustrated woman in desperate search for a man, any man. As readers who have identified closely with this heroine, we must admit in fairness that the joke's been on us. And I don't think we can altogether escape the haunting suspicion that we are to recognize in Mrs. Parker's waltzer something of a self-portrait of the reader."

II
IMPLICATIONS

"The Waltz" gives rise to many questions concerning relationships among people; some of these matters are raised in the following statements. Discuss them in the light of the selection and of your own experiences.

1. People should not hide their true feelings; it is always best to be honest about what you think and feel.

2. "White lies" about one's true feelings are justified when they are told in order to avoid hurting someone else.

3. When individuals agree to do something that they don't really want to do, it is usually because they are afraid to stand alone.

4. "Tact" is just a polite word for lying.

5. If everyone could read everyone else's mind, it would be impossible for people to live together happily.

6. Our feelings toward others depend a great deal upon how they feel about us.

7. It is impossible to know whether or not you really like a person on your first meeting.

III
TECHNIQUES

Comedy

One analyst of laughter has maintained that wit makes us laugh by leading us to a goal and then either leaving us flat or taking us somewhere else. A brief illustration may be seen in the following line from Josh Billings, one of the best of America's nineteenth-century wits: "Remember the poor—it costs nothing." Or, consider this example from "The Waltz": "For God's sake, don't *kick*, you idiot; this is only second down."

Wit, which tends to be hard and critical, is usually rapid and sharp; it is associated primarily with the intellect. Humor, by contrast, tends to be sympathetic; it is associated with the heart.

Show that on the whole "The Waltz" is either a witty or a humorous sketch.

Sympathy and Detachment

If a witty writer is going to take a reader somewhere where he hadn't intended to go, it is obvious that he must first gain the reader's sympathies in some way. Assuming that Dorothy Parker succeeds in taking at least some readers to a place where they hadn't intended to go, how does she manage to gain their sympathies?

What effect does the reader's sex have on his or her sympathies? Why might girls find the story funnier than boys?

IV
WORDS

Select the word that seems most effective in the context given below. Support your choice and discuss how the word you selected differs from the others. Notice how the tone determines the appropriateness of a word.

1. . . . that kick was (1) *impromptu* (2) *unpremeditated* (3) *offhand*.

2. I've led no (1) *sheltered* (2) *protected* (3) *cloistered* life.

3. Maybe he didn't do it (1) *spitefully* (2) *maliciously* (3) *intentionally*. . . .

4. . . . locked in his (1) *noxious* (2) *baneful* (3) *pernicious* embrace. . . .

5. With a (1) *gigantic* (2) *enormous* (3) *immense* effort of will, I (1) *modulated* (2) *altered* (3) *varied* my voice.

Like the previous selection, "The Vanishing American" is,
in part at least, an attempt to level some rather serious criticism.
It differs, however, from Dorothy Parker's sketch in two important ways—
for one thing, it is a *fantasy;* see if you can determine for yourself
what the other important difference is.

The Vanishing American

CHARLES BEAUMONT

He got the notion shortly after five o'clock;
at least, a part of him did, a small part hidden
down beneath all the conscious cells—*he* didn't
get the notion until some time later. At exactly
5 P.M. the bell rang. At two minutes after, the
chairs began to empty. There was the vast
slamming of drawers, the straightening of
rulers, the sound of bones snapping and mouths
yawning and feet shuffling tiredly.

Mr. Minchell relaxed. He rubbed his hands
together and relaxed and thought how nice it
would be to get up and go home, like the
others. But of course there was the tape, only
three-quarters finished. He would have to stay.

He stretched and said good night to the
people who filed past him. As usual, no one answered. When they had gone, he set his fingers
pecking again over the keyboard. The click-
clicking grew loud in the suddenly still office,
but Mr. Minchell did not notice. He was lost
in the work. Soon, he knew, it would be time
for the totaling, and his pulse quickened at
the thought of this.

He lit a cigarette. Heart tapping, he drew in
smoke and released it.

He extended his right hand and rested his
index and middle fingers on the metal bar
marked TOTAL. A mile-long ribbon of paper
lay gathered on the desk, strangely festive. He
glanced at it, then at the manifest sheet. The

figure 18037448 was circled in red. He pulled
breath into his lungs, locked it there; then he
closed his eyes and pressed the TOTAL bar.

There was a smooth low metallic grinding,
followed by absolute silence.

Mr. Minchell opened one eye, dragged it
from the ceiling on down to the adding
machine.

He groaned, slightly.

The total read: 18037447.

"God." He stared at the figure and thought
of the fifty-three pages of manifest, the three
thousand separate rows of figures that would
have to be checked again. "God."

The day was lost, now. Irretrievably. It was
too late to do anything. Madge would have
supper waiting, and F.J. didn't approve of overtime; also——

He looked at the total again. At the last two
digits.

He sighed. Forty-seven. And thought,
startled: Today, for the Lord's sake, is my
birthday! Today I am forty—what? forty-
seven. And that explains the mistake, I suppose. Subconscious kind of thing . . .

Slowly he got up and looked around the deserted office.

Then he went to the dressing room and got
his hat and his coat and put them on, carefully.

"Pushing fifty now . . ."

The outside hall was dark. Mr. Minchell
walked softly to the elevator and punched the
down button. "Forty-seven," he said, aloud;

Reprinted by permission of G. P. Putnam's Sons, Inc. from
The Hunger and Other Stories by Charles Beaumont. Copyright
1957 by Charles Beaumont.

then, almost immediately, the light turned red
and the thick door slid back noisily. The elevator operator, a bird-thin, tan-fleshed girl, swiveled her head, looking up and down the hall.
"Going down," she said.

"Yes," Mr. Minchell said, stepping forward.

"Going down." The girl clicked her tongue
and muttered, "Damn kids." She gave the lattice gate a tired push and moved the smooth
wooden-handled lever in its slot.

Odd, Mr. Minchell decided, was the word
for this particular girl. He wished now that he
had taken the stairs. Being alone with only one
other person in an elevator had always made
him nervous: now it made him very nervous.
He felt the tension growing. When it became
unbearable, he cleared his throat and said,
"Long day."

The girl said nothing. She had a surly look,
and she seemed to be humming something deep
in her throat.

Mr. Minchell closed his eyes. In less than a
minute—during which time he dreamed of the
cable snarling, of the car being caught between
floors, of himself trying to make small talk with
the odd girl for six straight hours—he opened
his eyes again and walked into the lobby,
briskly.

The gate slammed.

He turned and started for the doorway. Then
he paused, feeling a sharp increase in his heart-
beat. A large, red-faced, magnificently groomed
man of middle years stood directly beyond the
glass, talking with another man.

Mr. Minchell pushed through the door, with
effort. He's seen me now, he thought. If he asks
any questions, though, or anything, I'll just say
I didn't put it on the time card; that ought to
make it all right. . . .

He nodded and smiled at the large man.
"Good night, Mr. Diemel."

The man looked up briefly, blinked, and returned to his conversation.

Mr. Minchell felt a burning come into his
face. He hurried on down the street. Now the
notion—though it was not even that yet,
strictly: it was more a vague feeling—swam up

"*You're all fired!*"

from the bottom of his brain. He remembered
that he had not spoken directly to F.J. Diemel
for over ten years, beyond a good morning. . . .

Ice-cold shadows fell off the tall buildings,
staining the streets, now. Crowds of shoppers
moved along the pavement like juggernauts,
exhaustedly, but with great determination. Mr.
Minchell looked at them. They all had furtive
appearances, it seemed to him, suddenly, even
the children, as if each was fleeing from some
hideous crime. They hurried along, staring.

But not, Mr. Minchell noticed, at him.
Through him, yes. Past him. As the elevator
operator had done, and now F.J. And had anyone said good night?

He pulled up his coat collar and walked toward the drugstore, thinking. He was forty-
seven years old. At the current life-expectancy
rate, he might have another seventeen or eighteen years left. And then death.

If you're not dead already.

He paused and for some reason remembered a story he'd once read in a magazine. Something about a man who dies and whose ghost takes up his duties, or something; anyway, the man didn't know he was dead—that was it. And at the end of the story, he runs into his own corpse.

Which is pretty absurd: he glanced down at his body. Ghosts don't wear $36 suits, nor do they have trouble pushing doors open, nor do their corns ache like blazes, and what the devil is wrong with me today?

He shook his head.

It was the tape, of course, and the fact that it was his birthday. That was why his mind was behaving so foolishly.

He went into the drugstore. It was an immense place, packed with people. He walked to the cigar counter, trying not to feel intimidated, and reached into his pocket. A small man elbowed in front of him and called loudly: "Gimme coupla nickels, will you, Jack?" The clerk scowled and scooped the change out of his cash register. The small man scurried off. Others took his place. Mr. Minchell thrust his arm forward. "A pack of Luckies, please," he said. The clerk whipped his fingers around a pile of cellophaned packages and, looking elsewhere, droned: "Twenty-six." Mr. Minchell put his twenty-six cents exactly on the glass shelf. The clerk shoved the cigarettes toward the edge and picked up the money, deftly. Not once did he lift his eyes.

Mr. Minchell pocketed the Luckies and went back out of the store. He was perspiring now, slightly, despite the chill wind. The word "ridiculous" lodged in his mind and stayed there. Ridiculous, yes, for heaven's sake. Still, he thought—now just answer the question—isn't it true? Can you honestly say that that clerk saw you?

Or that anyone saw you today?

Swallowing dryly, he walked another two blocks, always in the direction of the subway, and went into a bar called the Chez When. One

drink would not hurt, one small, stiff, steadying shot.

The bar was a gloomy place, and not very warm, but there was a good crowd. Mr. Minchell sat down on a stool and folded his hands. The bartender was talking animatedly with an old woman, laughing with boisterous good humor from time to time. Mr. Minchell waited. Minutes passed. The bartender looked up several times, but never made a move to indicate that he had seen a customer.

Mr. Minchell looked at his old gray overcoat, the humbly floraled tie, the cheap sharkskin suit-cloth, and became aware of the extent to which he detested this ensemble. He sat there and detested his clothes for a long time. Then he glanced around. The bartender was wiping a glass, slowly.

All right, the hell with you. I'll go somewhere else.

He slid off the stool. Just as he was about to turn he saw the mirrored wall, pink-tinted and curved. He stopped, peering. Then he almost ran out of the bar.

Cold wind went into his head.

Ridiculous. The mirror was curved, you jackass. How do you expect to see yourself in curved mirrors?

He walked past high buildings, and now past the library and the stone lion he had once, long ago, named King Richard; and he did not look at the lion, because he'd always wanted to ride the lion, ever since he was a child, and he'd promised himself he would do that, but he never did.

He hurried on to the subway, took the stairs by twos, and clattered across the platform in time to board the express.

It roared and thundered. Mr. Minchell held onto the strap and kept himself from staring. No one watched him. No one even glanced at him when he pushed his way to the door and went out onto the empty platform.

He waited. Then the train was gone, and he was alone.

He walked up the stairs. It was fully night now, a soft, unshadowed darkness. He thought about the day and the strange things that were gouging into his mind and thought about all this as he turned down a familiar street which led to his familiar apartment.

The door opened.

His wife was in the kitchen, he could see. Her apron flashed across the arch, and back, and across. He called: "Madge, I'm home."

Madge did not answer. Her movements were regular. Jimmy was sitting at the table, drooling over a glass of pop, whispering to himself.

"I said——" Mr. Minchell began.

"Jimmy, get up and go to the bathroom, you hear? I've got your water drawn."

Jimmy promptly broke into tears. He jumped off the chair and ran past Mr. Minchell into the bedroom. The door slammed viciously.

"Madge."

Madge Minchell came into the room, tired and lined and heavy. Her eyes did not waver. She went into the bedroom, and there was a silence; then a sharp slapping noise, and a yelling.

Mr. Minchell walked to the bathroom, fighting down the small terror. He closed the door and locked it and wiped his forehead with a handkerchief. Ridiculous, he thought, and ridiculous and ridiculous. I am making something utterly foolish out of nothing. All I have to do is look in the mirror, and——

He held the handkerchief to his lips. It was difficult to breathe.

Then he knew that he was afraid, more so than ever before in a lifetime of being afraid.

Look at it this way, Minchell: why shouldn't *you vanish?*

"Young man, just you wait until your father gets here!"

He pushed the handkerchief against his mouth and leaned on the door and gasped.

"What do you mean, vanish?"

Go on, take a look. You'll see what I mean.

He tried to swallow, couldn't. Tried to wet his lips, they stayed dry.

"Lord——"

He slitted his eyes and walked to the shaving mirror and looked in.

His mouth fell open.

The mirror reflected nothing. It held nothing. It was dull and gray and empty.

Mr. Minchell stared at the glass, put out his hand, drew it back hastily.

He squinted. Inches away. There was a form now: vague, indistinct, featureless: but a form.

"Lord," he said. He understood why the elevator girl hadn't seen him, and why F.J. hadn't answered him, and why the clerk at the drugstore and the bartender and Madge . . .

"I'm not dead."

Of course you're not dead—not that way.

"—tan your hide, Jimmy Minchell, when he gets home."

Mr. Minchell suddenly wheeled and clicked the lock. He rushed out of the steam-filled bathroom, across the room, down the stairs, into the street, into the cool night.

A block from home he slowed to a walk.

Invisible! He said the word over and over, in a half-voice. He said it and tried to control the panic that pulled at his legs, and at his brain, and filled him.

Why?

A fat woman and a little girl passed by. Neither of them looked up. He started to call out and checked himself. No. That wouldn't do any good. There was no question about it now. He was invisible.

He walked on. As he did, forgotten things returned; they came and they left, too fast. He couldn't hold onto them. He could only watch, and remember. Himself as a youngster, reading: the Oz books, and Tarzan, and Mr. Wells. Himself, going to the University, wanting to teach, and meeting Madge; then not planning any more, and Madge changing, and all the dreams put away. For later. For the right time. And then Jimmy—little strange Jimmy, who ate filth and picked his nose and watched television, who never read books, never; Jimmy, his son, whom he would never understand . . .

He walked by the edge of the park now. Then on past the park, through a maze of familiar and unfamiliar neighborhoods. Walking, remembering, looking at the people and feeling pain because he knew that they could not see him, not now or ever again, because he had vanished. He walked and remembered and felt pain.

All the stagnant dreams came back. Fully. The trip to Italy he'd planned. The open sports car, bad weather be damned. The first-hand knowledge that would tell him whether he did or did not approve of bullfighting. The book . . .

Then something occurred to him. It occurred to Mr. Minchell that he had not just suddenly vanished, like that, after all. No; he had been vanishing gradually for a long while. Every time he said good morning to that bastard Diemel he got a little harder to see. Every time he put on this horrible suit he faded. The process of disappearing was set into action every time he brought his pay check home and turned it over to Madge, every time he kissed her, or listened to her vicious unending complaints, or decided against buying that novel, or punched the adding machine he hated so, or . . .

Certainly.

He had vanished for Diemel and the others in the office years ago. And for strangers right afterwards. Now even Madge and Jimmy couldn't see him. And he could barely see himself, even in a mirror.

It made terrible sense to him. *Why* shouldn't *you disappear?* Well, why, indeed? There wasn't any very good reason, actually. None. And this, in a nightmarish sort of a way, made it as brutally logical as a perfect tape.

Then he thought about going back to work tomorrow and the next day and the day after that. He'd have to, of course. He couldn't let Madge and Jimmy starve; and, besides, what else would he do? It wasn't as if anything important had changed. He'd go on punching the clock and saying good morning to people who didn't see him, and he'd run the tapes and come home beat, nothing altered, and someday he'd die and that would be that.

All at once he felt tired.

He sat down on a cement step and sighed. Distantly he realized that he had come to the library. He sat there, watching the people, feeling the tiredness seep through him, thickly.

Then he looked up.

Above him, black and regal against the sky, stood the huge stone lion. Its mouth was open, and the great head was raised proudly.

Mr. Minchell smiled. King Richard. Memories scattered in his mind: old King Richard, well, my God, here we are.

He got to his feet. Fifty thousand times, at least, he had passed this spot, and every time he had experienced that instant of wild craving. Less so of late, but still, had it ever completely gone? He was amazed to find that now the childish desire was welling up again, stronger than ever before. Urgently.

He rubbed his cheek and stood there for several minutes. It's the most ridiculous thing in the world, he thought, and I must be going out of my mind, and that must explain everything. But, he inquired of himself, even so, why not?

After all, I'm invisible. No one can see me. Of course, it didn't have to be this way, not really. I don't know, he went on, I mean, I believed that I was doing the right thing. Would it have been right to go back to the University and the hell with Madge? I couldn't change that, could I? Could I have done anything about that, even if I'd known?

He nodded sadly.

All right, but don't make it any worse. Don't for God's sake *dwell* on it!

To his surprise, Mr. Minchell found that he was climbing up the concrete base of the statue. It ripped the breath from his lungs—and he saw that he could much more easily have gone up a few extra steps and simply stepped on— but there didn't seem anything else to do but just this, what he was doing. Once upright, he passed his hand over the statue's flank. The surface was incredibly sleek and cold, hard as a lion's muscles ought to be, and tawny.

He took a step backwards. Lord! Had there ever been such power? Such marvelous downright power and . . . majesty, as was here? From stone—no, indeed. It fooled a good many people, but it did not fool Mr. Minchell. He knew. This lion was no mere library decoration. It was an animal, of deadly cunning and fantastic strength and unbelievable ferocity. And it didn't move for the simple reason that it did not care to move. It was waiting. Someday it would see what it was waiting for, its enemy, coming down the street. Then look out, people!

He remembered the whole yarn now. Of everyone on Earth, only he, Henry Minchell, knew the secret of the lion. And only he was allowed to sit astride this mighty back.

He stepped onto the tail, experimentally. He hesitated, gulped, and swung forward, swiftly, on up to the curved rump.

Trembling, he slid forward, until finally he was over the shoulders of the lion, just behind the raised head.

His breath came very fast.

He closed his eyes.

It was not long before he was breathing regularly again. Only now it was the hot, fetid air of the jungle that went into his nostrils. He felt the great muscles ripple beneath him and he listened to the fast crackle of crushed foliage, and he whispered:

"Easy, fellow."

The flying spears did not frighten him. He sat straight, smiling, with his fingers buried in the rich, tawny mane of King Richard, while the wind tore at his hair. . . .

Then, abruptly, he opened his eyes.

The city stretched before him, and the people, and the lights. He tried quite hard not to cry, because he knew that forty-seven-year-old men never cried, not even when they had vanished, but he couldn't help it. So he sat on the stone lion and lowered his head and cried.

He didn't hear the laughter at first.

When he did hear it, he thought that he was dreaming. But it was true: somebody was laughing.

He grasped one of the statue's ears for balance and leaned forward. He blinked. Below, some fifteen feet, there were people. Young people. Some of them with books. They were looking up and smiling and laughing.

Mr. Minchell wiped his eyes.

A slight horror came over him, and fell away. He leaned farther out.

One of the boys waved and shouted: "Ride him, Pop!"

Mr. Minchell almost toppled. Then, without understanding, without even trying to understand—merely knowing—he grinned, widely, showing his teeth, which were his own and very white.

"You . . . see me?" he called.

The young people roared.

"You do!" Mr. Minchell's face seemed to melt upwards. He let out a yell and gave King Richard's shaggy stone mane an enormous hug.

Below, other people stopped in their walking and a small crowd began to form. Dozens of eyes peered sharply, quizzically.

A woman in gray furs giggled.

A thin man in a blue suit grunted something about these damned exhibitionists.

"You pipe down," another man said. "Guy wants to ride the god-damn lion it's his own business."

There were murmurings. The man who had said pipe down was small and he wore black-rimmed glasses. "I used to do it all the time." He turned to Mr. Minchell and cried: "How is it?"

Mr. Minchell grinned. Somehow, he realized, in some mysterious way, he had been given a second chance. And this time he knew what he would do with it. "Fine!" he shouted, and stood up on King Richard's back and sent his derby spinning out over the heads of the people. "Come on up!"

"Can't do it," the man said. "Got a date." There was a look of profound admiration in his eyes as he strode off. Away from the crowd he stopped and cupped his hands and cried: "I'll be seeing you!"

"That's right," Mr. Minchell said, feeling the cold new wind on his face. "You'll be seeing me."

Later, when he was good and ready, he got down off the lion.

I
SOME NOT SO FANTASTIC SYMBOLS

Although "The Vanishing American" seems quite fantastic on the surface, one does not have to go very far beneath its surface to find a great deal of realism. The key elements in the fantasy are Mr. Minchell's invisibility and his ride on the lion.

All of us—the psychology books say—seek recognition. Mr. Minchell, though he has nearly forgotten this human need, does in fact want to be recognized as a successful human being on some level. By making him turn invisible Beaumont hits upon a perfect and highly humorous way of symbolizing the fact that his "hero" has failed to achieve any success that would bring him recognition.

And then there's the ride on the library lion. Somehow that ride is a beginning for Minchell. Just as the invisibility symbolizes the fact that he has deserved no recognition, the lion ride is an excellent symbol for. . . What? Try to express in your own words what Minchell's ride means. Also try to explain why lion-riding is an especially appropriate symbol for the meaning the author wants to convey.

II
IMPLICATIONS

Discuss each of the following items.

1. Analyze the meaning of the title of the story. It has meaning on more than one level.

2. Recall what Mr. Minchell had wanted to do with his life. In what ways do you think this path would have led him to greater recognition and self-satisfaction?

3. As you no doubt realize, this story has some important implications for modern American life. We live in a technological society in which buttons, keyboards, tapes, and the machines they control become increasingly important each year. Each year, therefore, we need more Mr. Minchells. Aside from taking rides on library lions, how are such individuals going to achieve a significant measure of self-respect and recognition?

4. Work involving little mental or emotional satisfaction is of course nothing new. What is new is the fact that modern man has much more leisure time than his predecessors. What do you think are some of the most satisfying ways he can spend this leisure time? How do you suppose Mr. Minchell spent his leisure time?

III
TECHNIQUES

Comedy

A satirist may be defined as one who uses laughter to criticize human institutions and humanity. Satirists, however, may use a great number of different weapons to make their criticisms. Dorothy Parker, on the whole, tends to make use of wit. Which of the following would you say are Charles Beaumont's chief weapons?

1. humor

2. symbolism

3. invective

4. nonsense

5. exaggeration

6. understatement

Sympathy and Detachment

Most readers are not likely to identify very closely with a forty-seven-year-old man who has wasted his life; yet it is important for Beaumont's purposes that the reader not be too detached from him. What are some of the factors that cause the reader to sympathize with Mr. Minchell and that keep him from being excessively detached from the hero's problems?

The selections you have read up to now have depended,
for the most part, on either humor or wit for their comic effects.
In the following three pieces the comic writers are concerned
less with humor and wit than with pure fun—nonsense.

Ring Lardner got his start in writing as a sports reporter
and later was editor of a baseball weekly; he wrote many amusing pieces
on the sports scene, including some on what he called the baseball
"world serious" (world series). In his late career he published
a number of stories that are ranked by many critics as among America's best
modern fiction, including the much-anthologized "Haircut" and "The Love Nest."
Although he was fundamentally a satirist and has been called
"a great pessimist," he was also author of a good deal of nonsense,
one example of which is the following brief play.

Thompson's Vacation

PLAY IN TWO ACTS

RING LARDNER

Characters

THOMPSON, *a plain citizen*

HAINES, *another*

DILLON, *another*

Act I

August 28. The smoking car of a city-bound suburban train. THOMPSON *is sitting alone.* HAINES *comes in, recognizes him and takes the seat beside him.*

HAINES: Hello there, Thompson.
THOMPSON: Hello, Mr. Haines.
HAINES: What's the good word?

THOMPSON: Well—
HAINES: How's business?
THOMPSON: I don't know. I've been on a vacation for two weeks.
HAINES: Where was you?
THOMPSON: Atlantic City.
HAINES: Where did you stop?
THOMPSON: At the Edgar.
HAINES: The Edgar! Who steered you to that joint?
THOMPSON: I liked it all right.
HAINES: Why didn't you go to the Wallace? Same prices and everything up to date. How did you happen to pick out a dirty old joint like the Edgar?
THOMPSON: I thought it was all right.
HAINES: What did you do to kill time down there?
THOMPSON: Oh, I swam and went to a couple of shows and laid around.
HAINES: Didn't you go up in the air?
THOMPSON: No.

Reprinted with the permission of Charles Scribner's Sons from *First and Last,* pp. 329-332, by Ring Lardner. Copyright 1934 Ellisa Lardner; renewal copyright © 1962 Ring Lardner, Jr.

HAINES: That's the only thing they is to do in Atlantic City, is go up in the air. If you didn't do that, you didn't do nothing.

THOMPSON: I never been up.

HAINES: That's all they is to do down there, especially in August, when it's so hot.

THOMPSON: They was generally always a breeze.

HAINES: Yes, I know what that breeze is in August. It's like a blast out of a furnace. Did you go in any of them cabarets?

THOMPSON: Yes, I was in the Mecca and the Garden.

HAINES: Wasn't you in the La Marne?

THOMPSON: No.

HAINES: If you wasn't in the La Marne, you didn't see nothing.

THOMPSON: I had some real beer in the Mecca.

HAINES: Say, that stuff they give you in the Mecca is dishwater. They's only one place in Atlantic City to get real beer. That's the Wonderland. Didn't you make the Wonderland?

THOMPSON: No.

HAINES: Then you didn't have no real beer. Did you meet many dames?

THOMPSON: Only a couple of them. But they was pips!

HAINES: Pips! You don't see no real pips down there in August. The time to catch the pips down there is—well, June, July, September, May, or any time in the fall or winter or spring. You don't see them there in August. Did you go fishing?

THOMPSON: No.

HAINES: Oh, they's great fishing around there! If you didn't go fishing, you didn't do nothing.

THOMPSON (*rising*): Well, here we are.

HAINES: I think you're a sucker to pick out August for a vacation. May or June or September, that's the time for a vacation.

THOMPSON: Well, see you again.

Act II

Four minutes later. A downtown subway express. THOMPSON *is hanging on a strap.* DILLON *enters and hangs on the next strap.*

DILLON: Hello there, Thompson.

THOMPSON: Hello.

DILLON: How's everything?

THOMPSON: All right, I guess.

DILLON: Ain't you been on a vacation?

THOMPSON: Yeah.

DILLON: What kind of a time did you have?

THOMPSON: Rotten.

DILLON: Where was you?

THOMPSON: Nowhere.

Curtain

Robert Benchley was drama editor of *The New Yorker* from 1929 till 1940. He was also in films, on the radio, and on the stage. Stephen Leacock, who is often credited with founding the modern school of nonsense humor, once said of Benchley: "As a writer of nonsense for nonsense's sake, he is unsurpassed."

Sporting Life in America: Dozing

ROBERT BENCHLEY

We Americans are a hardy race, and hardy races need a lot of sleep. "Sleep, that knits up the ravell'd sleave of care,"[1] Shakespeare has called it, and, except for the fact that it doesn't mean much, it is a pretty good simile. I often think of it myself just as I am dropping off into a light doze: "Sleep, that sleeves up the raveled care of . . . knit, that sleeps up the shaveled neeve of pfor—pff—prpf—orpffff" (*trailing off into a low whistle*).

One of the most charming manifestations of sleep which we, as a nation, indulge in as a pastime is the Doze. By the Doze I mean those little snatches of sleep which are caught now and then during the day, usually with the collar on and choking slightly, with the head inclined coyly to one side, during which there is a semiconscious attempt to appear as if we were really awake. It is in this department of sleep that we are really at our best.

Of course, there is one form of doze which, to the casual observer or tourist, gives the appearance of legitimate sleep. This is the short doze, or "quickie," which is taken just after the main awakening in the morning. The alarm rings, or the Lord High Chamberlain taps us on the shoulder (in the absence of a chamberlain a relative will do. And right here I would like to offer for examination that type of sadistic relative who takes actual delight in awakening people. They hover about with ghoulish anticipation until the minute arrives when they may legitimately begin their dirty work, and then, leering unpleasantly, they shake the sleeper roughly with a "Come, come! Time to get up!" and wait right there until he is actually out on the cold floor in his bare feet. There is something radically wrong with such people, and the sooner they are exposed as pathological cases the better it will be for the world). I'm sorry. I didn't mean to be nasty about it.

At any rate, we are awakened and look at the clock. There are five minutes before it is absolutely necessary to get out of bed. If we leave shaving until night, there might even be fifteen minutes. If we leave dressing until we get to the office, snatching our clothes from the chair and carrying them downtown on our arm, there might even be half an hour more for a good, health-giving nap. Who knows? Perhaps those few minutes of extra sleep might make us just ten times as efficient during the day! That is what we must think of—efficiency. We must sacrifice our petty opinions on the matter and think of the rest of the day and our efficiency. There is no doubt that fifteen minutes' more sleep would do wonders for us, no matter how little we really want to take it.

1. **Sleep . . . care,** Shakespeare, *Macbeth*, Act II, Sc. 2, l. 36.

By the time we have finished this line of argument we are out pretty fairly cold again, but not so cold that we are not conscious of anyone entering the room. We feel that they are going to say: "Come, come, don't go back to sleep again!" and we forestall this warning with a brisk "I know! I know! I'm just thinking!" This is said with one eye partially open and one tiny corner of the brain functioning. The rest of our powers add up to a total loss.

It is one of Nature's wonders how a man can carry on an argument with someone standing beside his bed and still be asleep to all intents and purposes. Not a very good argument, perhaps, and one in which many important words are missing or indistinct, but still an argument. It is an argument, however, which seldom wins, the state of justice in the world being what it is today.

Dozing before arising does not really come within the range of this treatise. What we are concerned with are those little lapses when we are fully dressed, when we fondly believe that no one notices. Riding on a train, for example.

There is the short-distance doze in a day coach, probably the most humiliating form of train sleeping. In this the elbow is rested on the window sill and the head placed in the hand in an attitude of thought. The glass feels very cool on the forehead and we rest it there, more to cool off than anything else. The next thing we know the forehead (carrying the entire head with it) has slid down the length of the slippery pane and we have received a rather nasty bang against the woodwork. They shouldn't keep their glass so slippery. A person is likely to get badly hurt that way.

However, back again goes the forehead against the pane in its original position, with the hand serving more or less as a buffer, until another skid occurs, this time resulting in an angry determination to give the whole thing up entirely and sit up straight in the seat. Some dozers will take four or five slides without whimpering, going back each time for more with apparently undiminished confidence in their ability to see the thing through.

It is a game that you can't beat, however, and the sooner you sit up straight in your seat, the sooner you will stop banging your head.

Dozing in a Pullman chair is not so dangerous, as one does not have the risk of the sliding glass to cope with, but it is even less lovely in its appearance. Here the head is allowed to sink back against the antimacassar—just for a minute to see if the headrest is really as comfortable as it seems. It is then but the work of a minute for the mouth to open slightly and the head to tip roguishly to the right, and there you are—as pretty a picture as one would care to see. You are very lucky if, when you come to and look about, you do not find your neighbors smiling indulgently at some little vagaries of breathing or eccentricities of facial expression which you have been permitting yourself.

The game in all this public dozing is to act, on awakening, as if you had known all along what you were doing. If your neighbors are smiling, you should smile back, as if to say: "Fooled you that time! You thought I was asleep, didn't you?"

If they are not quite so rude as to smile, but look quickly back at their reading on seeing your eyes open, you should assume a brisk, businesslike expression indicating that you have been thinking out some weighty business problem with your eyes closed, and, now that you have at last come on its solution, that it is snap-snap! back to work for you! If, after a furtive look around, you discover that no one has caught you at it, then it will do no harm to give it another try, this time until your collar chokes you into awakening with a strangling gasp.

The collar, however, is not always an impediment to public dozing. In the theater, for example, a good, stiff dress collar and shirt bosom have been known to hold the sleeper in an upright position when otherwise he might have plunged forward and banged his head on the back of the seat in front.

In my professional capacity as play reviewer I have had occasion to experiment in the various ways of sitting up straight and still snatching a few winks of health-giving sleep. I have found that by far the safest is to keep one's heavy overcoat on, especially if it is made of some good, substantial material which will hold a sagging torso erect within its folds. With a good overcoat, reënforced by a stiff dress shirt and a high collar, one may even go beyond the dozing stage and sink into a deep, refreshing slumber, and still not be made conspicuous by continual lurchings and plungings. Of course, if you are an uneasy sleeper and given to thrashing about, you will find that even a heavy overcoat will let you down once in a while. But for the average man, who holds approximately the same position after he has gone to sleep, I don't think that this method can go wrong. Its only drawback is that you are likely to get a little warm along about the middle of the second act.

If you don't want to wear your overcoat in the theater, the next best method is to fold the arms across the chest and brace the chin against the dress collar, exerting a slight upward pressure with the arms against the shirt front. This, however, can be used only for the lightest of dozes, as, once unconsciousness has set in, the pressure relaxes and over you go.

Dozing at a play, however refreshing, makes it a bit difficult to follow the argument on the stage, as occasionally the nap drags itself out into a couple of minutes and you awake to find a wholly fresh set of characters on the scene, or even a wholly fresh scene. This is confusing. It is therefore wise to have someone along with you who will alternate watches with you, dozing when you are awake and keeping more or less alert while you are dozing. In this way you can keep abreast of what has been happening.

This, unfortunately, is impossible in personal conversations. If you slip off into a quick coma late some evening when your *vis-à-vis*[2] is telling you about South America or a new solvent process, it is usually pretty difficult to pick up the thread where you dropped it. You may remember that the last words he was saying were "—which is situated at the mouth of the Amazon," but that isn't going to help you much if you come to just as he is asking you: "What would *you* say are?" As in the personal-conversation doze the eyes very seldom completely close (it is more of a turning back of the eyeballs than a closing of the lids), you may escape detection if you have a ready answer for the emergency. I find that "Well, I don't know," said very slowly and deliberately, will fit almost any question that has been asked you. "Yes" and "No" should never be offered, as they might make you sound even sillier than you look. If you say: "Well, I—don't—know," it will give you a chance to collect your wits (what few there are left) and may lead your questioner into answering the thing himself.

At any rate, it will serve as a stall. If there are other people present, some one of them is quite likely to come to your rescue and say something which will tip you off as to the general subject under discussion. From then on, you will have to fight your own battle. I can't help you.

The whole problem is one which calls for a great deal of thought. If we can develop some way in which a man can doze and still keep from making a monkey of himself, we have removed one of the big obstacles to human happiness in modern civilization. It goes without saying that we don't get enough sleep while we are in bed; so we have got to get a little now and then while we are at work or at play. If we can find some way to keep the head up straight, the mouth closed, and just enough of the brain working to answer questions, we have got the thing solved right there.

I am working on it right now, as a matter of fact, but I find it a little difficult to keep awake.

---

2. **vis-à-vis**\ˈvē·zĕ ˈvē\ person sitting opposite, face to face.

Everybody has his own favorite humorist, but if a poll were taken
to determine the favorite humorist of the humorists themselves,
who do you suppose would win the honor? So far no poll has been taken,
yet there is a feeling in many quarters that if one were,
the "humorists' humorist" would be S. J. Perelman, a former "gagman"
for Marx Brothers' films and a perennial contributor of sketches
to *The New Yorker* and *Holiday* magazines. Benchley once said
that when Perelman came on the scene he put all the other nonsense humorists
out of work. Dorothy Parker's opinion follows: "Mr. Perelman stands alone
in this day of humorists. Mr. Perelman—there he is. Robert Benchley,
who was probably nearest to Perelman, and Ring Lardner, who was nearest
to nobody, are gone, and so Mr. Perelman stands by himself.
Lonely he may be—but there he is."

Nothing but the Tooth

S. J. PERELMAN

I am thirty-eight years old, have curly brown hair and blue eyes, own a uke and a yellow roadster, and am considered a snappy dresser in my crowd. But the thing I want most in the world for my birthday is a free subscription to *Oral Hygiene,* published by Merwin B. Massol, 1005 Liberty Avenue, Pittsburgh, Pa. In the event you have been repairing your own teeth, *Oral Hygiene* is a respectable smooth-finish technical magazine circulated to your dentist with the compliments of his local supply company. Through its pages runs a recital of the most horrendous and fantastic deviations from the dental norm. It is a confessional in which dentists take down their back hair and stammer out the secrets of their craft. But every time I plunge into its crackling pages at my dentist's, just as I get interested in the story of the Man with the Alveolar Dentures or Thirty Reasons Why People Stay Away from Dentists, the nurse comes out slightly flushed and smoothing her hair to tell me that the doctor is ready.

Last Thursday, for example, I was head over heels in the question-and-answer department of *Oral Hygiene.* A frankly puzzled extractionist, who tried to cloak his agitation under the initials "J. S. G.," had put his plight squarely up to the editor: "I have a patient, a woman of 20, who has a full complement of teeth. All of her restorations are gold foils or inlays. She constantly grinds her teeth at night. How can I aid her to stop grinding them? Would it do any good to give her a vellum rubber bite?"[1] But before I could learn whether it was a bite or just a gentle hug the editor recommended, out popped Miss Inchbald with lipstick on her nose, giggling, "The Doctor is free now." "Free" indeed—"running amok" would be a better way to put it.

I had always thought of dentists as of the phlegmatic[2] type—square-jawed sadists in white aprons who found release in trying out new kinds of burs[3] on my shaky little incisors.[4]

----

1. **vellum rubber bite,** protection to prevent grinding of the teeth.
2. **phlegmatic**\flĕg ▲mă·tĭk\ calm, cool, slow to act.
3. **burs,** dentist drills.
4. **incisors**\ĭn ▲sī·zərz\ any of the front teeth.

One look at *Oral Hygiene* fixed that. Of all the inhibited, timorous, uncertain fumble-bunnies who creep the earth, Mr. Average Dentist is the worst. A filing clerk is a veritable sabre-toothed tiger by comparison. Faced with a decision, your dentist's bones turn to water and he becomes all hands and feet. He muddles through his ordinary routine with a certain amount of bravado, plugging a molar here with chewing gum, sinking a shaft in a sound tooth there. In his spare time he putters around his laboratory making tiny cement cup-cakes, substituting amber electric bulbs for ordinary bulbs in his waiting-room to depress patients, and jotting down nasty little innuendoes about people's gums in his notebook. But let an honest-to-goodness sufferer stagger in with his face out of drawing, and Mr. Average Dentist's nerves go to hell. He runs sobbing to the "Ask *Oral Hygiene*" department and buries his head in the lap of V. C. Smedley, its director. I dip in for a typical sample:

Question—A patient of mine, a girl, 18, returned from school recently with a weird story of lightning having struck an upper right cuspid tooth and checked the enamel on the labial surface nearly two-thirds of the way from the incisal edge toward the neck. The patient was lying on a bed looking out an open window during an electric storm, and this one flash put out the lights of the house, and at the same time, the patient felt a burning sensation (like a burning wire) along the cuspid tooth. She immediately put her tongue on the tooth which felt rough, but as the lights were out she could not see it so she went to bed. (A taste as from a burnt match accompanied the shock.)

Next morning she found the labial of the tooth black. Some of the color came off on her finger. By continually brushing all day with the aid of peroxide, salt, soda and vinegar she removed the remainder of the black after which the tooth was a yellow shade and there was some roughness on the labial surface.

Could the lightning have caused this and do you recommend smoothing the surface with discs?— R.D.L., D.D.S., Oregon.

Well, Doctor, let us take your story step by step. Miss Muffet told you the sensation was like a burning wire, and she tasted something like a burnt match. Did you think, by any chance, of looking into her mouth for either wire or matches? Did you even think of looking into her mouth? I see no mention of the fact in your letter. You state that she walked in and told you the story, that's all. Of course it never occurred to you that she had brought along her mouth for a reason. Then you say, "she removed the remainder of the black after which the tooth was a yellow shade." Would it be asking too much of you to make up your mind? Was it a tooth or a yellow shade? You're quite sure it wasn't a Venetian blind? Or a gaily striped awning? Do you ever take a drink in the daytime, Doctor?

Frankly, men, I have no patience with such idiotic professional behavior. An eighteen-year-old girl walks into a dentist's office exhibiting obvious symptoms of religious hysteria (stigmata,[5] etc.). She babbles vaguely of thunderstorms and is patently a confirmed drunkard. The dentist goes to pieces, forgets to look in her mouth, and scurries off to *Oral Hygiene* asking for permission to smooth her surface with discs. It's a mercy he doesn't take matters into his own hands and try to plough every fourth tooth under. This is the kind of man to whom we intrust our daughters' dentures.

There is practically no problem so simple that it cannot confuse a dentist. For instance, thumb-sucking. "Could you suggest a method to correct thumb and index finger sucking by an infant of one year?" flutters a Minnesota orthodontist, awkwardly digging his toe into the hot sand. Dr. Smedley, whose patience rivals Job's, has an answer for everything: "Enclose the hand by tying shut the end of the sleeve of a sleeping garment, or fasten a section of a pasteboard mailing tube to the sleeping garment in such a position as to prevent the bending of the elbow sufficiently to carry the thumb or index finger to the mouth." Now truly, Dr. Smedley, isn't that going all the way around

---

5. **stigmata**\\'stĭg▲mǎ•tə\\ plural of stigma; marks resembling wounds of Jesus.

Robin Hood's barn? Nailing the baby's hand to the highchair is much more cozy, or, if no nail is available, a smart blow with the hammer on Baby's fingers will slow him down. My grandfather, who was rather active in the nineties (between Columbus and Amsterdam Avenues—they finally got him for breaking and entering), always used an effective method to break children of this habit. He used to tie a Mills grenade to the baby's thumb with cobbler's waxed thread, and when the little spanker pulled out the detonating pin with his teeth, Grandpa would stuff his fingers into his ears and run like the wind. Ironically enough, the people with whom Grandpa now boards have the same trouble keeping him from biting his thumbs, but overcome it by making him wear a loose jacket with very long sleeves, which they tie to the bars.

I have always been the mildest of men, but you remember the old saying, "Beware the fury of a patient man." (I remembered it very well and put my finger on it instantly, page 269 of Bartlett's book of quotations.) For years I have let dentists ride rough-shod over my teeth; I have been sawed, hacked, chopped, whittled, bewitched, bewildered, tattooed, and signed on again; but this is cuspid's last stand. They'll never get *me* into that chair again. I'll dispose of my teeth as I see fit, and after they're gone, I'll get along. I started off living on gruel, and, by God, I can always go back to it again.

I
NONSENSE
AND OTHER COMIC MODES

Of the selections you have just read, Perelman's "Nothing but the Tooth" probably comes closest to pure nonsense. In this form of comedy there is no intention either of criticizing or of sympathizing with any particular person or group of persons. The laughter that nonsense evokes is usually described as "harmless." We laugh primarily at ridiculous or absurd ideas and situations, such as at the thought that a young girl could have a yellow shade in her mouth.

Some readers might think that "Thompson's Vacation" is largely nonsense, but on the other hand it may be viewed as a criticism of certain human attitudes exemplified by Mr. Thompson. Which of these two points of view would you take?

Finally, Benchley's essay has elements of nonsense, of sympathetic humor, and of critical wit. Can you point to instances of each? Which of the three do you consider the dominant element in the essay?

II
IMPLICATIONS

Discuss each of the following propositions.

1. "Thompson's Vacation" is an implicit criticism of the human tendency to judge oneself (or see oneself) in the light of the opinions of others.

2. Lardner intends to show the susceptibility of the average person to advertisers, politicians, and other molders of opinion.

3. Benchley's chief target is the idea that Americans are a hardy and supremely efficient people.

4. One of the underlying reasons for Benchley's appeal is that he champions the cause of the average person against those whose tastes are sophisticated and intellectual.

5. The comic effect of "Nothing but the Tooth" depends in part upon the fact that most of us feel a certain amount of fear or hostility toward dentists.

6. Since nonsense involves neither healthy criticism nor sympathetic understanding, it has little, if any, reason for existence.

III
TECHNIQUES

Comedy

In most of the selections in this unit, the comedy has stemmed from both *character* and *situation*, with a heavy emphasis in most cases upon the former. Upon which of these two elements do you think nonsense humorists depend most heavily?

Like writers of light verse, nonsense writers often show a great fondness for word play and many of their comical effects depend upon their handling of language. When Perelman writes, for example, ". . . this is cuspid's last stand," he creates a humorous effect by his shift in the key word of the phrase, "Custer's last stand." The shift is especially funny because "cuspid" and "Custer" sound so much alike and because "cuspid" is more appropriate in the context even though "Custer" is expected. How many other examples of word play can you find in the selections?

Sympathy and Detachment

In pure humor the reader's heart is involved and he normally sympathizes with one or more characters. In wit there is involvement of the reader's mind and a tendency to identify with superior characters or with the author. What is the pattern, so far as sympathy and detachment are concerned, in nonsense?

IV
WORDS

If you look up *furtive* in the dictionary, you will find it means "sly," "stolen," "secret." If you look up *sly,* you will find it means "shrewd," "crafty." If you look up *secret,* you will find it means "hidden." So it goes. To define a word the dictionary must use other words. A good dictionary, however, goes further by explaining the differences among meanings.

1. While synonyms have some meaning in common, each has its own suggestive meaning which is usually explained in the synonymy.

There are several ways to express a hiding or concealing of something: (a) *covert* applies to something done under cover and not admitted; (b) *furtive* implies slyness or fearful timidity; (c) *clandestine* implies concealment for some evil end. Decide which of these synonyms fits each of the sentences which follow.

a. The young man, after a _____ glance, looked the other way as if he were afraid.

b. She was too innocent to understand the _____ glances of the villain.

c. He kept to himself as if there were something _____ about his plans.

2. To say something is *obscure* is to imply that meaning is hidden or withheld. Other synonyms expressing the same general meaning are (a) enigmatic, (b) cryptic, (c) ambiguous. Using the synonymy in your dictionary, decide which synonym fits and explain the suggestive meaning of each in context.

a. He made some *obscure* remark that no one understood.

b. The play shall remain *obscure* to those unwilling to seek its true meaning.

c. The *obscure* passage may be interpreted in several ways.

FINAL REFLECTIONS

The Comic Imagination

The writers represented in this unit have focused on the absurdities of Americans as individuals and as a group. They have exposed our weaknesses and have invited us to laugh at them. It is worth pointing out, too, that American comedy has always tended to play up sympathy and play down cruelty. Put in another way, one might say that American comedy is essentially optimistic rather than pessimistic. In this respect it tends to reflect the basically optimistic outlook of American society as a whole.

The optimism, the sympathetic emphasis of American comedy, is not, however, a loose and lazy optimism which bids us to do nothing because all things are ultimately for the best in this best of all possible societies. Although the prevailing spirit of American comedy has been sympathetic, we should not overlook the fact that it has criticized real faults. Humorists call attention to our foibles and invite us to laugh at them, but they do not invite us to forget them.

IMPLICATIONS

Recall the selections in this unit and use illustrations from them to support your evaluation of each of the following statements. You may also call upon your own experience, where applicable.

1. Americans resist rules and regulations of all kinds and enjoy "cutting up" authorities.

2. Young Americans are more impulsive and take things far less seriously than their elders.

3. In American society women are far more likely to avoid the ruts of conformity than men.

4. There is still a great deal of the Puritan in the American character; we do not generally enjoy seeing others having fun.

5. In a technological and automated society such as ours, the responses of individuals tend to become automatic and standardized.

6. Americans have an unusually strong sympathy for the underdog.

7. Americans tend to identify with the common man and to be suspicious of all those who for one reason or another stand above the average.

TECHNIQUES

Comedy

Each of the following quotations makes some statement about comedy. Study each statement to determine what it means, and then be prepared to point out two or three selections that show the statement to be either true or false.

1. ". . . *too much* of anything, if plausibly brought in and playfully received, is comic."

2. "Humor is meant to blow up evil and make fun of the follies of life."

3. "Why we laugh is generally because we have seen or heard something that is at variance with custom."

4. "The true humorist must be an optimist."

5. ". . . humor is the best that lies closest to the familiar, to that part of the familiar which is humiliating, distressing, even tragic."

Sympathy and Detachment

You have seen that in order for a comedy to be successful an author must succeed in winning some measure of sympathy from his readers for his characters or with the situation he presents. On the other hand, he also wants the reader to remain somewhat detached; for if the reader is too sympathetic—if he identifies fully with a character—he may not enjoy seeing that character as an object of ridicule. In other words, the author must maintain a rather delicate balance between sympathy and detachment; the reader must be *involved*, but he must be involved playfully, not seriously.

Look over two or three of the selections which you liked particularly and try to determine how the author captured your sympathy and managed to turn it in a playful direction. (You can probably do this merely by examining the beginning of the selection.) If you wish, you might also choose some selections you didn't like and try to determine why the author failed to attract your sympathies for his characters or his situation.

O. Henry

O. Henry (1862–1910), a pseudonym for William Sydney Porter, has become synonymous with the surprise-ending short story. Born in North Carolina, he left school early and went first to Austin and then to Houston, Texas, working at various jobs, including teller at a bank, until he became editor of a weekly, *Rolling Stone,* which soon after went out of business. Fleeing from charges of embezzlement at the Austin bank, O. Henry went first to New Orleans, then to Honduras. In 1897 he returned to Austin and was sentenced to five years in a federal prison at Columbus, Ohio. In prison he wrote stories under a variety of names, but finally settled upon O. Henry as a pseudonym. When he was released, O. Henry first moved to Pittsburgh and then to New York where he settled down to writing stories for magazines, later collected under such titles as *Cabbages and Kings, The Four Million,* and *The Gentle Grafter.* His stories are characterized by an empathy for the underdog, humor, and pathos.

J. Frank Dobie

J. Frank Dobie (1888–1964), colorful chronicler of Texas history and folklore, was born on a Texas ranch in 1888. A graduate of Southwestern University, he was for most of his life a college professor, chiefly at the University of Texas. His works include *Longhorns, Mustangs, Coronado's Children, Up the Trail from Texas, Tales of Old-Time Texas, A Texan in England.*

Ludwig Bemelmans

Ludwig Bemelmans (1898–1962) was a prolific writer of books for children and adults and a painter of some renown. Born in the Austrian Tyrol, Bemelmans came to the United States in 1914 at the age of sixteen. He worked in various hotels and studied painting until he settled to writing and illustrating stories and articles for a number of magazines and, finally, his own books. Among his famous stories are those about Madeline, a small girl who lived in a convent school in Paris: *Madeline* and *Madeline's Rescue.*

Cornelia Otis Skinner

An actress and monologuist, Cornelia Otis Skinner (1901–   ) has been a Broadway star and has appeared on radio, television, and in motion pictures. She is also famous for her writings. In 1942 she coauthored (with Emily Kimbrough) the best-selling *Our Hearts Were Young and Gay*. Born into a theatrical family, Miss Skinner spent her early childhood accompanying her actor father, Otis Skinner, on his tours in America and in Europe. The story of this life she has told in *Family Circle*. Of her other collections of essays or personal reminiscences, the most recently published is *Elegant Wits and Grand Horizontals* (1962).

Emily Kimbrough

Emily Kimbrough (1899–) was collaborator with Cornelia Otis Skinner on *Our Hearts Were Young and Gay*. A Hoosier by birth, Miss Kimbrough grew up in Chicago and has for many years lived in New York. Her first job was editor of a fashion magazine for Marshall Field & Company. Later she became fashion editor and then managing editor of *The Ladies' Home Journal*. The story of her trip to Europe was only the first of many gay and hilarious accounts of her travels. Recent volumes include *And a Right Good Crew, Forty Plus and Fancy Free, Pleasure by the Busload,* and *Water, Water, Everywhere.*

Ogden Nash

Ogden Nash (1902–) is a master of humorous verse—visual and auditory. He taught at Newport, Rhode Island, for one year and then worked several years in a publishing company. Somewhat sophisticated in style, often published in *The New Yorker*, Nash pushes, struggles, triumphs in the eventual rhyme. Occasionally bitter, Nash's verses are usually humorous. He has written the lyrics for two musical comedies. Among his best-known collections of verse are *I'm a Stranger Here Myself, Parents Keep Out, You Can't Get There from Here.*

Conrad Aiken

Conrad Aiken (1889–), who was born in Savannah, Georgia, and educated in New England private schools and at Harvard, has devoted his life to writing. In 1930 his *Selected Poems* was awarded the Pulitzer Prize for poetry and in 1954 *Collected Poems* received the National Book Award. In addition, he has written short stories for *The New Yorker*, *Scribner's*, and *Esquire* and published four novels, among them *King Coffin*, a study of criminal neuroses.

e. e. cummings

Edward Estlin Cummings (1894–1962) was born in Massachusetts and educated at Harvard University. During World War I, he went to France as an ambulance driver and later joined the American forces as a private. After a brief imprisonment in France, Cummings wrote *The Enormous Room*, a full-length story which gained him a small but substantial reputation. It is, however, through his poetry—and his unconventionalities—that most readers today know him. Cummings' poetry was marked by experimentation with technique and typography. Through form as well as through meaning, Cummings attempted to give his readers certain experiences—humorous, ironic, cynical.

Richard Armour

Richard Armour (1906–), though long a professor in a girls' college, happily married, and the father of daughters, has made a career out of poking fun at the female—and survived. His writings, serious and funny, and his humorous verse have dealt with such diverse subjects as Coleridge, Shakespeare, parents, the classics. His series, "It All Started with . . ." has included Columbus, Europe, Eve, and Karl Marx. He has written thousands of verses, some of them collected in such volumes as *Light Armour* and *Nights with Armour*. Armour has taught English at many colleges and universities, most recently at Scripps College.

David McCord

David McCord (1897–), a New Yorker by birth, earned his bachelor's and master's degrees at Harvard. He once served on the staff of the Boston *Evening Transcript*. He has written prose and poetry and published a number of volumes. His work has also appeared in *The New Yorker, Saturday Review, Atlantic,* and *Harper's*. He has edited collections of British and American poetry and poems for children and has had a number of one-man shows of his watercolors.

Phyllis McGinley

Phyllis McGinley (1905–) was born in Oregon and grew up in the West. She attended the

Universities of Utah and California and then taught one year in Utah. Bent on a writing career, she moved to New York, held a succession of jobs, including writing for *Town and Country.* Her first children's book, *The Horse Who Lived Upstairs,* was published in 1944 and since that time she has written many others. She is known chiefly for her verse, much of which is published in *The New Yorker.* Among her collections of verse, two of the best-known volumes are *A Short Walk from the Station* and *The Love Letters of Phyllis McGinley.* In 1961 she became the first writer of light verse to win the Pulitzer Prize.

Dorothy Parker

Dorothy Parker (1893–   ), New Jersey-born satiric poet and short-story writer, worked as drama critic and book critic for New York magazines. In 1927 her first book of verse, *Enough Rope,* was a best seller. As a free-lance writer, she continued to write sardonic, satiric verse and a great many short stories, marked by their diversity, many revealing a strong social consciousness.

Countée Cullen

Countée Cullen's (1903–1946) first book of poems, *Color,* appeared in 1925; it immediately marked him as a gifted writer. It was soon followed by other collections, ending ultimately with the volume entitled *On These I Stand,* a collection of the poems Cullen thought his best. The volume was published in 1947, a year after his untimely death.

Max Shulman

A Minnesotan by birth, Max Shulman (1919–   ) attended the University of Minnesota, writing a humor column for the campus newspaper and editing the campus humor magazine. A year out of college his first novel, *Barefoot Boy with Cheek,* lampooning college life, was published. He has written several other humorous, satiric novels, coauthored two successful musical comedies, and a television series. The series centered on the main figure of his novel, *The Many Loves of Dobie Gillis.* Recent novels include *I Was a Teen-Age Dwarf* and *Rally Round the Flag, Boys!*

Charles Beaumont

Charles Beaumont (1929–   ), a prolific writer of short stories and articles, has also written several

scores of television plays and scripts for motion pictures. He writes under three pseudonyms in addition to his own name. Several of his books have been written with coauthors. Recent books are *The Intruder, The Hunger, Night Ride, Omnibus of Speed,* and *Remember? Remember?*

Ring Lardner

Although Ring Lardner (1885–1933) studied engineering, he became a newspaperman instead—first in South Bend, Indiana, later in Chicago and New York. He wrote a sports column for the Chicago *Tribune* and printed there his first "You know me, Al" sketches, published later in a collection under that title. His favorite subjects were baseball players and boxers, and his style was a racy vernacular, humorous, sometimes cynical. For a brief period he was editor of the publication *Sporting News.*

Robert Benchley

A versatile humorist, Robert Benchley (1889–1945) achieved fame as an essayist, editor, and motion picture actor. Benchley, born in Massachusetts, took an A.B. at Harvard in 1912. He worked for the advertising department in the Curtis Publishing Co. for two years and then did a stint in personnel work in Boston. Later he became editor of various newspapers in New York and Washington. After World War I, he served briefly as editor of the magazine, *Vanity Fair,* and then for almost a decade as drama editor for the old *Life.* He wrote many poems and humorous essays. Some of the latter became the subject of motion picture shorts in which he starred. His many books include two which were posthumously published, *Benchley—or Else* and *Chips Off the Old Benchley.*

S. J. Perelman

S. J. Perelman (1904–   ) graduated from Brown University in 1925. He wrote first for the humor magazine, *Judge,* and later contributed to *The New Yorker* and the old *Life.* In recent years he has written chiefly for *The New Yorker* and *Holiday.* As a master of the *gag,* Perelman has written a great many motion pictures and a successful musical comedy. His accounts of two round-the-world trips were published as *Westward Ha!* and *The Swiss Family Perelman.*

MARK TWAIN

SAMUEL LANGHORNE CLEMENS

1835–1910

The evolution of Sam Clemens of Hannibal, Missouri, into Mark Twain, the internationally known literary artist, was a gradual process and, in some respects, accidental. When Clemens at the age of fourteen went to work as an apprentice to the publisher of the *Missouri Courier,* he had little thought of a career; his father had died and the sons had no choice but to support the family. Yet many years later Clemens wrote: "I became a printer and began to add one link after another to the chain which was to lead me into the literary profession." These "links" took him from Missouri to the East, then to Nevada and California, to Hawaii, to Europe, back to Buffalo, to Hartford, nine more years in Europe, and finally two lonely years in Redding, Connecticut—a crowded, busy, boisterous lifetime that brought him riches and fame. When Oxford University granted him an honorary degree in 1907, no one, looking back at his achievement, could have been more surprised than Sam Clemens himself at the distance he had come from that Mississippi River town.

Before personal unhappiness and financial disaster robbed Twain of his youthful enthusiasm, he produced two novels which alone would have made him a classic in American Literature. They are built on the loose frame of his autobiographical volumes: a disjointed plot sprinkled with tall tales, extravagant excursions, sharp satire, and moral instruction. The Adventures of Tom Sawyer captured the imagination of most of America when it appeared in 1876. The Adventures of Huckleberry Finn, published in 1885, has become quite literally a world favorite.

Hannibal in the 1830's was a paradise for a young boy. "I can call back the solemn twilight and mystery of the deep woods, the earthy smells, the faint odors of the wild flowers, the sheen of rain-washed foliage," he wrote in his *Autobiography*. Nor did the hectic life on the waterfront ever quite leave his memory. It infected him with restlessness and the sweet smell of romantic journeys. At the age of seventeen, Sam left his brother's newspaper to discover for himself what the world had to offer. As a journeyman printer he wandered along the East coast and through the Middle West, never in want of work, occasionally contributing letters and humorous sketches to various papers, signing them "Grumbler" or "Rumbler" or "Thomas Jefferson Snodgrass."

After reading travel books on South America, he set out for the Amazon and the Orinoco. But once again the great Mississippi entered his life. On the boat to New Orleans he met Horace Bixby, the river pilot, and in a short time the young Sam Clemens was apprenticed to him as a "cub," eager to "learn the river" and eventually to earn his own exalted place on a magnificent steamboat. "After a year and a half of hard study," he recalled later, "the United States Inspectors rigorously examined me through a couple of long sittings and decided that I knew every inch of the Mississippi—thirteen hundred miles in the dark and in the day." For three years Clemens was a licensed pilot, watching more closely than perhaps he realized the motley crowds aboard—gamblers, prospectors, Southern planters, slave traders, harlots. His ear for local speech and his eye for melodramatic detail were given the best training they could have had.

But like the rest of America he was on the move. His brother Orion had been appointed Secretary to the Territory of Nevada and urged Sam to join him there. After a few weeks of Civil War service as a hopelessly bad Confederate soldier, Clemens turned westward, as prospector and miner. The lure of sudden wealth in the Nevada mountains was irresistible. Within a year he was back in Virginia City

as a reporter on the *Territorial Enterprise,* wiser but no richer. Now twenty-five, he realized he was happier in journalism than anywhere else, and his talent for writing humorous and satiric sketches had a chance to bloom. Sam Clemens signed his contributions with the pseudonym Mark Twain, a name he said he stole from a Captain Isaiah Sellers who used to write for the New Orleans *Picayune* and who had recently died. More likely it was a recollection from his river days, since "mark twain" was the leadsman's call telling the pilot that his ship was in two fathoms of water and therefore safe. As Mark Twain, Sam Clemens began a third and wildly successful career, but in 1862 he was still not a literary artist nor trying to be.

From Virginia City to San Francisco to Sacramento as journalist, and then to the Sandwich Islands (now called Hawaii) as travel correspondent, the talented Mark Twain was gaining a reputation as one of the wittiest men on the West coast. He had always been a natural storyteller, a showman who genuinely enjoyed entertaining an audience with tall tales and whimsical anecdotes. It was natural for him to try the lecture platform after his travels to Hawaii. His success was instantaneous. He gave his first lecture in San Francisco at the age of thirty and continued to delight audiences all over the world well past his seventieth year, earning as much as $1,600 in one night. Before he left for the East, Mark Twain was hailed as "The Humorist of the Pacific Slope," a reputation built in part on his newspaper column but chiefly on his hilarious public lectures. One printed story, however, preceded him in the East and prepared the way for his arrival. Artemus Ward had persuaded him to write a tale about a jumping frog which Twain had heard in an Angel Camp tavern in Calaveras County. The New York *Saturday Press* published "The Celebrated Jumping Frog" in 1865; it was the beginning of literary fame, though Twain refused to call it that. He was, he said, a successful lecturer at best, a roving journalist at worst.

This roving spirit next took him eastward, to New York and Europe. He boarded the *Quaker City* in 1867 for a five-month tour of France, Italy, and the Holy Land. To meet expenses he accepted a commission to write letters periodically to the *Alta California* and the New York *Tribune.* In them Twain poured out a seemingly endless series of critical opinions based on American superiority to all things European. He knew well how to entertain the American reader. French manners, Italian guides, Greek ruins, Near Eastern monuments struck him as equally ridiculous. On his return he was besieged with offers. "I have 18 invitations to lecture, at $100 each, in various parts of the Union," he wrote his mother. "Have declined them all. I am for business now. Belong on the *Tribune* staff, and shall write occasionally." Business, little did he know at the time, meant literature, not journalism. New York publishers insisted the *Quaker City* letters cried out for republication, and they offered Twain an irresistible contract. "I had made my mind up to *one* thing," he told his friends. "I wasn't going to touch a book unless there was *money* in it, and a good deal of it. I told them so." Money there was; too much of it. *The Innocents Abroad* appeared in 1869, an immediate best seller. Twain had been persuaded, moreover, to edit his letters, to rewrite some and destroy others. What began as journalism was soon shaped into literature. His newest career was launched.

To make money making people laugh, however, struck some of Twain's friends as an "unliterary" ambition, so he continued to call his work journalism. He bought a third interest in the Buffalo *Express* and married Olivia Langdon on the strength of *The Innocents Abroad* sales, hoping to settle down to a more sedate domestic life and to contribute nothing more than occasional satiric letters or humorous sketches to New York papers. Then he moved his family to Hartford, Connecticut. Harriet Beecher Stowe, of *Uncle Tom's Cabin* fame, was a near neighbor; William Dean Howells, editor of the *Atlantic Monthly,* became an inti-

mate friend, as did the Reverend Joseph Twichell of Hartford. Twain was surrounded by helpful critics. Howells asked for contributions to his magazine and Twain wrote him: "Twichell and I have had a long walk in the woods and I got to telling him about old Mississippi days of steamboating glory and grandeur as I saw them (during 5 years) from the pilot-house. He said 'What a virgin subject to hurl into a magazine!' I hadn't thought of that before. Would you like a series of papers to run . . . about 4 months, say?" Howells knew where Twain's strength lay and he urged him to begin his reminiscences. The appearance of these papers in the *Atlantic Monthly* in 1875 brought such instant praise and so many demands for more of his vivid prose that Twain was ready to admit that he had become a man of letters, almost against his will. The West had nourished the ambitious Sam Clemens. Mark Twain the artist was born in New England.

A newspaper friend of Twain's drew this impression of the 1865 San Francisco earthquake. It was one of Mark Twain's favorite drawings.

What of that West had he captured in his pages—its brash, overconfident youthfulness, its growing pains, its glorious abandon? His recipe for autobiographical writing smacks of the lawless frontier attitudes: "Start at no particular time of your life; wander at your free will all over your life; talk only about the thing which interests you for the moment; drop it the minute its interest threatens to pale, and turn your talk upon the new and more interesting thing that has intruded itself into your mind meantime." *Roughing It* (1872) was assembled in this way, a series of tall tales, brilliant descriptions, humorous anecdotes, and character studies, held together loosely by a first-person narrator, Twain himself. *Life on the Mississippi,* published ten years later, and his *Autobiography,* published after his death, continue the pattern. But reminiscence alone is not enough to make a great writer. Sam Clemens loved the Western brand of humor: the prac-

tical joke, the extravagant, improbable tale, the Indian and Negro legends, the coarse and ribald story. He not only preserved these for posterity but he also learned to preserve Western dialect speech, so easy to mimic on the lecture platform but so difficult to record. What is more, Twain as he matured let his satiric bent develop freely. *The Innocents Aboard* is full of healthy criticism of European culture. When he came to recall his early life in Missouri, Nevada, and California, he did not spare his native subjects: reckless speculators, brash politicians, brutal desperados, hypocritical ministers. He loved the life he lived in the West, but he could also look at it realistically. Indeed, by the time he died, in 1910, Twain had produced at least a half-dozen sharply satiric, even bitter, fictional studies of his society, beginning with *The Gilded Age* and ending with one of the most pessimistic stories written in the twentieth century, *The Mysterious Stranger.*

The reasons for this pessimism are numerous. Financial success came so easily that he squandered his money. The failure of the Paige typesetter and the bankruptcy of his publishing company sent him into enormous debt which only a grueling round-the-world lecture tour could erase. His daughter Susan died while he was living in England. A few years after his return, his wife died and then his daughter Jean. He faced the loneliness of old age with a firm conviction that "the damned human race" deserved all the misery it had brought on itself. No wonder that he could give one of his characters, Pudd'nhead Wilson, these black thoughts: "Whoever has lived long enough to find out what life is, knows how deep a debt of gratitude we owe to Adam, the first great benefactor of our age. He brought death into the world."

Before personal unhappiness and financial disaster robbed Twain of his youthful enthusiasm, however, he produced two novels which alone would have made him a classic in American literature. They are built on the loose frame of his autobiographical volumes: a disjointed plot sprinkled with tall tales, extravagant excursions, sharp satire, and moral instruction. *The Adventures of Tom Sawyer* captured the imagination of most of America when it appeared in 1876. *The Adventures of Huckleberry Finn,* published in 1885, has become quite literally a world favorite. They are boys' books seemingly, melodramatic adventure stories told by a master storyteller. But beneath the surface lies more serious criticism of man's foibles than some readers suspect. Twain had written plenty of social history and moral criticism. Now he tried to embody his feelings in imaginative characters, to shape a story around them, to disentangle his own life from Tom and Huck so that they could stand as free of their creator as Hamlet or Silas Marner. Twain did not wholly succeed; it is not difficult to trace characters and plot to specific incidents in Sam Clemens' life. But these parallels are unimportant. What is more essential is the universality Twain gives his story, the intense honesty with which he describes young boys growing into manhood, the depth of feeling he is able to give to the moral crises all youths have to cope with sometime in their lives.

Tom Sawyer may well have been intended to entertain and to do little more. It entertains supremely well, being packed with midnight incantations, a cruel murder, blackmail, witchery, a court trial, and the expected happy ending. The mastermind is Tom himself, mischievous, clever, romantically imaginative. *Huckleberry Finn,* intended as a sequel, is infinitely more complex a story, and Twain almost abandoned the manuscript in despair several times during its creation. Huck's moral awareness is the heart of the novel, the center of the action. The greatest difficulty Twain faced was to untangle Huck and his friend Jim, the runaway slave, from a plot that threatened to swamp the hero and the story's moral at the same time. The plot suffers; some critics feel the ending is grotesquely mismanaged. But Huck emerges nevertheless a believable adolescent who is confronted by the moral decisions which test most of us. His decisions run counter to the society in which he lived and they were both a challenge to and a commentary on the values of that society.

Twain describes life on the raft in brutal contrast to life ashore. Huck is quick to see that each time he becomes entangled in "civilized" life in the riverbank towns he confronts violence or hypocrisy and has to flee to the raft and his friend Jim for safety. Twain lavishes his creative powers on the Negro, faithful Jim, the inherently good man who loves Huck no matter how the young boy treats him. In time, Huck comes to understand what brotherhood means, not through Sunday school texts but through the blunt realities of frontier life. And after his baptism on the river, he fears what civilized life can bring. "I reckon," he concludes, "I got to light out for the Territory ahead of the rest, because Aunt Sally she's going to adopt me and sivilize me, and I can't stand it. I been there before." Huck's cry is Sam Clemens' cry, for the freedom of childhood, for the romantic dream of the open road that somehow, in our growing up, has escaped us. It is our good fortune that a Mark Twain came into being to recollect that childhood.

This story is not original
with Twain. We are told that he first
heard it from a man named Ben Coon in a western
mining camp and that he probably read
Henry Leland's "Frogs Shot without Powder"
in the New York journal, *Spirit of the Times.*
But this version, at least, is his own,
particularly the leisurely way in which he moves
into the story and the manner in which he builds
suspense. When it appeared in the New York
Saturday Press on November 18, 1865,
Mark Twain's name became literary news.
Even so eminent a New Englander
as James Russell Lowell was ready to call it
"the finest piece of humorous literature
yet produced in America." With Bret Harte,
Twain became a spokesman for Western culture,
almost, one could say, against his will.
"The Jumping Frog" was, after all, only
a tall tale written down, oral history
now made "literary."

The Celebrated Jumping Frog of Calaveras County

In compliance with the request of a friend of mine who wrote me from the East, I called on good-natured, garrulous old Simon Wheeler and inquired after my friend's friend, Leonidas W. Smiley, as requested to do, and I hereunto append the result. I have a lurking suspicion that *Leonidas W.* Smiley is a myth, that my friend never knew such a personage, and that he only conjectured that if I asked old Wheeler about him, it would remind him of his infamous *Jim* Smiley and he would go to work and bore me to death with some exasperating reminiscence of him as long and as tedious as it should be useless to me. If that was the design, it succeeded.

I found Simon Wheeler dozing comfortably by the barroom stove of the dilapidated tavern in the decayed mining camp of Angel's, and I noticed that he was fat and bald-headed and had an expression of winning gentleness and simplicity upon his tranquil countenance. He roused up and gave me good day. I told him that a friend of mine had commissioned me to make some inquiries about a cherished companion of his boyhood named *Leonidas W.* Smiley—*Rev. Leonidas W.* Smiley, a young minister of the Gospel, who he had heard was at one time a resident of Angel's Camp. I added that if Mr. Wheeler could tell me anything about this Rev. Leonidas W. Smiley, I would feel under many obligations to him.

Simon Wheeler backed me into a corner and blockaded me there with his chair, and then sat down and reeled off the monotonous narrative which follows this paragraph. He never smiled, he never frowned, he never changed his voice from the gentle-flowing key to which he tuned his initial sentence, he never betrayed the slightest suspicion of enthusiasm, but all through the interminable narrative there ran a vein of impressive earnestness and sincerity which showed me plainly that, so far from his imagining that there was anything ridiculous or funny about his story, he regarded it as a really important matter and admired its two heroes as men of transcendent genius in *finesse.*[1] I let him go on in his own way and never interrupted him once.

"Rev. Leonidas W. H'm, Reverend Le—— Well, there was a feller here once by the name of *Jim* Smiley, in the winter of '49—or maybe it was the spring of '50—I don't recollect exactly, somehow, though what makes me think it was one or the other is because I remember

From *In Defense of Harriet Shelley and Other Stories.* Reprinted with the permission of Harper & Row, Publishers, Inc.

1. **finesse**\fĭ ▲nĕs\ clever maneuvering.

the big flume[2] warn't finished when he first come to the camp; but anyway, he was the curiousest man about always betting on anything that turned up you ever see, if he could get anybody to bet on the other side, and if he couldn't he'd change sides. Any way that suited the other man would suit *him*—any way just so's he got a bet, *he* was satisfied. But still he was lucky, uncommon lucky; he most always come out winner. He was always ready and laying for a chance; there couldn't be no solit'ry thing mentioned but that feller'd offer to bet on it and take ary side you please, as I was just telling you. If there was a horse-race, you'd find him flush or you'd find him busted at the end of it; if there was a dog-fight, he'd bet on it; if there was a cat-fight, he'd bet on it; if there was a chicken-fight, he'd bet on it; why, if there was two birds setting on a fence, he would bet you which one would fly first; or if there was a camp-meeting, he would be there reg'lar to bet on Parson Walker, which he judged to be the best exhorter about here, and so he was too, and a good man. If he even see a straddle-bug[3] start to go anywheres, he would bet you how long it would take him to get to—to wherever he was going to, and if you took him up, he would foller that straddle-bug to Mexico but what he would find out where he was bound for and how long he was on the road. Lots of the boys here has seen that Smiley and can tell you about him. Why, it never made no difference to *him*—he'd bet on *any* thing—the dangdest feller. Parson Walker's wife laid very sick once for a good while, and it seemed as if they warn't going to save her; but one morning he come in and Smiley up and asked him how she was, and he said she was considerable better—thank the Lord for his inf'nite mercy—and coming on so smart that with the blessing of Prov'dence she'd get well yet; and Smiley, before he thought, says, 'Well, I'll resk two-and-a-half she don't anyway.'

"Thish-yer Smiley had a mare—the boys called her the fifteen-minute nag but that was only in fun, you know, because of course she was faster than that—and he used to win money on that horse, for all she was so slow and always had the asthma, or the distemper, or the consumption, or something of that kind. They used to give her two or three hundred yards' start and then pass her under way, but always at the fag end of the race she'd get excited and desperate like, and come cavorting and straddling up and scattering her legs around limber, sometimes in the air and sometimes out to one side among the fences, and kicking up m-o-r-e dust and raising m-o-r-e racket with her coughing and sneezing and blowing her nose—and *always* fetch up at the stand just about a neck ahead, as near as you could cipher[4] it down.

"And he had a little small bull-pup, that to look at him you'd think he warn't worth a cent but to set around and look ornery and lay for a chance to steal something. But as soon as money was up on him he was a different dog; his under-jaw'd begin to stick out like the fo'castle[5] of a steamboat and his teeth would uncover and shine like the furnaces. And a dog might tackle him and bully-rag[6] him, and bite him and throw him over his shoulder two or three times, and Andrew Jackson—which was the name of the pup—Andrew Jackson would never let on but what *he* was satisfied and hadn't expected nothing else—and the bets being doubled and doubled on the other side all the time, till the money was all up; and then all of a sudden he would grab that other dog jest by the j'int of his hind leg and freeze to it—not chaw, you understand, but only just grip and hang on till they throwed up the sponge, if it was a year. Smiley always come out winner on that pup till he harnessed a dog once that didn't have no hind legs, because they'd been sawed off in a circular saw, and when the thing had gone along far enough and the money was all up and he come to make a snatch for his pet holt, he see in a minute how he'd been imposed

---

2. **flume**\flūm\ channel for conveying water used for power, transportation, or irrigation.
3. **straddle-bug**, long-legged insect.
4. **cipher**, write.
5. **fo'castle** (forecastle)\fōk•səl\ upper deck of a ship.
6. **bully-rag**, to torment or harass.

Poster used by Mark Twain for a Brooklyn lecture, about 1869.

on and how the other dog had him in the door, so to speak, and he 'peared suprised, and then he looked sorter discouraged-like and didn't try no more to win the fight, and so he got shucked[7] out bad. He gave Smiley a look, as much as to say his heart was broke, and it was *his* fault for putting up a dog that hadn't no hind legs for him to take holt of, which was his main dependence in a fight, and then he limped off a piece and laid down and died. It was a good pup, was that Andrew Jackson, and would have made a name for hisself if he'd lived, for the stuff was in him and he had genius—I know it, because he hadn't no opportunities to speak of, and it don't stand to reason that a dog could make such a fight as he could under them circumstances if he hadn't no talent. It always makes me feel sorry when I think of that last fight of his'n and the way it turned out.

"Well, thish-yer Smiley had rat-tarriers, and chicken cocks, and tomcats and all them kind of things till you couldn't rest, and you couldn't fetch nothing for him to bet on but he'd match you. He ketched a frog one day and took him home, and said he cal'lated to educate him; and so he never done nothing for three months but set in his back yard and learn that frog to jump. And you bet you he *did* learn him, too. He'd give him a little punch behind, and the next minute you'd see that frog whirling in the air like a doughnut—see him turn one summerset, or maybe a couple if he got a good start, and come down flat-footed and all right, like a cat. He got him up so in the matter of ketching flies, and kep' him in practice so constant, that he'd nail a fly every time as fur as he could see him. Smiley said all a frog wanted was education and he could do 'most anything—and I believe him. Why, I've seen him set Dan'l Webster down here on this floor—Dan'l Webster was the name of the frog—and sing out, 'Flies, Dan'l, flies!' and quicker'n you could wink he'd spring straight up and snake a fly off'n the counter there, and flop down on the floor ag'in as solid as a gob of mud, and fall to scratching the side of his head with his hind foot as indifferent as if he hadn't no idea he'd been doin' any more'n any frog might do. You never see a frog so modest and straight-for'ard as he was, for all he was so gifted. And when it come to fair and square jumping on a dead level, he could get over more ground at one straddle than any animal of his breed you ever see. Jumping on a dead level was his strong suit, you understand; and when it come to that, Smiley would ante up money on him as long as he had a red. Smiley was monstrous proud of his frog, and well he might be for fellers that had traveled and been everywheres all said he laid over any frog that ever *they* see.

"Well, Smiley kep' the beast in a little lattice box, and he used to fetch him down-town sometimes and lay for a bet. One day a feller—a

---

7. **shucked**\shəkt\ stripped, cast off.

stranger in the camp, he was—come acrost him with his box and says:

" 'What might it be that you've got in the box?'

"And Smiley says, sorter indifferent-like, 'It might be a parrot, or it might be a canary, maybe, but it ain't—it's only just a frog.'

"And the feller took it and looked at it careful, and turned it round this way and that, and says, 'H'm—so 'tis. Well, what's *he* good for?'

" 'Well,' Smiley says, easy and careless, 'he's good enough for *one* thing, I should judge—he can outjump any frog in Calaveras County.'

"The feller took the box again and took another long, particular look, and give it back to Smiley and says, very deliberate, 'Well,' he says, 'I don't see no p'ints about that frog that's any better'n any other frog.'

" 'Maybe you don't,' Smiley says. 'Maybe you understand frogs and maybe you don't understand 'em; maybe you've had experience and maybe you ain't only a amature, as it were. Anyways, I've got *my* opinion, and I'll resk forty dollars that he can outjump any frog in Calaveras County.'

"And the feller studied a minute and then says, kinder sad-like, 'Well, I'm only a stranger here and I ain't got no frog; but if I had a frog, I'd bet you.'

"And then Smiley says, 'That's all right—that's all right—if you'll hold my box a minute, I'll go and get you a frog.' And so the feller took the box and put up his forty dollars along with Smiley's, and set down to wait.

"So he set there a good while thinking and thinking to himself, and then he got the frog out and prized his mouth open and took a teaspoon and filled him full of quail-shot—filled him pretty near up to his chin—and set him on the floor. Smiley he went to the swamp and slopped around in the mud for a long time, and finally he ketched a frog and fetched him in and give him to this feller, and says:

" 'Now, if you're ready, set him alongside of Dan'l, with his forepaws just even with Dan'l's, and I'll give the word.' Then he says, 'One—two—three—*git!*' and him and the feller touched up the frogs from behind, and the new frog hopped off lively, but Dan'l give a heave and hysted up his shoulders—so—like a Frenchman, but it warn't no use—he couldn't budge; he was planted as solid as a church, and he couldn't no more stir than if he was anchored out. Smiley was a good deal surprised, and he was disgusted too, but he didn't have no idea what the matter was, of course.

"The feller took the money and started away, and when he was going out at the door, he sorter jerked his thumb over his shoulder—so—at Dan'l and says again, very deliberate, 'Well,' he says, '*I* don't see no p'ints about that frog that's any better'n any other frog.'

"Smiley he stood scratching his head and looking down at Dan'l a long time, and at last he says, 'I do wonder what in the nation that frog throw'd off for—I wonder if there ain't something the matter with him—he 'pears to look mighty baggy, somehow.' And he ketched Dan'l by the nap of the neck and hefted him, and says, 'Why, blame my cats if he don't weigh five pound!' and turned him upside down and he belched out a double handful of shot. And then he see how it was, and he was the maddest man—he set the frog down and took out after that feller, but he never ketched him. And—"

[Here Simon Wheeler heard his name called from the front yard and got up to see what was wanted.] And turning to me as he moved away, he said: "Just set where you are, stranger, and rest easy—I ain't going to be gone a second."

But, by your leave, I did not think that a continuation of the history of the enterprising vagabond *Jim* Smiley would be likely to afford me much information concerning the Rev. *Leonidas W.* Smiley and so I started away.

At the door I met the sociable Wheeler returning, and he buttonholed me and recommenced:

"Well, thish-yer Smiley had a yaller one-eyed cow that didn't have no tail, only just a short stump like a bannanner, and—"

However, lacking both time and inclination, I did not wait to hear about the afflicted cow but took my leave.

Twain began his autobiography in 1897
and kept working on it from time to time
until his death in 1910. As one would expect,
the manuscript he left was a grab bag
of reminiscences, portraits of friends, business
ventures, visits to Europe, his uncle's farm,
and much else, written in Vienna and Florence
and several American cities. In 1924,
Albert Bigelow Paine published about half
of the surviving pages, calling it *Mark Twain's
Autobiography*. In 1940, Bernard De Voto used
about half of the remainder to publish what is
really a third volume of the autobiography,
though he calls it *Mark Twain in Eruption*.
Finally, Charles Neider put the unwieldy
manuscript into proper sequence and published,
in 1959, *The Autobiography of Mark Twain:
Including Chapters Now Published for the First
Time*. Chapter 30 of this edition recalls a visit
Twain made in 1867 to Washington, immediately
after his return from Europe on the *Quaker City*.
The book he refers to in the first sentence
is *The Innocents Abroad*.

I Sell a Dog

I was out of money and I went down to
Washington to see if I could earn enough there
to keep me in bread and butter while I should
write the book. I came across William Swinton, brother of the historian, and together we
invented a scheme for our mutual sustenance;
we became the fathers and originators of what
is a common feature in the newspaper world
now, the syndicate. We became the old original
first Newspaper Syndicate on the planet; it was
on a small scale but that is usual with untried
new enterprises. We had twelve journals on our

list; they were all weeklies, all obscure and poor
and all scattered far away among the back settlements. It was a proud thing for those little
newspapers to have a Washington correspondent and a fortunate thing for us that they felt
in that way about it. Each of the twelve took
two letters a week from us, at a dollar per letter;
each of us wrote one letter per week and sent
off six duplicates of it to these benefactors, thus
acquiring twenty-four dollars a week to live on,
which was all we needed in our cheap and
humble quarters.

Swinton was one of the dearest and loveliest
human beings I have ever known, and we led
a charmed existence together, in a contentment
which knew no bounds. Swinton was refined by
nature and breeding; he was a gentle man by
nature and breeding; he was highly educated;
he was of a beautiful spirit; he was pure in
heart and speech. He was a Scotchman and a
Presbyterian; a Presbyterian of the old and
genuine school, being honest and sincere in his
religion and loving it and finding serenity and
peace in it. He hadn't a vice, unless a large and
grateful sympathy with Scotch whiskey may be
called by that name. I didn't regard it as a vice,
because he was a Scotchman, and Scotch
whiskey to a Scotchman is as innocent as milk
is to the rest of the human race. In Swinton's
case it was a virtue and not an economical one.
Twenty-four dollars a week would really have
been riches to us if we hadn't had to support
that jug; because of the jug we were always
sailing pretty close to the wind, and any tardi-
ness in the arrival of any part of our income
was sure to cause some inconvenience.

I remember a time when a shortage occurred; we had to have three dollars and we
had to have it before the close of the day. I
don't know now how we happened to want all
that money at one time; I only know we had to
have it. Swinton told me to go out and find it
and he said he would also go out and see what
he could do. He didn't seem to have any doubt
that we would succeed but I knew that that
was his religion working in him; I hadn't the
same confidence; I hadn't any idea where to

turn to raise all that bullion and I said so. I think he was ashamed of me, privately, because of my weak faith. He told me to give myself no uneasiness, no concern; and said in a simple, confident, and unquestioning way, "The Lord will provide." I saw that he fully believed the Lord would provide but it seemed to me that if he had had my experience—But never mind that; before he was done with me his strong faith had had its influence and I went forth from the place almost convinced that the Lord really would provide.

I wandered around the streets for an hour, trying to think up some way to get that money, but nothing suggested itself. At last I lounged into the big lobby of the Ebbitt House, which was then a new hotel, and sat down. Presently a dog came loafing along. He paused, glanced up at me and said with his eyes, "Are you friendly?" I answered with my eyes that I was. He gave his tail a grateful wag and came forward and rested his jaw on my knee and lifted his brown eyes to my face in a winningly affectionate way. He was a lovely creature, as beautiful as a girl, and he was made all of silk and velvet. I stroked his smooth brown head and fondled his drooping ears and we were a pair of lovers right away. Pretty soon Brig.-Gen. Miles, the hero of the land, came strolling by in his blue and gold splendors, with everybody's admiring gaze upon him. He saw the dog and stopped, and there was a light in his eye which showed that he had a warm place in his heart for dogs like this gracious creature; then he came forward and patted the dog and said,

"He is very fine—he is a wonder; would you sell him?"

I was greatly moved; it seemed a marvelous thing to me, the way Swinton's prediction had come true.

I said, "Yes."

The General said, "What do you ask for him?"

"Three dollars."

The General was manifestly surprised. He said, "Three dollars? Only three dollars? Why that dog is a most uncommon dog; he can't possibly be worth less than fifty. If he were mine, I wouldn't take a hundred for him. I'm afraid you are not aware of his value. Reconsider your price if you like, I don't wish to wrong you."

But if he had known me he would have known that I was no more capable of wronging him that he was of wronging me. I responded with the same quiet decision as before.

"No, three dollars. That is his price."

"Very well, since you insist upon it," said the General, and he gave me three dollars and led the dog away and disappeared upstairs.

In about ten minutes a gentle-faced, middle-aged gentleman came along and began to look around here and there and under tables and everywhere, and I said to him, "Is it a dog you are looking for?"

His face had been sad before and troubled; but it lit up gladly now and he answered, "Yes—have you seen him?"

"Yes," I said, "he was here a minute ago and I saw him follow a gentleman away. I think I could find him for you if you would like me to try."

I have seldom seen a person look so grateful, and there was gratitude in his voice too when he conceded that he would like me to try. I said I would do it with great pleasure but that as it might take a little time I hoped he would not mind paying me something for my trouble. He said he would do it most gladly—repeating that phrase "most gladly"—and asked me how much.

I said, "Three dollars."

He looked surprised, and said, "Dear me, it is nothing! I will pay you ten, quite willingly."

But I said, "No, three is the price," and I started for the stairs without waiting for any further argument, for Swinton had said that that was the amount that the Lord would provide and it seemed to me that it would be sacrilegious to take a penny more than was promised.

I got the number of the General's room from the office clerk as I passed by his wicket, and when I reached the room I found the General there caressing his dog and quite happy. I said, "I am sorry, but I have to take the dog again."

He seemed very much surprised and said, "Take him again? Why, he is my dog; you sold him to me and at your own price."

"Yes," I said, "it is true—but I have to have him, because the man wants him again."

"What man?"

"The man that owns him; he wasn't my dog."

The General looked even more surprised than before, and for a moment he couldn't seem to find his voice; then he said, "Do you mean to tell me that you were selling another man's dog —and knew it?"

"Yes, I knew it wasn't my dog."

"Then why did you sell him?"

I said, "Well, that is a curious question to ask. I sold him because you wanted him. You offered to buy the dog; you can't deny that. I was not anxious to sell him—I had not even thought of selling him—but it seemed to me that if it could be any accommodation to you—"

He broke me off in the middle, and said, "*Accommodation* to me? It is the most extraordinary spirit of accommodation I have ever heard of—the idea of your selling a dog that didn't belong to you—"

I broke him off there and said, "There is no relevance about this kind of argument; you said yourself that the dog was probably worth a hundred dollars. I only asked you three; was there anything unfair about that? You offered to pay more, you know you did. I only asked you three; you can't deny it."

"Oh, what in the world has that to do with it! The crux of the matter is that you didn't own the dog—can't you see that? You seem to think that there is no impropriety in selling property that isn't yours provided you sell it cheap. Now then—"

I said, "Please don't argue about it any more. You can't get around the fact that the price was perfectly fair, perfectly reasonable—considering that I didn't own the dog—and so arguing about it is only a waste of words. I have to have him back again because the man wants him; don't you see that I haven't any choice in the matter? Put yourself in my place. Suppose you had sold a dog that didn't belong to you; suppose you—"

"Oh," he said, "don't muddle my brains any more with your idiotic reasoning! Take him along and give me a rest."

So I paid back the three dollars and led the dog downstairs and passed him over to his owner and collected three for my trouble.

I went away then with a good conscience, because I had acted honorably; I never could have used the three that I sold the dog for, because it was not rightly my own, but the three I got for restoring him to his rightful owner was righteously and properly mine, because I had earned it. That man might never have gotten that dog back at all, if it hadn't been for me. My principles have remained to this day what they were then. I was always honest; I know I can never be otherwise. It is as I said in the beginning—I was never able to persuade myself to use money which I had acquired in questionable ways.

Now then, that is the tale. Some of it is true.

I

THE ART OF FINESSE

Simon Wheeler admires the two heroes of the "Jumping Frog" tale as "men of transcendent genius in *finesse*." We may perhaps not agree that they deserve to be called "transcendent geniuses," but we can agree that each is engaged in the art of trying to outsmart the other. What Twain called *finesse*, we today might call "one-upmanship."

In the passage from *Autobiography*, we see that Twain himself was a master of the art of finesse.

II

IMPLICATIONS

Discuss the following statements.

1. Twain's heroes of the art of finesse have much in common with the Yankee peddler, as seen in O. Henry's "Jeff Peters as a Personal Magnet."

2. Finesse is most entertaining and humorous when it is practiced against persons like Jim Smiley and Brig.-Gen. Miles.

This excerpt from the first volume
of Twain's first best seller can hardly do
more than suggest the pleasures he and his
friends derived from playing the "innocents"
across Europe and in the Near East. Twain was
ready, in his breezy Western manner,
to criticize everything from his fellow
passengers and the sights of Europe to the food,
the lodging, and the guides. Especially
the guides. He and the doctor baited them
cruelly, calling all of them Ferguson
because they could not remember their names.
The enthusiasm of the Italian guides for their
country's landmarks lent itself easily
to Twain's broad humor.

FROM

The Innocents Abroad

In this place I may as well jot down a chapter concerning those necessary nuisances, European guides. Many a man has wished in his heart he could do without his guide; but knowing he could not, has wished he could get some amusement out of him as a remuneration for the affliction of his society. We accomplished this latter matter, and if our experience can be made useful to others they are welcome to it.

Guides know about enough English to tangle everything up so that a man can make neither head nor tail of it. They know their story by heart—the history of every statue, painting, cathedral, or other wonder they show you. They know it and tell it as a parrot would—and if you interrupt, and throw them off the track, they have to go back and begin over again. All their lives long, they are employed in show-ing strange things to foreigners and listening to their bursts of admiration. It is human nature to take delight in exciting admiration. It is what prompts children to say "smart" things, and do absurd ones, and in other ways "show off" when company is present. It is what makes gossips turn out in rain and storm to go and be the first to tell a startling bit of news. Think, then, what a passion it becomes with a guide, whose privilege it is, every day, to show to strangers wonders that throw them into perfect ecstasies of admiration! He gets so that he could not by any possibility live in a soberer atmosphere. After we discovered this, we *never* went into ecstasies any more—we never admired anything—we never showed any but impassible faces and stupid indifference in the presence of the sublimest wonders a guide had to display. We had found their weak point. We have made good use of it ever since. We have made some of those people savage, at times, but we have never lost our own serenity.

The doctor asks the questions, generally, because he can keep his countenance, and look more like an inspired idiot, and throw more imbecility into the tone of his voice than any man that lives. It comes natural to him.

The guides in Genoa are delighted to secure an American party, because Americans so much wonder, and deal so much in sentiment and emotion before any relic of Columbus. Our guide there fidgeted about as if he had swallowed a spring mattress. He was full of animation—full of impatience. He said:

"Come wis me, genteelmen!—come! I show you ze letterwriting by Christopher Colombo! —write it himself!—write it wis his own hand! —come!"

He took us to the municipal palace. After much impressive fumbling of keys and opening of locks, the stained and aged document was spread before us. The guide's eyes sparkled. He danced about us and tapped the parchment with his finger:

"What I tell you, genteelmen! Is it not so? See! handwriting Christopher Colombo!— write it himself!"

From *The Innocents Abroad*, Vol. I. Reprinted with the permission of Harper & Row, Publishers, Inc.

We looked indifferent—unconcerned. The doctor examined the document very deliberately, during a painful pause. Then he said, without any show of interest:

"Ah—Ferguson—what—what did you say was the name of the party who wrote this?"

"Christopher Colombo! ze great Christopher Colombo!"

Another deliberate examination.

"Ah—did he write it himself, or—or how?"

"He write it himself!—Christopher Colombo! he's own handwriting, write by himself!"

Then the doctor laid the document down and said:

"Why, I have seen boys in America only fourteen years old that could write better than that."

"But zis is ze great Christo—"

"I don't care who it is! It's the worst writing I ever saw. Now you mustn't think you can impose on us because we are strangers. We are not fools, by a good deal. If you have got any specimens of penmanship of real merit, trot them out!—and if you haven't, drive on!"

We drove on. The guide was considerably shaken up, but he made one more venture. He had something which he thought would overcome us. He said:

"Ah, genteelmen, you come wis me! I show you beautiful, oh, magnificent bust Christopher Colombo!—splendid, grand, magnificent!"

He brought us before the beautiful bust—for it *was* beautiful—and sprang back and struck an attitude:

"Ah, look, genteelmen!—beautiful, grand,—bust Christopher Colombo!—beautiful bust, beautiful pedestal!"

The doctor put up his eyeglass—procured for such occasions:

"Ah—what did you say this gentleman's name was?"

"Christopher Colombo!—ze great Christopher Colombo!"

"'Christopher Colombo! ze great Christopher Colombo!' Well, what did *he* do?"

"Discover America!—discover America, oh, ze devil!"

"Discover America. No—that statement will hardly wash. We are just from America ourselves. We heard nothing about it. Christopher Colombo—pleasant name—is—is he dead?"

"Oh, *corpo di Baccho!*[1]—three hundred years!"

"What did he die of?"

"I do not know!—I cannot tell."

"Smallpox, think?"

"I do not know, genteelmen!—I do not know *what* he die of!"

"Measles, likely?"

"Maybe—maybe—I do *not* know—I think he die of somethings."

"Parents living?"

"Im-posseeble!"

"Ah—which is the bust and which is the pedestal?"

"Santa Maria!—zis ze bust!—zis ze pedestal!"

"Ah, I see, I see—happy combination—very happy combination, indeed. Is—is this the first time this gentleman was ever on a bust?"

That joke was lost on the foreigner—guides cannot master the subtleties of the American joke.

We have made it interesting for this Roman guide. Yesterday we spent three or four hours in the Vatican again, that wonderful world of curiosities. We came very near expressing interest, sometimes—even admiration—it was very hard to keep from it. We succeeded though. Nobody else ever did, in the Vatican museums. The guide was bewildered—nonplussed. He walked his legs off, nearly, hunting up extraordinary things, and exhausted all his ingenuity on us, but it was a failure; we never showed any interest in anything. He had reserved what he considered to be his greatest wonder till the last—a royal Egyptian mummy, the best-preserved in the world, perhaps. He took us there. He felt so sure, this time, that some of his old enthusiasm came back to him:

---

1. **corpo di Baccho**\ˈkor·pō dē ˈbak·kō\ mild curse, lit. body of Bacchus, mythical god of wine and revelry.

"See, genteelmen!—Mummy! Mummy!"

The eyeglasses came up as calmly, as deliberately as ever.

"Ah,—Ferguson—what did I understand you to say the gentleman's name was?"

"Name?—he got no name!—Mummy!—'Gyptian mummy!"

"Yes, yes. Born here?"

"No! 'Gyptian mummy!"

"Ah, just so. Frenchman, I presume?"

"No!—*not* Frenchman, not Roman!—born in Egypta!"

"Born in Egypta. Never heard of Egypta before. Foreign locality, likely. Mummy—mummy. How calm he is—how self-possessed. Is, ah—is he dead?"

"Oh, *sacré bleu,*[2] been dead three thousan' year!"

The doctor turned on him savagely:

"Here, now, what do you mean by such conduct as this? Playing us for Chinamen because we are strangers and trying to learn! Trying to impose your vile second-hand carcasses on *us!* —thunder and lightning, I've a notion to—to— if you've got a nice *fresh* corpse, fetch him out! —or, by George, we'll brain you!"

We make it exceedingly interesting for this Frenchman. However, he has paid us back, partly, without knowing it. He came to the hotel this morning to ask if we were up, and he endeavored as well as he could to describe us, so that the landlord would know which persons he meant. He finished with the casual remark that we were lunatics. The observation was so innocent and so honest that it amounted to a very good thing for a guide to say.

There is one remark (already mentioned) which never yet has failed to disgust these guides. We use it always, when we can think of nothing else to say. After they have exhausted their enthusiasm pointing out to us and praising the beauties of some ancient bronze image or broken-legged statue, we look at it stupidly and in silence for five, ten, fifteen minutes—as long as we can hold out, in fact— and then ask:

"Is—is he dead?"

That conquers the serenest of them. It is not what they are looking for—especially a new guide. Our Roman Ferguson is the most patient, unsuspecting, long-suffering subject we have had yet. We shall be sorry to part with him. We have enjoyed his society very much. We trust he has enjoyed ours, but we are harassed with doubts. . . .

---

2. **sacré bleu**\\^sa·krä ˈblʊ\\ literally "sacred blue," a reference to the Blessed Mother and hence a mild curse.

To Twain, the stage driver was a romantic figure, the "river pilot" of the West.

CALIFORNIA STAGE-DRIVER.

So slight a sketch as this
would hardly be worth reprinting
were it not so memorable an example
of the burlesque humor that delighted
Twain's newspaper audience in the 1860's.
On his way east, via Panama, he wrote
a series of letters for the San Francisco
Alta California; and in one of them
he incorporated this satire of the Little Rollo
books, stories about a boy named Rollo
devised by Jacob Abbott to teach honesty
and self-improvement. Twain loathed
the goody-goody characters in Abbott's work
and so tried, here, to turn the familiar
pattern upside down.

The Story of
the Bad Little Boy
Who Didn't Come
to Grief

Once there was a bad little boy whose name was Jim—though, if you will notice, you will find that bad little boys are nearly always called James in your Sunday-school books. It was strange, but still it was true, that this one was called Jim.

He didn't have any sick mother, either—a sick mother who was pious and had the consumption, and would be glad to lie down in the grave and be at rest but for the strong love she bore her boy, and the anxiety she felt that the world might be harsh and cold toward him when she was gone. Most bad boys in the

Sunday books are named James, and have sick mothers, who teach them to say, "Now, I lay me down," etc., and sing them to sleep with sweet, plaintive voices, and then kiss them good night, and kneel down by the bedside and weep. But it was different with this fellow. He was named Jim, and there wasn't anything the matter with his mother—no consumption, nor anything of that kind. She was stout rather than otherwise, and she was not pious; moreover, she was not anxious on Jim's account. She said if he were to break his neck it wouldn't be much loss. She always spanked Jim to sleep, and she never kissed him good night; on the contrary, she boxed his ears when she was ready to leave him.

Once this little bad boy stole the key of the pantry, and slipped in there and helped himself to some jam, and filled up the vessel with tar, so that his mother would never know the difference; but all at once a terrible feeling didn't come over him, and something didn't seem to whisper to him, "Is it right to disobey my mother? Isn't it sinful to do this? Where do bad little boys go who gobble up their kind good mother's jam?" and then he didn't kneel down all alone and promise never to be wicked any more, and rise up with a light, happy heart, and go and tell his mother all about it, and beg her forgiveness, and be blessed by her with tears of pride and thankfulness in her eyes. No; that is the way with all other bad boys in the books; but it happened otherwise with this Jim, strangely enough. He ate that jam, and said it was bully, in his sinful vulgar way; and he put in the tar, and said that was bully also, and laughed, and observed "that the old woman would get up and snort" when she found it out; and when she did find it out, he denied knowing anything about it, and she whipped him severely, and he did the crying himself. Everything about this boy was curious—everything turned out differently with him from the way it does to the bad Jameses in the books.

Once he climbed up in Farmer Acorn's apple tree to steal apples, and the limb didn't break,

Reprinted with the permission of Harper & Row, Publishers, Inc.

and he didn't fall and break his arm, and get torn by the farmer's great dog, and then languish on a sickbed for weeks, and repent and become good. Oh, no; he stole as many apples as he wanted and came down all right; and he was all ready for the dog, too, and knocked him endways with a brick when he came to tear him. It was very strange—nothing like it ever happened in those mild little books with marbled backs, and with pictures in them of men with swallow-tailed coats and bell-crowned hats, and pantaloons that are short in the legs, and women with the waists of their dresses under their arms, and no hoops on. Nothing like it in any of the Sunday-school books.

Once he stole the teacher's penknife, and, when he was afraid it would be found out and he would get whipped, he slipped it into George Wilson's cap—poor Widow Wilson's son, the moral boy, the good little boy of the village, who always obeyed his mother, and never told an untruth, and was fond of his lessons, and infatuated with Sunday-school. And when the knife dropped from the cap, and poor George hung his head and blushed, as if in conscious guilt, and the grieved teacher charged the theft upon him, and was just in the very act of bringing the switch down upon his trembling shoulders, a white-haired improbable justice of the peace did not suddenly appear in their midst, and strike an attitude and say, "Spare this noble boy—there stands the cowering culprit! I was passing the school at recess, and, unseen myself, I saw the theft committed!" And then Jim didn't get whaled, and the venerable justice didn't read the tearful school a homily, and take George by the hand and say such a boy deserved to be exalted, and then tell him to come and make his home with him, and sweep out the office, and make fires, and run errands, and chop wood, and study law, and help his wife do household labors, and have all the balance of the time to play, and get forty cents a month, and be happy. No; it would have happened that way in the books, but it didn't happen that way to Jim. No

meddling old clam of a justice dropped in to make trouble, and so the model boy got thrashed, and Jim was glad of it because, you know, Jim hated moral boys. Jim said he was "down on them milksops."[1] Such was the coarse language of this bad, neglected boy.

But the strangest thing that ever happened to Jim was the time he went boating on Sunday, and didn't get drowned, and that other time that he got caught out in the storm when he was fishing on Sunday, and didn't get struck by lightning. Why, you might look, and look, all through the Sunday-school books from now till next Christmas, and you would never come across anything like this. Oh, no; you would find that all the bad boys who get caught in storms when they are fishing on Sunday infallibly get struck by lightning. Boats with bad boys in them always upset on Sunday, and it always storms when bad boys go fishing on the Sabbath. How this Jim ever escaped is a mystery to me.

This Jim bore a charmed life—that must have been the way of it. Nothing could hurt him. He even gave the elephant in the menagerie a plug of tobacco, and the elephant didn't knock the top of his head off with his trunk. He browsed around the cupboard after essence of peppermint, and didn't make a mistake and drink *aqua fortis*.[2] He stole his father's gun and went hunting on the Sabbath, and didn't shoot three or four of his fingers off. He struck his little sister on the temple with his fist when he was angry, and she didn't linger in pain through long summer days, and die with sweet words of forgiveness upon her lips that redoubled the anguish of his breaking heart. No; she got over it. He ran off and went to sea at last, and didn't come back and find himself sad and alone in the world, his loved ones sleeping in the quiet churchyard, and the vine-embowered home of his boyhood tumbled down and gone to decay. Ah, no; he came home drunk

---

1. **milksops,** unmanly boys or men.
2. **aqua fortis,** literally "strong water"; a vile medicine or an acid.

as a piper, and got into the station-house the first thing.

And he grew up and married, and raised a large family, and brained them all with an ax one night, and got wealthy by all manner of cheating and rascality; and now he is the infernalest wickedest scoundrel in his native village, and is universally respected, and belongs to the legislature.

So you see there never was a bad James in the Sunday-school books that had such a streak of luck as this sinful Jim with the charmed life.

I
THE TASK OF THE SATIRIST

Certain classes of Americans in Twain's time thought that European products and institutions were greatly superior to their American counterparts; apparently most Americans of his time also loved to read about paragons of virtue, for Abbott's Rollo books (of which there were twenty-eight volumes!) had enormous circulations. Both in the admiration of the Rollo-type and in the adulation of things European, Twain saw something that was *uncritical* and *excessive* on the part of his fellow Americans. He felt it was his task as a satirist to cut such tendencies down to size. Of course, on another level Twain is directly criticizing certain aspects of Europe and good little boys, but his indirect criticism of Americans is equally if not more important.

II
IMPLICATIONS

Discuss the following propositions.

1. In both selections Twain adopts the values of the American frontiersman as opposed to those of the cultured, metropolitan "easterner."

2. There seems to be a natural human tendency to criticize those who carry things to excess, even if it is virtue that is excessive.

3. One of the chief functions of the satirist is to restore *balance* to our view of things.

4. A satire will strike a given reader as funny only if he shares in the first place the same point of view as the author.

5. The danger of a satire like *The Innocents Abroad* is that it might lead to self-complacency on the part of Americans who shared Twain's point of view.

III
TECHNIQUES
Comedy and Sympathy and Detachment

The comedy in the four Twain selections you have just read might readily be called a comedy of irreverence; that is to say, Twain consistently cuts up things that many persons respect. Note, for example, that the names of the bull-pup and of the frog in "The Jumping Frog" are Andrew Jackson and Dan'l Webster, respectively. Similarly, at the end of the "Bad Little Boy" Jim "brains" his whole family with an ax. For most of Twain's readers, Jackson and Webster were revered men, and presumably most of his readers loved and respected their own wives and children. What other venerated persons or things does Twain treat irreverently? How can such irreverence be funny?

In trying to answer the last question, consider carefully what you have learned from the previous unit regarding sympathy and detachment. Note whom the reader stands with in each of the four selections and how this affects his enjoyment.

Tom Sawyer and Huck Finn are,
without question, Twain's most famous
characters, and rightly so. They are the epitome
of young-boy rebellion and light-hearted
independence, the kind of youth
Twain enjoyed in Hannibal. In *The Adventures
of Huckleberry Finn*, the main action is centered
on Huck's escape from his father's clutches
and Negro Jim's escape from his owner, Miss
Watson. Together they float down the Mississippi
on a raft, hoping to leave it at Cairo and take
a steamboat up the Ohio into free territory.
But one night the raft capsizes, and they
are separated. Huck swims ashore and, assuming
the name George Jackson, he seeks shelter
with a family called Grangerford who happen
to be feuding with their neighbors,
the Shepherdsons. The temporary separation
of Huck and Jim allows Twain to focus
on a second major element of the novel—
the social satire of the towns
and people along the river.

FROM

The Adventures
of Huckleberry Finn

CHAPTER XVII

In about half a minute somebody spoke out of a window, without putting his head out, and says:

"Be done, boys! Who's there?"

I says:

"It's me."

"Who's me?"

"George Jackson, sir."

Reprinted from *The Adventures of Huckleberry Finn*, by Mark Twain, with the permission of Harper & Row, Publishers, Inc.

"What do you want?"

"I don't want nothing, sir. I only want to go along by, but the dogs won't let me."

"What are you prowling around here this time of night, for—hey?"

"I warn't prowling around, sir; I fell overboard off of the steamboat."

"Oh, you did, did you? Strike a light there, somebody. What did you say your name was?"

"George Jackson, sir. I'm only a boy."

"Look here; if you're telling the truth, you needn't be afraid—nobody'll hurt you. But don't try to budge; stand right where you are. Rouse out Bob and Tom, some of you, and fetch the guns. George Jackson, is there anybody with you?"

"No, sir, nobody."

I heard the people stirring around in the house, now, and see a light. The man sung out:

"Snatch that light away, Betsy, you old fool—ain't you got any sense? Put it on the floor behind the front door. Bob, if you and Tom are ready, take your places."

"All ready."

"Now, George Jackson, do you know the Shepherdsons?"

"No, sir—I never heard of them."

"Well, that may be so, and it mayn't. Now, all ready. Step forward, George Jackson. And mind, don't you hurry—come mighty slow. If there's anybody with you, let him keep back—if he shows himself he'll be shot. Come along, now. Come slow; push the door open, yourself—just enough to squeeze in, d' you hear?"

I didn't hurry, I couldn't if I'd a wanted to. I took one slow step at a time, and there warn't a sound, only I thought I could hear my heart. The dogs were as still as the humans, but they followed a little behind me. When I got to the three log doorsteps, I heard them unlocking and unbarring and unbolting. I put my hand on the door and pushed it a little and a little more, till somebody said, "There, that's enough—put your head in." I done it, but I judged they would take it off.

The candle was on the floor, and there they all was, looking at me, and me at them, for about a quarter of a minute. Three big men with guns pointed at me, which made me wince, I tell you; the oldest, gray and about sixty, the other two thirty or more—all of them fine and handsome—and the sweetest old gray-headed lady, and back of her two young women which I couldn't see right well. The old gentleman says:

"There—I reckon it's all right. Come in."

As soon as I was in, the old gentleman he locked the door and barred it and bolted it, and told the young men to come in with their guns, and they all went in a big parlor that had a new rag carpet on the floor, and got together in a corner that was out of range of the front windows—there warn't none on the side. They held the candle, and took a good look at me, and all said, "Why *he* ain't a Shepherdson—no, there ain't any Shepherdson about him." Then the old man said he hoped I wouldn't mind being searched for arms, because he didn't mean no harm by it—it was only to make sure. So he didn't pry into my pockets, but only felt outside with his hands, and said it was all right. He told me to make myself easy and at home, and tell all about myself; but the old lady says:

"Why bless you, Saul, the poor thing's as wet as he can be; and don't you reckon it may be he's hungry?"

"True for you, Rachel—I forgot."

So the old lady says to the Negro woman:

"Betsy, you fly around and get him something to eat, as quick as you can, poor thing; and one of you girls go and wake up Buck and tell him—Oh, here he is himself. Buck, take this little stranger and get the wet clothes off from him and dress him up in some of yours that's dry."

Buck looked about as old as me—thirteen or fourteen or along there, though he was a little bigger than me. He hadn't on anything but a shirt, and he was very frowsy-headed.[1] He come in gaping and digging one fist into his eyes, and he was dragging a gun along with the other one. He says:

"Ain't they no Shepherdsons around?"

They said, no, 'twas a false alarm.

"Well," he says, "if they'd a ben some, I reckon I'd a got one."

They all laughed, and Bob says:

"Why, Buck, they might have scalped us all, you've been so slow in coming."

"Well, nobody come after me, and it ain't right. I'm always kep' down; I don't get no show."

"Never mind, Buck, my boy," says the old man, "you'll have show enough, all in good time, don't you fret about that. Go 'long with you now, and do as your mother told you."

When we got up stairs to his room, he got me a coarse shirt and a roundabout and pants of his, and I put them on. While I was at it he asked me what my name was, but before I could tell him, he started to telling me about a blue jay and a young rabbit he had catched in the woods day before yesterday, and he asked me where Moses was when the candle went out. I said I didn't know; I hadn't heard about it before, no way.

"Well, guess," he says.

"How'm I going to guess," says I, "when I never heard tell about it before?"

"But you can guess, can't you? It's just as easy."

"*Which* candle?" I says.

"Why, any candle," he says.

"I don't know where he was," says I; "where was he?"

"Why he was in the *dark!* That's where he was!"

"Well, if you knowed where he was, what did you ask me for?"

"Why, blame it, it's a riddle, don't you see? Say, how long are you going to stay here? You got to stay always. We can just have booming times—they don't have no school now. Do you own a dog? I've got a dog—and he'll go in the river and bring out chips that you throw in. Do you like to comb up, Sundays, and all that kind of foolishness? You bet I don't, but ma she makes me. Confound these ole britches, I

---

1. **frowsy-headed,** having unkempt hair.

reckon I'd better put 'em on, but I'd ruther not, it's so warm. Are you all ready? All right— come along, old hoss."

Cold corn-pone,[2] cold corn-beef, butter and butter-milk—that is what they had for me down there, and there ain't nothing better that ever I've come across yet. Buck and his ma and all of them smoked cob pipes, except the Negro woman, which was gone, and the two young women. They all smoked and talked, and I eat and talked. The young women had quilts around them, and their hair down their backs. They all asked me questions, and I told them how pap and me and all the family was living on a little farm down at the bottom of Arkansaw, and my sister Mary Ann run off and got married and never was heard of no more, and Bill went to hunt them and he warn't heard of no more, and Tom and Mort died, and then there warn't nobody but just me and pap left, and he was just trimmed down to nothing, on account of his troubles; so when he died I took what there was left, because the farm didn't belong to us, and started up the river, deck passage, and fell overboard; and that was how I come to be here. So they said I could have a home there as long as I wanted it. Then it was most daylight, and everybody went to bed, and I went to bed with Buck, and when I waked up in the morning, drat it all, I had forgot what my name was. So I laid there about an hour trying to think, and when Buck waked up, I says:

"Can you spell, Buck?"

"Yes," he says.

"I bet you can't spell my name," says I.

"I bet you what you dare I can," says he.

"All right," says I, "go ahead."

"G-o-r-g-e J-a-x-o-n—there now," he says.

"Well," says I, "you done it, but I didn't think you could. It ain't no slouch of a name to spell—right off without studying."

I set it down, private, because somebody might want *me* to spell it, next, and so I wanted to be handy with it and rattle it off like I was used to it.

It was a mighty nice family, and a mighty nice house, too. I hadn't seen no house out in the country before that was so nice and had so much style. It didn't have an iron latch on the front door, nor a wooden one with a buckskin string, but a brass knob to turn, the same as houses in a town. There warn't no bed in the parlor, not a sign of a bed; but heaps of parlors in towns has beds in them. There was a big fireplace that was bricked on the bottom, and the bricks was kept clean and red by pouring water on them and scrubbing them with another brick; sometimes they washed them over with red water-paint that they call Spanish-brown, same as they do in town. They had big brass dog-irons that could hold up a sawlog. There was a clock on the middle of the mantel-piece, with a picture of a town painted on the bottom half of the glass front, and a round place in the middle of it for the sun, and you could see the pendulum swing behind it. It was beautiful to hear that clock tick; and sometimes when one of these peddlers had been along and scoured her up and got her in good shape, she would start in and strike a hundred and fifty before she got tuckered out. They wouldn't took any money for her.

Well, there was a big outlandish parrot on each side of the clock, made out of something like chalk, and painted up gaudy. By one of the parrots was a cat made of crockery, and a crockery dog by the other; and when you pressed down on them they squeaked, but didn't open their mouths nor look different nor interested. They squeaked through underneath. There was a couple of big wild-turkey-wing fans spread out behind those things. On a table in the middle of the room was a kind of a lovely crockery basket that had apples and oranges and peaches and grapes piled up in it which was much redder and yellower and prettier than real ones is, but they warn't real because you could see where pieces had got chipped off and showed the white chalk or whatever it was, underneath.

---

2. **corn-pone,** corn bread often made without milk or eggs.

This table had a cover made out of beautiful oil-cloth, with a red and blue spread-eagle painted on it, and a painted border all around. It come all the way from Philadelphia, they said. There was some books too, piled up perfectly exact, on each corner of the table. One was a big family Bible, full of pictures. One was "Pilgrim's Progress," about a man that left his family it didn't say why. I read considerable in it now and then. The statements was interesting, but tough. Another was "Friendship's Offering," full of beautiful stuff and poetry; but I didn't read the poetry. Another was Henry Clay's Speeches, and another was Dr. Gunn's Family Medicine, which told you all about what to do if a body was sick or dead. There was a Hymn Book, and a lot of other books. And there was nice split-bottom chairs, and perfectly sound, too—not bagged down in the middle and busted, like an old basket.

They had pictures hung on the walls—mainly Washingtons and Lafayettes, and battles, and Highland Marys, and one called "Signing the Declaration." There was some that they called crayons, which one of the daughters which was dead made her own self when she was only fifteen years old. They was different from any pictures I ever see before; blacker, mostly, than is common. One was a woman in a slim black dress, belted small under the arm-pits, with bulges like a cabbage in the middle of the sleeves, and a large black scoop-shovel bonnet with a black veil, and white slim ankles crossed about with black tape, and very wee black slippers, like a chisel, and she was leaning pensive on a tombstone on her right elbow, under a weeping willow, and her other hand hanging down her side holding a white handkerchief and a reticule, and underneath the picture it said "Shall I Never See Thee More Alas." Another one was a young lady with her hair all combed up straight to the top of her head, and knotted there in front of a comb like a chair-back, and she was crying into a handkerchief and had a dead bird laying on its back in her other hand with its heels up, and underneath the picture it said "I Shall Never Hear Thy Sweet Chirrup More Alas." There was one where a young lady was at a window looking up at the moon, and tears running down her cheeks; and she had an open letter in one hand with black sealing-wax showing on one edge of it, and she was mashing a locket with a chain to it against her mouth, and underneath the picture it said "And Art Thou Gone Yes Thou Art Gone Alas." These was all nice pictures, I reckon, but I didn't somehow seem to take to them, because if ever I was down a little, they always give me the fan-tods. Everybody was sorry she died, because she had laid out a lot more of these pictures to do, and a body could see by what she had done what they had lost. But I reckoned, that with her disposition, she was having a better time in the graveyard. She was at work on what they said was her greatest picture when she took sick, and every day and every night it was her prayer to be allowed to live till she got it done, but she never got the chance. It was a picture of a young woman in a long white gown, standing on the rail of a bridge all ready to jump off, with her hair all down her back, and looking up to the moon, with the tears running down her face, and she had two arms folded across her breast, and two arms stretched out in front, and two more reaching up towards the moon—and the idea was, to see which pair would look best and then scratch out all the other arms; but, as I was saying, she died before she got her mind made up, and now they kept this picture over the head of the bed in her room, and every time her birthday come they hung flowers on it. Other times it was hid with a little curtain. The young woman in the picture had a kind of a nice sweet face, but there was so many arms it made her look too spidery, seemed to me.

This young girl kept a scrap-book when she was alive, and used to paste obituaries and accidents and cases of patient suffering in it out of the *Presbyterian Observer*, and write poetry after them out of her own head. It was very good poetry. This is what she wrote about a boy by the name of Stephen Dowling Bots that fell down a well and was drownded:

ODE TO STEPHEN DOWLING BOTS, DEC'D.

And did young Stephen sicken,
    And did young Stephen die?
And did the sad hearts thicken,
    And did the mourners cry?

No; such was not the fate of
    Young Stephen Dowling Bots;
Though sad hearts round him thickened,
    'Twas not from sickness' shots.

No whooping-cough did rack his frame,
    Nor measles drear, with spots;
Not these impaired the sacred name
    Of Stephen Dowling Bots.

Despised love struck not with woe
    That head of curly knots,
Nor stomach troubles laid him low,
    Young Stephen Dowling Bots.

O no. Then list with tearful eye,
    Whilst I his fate do tell.
His soul did from this cold world fly,
    By falling down a well.

They got him out and emptied him;
    Alas it was too late;
His spirit was gone for to sport aloft
    In the realms of the good and great.

If Emmeline Grangerford could make poetry like that before she was fourteen, there ain't no telling what she could a done by-and-by. Buck said she could rattle off poetry like nothing. She didn't ever have to stop to think. He said she would slap down a line, and if she couldn't find anything to rhyme with it she would just scratch it out and slap down another one, and go ahead. She warn't particular, she could write about anything you choose to give her to write about, just so it was sadful. Every time a man died, or a woman died, or a child died, she would be on hand with her "tribute" before he was cold. She called them tributes. The neighbors said it was the doctor first, then Emmeline, then the undertaker—the undertaker never got in ahead of Emmeline but once, and then she hung fire on a rhyme for the dead person's name, which was Whistler. She warn't ever the same, after that; she never complained, but she kind of pined away and did not live long. Poor thing, many's the time I made myself go up to the little room that used to be hers and get out her poor old scrap-book and read in it when her pictures had been aggravating me and I had soured on her a little. I liked all that family, dead ones and all, and warn't going to let anything come between us. Poor Emmeline made poetry about all the dead people when she was alive, and it didn't seem right that there warn't nobody to make some about her, now she was gone; so I tried to sweat out a verse or two myself, but I couldn't seem to make it go, somehow. They kept Emmeline's room trim and nice and all the things fixed in it just the way she liked to have them when she was alive, and nobody ever slept there. The old lady took care of the room herself, and she sewed there a good deal and read her Bible there, mostly.

Well, as I was saying about the parlor, there was beautiful curtains on the windows: white, with pictures painted on them, of castles with vines all down the walls, and cattle coming down to drink. There was a little old piano, too, that had tin pans in it, I reckon, and nothing was ever so lovely as to hear the young ladies sing, "The Last Link is Broken" and play "The Battle of Prague" on it. The walls of all the rooms was plastered, and most had carpets on the floors, and the whole house was whitewashed on the outside.

It was a double house, and the big open place betwixt them was roofed and floored, and sometimes the table was set there in the middle of the day, and it was a cool, comfortable place. Nothing couldn't be better. And warn't the cooking good, and just bushels of it too!

CHAPTER XVIII

Col. Grangerford was a gentleman, you see. He was a gentleman all over; and so was his family. He was well born, as the saying is, and that's worth as much in a man as it is in a horse, so the Widow Douglas said, and nobody

Hannibal, Missouri, Twain's childhood home and the setting for many of Tom Sawyer's and Huck Finn's adventures.

ever denied that she was of the first aristocracy in our town; and pap he always said it, too, though he warn't no more quality than a mudcat, himself. Col. Grangerford was very tall and very slim, and had a darkish-paly complexion, not a sign of red in it anywheres; he was clean-shaved every morning, all over his thin face, and he had the thinnest kind of lips, and the thinnest kind of nostrils, and a high nose, and heavy eyebrows, and the blackest kind of eyes, sunk so deep back that they seemed like they was looking out of caverns at you, as you may say. His forehead was high, and his hair was black and straight, and hung to his shoulders. His hands was long and thin, and every day of his life he put on a clean shirt and a full suit from head to foot made out of linen so white it hurt your eyes to look at it; and on Sundays he wore a blue tail-coat with brass buttons on it. He carried a mahogany cane with a silver head to it. There warn't no frivolishness about him, not a bit, and he warn't ever loud. He was as kind as he could be—you could feel that, you know, and so you had confidence. Sometimes he smiled, and it was good to see; but when he straightened himself up like a liberty-pole, and the lightning begun to flicker out from under his eyebrows you wanted to climb a tree first, and find out what the matter was afterwards. He didn't ever have to tell anybody to mind their manners—everybody was always good mannered where he was. Everybody loved to have him around, too; he was sunshine most always—I mean he made it seem like good weather. When he turned into a cloud-bank it was awful dark for a half a minute and that was enough; there wouldn't nothing go wrong again for a week.

When him and the old lady come down in the morning, all the family got up out of their chairs and give them good-day, and didn't set down again till they had set down. Then Tom and Bob went to the sideboard where the decanters was, and mixed a glass of bitters and handed it to him, and he held it in his hand and waited till Tom's and Bob's was mixed, and then they bowed and said "Our duty to you, sir, and madam;" and *they* bowed the least bit in the world and said thank you, and so they drank, all three, and Bob and Tom poured a spoonful of water on the sugar and the mite of whisky or apple brandy in the bottom of their tumblers, and give it to me and Buck, and we drank to the old people too.

Bob was the oldest, and Tom next. Tall, beautiful men with very broad shoulders and brown faces, and long black hair and black eyes. They dressed in white linen from head to foot, like the old gentleman, and wore broad Panama hats.

Then there was Miss Charlotte, she was twenty-five, and tall and proud and grand, but as good as she could be, when she warn't stirred up; but when she was, she had a look that would make you wilt in your tracks, like her father. She was beautiful.

So was her sister, Miss Sophia, but it was a different kind. She was gentle and sweet, like a dove, and she was only twenty.

Each person had their own servant to wait on them—Buck, too. My servant had a monstrous easy time, because I warn't used to having anybody do anything for me, but Buck's was on the jump most of the time.

This was all there was of the family, now; but there used to be more—three sons; they got killed; and Emmeline that died.

The old gentleman owned a lot of farms, and over a hundred Negroes. Sometimes a stack of people would come there, horseback, from ten or fifteen mile around, and stay five or six days, and have such junketings round about and on the river, and dances and picnics in the woods, day-times, and balls at the house, nights. These people was mostly kin-folks of the family. The men brought their guns with them. It was a handsome lot of quality, I tell you.

There was another clan of aristocracy around there—five or six families—mostly of the name of Shepherdson. They was as high-toned, and well born, and rich and grand, as the tribe of Grangerfords. The Shepherdsons and the Grangerfords used the same steamboat landing, which was about two mile above our house; so sometimes when I went up there with a lot of our folks I used to see a lot of the Shepherdsons there, on their fine horses.

One day Buck and me was away out in the woods, hunting, and heard a horse coming. We was crossing the road. Buck says:

"Quick! Jump for the woods!"

We done it, and then peeped down the woods through the leaves. Pretty soon a splendid young man come galloping down the road, setting his horse easy and looking like a soldier. He had his gun across his pommel. I had seen him before. It was young Harney Shepherdson. I heard Buck's gun go off at my ear, and Harney's hat tumbled off from his head. He grabbed his gun and rode straight to the place where we was hid. But we didn't wait. We started through the woods on a run. The woods warn't thick, so I looked over my shoulder, to dodge the bullet, and twice I seen Harney cover Buck with his gun; and then he rode away the way he come—to get his hat, I reckon, but I couldn't see. We never stopped running till we got home. The old gentleman's eyes blazed a minute—'twas pleasure, mainly, I judged—then his face sort of smoothed down, and he says, kind of gentle:

"I don't like that shooting from behind a bush. Why didn't you step into the road, my boy?"

"The Shepherdsons don't, father. They always take advantage."

Miss Charlotte she held her head up like a queen while Buck was telling his tale, and her nostrils spread and her eyes snapped. The two young men looked dark, but never said nothing. Miss Sophia she turned pale, but the color come back when she found the man warn't hurt.

Soon as I could get Buck down by the corn-cribs under the trees by ourselves, I says:

"Did you want to kill him, Buck?"

"Well, I bet I did."

"What did he do to you?"

"Him? He never done nothing to me."

"Well, then, what did you want to kill him for?"

"Why nothing—only it's on account of the feud."

"What's a feud?"

"Why, where was you raised? Don't you know what a feud is?"

"Never heard of it before—tell me about it."

"Well," says Buck, "a feud is this way. A man has a quarrel with another man, and kills him; then that other man's brother kills *him;* then the other brothers, on both sides, goes for one another; then the *cousins* chip in—and by-and-by everybody's killed off, and there ain't no more feud. But it's kind of slow, and takes a long time."

"Has this one been going on long, Buck?"

"Well I should *reckon!* it started thirty year ago, or som'ers along there. There was trouble 'bout something and then a lawsuit to settle it; and the suit went agin one of the men, and so he up and shot the man that won the suit—which he would naturally do, of course. Anybody would."

"What was the trouble about, Buck?—land?"

"I reckon maybe—I don't know."

"Well, who done the shooting?—was it a Grangerford or a Shepherdson?"

"Laws, how do *I* know? it was so long ago."

"Don't anybody know?"

"Oh, yes, pa knows, I reckon, and some of the other old folks; but they don't know, now, what the row was about in the first place."

"Has there been many killed, Buck?"

"Yes—right smart chance of funerals. But they don't always kill. Pa's got a few buck-shot in him; but he don't mind it 'cuz he don't weigh much anyway. Bob's been carved up some with a bowie, and Tom's been hurt once or twice."

"Has anybody been killed this year, Buck?"

"Yes, we got one and they got one. 'Bout three months ago, my cousin Bud, fourteen year old, was riding through the woods, on t'other side of the river, and didn't have no weapon with him, which was blame' foolishness, and in a lonesome place he hears a horse a-coming behind him, and sees old Baldy Shepherdson a-linkin' after him with his gun in his hand and his white hair a-flying in the wind; and 'stead of jumping off and taking to the brush, Bud 'lowed he could outrun him; so they had it, nip and tuck, for five mile or more, the old man a-gaining all the time; so at last Bud seen it warn't any use, so he stopped and faced around so as to have the bullet holes in front, you know, and the old man he rode up and shot him down. But he didn't git much chance to enjoy his luck, for inside of a week our folks laid *him* out."

"I reckon that old man was a coward, Buck."

"I reckon he *warn't* a coward. Not by a blame' sight. There ain't a coward amongst them Shepherdsons—not a one. And there ain't no cowards amongst the Grangerfords, either. Why, that old man kep' up his end in a fight one day, for a half an hour, against three Grangerfords, and come out winner. They was all a-horseback; he lit off of his horse and got behind a little wood-pile, and kep' his horse before him to stop the bullets; but the Grangerfords staid on their horses and capered around the old man, and peppered away at him, and he peppered away at them. Him and his horse both went home pretty leaky and crippled, but the Grangerfords had to be *fetched* home—and one of 'em was dead, and another died the next day. No, sir, if a body's out hunting for cowards, he don't want to fool away any time amongst them Shepherdsons, becuz they don't breed any of that *kind.*"

Next Sunday we all went to church, about three mile, everybody a-horseback. The men took their guns along, so did Buck, and kept them between their knees or stood them handy against the wall. The Shepherdsons done the same. It was pretty ornery preaching—all about brotherly love, and such-like tiresomeness; but everybody said it was a good sermon, and they all talked it over going home, and had such a powerful lot to say about faith, and good works, and free grace, and prefore-ordestination, and I don't know what all, that it did seem to me to be one of the roughest Sundays I had run across yet.

About an hour after dinner everybody was dozing around, some in their chairs and some in their rooms, and it got to be pretty dull. Buck and a dog was stretched out on the grass in the sun, sound asleep. I went up to our room, and judged I would take a nap myself. I found that sweet Miss Sophia standing in her door, which was next to ours, and she took me in her room and shut the door very soft, and asked me if I liked her, and I said I did; and she asked me if I would do something for her and not tell anybody, and I said I would. Then she said she'd forgot her Testament, and left it in the seat at church, between two other books and would I slip out quiet and go there and fetch it to her, and not say nothing to nobody. I said I would. So I slid out and slipped off up the road, and there warn't anybody at the church, except maybe a hog or two, for there warn't any lock on the door, and hogs likes a puncheon floor in summer-time because it's cool. If you notice, most folks don't go to church only when they've got to; but a hog is different.

Says I to myself something's up—it ain't natural for a girl to be in such a sweat about a Testament; so I give it a shake, and out drops a little piece of paper with *"Half-past two"* wrote on it with a pencil. I ransacked it, but couldn't find anything else. I couldn't make anything out of that, so I put the paper in the book again, and when I got home and up stairs, there was Miss Sophia in her door waiting for me. She pulled me in and shut the door; then she looked in the Testament till she found the paper, and as soon as she read it she looked glad; and before a body could think, she grabbed me and give me a squeeze, and said I was the best boy in the world, and not to tell anybody. She was mighty red in the face, for a minute, and her eyes lighted up and it made her powerful pretty. I was a good deal astonished, but when I got my breath I asked her what the paper was about, and she asked me if I had read it, and I said no, and she asked me if I could read writing, and I told her "no, only coarse-hand," and then she said the paper warn't anything but a book-mark to keep her place, and I might go and play now. . . .

I don't want to talk much about the next day. I reckon I'll cut it pretty short. I waked up about dawn, and was agoing to turn over and go to sleep again, when I noticed how still it was—didn't seem to be anybody stirring. That warn't usual. Next I noticed that Buck was up and gone. Well, I gets up, a-wondering, and goes down stairs—nobody around; everything as still as a mouse. Just the same outside; thinks I, what does it mean? Down by the wood-pile I comes across my Jack, and says:

"What's it all about?"

Says he:

"Don't you know, Mars Jawge?"

"No," says I, "I don't."

"Well, den, Miss Sophia's run off! 'deed she has. She run off in de night, sometime—nobody don't know jis' when—run off to git married to dat young Harney Shepherdson, you know—leastways, so dey 'spec. De fambly foun' it out, 'bout half an hour ago—maybe a little mo'—en' I *tell* you dey warn't no time los'. Sich another hurryin' up guns en hosses *you* never see! De women folks has gone for to stir up de relations, en ole Mars Saul en de boys tuck dey guns en rode up de river road for to try to ketch dat young man en kill him 'fo' he kin git acrost de river wid Miss Sophia. I reck'n dey's gwyne to be mighty rough times."

"Buck went off 'thout waking me up."

"Well I reck'n he *did!* Dey warn't gwyne to mix you up in it. Mars Buck he loaded up his gun en 'lowed he's gwyne to fetch home a Shepherdson or bust. Well, dey'll be plenty un 'm dah, I reck'n, en you bet you he'll fetch one ef he gits a chanst."

I took up the river road as hard as I could put. By-and-by I begin to hear guns a good ways off. When I come in sight of the log store and the wood-pile where the steamboats lands,

I worked along under the trees and brush till I got to a good place, and then I clumb up into the forks of a cotton-wood that was out of reach, and watched. There was a wood-rank four foot high, a little ways in front of the tree, and first I was going to hide behind that; but maybe it was luckier I didn't.

There was four or five men cavorting around on their horses in the open place before the log store, cussing and yelling, and trying to get at a couple of young chaps that was behind the wood-rank alongside of the steamboat landing —but they couldn't come it. Every time one of them showed himself on the river side of the wood-pile he got shot at. The two boys was squatting back to back behind the pile, so they could watch both ways.

By-and-by the men stopped cavorting around and yelling. They started riding towards the store; then up gets one of the boys, draws a steady bead over the wood-rank, and drops one of them out of his saddle. All the men jumped off of their horses and grabbed the hurt one and started to carry him to the store; and that minute the two boys started on the run. They go half-way to the tree I was in before the men noticed. Then the men see them, and jumped on their horses and took out after them. They gained on the boys, but it didn't do no good, the boys had too good a start; they got to the wood-pile that was in front of my tree, and slipped in behind it, and so they had the bulge on the men again. One of the boys was Buck, and the other was a slim young chap about nineteen years old.

The men ripped around awhile, and then rode away. As soon as they was out of sight, I sung out to Buck and told him. He didn't know what to make of my voice coming out of the tree, at first. He was awful surprised. He told me to watch out sharp and let him know when the men come in sight again; said they was up to some devilment or other—wouldn't be gone long. I wished I was out of that tree, but I dasn't come down. Buck begun to cry and rip, and 'lowed that him and his cousin Joe (that was the other young chap) would

make up for this day, yet. He said his father and his two brothers was killed, and two or three of the enemy. Said the Shepherdsons laid for them, in ambush. Buck said his father and brothers ought to waited for their relations— the Shepherdsons was too strong for them. I asked him what was become of young Harney and Miss Sophia. He said they'd got across the river and was safe. I was glad of that; but the way Buck did take on because he didn't manage to kill Harney that day he shot at him—I hain't ever heard anything like it.

All of a sudden, bang! bang! bang! goes three or four guns—the men had slipped around through the woods and come in from behind without their horses! The boys jumped for the river—both of them hurt—and as they swum down the current the men run along the bank shooting at them and singing out, "Kill them, kill them!" It made me so sick I most fell out of the tree. I ain't agoing to tell *all* that happened—it would make me sick again if I was to do that. I wished I hadn't ever come ashore that night, to see such things. I ain't ever going to get shut of them—lots of times I dream about them.

I staid in the tree till it begun to get dark, afraid to come down. Sometimes I heard guns away off in the woods; and twice I seen little gangs of men gallop past the log store with guns; so I reckoned the trouble was still agoing on. I was mighty down-hearted; so I made up my mind I wouldn't ever go anear that house again, because I reckoned I was to blame, somehow. I judged that that piece of paper meant that Miss Sophia was to meet Harney somewheres at half-past two and run off; and I judged I ought to told her father about that paper and the curious way she acted, and then maybe he would a locked her up and this awful mess wouldn't ever happened.

When I got down out of the tree, I crept along down the river bank a piece, and found the two bodies laying in the edge of the water, and tugged at them till I got them ashore; then I covered up their faces, and got away as quick as I could. I cried a little when I was covering up Buck's face, for he was mighty good to me.

It was just dark, now. I never went near the house, but struck through the woods and made for the swamp. Jim warn't on his island, so I tramped off in a hurry for the crick, and crowded through the willows, red-hot to jump aboard and get out of that awful country—the raft was gone! My souls, but I was scared! I couldn't get my breath for most a minute. Then I raised a yell. A voice not twenty-five foot from me, says—

"Good lan'! is dat you, honey? Doan' make no noise."

It was Jim's voice—nothing ever sounded so good before. I run along the bank a piece and got aboard, and Jim he grabbed me and hugged me, he was so glad to see me. He says—

"Laws bless you, chile, I 'uz right down sho' you's dead agin. Jack's been heah, he say he reck'n you's ben shot, kase you didn' come home no mo'; so I's jes' dis minute a startin' de raf' down towards de mouf er de crick, so's to be all ready for to shove out en leave soon as Jack comes agin en tells me for certain you *is* dead. Lawsy, I's mighty glad to git you back agin, honey."

I says—

"All right—that's mighty good; they won't find me, and they'll think I've been killed, and floated down the river—there's something up there that'll help them to think so—so don't you lose no time, Jim, but just shove off for the big water as fast as ever you can."

I never felt easy till the raft was two mile below there and out in the middle of the Mississippi. Then we hung up our signal lantern, and judged that we was free and safe once more. I hadn't had a bite to eat since yesterday; so Jim he got out some corn-dodgers and butter-milk, and pork and cabbage, and greens—there ain't nothing in the world so good, when it's cooked right—and whilst I eat my supper we talked, and had a good time. I was powerful glad to get away from the feuds, and so was Jim to get away from the swamp. We said there warn't no home like a raft, after all. Other places do seem so cramped up and smothery, but a raft don't. You feel mighty free and easy and comfortable on a raft.

I
FREEDOM AND SLAVERY

Although the main emphasis in this selection is on social criticism of the riverbank society, there is clearly a connection between this criticism and what may be the major theme of the novel as a whole, freedom. An important contrast between Huck and the Grangerford family is that Huck is essentially free whereas the lives of the Grangerfords are enmeshed in restrictions. Virtually everything they do *must* be done, and must be done in certain prescribed ways. In short, they have become slaves to a tradition which they follow unquestioningly, even when it is irrational. Thus Buck, for instance, dies in a tradition called a feud, without even knowing the source of the quarrel or why he is fighting.

II
IMPLICATIONS

Twain's social criticism in this selection is largely *indirect;* that is, his narrator, Huck, says one thing but the reader understands Twain to mean something else. Below are four statements made by Huck. For each statement discuss both Huck's attitude and the contrasting attitude of Twain.

1. Everybody was sorry she [Emmeline Grangerford] died. . . . But I reckoned, that with her disposition, she was having a better time in the graveyard.

2. Buck said she [Emmeline] could rattle off poetry like nothing. She didn't ever have to stop to think.

3. Next Sunday we all went to church. . . . The men took their guns along. . . . It was pretty ornery preaching—all about brotherly love, and such-like tiresomeness; but everybody said it was a good sermon, and they all talked it over going home, and had such a powerful lot to say about faith, and good works. . . .

4. . . . there warn't anybody at the church, except maybe a hog or two. . . . If you notice, most folks don't go to church only when they've got to; but a hog is different.

III
TECHNIQUES
Comedy and Sympathy and Detachment

Twain's comic technique in this selection rests heavily on a device called *irony of statement.* Huck, the narrator, makes statements usually showing either approval or neutrality toward a given thing, but these attitudes are in marked contrast with those of Twain. Thus there is a contrast in the statements between what is said and what is meant. This is irony of statement.

In his description of the parlor furnishings, for example, Huck says that the clock is "beautiful" and that the fruits in the crockery basket are "prettier than real ones is." Huck, in short, approves of both. But how does Twain feel about them? The fact is that Twain thinks both the clock and the fruits are pretentious and useless, tokens of the kind of life the Grangerfords live, a life in which appearances are more important than realities, in which the importance is placed on the shadow rather than the substance.

But how does the reader know what Twain thinks, how does he know that there is a contrast between the feelings of the author and the feelings of the narrator?

It is true that Twain never reveals his attitudes directly; nevertheless it is possible for the reader to infer the author's attitude from what Huck says and from the things he chooses to notice. Concerning the "pretty" fruits, for example, Huck notices not only that they are "prettier than real ones" but also that "they warn't real because you could see where pieces had got chipped off and showed the white chalk or whatever it was, underneath." Why should Huck mention this detail? The best answer seems to be because the detail gives the reader a key to the author's attitude.

Ironies such as these demand a good deal of the reader, especially with regard to his nearness to or distance from the characters in the work of fiction. In this case, for instance, the reader must sympathize with Huck and yet at the same time remain sufficiently detached from him to see the contrast between his attitudes and the attitudes of his creator.

IV
WORDS

A. 1. The first paragraph of "The Celebrated Jumping Frog of Calaveras County" contains such literary words as *garrulous, append, personage, conjectured, infamous, reminiscence, tedious.* Find several synonyms for each word. Rewrite the paragraph using more conversational words, and then rewrite the paragraph using colloquial and slang terms. Explain how your revisions differ from and change the original.

2. Find a simple synonym for each word below. *sustenance, remuneration, dogmatic, savant, venerable, thesaurus.*

3. Many of our more literary words are borrowed words—words that came into the language directly from Latin or Greek or by way of French. Look up the origin of the words in number two above. Find a more learned or literary synonym for the following native words.

dark, forgive, greed, kind (adj.), *start* (v.), *sharp, angry, deep.*

B. Dialects attracted American writers from almost the beginning of American literature. Mark Twain, breaking away from the rhetorical flourish of contemporary English writers, wrote American colloquial speech, attempting to represent the speech of the far westerner in "The Jumping Frog of Calaveras County," *Roughing It,* and the varieties of speech found in Pike County, Mississippi, in *The Adventures of Huckleberry Finn.* In the beginning of this novel, Twain explains to his readers that he used several dialects: the Missouri Negro dialect, the backwoods speech, and varieties of Pike County dialects.

1. Study the selections carefully. Make a list of pronunciation items, such as: use of "r" after vowels as in *idear;* "thish-yer" for "this here"; "jest" for "just" and so on. If you wish to make your description more accurate, use the pronunciation symbols found in your dictionary or the International Phonetic Alphabet system.

2. Make another list of vocabulary items, for example: *carry* for "escort," *cipher* for "write." What is a "straddle-bug"? Do you find any other regional names for objects, such as "corn-pone"?

3. Look for examples of meanings now obsolete, as in "I judged they would take it off." Using context as a guide, define the various vocabulary terms.

JAMES THURBER

1894–1961

Among twentieth-century humorists, James Thurber has an untouchable reputation. Being both artist and writer, he recorded his particular view of life in witty essays, informal autobiography, fables and short stories, satires, drama, and unforgettable line drawings. From his early years in Columbus, Ohio, to his last in West Cornwall, Connecticut, he looked out on the world with such surface calm that it was often taken for tolerance. But anyone who has read widely in his work knows that whimsy is a deceptive cover for a biting wit. He can deflate man's pretensions in both subtle prose and inspired drawing; beneath the calm exterior lies controlled anger. "One thing let's get straight," he told a *Life* reporter; "I'm not mild and gentle. Let the meek inherit the earth—they have it coming to them. I get up mad at something every morning and I think I should."

Yet it is the zany and whimsical pose that first made Thurber's reputation, not the exasperated cynicism. He wrote frequently about his boyhood in Columbus and his indulgent, peculiar family. He claimed he was born "on

JAMES THURBER, *photo by Douglas Glass*

A tall, lanky man with bushy hair, Thurber one day said, "Everyone thinks I look like the man I draw—bald and five feet one. Actually I draw the spirit of the man I am—and I'm a pussycat." His readers knew what he meant: independent, self-assured, curious, intelligent, not above purring when something pleased him, but quick to strike at irritants and intrusions. It is difficult to be neutral to his work. He engages our minds and imaginations, but above all he helps us to laugh at human behavior. And without laughter our lives would be harder to endure.

377

a night of wild portent and high wind. . . . The house, which is still standing, bears no tablet or plaque of any description, and is never pointed out to visitors." Once when his mother was "walking past the place with an old lady from Fostoria, Ohio, [she] said to her, 'My son James was born in that house,' to which the old lady, who was extremely deaf, replied, 'Why, on the Tuesday morning train, unless my sister is worse.' Mrs. Thurber let it go at that."

All the Thurbers "let things go at that." Bewildered but undaunted, they had secret lives and endured cold reality by ignoring it, or laughing at it. Thurber began writing at the age of ten. *Horse Sandusky, the Intrepid Boy Scout* was, if he remembered correctly, his first work. He started drawing a few years later. His family, for the most part, ignored his amateurish work, except perhaps "Aunt Lou, who wrote sixteen-stress verse, with hit-and-miss rhymes, in celebration of people's birthdays or on occasion of great national disaster." In 1913 he entered Ohio State University but left, when World War I broke out, to spend a year as a code clerk in the State Department in Washington and eventually in Paris. On his return to Columbus he earned his degree and then joined the staff of the Columbus *Dispatch*.

From Columbus he moved to the Paris edition of the Chicago *Tribune* and finally to the New York *Evening Post*. At a party in 1927, he met E. B. White, soon to become one of America's wittiest essayists and Thurber's intimate friend. Through White he was introduced to the intrepid Harold Ross who had founded *The New Yorker* magazine a few years before. Always quick to spot original talent, Ross soon had White writing the "Talk of the Town" columns and Thurber acting as managing editor. The combination was inspired, though Thurber claims he had to work himself down to a regular staff job before he felt at ease on the magazine.

His first drawings in *The New Yorker* appeared in 1931. By that time he and E. B. White had published a successful satire, *Is Sex Necessary?* aimed at demolishing the pseudopsycho-

logical treatises of the day. Thurber's drawings in this collection of essays helped the demolition more than anyone anticipated. He later recalled that they were at first a "form of nervous relaxation. I did them swiftly, almost absently, and threw them away. It was years before I learned to my astonishment that they could be sold. Then I tried to draw slowly and carefully but my colleague, E. B. White, put a stop to that. 'If you ever became good,' he said, 'you'd be mediocre.' I went back to rapidity."

Thurber's prose is another matter. He was known to rewrite a piece as often as twenty-five times until he had caught exactly the right tone, casual yet exact, tender but always sharp. By the mid-1930's he had left *The New Yorker* staff to become a free-lance contributor, devoting his creative energies to almost twenty volumes of magazine pieces in the next twenty years. *The Owl in the Attic* (1931) and *The Seal in the Bedroom* (1932) concentrated on drawings. *My Life and Hard Times* (1933) is autobiography clearly enough and, as he reminds us in the preface, it is his "own personal time, circumscribed by the short boundaries of his pain and his embarrassment, in which what happens to his digestion, the rear axle of his car, and the confused flow of his relationships with six or eight persons and two or three buildings is of greater importance than what goes on in the nation or the universe." The world, he admits, is in bad shape; but he is in worse.

Thurber writes with such conviction that we seldom stop to question the relevance of his material or the truth of his revelations. More than likely we identify ourselves at once with the follies of humanity he finds so funny in reviewing the past, so confusing in living the present. Not just Thurber but many men have experienced the frustrations he describes. Domestic disaster is universal; the battle of the sexes has intrigued writers for centuries; bewilderment is a public as well as a private hazard. In other words, he knows the weaknesses of our civilization almost more acutely than he has a right to.

Since Thurber defines humor as "a kind of emotional chaos told about calmly and quietly in retrospect," it is not difficult to see the pattern his books were to follow after the success of *My Life and Hard Times.* In 1935 he published *The Middle-Aged Man on the Flying Trapeze,* a collection of short stories and autobiographical essays. His subjects are pet dogs, old aunts, bad plays, social bores, parlor games, hired men, grade schools, traffic cops, and overcoats. The daring young man grown cautious? Not at all. Thurber once admitted he was unable "to maintain a consistent attitude toward life or reality, or toward anything else." What he was trying to do here was voice strong opinions about the unsensational but frequently unsettling aspects of daily life, and he made no attempt to organize the book around topics or people. He simply let himself ramble.

But with Thurber, rambling was always, contradictory though it sounds, controlled. The chaos of the event is the essence of the piece, and "what happens" strikes one on first reading as somewhat fantastic or at least outrageous. Disorder *seems* rampant. The artistry of the writing is the reward of a second reading. As Thurber recalled the experience "calmly and quietly in retrospect," he fit the pieces together, he polished each phrase. It was the only way he could work. "I don't think too clearly," he admitted; "too many thoughts bump into one another. Trains of thought run on a track of the Central Nervous System—the New York Central Nervous System, to make it worse."

Let Your Mind Alone (1937) assured Thurber a lasting reputation in American letters, if there was any doubt by this time. He was weary of the "inspirational" books and said so boldly in such essays as "The Case for the Daydreamer," "The Conscious vs. the Unconscious," and "Destructive Forces in Life." He begins one piece: "With the disappearance of the gas mantle and the advent of the short circuit, man's tranquility began to be threatened by everything he put his hand on"; and before long he is deep into an attack on Dr. Bisch, the Be-Glad-You're-Neurotic man. Another essay reveals Thurber's twitching annoyance before we are beyond even the first sentence: "I hardly know where to begin in trying to summarize for you a pamphlet called 'The Technique of Good Manners,' by one Mary Perin Barker, which has fallen into my hands." Not all of the pieces, of course, are safety valves on Thurber's blood pressure. Humor for its own sake filters through his reminiscences of Columbus, Ohio, friends, of dogs he had known and bizarre animals he wished he had known, of books he found amusing. Nothing was too slight to be unusable.

In 1940, turning momentarily from his drawings and magazine essays, Thurber became a successful playwright when he collaborated with Elliot Nugent, one of America's leading actors at the time, in writing *The Male Animal,* one of the most delightful, satiric comedies of the season. The play had a very successful Broadway run and was later made into a hilarious, popular motion picture. In this new medium Thurber admirers found the elements they had come to expect from him: the battle of the sexes, beast fable, social satire, and sharp wit poking at the essential madness of things. Set on the campus of a large midwestern university, *The Male Animal* irreverently questions the whole educational function of the university where football is more important than education, deftly exploits the amusing domestic triangle involving a professor of English, his lovely wife, and a football all-American, and forcefully binds these two conflicts together in the seriously treated theme of academic freedom.

But in spite of his Broadway and Hollywood successes, and in spite of his failing eyesight, his chief work continued to be his drawings, stories, and essays. In the last two decades of his life he continued to collect his *New Yorker* essays and stories: *My World—and Welcome to It* (1942), *Alarms and Diversions* (1957), *Lanterns and Lances* (1961). In the preface to this last volume, published the year he died, Thurber could not resist saying that though he attempted to "throw a few lantern beams here and there" he also wanted to "cast a few lances at the people and ideas that have disturbed me, and I make no apology for their seriousness." Precocious children, argumentative women, newspaper advertising, insomnia, and the decay of the English language set Thurber's teeth on edge. Listening to his fuming is worth the price of the book.

But a humorist's reputation is not built on satiric criticisms alone, and Thurber knew it. Taken as a whole, his work is humane and understanding. He never felt superior to his subject; indeed he was often self-deprecating, assuring us that he was as guilty as any of us of foolish behavior. Left alone, man is a reasonable animal, he would argue; but face him in groups and the trouble begins. Mass advertising, mass media, any attempt to regulate his mind or shape his opinion roused Thurber to violent action. Yet he was quick to forgive. A tall, lanky man with bushy hair, he one day said, "Everyone thinks I look like the man I draw—bald and 5 feet 1. Actually I draw the *spirit* of the man I am—and I'm a pussycat." His readers knew what he meant: independent, self-assured, curious, intelligent, not above purring when something pleased him, but quick to strike at irritants and intrusions. It is difficult to be neutral to James Thurber's work. He engages our minds and imaginations, but above all he helps us to laugh at human behavior. And without laughter our lives would be harder to endure.

Columbus, Ohio, provided
James Thurber with more material
than any writer could expect from his hometown.
My Life and Hard Times, from which the two
following pieces are taken, describes domestic
disasters, local eccentrics, draft boards,
family pets (especially Muggs, the Airedale),
and crises peculiar only to the Thurber family.
"Mistaken exits and entrances"
Thurber called them, autobiography
as it should be written: frank, honest,
and frequently hilarious.

The Night the Ghost Got In

The ghost that got into our house on the night of November 17, 1915, raised such a hullabaloo of misunderstandings that I am sorry I didn't just let it keep on walking, and go to bed. Its advent caused my mother to throw a shoe through a window of the house next door and ended up with my grandfather shooting a patrolman. I am sorry, therefore, as I have said, that I ever paid any attention to the footsteps.

They began about a quarter past one o'clock in the morning, a rhythmic, quick-cadenced walking around the dining-room table. My mother was asleep in one room upstairs, my brother Herman in another; grandfather was in the attic, in the old walnut bed which, as you will remember, once fell on my father. I had just stepped out of the bathtub and was busily rubbing myself with a towel when I heard the steps. They were the steps of a man walking rapidly around the dining-room table downstairs. The light from the bathroom shone down the back steps, which dropped directly into the dining-room; I could see the faint shine of plates on the plate-rail; I couldn't see the table. The steps kept going round and round the table; at regular intervals a board creaked, when it was trod upon. I supposed at first that it was my father or my brother Roy, who had gone to Indianapolis but were expected home at any time. I suspected next that it was a burglar. It did not enter my mind until later that it was a ghost.

After the walking had gone on for perhaps three minutes, I tiptoed to Herman's room. "Psst!" I hissed, in the dark, shaking him. "Awp," he said, in the low, hopeless tone of a despondent beagle—he always half suspected that something would "get him" in the night. I told him who I was. "There's something downstairs!" I said. He got up and followed me to the head of the back staircase. We listened together. There was no sound. The steps had ceased. Herman looked at me in some alarm: I had only the bath towel around my waist. He wanted to go back to bed, but I gripped his arm. "There's something down there!" I said. Instantly the steps began again, circled the dining-room table like a man running, and started up the stairs toward us, heavily, two at a time. The light still shone palely down the stairs; we saw nothing coming; we only heard the steps. Herman rushed to his room and slammed the door. I slammed shut the door at the stairs top and held my knee against it. After a long minute, I slowly opened it again. There was nothing there. There was no sound. None of us ever heard the ghost again.

The slamming of the doors had aroused mother: she peered out of her room. "What on earth are you boys doing?" she demanded. Herman ventured out of his room. "Nothing," he said, gruffly, but he was, in color, a light green. "What was all that running around downstairs?" said mother. So she had heard the steps, too! We just looked at her. "Burglars!" she shouted intuitively. I tried to quiet her by starting lightly downstairs.

He always half suspected that something would get him.

"Come on, Herman," I said.

"I'll stay with mother," he said. "She's all excited."

I stepped back onto the landing.

"Don't either of you go a step," said mother. "We'll call the police." Since the phone was downstairs, I didn't see how we were going to call the police—nor did I want the police—but mother made one of her quick, incomparable decisions. She flung up a window of her bedroom which faced the bedroom windows of the house of a neighbor, picked up a shoe, and whammed it through a pane of glass across the narrow space that separated the two houses. Glass tinkled into the bedroom occupied by a retired engraver named Bodwell and his wife. Bodwell had been for some years in rather a bad way and was subject to mild "attacks." Most everybody we knew or lived near had *some* kind of attacks.

It was now about two o'clock of a moonless night; clouds hung black and low. Bodwell was at the window in a minute, shouting, frothing a little, shaking his fist. "We'll sell the house and go back to Peoria," we could hear Mrs. Bodwell saying. It was some time before mother "got through" to Bodwell. "Burglars!" she shouted. "Burglars in the house!" Herman and I hadn't dared to tell her that it was not burglars but ghosts, for she was even more afraid of ghosts than of burglars. Bodwell at first thought that she meant there were burglars in his house, but finally he quieted down and called the police for us over an extension phone by his bed. After he had disappeared from the window, mother suddenly made as if to throw another shoe, not because there was further need of it but, as she later explained, because the thrill of heaving a shoe through a window glass had enormously taken her fancy. I prevented her.

The police were on hand in a commendably short time: a Ford sedan full of them, two on motorcycles, and a patrol wagon with about eight in it and a few reporters. They began banging at our front door. Flashlights shot streaks of gleam up and down the walls, across the yard, down the walk between our house and Bodwell's. "Open up!" cried a hoarse voice. "We're men from Headquarters!" I wanted to go down and let them in, since there they were, but mother wouldn't hear of it. "You haven't a stitch on," she pointed out. "You'd catch your death." I wound the towel around me again. Finally the cops put their shoulders to our big heavy front door with its thick beveled glass and broke it in: I could hear a rending of wood and a splash of glass on the floor of the hall. Their lights played all over the living-room and crisscrossed nervously in the dining-room, stabbed into hallways, shot up the front stairs and finally up the back. They caught me standing in my towel at the top. A heavy policeman bounded up the steps. "Who are you?" he demanded. "I live here," I said. "Well, whattsa matta, ya hot?" he asked. I was, as a matter of fact, cold; I went to my room and pulled on some trousers. On my way out, a cop stuck a gun into my ribs. "Whatta you doin' here?" he demanded. "I live here," I said.

The officer in charge reported to mother "No sign of nobody, lady," he said. "Musta got away—whatt'd he look like?" "There were two or three of them," mother said, "whooping and carrying on and slamming doors." "Funny,"

said the cop. "All ya windows and doors was locked on the inside tight as a tick."

Downstairs, we could hear the tromping of the other police. Police were all over the place; doors were yanked open, drawers were yanked open, windows were shot up and pulled down, furniture fell with dull thumps. A half-dozen policemen emerged out of the darkness of the front hallway upstairs. They began to ransack the floor: pulled beds away from walls, tore clothes off hooks in the closets, pulled suitcases and boxes off shelves. One of them found an old zither[1] that Roy had won in a pool tournament. "Looky here, Joe," he said, strumming it with a big paw. The cop named Joe took it and turned it over. "What is it?" he asked me. "It's an old zither our guinea pig used to sleep on," I said. It was true that a pet guinea pig we once had would never sleep anywhere except on the zither, but I should never have said so. Joe and the other cop looked at me a long time. They put the zither back on a shelf.

"No sign o' nuthin'," said the cop who had first spoken to mother. "This guy," he explained to the others, jerking a thumb at me, "was nekked. The lady seems historical." They all nodded, but said nothing; just looked at me. In the small silence we all heard a creaking in the attic. Grandfather was turning over in bed. "What's 'at?" snapped Joe. Five or six cops sprang for the attic door before I could intervene or explain. I realized that it would be bad if they burst in on grandfather unannounced, or even announced. He was going through a phase in which he believed that General Meade's men, under steady hammering by Stonewell Jackson, were beginning to retreat and even desert.

When I got to the attic, things were pretty confused. Grandfather had evidently jumped to the conclusion that the police were deserters from Meade's army, trying to hide away in his attic. He bounded out of bed wearing a long

---

1. **zither**, musical instrument with 30 to 40 strings stretched over a shallow box and played with the fingers.

Police were all over the place.

flannel nightgown over long woolen underwear, a nightcap, and a leather jacket around his chest. The cops must have realized at once that the indignant white-haired old man belonged in the house, but they had no chance to say so. "Back, ye cowardly dogs!" roared grandfather. "Back t' the lines, ye goddam, lily-livered cattle!" With that, he fetched the officer who found the zither a flat-handed smack alongside his head that sent him sprawling. The others beat a retreat, but not fast enough; grandfather grabbed Zither's gun from its holster and let fly. The report seemed to crack the rafters; smoke filled the attic. A cop cursed and shot his hand to his shoulder. Somehow, we all finally got downstairs again and locked the door against the old gentleman. He fired once or twice more in the darkness and then went back to bed. "That was grandfather," I explained to Joe, out of breath. "He thinks you're deserters." "I'll say he does," said Joe.

The cops were reluctant to leave without getting their hands on somebody besides grandfather; the night had been distinctly a defeat for them. Furthermore, they obviously didn't like the "layout"; something looked—and I can see their viewpoint—phony. They began to poke into things again. A reporter, a thin-faced, wispy man, came up to me. I had put on one of mother's blouses, not being able to find anything else. The reporter looked at me with mingled suspicion and interest. "Just what the hell is the real low down here, Bud?" he asked. I decided to be frank with him. "We had ghosts," I said. He gazed at me a long time as if I were a slot machine into which he had, without results, dropped a nickel. Then he walked away. The cops followed him, the one grandfather shot holding his now-bandaged arm, cursing and blaspheming. "I'm gonna get my gun back from that old bird," said the zither-cop. "Yeh," said Joe. "You—and who else?" I told them I would bring it to the station house the next day.

"What was the matter with that one policeman?" mother asked, after they had gone. "Grandfather shot him," I said. "What for?" she demanded. I told her he was a deserter. "Of all things!" said mother. "He was such a nice-looking young man."

Grandfather was fresh as a daisy and full of jokes at breakfast next morning. We thought at first he had forgotten all about what had happened, but he hadn't. Over his third cup of coffee, he glared at Herman and me. "What was the idee of all them cops tarryhootin' round the house last night?" he demanded. He had us there.

University Days

I passed all the other courses that I took at my University, but I could never pass botany. This was because all botany students had to spend several hours a week in a laboratory looking through a microscope at plant cells, and I could never see through a microscope. I never once saw a cell through a microscope. This used to enrage my instructor. He would wander around the laboratory pleased with the progress all the students were making in drawing the involved and, so I am told, interesting structure of flower cells, until he came to me. I would just be standing there. "I can't see anything," I would say. He would begin patiently enough, explaining how anybody can see through a microscope, but he would always end up in a fury, claiming that I could *too* see through a microscope but just pretended that I couldn't. "It takes away from the beauty of flowers anyway," I used to tell him. "We are not concerned with beauty in this course," he would say. "We are concerned solely with what I may call the *mechanics* of flars." "Well," I'd say, "I can't see anything." "Try it just once again," he'd say, and I would put my eye to the microscope and see nothing at all, except now and again a nebulous milky substance—a phenomenon of maladjustment. You were supposed to see a vivid, restless clockwork of sharply defined plant cells. "I see what looks like a lot of milk," I would tell him. This, he claimed, was the result of my not having adjusted the microscope properly, so he would readjust it for me, or rather, for himself. And I would look again and see milk.

I finally took a deferred pass, as they called it, and waited a year and tried again. (You had to pass one of the biological sciences or you couldn't graduate.) The professor had come back from vacation brown as a berry, bright-eyed, and eager to explain cell-structure again to his classes. "Well," he said to me, cheerily, when we met in the first laboratory hour of the semester, "we're going to see cells this time, aren't we?" "Yes, sir," I said. Students to right of me and to left of me and in front of me were seeing cells; what's more, they were quietly drawing pictures of them in their notebooks. Of course, I didn't see anything.

"We'll try it," the professor said to me, grimly, "with every adjustment of the microscope known to man. As God is my witness, I'll arrange this glass so that you see cells through it or I'll give up teaching. In twenty-two years of botany, I—" He cut off abruptly for he was beginning to quiver all over, like Lionel Barrymore, and he genuinely wished to hold onto his temper; his scenes with me had taken a great deal out of him.

So we tried it with every adjustment of the microscope known to man. With only one of

He was beginning to quiver all over like Lionel Barrymore.

them did I see anything but blackness or the familiar lacteal opacity,[1] and that time I saw, to my pleasure and amazement, a variegated constellation of flecks, specks, and dots. These I hastily drew. The instructor, noting my activity, came back from an adjoining desk, a smile on his lips and his eyebrows high in hope. He looked at my cell drawing. "What's that?" he demanded, with a hint of a squeal in his voice. "That's what I saw," I said. "You didn't, you didn't, you *did*n't!" he screamed, losing control of his temper instantly, and he bent over and squinted into the microscope. His head snapped up. "That's your eye!" he shouted. "You've fixed the lens so that it reflects! You've drawn your eye!"

Another course that I didn't like, but somehow managed to pass, was economics. I went to that class straight from the botany class, which didn't help me any in understanding either subject. I used to get them mixed up. But not as mixed up as another student in my economics class who came there direct from a physics laboratory. He was a tackle on the football team, named Bolenciecwcz. At that time Ohio State University had one of the best football teams in the country, and Bolenciecwcz was one of its outstanding stars. In order to be eligible to play it was necessary for him to keep up in his studies, a very difficult matter, for while he was not dumber than an ox he was not any smarter. Most of his professors were lenient and helped him along. None gave him more hints, in answering questions, or asked him simpler ones than the economics professor, a thin, timid man named Bassum. One day when we were on the subject of transportation and distribution, it came Bolenciecwcz's turn to answer a question. "Name one means of transportation," the professor said to him. No light came into the big tackle's eyes. "Just any means of transportation," said the professor. Bolenciecwcz sat staring at him. "That is," pursued the professor, "any medium, agency, or method of going from one place to another." Bolenciecwcz had the look of a man who is being led into a trap. "You may choose among steam,

Bolenciecwcz was trying to think..

horse-drawn, or electrically propelled vehicles," said the instructor. "I might suggest the one which we commonly take in making long journeys across land." There was a profound silence in which everybody stirred uneasily, including Bolenciecwcz and Mr. Bassum. Mr. Bassum abruptly broke this silence in an amazing manner. "Choo-choo-choo," he said, in a low voice, and turned instantly scarlet. He glanced appealingly around the room. All of us, of course, shared Mr. Bassum's desire that Bolenciecwcz should stay abreast of the class in economics, for the Illinois game, one of the hardest and most important of the season, was only a week off. "Toot, toot, too-tooooooot!" some student with a deep voice moaned, and we all looked encouragingly at Bolenciecwcz. Somebody else gave a fine imitation of a locomotive letting off steam. Mr. Bassum himself rounded off the little show. "Ding, dong, ding, dong," he said, hopefully. Bolenciecwcz was staring at the floor now, trying to think, his great brow furrowed, his huge hands rubbing together, his face red.

---

1. **lacteal opacity**\ˈlăk·tē·əl ō ˈpă·sĕd·ē\ milky matter.

"How did you come to college this year, Mr. Bolenciecwcz?" asked the professor. "*Chuff*a chuffa, *chuff*a chuffa."

"M'father sent me," said the football player.

"What on?" asked Bassum.

"I git an 'lowance," said the tackle, in a low, husky voice, obviously embarrassed.

"No, no," said Bassum. "Name a means of transportation. What did you *ride* here on?"

"Train," said Bolenciecwcz.

"Quite right," said the professor. "Now, Mr. Nugent, will you tell us——"

If I went through anguish in botany and economics—for different reasons—gymnasium work was even worse. I don't even like to think about it. They wouldn't let you play games or join in the exercises with your glasses on and I couldn't see with mine off. I bumped into professors, horizontal bars, agricultural students, and swinging iron rings. Not being able to see, I could take it but I couldn't dish it out. Also, in order to pass gymnasium (and you had to pass it to graduate) you had to learn to swim if you didn't know how. I didn't like the swimming pool, I didn't like swimming, and I didn't like the swimming instructor, and after all these years I still don't. I never swam but I passed my gym work anyway, by having another student give my gymnasium number (978) and swim across the pool in my place. He was a quiet, amiable blond youth, number 473, and he would have seen through a microscope for me if we could have got away with it, but we couldn't get away with it. Another thing I didn't like about gymnasium work was that they made you strip the day you registered. It is impossible for me to be happy when I am stripped and being asked a lot of questions. Still, I did better than a lanky agricultural student who was cross-examined just before I was. They asked each student what college he was in—that is, whether Arts, Engineering, Commerce, or Agriculture. "What college are you in?" the instructor snapped at the youth in front of me. "Ohio State University," he said promptly.

It wasn't that agricultural student but it was another a whole lot like him who decided to take up journalism, possibly on the ground that when farming went to hell he could fall back on newspaper work. He didn't realize, of course, that that would be very much like falling back full-length on a kit of carpenter's tools. Haskins didn't seem cut out for journalism, being too embarrassed to talk to anybody and unable to use a typewriter, but the editor of the college paper assigned him to the cow barns, the sheep house, the horse pavilion, and the animal husbandry department generally. This was a genuinely big "beat," for it took up five times as much ground and got ten times as great a legislative appropriation as the College of Liberal Arts. The agricultural student knew animals, but nevertheless his stories were dull and colorlessly written. He took all afternoon on each of them, on account of having to hunt for each letter on the typewriter. Once in a while he had to ask somebody to help him hunt. "C" and "L," in particular, were hard letters for him to find. His editor finally got pretty much annoyed at the farmer-journalist because his pieces were so uninteresting. "See here, Haskins," he snapped at him one day, "why is it we never have anything hot from you on the horse pavilion? Here we have two hundred head of horses on this campus—more than any other university in the Western Conference except Purdue—and yet you never get any real low down on them. Now shoot over to the horse barns and dig up something lively." Haskins shambled out and came back in about an hour; he said he had something. "Well, start it off snappily," said the editor. "Something people will read." Haskins set to work and in a couple of hours brought a sheet of typewritten paper to the desk; it was a two-hundred word story about some disease that had broken out among the horses. Its opening sentence was simple but arresting. It read: "Who has noticed the sores on the tops of the horses in the animal husbandry buildings?"

Ohio State was a land grant university and therefore two years of military drill was compulsory. We drilled with old Springfield rifles and studied the tactics of the Civil War even though the World War was going on at the time. At 11 o'clock each morning thousands of freshmen and sophomores used to deploy over the campus, moodily creeping up on the old chemistry building. It was good training for the kind of warfare that was waged at Shiloh but it had no connection with what was going on in Europe. Some people used to think there was German money behind it, but they didn't dare say so or they would have been thrown in jail as German spies. It was a period of muddy thought and marked, I believe, the decline of higher education in the Middle West.

As a soldier I was never any good at all. Most of the cadets were glumly indifferent soldiers, but I was no good at all. Once General Littlefield, who was commandant of the cadet corps, popped up in front of me during regimental drill and snapped, "You are the main trouble with this university!" I think he meant that my type was the main trouble with the university but he may have meant me individually. I was mediocre at drill, certainly—that is, until my senior year. By that time I had drilled longer than anybody else in the Western Conference, having failed at military at the end of each preceding year so that I had to do it all over again. I was the only senior still in uniform. The uniform which, when new, had made me look like an interurban railway conductor, now that it had become faded and too tight made me look like Bert Williams in his bellboy act. This had a definitely bad effect on my morale. Even so, I had become by sheer practice little short of wonderful at squad maneuvers.

One day General Littlefield picked our company out of the whole regiment and tried to get it mixed up by putting it through one movement after another as fast as we could execute them: squads right, squads left, squads on right into line, squads right about, squads left front into line, etc. In about three minutes one hundred and nine men were marching in one direction and I was marching away from them at an angle of forty degrees, all alone. "Company,

halt!" shouted General Littlefield, "That man is the only man who has it right!" I was made a corporal for my achievement.

The next day General Littlefield summoned me to his office. He was swatting flies when I went in. I was silent and he was silent too, for a long time. I don't think he remembered me or why he had sent for me, but he didn't want to admit it. He swatted some more flies, keeping his eyes on them narrowly before he let go with the swatter. "Button up your coat!" he snapped. Looking back on it now I can see that he meant me although he was looking at a fly, but I just stood there. Another fly came to rest on a paper in front of the General and began rubbing its hind legs together. The General lifted the swatter cautiously. I moved restlessly and the fly flew away. "You startled him!" barked General Littlefield, looking at me severely. I said I was sorry. "That won't help the situation!" snapped the General, with cold military logic. I didn't see what I could do except offer to chase some more flies toward his desk, but I didn't say anything. He stared out the window at the far-away figures of co-eds crossing the campus toward the library. Finally, he told me I could go. So I went. He either didn't know which cadet I was or else he forgot what he wanted to see me about. It may have been that he wished to apologize for having called me the main trouble with the university; or maybe he had decided to compliment me on my brilliant drilling of the day before and then at the last minute decided not to. I don't know. I don't think about it much any more.

I

THE CLASH OF TWO "WORLDS"

The main conflict in "The Night the Ghost Got In" is between groups rather than individuals, between the Thurber family on the one hand and the neighbors, police, and the reporter on the other. The latter represent the common-sense, "real" world; the former represent a zany, "unreal" world, a world in which—for one thing—ghosts really exist. One of the main sources of fun is the fact that when the two worlds clash, the zany world comes out victorious. The frustration and defeat of the common-sense world is well expressed by the "thin-faced, wispy" reporter who at the end of the episode asks, "Just what the hell is the real low-down here, Bud?" Why is "Bud's" answer, "We had ghosts," a fitting and proper climax?

Something of the same sort of clash may be observed in some of the episodes in "University Days." In the botany class episode, for example, all students easily see and draw plant cells—all students, that is, except young Thurber, who can see only "a nebulous milky substance" until a misadjustment of the microscope helps him to see his own eye.

II
IMPLICATIONS

Discuss the following statements concerning the two previous selections.

1. It is difficult to identify with members of the Thurber family because they are such "oddballs."

2. Among other things, "The Night the Ghost Got In" is a satire against the police force.

3. School life readily lends itself to satire because it offers so many situations that are remote from reality.

4. Thurber's criticism of the botany professor, the gym department, and the army general represents his way of striking back at those areas of university life in which he felt most inadequate personally.

5. Thurber's strong bias in favor of the liberal arts invalidates his criticism of other aspects of university life.

III
TECHNIQUES

Comedy

We have already noted that Thurber defines humor as "a kind of emotional chaos told about calmly and quietly in retrospect." What episodes in the preceding selections best exemplify this definition? What episodes—if any—do not seem to exemplify it? How well does the definition fit other instances of literary humor you may have read? Be prepared to offer examples.

Sympathy and Detachment

It has been argued that readers enjoy certain comedies because they allow them to do vicariously certain things that they would never permit themselves to do in reality. To what extent did you identify (perhaps subconsciously) with such characters as the mother and the grandfather, who —among other things—break the window of a neighbor and shoot a policeman? Contrast your feelings toward these two characters with your feelings toward the football tackle, Bolenciecwcz.

Whether you call it sympathy or identification, how does Thurber get his readers on the side of zanies like the members of his family? Why don't we instead identify or sympathize with the relatively normal persons in Thurber's stories?

Let Your Mind Alone
is subtitled *And Other More or Less
Inspirational Pieces.* The following essay
is surely one of the less inspirational;
in fact, unsettling would more accurately
describe it. Thurber believed that life's
frustrations are daily and inevitable,
but beware of the day, he seems
to warn us, when they get out of hand
through sheer numbers.

Nine Needles

"And the medicine chest after it!"

One of the more spectacular minor happenings of the past few years which I am sorry that I missed took place in the Columbus, Ohio, home of some friends of a friend of mine. It seems that a Mr. Albatross, while looking for something in his medicine cabinet one morning, discovered a bottle of a kind of patent medicine which his wife had been taking for a stomach ailment. Now, Mr. Albatross is one of those apprehensive men who are afraid of patent medicines and of almost everything else. Some weeks before, he had encountered a paragraph in a Consumers' Research bulletin which announced that this particular medicine was bad for you. He had thereupon ordered his wife to throw out what was left of her supply of the stuff and never buy any more. She had promised, and here now was another bottle of the perilous liquid. Mr. Albatross, a man given to quick rages, shouted the conclusion of the story at my friend: "I threw the bottle out the bathroom window and the medicine chest after it!" It seems to me that must have been a spectacle worth going a long way to see.

I am sure that many a husband has wanted to wrench the family medicine cabinet off the wall and throw it out the window, if only because the average medicine cabinet is so filled with mysterious bottles and unidentifiable objects of all kinds that it is a source of constant bewilderment and exasperation to the American male. Surely the British medicine cabinet and the French medicine cabinet and all the other medicine cabinets must be simpler and better ordered than ours. It may be that the American habit of saving everything and never throwing anything away, even empty bottles, causes the domestic medicine cabinet to become as cluttered in its small way as the American attic becomes cluttered in its major way. I have encountered few medicine cabinets in this country which were not pack-jammed with something between a hundred and fifty and two hundred different items, from dental floss to boracic acid, from razor blades to sodium perborate,[1] from adhesive tape to coconut oil. Even the neatest wife will put off clearing out the medicine cabinet on the ground that she has something else to do that is more important at the moment, or more diverting. It was in the apartment of such a wife and her husband that I became enormously involved with a medicine cabinet one morning not long ago.

I had spent the weekend with this couple—they live on East Tenth Street near Fifth Avenue—such a weekend as left me reluctant to rise up on Monday morning with bright and shining face and go to work. They got up and went to work, but I didn't. I didn't get up until about two-thirty in the afternoon. I had my face all lathered for shaving and the washbowl was full of hot water when suddenly I cut myself with the razor. I cut my ear. Very few men cut their ears with razors, but I do, possibly because I was taught the old Spencerian free-wrist movement[2] by my writing teacher in the grammar grades. The ear bleeds rather profusely when cut with a razor and is difficult to get at. More angry than hurt, I jerked open the door of the medicine cabinet to see if I could find a styptic[3] pencil and out fell, from the top shelf, a little black paper packet containing nine needles. It seems that this wife kept a little paper packet containing nine needles on the top shelf of the medicine cabinet. The packet fell into the soapy water of the washbowl, where the paper rapidly disintegrated, leaving nine needles at large in the bowl. I was, naturally enough, not in the best condition, either physical or mental, to recover nine needles from a washbowl. No gentleman who has lather on his face and whose ear is bleeding is in the best condition for anything, even something involving the handling of nine large blunt objects.

It did not seem wise to me to pull the plug out of the washbowl and let the needles go down the drain. I had visions of clogging up the plumbing system of the house, and also a vague fear of causing short circuits somehow or other (I know very little about electricity and I don't want to have it explained to me). Finally, I groped very gently around the bowl and eventually had four of the needles in the palm of one hand and three in the palm of the other—two I couldn't find. If I had thought quickly and clearly, I wouldn't have done that. A lathered man whose ear is bleeding and who has four wet needles in one hand and three in the other may be said to have reached the lowest known point of human efficiency. There is nothing he can do but stand there. I tried transferring the needles in my left hand to the palm of my right hand, but I couldn't get them off my left hand. Wet needles cling to you. In the end, I wiped the needles off onto a bath-towel which was hanging on a rod above the bathtub. It was the only towel that I could find. I had to dry my hands afterward on the bathmat. Then I tried to find the needles in the towel. Hunting for seven needles in a bathtowel is the most tedious occupation I have ever engaged in. I could find only five of them. With the two that had been left in the bowl, that meant there were four needles in all missing—two in the washbowl and two others lurking in the towel or lying in the bathtub under the towel. Frightful thoughts came to me of what might happen to anyone who used that towel or washed his face in the bowl or got into the tub, if I didn't find the missing needles. Well, I didn't find them. I sat down on the edge of the tub to think, and I decided finally that the only thing to do was wrap up the towel in a newspaper and take it away with me. I also decided to leave a note for my friends explaining as clearly as I could that I was

---

1. **sodium perborate**\ˈsō·dē·əm ˈpər ˈbō·rāt\ powdery substance used in mouthwash and dentifrices and as a bleaching agent.
2. **Spencerian movement,** named after Platt Rogers Spencer (1800–1864), American teacher of penmanship and author of textbooks on penmanship.
3. **styptic**\ˈstĭp·tĭk\ tending to stop bleeding.

afraid there were two needles in the bathtub and two needles in the washbowl, and that they better be careful.

I looked everywhere in the apartment, but I could not find a pencil, or a pen, or a typewriter. I could find pieces of paper, but nothing with which to write on them. I don't know what gave me the idea—a movie I had seen, perhaps, or a story I had read—but I suddenly thought of writing a message with a lipstick. The wife might have an extra lipstick lying around and, if so, I concluded it would be in the medicine cabinet. I went back to the medicine cabinet and began poking around in it for a lipstick. I saw what I thought looked like the metal tip of one, and I got two fingers around it and began to pull gently—it was under a lot of things. Every object in the medicine cabinet began to slide. Bottles broke in the washbowl and on the floor; red, brown, and white liquids spurted; nail files, scissors, razor blades, and miscellaneous objects sang and clattered and tinkled. I was covered with perfume, peroxide, and cold cream.

It took me half an hour to get the debris all together in the middle of the bathroom floor. I made no attempt to put anything back in the medicine cabinet. I knew it would take a steadier hand than mine and a less shattered spirit. Before I went away (only partly shaved) and abandoned the shambles, I left a note saying that I was afraid there were needles in the bathtub and the washbowl and that I had taken their towel and that I would call up and tell them everything—I wrote it in iodine with the end of a toothbrush. I have not yet called up, I am sorry to say. I have neither found the courage nor thought up the words to explain what happened. I suppose my friends believe that I deliberately smashed up their bathroom and stole their towel. I don't know for sure, because they have not yet called me up, either.

___

I
MAN VS. MEDICINE CHEST

The hero of "Nine Needles" is a character-type quite familiar to Thurber fans. Sometimes called by Thurber "the American male," he is basically an uncomplicated, easygoing person whose fondest desire is simply to be let alone. One of his chief problems, on the other hand, is that people (especially female people) and "things" won't let him alone. Take the medicine chest in this story. All the hero did was open it twice—hardly provocative actions; yet that was enough to cause the chest to "attack." Thus the hero is enmeshed in conflict, fighting against one of the thousands of situations that daily threaten his peace of mind.

II
IMPLICATIONS

Each of the following propositions is expressed in two forms. Choose the form that agrees more with your own opinion and be prepared to defend your point of view against its opposite.

1. It is (relatively easy/relatively hard) to identify with the hero of "Nine Needles."

2. Thurber's hero is a (good/poor) representative of the average American male.

3. Ultimately, the hero comes off (rather well/ rather poorly) in his battle against the medicine chest.

4. It is (the small things like medicine chests/ the large things like hydrogen bombs) that are the chief source of anxiety in the modern world.

5. Those who do not have peace of mind have largely (themselves/things outside themselves) to blame for their state.

In 1940, Thurber published
Fables for Our Time, drawings and texts
so wisely critical of man's behavior
and so pertinent that they are likely
to become classics of their kind.
These four, only a sample
of the collection, need no commentary.
They make their point unerringly.

The Very Proper Gander

Not so very long ago there was a very fine gander. He was strong and smooth and beautiful and he spent most of his time singing to his wife and children. One day somebody who saw him strutting up and down in his yard and singing remarked, "There is a very proper gander." An old hen overheard this and told her husband about it that night in the roost. "They said something about propaganda," she said. "I have always suspected that," said the rooster, and he went around the barnyard next day telling everybody that the very fine gander was a dangerous bird, more than likely a hawk in gander's clothing. A small brown hen remembered a time when at a great distance she had seen the gander talking with some hawks in the forest. "They were up to no good," she said. A duck remembered that the gander had once told him he did not believe in anything. "He said to hell with the flag, too," said the duck. A guinea hen recalled that she had once seen somebody who looked very much like the gander throw something that looked a great deal like a bomb. Finally everybody snatched up sticks and stones and descended on the gander's house. He was strutting in his front yard, singing to his children and his wife. "There he is!" everybody cried. "Hawk-lover! Unbeliever! Flag-hater! Bomb-thrower!" So they set upon him and drove him out of the country.

Moral: Anyone who you or your wife thinks is going to overthrow the government by violence must be driven out of the country.

The Shrike
and the Chipmunks

Once upon a time there were two chipmunks, a male and a female. The male chipmunk thought that arranging nuts in artistic patterns was more fun than just piling them up to see how many you could pile up. The female was all for piling up as many as you could. She told her husband that if he gave up making designs with the nuts there would be room in their large cave for a great many more and he would soon become the wealthiest chipmunk in the woods. But he would not let her interfere with his designs, so she flew into a rage and left him. "The shrike will get you," she said, "because you are helpless and cannot look after yourself." To be sure, the female chipmunk had not been gone three nights before the male had to dress for a banquet and could not find his studs or shirt or suspenders. So he couldn't go to the banquet, but that was just as well, because all the chipmunks who did go were attacked and killed by a weasel.

The next day the shrike began hanging around outside the chipmunk's cave, waiting to catch him. The shrike couldn't get in because the doorway was clogged up with soiled laundry and dirty dishes. "He will come out for a walk after breakfast and I will get him then," thought the shrike. But the chipmunk slept all day and did not get up and have breakfast until after dark. Then he came out for a breath of air before beginning work on a new design. The shrike swooped down to snatch up the chipmunk, but could not see very well on account of the dark, so he batted his head against an alder branch and was killed.

A few days later the female chipmunk returned and saw the awful mess the house was in. She went to the bed and shook her husband.

"What would you do without me?" she demanded. "Just go on living, I guess," he said. "You wouldn't last five days," she told him. She swept the house and did the dishes and sent out the laundry, and then she made the chipmunk get up and wash and dress. "You can't be healthy if you lie in bed all day and never get any exercise," she told him. So she took him for a walk in the bright sunlight and they were both caught and killed by the shrike's brother, a shrike named Stoop.

Moral: Early to rise and early to bed makes a male healthy and wealthy and dead.

The Glass
in the Field

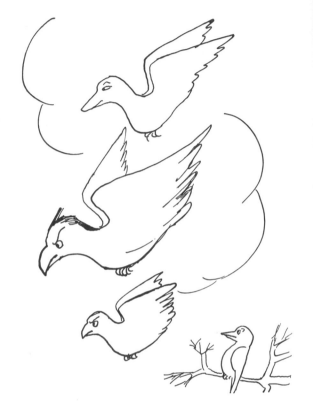

A short time ago some builders, working on a studio in Connecticut, left a huge square of plate glass standing upright in a field one day. A goldfinch flying swiftly across the field struck the glass and was knocked cold. When he came to he hastened to his club, where an attendant bandaged his head and gave him a stiff drink. "What the hell happened?" asked a sea gull. "I was flying across a meadow when all of a sudden the air crystallized on me," said the goldfinch. The sea gull and a hawk and an eagle all laughed heartily. A swallow listened gravely. "For fifteen years, fledgling and bird, I've flown this country," said the eagle, "and I assure you there is no such thing as air crystallizing. Water, yes; air, no." "You were probably struck by a hailstone," the hawk told the goldfinch. "Or he may have had a stroke," said the sea gull. "What do you think, swallow?" "Why, I—I think maybe the air crystallized on him," said the swallow. The large birds laughed so loudly that the goldfinch became annoyed and bet them each a dozen worms that they couldn't follow the course he had flown across the field without encountering the hardened atmosphere. They all took his bet; the swallow went along to watch. The sea gull, the eagle, and the hawk decided to fly together over the route the goldfinch indicated. "You come, too," they said to the swallow. "I—I— well, no," said the swallow. "I don't think I will." So the three large birds took off together and they hit the glass together and they were all knocked cold.

Moral: He who hesitates is sometimes saved.

The Owl
Who Was God

Once upon a starless midnight there was an owl who sat on the branch of an oak tree. Two ground moles tried to slip quietly by, unnoticed. "You!" said the owl. "Who?" they quavered, in fear and astonishment, for they could not believe it was possible for anyone to see them in that thick darkness. "You two!" said the owl. The moles hurried away and told the other creatures of the field and forest that the owl was the greatest and wisest of all animals because he could see in the dark and because he could answer any question. "I'll see about that," said a secretary bird, and he called on the owl one night when it was again very dark. "How many claws am I holding up?" said the secretary bird. "Two," said the owl, and that was right. "Can you give me another expression for 'that is to say' or 'namely'?" asked the secretary bird. "To wit," said the owl. "Why does a lover call on his love?" asked the secretary bird. "To woo," said the owl.

The secretary bird hastened back to the other creatures and reported that the owl was indeed the greatest and wisest animal in the world because he could see in the dark and because he could answer any question. "Can he see in the daytime, too?" asked a red fox. "Yes," echoed a dormouse and a French poodle. "Can he see in the daytime, too?" All the other creatures laughed loudly at this silly question, and they set upon the red fox and his friends and drove them out of the region. Then they sent a messenger to the owl and asked him to be their leader.

When the owl appeared among the animals it was high noon and the sun was shining brightly. He walked very slowly, which gave him an appearance of great dignity, and he peered about him with large, staring eyes, which gave him an air of tremendous importance. "He's God!" screamed a Plymouth Rock hen. And the others took up the cry "He's God!" So they followed him wherever he went and when he began to bump into things they began to bump into things, too. Finally he came to a concrete highway and he started up the middle of it and all the other creatures followed him. Presently a hawk, who was acting as outrider, observed a truck coming toward them at fifty miles an hour, and he reported to the secretary bird and the secretary bird reported to the owl. "There's danger ahead," said the secretary bird. "To wit?" said the owl. The secretary bird told him. "Aren't you afraid?" he asked. "Who?" said the owl calmly, for he could not see the truck. "He's God!" cried all the creatures again, and they were still crying "He's God!" when the truck hit them and ran them down. Some of the animals were merely injured, but most of them, including the owl, were killed.

Moral: You can fool too many of the people too much of the time.

I
CRITICISM CLOSE TO HOME

Those who judge Thurber himself to be a relatively meek and gentle man like the character in "Nine Needles" are often startled by the acid, almost cynical, comments of some of the satires in *Fables for Our Time*. Of course the characters are all disguised as animals, but there can be no question that Thurber's target is human nature; note, for example, that the morals to "The Owl Who Was God" and "The Very Proper Gander" refer directly to human beings and not to the animals who illustrate the point. Indeed, one of the chief characteristics of the morals of Thurber's fables is that they can be applied so frequently to ourselves and to those we know best.

II
IMPLICATIONS

Identify the fable or fables that bear upon the following statements and discuss both Thurber's and your own attitude toward each proposition.

1. Human beings are far too ready to follow; far too slow to lead.

2. He who would live a quiet life and escape criticism had best be a conformist.

3. Faith should never be so blind as to be completely out of touch with Reason.

4. Self-confidence should have narrow boundaries—It is far better to be too unsure of yourself than to be too sure.

5. Human beings readily react to the improbable by dismissing it rather than by seeking to discover its causes.

III
TECHNIQUES

Comedy

Mark Twain once observed that a humorist had to preach if he would "live forever." (He also added, "By forever, I mean thirty years.") Do you believe that a humorist must preach in order to secure a lasting reputation? In answering this question compare "Nine Needles," in which Thurber does not "preach," with the fables, in which he does. Is either one more likely to endure than the other? If you think that the fables are likely to endure longer, would you say it is because they preach, or for some other reason?

Sympathy and Detachment

We have observed that the reader must retain some degree of detachment in order to appreciate fully some of the ironies in *Huck Finn*. In which of the Thurber selections—"Nine Needles" or the fables—is detachment more important?

THE STRUGGLE FOR JUSTICE

"With liberty and justice for all." Every time we Americans recite the Pledge of Allegiance, we use the word "justice." What, precisely, do we mean by this word? How do we discriminate between what is just and what is unjust?

In trying to answer these questions, it is natural to think of the judicial department of the government and of the courts. It is true—in America, at least—that juries and judges are charged with the duty of deciding what is just and unjust in a given case. Consequently, we may feel that a person is given

justice when he is treated according to laws and certain legal procedures. In part, justice may be defined as equal treatment under the law.

But the word "law" itself raises several problems. Where does the law come from? Are laws always just? Do they, for example, always protect the rights of minority groups? On the other hand, do they always protect the rights of the majority against a minority that has power and influence?

It is obvious that legal codes are formed to some extent both by majority and minority pressures. It is equally obvious that there have always been laws which some persons have considered unjust. Before 1920, for example, women were not guaranteed the right to vote in the United States. Today, we would agree that women were treated unjustly by the laws which denied them voting privileges.

The fact that some laws have been considered unjust raises a fundamental question: How do we determine whether or not any given law is "just?" If we say, for instance, that the laws that prohibited women from voting were not "just" laws, upon what standard are we basing our idea of justice? Certainly, we are using some standard other than the law itself.

In the Declaration of Independence, Thomas Jefferson named some of these extralegal standards when he spoke of "the laws of nature and of nature's God." According to Jefferson's view, justice is based not upon man-made laws only, but especially upon what we might call natural and supernatural "laws." These standards, he affirmed, are the standards upon which legal codes should be based; and if man-made laws are not based upon such standards, men have the right to revolt against them. That, of course, is exactly what Jefferson and many of his fellow-Americans did; our country was born partly because certain men believed that English laws of the time were unjust.

Our history has been and continues to be characterized by struggles led by individuals who have felt themselves and their groups unjustly treated. THE STRUGGLE FOR JUSTICE is a theme that runs throughout American history and it is natural that American writers have made it the theme of many stories, essays, and poems. The selections in the following unit deal with this struggle. Some are concerned with historical struggles of groups of people; others with the struggles of individuals against other individuals or against "the tyranny of the majority." As you read these selections you may find opinions or points of view with which you may disagree, but try to remember—as James Madison pointed out—that justice is secured neither by destroying liberty nor by giving every citizen the same opinions.

One of the earliest and most horrible acts of injustice in America
was the hanging of a number of citizens as witches in Salem, Massachusetts,
in 1692. Though this episode occurred over two centuries ago,
mob reactions and suspicions of one's neighbors have produced incidents
in modern history that closely parallel the events in Salem.

Trials at Salem

STEPHEN VINCENT BENÉT

Salem Village had got a new minister—the Reverend Samuel Parris, ex-merchant in the West Indies. The most important thing about Samuel Parris was the fact that he brought with him to Salem Village two West Indian servants —a man known as John Indian and a woman named Tituba. And when he bought those two or their services in the West Indies, he was buying a rope that was to hang nineteen men and women of New England—so odd are the links in the circumstantial chain.

Perhaps the nine-year-old Elizabeth Parris, the daughter of the parsonage, boasted to her new friends of the odd stories Tituba told and the queer things she could do. Perhaps Tituba herself let the report of her magic powers be spread about the village. She must have been as odd and imagination-stirring a figure as a parrot or a tame monkey in the small New England town. And the winters were long and white—and any diversion a godsend.

In any case, during the winter of 1691–92 a group of girls and women began to meet nightly at the parsonage, with Tituba and her fortune telling as the chief attraction. Elizabeth Parris, at nine, was the youngest; then came Abigail Williams, eleven, and Ann Putnam, twelve. The rest were older—Mercy Lewis, Mary Wolcott, and Elizabeth Hubbard were seventeen; Elizabeth Booth and Susan Sheldon,

eighteen; and Mary Warren and Sarah Churchill, twenty. Three were servants—Mercy Lewis had been employed by the Reverend George Burroughs, a previous minister of Salem Village, and now worked for the Putnams; Mary Warren was a maid at the John Procters'; Sarah Churchill, at the George Jacobs'. All, except for Elizabeth Parris, were adolescent or just leaving adolescence.

The elder women included a pair of gossipy, superstitious busybodies—Mrs. Pope and Mrs. Bibber; and young Ann Putnam's mother, Ann Putnam, Sr., who deserves a sentence to herself.

For the Putnams were a powerful family in the neighborhood and Ann Putnam, married at seventeen and now only thirty, is described as handsome, arrogant, temperamental, and high-strung. She was also one of those people who can cherish a grudge and revenge it.

The circle met—the circle continued to meet —no doubt with the usual giggling, whispering, and gossip. From mere fortune telling it proceeded to other and more serious matters— table rapping, perhaps, and a little West Indian voodoo—weird stories told by Tituba and weird things shown, while the wind blew outside and the big shadows flickered on the wall. Adolescent girls, credulous servants, superstitious old women—and the two enigmatic figures of Tituba, the West Indian, and Ann Putnam, Sr.

But soon the members of the circle began to show hysterical symptoms. They crawled under tables and chairs; they made strange sounds; they shook and trembled with nightmare fears. The thing became a village celebrity—and more. Something strange and out of nature was happening—who had ever seen normal young girls behave like these young girls? And no one—certainly not the Reverend Samuel Parris—even suggested that a mixed diet of fortune telling, ghost stories, and voodoo is hardly the thing for impressionable minds during a long New England winter. Hysteria was possession by an evil spirit; pathological lying, the devil putting words into one's mouth. The Reverend Samuel became very busy. Grave ministers were called in to look at the afflicted children. A Dr. Gregg gave his opinion. It was almost too terrible to believe, and yet what else could be believed? Witchcraft!

Meanwhile, one may suppose, the "afflicted children," like most hysterical subjects, enjoyed the awed stares, the horrified looks, the respectful questions that greeted them, with girlish zest. They had been unimportant girls of a little hamlet;[1] now they were, in every sense of the word, spot news. And any reporter knows what that does to certain kinds of people. They continued to writhe and demonstrate—and be the center of attention. There was only one catch about it. If they were really bewitched, somebody must be doing the bewitching.

On the twenty-ninth of February, 1692, in the midst of an appropriate storm of thunder and lightning, three women—Sarah Good, Sarah Osburn, and Tituba—were arrested on the deadly charge of bewitching the children.

The next day, March 1, two magistrates, Justice Hawthorne[2] and Justice Corwin, arrived with appropriate pomp and ceremony. The first hearing was held in the crowded meetinghouse of the village; and all Salem swarmed to it, as crowds in our time have swarmed to other sleepy little villages suddenly notorious.

The children—or the children and Tituba—had picked their first victims well. Sarah Good

and Sarah Osburn were old women of no particular standing in the community.

We can imagine that meetinghouse—and the country crowd within it—on that chill March day. At one end was the majesty of the law—and the "afflicted children," where all might see them and observe. Dressed in their best, very likely, and with solicitous relatives near at hand. Do you see Mercy Lewis? Do you see Ann Putnam? And then the whole crowd turned to one vast, horrified eye. For there was the accused—the old woman—the witch!

The justices—grim Justice Hawthorne in particular—had, evidently, arrived with their minds made up. For the first question addressed to Sarah Good was, bluntly:

"What evil spirit have you familiarity with?"

"None," said the piping old voice. But everybody in the village knew worthless Sarah Good. And the eye of the audience went from her to the deadly row of "afflicted children" and back again.

"Have you made no contracts with the devil?" proceeded the Justice.

"No."

The Justice went to the root of the matter at once.

"Why do you hurt these children?"

A rustle must have gone through the meetinghouse at that. Aye, that's it; the Justice speaks shrewdly; hark to the Justice! Aye, but look too! Look at the children! Poor things, poor things!

"I do not hurt them. I scorn it," said Sarah Good defiantly. But the Justice had her now; he was not to be brushed aside.

"Who, then, do you employ to do it?"

"I employ nobody."

"What creature do you employ then?" For all witches had familiars.

"No creature, but I am falsely accused." But the sweat must have been on the old woman's palms by now.

---

1. **hamlet,** a small village.
2. **Justice Hawthorne,** distant relative of Nathaniel Hawthorne. The Justice actually spelled his name Hathorne; the *w* was added by Nathaniel.

The Justice considered. There was another point, minor but illuminating.

"Why did you go away muttering from Mr. Parris, his house?"

"I did not mutter, but I thanked him for what he gave my child."

The Justice returned to the main charge, like any prosecuting attorney.

"Have you made no contract with the devil?"

"No."

It was time for Exhibit A. The Justice turned to the children. Was Sarah Good one of the persons who tormented them? Yes, yes!—and a horrified murmur running through the crowd. And then, before the awe-stricken eyes of all, they began to be tormented. They writhed; they grew stiff; they contorted; they were stricken moaning or speechless. Yet, when they were brought to Sarah Good and allowed to touch her, they grew quite quiet and calm. For, as everyone knew, a witch's physical body was like an electric conductor—it reabsorbed, on touch, the malefic force discharged by witchcraft into the bodies of the tormented. Everybody could see what happened and everybody saw. When the meetinghouse was quiet, the Justice spoke again.

"Sarah Good, do you not see now what you have done? Why do you not tell us the truth? Why do you torment these poor children?"

And with these words Sarah Good was already hanged. For all that she could say was, "I do not torment them." And yet everyone had seen her, with their own eyes.

Sarah Osburn's examination followed the same course, the same prosecutor's first question, the same useless denial, the same epileptic feats of the "afflicted children," the same end.

Then Tituba was examined and gave them their fill of marvels, prodigies, and horrors.

The West Indian woman, a slave in a strange land, was fighting for her life, and she did it shrewdly, and desperately. She admitted, repentantly, that she had tormented the children. But she had been forced to do so. By whom? By Goody Good and Goody Osburn and two other witches whom she hadn't yet been able to

TRIAL OF GEORGE JACOBS,
T. H. Matterson

recognize. Her voodoo knowledge aided her—she filled the open ears of Justices and crowd with tales of hairy familiars and black dogs, red cats and black cats and yellow birds, the phantasm of a woman with legs and wings. And everybody could see that she spoke the truth. For, when she was first brought in, the children were tormented at her presence; but as soon as she had confessed and turned King's evidence, she was tormented herself, and fearfully. To Boston Jail with her—but she had saved her neck.

The hearing was over; the men and women of Salem and its outlying farms went broodingly or excitedly back to their homes to discuss the fearful workings of God's providence. Here and there a common sense voice murmured a doubt of two—Sarah Good and Sarah Osburn were no great losses to the community; but still, to convict two old women of heinous crime on the testimony of greensick girls and a West Indian slave! But, on the whole, the villagers of Salem felt relieved. The cause of the plague had been found; it would be stamped out and the afflicted children recover. The Justices, no doubt, congratulated themselves on their prompt and intelligent action. The "afflicted children" slept, after a tiring day—they were not quite so used to such performances as they were to become.

As for the accused women, they went to Boston Jail—to be chained there while waiting trial and gallows.

Meanwhile, on an outlying farm, Giles Corey, a turbulent, salty old fellow of eighty-one, began to argue the case with his wife, Martha. He believed, fanatically, in the "afflicted children." She did not, and said so—even going so far as to say that the magistrates were blinded and she could open their eyes. It was one of those marital disputes that occur between strong-willed people. And it was to bring Martha Corey to the gallows and Giles Corey to an even stranger doom.

Yet now there was a lull, through which people whispered.

As for what went on in the minds of the "afflicted children," during that lull we may not say. But this much is evident. They had seen and felt their power. The hearing had been the greatest and most exciting event of their narrow lives. And it was so easy to do; they grew more and more ingenious with each rehearsal. You twisted your body and groaned —and grown people were afraid.

Add to this the three girl-servants, with the usual servants' grudges against present or former masters. Add to this that high-strung, dominant woman Ann Putnam, Sr., who could hold a grudge and remember it. Such a grudge as there might be against the Towne sisters, for instance—they were all married women of the highest standing, particularly Rebecca Nurse. So suppose—just suppose—that one of them were found out to be a witch? And hadn't Tituba deposed that there were other women, besides Good and Osburn, who made her torment the children?

On March 19 Martha Corey and Rebecca Nurse were arrested on the charge of witchcraft. On March 21 they were examined and committed. And with that the real reign of terror began.

Salem Village, as a community, was no longer sane.

Let us get it over quickly. The Salem witches ceased to be Salem's affair—they became a matter affecting the whole colony. Sir William Phips, the new governor, appointed a special court of oyer and terminer[3] to try the cases. And the hangings began.

On January 1, 1692, no one, except possibly the "circle children," had heard of Salem witches. On June 10 Bridget Bishop was hanged. She had not been one of the first accused, but she was the first to suffer. She had been married three times, kept a roadhouse on the road to Beverly where people drank rum and played shovelboard, and dressed, distinctively for the period, in a "black cap and black hat and red paragon bodice broidered and looped with diverse colors." But those seem to have been her chief offenses. When questioned, she said, "I never saw the devil in my life."

All through the summer the accusations, the arrests, the trials, came thick and fast till the jails were crowded. Nor were those now accused friendless old beldames like Sarah Good. They included Captain John Alden (son of Miles Standish's friend[4]), who saved himself by breaking jail, and the wealthy and prominent Englishes, who saved themselves by flight. The most disgraceful scenes occurred at the trial of the saintly Rebecca Nurse. Thirty-nine citizens of Salem were brave enough to sign a petition for her, and the jury brought in a verdict of "not guilty." The mob in the sweating courtroom immediately began to cry out, and the presiding judge as much as told the jury to reverse their verdict. They did so, to the mob's delight. Then the governor pardoned her. And "certain gentlemen of Salem"—and perhaps the mob—persuaded him into reversing his pardon. She was hanged on Gallows Hill on July 19 with Sarah Good, Sarah Wilds, Elizabeth How, and Susanna Martin.

Susanna Martin's only witchcraft seems to have been that she was an unusually tidy woman and had once walked a muddy road

---

3. **court of oyer and terminer**\'ōy·ər . . . ᴬtĕr·mə·nər\ a high court which hears and determines criminal cases.
4. **Miles Standish's friend**, John Alden, Sr., who with Standish founded Duxbury.

without getting her dress bedraggled. No, I am quoting from testimony, not inventing. As for Elizabeth How, a neighbor testified, "I have been acquainted with Goodwife How as a naybor for nine or ten years and I never saw any harm in her but found her just in her dealings and faithful to her promises . . . I never heard her revile any person but she always pitied them and said, 'I pray God forgive them now.'" But the children cried, "I am stuck with a pin. I am pinched," when they saw her—and she hanged.

It took a little more to hang the Reverend George Burroughs. He had been Salem Village's second minister—then gone on to a parish in Maine. And the cloth had great sanctity. But Ann Putnam and Mercy Lewis managed to doom him between them, with the able assistance of the rest of the troupe. Mr. Burroughs was unfortunate enough to be a man of unusual physical strength—anyone who could lift a gun by putting four fingers in its barrel must do so by magic arts. Also, he had been married three times. So when the ghosts of his first two wives, dressed in winding sheets, appeared in a sort of magic lantern show to Ann Putnam and cried out that Mr. Burroughs had murdered them— the cloth could not save him then.

Here and there in the records gleams a flash of frantic common sense. Susanna Martin laughs when Ann Putnam and her daughter go into convulsions at her appearance. When asked why, she says, "Well I may, at such folly. I never hurt this woman or her child in my life." John Procter, the prosperous farmer who employed Mary Warren, said sensibly, before his arrest, "If these girls are left alone, we will all be devils and witches. They ought all to be sent to the whipping post." He was right enough about it—but his servant helped hang him.

Judge, jury, and colony preferred to believe the writhings of the children; the stammerings of those whose sows had died inexplicably; the testimony of such as Bernard Peach, who swore that Susanna Martin had flown in through his window, bent his body into the shape of a "Whoope," and sat upon him for an hour and a half.

One hanging on June 10, five or July 19, five on August 19, eight on September 22, including Mary Easty and Martha Corey. And of these the Reverend Noyes remarked, with unction, "What a sad thing it is to see eight firebrands of hell hanging there!" But for stubborn Giles Corey a different fate was reserved.

The old man had begun by believing in the whole hocus-pocus. He had quarreled with his wife about it. He had seen her arrested as a witch, insulted by the magistrates, condemned to die. Two of his sons-in-law had testified against her; he himself had been closely questioned as to her actions and had made the deposition of a badgered and simple man. Yes, she prayed a good deal; sometimes he couldn't hear what she said—that sort of thing. The memory must have risen to haunt him when she was condemned. Now he himself was in danger.

Well, he could die as his wife would. But there was the property—his goods, his prospering lands. By law, the goods and property of those convicted of witchcraft were confiscated by the state and the name attainted. With a curious, grim heroism, Giles Corey drew up a will leaving that property to the two sons-in-law who had not joined in the prevailing madness. And then at his trial, he said, "I will not plead. If I deny, I am condemned already in courts where ghosts appear as witnesses and swear men's lives away."

A curious, grim heroism? It was so. For those who refused to plead either guilty or not guilty in such a suit were liable to the old English punishment called *peine forte et dure.*[5] It consisted in heaping weights or stones upon the unhappy victim till he accepted a plea—or until his chest was crushed. And exactly that happened to old Giles Corey. They heaped the stones upon him until they killed him—and two

---

5. **peine forte et dure**\pĕn fȯr·tĕ dūr\ lit. severe and strong punishment; a form of punishment by pressing under heavy weights.

days before his wife was hanged, he died. But his property went to the two loyal sons-in-law, without confiscation—and his name was not attainted. So died Giles Corey, New England to the bone.

And then, suddenly and fantastically as the madness had come, it was gone.

The "afflicted children," at long last, had gone too far. They had accused the governor's lady. They had accused Mrs. Hall, the wife of the minister at Beverly and a woman known throughout the colony for her virtues. And there comes a point when driven men and women revolt against blood and horror. It was that which ended Robespierre's[6] terror—it was that which ended the terror of the "afflicted children." The thing had become a *reductio ad absurdum*.[7] If it went on, logically, no one but the "afflicted children" and their protégées would be left alive.

In 1706 Ann Putnam made public confession that she had been deluded by the devil in testifying as she had. She had testified in every case but one. And in 1711 the colony of Massachusetts paid fifty pounds to the heirs of George Burroughs, twenty-one pounds to the heirs of Giles Corey—five hundred and seventy-eight pounds in all to the heirs of various victims. An expensive business for the colony, on the whole.

What happened to the survivors? Well, the Reverend Samuel Parris quit Salem Village to go into business in Boston and died at Sudbury in 1720. And Ann Putnam died in 1716 and from the stock of the Putnams sprang Israel Putnam, the Revolutionary hero. And from the stock of the "Witches," the Nurses and the others, sprang excellent and distinguished people of service to state and nation. And hanging Judge Hawthorne's descendant was Nathaniel Hawthorne.

We have no reason to hold Salem up to obloquy. It was a town, like another, and a strange madness took hold of it. But it is not a stranger thing to hang a man for witchcraft than to hang him for the shape of his nose or the color of his skin. We are not superstitious, no. Well, let us be a little sure we are not. For persecution follows superstition and intolerance as fire follows the fuse. And once we light that fire we cannot foresee where it will end or what it will consume—any more than they could in Salem two hundred and sixty-seven years ago.

I
INSANITY AND JUSTICE

Laws in themselves never guarantee justice; there must also be fair and sane administration of the laws. If judges and juries are irrational, no amount of law can protect the individual citizen. Injustice was done at Salem largely because the community, the citizens themselves, had temporarily lost their sanity, their ability to distinguish between the real and the unreal.

In communities and even in nations mass madness is not nearly as uncommon as most of us would like to believe. Especially in a nation where extremes of opinion are allowed, there is always likely to be some "community," some group, which stands upon beliefs that are not grounded in reality. Benét puts his finger on two of the causes leading to irrational belief and conduct—superstition and intolerance. What modern instances of group insanity can you point to and to what extent are they rooted in either superstition or intolerance?

II
IMPLICATIONS

Resolved: "When a group or a community within our nation shows that it cannot distinguish between what is real and what is unreal (as in Salem in 1692), some force outside of that group or community should step in and take charge until sanity has been restored."

Debate this proposition on either the affirmative or the negative side. As you think about your case, consider the following questions.

1. What standard or standards can one use to determine whether or not a given group is "sane"?

---

6. **Robespierre**\ro 'bĕs ▲pyăr\ French revolutionist responsible for much of the reign of terror.
7. **reductio ad absurdum**\rē ▲dŭk•shē•ō ăd ăb ▲sər•dəm\ proof of the falsity of a conclusion by reducing it to absurdity.

2. Who can be entrusted with making this kind of a decision?

3. Will the control of a group by outside pressure destroy freedom of opinion?

4. Can true democracy flourish only when extremes of opinion are tolerated?

5. If certain types of groups are not controlled, might they destroy democracy entirely?

III
TECHNIQUES

This unit examines *intention* and *theme* in literature. These two elements are sometimes very closely related; in an essay, for example, the author's intention may be to define and express his theme. Our discussions of intention, however, will generally explore how the reader can learn what the author's intention is. When we discuss theme, we will be concerned with the author's methods of stating and developing his theme.

Intention

We often feel that we have grasped the "true" meaning of a work of literature when the meaning we infer and the meaning the writer intended are identical. This feeling, however, may raise a vexing question: "How do we know what a writer's intention is?"

First of all, it is usually impractical and often impossible to get at the writer's intention by asking him in person or by reading what he may have said about it in some other work.

It is usually best, then—or at least most convenient—to judge a writer's intentions by looking at the work itself rather than at some source outside the work. There are usually many clues to intention within the work itself. In Benét's article, let us observe one of the simplest—*the writer's choice of words.*

In his third, fourth, and fifth paragraphs Benét names the girls and women who met with Tituba. His description of the younger members of the circle is relatively neutral; he does little but mention their names and ages. In the fourth paragraph, however, where he takes up the older members, he calls Mrs. Pope and Mrs. Bibber, "a pair of gossipy, superstitious busybodies." His description of Ann Putnam, Sr., in the next paragraph is even stronger; among other things, he notes that she is "arrogant" and that she "can cherish a grudge and revenge it."

From words like "arrogant," "busybody," and "gossipy," we can judge that Benét's intention is certainly not to treat these women sympathetically.

The contrast between Benét's neutral description of the younger members and his criticism of the older ones does not necessarily mean that he considers the former group blameless; it does, however, show effectively that he believes the older women should have known better. He has placed the primary responsibility on their shoulders.

But there is one other important caution concerning a writer's choice of words as a means of grasping his intention: We must be sure that he "means what he says," that he is not speaking ironically. When in Shakespeare's *Julius Caesar* Antony calls Brutus, "an honorable man," we know that Antony does not mean what he says. How do you know that Benét means what he says when he calls the older women "gossipy, superstitious busybodies"?

Benét's intention of creating an unsympathetic picture of the older women is only a minor aspect of his overall intention. What was his major intention in "Trials at Salem"? What evidence from the essay supports your opinion?

Theme

Theme may be defined as the *central idea* in a work of literature. In nonfiction theme often takes the form of a *thesis;* that is, a position or proposition to be proved or supported by evidence.

How may an author's theme be expressed by a reader? A popular way of expressing theme is choosing a single word or phrase to describe the central idea. However, it may be difficult to decide what single word to use. Consider "Trials at Salem." Which of the following words most adequately describes its theme: "superstition," "injustice," "persecution," "community insanity," or "intolerance"? Even assuming that you can choose one of these words as somehow more appropriate than the others, you will probably agree that you haven't given a very clear indication of Benét's central idea.

The adequate expression of a theme almost always requires more than a single word. Indeed especially in nonfiction, it usually must be expressed in a complete sentence. Hence, Benét's theme might be stated as follows: "Community insanity, which grows out of superstition and intolerance, leads to injustice and persecution."

Hamlin Garland, who was himself raised on a Midwestern farm,
speaks with authority of the life of prairie farmers in the late 1800's.
As you read the following story, consider how its title serves
to point up the author's intention and theme.

Under the Lion's Paw

HAMLIN GARLAND

I

It was the last of autumn and first day of winter coming together. All day long the ploughmen on their prairie farms had moved to and fro in their wide level fields through the falling snow, which melted as it fell, wetting them to the skin—all day, notwithstanding the frequent squalls of snow, the dripping, desolate clouds, and the muck of the furrows, black and tenacious as tar.

Under their dripping harness the horses swung to and fro silently, with that marvellous uncomplaining patience which marks the horse. All day the wild geese, honking wildly, as they sprawled sidewise down the wind, seemed to be fleeing from an enemy behind, and with neck outthrust and wings extended, sailed down the wind, soon lost to sight.

Yet the ploughman behind his plough, though the snow lay on his ragged great-coat, and the cold clinging mud rose on his heavy boots, fettering him like gyves,[1] whistled in the very beard of the gale. As day passed, the snow, ceasing to melt, lay along the ploughed land, and lodged in the depth of the stubble, till on each slow round the last furrow stood out black and shining as jet between the ploughed land and the gray stubble.

When night began to fall, and the geese, flying low, began to alight invisibly in the near corn-field, Stephen Council was still at work "finishing a land." He rode on his sulky plough when going with the wind, but walked when facing it. Sitting bent and cold but cheery under his slouch hat, he talked encouragingly to his four-in-hand.

"Come round there, boys!—Round agin! We got t' finish this land. Come in there, Dan! *Stiddy*, Kate,—stiddy! None o' y'r tantrums, Kittie. It's purty tuff, but got a be did. *Tchk! tchk!* Step along, Pete! Don't let Kate git y'r single-tree on the wheel. *Once* more!"

They seemed to know what he meant, and that this was the last round, for they worked with greater vigor than before.

"Once more, boys, an' then, sez I, oats an' a nice warm stall, an' sleep f'r all."

By the time the last furrow was turned on the land it was too dark to see the house, and the snow was changing to rain again. The tired and hungry man could see the light from the kitchen shining through the leafless hedge, and he lifted a great shout, "Supper f'r a half a dozen!"

It was nearly eight o'clock by the time he had finished his chores and started for supper. He was picking his way carefully through the mud, when the tall form of a man loomed up before him with a premonitory cough.

"Waddy ye want?" was the rather startled question of the farmer.

Reprinted by permission of Mrs. Constance Garland Doyle and Mrs. Isabel Garland Lord.

1. **fettering,** binding or shackling the feet. **gyves**\jaivz\ another word for fetter or chain.

"Well, ye see," began the stranger, in a deprecating tone, "we'd like t' git in fr the night. We've tried every house fr the last two miles, but they hadn't any room fr us. My wife's jest about sick, 'n' the children are cold and hungry —"

"Oh, y' want 'o stay all night, eh?"

"Yes, sir; it 'ud be a great accom—"

"Waal, I don't make it a practice t' turn anybuddy way hungry, not on sech nights as this. Drive right in. We ain't got much, but sech as it is—"

But the stranger had disappeared. And soon his steaming, weary team, with drooping heads and swinging single-trees, moved past the well to the block beside the path. Council stood at the side of the "schooner"[2] and helped the children out—two little half-sleeping children— and then a small woman with a babe in her arms.

"There ye go!" he shouted jovially, to the children. "*Now* we're all right! Run right along to the house there, an' tell Mam' Council you wants sumpthin' t' eat. Right this way, Mis'— keep right off t' the right there. I'll go an' git a lantern. Come," he said to the dazed and silent group at his side.

"Mother," he shouted, as he neared the fragrant and warmly lighted kitchen, "here are some wayfarers an' folks who need sumpthin' t' eat an' a place t' snooze." He ended by pushing them all in.

Mrs. Council, a large, jolly, rather coarse-looking woman, took the children in her arms. "Come right in, you little rabbits. 'Most asleep, hey? Now here's a drink o' milk fr each o' ye. I'll have s'm tea in a minute. Take off y'r things and set up t' the fire."

While she set the children to drinking milk, Council got out his lantern and went out to the barn to help the stranger about his team, where his loud, hearty voice could be heard as it came and went between the haymow[3] and the stalls.

The woman came to light as a small, timid, and discouraged-looking woman, but still pretty, in a thin and sorrowful way.

"Land sakes! An' you've travelled all the way from Clear Lake t'-day in this mud! Waal! waal! No wonder you're all tired out. Don't wait fr the men, Mis'—" She hesitated, waiting for the name.

"Haskins."

"Mis' Haskins, set right up to the table an' take a good swig o' tea whilst I make y' s'm toast. It's green tea, an' it's good. I tell Council as I git older I don't seem to enjoy Young Hyson n'r Gunpowder.[4] I want the reel green tea, jest as it comes off'n the vines. Seems t' have more heart in it, some way. Don't s'pose it has. Council says it's all in m' eye."

Going on in this easy way, she soon had the children filled with bread and milk and the woman thoroughly at home, eating some toast and sweet-melon pickles, and sipping the tea.

"See the little rats!" she laughed at the children. "They're full as they can stick now, and they want to go to bed. Now, don't git up, Mis' Haskins; set right where you are an' let me look after 'em. I know all about young ones, though I'm all alone now. Jane went an' married last fall. But, as I tell Council, it's lucky we keep our health. Set right there, Mis' Haskins; I won't have you stir a finger."

It was an unmeasured pleasure to sit there in the warm, homely kitchen, the jovial chatter of the housewife driving out and holding at bay the growl of the impotent, cheated wind.

The little woman's eyes filled with tears which fell down upon the sleeping baby in her arms. The world was not so desolate and cold and hopeless, after all.

"Now I hope Council won't stop out there and talk politics all night. He's the greatest man to talk politics an' read the *Tribune*—How old is it?"

She broke off and peered down at the face of the babe.

"Two months 'n' five days," said the mother, with a mother's exactness.

---

2. **schooner,** covered wagon.
3. **haymow,** a part of the barn where the hay is stored.
4. **Young Hyson . . . Gunpowder,** kinds of tea.

"Ye don't say! I want 'o know! The dear little pudzy-wudzy!" she went on, stirring it up in the neighborhood of the ribs with her fat forefinger.

"Pooty tough on 'oo to go gallivant'n' 'cross lots this way—"

"Yes, that's so; a man can't lift a mountain," said Council, entering the door. "Mother, this is Mr. Haskins, from Kansas. He's been eat up 'n' drove out by grasshoppers."

"Glad t' see yeh!—Pa, empty that wash-basin 'n' give him a chance t' wash."

Haskins was a tall man, with a thin, gloomy face. His hair was a reddish brown, like his coat, and seemed equally faded by the wind and sun, and his sallow face, though hard and set, was pathetic somehow. You would have felt that he had suffered much by the line of his mouth showing under his thin, yellow mustache.

"Hain't Ike got home yet, Sairy?"

"Hain't seen 'im."

"W-a-a-l, set right up, Mr. Haskins; wade right into what we've got; 'tain't much, but we manage to live on it—she gits fat on it," laughed Council, pointing his thumb at his wife.

After supper, while the women put the children to bed, Haskins and Council talked on, seated near the huge cooking-stove, the steam rising from their wet clothing. In the Western fashion Council told as much of his own life as he drew from his guest. He asked but few questions, but by and by the story of Haskins' struggles and defeat came out. The story was a terrible one, but he told it quietly, seated with his elbows on his knees, gazing most of the time at the hearth.

"I didn't like the looks of the country, anyhow," Haskins said, partly rising and glancing at his wife. "I was ust t' northern Ingyannie,[5] where we have lots o' timber 'n' lots o' rain, 'n' I didn't like the looks o' that dry prairie. What galled me the worst was goin' s' far away acrosst so much fine land layin' all through here vacant."

"And the 'hoppers eat ye four years, hand runnin', did they?"

"Eat! They wiped us out. They chawed everything that was green. They jest set around waitin' f'r us to die t' eat us, too. My God! I ust t' dream of 'em sittin' 'round on the bedpost, six feet long, workin' their jaws. They eet the forkhandles. They got worse 'n' worse till they jest rolled on one another, piled up like snow in winter. Well, it ain't no use. If I was t' talk all winter I couldn't tell nawthin'. But all the while I couldn't help thinkin' of all that land back here that nobuddy was usin' that I ought 'o had 'stead o' bein' out there in that cussed country."

"Waal, why didn't ye stop an' settle here?" asked Ike, who had come in and was eating his supper.

"Fer the simple reason that you fellers wantid ten 'r fifteen dollars an acre fer the bare land, and I hadn't no money fer that kind o' thing."

"Yes, I do my own work," Mrs. Council was heard to say in the pause which followed. "I'm a gettin' purty heavy t' be on m' laigs all day, but we can't afford t' hire, so I keep rackin'[6] around somehow, like a foundered horse.[7] S' lame—I tell Council he can't tell how lame I am, f'r I'm jest as lame in one laig as t'other." And the good soul laughed at the joke on herself as she took a handful of flour and dusted the biscuit-board to keep the dough from sticking.

"Well, I hain't *never* been very strong," said Mrs. Haskins. "Our folks was Canadians an' small-boned, and then since my last child I hain't got up again fairly. I don't like t' complain. Tim has about all he can bear now—but they was days this week when I jest wanted to lay right down an' die."

"Waal, now, I'll tell ye," said Council, from his side of the stove, silencing everybody with his good-natured roar, "I'd go down and *see* Butler, *anyway*, if I was you. I guess he'd let you have his place purty cheap; the farm's all run down. He's ben anxious t' let t' somebuddy next year. It 'ud be a good chance fer you. Any-

---

5. **Ingyannie,** Indiana.
6. **rackin',** stretching and straining.
7. **foundered horse,** horse disabled or gone lame.

how, you go to bed and sleep like a babe. I've got some ploughin' t' do, anyhow, an' we'll see if somethin' can't be done about your case. Ike, you go out an' see if the horses is all right, an' I'll show the folks t' bed."

When the tired husband and wife were lying under the generous quilts of the spare bed, Haskins listened a moment to the wind in the eaves, and then said, with a slow and solemn tone,

"There are people in this world who are good enough t' be angels, an' only haff t' die to *be* angels."

II

Jim Butler was one of those men called in the West "land poor." Early in the history of Rock River he had come into the town and started in the grocery business in a small way, occupying a small building in a mean part of the town. At this period of his life he earned all he got, and was up early and late sorting beans, working over butter, and carting his goods to and from the station. But a change came over him at the end of the second year, when he sold a lot of land for four times what he paid for it. From that time forward he believed in land speculation as the surest way of getting rich. Every cent he could save or spare from his trade he put into land at forced sale, or mortgages on land, which were "just as good as the wheat," he was accustomed to say.

Farm after farm fell into his hands, until he was recognized as one of the leading landowners of the county. His mortgages were scattered all over Cedar County, and as they slowly but surely fell in he sought usually to retain the former owner as tenant.

He was not ready to foreclose; indeed, he had the name of being one of the "easiest" men in the town. He let the debtor off again and again, extending the time whenever possible.

"I don't want y'r land," he said. "All I'm after is the int'rest on my money—that's all. Now, if y' want o' stay on the farm, why, I'll give y' a good chance. I can't have the land layin' va-

cant." And in many cases the owner remained as tenant.

In the meantime he had sold his store; he couldn't spend time in it; he was mainly occupied now with sitting around town on rainy days smoking and "gassin' with the boys," or in riding to and from his farms. In fishing-time he fished a good deal. Doc Grimes, Ben Ashley, and Cal Cheatham were his cronies on these fishing excursions or hunting trips in the time of chickens or partridges. In winter they went to Northern Wisconsin to shoot deer.

In spite of all these signs of easy life Butler persisted in saying he "hadn't enough money to pay taxes on his land," and was careful to convey the impression that he was poor in spite of his twenty farms. At one time he was said to be worth fifty thousand dollars, but land had been a little slow of sale of late, so that he was not worth so much.

A fine farm, known as the Higley place, had fallen into his hands in the usual way the previous year, and he had not been able to find a tenant for it. Poor Higley, after working himself nearly to death on it in the attempt to lift the mortgage, had gone off to Dakota, leaving the farm and his curse to Butler.

This was the farm which Council advised Haskins to apply for; and the next day Council hitched up his team and drove down town to see Butler.

"You jest let *me* do the talkin'," he said. "We'll find him wearin' out his pants on some salt barrel somew'ers; and if he thought you *wanted* a place he'd sock it to you hot and heavy. You jest keep quiet; I'll fix 'im."

Butler was seated in Ben Ashley's store telling fish yarns when Council sauntered in casually.

"Hello, But; lyin' agin, hey?"

"Hello, Steve! how goes it?"

"Oh, so-so. Too dang much rain these days. I thought it was goin' t' freeze up f'r good last night. Tight squeak if I get m' ploughin' done. How's farmin' with *you* these days?"

"Bad. Ploughin' ain't half done."

"It 'ud be a religious idee f'r you t' go out an' take a hand y'rself."

"I don't haff to," said Butler, with a wink.

"Got anybody on the Higley place?"

"No. Know of anybody?"

"Waal, no; not eggsackly. I've got a relation back t' Michigan who's ben hot an' cold on the idee o' comin' West f'r some time. *Might* come if he could get a good lay-out. What do you talk on the farm?"

"Well, I d' know. I'll rent it on shares or I'll rent it money rent."

"Waal, how much money, say?"

"Well, say ten per cent, on the price—two-fifty."

"Waal, that ain't bad. Wait on 'im till 'e thrashes?"

Haskins listened eagerly to his important question, but Council was coolly eating a dried apple which he had speared out of a barrel with his knife. Butler studied him carefully.

"Well, knocks me out of twenty-five dollars interest."

"My relation'll need all he's got t' git his crops in," said Council, in the safe, indifferent way.

"Well, all right; *say* wait," concluded Butler.

"All right; this is the man. Haskins, this is Mr. Butler—no relation to Ben—the hardest-working man in Cedar County."

On the way home Haskins said: "I ain't much better off. I'd like that farm; it's a good farm, but it's all run down, an' so 'm I. I could make a good farm of it if I had half a show. But I can't stock it n'r seed it."

"Waal, now, don't you worry," roared Council in his ear. "We'll pull y' through somehow till next harvest. He's agreed t' hire it ploughed, an' you can earn a hundred dollars ploughin' an' y' c'n git the seed o' me, an' pay me back when y' can."

Haskins was silent with emotion, but at last he said, "I ain't got nothin' t' live on."

"Now, don't you worry 'bout that. You jest make your headquarters at ol' Steve Council's. Mother'll take a pile o' comfort in havin' y'r wife an' children 'round. Y' see, Jane's married off latey, an' Ike's away a good 'eal, so we'll be

darn glad t' have y' stop with us this winter. Nex' spring we'll see if y' can't git a start agin." And he chirruped to the team, which sprang forward with the rumbling, clattering wagon.

"Say, looky here, Council, you can't do this. I never saw—" shouted Haskins in his neighbor's ear.

Council moved about uneasily in his seat and stopped his stammering gratitude by saying: "Hold on, now; don't make such a fuss over a little thing. When I see a man down, an' things all on top of 'm, I jest like t' kick 'em off an' help 'm up. That's the kind of religion I got, an' it's about the *only* kind."

They rode the rest of the way home in silence. And when the red light of the lamp shone out into the darkness of the cold and windy night, and he thought of this refuge for his children and wife, Haskins could have put his arm around the neck of his burly companion and squeezed him like a lover. But he contented himself with saying, "Steve Council, you'll git y'r pay f'r this some day."

"Don't want any pay. My religion ain't run on such business principles."

The wind was growing colder, and the ground was covered with a white frost, as they turned into the gate of the Council farm, and the children came rushing out, shouting, "Papa's come!" They hardly looked like the same children who had sat at the table the night before. Their torpidity, under the influence of sunshine and Mother Council, had given way to a sort of spasmodic cheerfulness, as insects in winter revive when laid on the hearth.

III

Haskins worked like a fiend, and his wife, like the heroic woman that she was, bore also uncomplainingly the most terrible burdens. They rose early and toiled without intermission till the darkness fell on the plain, then tumbled into bed, every bone and muscle aching with fatigue, to rise with the sun next morning to the same round of the same ferocity of labor.

The eldest boy drove a team all through the spring, ploughing and seeding, milked the cows, and did chores innumerable, in most ways taking the place of a man.

An infinitely pathetic but common figure—this boy on the American farm, where there is no law against child labor. To see him in his coarse clothing, his huge boots, and his ragged cap, as he staggered with a pail of water from the well, or trudged in the cold and cheerless dawn out into the frosty field behind his team, gave the city-bred visitor a sharp pang of sympathetic pain. Yet Haskins loved his boy, and would have saved him from this if he could, but he could not.

By June the first year the result of such Herculean[8] toil began to show on the farm. The yard was cleaned up and sown to grass, the garden ploughed and planted, and the house mended.

Council had given them four of his cows.

"Take 'em an' run 'em on shares. I don't want 'o milk s' many. Ike's away s' much now, Sat'd'ys an' Sund'ys, I can't stand the bother anyhow."

Other men, seeing the confidence of Council in the newcomer, had sold him tools on time; and as he was really an able farmer, he soon had round him many evidences of his care and thrift. At the advice of Council he had taken the farm for three years, with the privilege of re-renting or buying at the end of the term.

"It's a good bargain, an' y' want 'o nail it," said Council. "If you have any kind ov a crop, you c'n pay y'r debts, an' keep seed an' bread."

The new hope which now sprang up in the heart of Haskins and his wife grew great almost as a pain by the time the wide field of wheat began to wave and rustle and swirl in the winds of July. Day after day he would snatch a few moments after supper to go and look at it.

"Have ye seen the wheat t'-day, Nettie?" he asked one night as he rose from supper.

"No, Tim, I ain't had time."

"Well, take time now. Le's go look at it."

She threw an old hat on her head—Tommy's hat—and looking almost pretty in her thin, sad way, went out with her husband to the hedge.

"Ain't it grand, Nettie? Just look at it."

It was grand. Level, russet here and there, heavy-headed, wide as a lake, and full of multitudinous whispers and gleams of wealth, it stretched away before the gazers like the fabled field of the cloth of gold.[9]

"Oh, I think—I *hope* we'll have a good crop, Tim; and oh, how good the people have been to us!"

"Yes; I don't know where we'd be t'-day if it hadn't ben f'r Council and his wife."

"They're the best people in the world," said the little woman, with a great sob of gratitude.

"We'll be in the field on Monday, sure," said Haskins, gripping the rail on the fence as if already at the work of the harvest.

The harvest came, bounteous, glorious, but the winds came and blew it into tangles, and the rain matted it here and there close to the ground, increasing the work of gathering it threefold.

Oh, how they toiled in those glorious days! Clothing dripping with sweat, arms aching, filled with briers, fingers raw and bleeding, backs broken with the weight of heavy bundles, Haskins and his man toiled on. Tommy drove the harvester, while his father and a hired man bound on the machine. In this way they cut ten acres every day, and almost every night after supper, when the hand went to bed, Haskins returned to the field shocking the bound grain in the light of the moon. Many a night he worked till his anxious wife came out at ten o'clock to call him in to rest and lunch.

At the same time she cooked for the men, took care of the children, washed and ironed, milked the cows at night, made the butter, and sometimes fed the horses and watered them while her husband kept at the shocking.

No slave in the Roman galleys could have toiled so frightfully and lived, for this man thought himself a free man, and that he was working for his wife and babes.

---

8. **Herculean** \\'hər·kyə ᴧlē·ən\\ work requiring superhuman strength like that of Hercules.
9. **cloth of gold**, Golden Fleece rescued by Jason.

When he sank into his bed with a deep groan of relief, too tired to change his grimy, dripping clothing, he felt that he was getting nearer and nearer to a home of his own, and pushing the wolf of want a little farther from his door.

There is no despair so deep as the despair of a homeless man or woman. To roam the roads of the country or the streets of the city, to feel there is no rood of ground on which the feet can rest, to halt weary and hungry outside lighted windows and hear laughter and song within,—these are the hungers and rebellions that drive men to crime and women to shame.

It was the memory of this homelessness, and the fear of its coming again, that spurred Timothy Haskins and Nettie, his wife, to such ferocious labor during that first year.

IV

" 'M, yes; 'm, yes; first-rate," said Butler, as his eye took in the neat garden, the pig-pen, and the well-filled barnyard. "You're gitt'n' quite a stock around yeh. Done well, eh?"

Haskins was showing Butler around the place. He had not seen it for a year, having spent the year in Washington and Boston with Ashley, his brother-in-law, who had been elected to Congress.

"Yes, I've laid out a good deal of money durin' the last three years. I've paid out three hundred dollars f'r fencin'."

"Um—h'm! I see, I see," said Butler, while Haskins went on:

"The kitchen there cost two hundred; the barn ain't cost much in money, but I've put a lot o' time on it. I've dug a new well, and I—"

"Yes, yes, I see. You've done well. Stock worth a thousand dollars," said Butler, picking his teeth with a straw.

"About that," said Haskins, modestly. "We begin to feel's if we was gitt'n' a home f'r ourselves; but we've worked hard. I tell you we begin to feel it, Mr. Butler, and we're goin' t' begin to ease up purty soon. We've been kind o' plannin' a trip back t' *her* folks after the fall ploughin's done."

"*Eggs*-actly!" said Butler, who was evidently thinking of something else. "I suppose you've kind o' calc'lated on stayin' here three years more?"

"Well, yes. Fact is, I think I c'n buy the farm this fall, if you'll give me a reasonable show."

"Um—m! What do you call a reasonable show?"

"Well, say a quarter down and three years' time."

Butler looked at the huge stacks of wheat, which filled the yard, over which the chickens were fluttering and crawling, catching grasshoppers, and out of which the crickets were singing innumerably. He smiled in a peculiar way as he said, "Oh, I won't be hard on yeh. But what did you expect to pay f'r the place?"

"Why, about what you offered it for before, two thousand five hundred, or *possibly* three thousand dollars," he added quickly, as he saw the owner shake his head.

"This farm is worth five thousand and five hundred dollars," said Butler, in a careless and decided voice.

"*What!*" almost shrieked the astounded Haskins. "What's that? Five thousand? Why, that's double what you offered it for three years ago."

"Of course, and it's worth it. It was all run down then; now it's in good shape. You've laid out fifteen hundred dollars in improvements, according to your own story."

"But *you* had nothin' t' do about that. It's my work an' my money."

"You bet it was; but it's my land."

"But what's to pay me for all my—"

"Ain't you had the use of 'em?" replied Butler, smiling calmly into his face.

Haskins was like a man struck on the head with a sandbag; he couldn't think; he stammered as he tried to say: "But—I never'd git the use—You'd rob me! More'n that: you agreed—you promised that I could buy or rent at the end of three years at—"

"That's all right. But I didn't say I'd let you carry off the improvements, nor that I'd go on renting the farm at two-fifty. The land is doubled in value, it don't matter how; it don't enter into the question; an' now you can pay me five hundred dollars a year rent, or take it on your own terms at fifty-five hundred, or—git out."

He was turning away when Haskins, the sweat pouring from his face, fronted him, saying again:

"But *you've* done nothing to make it so. You hain't added a cent. I put it all there myself, expectin' to buy. I worked an' sweat to improve it. I was workin' for myself an' babes—"

"Well, why didn't you buy when I offered to sell? What y' kickin' about?"

"I'm kickin' about payin' you twice f'r my own things,—my own fences, my own kitchen, my own garden."

Butler laughed. "You're too green t' eat, young feller. *Your* improvements! The law will sing another tune."

"But I trusted your word."

"Never trust anybody, my friend. Besides, I didn't promise not to do this thing. Why, man, don't look at me like that. Don't take me for a thief. It's the law. The reg'lar thing. Everybody does it."

"I don't care if they do. It's stealin' jest the same. You take three thousand dollars of my money—the work o' my hands and my wife's." He broke down at this point. He was not a strong man mentally. He could face hardship, ceaseless toil, but he could not face the cold and sneering face of Butler.

"But I don't take it," said Butler, coolly. "All you've got to do is to go on jest as you've been a-doin', or give me a thousand dollars down, and a mortgage at ten per cent on the rest."

Haskins sat down blindly on a bundle of oats near by, and with staring eyes and drooping head went over the situation. He was under the lion's paw. He felt a horrible numbness in his heart and limbs. He was hid in a mist, and there was no path out.

Butler walked about, looking at the huge stacks of grain, and pulling now and again a few handfuls out, shelling the heads in his hands and blowing the chaff away. He hummed

a little tune as he did so. He had an accommodating air of waiting.

Haskins was in the midst of the terrible toil of the last year. He was walking again in the rain and the mud behind his plough; he felt the dust and dirt of the threshing. The ferocious husking-time, with its cutting wind and biting, clinging snows, lay hard upon him. Then he thought of his wife, how she had cheerfully cooked and baked, without holiday and without rest.

"Well, what do you think of it?" inquired the cool, mocking, insinuating voice of Butler.

"I think you're a thief and a liar!" shouted Haskins, leaping up. "A black-hearted houn'!" Butler's smile maddened him; with a sudden leap he caught a fork in his hands, and whirled it in the air. "You'll never rob another man, damn ye!" he grated through his teeth, a look of pitiless ferocity in his accusing eyes.

Butler shrank and quivered, expecting the blow; stood, held hypnotized by the eyes of the man he had a moment before despised—a man transformed into an avenging demon. But in the deadly hush between the lift of the weapon and its fall there came a gush of faint, childish laughter and then across the range of his vision, far away and dim, he saw the sun-bright head of his baby girl, as, with the pretty, tottering run of a two-year-old, she moved across the grass of the dooryard. His hands relaxed; the fork fell to the ground; his head lowered.

"Make out y'd deed an' mor'gage, an git off'n my land, an' don't ye never cross my line agin; if y' do, I'll kill ye."

Butler backed away from the man in wild haste, and climbing into his buggy with trembling limbs drove off down the road, leaving Haskins seated dumbly on the sunny pile of sheaves, his head sunk into his hands.

I

LOCAL COLOR WRITING AND REGIONALISM

Previous to the Civil War, New York and New England were the dominant centers of American literature. Soon after the War, however, a tendency toward decentralization was marked. Many writers tried to capture the local color of the region in which they lived by reporting its speech, customs, and geographical details. Such writers are often called "local colorists" or "regionalists."

Today, the term "local colorist" is chiefly used to denote those writers who capitalize on the oddities of setting with little or no attention to deeper and more universal values. The term "regionalist," by contrast, is reserved for writers who, though they concentrate on a given geographical area, do so with an eye to revealing deeper and larger aspects of human nature.

Using these definitions, classify "Under the Lion's Paw" as local color or as regionalist literature. Specifically, are Garland's characters solid individuals, or merely Midwestern "types"?

II
IMPLICATIONS

The following represent possible reactions to the story. Compare each reaction with your own, and discuss why you agree or disagree with them.

1. Haskins "got what he deserved." He should have been intelligent enough to protect himself against a man like Butler.

2. The story should have ended with Haskins killing Butler.

3. The appearance of the child at the end of the story is a "trick"; it cheapens the story because the only motive for the child's appearance is the author's desire not to have Haskins become a murderer.

4. The whole story was unrealistic; it was impossible to believe that Butler would actually have had the law on his side.

III
TECHNIQUES

Intention

A writer reveals his intention not only by his choice of words but also by his *choice of incidents.* Try to determine how the following incidents reveal Garland's intentions.

1. Council plowing his field.

2. The appearance of the Haskins family and the conversations between the Haskinses and the Councils.

3. The appearance of Butler and the conversation between him and the other two men.

4. The conversation between Haskins and Council that follows the above incident.

5. The details and conversation concerning the result of the first year's work on the farm.

6. The final conversation between Haskins and Butler.

Theme

The nature and relative importance of a theme in a short story may be highlighted by a reference to it or to some aspect of it in the title of the story. Considering the story itself and its title, state the theme of "Under the Lion's Paw."

Do you agree or disagree with the notion that Garland was primarily interested in getting across the theme, as opposed to such other things as (1) drawing a vivid portrait of farm life in the Midwest, (2) telling an exciting story, or (3) creating a number of convincing and interesting characters?

IV
WORDS

A. In each of the following phrases, substitute the word in the parentheses for the italicized word. Explain the difference in meaning between the italicized word and the possible synonym.

(1) *credulous* (superstitious) servants; (2) *enigmatic* (obscure) figure; (3) *circumstantial* (presumptive) chain; (4) *revile* (scold) any person; (5) *badgering* (riding) of the regulars; (6) *infuriated* (enraged) masses; (7) *tenacious* (sturdy) as tar.

B. Usage depends on the situation. Such a statement as "we haven't much" would be acceptable in most situations but "we ain't got much" would not. A speaker who habitually uses such structures "see if the horses is all right," "I likes to do that," "ain't seen them people," we consider uneducated. Which of the following statements would be acceptable in most situations? Which would not? Which are ungrammatical?

(a) I'm all whipped out; (b) I'm so very tired; (c) I ain't got no energy; (d) I haven't any energy left; (e) I am extremely exhausted; (f) My energy state is presently at a depressed level.

The following selection, by the contemporary author Jesse Stuart,
is a chapter from a biography entitled *Clearing in the Sky*. As you read it
you will find that it has many parallels with Garland's
"Under the Lion's Paw," but it also differs in a number of ways
from the Garland story. Look especially for the contrast in the styles
of the two authors and for the contrast in the reactions
of the protagonists.

Testimony of Trees

JESSE STUART

We had just moved onto the first farm we had ever owned when Jake Timmins walked down the path to the barn where Pa and I were nailing planks on a barn stall. Pa stood with a nail in one hand and his hatchet in the other while I stood holding the plank. We watched this small man with a beardy face walk toward us. He took short steps and jabbed his sharpened sourwood cane into the ground as he hurried down the path.

"Wonder what he's after?" Pa asked as Jake Timmins came near the barn.

"Don't know," I said.

"Howdy, Mick," Jake said as he leaned on his cane and looked over the new barn that we had built.

"Howdy, Jake," Pa grunted. We had heard how Jake Timmins had taken men's farms. Pa was nervous when he spoke, for I watched the hatchet shake in his hand.

"I see ye're a-putting improvements on yer barn," Jake said.

"A-tryin' to get it fixed for winter," Pa told him.

"I'd advise ye to stop now, Mick," he said. "Jist want to be fair with ye so ye won't go ahead and do a lot of work fer me fer nothing."

"How's that, Jake?" Pa asked.

"Ye've built yer barn on my land, Mick," he said with a little laugh.

"Ain't you a-joking, Jake?" Pa asked him.

"Nope, this is my land by rights," he told Pa as he looked our new barn over. "I hate to take this land with this fine barn on it, but it's mine and I'll haf to take it."

"I'm afraid not, Jake," Pa said. "I've been around here since I was a boy. I know where the lines run. I know that ledge of rocks with that row of oak trees a-growing on it is the line!"

"No it hain't, Mick," Jake said. "If it goes to court, ye'll find out. The line runs from that big dead chestnut up there on the knoll, straight across this holler to the top of the knoll up there where the twin hickories grow."

"But that takes my barn, my meadow, my garden," Pa said. "That takes ten acres of the best land I have. It almost gets my house!"

The hatchet quivered in Pa's hand and his lips trembled when he spoke.

"Tim Mennix sold ye land that belonged to me," Jake said.

"But you ought to a-said something about it before I built my house and barn on it," Pa told Jake fast as the words would leave his mouth.

"Sorry, Mick," Jake said, "but I must be a-going. I've given ye fair warning that ye air a-building on my land!"

From *Clearing in the Sky* by Jesse Stuart. Copyright 1950
McGraw-Hill Book Company. Used by permission.

"But I bought this land," Pa told him. "I'm a-goin' to keep it."

"I can't hep that," Jake told Pa as he turned to walk away. "Don't tear this barn down fer it's on my property!"

"Don't worry, Jake," Pa said. "I'm not a-tearing this barn down. I'll be a-feeding my cattle in it this winter!"

Jake Timmins walked slowly up the path the way he had come. Pa and I stood watching him as he stopped and looked our barn over; then he looked at our garden that we had fenced and he looked at the new house that we had built.

"I guess he'll be a-claiming the house too," Pa said.

And just as soon as Jake Timmins crossed the ledge of rocks that separated our farms Pa threw his hatchet to the ground and hurried from the barn.

"Where are you a-going, Pa?" I asked.

"To see Tim Mennix."

"Can I go too?"

"Come along," he said.

We hurried over the mountain path toward Tim Mennix's shack. He lived two miles from us. Pa's brogan shoes[1] rustled the fallen leaves that covered the path. October wind moaned among the leafless treetops. Soon as we reached the shack we found Tim cutting wood near his woodshed.

"What's the hurry, Mick?" Tim asked Pa who stood wiping sweat from his October-leaf-colored face with his blue bandanna.

"Jake Timmins is a-tryin' to take my land," Pa told Tim.

"Ye don't mean it?"

"I do mean it," Pa said. "He's just been to see me and he said the land where my barn, garden, and meadow were belonged to him. Claims about ten acres of the best land I got. I told him I bought it from you and he said it didn't belong to you to sell."

"That ledge of rocks and the big oak trees that grow along the backbone of the ledge has been the line fer seventy years," Tim said. "But

lissen, Mick, when Jake Timmins wants a piece of land, he takes it."

"People told me he's like that," Pa said. "I was warned against buying my farm because he's like that. People said he'd steal all my land if I lived beside him ten years."

"He'll have it before then, Mick," Tim Mennix told Pa in a trembling voice. "He didn't have but an acre to start from. That acre was a bluff where three farms jined and no one fenced it in because it was worthless and they didn't want it. He had a deed made fer this acre and he's had forty lawsuits when he set his fence over on other people's farms and took their land, but he goes to court and wins every time."

"I'll have the County Surveyor, Finn Madden, to survey my lines," Pa said.

"That won't hep any," Tim told Pa. "There's been more people kilt over the line fences that he's surveyed than has been kilt over any other one thing in this county. Surveyor Finn Madden's a good friend to Jake."

"But he's the County Surveyor," Pa said. "I'll haf to have him."

"Jake Timmins is a dangerous man," Tim Mennix warned Pa. "He's dangerous as a loaded double-barrel shotgun with both hammers cocked."

"I've heard that," Pa said. "I don't want any trouble. I'm a married man with a family."

When we reached home, we saw Jake upon the knoll at the big chestnut tree sighting across the hollow to the twin hickories on the knoll above our house. And as he sighted across the hollow, he walked along and drove stakes into the ground. He set one stake in our front yard, about five feet from the corner of our house. Pa started out on him once but Mom wouldn't let him go. Mom said let the law settle the dispute over the land.

And that night Pa couldn't go to sleep. I was awake and heard him a-walking the floor when the clock struck twelve. I knew that Pa was worried, for Jake was the most feared man

---

1. **brogan shoes**, coarse leather work shoes.

among our hills. He had started with one acre and now had over four hundred acres that he had taken from other people.

Next day Surveyor Finn Madden and Jake ran a line across the hollow just about on the same line that Jake had surveyed with his own eyes. And while Surveyor Finn Madden looked through the instrument, he had Jake set the stakes and drive them into the ground with a poleax. They worked at the line all day. And when they had finished surveying the line, Pa went up on the knoll at the twin hickories behind our house and asked Surveyor Finn Madden if his line was right.

"Surveyed it right with the deed," he told Pa. "Tim Mennix sold you land that didn't belong to him."

"Looks like this line would've been surveyed before I built my barn," Pa said.

"Can't see why it wasn't," he told Pa. "Looks like you're a-losing the best part of your farm, Mick."

Then Surveyor Finn Madden, a tall man with a white beard, and Jake Timmins went down the hill together.

"I'm not so sure that I'm a-losing the best part of my farm," Pa said. "I'm not a-goin' to sit down and take it! I know Jake's a land thief and it's time his stealing land is stopped."

"What are you a-goin' to do, Pa?" I asked.

"Don't know," he said.

"You're not a-goin' to hurt Jake over the land, are you?"

He didn't say anything but he looked at the two men as they turned over the ledge of rocks and out of sight.

"You know Mom said the land wasn't worth hurting anybody over," I said.

"But it's my land," Pa said.

And that night Pa walked the floor. And Mom got out of bed and talked to him and made him go to bed. And that day Sheriff Eif Whiteapple served a notice on Pa to keep his cattle out of the barn that we had built. The notice said that the barn belonged to Jake Timmins. Jake ordered us to put our chickens up, to keep them off his garden when it was our

garden. He told us not to let anything trespass on his land and his land was on the other side of the stakes. We couldn't even walk in part of our yard.

"He'll have the house next if we don't do something about it," Pa said.

Pa walked around our house in a deep study. He was trying to think of something to do about it. Mom talked to him. She told him to get a lawyer and fight the case in court. But Pa said something had to be done to prove that the land belonged to us, though we had a deed for our land in our trunk. And before Sunday came, Pa dressed in his best clothes.

"Where're you a-going, Mick?" Mom asked.

"A-goin' to see Uncle Mel," he said. "He's been in a lot of line-fence fights and he could give me some good advice!"

"We hate to stay here and you gone, Mick," Mom said.

"Just don't step on property Jake laid claim to until I get back," Pa said. "I'll be back soon as I can. Some time next week you can look for me."

Pa went to West Virginia to get Uncle Mel. And while he was gone, Jake Timmins hauled wagonloads of hay and corn to the barn that we had built. He had taken over as if it were his own and as if he would always have it. We didn't step beyond the stakes where Surveyor Finn Madden had surveyed. We waited for Pa to come. And when Pa came, Uncle Mel came with him carrying a long-handled double-bitted ax and a turkey of clothes across his shoulder. Before they reached the house, Pa showed Uncle Mel the land Jake Timmins had taken.

"Land hogs air pizen as copperhead snakes," Uncle Mel said, then he fondled his long white beard in his hand. Uncle Mel was eighty-two years old, but his eyes were keen as sharp-pointed briers and his shoulders were broad and his hands were big and rough. He had been a timber cutter all his days and he was still a-cuttin' timber in West Virginia at the age of eighty-two. "He can't do this to ye, Mick!"

Uncle Mel was madder than Pa when he looked over the new line that they had surveyed from the dead chestnut on one knoll to the twin hickories on the other knoll.

"Anybody would know the line wouldn't go like that," Uncle Mel said. "The line would follow the ridge."

"Looks that way to me too," Pa said.

"He's a-stealin' yer land, Mick," Uncle Mel said. "I'll hep ye get yer land back. He'll never beat me. I've had to fight too many squatters a-tryin' to take my land. I know how to fight 'em with the law."

That night Pa and Uncle Mel sat before the fire and Uncle Mel looked over Pa's deed. Uncle Mel couldn't read very well and when he came to a word he couldn't read, I told him what it was.

"We'll haf to have a court order first, Mick," Uncle Mel said. "When we get the court order, I'll find the line."

I didn't know what Uncle Mel wanted with a court order, but I found out after he got it. He couldn't chop on a line tree until he got an order from the court. And soon as Pa got the court order and gathered a group of men for witnesses, Uncle Mel started work on the line fence.

"Sixteen rods from the dead chestnut due north," Uncle Mel said, and we started measuring sixteen rods due north.

"That's the oak tree, there," Uncle Mel said. It measured exactly sixteen rods from the dead chestnut to the black oak tree.

"Deed said the oak was blazed," Uncle Mel said, for he'd gone over the deed until he'd memorized it.

"See the scar, men," Uncle Mel said.

"But that was done seventy years ago," Pa said.

"Funny about the testimony of trees," Uncle Mel told Pa, Tim Mennix, Orbie Dorton, and Dave Sperry. "The scar will allus stay on the outside of a tree well as on the inside. The silent trees will keep their secrets."

Uncle Mel started chopping into the tree. He swung his ax over his shoulder and bit out a slice of wood every time he struck. He cut a neat block into the tree until he found a dark place deep inside the tree.

"Come, men, and look," Uncle Mel said. "Look at that scar. It's as pretty a scar as I ever seen in the heart of a tree!"

And while Uncle Mel wiped sweat with his blue bandanna from his white beard, we looked at the scar.

"It's a scar, all right," Tim Mennix said, since he had been a timber cutter most of his life and knew a scar on a tree.

"Think that was cut seventy years ago," Orbie Dorton said. "That's when the deed was made and the old survey was run."

"We'll see if it's been seventy years ago," Uncle Mel said as he started counting the rings in the tree. "Each ring is a year's growth."

We watched Uncle Mel pull his knife from his pocket, open the blade, and touch each ring with his knife-blade point as he counted the rings across the square he had chopped into the tree. Uncle Mel counted exactly seventy rings from the bark to the scar.

"Ain't it the line tree, boys?" Uncle Mel asked.

"Can't be anything else," Dave Sperry said.

And then Uncle Mel read the deed, which called for a mulberry thirteen rods due north from the black oak. We measured to the mulberry and Uncle Mel cut his notch to the scar and counted the rings. It was seventy rings from the bark to the scar. Ten more rods we came to the poplar the deed called for, and he found the scar on the outer bark and inside the tree. We found every tree the deed called for but one, and we found its stump. We surveyed the land from the dead chestnut to the twin hickories. We followed it around the ledge.

"We have the evidence to take to court," Uncle Mel said. "I'd like to bring the jurymen right here to this line fence to show 'em."

"I'll go right to town and put this thing in court," Pa said.

"I'll go around and see the men that have lost land to Jake Timmins," Uncle Mel said. "I want 'em to be at the trial."

Before our case got to court, Uncle Mel had shown seven of our neighbors how to trace their lines and get their land back from Jake Timmins. And when our trial was called, the courthouse was filled with people who had lost land and who had disputes with their neighbors over line fences, attending the trial to see if we won. Jake Timmins, Surveyor Finn Madden, and their lawyer, Henson Stapleton, had produced their side of the question before the jurors and we had lawyer Sherman Stone and our witnesses to present our side, while all the landowners Jake Timmins had stolen land from listened to the trial. The foreman of the jury asked that the members of the jury be taken to the line fence.

"Now here's the way to tell where a line was blazed on saplings seventy years ago," Uncle Mel said, as he showed them the inner mark on the line oak; then he showed them the outward scar. Uncle Mel took them along the line fence and showed them each tree that the deed called for all but the one that had fallen.

"It's plain as the nose on your face," Uncle Mel would say every time he explained each line tree. "Too many land thieves in this county and a county surveyor the devil won't have in hell."

After Uncle Mel had explained the line fence to the jurors, they followed Sheriff Whiteapple and his deputies back to the courtroom. Pa went with them to get the decision. Uncle Mel waited at our house for Pa to return.

"That land will belong to Mick," Uncle Mel told us. "And the hay and corn in that barn will belong to him."

When Pa came home, there was a smile on his face.

"It's yer land, ain't it, Mick?" Uncle Mel asked.

"It's still my land," Pa said, "and sixteen men are now filing suits to recover their land. Jake Timmins won't have but an acre left."

"Remember the hay and corn he put in yer barn is yourn," Uncle Mel said.

Uncle Mel got up from his chair, stretched his arms. Then he said, "I must be back on my way to West Virginia."

"Can't you stay longer with us, Uncle Mel?" Pa said.

"I must be a-gettin' back to cut timber," he said. "If ye have any more land troubles, write me."

We tried to get Uncle Mel to stay longer. But he wouldn't stay. He left with his turkey of clothes and his long-handled, double-bitted ax across his shoulder. We waved good-by to him as he walked slowly down the path and out of sight on his way to West Virginia.

I
"THE PURSUIT OF HAPPINESS"

America was founded on the belief that all men are entitled to certain "unalienable rights," among which are "life, liberty, and the pursuit of happiness." When we say that a government ought to guarantee individuals the right to pursue happiness, what do we mean? What rights must a man have in order to be able to "pursue happiness"?

Because each of us tends to define "happiness" a little differently, we may also disagree to some extent on the rights needed to pursue it. In early America, however, one of the guarantees thought essential to secure happiness was the right to obtain and hold one's own property. You have just read two selections in which this right was threatened by unscrupulous men, both of whom claimed to have the law on their side. Assuming that the law should protect the rights of individuals, how did it happen in these two cases that this purpose of the law was perverted?

II
IMPLICATIONS

Discuss the following questions in terms of "Under the Lion's Paw" and "Testimony of Trees."

1. In which selection does the setting and the dialogue seem more convincing to you? Can you tell why?

2. Compare and contrast Timothy Haskins with Mick Stuart. What is the essential difference between them?

3. Compare the motives of the "villains" in each selection. Would you describe them as "natural" human motives?

4. Which character seemed more realistic—Butler or Jake Timmins?

5. What roles do Mrs. Haskins and Mrs. Stuart play in the tales? Do you think they are essential characters? If not, why did the authors use them?

III
TECHNIQUES

Intention

In a story like "Under the Lion's Paw," told in part by the author himself, we usually feel confident that we can take his comments on the action at face value. In "Testimony of Trees," however, we get the action through the report of a young boy, the son of Mick Stuart. Since he is likely to favor his own father, how do we know that he is giving us a "straight" story, that he truly reflects the author's intention? To what extent do we actually have to depend upon him?

IV
WORDS

Usage levels fall into two broad classifications: standard and nonstandard. Standard usage includes *formal* or *literary* (spoken and written communication for a select educated group) and *informal* (speech and writing used in personal, casual situations, including regionalisms and slang words, as well as more liberal grammar). Generally we classify written work according to the appropriateness of usage, diction, and types of sentences. But when we come to informal speech, we are confronted with numerous dialects.

Study carefully "Under the Lion's Paw" and "Testimony of Trees," listing variants in pronunciation, vocabulary, and grammar. Again, be careful about judging a pronunciation such as "git" for the word *get*, or "jist" for the word *just* as nonstandard. Both occur in the speech of educated people. Britishers, for example, pronounce ate "et." Review your lists for examples of nonstandard usages and then for standard but regional variants.

That justice must often be fought for is clear from the history
of the women's rights movement, and that such a struggle can succeed
is shown in the life story of Susan B. Anthony, "The Napoleon of Feminism."
You may be surprised to learn of the contrast between the rights
that women had in the mid-nineteenth century and the rights they have today.
That the situation could alter so dramatically is testimony that change
can occur within a democratic society without serious damage
to social stability. "Susan B. Anthony" is one of ninety-two biographies
presented in Louis Untermeyer's *Makers of the Modern World.*

Susan B. Anthony

LOUIS UNTERMEYER

*That women might own
and possess their own souls.*

What is perhaps the most radical alteration of social relationships in the last century is already so taken for granted that its newness is generally overlooked. Yet less than one hundred years ago women had no rights. The first organized demand occurred as late as 1848 and asked for such essentials as the right "to have personal freedom, to acquire an education, to earn a living, to claim her wages, to own property, to make contracts, to bring suit, to testify in court, to obtain a divorce for just cause, to possess her children, to claim a fair share of the accumulations during marriage." Only one college in the United States admitted women; there were no women doctors or lawyers in the country. Married women literally "belonged" to their husbands as slaves or chattels. If they earned money or inherited it, legally it was not theirs but their husbands'. Single women had to be represented by male guardians. Obviously, no woman was entitled to vote. Except in ancient Egypt and under Roman law, this approximately had been the status of women from the beginnings of time.

The dogged seventy-five-year campaign of prodding, petitioning, and pleading that emancipated modern woman owed its strength and its strategy to Susan Brownell Anthony, sometimes called "the Napoleon of Feminism." She was born February 15, 1820, in Adams, Massachusetts, the second child in a family of eight. Her father, Daniel Anthony, was a man of strong intellect and liberal inclinations. Though a Quaker, he was not a conformist. For his wife he picked Lucy Read, who was not only a Baptist but a young woman of lively disposition. However, when she became Mrs. Anthony she observed all the Quaker customs. Susan was brought up in a household that, in her childhood, wore Quaker clothes, spoke in Quaker terms, and proscribed frivolity. Though Daniel was a prosperous mill owner, it was incumbent on his wife to do all her own work, including farm chores, as well as board and serve the mill hands who lived with them from time to time. The children, particularly the older girls, were trained early in household accomplishments. But their education was far from neglected. Before she was five, precocious Susan could read and write. As her schooling progressed, whenever she came to a subject in which she was interested (such as more and more advanced arithmetic) she insisted on being taught it—even though it was nothing that girls were supposed to know. The early learning was obtained at home from a governess. In her teens, Susan was sent to an inexpensive finishing school near Philadelphia, Miss Deborah Moulson's Select Seminary for Females. Miss Moulson's task, as she saw it, was to mold her pupils in the prevailing forms, rather than direct an inquisitive spirit, and Susan's inquiring mind was bound to rebel.

Daniel Anthony went bankrupt in the panic of 1838. He was forced to move his family from Battenville, New York, where they had been living for more than ten years, to the aptly named town of Hardscrabble, where he had a farm. All other means of surviving failed; Daniel found employment with the New York Life Insurance Company and was a salaried worker for them for the rest of his life.

Susan was not unhappy to be taken out of Miss Moulson's Seminary; her main concern was to help in the financial emergency. Due to the depression, probably for the first time numbers of young women from formerly well-to-do homes were thinking the same thing, and the more courageous—or more desperate—were moving into the world of men's concerns. Susan's first step, however, was in a field where women had been tolerated for some time: the teaching profession. She served as assistant

principal of a boarding school, succeeding a man who had been paid $10 a week. Not being a man, Susan was given a salary of $2.50 a week.

Better teaching posts followed, culminating in a position as the principal of the girls' department in the Canajoharie Academy.[1] Living away from home, in a free environment, with money of her own to spend on a few indulgences, Susan broke away from her Quaker ways and repressions. Tall, broad-shouldered, vigorous, she attracted suitors, but none suited her. She was conceded to be "the smartest woman in Canajoharie"; her sympathies were with the extreme Abolitionists; she had become interested in the temperance movement, a genuine social problem during that hard-drinking period. For some time she had questioned the inequalities in employment of women, not only in the teaching field but from what she had seen in her own father's mills. She waited only for the opportunity to help right the prevailing wrongs.

It was through her own family that in 1848 she heard about the Seneca Falls Convention, derided as "The Hen Convention," called by Elizabeth Cady Stanton and Lucretia Mott to discuss the social, civil, and religious rights of women. Preferring to throw her now impatient energy into the temperance fight, Susan joined the Daughters of Temperance, sparked her local Canajoharie branch, spread out as an organizer up to state level, finally gave up her teaching position and devoted herself to the Woman's State Temperance Society. Not an eloquent speaker, she became a convincing one. Her main gift was for organization. It was dismaying to find that her work was being blocked, not by an indifferent public, but by the opposition of the men's temperance society. The men would not allow the women to work with them—at that time women might be seen but not heard at a public meeting—and were afraid they would do disservice to the whole

---

1. **Canajoharie**\kă·na·jo ▲hă·rǐ\ **Academy**, located in Montgomery County, east New York, on the Mohawk River.

temperance cause by raising the diverting question of women's rights. Susan, who had embarked on her fifty-year friendship with Elizabeth Stanton, was beginning to be swayed by her friend's reiteration that the fight for women's rights was really the main fight. She shifted her focus of attention for the last time. Susan carried one of her earliest bids for recognition into the New York State Teachers' Association and succeeded in forcing through a vote that permitted female teachers to "share in all the privileges and deliberations" of the organization.

By 1853, the women's rights cause had become her main absorbing interest. At first she was junior to Elizabeth Stanton in age and leadership; gradually she became the guiding mind of the crusade. Much of the time Susan lived with Elizabeth and her lawyer husband, so that the two friends could write speeches, organize groups, draft petitions, and agitate the country between household chores. Susan was already termed an old maid, but Mrs. Stanton mothered seven children. Since Mrs. Stanton was the better speaker, Susan frequently minded the home so that Elizabeth could campaign.

For several years, the leaders in the movement dramatized their protest against the stifling constraint of corsets and other oppressive clothing by appearing in public in "bloomers," loose trousers that were gathered at the ankles. Susan cut off her lustrous brown hair for further effect. Soon it became evident that the sensationalism of the costumes drew attention away from basic issues, and the feminists, more publicized than they had ever been, went back to layers and layers of floor-sweeping skirts.

Still the work lagged, mainly through lack of funds. The root of the difficulty, Susan saw, was that few women had money to call their own. A radical remedy was needed: a campaign to force the New York State legislature to alter the status of women. Susan threatened to bring the matter up again year after year until the laws were changed. It took ten years, ten years wearing the same old clothes, slogging away at

Susan B. Anthony photographed near the end of her life.

tedious details, traveling about in all weathers under adverse conditions, in all kinds of conveyances, carrying arguments into other states where word about her had spread. In 1860, the first great change was accomplished. By New York State law, a married woman thenceforward could control her own property, her own earnings, would have joint guardianship over her children, and be granted many of the economic demands raised by Susan and her co-workers. Several other states were forced by strong women's rights groups to take similar action.

In between victories were many defeats and bitter, merciless opposition. The onslaughts were vicious: a typical volume, written by a noted minister, was entitled *Woman's Suffrage: the Reform Against Nature.* Many of the attacks were spiteful and personally wounding. The *New York World* reported gleefully that "Susan is lean, cadaverous, and intellectual, with the

423

proportions of a file, and the voice of a hurdy-gurdy."[2]

Meanwhile, the Civil War was embroiling the nation. Immediately upon Lincoln's election the extreme Abolitionists, with whom Susan had always identified herself, had campaigned—at first against Lincoln who was trying to prevent the war—for immediate emancipation. During the war the women's rights fight was suspended. The New York State legislature took advantage of the situation by repealing that part of the law they had passed two years earlier covering women's rights over children. Susan was immobilized on her father's farm. In her journal she noted: "Tried to interest myself in a sewing society; but little intelligence among them." Besides the farm work, she passed the time reading Elizabeth Barrett Browning and George Eliot, storing up energy towards the next battle. The call for it sounded in the clanging notes of the Emancipation Proclamation. Free the women as well as the slaves, Susan demanded. Let this be a government of the people, by the people, including women, she insisted—assuming that women are people.

Arguing that women's rights could be tied in with Negro rights, Elizabeth Stanton and Susan organized large numbers of women to campaign for a constitutional amendment abolishing slavery; the signatures they succeeded in getting to a petition helped effect the passage of the Thirteenth Amendment. It was with dismay, then, that they read the proposed Fourteenth Amendment and learned that civil rights were reserved for previously disenfranchised *male* citizens only. If they could have that one word struck out of the amendment, then all women, white as well as Negro, would win the vote at one stroke. The amendment, however, was passed as written.

Susan retired to home ground, concentrating on the votes-for-women issue in Albany. It was at this time that the famous exchange of discourtesies took place between her and Horace Greeley.

"Miss Anthony," said Greeley with deadly suavity, "you are aware that the ballot and the bullet go together. If you vote, are you also prepared to fight?"

"Certainly, Mr. Greeley," Susan retorted. "Just as you fought in the last war—at the point of a goose-quill."

Greeley and other opponents blocked the drive for votes for women in the New York State legislature. Discouraging years followed. Susan briefly edited a newspaper, called *Revolution.* Its motto was: "Men, their rights, and nothing more; Women, their rights, and nothing less." The paper was finally forced to suspend, and although it took years for her to do it, Susan personally paid off the newspaper's debt of ten thousand dollars. During all this time, she lived on a bit of money left her by her father and on lecture earnings. She often spent her last cent to enable women with no money at all to attend conventions and participate in the work. She was a party to a suit in 1872 to test the Fourteenth and Fifteenth Amendments. She cast a vote in the Presidential election of that year, was tried for violating the constitution, was fined $100 and costs. She refused to pay. On and off she worked on the monumental *History of Woman Suffrage,* the first three volumes with the collaboration of Mrs. Stanton and Matilda Joslyn Gage, the last two with Ida Husted Harper.

By now, the organization which she headed was called the National American Woman Suffrage Association. As Mrs. Rheta Childe Dorr explained in *Susan B. Anthony: The Woman Who Changed the Mind of a Nation,* "To her the whole object of the woman suffrage movement was sex equality, the wiping out of every arbitrary distinction in law and custom, that women, as she phrased it, might own and possess their own souls." In 1883, she took the first vacation she ever had, went to Europe, and found herself famous, particularly in England, where the feminist movement was just gaining momentum.

---

2. **hurdy-gurdy**\ˈhər·dē ▲gər·dē\ a musical instrument played by turning a crank.

When she was seventy, her sister Mary, retiring as a school teacher, urged her to make a home with her in Rochester. Neither had enough money to furnish the house they had inherited there. As a tribute to her, the Political Equality League of Rochester furnished the house. But Susan was too busy to stay in it. Not before she was eighty did she retire as president of the Woman Suffrage Association. Completing the *History of Woman Suffrage*, she emphasized her final demand that American women must get the vote through an amendment to the federal constitution, not through state laws.

In 1904, when the International Woman Suffrage Alliance was formed, she was automatically acknowledged by the women of the world as their undisputed leader. Early in 1906, she attended what she suspected would be her last convention and told the delegates: "The fight must not stop. You must see it does not stop!" On her eighty-sixth birthday, she insisted on going to Washington to attend a dinner in her honor and ended her remarks by insisting, "Failure is impossible."

It was success, however, that seemed impossible. When, as the result of a cold caught on the trip to Washington, she died on March 13, 1906, though the country flew its flags at half-mast in grief at her passing, she was eulogized as "The Champion of a Lost Cause."

Thirteen years later, on May 21, 1919, the lost cause was won; an amendment giving women the full rights of citizenship was added to the United States Constitution. It was called the Susan B. Anthony Amendment.

I
TOLERATION OF EXTREME OPINIONS

It is probably natural in a stable society that we should hold in suspicion those who have extreme opinions. In her day Susan Anthony was a member of a small minority. People everywhere—including women—dismissed her opinions without granting her a fair hearing. Today, we wonder at the intolerance of her contemporaries, and we can see that yesterday's "radicalism" sometimes becomes tomorrow's "common sense." Thus, Miss Anthony's story illustrates the importance of tolerating views that differ from widely accepted opinions.

II
IMPLICATIONS

The history of women's rights has implications for many present-day struggles for justice. Select some contemporary group that claims to be seeking a greater measure of justice and discuss its similarities to and differences from the women's rights movement. What lessons might this group learn from the story of Miss Anthony and her fellow-workers?

III
TECHNIQUES

Intention

Untermeyer set out to write a brief biography. Thus, he had to select the incidents that would carry out his intentions with great care. How do the following incidents reveal Untermeyer's intentions particularly well?

1. Susan's job as teacher.
2. Susan's interests in temperance and slavery.
3. Susan's exchange with Horace Greeley.
4. The last few years of her life.
5. Her early home life.

Theme

Untermeyer's subject is Miss Anthony, but it would be awkward to say that she is his "theme." If "theme" is defined as the central idea, what in your opinion is the theme of this work?

Edwin Markham was inspired to write his famous poem,
"The Man with the Hoe," after seeing Jean François Millet's
world-famous painting of a French peasant standing in a field, leaning
on his hoe. It has been said that no poem ever published in America
has had the instant and lasting popularity of "The Man with the Hoe."
See if you can tell why this poem should have such broad
and enduring appeal.

The Man with the Hoe

WRITTEN AFTER SEEING MILLET'S WORLD-FAMOUS PAINTING

*God made man in His own image;
in the image of God made He him.*—Genesis.

Bowed by the weight of centuries he leans
Upon his hoe and gazes on the ground,
The emptiness of ages in his face,
And on his back the burden of the world.
Who made him dead to rapture and despair,   5
A thing that grieves not and that never hopes,
Stolid and stunned, a brother to the ox?
Who loosened and let down this brutal jaw?
Whose was the hand that slanted back this brow?
Whose breath blew out the light within this brain?   10

Is this the thing the Lord God made and gave
To have dominion over sea and land;
To trace the stars and search the heavens for power;
To feel the passion of eternity?
Is this the Dream He dreamed who shaped the suns   15
And pillared the blue firmament with light?
Down all the stretch of hell to its last gulf
There is no shape more terrible than this—
More tongued with cries against the world's blind greed—
More filled with signs and portents for the soul—   20
More fraught with menace to the universe.

What gulfs between him and the seraphim![1]
Slave of the wheel of labor, what to him
Are Plato and the swing of Pleiades?[2]

---

1. **seraphim**\ˈsĕr•ə•fĭm\ the highest order of angels.
2. **Pleiades**\ˈplē•ə•dēz\ in Greek mythology the seven daughters of Atlas transformed by Zeus into a group of stars near the constellation Orion.

What the long reaches of the peaks of song,   25
The rift of dawn, the reddening of the rose?
Through this dread shape the suffering ages look;
Time's tragedy is in that aching stoop;
Through this dread shape humanity betrayed,
Plundered, profaned, and disinherited,   30
Cries protest to the Powers that made the world,
A protest that is also prophecy.

O masters, lords and rulers in all lands,
Is this the handiwork you give to God,
This monstrous thing distorted and soul-quenched?   35
How will you ever straighten up this shape;
Touch it again with immortality;
Give back the upward looking and the light;
Rebuild in it the music and the dream;
Make right the immemorial infamies,   40
Perfidious wrongs, immedicable woes?

O masters, lords and rulers in all lands,
How will the future reckon with this Man?
How answer his brute question in that hour
When whirlwinds of rebellion shake the world?   45
How will it be with kindoms and with kings—
With those who shaped him to the thing he is—
When this dumb Terror shall reply to God,
After the silence of the centuries?

EDWIN MARKHAM

IMPLICATIONS

1. What mental picture of the hoeman does the reader get from the first stanza? Which of the following does the picture make you feel: despair, anger, indifference, sadness?

2. What is the answer to the questions asked in the first stanza of the poem? What is the relationship between those questions and the questions in the second stanza?

3. In the second stanza the poet says that the enslaved hoeman is "fraught with menace to the universe." What does this mean? Can you cite any evidence to support or deny the idea?

4. What is your own opinion of Markham's belief that the "masters, lords and rulers" are responsible for the condition of the hoeman? Are there other things or persons that might also be responsible? If so, name them.

5. Describe the prophecy the author makes in the final stanza. Is the prophecy justified by what the author has said previously or is he, perhaps, only playing on the human wish to see wrongs righted?

A little over a generation after the appearance
of "The Man with the Hoe," Carl Sandburg published a book of poems
about the "common man," entitled *The People, Yes* (1936). Having worked
as a milkman, a porter in a barbershop, a sceneshifter,
a truck handler, a dishwasher, a harvest hand, a janitor, and a salesman,
Carl Sandburg is well qualified to speak about "the people."
"The People Will Live On" is the last poem in *The People, Yes.*
As you read it, pay close attention to the comparisons and contrasts
between Markham's and Sandburg's views on the common man.

The People Will Live On

107

The people will live on.
The learning and blundering people will live on.
      They will be tricked and sold and again sold
And go back to the nourishing earth for rootholds,
      The people so peculiar in renewal and comeback,   5
      You can't laugh off their capacity to take it.
The mammoth rests between his cyclonic[1] dramas.

The people so often sleepy, weary, enigmatic,
is a vast huddle with many units saying:
      "I earn my living.   10
      I make enough to get by
      and it takes all my time.
      If I had more time
      I could do more for myself
      and maybe for others.   15
      I could read and study
      and talk things over
      and find out about things.
      It takes time.
      I wish I had the time."   20

The people is a tragic and comic two-face:
hero and hoodlum: phantom and gorilla twisting to moan with a gargoyle[2] mouth: "They
buy me and sell me . . . it's a game . . .
sometime I'll break loose . . ."   25

---

1. **cyclonic**\sai ᴬklɔ‧nĭk\ having the nature of a cyclone.
2. **gargoyle**\ᴬgɔr ˈgoil\ a grotesquely carved figure.

Once having marched
Over the margins of animal necessity,
Over the grim line of sheer subsistence
    Then man came
To the deeper rituals of his bones,   30
To the lights lighter than any bones,
To the time for thinking things over,
To the dance, the song, the story,
Or the hours given over to dreaming,
    Once having so marched.   35

Between the finite limitations of the five senses
and the endless yearnings of man for the beyond
the people hold to the humdrum bidding of work and food
while reaching out when it comes their way
for lights beyond the prison of the five senses,   40
for keepsakes lasting beyond any hunger or death.
    This reaching is alive.
The panderers and liars have violated and smutted it.
    Yet this reaching is alive yet
    for lights and keepsakes.   45

    The people know the salt of the sea
    and the strength of the winds
    lashing the corners of the earth.
    The people take the earth
    as a tomb of rest and a cradle of hope.   50
    Who else speaks for the Family of Man?
    They are in tune and step
    with constellations of universal law.

    The people is a polychrome,[3]
    a spectrum and a prism   55
    held in a moving monolith,[4]
    a console organ of changing themes,
    a clavilux[5] of color poems
    wherein the sea offers fog
    and the fog moves off in rain   60
    and the labrador sunset shortens
    to a nocturne of clear stars
    serene over the shot spray
    of northern lights.

---

3. **polychrome,** many colored.
4. **monolith,** a great stone in the form of a column.
5. **clavilux**\ˈklä·və ˈləks\ an instrument which throws patterns of light
and color upon a screen.

The steel mill sky is alive.   65
The fire breaks white and zigzag
shot on a gun-metal gloaming.
Man is a long time coming.
Man will yet win.
Brother may yet line up with brother: 70

This old anvil laughs at many broken hammers.
There are men who can't be bought.
The fireborn are at home in fire.
The stars make no noise.
You can't hinder the wind from blowing.   75
Time is a great teacher.
Who can live without hope?

In the darkness with a great bundle of grief
    the people march.
In the night, and overhead a shovel of stars for   80
    keeps, the people march:
                    "Where to? what next?"

CARL SANDBURG

I
"CONSTELLATIONS OF UNIVERSAL LAW"

Sandburg sees the people marching "In the darkness with a great bundle of grief," yet he also sees them ". . . in tune and step with constellations of universal law." Markham does not speak directly of "universal law," yet it is obvious that he, too, believes in some such concept. He presumably condemns the "lords and rulers of all lands" for not obeying universal laws.

How would you describe the "universal law" to which these poets appeal? What signs—if any—in each poem point to the possibility that a spiritual force is the arbiter of such law? Finally, if there is such a thing as universal law, why is it that it is so readily ignored, and why aren't our laws modeled more closely to it?

II
IMPLICATIONS

Discuss the truth or falsity of the following propositions.

1. The poor and the ignorant are always exploited by the wealthy and the more intelligent.

2. The difficulty of earning a living is no excuse for ignoring the finer things in life.

3. Life without hope isn't worth living.

4. The ability to endure almost any hardship is the chief virtue of the people.

5. Man will someday build a near-perfect world marked by justice for all.

The Lottery

SHIRLEY JACKSON

The morning of June 27th was clear and sunny, with the fresh warmth of a full-summer day; the flowers were blossoming profusely and the grass was richly green. The people of the village began to gather in the square, between the post office and the bank, around ten o'clock; in some towns there were so many people that the lottery took two days and had to be started on June 26th, but in this village, where there were only about three hundred people, the whole lottery took less than two hours, so it could begin at ten o'clock in the morning and still be through in time to allow the villagers to get home for noon dinner.

The children assembled first, of course. School was recently over for the summer, and the feeling of liberty sat uneasily on most of them; they tended to gather together quietly for a while before they broke into boisterous play, and their talk was still of the classroom and the teacher, of books and reprimands. Bobby Martin had already stuffed his pockets full of stones, and the other boys soon followed his example, selecting the smoothest and roundest stones; Bobby and Harry Jones and Dickie Delacroix[1]—the villagers pronounced this name "Dellacroy"—eventually made a great pile of stones in one corner of the square and guarded it against the raids of the other boys.

The girls stood aside, talking among themselves, looking over their shoulders at the boys, and the very small children rolled in the dust or clung to the hands of their older brothers or sisters.

Soon the men began to gather, surveying their own children, speaking of planting and rain, tractors and taxes. They stood together, away from the pile of stones in the corner, and their jokes were quiet and they smiled rather than laughed. The women, wearing faded house dresses and sweaters, came shortly after their menfolk. They greeted one another and exchanged bits of gossip as they went to join their husbands. Soon the women, standing by their husbands, began to call to their children, and the children came reluctantly, having to be called four or five times. Bobby Martin ducked under his mother's grasping hand and ran, laughing, back to the pile of stones. His father spoke up sharply, and Bobby came quickly and took his place between his father and his oldest brother.

The lottery was conducted—as were the square dances, the teen-age club, the Halloween program—by Mr. Summers, who had time and energy to devote to civic activities. He was a round-faced, jovial man and he ran the coal business, and people were sorry for him, because he had no children and his wife was a

1. Delacroix\dĕ 'la ▲krwa\.

scold. When he arrived in the square, carrying the black wooden box, there was a murmur of conversation among the villagers, and he waved and called, "Little late today, folks." The postmaster, Mr. Graves, followed him, carrying a three-legged stool, and the stool was put in the center of the square and Mr. Summers set the black box down on it. The villagers kept their distance, leaving a space between themselves and the stool, and when Mr. Summers said, "Some of you fellows want to give me a hand?" there was a hesitation before two men, Mr. Martin and his oldest son, Baxter, came forward to hold the box steady on the stool while Mr. Summers stirred up the papers inside it.

The original paraphernalia[2] for the lottery had been lost long ago, and the black box now resting on the stool had been put into use even before Old Man Warner, the oldest man in town, was born. Mr. Summers spoke frequently to the villagers about making a new box, but no one liked to upset even as much tradition as was represented by the black box. There was a story that the present box had been made with some pieces of the box that had preceded it, the one that had been constructed when the first people settled down to make a village here. Every year, after the lottery, Mr. Summers began talking again about a new box, but every year the subject was allowed to fade off without anything's being done. The black box grew shabbier each year; by now it was no longer completely black but splintered badly along one side to show the original wood color, and in some places faded or stained.

Mr. Martin and his oldest son, Baxter, held the black box securely on the stool until Mr. Summers had stirred the papers thoroughly with his hand. Because so much of the ritual had been forgotten or discarded, Mr. Summers had been successful in having slips of paper substituted for the chips of wood that had been used for generations. Chips of wood, Mr. Summers had argued, had been all very well when the village was tiny, but now that the population was more than three hundred and likely to keep on growing, it was necessary to use something that would fit more easily into the black box. The night before the lottery, Mr. Summers and Mr. Graves made up the slips of paper and put them in the box, and it was then taken to the safe of Mr. Summers' coal company and locked up until Mr. Summers was ready to take it to the square next morning. The rest of the year, the box was put away, sometimes one place, sometimes another; it had spent one year in Mr. Graves's barn and another year underfoot in the post office, and sometimes it was set on a shelf in the Martin grocery and left there.

There was a great deal of fussing to be done before Mr. Summers declared the lottery open. There were the lists to make up—of heads of families, heads of households in each family, members of each household in each family. There was the proper swearing-in of Mr. Summers by the postmaster, as the official of the lottery; at one time, some people remembered, there had been a recital of some sort, performed by the official of the lottery, a perfunctory, tuneless chant that had been rattled off duly each year; some people believed that the official of the lottery used to stand just so when he said or sang it, others believed that he was supposed to walk among the people, but years and years ago this part of the ritual had been allowed to lapse. There had been, also, a ritual salute, which the official of the lottery had had to use in addressing each person who came up to draw from the box, but this also had changed with time, until now it was felt necessary only for the official to speak to each person approaching. Mr. Summers was very good at all this; in his clean white shirt and blue jeans, with one hand resting carelessly on the black box, he seemed very proper and important as he talked interminably to Mr. Graves and the Martins.

Just as Mr. Summers finally left off talking and turned to the assembled villagers, Mrs. Hutchinson came hurriedly along the path to

---

2. **paraphernalia**\ˈpăr•ə•fə(r) ˈnāl•yə\ furnishings, apparatus, equipment.

the square, her sweater thrown over her shoulders, and slid into place in the back of the crowd. "Clean forgot what day it was," she said to Mrs. Delacroix, who stood next to her, and they both laughed softly. "Thought my old man was out back stacking wood," Mrs. Hutchinson went on, "and then I looked out the window and the kids were gone, and then I remembered it was the twenty-seventh and came a-running." She dried her hands on her apron, and Mrs. Delacroix said, "You're in time, though. They're still talking away up there."

Mrs. Hutchinson craned her neck to see through the crowd and found her husband and children standing near the front. She tapped Mrs. Delacroix on the arm as a farewell and began to make her way through the crowd. The people separated good-humoredly to let her through; two or three people said, in voices just loud enough to be heard across the crowd, "Here comes your Missus, Hutchinson," and "Bill, she made it after all." Mrs. Hutchinson reached her husband, and Mr. Summers, who had been waiting, said cheerfully, "Thought we were going to have to get on without you, Tessie." Mrs. Hutchinson said, grinning, "Wouldn't have me leave m'dishes in the sink, now, would you, Joe?," and soft laughter ran through the crowd as the people stirred back into position after Mrs. Hutchinson's arrival.

"Well, now," Mr. Summers said soberly, "guess we better get started, get this over with, so's we can go back to work. Anybody ain't here?"

"Dunbar," several people said. "Dunbar, Dunbar."

Mr. Summers consulted his list. "Clyde Dunbar," he said. "That's right. He's broke his leg, hasn't he? Who's drawing for him?"

"Me, I guess," a woman said, and Mr. Summers turned to look at her. "Wife draws for her husband," Mr. Summers said. "Don't you have a grown boy to do it for you, Janey?" Although Mr. Summers and everyone else in the village knew the answer perfectly well, it was the business of the official of the lottery to ask such questions formally. Mr. Summers waited with

an expression of polite interest while Mrs. Dunbar answered.

"Horace's not but sixteen yet," Mrs. Dunbar said regretfully. "Guess I gotta fill in for the old man this year."

"Right," Mr. Summers said. He made a note on the list he was holding. Then he asked, "Watson boy drawing this year?"

A tall boy in the crowd raised his hand. "Here," he said. "I'm drawing for m'mother and me." He blinked his eyes nervously and ducked his head as several voices in the crowd said things like "Good fellow, Jack," and "Glad to see your mother's got a man to do it."

"Well," Mr. Summers said, "guess that's everyone. Old Man Warner make it?"

"Here," a voice said, and Mr. Summers nodded.

A sudden hush fell on the crowd as Mr. Summers cleared his throat and looked at the list. "All ready?" he called. "Now, I'll read the names—heads of families first—and the men come up and take a paper out of the box. Keep the paper folded in your hand without looking at it until everyone has had a turn. Everything clear?"

The people had done it so many times that they only half listened to the directions; most of them were quiet, wetting their lips, not looking around. Then Mr. Summers raised one hand high and said, "Adams." A man disengaged himself from the crowd and came forward. "Hi, Steve," Mr. Summers said, and Mr. Adams said, "Hi, Joe." They grinned at one another humorlessly and nervously. Then Mr. Adams reached into the black box and took out a folded paper. He held it firmly by one corner as he turned and went hastily back to his place in the crowd, where he stood a little apart from his family, not looking down at his hand.

"Allen," Mr. Summers said. "Anderson. . . . Bentham."

"Seems like there's no time at all between lotteries any more," Mrs. Delacroix said to Mrs. Graves in the back row. "Seems like we got through with the last one only last week."

"Time sure goes fast," Mrs. Graves said.

"Clark. . . . Delacroix."

"There goes my old man," Mrs. Delacroix said. She held her breath while her husband went forward.

"Dunbar," Mr. Summers said, and Mrs. Dunbar went steadily to the box while one of the women said, "Go on, Janey," and another said, "There she goes."

"We're next," Mrs. Graves said. She watched while Mr. Graves came around from the side of the box, greeted Mr. Summers gravely, and selected a slip of paper from the box. By now, all through the crowd there were men holding the small folded papers in their large hands, turning them over and over nervously. Mrs. Dunbar and her two sons stood together, Mrs. Dunbar holding the slip of paper.

"Harburt. . . . Hutchinson."

"Get up there, Bill," Mrs. Hutchinson said, and the people near her laughed.

"Jones."

"They do say," Mr. Adams said to Old Man Warner, who stood next to him, "that over in the north village they're talking of giving up the lottery."

Old Man Warner snorted. "Pack of crazy fools," he said. "Listening to the young folks, nothin's good enough for *them*. Next thing you know, they'll be wanting to go back to living in caves, nobody work any more, live *that* way for a while. Used to be a saying about 'Lottery in June, corn be heavy soon.' First thing you know, we'd all be eating stewed chickweed and acorns. There's *always* been a lottery," he added petulantly. "Bad enough to see young Joe Summers up there joking with everybody."

"Some places have already quit lotteries," Mrs. Adams said.

"Nothing but trouble in *that*," Old Man Warner said stoutly. "Pack of young fools."

"Martin." And Bobby Martin watched his father go forward. "Overdyke. . . . Percy."

"I wish they'd hurry," Mrs. Dunbar said to her older son. "I wish they'd hurry."

"They're almost through," her son said.

"You get ready to run tell Dad," Mrs. Dunbar said.

Mr. Summers called his own name and then stepped forward precisely and selected a slip from the box. Then he called, "Warner."

"Seventy-seventh year I been in the lottery," Old Man Warner said as he went through the crowd. "Seventy-seventh time."

"Watson." The tall boy came awkwardly through the crowd. Someone said, "Don't be nervous, Jack," and Mr. Summers said, "Take your time, son."

"Zanini."

After that, there was a long pause, a breathless pause, until Mr. Summers, holding his slip of paper in the air, said, "All right, fellows." For a minute, no one moved, and then all the slips of paper were opened. Suddenly, all the women began to speak at once, saying, "Who is it?," "Who's got it?," "Is it the Dunbars?," "Is it the Watsons?" Then the voices began to say, "It's Hutchinson. It's Bill." "Bill Hutchinson's got it."

"Go tell your father," Mrs. Dunbar said to her older son.

People began to look around to see the Hutchinsons. Bill Hutchinson was standing quiet, staring down at the paper in his hand. Suddenly, Tessie Hutchinson shouted to Mr. Summers, "You didn't give him time enough to take any paper he wanted. I saw you. It wasn't fair."

"Be a good sport, Tessie," Mrs. Delacroix called, and Mrs. Graves said, "All of us took the same chance."

"Shut up, Tessie," Bill Hutchinson said.

"Well, everyone," Mr. Summers said, "that was done pretty fast, and now we've got to be hurrying a little more to get done in time." He consulted his next list. "Bill," he said, "you draw for the Hutchinson family. You got any other households in the Hutchinsons?"

"There's Don and Eva," Mrs. Hutchinson yelled. "Make *them* take their chance!"

"Daughters draw with their husbands' families, Tessie," Mr. Summers said gently. "You know that as well as anyone else."

"It wasn't *fair*," Tessie said.

"I guess not, Joe," Bill Hutchinson said regretfully. "My daughter draws with her husband's family, that's only fair. And I've got no other family except the kids."

"Then, as far as drawing for families is concerned, it's you," Mr. Summers said in explanation, "and as far as drawing for households is concerned, that's you, too. Right?"

"Right," Bill Hutchinson said.

"How many kids, Bill?" Mr. Summers asked formally.

"Three," Bill Hutchinson said. "There's Bill, Jr., and Nancy, and little Dave. And Tessie and me."

"All right, then," Mr. Summers said. "Harry, you got their tickets back?"

Mr. Graves nodded and held up the slips of paper. "Put them in the box, then," Mr. Summers directed. "Take Bill's and put it in."

"I think we ought to start over," Mrs. Hutchinson said, as quietly as she could. "I tell you it wasn't *fair*. You didn't give him time enough to choose. *Every*body saw that."

Mr. Graves had selected the five slips and put them in the box, and he dropped all the papers but those onto the ground, where the breeze caught them and lifted them off.

"Listen, everybody," Mrs. Hutchinson was saying to the people around her.

"Ready, Bill?" Mr. Summers asked, and Bill Hutchinson, with one quick glance around at his wife and children, nodded.

"Remember," Mr. Summers said, "take the slips and keep them folded until each person has taken one. Harry, you help little Dave." Mr. Graves took the hand of the little boy, who came willingly with him up to the box. "Take a paper out of the box, Davy," Mr. Summers said. Davy put his hand into the box and laughed. "Take just one paper," Mr. Summers said. "Harry, you hold it for him." Mr. Graves took the child's hand and removed the folded paper from the tight fist and held it while little Dave stood next to him and looked up at him wonderingly.

"Nancy next," Mr. Summers said. Nancy was twelve, and her school friends breathed heavily as she went forward, switching her skirt, and took a slip daintily from the box. "Bill, Jr.," Mr. Summers said, and Billy, his face red and his feet over-large, nearly knocked the box over as he got a paper out. "Tessie," Mr. Summers said. She hesitated for a minute, looking around defiantly, and then set her lips and went up to the box. She snatched a paper out and held it behind her.

"Bill," Mr. Summers said, and Bill Hutchinson reached into the box and felt around, bringing his hand out at last with the slip of paper in it.

The crowd was quiet. A girl whispered, "I hope it's not Nancy," and the sound of the whisper reached the edges of the crowd.

"It's not the way it used to be," Old Man Warner said clearly. "People ain't the way they used to be."

"All right," Mr. Summers said. "Open the papers. Harry, you open little Dave's."

Mr. Graves opened the slip of paper and there was a general sigh through the crowd as he held it up and everyone could see that it was blank. Nancy and Bill, Jr., opened theirs at the same time, and both beamed and laughed, turning around to the crowd and holding their slips of paper above their heads.

"Tessie," Mr. Summers said. There was a pause, and then Mr. Summers looked at Bill Hutchinson, and Bill unfolded his paper and showed it. It was blank.

"It's Tessie," Mr. Summers said, and his voice was hushed. "Show us her paper, Bill."

Bill Hutchinson went over to his wife and forced the slip of paper out of her hand. It had a black spot on it, the black spot Mr. Summers had made the night before with the heavy pencil in the coal-company office. Bill Hutchinson held it up, and there was a stir in the crowd.

"All right, folks," Mr. Summers said. "Let's finish quickly."

Although the villagers had forgotten the ritual and lost the original black box, they still remembered to use stones. The pile of stones the boys had made earlier was ready; there were stones on the ground with the blowing scraps of paper that had come out of the box.

Mrs. Delacroix selected a stone so large she had to pick it up with both hands and turned to Mrs. Dunbar. "Come on," she said. "Hurry up."

Mrs. Dunbar had small stones in both hands, and she said, gasping for breath, "I can't run at all. You'll have to go ahead and I'll catch up with you."

The children had stones already, and someone gave little Davy Hutchinson a few pebbles.

Tessie Hutchinson was in the center of a cleared space by now, and she held her hands out desperately as the villagers moved in on her. "It isn't fair," she said. A stone hit her on the side of the head.

Old Man Warner was saying, "Come on, come on, everyone." Steve Adams was in the front of the crowd of villagers, with Mrs. Graves beside him.

"It isn't fair, it isn't right," Mrs. Hutchinson screamed, and then they were upon her.

I
TRADITIONS—
BLIND, FROZEN AND UNJUST

At one point in the story Old Man Warner recalls an old saying, "Lottery in June, corn be heavy soon." The proverb seems to imply some causal connection between the holding of the lottery and the growth of the corn. We would say that any such connection was purely superstitious. But we *know* what makes corn grow.

Perhaps in the distant past your primitive ancestors, knowing nothing about science, soil, fertilization, or the effect of rain upon crops, attributed the growth of corn to spirits. When the spirits were pleased, they made his corn grow; when they were displeased, they caused his corn to die. When the corn didn't grow, your ancestors probably believed that some member of the community had displeased the spirits. To appease them, the guilty member (or someone else) had to be sacrificed.

Soon someone had to be sacrificed every year in order to ensure good crops.

Eventually your ancestors learn what really causes corn to grow, but by that time the ceremonial sacrifice has been going on for generations. They still believe in the spirits and are fearful of disturbing them. The sacrifice goes on.

As time passes your people forget the original purpose of the sacrifice. All they know is "There's *always* been a sacrifice." And so the tradition goes on—with perhaps some modifications—even though it is totally senseless and horrible. Year after year after year the blind, frozen, unjust tradition goes on.

Miss Jackson is not suggesting that there is a civilized community in which a lottery of the sort she describes is actually practiced; but she is implying that traditions similar to lotteries are practiced and that they can produce tragic consequences.

II
IMPLICATIONS

All of the following statements have some relation to the story you have just read. Discuss their meaning and implications.

1. Traditions are good because they tend to bind people together.

2. Self-preservation is the most powerful instinct in man.

3. People enjoy being part of terrible events, as long as they can remain only spectators.

4. No traditional belief or custom should be accepted by an individual until he has examined it and its possible consequences thoroughly.

5. Traditions crush individuality and make human beings slaves to society.

6. Every time a test is given, somebody will be chosen to fail. This is similar to the situation in "The Lottery."

III
TECHNIQUES

Intention

Miss Jackson does not intrude in her story to let the reader know her opinion of the custom she depicts. Nevertheless, we feel quite certain that her attitude is one of condemnation. *How* has she managed to communicate this part of her intention?

Theme

It is not uncommon for a person to read "The Lottery" and not realize its theme. By not giving us more clues to the meaning of her story, Miss Jackson took the risk of baffling some of her readers. Why do you suppose she was willing to take this risk? Did she gain anything by not entering into her story herself to make her theme more explicit?

IV
WORDS

A. Using what you know about context clues, work out the meaning of the italicized words below.

1. . . . then he *fondled* his long white beard in his hand.

2. The dogged seventy-five-year campaign of prodding, petitioning, and pleading that *emancipated* modern woman.

3. Her father was a man of strong intellect and liberal *inclinations*.

4. Though Daniel was a prosperous mill owner, it was *incumbent* on his wife to do all her own work. . . .

5. Before she was five, *precocious* Susan could read and write.

6. Living away from home, in a free environment, with money of her own to spend on a few *indulgences*. . . .

7. Civil rights were reserved for previously *disenfranchised* male citizens only.

8. She was *eulogized* as "The champion of a lost cause."

9. The original *paraphernalia* for the lottery had been lost long ago.

10. There had been a recital of some sort . . . a *perfunctory* tuneless chant that had been rattled off duly each year.

B. If synonyms had exactly the same meaning, writers would have no need of them. A good writer selects the right synonym. But a writer must strive for even greater accuracy in his choice of antonyms. An antonym is a word that means the opposite of another word; for example, *good* is the antonym of *bad*, *wet* of *dry*, *poor* of *rich*. The proper selection of an antonym shows precise thought. For example, *wild* and *savage* are sometimes used as synonyms, yet the antonym of *wild* in "a wild shot" is *controlled* and that of *savage* is *civilized*. Common words have acquired more than one meaning and an additional set of synonyms and antonyms for each meaning. Give one synonym and one antonym for each meaning. For example:

	synonym	antonym
a *clear* day	cloudless	cloudy
a *clear* style	lucid	obscure

1. *fast* living — hard and *fast* rules
fast-acting medicine — *fast*-thinking person

2. a *clean* miss — a *clean* copy
a *clean* shirt — a *clean* edge

3. *hard* work — *hard* agreement
hard heart — *hard* water

4. *bright* light — *bright* idea — *bright* child

5. *dead* faint — *dead* center — *dead* ball

6. *high* note — *high* winds — *high* and dry

C. Linguists have found three main dialect areas in the United States: Northern, Midland, and Southern. These dialects reveal differences in pronunciation, vocabulary, and grammar. A dialect does not mean a foreign accent or refer to a nonstandard level. Each speaker, educated or uneducated, has a dialect. Survey your own dialect for regionalisms, or names for certain objects. Which do you use?

1. garment worn by men: trousers, pants, breeches.

2. a fixture that controls flow of water: tap, hydrant, faucet, spigot, cock.

3. a variety of beans: green beans, snap beans, beans.

4. piece of furniture with drawers for storing clothes: chest of drawers, dresser, bureau, chifferobe.

5. strong cold wind from the north: norther, blue norther, nor'easter.

6. a pan for frying: skillet, spider, fry pan.

7. a nutlike seed: goobers, grubies, peanuts, pinders.

8. which of these phrases do you use?

a. He *caught, took, take, ketched* cold.

b. She is *fixing, making, getting* supper.

c. Please *cook, boil, steep, make* some tea.

d. Will you *look after, tend, mind, take care of, see after* the baby?

e. He is going to *escort, take, carry, drag, accompany* her.

f. It is a quarter *of, to, till* ten.

THE STRUGGLE FOR JUSTICE

It has been said, "All that is necessary for evil to succeed in the world is that enough good men do nothing." Like all great goods, justice rarely comes without a struggle, and the resulting drama becomes the natural concern of the aware and sensitive recorders among us—notably, the writers and the artists. This gallery displays something of the pictorial range of painters' concern for the struggle for justice.

LAW VERSUS MOB RULE
John Steuart Curry

The vigor of the young nation was not a steadfast blessing. Faced with an affront to their young societies, citizens intense in their efforts to carve out a life in a new land, became, all too easily, a mob bent on destroying whatever threatened them. From the halls of the United States Department of Justice comes the fresco depicting the mastery of reason over the mob.

Angry over social injustices, the contemporary humorist William Gropper laces the legislature with a searing comment about the character and purpose of its members. Millions of Americans of different attitudes have defended the rights of such loyal opposition. A free society not only tolerates but needs such controversy.

THE OPPOSITION
William Gropper

Even within the courts
the struggle for justice
has many sides.
In the 1920's the trial
of two Italian immigrants
accused of robbery
and murder
stirred up passions
throughout the country.
Because the accused men
held what were considered
dangerous political
beliefs, there
were many Americans
who felt that the trial
was a cover
for political persecution.
After the men were
convicted and executed,
Ben Shahn's
forceful painting
was only one
of many protests.

THE PASSION
OF SACCO AND VANZETTI
Ben Shahn
1931–32, Tempera, Collection of
the Whitney Museum of American
Art, New York, Gift of Edith and
Milton Lowenthal in memory of
Juliana Force

Wh   hat gallery of this theme in America could be complete
without a spirited scene from the Revolutionary War?
The painter, John Trumbull, a school teacher
in Connecticut before the war, had hoped
to become the acclaimed Chronicler
of the Struggle for Justice
that began in 1776.

The contemporary American painter Jacob Lawrence
has created a stark, semiabstract painting
on this vital struggle for justice.
Notice how the bayonets
and sharp triangular shapes add tension
and an air of conflict to the scene.

GEORGE WASHINGTON CROSSING THE DELAWARE, NO. 46
Jacob Lawrence

Not without cynical humor,
           are the many election scenes painted
     by that recorder of Young America, George Caleb Bingham.
       The rough and tumble excesses of COUNTY ELECTION
             may not have been all order and reason
         but they were part of the pattern of political justice
             for which the new nation was struggling.

COUNTY ELECTION
George Caleb Bingham

THE WOUNDED DRUMMER BOY
Eastman Johnson

Grace under pressure,"
was the novelist Hemingway's definition
for courage. It might seem
that during the Civil War,
Eastman Johnson said something similar
in his painting of THE WOUNDED DRUMMER
BOY. The youth saw the battle as a fight
for justice, and he was not easily put off.

The pilgrims seeking their place
in the sun are a poignant observation
that the struggle for justice
is never over.

MINORITIES 1939
William Gropper

Six War Poems

How does the topic of war fit into the consideration
of the struggle for justice? Some wars, of course, are fought,
more or less, to gain justice or to secure it. There is, however,
another way of looking at war, particularly modern war: It often seems
to involve a kind of cosmic injustice—the mass slaughter of millions
of innocent men, women, and children. Poets have praised wars and they have
condemned them. But most important, perhaps, they have in many cases
gathered their impressions from first-hand experience. Of the following poets,
both MacLeish and Jarrell served with the armed forces of the United States,
and Alan Seeger died on a battlefield in World War I.

The Arsenal at Springfield

This is the Arsenal. From floor to ceiling,
    Like a huge organ, rise the burnished arms;
But from their silent pipes no anthem pealing
    Startles the villages with strange alarms.

Ah! what a sound will rise, how wild and dreary,   5
    When the death-angel touches those swift keys!
What loud lament and dismal Miserere[1]
    Will mingle with their awful symphonies!

I hear even now the infinite fierce chorus,
    The cries of agony, the endless groan,   10
Which, through the ages that have gone before us,
    In long reverberations reach our own.

On helm and harness rings the Saxon hammer,
    Through Cimbric[2] forest roars the Norseman's song,
And loud, amid the universal clamor,   15
    O'er distant deserts sounds the Tartar[3] gong.

---

1. **Miserere**\mĭ·zə ˄rar·ē\ the 51st Psalm in the Vulgate, the 50th in
the Douay Bible: the first word of the Latin Version; "Have mercy!"
This psalm is frequently recited in services for the dead.
2. **Cimbric**\˄sĭm·brĭk\ pertaining to Germanic people of central Europe
who were defeated in northern Italy, 101 B.C.
3. **Tartar**, refers to the Tartars who ruled Tartar, a region of Asia and
eastern Europe, in the thirteenth and fourteenth centuries and who
reached greatest power under Genghis Khan.

I hear the Florentine, who from his palace
    Wheels out his battle-bell with dreadful din,
And Aztec priests upon their teocallis[4]
    Beat the wild war-drums made of serpent's skin;   20

The tumult of each sacked and burning village;
    The shout that every prayer for mercy drowns;
The soldiers' revels in the midst of pillage;
    The wail of famine in beleaguered towns;

The bursting shell, the gateway wrenched asunder,   25
    The rattling musketry, the clashing blade;
And ever and anon, in tones of thunder,
    The diapason[5] of the cannonade.

Is it, O man, with such discordant noises,
    With such accursed instruments as these,   30
Thou drownest Nature's sweet and kindly voices,
    And jarrest the celestial harmonies?

Were half the power, that fills the world with terror,
    Were half the wealth bestowed on camps and courts,
Given to redeem the human mind from error,   35
    There were no need of arsenals or forts:

The warrior's name would be a name abhorred!
    And every nation, that should lift again
Its hand against a brother, on its forehead
    Would wear forevermore the curse of Cain!   40

Down the dark future, through long generations,
    The echoing sounds grow fainter and then cease;
And like a bell, with solemn, sweet vibrations,
    I hear once more the voice of Christ say, "Peace!"

Peace! and no longer from its brazen portals   45
    The blast of War's great organ shakes the skies!
But beautiful as songs of the immortals,
    The holy melodies of love arise.

HENRY WADSWORTH LONGFELLOW

---

4. **teocallis**\\'tē·ə ᴧkă·lēz\\ temples erected by ancient Mexicans and Central Americans.
5. **diapason**\\'dai·ə ᴧpā·sən\\ in general, a vast, majestic production of sound. Specifically, on an organ a principal flue stop extending through the instrument's complete scale.

Drypoint by Kerr Eby

I Have a Rendezvous with Death

I have a rendezvous with Death
At some disputed barricade,
When Spring comes back with rustling shade
And apple-blossoms fill the air—
I have a rendezvous with Death   5
When Spring brings back blue days and fair.

It may be he shall take my hand
And lead me into his dark land
And close my eyes and quench my breath—
It may be I shall pass him still.   10
I have a rendezvous with Death

On some scarred slope of battered hill,
When Spring comes round again this year
And the first meadow-flowers appear.

God knows 'twere better to be deep   15
Pillowed in silk and scented down,
Where Love throbs out in blissful sleep,
Pulse nigh to pulse, and breath to breath,
Where hushed awakenings are dear . . .
But I've a rendezvous with Death   20
At midnight in some flaming town,
When Spring trips north again this year,
And I to my pledged word am true,
I shall not fail that rendezvous.

ALAN SEEGAR

Eleven o' Clock News Summary

Fold up the papers now. It is hushed, it is late;
Now the quick day unwinds.
Yawning, empty the ashtrays into the grate.
Close the Venetian blinds.
Then turn, by custom, the dial a wave length lower.   5
This is the hour (directly upon the hour)
Briefly to hear
With half-attentive and habitual ear
Important news bulletins.

                             Our armies are valiant.   10
They have taken another ridge,
Another town, a fort, a strip, a salient.
They have held a bridge
(With heavy casualties). Our planes today,
According to a recent communique,   15
Struck (though the loss was high) at a vital border.
Remember to leave a note for the dairy order
And to set the thermostat at sixty-two.
We have captured an island at merely a moderate cost.
One of our submarines is overdue   20
And must be presumed lost.

In forests, in muddy fields, while winter fades,
Our troops are smashing through the Barricades,
They Push, they Storm, they Forge Ahead, they die
And lie on litters or unburied lie.   25
Static is bad tonight.
There—twiddle the knob a little to the right.

Here in the nation
Obedient curfews sound their midnight wails.
This is America's leading independent station.   30
Read the paper tomorrow for further details—
Details of death on the beaches, in the heat, in the cold,
Of death in gliders, in tanks, at a city's gate,
Death of young men who fancied they might grow old
But could not wait   35
(Being given, of course, no choice).

Well, snap the switch, turn off the announcer's voice,
Plump up the pillows on the green divan,
For day unwinds like a thread
And it is time now for a punctual man,   40
Drowsy, a little absent, warmed and fed,
To dim the light, turn down the blanketed bed,
And sleep, if he can.

From *Stones from a Glass House* by Phyllis McGinley. Originally appeared in *The New Yorker*. Copyright 1945 by Phyllis McGinley. Reprinted by permission of The Viking Press, Inc.

PHYLLIS MCGINLEY

Lines for an Interment

Now it is fifteen years you have lain in the meadow:
The boards at your face have gone through: the earth is
Packed down and the sound of the rain is fainter:
The roots of the first grass are dead.
It's a long time to lie in the earth with your honor: 5
The world, Soldier, the world has been moving on.
The girls wouldn't look at you twice in the cloth cap:
Six years old they were when it happened:
It bores them even in books: "Soissons[1] besieged!"
As for the gents they have joined the American Legion: 10
Belts and a brass band and the ladies' auxiliaries:
The Californians march in the OD silk.[2]
We are all acting again like civilized beings:
People mention it at tea . . .
The Facts of Life we have learned are Economic: 15
You were deceived by the detonations of bombs:
You thought of courage and death when you thought of warfare.
Hadn't they taught you the fine words were unfortunate?
Now that we understand we judge without bias:
We feel of course for those who had to die: 20
Women have written us novels of great passion
Proving the useless death of the dead was a tragedy.
Nevertheless it is foolish to chew gall:
The foremost writers on both sides have apologized:
The Germans are back in the Midi with cropped hair: 25
The English are drinking the better beer in Bavaria.
You can rest now in the rain in the Belgian meadow—
Now that it's all explained away and forgotten:
Now that the earth is hard and the wood rots:
Now you are dead . . .   30

ARCHIBALD MACLEISH

---

1. **Soissons**\swä ᴀsȯn\ a city in northeast France.
2. **OD silk**, olive drab.

Published by Houghton Mifflin Company and reprinted with their permission.

Losses

It was not dying: everybody died.
It was not dying: we had died before
In the routine crashes—and our fields
Called up the papers, wrote home to our folks,
And the rates rose, all because of us.   5
We died on the wrong page of the almanac,
Scattered on mountains fifty miles away;
Diving on haystacks, fighting with a friend,
We blazed up on the lines we never saw.
We died like ants or pets or foreigners.   10
(When we left high school nothing else had died
For us to figure we had died like.)

In our new planes, with our new crews, we bombed
The ranges by the desert or the shore,
Fired at towed targets, waited for our scores—   15
And turned into replacements and woke up
One morning, over England, operational.
It wasn't different: but if we died
It was not an accident but a mistake
(But an easy one for anyone to make).   20
We read our mail and counted up our missions—
In bombers named for girls, we burned
The cities we had learned about in school—
Till our lives wore out; our bodies lay among
The people we had killed and never seen.   25
When we lasted long enough they gave us medals;
When we died they said, "Our casualties were low."
They said, "Here are the maps"; we burned the cities.

It was not dying—no, not ever dying;
But the night I died I dreamed that I was dead,   30
And the cities said to me: "Why are you dying?
We are satisfied, if you are; but why did I die?"

RANDALL JARRELL

———————

Reprinted by permission of Randall Jarrell.

Looking

Y̶ou have no word for soldiers to enjoy
The feel of, as an apple, and to chew
With masculine satisfaction. Not "good-by!"
"Come back!" or "careful!" Look, and let him go.
"Good-by!" is brutal, and "come back!" the raw   5
Insistence of an idle desperation
Since could he favor he would favor now.
He will be "careful!" if he has permission.
Looking is better. At the dissolution
Grab greatly with the eye, crush in a steel   10
Of study—Even that is vain. Expression,
The touch or look or word, will little avail.
The brawniest will not beat back the storm
Nor the heaviest haul your little boy from harm.

GWENDOLYN BROOKS

FOR DISCUSSION

The Arsenal at Springfield

The theme of Longfellow's poem might be summed up in a few words: "War is terrifying and morally wrong; it can be avoided through understanding and love." This thematic statement might then be broken down into four separate propositions, as follows: (1) War is terrifying. (2) War is morally wrong. (3) War can be avoided by increasing human understanding. (4) War can be avoided by increasing man's love of his fellows.

What is your opinion of the truth or falsity of each of these propositions? How might you expand or qualify some of them? Finally, what is your opinion of the *practicality* of propositions three and four?

I Have a Rendezvous with Death

If you liked this poem, perhaps one source of your enjoyment was the poem's structure. Of course, it is not necessary for a reader to be consciously aware of structure in order for him to respond to it. Observe how Seeger has structured the poem to convey his theme.

1. Extract for a moment lines 7 to 10 and lines 15 to 19. Observe that the remaining lines alternate between references to Death and to Spring: lines 1 and 2 deal with Death, lines 3 and 4 deal with Spring; line 5 deals with Death, line 6 with Spring, and so on. What is the result, emotionally, of the poet's having intimately linked Death and Spring?

2. Now consider lines 7 to 10 and lines 15 to 19. Do you see any relationship between them and the rest of the poem? Note particularly the possible comparisons between the latter section and *Spring*. How are these two sections linked by rhyme to each other and to the rest of the poem?

Structure in poetry—in all art—is not incidental; it is essential. It is essential because what art does is precisely to order and arrange, to impose a structure (and hence, a meaning) upon raw experience.

Eleven o'Clock News Summary

1. This poem is divided about equally between italicized and nonitalicized lines. The italicized portions represent a person thinking or speaking to himself, but it is obvious that his thoughts are being screened by the poet. Where is it most obvious that the poet has intruded her own thought rather than given the thought of the man?

2. The nonitalicized lines in this poem for the most part represent the voice of the news commentator, but again his words are being given to the reader through the poet. Where are you most conscious that you are being given the poet's thoughts rather than the newscaster's?

3. From your answers to the above questions you should see clearly that Miss McGinley intends to criticize the man listening to the news summary. Less obvious, and more interesting, however, is the question of what the man represents. Does the poet criticize a single individual, or is her intention a broader one?

Lines for an Interment

1. In the sixth line, MacLeish—addressing the dead soldier—says that "the world has been moving on." How does he prove his point?

2. Note especially the last instance of "progressive" movement—lines 25 and 26. Is MacLeish really trying to prove that the world has been moving on in a progressive sense? If not, in what sense was it "moving on"? in what direction?

3. In the last line of the poem MacLeish omits the word "that" (which he had used in the two previous lines). Is this a significant omission? Does it help you to see something about the direction of events since the war?

Losses

1. The bombing missions in World War II were flown for the most part by very young men. Randall Jarrell—himself only 27 when the United States entered the war—knew them very well, for he trained B-29 bomber crews. How does Jarrell emphasize the youth of the flyers in this poem?

2. It is not surprising that these young men should think lightly of death. Since they were too young to have experienced the death of anyone they knew intimately (in their experience it had only happened to "ants or pets or foreigners") and since they lived with death in training as well as in battle, it for them was something commonplace yet something *abstract*. What lines in the first stanza express this attitude particularly well? in the second stanza?

3. Through the first two stanzas of the poem Jarrell shows that the whole experience of war for the men was something abstract, something not quite real. How does the final stanza of the poem represent an ironic "awakening"?

Looking

1. Modern poets may use traditional verse forms, but often in an experimental way, shaping them to their own ends. The sonnet form seems to be so used here. This form is defined as a fourteen-line poem with five stresses to a line (usually iambic) and a fixed rhyme scheme. One of these fixed rhyme schemes is called the "Spenserian" (after the English poet, Edmund Spenser); it connects the quatrains—four line units—by interlacing the rhymes: *abab bcbc cdcd ee*. This type of sonnet usually deals with a single idea or emotion, and its final couplet is frequently used as a sort of summary of or conclusion for what has gone before.

Discuss "Looking" as a variation of the Spenserian sonnet form. What are its chief similarities to and differences from the "pure" Spenserian sonnet?

2. "Looking" expresses a distinctly feminine viewpoint on war. In what way or ways is it different from the masculine viewpoint of Seeger's or Jarrell's poems?

Though lawyers, lawmakers, and judges have a powerful influence
on justice, the ultimate decisions regarding guilt and innocence
are made in American society by the people themselves in their roles
as jurors. Reginald Rose's television drama, "Twelve Angry Men," focuses
on a group of citizens who are charged with the duty of determining
the fate of a nineteen-year-old boy accused of the murder of his father.
You will find that the characters are identified
only by a number. This is not a drawback on the television screen,
of course, but in reading the play you will need to take extra care to keep
the characters separate. To help you, a brief description of each juror is
given in the table at the beginning of the play. While you read the play,
refer to it as often as necessary. The chief characters are Juror Number 8,
who is the protagonist, and Juror Number 3, who is the antagonist.
Juror Number 10 also plays an important role as an antagonist.

Twelve Angry Men

REGINALD ROSE

Cast

FOREMAN
JURORS (Numbers 2–12)
JUDGE
GUARD

Description of Jurors

FOREMAN. *A small, petty man who is impressed
with the authority he has and handles himself quite formally. Not overly bright, but
dogged.*

JUROR NO. 2. *A meek, hesitant man who finds it
difficult to maintain any opinions of his own.
Easily swayed and usually adopts the opinion of the last person to whom he has spoken.*

JUROR NO. 3. *A very strong, very forceful, extremely opinionated man within whom can
be detected a streak of sadism. A humorless
man who is intolerant of opinions other than
his own and accustomed to forcing his wishes
and views upon others.*

JUROR NO. 4. *Seems to be a man of wealth and
position. A practiced speaker who presents
himself well at all times. Seems to feel a little
bit above the rest of the jurors. His only concern is with the facts in this case, and he is
appalled at the behavior of the others.*

JUROR NO. 5. *A naive, very frightened young
man who takes his obligations in this case
very seriously, but who finds it difficult to
speak up when his elders have the floor.*

JUROR NO. 6. *An honest but dull-witted man
who comes upon his decisions slowly and
carefully. A man who finds it difficult to create positive opinions, but who must listen to
and digest and accept those opinions offered
by others which appeal to him most.*

JUROR NO. 7. *A loud, flashy, gladhanded salesman type who has more important things to
do than to sit on a jury. He is quick to show
temper, quick to form opinions on things
about which he knows nothing. Is a bully
and, of course, a coward.*

JUROR NO. 8. *A quiet, thoughtful, gentle man.
A man who sees all sides of every question
and constantly seeks the truth. A man of*

strength tempered with compassion. Above all, a man who wants justice to be done and will fight to see that it is.

JUROR NO. 9. *A mild, gentle old man, long since defeated by life and now merely waiting to die. A man who recognizes himself for what he is and mourns the days when it would have been possible to be courageous without shielding himself behind his many years.*

JUROR NO. 10. *An angry, bitter man. A man who antagonizes almost at sight. A bigot who places no values on any human life save his own. A man who has been nowhere and is going nowhere and knows it deep within him.*

JUROR NO. 11. *A refugee from Europe who has come to this country in 1941. A man who speaks with an accent and who is ashamed, humble, almost subservient to the people around him, but who will honestly seek justice because he has suffered through so much injustice.*

JUROR NO. 12. *A slick, bright advertising man who thinks of human beings in terms of percentages, graphs and polls and has no real understanding of people. A superficial snob, but trying to be a good fellow.*

Act I

Fade in on a jury box. Twelve men are seated in it, listening intently to the voice of the JUDGE *as he charges them. We do not see the* JUDGE. *He speaks in slow, measured tones and his voice is grave. The camera drifts over the faces of the jurymen as the* JUDGE *speaks and we see that most of their heads are turned to camera's left.* NO. 7 *looks down at his hands.* NO. 3 *looks off in another direction, the direction in which the defendant would be sitting.* NO. 10 *keeps moving his head back and forth nervously. The* JUDGE *drones on.*

JUDGE. Murder in the first degree—premeditated homicide—is the most serious charge tried in our criminal courts. You've heard a long and complex case, gentlemen, and it is now your duty to sit down to try and separate the facts from the fancy. One man is dead. The life of another is at stake. If there is a reasonable doubt in your minds as to the guilt of the accused . . . then you must declare him not guilty. If, however, there is no reasonable doubt, then he must be found guilty. Whichever way you decide, the verdict must be unanimous. I urge you to deliberate honestly and thoughtfully. You are faced with a grave responsibility. Thank you, gentlemen.

There is a long pause.

CLERK (*Droning*). The jury will retire.

And now, slowly, almost hesitantly, the members of the jury begin to rise. Awkwardly, they file out of the jury box and off camera to the left. Camera holds on jury box, then fades out.

Fade in on a large, bare, unpleasant-looking room. This is the jury room in the county criminal court of a large Eastern city. It is about 4:00 P.M. The room is furnished with a long conference table and a dozen chairs. The walls are bare, drab and badly in need of a fresh coat of paint. Along one wall is a row of windows which look out on the skyline of the city's financial district. High on another wall is an electric clock. A washroom opens off the jury room. In one corner of the room is a water fountain. On the table are pads, pencils, ashtrays. One of the windows is open. Papers blow across the table and onto the floor as the door opens. Lettered on the outside of the door are the words "Jury Room." A uniformed GUARD *holds the door open. Slowly, almost self-consciously, the twelve jurors file in. The* GUARD *counts them as they enter the door, his lips moving, but no sound coming forth. Four or five of the jurors light cigarettes as they enter the room.* JUROR NO. 5 *lights his pipe, which he smokes constantly throughout the play.* JURORS NO.

2 and 12 go to the water fountain. NO. 9 *goes into the washroom, the door of which is lettered "Men." Several of the jurors take seats at the table. Others stand awkwardly around the room. Several look out the windows. These are men who are ill at ease, who do not really know each other to talk to and who wish they were anywhere but here.* NO. 7, *standing at window, takes out a pack of gum, takes a piece and offers it around. There are no takers. He mops his brow.*

NO. 7 *(To* NO. *6).* Y'know something? It's hot. *(*NO. *6 nods)* You'd think they'd at least air-condition the place. I almost dropped dead in court.

NO. 7 *opens the window a bit wider. The* GUARD *looks them over and checks his count. Then, satisfied, he makes ready to leave.*

GUARD. Okay, gentlemen. Everybody's here. If there's anything you want, I'm right outside. Just knock.

He exits, closing the door. Silently they all look at the door. We hear the lock clicking.

NO. 5. I never knew they locked the door.

NO. 10 *(Blowing nose).* Sure, they lock the door. What did you think?

NO. 5. I don't know. It just never occurred to me.

Some of the jurors are taking off their jackets. Others are sitting down at the table. They still are reluctant to talk to each other. FOREMAN *is at head of table, tearing slips of paper for ballots. Now we get a close shot of* NO. 8. *He looks out the window. We hear* NO. 3 *talking to* NO. 2.

NO. 3. Six days. They should have finished it in two. Talk, talk, talk. Did you ever hear so much talk about nothing?

NO. 2 *(Nervously laughing).* Well . . . I guess . . . they're entitled.

NO. 3. Everybody gets a fair trial. *(He shakes his head)* That's the system. Well, I suppose you can't say anything against it.

NO. *2 looks at him nervously, nods and goes*

over to water cooler. Cut to shot of NO. 8 *staring out window. Cut to table.* NO. 7 *stands at the table, putting out a cigarette.*

NO. 7 *(To* NO. *10).* How did you like that business about the knife? Did you ever hear a phonier story?

NO. 10 *(Wisely).* Well, look, you've gotta expect that. You know what you're dealing with.

NO. 7. Yeah, I suppose. What's the matter, you got a cold?

NO. 10 *(Blowing).* A lulu. These hot-weather colds can kill you.

NO. 7 *nods sympathetically.*

FOREMAN *(Briskly).* All right, gentlemen. Let's take seats.

NO. 7. Right. This better be fast. I've got tickets to *The Seven Year Itch* tonight. I must be the only guy in the whole world who hasn't seen it yet. *(He laughs and sits down)* Okay, your honor, start the show.

They all begin to sit down. The FOREMAN *is seated at the head of the table.* NO. 8 *continues to look out the window.*

FOREMAN *(To* NO. *8).* How about sitting down? *(*NO. *8 doesn't hear him)* The gentleman at the window.

NO. 8 *turns, startled.*

FOREMAN. How about sitting down?

NO. 8. Oh. I'm sorry.

He heads for a seat.

NO. 10 *(To* NO. *6).* It's tough to figure, isn't it? A kid kills his father. Bing! Just like that. Well, it's the element. They let the kids run wild. Maybe it serves 'em right.

FOREMAN. Is everybody here?

NO. 12. The old man's inside.

The FOREMAN *turns to the washroom just as the door opens.* NO. 9 *comes out, embarrassed.*

FOREMAN. We'd like to get started.

NO. 9. Forgive me, gentlemen. I didn't mean to keep you waiting.

FOREMAN. It's all right. Find a seat.

NO. 9 *heads for a seat and sits down. They look at the* FOREMAN *expectantly.*

FOREMAN. All right. Now, you gentlemen can handle this any way you want to. I mean, I'm not going to make any rules. If we want to discuss it first and then vote, that's one way. Or we can vote right now to see how we stand.

NO. 7. Let's vote now. Who knows, maybe we can all go home.

NO. 10. Yeah. Let's see who's where.

NO. 3. Right. Let's vote now.

FOREMAN. Anybody doesn't want to vote? (*He looks around the table. There is no answer*) Okay, all those voting guilty raise your hands.

Seven or eight hands go up immediately. Several others go up more slowly. Everyone looks around the table. There are two hands not raised, NO. 9's *and* NO. 8's. NO. 9's *hand goes up slowly now as the foreman counts.*

FOREMAN. . . . Nine . . . ten . . . eleven . . . That's eleven for guilty. Okay. Not guilty? (NO. 8's *hand is raised*) One. Right. Okay. Eleven to one, guilty. Now we know where we are.

NO. 3. Somebody's in left field. (*To* NO. 8) You think he's not guilty?

NO. 8 (*Quietly*). I don't know.

NO. 3. I never saw a guiltier man in my life. You sat right in court and heard the same thing I did. The man's a dangerous killer. You could see it.

NO. 8. He's nineteen years old.

NO. 3. That's old enough. He knifed his own father. Four inches into the chest. An innocent little nineteen-year-old kid. They proved it a dozen different ways. Do you want me to list them?

NO. 8. No.

NO. 10 (To NO. 8). Well, do you believe his story?

NO. 8. I don't know whether I believe it or not. Maybe I don't.

NO. 7. So what'd you vote not guilty for?

NO. 8. There were eleven votes for guilty. It's not so easy for me to raise my hand and send a boy off to die without talking about it first.

NO. 7. Who says it's easy for me?

NO. 8. No one.

NO. 7. What, just because I voted fast? I think the guy's guilty. You couldn't change my mind if you talked for a hundred years.

NO. 8. I don't want to change your mind. I just want to talk for a while. Look, this boy's been kicked around all his life. You know, living in a slum, his mother dead since he was nine. That's not a very good head start. He's a tough, angry kid. You know why slum kids get that way? Because we knock 'em on the head once a day, every day. I think maybe we owe him a few words. That's all.

He looks around the table. Some of them look back coldly. Some cannot look at him. Only NO. 9 nods slowly. NO. 12 doodles steadily. NO. 4 begins to comb his hair.

NO. 10. I don't mind telling you this, mister. We don't owe him a thing. He got a fair trial, didn't he? You know what that trial cost? He's lucky he got it. Look, we're all grown-ups here. You're not going to tell us that we're supposed to believe him, knowing what he is. I've lived among 'em all my life. You can't believe a word they say. You know that.

NO. 9 (To NO. 10 very slowly). I don't know that. What a terrible thing for a man to believe! Since when is dishonesty a group characteristic? You have no monopoly on the truth——

NO. 3 (Interrupting). All right. It's not Sunday. We don't need a sermon.

NO. 9. What this man says is very dangerous. . . .

NO. 8 puts his hand on NO. 9's arm and stops

him. Somehow his touch and his gentle expression calm the old man. He draws a deep breath and relaxes.

NO. 4. I don't see any need for arguing like this. I think we ought to be able to behave like gentlemen.

NO. 7. Right!

NO. 4. If we're going to discuss this case, let's discuss the facts.

FOREMAN. I think that's a good point. We have a job to do. Let's do it.

NO. 11 (With accent). If you gentlemen don't mind, I'm going to close the window. (He gets up and does so) (Apologetically). It was blowing on my neck.

NO. 10 blows his nose fiercely.

NO. 12. I may have an idea here. I'm just thinking out loud now, but it seems to me that it's up to us to convince this gentleman (Indicating NO. 8) that we're right and he's wrong. Maybe if we each took a minute or two, you know, if we sort of try it on for size . . .

FOREMAN. That sounds fair enough. Supposing we go once around the table.

NO. 7. Okay, let's start it off.

FOREMAN. Right. (To NO. 2) I guess you're first.

NO. 2 (Timidly). Oh. Well . . . (Long pause) I just think he's guilty. I thought it was obvious. I mean nobody proved otherwise.

NO. 8 (Quietly). Nobody has to prove otherwise. The burden of proof is on the prosecution. The defendant doesn't have to open his mouth. That's in the Constitution. The Fifth Amendment. You've heard of it.

NO. 2 (Flustered). Well, sure, I've heard of it. I know what it is. I . . . what I meant . . . well, anyway, I think he was guilty.

NO. 3. Okay, let's get to the facts. Number one, let's take the old man who lived on the second floor right underneath the room where the murder took place. At ten minutes after twelve on the night of the killing he heard loud noises in the upstairs apartment. He said it sounded like a fight. Then he heard the kid say to his father, "I'm gonna kill you." A second later he heard a body falling, and he ran to the door of his apartment, looked out, and saw the kid running down the stairs and out of the house. Then he called the police. They found the father with a knife in his chest.

FOREMAN. And the coroner fixed the time of death at around midnight.

NO. 3. Right. Now what else do you want?

NO. 4. The boy's entire story is flimsy. He claimed he was at the movies. That's a little ridiculous, isn't it? He couldn't even remember what pictures he saw.

NO. 3. That's right. Did you hear that? (*To* NO. 4) You're absolutely right.

NO. 10. Look, what about the woman across the street? If her testimony don't prove it, then nothing does.

NO. 12. That's right. She saw the killing, didn't she?

FOREMAN. Let's go in order.

NO. 10 (*Loud*). Just a minute. Here's a woman who's lying in bed and can't sleep. It's hot, you know. (*He gets up and begins to walk around, blowing his nose and talking*) Anyway, she looks out the window, and right across the street she sees the kid stick the knife into his father. She's known the kid all his life. His window is right opposite hers, across the el tracks,[1] and she swore she saw him do it.

NO. 8. Through the windows of a passing elevated train.

NO. 10. Okay. And they proved in court that you can look through the windows of a passing el train at night and see what's happening on the other side. They proved it.

NO. 8. I'd like to ask you something. How come you believed her? She's one of "them" too, isn't she?

NO. *10 walks over to* NO. *8.*

NO. 10. You're a pretty smart fellow, aren't you?

FOREMAN (*Rising*). Now take it easy.

NO. *3 gets up and goes to* NO. *10.*

NO. 3. Come on. Sit down. (*He leads* NO. *10 back to his seat*) What're you letting him get

you all upset for? Relax.

NO. *10 and* NO. *3 sit down.*

FOREMAN. Let's calm down now. (*To* NO. 5) It's your turn.

NO. 5. I'll pass it.

FOREMAN. That's your privilege. (*To* NO. 6) How about you?

NO. 6 (*Slowly*). I don't know. I started to be convinced, you know, with the testimony from those people across the hall. Didn't they say something about an argument between the father and the boy around seven o'clock that night? I mean, I can be wrong.

NO. 11. I think it was eight o'clock. Not seven.

NO. 8. That's right. Eight o'clock. They heard the father hit the boy twice and then saw the boy walk angrily out of the house. What does that prove?

NO. 6. Well, it doesn't exactly prove anything. It's just part of the picture. I didn't say it proved anything.

FOREMAN. Anything else?

NO. 6. No.

NO. *6 goes to the water fountain.*

FOREMAN (*To* NO. 7). All right. How about you?

NO. 7. I don't know, most of it's been said already. We can talk all day about this thing, but I think we're wasting our time. Look at the kid's record. At fifteen he was in reform school. He stole a car. He's been arrested for mugging.[2] He was picked up for knife-fighting. I think they said he stabbed somebody in the arm. This is a very fine boy.

NO. 8. Ever since he was five years old his father beat him up regularly. He used his fists.

NO. 7. So would I! A kid like that.

NO. 3. You're right. It's the kids. The way they are—you know? They don't listen. (*Bitter*) I've got a kid. When he was eight years old he ran away from a fight. I saw him. I was so ashamed, I told him right out, "I'm gonna make a man out of you or I'm gonna bust you

---

1. el tracks, elevated railroad.
2. mugging, assaulting and robbing someone.

up into little pieces trying." When he was fifteen he hit me in the face. He's big, you know. I haven't seen him in three years. Rotten kid! You work your heart out. . . . *(Pause)* All right. Let's get on with it.

Looks away embarrassed.

NO. 4. We're missing the point here. This boy —let's say he's a product of a filthy neighborhood and a broken home. We can't help that. We're not here to go into the reasons why slums are breeding grounds for criminals. They are. I know it. So do you. The children who come out of slum backgrounds are potential menaces to society.

NO. 10. You said it there. I don't want any part of them, believe me.

There is a dead silence for a moment, and then NO. 5 speaks haltingly.

NO. 5. I've lived in a slum all my life—

NO. 10. Oh, now wait a second!

NO. 5. I used to play in a back yard that was filled with garbage. Maybe it still smells on me.

FOREMAN. Now let's be reasonable. There's nothing personal—

NO. 5 stands up.

NO. 5. There is something personal!

Then he catches himself and, seeing everyone looking at him, sits down, fists clenched.

NO. 3 *(Persuasively)*. Come on, now. He didn't mean you, feller. Let's not be so sensitive. . . .

There is a long pause.

NO. 11. I can understand this sensitivity.

FOREMAN. Now let's stop the bickering. We're wasting time. *(To NO. 8)* It's your turn.

NO. 8. All right. I had a peculiar feeling about this trial. Somehow I felt that the defense counsel never really conducted a thorough cross-examination. I mean, he was appointed by the court to defend the boy. He hardly seemed interested. Too many questions were left unasked.

NO. 3 *(Annoyed)*. What about the ones that

were asked? For instance, let's talk about that cute little switch-knife. You know, the one that fine, upright kid admitted buying.

NO. 8. All right. Let's talk about it. Let's get it in here and look at it. I'd like to see it again, Mr. Foreman.

The FOREMAN looks at him questioningly and then gets up and goes to the door. During the following dialogue the FOREMAN knocks, the GUARD comes in, the FOREMAN whispers to him, the GUARD nods and leaves, locking the door.

NO. 3. We all know what it looks like. I don't see why we have to look at it again. *(To NO. 4)* What do you think?

NO. 4. The gentleman has a right to see exhibits in evidence.

NO. 3 *(Shrugging)*. Okay with me.

NO. 4 *(To NO. 8)*. This knife is a pretty strong piece of evidence, don't you agree?

NO. 8. I do.

NO. 4. The boy admits going out of his house at eight o'clock after being slapped by his father.

NO. 8. Or punched.

NO. 4. Or punched. He went to a neighborhood store and bought a switch-knife. The storekeeper was arrested the following day when he admitted selling it to the boy. It's a very unusual knife. The storekeeper identified it and said it was the only one of its kind he had in stock. Why did the boy get it? *(Sarcastically)* As a present for a friend of his, he says. Am I right so far?

NO. 8. Right.

NO. 3. You bet he's right. *(To all)* Now listen to this man. He knows what he's talking about.

NO. 4. Next, the boy claims that on the way home the knife must have fallen through a hole in his coat pocket, that he never saw it again. Now there's a story, gentlemen. You know what actually happened. The boy took the knife home and a few hours later stabbed his father with it and even remembered to wipe off the fingerprints.

The door opens and the GUARD walks in with

an oddly designed knife with a tag on it. NO. 4 *gets up and takes it from him. The* GUARD *exits.*

NO. 4. Everyone connected with the case identified this knife. Now are you trying to tell me that someone picked it up off the street and went up to the boy's house and stabbed his father with it just to be amusing?

NO. 8. No, I'm saying that it's possible that the boy lost the knife and that someone else stabbed his father with a similar knife. It's possible.

NO. 4 *flips open the knife and jams it into the table.*

NO. 4. Take a look at that knife. It's a very strange knife. I've never seen one like it before in my life. Neither had the storekeeper who sold it to him.

NO. 8 *reaches casually into his pocket and withdraws an object. No one notices this. He stands up quietly.*

NO. 4. Aren't you trying to make us accept a pretty incredible coincidence?

NO. 8. I'm not trying to make anyone accept it. I'm just saying it's possible.

NO. 3 (*Shouting*). And I'm saying it's not possible.

NO. 8 *swiftly flicks open the blade of a switch-knife and jams it into the table next to the first one. They are exactly alike. There are several gasps and everyone stares at the knife. There is a long silence.*

NO. 3 (*Slowly amazed*). What are you trying to do?

NO. 10 (*Loud*). Yeah, what is this? Who do you think you are?

NO. 5. Look at it! It's the same knife!

FOREMAN. Quiet! Let's be quiet.

They quiet down.

NO. 4. Where did you get it?

NO. 8. I got it last night in a little junk shop around the corner from the boy's house. It cost two dollars.

NO. 3. Now listen to me! You pulled a real smart trick here, but you proved absolutely zero. Maybe there are ten knives like that, so what?

NO. 8. Maybe there are.

NO. 3. The boy lied and you know it.

NO. 8. He may have lied. (*To* NO. *10*) Do you think he lied?

NO. 10 (*Violently*). Now that's a stupid question. Sure he lied!

NO. 8 (*To* NO. *4*). Do you?

NO. 4. You don't have to ask me that. You know my answer. He lied.

NO. 8 (*To* NO. *5*). Do you think he lied?

NO. 5 *can't answer immediately. He looks around nervously.*

NO. 5. I . . . I don't know.

NO. 7. Now wait a second. What are you, the guy's lawyer? Listen, there are still eleven of us who think he's guilty. You're alone. What do you think you're gonna accomplish? If you want to be stubborn and hang this jury, he'll be tried again and found guilty, sure as he's born.

NO. 8. You're probably right.

NO. 7. So what are you gonna do about it? We can be here all night.

NO. 9. It's only one night. A man may die.

NO. 7 *glares at* NO. 9 *for a long while, but has no answer.* NO. 8 *looks closely at* NO. 9 *and we can begin to sense a rapport between them. There is a long silence. Then suddenly everyone begins to talk at once.*

NO. 3. Well, whose fault is that?

NO. 6. Do you think maybe if we went over it again? What I mean is . . .

NO. 10. Did anyone force him to kill his father? (*To* NO. *3*) How do you like him? Like someone forced him!

NO. 11. Perhaps this is not the point.

NO. 5. No one forced anyone. But listen . . .

NO. 12. Look, gentlemen, we can spitball all night here.

NO. 2. Well, I was going to say—

NO. 7. Just a minute. Some of us've got better things to do than sit around a jury room.

NO. 4. I can't understand a word in here. Why do we all have to talk at once?

FOREMAN. He's right. I think we ought to get on with it.

NO. 8 has been listening to this exchange closely.

NO. 3 (*To* NO. 8). Well, what do you say? You're the one holding up the show.

NO. 8 (*Standing*). I've got a proposition to make.

We catch a close shot of NO. 5, *looking steadily at him as he talks.* NO. 5, *seemingly puzzled, listens closely.*

NO. 8. I want to call for a vote. I want you eleven men to vote by secret ballot. I'll abstain. If there are still eleven votes for guilty, I won't stand alone. We'll take in a guilty verdict right now.

NO. 7. Okay. Let's do it.

FOREMAN. That sounds fair. Is everyone agreed?

They all nod their heads. NO. 8 *walks over to the window, looks out for a moment and then faces them.*

FOREMAN. Pass these along.

The FOREMAN *passes ballot slips to all of them, and now* NO. 8 *watches them tensely as they begin to write. Fade out.*

Act II

Fade in on same scene, no time lapse. NO. 8 *stands tensely watching as the jurors write on their ballots. He stays perfectly still as one by one they fold the ballots and pass them along to the* FOREMAN. *The* FOREMAN *takes them, riffles through the folded ballots, counts eleven and now begins to open them. He reads each one out loud and lays it aside. They watch him quietly, and all we hear is his voice and the sound of* NO. 2 *sucking on a cough drop.*

FOREMAN. Guilty. Guilty. Guilty. Guilty. Guilty. Guilty. Guilty. Guilty. Guilty. (*He pauses at the tenth ballot and then reads it*) Not Guilty. (NO. 3 *slams down hard on the table. The* FOREMAN *opens the last ballot*) Guilty.

NO. 10 (*Angry*). How do you like that!

NO. 7. Who was it? I think we have a right to know.

NO. 11. Excuse me. This was a secret ballot. We agreed on this point, no? If the gentleman wants it to remain secret—

NO. 3 (*Standing up angrily*). What do you mean? There are no secrets in here! I know who it was. (*He turns to* NO. 5) What's the matter with you? You come in here and you vote guilty and then this slick preacher starts to tear your heart out with stories about a poor little kid who just couldn't help becoming a murderer. So you change your vote. If that isn't the most sickening—

NO. 5 stares at NO. 3, *frightened at this outburst.*

FOREMAN. Now hold it.

NO. 3. Hold it? We're trying to put a guilty man into the chair where he belongs—and all of a sudden we're paying attention to fairy tales.

NO. 5. Now just a minute . . .

NO. 11. Please. I would like to say something here. I have always thought that a man was entitled to have unpopular opinions in this country. This is the reason I came here. I wanted to have the right to disagree. In my own country, I am ashamed to say—

NO. 10. What do we have to listen to now—the whole history of your country?

NO. 7. Yeah, let's stick to the subject. (*To* NO. 5) I want to ask you what made you change your vote.

There is a long pause as NO. 7 *and* NO. 5 *eye each other angrily.*

NO. 9 (*Quietly*). There's nothing for him to tell you. He didn't change his vote. I did. (*There is a pause*) Maybe you'd like to know why.

NO. 3. No, we wouldn't like to know why.

FOREMAN. The man wants to talk.

NO. 9. Thank you. (*Pointing at* NO. 8) This gentleman chose to stand alone against us. That's his right. It takes a great deal of courage to stand alone even if you believe in something very strongly. He left the verdict up to us. He gambled for support and I gave it to him. I want to hear more. The vote is ten to two.

NO. 10. That's fine. If the speech is over, let's go on.

FOREMAN *gets up, goes to door, knocks, hands* GUARD *the tagged switch-knife and sits down again.*

NO. 3 (*To* NO. 5). Look, buddy, I was a little excited. Well, you know how it is. I . . . I didn't mean to get nasty. Nothing personal.

NO. *5 looks at him.*

NO. 7 (*To* NO. 8). Look, supposing you answer me this. If the kid didn't kill him, who did?

NO. 8. As far as I know, we're supposed to decide whether or not the boy on trial is guilty. We're not concerned with anyone else's motives here.

NO. 9. Guilty beyond a reasonable doubt. This is an important thing to remember.

NO. 3 (*To* NO. 10). Everyone's a lawyer. (*To* NO. 9) Supposing you explain what your reasonable doubts are.

NO. 9. This is not easy. So far, it's only a feeling I have. A feeling. Perhaps you don't understand.

NO. 10. A feeling! What are we gonna do, spend the night talking about your feelings? What about the facts?

NO. 3. You said a mouthful. (*To* NO. 9) Look, the old man heard the kid yell, "I'm gonna kill you." A second later he heard the father's body falling, and he saw the boy running out of the house fifteen seconds after that.

NO. 12. That's right. And let's not forget the woman across the street. She looked into the open window and saw the boy stab his father. She saw it. Now if that's not enough for you . . .

NO. 8. It's not enough for me.

NO. 7. How do you like him? It's like talking into a dead phone.

NO. 4. The woman saw the killing through the windows of a moving elevated train. The train had five cars, and she saw it through the windows of the last two. She remembers the most insignificant details.

Cut to close shot of NO. *12 who doodles a picture of an el train on a scrap of paper.*

NO. 3. Well, what have you got to say about that?

NO. 8. I don't know. It doesn't sound right to me.

NO. 3. Well, supposing you think about it. (*To* NO. *12*) Lend me your pencil.

NO. *12 gives it to him. He draws a tic-tac-toe square on the same sheet of paper on which* NO. *12 has drawn the train. He fills in an X, hands the pencil to* NO. *12.*

NO. 3. Your turn. We might as well pass the time.

NO. *12 takes the pencil.* NO. *8 stands up and snatches the paper away.* NO. *3 leaps up.*

NO. 3. Wait a minute!

NO. 8 (*Hard*). This isn't a game.

NO. 3 (*Angry*). Who do you think you are?

NO. 7 (*Rising*). All right, let's take it easy.

NO. 3. I've got a good mind to walk around this table and belt him one!

FOREMAN. Now, please. I don't want any fights in here.

NO. 3. Did ya see him? The nerve! The absolute nerve!

NO. 10. All right. Forget it. It don't mean anything.

NO. 6. How about sitting down.

NO. 3. This isn't a game. Who does he think he is?

He lets them sit him down. NO. *8 remains standing, holding the scrap of paper. He looks at it closely now and seems to be suddenly interested in it. Then he throws it back toward* NO. *3. It lands in center of table.* NO. *3 is angered again at this, but* NO. *4 puts his hand on his arm.* NO. *8 speaks now and his voice is more intense.*

NO. 8 (*To* NO. *4*). Take a look at that sketch. How long does it take an elevated train going at top speed to pass a given point?

NO. 4. What has that got to do with anything?

NO. 8. How long? Guess.

NO. 4. I wouldn't have the slightest idea.

NO. 8 (*To* NO. *5*). What do you think?

NO. 5. About ten or twelve seconds, maybe.

NO. 8. I'd say that was a fair guess. Anyone else?

NO. 11. I would think about ten seconds, perhaps.

NO. 2. About ten seconds.

NO. 4. All right. Say ten seconds. What are you getting at?

NO. 8. This. An el train passes a given point in ten seconds. That given point is the window of the room in which the killing took place. You can almost reach out of the window of that room and touch the el. Right? (*Several of them nod*) All right. Now let me ask you this. Did anyone here ever live right next to the el tracks? I have. When your window is open and the train goes by, the noise is almost unbearable. You can't hear yourself think.

NO. 10. Okay. You can't hear yourself think. Will you get to the point?

NO. 8. The old man heard the boy say, "I'm going to kill you," and one second later he heard a body fall. One second. That's the testimony, right?

NO. 2. Right.

NO. 8. The woman across the street looked through the windows of the last two cars of the el and saw the body fall. Right? The *last two* cars.

NO. 10. What are you giving us here?

NO. 8. An el takes ten seconds to pass a given point or two seconds per car. That el had been going by the old man's window for at least six seconds, and maybe more, *before the body fell*, according to the woman. The old man would have had to hear the boy say, "I'm going to kill you," while the front of the el was roaring past his nose. It's not possible that he could have heard it.

NO. 3. What d'ya mean! Sure he could have heard it.

NO. 8. Could he?

NO. 3. He said the boy yelled it out. That's enough for me.

NO. 9. I don't think he could have heard it.

NO. 2. Maybe he didn't hear it. I mean with the el noise . . .

NO. 3. What are you people talking about? Are you calling the old man a liar?

NO. 5. Well, it stands to reason.

NO. 3. You're crazy. Why would he lie? What's he got to gain?

NO. 9. Attention, maybe.

NO. 3. You keep coming up with these bright sayings. Why don't you send one in to a newspaper? They pay two dollars.

NO. *8 looks hard at* NO. *3 and then turns to* NO. *9.*

NO. 8 (*Softly*). Why might the old man have lied? You have a right to be heard.

NO. 9. It's just that I looked at him for a very long time. The seam of his jacket was split under the arm. Did you notice that? He was a very old man with a torn jacket, and he carried two canes. I think I know him better than anyone here. This a quiet, frightened, insignificant man who has been nothing all his life, who has never had recognition—his name in the newspapers. Nobody knows him after seventy-five years. That's a very sad thing. A man like this needs to be recognized. To be questioned, and listened to and quoted just once. This is very important.

NO. 12. And you're trying to tell us he lied about a thing like this just so that he could be important?

NO. 9. No. He wouldn't really lie. But perhaps he'd make himself believe that he heard those words and recognized the boy's face.

NO. 3 (*Loud*). Well, that's the most fantastic story I've ever heard. How can you make up a thing like that? What do you know about it?

NO. 9 (*Low*). I speak from experience.

There is a long pause. Then the FOREMAN *clears his throat.*

FOREMAN (*To* NO. 8). All right. Is there anything else?

NO. 8 *is looking at* NO. 9. NO. *2 offers the* FOREMAN *a box of cough drops. The* FOREMAN *pushes it away.*

NO. 2 (*Hesitantly*). Anybody . . . want a cough . . . drop?

FOREMAN (*Sharply*). Come on. Let's get on with it.

NO. 8. I'll take one. (NO. 2 *almost gratefully slides him one along the table*) Thanks.

NO. *2 nods and* NO. 8 *puts the cough drop into his mouth.*

NO. 8. Now. There's something else I'd like to point out here. I think we proved that the old man couldn't have heard the boy say, "I'm going to kill you," but supposing he really did hear it? This phrase: how many times has each of you used it? Probably hundreds. "If you do that once more, Junior, I'm going to murder you." "Come on, Rocky, kill him!" We say it every day. This doesn't mean that we're going to kill someone.

NO. 3. Wait a minute. The phrase was "I'm going to kill you," and the kid screamed it out at the top of his lungs. Don't try and tell me he didn't mean it. Anybody says a thing like that the way he said it—they mean it.

NO. 10. And how they mean it!

NO. 8. Well, let me ask you this. Do you really think the boy would shout out a thing like that so the whole neighborhood would hear it? I don't think so. He's much too bright for that.

NO. 10 (*Exploding*). Bright! He's a common, ignorant slob. He don't even speak good English!

NO. 11 (*Slowly*). He *doesn't* even speak good English.

NO. *10 stares angrily at* NO. *11, and there is silence for a moment. Then* NO. *5 looks around the table nervously.*

NO. 5. I'd like to change my vote to not guilty.

NO. *3 gets up and walks to the window, furious, but trying to control himself.*

FOREMAN. Are you sure?

NO. 5. Yes. I'm sure.

FOREMAN. The vote is nine to three in favor of guilty.

NO. 7. Well, if that isn't the end. (*To* NO. 5) What are you basing it on? Stories this guy (*Indicating* NO. 8) made up! He oughta write for *Amazing Detective Monthly.* He'd make a fortune. Listen, the kid had a lawyer, didn't he? Why didn't his lawyer bring up all these points?

NO. 5. Lawyers can't think of everything.

NO. 7. Oh, brother! (*To* NO. 8) You sit in here and pull stories out of thin air. Now we're supposed to believe that the old man didn't get up out of bed, run to the door and see the kid beat it downstairs fifteen seconds after the killing. He's only saying he did to be important.

NO. 5. Did the old man say he *ran* to the door?

NO. 7. Ran. Walked. What's the difference? He got there.

NO. 5. I don't remember what he said. But I don't see how he could run.

NO. 4. He said he *went* from his bedroom to the front door. That's enough, isn't it?

NO. 8. Where was his bedroom again?

NO. 10. Down the hall somewhere. I thought you remembered everything. Don't you remember that?

NO. 8. No. Mr. Foreman, I'd like to take a look at the diagram of the apartment.

NO. 7. Why don't we have them run the trial over just so you can get everything straight?

NO. 8. Mr. Foreman . . .

FOREMAN (*Rising*). I heard you.

The FOREMAN *gets up, goes to door during following dialogue. He knocks on door,* GUARD *opens it, he whispers to* GUARD, GUARD *nods and closes door.*

NO. 3 (*To* NO. 8). All right. What's this for? How come you're the only one in the room who wants to see exhibits all the time.

NO. 5. I want to see this one, too.

NO. 3. And I want to stop wasting time.

NO. 4. If we're going to start wading through

all that nonsense about where the body was found . . .

NO. 8. We're not. We're going to find out how a man who's had two strokes in the past three years, and who walks with a pair of canes, could get to his front door in fifteen seconds.

NO. 3. He said twenty seconds.

NO. 2. He said fifteen.

NO. 3. How does he know how long fifteen seconds is? You can't judge that kind of a thing.

NO. 9. He said fifteen. He was very positive about it.

NO. 3 (*Angry*). He's an old man. You saw him. Half the time he was confused. How could he be positive about . . . anything?

NO. 3 looks around sheepishly, unable to cover up his blunder. The door opens and the GUARD walks in, carrying a large pen-and-ink diagram of the apartment. It is a railroad flat. A bedroom faces the el tracks. Behind it is a series of rooms off a long hall. In the front bedroom is a diagram of the spot where the body was found. At the back of the apartment we see the entrance into the apartment hall from the building hall. We see a flight of stairs in the building hall. The diagram is clearly labeled and included in the information on it are the dimensions of the various rooms. The GUARD gives the diagram to the FOREMAN.

GUARD. This what you wanted?

FOREMAN. That's right. Thank you.

The GUARD nods and exits. NO. 8 goes to FOREMAN and reaches for it.

NO. 8. May I?

The FOREMAN nods. NO. 8 takes the diagram and sets it up on a chair so that all can see it. NO. 8 looks it over. Several of the jurors get up to see it better. NO. 3, NO. 10 and NO. 7, however, barely bother to look at it.

NO. 7 (*To NO. 10*). Do me a favor. Wake me up when this is over.

NO. 8 (*Ignoring him*). All right. This is the apartment in which the killing took place. The old man's apartment is directly beneath

it and exactly the same. (*Pointing*) Here are the el tracks. The bedroom. Another bedroom. Living room. Bathroom. Kitchen. And this is the hall. Here's the front door to the apartment. And here are the steps. (*Pointing to front bedroom and then front door*) Now, the old man was in bed in this room. He says he got up, went out into the hall, down the hall to the front door, opened it and looked out just in time to see the boy racing down the stairs. Am I right?

NO. 3. That's the story.

NO. 8. Fifteen seconds after he heard the body fall.

NO. 11. Correct.

NO. 8. His bed was at the window. It's (*Looking closer*) twelve feet from his bed to the bedroom door. The length of the hall is forty-three feet, six inches. He had to get up out of bed, get his canes, walk twelve feet, open the bedroom door, walk forty-three feet and open the front door—all in fifteen seconds. Do you think this possible?

NO. 10. You know it's possible.

NO. 11. He can only walk very slowly. They had to help him into the witness chair.

NO. 3. You make it sound like a long walk. It's not.

NO. 8 gets up, goes to the end of the room and takes two chairs. He puts them together to indicate a bed.

NO. 9. For an old man who uses canes, it's a long walk.

NO. 3 (*To NO. 8*). What are you doing?

NO. 8. I want to try this thing. Let's see how long it took him. I'm going to pace off twelve feet —the length of the bedroom.

He begins to do so.

NO. 3. You're crazy. You can't recreate a thing like that.

NO. 11. Perhaps if we could see it . . . this is an important point.

NO. 3 (*Mad*). It's a ridiculous waste of time.

NO. 6. Let him do it.

NO. 8. Hand me a chair. (*Someone pushes a*

chair to him) All right. This is the bedroom door. Now how far would you say it is from here to the door of this room?

NO. 6. I'd say it was twenty feet.

NO. 2. Just about.

NO. 8. Twenty feet is close enough. All right, from here to the door and back is about forty feet. It's shorter than the length of the hall, wouldn't you say that?

NO. 9. A few feet, maybe.

NO. 10. Look, this is absolutely insane. What makes you think you can—

NO. 8. Do you mind if I try it? According to you, it'll only take fifteen seconds. We can spare that. (*He walks over to the two chairs now and lies down on them*) Who's got a watch with a second hand?

NO. 2. I have.

NO. 8. When you want me to start, stamp your foot. That'll be the body falling. Time me from there. (*He lies down on the chairs*) Let's say he keeps his canes right at his bedside. Right?

NO. 2. Right!

NO. 8. Okay. I'm ready.

They all watch carefully. NO. 2 stares at his watch, waiting for the second hand to reach 60. Then, as it does, he stamps his foot loudly. NO. 8 begins to get up. Slowly he swings his legs over the edges of the chairs, reaches for imaginary canes and struggles to his feet. NO. 2 stares at the watch. NO. 8 walks as a crippled old man would walk, toward the chair which is serving as the bedroom door. He gets to it and pretends to open it.

NO. 10 (*Shouting*). Speed it up. He walked twice as fast as that.

NO. 8, not having stopped for this outburst, begins to walk the simulated forty-foot hallway.

NO. 11. This is, I think, even more quickly than the old man walked in the courtroom.

NO. 8. If you think I should go faster, I will.

He speeds up his pace slightly. He reaches the door and turns now, heading back, hob-bling as an old man would hobble, bent over his imaginary canes. They watch him tensely. He hobbles back to the chair, which also serves as the front door. He stops there and pretends to unlock the door. Then he pretends to push it open.

NO. 8 (*Loud*). Stop.

NO. 2. Right.

NO. 8. What's the time?

NO. 2. Fifteen . . . twenty . . . thirty . . . thirty-one seconds exactly.

NO. 11. Thirty-one seconds.

Some of the jurors ad-lib their surprise to each other.

NO. 8. It's my guess that the old man was trying to get to the door, heard someone racing down the stairs and *assumed* that it was the boy.

NO. 6. I think that's possible.

NO. 3 (*Infuriated*). Assumed? Now, listen to me, you people. I've seen all kinds of dishonesty in my day . . . but this little display takes the cake. (*To* NO. 4) Tell him, will you?

NO. 4 sits silently. NO. 3 looks at him and then he strides over to NO. 8.

NO. 3. You come in here with your heart bleeding all over the floor about slum kids and injustice and you make up these wild stories, and you've got some softhearted old ladies listening to you. Well I'm not. I'm getting real sick of it. (*To all*) What's the matter with you people? This kid is guilty! He's got to burn! We're letting him slip through our fingers here.

NO. 8 (*Calmly*). Our fingers. Are you his executioner?

NO. 3 (*Raging*). I'm one of 'em.

NO. 8. Perhaps you'd like to pull the switch.

NO. 3 (*Shouting*). For this kid? You bet I'd like to pull the switch!

NO. 8. I'm sorry for you.

NO. 3 (*Shouting*). Don't start with me.

NO. 8. What it must feel like to want to pull the switch!

NO. 3. Shut up!

NO. 8. You're a sadist.

NO. 3 (*Louder*). Shut up!

NO. 8 (*Strong*). You want to see this boy die because you personally want it—not because of the facts.

NO. 3 (*Shouting*). Shut up!

He lunges at NO. 8, but is caught by two of the jurors and held. He struggles as NO. 8 watches calmly.

NO. 3 (*Screaming*). Let me go! I'll kill him. I'll kill him!

NO. 8 (*Softly*). You don't really mean you'll kill me, do you?

NO. 3 stops struggling now and stares at NO. 8. All the jurors watch in silence as we fade out.

Act III

Fade in on same scene. No time lapse. NO. 3 glares angrily at NO. 8. He is still held by two jurors. After a long pause, he shakes himself loose and turns away. He walks to the windows. The other jurors stand around the room now, shocked by this display of anger. There is silence. Then the door opens and the GUARD enters. He looks around the room.

GUARD. Is there anything wrong, gentlemen? I heard some noise.

FOREMAN. No. There's nothing wrong. (*He points to the large diagram of the apartment*) You can take that back. We're finished with it.

The GUARD nods and takes the diagram. He looks curiously at some of the jurors and exits. The jurors still are silent. Some of them slowly begin to sit down. NO. 3 still stands at the window. He turns around now. The jurors look at him.

NO. 3 (*Loud*). Well, what are you looking at?

They turn away. He goes back to his seat now. Silently the rest of the jurors take their seats. NO. 12 begins to doodle. NO. 10 blows his nose, but no one speaks. Then, finally—

NO. 4. I don't see why we have to behave like children here.

NO. 11. Nor do I. We have a responsibility. This is a remarkable thing about democracy. That we are . . . what is the word? . . . Ah, notified! That we are notified by mail to come down to this place and decide on the guilt or innocence of a man we have not known before. We have nothing to gain or lose by our verdict. This is one of the reasons why we are strong. We should not make it a personal thing.

There is a long, awkward pause.

NO. 12. Well—we're still nowhere. Who's got an idea?

NO. 6. I think maybe we should try another vote. Mr. Foreman?

FOREMAN. It's all right with me. Anybody doesn't want to vote?

He looks around the table.

NO. 7. All right, let's do it.

NO. 3. I want an open ballot. Let's call out our votes. I want to know who stands where.

FOREMAN. That sounds fair. Anyone object? (*No one does*) All right. I'll call off your jury numbers.

He takes a pencil and paper and makes marks now in one of two columns after each vote.

FOREMAN. I vote guilty. No. 2?

NO. 2. Not guilty.

FOREMAN. No. 3?

NO. 3. Guilty.

FOREMAN. No. 4?

NO. 4. Guilty.

FOREMAN. No. 5?

NO. 5. Not guilty.

FOREMAN. No. 6?

NO. 6. Not guilty.

FOREMAN. No. 7?

NO. 7. Guilty.

FOREMAN. No. 8?

NO. 8. Not guilty.

FOREMAN. No. 9?

NO. 9. Not guilty.

FOREMAN. No. 10?

NO. 10. Guilty.

FOREMAN. No. 11?

NO. 11. Not guilty.

FOREMAN. No. 12?

NO. 12. Guilty.

NO. 4. Six to six.

NO. 10 (*Mad*). I'll tell you something. The crime is being committed right in this room.

FOREMAN. The vote is six to six.

NO. 3. I'm ready to walk into court right now and declare a hung jury. There's no point in this going on any more.

NO. 7. I go for that, too. Let's take it in to the judge and let the kid take his chances with twelve other guys.

NO. 5 (*To* NO. 7). You mean you still don't think there's room for reasonable doubt?

NO. 7. No, I don't.

NO. 11. I beg your pardon. Maybe you don't understand the term "reasonable doubt."

NO. 7 (*Angry*). What do you mean I don't understand it? Who do you think you are to talk to me like that? (*To all*) How do you like this guy? He comes over here running for his life, and before he can even take a big breath he's telling us how to run the show. The arrogance of him!

NO. 5 (*To* NO. 7). Wait a second. Nobody around here's asking where you came from.

NO. 7. I was born right here.

NO. 5. Or where your father came from. . . . (*He looks at* NO. 7, *who doesn't answer but looks away*) Maybe it wouldn't hurt us to take a few tips from people who come running here! Maybe they learned something we don't know. We're not so perfect!

NO. 11. Please—I am used to this. It's all right. Thank you.

NO. 5. It's not all right!

NO. 7. Okay, okay, I apologize. Is that what you want?

NO. 5. That's what I want.

FOREMAN. All right. Let's stop the arguing. Who's got something constructive to say?

NO. 2 (*Hesitantly*). Well, something's been bothering me a little . . . this whole business about the stab wound and how it was made, the downward angle of it, you know?

NO. 3. Don't tell me we're gonna start that. They went over it and over it in court.

NO. 2. I know they did—but I don't go along with it. The boy is five feet eight inches tall. His father was six two. That's a difference of six inches. It's a very awkward thing to stab *down* into the chest of someone who's half a foot taller than you are.

NO. 3 *jumps up, holding the knife.*

NO. 3. Look, you're not going to be satisfied till you see it again. I'm going to give you a demonstration. Somebody get up.

He looks around the table. NO. 8 *stands up and walks toward him.* NO. 3 *closes the knife and puts it in his pocket. They stand face to face and look at each other for a moment.*

NO. 3. Okay. (*To* NO. 2) Now watch this. I don't want to have to do it again. (*He crouches down now until he is quite a bit shorter than* NO. 8) Is that six inches?

NO. 12. That's more than six inches.

NO. 3. Okay, let it be more.

He reaches into his pocket and takes out the knife. He flicks it open, changes its position in his hand and holds the knife aloft, ready to stab. He and NO. 8 *look steadily into each other's eyes. Then he stabs downward, hard.*

NO. 2 (*Shouting*). Look out!

He stops short just as the blade reaches NO. 8's *chest.* NO. 3 *laughs.*

NO. 6. That's not funny.

NO. 5. What's the matter with you?

NO. 3. Now just calm down. Nobody's hurt, are they?

NO. 8 (*Low*). No. Nobody's hurt.

NO. 3. All right. There's your angle. Take a look at it. Down and in. That's how I'd stab a taller man in the chest, and that's how it was done. Take a look at it and tell me I'm wrong.

NO. 2 *doesn't answer.* NO. 3 *looks at him for*

a moment, then jams the knife into the table and sits down. They all look at the knife.

NO. 6. Down and in. I guess there's no argument.

NO. *8 picks the knife out of the table and closes it. He flicks it open and, changing its position in his hand, stabs downward with it.*

NO. 8 (*To* NO. *6*). Did you ever stab a man?

NO. 6. Of course not.

NO. 8 (*To* NO. *3*). Did you?

NO. 3. All right, let's not be silly.

NO. 8. Did you?

NO. 3 (*Loud*). No, I didn't!

NO. 8. Where do you get all your information about how it's done?

NO. 3. What do you mean? It's just common sense.

NO. 8. Have you ever seen a man stabbed?

NO. 3 (*Pauses and looks around the room nervously*). No.

NO. 8. All right. I want to ask you something. The boy was an experienced knife fighter. He was even sent to reform school for knifing someone, isn't that so?

NO. 12. That's right.

NO. 8. Look at this. (NO. *8 closes the knife, flicks it open and changes the position of the knife so that he can stab overhanded*) Doesn't it seem like an awkward way to handle a knife?

NO. 3. What are you asking me for?

NO. *8 closes the blade and flicks it open, holds it ready to slash underhanded.*

NO. 5. Wait a minute! What's the matter with me? Give me that.

He reaches out for the knife.

NO. 8. Have you ever seen a knife fight?

NO. 5. Yes, I have.

NO. 8. In the movies?

NO. 5. In my back yard. On my stoop. In the vacant lot across the street. Too many of them. Switch-knives came with the neighborhood where I lived. Funny I didn't think of it before. I guess you try to forget those things. (*Flicking the knife open*) Anyone who's ever used a switch-knife would never have stabbed downward. You don't handle a switch-knife that way. You use it underhanded.

NO. 8. Then he couldn't have made the kind of wound which killed his father.

NO. 5. No. He couldn't have. Not if he'd ever had any experience with switch-knives.

NO. 3. I don't believe it.

NO. 10. Neither do I. You're giving us a lot of mumbo jumbo.

NO. 8 (*To* NO. *12*). What do you think?

NO. 12 (*Hesitantly*). Well . . . I don't know.

NO. 8 (*To* NO. *7*). What about you?

NO. 7. Listen, I'll tell you something. I'm a little sick of this whole thing already. We're getting nowhere fast. Let's break it up and go home. I'm changing my vote to not guilty.

NO. 3. You're what?

NO. 7. You heard me. I've had enough.

NO. 3. What do you mean, you've had enough? That's no answer.

NO. 11 (*Angry*). I think perhaps you're right. This is not an answer. (*To* NO. *7*) What kind of a man are you? You have sat here and voted guilty with everyone else because there are some theater tickets burning a hole in your pocket. Now you have changed your vote for the same reason. I do not think you have the right to play like this with a man's life. This is an ugly and terrible thing to do.

NO. 7. Now wait a minute . . . you can't talk like that to me.

NO. 11 (*Strong*). I can talk like that to you! If you want to vote not guilty, then do it because you are convinced the man is not guilty. If you believe he is guilty, then vote that way. Or don't you have the . . . the . . . guts—the guts to do what you think is right?

NO. 7. Now listen . . .

NO. 11. Is it guilty or not guilty?

NO. 7 (*Hesitantly*). I told you. Not . . . guilty.

NO. 11 (*Hard*). Why?

NO. 7. I don't have to—

NO. 11. You have to! Say it! Why?

They stare at each other for a long while.

NO. 7 (*Low*). I . . . don't know . . . he's guilty.

NO. 8 (*Fast*). I want another vote.

FOREMAN. Okay, there's another vote called for. I guess the quickest way is a show of hands. Anybody object? (*No one does*) All right. All those voting not guilty, raise your hands.

NUMBERS *2, 5, 6, 7, 8, 9 and 11 raise their hands immediately. Then, slowly,* NO. *12 raises his hand. The* FOREMAN *looks around the table carefully and then he too raises his hand. He looks around the table, counting silently.*

FOREMAN. Nine. (*The hands go down*) All those voting guilty.

NUMBERS *3, 4 and 10 raise their hands.*

FOREMAN. Three. (*They lower their hands*) The vote is nine to three in favor of acquittal.

NO. 10. I don't understand you people. How can you believe this kid is innocent? Look, you know how those people lie. I don't have to tell you. They don't know what the truth is. And lemme tell you, they—(NO. *5 gets up from table, turns his back to it and goes to window*)—don't need any real big reason to kill someone either. You know, they get drunk, and *bang,* someone's lying in the gutter. Nobody's blaming them. That's how they are. You know what I mean? Violent!

NO. *9 gets up and does the same. He is followed by* NO. *11.*

NO. 10. Human life don't mean as much to them as it does to us. Hey, where are you going? Look, these people are drinking and fighting all the time, and if somebody gets killed, so somebody gets killed. They don't care. Oh, sure, there are some good things about them, too. Look, I'm the first to say that.

NO. *8 gets up, and then* NO. *2 and* NO. *6 follow him to the window.*

NO. 10. I've known a few who were pretty decent, but that's the exception. Most of them, it's like they have no feelings. They can do anything. What's going on here?

The FOREMAN *gets up and goes to the windows, followed by* NO. *7 and* NO. *12.*

NO. 10. I'm speaking my piece, and you—Listen to me! They're no good. There's not a one of 'em who's any good. We better watch out. Take it from me. This kid on trial . . .

NO. *3 sits at table toying with the knife and* NO. *4 gets up and starts for the window. All have their backs to* NO. *10.*

NO. 10. Well, don't you know about them? Listen to me! What are you doing? I'm trying to tell you something. . . .

NO. *4 stands over him as he trails off. There is a dead silence. Then* NO. *4 speaks softly.*

NO. 4. I've had enough. If you open your mouth again, I'm going to split your skull.

NO. *4 stands there and looks at him. No one moves or speaks.* NO. *10 looks at him, then looks down at the table.*

NO. 10 (*Softly*). I'm only trying to tell you . . .

There is a long pause as NO. *4 stares down at* NO. *10.*

NO. 4 (*To all*). All right. Sit down everybody.

They all move back to their seats. When they are all seated, NO. *4 then sits down.*

NO. 4 (*Quietly*). I still believe the boy is guilty of murder. I'll tell you why. To me, the most damning evidence was given by the woman across the street who claimed she actually saw the murder committed.

NO. 3. That's right. As far as I'm concerned, that's the most important testimony.

NO. 8. All right. Let's go over her testimony. What exactly did she say?

NO. 4. I believe I can recount it accurately. She said that she went to bed at about eleven o'clock that night. Her bed was next to the open window, and she could look out of the window while lying down and see directly into the window across the street. She tossed and turned for over an hour, unable to fall asleep. Finally she turned toward the window at about twelve-ten and, as she looked out, she saw the boy stab his father. As far as I can see, this is unshakable testimony.

NO. 3. That's what I mean. That's the whole case.

NO. *4 takes off his eyeglasses and begins to polish them, as they all sit silently watching him.*

NO. 4 (*To the jury*). Frankly, I don't see how you can vote for acquittal. (*To* NO. *12*) What do you think about it?

NO. 12. Well . . . maybe . . . there's so much evidence to sift.

NO. 3. What do you mean, maybe? He's absolutely right. You can throw out all the other evidence.

NO. 4. That was my feeling.

NO. *2, polishing his glasses, squints at clock, can't see it.* NO. *6 watches him closely.*

NO. 2. What time is it?

NO. 11. Ten minutes of six.

NO. 2. It's late. You don't suppose they'd let us go home and finish it in the morning. I've got a kid with mumps.

NO. 5. Not a chance.

NO. 6 (*To* NO. *2*). Pardon me. Can't you see the clock without your glasses?

NO. 2. Not clearly. Why?

NO. 6. Oh, I don't know. Look, this may be a dumb thought, but what do you do when you wake up at night and want to know what time it is?

NO. 2. What do you mean? I put on my glasses and look at the clock.

NO. 6. You don't wear them to bed.

NO. 2. Of course not. No one wears eyeglasses to bed.

NO. 12. What's all this for?

NO. 6. Well, I was thinking. You know the woman who testified that she saw the killing wears glasses.

NO. 3. So does my grandmother. So what?

NO. 8. Your grandmother isn't a murder witness.

NO. 6. Look, stop me if I'm wrong. This woman wouldn't wear her eyeglasses to bed, would she?

FOREMAN. Wait a minute! Did she wear glasses at all? I don't remember.

NO. 11 (*Excited*). Of course she did! The woman wore bifocals. I remember this very clearly. They looked quite strong.

NO. 9. That's right. Bifocals. She never took them off.

NO. 4. She did wear glasses. Funny. I never thought of it.

NO. 8. Listen, she wasn't wearing them in bed. That's for sure. She testified that in the midst of her tossing and turning she rolled over and looked casually out the window. The murder was taking place as she looked out, and the lights went out a split second later. She couldn't have had time to put on her glasses. Now maybe she honestly thought she saw the boy kill his father. I say that she saw only a blur.

NO. 3. How do you know what she saw? Maybe she's far-sighted.

He looks around. No one answers.

NO. 3 (*Loud*). How does he know all these things?

There is silence.

NO. 8. Does anyone think there still is not a reasonable doubt?

He looks around the room, then squarely at NO. *10.* NO. *10 looks down and shakes his head no.*

NO. 3 (*Loud*). I think he's guilty!

NO. 8 (*Calmly*). Does anyone else?

NO. 4 (*Quietly*). No. I'm convinced.

NO. 8 (*To* NO. *3*). You're alone.

NO. 3. I don't care whether I'm alone or not! I have a right.

NO. 8. You have a right.

There is a pause. They all look at NO. *3.*

NO. 3. Well, I told you I think the kid's guilty. What else do you want?

NO. 8. Your arguments.

They all look at NO. *3.*

NO. 3. I gave you my arguments.

NO. 8. We're not convinced. We're waiting to hear them again. We have time.

NO. *3 runs to* NO. *4 and grabs his arm.*

NO. 3 (*Pleading*). Listen. What's the matter with you? You're the guy. You made all the arguments. You can't turn now. A guilty man's gonna be walking the streets. A murderer. He's got to die! Stay with me.

NO. 4. I'm sorry. There's a reasonable doubt in my mind.

NO. 8. We're waiting.

NO. *3 turns violently on him.*

NO. 3 (*Shouting*). Well, you're not going to intimidate me! (*They all look at* NO. *3*) I'm entitled to my opinion! (*No one answers him*) It's gonna be a hung jury! That's it!

NO. 8. There's nothing we can do about that, except hope that some night, maybe in a few months, you'll get some sleep.

NO. 5. You're all alone.

NO. 9. It takes a great deal of courage to stand alone.

NO. *3 looks around at all of them for a long time. They sit silently, waiting for him to speak, and all of them despise him for his stubbornness. Then, suddenly, his face contorts as if he is about to cry, and he slams his fist down on the table.*

NO. 3 (*Thundering*). All right!

NO. *3 turns his back on them. There is silence for a moment and then the* FOREMAN *goes to the door and knocks on it. It opens. The* GUARD *looks in and sees them all standing. The* GUARD *holds the door for them as they begin slowly to file out.* NO. *8 waits at the door as the others file past him. Finally he and* NO. *3 are the only ones left.* NO. *3 turns around and sees that they are alone. Slowly he moves toward the door. Then he stops at the table. He pulls the switch-knife out of the table and walks over to* NO. *8 with it. He holds it in the approved knife-fighter fashion and looks long and hard at* NO. *8, pointing the knife at his belly.* NO. *8 stares back. Then* NO.

3 turns the knife around. NO. *8 takes it by the handle.* NO. *3 exits.* NO. *8 closes the knife, puts it away and, taking a last look around the room, exits, closing the door. The camera moves in close on the littered table in the empty room, and we clearly see a slip of crumpled paper on which are scribbled the words "Not guilty."*

Fade out.

I

A CORNERSTONE OF JUSTICE

Of all man's attempts to find some way to determine justice fairly, the jury system is perhaps the best. It is based upon the idea of a jury of one's peers, a jury of one's equals; thus it is essentially a democratic institution. It is believed that such a jury is likely to be the most impartial way of determining justice.

As you saw in this play, however, the ideal of the impartial jury is not always reached in practice. Which of the jurors are not impartial? What causes their partiality in each case? How did these men get on the jury in the first place?

II

IMPLICATIONS

The following statements are generalities that might or might not be based on this play. In discussing them, draw on your own experience as well as your understanding of the play.

1. In reality, the decisions of juries are determined by two or three strong men, not by all twelve.

2. When men are publicly committed to a belief or opinion, it is extremely difficult to get them to change their minds.

3. In practice, a member of a minority group is much less likely to get a fair trial by jury than a member of a majority group.

4. One's first impressions and opinions are far more likely to be ruled by emotion than by reason.

5. It is easy to stand alone when one is emotionally convinced of the rightness of his beliefs.

TECHNIQUES

Intention

Just as an author might have more than one theme in a given work, so, too, might he have more than one intention. Below is a list of intentions that Reginald Rose *might* have had. What evidence can you offer to show that each of these was or was not one of his intentions? Which—if any—might you classify as *major* intentions, and which—if any—might you classify as *minor* intentions? Be prepared to defend your opinions.

1. To create a gallery of psychological character studies.

2. To show how the rational man triumphs over the irrational.

3. To examine and criticize the institution of trial by jury.

4. To create a dramatically intense and unstable situation and to bring it through a series of complications to a relatively stable situation.

5. To illustrate how emotions and prejudices affect the decisions of juries.

Irony

On a number of occasions in the play Rose makes use of *irony*. For example, when No. 3 says, "I'll kill him. I'll kill him!" his statement is ironic in that it contrasts with his earlier statement that those who say, "I'll kill you," mean it and will follow through with the threat.

A somewhat different sort of irony occurs when No. 10 says, "The crime is being committed right in this room." In this case the contrast is between what 10 intends his statement to mean—that the jurors are committing a crime by moving toward the verdict of "not guilty"—and what it *does* mean for the reader—that 10 is committing a crime by declaring the boy guilty purely on the basis of prejudice.

In both of these examples the essential element is a *contrast*. In fact, irony may be defined as a contrast between what is expected or intended and what is actual or real. On the basis of this definition and of the two examples given, try to detect the irony in the following statements:

1. NO. 3: Everybody gets a fair trial. . . . That's the system.

2. NO. 3: He's an old man. You saw him. Half the time he was confused. How could he be positive about . . . anything?

3. NO. 11: We have nothing to gain or lose by our verdict. This is one of the reasons why we are strong.

4. NO. 10: Human life don't mean as much to them as it does to us.

5. NO. 10: Bright! He's a common, ignorant slob. He don't even speak good English!

Why might an author wish to use irony? What specifically does Rose gain by using it?

FINAL REFLECTIONS

The Struggle for Justice

As one looks back on the American past, he cannot help feeling that the struggle for justice has had positive results: Women have achieved a much higher status than they had in the nineteenth century; the worker and the farmer are in a much better position than their ancestors; slavery has been abolished; and, in fact, our laws and Constitution guarantee a much greater measure of freedom to every individual than he would have known two hundred years ago. Yet we know that the struggle for justice remains a lively one at the present time and promises to continue in the future.

The writers you have read have tended to focus on some of the social and psychological factors that have prevented the realization of "liberty and justice *for all*." Some of these factors have been listed below. Choose one or more of them and be prepared to discuss at least one concrete instance of how it (or they) has resulted in an injustice done to some specific individual or group.

1. Black-and-white thinking.

2. Perversion of the law.

3. Prejudice.

4. Traditionalism or conformity resulting from insecurity.

5. Inertia—the failure of a group or individual to press for his rights.

6. Pressure groups working against justice.

You have also seen that it is pointless to define justice as "equal treatment under the law," when the laws themselves are unjust. This fact raises some fundamental questions: (1) By what standard may one judge whether or not a law is just? (2) How can a reasonable agreement on such a standard be reached? (3) How does one go about changing a law that he considers unjust? Select one, two, or all three of these questions and be prepared to discuss it (them). Be sure to bring your reading to bear on your discussion.

IMPLICATIONS

Below are five statements dealing with justice. After each statement is a list of some of the selections you have read. Be prepared to discuss each statement in the light of *each* of the selections listed.

1. So far as justice is concerned, the individual is very much at the mercy of society.

"Trials at Salem"
"Under the Lion's Paw"
"Testimony of Trees"
"Susan B. Anthony"
"The Man with the Hoe"
"Twelve Angry Men"

2. There would be a great deal more justice in the world if human beings were more charitable to each other.

"Arsenal at Springfield"
"Lines for an Interment"
"Losses"
"Twelve Angry Men"

3. Guilty, insecure people tend to band together and to seek scapegoats on whom they can inflict unjust punishments.

"Trials at Salem"
"Susan B. Anthony"
"The Lottery"
"Twelve Angry Men"

4. In general, the common man is reluctant to fight for justice; too often he tends merely to accept his lot without protest.

"Under the Lion's Paw"
"Testimony of Trees"
"The People Will Live On"

"The Lottery"
"The Man with the Hoe"
"Looking"

5. "Universal law" has generally been on the side of the common man and minority groups, but this fact has not helped them very much in their struggle to achieve identity and justice.

"The People Will Live On"
"Lines for an Interment"
"Losses"
"I Have a Rendezvous with Death"
"Susan B. Anthony"
"The Man with the Hoe"
"The Arsenal at Springfield"

TECHNIQUES

Intention

We have seen that a reader can best grasp a writer's intention by focusing on the work itself and by paying close attention to such matters as word-choice, choice of incidents and details, and the amount of attention or development given to incidents and details. We have also touched from time to time on how the reader knows whether or not a writer "means what he says." At this time let us take up this matter in some detail.

Consider the following situation: Three boys are discussing a fourth boy, Jack. The first boy says, "Jack's a tank." The second says, "Jack is 25 pounds overweight." The third says, "Jack's a toothpick." Suppose you know Jack and, in fact, he *is* 25 pounds overweight. You could then classify the statements of the boys as follows:

Exaggeration (Overstatement): "Jack's a tank."
Objective Statement: "Jack is 25 pounds overweight."
Understatement: "Jack's a toothpick."

Although our example is a crude one, the fact is that there is nothing unusual about such uses of language, and there are some very good reasons why writers use both exaggeration and understatement as well as objective statement. Exaggeration may often produce a strong and immediate effect on a reader, and it is commonly found in satire and in propagandist literature. Objective statement is the characteristic mode of expression of the reporter, the scientist, the historian, the philosopher, and of some literary essayists, all of whose main intention usually is to communicate information simply and clearly. Finally, understatement is used in much poetry and in most forms of serious modern fiction. It often helps to get a reader *inside* a poem or a story; it forces him to *participate* by placing on him the task of determining what the writer really means.

Of course, writers on occasion may use any of these forms of statement in any literary work—a poet may exaggerate, a satirist may use understatement, both may use objective statement, and so on. The type of statement any writer actually uses depends more upon his major purpose, upon the immediate context, and upon his style than upon the type of writing he is doing. By paying close attention to these points as well as to word choice, selection and importance of incidents and details, the reader will develop the ability to grasp the writer's intention.

Try to pick from the works in this unit at least one selection that employs a fair amount of exaggeration, one that uses objective statement, mainly, and one that makes extensive use of understatement. Discuss how you know which method the writer is using and why he may have chosen to use that method.

Theme

We have defined "theme" as the central idea in a literary work. We have also discovered that many literary works contain a number of themes and that if the work is to have unity, the final expression of the central idea should take account of subordinate themes. In Benét's "Trials at Salem," we noted that no single word expressed its theme adequately; we needed at least a full sentence to express the central idea fully.

To put it in another way, an adequate expression of theme requires a certain amount of *modification and qualification*. In fiction the task of expressing theme is likely to be still more complicated. The reader has to consider not only subordinate ideas, but also elements like character, setting, incident; indeed, the total pattern of organization. These elements modify and qualify fictional themes to such an extent that it has been said that the precise theme of most fictional works can be found only by reading the work itself.

The essential point is that *theme* is not merely something that is "tacked on" to a piece of fiction; it is something integral, something woven into the

total pattern. And it cannot be extracted from that total pattern as if it were one of several teeth.

In spite of this, however, shorthand expressions of theme do have value. They may help a reader tell someone else what a given work of fiction is "about" in a general way. Expressions of theme also help the reader unify his impressions and test his understanding of a story or poem.

Below are given five simple statements about human nature. After each statement are listed two selections for which the statement might be considered at least *a* theme. Discuss in each case why you consider the statement to be an inadequate expression of the central idea of the works involved.

1. Superstitions and blind traditions make individuals commit unjust acts ("Trials at Salem" and "The Lottery").

2. The common man will allow himself to be pushed around a good deal without fighting back ("The Man with the Hoe" and "The People Will Live On").

3. People usually show very little concern for matters that do not affect them directly ("Eleven o'Clock News Summary" and "Losses").

4. Laws alone do not guarantee that human beings will show respect for the rights of others ("Under the Lion's Paw" and "Testimony of Trees").

5. People in general are very ready to make judgments against others on the basis of emotions alone ("Twelve Angry Men").

BIOGRAPHICAL NOTES

Hamlin Garland

Hamlin Garland (1860–1940), born in Wisconsin and reared in Iowa and the Dakotas, was himself a child of the middle border—the prairie lands of the Midwest of which he wrote. Except for three propaganda novels which appeared in the 1890's, the farms and people of the prairies were the themes for Garland's realistic, yet romantic writings. Among his early books were collections of short stories, *Main-Travelled Roads* (1891), *Prairie Folks* (1893), and *Wayside Courtships* (1897).

Probably his best books are two autobiographical works: *A Son of the Middle Border* (1917) and *A Daughter of the Middle Border* (1921), which was awarded a Pulitzer Prize.

Jesse Stuart

Jesse Stuart (1907–   ), living today on the hill farm where he was born, continues writing about the Kentucky people and places he loves. Though he could attend school only irregularly as a boy, because he was needed to help with the farm chores, he finally finished high school and saved enough money to go to college. Returning home, he taught first in a rural school, then in a high school, and later served as a principal and county superintendent. He recounts these experiences in *The Thread That Runs So True*. A prolific short-story writer, Stuart has also written such novels as *Trees of Heaven, Taps for Private Tussie,* and *Hie to the Hunter.*

Louis Untermeyer

Louis Untermeyer (1885–   ) is a poet in his own right, although most famous for his editing of many volumes of verse. In addition, he has written many brief biographies and extensive critical essays. Untermeyer was born and grew up in the East. He left school at seventeen to enter his father's jewelry manufacturing firm. Twenty years later, as vice-president, he resigned to devote himself to writing and lecturing. His productivity in the years since has been extremely high; he has edited more than a dozen anthologies and written more than twenty-five volumes of verse.

Edwin Markham

Edwin Markham's (1852–1940) fame rests largely on the single poem, "The Man with the Hoe." First published in the San Francisco *Examiner*, the poem brought an immediate response from the American people who at that time were very much concerned about the living and working conditions of the common worker. Two years after the publication of *The Man with the Hoe and Other Poems* in 1899, Markham gave up his teaching career in California and moved to New York. He published four more volumes of poetry, the last, *New Poems*, on his eightieth birthday.

Carl Sandburg

Carl Sandburg (1878–   ), son of Swedish emigrants, was born in Galesburg, Illinois. He left school at thirteen and worked at a variety of odd jobs until he enlisted in the infantry in the Spanish-American War. Afterwards he attended Lombard College, where his writing was encouraged by one of the professors who paid for the publication of Sandburg's first volume of verse. After four years he went to Milwaukee as a news reporter and later became secretary to the mayor. In 1912 he moved to Chicago and there his poems were printed in the new *Poetry: A Magazine of Verse*. His writing over the years has been prolific. He has written many volumes of verse, including poems such as "Chicago" that have become world famous. Long an admirer of Lincoln, Sandburg wrote the magnificent biography, *The Prairie Years*, two volumes, and *The War Years,* four volumes. He has also written several children's books and collected a number of folk tales and folk songs.

Shirley Jackson

Shirley Jackson (1919–1965) was born in California and attended Syracuse University in the East where she met her husband. Mother of four lively children, she has described their hectic and hilarious life in *Life Among the Savages* and *Raising Demons*. In quite another vein are other novels, *The Bird's Nest* and *The Haunting of Hill House*. Of all her writings, "The Lottery" is among the best known. When it first appeared in *The New Yorker*, the reaction was immediate and widespread.

Henry Wadsworth Longfellow

Henry Wadsworth Longfellow (1807–1882), one of the "Cambridge Poets" (with James Russell Lowell and Oliver Wendell Holmes), enjoyed great popularity as a poet during his lifetime. After he was graduated from Bowdoin College, where he had been a classmate of Nathaniel Hawthorne, Longfellow traveled widely in Europe, studying languages and literature. Returning to Bowdoin he became one of America's first professors of modern languages. After a few years at Bowdoin, Longfellow again traveled in Europe and then joined the faculty at Harvard, where he remained for eighteen years, resigning his position then to devote his full attention to writing. His best-loved poems today are those on American themes.

Alan Seeger

Alan Seeger (1888–1916), born and reared in New York, attended Harvard College and, in his senior year, edited the *Harvard Monthly*. Always a nonconformist, Seeger rebelled against the conventions of the time and finally moved to Paris in 1912. He enlisted in the Foreign Legion at the beginning of World War I and was killed in 1916. *Collected Poems,* published in 1916, includes his only famous poem, "I Have a Rendezvous with Death."

Randall Jarrell

Randall Jarrell (1914–1965), poet, critic, and teacher, was born in Nashville and grew up to earn two degrees at Vanderbilt University in Nashville. He went on to teach at Kenyon College and the University of Tennessee. His first book of poetry, *Blood for a Stranger,* was published in 1942. His experiences in the Air Corps were recounted in *Little Friend, Little Friend,* published in 1945. After the war he was briefly the editor of *Nation* and a professor at Sarah Lawrence College. In 1947 he moved to the University of North Carolina and a year later his volume of verse entitled *Losses* was published. While continuing to teach and to write poetry, Jarrell turned to the novel and to literary criticism.

Gwendolyn Brooks

Gwendolyn Brooks (1917–   ), in 1950, became the first Negro woman to win a Pulitzer Prize. She won the award for her second volume of verse, *Annie Allen.* Her first book of poems, *A Street in Bronzeville,* had appeared in 1945. One critic has characterized Miss Brooks' style as an "individual staccato manner—the partial statement, the deliberately broken scansion, the startling, particularized image."

Reginald Rose

Reginald Rose (1921–   ) is one of the most sought-after writers of television scripts in recent years. A camp counselor, public relations worker for a motion picture company, advertising account executive, and copy chief—these were his jobs before he turned to television. "The Bus to Nowhere" was his first television play (1951). In addition to many adaptations, he has written a number of original scripts. Two, *Crime in the Streets* and *Twelve Angry Men,* were made into motion pictures. A collection of his best work appears in *Six Television Plays* (1956).

WALT WHITMAN

1819–1892

From the outset, any reader of Leaves of Grass *must recognize that Whitman's attempts to catalog America stem from a fervent belief in every man's worth no matter how lowly, an equally idealistic belief in the power of love to weld a free society, and the strongly Emersonian doctrine that by studying nature we come to understand both man and God . . . . The blade or leaf of grass is everywhere, like the common man. In it Whitman finds the symbol of growth, continuity, equality, even divine power.*

"Camerado," the poet announces in a voice rich with prophecy, "this is no book,/ Who touches this touches a man." The book is *Leaves of Grass*. The man is Walt Whitman, one of America's most articulate spokesmen. The time is 1860, on the eve of a great conflict. To touch this volume is to become absorbed in it and by it, to know the poet almost more intimately than we know our friends. In the history of American letters, both the book and the man are unique.

Walt Whitman began life so inauspiciously that fame seemed an unlikely prospect, particularly as a poet. The second of nine children, Walt was born on a farm near Huntington, Long Island, but the family moved to Brooklyn, near the ferry slip, before he was three. His father was a morose and luckless carpenter, his mother a self-centered housewife who fretted over her sickly children. When Whitman was ten years old, he quit school to work as office boy for a lawyer, finding the streets of Brooklyn and the spires of Manhattan, across the river, more exciting than life at home or in the classroom. Like many boys of his age, he was attracted to printing and newspaper work, so he learned the trade and by the time he was thirteen he was a full-fledged compositor on the Long Island *Star*. The reading he did not accomplish in school he did as a printer, enough apparently to qualify him as a teacher for three years, between the ages of seventeen and twenty, in the public schools of Norwich and Smithtown.

Tired of teaching, he returned to journalism and typesetting in Huntington, Jamaica, and finally New York City. He tried his hand at writing editorials, then fictional prose and some verse, finally political writing when he offered to electioneer for Martin Van Buren, all unfortunately with middling success. One of his bosses called him "the laziest fellow who ever undertook to edit a city paper." Walt did not deny it. The little taste he had had of writing as a free lance—he published a temperance novel in 1842—made the routine of the city desk a chore. Still he accepted the coveted post of editor of the Brooklyn *Daily Eagle* in 1846, at the age of twenty-seven, and kept it for almost two years before a political argument with the owner led to dismissal. Undismayed, Whitman with his brother Jeff boarded ship for New Orleans to work on the *Crescent*, at the invitation of the founder of the paper. He stayed less than four months. Jeff was homesick and Walt longed for the political activity of New York City. On his return he became editor of the Brooklyn *Freeman* and an ardent Freesoiler, but within the year he had left that post as well.

Surprisingly he returned to his parents' house in Brooklyn and supported himself, as did his father and brothers, by carpentry. His brother George recalled that Walt "wrote a little, worked a little, loafed a little." Part of what he wrote he turned into lectures or sold to newspapers, including his first free-verse poem, a political jibe he called "Blood Money." What was germinating during these years was, of course, *Leaves of Grass*. It was published on July 4, 1855, a slim green volume from the print shop of Andrew and James Rome, where Whitman had set the type himself. No name appeared on the title page, only the author's portrait; and the twelve poems were printed without titles. In the middle of the longest poem, however, the one he called "Song of Myself" in later versions, there was the line: "Walt Whitman, an American, one of the roughs, a kosmos." The poems needed no signature; their maker was literally part of them.

One of the first copies of his new book went immediately to Ralph Waldo Emerson, whose famous essays and lectures were one of his chief inspirations. Emerson not only read it through but wrote at once to say he thought it "the most extraordinary piece of wit and wisdom that America has yet produced." Whitman carried the letter around in his pocket all summer. When he came in 1856 to prepare the second edition, he ill-advisedly stamped in gold letters on the backstrip of the volume the words "I Greet You at the Beginning of a Great Career—R. W. Emerson," printed the text of the whole letter at the end of the book, and followed it with his own reply addressed to the "Master." If Emerson was disturbed by these liberties, Whitman was not. He knew he had written a unique book and he was ready to make America recognize it.

The reviewers of the first edition had not been unkind, though most of them found the language reckless and indecent for poetry, one of them saying "That he was one of the roughs was ... tolerably plain; but that he was a kosmos is a piece of news we were hardly prepared for." Not to be stopped in his grasping for critical approval as well as popularity, Whitman ventured to review, anonymously, his own work. "Very devilish to some, and very divine to some, will appear these new poems, the Leaves of Grass," he wrote in the Brooklyn *Times*; "an attempt as they are, of a live, naive, masculine, tenderly affectionate, rowdyish, contemplative, sensual, moral, susceptible and imperious person, to cast into literature not only his own grit and arrogance, but his own flesh and form."

Between 1855 and 1892, the year of his death, Whitman prepared nine separate editions of

Leaves of Grass. It grew from a ninety-five-page book of twelve poems to a collection of almost four hundred which has been printed many times in this century. Recognition, however, was long in coming. Whitman should have liked to divide his day between literary hackwork and literature, and he tried doing it between 1855 and 1860. He was even persuaded to edit the Brooklyn *Daily Times* for two years while preparing a third edition of his book. It was during these days that he frequented Pfaff's bar and restaurant on Broadway just above Bleeker Street, dressed in his familiar broad-brimmed hat and working-men's clothes, bright red or blue, exuding robustness among the writers and publishers and would-be Bohemians of the city.

When his brother George was reported wounded in 1862, Walt left for the war front in Virginia to find him. He discovered his brother was recovering but that hundreds of other soldiers were in need of attention in the Army hospitals. Taking part-time work in the paymaster's office, he settled in Washington as a volunteer nurse, writing letters for the men, bringing them medicines, reading to them, listening to their stories, and when necessary burying the dead. Early in 1865 he accepted a clerkship in the Indian Bureau in the Department of the Interior, but he was dismissed within six months, according to his own report, because his superior found a copy of *Leaves of Grass* in Whitman's desk, read it, and declared it an "indecent book." His friends interceded for him, finding him another job at once in the Attorney General's office which he kept until 1874 when continued ill-health following a paralytic stroke forced him to join his brother George in Camden, New Jersey.

Whitman was prepared for disapproval from critics who charged him with crudities because they could not get used to his long line and from the general reader who was offended by his "unpoetic" language, his frankness, his symbolic structure. No writer is content to wait for a posthumous reputation, but Whitman was more resigned than most poets to being sixty

Walt Whitman's birthplace, West Hills, L. I.

years ahead of his time. Surprisingly, the Victorian poets—Tennyson and Swinburne and the Rossettis—were quick to realize his worth and send him encouragement long before his countrymen knew what new ground he was tilling.

Whitman spent the last two decades of his life in New Jersey with relatives or friends, lecturing occasionally, giving public readings, on one occasion traveling as far west as Nevada. The 1881 edition of *Leaves of Grass,* in which he gave most of his poems their final revision and their permanent titles, brought him enough income to buy a small house in Camden, but he was never far from the brink of poverty. He published a collection of prose essays in 1882 as *Specimen Days and Collect.* Ten years later he readied *Complete Prose Works* for the printer as well as the ninth and last edition of *Leaves of Grass*, signing it on his deathbed. The house on Mickle Street in Camden became a shrine shortly after Whitman's death, but one wonders if Walt would not have preferred the honor being paid to his one great book.

"Remember the book arose," he had written to Richard Bucke, his friend and biographer, "out of my life in Brooklyn and New York . . . absorbing a million people with an intimacy, an eagerness, an abandon probably never equalled." His book began there, it is true, and if Whitman exaggerates his absorptive powers we can overlook the fact for the spirit. But *Leaves of Grass* grew into the unique volume it is because of various influences. Emerson's example of irregular, frequently unrhymed verse was primary, as well as his faith in the democratic process as universal law and his calling for a poet who could embody America in all its variety. "I was simmering, simmering, simmering," Whitman admitted; "Emerson brought me to a boil." From the outset, any reader of *Leaves of Grass* must recognize that Whitman's attempts to catalog America stem from a fervent belief in every man's worth no matter how lowly, an equally idealistic belief in the power of love to weld a free society, and the strongly Emersonian doctrine that by studying nature we come to understand both man and God. Whitman begins his longest poem:

I celebrate myself, and sing myself,
And what I assume you shall assume,
For every atom belonging to me as good belongs
  to you.

I loafe and invite my soul,
I lean and loafe at ease observing a spear of summer grass.

The blade or leaf of grass is everywhere, like the common man. In it Whitman finds the symbol of growth, continuity, equality, even divine power, and expresses it succinctly:

Or I guess it is a uniform hieroglyphic,
And it means, Sprouting alike in broad zones and
  narrow zones,
Growing among black folks as among white,
Kanuck, Tuckahoe, Congressman, Cuff; I give
  them the same, I receive them the same.

The lines could never have been Emerson's, but the essence is his philosophy.

But philosophy is not Whitman's strength. If he appeals to the popular mind, and that was his aim, he does it concretely, forcefully, dramatically. His free verse was a distinct break from the tidy meters of his predecessors, that "copious dribble" of conventional sentimentalists, as he called them. He felt that Nature looked on all "fixed-up poetry and art as something almost impertinent," and he wished above all to be natural. John Greenleaf Whittier is said to have thrown his copy of *Leaves of Grass* into the fire. Little did he know that by the mere publication of that volume, Whitman had begun the destruction of the genteel tradition of poetry, the work of Longfellow and Whittier and the lesser talents who followed them. His revolution in language and meter came from his love for opera, oratory, and the ocean just as much as his devotion to Emerson's essays. The free translations of Italian librettos taught him what aria and recitative could do for poetry in which line length is not rigidly controlled. The openness of oratorical style, its use of exhortation to lift the audience to action or thought brought new vigor to his lines and broke down the distinction between prose and poetry. His adolescence on the shores of Long Island, on Whitman's own admission, played a large part in bringing the ebb and flow of the sea into his poetic rhythms.

Add to these influences his knowledge of the King James version of the Bible, his remarkable ear for retaining the slang of the street, a sharp memory for color and detail, his eager desire to merge all of life—the spiritual, the physical, the sexual—into one great poem, and it is no surprise that American readers took some years to adjust to his work. His contemporaries read his "I" as wholly personal when he frequently meant it symbolically, as "poet" or "spokesman" or "maker" for the spirit of the people. They damned his language so long that he was led to admit.

The spotted hawk swoops by and accuses me, he
  complains of my gab and my loitering.

I too am not a bit tamed, I too am untranslatable,
I sound my barbaric yawp over the roofs of the
  world.

But they could not kill his book. His unshaken faith in love as the key to man's survival, to the success of democracy, to our knowledge of God gave him the strength to pursue his own light. Now we look on *Leaves of Grass* as germinal to the best of modern poetry.

The following two poems are a kind of signature written by the poet for his book *Leaves of Grass*. In them he announces his poetic intentions and his relationship to the artists of the future in language unmistakably his own.

One's-Self I Sing

One's-self I sing, a simple separate person,
Yet utter the word Democratic, the word En-Masse.

Of physiology from top to toe I sing,
Not physiognomy[1] alone nor brain alone is worthy for the Muse.[2]
I say the Form complete is worthier far,
The Female equally with the Male I sing.

Of Life immense in passion, pulse, and power,
Cheerful, for freest action form'd under the laws divine,
The Modern Man I sing.

---

1. **physiognomy**\'fĭ·zē ▲ŏg·nə•mē\ features that reveal character.
2. **Muse,** spirit that inspires poets.

Poets to Come

Poets to come! orators, singers, musicians to come!
Not to-day is to justify me and answer what I am for,
But you, a new brood, native, athletic, continental, greater than before
　　　　　known,
Arouse! for you must justify me.　　　　　　　　　　　　　　　5

I myself but write one or two indicative words for the future,
I but advance a moment only to wheel and hurry back in the darkness.

I am a man who, sauntering along without fully stopping, turns a
　　　　　casual look upon you and then averts his face,
Leaving it to you to prove and define it,　　　　　　　　　　10
Expecting the main things from you.

IMPLICATIONS

One's-Self I Sing

1. Whitman announces in his opening lines that he shall sing of one man and of all men simultaneously. How would you explain this apparent contradiction?

2. List and discuss the other themes about which Whitman promises to sing.

Poets to Come

1. Note that Whitman groups poets with orators, singers, musicians; and he addresses here the *next* generation or "brood," as he calls them. If the poets to come are "native, athletic, and continental," how will they "justify" Whitman?

2. How do you interpret "the main things" in the last stanza?

Whitman printed this poem without a title
in the first edition of *Leaves of Grass,* but the next year
he called it "Poem of the Child That Went Forth, and Always Goes Forth
Forever and Forever." In the following decades he rewrote it many times
before settling on this final (1881) version. As it now stands, the poem is
a celebration of life in mid-nineteenth-century America, originally seen
through the eyes of a young child and now recollected by the mature poet.
Whitman may have had his own childhood in mind in this poem,
but you will limit your pleasure if you read it biographically.
"Third-month" is the Quaker way of designating March.

There Was a Child
Went Forth

There was a child went forth every day,
And the first object he look'd upon, that object he became,
And that object became part of him for the day or a certain part of the day,
Or for many years or stretching cycles of years.

The early lilacs became part of this child,   5
And grass and white and red morning-glories, and white and red clover, and
        the song of the phœbe-bird,[1]
And the Third-month lambs and the sow's pink-faint litter, and the mare's foal
        and the cow's calf,
And the noisy brood of the barnyard or by the mire of the pond-side,
And the fish suspending themselves so curiously below there, and the beautiful
        curious liquid,
And the water-plants with their graceful flat heads, all became part of him. 10

The field-sprouts of Fourth-month and Fifth-month became part of him,
Winter-grain sprouts and those of the light-yellow corn, and the esculent[2] roots
        of the garden,
And the apple-trees cover'd with blossoms and the fruit afterward, and wood-
        berries, and the commonest weeds by the road,
And the old drunkard staggering home from the outhouse of the tavern whence
        he had lately risen,
And the schoolmistress that pass'd on her way to the school,   15
And the friendly boys that pass'd, and the quarrelsome boys,
And the tidy and fresh-cheek'd girls, and the barefoot negro boy and girl,
And all the changes of city and country wherever he went.

---

1. **phoebe**\ˈfē·bē\ **bird,** an American flycatcher.
2. **esculent**\ˈĕs·kyə·lənt\ edible.

His own parents, he that had father'd him and she that had conceiv'd him in her
        womb and birth'd him,
They gave this child more of themselves than that,   20
They gave him afterward every day, they became part of him.

The mother at home quietly placing the dishes on the supper-table,
The mother with mild words, clean her cap and gown, a wholesome odor falling
        off her person and clothes as she walks by,
The father, strong, self-sufficient, manly, mean, anger'd, unjust,
The blow, the quick loud word, the tight bargain, the crafty lure,   25
The family usages, the language, the company, the furniture, the yearning and
        swelling heart,
Affection that will not be gainsay'd, the sense of what is real, the thought if
        after all it should prove unreal,
The doubts of day-time and the doubts of night-time, the curious whether and
        how,
Whether that which appears so is so, or is it all flashes and specks?
Men and women crowding fast in the streets, if they are not flashes and specks
        what are they?   30
The streets themselves and the façades[3] of houses, and goods in the windows,
Vehicles, teams, the heavy-plank'd wharves, the huge crossing at the ferries,
The village on the highland seen from afar at sunset, the river between,
Shadows, aureola[4] and mist, the light falling on roofs and gables[5] of white or
        brown two miles off,
The schooner near by sleepily dropping down the tide, the little boat slack-tow'd
        astern,   35
The hurrying tumbling waves, quick-broken crests, slapping,
The strata of color'd clouds, the long bar of maroon-tint away solitary by itself,
        the spread of purity it lies motionless in,
The horizon's edge, the flying sea-crow, the fragrance of salt marsh and shore
        mud,
These became part of that child who went forth every day, and who now goes,
        and will always go forth every day.

---

3. **façades**\fə ˈsadz\ fronts of buildings.
4. **aureola**\ɔ ˈrē·ə·lə\ radiance or halo.
5. **gables,** sections of walls extending upward from level of the eaves of a sloped roof.

IMPLICATIONS

1. Whitman's long, open line is designed for the kind of catalog he gives us here. The child looks about and what he sees we see. What does the poet mean when he says all these sights "became part of this child"?

2. The third stanza has many elements that apparently, to say the least, have little in common:
winter-grain sprouts, old drunkards, and quarrelsome boys. Why should Whitman try to combine them?

3. How does the poet move naturally from "men and women crowding fast in the streets" to "the horizon's edge"?

4. What meaning has "go forth" taken on by the time you reach the end of the poem?

In the following poem Whitman proclaims the power and urgency of the giant steam engines that were beginning to change the face of America. A picture of the locomotive in the 1870's (the poem was written in 1876) will explain such a phrase as "thy great protruding head-light."

To a Locomotive in Winter

Thee for my recitative,[1]
Thee in the driving storm even as now, the snow, the winter-day declining,
Thee in thy panoply,[2] thy measur'd dual throbbing and thy beat convulsive,
Thy black cylindric body, golden brass and silvery steel,
Thy ponderous side-bars, parallel and connecting rods, gyrating,[3] shuttling at
                     thy sides,   5
Thy metrical, now swelling pant and roar, now tapering in the distance,
Thy great protruding head-light fix'd in front,
Thy long, pale, floating vapor-pennants, tinged with delicate purple,
The dense and murky clouds out-belching from thy smoke-stack,
Thy knitted frame, thy springs and valves, the tremulous twinkle of thy wheels, 10
Thy train of cars behind, obedient, merrily following,
Through gale or calm, now swift, now slack, yet steadily careering;
Type of the modern—emblem of motion and power—pulse of the continent,
For once come serve the Muse and merge in verse, even as here I see thee,
With storm and buffeting gusts of wind and falling snow,   15
By day thy warning ringing bell to sound its notes,
By night thy silent signal lamps to swing.

Fierce-throated beauty!
Roll through my chant with all thy lawless music, thy swinging lamps at night,
Thy madly-whistled laughter, echoing, rumbling like an earthquake, rousing all, 20
Law of thyself complete, thine own track firmly holding,
(No sweetness debonair of tearful harp or glib piano thine,)
Thy trills of shrieks by rocks and hills return'd,
Launch'd o'er the prairies wide, across the lakes,
To the free skies unpent and glad and strong.   25

---

1. **recitative**\'rĕ·sə·tə ˄tēv\ recital of details, a narrative; term borrowed from opera, where it denotes a narrative text sung in a nonmetric style—in speech rhythms.
2. **panoply**\˄pă·nə·plē\ complete covering for protection.
3. **gyrating**\ji·rāt·iŋ\ turning in a spiral motion.

IMPLICATIONS

1. What words make this poem vibrate with as much life as the steam engine contains?

2. Why is a locomotive "type of the modern"? What did it symbolize in the 1870's?

3. "Roll through my chant with all thy lawless music" suggests identification of Whitman's poetic ideas with the locomotive itself. Could there be other reasons than mere admiration that led Whitman to choose the locomotive as his subject?

These two brief poems are among Whitman's most popular.
They make their points directly and memorably. Written during the Civil War,
they share a religious feeling, a striving of the individual man
for understanding and love. Man's soul, in the vast oceans of space
around it, must seek anchorage somewhere. In the first poem,
Whitman seeks the answer in the "mystical moist night-air"; in the second,
he hopes to learn from the patient spider. Both poems must be read
for what they suggest as well as what they describe.

When I Heard the Learn'd Astronomer

When I heard the learn'd astronomer,
When the proofs, the figures, were ranged in columns before me,
When I was shown the charts and diagrams, to add, divide, and measure them,
When I sitting heard the astronomer where he lectured with much applause in
        the lecture-room,
How soon unaccountable I became tired and sick,
Till rising and gliding out I wander'd off by myself,
In the mystical moist night-air, and from time to time,
Look'd up in perfect silence at the stars.

A Noiseless Patient Spider

A noiseless patient spider,
I mark'd where on a little promontory[1] it stood isolated,
Mark'd how to explore the vacant vast surrounding,
It launch'd forth filament, filament, filament, out of itself,
Ever unreeling them, ever tirelessly speeding them.   5

And you O my soul where you stand,
Surrounded, detached, in measureless oceans of space,
Ceaselessly musing, venturing, throwing, seeking the spheres to connect them,
Till the bridge you will need be form'd, till the ductile[2] anchor hold,
Till the gossamer[3] thread you fling catch somewhere, O my soul.   10

---

1. **promontory**\ˈprŏ•mən ˈtō•rē\ high point of land projecting outward, usually into the sea.
2. **ductile**\ˈdək•təl\ capable of being drawn out or molded.
3. **gossamer**\ˈgŏ•sə•mər\ fine strands of spider's silk that float in the air or are loosely suspended from something.

IMPLICATIONS

When I Heard the Learn'd Astronomer

1. Whitman looks in two directions in this poem and chooses one as the shorter road to an understanding of God and nature. How would you identify these two outlooks?

2. What is the cumulative effect of words like "proofs," "figures," "charts," "diagrams"?

3. What connection is there between "applause" in line 4 and "accountable" in line 5?

4. Why is the night air "mystical" and what is implied in this word? How is the implication reinforced in the "perfect silence" of the last line?

A Noiseless Patient Spider

1. As in "When I Heard the Learn'd Astronomer," Whitman divides this brief poem between two subjects, only here it is a comparison between the spider and the poet's soul, dissimilar though they may seem at first. What are the attributes he admires in the spider?

2. Does the repetition of the word "filament" help to underscore these attributes? Note that the filament comes "out of itself," meaning out of the spider's body. Why is this important in the next stanza?

3. The soul in vast oceans of space is a familiar poetic way of speaking of the spirit of man "surrounded" by the body yet "living" in another element. How do the verbs "musing, venturing, throwing" connect the soul and the spider?

4. What sort of thread is a "gossamer" thread? Does the poet succeed in applying it to both the spider and the soul?

In the spring of 1865, Whitman published privately
a small collection of war poems which he called *Drum Taps*.
In the following autumn he added to it a group he called
Sequel to Drum Taps, including four poems dedicated to the memory
of Abraham Lincoln. Both collections were incorporated into *Leaves of Grass*
in 1871. In the two poems that follow, Whitman shows himself to
be an acute observer and communicator of the
fleeting glamor and the deep misery of war.

Cavalry Crossing a Ford

A line in long array where they wind betwixt green islands,
They take a serpentine course, their arms flash in the sun—hark to the musical
      clank,
Behold the silvery river, in it the splashing horses loitering stop to drink,
Behold the brown-faced men, each group, each person a picture, the negligent
      rest on the saddles,
Some merge on the opposite bank, others are just entering the ford—while,
Scarlet and blue and snowy white,
The guidon flags flutter gayly in the wind.

A March
in the Ranks Hard-Prest,
and the Road Unknown

A march in the ranks hard-prest, and the road unknown,
A route through a heavy wood with muffled steps in the darkness,
Our army foil'd with loss severe, and the sullen remnant retreating,
Till after midnight glimmer upon us the lights of a dim-lighted building,
We come to an open space in the woods, and halt by the dim-lighted building,   5
'Tis a large old church at the crossing roads, now an impromptu hospital,
Entering but for a minute I see a sight beyond all the pictures and poems ever
      made,
Shadows of deepest, deepest black, just lit by moving candles and lamps,
And by one great pitchy torch stationary with wild red flame and clouds of
      smoke,
By these, crowds, groups of forms vaguely I see on the floor, some in the pews
      laid down,   10
At my feet more distinctly a soldier, a mere lad, in danger of bleeding to death,
      (he is shot in the abdomen,)

I stanch the blood temporarily, (the youngster's face is white as a lily,)
Then before I depart I sweep my eyes o'er the scene fain to absorb it all,
Faces, varieties, postures beyond description, most in obscurity, some of them
        dead,
Surgeons operating, attendants holding lights, the smell of ether, the odor of
        blood,   15
The crowd, O the crowd of the bloody forms, the yard outside also fill'd,
Some on the bare ground, some on planks or stretchers, some in the death-spasm
        sweating,
An occasional scream or cry, the doctor's shouted orders or calls,
The glisten of the little steel instruments catching the glint of the torches,
These I resume as I chant, I see again the forms, I smell the odor,   20
Then hear outside the orders given, *Fall in, my men, fall in;*
But first I bend to the dying lad, his eyes open, a half-smile gives he me,
Then the eyes close, calmly close, and I speed forth to the darkness,
Resuming, marching, ever in darkness marching, on in the ranks,
The unknown road still marching.   25

IMPLICATIONS

"Cavalry Crossing a Ford"

1. Whitman piles up vivid sense impressions. To which senses does he appeal in this poem? Which sense seems to be the dominant one?

2. What is the dominant impression Whitman gives the scene? Is it weariness, boredom, gaiety, or peacefulness? Explain your answer.

3. Compare this scene with the one in "A March in the Ranks Hard-Prest."

"A March in the Ranks Hard-Prest"

1. The visual setting, across which the poet's eyes travel with anguish, is the heart of this poem. What specific details does Whitman use to build up this sense of anguish?

2. To the visual effects, Whitman adds details which affect our other senses. Beginning with "muffled steps," move through the poem and list other sensory impressions. Do they complement the visual images?

3. Whitman might easily have added dialogue to this poem. How would it have affected the mood?

4. The poem begins with "a march in the ranks" and ends with "still marching." We might call this format an "envelope" design, in which the "flap" is brought down to "seal" the poem. Why do you think Whitman uses this device?

Originally called "Sun-Down Poem," this poem
is one of Whitman's most successful attempts to blend past,
present, and future. The basic symbol of the ferry works so well
because it literally ties one shore to another and figuratively joins
one generation to the next. The poem begins on the factual level;
Whitman always enjoyed the East River journey from Manhattan to Brooklyn.
But he soon projects his thoughts into the future, identifies himself
(in his own mind) with all future travelers, and thus makes the poem itself
into a ferry, shuttling across the river of time. When he speaks
of the water as the "float forever held in solution" (Section 5),
he means the flow of life as well as of the East River.

Crossing Brooklyn Ferry

1

Flood-tide below me! I see you face to face!
Clouds of the west—sun there half an hour high—I see you also face to face.

Crowds of men and women attired in the usual costumes, how curious you are
               to me!
On the ferry-boats the hundreds and hundreds that cross, returning home, are
               more curious to me than you suppose,
And you that shall cross from shore to shore years hence are more to me, and
               more in my meditations, than you might suppose.   5

2

The impalpable sustenance[1] of me from all things at all hours of the day,
The simple, compact, well-join'd scheme, myself disintegrated, every one
               disintegrated yet part of the scheme,
The similitudes of the past and those of the future,
The glories strung like beads on my smallest sights and hearings, on the walk
               in the street and the passage over the river,
The current rushing so swiftly and swimming with me far away,   10
The others that are to follow me, the ties between me and them,
The certainty of others, the life, love, sight, hearing of others.

Others will enter the gates of the ferry and cross from shore to shore,
Others will watch the run of the flood-tide,
Others will see the shipping of Manhattan north and west, and the heights of
               Brooklyn to the south and east,   15
Others will see the islands large and small;
Fifty years hence, others will see them as they cross, the sun half an hour high,

---

1. **impalpable sustenance,** something not perceived by sense of touch.

A hundred years hence, or ever so many hundred years hence, others will see them,

Will enjoy the sunset, the pouring-in of the flood-tide, the falling-back to the sea of the ebb-tide.

3

It avails not, time nor place—distance avails not,   20

I am with you, you men and women of a generation, or ever so many, generations hence,

Just as you feel when you look on the river and sky, so I felt,

Just as any of you is one of a living crowd, I was one of a crowd,

Just as you are refresh'd by the gladness of the river and the bright flow, I was refresh'd,

Just as you stand and lean on the rail, yet hurry with the swift current, I stood yet was hurried,   25

Just as you look on the numberless masts of ships and the thick-stemm'd pipes of steamboats, I look'd.

I too many and many a time cross'd the river of old,

Watched the Twelfth-month[2] sea-gulls, saw them high in the air floating with motionless wings, oscillating their bodies,

Saw how the glistening yellow lit up parts of their bodies and left the rest in strong shadow,

Saw the slow-wheeling circles and the gradual edging toward the south,   30

Saw the reflection of the summer sky in the water,

Had my eyes dazzled by the shimmering track of beams,

Look'd at the fine centrifugal spokes of light round the shape of my head in the sunlit water,

Look'd on the haze on the hills southward and south-westward,

Look'd on the vapor as it flew in fleeces tinged with violet,   35

Look'd toward the lower bay to notice the vessels arriving,

Saw their approach, saw aboard those that were near me,

Saw the white sails of schooners and sloops, saw the ships at anchor,

The sailors at work in the rigging or out astride the spars,

The round masts, the swinging motion of the hulls, the slender serpentine pennants,   40

The large and small steamers in motion, the pilots in their pilot-houses,

The white wake left by the passage, the quick tremulous whirl of the wheels,

The flags of all nations, the falling of them at sunset,

The scallop-edged waves in the twilight, the ladled cups, the frolicsome crests and glistening,

The stretch afar growing dimmer and dimmer, the gray walls of the granite storehouses by the docks,   45

———

2. **Twelfth-month**, after 1860 Whitman used the Quaker names for the months.

On the river the shadowy group, the big steam-tug closely flank'd on each side
      by the barges, the hay-boat, the belated lighter,[3]
On the neighboring shore the fires from the foundry chimneys burning high and
      glaringly into the night,
Casting their flicker of black contrasted with wild red and yellow light over the
      tops of houses, and down into the clefts of streets.

4

These and all else were to me the same as they are to you,
I loved well those cities, loved well the stately and rapid river,   50
The men and women I saw were all near to me,
Others the same—others who look back on me because I look'd forward to
      them,
(The time will come, though I stop here to-day and to-night.)

5

What is it then between us?
What is the count of the scores or hundreds of years between us?   55

Whatever it is, it avails not—distance avails not, and place avails not,
I too lived, Brooklyn of ample hills was mine,
I too walk'd the streets of Manhattan island, and bathed in the waters around it,
I too felt the curious abrupt questionings stir within me.
In the day among crowds of people sometimes they came upon me,   60
In my walks home late at night or as I lay in my bed they came upon me,
I too had been struck from the float forever held in solution,
I too had receiv'd identity by my body,
That I was I knew was of my body, and what I should be I knew I should be
      of my body.

6

It is not upon you alone the dark patches fall,   65
The dark threw its patches down upon me also,
The best I had done seem'd to me blank and suspicious,
My great thoughts as I supposed them, were they not in reality meagre?
Nor is it you alone who know what it is to be evil,
I am he who knew what it was to be evil.   70
I too knitted the old knot of contrariety,[4]
Blabb'd, blush'd, resented, lied, stole, grudg'd,
Had guile, anger, lust, hot wishes I dared not speak,

---

3. **lighter,** barge.
4. **knot of contrariety,** used in logic to refer to a statement so closely related to another that
though both may be false both cannot be true.

Was wayward, vain, greedy, shallow, sly, cowardly, malignant,
The wolf, the snake, the hog, not wanting in me, 75
The cheating look, the frivolous word, the adulterous wish, not wanting,
Refusals, hates, postponements, meanness, laziness, none of these wanting,
Was one with the rest, the days and haps of the rest,
Was call'd by my nighest name by clear loud voices of young men as they saw
        me approaching or passing,
Felt their arms on my neck as I stood, or the negligent leaning of their flesh
        against me as I sat, 80
Saw many I loved in the street or ferry-boat or public assembly, yet never told
        them a word,
Lived the same life with the rest, the same old laughing, gnawing, sleeping,
Play'd the part that still looks back on the actor or actress,
The same old role, the role that is what we make it, as great as we like,
Or as small as we like, or both great and small. 85

7

Closer yet I approach you,
What thought you have of me now, I had as much of you—I laid in my stores
        in advance,
I consider'd long and seriously of you before you were born.

Who was to know what should come home to me?
Who knows but I am enjoying this? 90
Who knows, for all the distance, but I am as good as looking at you now, for all
        you cannot see me?

8

Ah, what can ever be more stately and admirable to me than mast-hemm'd
        Manhattan?
River and sunset and scallop-edg'd waves of flood-tide?
The sea-gulls oscillating their bodies, the hay-boat in the twilight, and the
        belated lighter?
What gods can exceed these that clasp me by the hand, and with voices I love
        call me promptly and loudly by my nighest name as I
        approach? 95

What is more subtle than this which ties me to the woman or man that looks in
        my face?
Which fuses me into you now, and pours my meaning into you?

We understand then do we not?
What I promis'd without mentioning it, have you not accepted?

What the study could not teach—what the preaching could not accomplish is
        accomplish'd, is it not?   100

9

Flow on, river! flow with the flood-tide, and ebb with the ebb-tide!
Frolic on, crested and scallop-edg'd waves!
Gorgeous clouds of the sunset! drench with your splendor me, or the men and
        women generations after me!
Cross from shore to shore, countless crowds of passengers!
Stand up, tall masts of Mannahatta! stand up, beautiful hills of Brooklyn!   105
Throb, baffled and curious brain! throw out questions and answers!
Suspend here and everywhere, eternal float of solution!
Gaze, loving and thirsting eyes, in the house or street or public assembly!
Sound out, voices of young men! loudly and musically call me by my nighest
        name!
Live, old life! play the part that looks back on the actor or actress!   110
Play the old role, the role that is great or small according as one makes it!
Consider, you who peruse me, whether I may not in unknown ways be looking
        upon you;
Be firm, rail over the river, to support those who lean idly, yet haste with the
        hasting current;
Fly on, sea-birds! fly sideways, or wheel in large circles high in the air;
Receive the summer sky, you water, and faithfully hold it till all downcast eyes
        have time to take it from you!   115
Diverge, fine spokes of light, from the shape of my head, or any one's head, in
        the sunlit water!
Come on, ships from the lower bay! pass up or down, white-sail'd schooners,
        sloops, lighters!
Flaunt away, flags of all nations; be duly lower'd at sunset!
Burn high your fires, foundry chimneys! cast black shadows at nightfall! cast
        red and yellow light over the tops of the houses!
Appearances, now or henceforth, indicate what you are,   120
You necessary film, continue to envelop the soul,
About my body for me, and your body for you, be hung our divinest aromas,
Thrive, cities—bring your freight, bring your shows, ample and sufficient rivers,
Expand, being than which none else is perhaps more spiritual,
Keep your places, objects than which none else is more lasting.   125

You have waited, you always wait, you dumb, beautiful ministers,
We receive you with free sense at last, and are insatiate henceforward,
Not you any more shall be able to foil us, or withhold yourselves from us,
We use you, and do not cast you aside—we plant you permanently within us,
We fathom you not—we love you—there is perfection in you also,   130
You furnish your parts toward eternity,
Great or small, you furnish your parts toward the soul.

1. From the very beginning of this poem, Whitman speaks not only of the present but of the future, especially in lines 5, 8, and 11. But the phrase "impalpable sustenance of me" (line 6) is also vital to this idea. What do these words mean?

2. Does the repetition of the words "just as" in Section 3 help to reinforce the connection Whitman sees between the present and future generations? Or in other words, does the verse form assist in establishing the main idea of the poem?

3. In the opening of Section 5, Whitman asks: "What is it then between us?" Why should he say here "distance avails not, and place avails not"?

4. Through ordinary human failings and vices, Whitman wishes to seek attachment, figuratively, to the next generation. What are some of these vices he has in common with us?

5. In Section 8, the poet asks "We understand then do we not?" Can you answer him? What did he "promise"? How have we "accepted"?

6. A vital line of this poem, after the long catalog of Section 9, is: "You have waited, you always wait, you dumb, beautiful ministers." Obviously, Whitman does not mean preachers or clerics. How is he using "ministers" here and what meanings do you give to the word?

7. Now reread the poem for its visual beauties. Do you think Whitman is only photographing the Brooklyn ferry?

TECHNIQUES

Free Verse

When we speak of the rhythm of a line of poetry or prose, we mean the natural rise and fall of language in wavelike motion. By meter we mean carefully arranged rhythm, with the accents spaced in patterned intervals of time. Poe, Longfellow, Lowell used meter to limit their lines and stanzas. "I lift mine eyes and all the windows blaze" is a strictly ordered five-beat line; Longfellow follows it with thirteen other five-beat lines to form a sonnet. His rhyme scheme is equally patterned, thus adding a further limit to the shape of the poem.

Whitman wished to forsake meter and rhyme. He writes what we now call free verse; though many poets feel free verse is not verse at all, since its only distinction from rhythmical prose is the arrangement into lines, each one usually capitalized. Whitman, however, liked the liberation of free verse. It gave him more scope, more expansiveness, and he never worried about metrical count. That is not to say he writes in paragraphs or rejects any controls that would give his stanzas unity.

You may find Whitman's verse more difficult to analyze than Longfellow's sonnets, but look closely at his poems to see if he does not use some of these devices to give his work controlling form:

a. End-stopped lines. The end of the line corresponds with the natural pause in speech. Invariably the line ends with a mark of punctuation.

b. Parallel constructions. Whole phrases or a single word are repeated at the beginning of each line. Occasionally Whitman merely repeats a grammatical form in parallel: noun-verb, or noun-verb-object.

c. Single sentence stanzas.

d. Repetition. Whitman is especially fond of the participial form of the verb. The locomotive, for example, is "declining," "throbbing," "gyrating," and so on.

e. Recurring symbols.

f. Alliteration (repetition of initial consonants) and assonance (repetition of vowel sounds).

Theme

Nine poems are only a small sampling of *Leaves of Grass,* but these nine serve well to illustrate Whitman's main themes and various facets of his art. To this list, a mere beginning, add your own reactions to reading Whitman, the ideas you take away from his poems. Are you willing to accept these six?

1. America is crowds at the same time it is single individuals. The poet must see and know both.

2. Poetry is timely but it is also eternal, for all time.

3. We are what we observe; we become what we partake of.

4. The poet must write for the Modern Man.

5. Clock time and eternal time are not the same thing, yet the poet can live in both.

6. The mystical attitude adds as much to poetry as the observant eye.

STEPHEN CRANE

1871–1900

Edgar Allan Poe and Stephen Crane had much in common. Both men were erratic writers: they experimented in prose and poetry with new styles and subjects; they attempted to live by their writing and frequently knew poverty because of it; they died young, having in a sense burned themselves out. What is more, the lives of both men started sentimental legends of wasted talent. It is an image too many readers enjoy perpetuating, even though the facts of honest biographies have exposed these myths. What we know now of Poe's personal life, his fragile health, his enormous powers of concentration even on hackwork helps to correct the popular belief that he wrote only under the influence of dope or alcohol. Crane's biography explains even more clearly what forces shaped his literary work, where he found his subjects, and how he developed his style.

Crane was a writer of such remarkable natural talent that he sprang at once into literary prominence. Before he was twenty-three, he had written two novels of major importance in the development of American fiction, yet his

To the day of his death, Crane had not forsaken the creed he lived by: "You can never do anything good aesthetically . . . unless it has at one time meant something important to you." That is not to say that Crane believed an artist must experience every event he describes realistically. Much of his best work was imagined. He was, however, talking of his own formula for fiction: taking a germ of an experience and then letting it grow in the mind, writing from the truth of the experience but always expressing that truth with acute feelings, acutely expressed.

adolescence was much like that of other young men of his day. He was born in 1871 in Newark, New Jersey, but the family finally settled in Port Jervis, New York. It was a large family and the father, a Methodist minister, died when Crane was nine years old. Stephen, the youngest, had more schooling than the rest of the fourteen children but even that was limited. Two years at a military academy in Claverack, New York, preceded a fall term at Lafayette College, a spring term at Syracuse University. He cared little for reading and preferred baseball to the lecture room, so after one year of college he was eager to leave for the active life of the world. Since both parents were writers and two of his brothers newspaper reporters, he, too, wanted to get on with his writing, as a free-lance reporter for various newspapers in New York City and, when time allowed, as a novelist.

Crane came to know New York through its slums and street life, particularly in the Bowery. He thought that "one could train one's mind to observe and a man should be able to say something worthwhile about any event." His first Bowery tales were just that: honest recording of brutal poverty. When he came to write *Maggie: A Girl of the Streets* (1893), he went even further, for this short novel records slum life with the realistic accuracy of a camera. Although *Maggie* is an immature work in conception and execution, it marks a significant step in the development of American fiction. It is a plain story of Maggie Johnson and her brother Jimmie in Rum Alley, a tenement district of New York City. The young girl is driven out of her home by a drunken mother; she falls in love with a bartender named Pete, a friend of Jimmie, who leaves her to make a living as best she can. Eventually she ends her short life by drowning herself, the helpless victim of her sordid surroundings. Crane tells her story without softening its harshness and without judging his characters. The dialogue reflects as closely as possible this world of unrelieved depression. "It is inevitable that you will be greatly shocked by the book," Crane wrote his

friend Hamlin Garland, "but continue please with all possible courage to the end. For it tries to show that environment is a tremendous thing in the world and frequently shapes lives regardless."

The word "environment" is the key to Crane's attitude. *Maggie* could easily have been reduced to a pious moral: "Poverty is the source of sin," but that was scarcely why Crane wanted to tell the story. Pete and Jimmie and the drunken mother are to blame for Maggie's death, but the real villain is the Bowery. Crane had learned from Garland that honest realism is the only right method for fiction, and the closer a novelist approaches the method of science—observation, analysis, careful judgment —the more faithful, so they believed, he is to life. What his observations of tenement life had shown to Crane depressed him utterly, and he wanted his readers to "feel" the weight of this environment in his story of a helpless girl. *Maggie* remained generally unread, however, until his second novel, *The Red Badge of Courage* (1895), made him an overnight success.

The American Civil War had long interested Crane. Obviously unable to observe his material at first hand, he immersed himself in Mathew Brady's remarkable photographs, in such books as *Battles and Leaders of the Civil War* and Colonel Wilbur F. Hinman's *Corporal Si Klegg and His "Pards,"* and in the war reminiscences of his brother William. Just three months after *Maggie* had been printed, he wrote a first draft of *The Red Badge of Courage*. He told a friend that "I have spent ten nights writing a story of the war on my own responsibility but I am not sure my facts are real and the books won't tell me what I want to know so I must do it all over again, I guess." A second draft followed several months later, and he continued to polish it for over a year before selling it to the Philadelphia *Press* for serializing. Just before his twenty-fourth birthday, in 1895, D. Appleton and Company published *The Red Badge* as a book.

His reputation was made. Though it was a war novel by a man who had never been to war, it was praised in England as well as in America for its unvarnished realism, its unheroic hero, and its smell of gunpowder. Crane had dared to be truthful. He had wiped away the glamor of combat and replaced it with a simple story of one confused soldier, trying to be brave but frightened to near hysteria during his baptism of fire. The battle is Chancellorsville; the soldier is Henry Fleming. But names and places are less important than the details of the action. As realist, Crane was adding another dimension to his fiction.

We call it impressionism. Joseph Conrad, the English novelist, was to define it several years after *The Red Badge* had appeared: "By the power of the written word, to make you hear, to make you feel—it is, before all, to make you *see*." Crane had tried to make us see the Bowery through Maggie's weary eyes. His readers were not ready for the truth. Or perhaps Crane was not ready for the supreme effort, to make us feel as well as see Maggie's suicide. Though her death takes place in a real world, one we can believe in, her suicide is still remote to us as readers because we do not enter Maggie's mind and heart. *The Red Badge,* by contrast, succeeds because it focuses on Henry's psychological problems as well as his physical discomforts. Crane never tries to paint the whole battlefield. We see only what Henry sees, and we soon come to realize that the hero is fighting himself as well as the enemy, that he is assailed with doubts about his own bravery. War can be presented realistically; that is no problem. What the impressionistic method adds to realism is the feeling of being there, of discovering and mastering fear *along with* Henry Fleming. Call it identification, if you wish, or rapport or empathy. The labels do not matter.

What matters is the success of Crane's simple plot, his accurate descriptions, and his determination to write nothing but what could have happened to his most unheroic hero. The style is disjointed because Henry's impressions are disjointed. The images are sometimes blurred, at other times as hard and flashing as swords. The action itself is so slight as to be

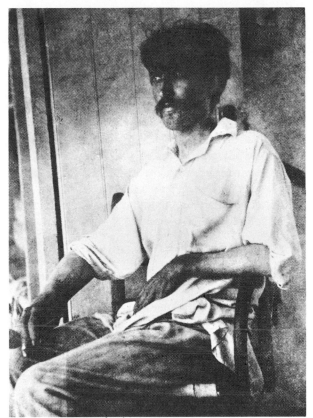

Rare informal photograph of Crane.

lost in the sense impressions, but all the time Crane is piling up these impressions to reinforce his theme; and his main theme is neither the miseries of war nor the nature of fear but spiritual growth, self-recognition, development of conscience as well as courage.

The remaining five years of Crane's life were crowded with activity. In 1895 he also published *The Black Riders,* a volume of poems. His reputation was reinforced in 1896 with a new novel, *George's Mother,* and a collection of tales, *The Little Regiment and Other Episodes of the American Civil War.* Two more novels, four collections of sketches and tales, and a second volume of poems appeared before he succumbed to tuberculosis in 1900. His premature death was the cause of much grief among American critics, but fellow writers who knew Crane in England during his last years had sensed a certain self-destructiveness in this young American and saw clearly that he was writing too much too fast. Much of this writing was done to earn a living, on assignments as roving correspondent. Bacheller's Syndicate sent him in 1895 to Nebraska, Arizona, Texas, and Mexico. In 1897 he was on his way from Florida to Cuba when his ship, the *Commodore*, sank and he spent thirty hours at sea in a dinghy. Later the same year he was sent to Athens to report the Greco-Turkish war for the New York *Journal*. In 1898, another war, the Spanish-American, took his energy and, ultimately, his health.

To the day of his death, Crane had not forsaken the creed he lived by: "You can never do anything good aesthetically . . . unless it has at one time meant something important to you." That is not to say that Crane believed an artist must experience every event he describes realistically; if he had believed that, he would have been denying the imagination. Much of his best work was imagined. He was, however, talking of his own formula for fiction: taking a germ of an experience and then letting it grow in the mind, writing from the truth of experience but always expressing that truth with acute feelings, acutely expressed. After the shipwreck off the coast of Florida, he transmuted his experiences into one of his best short stories, "The Open Boat." After seeing a Nebraska hotel painted a screaming blue, he used the image as the focus of his violent story, "The Blue Hotel." Had he done no more, he would have remained a reporter, a roving journalist, who also wrote fiction. Crane's artistry lies in the immediacy

of these descriptions, in the intensity of these feelings and of the imagination.

When Crane describes Scratchy Wilson in "The Bride Comes to Yellow Sky," he calls on his memories of the West. We not only see Scratchy, we hear him:

The man's face flamed in a rage begot of whisky. His eyes, rolling, and yet keen for ambush, hunted the still doorways and windows. He walked with the creeping movement of the midnight cat. As it occurred to him, he roared menacing information. The long revolvers in his hands moved with an electric swiftness. The little fingers of each hand played sometimes in a musician's way. . . . The only sounds were his terrible invitations. The calm adobes preserved their demeanour at the passing of this small thing in the middle of the street.

When he tells us, in "A Mystery of Heroism," what artillery fire does to men and houses, we can almost smell the burning powder:

A shell struck the grey ruins of the house, and as, after the roar, the shattered wall fell in fragments, there was a noise which resembled the flapping of shutters during a wild gale of winter. Indeed, the infantry paused in the shelter of the bank appeared as men standing upon a shore contemplating a madness of the sea . . . and after the flare, the smoke, the dust, the wrath of this blow were gone, it was possible to see white legs stretched horizontally upon the ground.

This is what is meant by transmutation: observation filtered through the imagination. A conscious artist like Crane worked valiantly to achieve the realistic, honest picture described in such accurate language as to make the impression indelible. With his work, modern American fiction was established.

In a volume called
*The Little Regiment and Other Episodes
of the American Civil War* (1896),
Crane published six stories,
of which this is one of the best. All of them
were imagined, written before he had a chance
to witness actual warfare. One critic
has called this story "pure, concentrated
Crane." He probably had in mind
the intensity of the description, especially
the sounds and smells of battle; the simple
but accurate dialogue; the irony of the title;
and the brutal anticlimax of the last paragraph.
Crane makes us feel that we are there,
in the midst of it all, and he lets us
fathom for ourselves the "mystery"
of Fred Collins' "heroism."

A Mystery of Heroism

The dark uniforms of the men were so coated with dust from the incessant wrestling of the two armies that the regiment almost seemed a part of the clay bank which shielded them from the shells. On the top of the hill a battery was arguing in tremendous roars with some other guns, and to the eye of the infantry the artillery-men, the guns, the caissons, the horses, were distinctly outlined upon the blue sky. When a piece was fired, a red streak as round as a log flashed low in the heavens, like a monstrous bolt of lightning. The men of the battery wore white duck trousers, which somehow empha-sized their legs; and when they ran and crowded in little groups at the bidding of the shouting officers, it was more impressive than usual to the infantry.

Fred Collins, of A Company, was saying: "Thunder! I wisht I had a drink. Ain't there any water round here?" Then somebody yelled: "There goes th' bugler!"

As the eyes of half the regiment swept in one machine-like movement, there was an instant's picture of a horse in a great convulsive leap of a death-wound and a rider leaning back with a crooked arm and spread fingers before his face. On the ground was the crimson terror of an exploding shell, with fibres of flame that seemed like lances. A glittering bugle swung clear of the rider's back as fell headlong the horse and the man. In the air was an odour as from a conflagration.

Sometimes they of the infantry looked down at a fair little meadow which spread at their feet. Its long green grass was rippling gently in a breeze. Beyond it was the grey form of a house half torn to pieces by shells and by the busy axes of soldiers who had pursued fire-wood. The line of an old fence was now dimly marked by long weeds and by an occasional post. A shell had blown the well-house to frag-ments. Little lines of grey smoke ribboning upward from some embers indicated the place where had stood the barn.

From beyond a curtain of green woods there came the sound of some stupendous scuffle, as if two animals of the size of islands were fight-ing. At a distance there were occasional appear-ances of swift-moving men, horses, batteries, flags, and with the crashing of infantry volleys were heard, often, wild and frenzied cheers. In the midst of it all Smith and Ferguson, two privates of A Company, were engaged in a heated discussion which involved the greatest questions of the national existence.

The battery on the hill presently engaged in a frightful duel. The white legs of the gunners scampered this way and that way, and the offi-cers redoubled their shouts. The guns, with their demeanours of stolidity and courage, were typical of something infinitely self-possessed in this clamour of death that swirled around the hill.

One of a "swing" team was suddenly smitten quivering to the ground, and his maddened brethren dragged his torn body in their struggle to escape from this turmoil and danger. A young soldier astride one of the leaders swore and fumed in his saddle and furiously jerked at the bridle. An officer screamed out an order so violently that his voice broke and ended the sentence in a falsetto[1] shriek.

The leading company of the infantry regiment was somewhat exposed, and the colonel ordered it moved more fully under the shelter of the hill. There was the clank of steel against steel.

A lieutenant of the battery rode down and passed them, holding his right arm carefully in his left hand. And it was as if this arm was not at all a part of him, but belonged to another man. His sober and reflective charger went slowly. The officer's face was grimy and perspiring, and his uniform was tousled as if he had been in direct grapple with an enemy. He smiled grimly when the men stared at him. He turned his horse toward the meadow.

Collins, of A Company, said: "I wisht I had a drink. I bet there's water in that there ol' well yonder!"

"Yes; but how you goin' to git it?"

For the little meadow which intervened was now suffering a terrible onslaught of shells. Its green and beautiful calm had vanished utterly. Brown earth was being flung in monstrous handfuls. And there was a massacre of the young blades of grass. They were being torn, burned, obliterated. Some curious fortune of the battle had made this gentle little meadow the object of the red hate of the shells, and each one as it exploded seemed like an imprecation in the face of a maiden.

The wounded officer who was riding across this expanse said to himself: "Why, they couldn't shoot any harder if the whole army was massed here!"

A shell struck the grey ruins of the house, and as, after the roar, the shattered wall fell in fragments, there was a noise which resembled the flapping of shutters during a wild gale of winter. Indeed, the infantry paused in the shelter of the bank appeared as men standing upon a shore contemplating a madness of the sea. The angel of calamity had under its glance the battery upon the hill. Fewer white-legged men laboured about the guns. A shell had smitten one of the pieces, and after the flare, the smoke, the dust, the wrath of this blow were gone, it was possible to see white legs stretched horizontally upon the ground. And at the interval to the rear where it is the business of battery horses to stand with their noses to the fight, awaiting the command to drag their guns out of the destruction, or into it, or wheresoever these incomprehensible humans demanded with whip and spur—in this line of passive and dumb spectators, whose fluttering hearts yet would not let them forget the iron laws of man's control of them—in this rank of brute-soldiers there had been relentless and hideous carnage. From the ruck of bleeding and prostrate horses, the men of the infantry could see one animal raising its stricken body with its forelegs and turning its nose with mystic and profound eloquence toward the sky.

Some comrades joked Collins about his thirst. "Well, if yeh want a drink so bad, why don't yeh go git it?"

"Well, I will in a minnet, if yeh don't shut up!"

A lieutenant of artillery floundered[2] his horse straight down the hill with as little concern as if it were level ground. As he galloped past the colonel of the infantry, he threw up his hand in swift salute. "We've got to get out of that," he roared angrily. He was a black-bearded officer, and his eyes, which resembled beads, sparkled like those of an insane man. His jumping horse sped along the column of infantry.

The fat major, standing carelessly with his sword held horizontally behind him and with his legs far apart, looked after the receding horseman and laughed. "He wants to get back with orders pretty quick, or there'll be no batt'ry left," he observed.

The wise young captain of the second company hazarded to the lieutenant-colonel that

---

1. **falsetto,** high, artificial tone of voice.
2. **floundered,** moved in awkward, struggling motion.

the enemy's infantry would probably soon attack the hill, and the lieutenant-colonel snubbed him.

A private in one of the rear companies looked out over the meadow, and then turned to a companion and said, "Look there, Jim!" It was the wounded officer from the battery, who some time before had started to ride across the meadow, supporting his right arm carefully with his left hand. This man had encountered a shell, apparently, at a time when no one perceived him, and he could now be seen lying face downward with a stirruped foot stretched across the body of his dead horse. A leg of the charger extended slantingly upward, precisely as stiff as a stake. Around this motionless pair the shells still howled.

There was a quarrel in A Company. Collins was shaking his fist in the faces of some laughing comrades. "Dern yeh! I ain't afraid t' go. If yeh say much, I will go!"

"Of course, yeh will! You'll run through that there medder, won't yeh?"

Collins said, in a terrible voice: "You see now!"

At this ominous threat his comrades broke into renewed jeers.

Collins gave them a dark scowl, and went to find his captain. The latter was conversing with the colonel of the regiment.

"Captain," said Collins, saluting and standing at attention—in those days all trousers bagged at the knees—"Captain, I want t' get permission to go git some water from that there well over yonder!"

The colonel and the captain swung about simultaneously and stared across the meadow. The captain laughed. "You must be pretty thirsty, Collins?"

"Yes, sir, I am."

"Well—ah," said the captain. After a moment, he asked, "Can't you wait?"

"No, sir."

The colonel was watching Collins's face. "Look here, my lad," he said, in a pious sort of voice—"Look here, my lad"—Collins was not

a lad—"don't you think that's taking pretty big risks for a little drink of water?"

"I dunno," said Collins uncomfortably. Some of the resentment toward his companions, which perhaps had forced him into this affair, was beginning to fade. "I dunno w'ether 'tis."

The colonel and the captain contemplated him for a time.

"Well," said the captain finally.

"Well," said the colonel, "if you want to go, why, go."

Collins saluted. "Much obliged t' yeh."

As he moved away the colonel called after him. "Take some of the other boys' canteens with you, an' hurry back, now."

"Yes, sir, I will."

The colonel and the captain looked at each other then, for it had suddenly occurred that they could not for the life of them tell whether Collins wanted to go or whether he did not.

They turned to regard Collins, and as they perceived him surrounded by gesticulating comrades, the colonel said: "Well, by thunder! I guess he's going."

Collins appeared as a man dreaming. In the midst of the questions, the advice, the warnings, all the excited talk of his company mates, he maintained a curious silence.

They were very busy in preparing him for his ordeal. When they inspected him carefully, it was somewhat like the examination that grooms give a horse before a race; and they were amazed, staggered, by the whole affair. Their astonishment found vent in strange repetitions.

"Are yeh sure a-goin'?" they demanded again and again.

"Certainly I am," cried Collins at last, furiously.

He strode sullenly away from them. He was swinging five or six canteens by their cords. It seemed that his cap would not remain firmly on his head, and often he reached and pulled it down over his brow.

There was a general movement in the compact column. The long animal-like thing moved slightly. Its four hundred eyes were turned upon the figure of Collins.

"Well, sir, if that ain't th' derndest thing! I never thought Fred Collins had the blood in him for that kind of business."

"What's he goin' to do, anyhow?"

"He's goin' to that well there after water."

"We ain't dyin' of thirst, are we? That's foolishness."

"Well, somebody put him up to it, an' he's doin' it."

"Say, he must be a desperate cuss."

When Collins faced the meadow and walked away from the regiment, he was vaguely conscious that a chasm, the deep valley of all prides, was suddenly between him and his comrades. It was provisional, but the provision was that he return as a victor. He had blindly been led by quaint emotions, and laid himself under an obligation to walk squarely up to the face of death.

But he was not sure that he wished to make a retraction, even if he could do so without shame. As a matter of truth, he was sure of very little. He was mainly surprised.

It seemed to him supernaturally strange that he had allowed his mind to manœuvre his body into such a situation. He understood that it might be called dramatically great.

However, he had no full appreciation of anything, excepting that he was actually conscious of being dazed. He could feel his dulled mind groping after the form and colour of this incident. He wondered why he did not feel some keen agony of fear cutting his sense like a knife. He wondered at this, because human expression had said loudly for centuries that men should feel afraid of certain things, and that all men who did not feel this fear were phenomena—heroes.

He was, then, a hero. He suffered that disappointment which we would all have if we discovered that we were ourselves capable of those deeds which we most admire in history and legend. This, then, was a hero. After all, heroes were not much.

No, it could not be true. He was not a hero.

Heroes had no shames in their lives, and, as for him, he remembered borrowing fifteen dollars from a friend and promising to pay it back the next day, and then avoiding that friend for ten months. When, at home, his mother had aroused him for the early labour of his life on the farm, it had often been his fashion to be irritable, childish, diabolical; and his mother had died since he had come to the war.

He saw that, in this matter of the well, the canteens, the shells, he was an intruder in the land of fine deeds.

He was now about thirty paces from his comrades. The regiment had just turned its many faces toward him.

From the forest of terrific noises there suddenly emerged a little uneven line of men. They fired fiercely and rapidly at distant foliage on which appeared little puffs of white smoke. The spatter of skirmish firing was added to the thunder of the guns on the hill. The little line of men ran forward. A colour-sergeant fell flat with his flag as if he had slipped on ice. There was hoarse cheering from this distant field.

Collins suddenly felt that two demon fingers were pressed into his ears. He could see nothing but flying arrows, flaming red. He lurched from the shock of this explosion, but he made a mad rush for the house, which he viewed as a man submerged to the neck in a boiling surf might view the shore. In the air little pieces of shell howled, and the earthquake explosions drove him insane with the menace of their roar. As he ran the canteens knocked together with a rhythmical tinkling.

As he neared the house, each detail of the scene became vivid to him. He was aware of some bricks of the vanished chimney lying on the sod. There was a door which hung by one hinge.

Rifle bullets called forth by the insistent skirmishers came from the far-off bank of foliage. They mingled with the shells and the pieces of shells until the air was torn in all directions by hootings, yells, howls. The sky was full of fiends who directed all their wild rage at his head.

When he came to the well, he flung himself face downward and peered into its darkness. There were furtive silver glintings some feet from the surface. He grabbed one of the canteens and, unfastening its cap, swung it down by the cord. The water flowed slowly in with an indolent gurgle.

And now, as he lay with his face turned away, he was suddenly smitten with the terror. It came upon his heart like the grasp of claws. All the power faded from his muscles. For an instant he was no more than a dead man.

The canteen filled with a maddening slowness, in the manner of all bottles. Presently he recovered his strength and addressed a screaming oath to it. He leaned over until it seemed as if he intended to try to push water into it with his hands. His eyes as he gazed down into the well shone like two pieces of metal, and in their expression was a great appeal and a great curse. The stupid water derided him.

There was the blaring thunder of a shell. Crimson light shone through the swift-boiling smoke and made a pink reflection on part of the wall of the well. Collins jerked out his arm and canteen with the same motion that a man would use in withdrawing his head from a furnace.

He scrambled erect and glared and hesitated. On the ground near him lay the old well bucket, with a length of rusty chain. He lowered it swiftly into the well. The bucket struck the water and then, turning lazily over, sank. When, with hand reaching tremblingly over hand, he hauled it out, it knocked often against the walls of the well and spilled some of its contents.

In running with a filled bucket, a man can adopt but one kind of gait. So, through this terrible field over which screamed practical angels of death, Collins ran in the manner of a farmer chased out of a dairy by a bull.

His face went staring white with anticipation—anticipation of a blow that would whirl him around and down. He would fall as he had seen other men fall, the life knocked out of them so suddenly that their knees were no more quick to touch the ground than their heads. He saw the long blue line of the regiment, but his comrades were standing looking at him from the edge of an impossible star. He was aware of some deep wheel-ruts and hoofprints in the sod beneath his feet.

The artillery officer who had fallen in this meadow had been making groans in the teeth of the tempest of sound. These futile cries, wrenched from him by his agony, were heard only by shells, bullets. When wild-eyed Collins came running, this officer raised himself. His face contorted and blanched from pain, he was about to utter some great beseeching cry. But suddenly his face straightened, and he called: "Say, young man, give me a drink of water, will you?"

Collins had no room amid his emotions for surprise. He was mad from the threats of destruction.

"I can't!" he screamed, and in his reply was a full description of his quaking apprehension. His cap was gone and his hair was riotous. His clothes made it appear that he had been dragged over the ground by the heels. He ran on.

The officer's head sank down, and one elbow crooked. His foot in its brass-bound stirrup still stretched over the body of his horse, and the other leg was under the steed.

But Collins turned. He came dashing back. His face had now turned grey, and in his eyes was all terror. "Here it is! Here it is!"

The officer was as a man gone in drink. His arm bent like a twig. His head drooped as if his neck were of willow. He was sinking to the ground, to lie face downward.

Collins grabbed him by the shoulder. "Here it is. Here's your drink. Turn over. Turn over, man, for God's sake!"

With Collins hauling at his shoulder, the officer twisted his body and fell with his face turned toward that region where lived the unspeakable noises of the swirling missiles. There was the faintest shadow of a smile on his lips as he looked at Collins. He gave a sigh, a little primitive breath like that from a child.

Collins tried to hold the bucket steadily, but his shaking hands caused the water to splash all over the face of the dying man. Then he jerked it away and ran on.

The regiment gave him a welcoming roar. The grimed faces were wrinkled in laughter.

His captain waved the bucket away. "Give it to the men!"

The two genial, skylarking young lieutenants were the first to gain possession of it. They played over it in their fashion.

When one tried to drink, the other teasingly knocked his elbow. "Don't Billie! You'll make me spill it," said the one. The other laughed.

Suddenly there was an oath, the thud of wood on the ground, and a swift murmur of astonishment among the ranks. The two lieutenants glared at each other. The bucket lay on the ground, empty.

I
MEN AT WAR

Every paragraph of this story of Fred Collins drenches us with the sights, sounds, and smells of the battlefield. Crane intensifies his descriptions with phrases like "fibres of flame that seemed like lances," "the ruck of bleeding and prostrate horses," and "earthquake explosions drove him insane with the menace of their roar." He wants us to contemplate the senseless slaughter in the most vivid language he can manage.

But we, like the author, are only observers. Fred Collins is the participant. He and his fellow soldiers talk in the simplest kind of language. In the midst of the agony and carnage around him, Collins wants—of all things—a drink of water. Crane's problem is to make us see that this ordinary gesture—taking empty canteens to the well—is connected directly with the romantic idea of "a mystery of heroism."

II
IMPLICATIONS

Discuss the following propositions as we move from the first page to the last of this story.

1. Collins' thirst is literally of more concern to him than the death of the bugler.

2. Collins' heroism is merely a foolish dare triggered by a joke.

3. It is only as he begins to *think* about his action, that Collins contemplates "heroism" but rejects it.

4. Collins performs heroically almost without knowing it.

5. The trip back is for Collins the heroic gesture because he masters his fear, especially when he stops to give a dying man water rather than rush on to safety.

6. The essence of Collins' heroism is not to be without fears but rather to conquer them.

III
TECHNIQUES
Intention and Theme

Without the last four paragraphs, this story would lose much of its bite. When the captain "waved the bucket away" and the lieutenant spills the precious water on the ground, what is Crane saying about life? Could he be saying that life is often brutal in its treatment of man's heroic gestures, either out of ignorance (the lieutenants could not have known what the victory "cost" Collins) or out of vindictiveness (life is determined to "defeat" man no matter how he tries to rise above it)? If this is the point of the story, then heroism is indeed a mystery, because Collins must be saying that his risking his life was futile after all, not worth the victory over fear.

Or could a wholly different intention have been in Crane's mind as he wrote these last paragraphs? Could he have felt that since Collins chose to make a foolish, even a stupid, gesture in running to the well for water, he deserved exactly what happens: a waste of effort? Is the story far more pessimistic—even fatalistic—than we realize at first?

Which way do you read it: Collins achieves heroic stature by facing death and his own fears; Collins acts stupidly and the ironic spilling of his prize is all he deserves; life will diminish man's heroic acts no matter what he does to protect them? What would Crane have risked by giving Collins additional dialogue after the last sentence: "The bucket lay on the ground empty." Could the word *empty* be the clue to the author's intention?

Although this story
was written while Crane lived in England,
its beginnings lay in his tour of the Southwest
in 1895. Always alert to local color,
he had visited San Antonio and the Rio Grande,
hoping to collect short-story material.
The central dramatic incident is invented,
but the frontier code, the atmosphere,
the language the characters speak
ring true to what history records
of these days in the West. As with "A Mystery
of Heroism," the whole story hinges
on the last paragraphs; but here Crane
works harder at creating two sharply different
points of view: those of Jack Potter,
the marshal of Yellow Sky, and Scratchy Wilson,
the town drunk. As he brings them together,
these viewpoints inevitably clash,
yet not as we expected.

The Bride Comes to Yellow Sky

I

The great Pullman was whirling onward with such dignity of motion that a glance from the window seemed simply to prove that the plains of Texas were pouring eastward. Vast flats of green grass, dull-hued spaces of mesquit[1] and cactus, little groups of frame houses, woods of light and tender trees, all were sweeping into the east, sweeping over the horizon, a precipice.

A newly married pair had boarded this coach at San Antonio. The man's face was reddened from many days in the wind and sun, and a direct result of his new black clothes was that his brick-coloured hands were constantly performing in a most conscious fashion. From time to time he looked down respectfully at his attire. He sat with a hand on each knee, like a man waiting in a barber's shop. The glances he devoted to other passengers were furtive and shy.

The bride was not pretty, nor was she very young. She wore a dress of blue cashmere, with small reservations of velvet here and there, and with steel buttons abounding. She continually twisted her head to regard her puff sleeves, very stiff, straight, and high. They embarrassed her. It was quite apparent that she had cooked, and that she expected to cook, dutifully. The blushes caused by the careless scrutiny of some passengers as she had entered the car were strange to see upon this plain, under-class countenance, which was drawn in placid, almost emotionless lines.

They were evidently very happy. "Ever been in a parlour-car before?" he asked, smiling with delight.

"No," she answered; "I never was. It's fine, ain't it?"

"Great! And then after a while we'll go forward to the diner, and get a big lay-out. Finest meal in the world. Charge a dollar."

"Oh, do they?" cried the bride. "Charge a dollar? Why, that's too much—for us—ain't it, Jack?"

"Not this trip, anyhow," he answered bravely. "We're going to go the whole thing."

Later he explained to her about the trains. "You see, it's a thousand miles from one end of Texas to the other; and this train runs right across it, and never stops but four times." He had the pride of an owner. He pointed out to her the dazzling fittings of the coach; and in truth her eyes opened wider as she contemplated the sea-green figured velvet, the shining brass, silver, and glass, the wood that gleamed as darkly brilliant as the surface of a pool of oil. At one end a bronze figure sturdily held a support for a separated chamber, and at convenient places on the ceiling were frescos in olive and silver.

---

1. **mesquit**\mĕs ᴧkēt\ small shrub that yields sweet pods.

To the minds of the pair, their surroundings reflected the glory of their marriage that morning in San Antonio; this was the environment of their new estate; and the man's face in particular beamed with an elation that made him appear ridiculous to the Negro porter. This individual at times surveyed them from afar with an amused and superior grin. On other occasions he bullied them with skill in ways that did not make it exactly plain to them that they were being bullied. He subtly used all the manners of the most unconquerable kind of snobbery. He oppressed them; but of this oppression they had small knowledge, and they speedily forgot that infrequently a number of travellers covered them with stares of derisive enjoyment. Historically there was supposed to be something infinitely humorous in their situation.

"We are due in Yellow Sky at 3:42," he said, looking tenderly into her eyes.

"Oh, are we?" she said, as if she had not been aware of it. To evince surprise at her husband's statement was part of her wifely amiability. She took from a pocket a little silver watch; and as she held it before her, and stared at it with a frown of attention, the new husband's face shone.

"I bought it in San Anton' from a friend of mine," he told her gleefully.

"It's seventeen minutes past twelve," she said, looking up at him with a kind of shy and clumsy coquetry. A passenger, noting this play, grew excessively sardonic, and winked at himself in one of the numerous mirrors.

At last they went to the dining-car. Two rows of Negro waiters, in glowing white suits, surveyed their entrance with the interest, and also the equanimity, of men who had been forewarned. The pair fell to the lot of a waiter who happened to feel pleasure in steering them through their meal. He viewed them with the manner of a fatherly pilot, his countenance radiant with benevolence. The patronage, entwined with the ordinary deference, was not plain to them. And yet, as they returned to their coach, they showed in their faces a sense of escape.

To the left, miles down a long purple slope, was a little ribbon of mist where moved the keening Rio Grande. The train was approaching it at an angle, and the apex was Yellow Sky. Presently it was apparent that, as the distance from Yellow Sky grew shorter, the husband became commensurately restless. His brick-red hands were more insistent in their prominence. Occasionally he was even rather absent-minded and far-away when the bride leaned forward and addressed him.

As a matter of truth, Jack Potter was beginning to find the shadow of a deed weigh upon him like a leaden slab. He, the town marshal of Yellow Sky, a man known, liked, and feared in his corner, a prominent person, had gone to San Antonio to meet a girl he believed he loved, and there, after the usual prayers, had actually induced her to marry him, without consulting Yellow Sky for any part of the transaction. He was now bringing his bride before an innocent and unsuspecting community.

Of course people in Yellow Sky married as it pleased them, in accordance with a general custom; but such was Potter's thought of his duty to his friends, or of their idea of his duty, or of an unspoken form which does not control men in these matters, that he felt he was heinous. He had committed an extraordinary crime. Face to face with this girl in San Antonio, and spurred by his sharp impulse, he had gone headlong over all the social hedges. At San Antonio he was like a man hidden in the dark. A knife to sever any friendly duty, any form, was easy to his hand in that remote city. But the hour of Yellow Sky—the hour of daylight—was approaching.

He knew full well that his marriage was an important thing to his town. It could only be exceeded by the burning of the new hotel. His friends could not forgive him. Frequently he had reflected on the advisability of telling them by telegraph, but a new cowardice had been upon him. He feared to do it. And now the train was hurrying him toward a scene of amazement, glee, and reproach. He glanced out of the window at the line of haze swinging slowly in toward the train.

Yellow Sky had a kind of brass band, which played painfully, to the delight of the populace. He laughed without heart as he thought of it. If the citizens could dream of his prospective arrival with his bride, they would parade the band at the station and escort them, amid cheers and laughing congratulations, to his adobe home.

He resolved that he would use all the devices of speed and plainscraft in making the journey from the station to his house. Once within that safe citadel, he could issue some sort of vocal bulletin, and then not go among the citizens until they had time to wear off a little of their enthusiasm.

The bride looked anxiously at him. "What's worrying you, Jack?"

He laughed again. "I'm not worrying, girl; I'm only thinking of Yellow Sky."

She flushed in comprehension.

A sense of mutual guilt invaded their minds and developed a finer tenderness. They looked at each other with eyes softly aglow. But Potter often laughed the same nervous laugh; the flush upon the bride's face seemed quite permanent.

The traitor to the feelings of Yellow Sky narrowly watched the speeding landscape. "We're nearly there," he said.

Presently the porter came and announced the proximity of Potter's home. He held a brush in his hand, and, with all his airy superiority gone, he brushed Potter's new clothes as the latter slowly turned this way and that way. Potter fumbled out a coin and gave it to the porter, as he had seen others do. It was a heavy and muscle-bound business, as that of a man shoeing his first horse.

The porter took their bag, and as the train began to slow they moved forward to the hooded platform of the car. Presently the two engines and their long string of coaches rushed into the station of Yellow Sky.

"They have to take water here," said Potter, from a constricted throat and in mournful cadence, as one announcing death. Before the train stopped his eye had swept the length of the platform, and he was glad and astonished to see there was none upon it but the station-agent, who, with a slightly hurried and anxious air, was walking toward the water-tanks. When the train had halted, the porter alighted first, and placed in position a little temporary step.

"Come on, girl," said Potter, hoarsely. As he helped her down they each laughed on a false note. He took the bag from the Negro, and bade his wife cling to his arm. As they slunk rapidly away, his hang-dog glance perceived that they were unloading the two trunks, and also that the station-agent, far ahead near the baggage-car, had turned and was running toward him, making gestures. He laughed, and groaned as he laughed, when he noted the first effect of his marital bliss upon Yellow Sky. He gripped his wife's arm firmly to his side, and they fled. Behind them the porter stood, chuckling fatuously.

II

The California express on the Southern Railway was due at Yellow Sky in twenty-one minutes. There were six men at the bar of the Weary Gentleman saloon. One was a drummer[2] who talked a great deal and rapidly; three were Texans who did not care to talk at that time; and two were Mexican sheep-herders, who did not talk as a general practice in the Weary Gentleman saloon. The barkeeper's dog lay on the board walk that crossed in front of the door. His head was on his paws, and he glanced drowsily here and there with the constant vigilance of a dog that is kicked on occasion. Across the sandy street were some vivid green grass-plots, so wonderful in appearance, amid the sands that burned near them in a blazing sun, that they caused a doubt in the mind. They exactly resembled the grass mats used to represent lawns on the stage. At the

---

2. **drummer,** traveling salesman.

cooler end of the railway station, a man without a coat sat in a tilted chair and smoked his pipe. The fresh-cut bank of the Rio Grande circled near the town, and there could be seen beyond it a great plum-coloured plain of mesquit.

Save for the busy drummer and his companions in the saloon, Yellow Sky was dozing. The new-comer leaned gracefully upon the bar, and recited many tales with the confidence of a bard who has come upon a new field.

"—and at the moment that the old man fell downstairs with the bureau in his arms, the old woman was coming up with two scuttles[3] of coal, and of course—"

The drummer's tale was interrupted by a young man who suddenly appeared in the open door. He cried: "Scratchy Wilson's drunk, and has turned loose with both hands." The two Mexicans at once set down their glasses and faded out of the rear entrance of the saloon.

The drummer, innocent and jocular, answered: "All right, old man. S'pose he has? Come in and have a drink, anyhow."

But the information had made such an obvious cleft in every skull in the room that the drummer was obliged to see its importance. All had become instantly solemn. "Say," said he, mystified, "what is this?" His three companions made the introductory gesture of eloquent speech; but the young man at the door forestalled them.

"It means, my friend," he answered, as he came into the saloon, "that for the next two hours this town won't be a health resort."

The barkeeper went to the door, and locked and barred it; reaching out of the window, he pulled in heavy wooden shutters, and barred them. Immediately a solemn, chapel-like gloom was upon the place. The drummer was looking from one to another.

"But say," he cried, "what is this, anyhow? You don't mean there is going to be a gun-fight?"

"Don't know whether there'll be a fight or not," answered one man, grimly; "but there'll be some shootin'—some good shootin'."

The young man who had warned them waved his hand. "Oh, there'll be a fight fast enough, if any one wants it. Anybody can get a fight out there in the street. There's a fight just waiting."

The drummer seemed to be swayed between the interest of a foreigner and a perception of personal danger.

"What did you say his name was?" he asked.

"Scratchy Wilson," they answered in chorus.

"And will he kill anybody? What are you going to do? Does this happen often? Does he rampage around like this once a week or so? Can he break in that door?"

"No; he can't break down that door," replied the barkeeper. "He's tried it three times. But when he comes you'd better lay down on the floor, stranger. He's dead sure to shoot at it, and a bullet may come through."

Thereafter the drummer kept a strict eye upon the door. The time had not yet been called for him to hug the floor, but, as a minor precaution, he sidled near to the wall. "Will he kill anybody?" he said again.

The men laughed low and scornfully at the question.

"He's out to shoot, and he's out for trouble. Don't see any good in experimentin' with him."

"But what do you do in a case like this? What do you do?"

A man responded: "Why, he and Jack Potter—"

"But," in chorus the other men interrupted, "Jack Potter's in San Anton'."

"Well, who is he? What's he got to do with it?"

"Oh, he's the town marshal. He goes out and fights Scratchy when he gets on one of these tears."

"Wow!" said the drummer, mopping his brow. "Nice job he's got."

The voices had toned away to mere whisperings. The drummer wished to ask further questions, which were born of an increasing anxiety and bewilderment; but when he attempted

---

3. **scuttles**\\ˈskət·əlz\\ metal pails for carrying coal.

them, the men merely looked at him in irritation and motioned him to remain silent. A tense waiting hush was upon them. In the deep shadows of the room their eyes shone as they listened for sounds from the street. One man made three gestures at the barkeeper; and the latter, moving like a ghost, handed him a glass and a bottle. The man poured a full glass of whisky, and set down the bottle noiselessly. He gulped the whisky in a swallow, and turned again toward the door in immovable silence. The drummer saw that the barkeeper, without a sound, had taken a Winchester from beneath the bar. Later he saw this individual beckoning to him, so he tiptoed across the room.

"You better come with me back of the bar."

"No, thanks," said the drummer, perspiring; "I'd rather be where I can make a break for the back door."

Whereupon the man of bottles made a kindly but peremptory gesture. The drummer obeyed it, and, finding himself seated on a box with his head below the level of the bar, balm was laid upon his soul at sight of various zinc and copper fittings that bore a resemblance to armour-plate. The barkeeper took a seat comfortably upon an adjacent box.

"You see," he whispered, "this here Scratchy Wilson is a wonder with a gun—a perfect wonder; and when he goes on the war-trail, we hunt our holes—naturally. He's about the last one of the old gang that used to hang out along the river here. He's a terror when he's drunk. When he's sober he's all right—kind of simple—wouldn't hurt a fly—nicest fellow in town. But when he's drunk—whoo!"

There were periods of stillness. "I wish Jack Potter was back from San Anton'," said the barkeeper. "He shot Wilson up once—in the leg—and he would sail in and pull out the kinks in this thing."

Presently they heard from a distance the sound of a shot, followed by three wild yowls. It instantly removed a bond from the men in the darkened saloon. There was a shuffling of feet. They looked at each other. "Here he comes," they said.

III

A man in a maroon-coloured flannel shirt, which had been purchased for purposes of decoration, and made principally by some Jewish women on the East Side of New York, rounded a corner and walked into the middle of the main street of Yellow Sky. In either hand the man held a long, heavy, blue-black revolver. Often he yelled, and these cries rang through a semblance of a deserted village, shrilly flying over the roofs in a volume that seemed to have no relation to the ordinary vocal strength of a man. It was as if the surrounding stillness formed the arch of a tomb over him. These cries of ferocious challenge rang against walls of silence. And his boots had red tops with gilded imprints, of the kind beloved in winter by little sledding boys on the hillsides of New England.

The man's face flamed in a rage begot of whisky. His eyes, rolling, and yet keen for ambush, hunted the still doorways and windows. He walked with the creeping movement of the midnight cat. As it occurred to him, he roared menacing information. The long revolvers in his hands were as easy as straws; they were moved with an electric swiftness. The little fingers of each hand played sometimes in a musician's way. Plain from the low collar of the shirt, the cords of his neck straightened and sank, straightened and sank, as passion moved him. The only sounds were his terrible invitations. The calm adobes preserved their demeanour at the passing of this small thing in the middle of the street.

There was no offer of fight—no offer of fight. The man called to the sky. There were no attractions. He bellowed and fumed and swayed his revolvers here and everywhere.

The dog of the barkeeper of the Weary Gentleman saloon had not appreciated the advance of events. He yet lay dozing in front of his master's door. At sight of the dog, the man paused and raised his revolver humorously. At sight of the man, the dog sprang up and walked diagonally away, with a sullen head, and growling. The man yelled, and the dog broke into a gallop. As it was about to enter an alley, there was a loud noise, a whistling, and something spat the ground directly before it. The dog screamed, and, wheeling in terror, galloped headlong in a new direction. Again there was a noise, a whistling, and sand was kicked viciously before it. Fear-stricken, the dog turned and flurried like an animal in a pen. The man stood laughing, his weapons at his hips.

Ultimately the man was attracted by the closed door of the Weary Gentleman saloon. He went to it and, hammering with a revolver, demanded drink.

The door remaining imperturbable, he picked a bit of paper from the walk, and nailed it to the framework with a knife. He then turned his back contemptuously upon this popular resort and, walking to the opposite side of the street and spinning there on his heel quickly and lithely, fired at the bit of paper. He missed it by a half-inch. He swore at himself, and went away. Later he comfortably fusilladed[4] the windows of his most intimate friend. The man was playing with this town; it was a toy for him.

But still there was no offer of fight. The name of Jack Potter, his ancient antagonist, entered his mind, and he concluded that it would be a glad thing if he should go to Potter's house, and by bombardment induce him to come out and fight. He moved in the direction of his desire, chanting Apache scalp-music.

When he arrived at it, Potter's house presented the same still front as had the other adobes. Taking up a strategic position, the man howled a challenge. But this house regarded him as might a great stone god. It gave no sign. After a decent wait, the man howled further challenges, mingling with them wonderful epithets.

Presently there came the spectacle of a man churning himself into deepest rage over the immobility of a house. He fumed at it as the winter wind attacks a prairie cabin in the North. To the distance there should have gone the sound of a tumult like the fighting of two hundred Mexicans. As necessity bade him, he paused for breath or to reload his revolvers.

IV

Potter and his bride walked sheepishly and with speed. Sometimes they laughed together shamefacedly and low.

"Next corner, dear," he said finally.

They put forth the efforts of a pair walking bowed against a strong wind. Potter was about to raise a finger to point the first appearance of the new home when, as they circled the corner, they came face to face with a man in a maroon-coloured shirt, who was feverishly pushing cartridges into a large revolver. Upon the instant the man dropped his revolver to the ground and, like lightning, whipped another from its holster. The second weapon was aimed at the bridegroom's chest.

There was a silence. Potter's mouth seemed to be merely a grave for his tongue. He exhibited an instinct to at once loosen his arm from the woman's grip, and he dropped the bag to the sand. As for the bride, her face had gone as yellow as old cloth. She was a slave to hideous rites, gazing at the apparitional snake.

The two men faced each other at a distance of three paces. He of the revolver smiled with a new and quiet ferocity.

"Tried to sneak up on me," he said. "Tried to sneak up on me!" His eyes grew more baleful. As Potter made a slight movement, the man thrust his revolver venomously forward. "No; don't you do it, Jack Potter. Don't you move a finger toward a gun just yet. Don't you move an eyelash. The time has come for me to settle with you, and I'm goin' to do it my own way, and loaf along with no interferin'. So if you don't want a gun bent on you, just mind what I tell you."

---

4. **fusilladed**\ˈfyü·sə ˈlād·əd\ fired a number of shots in rapid succession.

Potter looked at his enemy. "I ain't got a gun on me Scratchy," he said. "Honest, I ain't." He was stiffening and steadying, but yet somewhere at the back of his mind a vision of the Pullman floated: the sea-green figured velvet, the shining brass, silver, and glass, the wood that gleamed as darkly brilliant as the surface of a pool of oil—all the glory of the marriage, the environment of the new estate. "You know I fight when it comes to fighting, Scratchy Wilson; but I ain't got a gun on me. You'll have to do all the shootin' yourself."

His enemy's face went livid. He stepped forward, and lashed his weapon to and fro before Potter's chest. "Don't you tell me you ain't got no gun on you, you whelp.[5] Don't tell me no lie like that. There ain't a man in Texas ever seen you without no gun. Don't take me for no kid." His eyes blazed with light, and his throat worked like a pump.

"I ain't takin' you for no kid," answered Potter. His heels had not moved an inch backward. "I'm takin' you for a damn fool. I tell you I ain't got a gun, and I ain't. If you're goin' to shoot me up, you better begin now; you'll never get a chance like this again."

So much enforced reasoning had told on Wilson's rage; he was calmer. "If you ain't got a gun, why ain't you got a gun?" he sneered. "Been to Sunday-school?"

"I ain't got a gun because I've just come from San Anton' with my wife. I'm married," said Potter. "And if I'd thought there was going to be any galoots like you prowling around when I brought my wife home, I'd had a gun, and don't you forget it."

"Married!" said Scratchy, not at all comprehending.

"Yes, married. I'm married," said Potter, distinctly.

"Married?" said Scratchy. Seemingly for the first time, he saw the drooping, drowning woman at the other man's side. "No!" he said. He was like a creature allowed a glimpse of another world. He moved a pace backward, and his arm, with the revolver, dropped to his side. "Is this the lady?" he asked.

"Yes; this is the lady," answered Potter.

There was another period of silence.

"Well," said Wilson at last, slowly, "I s'pose it's all off now."

"It's all off if you say so, Scratchy. You know I didn't make the trouble." Potter lifted his valise.

"Well, I 'low it's off, Jack," said Wilson. He was looking at the ground. "Married!" He was not a student of chivalry; it was merely that in the presence of this foreign condition he was a simple child of the earlier plains. He picked up his starboard revolver, and, placing both weapons in their holsters, he went away. His feet made funnel-shaped tracks in the heavy sand.

I

STORY IN FOUR ACTS

Crane breaks this story into four distinct parts, and he handles them as deftly as though they were four acts of a drama. The first sets the scene: the timid newlyweds, still strangers to each other, wonder how to confront the hometown after their "daring" decision to get married. The second section sets another kind of scene, this time from the hometown's point of view, only the local rowdy is the main character and a more serious confrontation is at hand. In the third section, Crane shifts his focus to Scratchy Wilson himself. Crane is still the narrator, even though we now see Yellow Sky through Scratchy's eyes. As his rage mounts, Scratchy comes face to face not with Potter himself but with Potter's house. The fourth section is inevitable: the two adversaries must meet, and naturally they must meet unequally armed if Crane wishes to avoid bloodshed. The brandished pistols are menacing, without doubt, but Potter has a secret weapon, a single word: married. Now we see and feel the impact of the title as the retreating Scratchy Wilson makes "funnel-shaped

---

5. **whelp,** young man, usually used with unfavorable connotation.

tracks in the heavy sand." Has Crane cheated us of the rousing climax we might expect, or is he striving for more subtle effects, thus risking an anticlimax without fear of diminishing his story?

II
IMPLICATIONS

Crane often suggests more than he says. What do the following statements from the story reveal about the characters and the situation?

1. She continually twisted her head to regard her puff sleeves, very stiff, straight, and high.

2. He had committed an extraordinary crime. Face to face with this girl in San Antonio, and spurred by his sharp impulse, he had gone headlong over all the social hedges.

3. He gripped his wife's arm firmly to his side, and they fled. Behind them the porter stood, chuckling fatuously.

4. "Don't know whether there'll be a fight or not, but there'll be some shootin'—some good shootin'."

5. "Oh, he's the town marshal. He goes out and fights Scratchy when he gets on one of these tears."

6. The drummer saw that the barkeeper, without a sound, had taken a Winchester from beneath the bar.

7. Presently there came the spectacle of a man churning himself into deepest rage over the immobility of a house.

8. Potter's mouth seemed to be merely a grave for his tongue.

9. As for the bride, her face had gone as yellow as old cloth.

10. Seemingly for the first time, he saw the drooping, drowning woman at the other man's side.

III
TECHNIQUES
Intention and Theme

Like "A Mystery of Heroism," this story turns on the irony of the last paragraphs. The threatening man, gun in hand, is defeated by his unarmed enemy, and defeated not physically but spiritually, which is worse. Scratchy expected to encounter gunfire (he was ready for that; the whole town was ready), but he meets instead a marshal more resolute than ever. Potter is a new man. Marriage

has transformed him, not only in his own eyes but in Scratchy's eyes as well. Marriage, to Scratchy Wilson, is "another world," a "foreign condition." The one word—"married"—is like a blow aimed squarely at Scratchy's jaw. All he can say is "I s'pose it's all off now" and slump away through "the heavy sand."

What reaction do you think Crane expects from his reader: surprise, relief, laughter? What other endings could he have given this story? If "The Bride Comes to Yellow Sky" sets out to illustrate "what innocence can do if it has the opportunity," as one critic believes, could Crane have chosen any other ending?

IV
WORDS

A. Using what you have learned about context clues, determine the meaning of the following italicized words.

1. . . . he was vaguely conscious that a *chasm*, the deep valley of all prides, was suddenly between him and his comrades.

2. To *evince* surprise at her husband's statement was part of her wifely *amiability*.

3. . . . as the distance from Yellow Sky grew shorter, the husband became *commensurately* restless.

4. The train was approaching it at an angle, and the *apex* was Yellow Sky.

5. . . . spinning there on his heel quickly and *lithely,* fired at the bit of paper.

B. 1. Many antonyms are derived forms with one of the negative affixes: *in-, non-, dis-, mis-, un-, -less.* The antonym of subversive might be "non-subversive"; *adequate,* inadequate; *exalted,* unexalted. Yet not all words have a clear-cut negative affix. For example, antonyms for *moral* might be *unmoral, immoral, amoral;* for *American, non-American* and *un-American.* Do these words carry the same implications?

2. For the words listed below, form negative words. Define negative forms that differ in meaning.

(a) the guns were *typical;* (b) guilty of *human* feelings; (c) the last *divisible* parts; (d) *similar* reaction; (e) *impassioned* plea; (f) *respectful* answer.

C. The function of language, written and spoken, is to communicate. Good English is English which communicates most completely and accurately in a specific situation. A speaker or writer adjusts his language to his subject, his audience, and to himself. Yet in the social and in the business worlds your success depends largely on how well you speak "good English." Survey your use of the spoken language. What do you say?

1. *waked up* or *woke up*; he *has proved, has proven* his case; he *couldn't help but feel* as he did, he *couldn't help feeling* as he did.

2. the girl *has got, has gotten* herself a boyfriend; he went no *farther, further* than the next town; neither of the moves *justify, justifies* the end result.

3. he was *enthused, enthusiastic* about the trip; the crowd *derided, ridiculed* him; inside that safe *citadel, fort.*

Again, good English is that which is most appropriate to the situation, the listener, and the speaker himself. Nonstandard usage is inappropriate most of the time. Use of standard usage, on the other hand, is appropriate most of the time. From a daily newspaper, find examples of each level of usage. What was the purpose of each writer?

When first published Crane's poems did not please many readers, because the lines were not like the popular poetry of the day. Yet Crane thought of them as a more ambitious effort than his famous novel *The Red Badge of Courage,* because they gave his ideas of life as a whole. These ideas were frequently bitter, always antiheroic, not unlike some of his short stories. The form of these remarkable poems owes much to Crane's knowledge of the Bible and to his admiration for Walt Whitman and Emily Dickinson.

A Man Saw a Ball of Gold in the Sky

A man saw a ball of gold in the sky.
He climbed for it,
And eventually he achieved it—
It was clay.

Now this is the strange part: 5
When the man went to earth
And looked again,
Lo, there was the ball of gold.
Now this is the strange part:
It was a ball of gold.   10
Ay, by the heavens it was a ball of gold.

God Fashioned
the Ship of the World

God fashioned the ship of the world carefully.
With the infinite skill of an All-Master
Made He the hull and the sails,
Held He the rudder
Ready for adjustment.   5
Erect stood He, scanning His work proudly.
Then—at fateful time—a wrong called,
And God turned, heeding.
Lo, the ship, at this opportunity, slipped slyly,
Making cunning noiseless travel down the ways.   10
So that, for ever rudderless, it went upon the seas
Going ridiculous voyages,
Making quaint progress,
Turning as with serious purpose
Before stupid winds.   15
And there were many in the sky
Who laughed at this thing.

The Wayfarer

The wayfarer,
Perceiving the pathway to truth,
Was struck with astonishment.
It was thickly grown with weeds.
"Ha," he said,   5
"I see that no one has passed here
In a long time."
Later he saw that each weed
Was a singular knife.
"Well," he mumbled at last,   10
"Doubtless there are other roads."

The Book of Wisdom

I met a seer.
He held in his hands
The book of wisdom.
"Sir," I addressed him,
"Let me read."   5
"Child—" he began.
"Sir," I said.
"Think not that I am a child,
For already I know much
Of that which you hold;   10
Aye, much."

He smiled.
Then he opened the book
And held it before me.
Strange that I should have grown so suddenly blind.   15

A Man Said to the Universe

A man said to the universe:
"Sir, I exist!"
"However," replied the universe,
"The fact has not created in me
A sense of obligation."

LINES ON LIFE

Reviewers used harsh language to damn these poems when they first appeared. But Crane ignored critical opinions about his poems; in fact, he called them "lines" rather than poetry. His poems are closely connected with his novels and short stories. They use the familiar reversals, the ironic conclusions, and the flat, direct language of his dialogue. What is more, they are sincere and honest statements that reflect Crane's constant concern over the bitter realities of our lives.

II
IMPLICATIONS
Discuss the following interpretations.

A Man Saw a Ball of Gold
in the Sky

1. Beauty is in the eye of the beholder.
2. There is more joy in expectation than in fulfillment.
3. Even in the face of facts men cling to illusions.

God Fashioned
the Ship of the World

1. Men's lives are meaningless and without direction.
2. Man is an absurd creature, the laughing stock of the universe.

The Wayfarer

1. All men are wayfarers and this poem is a universal indictment. Crane was not the first to suggest that the path to truth is difficult, but what is he trying to suggest by "thickly grown with weeds" and then "each weed/ Was a singular knife"? Why "singular"?
2. The wayfarer "mumbles" a weak assurance, but the poet is skeptical. What would you tell the wayfarer: there is only one road to truth? all roads to truth are overgrown with weeds? each man must kill the weeds by himself?

The Book of Wisdom

1. Why are we told nothing about this "seer" and his "book of wisdom"?
2. How does the last line of the poem connect with the word "child"? How does it connect with the word "seer"?
3. What does the word "blind" suggest here in addition to "unable to see"?

A Man Said to the Universe

1. Shall we read "God" for universe, or is the whole point of the poem that the universe is Godless?
2. If we substitute "nature" for universe, what does this do to our idea of "Mother Nature" as a kindly benefactor?

INDEPENDENT SPIRIT

The Declaration of Independence asserts, "We hold these truths to be self-evident: that all men are created equal, that they are endowed by their Creator with certain unalienable rights, that among these are life, liberty, and the pursuit of happiness." In these words our founding fathers set forth the

ANDREW JACKSON, *Thomas Scully*

"Old Hickory," lawyer, judge, general, Representative, Senator, and seventh president of the United States. He is an outstanding example of an American who started in humble circumstances and traveled far by his own hard efforts.

517

most fundamental American doctrine—the unalienable rights of the individual person. Later, when the Constitution defined some of these rights in the Bill of Rights, they were recognized as the civil rights of every citizen. Consequently, the individual American was guaranteed by law the right to be different, to be uncommon, to be independent, to follow "a different drummer" as long as he respected the God-given rights of others.

The lazy, the indifferent, the untalented, the follower need not practice these rights, but the opportunities for breaking the common patterns of the Old World were everywhere. The wild frontiers of the seventeenth, eighteenth, and nineteenth centuries fostered self-reliance, responsibility, and independence. American society, shorn of the rigid European class distinctions based upon inherited position, rewarded achievement and personal quality. Every man was freed to pursue his own dreams— to go wherever the limits of his ambition and talent led.

While the spirit of independence and self-determination cannot account for the whole of the American character, it constitutes the most essential key to understanding that character. At their best, Americans have been an independent breed, mistrusting tradition and established procedures. They are fond of improvising, of trying new ways, of creating innovations.

As the tension between this spirit and mass culture, "big" business, "big" labor, and "big" government mounts in our society, more and more we come to value those persons who have accepted the challenge of freedom, who have through originality of talent and temper raised themselves above the "common herd." These independent spirits, recognized in almost every sector of American life, remind us of the best that is in us and in our heritage.

It is only natural that American writers have consistently celebrated the exploits of these independent spirits. Some writers have literally created such heroes out of their own imaginations; other writers have greatly strengthened the position of real life heroes through vivid portraits of their lives in fiction, nonfiction, or poetry. But whether these embodiments of the independent spirits are imagined or real, the writer guarantees their places in our national awareness. In the face of charges that Americans are conformists and organization men, the writer performs a crucial role in reminding us of our national heritage, the independent spirit.

Though there is some question whether or not
a real Paul Bunyan ever lived, there is no doubt about that
famous early American hero, Johnny Appleseed. Born John Chapman in 1774
in Massachusetts, he left his native state early in life and traveled
through the Pennsylvania, Ohio, and Indiana frontier planting nurseries,
healing, and preaching. The profits he made from selling apple seeds
were spent on copies of the works of Emanuel Swedenborg,
a Swedish religious thinker. As you read, try to figure out
why this one individual has captured the imagination of the American
people. Had you met him when he lived, would you have thought him
a person likely to be remembered?

The Apple-Barrel
of Johnny Appleseed

On the mountain peak, called "Going-To-The-Sun,"
I saw gray Johnny Appleseed at prayer
Just as the sunset made the old earth fair.
Then darkness came; in an instant, like great smoke,
The sun fell down as though its great hoops broke   5
And dark rich apples, poured from the dim flame
Where the sun set, came rolling toward the peak,
A storm of fruit, a mighty cider-reek,
The perfume of the orchards of the world,
From apple-shadows: red and russet domes   10
That turned to clouds of glory and strange homes
Above the mountain tops for cloud-born souls:—
Reproofs for men who build the world like moles,
Models for men, if they would build the world
As Johnny Appleseed would have it done—   15
Praying, and reading the books of Swedenborg[1]
On the mountain top called "Going-To-The-Sun."

VACHEL LINDSAY

JOHNNY APPLESEED, *Gropper*

---

1. **Swedenborg**, 1688–1772, Swedish scientist, philosopher, and religious writer.

Few American heroes mean so much to us
as the heroic farmers who fought in the Revolution.
The "minutemen," as they were called, personify the great courage
and determination of the common man in the face of threats
to his liberty. When a statue was raised in honor of these farmers,
the best-known American man-of-letters, Ralph Waldo Emerson,
was asked to write a poem to celebrate the occasion.

Concord Hymn

SUNG AT THE COMPLETION
OF THE BATTLE MONUMENT,
JULY 4, 1837

By the rude bridge that arched the flood,
   Their flag to April's breeze unfurled,
Here once the embattled farmers stood
   And fired the shot heard round the world.

The foe long since in silence slept;   5
   Alike the conqueror silent sleeps;
And Time the ruined bridge has swept
   Down the dark stream which seaward creeps.

On this green bank, by this soft stream,
   We set to-day a votive[1] stone;   10
That memory may their dead redeem,
   When, like our sires, our sons are gone.

Spirit, that made those heroes dare
   To die, and leave their children free,
Bid Time and Nature gently spare   15
   The shaft we raise to them and thee.

RALPH WALDO EMERSON

------

1. **votive**\ˈvō·tĭv\ dedicated in fulfillment of a vow or
in gratitude.

RETREAT OF THE BRITISH
FROM CONCORD,
Alonzo Chappel

I
HEROIC DIVERSITY IN AMERICA

An itinerant preacher and a band of New England farmers: We see in such figures a strictly democratic tendency, a tendency to recognize and praise merit in anyone, regardless of his station in life. Freed from an aristocracy of birth perpetuated by pomp and title, America opened its doors to diversity and individuality. And so the roving Johnny Appleseed and the simple, common farmer became early ideals of the independent spirit.

II
IMPLICATIONS

Answer the following questions either orally or in writing.

1. What are the similarities and differences between Johnny Appleseed, the hero who planted trees, and Paul Bunyan, the hero who chopped them down?

2. Why might Paul Bunyan have become a more popular hero than Johnny Appleseed in twentieth-century America?

3. Long before Lexington and Concord, battles were fought and won by common people, but the credit for victory was usually given to their leaders. What is the special significance of the fact that a *group* of persons remain the great heroes of the first battles of our Revolutionary War?

III
TECHNIQUES

Selection of Significant Detail
and Tone

1. Selection of detail is an even more important technical problem in poetry than in prose, because poetry is usually very compressed. With this in mind, consider the relevance of the fact that Lindsay uses a mountain top called "Going-To-The-Sun" as the setting for his poem. Also, what is the effect of his mentioning it both at the beginning and at the end of the poem?

2. Among the significant details in poetry are the sounds the poet chooses. His choice of sounds will depend partly upon the tone he is trying to create. Emerson, for example, strives for a tone of quiet reverence. Note how his choice of voiceless "s" and "f" consonants helps him to achieve this tone. Still another consonant is used frequently, particularly in the first and second stanzas. What is it? Would you describe it as a harsh or a soft sound?

INDEPENDENT SPIRIT

Moses, Achilles, Aeneas, Roland, King Arthur—you can know a people by their heroes. Over the years Americans, for the most part, have come to admire those men and women whose achievements have exemplified our independent spirit. Consider this small sample of independent spirits in this gallery. The group ranges from Revolutionary leaders through modern adventurers, from war heroes to pioneer women, from legendary figures to a modern scientist. Beloved for different reasons and of unequal fame, the Americans in this gallery can tell you much about the variety of directions in which the independent spirit has expressed itself.

George Washington is the man whose nobility and vision in a formative period guided an infant nation toward greatness. The unusual early American wood sculpture seems comic until you consider the painstaking effort an untrained hand put into creating this historic memorial to a beloved hero.

CARVED MINIATURE
OF GEORGE WASHINGTON
ON HORSEBACK
Unknown American

Nobly carved in marble by
a much more competent hand,
Sam Adams, the explosive
Revolutionary leader,
is displayed in
the nation's Capitol
for all Americans.

JOHN ADAMS
Gilbert Stuart

The second President of the United States,
John Adams, like all of the leaders
in those crucial times, has a lasting place
among those free and courageous men
who lived what they believed
regardless of personal cost.

SAMUEL ADAMS

MASSACHUSETTS

STATUE
OF SAMUEL ADAMS
Anne Whitney

523

DANIEL WEBSTER
Frank McCarthy

Like Washington, the great orator and statesman
Daniel Webster has an image enhanced with myth.
While the painting is realistic enough,
the well-known story by Stephen Vincent Benét,
"The Devil and Daniel Webster,"
shows the hero-worshipping legend.

One more legendary figure
from the Revolutionary War who typified
the independent spirit of the times was Paul
Revere, whose midnight ride to give alarm was
probably, in point of fact, a failure. Yet it gave rise
to a lasting legend memorialized
in painting and verse. Actually, Revere is entitled
to a more stable place in our hall of fame
as a master silversmith.

MIDNIGHT RIDE OF PAUL REVERE
Grant Wood

RETURN OF PRIVATE DAVIS
John Steuart Curry
Courtesy of Alonzo Cudworth Post No. 23,
Milwaukee, Wisconsin

The wars of contemporary history proclaim that the spirit of liberty
nurtured by our forefathers has not died.
The sensitive regional painter, John Steuart Curry,
pictures the RETURN OF PRIVATE DAVIS to his prairie home.
On this theme, a monument in Washington
commemorates the tomb of the Unknown Soldier.

After her mysterious death in 1937, a gallant lady, Amelia Earhart, joined the ranks of fabled Americans. Among many firsts, she was the first woman to fly over the Atlantic Ocean and to cross the United States alone. Her plane disappeared in the Pacific during her attempt to fly around the world.

AMELIA
EARHART
*Bernard
Fuchs*

A PORTRAIT
OF ALBERT EINSTEIN
Antonio Frasconi

The monumental German-born scientist Albert Einstein conceived mathematical theories and calculations which opened the realms of nuclear power and outer space for human entrance. The brooding woodcut is a sensitive tribute to his greatness.

But long before Dr. Einstein, a courageous woman helped open the American frontier: THE PRAIRIE WIFE, collective symbol of the thousands of uncelebrated independent spirits.

THE PRAIRIE WIFE
Harvey Dunn

SPIRIT OF THE INDIAN
Thomas Moran

Ironically, about the time the new
European-American had virtually eliminated
his primitive predecessor, he began to
romanticize him (and the cowboy) into a
favorite American symbol for independence.
The American Indian—the noble savage—
the two final paintings
praise the superb woodsman
and brave warrior,
free as the wind,
a beloved enemy.

THE LAST SCALP
Carl Hassman

Of all the legendary American heroes, probably none is more famous
than the giant logger, Paul Bunyan. As you read the following key episode
from his early life, consider what spirit transforms him
from a simple Canadian student into a potentially great American hero?
"The Winter of the Blue Snow" is the first chapter of *Paul Bunyan*,
a series of Bunyan tales, written by James Stevens, who is probably
the best-known perpetuator of Bunyan lore.

The Winter of the Blue Snow

JAMES STEVENS

Paul Bunyan was the one historian of the useful and the beautiful; other writers of history tell only of terrible and dramatic events. Therefore the chronicles of Paul Bunyan, the mighty logger, the inventor of the lumber industry, the leader-hero of the best band of bullies, the finest bunch of savages, that ever tramped the continent, the master orator of a land that has since grown forests of orators—his chronicles alone tell of the Winter of the Blue Snow.

The blue snow fell first in the North. It fell scantily in its earlier hours, its sapphire flakes floating down on the waves of a mild winter wind, and glittering in an ashen gold light, a sober pale radiance which shimmered through silver mists. There was poetry in the spectacle of these hours. And then the hard gray ground of a peopleless land was hidden under a blanket of dark blue. And the nameless frozen lakes and rivers, the silent valleys and the windy hills of the country were all spread over with a sky-dyed snow. When the last light of this day went out, the boughs of the great pines were creaking under heavy wet masses of snow like torn bales of blue cotton. There was a rush in the snowfall now, as a fiercer wind whipped it on; its heavy flakes were driven down in thick,

whirling clusters, in streaming veils, leaping lines and dashing columns; and there were cloudlike swarms of the blue flakes, which settled slowly, floating easily in the hard wind. This wind got so strong that it shivered the timber, and the piles of blue snow which had gathered on the pine boughs were shaken down. Most of this snow fell into blue mounds around the trees, but some of it fell on the fauna[1] of the forest, adding to their troublement.

At the time of the Winter of the Blue Snow, the forest creatures of this land lived a free and easy life. Man was not there to embarrass them with accusations of trespass and to slay them for their ignorance of the crime. Their main problem was the overcrowding of the forests. The vast moose herds, who populated the woods so densely that traffic through their favorite timber was dangerous, made the matter of getting food a simple one for the carnivorous animals. There were many moose to spare, and the elders of the herds, like most prolific parents, never became frantically resentful over the loss of an offspring. The moose themselves, of course, lived easily on the crisp, juicy moose grass which grew so plenteously in these regions before the blue snow. So the carnivorous creatures of the forests lived a fast and furious

1. **fauna**\ˈfȯ·nə\ the animals of a particular area and time.

life; and it is certain that if they were capable of praise, they had good praises for the moose meat which they got with such little difficulty. The coal-black bruins[2] of the North were an especially happy crowd. Theirs was a gay, frolicsome life in the summer time, when the big bruins danced and galloped through sunny valleys and the small ones had rolling races on shady hillsides. In the fall, all fat and drowsy from moose meat, the bruins would go to sleep in their warm caves and dream pleasantly all winter.

They were all dreaming now; and the blue snow would no doubt have fallen and melted away without their knowledge had it not been for the moose herds which crowded the forest aisles. Moose at that time did not have it in them to enjoy wonder, and they had not learned to combat fear, for they were never afraid. Still, they had some imagination, and the moose trembled when the first blue snowflakes fell among them. They kept up an appearance of unconcern at first, eating moose moss as usual; but they sniffed gingerly at the blue streaks in it, and they stole furtive glances at each other as they bravely ate. This strange snowfall was certainly breeding fear of it in the hearts of all the moose, but each one seemed determined to be the last one to show it. However, as the day-end got near, and the wind grew more boisterous, shaking snow masses from the trees, some of the moose had fits of trembling and eye-rolling which they could not conceal. When a heap of snow dropped on the back of some timid moose, he would twist his head sharply and stare with bulging eyes at the mysteriously fearsome color, then he would prance wildly until the unwelcome snow was bucked from his shivering back. When the early shadows of evening came among the trees, the moose all had a heavy darkness of fear in their hearts. Little was needed to put them in a panic.

It was a great bull moose, a herd king, who forgot the example he owed to his weaker kindred and unloosed a thunderous bellow of terror which started the moose flight, the first memorable incident of the Winter of the Blue Snow. An overladen bough cracked above him; it fell and straddled him from quivering tail to flailing horns, burying him under its wet blue load. He reared out roaring, and his own herd echoed the cry; then a storm of moose bellows crashed through the forest. This tumult died, but there followed the earth-shaking thunder of a stampede.

The bruins, awakened from their pleasant dreams, came out from their caves and blinked at the hosts of terrified moose which were galloping past. The earth-shaking uproar of the flight at last thoroughly aroused the bruins, and they began to sniff the air uneasily. Then they noticed the blue snow; and now in front of every cave crowds of bruins were staring down at the snow; and each bruin was swaying heavily, lifting his left front foot as he swayed to the right, and lifting his right front foot as he swayed to the left. The bruins had no courage either, and, once they had got sleep out of their heads, nearly all of them took out after the moose herds. The wind roared louder with every passing minute this night. And the flakes of the blue snow were as dense as the particles of a fog. At dawn a blue blizzard was raging. But the fauna of the forest plunged tirelessly on, seeking a refuge of white snow.

And Niagara, made faithless by the Blue Terror, galloped behind them—Niagara, the great moose hound, bread-winner for the student of history, Paul Bunyon (his real name), and his companion also.

Paul Bunyon lived at Tonnere Bay.[3] He dwelt in a cave that was as large as ten Mammoth Caves and which had a roof loftier than any tower or spire. But this cave was none too vast for Paul Bunyon, the one man of this region, but one man as great as a city of ordinary men. His tarpaulins and blankets covered one-fourth of the cave floor; his hunting clothes, traps and seines filled another quarter; and the rest of the space was occupied by a fireplace and his papers and books.

2. **bruins**\ˈbrü·ĭnz\ bears, especially brown bears.
3. **Tonnere**\tō ˈnĕr\ **Bay**.

PAUL BUNYON, *Gropper*

For Paul Bunyon was a student now. There had been a time when he had gone forth in the hunting and fishing season to gather the huge supplies of provender[4] which he required, but now his days and nights were all spent with his books. Paul Bunyon's favorite food was raw moose meat, and after he found Niagara in the Tall Wolf country he no longer needed to hunt. Each night Niagara trotted out in the darkness and satisfied his own hunger, then he carried mouthfuls of moose to the cave until he had a day's supply of meat for his master. Niagara

was ever careful not to frighten the moose herds; he hunted stealthily and with quiet. The moose at night were only conscious of a dark cloud looming over them, then numbers of the herds would disappear without painful sound. The moose, if they had thought about it, would have been only thankful to Niagara for lessening the congestion of the forests.

So Paul Bunyon fared well on the moose meat which Niagara brought him, and he lived con-

_____

4. **provender**\\ˈprŏ·vən·dər\\ food.

tentedly as a student in his cave at Tonnere Bay. Each day he studied, and far into the night he figured. Taking a trimmed pine tree for a pencil, he would char its end in the fire and use the cave floor for a slate. He was not long in learning all the history worth knowing, and he became as good a figurer as any man could be.

Vague ambitions began to stir in his soul after this and he often deserted his studies to dream about them. He knew he would not spend his days forever in the cave at Tonnere Bay. Somewhere in the future a great Work was waiting to be done by him. Now it was only a dream; but he was sure that it would be a reality; and he came to think more and more about it. The books were opened less and less; the pine tree pencil was seldom brought from its corner. Paul Bunyon now used another pine tree which still had its boughs; it was a young one, and he brushed his curly black beard with it as he dreamed. But he was still a contented man at the time of the Winter of the Blue Snow, for his dreams had not yet blazed up in a desire for any certain attainment.

On the first day of the blue snow, Paul Bunyon was in a particularly contented mood. He sat all that day before his fire; so charmed with drowsy thoughts was he that he did not once look out. It had been dark a long time before he rolled into his blankets. He awoke at the dawn of a day that had scarcely more light than the night. He was cold, and he got up to throw an armful of trees on the fire. Then he saw the blue drifts which had piled up before the cave, and he saw the fog of the blue blizzard. He heard the roar of a terrific wind, too, and he knew that the storm was perilous as well as strange. But Paul Bunyon thought gladly of the blue snow, for it was a beautiful event, and the historians he liked most would write wonderful books about it.

He kicked the drifts away from the cave entrance, but the usual pile of slain moose was not under them. Paul Bunyon was a little worried, as he thought that Niagara might have lost himself in the blue blizzard. The possibility that the unnatural color of the storm might send the fauna of the forest, and Niagara as well, into panicky flight did not occur to him. He was sure that Niagara would return with a grand supply of moose meat when the blue blizzard had passed.

But the moose herds were now far to the North, fleeing blindly from the blue snow. The bruins galloped after them. Before the day was over, Niagara had overtaken the bruins and was gaining on the moose. At nightfall his lunging strides had carried him far ahead of all the fauna of the forest. He galloped yet faster as he reached the blacker darkness of the Arctic winter. Now the darkness was so heavy that even his powerful eyes could not see in it. . . . Niagara at last ran head-on into the North Pole; the terrific speed at which he was traveling threw his body whirling high in the air; when Niagara fell he crashed through ninety feet of ice, and the polar fields cracked explosively as his struggles convulsed the waters under them. . . . Then only mournful blasts of wind sounded in the night of the Farthest North.

The moose were wearied out before they reached the white Arctic, and hordes of them fell and perished in the blizzard; many others died from fright, and only a tiny remnant of the great herds survived. Some of the bruins reached the polar fields, and they have lived there since. Their hair had turned white from fright, and their descendants still wear that mark of fear. Others were not frightened so much, and their hair only turned gray. They did not run out of the timber, and their descendants, the silver-tip grizzlies, still live in the Northern woods. The baby bruins were only scared out of their growth, and their black descendants now grow no larger than the cubs of Paul Bunyon's time.

Being ignorant of this disaster, Paul Bunyon was comfortable enough while the blizzard lasted. He had a good store of trees on hand and his cave was warm in the storm. He got hungry in the last days; but this emotion, or any emotion, for that matter, could have but little power over him when he was dreaming.

And he dreamed deeply now of great enter-prises; his dreams were formless, without any substance of reality; but they had brilliant colors, and they made him very hopeful.

The sun shone at last from a whitish blue sky, and the strange snow fell no more. A snapping cold was in the land; and pine boughs were bangled and brocaded with glittering blue crystals, and crusty blue snow crackled underfoot.

Paul Bunyon strapped on his snow shoes and started out through the Border forests in search of Niagara. His was a kingly figure as he mushed through the pine trees, looming above all but the very tallest of them. He wore a wine-red hunting cap, and his glossy hair and beard shone under it with a blackness that blended with the cap's color perfectly. His unique eyebrows were black also; covering a fourth of his forehead above the eyes, they narrowed where they arched down under his temples, and they ended in thin curls just in front of his ears. His mustache had natural twirls and he never disturbed it. He wore a yellow muffler this morning under his virile curly beard. His mackinaw[5] coat was of huge orange and purple checks. His mackinaw pants were sober-seeming, having tan and light gray checks, but some small crimson dots and crosses brightened them. Green wool socks showed above his black boots, which had buckskin laces and big brass eyelets and hooks. And he wore striped mittens of white and plum color. Paul Bunyon was a gorgeous picture this morning in the frozen fields and forests, all covered with blue snow which sparkled in a pale gold light.

That day and the next, and for five more days, he searched in vain for Niagara; and neither did he see any moose herds in the woods. Only the frost crackles broke the silences of the deserted blue forests. And at last Paul Bunyon returned to his cave, feeling depressed and lonely. He had not thought that the companionship of Niagara could mean so much to him. In his mood of depression he forgot his hunger and made no further effort to find food.

Lonely Paul Bunyon lay sleepless in his blankets this night, his eyes gleaming through hedgelike eyelashes as their gaze restlessly followed the red flares that shot from the fire and streaked the walls and roof of the cave. He did not realize that his first creative idea was now struggling for birth. He could yet feel no shape of it. He was only conscious of an unaccustomed turmoil of mind. Wearied with fruitless thought, he at last fell into a doze. But Paul Bunyon was not fated to sleep this night. A sustained crashing roar, as of the splintering of millions of timbers, brought him up suddenly; it was hushed for a short second; then a thudding boom sounded from Tonnere Bay. Paul Bunyon leaped to the cave door, and in the moonlight he saw a white wave of water rolling over the blue beach. It came near to the cave before it stopped and receded. He pulled on his boots, and two strides brought him down to the bay. It had been covered with ice seven feet thick, and the cakes of this broken ice were now tossing on heaving waters. Now Paul Bunyon saw two ears show sometimes above the billows; they were of the shape of moose ears, but enormous as his two forefingers. Paul Bunyon waded out into the waters, and he reached these ears a mile from shore. He seized them without fear and he lifted . . . now a head with closed eyes appeared . . . shoulders and forelegs . . . body and hips . . . rear legs and curled tail. It was a calf, newborn apparently, though it was of such a size that Paul Bunyon had to use both arms to carry it.

"*Nom d'un nom!*" exclaimed Paul Bunyon. "*Pauvre petite bleue bête!*"[6]

For this great baby calf was of a bright blue hue which was neither darker nor lighter than the color of the beautiful strange snow. A blue baby ox calf. For such was its sex. Its ears drooped pitifully, and its scrawny, big-jointed legs hung limply below Paul Bunyon's arms. A spasmodic shiver ran from its head to its tail, and its savior was glad to feel this shiver, for

---

5. mackinaw, thick, short, double-breasted woolen coat with a plaid pattern.
6. Nom d'un nom\nōm də nōm\ lit. name of a name; "by Jove." Pauvre petite bleue bête\⌃pō·vrə pĕ ⌃tēt blə bĕt\ poor little blue beast.

it showed that life remained. Paul Bunyon was touched with a tenderness that drove out his loneliness. "*Ma bête,*" he said. "*Mon cher bleu bébé ausha.*"[7]

He turned back through the waters, and the ice cakes pounded each other into bits as they rolled together in his wake. In thirty seconds Paul Bunyon was back in his cave. He spread out his blankets in front of the fire, and he laid Bébé upon them.

Through the night Paul Bunyon worked over the blue ox calf, nursing him back to warm life; and in the morning Bébé was breathing regularly and seemed to rest. Paul Bunyon leaned over to hear his exhalations, and the blue ox calf suddenly opened his mouth and caressed Paul Bunyon's neck with his tongue. Paul Bunyon then discovered that he was ticklish in this region, for the caress impelled him to roll and laugh. The serious student Paul Bunyon had never laughed before; and he now enjoyed the new pleasure to the utmost.

"*Eh, Bébé!*" he chuckled. "*Eh, Bébé! Sacré bleu! Bon bleu, mon cher!*"[8] Bébé raised his eyelids with astonishment upon hearing this cave-shaking chuckle, revealing large, bulging orbs which were of even a heavenlier blue than his silken hair. Such affection and intelligence shone in his eyes that Paul Bunyon wished he would keep his eyes opened. But Bébé was weary and weak, and he closed them again.

He is hungry, thought Paul Bunyon; and he went out to find him food. None of the animals he knew about could supply milk for such a calf as this blue Bébé. But he was newborn and his parents should be somewhere in the neighborhood. Paul Bunyon stepped up on the cliff over which Bébé had bounced when he fell into Tonnere Bay. From here a wide swath of smashed timber ran straight up the side of the tallest Northern mountain. It was here that Bébé had made his thunderous roll of the night before.

Six strides brought Paul Bunyon to the mountain-top. One of its jagged peaks was broken off, showing where Bébé had stumbled over it and fallen. Then Paul Bunyon followed the calf tracks down the land side of the mountain. For two hours he trailed them, but they grew fainter as he went on, and in the Big Bay country the last fall of the blue snow had covered them. Paul Bunyon now had no doubt that Bébé's mother had been frightened by the strange color of the snow and that his blueness was a birthmark. Like Niagara and the fauna of the forest, the parents had stampeded, forgetting the little one. It was no use to search for them.

Paul Bunyon circled back through the forest and gathered a great load of moose moss before he returned to the cave. This rich food would meet the lack of milk. Bébé was asleep before the fireplace when Paul Bunyon returned, and he still slumbered while his friend prepared him some moose moss soup. But when a kettle full of steaming odorous food was set before him, he opened his eyes with amazing energy and sat up. It was then that Bébé first showed the depth and circumstance of his natural appetite, an appetite which was to have its effect on history. He drank most of the moose moss soup at three gulps, he seized the rim of the kettle in his teeth and tilted it up until even the last ten gallons were drained out of it; then, looking roguishly at Paul Bunyon the while, he bit off a large section of the kettle rim and chewed it down, switching his pretty tail to show his enjoyment.

"*Eh, Bébé!*" roared Paul Bunyon, doubling up with laughter for the second time in his life. And he praised the blue snow for giving him such a creature, and did not mourn Niagara, who had never been amusing. But now, as Paul Bunyon doubled over for another rare roar of laughter, he got one more surprise. He was struck with terrifical force from the rear and knocked flat. Paul Bunyon hit the cave floor so hard that its walls were shaken, and a cloud of stones dropped from the roof, covering him from his hips to his thighs. Paul Bunyon dug

---

7. **Mon cher bleu bébé ausha**\mōn chĕr blə bābā ō ᵃsha\ my dear blue baby.
8. **Sacré bleu**\ᵃsa·crā blə\ a mild oath, lit. sacred blue. **Bon bleu**\bōn blə\ good blue.

himself out with no displeasure. He was marveling too much to be wrathful.

There is strength in this baby animal, he thought; surely he has the muscle and energy for great deeds; for that was such a tremendous butting he gave me that I am more comfortable standing than sitting. So he stood and admired this strong and energetic ox calf, who was calmly seated on his haunches before the fireplace, now throwing his head to the right as he licked his right shoulder, now throwing his head to the left as he licked his left shoulder. While Paul Bunyon admired, he pondered; then, even as Bébé had given him his first laugh, the ox calf now showed him the outline of his first real idea. The thought struck him that his student's life was finally over; there was nothing more for him to learn; there was everything for him to do. The hour for action was at hand.

Indeed, if he was to keep this blue ox calf, action was truly necessary. Bébé had shown that his super-abundance of vitality made him dangerous as well as delightful and amusing. This inexhaustible energy of his must be put to work; this vast store of power in an ox-hide should be developed and harnessed to give reality to some one of Paul Bunyon's vague dreams.

Soon the well-fed blue ox calf lay down and slept contentedly. But Paul Bunyon did not sleep. One after another, occupations, enterprises and industries which would be worthy of his knowledge and his extraordinary mental and physical powers, and which would also offer labor great enough for Bébé when he was grown, were considered by Paul Bunyon; but nothing that he thought about satisfied him in the least. Certainly he would have to invent something new; and as he thought of invention, his imagination blazed up like a fire in a dry forest. He was so unused to it that it got out of control, and its smoky flames hid his idea rather than illuminating it.

Wearied at last, he lay on his side, for he remembered his bruises, and he fell into a troubled doze. Now he dreamed and saw great blazing letters which formed the words REAL AMERICA. He sat up, and his bruises gave him such sudden pain that the dream vanished utterly. But he dreamed again before morning. In this second dream he saw no words, but a forest. A flame like a scythe blade sheared through the trees and they fell. Then Paul Bunyon saw in his dream a forest of stumps, and trees were fallen among them.

For many days Paul Bunyon thought about these dreams as he gathered moose moss for Bébé and seined fish from the bay for himself. And for many nights he tried to dream again, but his sleep was the untroubled sleep of the weary.

Bébé grew wonderfully as the weeks went by, and the moose moss made him saucy as well as fat. His bulging blue eyes got a jovial look that was never to leave them. His bellow already had bass tones in it. He would paw and snort and lift his tail as vigorously as any ordinary ox ten times his age. His chest deepened, his back widened, muscle-masses began to swell and quiver under the fat of his shoulders and haunches. The drifts of the beautiful unnatural snow melted away in streams of blue water, and the marvelous color of this historical winter vanished, but the glittering blue of Bébé's silken hair remained. His tail brush was of a darker blue; it looked like a heavily foliaged cypress bough in purple twilight; and Bébé was proud of this wonderful tail brush that belonged to him, for he would twist it from behind him and turn his head and stare at it by the hour.

Now spring came and Paul Bunyon determined to start out with his blue ox calf and try to find the meanings of his dreams. The bright warm hours of these days gave him a tormenting physical restlessness; and his imagination ranged through a thousand lands, playing over a thousand activities. It was certainly the time to begin a Life Work.

Each day Paul Bunyon pondered his two dreams without finding substantial meaning in them. The first one indicated that he should go to Real America; and this Paul Bunyon finally resolved to do, hoping that he would discover the Work that was meant for him and the blue ox calf. He knew that he could not fare worse in that land, for few of the fauna of his native country had returned with the spring, and Paul Bunyon could not live well on a fish diet. Bébé's growing appetite, too, made some move a necessity, for the blue snow had killed the moose grass, and moose moss was a dry food without nourishment in the summer. The more Paul Bunyon thought about Real America, the better he liked the idea of going there. Moose and grass, at least, were to be found across the Border. And no doubt Real America was his Land of Opportunity.

So one fine day Paul Bunyon and Bébé came down to the Border. The blue ox calf frolicked with his master and bellowed happily when he saw the green grass and clover on the hills of Real America. He was for rushing over at once, but Paul Bunyon, the student, was not unmindful of his duty to his new country; he would not enter it without fitting ceremonies and pledges, though Bébé butted him soundly in resenting the delay.

Now Paul Bunyon lifted his hands solemnly and spoke in the rightful language of Real America.

"In becoming a Real American, I become Paul *Bunyan*," he declared. "I am Paul *Bunyon* no more. Even so shall my blue ox calf be called Babe, and Bébé no longer. We are now Real Americans both, hearts, souls and hides."

After uttering these words with feeling and solemnity, an emotion more expansive, more uplifting and more inspiring than any he had ever known possessed Paul Bunyon and transfigured him. His chest swelled, his eyes danced and glittered, and his cheeks shone rosily through the black curls of his beard.

"And I'm glad of it!" he roared. "By the holy old mackinaw, and by the hell-jumping, high-tailed, fuzzy-eared, whistling old jeem cris and seventeen slippery saints, I'm *proud* of it, too! Gloriously proud!"

Then he felt amazed beyond words that the simple fact of entering Real America and becoming a Real American could make him feel so exalted, so pure, so noble, so good. And an indomitable conquering spirit had come to him also. He now felt that he could whip his weight in wildcats, that he could pull the clouds out of the sky, or chew up stones, or tell the whole world anything.

"Since becoming a Real American," roared Paul Bunyan, "I can look any man straight in the eye and tell him to go to hell! If I could meet a man of my own size, I'd prove this instantly. We may find such a man and celebrate our naturalization in a Real American manner. We shall see. Yay, Babe!"

Then the two great Real Americans leaped over the Border. Freedom and Inspiration and Uplift were in the very air of this country, and Babe and Paul Bunyan got more noble feelings in every breath. They were greatly exhilarated physically at first; and they galloped over valleys and hills without looking about them, but only breathing this soul-flushing air and roaring and bellowing their delight in it.

But before the day was over, Paul Bunyan discovered that Real America had its sober, matter-of-fact side also. A whisper stirred in his heart: "To work! Take advantage of your opportunity!" The whisper got louder and more insistent every moment; and at last the idea it spoke possessed Paul Bunyan, and he sat down to ponder it, letting Babe graze and roll on the clover-covered hills.

Now the whisper became an insistent cry: "Work! Work! Work!" Paul Bunyan looked up, and he seemed to see the word shining among the clouds; he looked down then into the vast valley, and he seemed to see—by the holy old mackinaw! he did see—the forest of his second dream! And now he knew it: his Life Work was to begin here.

For many days and nights Paul Bunyan pondered on the hillside before the Great Idea came to him. Like all Great Ideas, it was simple enough, once he had thought of it. Real

America was covered with forests. A forest was composed of trees. A felled and trimmed tree was a log. Paul Bunyan threw aside his pine tree beard brush and jumped to his feet with a great shout.

"What greater work could be done in Real America than to make logs from trees?" he cried. "Logging! I shall invent this industry and make it the greatest one of all time! I shall become a figure as admired in history as any of the great ones I have read about."

Paul Bunyan then delivered his first oration. The blue ox calf was his only listener; and this was a pity, for Paul Bunyan's first oratorical effort, inspired as it was, surely was one of his noblest ones. But we know the outline of this oration, if not the words. It dealt mainly with the logging method which he had devised in the moment, the one which he used in his first work. So he told of his plan to uproot the trees by hand, and to transport the logs overland, binding a bundle of them on one side of Babe, and hanging a sack of rocks from the other side for ballast. It was months after this that he made his first improvement, the using of a second bundle of logs, instead of rocks, for ballast. And at this moment Paul Bunyan, for all his foresight and imagination, could not have dreamed of the superb tools and marvelous logging methods that he was to originate, or of the countless crews of little loggers that he was to import from France, Ireland, Scotland and Scandinavia, or of the tremendous river drives and the mammoth camp life he was to create. He would have been bewildered then by the fact that he would some day need a foreman as grand as himself for his Life Work; and the notion that he would some day need help in his figuring would have seemed like a far-fetched jest.

No; in this first oration, imaginative and eloquent as it must have been, Paul Bunyan only spoke of simple work for himself and Babe. But he only tells us that the oration was not a long one, for the call to Work came more insistently as he ended each period. At last he had to an-

swer this powerful call. He commanded, "Yay, Babe!" and the baby blue ox and Paul Bunyan descended into the valley to begin the first logging in the Real American woods.

I
THE MAKING OF A HERO
Like Hercules of the ancient Greeks and Samson of the Israelites, Paul Bunyan is a hero in the strong-man tradition. But, as you can see clearly in this selection, it is not strength alone that makes Bunyan a hero. Before he performs heroic deeds, he needs a personal vision, a sense of purpose that will allow him to put his strength to good use. He dares to dream his own dream, simple but new. The connection between heroic acts and a vision of "Life Work" is a very close one. You can probably think of a great many heroes who—like Paul Bunyan—would never have become great men if they hadn't developed a dream of their own and a sense of mission in life.

II
IMPLICATIONS
What does each of the following quotations reveal about Bunyan and his spirit?

1. . . . he was still a contented man at the time of the Winter of the Blue Snow, for his dreams had not yet blazed up in a desire for any certain attainment.

2. The thought struck him that his student's life was finally over; there was nothing more for him to learn; there was everything for him to do. The hour for action was at hand.

3. In this second dream he saw no words, but a forest. A flame like a scythe blade sheared through the trees and they fell. Then Paul Bunyon saw in his dream a forest of stumps, and trees were fallen among them.

4. Then he felt amazed beyond words that the simple fact of entering Real America and becoming a Real American could make him feel so exalted, so pure, so noble, so good.

5. . . . Paul Bunyan discovered that Real America had its sober, matter-of-fact side also. A whisper stirred in his heart: "To work! Take advantage of your opportunity!"

6. Like all Great Ideas, it was simple enough, once he had thought of it.

III
TECHNIQUES

Especially in brief biographical essays and poems of the sort that appear in this unit, the details an author chooses to include in his biographical portrait are of the greatest importance. Clearly, the writer cannot tell the whole story of his subject in a brief space, and the reader should never assume that he is getting the whole truth. The reader can get some notion of how objective or slanted a biography is, however, if he will pay close attention to the details upon which the writer focuses and to the writer's attitude toward his subject. We will discuss these two aspects of technique—selection of significant detail and tone—in this unit.

Selection of Significant Detail

James Stevens was familiar with the oral Bunyan legends and used some folk elements in his stories, but he also frankly admitted that he called upon his own imagination for many important details. Let us look at the specific portrait of Bunyan that Stevens creates through the details he chooses to use.

First, note that though Paul is a giant, taller than all but the very tallest pine trees, Stevens does not make very much of Paul's size and strength; as a matter of fact, Babe, the great blue ox (who was created by Stevens), is obviously intended to play the role of laborer. This is not to say that Paul's great size and strength are unimportant, but it is clear from the greater number of details dealing with him as an independent thinker and dreamer that Stevens's Bunyan is much more than a strong man.

The details at the beginning and end of this selection reveal that this Paul Bunyan has to do with "the beautiful and useful"; he is eloquent, imaginative, inventive. He is, in fact, primarily a symbol of American energy and "know-how."

Tone

"Tone," in fiction, usually refers to the author's attitude toward his material. Just as a speaker's tone of voice shows his attitude, so a writer reveals his attitude toward his subject in various ways. Some of the devices that communicate tone in writing are very simple, such as the use of capital letters, italics, or exclamation points to indicate emphasis. A somewhat more subtle means of emphasizing a point is to place it in a strategic position, especially at the end of a paragraph or section of a work. Word choice also commonly reveals an author's attitude toward his subject; consider, for example, the contrast in connotation between "fuzz," "cop," and "law-enforcement officer," all of which may be used to refer to a policeman.

As one indication of Stevens's tone, note his use of capital letters in "Great Idea" and other such phrases. As you know, proper nouns and adjectives are normally used to denote specific persons, places, and things: George Washington, the Alamo, the Ford Motor Company. By using capital letters for the phrase, "Great Idea," Stevens means to convey that Bunyan's idea is unique, the only one of its kind—or at least the first one of its kind.

In "REAL AMERICA" Stevens goes a step further, capitalizing every letter of the phrase. The capitalization of the word "real" would seem to set off Canada—Paul's birthplace—from the United States; but since there is no serious criticism of Canada in the story, it is unlikely that Stevens wants us to think of Canada as a "false America." It is more likely that he means that REAL AMERICA is a place where a man can be a REAL MAN, a he-man.

The frequency with which the author repeats such phrases as "Real America" and "Real American" tends to show that he is deeply committed to this idea. His tone is serious; he cares for his hero and the values he stands for—he cares for the rugged American and the North Woods, where the American Bunyan dreams his dreams and performs his heroic and Herculean deeds.

No one can trace any aspect of American culture back very far
without bumping into Benjamin Franklin, for he seems to have dabbled
in most fields. He was a scientist, an inventor, an oculist, an "Emily Post,"
a public servant, a diplomat, and more. Americans like to think of him
as the first typical American. If this is true, what are the qualities,
then, that Americans like to think they typically possess?

Benjamin Franklin: Multiple Genius

DONALD CULROSS PEATTIE

When the public opened its favorite almanac for the year 1733 it discovered, among the usual weather predictions and herb remedies, that a new inmate had come to the American household. By name Poor Richard, he was poor only in purse, not in wit, good cheer, or good sense, and his sayings were to make men smile now as then. "Three removes are as bad as a fire." "Keep thy shop and it will keep thee." "Fish and visitors smell in three days." "A house without a wife and fire-light is like a body without soul or sprite." This threadbare scholar who made the almanac's astronomical calculations and interlarded them with confidences about his wife and hard times supposedly handed in his copy to the printer, one Benjamin Franklin.

With each succeeding year the fame of Poor Richard's *Almanac* grew by leaps and chuckles. Soon 10,000 copies a year were sold—one to every hundred Americans, with probably ten times that many readers. Some of these wrote Richard to ask how he kept up the pretense of being poor. He answered that Benjamin Franklin made off with most of the profits. Somewhat as Charlie McCarthy does with Bergen today, Richard took his revenge on the author of his being; "Ben raps his poll, and fancies wit will come; but all in vain, there's nobody at home."

A new kind of laughter had been born to print—American humor, dry, crackling, quizzical, the wit that made Artemus Ward, Mark Twain, Will Rogers. And for the first time a genuine American had appeared in fiction, as Yankee as Y. Doodle, Esq. Every reader could find something of himself in Poor Richard.

The reason for that was that Benjamin Franklin, printer, editor, author, humorist, moralist, and businessman, was in himself a whole crowd of men. But Poor Richard and Benjamin Franklin are far from being one and the same person. Richard was economical; Ben enjoyed his money when he had it, though he was the same generous, contented man without it; Richard recommended temperance and silence whereas Ben loved wines and talk. Richard pointed out the virtue of orderliness; Ben found it easier to remember where he put things than to tidy them. These are some of the human foibles of the most human of great men, Ben-of-all-trades.

Franklin was born in Boston, in 1706, of what he called the "middling people." His father was a candlemaker, whose fathers before him had been honest yeomen of Oxfordshire. Ben's mother was a tidy Nantucket woman, and her mother had come to this country as a "bound-out girl" or indentured servant. Ben grew rich and Ben grew famous without ever feeling that he need rise higher than the honest folk who made him. By his life he ennobled his ancestors.

No learned man ever learned less from school. He had only two years of formal education, did poorly in Latin, and failed in arithmetic—the two subjects by which teachers then judged a boy's mental powers. Later he taught himself mathematics; he taught himself French, Spanish, and Italian, and found they made Latin easy. In fact, Franklin taught himself almost everything that ever entered his encyclopedic mind. Except printing; that he learned during an apprenticeship to his brother James, who was then the best printer in America. The boy was soon an expert, too. Jealousy in James and independence in Ben led James to raining blows on his younger brother. That's how James came to advertise for a "likely lad" to learn the printing trade.

But the likeliest lad in all America was then tramping the streets of Philadelphia, a sixteen-year-old runaway looking for work. When he found it, he meant to—and did—pull himself hand over hand up the ladder.

Ten years later Benjamin Franklin was the best and biggest printer in America, producing almanacs, religious books, text books, reprints of classics, and the finest in current English literature. He did all the government printing for Pennsylvania, Delaware, Maryland and New Jersey. He had founded the first German-language newspaper in this country, and was editing the magazine that became the *Saturday Evening Post*. The runaway waif was now in easy circumstances and the head of a family.

And within twenty years Ben Franklin had become Philadelphia's most prominent citizen, clerk of the colony's Assembly, alderman of the city's Common Council, organizer of the first fire brigade, too. Ten years more, and he was Grand Master of the Pennsylvania Masons, founder of the Philadelphia Academy, (Pennsylvania's first college), the colony's postmaster and its most potent politician behind the scenes. He had originated the American Philosophical Society, formed to link native scientists together; on its rolls are many of the most famous names in our scientific history, and today it annually distributes hundreds of thousands of dollars for grants-in-aid to research. Incidentally, Franklin had invented a stove, which gave twice as much heat for a quarter of the fuel and made his name as much a household word as even Poor Richard.

BEN FRANKLIN, *Duplessis*

Then when he was forty, comfortably settled, with all the importance that a big frog in a small pond could wish for, world fame burst upon him. From a traveling "professor" he purchased a bit of parlor magic, as it was then considered, a jar for condensing electricity produced by hand friction. Only a small boy would have taken the "magic" apart to see what made it work, and only a philosopher would have succeeded. With so much of both in him, Ben Franklin in a few months found out more about the mysterious science of electricity than had all the scientists from Aristotle to Newton. As sparks literally and figuratively flew from his woodshed-laboratory, the crowds had to be roped back with chains.

Franklin was the first man ever to understand that electricity is a current, the first to conduct an electric current where he wished, the first to grasp the concept that electricity is energy. Before him, no man ever turned a wheel by electricity, or made a bell ring by it. He invented the words, still unimproved in the electrician's vocabulary: storage battery, charged, uncharged, conductor, nonconductor, condenser, positive electricity, negative electricity. The words imply how much he discovered that was new. They sound self-explanatory now, but that is because Ben explained them to himself and the world.

Franklin's experiments literally electrified European scientific circles. They brought him membership in learned societies and honorary degrees from the greatest universities, carrying with them the title of "Doctor" Franklin. But more, the spark of Franklin's genius had touched off the humming dynamo of the electrical age. Ben wished that he could wake up every hundred years after his death and see how his country was getting on. Could he do so now, he would find his people reading by electric lights, telephoning on electric wire, and watching and listening to concerts, news and sports events by electrical waves. And he would chuckle with delight before sleeping again.

When Franklin was appointed Postmaster for all the American colonies in 1753, his genius for administration found scope. Mails were few, slow, and irregular, the balance sheets were in red ink, and the regulations in red tape. Franklin substituted a system of accounting that the simplest postmaster could put into practice. In a short time his department showed a profit, and he had the mails traveling day and night, every day in the year, between the principal cities. Franklin's improved postal communications did more than anything else to link together the colonies for their approaching struggles.

As postmaster, he also took on the task of quartermaster when Braddock[1] came over with his Redcoats to repel the French and Indians. Braddock found himself unable to assemble transport trains, but Franklin in two weeks collected 150 wagons, complete with horses and drivers, loaded them with supplies, and sent them to the astounded, grateful commander. And when, after Braddock's ill-starred campaign, the colony lay open to French vessels by sea and Indians on the frontier, Ben Franklin was alert to its unpreparedness. He organized the first militia, serving in it himself as a common soldier who shouldered a musket and paced on guard duty. He got up a lottery and bought cannon with the proceeds. He worried the Assembly into arming the colony.

But though no Quaker, Franklin was no vigilante[2] either. When some hot heads on the frontier revenged themselves for redskin outrages by butchering the women and children of peaceful, Christianized Indians, and these redmen, fleeing to Philadelphia, were pursued by a howling mob, the Governor called on Franklin to take command of the militia and quell the riot with it. Instead, Franklin went out, unarmed, to meet the violent crowd, and with words alone turned it back. As he wrote smilingly to a friend in London: "Within twenty-four hours your old friend was a common soldier, a councillor, a kind of dictator, an ambassador to a country mob and, on his returning home, a nobody again."

This nobody was sent, in 1764, to London to stand up to Parliament, King, and the ruling Tory class, for the rights first of Pennsylvania, then of Massachusetts too, and finally of all the colonies. Franklin's famous appearance before Parliament in 1766, to fight the hated Stamp Act, was a model of how to answer a legislative committee. Never growing angry, always replying in two or three clear sentences, unshakably grounded in his facts, Franklin in one day answered 174 questions, and to Parliament's own complete astonishment it repealed the Stamp Act in short order. Franklin's testimony, circulated in print all over Europe and Amer-

1. **Braddock**, Edward, 1695–1755, Commander-in-Chief of British forces in America.
2. **vigilante** \'vĭ·jə ▲län·tē\ a member of a volunteer citizens committee to suppress and punish crime.

PRIDE BREAKFASTED WITH PLENTY, DINED WITH POVERTY, AND SUPPED WITH INFAMY.

PRIDE THAT DINES ON VANITY SUPS ON CONTEMPT.

Poor Richard's way to wealth

ica, made him overnight one of the great practical politicians of the age. The world, for the first time, heard the true voice of America.

After eleven years of diplomatic experience, Franklin escaped from England just as the mother country and her colonies came to blows. When in the hot first days of July 1776, the Continental Congress assembled in Philadelphia, Franklin was appointed, with Adams and Jefferson, to draw up the Declaration of Independence. Jefferson is the foremost author of it. Franklin modified the wording, making it calmer and more exact in many places.

Now what the new-born nation needed was recognition by foreign powers, above all by France, then the hereditary foe of England. France must be persuaded to lend money and send arms to the ill-prepared bankrupt states. To Franklin fell this task of wheedling vast sums out of the depleted treasury of the indecisive Louis XVI, to be loaned to a nation without credit or security, an infant nation that seemed, from day to day, about to breathe its last. All this Franklin accomplished; even when Arnold was defeated at Quebec, and Washington at Long Island, even when the British took Philadelphia, Franklin could get fresh loans. And this in spite of the jealousy and obstructions of some of his fellow American commissioners, in spite of the suavity of the British ambassador at Paris, and the spies that he introduced right into Franklin's secret negotiations. Where other emissaries were failing to get recognition or aid from Holland, Spain, and Prussia, Franklin succeeded in France. He did this because he was Benjamin Franklin, the "good Doctor," and because honest and candid men found him candid and honest, scheming men found him wilier than they, learned men

541

found him scholarly, and simple men found him one of themselves.

In more than 150 years of American diplomacy, Benjamin Franklin is probably the most consummate diplomat we have ever had. He possessed the two great qualifications an American ambassador must have—popularity in the land to which he is accredited, and an instinctive awareness, even when out of communication, of what the folks back home are thinking. To him more than to any other man, Washington and Lafayette not excepted, was due the treaty of alliance with France which cheered the troops at Valley Forge and brought victory to the American Revolution. When Franklin was at last presented at Versailles[3] as the ambassador of a recognized nation, he appeared, not in the satin and wig and sword of fashion, but in his old brown coat, carrying his walking stick, wearing his square-rimmed spectacles. This he did because the world wanted it; the legend of the good old Doctor was already firm, and what could he do but dress to look like the man who was appearing on every fan and snuff box?

After Yorktown, Franklin was still needed abroad for the peace negotiations. He countered every foxy twist and turn of foreign diplomacy, got America the boundaries she asked for—west to the Mississippi. Franklin won the peace as definitely as Washington won the war.

The roar of cannon announced his return to the United States. Bells rocked their steeples. Every organization in Philadelphia turned out to greet the greatest civilian hero of the American Revolution. The Union Fire Company, which he had founded 50 years before, contained only four other members of the original roll call, but they were there to welcome him, and Franklin told them that he would have his bucket and axe in order by the next meeting.

Elected to the Pennsylvania legislature, he was soon in its president's chair. There, though conservatives had voted him in and though he was rich and old now, he remained what he had been when a poor young man—a liberal, vigilant to protect minorities, foe of vengeful and class legislation, putting human rights ahead of property rights.

These principles he brought with him to the convention that met in 1787 to draw up a constitution for the United States. Long ago Franklin had declared that the colonies should form a union; now the living spirit of our nation was to be given a body. But tempers waxed hot those blistering days; over and over, Franklin's good humor and tact restored better feeling—like Lincoln, he had a habit of turning away wrath by telling a funny story. Thus he did much to keep the convention from failure by disunity; he successfully fought property as a qualification for voting or office-holding, and in the end it was he who unsnarled the worst knot in the convention: the big states wanted representation proportional to population, and the little states wanted equal votes for all. For weeks the delegates had been deadlocked over this question. Then Franklin got up and proposed the compromise that is built into our system of government today—proportional representation in the House, but equal in the Senate.

Yet those far-seeing eyes of Franklin's were beginning to fail; so, ever ingenious, he invented bifocal lenses. He was getting too old to climb up for a book he might want on the top shelf, so he devised the hook and pole still used today in libraries and groceries. He was eighty-four when death came in 1790, a not unwelcome visitor.

Behind him he left invested funds for charitable and educational institutions, in Boston and Philadelphia, which have been used to benefit scholars and research ever since; by 1991 this little nest-egg of Franklin's will have grown to four million dollars. A bit of it was willed to provide silver medals for outstanding boy scholars in the high-schools of his native Boston. About thirty medals a year are awarded, and since 1793 some 4,500 have been received

---

3. **Versailles**\věr ▲sai\ famous palace built by Louis XIV.

by proud youngsters. The boy who lived to become a printer, editor, humorist, inventor, scientist, businessman, legislator, diplomat, philanthropist, patriot, and multiple genius is thus still hopefully looking for some American lad of today to fill his square-buckled shoes.

I

THE ALL-AROUND MAN

Henry David Thoreau once wrote, "I have never yet met a man who was quite awake." If he had met Ben Franklin, do you think he would have modified his statement? Most people probably feel that they could accomplish much more if they used more of the energy they have. And perhaps this is one of the reasons Americans admire all-around men like Ben Franklin, men who live up to their full potential and achieve first rank in a wide range of endeavors. What other reasons can you offer for American admiration of the all-around man?

II

IMPLICATIONS

Discuss the following statements in the light of your experience and of the selection.

1. It was easier to become an all-around man in Franklin's time than it is in the more complex society in which we now live.

2. It is much wiser for a person to channel his energies into a special field than to attempt to become an all-around man like Franklin.

3. Franklin was probably born with greater talent and energy than other people; otherwise he could not have succeeded in so many diverse fields.

4. Franklin's life disproves the old adage, "Jack of all trades, master of none."

5. Franklin's story shows that a person can achieve success in many fields despite a lack of education.

III

TECHNIQUES

Selection of Significant Detail

Mr. Peattie set himself the difficult task of portraying the many-sidedness of Franklin's character in a relatively brief space. The danger in such presentations is that they are likely to consist of a series of oversimplified generalities unsupported by evidence and dramatized details which allow the reader to form a concrete image of the subject.

Discuss whether Peattie avoided these dangers by showing whether or not he offered sufficient evidence or good concrete images to support the following general statements:

1. . . . he was poor only in purse, not in wit, good cheer, or good sense. . . .

2. Benjamin Franklin . . . was in himself a whole crowd of men.

3. In fact, Franklin taught himself almost everything that ever entered his encyclopedic mind.

4. . . . when he was forty . . . world fame burst upon him.

5. Franklin's experiments literally electrified European scientific circles.

6. . . . Benjamin Franklin is probably the most consummate diplomat we have ever had.

7. . . . Franklin's good humor and tact restored better feeling [at the 1787 convention]. . . .

Tone

Essays may be divided into two broad categories: *formal* and *informal*. Tone is one of the main standards used to make this division. The formal essay has a serious, dignified tone; the informal essay has a more intimate, lighter tone.

This essay would be classified as informal. Note, for example, that the author frequently refers to Franklin as *Ben* rather than *Benjamin*. Early in the essay he draws a comparison between Poor Richard and Edgar Bergen's dummy, Charlie McCarthy. Such a comparison would clearly be out of place in a formal essay, for it would work against its dignity of tone. What other word choices or details reveal that this is an informal essay?

Lincoln was so clearly a man of the people, so clearly one of us,
that we may wonder how it was that he accomplished so much and we
so little. Baffled by his humility and simplicity, we may ask whether,
perhaps, he was one of those who have greatness thrust upon them; whether,
if it had not been for such events as the Civil War and the assassination,
he might have been just another president. To put it simply, was Lincoln
a shaper of events, or was he shaped by them? The following account
should give some basis for answering this question. It is the last chapter
of Paul Horgan's *Citizen of New Salem,* a biographical sketch which traces Lincoln's
transformation from a twenty-one-year-old flatboatman to a twenty-eight-year-old
State Assemblyman and counselor-at-law. The transformation took place
in the small frontier town of New Salem, Illinois.

Lincoln Becomes a Lawyer

PAUL HORGAN

I*f you are resolutely determined to make a lawyer of yourself, the thing is more than half-done already. . . .*

What if there was no one at New Salem[1] to teach him the law—no one to "read with," as he said? If a man must do it alone, he could do so. The main thing was to get the necessary books and read them, and study their principal features. What did it matter if New Salem was a small town which "never had three hundred people living in it?" All that mattered were the books and his capacity for understanding them. These would be "just the same" wherever he might be. Surely his own resolution to succeed must be "more important than any other one thing?"

The stage fare from New Salem to Springfield was a dollar and a half. The assemblyman rode in a farmer's wagon or walked to Springfield to borrow law books from Attorney Stuart. He went more than once, and one day at an auction he bought a copy of Blackstone's *Commentaries on the Common Law.* Back home it

was now the law books—Chitty or Blackstone[2] —which he took everywhere with him. The neighbors saw him and remembered how he studied wherever he could—"in some nook in a store," or at "the foot of a hay-stack," or "sometimes lying on his back, putting his feet up the tree. . . ." They were used to him and let him be, though to an occasional observer he was a sight. Russell Godbey, the farmer, for whom he did odd jobs, found him one day sitting barefoot at the top of a woodpile with a book. It might seem a curious thing for a farm hand to be doing, and the farmer asked,

"What are you reading?"

"I am not reading," replied the farm hand, "I am studying."

"Studying what?"

"Law, sir," said the farm hand with emphasis. Russell Godbey said it was really too much for him, as he looked at the law student, "sitting there proud as Cicero." Going on his way,

---

1. **New Salem,** village in central Illinois, now reconstructed and located on the outskirts of Springfield.
2. **Chitty or Blackstone.** Joseph Chitty, author of *Chitty on Contracts;* Sir William Blackstone, author of *Commentaries on the Laws of England,* which influenced jurisprudence in United States.

"Great God Almighty!" exploded Mr. Godbey.

During the spring and summer of 1835 New Salem had its own excitements. Samuel Hill built a carder[3] and storehouse for wool. The carding machine was powered from a treadmill walked by oxen on a tilted wooden wheel with cleats—a late marvel of the mechanic arts. A new sound—the friction of moving wood, the muffled knock of hooves on wood—entered the village day. On August seventeenth at night a tornado came tubing and screaming over the prairie and in its wake Matthew S. Marsh saw fences flat, trees uprooted, and corn beaten down. At daylight he went to put up his fence and saw to his amazement how "two great wolves walked along unconcerned within 50 yards of me." Eight days later at her father's farm northeast of New Salem, after an illness of six weeks, young Anne Rutledge died.

The law student knew her well, as he knew all her family. She was the third of nine children, and as a boarder at her father's New Salem tavern in 1833 he had surely seen her. She was vivacious and pretty, with auburn hair and blue eyes. At quilting bees she was faster than anyone with her needle, and in the other household arts she was accomplished. She would make someone a good wife.

In 1832 she became engaged to a prosperous young farmer and storekeeper who went east to arrange his affairs with a promise to return and marry Miss Rutledge. Time passed while his letters dwindled and finally ceased. She grieved. The law student saw her so, and certain neighbors wondered if he might be ready to fall in love. A few became sure for all their lives that he courted her and that she was prepared to accept him. She hesitated, but at last wrote to break her engagement. No answer came. Torn between desires, she fell ill and within a few weeks was dying of fever. One of her brothers said she kept asking for the law student and at the last she was allowed to be alone with him. A few days later she lost consciousness and on August twenty-fifth she died. They buried her in Concord graveyard.

New Salem sorrowed for Anne. Some said long afterward that the law student sorrowed more than anyone—that once again they feared for his reason. Slicky Greene reported that when the snows or rains fell, the law student was filled with "indescribable grief" at the thought of how they fell on her small resting place in the country graveyard. His inclination to occasional low spirits seemed to be increased by her death. She used to sing hymns to him. The last one she ever sang was "Vain Man, thy fond pursuits forbear." Sometimes, even where advantage lay, human pursuits seemed futile. Where of advantage there was none, depression could the more easily enter a man. "Woefully abstracted," said a friend, the law student would range along the river and into the woods. Neighbors kept an eye on him especially on "damp, stormy days, under the belief that dark and gloomy weather might produce such a depression of spirits as to induce him to take his own life."

It was one thing to be given "the hypo," as he called it, by fugitive annoyances; quite another to be lost to the whole daily world. Finally he was persuaded to stay for a few weeks with the jolly justice of the peace, Judge Bowling Green, beyond the little hills north of New Salem. Judge Green loved to laugh with all his three hundred pounds. The shape of his belly earned him the nickname of "Pot." He was good for the law student. The ordinary matters of life proceeded. The law student tended the post office, though someone complained that he neglected his duties at this time. He studied. He surveyed a ten-acre lot of timber. He wrote to the Governor of Illinois to endorse an applicant for the post of public auditor. On December seventh, 1835, he was counted present at the opening of a special session of the Assembly in Vandalia.[4] On March twenty-fourth, 1836, his name was entered on the record of the Sangamon[5] Circuit

---

3. **carder,** place for combing and cleansing wool.
4. **Vandalia**\văn ˄dā·lyə\ city in south-central Illinois; capital of Illinois 1820–36.
5. **Sangamon**\˄săŋ·gă·mən\ county in central Illinois.

Court as a man of good moral character. This was the first of three steps leading to the license to practice law. The law student was coming back to himself. Years afterward, Isaac Cogsdale, formerly of New Salem, said he heard him say of Anne Rutledge, "I loved her dearly . . ."

Throughout the spring he was active as deputy surveyor, but in May he lost his other position when the post office of New Salem was discontinued by the government. The village had ceased to grow—had even begun to decline. Families moved away. A number of them founded the town of Petersburg which the deputy surveyor had laid out in February. Perhaps the future lay elsewhere.

A daguerrotype of Lincoln taken when he was thirty-six.

In early summer an old excitement came back in the air, for it was again a campaign year, and the assemblyman announced his stand for reëlection on June thirteenth. "All," he said, should share the privileges of the government "who assist in bearing its burthens." He believed all whites who bore arms and paid taxes should vote, not excluding females—though he could not have imagined women

in the army. He declared further that he went for "distributing the proceeds of the sales of the public lands to the several states."

From July fourth, when the campaign opened at Petersburg, to the thirtieth, when it ended at Springfield two days before the election, the candidate toured the district with his rivals. They came to meetings on horseback, riding into a grove in the forenoon, when the opposing candidates took turns speaking until all were done. If a fight broke out that seemed to depart from fair play, the tall candidate from New Salem stepped in to shake the fighters apart. He spoke in groves and on farms, supporting the Whig position. On July twenty-ninth he spoke at the farm of Isaac Spear, six miles southeast of Springfield, where the campaign would wind up.

Moving on, he rode past the new house of old George Forquer, who was running against him. On top of the house—it was regarded as the finest house in Springfield—he saw, for the first time, a lightning rod.

What a contraption. He never saw the like. It led him to speculate about electrical conduction. It gave him thoughts about the owner.

George Forquer had until recently been a Whig himself, but now he was running as a Democrat, and what was more, as a new Democrat who had been given the post of register of the Land Office at a fine salary—three thousand dollars a year. No wonder he could build a new frame house with a lightning rod on top. It was enough to give a man the hypo. The New Salem candidate rode on to Springfield.

There the next day he took his turn and made his speech. He was the last. When he was done, the crowd began to go. Democratic Land Office Register George Forquer rose to detain the crowd and they turned back to listen.

He was sorry, he said, but of his opponent, who had just spoken, he must say that "the young man would have to be taken down."

The Democrat, as an elderly and prominent man, had much to say and he said it at length, and with every air of superiority. The New Salem candidate stood aside, listening intently and with growing excitement. His chance for rebuttal came, and he took the platform again, made another speech, and ended with this:

"Mr. Forquer commenced his speech by announcing that the young man would have to be taken down. It is for you, citizens, not for me to say whether I am up or down. The gentleman has seen fit to allude to my being a young man; but he forgets that I am older in years than I am in the tricks and trades of politicians. I desire to live, and I desire place and distinction; but I would rather die now, than, like the gentleman, live to see the day that I would change my politics for an office worth three thousand dollars a year, and then feel compelled to erect a lightning rod to protect a guilty conscience from an offended God."

"*Wonderful,*" said a witness, the effect of this reply was wonderful, something he would never forget. The public was captivated by it. Two days later, on August first, the young man from New Salem—he was twenty-seven—was reëlected by the highest vote out of the field of seventeen candidates. On December fifth, then, he was present when the Tenth General Assembly of Illinois met in Vandalia.

He came there with his desired goal more clearly in sight, for on September ninth he had applied for a license to practice law in all the courts of the state, and this had been granted to him on the same day. It was the second official step which would lead him to the work he wanted. Only one more remained. But before he could take it, he must serve the Assembly in his elected duty. Because of their height, he and the other eight members of the Sangamon delegation were nicknamed the Long Nine.

In his current term, as in his previous one, the assemblyman met with a wide range of affairs in the bills proposed, the debates which resulted, the hearings which were required, and the disposals made. All these reflected the needs and aspirations, the concerns and the natures of the men and women whose lives they sought to govern for the better.

The assemblyman took part in the vote on such matters as the works of human justice and dignity which appeared in bills on the establishment of circuit courts, and on the powers of justices of the peace, and on legislative procedures, and on the delineation of voting districts and precincts. With his fellow members he voted on the election of the United States Senator. He considered as a committee member the problems inseparable from the disposition of public monies, and with scarcely a half-cent piece in his pocket, he voted on questions of taxation, of banking, and of incorporation of insurance companies and railroads. The Assembly was much occupied with the development of travel and the needs of people coming and going. He considered and helped to decide upon proposals dealing with public roads, toll bridges, canals, and river navigation. Education was public business, and the assemblyman worked on schools in general and schools for orphans. Much of the common concern had to do with the homely life of work, household and sustenance. He was on the record of legislation covering cattle marks and brands, the regulation of mills and millers, the "Little Bull Law" which meant to govern breeding of cattle but which was repealed as inequitable, the killing of wolves and the determination of bounties therefor, and—an act which reflected with intimacy and compassion the poverty, the need and the terms of the farmer's life—a bill to declare exempt from legal attachment one work horse or a yoke of oxen, so that daily work might continue. The Assembly took account of human trouble, and the assemblyman acted with his associates on bills looking to the relief of debtors, and bills against gaming, and bills regulating the penitentiary.

It was a broad experience of man and man's ways of constantly reshaping himself as a social being. In his first term the assemblyman had been "silent, observant, studious," as a contemporary said. In the new term, he was, of those his own age and length of service, "the smartest parliamentarian and cunningest 'log-roller.'" These knacks of his enlivened his efforts in the second term to secure the removal of the state capital from Vandalia. Many towns were after the prize, but Springfield was the leader. The assemblyman led the fight and on the last day of February, 1837, he saw the bill he backed win the approval of the majority. On March first he saw another achievement when in the office of the clerk of the Supreme Court of Illinois his name was entered upon the roll of attorneys as a member of the State Bar. It was the third and final qualification toward which he had worked.

Before the term was over on March sixth, the assemblyman, with Dan Stone, his fellow townsman, filed dissent from a resolution adopted by the House. The House resolution went on record against the abolition of slavery. The Sangamon assemblyman and his colleague made a joint statement saying that "the institution of slavery is founded on both injustice and bad policy." In the temper of the time, however, they added that "the promulgation of abolition doctrines tends rather to increase than abate its evils." With this moral act, the assemblyman was ready for the adjournment of the House on March sixth.

During this term his self-image found words; for he told Joshua Fry Speed of Springfield that he aimed—it could only be the pinnacle of fame —he aimed at the "great distinction" of being known as "the DeWitt Clinton of Illinois." Governor Clinton of New York was dead since 1828, but he was remembered. Six feet tall, of noble proportions, he was known as "Magnus Apollo." Like the assemblyman, he had started his career in the state legislature. He had gone on to become United States senator, mayor of New York City, governor of New York State, father of the Erie Canal, and a champion of public education. Joshua Speed could be excused if he smiled kindly at the hope of any-one to equal such an illustrious record. On

March seventh and eighth the assemblyman, in his short clawhammer coat and his hiked up pantaloons, made his way home to New Salem.

He had come there the first time on the heels of a hard winter. This, of 1836–1837, was another such, when weeks of rain left puddles and snow melted to slush. Suddenly one day came a violent freeze and the countryside was fixed in ice. Chickens and geese were frozen fast to the ground. Travellers, caught by the shift of wind which brought the freeze, were endangered, and some died. Washington Crowder, riding to Springfield, was overtaken by the storm. Coming to a store he tried to dismount, but—as a local account of the marvel said—"was unable to dismount, his overcoat holding him as firmly as though it had been made of sheet iron." He called for help. Two men heard him and came out of the store. They tried to lift him down, but his clothes were frozen to the saddle. They loosened the girth and "then carried man and saddle to the fire and thawed them asunder."

Home again in New Salem, the assemblyman contained a new resolve. It would not be long until he should make it known.

New Salem had been his school, his academy, his college. There he had learned how to use language correctly and beautifully; how to speak and debate in public; how to study; how to plan towns; how to write laws by reading law; how to live amidst people and how to respect their common concerns and forgive their uncommon ones. There it was he had left the forest and the river, which had also taught him much, and had found the world. Like all others, he had to find out where to look for it, but it was there to be seen, if he would look, in a hamlet in a wood above a river. In all his young life he had worked to overcome disadvantages, and as they enlarged, so did he, in spirit, patience and strength, among his neighbors of New Salem. They had suffered him when he suffered, and laughed for him when he reached for their funny-bones, and allowed him his hopes, and voted for him when he asked them to. As he was, so had New Salem helped to make him.

On April twelfth the Springfield paper carried an announcement that the assemblyman —once a flatboatman, a store clerk, a militia captain, a candidate, a postmaster, a deputy surveyor, a law student, and now a full attorney at law—would, with J. T. Stuart, "practice conjointly in the courts of this Judicial Circuit Office No. 4 Hoffman's Row upstairs."

The resolve made, it was time to go.

On April fifteenth, 1837, he borrowed from Judge Bowling Green a small pony with a worn-out saddle. In the saddle bags he put his copy of Blackstone, a copy of the compiled laws of Illinois for 1833, three volumes of session laws, two small miscellaneous books, and some underclothes. When he mounted the pony his long legs nearly reached the ground. His fortune consisted of about seven dollars in his pocket. A friend declared that "superficially he seemed like a farm hand in search of employment." So it was he rode off to Springfield, leaving New Salem which, in two years, like the store he had once owned with William Berry, would "wink out."

Springfield numbered fewer than a thousand people but it was a lively town and promised, as the new state capital, to be livelier, after the State House was built. Business houses defined the public square, which like all the streets was dust in summer and thick with mud in winter. Street crossings consisted of slabs of wood. A few small brick buildings contained stores and offices, which were furnished with the barest conveniences. Six stores, a merchant's mill for custom work, and three country taverns completed the public buildings. Yet residents could show style. Some went richly dressed in fine carriages. Little luxuries were imported, and gave tone to literary evenings and political dinners. If the frontier was just down the street, cultivated life could be found just indoors.

The new attorney and counselor at law from New Salem rode into Springfield on April fifteenth and went to the only cabinet-maker in town to inquire for a single bedstead. He then saw the store of Joshua Speed. He tied his pony and unsaddled it and went in, hauling the saddle bags which he threw on the counter. What, he asked, would the mattress and bedding for a single bedstead cost?

Joshua Speed took his slate and pencil and worked out some figures. The total, he stated, would come to seventeen dollars.

"It is probably cheap enough," said the attorney, "but I want to say that, cheap as it is, I have not the money to pay." They looked at each other. "But," he continued, "if you will credit me until Christmas, and my experiment here as a lawyer is a success, I will pay you then." The tone of his voice, thought Speed, was so melancholy that he felt for him. The attorney said, "If I fail in that I will probably never pay you at all."

Speed looked at him and said to himself that he had never seen so gloomy and melancholy a face in his life. He said to him,

"So small a debt seems to affect you so deeply, I think I can suggest a plan by which you will be able to attain your end without incurring any debt. I have a very large room and a very large double bed in it, which you are perfectly willing to share with me if you choose."

"Where is your room?" asked the attorney.

Speed pointed to the stairs leading from the store to his room.

"Upstairs," he said.

The attorney said nothing, threw his saddlebags over his arm, went upstairs and set them on the floor, and at once returned. Speed said his face was "beaming with pleasure and smiles."

"Well, Speed," he exclaimed, "I'm moved."

The satisfaction of this youthful attainment of a momentous stage could not last.

But for now—while still lost in the inexorable future were the circuit and the Congress and the White House and Ford's Theatre and a lodging in the world's heart—it was enough for the former citizen of New Salem.

I

EVENTS AND THE MAN

It is possible that Lincoln would never have become quite as famous as he has without the political, social, and moral challenges with which history confronted him. On the other hand, Mr. Horgan's treatment of his formative years clearly illustrates that Lincoln was not merely a pawn in the hands of history. He was a resourceful man with a tremendous capacity for growing through experience; he possessed an unusually large measure of determination and courage; and he was self-lessly devoted to causes larger than himself, to liberty and honor, justice, and truth.

All of us are shaped by events, and Lincoln was no exception. What was exceptional about him was his willingness and ability to meet the challenges of his time; he never turned his back on events or on the momentous decisions they forced him to make. He never let *them* defeat *him*.

II

IMPLICATIONS

Discuss in full the meaning of each of the following quotations; also discuss their relevance to the idea of Lincoln as a self-made man.

1. *If you are resolutely determined . . . the thing is more than half-done already. . . .*

2. In his first term the assemblyman [Lincoln] had been "silent, observant, studious."

3. During this term [his second] his self-image found words; . . . he aimed at the "great distinction" of being known as "the DeWitt Clinton of Illinois."

4. New Salem had been his school, his academy, his college.

5. In all his young life he had worked to overcome disadvantages, and as they enlarged, so did he. . . .

III

TECHNIQUES

Tone

A writer's style is not a fixed, unvarying thing. The fact is that the writer's attitude toward his subject, his tone, will sometimes cause a great deal of variation in his style. Discuss this topic with reference to the two paragraphs below, both of which were written by Horgan. Some of the specifics you should be prepared to discuss are the

following: (1) vocabulary level, (2) average sentence length, and (3) grammatical complexity. Also, how would you describe Horgan's tone in each instance and do you think his Lincoln tone is appropriate, considering the man he was writing about?

1. Ever since the eighteenth century the raising and tending of large herds of beef cattle had been practiced on the Texas river's wide, flat borderlands. All descended from animals brought to Mexico in the sixteenth century by Spaniards, there were several types of cattle on the river plains, of which the most distinctive had tremendously long horns doubled up and backward for half their length; heavy thin heads; tall legs, and narrow, powerful flanks. They were haired in various colors, with white patches. By the hundred thousand, wild cattle roved at large over the uninhabited land on both sides of the border, and constituted its prevailing form of wealth. As such they were always prizes for Indians, Mexicans and Americans who in an unbroken tradition of border violence raided the herds—preferably those already gathered into ownership by other men—and drove away thousands of animals to sell on the hoof, or to kill for their hides which were bailed and sold to traders, while the carcasses were left to carrion, and the bones to workers who gathered them up and hauled them for sale as fertilizer to Texas farming towns.

2. It was one thing to be given "the hypo," as he called it, by fugitive annoyances; quite another to be lost to the whole daily world. Finally he was persuaded to stay for a few weeks with the jolly justice of the peace, Judge Bowling Green, beyond the little hills north of New Salem. Judge Green loved to laugh with all his three hundred pounds. The shape of his belly earned him the nickname of "Pot." He was good for the law student. The ordinary matters of life proceeded. The law student tended the post office, though someone complained that he neglected his duties at this time. He studied. He surveyed a ten-acre lot of timber. He wrote to the Governor of Illinois to endorse an applicant for the post of public auditor. On December seventh, 1835, he was counted present at the opening of a special session of the Assembly in Vandalia. On March twenty-fourth, 1836, his name was entered on the record of the Sangamon Circuit Court as a man of good moral character. This was the first of three steps leading to the license to practice law. The law student was coming back to himself. Years afterward, Isaac Cogsdale, formerly of New Salem, said he heard him say of Anne Rutledge, "I loved her dearly. . . ."

IV
WORDS

A. Using what you know about context clues and word parts, determine the meaning of the italicized words. Be prepared to discuss the clues that helped you.

1. . . . his *chronicles* alone tell of the Winter of the Blue Snow.

2. . . . the polar fields cracked explosively as his struggle *convulsed* the waters under them.

3. . . . her mother had come to this country as a "bound-out girl" or *indentured* servant.

4. To Franklin fell this task of *wheedling* vast sums out of the depleted treasury. . . .

5. . . . scheming men found him *wilier* than they. . . .

6. "The gentleman has seen fit to *allude* to my being a young man. . . ."

7. The assemblyman took part in the vote. . . on the *delineation* of voting districts and precincts.

8. . . . "the *promulgation* of abolition doctrines tends rather to increase than *abate* its evils."

B. Words that have more than one meaning may also have different sets of synonyms and antonyms. The most comprehensive treatment of synonyms and antonyms may be found in *Webster's Dictionary of Synonyms.* This book contains a survey of the history of English synonymy, a discussion of the definitions of *synonym* and *antonym*, and entries for synonyms, carefully distinguishing the differences in implications, connotations, and applications. You will find this book and a collegiate-size dictionary helpful in doing the exercises that follow. Following each italicized word are several meanings of the word and an antonym that opposes one of the meanings. Find the meaning for which the antonym is opposite.

Example: *dull* 1. gloomy 2. dusky 3. obtuse
Antonym: *keen* Answer: *obtuse*

1. *obstruct* 1. block or close 2. check or impede 3. cut off sight of Antonym: *advance*

2. *prolific* 1. abundant reproduction 2. capable of reproduction Antonym: *barren*

3. *casual* 1. happening by chance 2. unconcerned 3. extemporaneous Antonym: *deliberate*

4. *confirm* 1. establish 2. ratify 3. verify Antonym: *contradict*

5. *elevation* 1. altitude 2. promotion Antonym: *degradation*

6. *copy* 1. imitate 2. model or pattern 3. subject matter Antonym: *originate*

7. *effervescent* 1. lively and high spirited 2. animated 3. brazen Antonym: *subdued*

C. It is interesting to compare two broad dialects of English, American and British. Through the years Americans have adapted English to their needs by coining new words, by finding words to label topographical features, by dropping certain features of British English, and by retaining others that were disappearing in British English.

1. Look up the etymology of *fen, moor, bluff, pond, beech, hemlock, barn, bee* (as in "spelling bee"). Which are of British origin but with new meanings in American English? Which are familiar in British English but have become obsolete in American English?

2. In *My Fair Lady*, Henry Higgins thinks about throwing the "baggage" out. Which sense of the word *baggage* does he mean?

3. What is the American word for the British *chemist, lift, bonnet, wireless, "telly"*?

4. Look up the term *Americanism.*

Most of America's military heroes have been victorious,
but by a curious irony the man who may well be the most beloved
military hero in our history was a defeated general. Throughout the South,
schools are named for him, as are towns, public parks, and children.
Though he was a Confederate general, he has equally won the admiration
of the North. Try to see the qualities of this man that have won the respect
both of his friends and of his foes.

Lee in Battle

GAMALIEL BRADFORD, JR.

We like to imagine the master mind in a great conflict controlling everything, down to the minutest detail. But with vast modern armies this is far from being the case, even with the elaborate electrical facilities of today; and in Lee's time those facilities were much less complete. Lee himself indicated the difficulty humorously when he was remonstrated with for taking risks, and answered, "I wish someone would tell me my proper place in battle. I am always told I should not be where I am." And he expressed it with entire seriousness when he said, "During the battle my direction is of more harm than use; I must then rely on my division and brigade commanders. I think and I act with all my might to bring up my troops to the right place at the right moment; after that I have done my duty."

Some critics hold that Lee was inclined to carry the principle much too far. What impresses me in this, as in other things, is the nice balance of his gifts. Persons by nature predisposed to direct others almost always seek to direct them in everything. How wise and constant Lee's direction was, where he thought it needed, is shown by his son's remark: "We were always fully instructed as to the best way to get to Lexington, and, indeed, all the roads of life were carefully marked out for us by him." Yet the instant he reached the limit of what he felt to be his province, he drew back and left decision to others whom he knew to be, by nature or position, better qualified.

The amount of Lee's direction and influence seems to have varied greatly in different battles. At Fredericksburg[1] he adopted a central position whence he could survey the whole field. Colonel Long's remarks in describing this must have given Longstreet exquisite pleasure. "In the battle Longstreet had his headquarters at the same place, so that Lee was able to keep his hand on the rein of his 'old war horse' and to direct him where to apply his strength." At Antietam[2] critics are agreed that Lee's management of things was perfect. "He utilized every available soldier; throughout the day he controlled the Confederate operations over the whole field." On the other hand, in the Peninsular battles, owing perhaps to imperfect organization and staff arrangements, his hold on the machine was much less complete; and at Gettysburg the vast extension of his lines made immediate personal direction almost impossible, with results that were disastrous.

1. **Fredericksburg,** a Virginia city in Spotsylvania County; site of major Confederate victory December 11–15, 1862.
2. **Antietam**\ăn ᴧtē·tăm\ village in Maryland, 3 miles north of which a battle was fought at Sharpsburg, 1862.

Reprinted from *Lee, the American* by Gamaliel Bradford, Jr. by permission of Houghton Mifflin Company.

It is at Gettysburg that we get one of the most vivid of the few pictures left us of Lee in the very midst of the crash and tumult of conflict. It is from the excellent pen of General Alexander, who says that the commander-in-chief rode up entirely alone, just after Pickett's charge, "and remained with me for a long time. He then probably first appreciated the extent of the disaster, as the disorganized stragglers made their way back past us. . . . It was certainly a momentous thing to him to see that superb attack end in such a bloody repulse. But, whatever his emotions, there was no trace of them in his calm and self-possessed bearing. I thought at that time his coming there very imprudent, and the absence of all his staff officers and couriers strange. It could only have happened by his express intention. I have since thought it possible that he came, thinking the enemy might follow in pursuit of Pickett, personally to rally stragglers about our guns and make a desperate defense. He had the instincts of a soldier within him as strongly as any man. . . . No soldier could have looked on at Pickett's charge and not burned to be in it. To have a personal part in a close and desperate fight at that moment would, I believe, have been at heart a great pleasure to General Lee, and possibly he was looking for one."

And I ask myself how much of that born soldier's lust for battle, keen enjoyment of danger and struggle and combat, Lee really had. Certainly there is little record of his speaking of any such feeling. At various times he expressed a keen sense of all the horrors of war. "You have no idea of what a horrible sight a battlefield is." And again, "What a cruel thing is war; to separate and destroy families and friends, and mar the purest joys and happiness God has granted us in this world; to fill our hearts with hatred instead of love for our neighbors, and to devastate the fair face of this beautiful world." One vivid sentence, spoken in the midst of the slaughter of Fredericksburg, lights the man's true instincts like a flash: "It is well that war is so terrible, or else we might grow too fond of it."

As to Lee's personal courage, of course the only point to be discussed is the peculiar quality of it. Judging from his character generally and from all that is recorded of him, I should not take his courage to consist in a temperamental indifference to danger, a stolid disregard of its very existence, such as we find perhaps in Grant or Wellington. Though far from being a highly nervous organization, Lee was sensitive, imaginative; and I take it that he had to accustom himself to being under fire and was always aware of any elements of peril there might be about him.

Testimony to his entire coolness in battle is of course abundant. I do not know that there is any more striking general statement than that of Cooke in reference to the second battle of Bull Run: "The writer of these pages chanced to be near the commander at this moment and was vividly impressed by the air of unmoved calmness which marked his countenance and demeanor. Nothing in the expression of his face, and no hurried movement, indicated excitement or anxiety. Here, as on many other occasions, Lee impressed the writer as an individual gifted with the most surprising faculty of remaining cool and unaffected in the midst of circumstances calculated to arouse the most phlegmatic."[3] A concrete instance of his self-possession in the midst of turmoil is narrated by a Union soldier: "A prisoner walked up to him and told him a Rebel had stolen his hat. In the midst of his orders he stopped and told the Rebel to give back the hat and saw that he done it, too."

I am not aware that Lee was wounded at any time during the war, or indeed in his life, except slightly at Chapultepec.[4] His hands were severely injured just before Antietam, but this was by the falling of his horse. He was, however, again and again under fire. At Antietam, A. P. Hill, who was close to the general, had his horse's forelegs shot off. On another occasion,

3. **phlegmatic**\flĕg ▲mă•tĭk\ apathetic, impassive.
4. **Chapultepec**\cha ▲pūl•tə•pĕk\ a rocky hill 3 miles south of Mexico City; the site of a battle, Sept. 12–13, 1847, in war with Mexico.

LEE AND HIS GENERALS,
Charles Hoffbauer

when Lee was sitting with Stuart and his staff, "a shell fell plump in their midst, burying in the earth with itself one of General Lee's gauntlets,[5] which lay on the ground only a few feet from the general himself." In 1864 Lee was inspecting the lines below Richmond, and the number of soldiers gathered about him drew the enemy's fire rather heavily. The general ordered the men back out of range and he himself followed at his leisure; but it was observed that he stopped to pick up something. A fledgling sparrow had fallen from its nest, and he took it from the ground and tenderly replaced it, with the bullets whistling about him.

As the following incident shows, Lee was extremely solicitous about the unnecessary exposure of his men. Once, when he was watching the effect of the fire on an advanced battery, a staff officer rode up to him by the approach which was least protected. The general reprimanded him for his carelessness, and when the young man urged that he could not seek cover himself while his chief was in the open, Lee answered sharply, "It is my duty to be here. Go back the way I told you, sir." At another time Lee had placed himself in a very exposed position, to the horror of all his officers. They could not prevail upon him to come down, so finally General Gracie stepped forward and interposed himself between his commander and the enemy. "Why, Gracie," protested Lee, "you will certainly be killed." "It is better, General, that I should be killed than you. When you get down, I will." Lee smiled and got down.

When things became really critical, Lee completely threw aside all caution. In the terrific battles of the Wilderness, where at times it seemed as if Grant would succeed in breaking through, the Confederate general repeatedly (on three separate occasions, as it appears) rushed to the front to rally his men and charge, like Ney or Murat,[6] at the head of them. "Go

---

5. **gauntlets**\gŏnt·lĭts\ gloves with a long extension over the wrist.
6. **Ney or Murat.** Michel Ney\nā\ French soldier in the Revolutionary and Napoleonic armies; Joachim Murat, 1767–1815, French cavalry commander who aided Napoleon in a *coup d'état*\'kū·dā ᵃta\.

back, General Lee, go back!" shouted the soldiers. But he would not go back till they had promised to do as much for him as they could have done with him. And they did as much. No men could have done more.

It was this occasional fury of combativeness which made Longstreet[7] assert that the general was sometimes unbalanced, not by any personal exposure or excitement, but by critical situations affecting the army as a whole. Longstreet, defending his own conduct at Gettysburg, urges that Lee was particularly overwrought at the time of that battle. In what is, to say the least, peculiar phraseology, he writes of his commander: "That he was excited and off his balance was evident on the afternoon of the first, and that he labored under that oppression till blood enough was shed to appease him." The suggestion that Lee required blood to appease him is grotesque, and his loyal admirers ridicule the idea that at Gettysburg he was unbalanced. But there is evidence besides Longstreet's that, once in a fight, he hated to give it up and perhaps occasionally allowed his ardor to overcome his discretion. The Prussian officer Scheibert remarks that while at Chancellorsville Lee was admirably calm, at Gettysburg he was restless and uneasy. General Anderson bears witness that at Gettysburg his chief was "very much disturbed and depressed."

The most heroic picture that is left us of Lee high-wrought by the excitement of battle and determined to fight to the end is the account, received by Henderson from a reliable eyewitness, of the chief's decision to remain north of the Potomac after Antietam. General after general rode up to the commander's headquarters, all with the same tale of discouragement and counsel of retreat. Hood was quite unmanned. "My God!" cried Lee to him, with unwonted vehemence, "where is the splendid division you had this morning?" "They are lying on the field where you sent them," answered Hood. Even Jackson did not venture to suggest anything but withdrawal. There were a few moments of oppressive silence. Then Lee

rose erect in his stirrups and said, "Gentlemen, we will not cross the Potomac tonight. You will go to your respective commands, strengthen your lines, send two officers from each brigade towards the ford to collect your stragglers and bring them up. Many have come in. I have had the proper steps taken to collect all the men who are in the rear. If McClellan[8] wants to fight in the morning, I will give him battle. Go!" They went, and in this case, at least, Lee's glorious audacity was justified; for he proved to all the world that McClellan did not dare attack him again.

However Lee's judgment may have been affected by the excitement of battle, it made little alteration in his bearing or manner. Fremantle tells us that the general's dress was always neat and clean, and adds, "I observed this during the three days fight at Gettysburg, when every one else looked and was extremely dirty." Stress of conflict sometimes seems to alter men's natures. Odd stories are told in the war books of officers quite saintly in common converse who in battle would swear like reprobates. Lee's politeness was always exquisite. It was only very, very rarely that some untoward incident stirred either his temper or his speech. "Probably no man ever commanded an army and, at the same time, so entirely commanded himself as Lee," says the cool-blooded Alexander. "This morning [after Chancellorsville] was almost the only occasion on which I ever saw him out of humor."

Nor was it only a question of mere politeness. Lee was as tender and sympathetic to man and beast in the fury of combat, in the chaos of defeat, as he could have been in his own domain at Arlington. After the great charge on the third day at Gettysburg, an officer rode up to him lashing an unwilling horse. "Don't whip him,

7. **Longstreet,** James, 1821–1904, Confederate brigadier general; his delay in carrying out Lee's orders to attack at Gettysburg has been said to have caused the Confederate defeat.
8. **McClellan,** George Brinton, 1826–1885, commanded U. S. Army at Antietam; defeated by Lincoln in presidential election in 1864.

Captain, don't whip him," protested the general. "I have just such another foolish beast myself, and whipping doesn't do any good." And as the tumult of disaster increased, the sympathy took larger forms of magnanimity than mere prevention of cruelty to animals. There was no faultfinding, no shifting of perhaps deserved blame to others, nothing but calmness, comfort, cheerfulness, confidence. "All will come right in the end; we'll talk of it afterwards, but in the meantime all good men must rally." "Never mind, General. All this has been my fault. It is I that have lost this fight, and you must help me out of it the best way you can."

So, with incomparable patience, tact, and energy, the great soldier held his army together after defeat and kept it in a temper and condition which went far to justify Meade's reluctance to follow up his success. Only, to complete the picture, one should turn to General Imboden's brief sketch, taken after the work was done and natural human exhaustion and despair claimed some little right over even a hero's nerve and brain. It must be remembered that this was a man fifty-six years old. Toward midnight Lee rode up to Imboden's command. "When he approached and saw us, he spoke, reined up his horse and endeavored to dismount. The effort to do so betrayed so much physical exhaustion that I stepped forward to assist him, but before I reached him, he had alighted. He threw his arm across his saddle to rest himself and fixing his eyes upon the ground, leaned in silence upon his equally weary horse; the two formed a striking group, as motionless as a statue. After some expressions as to Pickett's charge, etc., he added in a tone almost of agony, 'Too bad! Too bad! Oh, too bad!'"

With the portrait of Lee himself in the shock of battle we should put a background of his soldiers and their feeling as he came among them. We have already heard their passionate cry when he rushed to put himself at their head and charge into the thickest of the fight. "Go back, General Lee! Go back!" General Gordon, who loved to throw a high light of eloquence on all such scenes, describes this one with peculiar vividness, giving his own remonstrance, "These men are Georgians, Virginians, and Carolinians. They have never failed you on any field. They will not fail you now. Will you, boys?" and the enthusiastic answer, "No, no, no!" Those who like the quiet truth of history, even when it chills, will be interested in an eyewitness's simple comment on this picturesque narrative. "Gordon says, 'We need no such encouragement.' At this some of our soldiers called out, 'No, no!' Gordon continuing, said, 'There is not a soldier in the Confederate army who would not gladly lay down his life to save you from harm'; but the men did not respond to this last proposition."

It cannot be doubted, however, that Lee's personal influence in critical moments was immense. On one occasion, just before battle, there was heard to pass from mouth to mouth as a sort of watchword the simple comment, "Remember, General Lee is looking at us." Stuart's aide, Von Borcke, describes a scene which is immensely effective as showing how little the general relied on words, and how little he needed to. Lee was riding through the ranks before a charge. "He uttered no word. He simply removed his hat and passed bareheaded along the line. I had it from one who witnessed the act. 'It was,' said he, 'the most eloquent address ever delivered.' And a few minutes later he heard a youth, crying and reloading his musket, shout through his tears that 'any man who would not fight after what General Lee said was a damned coward.'"

Perhaps the most splendid battlepiece of Lee in the midst of his fighting soldiers is Colonel Marshall's account of the triumphant advance on the third day at Chancellorsville. The enemy were retiring and the troops swept forward through the tumult of battle and the smoke of woods and dwellings burning about them. Everywhere the field was strewn with the wounded and dying of both armies. "In the midst of this scene General Lee, mounted upon that horse which we all remember so well, rode to the front of his advancing battalions. His presence was the signal for one of those uncontrollable outbursts of enthusiasm which none can appreciate who have not witnessed them. The fierce soldiers, with their faces blackened with the smoke of battle, the wounded, crawling with feeble limbs from the fury of the devouring flames, all seemed possessed with a common impulse. One long unbroken cheer, in which the feeble cry of those who lay helpless on the earth blended with the strong voices of those who still fought, rose high above the roar of battle, and hailed the presence of the victorious chief. He sat in the full realization of all that soldiers dream of—triumph."

This was victory. But there came a day of defeat, when the Army of Northern Virginia, after four years of fighting and triumphing and suffering, shrunk almost to nothing, saw their great commander ride away to make his submission to a generous conqueror. Their love, their loyalty, their confidence, were no less than they had ever been. If he said further fighting was useless and inhuman, it must be so.

But this very absolute confidence increased the weight of the terrible decision. All these thousands trusted him to decide for them. He must decide rightly. What the burden was we can only imagine, never know. But under the noble serenity maintained by habitual effort, good observers detected signs of the struggle that must be taking place. "His face was still calm, but his carriage was no longer erect, as his soldiers had been used to see it. The trouble of those last days had already ploughed great furrows in his forehead. His eyes were red as if with weeping; his cheeks sunken and haggard; his face colorless. No one who looked upon him then, as he stood there in full view of the disastrous end, can ever forget the intense agony written upon his features. And yet he was calm, self-possessed, and deliberate." So great was his anguish that it wrung a wish to end it all, even from a natural self-control complete as his. "How easily I could get rid of this and be at rest. I have only to ride along the lines and all will be over. But," he quickly added, "it is our duty to live, for what will become of the women and children of the South if we are not here to support and protect them?"

So the decision had to be made. And he made it. "Then there is nothing left me but to go and see General Grant, and I would rather die a thousand deaths." His officers protested passionately, "Oh, General, what will history say of the surrender of the army in the field?" "Yes, I know, they will say hard things of us; they will not understand how we were overwhelmed by numbers; but that is not the question, Colonel; the question is, is it right to surrender this army? If it is right, then I will take all the responsibility."

The scene that ensued has been described often: the plain farmhouse room; the officers curious, yet respectful; the formal conversation, as always painfully unequal to the huge event it covered; the short, ungainly, ill-dressed man, as dignified in his awkwardness almost as the royal, perfectly appointed figure that conferred with him. Lee bore himself nobly, say his admirers; nobly, but a little coldly, say his opponents. And who shall blame him? Then it was over. One moment he paused at the door, as he went out, waiting for his horse, and as he paused, looking far into the tragic future or the tragic past, he struck his gauntleted hands together in a gesture of immense despair, profoundly significant for so self-contained a man. Then he rode away, back to his children, back to the Army of Northern Virginia, who had seen him daily for three years and now would never see him any more.

I

THE SPREAD OF FAME

There are several reasons for the growth and spread of Lee's fame. For one thing, many Americans admire him as an underdog and as a champion of a Lost Cause. More important, Lee proved himself worthy of deep respect and admiration, for he had the courage to follow the direction of his own unique talents and temper. But in addition to these factors, some credit for the spread of Lee's fame must be given to the many writers—South and North—who have told his story. For regardless of his greatness, Lee could not have achieved national reputation and recognition unless people everywhere knew about him. Thus the writer steps into the role of spreader of fame.

II
IMPLICATIONS

Part of Lee's great fame is due to his great character. Discuss those of his character traits that are revealed in the following incidents and quotations.

1. "What a cruel thing is war; to separate and destroy families and friends, and mar the purest joys and happiness God has granted us in this world; to fill our hearts with hatred instead of love for our neighbors, and to devastate the fair face of this beautiful world."

2. Lee's replacing a fallen sparrow in its nest during the heat of battle.

3. Lee's leading army charges at the battles of the Wilderness.

4. "Never mind, General. All this has been my fault. It is I that have lost this fight, and you must help me out of it the best way you can."

5. Lee's riding bare-headed along the lines before a charge.

6. "How easily I could get rid of this and be at rest. I have only to ride along the lines and all will be over. But it is our duty to live, for what will become of the women and children of the South if we are not here to support and protect them?"

7. ". . . the question is, is it right to surrender this army? If it is right, then I will take all the responsibility."

III
TECHNIQUES
Selection of Significant Detail

Bradford creates a favorable portrait of General Lee largely by selecting details that show him to be of noble character. You may have noticed, however, that some negative comments are introduced here and there. Point out two or three instances of unfavorable comments on Lee and discuss (1) how the author handles them, (2) how they affect his total portrait, and (3) how objective or slanted you think his essay is.

Tone

The simplest way for an author to reveal his attitude toward his subject is by direct statement. Such statements, if they are to carry weight with the reader, ought to be supported in some way by the author's reasons for holding that attitude or by evidence supporting the validity of the attitude.

In the following quotations, Bradford makes some direct statements about Lee and/or reveals his attitude toward the General. In each case what is Bradford's attitude? Also locate the quotation and determine whether or not the author backs up his statement with reasons or evidence. (The quotations are in the order of their appearance.)

1. What impresses me . . . is the nice balance of his gifts.

2. Though far from being a highly nervous organization, Lee was sensitive, imaginative. . . .

3. The suggestion that Lee required blood to appease him is grotesque, and his loyal admirers ridicule the idea that at Gettysburg he was unbalanced.

4. There was no faultfinding, no shifting of perhaps deserved blame to others, nothing but calmness, comfort, cheerfulness, confidence.

5. So, with incomparable patience, tact, and energy, the great soldier held his army together. . . .

American Individualists in Narrative Poetry

The American tradition of individualism
is reflected in the great diversity of our heroes. Each of the men
in the following narrative poems, for example, has been regarded as a hero
by a great many Americans—yet it would be difficult to find two
more markedly dissimilar individuals.

Abraham Davenport

"The famous Dark Day of New England, May 19, 1780, was a physical puzzle for many years to our ancestors, but its occurrence brought something more than philosophical speculation into the minds of those who passed through it. The incident of Colonel Abraham Davenport's sturdy protest is a matter of history" (Whittier).

In the old days (a custom laid aside
With breeches and cocked hats) the people sent
Their wisest men to make the public laws.
And so, from a brown homestead, where the Sound
Drinks the small tribute of the Mianas,   5
Waved over by the woods of Rippowams,
And hallowed by pure lives and tranquil deaths,
Stamford sent up to the councils of the State
Wisdom and grace in Abraham Davenport.

'Twas on a May-day of the far old year   10
Seventeen hundred eighty, that there fell
Over the bloom and sweet life of the Spring,
Over the fresh earth and the heaven of noon,
A horror of great darkness, like the night
In day of which the Norland sagas tell,—   15
The Twilight of the Gods. The low-hung sky
Was black with ominous clouds, save where its rim
Was fringed with a dull glow, like that which climbs
The crater's sides from the red hell below.
Birds ceased to sing, and all the barn-yard fowls   20
Roosted; the cattle at the pasture bars
Lowed, and looked homeward; bats on leathern wings
Flitted abroad; the sounds of labor died;
Men prayed, and women wept; all ears grew sharp
To hear the doom-blast of the trumpet shatter   25

The black sky, that the dreadful face of Christ
Might look from the rent clouds, not as he looked
A loving guest at Bethany, but stern
As Justice and inexorable Law.

Meanwhile in the old State House, dim as ghosts   30
Sat the lawgivers of Connecticut,
Trembling beneath their legislative robes.
"It is the Lord's Great Day! Let us adjourn,"
Some said; and then, as if with one accord,
All eyes were turned to Abraham Davenport.   35
He rose, slow cleaving with his steady voice
The intolerable hush. "This well may be
The Day of Judgment which the world awaits;
But be it so or not, I only know
My present duty, and my Lord's command   40
To occupy till He come. So at the post
Where He hath set me in his providence,
I choose, for one, to meet Him face to face,—
No faithless servant frightened from my task,
But ready when the Lord of the harvest calls;   45
And therefore, with all reverence, I would say,
Let God do his work, we will see to ours.
Bring in the candles." And they brought them in.

Then by the flaring lights the Speaker read,
Albeit with husky voice and shaking hands,   50
An act to amend an act to regulate
The shad and alewive fisheries. Whereupon
Wisely and well spake Abraham Davenport,
Straight to the question, with no figures of speech
Save the ten Arab signs, yet not without   55
The shrewd dry humor natural to the man:
His awe-struck colleagues listening all the while,
Between the pauses of his argument,
To hear the thunder of the wrath of God
Break from the hollow trumpet of the cloud.   60

And there he stands in memory to this day,
Erect, self-poised, a rugged face, half seen
Against the background of unnatural dark,
A witness to the ages as they pass,
That simple duty hath no place for fear.   65
JOHN GREENLEAF WHITTIER

John Henry

John Henry was a little baby,
　Setting on his mammy's knee,
Said "The Big Bend Tunnel on the C. & O. Road
　Is gonna be the death of me,
　　Lawd, gonna be the death of me."　　　　　5

One day his captain told him,
　How he had bet a man
That John Henry could beat his steam drill down,
　Cause John Henry was the best in the land,
　　John Henry was the best in the land.　　　10

John Henry walked in the tunnel,
　His captain by his side;
The mountain so tall, John Henry so small,
　He laid down his hammer and he cried,
　　Laid down his hammer and he cried.　　　15

John Henry kissed his hammer;
　White man turned on the steam;
Shaker held John Henry's steel;
　Was the biggest race the world had ever seen,
　　Lawd, biggest race the world ever seen.　　20

John Henry on the right side
　The steam drill on the left,
"Before I'll let your steam drill beat me down,
　I'll hammer my fool self to death,
　　Hammer my fool self to death."　　　　　25

Captain heard a mighty rumbling,
　Said, "The mountain must be caving in."
John Henry said to the captain,
　"It's my hammer sucking de wind,
　　My hammer sucking de wind."　　　　　　30

John Henry said to his captain,
　"A man ain't nothin' but a man,
But before I'll let dat steam drill beat me down,
　I'll die wid my hammer in my hand,
　　Lawd, die wid my hammer in my hand."　　35

John Henry hammering on the mountain,
　The whistle blew for half-past two,
The last words his captain heard him say,
　"I've done hammered my insides in two,
　　Lawd, I've hammered my insides in two."　　40

561

The hammer that John Henry swung
It weighed over twelve pound,
He broke a rib in his left-hand side
And his intrels fell on the ground,
Lawd, his intrels fell on the ground.   45

They took John Henry to the river,
And buried him in the sand,
And every locomotive come a-roaring by,
Says, "There lies that steel-drivin' man,
Lawd, there lies that steel-drivin' man!"   50

ANONYMOUS

I
AGAINST GREAT ODDS

Although they were certainly very different from each other, Abraham Davenport and John Henry have in common the fact that they had the courage to assert themselves against great odds: Abraham Davenport stood calm against the threat of imminent catastrophe; John Henry pitted his human strength against a steam drill.

II
IMPLICATIONS

Discuss each of the following propositions in terms of your experience and the poems above.

1. The one essential quality of all independent spirits is courage.

2. The cause that a person fights for makes very little difference in our admiration of him; that is, we can have intense admiration for a man even if we disapprove of what he is fighting for.

3. Being an underdog in a struggle will tend to increase rather than decrease a hero's stature.

4. A person like John Henry whose life ends tragically appeals to more people than those persons who lead generally happy lives.

5. Most American heroes tend to be nonconformists of one sort or another.

III
TECHNIQUES
Selection of Significant Detail

Sometimes details are significant by virtue of the fact that they modify the author's meaning or the effect of his work in important ways. Two such details are listed below; discuss how they modify the portrait of the hero in each case.

1. The fact that the question debated in the State House is "An act to amend an act to regulate / The shad and alewive fisheries."

2. The fact that John Henry predicts as a young boy that the Big Bend Tunnel will be the death of him.

Tone

"John Henry" contains a good deal of repetition. What is the function of this repetitive phrasing so far as the author's attitude is concerned?

The cowboy is not only the hero of countless television programs, movies, and novels in the United States, but he is also probably the single best-known American figure around the world. What was the real cowboy like and what is the basis of his broad and enduring popularity? These are two of the interesting questions that Professor Fishwick attempts to answer in the following excerpt from his chapter on the cowboy in his book, *American Heroes: Myth and Reality.*

Don't Fence Me In: The Cowboy

MARSHALL W. FISHWICK

Rousseau's[1] "natural man," that romantic symbol of freedom which captivated the eighteenth century, triumphantly entered the American forests as the buck-skin clad hunter, only to emerge on the Great Plains a century later as the American cowboy. Somewhere between the Alleghenies and the Rockies the followers of Daniel Boone traded coonskins for sombreros,[2] long rifles for six-shooters, and moccasins for spurs—without losing their fascination for the hero-loving American public.

The two symbolic figures, hunter and cowboy, made similar appeals to the trait valued above all others in American culture: freedom. The hunter wasn't happy unless he had what Daniel Boone called elbow room; which translated into the twentieth century terms became a popular cowboy ditty, "Don't Fence Me In." There was something nostalgic about it. For only two decades had the cowboy roamed hundreds of miles with no fences to hamper him or his herd. By 1954 those days were as distant as speculation over the morals of Grover Cleveland or the feasibility of eating tomatoes. With the coming of barbed wire and homesteaders in the 1870's, the open range quickly disappeared in fact, but not in fancy. On the back of Old Paint, the Cowboy has ridden through whole libraries of serious literature, hundreds of light

novels, box-car loads of pulp paper, and miles of celluloid (mostly grade B, alas), a world symbol of twentieth century America.

Today, with much less freedom but much better publicity than cowboys who went before him, he rides through the fictional world. No other occupation in America has developed so virulent a tradition. The American G.I.'s found this out during World War II. In remote places they discovered they were expected not to shoot the way the sergeant had taught them, but from the hip; to abandon their jeeps if a horse of any description were available; to ignore posture drills, and let their legs assume a normal bowed position; and to toss army tactics aside and track down enemy bad men in posses. The popular magazines and movies had done their job well. The cowboy legend preceded the American army around the world. This is even more noteworthy since the west's open ranges were gone forever before the turn of the century. Conditions have altered radically, but not the notion of the prairie paradise.

In analyzing the cowboy we are dealing not so much with individuals as with a recognizable type; not with an historical reality, but with a fictional ideal. This was precisely the case, in

---

1. **Rousseau**\ˈrü·sō\ Jean Jacques (1712–1778), French writer and philosopher.
2. **sombreros**\sŏm ˈbrā·rōz\ broad-brimmed hats, usually of felt.

the age of the Enlightenment, with Rousseau's natural man, and the trailblazer on the early American frontier. Most Americans feel that the west is governed by a compelling and unwritten code, a "spirit" unlike that east of the Mississippi. The cowboy epitomizes this code and spirit. That this is an oversimplification is beside the point; that many Americans believe it is central.

During the American Revolution, "cowboy" was a term applied to the Tories who organized raids on the Whigs' cattle. It was spoken in scorn rather than admiration. In the 1830's hired workmen called cowboys, much closer to current conceptions of the word, began to round up stray cattle in the Rio Grande country, and drive them to interior market towns. Some of the more daring ones drove their herds overland to Shreveport, Louisiana, there to be shipped down the river on flatboats to New Orleans. Thus their feats became widely known.

Major expansion in the cattle business came after the annexation of Texas in 1845. The number of cattle increased about 30% annually, with an equivalent increase in the herders. By the time of the 1849 California gold rush there was a less spectacular but more solid one underway on the Texas plains. There the gold was on the hoof. The editor of *DeBow's Review*[3] noted in 1850 that these Texas herds were "happier and prettier than those pastured by Virgil in his pastoral, enlivening the otherwise oppressive loneliness of the scene."

Most Easterners did not share this writer's enthusiasm for the little-known topography of the West. On many maps the plains appeared as the Great American Desert, which made the deeds of those who thrived there seem even more heroic. No less a figure than Daniel Webster, speaking in 1838 against a bill to establish a mail route between Independence, Missouri, and the mouth of the Columbia River, asked in the Senate: "To what use could we ever hope to put these great deserts or the endless mountain ranges, impregnable and cov-

ered to their very base with eternal snow? What use have we for such a country? Mr. President, I will never vote one cent from the public treasury to place the Pacific coast one inch nearer to Boston than it now is."

John C. Frémont's widely-read reports of his western exploration (actually written by his wife, and incidentally serving to make a hero of Frémont's scout Kit Carson) helped dispel the notion that the plains were an uninhabited desert; of course the dramatic exodus caused by the gold rush increased America's knowledge about the west enormously. The development of the cattle business, and popular interest in the cowboys who made it possible, stopped abruptly with the Civil War. In April, 1861, Lincoln declared a blockade on Southern ports and prohibited all commercial dealing with the rebels. During the war the open range could not compete with the firing range. Young Texans who had mastered the art of rounding up cattle went off to round up Yankees.

In 1861 the total number of cowboys was small, and there was still no recognizable stereotype. Most of the early men on the range had been Mexicans, admittedly skillful horsemen, but (according to Anglos in the Southwest) untrustworthy and hard on the stock. Since the standing of Mexicans in Alamo-obsessed Texas was not far above that of the longhorns which were coming into prominence, Mexicans had not been considered very heroic. The cowboy grew in stature after Appomattox; the two decades that followed were his golden years. Herds too vast to be counted grazed on the open pasture which extended from the Rio Grande to Canada, and from Kansas to the Rockies. Here was the famous sea of grass. The cowboys who drove their herds northward to be marketed were masters of it. If their lives were far from romantic, their duties and exploits brought them suddenly and dramatically into their own.

---

3. **DeBow's Review**, *Commercial Review of the South and Southwest* published in New Orleans, founded by James Dunwoody Brownson DeBow, 1820–67.

With relatively light rainfall, high summer temperatures, violent winters, and fine grained soils, the Great Plains constitute an area in which a few inches of rain can make the difference between a thriving region and a dustbowl. A major wet period on the plains coincided with the post-war expansion. Abnormally good grass and crops enticed the new adventurers westward. Few thought of what might happen in the dry years; no one had any way of telling when, if ever, they might come.

The result was a major cattle boom. Between 1860 and 1880 the human population tripled in Texas, and jumped from 107,000 to nearly a million in Kansas. The increase in cattle was even more spectacular. In the 1870's the number of head soared from 11,000 to 520,000 in Wyoming; 26,000 to 430,000 in Montana; and 71,000 to 791,000 in Colorado. This was the Great American Barbecue.

Tycoons and combinations appeared equaling in magnitude those of the Robber Baron East. The Prairie Land and Cattle Company grabbed off 790 square miles of land. Charles Goodnight's J. A. Ranch got over a million acres. The Capitol Freehold Company, in return for a promise to build a state capitol, was given 3,000,000 acres on which to graze 160,000 head of cattle within 1500 miles of barbed wire. The range cattle business was king-size from the first.

Unadorned truth would have been sufficient to start a boom. After western editors and boosters (never noted for understatement), had had their say, the notion that fortunes in beef were plentiful had moved on past the east coast to the other side of the Atlantic. All over Europe, drawing rooms buzzed with cowboy stories. Club members who scarcely knew the difference between a steer and a heifer discussed it. The flow of wealth from across the Atlantic encouraged overstocking and brought the day of reckoning nearer.

Across the roads and trails west went caravans of covered wagons headed for the New Promised Land—which was gradually moving from the wet to the dry years of its cycle. "This is it, Ma! We'll be big-time cattlemen before you know it!" gloated the men who held the reins. They could not know that they were destined to turn the grassy plains into the Dust Bowl; to drive their children's children, the future Ma and Pa Joads, to a land where the grapes of wrath were sown.

Woolaroc Museum, Bartlesville, Oklahoma

We are not concerned here with the 1873 panic and the economic, physical, and social factors which brought disaster to the boom land, littering the plains with the bones of cattle. Despite this collapse, the saga of the American cowboy gripped the American imagination. Writers, executives, and directors have dedicated themselves to the remunerative principle that old cowboy tales and deeds shall not die, nor even slightly fade away. They have added to the glory and guts of the historical cowboy, making him into what Omar Barker[4] calls a "fictitious hero," a guitar-strumming, movie set outdoors man, a pale imitation of the man who was once content to punch cattle.

Everyone (but especially 25,000,000 juvenile Americans) knows what the cowboy looks like. Physically he is tall, tanned, sinewy, a man at home in the great outdoors. Weather-beaten and rough, this child of nature is innately handsome, despite eyes squinted from work in the glaring sun and legs bowed from a life in the saddle. He is never far away from his horse, who has almost human intelligence. The two of them form the most enduring team in American mythology. This helps explain the growing horse cult in a highly mechanized America. Details of his uniform vary little. On his head is a broad-brimmed felt hat, white if he's a good guy, black if he is shady. Tied around his neck is a colored silk handkerchief, to be pulled over his face during a dust storm. A handsome loose flannel shirt (elaborately embroidered if a technicolor movie camera is lurking nearby) covers his manly chest. To his pants, which fit him not like trousers but a glove, might be attached leather chaps, to ease the strain of continuous riding. Since he must carry the law with him on his hip, a gun and holster are standard equipment. If he intends to make a place for himself with he-men, he will have two guns, symbols of quick and decisive action. These six-shooters, of heavy caliber, can be depended on to open a path for daylight through the body of any hostile critter,[5] man or beast. On his feet are tight-fitting, high-heeled boots which go into the stirrups. They make him out of place when walking like the lowly pedestrian. On these boots are spurs, which guide his horse while his hands are occupied with lasso or revolver.

All these things are functional for the cowboy, his best solutions to daily problems. But to the outsider, who has little use for any of them, they seem bizarre and dangerous. They put the cowboy in a different world. They mark him as a man who can cope with the lonely, grieving plains; with the shotlike sleet and smothering snow of winter; or the blistering heat and searing dryness of summer. Here is a real he-man dressed for the part, called by an awed Englishman "a species of centaur, half horse, half man, with immense rattling spurs, tanned skin, and dare-devil, ferocious face."

You will find him (say his admirers) modest, truthful, brave, enduring, democratic, fun-loving, and highly individualistic. He is the model of all who believe that life in God's outdoors, close to the "real" things, is desirable; a good man to have with you, and demon when against you; a man to be tampered with only when you are reconciled to picking lead slugs out of your carcass on short notice.

As a class, cowboys have always presented a discouraging field for missionaries. For years there was "no Sunday west of the Kaw[6] and no God west of the Pecos." A traditional specialty, once the long drive was over and the long-earned rest won, was raising hell. Naturally some excuse had to be advanced for such carryings-on in a nation where blue laws endured and the ghost of Calvin still stalked the land. An ample one existed in the effects of isolation and solitude upon the cowboy. If they did not condone, they at least explained his lawlessness. The unbroken quiet of the plains, a sort of perpetual solitary confinement, could be oppressive, almost unbearable. Like a heavy weight, the silent space bore down upon the mind. A man felt like crying aloud to break through the wall of padded loneliness surrounding him, but knew it would do no good. Not everyone could stand it. Some went mad.

So the cowboys shot up the town when they could get there and turned pleasure and vice into synonymous terms. To the usual sins were added as many new ones as conditions would permit. In his *Sketches of the Cattle Trail* (1874), McCoy pictured the cowboys reveling in pockets of iniquity with "men who lived a

---

4. **Omar Barker,** editor of *Legends and Tales of the Old West.*
5. **critter,** dialect word for creature, especially a cow or steer.
6. **Kaw,** the Kansas River.

YOUNG OMAHA, WAR EAGLE, LITTLE MISSOURI,
AND PAWNEE, *by Charles Bird King.*
*In addition to the hunter and cowboy, the
American Indian has been considered represen-
tative of Rousseau's "natural man." Charles
Bird King has given each subject a regal
bearing befitting a "noble savage."*

soulless, aimless life, dependent upon the turn
of a card for a living; blear-eyed and dissipated,
life had long since become for them worse than
a total blank." What could seem more shocking, and actually more enticing, to the sedate,
law-abiding, urban East? The West's "beautiful
bibulous Babylons[7] of the Plains," as one writer
called them, became symbols of escape. Many
a tourist dollar was, and is, spent in order to
indulge in a little authentic western revelry,
no holds barred. Such towns as Las Vegas,
Tombstone, and Reno have capitalized on it
for years.

This fascination of the wide-open land is no
new thing. On January 1, 1878, the editor of the
Washington *Star* reported that "those nomads
of regions remote from the restraints of normal
life" were actually laws unto themselves. There

cowboys "loiter sometimes for months, and
share the boughten dalliances of fallen
women." How many readers could attribute
trips or moves west to such editorials as these,
can never be computed. Oh, for a life on the
distant plains, where a man can let off a little
steam without ending up in a police court!

In his own bully way Theodore Roosevelt
was as good a publicist for the strenuous life,

7. **bibulous**\ˈbĭb·yū·ləs\ addicted to alcohol. **Babylons,**
cities of great wealth, luxury, wickedness.

and the cowboy who lived it, as anyone. He admired the cowboy, as his book on *Ranch Life and the Hunting Trail* (1888) showed. Roosevelt called him "the grim pioneer of our race," who "prepares the way for the civilization from before whose face he must disappear. Hard and dangerous though this is, it has a wild attraction that strongly draws to it his bold, free spirit." Such passages, repeated in many twentieth century books, established the general picture of the cowboy. None of them succeeded in making historical individuals into cowboy heroes. No Daniel Boones or Kit Carsons of the range emerged, and none exists in our heroic portrait gallery. . . .

Being "western" is, for thousands of writers, real estate men, restaurant owners, tourist specialists, and showmen, not only a preference but a vocation. One wonders where genuine love of the region stops and mere concern with the pocketbook begins. The greatest western publicist that ever lived was a man who died debt-ridden and harassed by creditors—"Buffalo Bill" Cody. By living so dramatically the role of plains hero, he convinced people that the west, and the cowboy who set its tone and pace, was heroic.

In order to bolster up this notion a good many towns annually stage an Old West Week and get their regional trappings out for the stereotyped saturnalia.[8] It is, in effect, an open season—on tourists. Commenting on the way the local burghers whoop it up, Bernard DeVoto writes: "The realtor, the bank cashier, and the soda jerk sport big hats, chromatic shirts,[9] short neckties painted with longhorns, and high-water Levi's. They pitch about on the high heels of unfamiliar riding boots and trip over three inch silver spurs that match their belt buckles. For the duration of Old West Week they are going to be cowpokes, bronzed horsemen, cattle barons. And that is what in fantasy they tend to be all year long. Here is make-believe on a national scale."

Those who cannot go to see the elaborate pageant can get in via radio, television, or mo-

tion picture instead. The Western generally considered the ancestor of all others was made in the East, near Dover, New Jersey. Called *The Great Train Robbery* (1903), it featured "Broncho Billy" Anderson, a protégé of Buffalo Bill. A decade later Thomas Ince was making Westerns out West, using real cowboys and Indians. In this locale William S. Hart rode "Pinto Ben" into stardom, as movies usurped the place of the dime novel in America.

The Covered Wagon (1923) was the first cowboy epic. It was based on a novel by Emerson Hough. . . . Directed by James Cruze and filmed near Snake Valley, Nevada, *The Covered Wagon* was free from staginess, and was much praised as a uniquely American production dramatizing the idea of Manifest Destiny.

Since then thousands of Westerns have come from Hollywood. Many have been "oaters," designed for friendly Saturday runs in little towns. Others, like *High Noon, Yellow Sky, Shane, The Gunfighters,* and *Hondo,* have been much more. The better ones reveal artistic conventions as rigid as those in a Greek temple, a classical sonata,[10] or a medieval morality play.

The Great American horse opera involves rapid action, the struggle of right and wrong, and the triumph of justice. It bristles with violence, which allows the hero to show his caliber. The actual drama and setting, though important, are always subordinate to the cowboy; they simply present opportunities for the definition of his code and character. Like a sacrament, the drama is repeated *ad infinitum* to reaffirm the audience's child-like faith in its idol.

The setting is Hangman's Hill or Go-to-Hell Gulch. The time is invariably about 1870; everyone prepares to do what he or she "has to do." The villain is very bad, the heroine very good; the hero must see that the twain never meet. In this he is ably assisted by his horse, a hero in his own right. Good and Evil finally clash

8. **saturnalia**\să·tər ▲nā·lyə\ extravagant celebration.
9. **chromatic shirts,** shirts of many colors.
10. **sonata**\sə ▲na·tə\ an instrumental composition which consists of an exposition, a development, and a recapitulation.

head on. Everybody on and off the screen holds his breath. Guns blaze. The smoke clears. Destiny is suspended for a fleeting instant.

The hero wins—he must. Defender of the purity of his own image, he is unconquerable. He fights not for laws or women or property, but to prove what he is: the last gentleman. In him not only the code of the Old West, but that of the Old South, flowers.

Only when one understands this can he explain the national appeal of the cowboy in a nation with the Mason and Dixon line drawn across its middle. The ranch is really a duplication of the plantation, without slaves. Free of this stigma, the Southern dream was purged and revitalized on the grass frontier. It is no accident that the novel that best explicated the modern cowboy ideal was called *The Virginian*.

The regenerated myth of the ante-bellum South, as David Davis has noted, could and did take advantage of certain western features: "It could focus all energies on its former role of opposing the peculiar social and economic philosophy of the Northeast. This took the form of something more fundamental than mere agrarianism or primitivism. Asserting the importance of values beyond the utilitarian and material, this transplanted Southern philosophy challenged the doctrine of enlightened self-interest and the belief that leisure time is sin."

The most important thing that the South contributed, however, was a foundation for the cowboy's code which basically is nothing more than a democratic version of the Southern gentleman's "honor."

The cowboy movie is the only American art form in which the notion of honor retains its full strength. "The Westerner," Robert Warshow comments, "seeks not to extend his dominion but only to assert his personal value. . . . Since he is not a murderer but a man of virtue, and since he is always prepared for defeat, he retains his inner invulnerability. His story need not end with his death (and usually does not); but what we finally respond to is not his victory but his defeat." Most good westerns are seemingly comic but basically tragic.

If there were one archetypal[11] movie, it was *The Virginian*, made in 1929 and starring Gary Cooper. Taken from Owen Wister's novel, it depicted the adventures of a chivalric cowboy who wooed and won Molly Wood, a pretty schoolteacher from Vermont. He would not violate the accepted forms of western combat. To the villain's taunts he merely replied, "When you call me that—smile!" But he knew, as do we, that sooner or later Trampas would "ask for it." The hero would then see that he got it. That was the whole point of his being there. . . .

As a purely literary hero Pecos Bill has done well. Getting into print in 1923, he has in three decades driven off his less virile legendary rivals. He is today the best-known literary hero of the cowboy country. Primarily the brainchild of Edward ("Tex") O'Reilly, publicist and author of the Southwest, Bill dates from O'Reilly's 1923 article in the *Century Magazine*. The article reveals in what pattern O'Reilly intends to construct this oversized literary cowboy; for he judges it "highly probable that Paul Bunyan and Pecos Bill, mythical cowboy of the Southwest, were blood brothers. At all events, they can meet on one common ground: they were both fathered by a liar."

His model was Paul Bunyan. The reader also confronts a number of the episodes usually recorded as the exploits of a real-life Texas hero, Bigfoot Wallace. Pecos does humorously what Bigfoot did in deadly earnest, and with less of a flair for the spectacular and Bunyanesque. There is also something of the Crockett and Fink sagas in the Pecos stories that O'Reilly and others have constructed. Pecos Bill is a prefabricated hero, put together with parts from many other American sources and traditions. Like Bunyan, whom he meets and fights, Pecos Bill depends heavily on his retinue, which includes such fascinating creatures as Alkali Ike, One Lung Lyon, Bean-Hole Brown, Bullfrog

---

11. **archetypal**\ˈär·kə ˈtaiˑpəl\ pertaining to the original pattern or model from which all things of the same type are copies.

Doyle, and Bronco Jones. Essentially Pecos Bill is a knavish blusterer, a picaresque hero who (like Davy Crockett, Mike Fink, and Paul Bunyan) passes from place to place, adventure to adventure. He has the cowboy's steel-grey eyes, sense of humor, weather-beaten countenance, quick trigger finger, and outdoor psychology. There must be a horse, naturally, and O'Reilly named it Widow Maker. An educated critter, Widow Maker has twenty-seven gaits (twenty-three forward and four reverse). Unlike most old-time cowboys, Bill also has a regular girl, Slue Foot Sue, who rode down the Rio Grande on a catfish, demonstrating that she was "a true girl of the west."

One of Pecos' great moments came when he appeared in Walt Disney's 1948 movie, *Melody Time.* The effort won him many new admirers who had not heard of Pecos before going to the theater. Simultaneously, but not accidentally, various advertisements featuring Pecos Bill appeared in *Time, Newsweek* and the *Saturday Evening Post.* If the hero-makers continue to concentrate on him, his reputation will grow in the years ahead. He will benefit from his connection with Paul Bunyan and from the fine writing which O'Reilly lavished on him as a birthright. After all, a hero who wants to join "not one of these ordinary cow-stealin', Mexican-shootin' bunches of amateurs, but a real hard herd of hand-picked hellions that make murder a fine art and take some proper pride in their slaughter," is not to be dismissed. We would not rank him in importance with Paul Bunyan, the nearest American approach to a folk hero. "The virility of the Bunyan legend," observes Frank Shay, "has so choked out the other heroes that today not one in a hundred old-time cowboys ever heard of Pecos Bill."

The radio, movies, ad men and television might revise things. We shall have to wait and see. Watch out Paul—Pecos is coming!

"If we could dispel the haze," writes Walter P. Webb in *The Great Plains,* "we could view western life as it was in reality—logical, perfectly in accord ultimately with the laws laid down by the inscrutable Plains." We can never get rid of the romantic haze that has settled permanently on the western horizon; and most of us wouldn't want to, even if we could. We like to conjure up our untarnished knights roaming about in their domains, where they make the laws and punish the wicked. We like to read about it, see it on the screen, describe it to our children. It is a world in which none of our little problems and dissatisfactions occur. There everyone knows what he is supposed to do, and does it. We have never permanently lost the tranquility and finality of the Medieval Synthesis as long as the tradition of the cowboy's west exists. Thus the editor of *Ranch Romances* writes, "We aim to lead our readers away from the complexities of civilization into a world of simple feeling and direct emotion." The formula sells millions of pulp magazines each month.

The American cowboy symbolizes a freedom, individuality, and closeness to nature which for many has become a mirage. He is a safety valve for our souls. When things get too bad, we slip into a movie house, or into a chair with the latest cowboy magazine or novel, and vicariously hit the trail. We become free agents in space and time, and for a while leave our world behind. "As I sat in the movie house it was evident that Bill Hart was being loved by all there," wrote Sherwood Anderson in *A Story Teller's Tale.* "I also wanted to be loved —to be a little dreaded and feared, too, perhaps. Ah! There goes Sherwood Anderson! Treat him with respect. He is a bad man when he is aroused. But treat him kindly and he will be as gentle with you as any cooing dove."

The cowboy legend, so appealing to mechanized and urbanized America, is spreading rapidly. Every fourth Hollywood movie deals with it, and many reach foreign audiences. Cowboy interpreters are receiving academic recognition. A few years ago the Texas historian J. Frank Dobie was called to Cambridge University to explain life on the range. After his year's visit the faculty solemnly awarded an honorary M.A. to this *Petastus inter togatas homines:* "sombrero wearer among the men with togas."

The cowboy is holding up well under all this admiration and examination; he makes an excellent hero. He is a horseback man, always the breed of heroes throughout history. As wholesome as a glass of Grade A pasteurized milk, he boasts a virile code and outlook. He has those virtues our culture most admires, and displays them on all occasions. With him the love of freedom is a passion, and the willingness to accept his responsibility a dogma. To his code, his horse, and his cattle, he is always faithful.

He quickens young America's belief in personal strength and ingenuity. The western movies are little courses in citizenship; modern morality plays. Parents send junior off to the Saturday matinee, knowing that virtue will triumph and the forces of darkness will be squelched. Like knights of old, cowboys seek combat for fair ladies. With so sound a function, they need not fear extinction.

The open range has gone forever. Only an imaginary trail winds its way through what was once the unbroken sea of grass. All that is left of the golden moment is a group of names on the land: Bitterroot, Rawhide Creek, Whoopup, Chugwater, Tensleep, Wounded Knee, Tombstone, Medicine Bow, and Horse Thief Creek.

Heartfelt and descriptive, they endure. So does the memory and the dream.

I
THE WRITER AS CRITIC
AND ANALYST

You have previously noted the roles writers may play in creating a hero (Paul Bunyan) and in broadcasting and perpetuating our memory of real heroes (Lee and Lincoln). In the foregoing selection you see the writer in still another role with respect to American heroes: Professor Fishwick takes on the task of critic and analyst of the cowboy hero. He attempts to separate fact from fancy in cowboy lore and to explain the reasons for the cowboy's appeal to us. Whether or not you agree with Professor Fishwick's estimates should depend not upon your emotions, but rather upon whether you can disprove his arguments or counter them with better arguments of your own.

II
IMPLICATIONS

The following questions give you the opportunity to express your own opinions on the cowboy, but you are first asked to consider the author's views. Try to give a fair and complete statement of Professor Fishwick's position.

1. According to Professor Fishwick, why has the cowboy become such a popular American hero? Do you agree or disagree with him, and why? If you disagree, try to offer a better explanation of your own.

2. According to the author, what are some of the major differences between real and romanticized cowboys? Do you feel he defends his opinions convincingly? Why, or why not?

3. For what reasons could the cowboys justify living according to a different moral code from others? Do you think this is sufficient justification for their bad conduct? Why, or why not?

4. For what reasons might you agree or disagree with Fishwick's opinion that "most of us" wouldn't get rid of the "romantic haze" surrounding the cowboy, even if we could?

5. Describe Fishwick's final estimate of the cowboy as hero. Do you agree or disagree with him?

III
TECHNIQUES

Tone

Study the word choices and the phrasing of the passages below and try to determine how you might best describe Professor Fishwick's tone. Also, does he use this particular tone consistently throughout the essay, or can you find places where he shifts to a different tone? If you find shifts, are they natural and justified?

1. During the war the open range could not compete with the firing range. Young Texans who had mastered the art of rounding up cattle went off to round up Yankees.

2. A handsome loose flannel shirt (elaborately embroidered if a technicolor movie camera is lurking nearby) covers his manly chest.

3. These six-shooters, of heavy caliber, can be depended on to open a path for daylight through the body of any hostile critter, man or beast.

4. He is the model of all who believe that life in God's outdoors, close to the "real" things, is desirable; a good man to have with you, and demon when against you; a man to be tampered with only when you are reconciled to picking lead slugs out of your carcass on short notice.

5. As a class, cowboys have always presented a discouraging field for missionaries.

6. Oh, for a life on the distant plains, where a man can let off a little steam without ending up in a police court!

IV
WORDS

A. Using what you know about context clues and word parts, determine the meaning of the italicized words.

1. Persons by nature *predisposed* to direct others almost always seek to direct them in everything.

2. Yet the instant he reached the limit of . . . his *province*, he drew back. . . .

3. . . . Lee was extremely *solicitous* about the unnecessary exposure of his men.

4. . . . the sympathy took larger forms of *magnanimity* than mere prevention of cruelty to animals.

5. . . . Frémont's widely-read reports . . . helped *dispel* the notion that the plains were an uninhabited desert. . . .

B. From the following list of words, choose an antonym for each italicized word in the sentences that follow.

renounce	fair	mature
condemn	evasive	diffident
unrelenting	abdicate	perverse
incidentally	righteousness	effeminate

1. He *arrogated* to Congress the power to decide.

2. He viewed with *complacence* the scene.

3. The commander was *clement* when he could be.

4. His *candid* approach was refreshing.

5. The leader's *complaisant* manner surprised the committee.

6. The law was repealed as *inequitable*.

7. A *fledgling* sparrow had fallen from its nest.

8. This child of nature is *innately* handsome.

9. The cowboys revelled in pockets of *iniquity*.

10. They did not *condone* his lawlessness.

11. The movies *usurped* the place of the dime novel.

12. He has driven off his less *virile* rivals.

C. When speakers of a language become separated, the language of each group begins to change. So it was with American and British English. Americans found new words to describe life in the new country; for example, Americans coined the words *backwoods, corn bread, schooner, ice cream, elbow room.* Many words still current in America are seldom used in England today: *slim* ("slim possibility"), *drouth* ("rainless period"), *homely* ("unattractive"), *chore* ("task"), *deck* ("of cards"). These differences in vocabulary and idiom between American and British English are most striking in slang and technical vocabularies. In the language of automotive trades, the British *gear lever* is the American *gearshift; gear set,* American *transmission; wing, fender; silencer, muffler; dynamo, generator.*

1. The early settlers also adopted many terms from other languages, especially the Algonquian language family. Look up the history of these words: *chipmunk, woodchuck, moose, succotash, Tammany.* Americans borrowed from other languages, as well. Check the source of *prairie, key, bayou, cache, levee, rapids, noodle.*

2. The men of the West found language as well as life uninhibited. Look up these now unfamiliar words once used by the tamers of the West: *rambunctious, hornswoggle, cahoots, bodacious, backslider, lickspittle.*

3. Select several pages in the *Dictionary of Americanisms.* Make a list of words which appeared for the first time between 1700–1800; between 1800–1850. Note the source of each new word. What do these words reveal about American life and culture?

For the most part, the independent spirits
we have discussed have been recognized
as such during their own lifetimes. Sometimes,
however, a man will gain most of his fame after he is dead.
This is especially true for the man whose ideas are far in advance
of his time. This was the case for the subject
of the following essay, Louis Sullivan, an American who is
now recognized as "the father of modern architecture."

Crisis in Chicago

ELINOR RICHEY

Recently a truck has been plying back and forth between a Chicago warehouse and a railroad platform transporting curious crates tagged for shipping to destinations throughout America and Europe. This cargo—the last remains of Louis Sullivan's razed Garrick Theater Building—is bound for the scores of museums and universities that requested ornamental detail from the masterpiece of the "father of modern architecture."

It might be wondered why a building so highly prized that its fragments are being divided among the art showcases of the world was demolished. Had the building deteriorated structurally? Or did it stand in the way of some vital public project? No, experts said the 68-year-old building was sounder than most new construction and good for two centuries more. The building was destroyed because its owner decided that the space could be more profitably used for a parking garage.

The Garrick is one of a dozen Sullivan buildings felled in Chicago during the past five years, along with a score of other distinguished examples of the late nineteenth-century "Chicago School" of architecture of which Sullivan

was leader. His most famous residential design, Babson Mansion in suburban Riverside, was offered free if devoted to public use, but found no taker to save it from the rubble heap. Only the Garrick demolition stirred any local opposition. A small group of devotees fought to preserve it as a culture center, and persuaded its owner to offer it at the bargain price of $1.5 million. But Chicago could not be persuaded to buy. Currently, demolition rumors hover over other Sullivan buildings, including his famed Stock Exchange.

Alarmed over what it terms "the crisis in Chicago," the architectural press has urged Chicago to cherish the art that it fathered. These appeals are well-meant, but uninformed. The fact is, Chicago never accepted its native school of architecture. The acclaim given to the revolutionary style that developed after the Chicago fire came from without. At home the work went unhonored—then as now.

Chicago is not alone in this prejudice which has had such a pernicious effect upon the nation's cultural growth. Always there has been an American tendency to reject the home-grown in favor of the import—a deep-seated inferiority complex remaining from colonialism. This bias has thwarted taste development, and into this vacuum has welled a passion for newness. Across the country, clearance projects are sweeping out good architecture along with bad to make way for mammoth new developments. We are losing some of our finest architectural monuments in the name of "progress."

If not unique, Chicago's aesthetic blind spot does appear especially acute, and, considering the caliber of what it has thwarted and destroyed, the Chicago situation is tragic. The queer, twisted saga of Chicago and its genius contains a timely object lesson for us all—a warning of how costly such prejudice can be. There are other Garricks among us now. There may be other Sullivans.

Louis Sullivan

Replacement of his "proud and soaring" tower by a parking garage gives the Sullivan story almost startling poetic unity. The witty, elegant master, whose goal it was to express the American condition in architecture, would have wryly savored this irony. He would have perceived that the American condition, especially the Chicago condition, has been expressed instead in the automobile—transient and disposable.

Yes, to capture the American spirit in architecture was the Lernaean Hydra[1] he wrestled with. It was by chance that his battlefield was Chicago. Louis Sullivan was born in 1856 to Boston immigrant parents, an Irish dancing-master father and Swiss musician mother, who early recognized their son's remarkable mind. As a schoolboy, he decided where he would direct it. Walking the streets of Victorian Boston, he felt the architecture spoke nothing of the spirit of the times—an age of burgeoning science and technology—but belonged to the past of his history books. He dreamed of creating an architecture suited to his own day and to America.

Enrolling for architectural studies at Massachusetts Institute of Technology, he was disappointed. No wonder architecture had suggested the past, he realized—it *was* the past, frozen in stone. As preparation for designing nineteenth-century buildings, students diligently traced Greek and Roman orders. Getting no answer as to why architecture had to imitate, he left and matriculated at the Beaux Arts in Paris, where he found the same academic idolatry. Obviously the whole problem of building needed rethinking. He decided to be his own teacher. Back in America, he assigned himself prodigious readings in science and philosophy. His singleness of purpose precluded intimate friendships, making him emotionally dependent upon his family.

His parents had moved to Chicago, and he joined them there in the mid-1870s when Chicago was emerging from the great fire. Practical builders had flocked there and construction was blatant and rushing. Chicago had set itself up as commissary for the expanding West and was worried lest St. Louis grab its trade. The builders were grappling with thorny technical problems. They had to build deep to cope with the lakeside's marshy soil, and a real estate spiral impelled them to build tall to make the

1. **Lernaean Hydra**\ˈlər·nē·ən ˈhai·drə\ in Greek mythology, a nine-headed serpent that grew two heads for each one cut off.

most of premium space. Iron, newly abundant through industrialization, was directed toward these requirements.

Thrilled by this technical progress, Sullivan took a drafting job and plunged into the problems. During the next few years he moved from one architectural firm to another, his practical experience fermenting with nightly reading and study. After a succession of masters came Dankmar Adler, a German engineer-architect in demand for his technical ability. Adler divined rare talent in his employee and gave him a free hand. By the time he was twenty-five, Sullivan was full partner in the firm of Adler & Sullivan.

In 1885, Chicago experiments with metal reached a dramatic climax. William Jenney built the ten-story Home Insurance Building on a framework of iron and steel that assumed the entire support burden. Sullivan realized with excitement that if metal bore the weight, a building was free to follow any form. Already he had been reaching toward a new style. Chicago builders by stressing practicality—by omitting adornment, baring structural facts and increasing light with big windows and bays—unconsciously had given buildings a new look. While approving of this rationale, Sullivan was offended by its rawness. He had tried to inject compositional motif and rhythms into this utilitarian work.

Still, he recognized this simplicity to be only a chipping away at the old, instead of something new. The way had opened for something new. Every commission was a fervent exploration. Musing over his drafting board, he perceived that form and function are interdependent. Why not mold building material and space into a single plastic reality? Function would determine the form, which in turn would express the function "as the oak tree expresses the function oak, the pine tree the function pine." He had arrived at the first new architectural theory since the Gothic cathedral.

Adler's *expertise* in acoustics won the firm the commission for the Auditorium Hotel. Sul-

livan's artistry made it an architectural triumph. The combination of theater, hotel, and office building required a design of unprecedented complexity, and Sullivan reasonably might have evaded applying functionalism to a tri-function structure. He elected to face it, and spent three years wrestling with the conflicting demands. Technical considerations alone were staggering. He often neared collapse. But out of his travail came a statement of architectural serenity. Inside the theater, concentric arches visually expressed the function of a great hearing trumpet. He hadn't solved all of his problems—notably motif—but he had learned many things.

In designing a St. Louis skyscraper the next year, he truly found himself. With his Wainwright Building he seized full advantage of the steel frame. Taking tallness as the feature for expression, he employed a system of closely ranked piers to achieve a statement of soaring

Wainwright Building, St. Louis, Missouri

exultation. Frank Lloyd Wright, then a young Adler & Sullivan draftsman, later recalled: "The skyscraper as a new thing beneath the sun was born. Until Louis Sullivan showed the way, high buildings lacked unity. They were built-up layers. All were fighting height instead of gracefully and honestly accepting it."

Next came the Garrick, a superbly integrated composition in which he strengthened the upward sweep. He also made it a showcase for the building ornament he had been designing for skeleton construction, accenting the exterior with a web-like detail of terra-cotta leaf and vine. "Ornament must be of, not on, a building," he believed.

Success seemed to have arrived, and Sullivan expanded. Always well-tailored, now he grew a Vandyke beard and became something of a *bon vivant*[2] about town. A coterie[3] of young architects clustered about him. Besides Wright, there were Walter Burley Griffin, William Purcell, and George Elmslie. They watched fascinated as Sullivan applied functionalism to a succession of problems. They began introducing it into their work. Sullivan's ideas spread to other cities. Avant-garde[4] critics hailed the budding style a new American expression and suggested it as the building style for Chicago's coming Columbian Exposition.

There was another reaction to Sullivan, however. Many of his colleagues scoffed at his preoccupation with "the spirit" of a building. They thought it absurd to seek a new architecture. Why improve on the rich heritage of Europe which was handily compiled in the copy books they kept for tips on how to "dress up" a building? When inspecting Sullivan's newest innovation, they demanded, "What's your authority for *that?*" and smiled at Sullivan's lofty, "I am."

Daniel Burnham of Burnham & Root was especially exasperated with Sullivan. He assured Sullivan he was wasting his time "because architecture is going the other way." The astute Burnham had sniffed out a new aesthetic development in Chicago. He had detected the at-

titude among businessmen that while local architecture had served its purpose, now that they were up in the world they deserved something better. Significantly, they had begun referring to each other as kings of this, barons of that. Many of them *had* come quite a way. The stockyard kings Swift and Armour had arrived in the 1860s each with only a few dollars in his pocket, and a certain millionaire hosteler was hoping no one remembered he had walked into town a bankrupt backwoods tailor. In the latest census, Chicago had shot past Philadelphia, the city long ranked second to New York. Chicago reacted with a burst of pride that surged exuberantly past its mark and proclaimed itself first. Loudly it boasted about being first in railroading, first in grain and lumber sales, in farm machinery, and in slaughtered hogs. It claimed to publish the "greatest newspaper" and to be "boss town of America." In short, Chicago announced itself greater than New York.

Actually, it did not believe this. Deep down, Chicago feared that it was in every way inferior. Its shrill braggadocio[5] gave it away, as did its mania for New York goods. "Bought in New York" became Chicago's status symbol, proof one had arrived. This was reflected at first in clothes, jewelry and furnishings, and then architecture. To be "really artistic" a residence, a church, even an office building, required a New York architect. Since the New Yorkers were working almost exclusively in English Gothic and French Renaissance, castles and chateaux were popping up over the Chicago flats.

Money was no object in furnishing these proud villas. Their murky interiors overflowed with scimitars[6] and swords, wax flowers and stuffed birds, seashell collections, engravings

2. **bon vivant**\bŏn vē ▲văn\ one who enjoys good living.
3. **coterie**\▲kō•tə 'rē\ small, exclusive group bound by similar interests.
4. **Avant-garde**\a 'vant ▲gard\ group considered most extreme or daring.
5. **braggadocio**\'brä•gə ▲dō•shē•ō\ empty boasting.
6. **scimitars**\▲sĭ•mə•tərsz\ curved sabers used chiefly by Arabs and Turks.

of "The Lion's Bride," photographs of the Taj Mahal, tinkling chimes, bronze Venus de Milos with clock in stomach.

Burnham felt Chicago architects ought to keep up with all of this. He was boning up on castles, hoping to ride the trend. Already he had scored a hit with his 13-story Woman's Temple, fashioning its top three floors into a replica of a famous French chateau.

Burnham's obliging spirit was rewarded. When Chicago named the planning team for the Columbian Exposition, he got the plum job of director of construction. Anxious to please, he considered assigning all of the fair buildings to New York men. His colleagues' protests caused him to split the work equally between Chicago and New York. But he left style selection to the Easterners, who included palace specialists Charles McKim, William Mead, and Stanford White. To represent industrial America on its four-hundredth anniversary they chose Roman classic, the style Rome borrowed from the Greeks.

The only discordant note in this dulcet symphonia[7] was struck by Sullivan. His firm had drawn a commission, but he obstinately refused to observe the rules. He insisted upon employing his own style and declared he would color his buildings. Burnham hastily decided to relocate Sullivan's building in an inconspicuous position.

Discerning opinion at the fair held the discordant note the only one worth listening to. American and European critics scorned the imitation classic, while praising the originality and honesty of Sullivan's Transportation Building with its open wall forms and dynamic arched doorway. Montgomery Schuyler observed in *Architecture Record:* "Arcadian architecture is one thing, American another; men bring back not the mastodon[8] nor we those times." An English critic jeered the copywork as "well-studded-Parisian." A French museum voted Sullivan three medals for his Transportation Building and devoted an exhibition to models of his work. This set off a flurry of Sulli-

Carson, Pirie, Scott & Company Building, Chicago, Illinois

van shows all over Europe, including one in Moscow.

But public reaction was something else again. Most visitors were delighted with the dazzling palaces, taking them for the latest style in public buildings. They returned to Main Streets all over America carrying visions that would be translated into churches, banks, courthouses, railroad stations. Most of these built-to-last soot-catchers remain today, obtruding for their blackness as formerly for their whiteness.

For Chicago, already suspicious of its local products, the fair was proof that tradition was the thing. Before the exposition closed, Doric columns were being deployed across the city.

For Sullivan the exposition was a different sort of turning point. Soon after it closed, his partner Adler was lured into an industrial job,

---

7. **symphonia,** symphony.
8. **mastodon**\\ˈmăs•tə•dŏn\\ any one of numerous extinct mammals; something of unusually large size.

leaving Sullivan alone. Bemedaled and proud, he sat in his tower offices of the Auditorium Hotel awaiting the commissions that went to men willing to truckle to Chicago's new infatuation with classicism. First he was bewildered, then shocked. Like a crown prince unwarned of the *coup d'état*,[9] he didn't know how his kingdom had vanished.

But vanished it had. Before the fair he designed more than a hundred buildings. In the three remaining decades of his life, his work, excepting commissions already obtained (including his famous Carson Pirie Store), would consist of a couple of Chicago store fronts, a Chicago residence, and a handful of small town assignments. Most of the latter were small banks across the Midwest. In his years of artistic maturity America's most original genius found his only appreciation in Gopher Prairie. Today these charming little designs still shine like jewels in the somber county seats—the best preserved of all Sullivan's many buildings.

For Sullivan there was no adjusting. It was incredible that America would reject the honest architecture he believed in like a religion in favor of snobbish copywork. He watched Chicago expand in confusion, erecting its homes and offices in mimicry of every academic fad that wafted by. He was given no part in the building, nor were the principles to which he had devoted his life. Adjust? He could only mute this mockery with alcohol. He lost his staff, his offices, his home, his books, and personal possessions. Returning to find the man he called master deserted and destitute, Wright wrote: "Popular timidity and prejudice encouraged by jealousy had built a wall of ignorance about him so high that the wall blinded his countrymen and wasted him." Sullivan died in 1924 in a shabby rented room.

But the rallying power of crushed truth was proved. Functional architecture did not die. Its verities were nourished in Europe, where Sullivan's flowing ornament influenced Belgium's *L'Art Nouveau* and his open wall forms and structural honesty gave sustenance to Germany's Bauhaus School of Architecture. Wright, moving about the world, scattered seeds that slowly began to grow.

In the mid-1920s, modern architecture returned to America. New York, which had scoffed at Chicago functional, applauded the new functional it was importing from abroad. Hailed as the new expression of the modern age, the International Style overnight became a conquering force. Wright moved from eclipse to prominence. Architectural scholars, documenting the new functional style, recognized the now dead Sullivan as its pioneer.

Quick to copy New York's enthusiasm, Chicago adopted the new style for its construction boom. During the last three years of the 1920s, it built a billion dollar's worth of modern towers, even constructing a skyscraper opera house ("the world's tallest opera house"). Proudly showing off its modern architecture, Chicago did not realize that it had welcomed home the descendant of a native.

The new modern did have a difference—but not in its favor. Practitioners of the International Style had lifted from Sullivan's functional theory only its physical aspect, ignoring the aesthetic function Sullivan held equally vital. Many of these sternly utilitarian structures were no more than machines for living, as in fact their creators claimed them to be. Barren, monotonous agents of congestion, they ignored the needs and aspirations of the human spirit. The style which Sullivan intended for furthering man's freedom was often perverted to cage him. Some of this graph paper harshness has been relieved, but much remains entrenched in our architecture.

Hopefully, growing numbers of architects are realizing that a building which starves man's psychological needs fails as surely as that which ignores his physiology. Many critics consider the International Style to have been a retrogressive trip into the backwaters of modernism—a trip Sullivan could have saved us.

---

9. **coup d'état**\\'kü·dā ˄ta\\ sudden seizure of government.

Chicago, which vanquished Sullivan's broad functionalism, has been a prime victim of the restricting kind. The ranks of uninspired façades[10] in Chicago's Loop are a forceful sermon on the limitations of the merely serviceable.

Among trends growing in reaction to the sterility is what machine-for-living adherents have dubbed "the new romanticism." Led by Edward Durell Stone, designer of the American Embassy at New Delhi, these men seek to broaden functionalism to include pleasure-giving as well as utility. Stone frankly courts elegance in his designs and has reintroduced building ornament, which the International Style tabooed. His work has been characterized as following in the Sullivan tradition.

Stone's first Chicago building is nearing completion on the University of Chicago campus. The block-long design beguiles the eye with molded colonnades and a stunning hexagon pattern incised over the entire limestone exterior.

Ironically, this Sullivanesque building stands on the Midway, scene of the Columbian Exposition seventy years ago. This original design has for companions a veritable zoo of academic styles. Sullivan underestimated when he predicted that the damage wrought by the fair would last fifty years. It will last many, many more. "Error, wounded, writhes in pain," and if it happens to be architectural error it writhes and writhes and writhes.

I
THE HERO IN ADVANCE
OF HIS TIMES

Louis Sullivan certainly deserves to be ranked among America's greatest independent spirits in the arts. He had brilliant ideas; he was selflessly dedicated to his principles, and he fought hard and courageously for them against great odds. But

---

10. façades\fə ᵂsadz\ principal faces or fronts of buildings.

recognition by his countrymen was largely denied him during his lifetime. His experience, however, is far from unique—many of the greatest artists in all fields have been fully recognized only after their deaths. What are some of the important factors that contributed to Sullivan's lack of recognition during his life? What has contributed to his later recognition?

II
IMPLICATIONS

Discuss the following propositions in the light of this selection and of your own experience.

1. The American desire for progress constantly threatens to destroy treasures of our past.

2. Americans tend to favor the import over the home-grown, especially in the arts.

3. Human beings like the comfortable and the familiar and therefore are quite reluctant to accept novel things.

4. An artist can never hope to achieve broad popular recognition in America because the average person is not able to understand or appreciate fully artistic contributions.

5. Louis Sullivan's experience points up the fact that there is a wide gulf in American life between the "highbrow" and the "lowbrow."

III
TECHNIQUES
Selection of Significant Detail

One of the most significant details in any piece of writing is its title. Because of its prominent position, it receives heavy emphasis; indeed, as you know from your own reading, a title will often determine whether or not a reader will read a given article in the first place.

Do you think Miss Richey's title is well-chosen? In answering this question, make a list of the things that a good title should do.

Tone

There is no doubt about Miss Richey's attitude toward Sullivan, but how would you describe her attitude toward the persons or factors that prevented him from gaining proper recognition? Is she bitter, flippant, condescending, forgiving, or what? Whatever you may decide her tone is, be sure that you can point to some examples to prove your case.

One of the most widely read books of the last decade is
Harper Lee's Pulitzer-Prize-winning novel, *To Kill a Mockingbird,*
from which the following selection is taken. Though there are
many reasons for the book's immense popularity, one of the main ones
is the independent spirit of the central character,
Atticus Finch.
Although our selection is Chapter 10 of the novel,
it is a self-contained story and needs little introduction.
The tale is set in Maycomb, a small Alabama town. The narrator is
Atticus's daughter, Scout (Jean Louise) Finch, who is about eight
when this episode occurs. Her brother, Jem, an important character
in this episode, is four years older. Most of the other characters
are neighbors of the Finches; Calpurnia is their maid.

To Kill a Mockingbird

HARPER LEE

CHAPTER 10

Atticus was feeble: he was nearly fifty. When Jem and I asked him why he was so old, he said he got started late, which we felt reflected upon his abilities and manliness. He was much older than the parents of our school contemporaries, and there was nothing Jem or I could say about him when our classmates said, "*My* father—"

Jem was football crazy. Atticus was never too tired to play keep-away, but when Jem wanted to tackle him Atticus would say, "I'm too old for that, son."

Our father didn't do anything. He worked in an office, not in a drugstore. Atticus did not drive a dump-truck for the county, he was not the sheriff, he did not farm, work in a garage, or do anything that could possibly arouse the admiration of anyone.

Besides that, he wore glasses. He was nearly blind in his left eye, and said left eyes were the tribal curse of the Finches. Whenever he wanted to see something well, he turned his head and looked from his right eye.

He did not do the things our schoolmates' fathers did: he never went hunting, he did not play poker or fish or drink or smoke. He sat in the livingroom and read.

With these attributes, however, he would not remain as inconspicuous as we wished him to: that year, the school buzzed with talk about him defending Tom Robinson, none of which was complimentary. After my bout with Cecil Jacobs when I committed myself to a policy of cowardice, word got around that Scout Finch wouldn't fight any more, her daddy wouldn't let her. This was not entirely correct: I wouldn't fight publicly for Atticus, but the family was private ground. I would fight anyone from a third cousin upwards tooth and nail. Francis Hancock, for example, knew that.

When he gave us our air-rifles Atticus wouldn't teach us to shoot. Uncle Jack instructed us in the rudiments thereof; he said Atticus wasn't interested in guns. Atticus said to Jem one day, "I'd rather you shot at tin cans in the back yard, but I know you'll go after birds. Shoot all the bluejays you want, if you can hit 'em, but remember it's a sin to kill a mockingbird."

That was the only time I ever heard Atticus say it was a sin to do something, and I asked Miss Maudie about it.

"Your father's right," she said. "Mockingbirds don't do one thing but make music for us to enjoy. They don't eat up people's gardens, don't nest in corncribs, they don't do one thing but sing their hearts out for us. That's why it's a sin to kill a mockingbird."

"Miss Maudie, this is an old neighborhood, ain't it?"

"Been here longer than the town."

"Nome, I mean the folks on our street are all old. Jem and me's the only children around here. Mrs. Dubose is close on to a hundred and Miss Rachel's old and so are you and Atticus."

"I don't call fifty very old," said Miss Maudie tartly. "Not being wheeled around yet, am I? Neither's your father. But I must say Providence was kind enough to burn down that old mausoleum of mine, I'm too old to keep it up—maybe you're right, Jean Louise, this is a settled neighborhood. You've never been around young folks much, have you?"

"Yessum, at school."

"I mean young grown-ups. You're lucky, you know. You and Jem have the benefit of your father's age. If your father was thirty you'd find life quite different."

"I sure would. Atticus can't do anything. . . ."

"You'd be surprised," said Miss Maudie. "There's life in him yet."

"What can he do?"

"Well, he can make somebody's will so airtight can't anybody meddle with it."

"Shoot . . ."

"Well, did you know he's the best checker-player in this town? Why, down at the Landing when we were coming up, Atticus Finch could beat everybody on both sides of the river."

"Good Lord, Miss Maudie, Jem and me beat him all the time."

"It's about time you found out it's because he lets you. Did you know he can play a Jew's Harp?"

This modest accomplishment served to make me even more ashamed of him.

"Well . . ." she said.

"Well, what, Miss Maudie?"

"Well nothing. Nothing—it seems with all that you'd be proud of him. Can't everybody play a Jew's Harp. Now keep out of the way of the carpenters. You'd better go home, I'll be in my azaleas and can't watch you. Plank might hit you."

I went to the back yard and found Jem plugging away at a tin can, which seemed stupid with all the bluejays around. I returned to the front yard and busied myself for two hours erecting a complicated breastworks at the side of the porch, consisting of a tire, an orange crate, the laundry hamper, the porch chairs, and a small U.S. flag Jem gave me from a popcorn box.

When Atticus came home to dinner he found me crouched down aiming across the street. "What are you shooting at?"

"Miss Maudie's rear end."

Atticus turned and saw my generous target bending over her bushes. He pushed his hat to the back of his head and crossed the street. "Maudie," he called, "I thought I'd better warn you. You're in considerable peril."

Miss Maudie straightened up and looked toward me. She said, "Atticus, you are a devil from hell."

When Atticus returned he told me to break camp. "Don't you ever let me catch you pointing that gun at anybody again," he said.

I wished my father was a devil from hell. I sounded out Calpurnia on the subject. "Mr. Finch? Why, he can do lots of things."

"Like what?" I asked.

Calpurnia scratched her head. "Well, I don't rightly know," she said.

Jem underlined it when he asked Atticus if he was going out for the Methodists and Atticus said he'd break his neck if he did, he was just too old for that sort of thing. The Methodists were trying to pay off their church mortgage, and had challenged the Baptists to a game of touch football. Everybody in town's father was playing, it seemed, except Atticus. Jem said he didn't even want to go, but he was unable to resist football in any form, and he stood gloomily on the sidelines with Atticus and me watching Cecil Jacobs's father make touchdowns for the Baptists.

One Saturday Jem and I decided to go exploring with our air-rifles to see if we could find a rabbit or a squirrel. We had gone about five hundred yards beyond the Radley Place when I noticed Jem squinting at something down the street. He had turned his head to one side and was looking out of the corners of his eyes.

"Whatcha looking at?"

"That old dog down yonder," he said.

"That's old Tim Johnson, ain't it?"

"Yeah."

Tim Johnson was the property of Mr. Harry Johnson who drove the Mobile bus and lived on the southern edge of town. Tim was a liver-colored bird dog, the pet of Maycomb.

"What's he doing?"

"I don't know, Scout. We better go home."

"Aw Jem, it's February."

"I don't care, I'm gonna tell Cal."

We raced home and ran to the kitchen.

"Cal," said Jem, "can you come down the sidewalk a minute?"

"What for, Jem? I can't come down the sidewalk every time you want me."

"There's somethin' wrong with an old dog down yonder."

Calpurnia sighed. "I can't wrap up any dog's foot now. There's some gauze in the bathroom, go get it and do it yourself."

Jem shook his head. "He's sick, Cal. Something's wrong with him."

"What's he doin', trying to catch his tail?"

"No, he's doin' like this."

Jem gulped like a goldfish, hunched his shoulders and twitched his torso. "He's goin' like that, only not like he means to."

"Are you telling me a story, Jem Finch?" Calpurnia's voice hardened.

"No Cal, I swear I'm not."

"Was he runnin'?"

"No, he's just moseyin' along, so slow you can't hardly tell it. He's comin' this way."

Calpurnia rinsed her hands and followed Jem into the yard. "I don't see any dog," she said.

She followed us beyond the Radley Place and looked where Jem pointed. Tim Johnson was not much more than a speck in the distance, but he was closer to us. He walked erratically, as if his right legs were shorter than his left legs. He reminded me of a car stuck in a sandbed.

"He's gone lopsided," said Jem.

Calpurnia stared, then grabbed us by the shoulders and ran us home. She shut the wood door behind us, went to the telephone and shouted, "Gimme Mr. Finch's office!"

"Mr. Finch!" she shouted. "This is Cal. I swear to God there's a mad dog down the street a piece—he's comin' this way, yes sir, he's—Mr. Finch, I declare he is—old Tim Johnson, yes sir . . . yessir . . . yes—"

She hung up and shook her head when we tried to ask her what Atticus had said. She rattled the telephone hook and said, "Miss Eula May—now ma'am, I'm through talkin' to Mr. Finch, please don't connect me no more—listen, Miss Eula May, can you call Miss Rachel and Miss Stephanie Crawford and whoever's got a phone on this street and tell 'em a mad dog's comin'? Please ma'am!"

Calpurnia listened. "I know it's February, Miss Eula May, but I know a mad dog when I see one. Please ma'am hurry!"

Calpurnia asked Jem, "Radleys got a phone?"

Jem looked in the book and said no. "They won't come out anyway, Cal."

"I don't care, I'm gonna tell 'em."

She ran to the front porch, Jem and I at her heels. "You stay in that house!" she yelled.

Calpurnia's message had been received by the neighborhood. Every wood door within our range of vision was closed tight. We saw no trace of Tim Johnson. We watched Calpurnia running toward the Radley Place, holding her skirt and apron above her knees. She went up to the front steps and banged on the door. She got no answer, and she shouted, "Mr. Nathan,

Mr. Arthur, mad dog's comin'! Mad dog's comin'!"

"She's supposed to go around in back," I said.

Jem shook his head. "Don't make any difference now," he said.

Calpurnia pounded on the door in vain. No one acknowledged her warning; no one seemed to have heard it.

As Calpurnia sprinted to the back porch a black Ford swung into the driveway. Atticus and Mr. Heck Tate got out.

Mr. Heck Tate was the sheriff of Maycomb County. He was as tall as Atticus, but thinner. He was long-nosed, wore boots with shiny metal eye-holes, boot pants and a lumber jacket. His belt had a row of bullets sticking in it. He carried a heavy rifle. When he and Atticus reached the porch, Jem opened the door.

"Stay inside, son," said Atticus. "Where is he, Cal?"

"He oughta be here by now," said Calpurnia, pointing down the street.

"Not runnin', is he?" asked Mr. Tate.

"Naw sir, he's in the twitchin' stage, Mr. Heck."

"Should we go after him, Heck?" asked Atticus.

"We better wait, Mr. Finch. They usually go in a straight line, but you never can tell. He might follow the curve—hope he does or he'll go straight in the Radley back yard. Let's wait a minute."

"Don't think he'll get in the Radley yard," said Atticus. "Fence'll stop him. He'll probably follow the road. . . ."

I thought mad dogs foamed at the mouth, galloped, leaped and lunged at throats, and I thought they did it in August. Had Tim Johnson behaved thus, I would have been less frightened.

Nothing is more deadly than a deserted, waiting street. The trees were still, the mockingbirds were silent, the carpenters at Miss Maudie's house had vanished. I heard Mr. Tate sniff, then blow his nose. I saw him shift his gun to the crook of his arm. I saw Miss Stephanie Crawford's face framed in the glass window of her front door. Miss Maudie appeared and stood beside her. Atticus put his foot on the rung of a chair and rubbed his hand slowly down the side of his thigh.

"There he is," he said softly.

Tim Johnson came into sight, walking dazedly in the inner rim of the curve parallel to the Radley house.

"Look at him," whispered Jem. "Mr. Heck said they walked in a straight line. He can't even stay in the road."

"He looks more sick than anything," I said.

"Let anything get in front of him and he'll come straight at it."

Mr. Tate put his hand to his forehead and leaned forward. "He's got it all right, Mr. Finch."

Tim Johnson was advancing at a snail's pace, but he was not playing or sniffing at foliage: he seemed dedicated to one course and motivated by an invisible force that was inching him toward us. We could see him shiver like a horse shedding flies; his jaw opened and shut; he was alist, but he was being pulled gradually toward us.

"He's lookin' for a place to die," said Jem.

Mr. Tate turned around. "He's far from dead, Jem, he hasn't got started yet."

Tim Johnson reached the side street that ran in front of the Radley Place, and what remained of his poor mind made him pause and seem to consider which road he would take. He made a few hesitant steps and stopped in front of the Radley gate; then he tried to turn around, but was having difficulty.

Atticus said, "He's within range, Heck. You better get him before he goes down the side street—Lord knows who's around the corner. Go inside, Cal."

Calpurnia opened the screen door, latched it behind her, then unlatched it and held onto the hook. She tried to block Jem and me with her body, but we looked out from beneath her arms.

"Take him, Mr. Finch." Mr. Tate handed the rifle to Atticus; Jem and I nearly fainted.

"Don't waste time, Heck," said Atticus. "Go on."

"Mr. Finch, this is a one-shot job."

Atticus shook his head vehemently: "Don't just stand there, Heck! He won't wait all day for you—"

"For God's sake, Mr. Finch, look where he is! Miss and you'll go straight into the Radley house! I can't shoot that well and you know it!"

"I haven't shot a gun in thirty years—"

Mr. Tate almost threw the rifle at Atticus. "I'd feel mighty comfortable if you did now," he said.

In a fog, Jem and I watched our father take the gun and walk out into the middle of the street. He walked quickly, but I thought he moved like an underwater swimmer: time had slowed to a nauseating crawl.

When Atticus raised his glasses Calpurnia murmured, "Sweet Jesus help him," and put her hands to her cheeks.

Atticus pushed his glasses to his forehead; they slipped down, and he dropped them in the street. In the silence, I heard them crack. Atticus rubbed his eyes and chin; we saw him blink hard.

In front of the Radley gate, Tim Johnson had made up what was left of his mind. He had finally turned himself around, to pursue his original course up our street. He made two steps forward, then stopped and raised his head. We saw his body go rigid.

With movements so swift they seemed simultaneous, Atticus's hand yanked a ball-tipped lever as he brought the gun to his shoulder.

The rifle cracked. Tim Johnson leaped, flopped over and crumpled on the sidewalk in a brown-and-white heap. He didn't know what hit him.

Mr. Tate jumped off the porch and ran to the Radley Place. He stopped in front of the dog, squatted, turned around and tapped his finger on his forehead above his left eye. "You were a little to the right, Mr. Finch," he called.

"Always was," answered Atticus. "If I had my 'druthers I'd take a shotgun."

He stooped and picked up his glasses, ground the broken lenses to powder under his heel, and went to Mr. Tate and stood looking down at Tim Johnson.

Doors opened one by one, and the neighborhood slowly came alive. Miss Maudie walked down the steps with Miss Stephanie Crawford.

Jem was paralyzed. I pinched him to get him moving, but when Atticus saw us coming he called, "Stay where you are."

When Mr. Tate and Atticus returned to the yard, Mr. Tate was smiling. "I'll have Zeebo collect him," he said. "You haven't forgot much, Mr. Finch. They say it never leaves you."

Atticus was silent.

"Atticus?" said Jem.

"Yes?"

"Nothin'."

"I saw that, One-Shot Finch!"

Atticus wheeled around and faced Miss Maudie. They looked at one another without saying anything, and Atticus got into the the sheriff's car. "Come here," he said to Jem. "Don't you go near that dog, you understand? Don't go near him, he's just as dangerous dead as alive."

"Yes sir," said Jem. "Atticus—"

"What, son?"

"Nothing."

"What's the matter with you, boy, can't you talk?" said Mr. Tate, grinning at Jem. "Didn't you know your daddy's—"

"Hush, Heck," said Atticus, "let's go back to town."

When they drove away, Jem and I went to Miss Stephanie's front steps. We sat waiting for Zeebo to arrive in the garbage truck.

Jem sat in numb confusion, and Miss Stephanie said, "Uh, uh, uh, who'da thought of a mad dog in February? Maybe he wasn't mad, maybe he was just crazy. I'd hate to see Harry Johnson's face when he gets in from the Mobile run and finds Atticus Finch's shot his dog. Bet he was just full of fleas from somewhere—"

Miss Maudie said Miss Stephanie'd be singing a different tune if Tim Johnson was still coming up the street, that they'd find out soon enough, they'd send his head to Montgomery.

Jem became vaguely articulate: "'d you see him, Scout? 'd you see him just standin' there? . . . 'n' all of a sudden he just relaxed all over, an' it looked like that gun was a part of him . . . an' he did it so quick, like . . . I hafta aim for ten minutes 'fore I can hit somethin'. . . ."

Miss Maudie grinned wickedly. "Well now, Miss Jean Louise," she said, "still think your father can't do anything? Still ashamed of him?"

"Nome," I said meekly.

"Forgot to tell you the other day that besides playing the Jew's Harp, Atticus Finch was the deadest shot in Maycomb County in his time."

"Dead shot . . ." echoed Jem.

"That's what I said, Jem Finch. Guess you'll change *your* tune now. The very idea, didn't you know his nickname was Ol' One-Shot when he was a boy? Why, down at the Landing when he was coming up, if he shot fifteen times and hit fourteen doves he'd complain about wasting ammunition."

"He never said anything about that," Jem muttered.

"Never said anything about it, did he?"

"No ma'am."

"Wonder why he never goes huntin' now," I said.

"Maybe I can tell you," said Miss Maudie. "If your father's anything, he's civilized in his heart. Marksmanship's a gift of God, a talent—oh, you have to practice to make it perfect, but shootin's different from playing the piano or the like. I think maybe he put his gun down when he realized that God had given him an unfair advantage over most living things. I guess he decided he wouldn't shoot till he had to, and he had to today."

"Looks like he'd be proud of it," I said.

"People in their right minds never take pride in their talents," said Miss Maudie.

We saw Zeebo drive up. He took a pitchfork from the back of the garbage truck and gingerly lifted Tim Johnson. He pitched the dog onto the truck, then poured something from a gallon jug on and around the spot where Tim fell. "Don't yawl come over here for a while," he called.

When we went home I told Jem we'd really have something to talk about at school on Monday. Jem turned on me.

"Don't say anything about it, Scout," he said.

"What? I certainly am. Ain't everybody's daddy the deadest shot in Maycomb County."

Jem said, "I reckon if he'd wanted us to know it, he'da told us. If he was proud of it, he'da told us."

"Maybe it just slipped his mind," I said.

"Naw, Scout, it's something you wouldn't understand. Atticus is real old, but I wouldn't care if he couldn't do anything—I wouldn't care if he couldn't do a blessed thing."

Jem picked up a rock and threw it jubilantly at the carhouse. Running after it, he called back: "Atticus is a gentleman, just like me!"

I

THE GENTLEMAN

Jem and Scout want very much to be able to think of their father as a hero. When he does perform a heroic act, the emotions of the children shift dramatically from disappointment with their father to overwhelming admiration. Yet if the need had not risen, it is doubtful that Atticus would have revealed his talent to his children even though he knew they wanted him to be like other fathers. Instead, he chose to follow his own convictions, to be true to himself. In so doing, Atticus taught Jem and Scout a far greater lesson than he could as a mere sharp-shooting hero.

II

IMPLICATIONS

Discuss each of the following propositions related to this selection.

1. Youngsters want their fathers to be heroic mainly so that they will not be looked down on by other children in the school or neighborhood.

2. Atticus appeals to hero-loving readers largely because of his modesty.

3. When Jem calls his father a gentleman, he is saying, in effect, that he loves and admires him even though Atticus has no special abilities.

4. "People in their right minds never take pride in their talents."

5. The main point of this story is that young boys want to be able to identify with their fathers.

III
TECHNIQUES
Selection of Significant Detail

Whether or not any given detail is to be counted as "significant" depends largely on the author's purpose. Assuming that one of the main purposes of Miss Lee in this chapter is to create a suspenseful situation, how would you evaluate the significance of (1) the talk about mockingbirds, (2) the peacefulness and "oldness" of the neighborhood, and (3) the several mentions of air-rifles.

Tone

When a writer uses a first-person narrator, as does Miss Lee, how can the reader discover the author's attitude toward his material? Clearly, we cannot assume that Miss Lee's judgments are identical to those of her young narrator; the author, for example, would not say, "Atticus was feeble"; nor would she agree with that opinion. Yet in spite of the fact that we have mainly to deal with Scout's words and opinions, we do feel that we also know Miss Lee's attitude toward her characters and situations.

One reason why we can judge the author's attitude is that we know it *is* her hand that determines what Scout sees. Miss Lee is the architect here, and we can discover how she feels about the structure she has built by inference from the structure itself. Thus, the very fact that she chose to include this chapter in her novel is evidence of the fact that she feels and wants her readers to feel that Atticus is heroic.

IV
WORDS

The major dialect areas of the United States reflect the movements of the settlers during the eighteenth and nineteenth centuries. After the Revolutionary War, settlers moved into Kentucky and Tennessee. These lands became crowded and the settlers moved further westward.

The completion of the Erie Canal in 1825 provided access to the midwest. What is now U.S. 40,

the National Road, opened the Ohio Valley and even today is a boundary for certain dialect features. By 1840, Illinois, Indiana, Michigan, and Ohio had been settled.

The Southern expansion centered around the Mississippi delta. Defeat of the Creek and Cherokee Indians opened Alabama, Arkansas, and Georgia for further settlement. During the 1840's the West Coast was settled. Later, the railroad made possible the settlement of other areas.

From these settlement patterns emerged three dialect areas: North, South, and Midland. The Northern area includes New England, upstate New York, metropolitan New York, the Hudson Valley, and northern Pennsylvania. The Midland consists of western New Jersey, Delaware, Maryland, central and southern Pennsylvania. The South generally includes Virginia, the Carolinas, Georgia, Florida, and Louisiana. Using state boundaries oversimplifies because dialect areas do not follow state lines.

Although the dialect areas along the coast are somewhat easily identified, the westward movement resulted in overlapping distribution of features. When we compare varieties of American English we find that differences in pronunciation, grammar, and vocabulary do not always occur in combination. Widespread education and mass media of communication have tended to level dialect differences. Nevertheless, you too may be a linguistic geographer by listening to and observing language habits of those about you. Study the following list of regional names for certain common objects.

	Northern	Midland	Southern
container for water	pail	bucket	bucket
small stream	brook	run	bayou
finished siding	clapboard		weather board

Here are additional vocabulary words peculiar to certain regions. Which do you use?

paper bag: sack, poke, tote bag
praying mantis: walking stick, devil's horse
sycamore: buttonwood, cottonball, buttonball, plane tree
chimney: flue, smokestack, funnel
overall: denims, blue jeans, Levi's, overalls

While the Geneva treaty of 1954 split the country of Viet Nam
into a Communist-controlled North and a non-Communist South, it also
provided a period of several months during which citizens could freely move
from one section of the country to the other. Some 600,000 north Vietnamese chose to take
the "Passage to Freedom." Most of these refugees passed through Haiphong,
the north Viet Nam port city where young Dr. Thomas A. Dooley was given
the staggering job of setting up and operating refugee camps. Here he
and his men did what they could for the refugees, delousing and vaccinating
them before they boarded ship for south Viet Nam. The following excerpt
from Dr. Dooley's first book, *Deliver Us from Evil*, tells part of
the story of this selfless, courageous, ingenious hero's
last days in Haiphong, "The Dying City."

The Dying City

THOMAS A. DOOLEY, M.D.

The months passed but the refugees continued to pour in week after week from all the provinces of north Indo-China. Some days we would get fewer than a hundred; other days there would be thousands. They came by boat, by land, by foot, by junks and sampans.

Camp de la Pagode was taken down in March and other camps were erected. During January and February, we had three huge camps with a total capacity of over 30,000.

Eventually all of my Navy corpsmen left except Norman Baker, the dauntless interpreter who did everything else but interpret.

It was at that luncheon given by Admiral Sabin that I made a clean breast of the Baker affair. "You see, sir," I said, "I speak French, and now I speak Vietnamese, so I hardly need an interpreter. But Baker is a wonderful all-around assistant. So I've been holding on to him under false pretenses."

"Well, well," the Admiral said, assuming a mock-serious expression. "I hate to disappoint you, but you weren't fooling us. I knew all along you were pulling a fast one."

It turned out there were a lot of other fast ones that he hadn't minded either. There had been complaints about my habit of lifting supplies from ships in the area. "Look what Dooley's done now—60 drums of oil and he just signed his name for it! Who the devil does that boy think he is?"

"Well," the Admiral would say, "I'm sure he wouldn't have taken the stuff if he hadn't needed it urgently."

Also, he had become inured to my rare but high-handed raids on ship personnel. For example, at a time when I was acutely short-handed, I requested that four volunteer corpsmen be given TAD (Temporary Additional Duty) with me. Since their Captain had no desire to release them, I sent a message directly to the Admiral. It must have reached him, for the four men were soon at work in my camps.

Many months after our talk on his flagship, I received a letter from Admiral Sabin commending me on having been awarded the Legion of Merit. In it he wrote: "The Book says the Lord will help those who help themselves

Reprinted from *Deliver Us from Evil* by Thomas A. Dooley, by permission of Farrar, Straus & Giroux, Inc. Copyright © 1956 by Thomas A. Dooley.

and it seems to me that, in the evacuation of Indo-China, you, Dr. Dooley, several times managed to give the Lord a nudge."

Not once did the Admiral fail to endorse my nudging. I had superb support from on high, and without it I would have been licked.

By April the push began to slow up. Evidently the new masters of north Viet Nam had plugged most of the remaining holes in their Curtain. The French Army was almost gone, along with its equipment, quonset huts, tanks, office furniture. Only a few hundred French soldiers were still encamped on the nail of the finger-like projection of Haiphong.[1] Operation Cockroach, my end of the more elegantly named Passage to Freedom, was entering its final stage. Once, when a helicopter was sent from a ship for me, the Communist perimeter was already so choking-close that the plane had to land on a small lot in town.

Haiphong was dying. Every day more shops and houses were deserted. Only a few civilian vehicles remained of the thick motor traffic we had found on arrival. The reeking bazaar which had fascinated me was burned "by accident." There was little doubt that it was the work of Viet Minh infiltrators.

The few officers of MAAG left, except an Air Force Major, Ralph Walker. Roger Ackley, replacing Mike Walker toward the end, brought some new ideas and the camp administration was revamped.

Major John McGowan, U. S. Army, was the Military Attaché who stayed on until the very last day. He was another excellent type of career officer who did his job with all his heart, withstood all discomforts and managed to retain his sense of humor. I was lucky to have men to work with like John McGowan. They were a constant inspiration—and a constant gig in the rear. When I felt myself slipping, becoming lazy, I would see other Americans in Haiphong doing their jobs well, and then guilt would get me. "Up and at 'em."

By now my evenings were spent either at the camps, talking to the refugees, by this time in their own language, or in town, at the aban-

doned bank building (the coolest place in town) where John and I would argue big subjects like Army versus Navy and bigger ones like wine and women. We would consider it a treat when relatives would get mail through to us and we would have a copy of *Time* or *Newsweek*. The Embassy in Saigon sent a plane up with our mail once or twice a month. This was always a great day.

We had used an amazing tonnage of DDT, plus thousands of gallons of Lindane,[2] and other insecticide solutions. The water systems had worked overtime and now I believed they should be put out to pasture in the green fields of North Carolina.

All the city people who intended to leave were leaving or had left. By this time, most of those remaining in the city could be assumed to be pro-Viet Minh, if not actually full-fledged Communists. It was now that real trouble began.

The Governor's staff and the Mayor's staff left, with only skeleton crews remaining. All was grim and silent on the streets. Violence became common in the "new society" about to install itself on the ruins of Haiphong. The first riots exploded in the second week of April.

It seems that several hundred Viet Minh trucks arrived with so-called refugees piled high in back. These refugees did not want to live in the camps; they wanted to move into the city, where there were hundreds of empty buildings.

As the trucks tried to drive across the Ha Ly Bridge leading to the city, the French stopped them and forbade them to enter, saying that the Viet Minh were not to take over completely until May 19, and that this was beating the Geneva deadline. The truck occupants argued that as refugees they could enter at any time.

Tempers became short on both sides. The bogus refugees pushed across the bridge and the French soldiers poured out tear-gas

---

1. **Haiphong**\ˆhai ˈfŏng\ chief port of north Viet Nam.
2. **Lindane**\ˈlĭn ˆdān\ an insecticide.

bombs. Hand-to-hand fights developed. Several of the "refugees" were killed, hundreds were wounded, including many soldiers; and the Red radio broadcasters in Hanoi had themselves another propaganda holiday. Such clashes became ever more frequent.

I had one more difficult task to perform. The shoeshine kids were still in the city, and still my friends and protectors. One time my camera was stolen when I foolishly left it in my truck, parked on a side street. I told the artful dodgers of my loss. They were furious to think that anyone would steal from their American doctor. I think they were also furious to think that other people were horning in on their own purloining territory. Within a few hours my camera was returned. They said they had found it. I wondered whether one of the lovable, larcenous kids had probably stolen it himself without knowing to whom it belonged.

The time had come for the shoeshine kids to go. I consoled them with assurances that the shoeshine business was certain to be lush in Saigon and that a good thief, like a religious man, finds it hard to survive in a police state.

What convinced them finally, I think, was the matter of shoes. The idea came to me in a flash one day. "Well," I said, "you might as well throw those kits away. There will be no more shoe-shining when the Viet Minh arrive. Or do you think you can shine canvas shoes?"

They looked at me suspiciously, and then at one another. I wasn't kidding! From their frequent forays behind the Bamboo Curtain, they had learned that canvas sneakers were standard equipment among the Viet Minh.

At that point they agreed to be vaccinated and dusted with DDT. One April morning, Baker and I boosted a few of them into a truck and went downtown to gather up the rest from the street corners. We gave them each a loaf of bread and a final delousing and watched them shoulder their shoeshine kits and file sullenly aboard the landing-craft. They arrived safely in Saigon, and I'm sure that city hasn't been the same since.

Dr. Tom Dooley and young patient.

On May 10 the Viet Minh staged another proof that the American doctor and Americans in general were hated by the population. Our green truck was stolen. It was a one-ton truck Doctor Amberson had gotten from the Haiphong Public Health people. They had received it from the French, who got it from the U.S.A. through American Aid. I used it for ten months, for every conceivable mission. It had been turned on its side in a riot and, in another demonstration, had had all its windows broken. The spare tire, the cap of the gasoline tank, the windshield and the light bulbs were missing towards the end. Baker's baboon had eaten most of the interior, yet the spunky little truck still ran. The monsoon rains had done their best to make it moldy. You couldn't sit down in it with clean trousers and come out looking the same. Yet the little chariot could go anywhere, haul anything, and was well known throughout the city. To make sure that no one forgot it, Mike Adler had the big American Aid insignia painted on its side.

On the tenth of May it was stolen from a parking space near the bank building. Late that night we found its charred and blackened chassis in the town square. The Viet Minh apparently had burned it in a public demonstration to illustrate to the Americans that they were despised and to the Vietnamese that the new Democratic Republic of Viet Minh would have nothing to do with anything "made in the U.S.A."

I was as depressed as if a friend had been murdered, and for a moment thought of having what was left of the chassis buried with military honors. USOM officials in Saigon probably are still filling out chits to account for ONE TRUCK, DODGE, ONE-TON, GREEN.

The Catholic Mission was now about empty. The nuns, the school children and all the priests except one very old native had been sent south. Sun-burned Father Lopez had packed up his bicycle and departed on the *General Brewster*, taking his one clean cassock and his intestinal worms with him. Father Felice, who always looked so jaundiced in spite of my vitamin pills, antibiotics and phenobarbital, left on an embassy plane in the last week of April.

I hated to see them go; they had become good friends. They were made with hearts of that proverbial precious metal and they had been wonderful to our small tribe of Americans. It was Father Felice who offered early Mass every morning in the Mission Church, usually full of barefoot chanting natives. He tells me he could usually determine when I arrived because of the way my boots squeaked as I made my way to the very front row.

The old native priest who was left in charge would say Mass until Haiphong fell, and intended to try to continue even after the Viet Minh took over. He knew that he might be made to suffer but he said that he was old and that a martyr's crown might ensure his entry into Heaven. Haiphong's last weeks found his Masses attended by a dwindling handful of the devout.

The pride of the Mission was their statue of Our Lady of Fatima. Several decades before, when Haiphong Catholics were in Rome on a pilgrimage, His Holiness the Pope had given it

to them with his blessing. It stood on an altar of its own just to the left of the main altar. It was an object of popular reverence, with flowers and burning candles always around it. Day and night peasants prayed before it.

There were many discussions about the advisability of removing the statue of Our Lady of Fatima. Should it be taken south when Father Lopez and Father Felice left Haiphong? Should it be kept until the very last possible day? Or should it be left to give comfort to the few who might, for one reason or another, remain behind?

In the end, the decision about the statue was made by an American, Norman Poulin. Roger Ackley was called back to Germany toward the very end and our embassy flew Norman up to succeed him. Norman spoke impeccable French. His job was to help wind up the final details of the evacuation. He was charged especially with getting out the American equipment that remained north, the tents, the few vehicles, some American Aid rice, and other products which USOM was determined not to leave behind for the use of the Viet Minh.

The last American embassy plane flew in on the eleventh of May, the main airport had gone to the enemy, so it landed on an abandoned military airstrip. The pilot of the plane had a message from Father Felice. He asked: "Is the statue of Fatima all right or have the Viet Minh defiled it?"

Norman met the plane and received this message. I was there hoping there would be a message for me to get on this plane and get the hell out of Indo-China. (There wasn't.) We held a short conference and made a quick decision. We sped to the Mission in the jeep, which was on its last legs. We buttonholed the poor old priest and tried to bamboozle him. "We want the statue. We want to send it south on the embassy plane."

The old priest shook his head. "Oh no, it must stay."

We failed to convince him and at last we pretended to agree. "Very well, perhaps it must stay."

Then, as he tottered back to his cubicle, we went into the church on the double. We climbed up on the little altar and literally kidnapped the statue. We wrapped it in an American Aid blanket which was on the jeep's floor and whisked it out to the airport. At this writing it is standing in a church built especially for the refugees, just outside Saigon. And that's how Our Blessed Lady of Fatima, with a boost from American Aid, made the Passage to Freedom.

When people ask when the heart of Haiphong stopped beating, the date I give them is the fourth of May. It was on the fourth of May that, according to the treaty, an advance echelon, the Viet Minh Committee of Experts, was allowed to enter the city. They were to go to the City Hall, the Governor's office, the public utilities plants and so on and learn how to take them over from the Vietnamese, the last of whom would leave on the sixteenth of May on the last boat out. Thus there would be no sudden cessation of water or electricity and, in theory at least, the turnover of the city would be smooth.

The Committee arrived, 480 strong, in brand-new, Russian-made Molotova trucks. They were impeccably dressed in high-collared grey uniforms, pith helmets and canvas shoes, and most of them spoke French very well.

They stopped me about four times daily, when I was trying to cross a street, or drive out to the camp or go down to the docks, but they were always polite and respectful. They said I was the only American they had ever met who could speak their language. Why had I learned it? Did I intend to stay on and try to help the "true people of Viet Nam" when the Democratic Republic established its offices? I replied that my job was just about over and that I expected to be leaving soon.

They sent a delegation out to the camp and gave me a bit of dialectical materialism.

"When you treat people in America," the leader asked, "do you make any distinction between Democrats and Republicans?"

"Certainly not!"

"Very well," he said. "There must be no distinction here between capitalistic dupes and the loyal people of Viet Nam."

Then the cheeky bastard ordered his men to divide up my pharmaceuticals and surgical supplies—half for me and half for the Democratic Republic of Viet Nam. And there wasn't a thing I could do about it.

I tried to be polite with the newcomers but perhaps I merely gave them the impression that I was afraid of them. And I was. I was constantly afraid that they would lock me up somewhere and hold me for investigation. Investigations can stretch out for years in Communist states, as many an American knows to his cost. And we were only four Americans in all of north Viet Nam.

The arrival of the Committee of Experts was not bad in itself. But trouble arose because, when they arrived, they brought several thousand armed bodyguards with them.

The bodyguards raised hell in the village. When they arrived, riots, fires, "spontaneous" anti-foreign demonstrations, and beatings of men and women who had been friendly to us became common. The newcomers cynically blamed all these things on the French.

There was a riot in front of the City Jail and the Committee of Experts demanded that all prisoners be released immediately. The French replied that they would not be released immediately. The French replied that they would be released on the sixteenth of May, according to the agreement, and not until then. This demonstration ended up in tear gas and firing on the crowd.

I climbed up in the steeple of the Mission one afternoon and looked all around the city. You could see little puffs and clouds of smoke in seven or eight parts of town, where demonstrations were being broken up with tear gas. The French used it frequently as the least violent method of dispersing mobs.

The forces of General Cogny, keeping cool heads, did a good job at keeping some semblance of order during these last weeks. As for me, I spent most of my time dodging riots, driving blocks out of my way to get to my objectives, so that I would not be stopped and questioned. A good deal of the time I spent just being afraid.

By the 10th of May we had taken down the tents of our camps and moved the remaining refugees into empty buildings in the city. It was on the twelfth of May that I saw my last grisly atrocity.

By this time the Viet Minh legally had all but a very small area on one side of Haiphong, but illegally they had just about all of it. Their strength was visible everywhere. They patrolled the main streets and waterways, and there were sentries at every intersection. They captured a young Vietnamese boy, a wild type of lad, who still wanted to escape from Viet Minh territory and dared to try.

He attempted to duck through back streets across the line of demarcation, known as the DMZ or Demilitarized Zone. Here he was apprehended by the Viets. They formed a circle around him and beat on his feet with the butts of their rifles. They continued this until the victim collapsed, then added more blows for good measure, all on the feet and ankles. This was what was to happen to runaways in the future!

The Viets stopped beating the boy only after he was unconscious. When he regained his senses, he found that he had been left alone and that the road was abandoned. He dragged his shattered, mangled feet into a nearby alley. There a rickshaw driver found him and somehow got him across to us on the free side.

I had no X-ray equipment but it was obvious that the damage was beyond repair. The feet and ankles felt like moist bags of marbles and were already gangrenous. I had only a few instruments left and a little procaine and penicillin. I did the best I could by disarticulating the ankles where they connect with the lower leg. Someone else would have to do a more thorough amputation job later. We managed to get the boy into a crash boat which took him out to a French LSM, waiting to sail for the south. He was crippled for life, but at least he was free.

Our last loading day was the twelfth of May, a dry hot morning. The shuffling of thousands of bare feet made acrid dust rise off the ground at the loading area. One could taste the dust. It made the tongue feel thick and the teeth gritty. There was little sound except for the chugging of the LST motors. We were still spraying the refugees with DDT.

A May morning in America means spring, softness, sweet odors, perhaps a cool misty rain. But here the heat of the Indo-China sun was intense, the glare of the river was blinding and the smell of the refugees was overpowering.

This was the last day of the last loading. Some 3,600 refugees would take the trip, first to the bay and then on to Saigon, huddled together with their cloth bags, their balance poles with household possessions at each end, their babies on mothers' hips. They were as desolate a slice of the human race as any that had preceded them. They walked slowly in line to be dusted with DDT, to accept a loaf of bread, or perhaps a few diapers and small bags of clothing. But to me they were not a mere mass of wretchedness. I had come to know their valiant hearts and stout spirit. Somehow, over the bitter months, without knowing how it happened, I had identified myself with their dream of life in freedom and their tragic destiny. They had become my suffering brothers.

Of course these last refugees were not really the last. There were still a couple of million behind the Bamboo Curtain who never had a chance. But we had done the best we could. And I hope the men who made the deal at that lovely Geneva lakeside are happy with the results.

I had been taught to believe in and do believe in God's love, His goodness, His mercy. And I knew that in some small degree at least these qualities can be shared by man. But I had seen very little of them in the last year.

"I must remember the things I have seen," I said to myself. "I must keep them fresh in memory, see them again in my mind's eye, live through them again and again in my thoughts. And most of all I must make good use of them in tomorrow's life."

I watched the last LCT pull away from the dock and, as I came to the full realization that it was all over, a quiet grief engulfed me. The boat headed downriver and an enormous sun was sinking in a burst of splendor.

I
SELF-SACRIFICE AND SELF-FULFILLMENT

Those who are pessimistic about human nature would have us believe that man is fundamentally a self-seeking animal always ready to step upon others in his egocentric drive toward self-fulfillment. Yet as the life of Tom Dooley admirably illustrates, the path to self-fulfillment may lie in quite an opposite direction. Dooley could have been a first-rate surgeon, able to afford a life of comparative ease and comfort; instead he followed a "different drummer," sacrificing this prospect in favor of aiding the suffering masses of Southeast Asia, which he did with great skill and ingenuity. That he became a nationally famous hero while still in his early thirties serves as proof that Americans everywhere have great admiration and respect for those who live lives of service and self-sacrifice.

II
IMPLICATIONS
Discuss each of the following.

1. Some persons will argue that even those who devote their lives to helping others are selfishly motivated. Discuss this notion, either pro or con, in reference to the life of Tom Dooley and his friends.

2. Aside from Dr. Dooley and his friends, what other evidence is offered in this selection showing that Americans are self-sacrificing?

3. Discuss the role faith played in Dr. Dooley's life.

4. What implicit comments does this selection make on such traditional American values as equality, independence, and optimism?

5. Discuss the full implications of Dr. Dooley's statement, "They had become my suffering brothers."

III
TECHNIQUES
Selection of Significant Detail and Tone

Describe and discuss the tone in which Dooley treats each of the following characters or details. Also discuss *why* the author chose to include each of them. How does his tone help you to understand his purpose for including the detail?

1. Major John McGowan
2. The shoeshine kids
3. The Dodge truck
4. The kidnapping of the statue
5. The young Vietnamese boy who was beaten

FINAL REFLECTIONS

Independent Spirit

It is nearly impossible to make generalizations about the American independent spirit. Our country was founded and built by diverse individuals, and thus it is not surprising that there is a broad diversity in the way this spirit manifests itself in America.

On the other hand, it is clear that there are certain persistent types of independent spirits which Americans admire. We admire the "rugged individualist," the self-made-man type. We admire "natural men" like the early Indian, our frontiersmen, and our cowboys. We admire self-sacrificing, self-effacing men like Johnny Appleseed, Tom Dooley, and the fictional Atticus Finch. And we admire the all-around man like Ben Franklin. As one studies these heroic types, he will see that each embodies a portion of the American dream that each man is free under law to develop himself in his own way to the limits of ambition and talent.

IMPLICATIONS

Discuss the following propositions in terms of the selections in this unit and of other reading you may have done.

1. The self-made man reflects the basic American belief in optimism and reinforces the idea that America is a land of opportunity.

2. The natural man shows that Americans value highly traits like independence and freedom.

3. Those Americans who sacrifice themselves for the sake of others show that Americans believe in cooperation, but they do not reflect our belief in individuality.

4. The all-around man is especially important in a free society because he stands as a symbol of diversity and of the fact that in a democracy man is free to develop himself to his fullest capacity.

5. American writers have helped to spread the fame of our heroes, but they have very little else to contribute to the hero-making process.

6. A study of American heroes will show that there is a split or division in American life between the mental and the physical.

TECHNIQUES

Selection of Significant Detail

As you have seen, the writer's purpose is an important consideration in weighing the significance of any given detail. That is, the reader should always ask himself why the writer chose to include the detail and how it contributes to the meaning he is trying to communicate. Pick three or four of the selections in this unit and state in a sentence or two what you think the writer's main intention was. Then discuss how several of the details he uses contribute to his overall intention.

Tone

Below you will find a list of words that may be used to describe a writer's tone. Select any five of these words and be prepared to cite a passage from one of the selections of this unit that illustrates this tone.

1. pompous	**7.** solemn
2. sarcastic	**8.** reverential
3. serious	**9.** condescending
4. playful	**10.** formal
5. ironic	**11.** intimate
6. matter-of-fact	**12.** bitter

BIOGRAPHICAL NOTES

James Stevens

James Stevens (1892–   ), American folklorist, was born in Iowa and spent his boyhood years in Iowa and Idaho. At 15 he left home and worked throughout the West, chiefly in jobs handling horses and mules. His first published writing was an article for H. L. Mencken, then editor of the old *American Mercury*. Later Stevens wrote a story on Paul Bunyan which was expanded into a series of stories and published as a book, *Paul Bunyan*, a milestone in the preservation of American folk figures. He has also written another volume on Bunyan, a novel, and several juvenile books.

Vachel Lindsay

Vachel Lindsay (1879–1931) was born in Springfield, Illinois. Interested in drawing, he studied at the Chicago Art Institute and the New York Art School. He could not sell his drawings, however, and finally began a walking tour of America, supporting himself by lecturing and reciting his poems. This was the first of many such tours, a life that was to pall and that later brought many frustrations to the poet. Weighted down by family responsibilities, debts, and worries, he was unable to improve upon his original body of work; at last he seemed to disintegrate, both as a poet and as a person. His most famous poems include "The Congo," "General William Booth Enters into Heaven," and "Abraham Lincoln Walks at Midnight."

Ralph Waldo Emerson

Lecturer, essayist, and poet, Ralph Waldo Emerson (1803–1882) was perhaps the most influential thinker in America during the nineteenth century. Born in Boston and educated at Harvard, he studied for the ministry but resigned his first pastorate because of doctrinal differences. After visiting Europe and forming lifelong friendships with Wordsworth and Carlyle, he settled in Concord, and soon drew about him a remarkable circle of friends, including A. B. Alcott, Margaret Fuller, and Thoreau. His first book, *Nature* (1836), contained the heart of his transcendental philosophy, which he soon applied to many areas of American life in lectures and essays such as "The American Scholar" and "Self-Reliance." His *Essays* (2 vol., 1841, 1844) won him an international reputation.

Donald Culross Peattie

Donald Culross Peattie (1898–   ) became interested in botanical studies while studying English literature at the University of Chicago. After a brief stint at a publishing house, Peattie entered Harvard to gain the scientific background he would need as a nature writer. In 1922, when he was graduated, he won the Witter Bynner Prize in poetry and published his first scientific papers. For many years he wrote a nature column for the Washington *Evening Star* and then the Chicago *Daily News*. Successful in combining two careers, Peattie has published a number of books, *Singing in the Wilderness, The Road of a Naturalist, Journey into America,* and two volumes about the natural history of trees in North America.

Paul Horgan

Born in Buffalo, New York, Paul Horgan (1903–   ) moved to New Mexico with his family in 1914 because of his father's health. Horgan's life was thereafter to alternate between the East, where he studied singing, and the West, where he served in various capacities at the New Mexico Military Institute. His first writing appeared in *Poetry,* and a short story was included in the 1931 O. Henry Memorial volume. His first published novel won the Harper Prize in 1933. Since then he has written many novels, plays, and short stories. In 1954 he published a two-volume history of the Rio Grande, *Great River,* which won both a Pulitzer Prize and the Bancroft Prize for History. His recent novel, *Things as They Are* (1964), has been acclaimed a modern classic.

Gamaliel Bradford, Jr.

Gamaliel Bradford, Jr. (1863–1932), was a descendent of William Bradford, Governor of the Plymouth Colony. His chief vehicle was biography. He called his work *psychography,* a term he gave to his condensed psychological character sketches. Although an invalid most of his life, he wrote a great deal, seeking always a place in the literary sun. His work has probably greatest significance as an early instance of what was to become psychoanalytical criticism.

John Greenleaf Whittier

Although he had almost no formal schooling, John Greenleaf Whittier (1807–1892) became a famous newspaper editor and one of the best-known and most loved of all American poets. He was also a vigorous champion of the abolitionist movement in the days before the Civil War. His best-known volume of poetry, *Snowbound,* appeared in 1866. Many of his poems deal with simple people and with the details of everyday life.

Marshall W. Fishwick

Marshall W. Fishwick (1923–   ) was born in Roanoke, Virginia, and earned his B.A. degree at the University of Virginia in Charlottesville. He later taught at Washington and Lee University in Lexington, Virginia. Dr. Fishwick has written several books on Virginia and the South, including a book on Robert E. Lee.

Elinor Richey

Elinor Richey was born in Mississippi but has been living recently in Chicago. She has a broad range of interests in current problems and has written on them for such magazines as the *Saturday Review,* the *Reporter,* and *Harpers.*

Harper Lee

The Pulitzer Prize in 1961 was awarded to Harper Lee (1926–   ) for *To Kill a Mockingbird,* a novel about two children who grow up in the South, learning the mores of the culture and the convictions of their lawyer father. An Alabaman, Miss Lee seems to be the prototype of Scout Finch, the young narrator of her best-selling novel, which has been made into a motion picture and translated into many languages.

Thomas A. Dooley

Tom Dooley (1927–1961) was a St. Louis-born doctor who became a writer because he had a story that he felt had to be told, the story of how he and a small group of fellow Americans devoted their lives to the less fortunate people of Southeast Asia. Dr. Dooley received his medical degree in 1953, and put his knowledge to work in "Operation Cockroach" in Viet Nam, while serving in the Navy. Later it became impossible for him to remain in the Navy and at the same time help the people of Southeast Asia; he therefore resigned from the Navy and formed a private group, Medico, which gave medical aid to the people of Laos and to other needy peoples in underdeveloped parts of the world.

HENRY DAVID THOREAU

1817-1862

Thoreau moved to Walden to simplify his life. "I wished to live deliberately," he wrote, "to front only the essential facts of life and see if I could not learn what it had to teach, and not, when I came to die, discover that I had not lived." But there were other reasons. He thought of himself as a philosopher and "to be a philosopher," he said, "is not merely to have subtle thoughts, nor even to found a school, but so to love wisdom as to live according to its dictates. . . . It is to solve some of the problems of life, not only theoretically but practically."

Few writers in America have felt a sense of place as strongly as Henry David Thoreau. He was born in Concord, Massachusetts, lived most of his life in and around the village, died, and was buried there. Yet he was not a hermit, in spite of his resolve at the age of twenty-eight to spend more than two years alone at Walden Pond, a mile and a half south of Concord. Thoreau's neighbors knew him as a strong-minded, restless individual, a man of dry wit, frank opinions, and unquestioned integrity. Clearly he was in love with life, but less with the bustle of Concord village than with the natural world of the fields and nearby ponds. He could do without the post office and the church more easily than he could give up his walks in the woods. "If a man does not keep pace with his companions," he once wrote, "perhaps it is because he hears a different drummer. Let him step to the music which he hears, however measured or far away. It is not important that he should mature as soon as an apple tree or an oak."

The "different drummer" Thoreau stepped to set him apart from Concord even before he returned from four years at Harvard College. He questioned authority when it was unreasonable or untested; he resented traditions when they were hollow gestures to the past; above all he fought his neighbors' "desperate haste to succeed and in such desperate enterprises." On graduation he applied for a teaching position in Concord but kept it only a few weeks. When a member of the school committee insisted Thoreau must not "spare the rod" on unruly pupils, he chose six of his students at random, whipped them soundly, and then resigned. Some months later he and his brother John opened a private school in Concord which prospered for about three years in spite of its progressive theories of education. The rod was abandoned; students were encouraged to make their own observations and form their own opinions, not merely parrot what they read in books; classes were held outdoors whenever possible so that the natural world could mix with the academic. Had it not been for John Thoreau's failing health, Henry might have devoted much of his life to teaching, since it provided him with the leisure to transact what he called "private business"—the writing of poetry, keeping his journals, reading, nature study, conversation.

After his brother's premature death in 1842, he resolved that making a living should never interfere with life itself, and so he spent the next twenty years earning only the minimum he needed, never letting work become an end in itself. He helped his father in the family's pencil factory; he lived with Ralph Waldo Emerson, the famous essayist, lecturer, and poet, and his wife as caretaker of their property; he worked in Concord as a gardener, surveyor, magazine editor, and curator of the lyceum; he lectured, with only fair success, from Bangor, Maine, to Philadelphia; he tutored the children of Emerson's brother William on Staten Island until homesickness drove him back to Concord. All the while, of course, he was confiding his inward life in his journals. What passed for the world's business— "desperate enterprises," that is—little interested him.

If Thoreau had written nothing else but his journals—he began them in 1837, just a few months after graduation from Harvard, and made the last entry a few months before his death—fame might have been even slower in coming than it was. For years he had mined the journals for lecture material and for the few essays he published in *The Dial*, at Emerson's suggestion. But it was not until 1845 that he made a decision which altered his life. Making his living in town was consuming more of his time than he had bargained for. "Actually," he was to write later, "the laboring man has not leisure for a true integrity day by day; he cannot afford to sustain the manliest relations to man; his labor would be depreciated in the market. He has no time to be anything but a machine." To escape the market and the machine, Thoreau conceived of building a cabin in comparative solitude and spending uninterrupted nights and days sorting out his philosophies. He considered Flint's Pond in nearby Lincoln, but he could not convince the owner of the land that his idea was sensible. Late in 1844, Emerson purchased some wood lots on the north shore of Walden Pond, and five months later Thoreau was borrowing an ax to build his own cabin there. For "rent," he would clear the fields for gardening and leave the cabin on the edge of the pine grove after he had finished his "experiment in living." On Independence Day, 1845, he moved in. He stayed slightly more than two years and two months.

Walden; or Life in the Woods is the record of that sojourn, and much more. The writing of this book and the reasons for writing it, however, are often misunderstood. Thoreau moved to Walden to simplify his life. "I wished to live deliberately," he wrote, "to front only the essential facts of life, and see if I could not learn what it had to teach, and not, when I came to die, discover that I had not lived." But there were other reasons. He thought of himself as a philosopher and "to be a philosopher," he said, "is not merely to have subtle thoughts, nor even to found a school, but so to

WALDEN;

OR,

LIFE IN THE WOODS.

By HENRY D. THOREAU,

AUTHOR OF "A WEEK ON THE CONCORD AND MERRIMACK RIVERS."

I do not propose to write an ode to dejection, but to brag as lustily as chanticleer in the morning, standing on his roost, if only to wake my neighbors up. — Page 92.

BOSTON:

TICKNOR AND FIELDS.

M DCCC LIV.

The original title page of Walden.

love wisdom as to live according to its dictates. . . . It is to solve some of the problems of life, not only theoretically but practically." He also wished to write a book. Not *Walden;* that was his second book. He and his brother John had made a memorable excursion in 1839 on the Concord and Merrimack Rivers, and he had delayed too long in publishing an account of the trip from the notes he had made in his journals. Possibly he had also felt the enmity of his fellow townspeople long enough. After he had refused to pay his church taxes in 1838,

he was looked upon as an extremist. Then, in 1844, when he and Edward Hoar let a cooking fire on the banks of Fairhaven Bay get out of hand and burn a hundred acres of Concord woodland, his reputation was thoroughly blackened.

His return to civilization in 1847 was dictated by equally practical considerations. Now that he had made his experiment, he had "several more lives to live, and could not spare any more time for that one." Emerson, moreover, was leaving in September for a lecture tour in England and had persuaded Thoreau once again to live in his Concord home and take care of his family. And his book was almost finished. He was eager to see it in print. Publishers in New York and Boston, alas, were not eager to accept it. It was 1849 before *A Week on the Concord and Merrimack Rivers* appeared, and then only at Thoreau's own expense. He had agreed to pay for a thousand copies. It was soon evident that the book was a total failure. The account of the voyage was vivid enough, but he bored some readers and offended others with his long digressions on history, ancient authors, philosophy, and especially religion. By 1853, the Boston publishers had sold only 219 copies. When they shipped the rest to Thoreau in October of that year he wrote in his journal: "They are something more substantial than fame, as my back knows, which has borne them up two flights of stairs to a place similar to that to which they trace their origin. . . . I have now a library of nearly nine hundred volumes, over seven hundred of which I wrote myself." Thoreau never lost his sense of humor, particularly about the eccentricities of his fellowmen or of life.

The publication of *Walden* is another story. Emerson persuaded Ticknor and Fields of Boston to print it. Before its appearance in August, 1854, excerpts appearing in the New York *Tribune* helped to spread the author's name. Even though the reviewers were not wholly satisfied, Thoreau was, with the general reception of the book and its sales. He knew he had written a masterpiece, and if it took several decades before America realized it he was prepared for that. Surprisingly he never attempted a sequel to the book, nor did he ever cull his journals for a third volume of any kind. The last eight years of his life were concentrated on brief travels—New Jersey, the Maine woods, Brooklyn (to meet Walt Whitman), Minnesota (to regain his health)—and on social issues on which he felt compelled to speak.

As early as 1849 he had published a remarkable essay called "On the Duty of Civil Disobedience" (it became Gandhi's [1869–1948] textbook during his passive resistance campaign in India), and he frequently lectured and debated on the Abolition movement, though he never formally joined any organizations. He forever remained the staunch individualist, standing apart from, but not above, his fellowmen, the better to observe them and their problems. When in 1859 he rose to defend another strong-minded man, Captain John Brown, a few days after the Harper's Ferry attack, he was advised by his Concord neighbors that such a defense was ill-timed. Thoreau assured them that he was not asking for advice but calling a meeting. When the selectmen refused to toll the bell for that meeting, he pulled the rope himself. Concord should have known by that time that Henry Thoreau made most of his decisions with little thought to their popularity and much to their necessity and their rightness.

Walden is based on similar assumptions. "I do not propose to write an ode to dejection," he writes on its title page, "but to brag as lustily as Chanticleer in the morning, standing on his roost, if only to wake my neighbors up." Whether they wished to be waked or not, we might add. He is not writing for the "strong and valiant natures, who will mind their own affairs whether in heaven or hell," nor is he addressing "those who are well employed, in whatever circumstances, and [who] know whether they are well employed or not," but

"the mass of men who are discontented and idly complaining of the hardness of their lot or of the times"—to these men Thoreau offers advice, inspiration, severe criticism, encouragement, even practical remedies. Modern critics see something of *Robinson Crusoe* in Thoreau's experiment in solitary life, something also of Jonathan Swift's *Gulliver's Travels* in his severe criticism of so-called civilization. Thoreau's contemporaries on reading *Walden* looked back to Emerson's essays, particularly "Self-Reliance," and to the sermons of Colonial New England preachers. But whatever comparisons are made, certain distinguishing characteristics set this book apart and give it a flavor of its own.

Thoreau first of all begins his opening sentence with the first-person pronoun and continues in that relaxed informal tone. We never lose sight of a humble citizen of Concord seeking to learn about life in observing nature and sharing his discoveries. Second, he warns us that he "would not have any one adopt [*his*] mode of living on any account." He is not advocating our leaving home to live on the edge of a pond in a timbered cabin. "I would have each one be very careful to find out and pursue *his own way*," he tells us more than once, so long as one knows where he is going and why. Finally, Thoreau's sense of humor (often missed by the hurried reader), his keen eye for the illustrative anecdote, his respect for the forces of nature, his alertness to the way language carefully shaped can reflect those forces, and above all his quality of "being," as Emerson called it, make *Walden* a unique experience. This book is not merely about nature, it *is* nature, captured. "I have travelled a good deal in Concord," he tells us with tongue in cheek early in the first chapter. We, too, can "travel" widely in Thoreau's world. Concord and Walden Pond have been reduced, in his prose, to a capsule of the human condition. He is writing not merely about life in 1840 but about us.

WALDEN

Thoreau divided his book
into eighteen chapters, the longest by far
being the first, called "Economy."
It is quite significant that he chose to begin
Walden with "Economy" and to devote more
than a quarter of the book to the chapter.
See if you can discover from the following
six excerpts some of the reasons
why economy was such a key concept
for Thoreau.

I. Economy

When I wrote the following pages, or rather the bulk of them, I lived alone, in the woods, a mile from any neighbor, in a house which I had built myself, on the shore of Walden Pond, in Concord, Massachusetts, and earned my living by the labor of my hands only. I lived there two years and two months. At present I am a sojourner in civilized life again.

I should not obtrude my affairs so much on the notice of my readers if very particular inquiries had not been made by my townsmen concerning my mode of life, which some would call impertinent, though they do not appear to me at all impertinent, but, considering the circumstances, very natural and pertinent. Some have asked what I got to eat; if I did not feel lonesome; if I was not afraid; and the like. Others have been curious to learn what portion of my income I devoted to charitable purposes; and some, who have large families, how many poor children I maintained. I will therefore ask those of my readers who feel no particular interest in me to pardon me if I undertake to answer some of these questions in this book. In most books, the *I*, or first person, is omitted; in this it will be retained; that, in respect to egotism, is the main difference. We commonly do not remember that it is, after all, always the first person that is speaking. I should not talk so much about myself if there were anybody else whom I knew as well. Unfortunately, I am confined to this theme by the narrowness of my experience. Moreover, I, on my side, require of every writer, first or last, a simple and sincere account of his own life, and not merely what he has heard of other men's lives; some such account as he would send to his kindred from a distant land; for if he has lived sincerely, it must have been in a distant land to me. Perhaps these pages are more particularly addressed to poor students. As for the rest of my readers, they will accept such portions as apply to them. I trust that none will stretch the seams in putting on the coat, for it may do good service to him whom it fits. . . .

I see young men, my townsmen, whose misfortune it is to have inherited farms, houses, barns, cattle, and farming tools; for these are more easily acquired than got rid of. Better if they had been born in the open pasture and suckled by a wolf, that they might have seen with clearer eyes what field they were called to labor in. Who made them serfs of the soil? Why should they eat their sixty acres, when man is condemned to eat only his peck of dirt? Why should they begin digging their graves as soon as they are born? They have got to live a man's life, pushing all these things before them, and get on as well as they can. How many a poor immortal soul have I met well nigh crushed and smothered under its load, creeping down the road of life, pushing before it a barn seventy-five feet by forty, its Augean stables[1] never cleansed, and one hundred acres of land, tillage, mowing, pasture, and wood-lot! The portionless, who struggle with no such unnecessary inherited encumbrances, find it labor enough to subdue and cultivate a few cubic feet of flesh.

But men labor under a mistake. The better part of the man is soon ploughed into the soil for compost. By a seeming fate, commonly called necessity, they are employed, as it says in an old book, laying up treasures which moth and rust will corrupt and thieves break through and steal. It is a fool's life, as they will find when they get to the end of it, if not before. . . .

When I consider my neighbors, the farmers of Concord, who are at least as well off as the other classes, I find that for the most part they have been toiling twenty, thirty, or forty years, that they may become the real owners of their farms, which commonly they have inherited with encumbrances, or else bought with hired money,—and we may regard one third of that toil as the cost of their houses,—but commonly they have not paid for them yet. It is true, the encumbrances sometimes outweigh the value of the farm, so that the farm itself becomes one great encumbrance, and still a man is found to inherit it, being well acquainted with it, as he says. On applying to the assessors, I am surprised to learn that they cannot at once name a dozen in the town who own their farms free and clear. If you would know the history of these homesteads, inquire at the bank where they are mortgaged. The man who has actually paid for his farm with labor on it is so rare that every neighbor can point to him. I doubt if there are three such men in Concord. What has been said of the merchants, that a very large majority, even ninety-seven in a hundred, are sure to fail, is equally true of the farmers. With regard to the merchants, however, one of them says pertinently that a great part of their failures are not genuine pecuniary failures, but merely failures to fulfil their engagements, because it is inconvenient; that is, it is the moral character that breaks down. But this puts an infinitely worse face on the matter, and

suggests, beside, that probably not even the other three succeed in saving their souls, but are perchance bankrupt in a worse sense than they who fail honestly. Bankruptcy and repudiation are the springboards from which much of our civilization vaults and turns its somersets, but the savage stands on the unelastic plank of famine. . . .

Near the end of March, 1845, I borrowed an axe and went down to the woods by Walden Pond, nearest to where I intended to build my house, and began to cut down some tall arrowy white pines, still in their youth, for timber. It is difficult to begin without borrowing, but perhaps it is the most generous course thus to permit your fellow-men to have an interest in your enterprise. The owner of the axe, as he released his hold on it, said that it was the apple of his eye; but I returned it sharper than I received it. It was a pleasant hillside where I worked, covered with pine woods, through which I looked out on the pond, and a small open field in the woods where pines and hickories were springing up. The ice in the pond was not yet dissolved, though there were some open spaces, and it was all dark colored and saturated with water. There were some slight flurries of snow during the days that I worked there; but for the most part when I came out on to the railroad, on my way home, its yellow sand heap stretched away gleaming in the hazy atmosphere, and the rails shone in the spring sun, and I heard the lark and pewee and other birds already come to commence another year with us. They were pleasant spring days, in which the winter of man's discontent was thawing as well as the earth, and the life that had lain torpid began to stretch itself. One day, when my axe had come off and I had cut a green hickory for a wedge, driving it with a stone, and had placed the whole to soak in a pond hole in order to swell the wood, I saw a striped snake run

---

1. **Augean**\ŏ ˈjē•ən\ **stables,** stables in which 3,000 oxen were kept, left uncleaned for 30 years; Hercules cleaned the stables in one day.

into the water, and he lay on the bottom, apparently without inconvenience, as long as I stayed there, or more than a quarter of an hour; perhaps because he had not yet fairly come out of the torpid state. It appeared to me that for a like reason men remain in their present low and primitive condition; but if they should feel the influence of the spring of springs arousing them, they would of necessity rise to a higher and more ethereal life. I had previously seen the snakes in frosty mornings in my path with portions of their bodies still numb and inflexible, waiting for the sun to thaw them. On the 1st of April it rained and melted the ice, and in the early part of the day, which was very foggy, I heard a stray goose groping about over the pond and cackling as if lost, or like the spirit of the fog.

So I went on for some days cutting and hewing timber, and also studs and rafters, all with my narrow axe, not having many communicable or scholar-like thoughts, singing to myself,—

> Men say they know many things;
> But lo! they have taken wings,—
> The arts and sciences,
> And a thousand appliances;
> The wind that blows
> Is all that anybody knows.

I hewed the main timbers six inches square, most of the studs on two sides only, and the rafters and floor timbers on one side, leaving the rest of the bark on, so that they were just as straight and much stronger than sawed ones. Each stick was carefully mortised or tenoned by its stump, for I had borrowed other tools by this time. My days in the woods were not very long ones; yet I usually carried my dinner of bread and butter, and read the newspaper in which it was wrapped, at noon, sitting amid the green pine boughs which I had cut off, and to my bread was imparted some of their fragrance, for my hands were covered with a thick coat of pitch. Before I had done I was more the friend than the foe of the pine tree, though I had cut down some of them, having become better ac-

quainted with it. Sometimes a rambler in the wood was attracted by the sound of my axe, and we chatted pleasantly over the chips which I had made.

By the middle of April, for I made no haste in my work, but rather made the most of it, my house was framed and ready for the raising. I had already bought the shanty of James Collins, an Irishman who worked on the Fitchburg Railroad, for boards. James Collins' shanty was considered an uncommonly fine one. When I called to see it he was not at home. I walked about the outside, at first unobserved from within, the window was so deep and high. It was of small dimensions, with a peaked cottage roof, and not much else to be seen, the dirt being raised five feet all around as if it were a compost heap. The roof was the soundest part, though a good deal warped and made brittle by the sun. Door-sill there was none, but a perennial passage for the hens under the door board. Mrs. C. came to the door and asked me to view it from the inside. The hens were driven in by my approach. It was dark, and had a dirt floor for the most part, dank, clammy, and aguish, only here a board and there a board which would not bear removal. She lighted a lamp to show me the inside of the roof and the walls, and also that the board floor extended under the bed, warning me not to step into the cellar, a sort of dust hole two feet deep. In her own words, they were "good boards overhead, good boards all around, and a good window,"—of two whole squares originally, only the cat had passed out that way lately. There was a stove, a bed, and a place to sit, an infant in the house where it was born, a silk parasol, gilt-framed looking-glass, and a patent new coffee-mill nailed to an oak sapling, all told. The bargain was soon concluded, for James had in the meanwhile returned. I to pay four dollars and twenty-five cents to-night, he to vacate at five to-morrow morning, selling to nobody else meanwhile: I to take possession at six. It were well, he said, to be there early, and anticipate certain indistinct but wholly unjust claims on the score of ground rent and fuel. This he assured me was the only encumbrance. At six I passed him and his family on the road. One large bundle held their all,—bed, coffee-mill, looking-glass, hens,—all but the cat; she took to the woods and became a wild cat, and, as I learned afterward, trod in a trap set for woodchucks, and so became a dead cat at last.

I took down this dwelling the same morning, drawing the nails, and removed it to the pond side by small car-loads, spreading the boards on the grass there to bleach and warp back again in the sun. One early thrush gave me a note or two as I drove along the woodland path. I was informed treacherously by a young Patrick that neighbor Seeley, an Irishman, in the intervals of the carting, transferred the still tolerable, straight, and drivable nails, staples, and spikes to his pocket, and then stood when I came back to pass the time of day, and look freshly up, unconcerned, with spring thoughts, at the devastation; there being a dearth of work, as he said. He was there to represent spectatordom, and help make this seemingly insignificant event one with the removal of the gods of Troy.[2]

I dug my cellar in the side of a hill sloping to the south, where a woodchuck had formerly dug his burrow, down through sumach[3] and blackberry roots, and the lowest stain of vegetation, six feet square by seven deep, to a fine sand where potatoes would not freeze in any winter. The sides were left shelving, and not stoned; but the sun having never shone on them, the sand still keeps its place. It was but two hours' work. I took particular pleasure in this breaking of ground, for in almost all latitudes men dig into the earth for an equable temperature. Under the most splendid house in the city is still to be found the cellar where they store their roots as of old, and long after the superstructure has disappeared posterity remark its dent in the earth. The house is still but a sort of porch at the entrance of a burrow.

At length, in the beginning of May, with the help of some of my acquaintances, rather to improve so good an occasion for neighborliness than from any necessity, I set up the frame of my house. No man was ever more honored in the character of his raisers than I. They are destined, I trust, to assist at the raising of loftier structures one day. I began to occupy my house on the 4th of July, as soon as it was boarded and roofed, for the boards were carefully feather-edged and lapped, so that it was perfectly impervious to rain, but before boarding I laid the foundation of a chimney at one end, bringing two cartloads of stones up the hill from the pond in my arms. I built the chimney after my hoeing in the fall, before a fire became necessary for warmth, doing my cooking in the mean while out of doors on the ground, early in the morning: which mode I still think is in some respects more convenient and agreeable than the usual one. When it stormed before my bread was baked, I fixed a few boards over the fire, and sat under them to watch my loaf, and passed some pleasant hours in that way. In those days, when my hands were much employed, I read but little, but the least scraps of paper which lay on the ground, my holder, or tablecloth, afforded me as much entertainment, in fact answered the same purpose as the Iliad.[4] . . .

Before winter I built a chimney, and shingled the sides of my house, which were already impervious to rain, with imperfect and sappy shingles made of the first slice of the log, whose edges I was obliged to straighten with a plane.

I have thus a tight shingled and plastered house, ten feet wide by fifteen long, and eight-feet posts, with a garret and a closet, a large window on each side, two trap doors, one door at the end, and a brick fireplace opposite. The exact cost of my house, paying the usual price for such materials as I used, but not counting the work, all of which was done by myself, was as follows; and I give the details because very

---

2. **gods of Troy,** probably an allusion to Virgil's *Aeneid,* in which the destruction of Troy is told.
3. **sumach, sumac**\ˈsü·măk\ any of a family of small trees, shrubs, and woody vines that produce small fleshy fruit and a milky juice.
4. **Iliad**\ˈĭl·ē·əd\ Greek epic composed by Homer, describing the siege of Troy and the terrible effects of Achilles' wrath.

few are able to tell exactly what their houses cost, and fewer still, if any, the separate cost of the various materials which compose them:—

Boards	$8 03½,	mostly shanty boards.
Refuse shingles for roof and sides	4 00	
Laths	1 25	
Two second-hand windows with glass	2 43	
One thousand old brick	4 00	
Two casks of lime	2 40	That was high.
Hair	0 31	More than I needed.
Mantle-tree iron	0 15	
Nails	3 90	
Hinges and screws	0 14	
Latch	0 10	
Chalk	0 01	
Transportation	1 40	I carried a good part on my back.
In all	$28 12½	

These are all the materials excepting the timber, stones, and sand, which I claimed by squatter's right. I have also a small woodshed adjoining, made chiefly of the stuff which was left after building the house.

I intend to build me a house which will surpass any on the main street in Concord in grandeur and luxury, as soon as it pleases me as much and will cost me no more than my present one. . . .

For more than five years I maintained myself solely by the labor of my hands, and I found, that by working about six weeks in a year, I could meet all the expenses of living. The whole of my winters, as well as most of my summers, I had free and clear for study. I have thoroughly tried school-keeping, and found that my expenses were in proportion, or rather out of proportion, to my income, for I was obliged to dress and train, not to say think and believe, accordingly, and I lost my time into the bargain. As I did not teach for the good of my fellow-men, but simply for a livelihood,

this was a failure. I have tried trade; but I found that it would take ten years to get under way in that, and that then I should probably be on my way to the devil. I was actually afraid that I might by that time be doing what is called a good business. When formerly I was looking about to see what I could do for a living, some sad experience in conforming to the wishes of friends being fresh in my mind to tax my ingenuity, I thought often and seriously of picking huckleberries; that surely I could do, and its small profits might suffice,—for my greatest skill has been to want but little,—so little capital is required, so little distraction from my wonted moods, I foolishly thought. While my acquaintances went unhesitatingly into trade or the professions, I contemplated this occupation as most like theirs; ranging the hills all summer to pick the berries which came in my way, and thereafter carelessly dispose of them; so, to keep the flocks of Admetus.[5] I also dreamed that I might gather the wild herbs, or carry evergreens to such villagers as loved to be reminded of the woods, even to the city, by hay-cart loads. But I have since learned that trade curses everything it handles; and though you trade in messages from heaven, the whole curse of trade attaches to the business.

As I preferred some things to others, and especially valued my freedom, as I could fare hard and yet succeed well, I did not wish to spend my time in earning rich carpets or other fine furniture, or delicate cookery, or a house in the Grecian or the Gothic style just yet. If there are any to whom it is no interruption to acquire these things, and who know how to use them when acquired, I relinquish to them the pursuit. Some are "industrious," and appear to love labor for its own sake, or perhaps because it keeps them out of worse mischief; to such I have at present nothing to say. Those who would not know what to do with more leisure than they now enjoy, I might advise to

5. Admetus\ad ˄mē·təs\ husband of Alcestis, who saved the life of Admetus by dying in his place; she was brought back from Hades by Hercules.

work twice as hard as they do,—work till they pay for themselves, and get their free papers. For myself I found that the occupation of a day-laborer was the most independent of any, especially as it required only thirty or forty days in a year to support one. The laborer's day ends with the going down of the sun, and he is then free to devote himself to his chosen pursuit, independent of his labor; but his employer, who speculates from month to month, has no respite from one end of the year to the other.

In short, I am convinced, both by faith and experience, that to maintain one's self on this earth is not a hardship but a pastime, if we will live simply and wisely; as the pursuits of the simpler nations are still the sports of the more artificial. It is not necessary that a man should earn his living by the sweat of his brow, unless he sweats easier than I do. . . .

I
ECONOMY AND LIFE

"Economy" can mean either thrifty management or merely the management of affairs, especially with regard to expenses. Thoreau uses it in both senses, but when he considers "expenses" he thinks not only of financial matters but also of expenses of time and energy and spirit. That he practiced economy in the building of his house is important, but of greater importance is the fact that he practiced economy in the building of his life. He was acutely conscious that the cost of anything should be measured by the amount of life that had to be exchanged for it.

One of the great "secrets" of Thoreau's life and practice of economy is that he knew better than most men what he wanted. In the main he wanted freedom, the leisure to "philosophize" and develop the inner man. He found freedom at Walden Pond, but he found it as well everywhere else he lived, for he was a wise economist.

II
IMPLICATIONS

Discuss what Thoreau might have said about each of the following statements. What do you say about them?

1. The more possessions a man has, the more difficult it is for him to practice economy.

2. Most of us today are overly concerned with the future, whereas we should be primarily concerned with the present.

3. Too much of our time is spent in trying to impress others; too little is spent in trying to satisfy our own inner needs.

4. It is foolish for a man to become a doctor, say, or a teacher, for such occupations leave one with too little time for oneself.

5. Self-discipline is a necessary preliminary to spiritual growth and realization.

6. Thoreau's modern-day counterpart is the beatnik.

III
TECHNIQUES

Style

In literature, "style" refers to *how* a writer says whatever he says. Naturally, how a man expresses his thoughts—in speech as well as in writing—can tell us a good deal about the man himself; to put it in the famous words of the French naturalist, George Buffon, "The style is the man himself."

Thoreau's style tells us much about him. One need not read very far in *Walden*, for example, to discover that its author was well acquainted with both Greek and Oriental literature. References to such things as "Augean stables" or the *Harivamsa* (p. 606) tell us that Thoreau was not simply an articulate vagabond but a well-read and well-educated man.

Thoreau is also very much a man of his time and place, and his references to his native environment far outweigh his references to antiquity. There is also much of the New England Yankee in two of the most salient characteristics of his style—its *economy* and its *concreteness*. Study the first paragraph of *Walden*, looking for these characteristics. On the basis of the economy and concreteness of his style as well as your knowledge of Thoreau himself, be prepared to discuss Buffon's statement on style.

II. Where I Lived, and What I Lived For

When first I took up my abode in the woods, that is, began to spend my nights as well as days there, which, by accident, was on Independence day, or the fourth of July, 1845, my house was not finished for winter, but was merely a defence against the rain, without plastering or chimney, the walls being of rough weather-stained boards, with wide chinks, which made it cool at night. The upright white hewn studs and freshly planed door and window casings gave it a clean and airy look, especially in the morning, when its timbers were saturated with dew, so that I fancied that by noon some sweet gum would exude from them. To my imagination it retained throughout the day more or less of this auroral[6] character, reminding me of a certain house on a mountain which I had visited a year before. This was an airy and unplastered cabin, fit to entertain a travelling god, and where a goddess might trail

her garments. The winds which passed over my dwelling were such as sweep over the ridges of mountains, bearing the broken strains, or celestial parts only, of terrestrial music. The morning wind forever blows, the poem of creation is uninterrupted; but few are the ears that hear it. Olympus[7] is but the outside of the earth everywhere.

The only house I had been the owner of before, if I except a boat, was a tent, which I used occasionally when making excursions in the summer, and this is still rolled up in my garret;[8] but the boat, after passing from hand to hand, has gone down the stream of time. With this more substantial shelter about me, I had made some progress toward settling in the world. This frame, so slightly clad, was a sort of crystallization around me, and reacted on the builder. It was suggestive somewhat as a picture in outlines. I did not need to go out doors to take the air, for the atmosphere within had lost none of its freshness. It was not so much within doors as behind a door where I sat, even in the rainiest weather. The Harivamsa[9] says, "An abode without birds is like a meat without seasoning." Such was not my abode, for I found myself suddenly neighbor to the birds; not by having imprisoned one, but having caged myself near them. I was not only nearer to some of those which commonly frequent the garden and the orchard, but to those wilder and more thrilling songsters of the forest which never, or rarely, serenade a villager,—the wood-thrush, the veery, the scarlet tanager, the field-sparrow, the whippoorwill, and many others.

I was seated by the shore of a small pond, about a mile and a half south of the village of Concord and somewhat higher than it, in the midst of an extensive wood between that town and Lincoln, and about two miles south of that

---

6. **auroral**\ə ˄rȯ·rəl\pertaining to the dawn.
7. **Olympus**\ō ˄lǐm·pəs\ a mountain in Thessaly considered to be the home of the gods.
8. **garret**\˄gă·rǐt\ set of rooms in an attic.
9. **Harivamsa**\'ha·rě ˄vam·sa\ a supplement to the great Hindu epic *Mahābhārata*.

our only field known to fame, Concord Battle Ground; but I was so low in the woods that the opposite shore, half a mile off, like the rest, covered with wood, was my most distant horizon. For the first week, whenever I looked out on the pond it impressed me like a tarn high up on the side of a mountain, its bottom far above the surface of other lakes, and, as the sun arose, I saw it throwing off its nightly clothing of mist, and here and there, by degrees, its soft ripples or its smooth reflecting surface was revealed, while the mists, like ghosts, were stealthily withdrawing in every direction into the woods, as at the breaking up of some nocturnal conventicle.[10] The very dew seemed to hang upon the trees later into the day than usual, as on the sides of mountains. . . .

Every morning was a cheerful invitation to make my life of equal simplicity, and I may say innocence, with Nature herself. I have been as sincere a worshipper of Aurora[11] as the Greeks. I got up early and bathed in the pond; that was a religious exercise, and one of the best things which I did. They say that characters were engraven on the bathing tub of king Tching-thang to this effect: "Renew thyself completely each day; do it again, and again, and forever again." I can understand that. Morning brings back the heroic ages. I was as much affected by the faint hum of a mosquito making its invisible and unimaginable tour through my apartment at earliest dawn, when I was sitting with door and windows open, as I could be by any trumpet that ever sang of fame. It was Homer's requiem; itself an Iliad and Odyssey in the air, singing its own wrath and wanderings. There was something cosmical about it; a standing advertisement, till forbidden, of the everlasting vigor and fertility of the world. The morning, which is the most memorable season of the day, is the awakening hour. Then there is least somnolence in us; and for an hour, at least, some part of us awakes which slumbers all the rest of the day and night. Little is to be expected of that day, if it can be called a day, to which we are not awakened by our Genius, but by the mechanical nudgings of some servitor, are not awakened by our own newly-acquired force and aspirations from within, accompanied by the undulations of celestial music, instead of factory bells, and a fragrance filling the air—to a higher life than we fell asleep from; and thus the darkness bear its fruit, and prove itself to be good, no less than the light. That man who does not believe that each day contains an earlier, more sacred, and auroral hour than he has yet profaned, has despaired of life, and is pursuing a descending and darkening way. After a partial cessation of his sensuous life, the soul of man, or its organs rather, are reinvigorated each day, and his Genius tries again what noble life it can make. All memorable events, I should say, transpire in morning time and in a morning atmosphere. The Vedas[12] say, "All intelligences awake with the morning." Poetry and art, and the fairest and most memorable of the actions of men, date from such an hour. All poets and heroes, like Memnon,[13] are the children of Aurora, and emit their music at sunrise. To him whose elastic and vigorous thought keeps pace with the sun, the day is a perpetual morning. It matters not what the clocks say or the attitudes and labors of men. Morning is when I am awake and there is a dawn in me. Moral reform is the effort to throw off sleep. Why is it that men give so poor an account of their day if they have not been slumbering? They are not such poor calculators. If they had not been overcome with drowsiness they would have performed something. The millions are awake enough for physical labor; but only one in a million is awake enough for effective intellectual exertion, only one in a hundred millions to a poetic or divine life. To be awake is to be alive. I have never yet met a man who was

10. **conventicle**\kən ▲věn·tǐ·kəl\ a secret religious assembly.
11. **Aurora**\ō ▲rō·rə\ the goddess of dawn.
12. **Vedas**\▲vā·dəz\ sacred literature of Hinduism written in Sanskrit.
13. **Memnon**\▲měm·nŏn\ a gigantic statue of an Egyptian king at Thebes, said to emit musical sound at sunrise.

quite awake. How could I have looked him in the face? . . .

I went to the woods because I wished to live deliberately, to front only the essential facts of life, and see if I could not learn what it had to teach, and not, when I came to die, discover that I had not lived. I did not wish to live what was not life, living is so dear; nor did I wish to practise resignation, unless it was quite necessary. I wanted to live deep and suck out all the marrow of life, to live so sturdily and Spartan-like as to put to rout all that was not life, to cut a broad swath and shave close, to drive life into a corner, and reduce it to its lowest terms, and, if it proved to be mean, why then to get the whole and genuine meanness of it, and publish its meanness to the world; or if it were sublime, to know it by experience, and be able to give a true account of it in my next excursion. For most men, it appears to me, are in a strange uncertainty about it, whether it is of the devil or of God, and have *somewhat hastily* concluded that it is the chief end of man here to "glorify God and enjoy him forever."

Still we live meanly, like ants; though the fable tells us that we were long ago changed into men; like pygmies we fight with cranes; it is error upon error, and clout upon clout, and our best virtue has for its occasion a superfluous and evitable wretchedness. Our life is frittered away by detail. An honest man has hardly need to count more than his ten fingers, or in extreme cases he may add his ten toes, and lump the rest. Simplicity, simplicity, simplicity! I say, let your affairs be as two or three, and not a hundred or a thousand; instead of a million count half a dozen, and keep your accounts on your thumb nail. In the midst of this chopping sea of civilized life, such are the clouds and storms and quicksands and thousand-and-one items to be allowed for, that a man has to live, if he would not founder and go to the bottom and not make his port at all, by dead reckoning, and he must be a great calculator indeed who succeeds. Simplify, simplify. Instead of three meals a day, if it be necessary eat but one; in-

stead of a hundred dishes, five; and reduce other things in proportion. Our life is like a German Confederacy, made up of petty states, with its boundary forever fluctuating, so that even a German cannot tell you how it is bounded at any moment. The nation itself, with all its so-called internal improvements, which, by the way are all external and superficial, is just such an unwieldy and overgrown establishment, cluttered with furniture and tripped up by its own traps, ruined by luxury and heedless expense, by want of calculation and a worthy aim, as the million households in the land; and the only cure for it as for them is in a rigid economy, a stern and more than Spartan simplicity of life and elevation of purpose. It lives too fast. Men think that it is essential that the *Nation* have commerce, and export ice, and talk through a telegraph, and ride thirty miles an hour, without a doubt, whether *they* do or not; but whether we should live like baboons or like men, is a little uncertain. If we do not get out sleepers, and forge rails, and devote days and nights to the work, but go to tinkering upon our *lives* to improve *them*, who will build railroads? And if railroads are not built, how shall we get to heaven in season? But if we stay at home and mind our business, who will want railroads? We do not ride on the railroad; it rides upon us. Did you ever think what those sleepers are that underlie the railroads? Each one is a man, an Irishman, or a Yankee man. The rails are laid on them, and they are covered with sand, and the cars run smoothly over them. They are sound sleepers, I assure you. And every few years a new lot is laid down and run over; so that, if some have the pleasure of riding on a rail, others have the misfortune to be ridden upon. And when they run over a man that is walking in his sleep, a supernumerary sleeper in the wrong position, and wake him up, they suddenly stop the cars, and make a hue and cry about it, as if this were an exception. I am glad to know that it takes a gang of men for every five miles to keep the sleepers down and level in their beds as it is, for this is a sign that they may sometime get up again.

Why should we live with such hurry and waste of life? We are determined to be starved before we are hungry. Men say that a stitch in time saves nine, and so they take a thousand stitches to-day to save nine to-morrow. As for *work*, we haven't any of any consequence. We have the Saint Vitus' dance,[14] and cannot possibly keep our heads still. If I should only give a few pulls at the parish bell-rope, as for a fire, that is, without setting the bell, there is hardly a man on his farm in the outskirts of Concord, notwithstanding that press of engagements which was his excuse so many times this morning, nor a boy, nor a woman, I might almost say, but would forsake all and follow that sound, not mainly to save property from the flames, but, if we will confess the truth, much more to see it burn, since burn it must, and we, be it known, did not set it on fire,—or to see it put out, and have a hand in it, if that is done as handsomely; yes, even if it were the parish church itself. Hardly a man takes a half hour's nap after dinner, but when he wakes he holds up his head and asks, "What's the news?" as if the rest of mankind had stood his sentinels. Some give directions to be waked every half hour, doubtless for no other purpose; and then, to pay for it, they tell what they have dreamed. After a night's sleep the news is as indispensable as the breakfast. "Pray tell me anything new that has happened to a man anywhere on this globe,"— and he reads it over his coffee and rolls, that a man has had his eyes gouged out this morning on the Wachito River,[15] never dreaming the while that he lives in the dark unfathomed mammoth cave of this world, and has but the rudiment of an eye himself.

For my part, I could easily do without the post-office. I think that there are very few important communications made through it. To speak critically, I never received more than one or two letters in my life—I wrote this some years ago—that were worth the postage. The penny-post is, commonly, an institution through which you seriously offer a man that penny for his thoughts which is so often safely offered in jest. And I am sure that I never read any memorable news in a newspaper. If we read of one man robbed, or murdered, or killed by accident, or one house burned, or one vessel wrecked, or one steamboat blown up, or one cow run over on the Western Railroad, or one mad dog killed, or one lot of grasshoppers in the winter,—we never need read of another. One is enough. If you are acquainted with the principle, what do you care for a myriad instances and applications? To a philosopher all *news*, as it is called, is gossip, and they who edit and read it are old women over their tea. Yet not a few are greedy after this gossip. . . .

I
THE DOCTRINE OF SIMPLICITY

Thoreau's advice to those who would live more satisfying lives is summed up in the injunction, "Simplify." He wants men to do away with what is not life, "to front only the essential facts of life." What these "essential facts" are becomes more and more clear as one reads on in *Walden*. Some of the essentials, however, as well as many of the nonessentials are spelled out here.

II
IMPLICATIONS

Discuss the following statements.

1. Thoreau's advice—to simplify—applies only to those who, like him, want to live the life of a thinker.

2. It is foolish to suppose that a modern nation like ours would prosper very long if it were to adopt the kind of "rigid economy" and "Spartan simplicity" that Thoreau recommends.

3. A civilization necessarily "pays for" every technological advance it makes; in a real sense there has been no progress since the beginning of time.

4. Times have changed to such an extent that many things Thoreau considered nonessential for his time are essential for ours.

---

14. **Saint Vitus' dance,** a nervous disorder in which there is involuntary movement of the muscles.
15. **Wachito River,** apparently a phonetic spelling of Ouachita\wa ▲chē·ta\ River, which rises in the Ouachita Mts. and flows southeast through southern Arkansas and northeastern Louisiana.

Chapters Three through Five
are called "Reading," "Sounds,"
and "Solitude," three reasons why Thoreau wanted
to escape to Walden Pond. In Chapter Six,
"Visitors," he turns his attention
to his former neighbors who visit from Concord
to inspect his new home. Two excerpts sample
his opinion of them. Chapter Seven, called
"The Bean-Field," is an account
of his major crops and how he tended them.
In Chapter Eight, "The Village," he says
he visited Concord to observe the habits
of busy men, "as curious to me as if they
had been prairie dogs." Two excerpts
illustrate what he means.

VI. Visitors

I think that I love society as much as most, and am ready enough to fasten myself like a bloodsucker for the time to any full-blooded man that comes in my way. I am naturally no hermit, but might possibly sit out the sturdiest frequenter of the bar-room, if my business called me thither.

I had three chairs in my house; one for solitude, two for friendship, three for society. When visitors came in larger and unexpected numbers there was but the third chair for them all, but they generally economized the room by standing up. It is surprising how many great men and women a small house will contain. I have had twenty-five or thirty souls, with their bodies, at once under my roof, and yet we often parted without being aware that we had come very near to one another. Many of our houses, both public and private, with their almost innumerable apartments, their huge halls and their cellars for the storage of wines and other munitions of peace, appear to me extravagantly large for their inhabitants. They are so vast and

magnificent that the latter seem to be only vermin which infest them. I am surprised when the herald blows his summons before some Tremont or Astor or Middlesex House, to see come creeping out over the piazza for all inhabitants a ridiculous mouse, which soon again slinks into some hole in the pavement.

One inconvenience I sometimes experienced in so small a house, the difficulty of getting to a sufficient distance from my guest when we began to utter the big thoughts in big words. You want room for your thoughts to get into sailing trim and run a course or two before they make their port. The bullet of your thought must have overcome its lateral and ricochet motion and fallen into its last and steady course before it reaches the ear of the hearer, else it may plough out again through the side of his head. Also, our sentences wanted room to unfold and form their columns in the interval. Individuals, like nations, must have suitable broad and natural boundaries, even a considerable neutral ground, between them. I have found it a singular luxury to talk across the pond to a companion on the opposite side. In my house we were so near that we could not begin to hear,—we could not speak low enough to be heard; as when you throw two stones into calm water so near that they break each other's undulations. If we are merely loquacious and loud talkers, then we can afford to stand very near together, cheek by jowl, and feel each other's breath; but if we speak reservedly and thoughtfully, we want to be farther apart, that all animal heat and moisture may have a chance to evaporate. If we would enjoy the most intimate society with that in each of us which is without, or above, being spoken to, we must not only be silent, but commonly so far apart bodily that we cannot possibly hear each other's voice in any case. Referred to this standard, speech is for the convenience of those who are hard of hearing; but there are many fine things which we cannot say if we have to shout. As the conversation began to assume a loftier and grander tone, we gradually shoved our chairs farther apart till they touched the wall in opposite corners, and then commonly there was not room enough.

My "best" room, however, my withdrawing room, always ready for company, on whose carpet the sun rarely fell, was the pine wood behind my house. Thither in summer days, when distinguished guests came, I took them, and a priceless domestic swept the floor and dusted the furniture and kept the things in order. . . .

Many a traveller came out of his way to see me and the inside of my house, and, as an excuse for calling, asked for a glass of water. I told them that I drank at the pond, and pointed thither, offering to lend them a dipper. Far off as I lived, I was not exempted from that annual visitation which occurs, methinks, about the first of April, when everybody is on the move; and I had my share of good luck, though there were some curious specimens among my visitors. Half-witted men from the almshouse and elsewhere came to see me; but I endeavored to make them exercise all the wit they had, and make their confessions to me; in such cases making wit the theme of our conversation; and so was compensated. Indeed, I found some of them to be wiser than the so-called *overseers* of the poor and selectmen of the town, and thought it was time that the tables were turned. With respect to wit, I learned that there was not much difference between the half and the whole. One day, in particular, an inoffensive, simple-minded pauper, whom with others I had often seen used as fencing stuff, standing or sitting on a bushel in the fields to keep cattle and himself from straying, visited me, and expressed a wish to live as I did. He told me, with the utmost simplicity and truth, quite superior, or rather *inferior,* to anything that is called humility, that he was "deficient in intellect." These were his words. The Lord had made him so, yet he supposed the Lord cared as much for him as for another. "I have always been so," said he, "from my childhood; I never had much mind; I was not like other children; I am weak in the head. It was the Lord's will, I suppose." And there he was to prove the truth of his words. He was a metaphysical puzzle[16] to me. I have rarely met a fellowman on such promising ground,—it was so simple and sincere and so true all that he said. And, true enough, in proportion as he appeared to humble himself was he exalted. I did not know at first but it was the result of a wise policy. It seemed that from such a basis of truth and frankness as the poor weak-headed pauper had laid, our intercourse might go forward to something better than the intercourse of sages. . . .

VIII. The Village

After hoeing, or perhaps reading and writing, in the forenoon, I usually bathed again in the pond, swimming across one of its coves for a stint, and washed the dust of labor from my person, or smoothed out the last wrinkle which study had made, and for the afternoon was absolutely free. Every day or two I strolled to the village to hear some of the gossip which is incessantly going on there, circulating either from mouth to mouth, or from newspaper to newspaper, and which, taken in homœopathic doses, was really as refreshing in its way as the rustle of leaves and the peeping of frogs. As I walked in the woods to see the birds and squirrels, so I walked in the village to see the men and boys; instead of the wind among the pines I heard the carts rattle. In one direction from my house there was a colony of musk-rats in the river meadows; under the grove of elms and buttonwoods in the other horizon was a village of busy men, as curious to me as if they had been prairie dogs, each sitting at the mouth of its burrow,

---

16. **metaphysical puzzle,** Thoreau means that the pauper's sincerity and simple wisdom on the one hand and his self-professed inferiority on the other are such contradictions that they cannot be explained by the accepted principles of philosophy.

or running out to a neighbor's to gossip. I went there frequently to observe their habits. The village appeared to me a great news room; and on one side, to support it, as once at Redding & Company's on State Street, they kept nuts and raisins, or salt and meal and other groceries. Some have such a vast appetite for the former commodity, that is, the news, and such sound digestive organs, that they can sit forever in public avenues without stirring, and let it simmer and whisper through them like the Etesian winds,[17] or as if inhaling ether, it only producing numbness and insensibility to pain, —otherwise it would often be painful to hear, —without affecting the consciousness. I hardly ever failed, when I rambled through the village, to see a row of such worthies, either sitting on a ladder sunning themselves, with their bodies inclined forward and their eyes glancing along the line this way and that, from time to time, with a voluptuous expression, or else leaning against a barn with their hands in their pockets, like caryatides, as if to prop it up. They, being commonly out of doors, heard whatever was in the wind. These are the coarsest mills, in which all gossip is first rudely digested or cracked up before it is emptied into finer and more delicate hoppers within doors. I observed that the vitals of the village were the grocery, the bar-room, the post-office, and the bank; and, as a necessary part of the machinery, they kept a bell, a big gun, and a fire-engine, at convenient places; and the houses were so arranged as to make the most of mankind, in lanes and fronting one another, so that every traveller had to run the gauntlet, and every man, woman, and child might get a lick at him. Of course, those who were stationed nearest to the head of the line, where they could most see and be seen, and have the first blow at him, paid the highest prices for their places; and the few straggling inhabitants in the outskirts, where long gaps in the line began to occur, and the traveller could get over walls or turn aside into cow-paths, and so escape, paid a very slight ground or window tax. Signs were hung out on all sides to allure him; some to catch him by the ap-

petite, as the tavern and victualling cellar; some by the fancy, as the dry goods store and the jeweller's; and others by the hair or the feet or the skirts, as the barber, the shoemaker, or the tailor. Besides, there was a still more terrible standing invitation to call at every one of these houses, and company expected about these times. For the most part I escaped wonderfully from these dangers, either by proceeding at once boldly and without deliberation to the goal, as is recommended to those who run the gauntlet, or by keeping my thoughts on high things, like Orpheus,[18] who, "loudly singing the praises of the gods to his lyre, drowned the voices of the Sirens,[19] and kept out of danger." Sometimes I bolted suddenly, and nobody could tell my whereabouts, for I did not stand much about gracefulness, and never hesitated at a gap in a fence. I was even accustomed to make an irruption into some houses, where I was well entertained, and after learning the kernels and very last sieve-ful of news, what had subsided, the prospects of war and peace, and whether the world was likely to hold together much longer, I was let out through the rear avenues, and so escaped to the woods again. . . .

One afternoon, near the end of the first summer, when I went to the village to get a shoe from the cobbler's, I was seized and put into jail, because, as I have elsewhere related, I did not pay a tax to, or recognize the authority of, the state which buys and sells men, women, and children, like cattle at the door of its senate-house. I had gone down to the woods for other purposes. But, wherever a man goes, men will pursue and paw him with their dirty institutions, and, if they can, constrain him to belong to their desperate odd-fellow society. It is true, I might have resisted forcibly with more or less

---

17. **Etesian winds**\ĭ ˄tē˙zhən\ northerly Mediterranean summer winds which recur annually.
18. **Orpheus**\˄ȯr·fē·əs\ in Greek mythology, his singing charmed even beasts, rocks, and trees.
19. **Sirens**\˄Sai·rĕnz\ mythological creatures, part beast and part woman, whose enchanting songs led sailors to shipwreck.

effect, might have run "amok" against society; but I preferred that society should run "amok" against me, it being the desperate party. However, I was released the next day, obtained my mended shoe, and returned to the woods in season to get my dinner of huckleberries on Fair Haven Hill. I was never molested by any person but those who represented the state. I had no lock nor bolt but for the desk which held my papers, not even a nail to put over my latch or windows. I never fastened my door night or day, though I was to be absent several days; not even when the next fall I spent a fortnight in the woods of Maine. And yet my house was more respected than if it had been surrounded by a file of soldiers. The tired rambler could rest and warm himself by my fire, the literary amuse himself with the few books on my table, or the curious, by opening my closet door, see what was left of my dinner, and what prospect I had of a supper. Yet, though many people of every class came this way to the pond, I suffered no serious inconvenience from these sources, and I never missed anything but one small book, a volume of Homer, which perhaps was improperly gilded, and this I trust a soldier of our camp has found by this time. I am convinced, that if all men were to live as simply as I then did, thieving and robbery would be unknown. . . .

I
A LOVER OR HATER OF HUMANKIND?

Some of Thoreau's criticism of human beings and human institutions in the foregoing selections is very strong. He speaks of men "pawing" him with their "dirty institutions," of "their desperate odd-fellow society," and of the resemblance of the villagers to prairie-dogs sitting at the mouths of their burrows. In his most famous essay, "Civil Disobedience," he calls the State "half-witted" and maintains that one "cannot without disgrace be associated with it." The town-clerk of Concord had a written statement by Thoreau which read as follows: "Know all men by these presents, that I, Henry Thoreau, do not wish to be regarded as a member of any incorporated society which I have not joined."

Such bitter criticism has led some to believe that Thoreau was essentially antisocial or even misanthropic. One of his biographers, however, defends him against such charges by saying that the truth was that Thoreau loved humanity too much to flatter it. What evidence can you find to show that Thoreau either essentially loved or essentially hated his fellow human beings?

II
IMPLICATIONS

Consider the following statements.

1. The fact that Thoreau thought one could best enjoy the most intimate society through silence and at a distance proves that he really cared very little for his fellowmen.

2. A man who uncompromisingly lives a life of principle is certain to be looked upon as a "kook."

3. It is not inconsistent for a person who loves humanity to criticize it mercilessly if he feels it is not acting in its own best interest.

4. A man who believes that it is a disgrace to be associated with the government of his nation ought to go live elsewhere.

5. It is our *duty* as human beings and as citizens to refuse to obey a law that we know to be unjust.

6. A man who lives apart from society for a considerable period of time must be either a misfit or a misanthrope.

7. Thoreau's frequent visits to Concord prove that his Walden experiment was essentially a failure.

"Brute Neighbors,"
the twelfth chapter of *Walden*,
could easily stand by itself;
it is a delightful reminiscence of birds
and animals Thoreau came to know almost as well
as he knew his Concord neighbors.
He opens the chapter with a humorous dialogue
between a "poet" and a "hermit" and concludes
with a charming account of a loon on the pond.
Between these two episodes are
the following paragraphs.

XII. Brute Neighbors

Why do precisely these objects which we behold make a world? Why has man just these species of animals for his neighbors; as if nothing but a mouse could have filled this crevice? I suspect that Pilpay & Co. have put animals to their best use, for they are all beasts of burden, in a sense, made to carry some portion of our thoughts. . . .

The mice which haunted my house were not the common ones, which are said to have been introduced into the country, but a wild native kind not found in the village. I sent one to a distinguished naturalist, and it interested him much. When I was building, one of these had its nest underneath the house, and before I had laid the second floor, and swept out the shavings, would come out regularly at lunch time and pick up the crumbs at my feet. It probably had never seen a man before; and it soon became quite familiar, and would run over my shoes and up my clothes. It could readily ascend the sides of the room by short impulses, like a squirrel, which it resembled in its motions. At length, as I leaned with my elbow on the bench one day, it ran up my clothes, and along my sleeve, and round and round the paper which held my dinner, while I kept the latter close, and dodged and played at bo-peep with it; and when at last I held still a piece of cheese between my thumb and finger, it came and nibbled it, sitting in my hand, and afterward cleaned its face and paws, like a fly, and walked away.

A phœbe[20] soon built in my shed, and a robin for protection in a pine which grew against the house. In June the partridge (*Tetrao umbellus'*), which is so shy a bird, led her brood past my windows, from the woods in the rear to the front of my house, clucking and calling to them like a hen, and in all her behavior proving herself the hen of the woods. The young suddenly disperse on your approach, at a signal from the mother, as if a whirlwind had swept them away, and they so exactly resemble the dried leaves and twigs that many a traveller has placed his foot in the midst of a brood, and heard the whir of the old bird as she flew off, and her anxious calls and mewing, or seen her trail her wings to attract his attention, without suspecting their neighborhood. The parent will sometimes roll and spin round before you in such a dishabille,[21] that you cannot, for a few moments, detect what kind of creature it is. The young squat still and flat, often running their heads under a leaf, and mind only their mother's directions given from a distance, nor will your approach make them run again and betray themselves. You may even tread on them, or have your eyes on them for a minute, without discovering them. I have held them in my open hand at such a time, and still their only care, obedient to their mother and their instinct, was to squat there without fear or trembling. So perfect is this instinct, that once, when I had laid them on the leaves again, and one accidentally fell on its side, it was found with the rest in exactly the same position ten minutes afterward. They are not callow like the young of most birds, but more perfectly developed and precocious even than chickens.

20. **phœbe**\ˈfē·bē\ an American flycatcher common in eastern United States.
21. **dishabille**\ˈdĭ·sə ˈbē\ state of being carelessly dressed.

The remarkably adult yet innocent expression of their open and serene eyes is very memorable. All intelligence seems reflected in them. They suggest not merely the purity of infancy, but a wisdom clarified by experience. Such an eye was not born when the bird was, but is coeval with the sky it reflects. The woods do not yield another such a gem. The traveller does not often look into such a limpid well. The ignorant or reckless sportsman often shoots the parent at such a time, and leaves these innocents to fall a prey to some prowling beast or bird, or gradually mingle with the decaying leaves which they so much resemble. It is said that when hatched by a hen they will directly disperse on some alarm, and so are lost, for they never hear the mother's call which gathers them again. These were my hens and chickens.

It is remarkable how many creatures live wild and free though secret in the woods, and still sustain themselves in the neighborhood of towns, suspected by hunters only. How retired the otter manages to live here! He grows to be four feet long, as big as a small boy, perhaps without any human being getting a glimpse of him. I formerly saw the raccoon in the woods behind where my house is built, and probably still heard their whinnering at night. Commonly I rested an hour or two in the shade at noon, after planting, and ate my lunch, and read a little by a spring which was the source of a swamp and of a brook, oozing from under Brister's Hill, half a mile from my field. The approach to this was through a succession of descending grassy hollows, full of young pitch-pines, into a larger wood about the swamp. There, in a very secluded and shaded spot, under a spreading white-pine, there was yet a clean firm sward to sit on. I had dug out the spring and made a well of clear gray water, where I could dip up a pailful without roiling it, and thither I went for this purpose almost every day in mid-summer, when the pond was warmest. Thither too the wood-cock led her brood, to probe the mud for worms, flying but a foot above them down the bank, while they ran in a troop beneath; but at last, spying me, she would leave her young and circle round and round me, nearer and nearer till within four or five feet, pretending broken wings and legs, to attract my attention, and get off her young, who would already have taken up their march, with faint wiry peep, single file through the swamp, as she directed. Or I heard the peep of the young when I could not see the parent bird. There too the turtle-doves sat over the spring, or fluttered from bough to bough of the soft white-pines over my head; or the red squirrel, coursing down the nearest bough, was particularly familiar and inquisitive. You only need sit still long enough in some attractive spot in the woods that all its inhabitants may exhibit themselves to you by turns.

I was witness to events of a less peaceful character. One day when I went out to my wood-pile, or rather my pile of stumps, I observed two large ants, the one red, the other much larger, nearly half an inch long, and black, fiercely contending with one another. Having once got hold they never let go, but struggled and wrestled and rolled on the chips incessantly. Looking farther, I was surprised to find that the chips were covered with such combatants, that it was not a *duellum,* but a *bellum,* a war between two races of ants, the red always pitted against the black, and frequently two red ones to one black. The legions of these Myrmidons[22] covered all the hills and vales in my wood-yard, and the ground was already strewn with the dead and dying, both red and black. It was the only battle which I have ever witnessed, the only battle-field I ever trod while the battle was raging; internecine war; the red republicans on the one hand, and the black imperialists on the other. On every side they were engaged in deadly combat, yet without any noise that I could hear, and human soldiers never fought so resolutely. I watched a couple that were fast locked in each other's embraces, in a little sunny valley amid the

---

22. **Myrmidons**\ ᴧmēr·mə·dŏnz\ an allusion to Homer's *Iliad;* the Greek hero Achilles led his army, the Myrmidons. They were his faithful unquestioning followers.

chips, now at noon-day prepared to fight till the sun went down, or life went out. The smaller red champion had fastened himself like a vise to his adversary's front, and through all the tumblings on that field never for an instant ceased to gnaw at one of his feelers near the root, having already caused the other to go by the board; while the stronger black one dashed him from side to side, and, as I saw on looking nearer, had already divested him of several of his members. They fought with more pertinacity than bull-dogs. Neither manifested the least disposition to retreat. It was evident that their battle-cry was Conquer or die.

In the mean while there came along a single red ant on the hillside of this valley, evidently full of excitement, who either had despatched his foe, or had not yet taken part in the battle; probably the latter, for he had lost none of his limbs; whose mother had charged him to return with his shield or upon it. Or perchance he was some Achilles, who had nourished his wrath apart, and had now come to avenge or rescue his Patroclus.[23] He saw this unequal combat from afar,—for the blacks were nearly twice the size of the red,—he drew near with rapid pace till he stood on his guard within half an inch of the combatants; then, watching his opportunity, he sprang upon the black warrior, and commenced his operations near the root of his right fore-leg, leaving the foe to select among his own members; and so there were three united for life, as if a new kind of attraction had been invented which put all other locks and cements to shame. I should not have wondered by this time to find that they had their respective musical bands stationed on some eminent chip, and playing their national airs the while, to excite the slow and cheer the dying combatants. I was myself excited somewhat even as if they had been men. The more you think of it, the less the difference. And certainly there is not the fight recorded in Concord history, at least, if in the history of America, that will bear a moment's comparison with this, whether for the numbers engaged in it, or for the patriotism and heroism displayed. For numbers and for carnage it was an Austerlitz[24] or Dresden. Concord Fight! Two killed on the patriots' side, and Luther Blanchard wounded! Why here every ant was a Buttrick,[25] —"Fire! for God's sake fire!"—and thousands shared the fate of Davis and Hosmer. There was not one hireling there. I have no doubt that it was a principle they fought for, as much as our ancestors, and not to avoid a three-penny tax on their tea; and the results of this battle will be as important and memorable to those whom it concerns as those of the battle of Bunker Hill, at least.

I took up the chip on which the three I have particularly described were struggling, carried it into my house, and placed it under a tumbler on my window-sill, in order to see the issue. Holding a microscope to the first-mentioned red ant, I saw that, though he was assiduously gnawing at the near fore-leg of his enemy, having severed his remaining feeler, his own breast was all torn away, exposing what vitals he had there to the jaws of the black warrior, whose breastplate was apparently too thick for him to pierce; and the dark carbuncles of the sufferer's eyes shone with ferocity such as war only could excite. They struggled half an hour longer under the tumbler, and when I looked again the black soldier had severed the heads of his foes from their bodies, and the still living heads were hanging on either side of him like ghastly trophies at his saddle-bow, still apparently as firmly fastened as ever, and he was endeavoring with feeble struggles, being without feelers and with only the remnant of a leg, and I know not how many other wounds, to divest himself of them; which at length, after half an hour more, he accomplished. I raised the glass, and he went off over the window-sill in that

---

23. **Patroclus**\pə ˈtra·kləs\ in the *Iliad*, Achilles' dear friend, killed by the Trojan hero Hector.
24. **Austerlitz**\ˈŏs·tər·lits\ town in Czechoslovakia and site of Napoleon's victory over Austrian and Russian armies, 1805.
25. **Buttrick**, Maj. John, leader of the provincials who turned back the British advance at the North Bridge, Concord, Mass., in 1775. Blanchard, Davis, and Hosmer were casualties in the skirmish.

crippled state. Whether he finally survived that combat, and spent the remainder of his days in some Hotel des Invalides,[26] I do not know; but I thought that his industry would not be worth much thereafter. I never learned which party was victorious, nor the cause of the war; but I felt for the rest of that day as if I had had my feelings excited and harrowed by witnessing the struggle, the ferocity and carnage, of a human battle before my door. . . .

⚜

No sampling of *Walden* could be satisfactory without these paragraphs from his last chapter. If we had any doubts why he left his hut to return to civilization, he dispels them here.

XVIII. Conclusion

I left the woods for as good a reason as I went there. Perhaps it seemed to me that I had several more lives to live, and could not spare any more time for that one. It is remarkable how easily and insensibly we fall into a particular route, and make a beaten track for ourselves. I had not lived there a week before my feet wore a path from my door to the pond-side; and though it is five or six years since I trod it, it is still quite distinct. It is true, I fear that others may have fallen into it, and so helped to keep it open. The surface of the earth is soft and impressible by the feet of men; and so with the paths which the mind travels. How worn and dusty, then, must be the highways of the world, how deep the ruts of tradition and conformity! I did not wish to take a cabin passage, but rather to go before the mast and on the deck of the world, for there I could best see the moonlight amid the mountains. I do not wish to go below now.

I learned this, at least, by my experiment; that if one advances confidently in the direction of his dreams, and endeavors to live the life which he has imagined, he will meet with a success unexpected in common hours. He will put some things behind, will pass an invisible boundary; new, universal, and more liberal laws will begin to establish themselves around and within him; or the old laws be expanded, and interpreted in his favor in a more liberal sense, and he will live with the license of a higher order of beings. In proportion as he simplifies his life, the laws of the universe will appear less complex, and solitude will not be solitude, nor poverty poverty, nor weakness weakness. If you have built castles in the air, your work need not be lost; that is where they should be. Now put the foundations under them. . . .

---

26. **Hotel des Invalides**\ō ᴬtĕl 'dä·zan·vă ᴬlēd\ in Paris, originally a hospital for veterans; now a museum containing the tomb of Napoleon.

I

"TO PASS AN INVISIBLE BOUNDARY"

The "invisible boundary" to which Thoreau refers in his "Conclusion" is that boundary that separates a man from his dreams and prevents his fullest self-realization. It is the boundary of the humdrum, created by convention and laziness of spirit. It is the boundary that we can cross through the kind of self-disciplined simplicity that Henry David Thoreau practiced in his lifetime.

In "Brute Neighbors" we see some aspects of nature through the eyes of a man who has passed the invisible boundary. Thoreau gives us the subtle details that only a great observer could have noticed. And he sees his "neighbors" honestly, not sentimentally—the ant episode reminds us that brute neighbors can be as brutal as human neighbors often are.

II
IMPLICATIONS

The following quotations are gathered from all the foregoing passages. Discuss the meaning of each and the relevance of any five to your own life and experience.

1. But men labor under a mistake. The better part of the man is soon plowed into the soil for compost.

2. . . . I made no haste in my work, but rather made the most of it. . . .

3. . . . my greatest skill has been to want but little. . . .

4. . . . trade curses everything it handles; and though you trade in messages from Heaven, the whole curse of trade attaches to the business.

5. . . . I am convinced . . . that to maintain one's self on this earth is not a hardship but a pastime, if we will live simply and wisely. . . .

6. Morning is when I am awake and there is a dawn in me. Moral reform is the effort to throw off sleep.

7. I have never yet met a man who was quite awake. How could I have looked him in the face?

8. Our life is frittered away by detail.

9. . . . if railroads are not built, how shall we get to heaven in season? But if we stay home and mind our business, who will want railroads? We do not ride on the railroad; it rides upon us.

10. . . . speech is for the convenience of those who are hard of hearing. . . .

11. It is remarkable how easily and insensibly we fall into a particular route, and make a beaten track for ourselves.

III
TECHNIQUES

Tone

In the previous unit we defined *tone* as the writer's attitude toward his material, and we likened it to the tone of voice in speaking. Our spoken words, however, not only reveal our attitude toward what we are talking about but also toward our listeners. The writer, too, presumably has an attitude toward his audience, and his words may reveal what that attitude is.

It is important to distinguish between the two sorts of tone we have been describing. When Thoreau speaks of the "dirty institutions" of men, his tone *toward his material* may properly be called hostile or even bitter; but he does not necessarily adopt the same tone *toward his audience*. Certainly those members of his audience who admire him do not feel that he is expressing hostility toward them; on the contrary they are far more likely to describe his tone toward his audience as friendly, honest, sincere.

Choose three or four of the quotations above—or any others from the Thoreau selections—and discuss the differences between Thoreau's attitude toward his material and his attitude toward his readers. Note especially which of the two attitudes seems to vary more and why.

EMILY DICKINSON

1830–1886

Emily Dickinson was no ordinary citizen of Amherst, Massachusetts. Born there in 1830, she lived so private a life that piecing together her biography from the letters she left behind, the reminiscences of her friends, and especially her poems has been a task that has led to a variety of conclusions. Surely she was "a strange and original genius," as the poet Conrad Aiken called her. Whether she was "the greatest woman poet who ever lived," as another critic calls her, is difficult to say. Emily Dickinson has been misrepresented, just as Poe and Whitman have been, partly through her own fault. "Biography," she said, "first convinces us of the fleeing of the biographied." But too little knowledge of the life she led in Amherst is equally as hazardous as reading intimate revelations into every line of her poetry.

In the *Atlantic Monthly* for April, 1862, Thomas Wentworth Higginson, a writer and former minister, published a "Letter to a Young Contributor," urging poets to forsake the old models and strive for new forms charged with life. Emily Dickinson wrote him at once, asking "Are you too deeply occupied to say if my verse is alive? The mind is so near itself it cannot see distinctly, and I have none to ask." She was thirty-one years old, the shy unmarried daughter of a prominent Amherst lawyer. She had published nothing. We think now that by this date she had written, privately, at least 300 poems. She sent Higginson four. He answered her promptly, urging her to send more and to tell him something about herself. Her answer is one of the most revealing letters she ever wrote; and with it began a long correspondence between a scholar and a teacher, as she chose to think of the relationship. Higginson was not the most perceptive of critics, and he tried too often to improve her unconventional style; but he offered her the friendship she needed. "You were not aware," she wrote years later, "that you saved my life." Nor was Emily aware that after first meeting her Higginson wrote his wife: "I never was with anyone who drained my nerve power so much. Without touching her she drew from me. I am glad not to live near her."

Higginson not only saved her life but her poetry as well, or at least he persuaded her to go on writing. She thanked him for "the surgery," saying "it was not so painful as I supposed." Probably he had found the four poems cryptic and irregular, perhaps even jarring to his ear. If he suggested that Emily smooth the meters and tidy up the rhymes, he could hardly have guessed that he was dealing with a "born" poet who was assured she knew how and why she broke the rules. She would continue to write as she must write. When Higginson came to edit Emily's poems after her death (he published three volumes beginning in 1890), he did indeed alter their roughness; but he also had the good sense to preserve the original manuscripts. To our ears, the half-rhymes, the broken syntax, the veiled meanings are intriguing rather than baffling. Even Higginson could say, following Emily's death, "After all, when a thought takes one's breath away, a lesson on grammar seems an impertinence."

Emily's letter of 1862 had more to say. In an almost childlike hand, she wrote Higginson: "I have a brother and sister; my mother does not care for thought; and father, too busy with his briefs to notice what we do. He buys me many books, but begs me not to read them, because he fears they joggle the mind." Edward Dickinson was a successful lawyer and for years the bursar of Amherst College. His spacious house on Main Street was scarcely the center of unrestrained gaiety, since the Puritan village offered little lightheartedness to anyone, except a few rowdy college students. The church was the center of activity, morally and physically. Card games, dancing, theater, concerts were nonexistent. The main social events were Commencement Week in August and the Cattle Show in October. Of the latter, Emily thought "The show is not the show,/ But they that go." The villagers thought otherwise.

Emily's mother was a nonentity; her only brother, Austin, was an image of his father. In Susan, Austin's wife, Emily found a confederate for a time, especially since she lived next door and enjoyed poetry. But when Susan betrayed Emily by sending one of her poems to the Springfield *Republican,* their friendship cooled. "Publication," she argued, "is the auction of the mind." To Lavinia, her younger sister, Emily was always devoted, increasingly as the family diminished in size and the two unmarried sisters were left to run the big house. As Emily became more and more a recluse, Lavinia served as her only link with the outside world. It was natural that Emily should leave her poems in her sister's care and just as natural that Lavinia should turn to Higginson when she resolved to collect them for publication in 1890. What no one suspected was the immense number Emily had written: over seventeen hundred.

What companions, what education had she, Higginson must have asked, for we have Emily's answer in the 1862 letter. "You ask of my companions. Hills, sir, and the sundown, and a dog as large as myself, that father bought me. They are better than beings because they know, but do not tell." The reply is typically elusive but not wholly accurate. Though she made few trips out of Amherst—to Boston to see a physician, to Philadelphia and Washington to visit friends—she received guests in her father's house, called on new neighbors, attended local parties, and church occasionally. She had eight years of schooling, first at Amherst Academy and then at Mount Holyoke Female Seminary. By 1862, however, she was seeing less of the townspeople and more of her garden where, at dusk, she could enjoy the solitude behind hemlock hedges. She had taken to wearing only white and to communicating with the neighbors by means of hand-picked bouquets or freshly baked bread, accompanied by a poem as greeting or as cryptic note. By 1870, her seclusion was overtly admitted: "I do not cross my father's ground to any house or town." Her reasons are only hinted at: domestic chores, and they were many, ill health, natural shyness, poetic composition, psychic withdrawal. Whatever the causes, her seclusion was her own choosing. It was a hermit's existence as far as the town knew, but Emily's private life was full of introspection and literary labor. "The soul selects her own society," she wrote, "then shuts the door."

Early biographers were quite certain that this life was emotionally frustrated to the point of despair. "I went to school," she wrote Higginson, "but in your manner of the phrase had no education. When a little girl, I had a friend who taught me Immortality; but venturing too near himself, he never returned. Soon after my tutor died, and for several years my lexicon was my own companion. Then I found one more, but he was not contented I be his scholar, so he left the land." The first "tutor" was Benjamin Newton, a young man too poor to marry who had worked in her father's law office, then moved to Worcester where he died at an early age. The second was the Reverend Charles Wadsworth of Philadelphia whom she may have met in 1854. He was considerably older than Emily and already married. He called on her in Amherst in 1860; of this we have record. But two years later he left for San Francisco and she did not see him again until 1880. It is extremely unlikely that Wadsworth could have encouraged Emily's passion, if that is what she felt toward him.

The great risk in reading her poems biographically—particularly the one beginning "My life closed twice before its close"—is not the uncertainty of fact but the limitations such narrow reading imposes on the poet's lines. Emily's subjects are fear, frustration, death, God, friendships, love, and the natural world around her. When she speaks in the first person—"I could not live with you," one poem begins—she does not necessarily record a personal experience, though the emotions which led to creating the poem may have begun there.

Rather she is writing of universal feelings—the agony of separation, the need for love, the fear of loneliness. Like Thoreau, Emily traveled widely without leaving the village where she was born; we could almost say without leaving her garden and her study. She withdrew from the world in order to know it better, to contemplate the human condition, man's relation to the things of this world. "To live is so startling," she wrote Higginson, "it leaves but little room for other occupations, though friends are, if possible, an event more fair." Her poems are life distilled, not the temporal happenings of Massachusetts in 1860, not even of the Civil War, but events common to all men: sorrow at the loss of a friend, joy at summer noon, despair at nightfall, the first crocus in spring, the shapes the snow takes in December, walks with her dog, small-town hypocrisy, the renunciation of hope, the nature of God. To all these subjects Emily brings intense personal reactions, quite oblivious of fashion or acceptability. She read deeply in Keats, Emerson, the Brownings, the Bible; but her forms are her own. When Higginson suggested she wait before publishing, he was thinking of the roughness, the starkness of her meter, not the revelation of private thoughts. "I smile when you suggest I delay to 'publish,'" she replied, "that being foreign to my thought."

Possibly publication would have spoiled her genius. The rebel in Emily Dickinson had an outlet in her poetry, a release she needed partly because of her family, partly because of her self-imposed solitude. Her poems were her confidante. She labored over them with love, rewriting, reshaping her thoughts into arresting metaphors, witty observations, acute revelations of sensory experience, always with the idea that an emotion captured, a thought well expressed, were more vital to the life of a poem than a listener soothed or a critic pleased. "Is my verse alive," not "Is my poetry good poetry," she asked of Higginson. The reader who discovers her genius will answer for her. Once exposed to her frankness, to the force of her lines, he does not easily forget them.

God and Nature

Like most poets, Emily Dickinson was alert to the world
around her, particularly the natural world. In these poems she speaks
of Nature as though it were a friend, or at least a confidante.
Since she sees God's presence in all of Nature, it is not surprising, then,
to find her also thinking of God in familiar terms. Had she published
these poems during her lifetime, she very likely would have drawn censure
for her brashness. As it is they remain private thoughts
which we, at last, can "overhear."

This Is My Letter to the World

This is my letter to the world
That never wrote to me,—
The simple news that nature told,
With tender majesty.

Her message is committed
To hands I cannot see;
For love of her, sweet countrymen,
Judge tenderly of me!

Poems, 1890

The Sky Is Low, the Clouds Are Mean

The sky is low, the clouds are mean,
A travelling flake of snow
Across a barn or through a rut
Debates if it will go.

A narrow wind complains all day
How some one treated him;
Nature, like us, is sometimes caught
Without her diadem.

Poems, 1890

A Little Madness in the Spring

A little madness in the Spring
Is wholesome even for the King,
But God be with the Clown,
Who ponders this tremendous scene—
This whole experiment of green,
As if it were his own!

From *The Single Hound.* Copyright 1914, 1942 by Martha
Dickinson Bianchi. Reprinted by permission of Little, Brown
and Company.

Some Keep the Sabbath Going to Church

Some keep the Sabbath going to church;
I keep it staying at home,
With a bobolink for a chorister,
And an orchard for a dome.

Some keep the Sabbath in surplice;   5
I just wear my wings,
And instead of tolling the bell for church,
Our little sexton sings.

God preaches,—a noted clergyman,—
And the sermon is never long;   10
So instead of getting to heaven at last
I'm going all along!

Poems, 1890

Lightly Stepped a Yellow Star

Lightly stepped a yellow star
To its lofty place,
Loosed the Moon her silver hat
From her lustral face.
All of evening softly lit
As an astral hall—
"Father," I observed to Heaven,
"You are punctual."

The Single Hound, 1914

I Never Saw a Moor

I never saw a moor,
I never saw the sea;
Yet know I how the heather looks,
And what a wave must be.

I never spoke with God,
Nor visited in heaven;
Yet certain am I of the spot
As if the chart were given.

Poems, 1890

I
PERSONAL CREEDS

These six poems reflect Emily Dickinson's deep respect for creation and the creator. No one had to teach her how to worship nor, for that matter, did she need a text. She wrote her own. With her discerning eye, she saw the evidence of God's power in the smallest creatures, the simplest gesture. In the transferring of these observations to poetry she sets forth her personal creed.

II
IMPLICATIONS
This Is My Letter to the World

1. Miss Dickinson says she writes a "letter" to the world to send nature's "message." Though we often use these two words interchangeably, they have distinct meanings here. Her "letter" is her poetry. What is nature's "message"?

The Sky Is Low, the Clouds Are Mean

1. Nature is personified here in the most human of terms. In what mood do we find her?

2. "Diadem" is the most vital word in the poem. What more does it suggest to you than "crown"? What would this poem lose if, instead of this last line, Miss Dickinson had written "Yielding to every whim"?

A Little Madness in the Spring

1. What words in this poem are carefully chosen for contrast?

2. The distance from king to clown is great. Is there an equally great distance between wholesome and mad?

3. Miss Dickinson had difficulty settling on the word "experiment" in the fifth line. She tried these lines first:
   a. This sudden legacy of green.
   b. This fair apocalypse of green.
   c. This whole apocalypse of green.
   d. This whole astonishment of green.
   e. This wild experiment of green.
Has she made the wisest choice? What does "experiment" suggest to you?

Some Keep the Sabbath Going to Church

1. How does Miss Dickinson contrast her church with the town's church?

2. Can one be "going to heaven" every Sunday? Can this be inferred from her last lines?

Lightly Stepped a Yellow Star

1. "Lustral" is an archaic word meaning "purified" as it is used here. "Astral" suggests the starry sky. What word do they prepare for later in the poem?

2. Miss Dickinson knows the effectiveness of repeating a single vowel or consonant in a poem. What consonant is repeated in a way that ties all these lines together more surely than even rhyme could do?

I Never Saw a Moor

We are asked to make a comparison between the two halves of this poem. Why is it vital that the poet has not *seen* a moor or sea?

Observations and Comment

Society perplexed Emily Dickinson.
She seldom felt comfortable in large groups of people,
and yet she had a keen ear and eye for society's deficiencies. In these poems
her comments are terse, accurate, and perceptive. The first two deal
with social behavior. The last three are more general observations
on the nature of language, revery, and happiness.

Much Madness Is Divinest Sense

Much madness is divinest sense
To a discerning eye;
Much sense the starkest madness.
'Tis the majority
In this, as all, prevails.
Assent, and you are sane;
Demur,—you're straightway dangerous,
And handled with a chain.

Poems, 1890

Go Not Too Near a House of Rose

Go not too near a house of rose,
The depredation of a breeze
Or inundation of a dew
Alarms its walls away;
Nor try to tie the butterfly,
Nor climb the bars of ecstasy.
In insecurity to lie
Is joy's insuring quality.

Letters, 1894

To Make a Prairie It Takes a Clover and One Bee

To make a prairie it takes a clover and one bee,—
One clover, and a bee
And revery.
The revery alone will do
If bees are few.

Poems, 1896

Success Is Counted Sweetest

Success is counted sweetest
By those who ne'er succeed.
To comprehend a nectar
Requires sorest need.

Not one of all the purple host   5
Who took the flag today
Can tell the definition
So clear, of victory,

As he, defeated, dying,
On whose forbidden ear   10
The distant strains of triumph
Break, agonized and clear.

Poems, 1890

A Word Is Dead

A word is dead
When it is said,
Some say.
I say it just
Begins to live
That day.

Poems, 1896

I
SOCIETY AND THE INDIVIDUAL

As a recluse, Emily Dickinson had little contact with the citizens of Amherst other than her close friends, neighbors, and family. Yet she must have been a good listener. She had strong opinions about

Success Is Counted Sweetest

Success is counted sweetest
By those who ne'er succeed.
To comprehend a nectar
Requires sorest need.

Not one of all the purple host   5
Who took the flag today
Can tell the definition
So clear, of victory,

As he, defeated, dying,
On whose forbidden ear   10
The distant strains of triumph
Break, agonized and clear.

Poems, 1890

A Word Is Dead

A word is dead
When it is said,
Some say.
I say it just
Begins to live
That day.

Poems, 1896

I
SOCIETY AND THE INDIVIDUAL

As a recluse, Emily Dickinson had little contact with the citizens of Amherst other than her close friends, neighbors, and family. Yet she must have been a good listener. She had strong opinions about society's decrees, what was fashionable and not fashionable, what the world expects of us, what we ask of ourselves. She would have shared with a man like Thoreau, had she known him, a strong distrust of majority opinion and mass media.

II
IMPLICATIONS
Much Madness Is Divinest Sense

1. What is the paradox, or apparent contradiction, on which this poem is built? To appreciate it you must be certain you understand how the poet uses the words "discerning" and "demur."

2. In line 5, the poet employs a casual parenthetical phrase: "as all." What do these two seemingly unimportant words add to the major statement of the poem?

Go Not Too Near a House of Rose

1. A "house of rose" is an inspired image for the opening line of this poem. Where are sibilant *s*'s repeated in the next lines?

2. More than the sounds, the implications of "house" of rose are important. "Walls" can be connected in a literal sense. But can one "alarm" walls away literally? How has the poet chosen an oblique way of suggesting that a rose is fragile?

3. How is tying a butterfly a clear restatement of the proposition of the first line?

4. "Rose" and "butterfly" are concrete nouns. What abstract word does the poet substitute for them?

5. Explain the poet's conclusion.

Success Is Counted Sweetest

1. Here Miss Dickinson reverses her usual tack. She states a proposition in the first two lines and then illustrates it. How are "nectar" and "need" closely tied to the opening lines?

2. Lines 5–12 are one sentence. The strains of triumph are agony for the dying man to hear, yet he knows better than any of the victors what victory means. How do you make a connection between this image and "nectar/need" of the first stanza?

Portraits

Emily Dickinson might not have thought of these four poems
as "portraits," but read as a group they demonstrate her immense power
for personifying a train or a bird or even the wind. One need not share
her enthusiasm for her subject to appreciate the sharpness
of her description and the intensity of the language. She makes us *see*
common objects as clearly as she does.

A Bird Came Down the Walk

A bird came down the walk;
He did not know I saw;
He bit an angle-worm in halves
And ate the fellow, raw.

And then he drank a dew 5
From a convenient grass,
And then hopped sidewise to the wall
To let a beetle pass.

He glanced with rapid eyes
That hurried all abroad,— 10
They looked like frightened beads, I thought;
He stirred his velvet head

Like one in danger; cautious,
I offered him a crumb,
And he unrolled his feathers 15
And rowed him softer home

Than oars divide the ocean,
Too silver for a seam,
Or butterflies, off banks of noon,
Leap, plashless, as they swim. 20

Poems, 1891

A Narrow Fellow in the Grass

A narrow fellow in the grass
Occasionally rides;
You may have met him,—did you not,
His notice sudden is.

The grass divides as with a comb, 5
A spotted shaft is seen;
And then it closes at your feet
And opens further on.

He likes a boggy acre,
A floor too cool for corn. 10
Yet when a child, and barefoot,
I more than once, at morn,

Have passed, I thought, a whip-lash
Unbraiding in the sun,—
When, stooping to secure it, 15
It wrinkled, and was gone.

Several of nature's people
I know, and they know me;
I feel for them a transport
Of cordiality; 20

But never met this fellow,
Attended or alone,
Without a tighter breathing,
And zero at the bone.

Poems, 1891

The Wind Tapped Like a Tired Man

The wind tapped like a tired man,
And like a host, "Come in,"
I boldly answered; entered then
My residence within

A rapid, footless guest,   5
To offer whom a chair
Were as impossible as hand
A sofa to the air.

No bone had he to bind him,
His speech was like the push   10
Of numerous humming-birds at once
From a superior bush.

His countenance a billow,
His fingers, if he pass
Let go a music, as of tunes   15
Blown tremulous in glass.

He visited, still flitting;
Then, like a timid man,
Again he tapped—'twas flurriedly—
And I became alone.   20

Poems, 1891

To fit its sides, and crawl between,
Complaining all the while   10
In horrid, hooting stanza;
Then chase itself down hill

And neigh like Boanerges;[1]
Then, punctual as a star,
Stop—docile and omnipotent—   15
At its own stable door.

Poems, 1891

---

1. **Boanerges**\ˈbō·ə ˈněr·jēz\ literally, sons of thunder; name given by Jesus to sons of Zebedee; used to refer to forceful preacher.

IMPLICATIONS

A Bird Came Down the Walk

1. Why is the kind of bird Miss Dickinson observes never made clear?

2. How do you know that the poet is more interested in the manner in which he flies away than in why he rejects the crumb?

A Narrow Fellow in the Grass

1. For four stanzas, this poem is chiefly description, and accurate description it is. "Spotted shaft" and "whip-lash" are not ordinary terms to describe a snake. Why are they memorable here?

2. The last stanza sets up opposition to the earlier noncommittal description. What is Miss Dickinson's feeling about the snake?

The Wind Tapped Like a Tired Man

1. The heart of this poem is movement; the wind is here and gone. Hence, what seems to be the author's main intention in this poem?

2. What similes (stated or implied) add extra dimensions to the movement and manners of the wind?

I Like to See It Lap the Miles

1. What image does Miss Dickinson use for the train? Why is it most appropriate?

2. Considering the image used for the train, one line seems out of place: "Complaining all the while/In horrid, hooting stanza." How do you explain it?

I Like to See It Lap the Miles

I like to see it lap the miles,
And lick the valleys up,
And stop to feed itself at tanks;
And then, prodigious, step

Around a pile of mountains,   5
And, supercilious, peer
In shanties by the sides of roads;
And then a quarry pare

627

Love

To be fully appreciated, these five poems
must *not* be read biographically. Emily Dickinson is talking here
of common feelings: absence, parting, arrival, life alone, life shared.
If she gives these ordinary occasions special meaning, it is more
as a responsive poet than as one particular woman in a New England town
in the mid-nineteenth century. She speaks of emotions
all of us feel and try to understand.

Elysium Is as Far as to

Elysium[1] is as far as to
The very nearest room,
If in that room a friend await
Felicity or doom.

What fortitude the soul contains,
That it can so endure
The accent of a coming foot,
The opening of a door!

Poems, 1890

----
1. **Elysium**\ĭ ᴧlĭzh·ē·əm\ in Greek mythology, land of
the blessed dead.

Alter? When the Hills Do

Alter? When the hills do.
Falter? When the sun
Question if his glory
Be the perfect one.

Surfeit? When the daffodil
Doth of the dew:
Even as herself, O friend!
I will of you!

Poems, 1890

It Might Have Been Lonelier

It might have been lonelier
Without the loneliness;
I'm so accustomed to my fate
Perhaps the other—peace—

Would interrupt the dark,   5
And crowd the little room—
Too scant, by cubits, to contain
The Sacrament of Him.

I am not used to hope:
I might intrude upon   10
Its sweet parade, blaspheme the place
Ordained to suffering.

It might be easier
To fail with land in sight
Than gain my blue peninsula—   15
To perish—of delight.

My Life Had Stood
a Loaded Gun

My life had stood a loaded gun
In corners, till a day
The owner passed—identified,
And carried me away.

And now we roam the sov'reign woods,   5
And now we hunt the doe—
And every time I speak for him
The mountains straight reply.

And do I smile, such cordial light
Upon the valley glow—   10
It is as a Vesuvian face
Had let its pleasure through.

And when at night, our good day done,
I guard my master's head,
'Tis better than the eider duck's   15
Deep pillow to have shared.

To foe of his I'm deadly foe,
None stir the second time
On whom I lay a yellow eye
Or an emphatic thumb.   20

Though I than he may longer live,
He longer must than I,
For I have but the art to kill—
Without the power to die.

We Learned
the Whole of Love

We learned the whole of love,
The alphabet, the words,
A chapter, then the mighty book—
Then revelation closed.

But in each other's eyes   5
An ignorance beheld
Diviner than the childhood's,
And each to each a child

Attempted to expound
What neither understood.   10
Alas, that wisdom is so large
And truth so manifold!

I
BEYOND FRIENDSHIP

The more we read of Emily Dickinson's life, the more remarkable it seems to us that this impressionable but shy Amherst lady could have known as much as she did about love and friendship. Some poems seem to be written directly to or for a particular person; yet we have no clues that she ever received encouragement from male visitors, or at least not the kind that could lead her to use words like "doom" and "fate" and the "alphabet" of love. This group of poems attests clearly to the great powers of a poet's imagination.

II
IMPLICATIONS

Elysium Is as Far as to

1. What is the author's opening definition of paradise? How is it related to the word "if" in the third line?

2. What part does anticipation play in joy?

Alter? When the Hills Do

1. The pattern of the poem is familiar: three questions, three answers. Why are the comparisons apt?

2. How do the strong rhymes help to bring the poem's force to bear on the most important word: you?

It Might Have Been Lonelier

1. Show how the first two lines are the inspiration of all that follows.

2. Do you believe she really means the last stanza? Would she rather live alone in the "little room" than together on the "blue peninsula"?

We Learned the Whole of Love

1. How is this poem built on a paradox?

2. Wisdom and truth are here more spiritual than intellectual. How could the language of the eyes be as necessary to the spirit as verbal language is to reading "the mighty book"?

My Life Had Stood a Loaded Gun

1. This poem is far more complex than the others in this group. The loaded gun as a symbol for the poet's life is easy enough, but what happens after the "owner" claims the gun?

2. Do "yellow eye" and "emphatic thumb" carry out the basic metaphor of life as a gun?

3. The last stanza is tricky. Read it carefully. The gun may outlive the owner; that is credible enough. But what impasse will develop if the owner dies and the gun (that is, the poet's life) cannot expire? What irony lies in placing "kill" so close to "die" in the last stanza?

Loss and Death

Emily Dickinson tried not to sentimentalize her life.
She could become coy on occasion, but she never became maudlin,
in spite of the long years she spent in solitude. These poems speak
a brutal truth about loneliness, one she felt from her heart,
and in their forthright language they impress on the reader
the cruelty of separation and the finality of death.

They Say That "Time Assuages"

They say that "time assuages,"—
Time never did assuage;
An actual suffering strengthens,
As sinews do, with age.

Time is a test of trouble,
But not a remedy.
If such it prove, it prove too
There was no malady.

Poems, 1896

My Life Closed Twice Before Its Close

My life closed twice before its close;
It yet remains to see
If Immortality unveil
A third event to me,

So huge, so hopeless to conceive,
As these that twice befell.
Parting is all we know of heaven,
And all we need of hell.

Poems, 1896

If You Were Coming in the Fall

If you were coming in the fall,
I'd brush the summer by
With half a smile and half a spurn,
As housewives do a fly.

If I could see you in a year,   5
I'd wind the months in balls,
And put them each in separate drawers,
Until their time befalls.

If only centuries delayed,
I'd count them on my hand,   10
Subtracting till my fingers dropped
Into Van Dieman's land.[1]

If certain, when this life was out
That yours and mine should be,
I'd toss it yonder like a rind,   15
And taste eternity.

---

1. **Van Dieman's**\văn ᴬdē·mənz\ **land,** former name for
Tasmania, a state of Australia, in the poet's day considered to be extremely remote from Amherst, Mass.

But now, all ignorant of the length
Of time's uncertain wing,
It goads me, like the goblin bee,
That will not state its sting.   20

Poems, 1890

Because I Could Not Stop for Death

Because I could not stop for Death,
He kindly stopped for me;
The carriage held but just ourselves
And Immortality.

We slowly drove, he knew no haste,   5
And I had put away
My labor, and my leisure too,
For his civility.

We passed the school where children played
Their lessons scarcely done;   10
We passed the fields of gazing grain,
We passed the setting sun.

We paused before a house that seemed
A swelling in the ground;
The roof was scarcely visible,   15
The cornice but a mound.

Since then 'tis centuries; but each
Feels shorter than the day
I first surmised the horses' heads
Were toward eternity.   20

Poems, 1890

I
IMPLICATIONS
They Say That "Time Assuages"

With what commonplace saying is the poet taking issue?

My Life Closed Twice Before Its Close

Miss Dickinson may be referring in line 1 to two loves she lost during her lifetime. Does it matter that we cannot be certain?

If You Were Coming in the Fall

How does the time "build" in this poem?

Because I Could Not Stop for Death

What metaphor has Miss Dickinson used for Death? How does she maintain it throughout the poem?

II
TECHNIQUES
Selection of Significant Details

A novelist has several hundred pages in which to build the atmosphere and setting for his narrative. A short-story writer must work faster in his relatively confining space. The poet, unless he is writing epics or dramas, is even more restrained and thus must make each word count. Emily Dickinson took upon herself the tightest of restrictions when she chose the four-line stanza, the two- or three-stanza poem. Her form is so miniature that she must register sharp, immediate impressions or her thought barely has a chance to expand.

Being the skillful worker she is, Miss Dickinson developed several devices to concentrate details rather than generalities in the reader's mind. Note first the poem "Some Keep the Sabbath Going to Church." Here she wisely groups details to give the reader a clear view of *her* church: bobolink, orchard, wings, bird song implied in singing sexton, God preaching, a short sermon. Now look at "The Wind Tapped Like a Tired Man." Here she casts her details into similes: like a tired man, like a host, like the push of numerous humming-birds, his fingers as of tunes, like a timid man. The reader must help the poet make these comparisons in his mind's eye.

If you inspect closely "I Like to See It Lap the Miles," you will notice how the details accumulate rapidly as the train rolls through the countryside:

from valleys to tanks, from a pile of mountains (not a range but a *pile*) to shanties, then on to quarries, and down hills to the stable door. Finally, turn to "If You Were Coming in the Fall." Here the poet chooses the homeliest details to describe the passage of time and uses them in unlikely, therefore arresting, ways: summer brushed away like a fly, months rolled into balls, centuries counted on fingers, life tossed away like the rind of fruit.

Choose the Dickinson poems which please you most and look at them closely, give them a second and third reading. John Crowe Ransom, a contemporary American poet, once said he enjoyed poetry for the logical irrelevancy of its local details. Miss Dickinson would have understood the paradox implied in a logical irrelevancy. Her local details may, at first glance, seem strange to you. What, for example, have a rose and a butterfly to do with ecstasy, you might ask. But give the poem a chance to assert itself on its own terms—above all, on its own terms, not yours—and you will discover the joys of connotations, those meanings that cluster around words beyond the standard dictionary meanings.

Roses have petals. Houses have walls. A "house of rose" is more than a "rose," because the phrase suggests all the fragility contained within a rose *just* as walls contain a house. And when Emily Dickinson writes that dew and breeze can alarm away the walls of this house, she is implying more than she could in a simple statement that a wind will destroy the petals of a rose. But she lets you make the inference. In the same way, she wants you to move from rose to butterfly to ecstasy. And when you have connected these three details, her last two lines become crystal clear. Fragile beauty is fleeting. "Nothing gold can stay," Robert Frost says. The details vary; the implications are often the same. Without carefully wrought details, poems are skim milk.

The pleasure of discovering significant details on your own is a main part of reading poetry. Look at the following poems and consider the specific adjectives and the important nouns in their lines:

"A Bird Came Down the Walk"
"A Narrow Fellow in the Grass"
"My Life Had Stood a Loaded Gun."

A mere listing is not enough. What are the connotations of these details, the suggested meanings behind the words?

THE SEARCH FOR VALUES

For all of us, much of life is routine. We get up in the morning. We dress and have breakfast. We go to school or to work. We relax in the evening. We go to bed. It is much the same round, day after day. There are a few accents—a trip, a special party, an occasional big event like a birth, a marriage, or a death. Now and then we may be especially happy or especially sad. But most of the time our feelings do not run to extremes.

There are many ways to view Andrew Wyeth's "Christina's World," but you should know that Christina was crippled and deeply unhappy: her world was isolated and stripped of promise.

A popular song of another generation asked, "Why was I born? Why am I living?" These are nagging questions, kept usually just below the surface of our minds. But they point to the real, human need for finding ways to tie the fragments of our lives together, to form patterns that will give our lives day-by-day significance, to give meaning to our lives by directing all our actions toward something which we value above all else.

This need to find meaning and values may well be more acute for Americans than for others because of certain factors in our background. Americans came from many parts of the world to find a new way of life, and each second generation found itself cut off—at least in part—from the customs, the beliefs, the patterns of life that were shared by its ancestors, who had perhaps lived for centuries in one place. The new American often gained more freedom, but he lost a great deal of security.

In time, the rich resources of America provided for many the opportunity to achieve material possessions and material security. But as this type of security became relatively commonplace, more and more people grew to realize that they had to find something more in order to achieve a real sense of fulfillment. Emerson wrote, "Things are in the saddle and ride mankind." Thoughtful men wanted mankind in the saddle, riding things; they knew that materialism was not the key to happiness.

By the twentieth century, materialism was only one of many concerns of thinking Americans. Large-scale wars at first, and later the harrowing, ever-present possibility of a nuclear holocaust, seemed to reduce man's stature; to some, he seemed no more than a pebble at the mercy of Chance. The "Age of Anxiety" was born; it is still very much alive today.

Though the typical person certainly suffers anxiety and is aware of nagging doubts about his life and its direction, it has been the writer, with his talent for observation and expression, who has made vivid for us modern man's search for values, who has put into words our feeling that man must seek fundamental values and live by them. Sometimes the writer has painted extremely gloomy and pessimistic pictures; yet even the most pessimistic portraits may bring knowledge and self-awareness and thus may lead to change rather than despair. More often, however, the writer has questioned and probed for positive answers to common human problems; he has sought values that will help man not only to endure but to prevail.

How should a man live? What should he value? There are
a variety of answers to questions like these, but most people would agree
that every person has a right to pursue happiness in his own way.
But what is happiness? The answer to this question is crucial,
for it depends upon our concept of the fundamental nature of man,
and it profoundly affects the way we order our lives.

Happiness

WILLIAM LYON PHELPS

No matter what may be one's nationality, sex, age, philosophy, or religion, everyone wishes either to become or to remain happy. Hence definitions of happiness are interesting. One of the best was given in my senior year at college by President Timothy Dwight: "The happiest person is the person who thinks the most interesting thoughts."

This definition places happiness where it belongs—within and not without. The principle of happiness should be like the principle of virtue; it should not be dependent on things, but be part of personality. Suppose you went to a member of a state legislature and offered him five hundred dollars to vote for a certain bill. Suppose he kicked you out of his office. Does that prove that he is virtuous? No; it simply proves that you can't buy him for five hundred. Suppose you went to the same man a month later and offered him a million dollars —that is, instead of making him a present, you make him and his family independent for life, for the best thing about having money is that if you have it you don't have to think about it. Suppose now, after listening to this offer, he should hesitate. That would mean he was already damned. He is not only not virtuous, he

knows nothing about virtue. Why? Because his virtue is dependent not on any interior standard but on the size of the temptation. If the temptation is slight, he can resist; if large, he weakens. Such virtue is like being brave when there is no danger, generous when you have nothing to give, cheerful when all is well, polite when you are courteously treated.

So far as it is possible—it is not always possible—happiness should be like virtue. It should be kept or lost, not by exterior circumstances but by an inner standard of life. Yet many people who read this article will lose their happiness before next Sunday, though I hope they recover it. But why lose it even for a season? There are people who carry their happiness as a foolish woman carries a purse of money in her hand while walking on a crowded thoroughfare. The first man who is quick with his fingers, nimble with his feet, and untrammelled by conscience can and will take the purse away and disappear with it. He will have separated the woman and her money. Now if one's happiness is like that, an exterior thing, dependent on an enemy's volition, on any one of a thousand accidents to which we are all exposed—the happiness can be lost.

If the happiest person is the person who thinks the most interesting thoughts, then the mind is more important than either of these tremendous blessings, wealth and health. I never indulge in slighting remarks about money, because if I did I should be a hypocrite. Money is a blessing; I should be glad to distribute a large sum to every one of my readers, of course reserving the usual commission. But money is not the chief factor in happiness. If it were, then everybody who had money would be happy and everyone without it would be unhappy; but there are so many wealthy people who are unhappy and so many poor people who are cheerful, that money, however important or desirable, is not the determining cause. It would be folly to speak slightingly of health. No one realizes what a blessing health is until one has lost it; then one has to devote time and energy and money to recover it. Anyone who is careless of his health is a traitor; because one's usefulness to do good in the world is usually seriously lessened by poor health. Yet even health is not the *sine qua non*. People without it think they would be perfectly happy if they were well. A man with a toothache imagines that everyone in the world without a toothache is happy; but it is not so. There are healthy people who are not happy; and there are invalids whose face, eyes, and conversation reveal an inner source of happiness that enables them to triumph over bodily ills. They have overcome the world, the flesh, and the devil.

I should be sorry to lose what money I have; but unfortunate as it might be, such a loss would not permanently destroy my happiness. I should be sorry to be run over by an automobile and lose my right leg; but such a loss would not permanently destroy my happiness. Why not? Because my happiness is centered neither in my purse nor my leg, but in my mind, my personality. The Irish dramatist St. John Ervine[1] lost a leg in the war. I asked him which he would prefer—to have two sound and healthy legs again and not to be able to write novels and plays, or to be as he is now, with only one leg, but an accomplished man of letters. He did not hesitate. He said there was no comparison possible; he would far rather be a one-legged writer than a two-legged something else. "And yet," he murmured thoughtfully, "I do miss that leg."

There is another important consideration. If the happiest person is the person who thinks the most interesting thoughts, then we grow happier as we grow older.

I know that such a statement runs counter to the generally expressed opinion. The majority of novels and poems and the common gossip of society assume that youth is the golden time of life.

When I was an undergraduate, a distinguished man addressed us; and he said emphatically: "Young gentlemen, make the most of these four years; for they are the happiest years you will ever know." The remark was given to us with that impressiveness that so often accompanies a falsehood. For it was a falsehood. My classmates and I have been out of college nearly forty years; most of us are happier now than then.

The belief that youth is the happiest time of life is founded on a fallacy—on a false definition of happiness. Many people think that to be free from physical pain and mental worry is perfection; knowing that as we grow older our physical pains and mental worries are apt to increase, they assume that youth is the happiest time of life. We are, of course, all animals; but we ought not to be merely animals. I suppose that in the case of animals youth is the happiest time of life; a puppy is happier than an old rheumatic hound; a young jackass braying in the pasture is presumably happier than an old donkey laboriously drawing a cart; but these are merely animals and lack man's greatest gift —the possibility of development.

Those who say that childhood is the happiest time are unconsciously postulating the animal definition: A child is happiest because he is healthy and has no worries; when he is cold, somebody covers him; when he is hungry, somebody feeds him; when he is sleepy, somebody puts him to bed. Yes, but when he is *not* sleepy, somebody puts him to bed. There is the

---

1. **St. John Ervine,** associated with the famous Abbey Theatre in Dublin.

shadow on the sunny years; there is the fly in the ointment.

Personally I had rather have a few worries and aches, and go to bed when I choose. A child is as dependent as a slave. If you would rather be a healthy, well-fed slave than an independent man, you will prefer childhood to maturity. A child is at the mercy of adults both physically and mentally. They are stronger than he and can force him to do whatever they wish; they are cleverer than he and can invariably outwit him.

There are some foolish people who say, "Well, I mean to grow old gracefully." It is impossible; it can't be done. Let us admit it because it is true; old people are not graceful. Grace belongs to youth and is its chief charm. The poet Browning hints that youth has beauty and grace because youth would be intolerable without it. Young people are decorative; that is why we like them. They are slender, agile, fair, and graceful, because nobody could stand them if they were otherwise. It would be horrible if boys and girls, knowing as little as they do, were also bald, grayheaded, fat, wrinkled, and double-chinned; then they would be unendurable. But nature has so arranged matters that young people are physically attractive until they acquire some brains and sense and are able to live by their wits; then they lose these superficial advantages. As responsibility grows, beauty and grace depart. The child sits on your knee and reaches for your watch. You smile, and say, "Nice baby, can't have de watch!" But when he is thirty and reaches for your watch, you put him in jail. More is expected of us, more is demanded of us as we grow older; nothing is more tragic therefore than a woman of mature years with the mind of a child. There is in civilized society no place for her.

It is also often said that as we grow older we lose our enthusiasms. This need not be true; it is never true with right-minded individuals. There is a fallacy lurking in such a statement. The fallacy is this: We confound the loss of the object that aroused the enthusiasm with the loss of enthusiasm—a very different thing. Things that excite children often fail to arouse mature men and women—which is not a sign that maturity has lost sensitiveness to excitement; it may have lost interest in childish things. When I was a child, the happiest day in the year was the Fourth of July. It was not illusory happiness; it was real; it was authentic bliss. Its cause? On the Fourth of July Mother allowed me to rise at midnight, go out on the street, and yell till daybreak. Think of it! I, who was usually forced to retire at eight, was out on a city street at three in the morning, shrieking and yelling! It was delirious joy. Now suppose you should tell me that tomorrow I may rise at midnight and yell till daybreak. I decline. Does that mean I have lost my happiness or my enthusiasm? No; it means that I don't care to rise at midnight. During the daytime of the glorious Fourth I used to shoot off firecrackers hour after hour with undiminished zeal. Every now and then I would see a very old man, about thirty-two, come along, and I would offer him an opportunity to share my delight. He always declined. "Poor fellow!" I reflected. "Life is over for him. He has lost his happiness." It never occurred to me that people over thirty had any fun. I supposed they had to go through the routine of life but had no pleasure in it.

The fact that a girl of three is enchanted by the gift of a doll, and the same girl at seventeen insulted by it, does not mean that the girl at seventeen has lost either her happiness or her enthusiasm; but that the enthusiasm, formerly aroused by dolls, is now stimulated by something else.

If the happiest person is the person who thinks the most interesting thoughts, we are bound to grow happier as we advance in years, because our minds have more and more interesting thoughts. A well-ordered life is like climbing a tower; the view halfway up is better than the view from the base, and it steadily becomes finer as the horizon expands.

Herein lies the real value of education. Advanced education may or may not make men and women more efficient; but it enriches personality, increases the wealth of the mind, and hence brings happiness. It is the finest insurance against old age, against the growth of physical disability, against the lack of animal delights. No matter how many there may be in our family, no matter how many friends we may have, we are in a certain sense forced to lead a lonely life, because we have all the days of our existence to live with ourselves. How essential it is then in youth to acquire some intellectual or artistic tastes, in order to furnish the mind, to be able to live inside a mind with attractive and interesting pictures on the walls. It is better to be an interesting personality than to be an efficient machine. The reason so many go to destruction by the alcoholic route is because they cannot endure themselves; the moment they are left alone with their empty minds they seek for a stimulant, for something to make them forget the waste places. Others rush off to the movies, run anywhere always seeking something to make them forget themselves.

Higher education, the cultivation of the mind, is more important for women than for men, because women are more often left alone. A large part of masculine activity is merely physical; men run around like dogs. But a woman, even in these emancipated days, is forced to be alone more than a man. Now take the instance of a girl who has been brought up happily in a large family, with plenty of neighbors and friends, whose bright days pass in happy activities and recreations; she is married to a surburbanite in New Jersey. Every morning he takes the 7:37 train to New York and does not return till the 6:48 in the evening. The young wife, rudely transplanted from a cheerful home, is placed in an empty house in a town where she knows no one, and is alone all day. Heaven help her if she has no mental interests, no ideas, no interesting thoughts. I have no desire to underestimate the worth of physical comfort or the charm of youth; but if happiness really and truly consisted in physical ease and freedom from care, then the happiest individual would not be either a man or a woman. It would be, I think, an American cow. American cows and American dogs are ladies and gentlemen of leisure; in Europe they hitch them up and make them draw loads. Take, therefore, an average day in the life of an American cow, and we shall see that it is not far from the commonly accepted ideal of human happiness. The cow rises in the morning, and with one flick of her tail her toilet is completed for the whole day. There is a distinct advantage over humanity. It takes the average woman—and it ought to—about three quarters of an hour every single day to arrange her appearance.

The cow does not have to brush her teeth; the cow does not have to bob her hair; the cow does not have to carry a compact; the cow does not have to select appropriate and expensive garments. One flick, and she is ready. And when she is ready, breakfast is ready.

She does not have to light the kitchen fire herself or to mourn because the cook has left without notice. The grass is her cereal breakfast and the dew thereupon is the cream. After eating for an hour or so, she gazes meditatively into the middle distance, querying first, whether that grass yonder is lusher and greener than this, and second, if it be so, whether peradventure it is worth the trouble to walk there and take it. Such an idea as that will occupy the mind of a cow for three hours.

After grazing, like Goethe,[2] without haste and without rest, she reaches by noon the edge of a stream. "Lo, here is water; what hinders me from descending and slaking my thirst?" She descends about waist-deep into the cooling stream; and after external and internal refreshment she walks with dignity to a spreading tree, and sits calmly down in the shade. There and then she begins to chew the cud. Cows are never perturbed by introspection or by worry.

---

2. Johann Wolfgang von **Goethe** (1749–1832), a great German poet. "Without haste and without rest" is a translation of a line from Goethe's poem of that title.

There are no agnostic cows, no Fundamentalist or Modernist[3] cows; cows do not worry about the income tax or the League of Nations; a cow does not lie awake at night wondering if her son is going to the devil in some distant city.

Cows have none of the thoughts that inflict upon humanity distress and torture. I have observed many cows, and there is in their beautiful eyes no perplexity; their serene faces betray no apprehension or alarm; they are never even bored. They have found some happy *via media*[4] by which they escape from Schopenhauer's[5] dilemma, who insisted that man had only the vain choice between the suffering of unsatisfied desire and the languor of ennui.

Well, since the daily life of an American cow is exactly the existence held up to us as ideal—physical comfort with no pains and no worries—wouldn't you like to be a cow? Very few human beings would be willing to change into cows, which must mean only one thing: Life, with all its sorrows, cares, perplexities, and heartbreaks, is more interesting than bovine placidity, hence more desirable. The more interesting it is, the happier it is. And the happiest person is the person who thinks the most interesting thoughts.

---

3. **agnostic**\ăg ˄nɔ•stĭk\ one who believes that truth may exist but is probably unknowable by man. **Fundamentalists,** Christians who hold that everything in the Bible is literally true. **Modernists,** those who are considered religious radicals by their opponents in that they question such matters as the authorship, the date of composition, and the authenticity of the Bible. The names, Fundamentalist and Modernist, first came into general usage in the 1920's.
4. **via media,** middle road.
5. **Schopenhauer's** \˄shō•pən 'hau•ər\ **dilemma.** A dilemma is the necessity of choosing between two equally undesirable alternatives. Here is one example of the human dilemma as Schopenhauer, the pessimistic German philosopher, saw it: "as soon as want and suffering permit rest to man, ennui (boredom) is at once so near that he necessarily requires diversion" which may again plunge him into want and suffering.

I
HAPPINESS AND THE NATURE OF MAN

Phelps points out that a person's definition of happiness depends in large measure on his conception of the essential nature of man. If one were to emphasize man's animal nature, he would define happiness largely in physical terms—what makes a cow happy would make a man happy. If one emphasizes the intellectual side of man's nature, as does Phelps, he naturally defines happiness in intellectual terms. If one stressed man's spiritual nature, how might he define happiness?

II
IMPLICATIONS

In the following statements, explain Phelps' meanings and discuss your opinion of them.

1. "The happiest person is the person who thinks the most interesting thoughts."

2. . . . , nature has so arranged matters that young people are physically attractive until they acquire some brains and sense and are able to live by their wits; then they lose these superficial advantages.

3. A well-ordered life is like climbing a tower; the view half-way up is better than the view from the base, and it steadily becomes finer as the horizon expands.

4. . . . we are in a certain sense forced to lead a lonely life, because we have all the days of our existence to live with ourselves.

III
TECHNIQUES

Structure

A literary work is in certain ways like a building. Both the architect's office building or house and the writer's essay, story, or poem have a *planned framework* or *structure*, and the materials used—the wood or the words—are arranged according to this planned framework.

This essay is well structured. Note, for example, that it both begins and ends with the author's favorite definition of happiness; this is certainly not an accident.

Within the essay there is also evidence of considerable planning. Consider, for instance, paragraphs 6 and 15. How do they relate to each other and to the essay as a whole? What other evidence of a planned framework or structure do you find?

THE SEARCH
FOR
VALUES

The artist, like the writer, is deeply sensitive
to the values of his society. He tends either to accept
and support them or to reject them with contempt and satire.
In either case, by his vivid responses to the values
upon which we operate, he dramatizes what is or what should be
and so plays a vital part in our search for values.
This gallery is divided among those who protest inadequate values,
those who suggest larger life goals,
and those who point poignantly to the search itself.

RED STAIRWAY
Ben Shahn

Like other contemporary painters in this gallery, Ben Shahn has devoted much
of his artistic life to exploring the tragic situations men have created
by blindly operating on short-term values. Yet as his contribution
to this gallery indicates, he is strangely optimistic about the human spirit.
THE RED STAIRWAY is packed with symbolism,
the crippled old man blindly, valiantly, climbing the blood-red stairs
which will deliver him after great effort only a small pointless distance from where he
starts. The broken wall of civilization is only a thin shell remaining
above endless rubble where a lone man works to move the stones with as little purpose
as the old man's climb. Is the artist suggesting that men give up?

Consider the elements within the LIGHT OF THE WORLD: the church to the left, the distant factory and fields, the dead tree, the hypnotised people on the checkered deck, and the bizarre structure holding the flashing globe. Where have men been, and where are they headed? Have men passed up beauty for a light that could go out? This is a picture which you must read for yourself.

LIGHT OF THE WORLD
Peter Blume
1932, Oil, Collection
of the Whitney Museum
of American Art, New York

Driftwood, emptiness, decay, and a shabby string of colored lights. What is it John Atherton would have us realize? What brings men here, and where should they be headed?

CHRISTMAS EVE
John Atherton
Collection, The Museum
of Modern Art, New York,
Purchase

These are the people who have nowhere to go but up. The artist has given us a portrait gallery
of human types characterized by famous paintings which tell us of their several goals.
From right to left the paintings are Boucher's MADAME DE POMPADOUR, romantic and feminine
and much more; a Daumier cartoon of social satire; Picasso's GIRL IN A MIRROR,
boldly abstract, defiant and searching; an old and realistic portrait
of a man like the merchants of the sixteenth-century Dutch painters, traditional and prosperous;
Grant Wood's AMERICAN GOTHIC, classic commentary on tightly held values
but with a serenity not to be mistaken; Millet's THE SOWER with its agricultural values;
and a modern piece of social, industrial protest.
Even the children hold their own painted hopes for life.
The paintings become metaphors to express the traditions and goals
of the people who have selected them.

WORKERS AND PAINTINGS
Honore Sharer
Collection, The Museum of Modern Art, New York, Gift of Lincoln Kirstein

A general
is welcomed home;
a group
has been gathered
for a formal banquet,
but the artist
has no mercy
in his satire.
In his own search
for values
he has found
these people
and their way
of life inadequate.

WELCOME HOME
Jack Levine

THE
PEACEABLE
KINGDOM
Edward Hicks

Early in the nineteenth century,
Edward Hicks was a traveling Quaker
preacher. Self-taught and full of simple hope,
he chose a passage from the Bible,
Isaiah 11: 6–9, as the basis
for THE PEACEABLE KINGDOM:
The wolf also shall dwell with the lamb,
and the leopard shall lie down with the kid;
and the calf and the young lion
and the fatling together;
and a little child shall lead them. . . .
They shall not hurt nor destroy
in all my holy mountain: For the earth
shall be full of the knowledge of the Lord,
As the waters cover the sea.

He filled his picture with his values, real and symbolic. In the background William Penn makes his treaty with the Indians.

Abstract and lyrical, the paintings of Feininger offer values more positive even than hope. He taught at the renowned industrial art school, the Bauhaus in Germany, where men search earnestly for applications for the values that they hold.

CHURCH OF THE MINORITIES (II), 1926
Lyonel Feininger

OUT FOR THE CHRISTMAS TREES
Grandma Moses

From a tradition fast disappearing
came the memory paintings of a rural childhood.
Simple, childlike, bright, and full of joy,
the pictures of Grandma Moses contain a set of values
hard to hold onto in today's world.

Through most of the nineteenth century, optimism was
the prevalent mood of Americans, but then came the First World War,
and some say we've never been the same since. Whatever the truth may be,
it is certain that many American writers of the 1920's and 1930's
were pessimistic. Unlike Phelps, who asks what happiness is, many of
these writers ask whether happiness is possible or life has meaning.
Their answers are often negative. One of the best-known postwar poets
was T. S. Eliot. In the following poem he pictures man of the mid-twenties
as empty of animal, intellectual, and spiritual values; he sees men
as essentially hollow, living in "death's dream kingdom." Note, too,
how his poetic method—sudden shifts, violent contrasts, apparent disunity—
tends to underscore the chaos of modern life. Because he uses many symbols
and allusions to history and literature, you may not get a very clear
understanding of this poem on your first reading, but it should be possible
to feel the emotional impact of what life is like in "death's dream kingdom."

The Hollow Men

T. S. ELIOT

A penny for the Old Guy

I

We are the hollow men
We are the stuffed men
Leaning together
Headpiece filled with straw. Alas!
Our dried voices, when   5
We whisper together
Are quiet and meaningless
As wind in dry grass
Or rats' feet over broken glass
In our dry cellar   10

Shape without form, shade without colour,
Paralysed force, gesture without motion;

Those who have crossed
With direct eyes, to death's other Kingdom
Remember us—if at all—not as lost   15
Violent souls, but only
As the hollow men
The stuffed men.

II

Eyes I dare not meet in dreams
In death's dream kingdom   20
These do not appear:
There, the eyes are
Sunlight on a broken column
There, is a tree swinging
And voices are   25
In the wind's singing
More distant and more solemn
Than a fading star.

Let me be no nearer
In death's dream kingdom   30
Let me also wear
Such deliberate disguises
Rat's coat, crowskin, crossed staves
In a field
Behaving as the wind behaves   35
No nearer—

Not that final meeting
In the twilight kingdom

III

This is the dead land
This is cactus land   40
Here the stone images[1]
Are raised, here they receive
The supplication of a dead man's hand
Under the twinkle of a fading star.

Is it like this   45
In death's other kingdom
Waking alone
At the hour when we are
Trembling with tenderness
Lips that would kiss   50
Form prayers to broken stone.

IV

The eyes are not here
There are no eyes here
In this valley of dying stars
In this hollow valley   55
This broken jaw of our lost kingdoms

In this last of meeting places
We grope together
And avoid speech
Gathered on this beach of the tumid[2] river   60

Sightless, unless
The eyes reappear
As the perpetual star
Multifoliate rose[3]
Of death's twilight kingdom   65
The hope only
Of empty men.

V

Here we go round the prickly pear
Prickly pear prickly pear
Here we go round the prickly pear   70
At five o'clock in the morning.

Between the idea
And the reality

T. S. ELIOT *Wyndham Lewis*

Between the motion
And the act   75
Falls the Shadow
                    For Thine is the Kingdom

Between the conception
And the creation
Between the emotion   80
And the response
Falls the Shadow
                    Life is very long

Between the desire
And the spasm   85
Between the potency

---

1. **stone images**, the idols, Wealth and Power, before which the poet felt America, after World War I, was bowing down.
2. **tumid**\ˈtū·məd\ **river**, the swollen river.
3. **Multifoliate**\məl·tĭ ˈfō·lē·ət\ **rose,** literally, the many leafed rose, perhaps many petaled. In religious symbolism a rose with many petals is the symbol of a soul unfolding spiritually. In Dante's *Paradise*, the multifoliate rose is his great metaphor for his vision of God.

And the existence
Between the essence
And the descent
Falls the Shadow   90

       For Thine is the Kingdom

For Thine is[4]
Life is
For Thine is the

This is the way the world ends   95
This is the way the world ends
This is the way the world ends
Not with a bang but a whimper.

I

THE PLIGHT OF MODERN MAN

Perhaps the two most significant characteristics of "the hollow men" are fear and impotence; and note that they are fearful and powerless with respect to *all* aspects of life. They are afraid to love, afraid to think, afraid to worship or face the afterlife. These fears are symbolized in Part V by the "Shadow" that falls between ideas and realities, emotions and responses, and so on. The shadow breaks the chain before fulfillment in much the same way as the Lord's Prayer is broken off just before it reaches the words, "the Power and the Glory."

II

IMPLICATIONS

Answer the following questions:

1. "A penny for the Old Guy" is what English children say when they go from door to door soliciting money for fireworks on Guy Fawkes Day (November 5). Look up Guy Fawkes or the Gunpowder Plot in a reference book and report your findings. How does knowledge of Fawkes help you to better understand the poem?

2. What is meant by a "lost violent soul"? Why are the hollow men not in this category?

3. Note as many instances as you can of the

hollow men's inability to communicate effectively. How is this inability related to their fate?

4. Could a man with sincere religious convictions be a hollow man in Eliot's sense?

III

TECHNIQUES

Symbolism

A symbol is an object or condition used to suggest something else. The moon, for example, may suggest romance, mystery, purity, imagination, and other things. The particular meaning or group of meanings that the symbol calls forth will depend upon how the writer handles the symbol, upon the contexts in which it occurs.

In the last stanza of Part IV, Eliot says that the hollow men are "Sightless, unless/ The eyes reappear/ As the perpetual star/ Multifoliate rose/ Of death's twilight kingdom. . . ." The condition of sightlessness is a symbol of the lack of vision of the hollow men—they do not "see" with imagination or spirit as a poet or a saint or prophet does. The lines say, however, that they might have such a vision if the eyes should reappear as "the perpetual star."

In trying to determine the symbolic meaning of this star the reader must call up those characteristics of stars that fit the present context. He might note that stars give light; they are in the heavens; and this star at least is "perpetual." Now especially in the context of this poem a perpetual light in the heavens can hardly fail to suggest God, or at least some aspect of divinity.

Since "Multifoliate rose" is an appositive to the perpetual star, it must suggest much the same meanings. Roses, of course, suggest brightness and beauty; and further support for thinking of the multifoliate rose as a symbol of divinity comes from the fact that this is what it symbolizes in the final portion of Dante's *Divine Comedy*, a famous poem of which Eliot was deeply fond.

1. Briefly, then, the lines suggest that the hollow men would cease to be hollow if they had spiritual vision. What are some of the advantages and disadvantages of the fact that the poet has chosen to communicate this idea symbolically rather than literally?

2. Discuss the symbolism of the earlier lines in Part IV, paying special attention to the meaning of "eyes" and to the physical setting.

---

4. **For Thine is,** note that the poem falters as from weariness. The hollow men cannot pray.

Poems by Robinson

Although Edwin Arlington Robinson was born in 1869
and began writing poems at a very early age, he was largely unknown
until the end of the First World War. It may be partly because he shared
the pessimistic spirit of many writers of the 1920's and 1930's
that he became known about that time as America's greatest living poet.
As you read the following poems, ask yourself about the parallels
and contrasts between his subjects and Eliot's "hollow men."

Miniver Cheevy

Miniver Cheevy, child of scorn,
   Grew lean while he assailed the seasons;
He wept that he was ever born,
   And he had reasons.

Miniver loved the days of old   5
   When swords were bright and steeds were prancing;
The vision of a warrior bold
   Would set him dancing.

Miniver sighed for what was not,
   And dreamed, and rested from his labors;   10
He dreamed of Thebes[1] and Camelot,[2]
   And Priam's neighbors.[3]

---

1. **Thebes**\thēbz\ the poet may have had in mind either of two ancient cities named Thebes. The more ancient (2000 B.C.) was in Egypt, its site marked by the magnificent ruins of Karnak and Luxor. The other ancient city of Thebes was in Greece and is frequently mentioned in Greek legends. It was destroyed, 336 B.C., by Alexander the Great.
2. **Camelot**\ˈcă·mə·lŏt\ was the beautiful rose-red city built for King Arthur by the magician Merlin.
3. **Priam's neighbors,** the kings of those neighboring cities in Asia Minor who helped Priam, king of Troy, resist the invading Greeks in the Trojan War, of which Homer tells in the *Iliad*.

Miniver mourned the ripe renown
    That made so many a name so fragrant;
He mourned Romance, now on the town,   15
    And Art, a vagrant.

Miniver loved the Medici,[4]
    Albeit he had never seen one;
He would have sinned incessantly
    Could he have been one.   20

Miniver cursed the commonplace
    And eyed a khaki suit with loathing;
He missed the mediaeval grace
    Of iron clothing.

Miniver scorned the gold he sought,   25
    But sore annoyed was he without it;
Miniver thought, and thought, and thought,
    And thought about it.

Miniver Cheevy, born too late,
    Scratched his head and kept on thinking;   30
Miniver coughed, and called it fate,
    And kept on drinking.

EDWIN ARLINGTON ROBINSON

---

4. **Medici**\ˈmĕ·də·chē\ a family of bankers and states-
men under whose tolerant rule Florence, Italy, became
one of the most beautiful cities in the world. In power
from the fifteenth to the eighteenth centuries, they were
patrons and protectors of the scholars and artists who
made Florence the very center of the Italian Renaissance.

Richard Cory

Whenever Richard Cory went down town,
    We people on the pavement looked at him:
He was a gentleman from sole to crown,
    Clean favored, and imperially slim.

And he was always quietly arrayed,   5
    And he was always human when he talked;
But still he fluttered pulses when he said,
    "Good-morning," and he glittered when he walked.

And he was rich—yes, richer than a king,
    And admirably schooled in every grace: 10
In fine, we thought that he was everything
    To make us wish that we were in his place.

So on we worked, and waited for the light,
    And went without the meat, and cursed the bread;
And Richard Cory, one calm summer night,   15
    Went home and put a bullet through his head.

EDWIN ARLINGTON ROBINSON

I
THE ALIENATED

Although Robinson's characters seem to share the fate of Eliot's hollow men, they differ from them in several ways. One important difference is that the Robinson character has dreams, even ideals often, but he has been cheated of their realization by fate or by the society in which he lives. Another important difference is that the hollow men exist in a group while the Robinson character usually has no one to share his burden. He is desperately, tragically, alone, alienated from the community. Who is responsible for this alienation—the individual himself, the society, or both?

II
IMPLICATIONS

Discuss each of the following statements in the light of these poems and of your own experience.

1. A person must be able to live with other human beings in order to be happy.

2. Cheevy's life shows that the fact that one has a strong sense of values is not enough to secure happiness.

3. Great pain and personal tragedy cannot be shared; where such things are concerned we are all, always, alone.

4. Wealth and material possessions are probably the least important factors in human happiness.

5. In the long run a given individual has only himself to blame if he is unhappy.

III
TECHNIQUES

Structure

1. Robinson's poems tend to be highly structured. Scan at least two stanzas of each poem and describe its rhyme and rhythm scheme. What regularities do you find? Are there any irregularities?

2. Notice also Robinson's stanza divisions. Explain how they serve to frame the thought structure of the poem.

Symbolism

Not only words and phrases but also actions may have symbolic significance. Cory's suicide, for example, might be regarded as a symbolic act, for it suggests a meaning beyond the act itself. Discuss the meaning of this suicide and the meanings of some of the other symbolic acts in the Robinson poems.

IV
WORDS

A. 1. Having discussed synonyms and antonyms previously, we should also consider *homonyms,* words that are identical in spelling and sound, but different in meaning. For example, *base* in the "base of the column" and *base* in "base remark" are alike in sound and spelling but different in origins and meanings. *Bay* in "a bay mare" and *bay* in "bay window" are also homonyms. Find several other examples.

2. Words that are alike in spelling but different in origin, meaning, and pronunciation are *homographs.* The word *tear* in "a tear fell from his eye" and *tear* in "a tear in his shirt" are homographs, as are *wind* in "wind the clock" and *wind* in "the wind from the east." List other examples.

3. *Homophones* are words which sound alike but differ in origin, meaning, and spelling. For each word, find another word that sounds just like it: *fair, break, minor, male, tale, right, bare, wait, plain, site.*

4. Now, if possible, find an antonym for each member of the pairs of homophones you listed for number three. You will find that some members of the pairs do not have antonyms.

5. Each of the following words has a homonym. Look up the origins and meanings of *bear, list, guy, mean, halter, hide, last, launch, mole, nob, palatine, palm, pan, scale.*

B. Every person has not one vocabulary but three vocabularies: a speaking vocabulary, words used when speaking with friends and with the public; a reading vocabulary, words we recognize in print; and a writing vocabulary, words we use in writing. The vocabularies are not identical; but certain words, what we might call general vocabulary, are common to all three. The guiding principle in one's choice of words is appropriateness. Is the word or phrase appropriate to the audience and to the situation? In previous exercises, we divided usage into two broad, general classes: *standard* and *nonstandard*. The term *nonstandard* generally refers to grammatical constructions, expressions and pronunciations rejected by most educated speakers. Unfortunately there is no universally recognized system of identifying the varieties of standard English. The different varieties indicate different styles for different occasions and different audiences. One variety is no better than another if each is appropriate to the subject and to the situation.

The varieties of standard English refer more to word choice than to pronunciation, spelling, or grammar. The guiding principle of word choice is appropriateness to the subject and to the situation. For example, synonyms or near synonyms sometimes indicate degrees of refinement. Classify these words as formal, general and/or informal: *fear, terror, trepidation; goodness, virtue, probity.*

Study your own vocabulary. Make a list of the words you have learned from your readings in this book. Take an essay you have written recently and classify the nouns you have used. Try substituting nouns from your "other" vocabularies.

The American writers of the generation that fought
World War I have been called "the lost generation." The term
refers to the fact that they felt they could no longer maintain
the traditional values of the past. Ernest Hemingway was
one of the chief spokesmen of this lost generation, and in this story
he gives the reader a glimpse of the effects of the First World War
on the men who fought it.

In Another Country

ERNEST HEMINGWAY

In the fall the war was always there, but we did not go to it any more. It was cold in the fall in Milan[1] and the dark came very early. Then the electric lights came on, and it was pleasant along the streets looking in the windows. There was much game hanging outside the shops, and the snow powdered in the fur of the foxes and the wind blew their tails. The deer hung stiff and heavy and empty, and small birds blew in the wind and the wind turned their feathers. It was a cold fall and the wind came down from the mountains.

We were all at the hospital every afternoon, and there were different ways of walking across the town through the dusk to the hospital. Two of the ways were alongside canals, but they were long. Always, though, you crossed a bridge across a canal to enter the hospital. There was a choice of three bridges. On one of them a woman sold roasted chestnuts. It was warm, standing in front of her charcoal fire, and the chestnuts were warm afterward in your pocket. The hospital was very old and very beautiful, and you entered through a gate and walked across a courtyard and out a gate on the other side. There were usually funerals starting from the courtyard. Beyond the old hospital were the new brick pavilions, and there we met every afternoon and were all very polite and interested in what was the matter, and sat in the machines[2] that were to make so much difference.

The doctor came up to the machine where I was sitting and said: "What did you like best to do before the war? Did you practice a sport?"

I said: "Yes, football."

"Good," he said. "You will be able to play football again better than ever."

My knee did not bend and the leg dropped straight from the knee to the ankle without a calf, and the machine was to bend the knee and make it move as in riding a tricycle. But it did not bend yet, and instead the machine lurched when it came to the bending part. The doctor said: "That will all pass. You are a fortunate young man. You will play football again like a champion."

In the next machine was a major who had a little hand like a baby's. He winked at me when the doctor examined his hand, which was between two leather straps that bounced up and down and flapped the stiff fingers, and said: "And will I too play football, captain-doctor?"

1. **Milan**\mĭ ▲lan\ a large industrial city in northern Italy.
2. **machines**, physical therapy machines for exercising the damaged muscles of the wounded.

He had been a very great fencer, and before the war the greatest fencer in Italy.

The doctor went to his office in the back room and brought a photograph which showed a hand that had been withered almost as small as the major's, before it had taken a machine course, and after was a little larger. The major held the photograph with his good hand and looked at it very carefully. "A wound?" he asked.

"An industrial accident," the doctor said.

"Very interesting, very interesting," the major said, and handed it back to the doctor.

"You have confidence?"

"No," said the major.

There were three boys who came each day who were about the same age I was. They were all three from Milan, and one of them was to be a lawyer, and one was to be a painter, and one had intended to be a soldier, and after we were finished with the machines, sometimes we walked back together to the Café Cova, which was next door to the Scala.[3] We walked the short way through the communist quarter because we were four together. The people hated us because we were officers, and from a wine shop some one called out, "A basso gli ufficiali!"[4] as we passed. Another boy who walked with us sometimes and made us five wore a black silk handkerchief across his face because he had no nose then and his face was to be rebuilt. He had gone out to the front from the military academy and had been wounded within an hour after he had gone into the front line for the first time. They rebuilt his face, but he came from a very old family and they could never get the nose exactly right. He went to South America and worked in a bank. But this was a long time ago, and then we did not any of us know how it was going to be afterward. We only knew then that there was always the war, but that we were not going to it any more.

We all had the same medals, except the boy with the black silk bandage across his face, and he had not been at the front long enough to get any medals. The tall boy with a very pale face who was to be a lawyer had been a lieutenant

of Arditi[5] and had three medals of the sort we each had only one of. He had lived a very long time with death and was a little detached. We were all a little detached, and there was nothing that held us together except that we met every afternoon at the hospital. Although, as we walked to the Cova through the tough part of town, walking in the dark, with light and singing coming out of the wine shops, and sometimes having to walk into the street when the men and women would crowd together on the sidewalk so that we would have had to jostle them to get by, we felt held together by there being something that happened that they, the people who disliked us, did not understand.

We ourselves all understood the Cova, where it was rich and warm and not too brightly lighted, and noisy and smoky at certain hours, and there were always girls at the tables and the illustrated papers on a rack on the wall. . . .

The boys at first were very polite about my medals and asked me what I had done to get them. I showed them the papers, which were written in very beautiful language and full of *fratellanza*[6] and *abnegazione*,[7] but which really said, with the adjectives removed, that I had been given the medals because I was an American. After that their manner changed a little toward me, although I was their friend against outsiders. I was a friend, but I was never really one of them after they had read the citations, because it had been different with them and they had done very different things to get their medals. I had been wounded, it was true; but we all knew that being wounded, after all, was really an accident. I was never ashamed of the ribbons, though, and sometimes, after the cocktail hour, I would imagine myself having done all the things they had done to get their medals; but walking home at night through the empty streets with the cold wind and all the shops

---

3. **Scala**\ˈskä·lä\ La Scala, a famous opera house in Milan.

4. **A basso gli ufficiali**, "Down with officers."

5. **Arditi**\är ˈdē·tē\ Italian storm troops.

6. **fratellanza**\frä·tə ˈlän·zə\ brotherhood.

7. **abnegazione**\ab·nəg·ə ˈzō·nē\ self-sacrifice.

closed, trying to keep near the street lights, I knew that I would never have done such things, and I was very much afraid to die, and often lay in bed at night by myself, afraid to die and wondering how I would be when I went back to the front again.

The three with the medals were like hunting hawks; and I was not a hawk, although I might seem a hawk to those who had never hunted; they, the three, knew better and so we drifted apart. But I stayed good friends with the boy who had been wounded his first day at the front, because he would never know now how he would have turned out; so he could never be accepted either, and I liked him because I thought perhaps he would not have turned out to be a hawk either.

The major, who had been the great fencer, did not believe in bravery, and spent much time while we sat in the machines correcting my grammar. He had complimented me on how I spoke Italian, and we talked together very easily. One day I had said that Italian seemed such an easy language to me that I could not take a great interest in it; everything was so easy to say. "Ah, yes," the major said. "Why, then, do you not take up the use of grammar?" So we took up the use of grammar, and soon Italian was such a difficult language that I was afraid to talk to him until I had the grammar straight in my mind.

The major came very regularly to the hospital. I do not think he ever missed a day, although I am sure he did not believe in the machines. There was a time when none of us believed in the machines, and one day the major said it was all nonsense. The machines were new then and it was we who were to prove them. It was an idiotic idea, he said, "a theory, like another." I had not learned my grammar, and he said I was a stupid impossible disgrace, and he was a fool to have bothered with me. He was a small man and he sat straight up in his chair with his right hand thrust into the machine and looked straight ahead at the wall while the straps thumped up and down with his fingers in them.

"What will you do when the war is over if it is over?" he asked me. "Speak grammatically!"

"I will go to the States."

"Are you married?"

"No, but I hope to be."

"The more of a fool you are," he said. He seemed very angry. "A man must not marry."

"Why, Signor Maggiore?"[8]

"Don't call me 'Signor Maggiore.'"

"Why must not a man marry?"

"He cannot marry. He cannot marry," he said angrily. "If he is to lose everything, he should not place himself in a position to lose that. He should not place himself in a position to lose. He should find things he cannot lose."

He spoke very angrily and bitterly, and looked straight ahead while he talked.

"But why should he necessarily lose it?"

"He'll lose it," the major said. He was looking at the wall. Then he looked down at the machine and jerked his little hand out from between the straps and slapped it hard against his thigh. "He'll lose it," he almost shouted. "Don't argue with me!" Then he called to the attendant who ran the machines. "Come and turn this damned thing off."

He went back into the other room for the light treatment and the massage. Then I heard him ask the doctor if he might use his telephone and he shut the door. When he came back into the room, I was sitting in another machine. He was wearing his cape and had his cap on, and he came directly toward my machine and put his arm on my shoulder.

"I am so sorry," he said, and patted me on the shoulder with his good hand. "I would not be rude. My wife has just died. You must forgive me."

"Oh——" I said, feeling sick for him. "I am *so* sorry."

He stood there biting his lower lip. "It is very difficult," he said. "I cannot resign myself."

He looked straight past me and out through the window. Then he began to cry. "I am utterly unable to resign myself," he said, and

---

8. **Signor Maggiore**\sē•nyōr ma ⁺jō•rē\ Mister Major.

choked. And then crying, his head up looking at nothing, carrying himself straight and soldierly, with tears on both his cheeks and biting his lip, he walked past the machines and out the door.

The doctor told me that the major's wife, who was very young and whom he had not married until he was definitely invalided out of the war, had died of pneumonia. She had been sick only a few days. No one expected her to die. The major did not come to the hospital for three days. Then he came at the usual hour, wearing a black band on the sleeve of his uniform. When he came back, there were large framed photographs around the wall, of all sorts of wounds before and after they had been cured by the machines. In front of the machine the major used were three photographs of hands like his that were completely restored. I do not know where the doctor got them. I always understood we were the first to use the machines. The photographs did not make much difference to the major because he only looked out of the window.

I

THE LOST GENERATION AND THE WAR

There are at least three important effects of the war on the characters in this story: (1) It has caused them wounds; (2) it has given them a sense of detachment from life; and (3) it has made them pessimistic and unhappy. These may all be considered characteristics of the lost generation, but an interesting question is, To what extent are they due to the war?

Why does Hemingway bring in the death of the major's wife, an event that has virtually nothing to do with the war?

II

IMPLICATIONS

Discuss the following questions in some detail.

1. Is the First World War a symptom of the loss of traditional values or is it the cause of the loss?

2. What does the first sentence of the story mean? In particular, what does "there" mean and why does the narrator use the adverb "always"?

3. The first photograph the doctor shows the major is a picture of an industrial wound rather than a war wound. What does this fact suggest regarding the author's conception of "wounds" in the story?

4. What is ironic about the fact that the major did not marry until he was "definitely invalided out of the war."

5. Who is the main character of this story—the major or the narrator?

6. What does the title of the story mean?

7. It is sometimes said that Hemingway was a believer in the philosophy known as "stoicism," one of whose basic ideas is stated below. Do you think that Hemingway would agree with this statement? Would any of his characters accept it, or might they be happier if they did?

"Ask not that events should happen as you will, but let your will be that events should happen as they do, and you shall have peace."

III

TECHNIQUES

Symbolism

Should such things as the dead animals, the hospital, and the machines be treated as symbols, or not? If the reader does decide to interpret them symbolically, how does he know whether he has the "right" interpretation?

1. Suppose that one person (A) supports the opinion that the hospital suggests a zoo because the men who go there are like dumb animals in that they communicate very little and are concerned chiefly with the body rather than with the mind or soul. Why might you agree or disagree with this person?

2. Another person (B) might point out that the story is set in Italy, a country that contains many very old and very beautiful churches. He might then note that the hospital is described as "very old and very beautiful." In addition he might point out that the soldiers do not go to this hospital—they walk around it and go instead to the "new brick pavilions" where the machines are kept.

Accordingly, then, the soldiers would be passing up or rejecting traditional Christian values (symbolized by the hospital) in favor of the values of the machine age (symbolized by the brick pavilions).

On what grounds might B argue that his interpretation is better than A's?

Traditionally, Americans have always looked to the future.
Complete happiness, prosperity, and fulfillment are the promises
of future progress, we earnestly believe. But will tomorrow be happier?
Will it be free of "hollow men" and "lost generations"? Can man escape
the past and start a new life?

The Million-Year Picnic

RAY BRADBURY

Somehow the idea was brought up by Mom that perhaps the whole family would enjoy a fishing trip. But they weren't Mom's words; Timothy knew that. They were Dad's words, and Mom used them for him somehow.

Dad shuffled his feet in a clutter of Martian pebbles and agreed. So immediately there was a tumult and a shouting, and very quickly the camp was tucked into capsules and containers, Mom slipped into traveling jumpers and blouse, Dad stuffed his pipe full with trembling hands, his eyes on the Martian sky, and the three boys piled yelling into the motorboat, none of them really keeping an eye on Mom and Dad, except Timothy.

Dad pushed a stud.[1] The water boat sent a humming sound up into the sky. The water shook back and the boat nosed ahead, and the family cried, "Hurrah!"

Timothy sat in the back of the boat with Dad, his small fingers atop Dad's hairy ones, watching the canal twist, leaving the crumbled place behind where they had landed in their small family rocket all the way from Earth. He remembered the night before they left Earth, the hustling and hurrying, the rocket that Dad had found somewhere, somehow, and the talk of a vacation on Mars. A long way to go for a vacation, but Timothy said nothing because of his younger brothers. They came to Mars and now, first thing, or so they said, they were going fishing.

Dad had a funny look in his eyes as the boat went up-canal. A look that Timothy couldn't figure. It was made of strong light and maybe a sort of relief. It made the deep wrinkles laugh instead of worry or cry.

So there went the cooling rocket, around a bend, gone.

"How far are we going?" Robert splashed his hand. It looked like a small crab jumping in the violet water.

Dad exhaled. "A million years."

"Gee," said Robert.

"Look, kids." Mother pointed one soft long arm. "There's a dead city."

They looked with fervent anticipation, and the dead city lay dead for them alone, drowsing in a hot silence of summer made on Mars by a Martian weatherman.

And Dad looked as if he was pleased that it was dead.

It was a futile spread of pink rocks sleeping on a rise of sand, a few tumbled pillars, one lonely shrine, and then the sweep of sand again. Nothing else for miles. A white desert around the canal and a blue desert over it.

Just then a bird flew up. Like a stone thrown across a blue pond, hitting, falling deep, and vanishing.

1. **stud**\stəd\ here, a rod or pin projecting from the motor of the boat.

657

Dad got a frightened look when he saw it. "I thought it was a rocket."

Timothy looked at the deep ocean sky, trying to see Earth and the war and the ruined cities and the men killing each other since the day he was born. But he saw nothing. The war was as removed and far off as two flies battling to the death in the arch of a great high and silent cathedral. And just as senseless.

William Thomas wiped his forehead and felt the touch of his son's hand on his arm, like a young tarantula, thrilled. He beamed at his son. "How goes it, Timmy?"

"Fine, Dad."

Timothy hadn't quite figured out what was ticking inside the vast adult mechanism beside him. The man with the immense hawk nose, sunburnt, peeling—and the hot blue eyes like agate marbles you play with after school in summer back on Earth, and the long thick columnar legs in the loose riding breeches.

"What are you looking at so hard, Dad?"

"I was looking for Earthian logic, common sense, good government, peace, and responsibility."

"All that up there?"

"No. I didn't find it. It's not there any more. Maybe it'll never be there again. Maybe we fooled ourselves that it was ever there."

"Huh?"

"See the fish," said Dad, pointing.

There rose a soprano clamor from all three boys as they rocked the boat in arching their tender necks to see. They *oohed* and *ahed*. A silver ring fish floated by them, undulating, and closing like an iris, instantly, around food particles, to assimilate them.

Dad looked at it. His voice was deep and quiet.

"Just like war. War swims along, sees food, contracts. A moment later—Earth is gone."

"William," said Mom.

"Sorry," said Dad.

They sat still and felt the canal water rush cool, swift, and glassy. The only sound was the motor hum, the glide of water, the sun expanding the air.

"When do we see the Martians?" cried Michael.

"Quite soon, perhaps," said Father. "Maybe tonight."

"Oh, but the Martians are a dead race now," said Mom.

"No, they're not. I'll show you some Martians, all right," Dad said presently.

Timothy scowled at that but said nothing. Everything was odd now. Vacations and fishing and looks between people.

The other boys were already engaged making shelves of their small hands and peering under them toward the seven-foot stone banks of the canal, watching for Martians.

"What do they look like?" demanded Michael.

"You'll know them when you see them." Dad sort of laughed, and Timothy saw a pulse beating time in his cheek.

Mother was slender and soft, with a woven plait of spun-gold hair over her head in a tiara, and eyes the color of the deep cool canal water where it ran in shadow, almost purple, with flecks of amber caught in it. You could see her thoughts swimming around in her eyes, like fish—some bright, some dark, some fast, quick, some slow and easy, and sometimes, like when she looked up where Earth was, being nothing but color and nothing else. She sat in the boat's prow, one hand resting on the side lip, the other on the lap of her dark blue breeches, and a line of sunburnt soft neck showing where her blouse opened like a white flower.

She kept looking ahead to see what was there, and, not being able to see it clearly enough, she looked backward toward her husband, and through his eyes, reflected then, she saw what was ahead; and since he added part of himself to this reflection, a determined firmness, her face relaxed and she accepted it and she turned back, knowing suddenly what to look for.

Timothy looked too. But all he saw was a straight pencil line of canal going violet through a wide shallow valley penned by low, eroded hills, and on until it fell over the sky's

Orion Nebula

edge. And this canal went on and on, through cities that would have rattled like beetles in a dry skull if you shook them. A hundred or two hundred cities dreaming hot summer-day dreams and cool summer-night dreams . . .

They had come millions of miles for this outing—to fish. But there had been a gun on the rocket. This was a vacation. But why all the food, more than enough to last them years and years, left hidden back there near the rocket? Vacation. Just behind the veil of the vacation was not a soft face of laughter, but something hard and bony and perhaps terrifying. Timothy could not lift the veil, and the two other boys were busy being ten and eight years old, respectively.

"No Martians yet. Nuts." Robert put his V-shaped chin on his hands and glared at the canal.

Dad had brought an atomic radio along, strapped to his wrist. It functioned on an old-fashioned principle: you held it against the bones near your ear and it vibrated singing or talking to you. Dad listened to it now. His face looked like one of those fallen Martian cities, caved in, sucked dry, almost dead.

Then he gave it to Mom to listen. Her lips dropped open.

"What——" Timothy started to question, but never finished what he wished to say.

For at that moment there were two titanic, marrow-jolting explosions that grew upon themselves, followed by a half dozen minor concussions.

Jerking his head up, Dad notched the boat speed higher immediately. The boat leaped and jounced and spanked. This shook Robert out of his funk[2] and elicited yelps of frightened but ecstatic joy from Michael, who clung to Mom's legs and watched the water pour by his nose in a wet torrent.

Dad swerved the boat, cut speed, and ducked the craft into a little branch canal and under an ancient, crumbling stone wharf that smelled of crab flesh. The boat rammed the wharf hard enough to throw them all forward, but no one was hurt, and Dad was already twisted to see if the ripples on the canal were enough to map their route into hiding. Water lines went across, lapped the stones, and rippled back to meet each other, settling, to be dappled by the sun. It all went away.

Dad listened. So did everybody.

Dad's breathing echoed like fists beating against the cold wet wharf stones. In the shadow, Mom's cat eyes just watched Father for some clue to what next.

Dad relaxed and blew out a breath, laughing at himself.

"The rocket, of course. I'm getting jumpy. The rocket."

Michael said, "What happened, Dad, what happened?"

"Oh, we just blew up our rocket, is all," said Timothy, trying to sound matter-of-fact. "I've heard rockets blow up before. Ours just blew."

"Why did we blow up our rocket?" asked Michael. "Huh, Dad?"

"It's part of the game, silly!" said Timothy.

"A game!" Michael and Robert loved the word.

"Dad fixed it so it would blow up and no one'd know where we landed or went! In case they ever came looking, see?"

"Oh boy, a secret!"

"Scared by my own rocket," admitted Dad to Mom. "I am nervous. It's silly to think there'll ever be any more rockets. Except *one*, perhaps,

if Edwards and his wife get through with *their* ship."

He put his tiny radio to his ear again. After two minutes he dropped his hand as you would drop a rag.

"It's over at last," he said to Mom. "The radio just went off the atomic beam. Every other world station's gone. They dwindled down to a couple in the last few years. Now the air's completely silent. It'll probably remain silent."

"For how long?" asked Robert.

"Maybe—your great-grandchildren will hear it again," said Dad. He just sat there, and the children were caught in the center of his awe and defeat and resignation and acceptance.

Finally he put the boat out into the canal again, and they continued in the direction in which they had originally started.

It was getting late. Already the sun was down the sky, and a series of dead cities lay ahead of them.

Dad talked very quietly and gently to his sons. Many times in the past he had been brisk, distant, removed from them, but now he patted them on the head with just a word and they felt it.

"Mike, pick a city."

"What, Dad?"

"Pick a city, Son. Any one of these cities we pass."

"All right," said Michael. "How do I pick?"

"Pick the one you like the most. You, too, Robert and Tim. Pick the city you like best."

"I want a city with Martians in it," said Michael.

"You'll have that," said Dad. "I promise." His lips were for the children, but his eyes were for Mom.

They passed six cities in twenty minutes. Dad didn't say anything more about the explosions; he seemed much more interested in having fun with his sons, keeping them happy, than anything else.

Michael liked the first city they passed, but this was vetoed because everyone doubted

---

2. funk\fəŋk\ depression.

quick first judgments. The second city nobody liked. It was an Earth Man's settlement, built of wood and already rotting into sawdust. Timothy liked the third city because it was large. The fourth and fifth were too small and the sixth brought acclaim from everyone, including Mother, who joined in the Gees, Goshes, and Look-at-thats!

There were fifty or sixty huge structures still standing, streets were dusty but paved, and you could see one or two old centrifugal fountains still pulsing wetly in the plazas. That was the only life—water leaping in the late sunlight.

"This is the city," said everybody.

Steering the boat to a wharf, Dad jumped out.

"Here we are. This is ours. This is where we live from now on!"

"From now on?" Michael was incredulous. He stood up, looking, and then turned to blink back at where the rocket used to be. "What about the rocket? What about Minnesota?"

"Here," said Dad.

He touched the small radio to Michael's blond head. "Listen."

Michael listened.

"Nothing," he said.

"That's right. Nothing. Nothing at all any more. No more Minneapolis, no more rockets, no more Earth."

Michael considered the lethal revelation and began to sob little dry sobs.

"Wait a moment," said Dad the next instant. "I'm giving you a lot more in exchange, Mike!"

"What?" Michael held off the tears, curious, but quite ready to continue in case Dad's further revelation was as disconcerting as the original.

"I'm giving you this city, Mike. It's yours."

"Mine?"

"For you and Robert and Timothy, all three of you, to own for yourselves."

Timothy bounded from the boat. "Look, guys, all for *us!* All of *that!*" He was playing the game with Dad, playing it large and playing it well. Later, after it was all over and

things had settled, he could go off by himself and cry for ten minutes. But now it was still a game, still a family outing, and the other kids must be kept playing.

Mike jumped out with Robert. They helped Mom.

"Be careful of your sister," said Dad, and nobody knew what he meant until later.

They hurried into the great pink-stoned city, whispering among themselves, because dead cities have a way of making you want to whisper, to watch the sun go down.

"In about five days," said Dad quietly, "I'll go back down to where our rocket was and collect the food hidden in the ruins there and bring it here; and I'll hunt for Bert Edwards and his wife and daughters there."

"Daughters?" asked Timothy. "How many?"

"Four."

"I can see that'll cause trouble later." Mom nodded slowly.

"Girls." Michael made a face like an ancient Martian stone image. "Girls."

"Are they coming in a rocket too?"

"Yes. If they make it. Family rockets are made for travel to the Moon, not Mars. We were lucky we got through."

"Where did you get the rocket?" whispered Timothy, for the other boys were running ahead.

"I saved it. I saved it for twenty years, Tim. I had it hidden away, hoping I'd never have to use it. I suppose I should have given it to the government for the war, but I kept thinking about Mars. . . ."

"And a picnic!"

"Right. This is between you and me. When I saw everything was finishing on Earth, after I'd waited until the last moment, I packed us up. Bert Edwards had a ship hidden, too, but we decided it would be safer to take off separately, in case anyone tried to shoot us down."

"Why'd you blow up the rocket, Dad?"

"So we can't go back, ever. And so if any of those evil men ever come to Mars they won't know we're here."

"Is that why you look up all the time?"

"Yes, it's silly. They won't follow us, ever. They haven't anything to follow with. I'm being too careful, is all."

Michael came running back. "Is this really our city, Dad?"

"The whole darn planet belongs to us, kids. The whole darn planet."

They stood there, King of the Hill, Top of the Heap, Ruler of All They Surveyed, Unimpeachable Monarchs and Presidents, trying to understand what it meant to own a world and how big a world really was.

Night came quickly in the thin atmosphere, and Dad left them in the square by the pulsing fountain, went down to the boat, and came walking back carrying a stack of paper in his big hands.

He laid the papers in a clutter in an old courtyard and set them afire. To keep warm, they crouched around the blaze and laughed, and Timothy saw the little letters leap like frightened animals when the flames touched and engulfed them. The papers crinkled like an old man's skin, and the cremation surrounded innumerable words:

"GOVERNMENT BONDS; Business Graph, 1999; Religious Prejudice: An Essay; The Science of Logistics; Problems of the Pan-American Unity; Stock Report for July 3, 1998; The War Digest . . ."

Dad had insisted on bringing these papers for this purpose. He sat there and fed them into the fire, one by one, with satisfaction, and told his children what it all meant.

"It's time I told you a few things. I don't suppose it was fair, keeping so much from you. I don't know if you'll understand, but I have to talk, even if only part of it gets over to you."

He dropped a leaf in the fire.

"I'm burning a way of life, just like that way of life is being burned clean of Earth right now. Forgive me if I talk like a politician. I am, after all, a former state governor, and I was honest and they hated me for it. Life on Earth never settled down to anything very good. Science ran too far ahead of us too quickly, and the people got lost in a mechanical wilder-

ness, like children making over pretty things, gadgets, helicopters, rockets; emphasizing the wrong items, emphasizing machines instead of how to run the machines. Wars got bigger and bigger and finally killed Earth. That's what the silent radio means. That's what we ran away from.

"We were lucky. There aren't any more rockets left. It's time you knew this isn't a fishing trip at all. I put off telling you. Earth is gone. Interplanetary travel won't be back for centuries, maybe never. But that way of life proved itself wrong and strangled itself with its own hands. You're young. I'll tell you this again every day until it sinks in."

He paused to feed more papers to the fire.

"Now we're alone. We and a handful of others who'll land in a few days. Enough to start over. Enough to turn away from all that back on Earth and strike out on a new line——"

The fire leaped up to emphasize his talking. And then all the papers were gone except one. All the laws and beliefs of Earth were burnt into small hot ashes which soon would be carried off in a wind.

Timothy looked at the last thing that Dad tossed in the fire. It was a map of the World, and it wrinkled and distorted itself hotly and went—flimpf—and was gone like a warm, black butterfly. Timothy turned away.

"Now I'm going to show you the Martians," said Dad. "Come on, all of you. Here, Alice." He took her hand.

Michael was crying loudly, and Dad picked him up and carried him, and they walked down through the ruins toward the canal.

The canal. Where tomorrow or the next day their future wives would come up in a boat, small laughing girls now, with their father and mother.

The night came down around them, and there were stars. But Timothy couldn't find Earth. It had already set. That was something to think about.

A night bird called among the ruins as they walked. Dad said, "Your mother and I will try to teach you. Perhaps we'll fail. I hope not. We've had a good lot to see and learn from. We planned this trip years ago, before you were born. Even if there hadn't been a war we would have come to Mars, I think, to live and form our own standard of living. It would have been another century before Mars would have been really poisoned by the Earth civilization. Now, of course——"

They reached the canal. It was long and straight and cool and wet and reflective in the night.

"I've always wanted to see a Martian," said Michael. "Where are they, Dad? You promised."

"There they are," said Dad, and he shifted Michael on his shoulder and pointed straight down.

The Martians were there. Timothy began to shiver.

The Martians were there—in the canal—reflected in the water. Timothy and Michael and Robert and Mom and Dad.

The Martians stared back up at them for a long, long silent time from the rippling water. . . .

I
THE SEARCH
FOR A NEW TOMORROW

On the surface it may seem as if this is a thoroughly pessimistic story: Bradbury condemns our way of life and predicts that the consequence of that life is self-destruction. On the other hand, at least one family is allowed to escape disaster, and the comments of the head of that family reveal what was wrong with the old life and suggest by implication the values upon which a new life can be built. Thus, for example, when one of his sons asks Mr. Thomas why he is looking so hard at

Earth, he says he is looking for logic, common sense, good government, peace, and responsibility. Such values will presumably be cornerstones of the family's future life on Mars, but there is also the suggestion that the same things may help to avert the disaster Bradbury predicts. The story thus can be read as a protest against the values of today, but also as an affirmation of those values that may help us to create a new tomorrow before it is too late.

II
IMPLICATIONS

Below are listed several quotations and situations from this story. Discuss them in terms of their meaning and your reactions to them.

1. The war [on Earth] was as removed and far off as two flies battling to the death in the arch of a great high and silent cathedral. And just as senseless.

2. The ceremonial burning of "all the laws and beliefs of Earth."

3. "Life on earth never settled down to anything very good."

4. The shiver and the silence as the Martians stare up at them from the canal.

5. "Science ran too far ahead of us too quickly, and the people got lost in a mechanical wilderness. . . ."

III
TECHNIQUES

Structure

One of the important aspects of the structure in many short stories is *suspense*. This is a device used to awaken and maintain the reader's interest in the outcome of the work. It may center in one or more of a number of issues: (1) The question of *what* will happen, (2) the question of *how* it will happen, (3) the question of *to whom* it will happen, and (4) the question of *when* something will happen. In this story the author provokes suspense in several ways—he raises the issue of the reasons for the trip, the somewhat mysterious behavior of the father, and the matter of what the Martians look like. Using any one of these, point out the place where the author first introduces it, how he develops it to maintain reader interest, and which of the four points mentioned above is/are concerned.

Protest and Affirmation
in Modern Poetry

One of the strongest directions in modern poetry has been
the tendency toward social criticism. But the criticism of most poets
has not been irresponsible and negative. For while poets have protested
against certain modern values or the lack of any values, they have also
tended to affirm new values or reaffirm tested values of the past.

On the morning of September 1, 1939,
the Nazi war machine moved into Poland. Two days later
England and France declared war on Germany,
and World War II had begun. What were some of the thoughts
that went through the mind of a poet at this fateful time? What values
did he feel were still worth cherishing in a chaotic world?
In the following poem the reader may glimpse into the mind of W. H. Auden
as he sat in a New York cafe on September 1, 1939.

September 1, 1939

I sit in one of the dives
On Fifty-second Street
Uncertain and afraid
As the clever hopes expire
Of a low dishonest decade:[1]   5
Waves of anger and fear
Circulate over the bright
And darkened lands of the earth,
Obsessing our private lives;
The unmentionable odour of death   10
Offends the September night.

Accurate scholarship can
Unearth the whole offence
From Luther until now
That has driven a culture mad,   15
Find what occurred at Linz,[2]
What huge imago made
A psychopathic god:[3]
I and the public know

---

1. **a low dishonest decade,** 1929–1939. These were the
years of the Great Depression which began with the
stock market crash of 1929.
2. **Linz**\lĭntz\ capital of upper Austria on the Danube
river west of Vienna. Hitler invaded Austria March 11,
1938, and annexed it two days later.
3. **a psychopathic**\sī·kə ˈpăth·ĭk\ **god,** here, a mentally
ill or unstable dictator, for example, Adolf Hitler.

What all schoolchildren learn,
Those to whom evil is done[4]
Do evil in return.

Exiled Thucydides[5] knew
All that a speech can say
About Democracy,
And what dictators do,
The elderly rubbish they talk
To an apathetic grave;[6]
Analysed all in his book,
The enlightenment driven away,
The habit-forming pain,
Mismanagement and grief:
We must suffer them all again.

Into this neutral air
Where blind skyscrapers use
Their full height to proclaim
The strength of Collective Man,
Each language pours its vain
Competitive excuse:
But who can live for long
In an euphoric dream;[7]
Out of the mirror they stare,
Imperialism's face
And the international wrong.

Faces along the bar
Cling to their average day:
The lights must never go out,
The music must always play,
All the conventions conspire
To make this fort assume
The furniture of home;
Lest we should see where we are,
Lost in a haunted wood,
Children afraid of the night
Who have never been happy or good.

The windiest militant trash
Important Persons shout
Is not so crude as our wish:
What mad Nijinsky[8] wrote
About Diaghilev[9]
Is true of the normal heart;
For the error bred in the bone

Of each woman and each man
Craves what it cannot have,
Not universal love
But to be loved alone.

From the conservative dark
Into the ethical life
The dense commuters come,
Repeating their morning vow;
"I *will* be true to the wife,
I'll concentrate more on my work,"
And helpless governors wake
To resume their compulsory game:
Who can release them now,
Who can reach the deaf,
Who can speak for the dumb?

Defenceless under the night
Our world in stupor lies;
Yet, dotted everywhere,
Ironic points of light
Flash out wherever the Just
Exchange their messages:
May I, composed like them
Of Eros[10] and of dust,
Beleaguered by the same
Negation and despair,
Show an affirming flame.

W. H. AUDEN

---

4. **those to whom evil is done.** Here, the poet may be suggesting that the Treaty of Versailles, dealing harshly with the defeated Germans, set the stage for other wars.
5. **Exiled Thucydides**\thū ˈsĭ·də·dēz\ considered the greatest historian of ancient times. After commanding an unsuccessful expedition, he went into exile. He was noted for his speeches, among them, Pericles' funeral oration.
6. **an apathetic**\ˈă·pə ˈthĕ·tĭk\ **grave.** Here, "grave" is a metonymy and stands for the soldier dead who lie in graves, indifferent now to the words of dictators.
7. **euphoric**\yū ˈfō·rĭk\ **dream**, a dream of unaccountable well-being and elation.
8. **Nijinsky**\nĭ ˈzhĭn·skē\ Waslaw (1890–1950), Russian dancer who appeared in Paris (1909) with Diaghilev's Ballet Russe but who later went insane.
9. **Diaghilev**\nĭ ˈdya·gĭ·lĕf\ Sergei Pavlovich (1872–1929), Russian ballet producer and art critic who introduced ballets adapted to orchestral works.
10. **Eros**\ˈĕr·əs\ the Greek god of love whom the Romans called Cupid.

Although Karl Shapiro himself served as a sergeant
in the South Pacific during the Second World War, he was,
nevertheless, able to sympathize with and understand the conscientious
objector, the man who refused to serve in the Armed Forces
on religious or moral grounds. At the conclusion of the following poem,
what justification does he give for defending the conscientious?

The Conscientious Objector

The gates clanged and they walked you into jail
More tense than felons but relieved to find
The hostile world shut out, the flags that dripped
From every mother's windowpane, obscene
The bloodlust sweating from the public heart,   5
The dog authority slavering at your throat.
A sense of quiet, of pulling down the blind
Possessed you. Punishment you felt was clean.

The decks, the catwalks, and the narrow light
Composed a ship. This was a mutinous crew   10
Troubling the captains for plain decencies,
A *Mayflower* brim with pilgrims headed out
To establish new theocracies to west,
A Noah's ark coasting the topmost seas
Ten miles above the sodomites and fish.   15
These inmates loved the only living doves.

Like all men hunted from the world you made
A good community, voyaging the storm
To no safe Plymouth or green Ararat;[1]
Trouble or calm, the men with Bibles prayed,   20
The gaunt politicals construed our hate.
The opposite of all armies, you were best
Opposing uniformity and yourselves;
Prison and personality were your fate.

You suffered not so physically but knew   25
Maltreatment, hunger, ennui of the mind.
Well might the soldier kissing the hot beach
Erupting in his face damn all your kind.

---

1. **Ararat**\ˈăr·ə·răt\ a mountain in Turkey where
Noah's Ark supposedly came to rest.

Yet you who saved neither yourselves nor us
Are equally with those who shed the blood   30
The heroes of our cause. Your conscience is
What we come back to in the armistice.

KARL SHAPIRO

e. e. cummings has long been identified as a critic
of materialistic values and of "man's inhumanity to man." These are
the objects of his criticism in the following poem; but though the poem
is satiric in tone and seems to be a rather general condemnation
of humanity, a close reading will reveal that cummings is also
commending the positive values of "a world of born."

pity this busy monster,
manunkind

pity this busy monster, manunkind,

not. Progress is a comfortable disease:
your victim (death and life safely beyond)

plays with the bigness of his littleness
—electrons deify one razorblade   5
into a mountainrange; lenses extend

unwish through curving wherewhen till unwish
returns on its unself.
                           A world of made
is not a world of born—pity poor flesh   10

and trees, poor stars and stones, but never this
fine specimen of hypermagical

ultraomnipotence. We doctors know

a hopeless case if—listen: there's a hell
of a good universe next door; let's go.   15

E. E. CUMMINGS

The bulk of the following poem is devoted
to a description of a juggling act, but the poet's main intention
is not descriptive. He is using the juggler and the audience's reaction
to his act to point up some important ideas about the way
most people live most of the time.

Juggler

A ball will bounce, but less and less. It's not
A light-hearted thing, resents its own resilience.
Falling is what it loves, and the earth falls
So in our hearts from brilliance,
Settles and is forgot.   5
It takes a skyblue juggler with five red balls
To shake our gravity up. Whee, in the air
The balls roll round, wheel on his wheeling hands,
Learning the ways of lightness, alter to spheres
Grazing his finger ends,   10
Cling to their courses there,
Swinging a small heaven about his ears.

But a heaven is easier made of nothing at all
Than the earth regained, and still and sole within
The spin of worlds, with a gesture sure and noble   15
He reels that heaven in,
Landing it ball by ball,
And trades it all for a broom, a plate, a table.

Oh, on his toe the table is turning, the broom's
Balancing up on his nose, and the plate whirls   20
On the tip of the broom! Damn, what a show, we cry:
The boys stamp, and the girls
Shriek, and the drum booms
And all comes down, and he bows and says goodbye.

If the juggler is tired now, if the broom stands   25
In the dust again, if the table starts to drop
Through the daily dark again, and though the plate
Lies flat on the table top,
For him we batter our hands
Who has won for once over the world's weight.   30

RICHARD WILBUR

Copyright, 1949, by Richard Wilbur. First published in *The
New Yorker*. Reprinted from his volume *Ceremony and Other
Poems* by permission of Harcourt, Brace & World, Inc.

As you might infer from lines seven and eight
in the following poem, Robinson Jeffers has been considered
one of the bitterest and most pessimistic of all modern poets. Yet even he—
who has called civilization a sickness and consciousness a disease—
is not without some measure of affirmation in his poetry.

To the Stone-Cutters

Stone-cutters fighting time with marble, you foredefeated
Challengers of oblivion
Eat cynical earnings, knowing rock splits, records fall down,
The square-limbed Roman letters
Scale in the thaws, wear in the rain. The poet as well   5
Builds his monument mockingly;
For man will be blotted out, the blithe earth die, the brave sun
Die blind and blacken to the heart:
Yet stones have stood for a thousand years, and pained thoughts found
The honey of peace in old poems.   10

ROBINSON JEFFERS

I

THE POET

AGAINST THE WORLD AS IT IS

Over eight hundred years ago the Persian poet Omar Khayyám wrote the following lines:

Ah Love! could Thou and I with Fate conspire
To grasp this sorry Scheme of Things entire,
    Would we not shatter it to bits—and then
Remold it nearer to the Heart's Desire!

The feeling expressed here is a familiar one in poetry. The poet has often protested against life as it is ("this sorry Scheme of Things") and expressed the hope that he could make it better ("Remold it nearer to the Heart's Desire"). Khayyám would begin by conspiring with Love and Fate to shatter to bits the world as it is.

The protest against life as it is echoes through the poems you have just read. Cummings, for example, protests against "a world of made," a world in which progress is judged in materialistic terms; Wilbur is protesting against human inertia. Underlying all the protest, however, you can detect, directly or indirectly, that the poet's concern is basically positive.

II

IMPLICATIONS

For each of the five poems, specify what the poet is protesting against and what—if anything—

he is affirming. Also discuss what the following lines have to do with his protest, his affirmation, or both.

1. May I, composed like them
   Of Eros and of dust,
   Beleaguered by the same
   Negation and despair,
   Show an affirming flame.   (W. H. Auden)

2.   Your conscience is
   What we come back to in the armistice.
                              (Karl Shapiro)

3.   A world of made
   is not a world of born. . . . (e. e. cummings)

4. For him we batter our hands
   Who has won for once over the world's
        weight.   (Richard Wilbur)

5. Yet stones have stood for a thousand years,
        and pained thoughts found
   The honey of peace in old poems.
                              (Robinson Jeffers)

III
TECHNIQUES

Figurative Language

The most common figures of speech are simile and metaphor. The former is usually defined as a stated comparison between two things, using *like* or *as*; a metaphor is defined as an implied comparison between two things.

It is important to note that the two things are never compared in all respects and important to see in just which respects they are being compared. Consider the following lines from the fifth stanza of Auden's "September 1, 1939":

> All the conventions conspire
> To make this fort assume
> The furniture of home;

"This fort" is clearly a metaphor involving a comparison between a fort and the cafe in which the speaker is seated. But a fort has many aspects—which should we compare with the cafe?

This is obviously a matter of the greatest importance. If a reader were to select the wrong aspect for comparison, he might completely mistake the poet's meaning. If the reader decides that the fort and cafe should be compared on the basis of physical appearance, for example, he will not understand the poet's true intention, which is not to call up a visual image at all but rather to call up the similarities in the protective qualities of the two things—just as a fort protects those within it from hostile and destructive forces without, so does the cafe protect those sitting in it from hostile ideas and realities that would shatter their complacency.

There is no magic way in which one can be certain he is selecting the proper actions, qualities, or sense appeals (or combinations of the three) for comparison, but the basic key is context. In Auden's poem, for example, the lines following those quoted clearly tell the basis on which the author wants the fort and cafe compared.

Some of the strongest social criticism in this century
has come from writers like Theodore Dreiser and Sinclair Lewis.
Lewis was especially strong in protesting against the narrowness of life
in the small midwestern towns of his time. The following story focuses
on a midwestern farmer who in spite of the fact that he has attained
comfort and security still does not feel completely happy.

Young Man Axelbrod

SINCLAIR LEWIS

The cottonwood is a tree of a slovenly and plebeian habit. Its woolly wisps turn gray the lawns and engender neighborhood hostilities about our town. Yet it is a mighty tree, a refuge and an inspiration; the sun flickers in its towering foliage, whence the tattoo of locusts enlivens our dusty summer afternoons. From the wheat-country out to the sagebrush plains between the buttes[1] and the Yellowstone it is the cottonwood that keeps a little grateful shade for sweating homesteaders.

In Joralemon we called Knute Axelbrod "Old Cottonwood." As a matter of fact, the name was derived not so much from the quality of the man as from the wide grove about his gaunt, white house and red barn. He made a comely row of trees on each side of the country road, so that a humble, daily sort of man, driving beneath them in his lumber-wagon, might fancy himself lord of a private avenue. And at sixty-five Knute was like one of his own cottonwoods, his roots deep in the soil, his trunk weathered by rain and blizzard and baking August noons, his crown spread to the wide horizon of day and the enormous sky of a prairie night.

This immigrant was an American even in speech. Save for a weakness about his j's and w's, he spoke the twangy Yankee English of the land. He was the more American because in his native Scandinavia he had dreamed of America as a land of light. Always through disillusion and weariness he beheld America as the world's nursery for justice, for broad, fair towns, and eager talk; and always he kept a young soul that dared to desire beauty.

As a lad Knute Axelbrod had wished to be a famous scholar, to learn the ease of foreign tongues, the romance of history, to unfold in the graciousness of wise books. When he first came to America he worked in a sawmill all day and studied all evening. He mastered enough book-learning to teach district school for two terms, then, when he was only eighteen, a great-hearted pity for faded little Lena Wesselius moved him to marry her. Gay enough, doubtless, was their hike by prairie-schooner to new farm-lands, but Knute was promptly caught in a net of poverty and family. From eighteen to fifty-eight he was always snatching children away from death or the farm away from mortgages.

He had to be content—and generously content he was—with the second-hand glory of his children's success and, for himself, with pilfered hours of reading—that reading of big, thick, dismal volumes of history and economics

1. **butte**\byūt\ an isolated hill or mountain rising abruptly above the surrounding land.

which the lone, mature learner chooses. Without ever losing his desire for strange cities and the dignity of towers he stuck to his farm. He acquired a half-section, free from debt, fertile, well-stocked, adorned with a cement silo, a chicken-run, a new windmill. He became comfortable, secure, and then he was ready, it seemed, to die; for at sixty-three his work was done, and he was unneeded and alone.

His wife was dead. His sons had scattered afar, one a dentist in Fargo, another a farmer in the Golden Valley. He had turned over his farm to his daughter and son-in-law. They had begged him to live with them, but Knute refused.

"No," he said, "you must learn to stand on your own feet. I vill not give you the farm. You pay me four hundred dollars a year rent, and I live on that and vatch you from my hill."

On a rise beside the lone cottonwood which he loved best of all his trees Knute built a tar-paper shack, and here he "bached it"; cooked his meals, made his bed—sometimes, sat in the sun, read many books from the Joralemon library, and began to feel that he was free of the yoke of citizenship which he had borne all his life.

For hours at a time he sat on a backless kitchen-chair before the shack, a wide-shouldered man, white-bearded, motionless; a seer despite his grotesquely baggy trousers, his collarless shirt. He looked across the miles of stubble to the steeple of the Jack-rabbit Forks church and meditated upon the uses of life. At first he could not break the rigidity of habit. He rose at five, found work in cleaning his cabin and cultivating his garden, had dinner exactly at twelve, and went to bed by afterglow. But little by little he discovered that he could be irregular without being arrested. He stayed abed till seven or even eight. He got a large, deliberate, tortoise-shell cat, and played games with it; let it lap milk upon the table, called it the Princess, and confided to it that he had a "sneaking idee" that men were fools to work so hard. Around this coatless old man, his stained waistcoat flapping about a huge

torso, in a shanty of rumpled bed and pine table covered with sheets of food-daubed newspaper, hovered all the passionate aspiration of youth and the dreams of ancient beauty.

He began to take long walks by night. In his necessitous life night had ever been a period of heavy slumber in close rooms. Now he discovered the mystery of the dark; saw the prairies wide-flung and misty beneath the moon, heard the voices of grass and cottonwoods and drowsy birds. He tramped for miles. His boots were dew-soaked, but he did not heed. He stopped upon hillocks, shyly threw wide his arms, and stood worshiping the naked, slumbering land.

These excursions he tried to keep secret, but they were bruited abroad. Neighbors, good, decent fellows with no nonsense about walking in the dew at night, when they were returning late from town, drunk, lashing their horses, and flinging whisky-bottles from their racing democrat wagons[2] saw him, and they spread the tidings that Old Cottonwood was "getting nutty since he give up his farm to that son-in-law of his and retired. Seen the old codger wandering around at midnight. Wish I had his chance to sleep. Wouldn't catch me out in the night air."

Any rural community from Todd Center to Seringapatam is resentful of any person who varies from its standard, and is morbidly fascinated by any hint of madness. The countryside began to spy on Knute Axelbrod, to ask him questions, and to stare from the road at his shack. He was sensitively aware of it, and inclined to be surly to inquisitive acquaintances. Doubtless that was the beginning of his great pilgrimage.

As a part of the general wild license of his new life,—really, he once roared at that startled cat, the Princess: "By gollies! I ain't going to brush my teeth tonight. All my life I've brushed 'em, and alvays wanted to skip a time vunce,"— Knute took considerable pleasure in degenerat-

---

2. **democrat wagons,** light farm wagons with two seats, usually drawn by two horses.

ing in his taste in scholarship. He wilfully declined to finish *The Conquest of Mexico,* and began to read light novels borrowed from the Joralemon library. So he rediscovered the lands of dancing and light wines, which all his life he had desired. Some economics and history he did read, but every evening he would stretch out in his buffalo-horn chair, his feet on the cot and the Princess in his lap, and invade Zenda[3] or fall in love with Trilby.[4]

Among the novels he chanced upon a highly optimistic story of Yale in which a worthy young man "earned his way through" college, stroked the crew, won Phi Beta Kappa,[5] and had the most entertaining, yet moral, conversations on or adjacent to "the dear old fence."

As a result of this chronicle, at about three o'clock one morning when Knute Axelbrod was sixty-four years of age, he decided that he would go to college! All his life he had wanted to. Why not do it?

When he awoke in the morning he was not so sure about it as when he had gone to sleep. He saw himself as ridiculous, a ponderous, oldish man among clean-limbed youths, like a dusty cottonwood among silver birches. But for months he wrestled and played with that idea of a great pilgrimage to the Mount of Muses;[6] for he really supposed college to be that sort of place. He believed that all college students, except for the wealthy idlers, burned to acquire learning. He pictured Harvard and Yale and Princeton as ancient groves set with marble temples, before which large groups of Grecian youths talked gently about astronomy and good government. In his picture they never cut classes or ate.

With a longing for music and books and graciousness such as the most ambitious boy could never comprehend, this thick-faced prairie farmer dedicated himself to beauty, and defied the unconquerable power of approaching old age. He sent for college catalogues and school-books, and diligently began to prepare himself for college.

He found Latin irregular verbs and the whimsicalities of algebra fiendish. They had

nothing to do with actual life as he had lived it. But he mastered them; he studied twelve hours a day, as once he had plodded through eighteen hours a day in the hay-field. With history and English literature he had comparatively little trouble; already he knew much of them from his recreative reading. From German neighbors he had picked up enough Plattdeutsch[7] to make German easy. The trick of study began to come back to him from his small school-teaching of forty-five years before. He began to believe that he could really put it through. He kept assuring himself that in college, with rare and sympathetic instructors to help him, there would not be this baffling search, this nervous strain.

But the unreality of the things he studied did disillusion him, and he tired of his new game. He kept it up chiefly because all his life he had kept up onerous labor without any taste for it. Toward the autumn of the second year of his eccentric life he no longer believed that he would ever go to college.

Then a busy little grocer stopped him on the street in Joralemon and quizzed him about his studies, to the delight of the informal club which always loafs at the corner of the hotel.

Knute was silent, but dangerously angry. He remembered just in time how he had once laid wrathful hands upon a hired man, and somehow the man's collarbone had been broken. He turned away and walked home, seven miles, still boiling. He picked up the Princess, and,

---

3. Zenda\ˈzĕn·də\ a place in the popular romance *Prisoner of Zenda* by Anthony Hope (1894).

4. Trilby, the heroine of a novel (1894) by George du Maurier. Under the hypnotic influence of Svengali, a Hungarian musician, Trilby became the greatest singer of the day.

5. Phi Beta Kappa\ˈfī ˈbē·tə ˈka·pə\ oldest Greek letter society in U. S., founded 1776 at College of William and Mary, Williamsburg, Va. It became a scholarship honor society.

6. Mount of Muses, here, Harvard University. Greek myth: The nine muses, daughters of Zeus, were believed to be the goddesses who inspired men to excel in the arts and sciences.

7. Plattdeutsch\ˈplat·doich\ the language of northern Germany.

with her mewing on his shoulder, tramped out again to enjoy the sunset.

He stopped at a reedy slough.[8] He gazed at a hopping plover without seeing it. He plucked at his beard. Suddenly he cried:

"I am going to college. It opens next veek. I t'ink that I can pass the examinations."

Two days later he had moved the Princess and his sticks of furniture to his son-in-law's house, had bought a new slouch hat, a celluloid collar, and a solemn suit of black, had wrestled with God in prayer through all of a star-clad night, and had taken the train for Minneapolis, on the way to New Haven.

While he stared out of the car-window Knute was warning himself that the millionaires' sons would make fun of him. Perhaps they would haze[9] him. He bade himself avoid all these sons of Belial[10] and cleave to his own people, those who "earned their way through."

At Chicago he was afraid with a great fear of the lightning flashes that the swift crowds made on his retina, the batteries of ranked motor-cars that charged at him. He prayed, and ran for his train to New York. He came at last to New Haven.

Not with gibing rudeness, but with politely quizzical eyebrows, Yale received him, led him through entrance examinations, which, after sweaty plowing with the pen, he barely passed, and found for him a room-mate. The room-mate was a large-browed, soft, white grub[11] named Ray Gribble, who had been teaching school in New England, and seemed chiefly to desire college training so that he might make more money as a teacher. Ray Gribble was a hustler; he instantly got work tutoring the awkward son of a steel man, and for board he waited on table.

He was Knute's chief acquaintance. Knute tried to fool himself into thinking he liked the grub, but Ray couldn't keep his damp hands off the old man's soul. He had the skill of a professional exhorter of young men in finding out Knute's motives, and when he discovered that Knute had a hidden desire to dabble in

gay, polite literature, Ray said in a shocked way:

"Strikes me a man like you, that's getting old, ought to be thinking more about saving your soul than about all these frills. You leave this poetry and stuff to these foreigners and artists, and you stick to Latin and math and the Bible. I tell you, I've taught school, and I've learned by experience."

With Ray Gribble, Knute lived grubbily, an existence of torn comforters and a smelly lamp, of lexicons and logarithm tables. No leisurely loafing by fireplaces was theirs. They roomed in West Divinity, where gather the theologues, the lesser sort of law students, a whimsical genius or two, and a horde of unplaced freshmen and "scrub seniors."[12]

Knute was shockingly disappointed, but he stuck to his room because outside of it he was afraid. He was a grotesque figure, and he knew it, a white-polled giant squeezed into a small seat in a classroom, listening to instructors younger than his own sons. Once he tried to sit on the fence. No one but "ringers" sat on the fence any more, and at the sight of him trying to look athletic and young, two upper-class men snickered, and he sneaked away.

He came to hate Ray Gribble and his voluble companions of the submerged tenth of the class, the hewers of tutorial wood.[13] It is doubtless safer to mock the flag than to question that best-established tradition of our democracy— that those who "earn their way through" college are necessarily stronger, braver, and more assured of success than the weaklings who talk by the fire. Every college story presents such a moral. But tremblingly the historian submits

8. **slough**\slū\ (British\slo\) a place of deep mud, a swamp.
9. **haze**\hāz\ to play abusive and humiliating tricks upon someone.
10. **sons of Belial**\bē ´lē•əl\ lawless, worthless, rebellious people. Belial was a devil.
11. **grub,** a drudge, one who does routine, boring work.
12. **unplaced freshmen and scrub seniors,** freshmen not living on campus and insignificant seniors.
13. **hewers of tutorial wood,** young men who paid their way by teaching slow students who could afford to pay them.

that Knute discovered that waiting on table did not make lads more heroic than did football or happy loafing. Fine fellows, cheerful and fearless, were many of the boys who "earned their way," and able to talk to richer classmates without fawning; but just as many of them assumed an abject respectability as the most convenient pose. They were pickers up of unconsidered trifles; they toadied to the classmates whom they tutored; they wriggled before the faculty committee on scholarships; they looked pious at Dwight Hall prayer-meetings to make an impression on the serious-minded; and they drank one glass of beer at Jake's to show the light-minded that they meant nothing offensive by their piety. In revenge for cringing to the insolent athletes whom they tutored, they would, when safe among their own kind, yammer about the "lack of democracy in colleges today." Not that they were so indiscreet as to do anything about it. They lacked the stuff of really rebellious souls. Knute listened to them and marveled. They sounded like young hired men talking behind his barn at harvest-time.

This submerged tenth hated the dilettantes[14] of the class even more than they hated the bloods.[15] Against one Gilbert Washburn, a rich esthete[16] with more manner than any freshman ought to have, they raged righteously. They spoke of seriousness and industry till Knute, who might once have desired to know lads like Washburn, felt ashamed of himself as a wicked, wasteful old man.

With the friends of his room-mate began Knute's series of disillusions. Humbly though he sought, he found no inspiration and no comradeship. He was the freak of the class, and aside from the submerged tenth, his classmates were afraid of being "queered" by being seen with him.

As he was still powerful, one who could take up a barrel of pork on his knees, he tried to find friendship among the athletes. He sat at Yale Field, watching the football tryouts, and tried to get acquainted with the candidates. They stared at him and answered his questions

Branford College, Yale University

grudgingly—beefy youths who in their simple-hearted way showed that they considered him plain crazy.

The place itself began to lose the haze of magic through which he had first seen it. Earth is earth, whether one sees it in Camelot or Joralemon or on the Yale campus—or possibly even in the Harvard yard![17] The buildings ceased to be temples to Knute; they became structures of brick or stone, filled with young men who lounged at windows and watched him amusedly as he tried to slip by.

---

14. **dilettantes**\ˈdĭ·lə·tantz\ the superficial students, the dabblers.
15. **the bloods,** aristocrats.
16. **esthete**\ˈĕs·thēt\ one with a deep love of the beautiful in art, music, poetry, etc.
17. **Harvard yard,** the grassy, tree-shaded quadrangle around which the older Harvard buildings and some important new ones stand; the center of student life.

The Gargantuan hall of Commons[18] became a tri-daily horror because at the table where he dined were two youths who, having uncommonly penetrating minds, discerned that Knute had a beard, and courageously told the world about it. One of them, named Atchison, was a superior person, very industrious and scholarly, glib in mathematics and manners. He despised Knute's lack of definite purpose in coming to college. The other was a play-boy, a wit and a stealer of street-signs, who had a wonderful sense for a subtle jest; and his references to Knute's beard shook the table with jocund mirth three times a day. So these youths of gentle birth drove the shambling, wistful old man away from Commons, and thereafter he ate at the lunch-counter at the Black Cat.

Lacking the stimulus of friendship, it was the harder for Knute to keep up the strain of studying the long assignments. What had been a week's pleasant reading in his shack was now thrown at him as a day's task. But he would not have minded the toil if he could have found one as young as himself. They were all so dreadfully old, the money-earners, the serious laborers at athletics, the instructors who worried over their life-work of putting marks in class-record books.

Then, on a sore, bruised day, Knute did meet one who was young.

Knute had heard that the professor who was the idol of the college had berated the too-earnest lads in his Browning class, and insisted that they read *Alice in Wonderland*. Knute floundered dustily about in a second-hand book-shop till he found an *Alice,* and he brought it home to read over his lunch of a hot-dog sandwich. Something in the grave absurdity of the book appealed to him, and he was chuckling over it when Ray Gribble came into the room and glanced at the reader.

"Huh!" said Mr. Gribble.

"That's a fine, funny book," said Knute.

"Huh! *Alice in Wonderland!* I've heard of it. Silly nonsense. Why don't you read something really fine, like Shakespeare or 'Paradise Lost'?"

"Vell—" said Knute, but that was all he could find to say.

With Ray Gribble's glassy eye on him, he could no longer roll and roar with the book. He wondered if indeed he ought not to be reading Milton's pompous anthropological misconceptions.[19] He went unhappily out to an early history class, ably conducted by Blevins, Ph.D.

Knute admired Blevins, Ph.D. He was so tubbed and eyeglassed and terribly right. But most of Blevins's lambs did not like Blevins. They said he was a "crank." They read newspapers in his class and covertly kicked one another.

In the smug, plastered classroom, his arm leaning heavily on the broad tablet-arm of his chair, Knute tried not to miss one of Blevins's sardonic proofs that the correct date of the second marriage of Themistocles was two years and seven days later than the date assigned by that illiterate ass, Frutari of Padua. Knute admired young Blevins's performance, and he felt virtuous in application to these hard, unnonsensical facts.

He became aware that certain lewd fellows of the lesser sort were playing poker just behind him. His prairie-trained ear caught whispers of "Two to dole," and "Raise you two beans." Knute revolved, and frowned upon these mockers of sound learning. As he turned back he was aware that the offenders were chuckling, and continuing their game. He saw that Blevins, Ph.D., perceived that something was wrong; he frowned, but he said nothing. Knute sat in meditation. He saw Blevins as merely a boy. He was sorry for him. He would do the boy a good turn.

When class was over he hung about Blevins's desk till the other students had clattered out. He rumbled:

---

18. **Gargantuan**\gar ⁺găn·tū·ən\ **hall of Commons** enormous dining-room suitable for the giant, Gargantua, the legendary figure adopted by Rabelais in his satirical writing.
19. **anthropological**\ăn·thrə·pə ⁺laj·ĭ·kəl\ **misconceptions,** mistaken ideas about the origin of man and his relation to God.

"Say, Professor, you're a fine fellow. I do something for you. If any of the boys make themselves a nuisance, you yust call on me, and I spank the son of a guns."

Blevins, Ph.D., spoke in a manner of culture and nastiness:

"Thanks so much, Axelbrod, but I don't fancy that will ever be necessary. I am supposed to be a reasonably good disciplinarian. Good day. Oh, one moment. There's something I've been wishing to speak to you about. I do wish you wouldn't try quite so hard to show off whenever I call on you during quizzes. You answer at such needless length, and you smile as though there were something highly amusing about me. I'm quite willing to have you regard me as a humorous figure, privately, but there are certain classroom conventions, you know, certain little conventions."

"Why, Professor!" wailed Knute. "I never make fun of you! I didn't know I smile. If I do, I guess it's yust because I am so glad when my stupid old head gets the lesson good."

"Well, well, that's very gratifying, I'm sure. And if you will be a little more careful——"

Blevins, Ph.D., smiled a toothy, frozen smile, and trotted off to the Graduates' Club, to be witty about old Knute and his way of saying "yust," while in the deserted classroom Knute sat chill, an old man and doomed. Through the windows came the light of Indian summer; clean, boyish cries rose from the campus. But the lover of autumn smoothed his baggy sleeve, stared at the blackboard, and there saw only the gray of October stubble about his distant shack. As he pictured the college watching him, secretly making fun of him and his smile, he was now faint and ashamed, now bull-angry. He was lonely for his cat, his fine chair of buffalo horns, the sunny doorstep of his shack, and the understanding land. He had been in college for about one month.

Before he left the classroom he stepped behind the instructor's desk and looked at an imaginary class.

"I might have stood there as a prof if I could have come earlier," he said softly to himself.

Calmed by the liquid autumn gold that flowed through the streets, he walked out Whitney Avenue toward the butte-like hill of East Rock. He observed the caress of the light upon the scarped rock,[20] heard the delicate music of leaves, breathed in air pregnant with tales of old New England. He exulted:

"I could write poetry now if I yust—if I yust could write poetry!"

He climbed to the top of East Rock, whence he could see the Yale buildings like the towers of Oxford, Long Island Sound, and the white glare of Long Island itself beyond the water. He marveled that Knute Axelbrod of the cottonwood country was looking across an arm of the Atlantic to New York State.

He noticed a freshman on a bench at the edge of the rock, and he became irritated. The freshman was Gilbert Washburn, the snob, the dilettante, of whom Ray Gribble had once said: "That guy is the disgrace of the class. He doesn't go out for anything, high stand or Dwight Hall or anything else. Thinks he's so doggone much better than the rest of the fellows that he doesn't associate with anybody. Thinks he's literary, they say, and yet he doesn't even heel the 'Lit,' like the regular literary fellows! Got no time for a loafing, mooning snob like that."

As Knute stared at the unaware Gil, whose profile was fine in outline against the sky, he was terrifically public-spirited and disapproving and that sort of moral thing. Though Gil was much too well dressed, he seemed moodily discontented.

"What he needs is to vork in a thrashing-crew and sleep in the hay," grumbled Knute almost in the virtuous manner of Gribble. "Then he vould know when he vas vell off, and not look like he had the earache. Pff!"

Gil Washburn rose, trailed toward Knute, glanced at him, hesitated, sat down on Knute's bench.

"Great view!" he said. His smile was eager.

---

20. **scarped rock,** steep rock rising nearly vertical.

That smile symbolized to Knute all the art of life he had come to college to find. He tumbled out of his moral attitude with ludicrous haste, and every wrinkle of his weathered face creased deep as he answered:

"Yes; I t'ink the Acropolis must be like this here."

"Say, look here, Axelbrod; I've been thinking about you."

"Yas?"

"We ought to know each other. We two are the class scandal. We came here to dream, and these busy little goats like Atchison and Giblets, or whatever your room-mate's name is, think we're fools not to go out for marks. You may not agree with me, but I've decided that you and I are precisely alike."

"What makes you t'ink I come here to dream?" bristled Knute.

"Oh, I used to sit near you at Commons and hear you try to quell jolly old Atchison whenever he got busy discussing the reasons for coming to college. That old, moth-eaten topic! I wonder if Cain and Abel didn't discuss it at the Eden Agricultural College. You know, Abel the mark-grabber, very pious and high stand, and Cain wanting to read poetry."

"Yes," said Knute, "and I guess Prof Adam say, 'Cain, don't you read this poetry; it von't help you in algebry.'"

"Of course. Say, wonder if you'd like to look at this volume of Musset[21] I was sentimental enough to lug up here today. Picked it up when I was abroad last year."

From his pocket Gil drew such a book as Knute had never seen before, a slender volume, in a strange language, bound in hand-tooled, crushed levant,[22] an effeminate bibelot[23] over which the prairie farmer gasped with luxurious pleasure. The book almost vanished in his big hands. With a timid forefinger he stroked the levant, ran through the leaves.

"I can't read it, but that's the kind of book I alvays t'ought there must be some like it," he sighed.

"Let me read you a little. It's French, poetry."

Gil read aloud. He made of the alien verses a music which satisfied Knute's sixty-five years of longing for he had never known what.

"That's—that's fine," he said.

"Listen!" cried Gil. "Ysaye[24] is playing up at Hartford tonight. Let's go hear him. We'll trolley up, make it in plenty of time. Tried to get some of the fellows to come, but they thought I was a nut."

What an Ysaye was, Knute Axelbrod had no notion; but "Sure!" he boomed.

When they got to Hartford they found that between them they had just enough money to get dinner, hear Ysaye from gallery seats, and return only as far as Meriden.

At Meriden Gil suggested:

"Let's walk back to New Haven, then. Can you make it?"

Knute had no knowledge as to whether it was four miles or forty back to the campus, but "Sure!" he said. For the last few months he had been noticing that, despite his bulk, he had to be careful, but tonight he could have flown.

In the music of Ysaye, the first real musician he had ever heard, Knute had found all the incredible things of which he had slowly been reading in William Morris[25] and "Idylls of the King."[26] Tall knights he had beheld, and slim princesses in white samite, the misty gates of forlorn towns, and the glory of the chivalry that never was.

They did walk, roaring down the road beneath the October moon, stopping to steal apples and to exclaim over silvered hills, taking a puerile and very natural joy in chasing a profane dog. It was Gil who talked, and Knute who listened, for the most part; but Knute was

21. **Musset**\myu ‸sā\ Alfred de Musset (1810–1857), a French poet and dramatist of the romantic period, an associate of Victor Hugo and his group.
22. **levant**, a superior grade of leather.
23. **bibelot**\Fr., bē ‸blō\ a small object of beauty and rarity.
24. **Ysaye**\ē ‸za·ē\ Eugene (1858–1931), Belgian, one of the greatest violinists of his time.
25. **William Morris** (1834–1896), an English poet who wrote of legendary heroes.
26. **Idylls of the King**, Alfred Tennyson's narrative poems based on the legends of King Arthur.

lured into tales of the pioneer days, of blizzards, of harvesting, and of the first flame of the green wheat. Regarding the Atchisons and Gribbles of the class both of them were youthfully bitter and supercilious. But they were not bitter long, for they were atavisms[27] tonight. They were wandering minstrels, Gilbert the troubadour with his man-at-arms.

They reached the campus at about five in the morning.

Fumbling for words that would express his feeling, Knute stammered:

"Vell, it vas fine. I go to bed now and I dream about——"

"Bed? Rats! Never believe in winding up a party when it's going strong. Too few good parties. Besides, it's only the shank of the evening. Besides, we're hungry. Besides—oh, besides! Wait here a second. I'm going up to my room to get some money, and we'll have some eats. Wait! Please do!"

Knute would have waited all night. He had lived sixty-five years and traveled fifteen hundred miles and endured Ray Gribble to find Gil Washburn.

Policemen wondered to see the celluloid-collared old man and the expensive-looking boy rolling arm in arm down Chapel Street in search of a restaurant suitable to poets. They were all closed.

"The Ghetto[28] will be awake by now," said Gil. "We'll go buy some eats and take 'em up to my room. I've got some tea there."

Knute shouldered through dark streets beside him as naturally as though he had always been a night-hawk, with an aversion to anything as rustic as beds. Down on Oak Street, a place of low shops, smoky lights, and alley mouths, they found the slum already astir. Gil contrived to purchase boxed biscuits, cream-cheese, chicken-loaf, a bottle of cream. While Gil was chaffering,[29] Knute stared out into the street milkily lighted by wavering gas and the first feebleness of coming day; he gazed upon Kosher[30] signs and advertisements in Russian letters, shawled women and bearded rabbis; and as he looked he gathered contentment

which he could never lose. He had traveled abroad tonight.

The room of Gil Washburn was all the useless, pleasant things Knute wanted it to be. There was more of Gil's Paris days in it than of his freshmanhood: cloisonné[31] on the mantelpiece, Persian rugs, a silver tea-service, etchings, and books. Knute Axelbrod of the tar-paper shack and piggy farm-yards gazed in satisfaction. Vast-bearded, sunk in an easy-chair, he clucked amiably while Gil lighted a fire and spread a wicker table.

Over supper they spoke of great men and heroic ideals. It was good talk, and not unspiced with lively references to Gribble and Atchison and Blevins, all asleep now in their correct beds. Gil read snatches of Stevenson and Anatole France;[32] then at last he read his own poetry.

It does not matter whether that poetry was good or bad. To Knute it was a miracle to find one who actually wrote it.

The talk grew slow, and they began to yawn. Knute was sensitive to the lowered key of their Indian-summer madness, and he hastily rose. As he said good-by he felt as though he had but to sleep a little while and return to this unending night of romance.

But he came out of the dormitory upon day. It was six-thirty of the morning, with a still, hard light upon red-brick walls.

"I can go to his room plenty times now; I find my friend," Knute said. He held tight the

---

27. **atavisms**\ˈă·tə·vĭ·zəms\ throwbacks to the days of knighthood and wandering minstrelsy.
28. **Ghetto**\ˈgĕ·tō\ a part of the city where the poorer Jewish families lived.
29. **chaffering**, here, exchanging small talk while he purchased food.
30. **Kosher**\ˈkō·shər\ **signs**, signs saying that in those shops food could be purchased which had been prepared for market according to Hebrew law, and could properly be eaten by the orthodox.
31. **cloisonné** multicolored ornament made of enamels poured into divided areas in a design outlined by bent wires secured to a metal base.
32. **Anatole France** (1844–1924), French novelist known for his taste for the classics, for legends, and for fairy stories.

volume of Musset, which Gil had begged him to take.

As he started to walk the few steps to West Divinity Knute felt very tired. By daylight the adventure seemed more and more incredible.

As he entered the dormitory he sighed heavily:

"Age and youth, I guess they can't team together long." As he mounted the stairs he said: "If I saw the boy again, he vould get tired of me. I tell him all I got to say." And as he opened his door, he added: "This is what I come to college for—this one night; I live for it sixty-five years. I go avay before I spoil it."

He wrote a note to Gil, and began to pack his telescope. He did not even wake Ray Gribble, sonorously sleeping in the stale air.

At five that afternoon, on the day-coach of a westbound train, an old man sat smiling. A lasting content was in his eyes, and in his hands a small book in French, though the curious fact is that this man could not read French.

I
THE ART OF LIFE

The physical, intellectual, and spiritual are not the only values in life. In this story still another, the aesthetic, is introduced. Lewis tells us that Knute "always kept a young soul that dared to desire beauty" and that his primary reason for going to college was to find "the art of life." In Knute's quest for truth and fulfillment, then, aesthetic values proved as important as values relating exclusively to body, mind, and soul.

II
IMPLICATIONS

Discuss the following propositions in terms of this story and your own experience.

1. College is probably the best place to learn "the art of life."

2. When Lewis says that Knute "dared" to desire beauty, he is implying that Knute's family

and neighbors would probably have disapproved strongly of his desire.

3. Concern for beauty and beautiful things almost invariably declines as one grows older.

4. Most people live unnecessarily narrow lives for fear of the opinions of others.

5. Discuss the following quotation from the American philosopher George Santayana in the light of this story.

"The appreciation of beauty and its embodiment in the arts are activities which belong to our holiday life, when we are redeemed for the moment from the shadow of evil and the slavery to fear, and are following the bent of our nature where it chooses to lead us."

III
TECHNIQUES

Structure

Structurally speaking, a short story may be divided into three basic parts: the *exposition,* the *complication,* and the *denouement.*

The exposition is that portion of the story in which the author supplies information about the characters' backgrounds and about events preceding the main action of the story.

The complication, the longest part of most stories, takes up the development of the conflict and of the personalities of the characters involved in the conflict. Tension steadily rises during this portion of the story.

The denouement resolves the conflict of the story; it typically begins at the climax and includes all of the elements that untie the plot.

If a story is told in normal time sequence, these elements will be in the order in which presented above. There is, however, no reason why an author can't change this order. He might, for example, use flashbacks to supply most of his exposition and begin at some point in the complication, even at the climax. "Young Man Axelbrod," however, is in normal order. Where do you think the exposition ends and the complication begins; and where does the complication end and the denouement begin?

Symbolism

1. Why does the author open the story with references to the cottonwood tree? What does it symbolize, and how does it relate to the main theme?

2. Why is the cottonwood an appropriate symbol? Inappropriate? Why, for instance, might it be a better or a poorer symbol than, say, a birch tree, or some other natural object?

IV
WORDS

A. Using context clues, signals, and hints, determine the meaning of the italicized words in the following.

1. Its wooly wisps turn gray the lawns and *engender* neighborhood hostilities.

2. These excursions he tried to keep secret, but they were *bruited* abroad.

3. He bade himself avoid all these sons of Belial and *cleave* to his own people. . . .

4. Fine fellows . . . who "earned their way" able to talk to richer classmates without *fawning;* but just as many of them assumed an *abject* respectability.

B. 1. Find the most appropriate synonym for the italicized word in each phrase.
comely (handsome, lovely, homely) row of trees
onerous (burdensome, arduous, weighty) labor
insolent (arrogant, contemptuous, submissive) athletes
sardonic (sinister, mocking, ironical) proofs
ludicrous (farcical, lugubrious, fantastic) haste
indigenous (endemic, exotic, frightening) night

2. Find the most appropriate antonym for the italicized word in each phrase.
covertly (openly, overtly, clearly) kick one another
voluble (curt, facile, stuttering) companions
jocund (staid, sportive, grave) mirth
puerile (youthful, callow, adult) joy

C. 1. English is full of phrases that may be replaced with a single word equivalent. These phrases are generally appropriate in conversation but in writing, general and especially formal, the single words are preferred. For example, "He tolerated the confusion" is more precise than "He put up with the confusion." Find single-word equivalents for the following phrases.

  a. on account of the fact that
  b. put an end to
  c. make fun of
  d. take part in
  e. do away with
  f. make away with
  g. cut down on

2. Another interesting feature of our language is the number of verb-particle combinations used in figurative and idiomatic senses. Familiar constructions are *pass out* (distribute), *give out* (exhaust), *hold up* (rob). Give a single verb equivalent for these phrases: *catch on, get through, pick up, put off, talk over, leave out, keep on, give up, give in.*

3. Look up the following verbs in your dictionary and list the idiomatic phrases: *come, pass, make, get, put.* What usage labels, if any, are indicated? Which phrases do you consider appropriate to informal writing, to general writing, to formal writing?

4. Good general writing is clear, precise, and lively. Review one of your compositions. Look for phrases that could be replaced with single word equivalents.

5. Study the dialogue of one selection. Discuss how the dialogue differs from the expository paragraphs.

The Traveler

WALLACE STEGNER

He was rolling in the first early dark down a snowy road, his headlights pinched between dark walls of trees, when the engine coughed, recovered, coughed again, and died. Down a slight hill he coasted in compression, working the choke, but at the bottom he had to pull over against the three-foot wall of plowed snow. Snow creaked under the tires as the car eased to a stop. The heater fan unwound with a final tinny sigh.

Here in its middle age this hitherto dependable mechanism had betrayed him, but he refused to admit immediately that he was betrayed. Some speck of dirt or bubble of water in the gas line, some momentary short circuit, some splash of snow on distributor points or plug connections—something that would cure itself before long. But turning off the lights and pressing on the starter brought no result; he held the choke out for several seconds, and got only the hopeful stink of gasoline; he waited and let the flooded carburetor rest and tried again, and nothing. Eventually he opened the door and stepped out onto the packed snow of the road.

It was so cold that his first breath turned to iron in his throat, the hairs in his nostrils webbed into instant ice, his eyes stung and watered. In the faint starlight and the bluish luminescence of the snow everything beyond a few yards away swam deceptive and without depth, glimmering with things half seen or imagined. Beside the dead car he stood with his head bent, listening, and there was not a sound. Everything on the planet might have died in the cold.

Indecisively seeking help, he walked to the top of the next rise, but the faintly-darker furrow of the road blurred and disappeared in the murk, the shadows pressed inward, there was no sign of a light. Back at the car he made the efforts that the morality of self-reliance demanded: trying to see by the backward diffusion of the headlamps, he groped over the motor feeling for broken wires or loose connections, until he had satisfied himself that he was helpless. He had known all along that he was.

His hands were already stung with cold, and around his ankles between low shoes and trouser cuffs he felt the chill like leg irons. When he had last stopped, twenty miles back, it had been near zero. It could be ten or fifteen below now. So what did he do, stranded in mid-journey fifty miles or more from his destination? He could hardly go in for help, leaving the sample cases, because the right rear door didn't lock properly. A little jiggling swung it

Reprinted from *The City of the Living*, published by Houghton Mifflin Company and used with their permission.

open. And all those drugs, some of them designed to cure anything—wonder drugs, sulphas, streptomycin, aureomycin, penicillin, pills and antitoxins and unguents—represented not only a value but a danger. They should not be left around loose. Someone might think they really *would* cure anything.

Not quite everything, he told the blue darkness. Not a fouled-up distributor or a cranky coil box. Absurdly, there came into his mind a fragment of an ancient hymn to mechanical transport:

If she runs out of dope, just fill her up with soap
And the little Ford will ramble right along.

He saw himself pouring a bottle of penicillin into the gas tank and driving off with the exhaust blowing happy smoke rings. A mock-heroic montage[1] of scientific discovery unreeled itself—white-coated scientists peering into microscopes, adjusting gauges, pipetting[2] precious liquids, weighing grains of powder on miniscule scales. Messenger boys sped with telegrams to the desks of busy executives. A group of observers stood beside an assembly line while the first tests were made. They broke a car's axle with sledges, gave it a drink of the wonder compound, and drove it off. They demolished the carburetor and cured it with one application. They yanked loose all the wires and watched the same magic set the motor purring.

But here he stood in light overcoat and thin leather gloves, without overshoes, and his car all but blocked the road, and the door could not be locked, and there was not a possibility that he could carry the heavy cases with him to the next farm or village. He switched on the headlights again and studied the roadside they revealed, and saw a rail fence, with cedars and spruces behind it. When more complex gadgets and more complex cures failed, there was always the lucifer match.

Ten minutes later he was sitting with the auto robe over his head and shoulders and his back against the plowed snowbank, digging the half melted snow from inside his shoes and gloating over the growing light and warmth of the fire. He had a supply of fence rails good for an hour. In that time, someone would come along and he could get a push or a tow. In this country, in winter, no one ever passed up a stranded motorist.

In the stillness the flames went straight upward; the heat was wonderfully pleasant on icy hands and numb ankles and stiffened face. He looked across the road, stained by horses, broken by wheel and runner tracks, and saw how the roadside acquired definition and sharp angles and shadows in the firelight. He saw too how he would look to anyone coming along: like a calendar picture.

But no one came along. Fifteen minutes stretched into a half hour, he had only two broken pieces of rail left, the fire sizzled half floating in the puddle of its melting. Restlessly he rose with the blanket around him and walked back up the road a hundred steps. Eastward, above jagged trees, he saw the sky where it lightened to moonrise, but here there was still only the blue glimmer of starlight on the snow. Something long-buried and forgotten tugged in him, and a shiver not entirely from cold prickled his whole body with goose flesh. There had been times in his childhood when he had walked home alone and been temporarily lost in nights like this. In many years he could not remember being out alone under such a sky. He felt spooked, his feet were chilled lumps, his nose leaked. Down the hill car and snow swam deceptively together; the red wink of the fire seemed inexpressibly far off.

Abruptly he did not want to wait in that lonely snow-banked ditch any longer. The sample cases could look after themselves, any motorist who passed could take his own chances. He would walk ahead to the nearest

---

1. **montage**\mŏn ▴tazh\ a composite picture made by combining several separate pictures.
2. **pipetting**\▴pai·pǝ·tĭŋ\ drawing into a glass tube by suction.

help, and if he found himself getting too cold on the way, he could always build another fire. The thought of action cheered him; he admitted to himself that he was all but terrified at the silence and the iron cold.

Locking the car doors, he dropped his key case in the snow, and panic stopped his pulse as he bent and frantically, with bare hand, brushed away the snow until he found it. The powdery snow ached and burned at his finger tips. He held them a last moment to the fire, and then, bundled like a squaw, with the blanket held across nose and mouth to ease the harshness of the cold in his lungs, he started up the road that looked as smooth as a table-cloth, but was deceptively rough and broken. He thought of what he had had every right to expect for this evening. By now, eight o'clock or so, he should have had a smoking supper, the luxury of a hot bath, the pleasure of a brandy in a comradely bar. By now he should be in pajamas making out sales reports by the bedlight, in a room where steam knocked comfortingly in the radiators and the help of a hundred hands was available to him at a word into the telephone. For all of this to be torn away suddenly, for him to be stumbling up a deserted road in danger of freezing to death, just because some simple mechanical part that had functioned for thirty thousand miles refused to function any longer, this was outrage, and he hated it. He thought of garage men and service station attendants he could blame. Ignoring the evidence of the flooded carburetor, he brooded about watered gas that could make ice in the gas line. A man was dependent on too many people; he was at everybody's mercy.

And then, on top of the second long rise, he met the moon.

Instantly the character of the night changed. The uncertain starlight was replaced at a step by an even flood of blue-white radiance. He looked across a snow meadow and saw how a rail fence had every stake and rider doubled in solid shadow, and how the edge of woods beyond was blackest India ink. The road ahead was drawn with a ruler, one bank smoothed by the flood of light, the other deeply shadowed. As he looked into the eye of the moon he saw the air shiver and glint with falling particles of frost.

In this White-Christmas night, this Good-King-Wenceslaus night, he went warily, not to be caught in sentimentality, and to an invisible audience he deprecated it profanely as a night in which no one would believe. Yet here it was, and he in it. With the coming of the moon the night even seemed to warm; he found that he could drop the blanket from across his face and drink the still air.

Along the roadside as he passed the meadow and entered woods again the moon showed him things. In moonlight openings he saw the snow stitched with tiny perfect tracks, mouse or weasel or the three-toed crowding tracks of partridge. These too, an indigenous[3] part of the night, came back to him as things once known and long forgotten. In his boyhood he had trapped and hunted the animals that made such tracks as these; it was as if his mind were a snowfield where the marks of their secret little feet had been printed long ago. With a queer tightening of the throat, with an odd pride, he read the trail of a fox that had wallowed through the soft snow from the woods, angling into the packed road and along it for a little way and out again, still angling, across the plowed bank, and then left a purposeful trail of clearly punched tracks, the hind feet out of line with the front, across the clean snow and into the opposite woods, from shadow across moonlight and into shadow again, mysterious.

Turning with the road, he passed through the stretch of woods and came into the open to see the moon-white, shadow-black buildings of a farm, and the weak bloom of light in a window.

His feet whined on the snow, dry as metal powder, as he turned in the loop of drive the county plow had cleared. But as he approached

_____

3. **indigenous**\in ᴬdĭ·jə·nəs\ **part,** a natural part.

the house doubt touched him. In spite of the light, the place looked unused, somehow. No dog welcomed him. The sound of his feet in the snow was alien, the hammer of his knuckles on the door an intrusion. Looking upward for some trace of telephone wires, he saw none, and he could not tell whether the quivering of the air that he thought he saw above the chimney was heat or smoke or the phantasmal falling frost.

"Hello?" he said, and knocked again. "Anybody home?" No sound answered him. He saw the moon glint on the great icicles along the eaves. His numb hand ached with the pain of knocking; he pounded with the soft edge of his fist.

Answer finally came, not from the door before which he stood, but from the barn, down at the end of a staggered string of attached sheds. A door creaked open against a snowbank and a figure with a lantern appeared, stood for a moment, and came running. The traveler wondered at the way it came, lurching and stumbling in the uneven snow, until it arrived at the porch and he saw that it was a boy of eleven or twelve. The boy set his lantern on the porch; between the upturned collar of his mackinaw and the down-pulled stocking cap his face was a pinched whiteness, his eyes enormous. He stared at the traveler until the traveler became aware of the blanket he still held over head and shoulders, and began to laugh.

"My car stopped on me, a mile or so up the road," he said. "I was just hunting a telephone or some place where I could get help."

The boy swallowed, wiped the back of his mitt across his nose. "Grandpa's sick!" he blurted, and opened the door.

Warmth rushed in their faces, cold rushed in at their backs, warm and cold mingled in an eddy of air as the door closed. The traveler saw a cot bed pulled close to the kitchen range, and on the cot an old man covered with a quilt, who breathed heavily and whose closed eyes did not open when the two came near. The gray-whiskered cheeks were sunken, the mouth open to expose toothless gums in a parody look of ancient mischief.

"He must've had a shock," the boy said. "I came in from chores and he was on the floor." He stared at the mummy under the quilt, and he swallowed.

"Has he come to at all?"

"No."

"Only the two of you live here?"

"Yes."

"No telephone?"

"No."

"How long ago did you find him?"

"Chore time. About six?"

"Why didn't you go for help?"

The boy looked down, ashamed. "It's near two miles. I was afraid he'd. . . ."

"But you left him. You were out in the barn."

"I was hitching up to go," the boy said. "I'd made up my mind."

The traveler backed away from the stove, his face smarting with the heat, his fingers and feet beginning to ache. He looked at the old man and knew that here, as at the car, he was helpless. The boy's thin anxious face told him how thoroughly his own emergency had been swallowed up in this other one. He had been altered from a man in need of help to one who must give it. Salesman of wonder cures, he must now produce something to calm this overworried boy, restore a dying man. Rebelliously, victimized by circumstances, he said, "Where were you going for help?"

"The Hill place. They've got a phone."

"How far are they from a town?"

"About five miles."

"Doctor there?"

"Yes."

"If I took your horse and—what is it, sleigh? —could someone at the Hills' bring them back, do you think?"

"Cutter. One of the Hill boys could, I should say."

"Or would you rather go, while I look after your Grandpa?"

"He don't know you," the boy said directly.

"If he should wake up he might . . . wonder . . . it might. . . ."

The traveler grudgingly gave up the prospect of staying in the warm kitchen while the boy did the work. And he granted that it was extraordinarily sensitive of the boy to know how it might disturb a man to wake from sickness in his own house and stare into the face of an utter stranger. "Yes," he said. "Well, I could call the doctor from the Hills'. Two miles, did you say?"

"About." The boy had pulled the stocking cap off so that his hair stood on end above his white forehead. He had odd eyes, very large and dark and intelligent, with an expectancy in them.

The traveler, watching him with interest, said, "How long have you lived with your grandfather?"

"Two years."

"Parents living?"

"No sir, that's why."

"Go to school?"

He got a queer sidling look. "Have to till you're sixteen."

"Is that the only reason you go?"

What he was trying to force out of the boy came out indirectly, with a shrugging of the shoulders. "Grandpa would take me out if he could."

"Would you be glad?"

"No sir," the boy said, but would not look at him. "I like school."

The traveler consciously corked his flow of questions. Once he himself had been an orphan living with his grandparents on a back farm; he wondered if this boy went as he had gone, knocking in imagination at all of life's closed doors.

The old man's harsh breathing filled the overwarm room. "Well," the traveler said, "maybe you'd better go finish hitching up. It's been thirty years since I harnessed a horse. I'll keep an eye on your Grandpa."

Pulling the stocking cap over his disheveled hair, the boy slid out the door. The traveler unbuttoned his overcoat and sat down beside the old man, felt the spurting, weak pulse, raised one eyelid with his thumb and looked without comprehension at the uprolled eye. He knew it was like feeling over a chilling motor for loose wires, and after two or three abortive motions he gave it up and sat contemplating the gray, sunken face, the unfamiliar face of an old man who would die, and thinking that the face was the only unfamiliar thing about the whole night. The kitchen smells, coffee and peanut butter and the mouldy, barky smell of wood from the woodbox, and the smell of the hot range and of paint baking in the heat, those were as familiar as light or dark. The spectacular night outside, the snowfields and the moon and the mysterious woods, the tracks venturing out across the snow from the protective eaves of firs and skunk spruce, the speculative, imagining expression of the boy's eyes, were just as familiar. He sat bemused, touching some brink as a man will walk along a cutbank trying to knock loose the crumbling overhang with an outstretched foot. The ways a man fitted in with himself and with other human beings were curious and complex.

And when he heard the jingle and creak outside, and buttoned himself into the overcoat again and wrapped his shoulders in the blanket and stepped out into the yard, there was a moment when the boy passed him the lines and they stood facing each other in the broken snow.

It was a moment like farewell, like a poignant parting. Touched by his pressing sense of familiarity and by a sort of compassion, the traveler reached out and laid his hand on the boy's shoulder. "Don't worry," he said. "I'll have someone back here right away. Your grandfather will be all right. Just keep him warm and don't worry."

He climbed into the cutter and pulled over his lap the balding buffalo robe he found there; the scallop of its felt edges was like a key that fitted a door. The horses breathed jets of steam in the moonlight, restlessly moving, jingling their harness bells, as the moment lengthened itself. The traveler saw how the boy, now that his anxiety was somewhat quieted, now that he had been able to unload part of his burden, watched him with a thousand questions in his face, and he remembered how he himself, thirty years ago, had searched the faces of passing strangers for something he could not name, how he had listened to their steps and seen their shadows lengthen ahead of them down roads that led to unimaginable places, and how he had ached with the desire to know them, who they were. But none of them had looked back at him as he tried now to look at this boy.

He was glad that no names had been spoken and no personal histories exchanged to obscure this meeting, for sitting in the sleigh above the boy's white upturned serious face he felt that some profound contact had unintentionally, almost casually, been made.

For half a breath he was utterly bewitched, frozen at the heart of some icy dream. Abruptly he slapped the reins across the backs of the horses; the cutter jerked and then slid smoothly out toward the road. The traveler looked back once, to fix forever the picture of himself standing silently watching himself go. As he slid into the road the horses broke into a trot. The icy flow of air locked his throat and made him let go the reins with one hand to pull the hairy, wool-smelling edge of the blanket all but shut across his face.

Along a road he had never driven he went swiftly toward an unknown farm and an unknown town, to distribute according to some wise law part of the burden of the boy's emergency and his own; but he bore in his mind, bright as moonlight over snow, a vivid wonder, almost an awe. For from that most chronic[4] and incurable of ills, identity, he had looked outward and for one unmistakable instant recognized himself.

---

4. **chronic**\ˈkrŏ·nĭk\ marked by long duration or frequent recurrence.

I
NO MAN IS AN ISLAND

In the last paragraph of this story—its moment of illumination—the narrator calls identity "that most chronic and incurable of ills." Offhand, you might wonder at such a statement—after all, isn't it good to have a sense of identity, a sense of who you are? As a matter of fact, isn't it precisely his identity that the traveler discovers?

Lost for thirty years, he searched in the wrong places. He looked inward for his identity—for those things that marked him off from others and made him unique. Identity, in this sense, could be called an illness, for it could lead to isolation from others and to the loss of such virtues as sympathy and compassion.

By looking outward, by loving—giving himself—the traveler discovers a deeper sense of his identity. He discovers not what separates him from others but what he has in common with them.

II
IMPLICATIONS

Discuss the following propositions.

1. The search for self-knowledge (or identity) is a lifelong one.

2. The stronger a person's sense of identity, the stronger his sense of values.

3. A man is dependent on too many people; he is at everybody's mercy.

4. The deeper one looks into himself, the more he will find he has in common with others.

III
TECHNIQUES

Structure

This story may be divided in half almost perfectly. The first half is devoted to the traveler, his car problem, and his loneliness; the second half brings in the boy and his dilemma. The parallel between the man's and the boy's situation is thus forced on the reader's attention. In what ways does the division of the story into two parts relate to the no-man-is-an-island theme?

Symbolism

1. What are some of the symbolic implications of the story's title?

2. Note all references to the moon or moonlight. What might they symbolize?

Although most of Herman Melville's novels and stories
were published between 1840 and 1860, it was not until this century
that his greatness was widely appreciated. Recognition came late,
primarily because he speaks more to the doubts, fears, and pessimism
of the twentieth century than to his own time. There were no hydrogen bombs
in Melville's day, of course, but to the individual, the power
of a lightning bolt was just as fearful. As you read the following story,
do not be concerned with the realism or the lack of it, but ponder
the universal qualities in the men and the situation.

The Lightning-Rod Man

HERMAN MELVILLE

What grand irregular thunder, thought I, standing on my hearth-stone among the Acroceraunian hills,[1] as the scattered bolts boomed overhead, and crashed down among the valleys, every bolt followed by zigzag irradiations, and swift slants of sharp rain, which audibly rang, like a charge of spearpoints, on my low shingled roof. I suppose, though, that the mountains hereabouts break and churn up the thunder, so that it is far more glorious here than on the plain. Hark!—some one at the door. Who is this that chooses a time of thunder for making calls? And why don't he, man-fashion, use the knocker, instead of making that doleful undertaker's clatter with his fist against the hollow panel? But let him in. Ah, here he comes. "Good day, sir:" an entire stranger. "Pray be seated." What is that strange-looking walking-stick he carries: "A fine thunder-storm sir."

"Fine?—Awful!"

"You are wet. Stand here on the hearth before the fire."

"Not for worlds!"

The stranger still stood in the exact middle of the cottage, where he had first planted himself. His singularity impelled a closer scrutiny. A lean, gloomy figure. Hair dark and lank, mattedly streaked over his brow. His sunken pitfalls of eyes were ringed by indigo halos,[2] and played with an innocuous sort of lightning: the gleam without the bolt. The whole man was dripping. He stood in a puddle on the bare oak floor: his strange walking-stick vertically resting at his side.

It was a polished copper rod, four feet long, lengthwise attached to a neat wooden staff, by insertion into two balls of greenish glass, ringed with copper bands. The metal rod terminated at the top tripodwise, in three keen tines, brightly gilt. He held the thing by the wooden part alone.

"Sir," said I, bowing politely, "have I the honor of a visit from that illustrious god, Jupiter Tonans?[3] So stood he in the Greek statue of old, grasping the lightning-bolt. If you be he, or his viceroy, I have to thank you for this noble storm you have brewed among our mountains. Listen: that was a glorious peal. Ah, to a lover of the majestic, it is a good thing to have the Thunderer himself in one's cottage.

---

1. **Acroceraunian**\ak·rō·sē ▲rōn·yən\ a mountain range in Albania opposite the southeast extremity of Italy, but here Melville is using the roots playfully to emphasize the literal subject of the story: *acer*, "bitter" and *ceraunia*, "thunderbolt." Melville's setting is New England; see notes 7 and 8.
2. **indigo**\▲ĭn·də·'gō\ **halos**\▲hā·loz\ violet-blue circles.
3. **Jupiter Tonans**, Jupiter the Thunderer.

The thunder grows finer for that. But pray be seated. This old rush-bottomed arm-chair, I grant, is a poor substitute for your evergreen throne on Olympus;[4] but, condescend to be seated."

While I thus pleasantly spoke, the stranger eyed me, half in wonder, and half in a strange sort of horror; but did not move a foot.

"Do, sir, be seated; you need to be dried ere going forth again."

I planted the chair invitingly on the broad hearth, where a little fire had been kindled that afternoon to dissipate the dampness, not the cold; for it was early in the month of September.

But without heeding my solicitation, and still standing in the middle of the floor, the stranger gazed at me portentously and spoke.

"Sir," said he, "excuse me; but instead of my accepting your invitation to be seated on the hearth there, I solemnly warn *you*, that you had best accept *mine,* and stand with me in the middle of the room. Good Heavens!" he cried, starting—"there is another of those awful crashes. I warn you, sir, quit the hearth."

"Mr. Jupiter Tonans," said I, quietly rolling my body on the stone, "I stand very well here."

"Are you so horridly ignorant, then," he cried, "as not to know, that by far the most dangerous part of a house, during such a terrific tempest as this, is the fire-place?"

"Nay, I did not know that," involuntarily stepping upon the first board next to the stone.

The stranger now assumed such an unpleasant air of successful admonition, that—quite involuntarily again—I stepped back upon the hearth, and threw myself into the erectest, proudest posture I could command. But I said nothing.

"For Heaven's sake," he cried, with a strange mixture of alarm and intimidation—"for Heaven's sake, get off the hearth! Know you not, that the heated air and soot are conductors;—to say nothing of those immense iron fire-dogs? Quit the spot—I conjure—I command you."

"Mr. Jupiter Tonans, I am not accustomed to be commanded in my own house."

"Call me not by that pagan name. You are profane in this time of terror."

"Sir, will you be so good as to tell me your business? If you seek shelter from the storm, you are welcome, so long as you be civil; but if you come on business, open it forthwith. Who are you?"

"I am a dealer in lightning-rods," said the stranger, softening his tone; "my special business is—— Merciful Heaven! what a crash!— Have you ever been struck—your premises, I mean? No? It's best to be provided,"—significantly rattling his metallic staff on the floor, —"by nature, there are no castles in thunderstorms; yet, say but the word, and of this cottage I can make a Gibraltar[5] by a few waves of this wand. Hark, what Himalayas of concussions!"

"You interrupted yourself; your special business you were about to speak of."

"My special business is to travel the country for orders for lightning-rods. This is my specimen rod;" tapping his staff; "I have the best of references"—fumbling in his pockets. "In Criggan last month, I put up three-and-twenty rods on only five buildings."

"Let me see. Was it not at Criggan last week, about midnight on Saturday, that the steeple, the big elm, and the assembly-room cupola were struck? Any of your rods there?"

"Not on the tree and cupola, but the steeple."

"Of what use is your rod, then?"

"Of life-and-death use. But my workman was heedless. In fitting the rod at the top of the steeple, he allowed a part of the metal to graze the tin sheeting. Hence the accident. Not my fault, but his. Hark!"

"Never mind. That clap burst quite loud enough to be heard without finger-pointing. Did you hear of the event at Montreal last year? A servant girl struck at her bed-side with

---

4. **Olympus**\ō ˈlĭm·pəs\ a high mountain in Greece, once believed to be the home of the gods.
5. **Gibraltar**\jə ˈbrɔl·tər\ famous rock fortress at the western entrance of the Mediterranean. Here, a safe refuge.

a rosary in her hand; the beads being metal. Does your beat extend into the Canadas?"

"No. And I hear that there, iron rods only are in use. They should have *mine*, which are copper. Iron is easily fused. Then they draw out the rod so slender, that it has not body enough to conduct the full electric current. The metal melts; the building is destroyed. My copper rods never act so. Those Canadians are fools. Some of them knob the rod at the top, which risks a deadly explosion, instead of imperceptibly carrying down the current into the earth, as this sort of rod does. *Mine* is the only true rod. Look at it. Only one dollar a foot."

"This abuse of your own calling in another might make one distrustful with respect to yourself."

"Hark! The thunder becomes less muttering. It is nearing us, and nearing the earth, too. Hark! One crammed crash! All the vibrations made one by nearness. Another flash. Hold."

"What do you?" I said, seeing him now instantaneously relinquishing his staff, lean intently forward towards the window, with his right fore and middle fingers on his left wrist.

But ere the words had well escaped me, another exclamation escaped him.

"Crash! only three pulses—less than a third of a mile off—yonder, somewhere in that wood. I passed three stricken oaks there, ripped out new and glittering. The oak draws lightning more than other timber, having iron in solution in its sap. Your floor here seems oak."

"Heart-of-oak. From the peculiar time of your call upon me, I suppose you purposely select stormy weather for your journeys. When the thunder is roaring, you deem it an hour peculiarly favorable for producing impressions favorable to your trade."

"Hark!—Awful!"

"For one who would arm others with fearlessness, you seem unbeseemingly timorous yourself. Common men choose fair weather for their travels: you choose thunder-storms; and yet——"

"That I travel in thunder-storms, I grant; but not without particular precautions, such as

only a lightning-rod man may know. Hark! Quick—look at my specimen rod. Only one dollar a foot."

"A very fine rod, I dare say. But what are these particular precautions of yours? Yet first let me close yonder shutters; the slanting rain is beating through the sash. I will bar up."

"Are you mad? Know you not that yon iron bar is a swift conductor? Desist."

"I will simply close the shutters, then, and call my boy to bring me a wooden bar. Pray, touch the bell-pull there."

"Are you frantic? That bell-wire might blast you. Never touch bell-wire in a thunder-storm, nor ring a bell of any sort."

"Nor those in belfries? Pray, will you tell me where and how one may be safe in a time like this? Is there any part of my house I may touch with hopes of my life?"

"There is; but not where you now stand. Come away from the wall. The current will sometimes run down a wall, and—a man being a better conductor than a wall—it would leave the wall and run into him. Swoop! *That* must have fallen very nigh. That must have been globular lightning."[6]

"Very probably. Tell me at once, which is, in your opinion, the safest part of this house?"

"This room, and this one spot in it where I stand. Come hither."

"The reasons first."

"Hark!—after the flash the gust—the sashes shiver—the house, the house!—Come hither to me!"

"The reasons, if you please."

"Come hither to me!"

"Thank you again, I think I will try my old stand—the hearth. And now, Mr. Lightning-rod man, in the pauses of the thunder, be so good as to tell me your reasons for esteeming this one room of the house the safest, and your own one stand-point there the safest spot in it."

6. **globular**\ˈglä·byū·lər\ **lightning,** ball lightning which consists of balls of fire as small as walnuts or as large as balloons that last three to five seconds. They fall swiftly from the clouds, exploding when they strike the earth. Sometimes they roll along the ground and do not explode until they hit an obstacle.

There was now a little cessation of the storm for a while. The Lightning-rod man seemed relieved, and replied:—

"Your house is a one-storied house, with an attic and a cellar; this room is between. Hence its comparative safety. Because lightning sometimes passes from the clouds to the earth, and sometimes from the earth to the clouds. Do you comprehend?—and I choose the middle of the room, because, if the lightning should strike the house at all, it would come down the chimney or walls; so, obviously, the further you are from them, the better. Come hither to me, now."

"Presently. Something you just said, instead of alarming me, has strangely inspired confidence."

"What have I said?"

"You said that sometimes lightning flashes from the earth to the clouds."

"Aye, the returning-stroke, as it is called; when the earth, being overcharged with the fluid, flashes its surplus upward."

"The returning-stroke; that is, from earth to sky. Better and better. But come here on the hearth and dry yourself."

"I am better here, and better wet."

"How?"

"It is the safest thing you can do—Hark, again!—to get yourself thoroughly drenched in a thunder-storm. Wet clothes are better conductors than the body; and so, if the lightning strike, it might pass down the wet clothes without touching the body. The storm deepens again. Have you a rug in the house? Rugs are non-conductors. Get one, that I may stand on it here, and you, too. The skies blacken—it is dusk at noon. Hark!—the rug, the rug!"

I gave him one; while the hooded mountains seemed closing and tumbling into the cottage.

"And now, since our being dumb will not help us," said I, resuming my place, "let me hear your precautions in traveling during thunder-storms."

"Wait till this one is passed."

"Nay, proceed with the precautions. You stand in the safest possible place according to your own account. Go on."

"Briefly, then. I avoid pine-trees, high houses, lonely barns, upland pastures, running water, flocks of cattle and sheep, a crowd of men. If I travel on foot—as to-day—I do not walk fast; if in my buggy, I touch not its back or sides; if on horseback, I dismount and lead the horse. But of all things, I avoid tall men."

"Do I dream? Man avoid man? and in danger-time, too."

"Tall men in a thunder-storm I avoid. Are you so grossly ignorant as not to know, that the height of a six-footer is sufficient to discharge an electric cloud upon him? Are not lonely Kentuckians, ploughing, smit in the unfinished furrow? Nay, if the six-footer stand by running water, the cloud will sometimes *select* him as its conductor to that running water. Hark! Sure, yon black pinnacle is split. Yes, a man is a good conductor. The lightning goes through and through a man, but only peels a tree. But sir, you have kept me so long answering your questions, that I have not yet come to business. Will you order one of my rods? Look at this specimen one? See: it is of the best copper. Copper's the best conductor. Your house is low; but being upon the mountains, that lowness does not one whit depress it. You mountaineers are most exposed. In mountainous countries the lightning-rod man should have most business. Look at the specimen, sir. One rod will answer for a house so small as this. Look over these recommendations. Only one rod, sir; cost, only twenty dollars. Hark! There go all the granite Taconics[7] and Hoosics[8] dashed together like pebbles. By the sound, that must have struck something. An elevation of five feet above the house, will protect twenty feet radius all about the rod. Only twenty dollars, sir—a dollar a foot. Hark!—Dreadful!—Will you order? Will you buy? Shall I put down your name? Think

---

7. **Taconics**\tə **̱**kon·ĭks\ a mountain ridge extending along the Massachusetts–New York border and into Vermont.
8. **Hoosics**\ **̱**hū·sĭks\ (usually spelled Hoosaks) a range of the Green Mountains in west Massachusetts.

of being a heap of charred offal, like a haltered horse burnt in his stall; and all in one flash!"

"You pretended envoy extraordinary and minister plenipotentiary[9] to and from Jupiter Tonans," laughed I; "you mere man who come here to put you and your pipestem between clay and sky, do you think that because you can strike a bit of green light from the Leyden jar,[10] that you can thoroughly avert the supernal bolt? Your rod rusts, or breaks, and where are you? Who has empowered you, you Tetzel,[11] to peddle round your indulgences[12] from divine ordinations? The hairs of our heads are numbered, and the days of our lives. In thunder as in sunshine, I stand at ease in the hands of my God. False negotiator, away! See, the scroll of the storm is rolled back; the house is unharmed; and in the blue heavens I read in the rainbow,[13] that the Deity will not, of purpose, make war on man's earth."

"Impious wretch!" foamed the stranger, blackening in the face as the rainbow beamed, "I will publish your infidel notions."

"Begone! move quickly! if quickly you can, you that shine forth into sight in moist times like the worm."

The scowl grew blacker on his face; the indigo-circles enlarged round his eyes as the storm-rings round the midnight moon. He sprang upon me, his tri-forked thing at my heart.

I seized it; I snapped it; I dashed it; I trod it; and dragging the dark lightning-king out of my door, flung his elbowed, copper sceptre after him.

But spite of my treatment, and spite of my dissuasive talk of him to my neighbors, the Lightning-rod man still dwells in the land; still travels in storm-time, and drives a brave trade with the fears of man.

I
THE ATTITUDE
OF THE RATIONAL FREE SPIRIT

The narrator in this story does not say that lightning is harmless, nor does he underrate its de-

structiveness; but he faces it without cowering, as a free spirit should. He never gives in to the counsels of fear from the salesman, for to do so would be to abandon reason and become a slave to irrational emotions.

II
IMPLICATIONS

Discuss each of the following questions.

1. Does the lightning-rod man still dwell in the land? Explain.

2. Argue by examples for or against the proposition that people faced by danger follow their emotions rather than their reason.

3. How do you reconcile the free spirit of the narrator with his belief in predestination?

III
TECHNIQUES

Symbolism

How can you decide whether or not this story should be interpreted symbolically? For one thing, you can ask some questions about the characters. Take the narrator, for example. Where does he live? What is his real name, his background? The fact that we have only vague answers to such questions suggests that the author doesn't care about them. It is not who the character is but what he stands for that is the primary consideration. What does the narrator stand for?

---

9. **minister plenipotentiary**\plĕ•nə•pə ᴬtĕnch•rē\ a person, especially a diplomat, who has been given full power to transact any business.
10. **Leyden**\lai•dən\ **jar**, a form of electrical condenser.
11. **Tetzel**\ᴬtĕt•səl\ Johann Tetzel (1465–1519), a German Dominican monk who debated with Martin Luther, then an Augustinian friar, the question of indulgences.
2. **indulgences**\ĭn ᴬdəl•jən•səz\ a Roman Catholic doctrine: "The remission in whole or part of temporal punishment due to sin, provided the sin has already been forgiven."—*Maryknoll Catholic Dictionary*.
13. **rainbow**, Genesis 9:11–17. After the Deluge, God made a covenant or solemn agreement with Noah that never again would such a flood engulf the earth. The rainbow was God's signature to that covenant. "I do set my bow in the cloud, and it shall be for a token of a covenant between me and the earth."

Can man's soul when it is once pinched by fear, sickened
by pain and sorrow, anguished by its own and the world's crimes—
can such a soul be renewed, reborn to a fresh awareness of
and faith in the world's fundamental beauty and goodness? Be alert
for the poet's shifting moods as she searches successfully for purpose
and meaning in life and the world.

Renascence

EDNA ST. VINCENT MILLAY

All I could see from where I stood
Was three long mountains and a wood;
I turned and looked another way,
And saw three islands in a bay.
So with my eyes I traced the line   5
Of the horizon, thin and fine,
Straight around till I was come
Back to where I'd started from;
And all I saw from where I stood
Was three long mountains and a wood.   10
Over these things I could not see;
These were the things that bounded me;
And I could touch them with my hand,
Almost, I thought, from where I stand.

And all at once things seemed so small   15
My breath came short, and scarce at all.
But, sure, the sky is big, I said;
Miles and miles above my head;
So here upon my back I'll lie
And look my fill into the sky.   20
And so I looked, and, after all,
The sky was not so very tall.
The sky, I said, must somewhere stop,
And—sure enough!—I see the top!
The sky, I thought, is not so grand;   25
I 'most could touch it with my hand!
And, reaching up my hand to try,
I screamed to feel it touch the sky.

I screamed, and—lo!—Infinity[1]
Came down and settled over me;   30
Forced back my scream into my chest,
Bent back my arm upon my breast,
And, pressing of the Undefined
The definition on my mind,[2]
Held up before my eyes a glass   35
Through which my shrinking sight did pass
Until it seemed I must behold
Immensity made manifold;
Whispered to me a word whose sound
Deafened the air for worlds around,   40
And brought unmuffled to my ears
The gossiping of friendly spheres,
The creaking of the tented sky,
The ticking of Eternity.

I saw and heard, and knew at last   45
The How and Why of all things, past
And present, and forevermore.
The universe, cleft to the core,
Lay open to my probing sense
That, sick'ning, I would fain pluck thence   50
But could not—nay! But needs must suck
At the great wound, and could not pluck

1. **Infinity**, when capitalized, as here, stands for God, the One, the First Cause.
2. **pressing of the Undefined/The definition on my mind**, revealing to my mind the meaning of that Being who can not be defined in the usual sense of the word because to define means to set limits (*Latin:* definire, to limit) and limits cannot be set to the Infinite.

My lips away till I had drawn
All venom out.—Ah, fearful pawn![3]
For my omniscience paid I toll[4]   55
In infinite remorse of soul.
All sin was of my sinning, all
Atoning mine, and mine the gall
Of all regret. Mine was the weight
Of every brooded wrong, the hate   60
That stood behind each envious thrust,
Mine every greed, mine every lust.
And all the while for every grief,
Each suffering, I craved relief
With individual desire—   65
Craved all in vain! And felt fierce fire
About a thousand people crawl;
Perished with each—then mourned for all!
A man was starving in Capri;[5]
He moved his eyes and looked at me;   70
I felt his gaze, I heard his moan,
And knew his hunger as my own.
I saw at sea a great fog bank
Between two ships that struck and sank;
A thousand screams the heavens smote;   75
And every scream tore through my throat.
No hurt I did not feel, no death
That was not mine; mine each last breath
That, crying, met an answering cry
From the compassion that was I.   80
All suffering mine, and mine its rod;[6]
Mine, pity like the pity of God.
Ah, awful weight! Infinity
Pressed down upon the finite Me!
My anguished spirit, like a bird,   85
Beating against my lips I heard;
Yet lay the weight so close about
There was no room for it without.
And so beneath the weight lay I
And suffered death, but could not die.   90

Deep in the earth I rested now;
Cool is its hand upon the brow
And soft its breast beneath the head
Of one who is so gladly dead.
And all at once, and over all,   95
The pitying rain began to fall;
I lay and heard each pattering hoof
Upon my lowly, thatchèd roof,

And seemed to love the sound far more
Than ever I had done before.   100
For rain it hath a friendly sound
To one who's six feet underground;
And scarce[7] the friendly voice or face:
A grave is such a quiet place.

The rain, I said, is kind to come   105
And speak to me in my new home.
I would I were alive again
To kiss the fingers of the rain,
To drink into my eyes the shine
Of every slanting silver line,   110
To catch the freshened, fragrant breeze
From drenched and dripping apple trees.
For soon the shower will be done,
And then the broad face of the sun
Will laugh above the rain-soaked earth   115
Until the world with answering mirth
Shakes joyously, and each round drop
Rolls, twinkling, from its grass-blade top.
How can I bear it; buried here,
While overhead the sky grows clear   120
And blue again after the storm?

O, multicolored, multiform
Belovèd beauty over me,
That I shall never, never see
Again! Spring silver, autumn gold,   125
That I shall never more behold!
Sleeping your myriad magics through,
Close sepulchered away from you!
O God, I cried, give me new birth,
And put me back upon the earth!   130
Upset each cloud's gigantic gourd[8]

---

3. **fearful pawn\pon** *Latin:* pedo, foot soldier. One of
the sixteen chessmen of least value and with greatest
limitation of movement on the chessboard. Here, an
insignificant person full of fear.
4. **For my omniscience paid I toll,** for my all-knowing
I paid a price. I had become one with all; I suffered
with all.
5. **Capri\ka ▲prē** an Italian island south of Naples.
6. **all suffering mine, and mine its rod.** In the moment
of attunement with the Infinite, the poet was at one
both with the sufferer and with that (the rod) which
caused the suffering.
7. **scarce,** here, the word means *seldom met.*
8. **gourd\gōrd** a plant that bears fruit with a shell
which is often dried and used to make dippers.

And let the heavy rain, down poured
In one big torrent, set me free,
Washing my grave away from me!

I ceased; and, through the breathless hush   135
That answered me, the far-off rush
Of herald wings came whispering
Like music down the vibrant string
Of my ascending prayer, and—crash!
Before the wild wind's whistling lash   140
The startled storm clouds reared on high
And plunged in terror down the sky,
And the big rain in one black wave
Fell from the sky and struck my grave.
I know not how such things can be   145
I only know there came to me
A fragrance such as never clings
To aught save happy living things;
A sound as of some joyous elf
Singing sweet songs to please himself,   150
And, through and over everything,
A sense of glad awakening.
The grass, a-tiptoe at my ear,
Whispering to me I could hear;
I felt the rain's cool finger tips   155
Brushed tenderly across my lips,
Laid gently on my sealèd sight,
And all at once the heavy night
Fell from my eyes and I could see—
A drenched and dripping apple tree,   160
A last long line of silver rain,
A sky grown clear and blue again.
And as I looked a quickening gust
Of wind blew up to me and thrust
Into my face a miracle   165
Of orchard breath, and with the smell—
I know not how such things can be!—
I breathed my soul back into me.

Ah! Up then from the ground sprang I
And hailed the earth with such a cry   170
As is not heard save from a man
Who has been dead, and lives again.
About the trees my arms I wound;
Like one gone mad I hugged the ground;
I raised my quivering arms on high;   175
I laughed and laughed into the sky,

Till at my throat a strangling sob
Caught fiercely, and a great heartthrob
Sent instant tears into my eyes;
O God, I cried, no dark disguise   180
Can e'er hereafter hide from me
Thy radiant identity!
Thou canst not move across the grass
But my quick eyes will see Thee pass,
Nor speak, however silently,   185
But my hushed voice will answer Thee.
I know the path that tells Thy way
Through the cool eve of every day;
God, I can push the grass apart
And lay my finger on Thy heart!   190

The world stands out on either side
No wider than the heart is wide;
Above the world is stretched the sky—
No higher than the soul is high.
The heart can push the sea and land   195
Farther away on either hand;
The soul can split the sky in two,
And let the face of God shine through.
But East and West will pinch the heart
That cannot keep them pushed apart;   200
And he whose soul is flat—the sky
Will cave in on him by and by.

I

THE REBIRTH OF THE SOUL

The feeling that one needs to be reborn spiritually often has its beginnings in the frustrations and failings of one's personal life, as well as in one's concern over the sufferings and crimes of humanity. And nearly always the rebirth involves some sort of suffering or atonement by which the soul is purged and washed clean.

1. What personal frustrations seem to beset the narrator?

2. What sufferings and crimes of the world trouble her? How do they affect her?

3. What does she suffer before she is reborn?

4. How does her rebirth change her?

II
IMPLICATIONS

Discuss the meaning of the following quotations and show how they relate to one another in telling the story of the narrator's rebirth.

1. And all I saw from where I stood
   Was three long mountains and a wood.
   Over these things I could not see;
   These were the things that bounded me;
   (lines 9–12)

2. I screamed, and—lo!—Infinity
   Came down and settled over me;
   (lines 29–30)

   . . . .

   Until it seemed I must behold
   Immensity made manifold;   (lines 37–38)

3. All suffering mine, and mine its rod;
   Mine, pity like the pity of God.
   Ah, awful weight! Infinity
   Pressed down upon the finite Me!
   (lines 81–84)

4. Before the wild wind's whistling lash
   The startled storm clouds reared on high
   And plunged in terror down the sky,
   And the big rain in one black wave
   Fell from the sky and struck my grave.
   (lines 140–144)

5. O God, I cried, no dark disguise
   Can e'er hereafter hide from me
   Thy radiant identity!   (lines 180–182)

   . . . .

   God, I can push the grass apart
   And lay my finger on Thy heart!
   (lines 189–190)

6. The world stands out on either side
   No wider than the heart is wide;
   Above the world is stretched the sky—
   No higher than the soul is high.
   (lines 191–194)

III
TECHNIQUES

Structure

Note the division of the poem into ten stanzas. Try to summarize the thought in each of them in a sentence or two in order to better see the planned framework of the poem. Also, compare the following: lines 1–16 with lines 151–160; lines 105–112 with lines 153–162; lines 1–28 with lines 187–202. Show how these comparisons argue for the idea that the poem was carefully planned.

Symbolism

1. What do the wind and the rain symbolize? Be prepared to argue for or against the notion that they are well-chosen symbols.

2. What does the poet's touching the sky symbolize?

3. What is the symbolic meaning of the "great wound"?

IV
WORDS

To develop large speaking, reading, and writing vocabularies, you must become interested in words, in how words acquire meanings, in how words change, and in how to add meanings to words you already know. The study of synonyms and antonyms helps sharpen your understanding of the distinctions that set words apart. Test your word knowledge by giving a synonym and antonym for the italicized words in each phrase.

> *stigma* of a fiction *monger*
> certain *alacrity* in his gait
> all had *furtive* appearances
> *fervent* explorations
> *inured* to my high-handed raids
> *bogus* refugees
> filed *sullenly* aboard
> *languid* with rest
> *precariously* rooted shrub
> *salient* characteristics

"Why was I born? Why am I living?" . . .
No other modern American writer has sought to answer
these haunting, universal questions so honestly and profoundly
as the Nobel-Prize-winning author, William Faulkner. Ironically,
though he exposes man's degradation and depravity in many of his stories,
Faulkner's works make a firm affirmation of his faith in the fundamental
nobility of man and the purposefulness of the universe. The following
two works, both by Faulkner, reflect this affirmation. "Race at Morning"
is a hunting story with a very unusual outcome, seen through the eyes
of a twelve-year-old boy. "Man Will Prevail" is Faulkner's Nobel Prize
Acceptance Speech. See what common elements you can find in the two.

Race at Morning

WILLIAM FAULKNER

I was in the boat when I seen him. It was jest dusk-dark; I had jest fed the horses and clumb back down the bank to the boat and shoved off to cross back to camp when I seen him, about half a quarter up the river, swimming; jest his head above the water, and it no more than a dot in that light. But I could see that rocking chair[1] he toted on it and I knowed it was him, going right back to that canebrake in the fork of the bayou[2] where he lived all year until the day before the season opened, like the game wardens had give him a calendar, when he would clear out and disappear, nobody knowed where, until the day after the season closed. But here he was, coming back a day ahead of time, like maybe he had got mixed up and was using last year's calendar by mistake. Which was jest too bad for him, because me and Mister Ernest would be setting on the horse right over him when the sun rose tomorrow morning.

So I told Mister Ernest and we et supper and fed the dogs, and then I help Mister Ernest in the poker game, standing behind his chair un-

til about ten o'clock, when Roth Edmonds said, "Why don't you go to bed, boy?"

"Or if you're going to set up," Willy Legate said, "why don't you take a spelling book to set up over? . . . He knows every cuss word in the dictionary, every poker hand in the deck and every whisky label in the distillery, but he can't even write his name . . . Can you?" he says to me.

"I don't need to write my name down," I said. "I can remember in my mind who I am."

"You're twelve years old," Walter Ewell said. "Man to man, now, how many days in your life did you ever spend in school?"

"He ain't got time to go to school," Willy Legate said. "What's the use in going to school from September to middle of November, when he'll have to quit then to come in here and do Ernest's hearing for him? And what's the use in going back to school in January, when in jest eleven months it will be November fifteenth

---

1. **rocking chair**, the twelve-pointed antlers or horns of a great stag.
2. **canebrake in the fork of the bayou**\ˈbai·ō\ a thicket of reeds and woody grasses on an island at the fork of the marshy, sluggish little river.

again and he'll have to start all over telling Ernest which way the dogs went?"

"Well, stop looking into my hand, anyway," Roth Edmonds said.

"What's that? What's that?" Mister Ernest said. He wore his listening button in his ear all the time, but he never brought the battery to camp with him because the cord would bound to get snagged ever time we run through a thicket.

"Willy says for me to go to bed!" I hollered.

"Don't you never call nobody 'mister'?" Willy said.

"I call Mister Ernest 'mister,'" I said.

"All right," Mister Ernest said. "Go to bed then. I don't need you."

"That ain't no lie," Willy said. "Deaf or no deaf, he can hear a fifty-dollar raise if you don't even move your lips."

So I went to bed, and after a while Mister Ernest come in and I wanted to tell him again how big them horns looked even half a quarter away in the river. Only I would 'a' had to holler, and the only time Mister Ernest agreed he couldn't hear was when we would be setting on Dan, waiting for me to point which way the dogs was going. So we jest laid down, and it wasn't no time Simon was beating the bottom of the dishpan with the spoon, hollering, "Raise up and get your four-o'clock coffee!" and I crossed the river in the dark this time, with the lantern, and fed Dan and Roth Edmondziz horse. It was going to be a fine day, cold and bright; even in the dark I could see the white frost on the leaves and bushes—jest exactly the kind of day that big old son of a gun laying up there in that brake would like to run.

Then we et, and set the stand-holder[3] across for Uncle Ike McCaslin to put them on the stands where he thought they ought to be, because he was the oldest one in camp. He had been hunting deer in these woods for about a hundred years, I reckon, and if anybody would know where a buck would pass, it would be him. Maybe with a big old buck like this one, that had been running the woods for what would amount to a hundred years in a deer's

life, too, him and Uncle Ike would sholy manage to be at the same place at the same time this morning—provided, of course, he managed to git away from me and Mister Ernest on the jump. Because me and Mister Ernest was going to git him.

Then me and Mister Ernest and Roth Edmonds set the dogs over, with Simon holding Eagle and the other old dogs on leash because the young ones, the puppies, wasn't going nowhere until Eagle let them, nohow. Then me and Mister Ernest and Roth saddled up, and Mister Ernest got up and I handed him up his pump gun and let Dan's bridle go for him to git rid of the spell of bucking he had to git shut of ever morning until Mister Ernest hit him between the ears with the gun barrel. Then Mister Ernest loaded the gun and give me the stirrup, and I got up behind him and we taken the fire road[4] up toward the bayou, the five big dogs dragging Simon along in front with his single-barrel britchloader slung on a piece of plow line across his back, and the puppies moiling along in ever'body's way. It was light now and it was going to be jest fine; the east already yellow for the sun and our breaths smoking in the cold still bright air until the sun would come up and warm it, and a little skim of ice in the ruts, and ever leaf and twig and switch and even the frozen clods frosted over, waiting to sparkle like a rainbow when the sun finally come up and hit them. Until all my insides felt light and strong as a balloon, full of that light cold strong air, so that it seemed to me like I couldn't even feel the horse's back I was straddle of—jest the hot strong muscles moving under the hot strong skin, setting up there without no weight atall, so that when old Eagle struck and jumped, me and Dan and Mister Ernest would go jest like

3. **stand-holder,** a wooden platform with four legs which can be driven into soft earth or into the bottom of a bayou or marsh. On it hunters wait for the game to be driven toward them so that they may have a chance to shoot. Here, the stand-holder is floated across the bayou and set up on the far side.
4. **fire road,** a fire break, a barrier of cleared land intended to stop a forest fire.

a bird, not even touching the ground. It was jest fine. When that big old buck got killed today, I knowed that even if he had put it off another ten years, he couldn't 'a' picked a better one.

And sho enough, as soon as we come to the bayou we seen his foot in the mud where he had come up out of the river last night, spread in the soft mud like a cow's foot, big as a cow's, big as a mule's, with Eagle and the other dogs laying into the leash rope now until Mister Ernest told me to jump down and help Simon hold them. Because me and Mister Ernest knowed exactly where he would be—a little canebrake island in the middle of the bayou, where he could lay up until whatever doe or little deer the dogs had happened to jump could go up or down the bayou in either direction and take the dogs on away, so he could steal out and creep back down the bayou to the river and swim it, and leave the country like he always done the day the season opened.

Which is jest what we never aimed for him to do this time. So we left Roth on his horse to cut him off and turn him over Uncle Ike's standers if he tried to slip back down the bayou, and me and Simon, with the leashed dogs, walked on up the bayou until Mister Ernest on the horse said it was fur enough; then turned up into the woods about half a quarter above the brake because the wind was going to be south this morning when it riz, and turned down toward the brake, and Mister Ernest give the word to cast them,[5] and we slipped the leash and Mister Ernest give me the stirrup again and I got up.

Old Eagle had done already took off because he knowed where that old son of a gun would be laying as good as we did, not making no racket atall yet, but jest boring on through the buck vines with the other dogs trailing along behind him, and even Dan seemed to know about that buck, too, beginning to souple up and jump a little through the vines, so that I taken my holt on Mister Ernest's belt already before the time had come for Mister Ernest to touch him. Because when we got strung out,

going fast behind a deer, I wasn't on Dan's back much of the time nohow, but mostly jest strung out from my holt on Mister Ernest's belt, so that Willy Legate said that when we was going through the wood fast, it looked like Mister Ernest had a boy-size pair of empty overhalls blowing out of his hind pocket.

So it wasn't even a strike, it was a jump. Eagle must 'a' walked right up behind him or maybe even stepped on him while he was laying there still thinking it was day after to-morrow. Eagle jest throwed his head back and up and said, "There he goes," and we even heard the buck crashing through the first of the cane. Then all the other dogs was hollering behind him, and Dan give a squat to jump, but it was against the curb[6] this time, not jest the snaffle,[7] and Mister Ernest let him down into the bayou and swung him around the brake and up the other bank. Only he never had to say, "Which way?" because I was already pointing past his shoulder, freshening my holt on the belt jest as Mister Ernest touched Dan with that big old rusty spur on his nigh heel, because when Dan felt it he would go off jest like a stick of dynamite, straight through whatever he could bust and over or under what he couldn't.

The dogs was already almost out of hearing. Eagle must 'a' been looking right up that big son of a gun's tail until he finally decided he better git on out of there. And now they must 'a' been getting pretty close to Uncle Ike's standers, and Mister Ernest reined Dan back and held him, squatting and bouncing and trembling like a mule having his tail roached,[8] while we listened for the shots. But never none come, and I hollered to Mister Ernest we better go on while I could still hear the dogs, and he let Dan off, but still there wasn't no shots, and now we knowed the race had done already

---

5. **to cast them,** to let the dogs run.
6. **curb,** a chain or strap on the upper part of the branches of a bit used to restrain a horse.
7. **snaffle,** a simple jointed bit.
8. **tail roached,** the removal of hair from the upper part of a mule's tail.

passed the standers; and we busted out of a thicket, and sho enough there was Uncle Ike and Willy standing beside his foot in a soft patch.

"He got through us all," Uncle Ike said. "I don't know how he done it. I just had a glimpse of him. He looked big as a elephant, with a rack[9] on his head you could cradle a yellin' calf in. He went right on down the ridge. You better get on, too; that Hog Bayou camp might not miss him."

So I freshened my holt and Mister Ernest touched Dan again. The ridge run due south; it was clear of vines and bushes so we could go fast, into the wind, too, because it had riz now, and now the sun was up too. So we would hear the dogs again any time now as the wind get up; we could make time now, but still holding Dan to a canter,[10] because it was either going to be quick, when he got down to the standers from that Hog Bayou camp eight miles below ourn, or a long time, in case he got by them too. And sho enough, after a while we heard the dogs; we was walking Dan now to let him blow a while, and we heard them, the sound coming faint up the wind, not running now, but trailing because the big son of a gun had decided a good piece back, probably, to put an end to this foolishness, and picked hisself up and souped out and put about a mile between hisself and the dogs—until he run up on them other standers from that camp below. I could almost see him stopped behind a bush, peeping out and saying, "What's this? What's this? Is this whole durn country full of folks this morning?" Then looking back over his shoulder at where old Eagle and the others was hollering along after him while he decided how much time he had to decide what to do next.

Except he almost shaved it too fine. We heard the shots; it sounded like a war. Old Eagle must 'a' been looking right up his tail again and he had to bust on through the best way he could. "Pow, pow, pow, pow" and then "Pow, pow, pow, pow," like it must 'a' been three or four ganged right up on him before

he had time even to swerve, and me hollering, "No! No! No! No!" because he was ourn. It was our beans and oats he et and our brake he laid in; we had been watching him every year, and it was like we had raised him, to be killed at last on our jump, in front of our dogs, by some strangers that would probably try to beat the dogs off and drag him away before we could even git a piece of the meat.

"Shut up and listen," Mister Ernest said. So I done it and we could hear the dogs; not just the others, but Eagle, too, not trailing no scent now and not baying no downed meat, neither, but running hot on sight long after the shooting was over. I jest had time to freshen my holt. Yes, sir, they was running on sight. Like Willy Legate would say, if Eagle jest had a drink of whisky he would ketch that deer; going on, done already gone when we broke out of the thicket and seen the fellers that had done the shooting, five or six of them, squatting and crawling around, looking at the ground and the bushes, like maybe if they looked hard enough, spots of blood would bloom out on the stalks and leaves like frogstools or hawberries.

"Have any luck, boys?" Mister Ernest said.

"I think I hit him," one of them said. "I know I did. We're hunting blood, now."

"Well, when you have found him, blow your horn and I'll come back and tote him in to camp for you," Mister Ernest said.

So we went on, going fast now because the race was almost out of hearing again, going fast, too, like not jest the buck, but the dogs, too, had took a new leash on life[11] from all the excitement and shooting.

We was in strange country now because we never had to run this fur before, we had always killed before now; now we had come to Hog Bayou that runs into the river a good fifteen miles below our camp. It had water in it, not to mention a mess of down trees and logs and

---

9. **rack**, antlers, horns.
10. **canter**, a three-beat trot, resembling but smoother and slower than a gallop.
11. **a new leash on life**, the boy means a new lease or hold on life.

such, and Mister Ernest checked Dan again, saying, "Which way?" I could just barely hear them, off to the east a little, like the old son of a gun had give up the idea Vicksburg or New Orleans, like he first seemed to have, and had decided to have a look at Alabama; so I pointed and we turned up the bayou hunting for a crossing, and maybe we could 'a' found one, except that I reckon Mister Ernest decided we never had time to wait.

We come to a place where the bayou had narrowed down to about twelve or fifteen feet, and Mister Ernest said, "Look out, I'm going to touch him," and done it.

I didn't even have time to freshen my holt when we was already in the air, and then I seen the vine—it was a loop of grapevine nigh as big as my wrist, looping down right across the middle of the bayou—and I thought he seen it, too, and was jest waiting to grab it and fling it up over our heads to go under it, and I know Dan seen it because he even ducked his head to jump under it. But Mister Ernest never seen it atall until it skun back along Dan's neck and hooked under the head of the saddle horn, us flying on through the air, the loop of the vine gitting tighter and tighter until something somewhere was going to have to give. It was the saddle girth.[12] It broke, and Dan going on and scrabbling up the other bank bare nekkid except for the bridle, and me and Mister Ernest and the saddle, Mister Ernest still setting in the saddle holding the gun, and me still holding onto Mister Ernest's belt, hanging in the air over the bayou in the tightened loop of that vine like in the drawed-back loop of a big rubber-banded slingshot, until it snapped back and shot us back across the bayou and flang us clear, me still holding onto Mister Ernest's belt and on the bottom now, so that when we lit I would 'a' had Mister Ernest and the saddle both on top of me if I hadn't clumb fast around the saddle and up Mister Ernest's side, so that when we landed, it was the saddle first, then Mister Ernest, and me on top, until I jumped up, and Mister Ernest

Copyright © 1963, Martin J. Dain

A hunter in the woods near Faulkner's home

still laying there with jest the white rim of his eyes showing.

"Mister Ernest!" I hollered, and then clumb down to the bayou and scopped my cap full of water and clumb back and throwed it in his face, and he opened his eyes and laid there on the saddle cussing me.

"God dawg it," he said, "why didn't you stay behind where you started out?"

---

12. **saddle girth,** the band or strap that encircles a horse's body to hold the saddle on his back.

"You was the biggest!" I said. "You would 'a' mashed me flat!"

"What do you think you done to me?" Mister Ernest said. "Next time, if you can't stay where you start out, jump clear. Don't climb up on top of me no more. You hear?"

"Yes, sir," I said.

So he got up then, still cussing and holding his back, and clumb down to the water and dipped some in his hand onto his face and neck and dipped some more up and drunk it, and I drunk some, too, and clumb back and got the saddle and the gun, and we crossed the bayou on the down logs. If we could jest ketch Dan; not that he would have went them fifteen miles back to camp, because, if anything, he would have went on by hisself to try to help Eagle ketch that buck. But he was about fifty yards away, eating buck vines, so I brought him back, and we taken Mister Ernest's galluses[13] and my belt and the whang leather[14] loop off Mister Ernest's horn and tied the saddle back on Dan. It didn't look like much, but maybe it would hold.

"Provided you don't let me jump him through no more grapevines without hollering first," Mister Ernest said.

"Yes, sir," I said. "I'll holler first next time— provided you'll holler a little quicker when you touch him next time too." But it was all right; we jest had to be a little easy getting up. "Now which-a-way?" I said. Because we couldn't hear nothing now, after wasting all this time. And this was new country, sho enough. It had been cut over and growed up in thickets we couldn't 'a' seen over even standing up on Dan.

But Mister Ernest never even answered. He jest turned Dan along the bank of the bayou where it was a little more open, and we could move faster again, soon as Dan and us got used to that homemade cinch strop and got a little confidence in it. Which jest happened to be east, or so I thought then, because I never paid no particular attention to east then because the sun—I don't know where the morning had

went, but it was gone, the morning and the frost, too—was up high now.

And then we heard him. No, that's wrong; what we heard was shots. And that was when we realized how fur we had come, because the only camp we knowed about in that direction was the Hollyknowe camp, and Hollyknowe was exactly twenty-eight miles from Van Dorn, where me and Mister Ernest lived—just the shots, no dogs nor nothing. If old Eagle was still behind him and the buck was still alive, he was too wore out now to even say, "Here he comes."

"Don't touch him!" I hollered. But Mister Ernest remembered that cinch strop, too, and he jest let Dan off the snaffle. And Dan heard them shots, too, picking his way through the thickets, hopping the vines and logs when he could and going under them when he couldn't. And sho enough, it was jest like before—two or three men squatting and creeping among the bushes, looking for blood that Eagle had done already told them wasn't there. But we never stopped this time, jest trotting on by. Then Mister Ernest swung Dan until we was going due north.

"Wait!" I hollered. "Not this way."

But Mister Ernest jest turned his face back over his shoulder. It looked tired, too, and there was a smear of mud on it where that 'ere grapevine had snatched him off the horse.

"Don't you know where he's heading?" he said. "He's done done his part, give everybody a fair open shot at him, and now he's going home, back to that brake in our bayou. He ought to make it exactly at dark."

And that's what he was doing. We went on. It didn't matter to hurry now. There wasn't no sound nowhere; it was that time in the early afternoon in November when don't nothing move or cry, not even birds, the peckerwoods and yellowhammers and jays, and it seemed to me like I could see all three of us—me and Mister Ernest and Dan—and Eagle, and the other

---

13. **galluses**\ˈgăl·əs·əs\ suspenders.
14. **whang leather,** rawhide leather.

dogs, and that big old buck, moving through the quiet woods in the same direction, headed for the same place, not running now but walking, that had all run the fine race the best we knowed how, and all three of us now turned like on a agreement to walk back home, not together in a bunch because we didn't want to worry or tempt one another, because what we had all three spent this morning doing was no play-acting jest for fun, but was serious, and all three of us was still what we was—that old buck that had to run, not because he was skeered, but because running was what he done the best and was proudest at; and Eagle and the dogs that chased him, not because they hated or feared him, but because that was the thing they done the best and was proudest at; and me and Mister Ernest and Dan, that run him not because we wanted his meat, which would be too tough to eat anyhow, or his head to hang on a wall, but because now we could go back and work hard for eleven months making a crop, so we would have the right to come back here next November—all three of us going back home now, peaceful and separate, until next year, next time.

Then we seen him for the first time. We was out of the cutover now; we could even 'a' cantered, except that all three of us was long past that. So we was walking, too, when we come on the dogs—the puppies and one of the old ones—played out, laying in a little wet swag,[15] panting, jest looking up at us when we passed. Then we come to a long open glade, and we seen the three other old dogs and about a hundred yards ahead of them Eagle, all walking, not making no sound; and then suddenly, at the fur end of the glade, the buck hisself getting up from where he had been resting for the dogs to come up, getting up without no hurry, big, big as a mule, tall as a mule, and turned, and the white underside of his tail for a second or two more before the thicket taken him.

It might 'a' been a signal, a good-by, a farewell. Still walking, we passed the other three old dogs in the middle of the glade, laying down, too; and still that hundred yards ahead

of them, Eagle, too, not laying down, because he was still on his feet, but his legs was spraddled and his head was down; maybe jest waiting until we was out of sight of his shame, his eyes saying plain as talk when we passed, "I'm sorry, boys, but this here is all."

Mister Ernest stopped Dan. "Jump down and look at his feet," he said.

"Nothing wrong with his feet," I said. "It's his wind has done give out."

"Jump down and look at his feet," Mister Ernest said.

So I done it, and while I was stooping over Eagle I could hear the pump gun go, "Snick-cluck. Snick-cluck. Snick-cluck" three times, except that I never thought nothing then. Maybe he was jest running the shells through to be sho it would work when we seen him again or maybe to make sho they was all buckshot. Then I got up again, and we went on, still walking; a little west of north now, because when we seen his white flag that second or two before the thicket hid it, it was on a beeline for that notch in the bayou. And it was evening, too, now. The wind had done dropped and there was a edge to the air and the sun jest touched the tops of the trees. And he was taking the easiest way, too, now, going straight as he could. When we seen his foot in the soft places he was running for a while at first after his rest. But soon he was walking, too, like he knowed, too, where Eagle and the dogs was.

And then we seen him again. It was the last time—a thicket, with the sun coming through a hole onto it like a searchlight. He crashed jest once; then he was standing there broadside to us, not twenty yards away, big as a statue and red as gold in the sun, and the sun sparking on the tips of his horns—they was twelve of them—so that he looked like he had twelve lighted candles branched around his head, standing there looking at us while Mister Ernest raised the gun and aimed at his neck, and the gun went, "Click. Snick-cluck. Click. Snick-cluck. Click. Snick-cluck" three times, and Mister

---

15. **wet swag,** a little wet depression.

Ernest still holding the gun aimed while the buck turned and give one long bound, the white underside of his tail like a blaze of fire, too, until the thicket and the shadows put it out; and Mister Ernest laid the gun slow and gentle back across the saddle in front of him, saying quiet and peaceful, and not much louder than jest breathing, "God dawg. God dawg."

Then he jogged me with his elbow and we got down, easy and careful because of that ere cinch strop, and he reached into his vest and taken out one of the cigars. It was busted where I had fell on it, I reckon, when we hit the ground. He throwed it away and taken out the other one. It was busted, too, so he bit off a hunk of it to chew and throwed the rest away. And now the sun was gone even from the tops of the trees and there wasn't nothing left but a big red glare in the west.

"Don't worry," I said. "I ain't going to tell them you forgot to load your gun. For that matter, they don't need to know we ever seed him."

"Much oblige," Mister Ernest said. There wasn't going to be no moon tonight neither, so he taken the compass off the whang leather loop in his buttonhole and handed me the gun and set the compass on a stump and stepped back and looked at it. "Jest about the way we're headed now," he said, and taken the gun from me and opened it and put one shell in the britch[16] and taken up the compass, and I taken Dan's reins and we started, with him in front with the compass in his hand.

And after a while it was full dark; Mister Ernest would have to strike a match ever now and then to read the compass, until the stars come out good and we could pick out one to follow, because I said, "How fur do you reckon it is?" and he said, "A little more than one box of matches." So we used a star when we could, only we couldn't see it all the time because the woods was too dense and we would git a little off until he would have to spend another match. And now it was good and late, and he stopped and said, "Get on the horse."

"I ain't tired," I said.

"Get on the horse," he said. "We don't want to spoil him."

Because he had been a good feller ever since I had knowed him, which was even before that day two years ago when maw went off with the Vicksburg roadhouse feller and the next day pap didn't come home neither, and on the third one Mister Ernest rid Dan up to the door of the cabin on the river he let us live in, so pap could work his piece of land and run his fish line, too, and said, "Put that gun down and come on here and climb up behind."

So I got in the saddle even if I couldn't reach the stirrups, and Mister Ernest taken the reins and I must 'a' went to sleep, because the next thing I knowed a buttonhole of my lumberjack was tied to the saddle horn with that ere whang cord off the compass, and it was good and late now and we wasn't fur, because Dan was already smelling water, the river. Or maybe it was the feed lot itself he smelled, because we struck the fire road not a quarter below it, and soon I could see the river, too, with the white mist laying on it soft and still as cotton. Then the lot, home; and up yonder in the dark, not no piece akchully, close enough to hear us unsaddling and shucking corn prob'ly, and sholy close enough to hear Mister Ernest blowing his horn at the dark camp for Simon to come in the boat and git us, that old buck in his brake in the bayou; home, too, resting, too, after the hard run, waking hisself now and then, dreaming of dogs behind him or maybe it was the racket we was making would wake him.

Then Mister Ernest stood on the bank blowing until Simon's lantern went bobbing down into the mist; then we clumb down to the landing and Mister Ernest blowed again now and then to guide Simon, until we seen the lantern in the mist, and then Simon and the boat; only it looked like ever time I set down and got still, I went back to sleep, because Mister Ernest

---

16. **britch,** breech, the part of the gun behind the barrel.

was shaking me again to git out and climb the bank into the dark camp, until I felt a bed against my knees and tumbled into it.

Then it was morning, tomorrow; it was all over now until next November, next year, and we could come back. Uncle Ike and Willy and Walter and Roth and the rest of them had come in yestiddy, soon as Eagle taken the buck out of hearing, and they knowed that deer was gone, to pack up and be ready to leave this morning for Yoknapatawpha,[17] where they lived, until it would be November again and they could come back again.

So, as soon as we et breakfast, Simon run them back up the river in the big boat to where they left their cars and pickups, and now it wasn't nobody but jest me and Mister Ernest setting on the bench against the kitchen wall in the sun; Mister Ernest smoking a cigar—a whole one this time that Dan hadn't had no chance to jump him through a grapevine and bust. He hadn't washed his face neither where that vine had throwed him into the mud. But that was all right, too; his face usually did have a smudge of mud or tractor grease or beard stubble on it, because he wasn't jest a planter; he was a farmer, he worked as hard as ara one of his hands and tenants—which is why I knowed from the very first that we would git along, that I wouldn't have no trouble with him and he wouldn't have no trouble with me, from that very first day when I woke up and maw had done gone off with that Vicksburg roadhouse feller without even waiting to cook breakfast, and the next morning pap was gone, too, and it was almost night the next day when I heard a horse coming up and I taken the gun that I had already throwed a shell into the britch when pap never come home last night, and stood in the door while Mister Ernest rid up and said, "Come on. Your paw ain't coming back neither."

"You mean he give me to you?" I said.

"Who cares?" he said. "Come on. I brought a lock for the door. We'll send the pickup back tomorrow for whatever you want."

So I come home with him and it was all right, it was jest fine—his wife had died about three years ago—without no women to worry us or take off in the middle of the night with a durn Vicksburg roadhouse jake without even waiting to cook breakfast. And we would go home this afternoon, too, but not jest yet; we always stayed one more day after the others left because Uncle Ike always left what grub they hadn't et, and the rest of the home-made corn whisky he drunk and that town whisky of Roth Edmondziz he called Scotch that smelled like it come out of a old bucket of roof paint; setting in the sun for one more day before we went back home to git ready to put in next year's crop of cotton and oats and beans and hay; and across the river yonder, behind the wall of trees where the big woods started, that old buck laying up today in the sun, too—resting today, too, without nobody to bother him until next November.

So at least one of us was glad it would be eleven months and two weeks before he would have to run that fur that fast again. So he was glad of the very same thing we was sorry of, and so all of a sudden I thought about how maybe planting and working and then harvesting oats and cotton and beans and hay wasn't jest something me and Mister Ernest done three hundred and fifty-one days to fill in the time until we could come back hunting again, but it was something we had to do, and do honest and good during the three hundred and fifty-one days, to have the right to come back into the big woods and hunt for the other fourteen; and the fourteen days that the old buck run in front of dogs wasn't jest something to fill his time until the three hundred and fifty-one when he didn't have to, but the running and the risking in front of guns and dogs was something he had to do for fourteen days to have the right not to be bothered for the other three hundred

---

17. **Yoknapatawpha**\ˈyɔk·nə·pə ˈtɔ·fə\ the fictitious county in northern Mississippi invented by William Faulkner as the scene of many of his stories.

and fifty-one. And so the hunting and the farming wasn't two different things atall—they was jest the other side of each other.

"Yes," I said. "All we got to do now is put in that next year's crop. Then November won't be no time away."

"You ain't going to put in the crop next year," Mister Ernest said. "You're going to school."

So at first I didn't even believe I had heard him. "What?" I said. "Me? Go to school?"

"Yes," Mister Ernest said. "You must make something out of yourself."

"I am," I said. "I'm doing it now. I'm going to be a hunter and a farmer like you."

"No," Mister Ernest said. "That ain't enough any more. Time was when all a man had to do was just farm eleven and a half months, and hunt the other half. But not now. Now just to belong to the farming business and the hunting business ain't enough. You got to belong to the business of mankind."

"Mankind?" I said.

"Yes," Mister Ernest said. "So you're going to school. Because you got to know why. You can belong to the farming and hunting business and you can learn the difference between what's right and what's wrong, and do right. And that used to be enough—just to do right. But not now. You got to know why it's right and why it's wrong, and be able to tell the folks that never had no chance to learn it; teach them how to do what's right, not just because they know it's right, but because they know now why it's right because you just showed them, told them, taught them why. So you're going to school."

"It's because you been listening to that durn Will Legate and Walter Ewell!" I said.

"No," Mister Ernest said.

"Yes!" I said. "No wonder you missed that buck yestiddy, taking ideas from the very fellers that let him git away, after me and you had run Dan and the dogs durn nigh clean to death! Because you never even missed him! You never forgot to load that gun! You had done already unloaded it a purpose! I heard you!"

"All right, all right," Mister Ernest said. "Which would you rather have? His bloody head and hide on the kitchen floor yonder and half his meat in a pickup truck on the way to Yoknapatawpha County, or him with his head and hide and meat still together over yonder in that brake, waiting for next November for us to run him again?"

"And git him, too," I said. "We won't even fool with no Willy Legate and Walter Ewell next time."

"Maybe," Mister Ernest said.

"Yes," I said.

"Maybe," Mister Ernest said. "The best word in our language, the best of all. That's what mankind keeps going on: Maybe. The best days of his life ain't the ones when he said 'Yes' beforehand: they're the ones when all he knew to say was 'Maybe.' He can't say 'Yes' until afterward because he not only don't know it until then, he don't want to know. 'Yes' until them. . . Step in the kitchen and make me a toddy. Then we'll see about dinner."

"All right," I said. I got up. "You want some of Uncle Ike's corn or that town whisky of Roth Edmondziz?"

"Can't you say Mister Roth or Mister Edmonds?" Mister Ernest said.

"Yes, sir," I said. "Well, which do you want? Uncle Ike's corn or that ere stuff of Roth Edmondziz?"

Man Will Prevail

WILLIAM FAULKNER

Nobel Prize Acceptance Speech,
Stockholm, December 10, 1950

I feel that this award was not made to me as a man, but to my work—a life's work in the agony and sweat of the human spirit, not for glory and least of all for profit, but to create out of the materials of the human spirit something which did not exist before. So this award is only mine in trust. It will not be difficult to find a dedica-

tion for the money part of it commensurate[1] with the purpose and significance of its origin. But I would like to do the same with the acclaim too, by using this moment as a pinnacle from which I might be listened to by the young men and women already dedicated to the same anguish and travail, among whom is already that one who will some day stand here where I am standing.

Our tragedy today is a general and universal physical fear so long sustained by now that we can even bear it. There are no longer problems of the spirit. There is only the question: When will I be blown up? Because of this, the young man or woman writing today has forgotten the problems of the human heart in conflict with itself which alone can make good writing because only that is worth writing about, worth the agony and the sweat.

He must learn them again. He must teach himself that the basest of all things is to be afraid; and, teaching himself that, forget it forever, leaving no room in his workshop for anything but the old verities and truths of the heart, the old universal truths lacking which any story is ephemeral[2] and doomed—love and honor and pity and pride and compassion and sacrifice. Until he does so, he labors under a curse. He writes not of love but of lust, of defeats in which nobody loses anything of value, of victories without hope and, worst of all, without pity or compassion. His griefs grieve on no

---

1. **commensurate**\kə ᐱmĕn·shə·rĭt\ suitable in measure and importance.
2. **ephemeral**\ə ᐱfĕm·rəl\ lasting for only a day, or for only a short time.

universal bones, leaving no scars. He writes not of the heart but of the glands.

Until he relearns these things, he will write as though he stood among and watched the end of man. I decline to accept the end of man. It is easy enough to say that man is immortal simply because he will endure: that when the last ding-dong of doom has clanged and faded from the last worthless rock hanging tideless in the last red and dying evening, that even then there will still be one more sound: that of his puny inexhaustible voice, still talking. I refuse to accept this. I believe that man will not merely endure: he will prevail. He is immortal, not because he alone among creatures has an inexhaustible voice, but because he has a soul, a spirit capable of compassion and sacrifice and endurance. The poet's, the writer's, duty is to write about these things. It is his privilege to help man endure by lifting his heart, by reminding him of the courage and honor and hope and pride and compassion and pity and sacrifice which have been the glory of his past. The poet's voice need not merely be the record of man, it can be one of the props, the pillars to help him endure and prevail.

I
"THE BUSINESS OF MANKIND"

In his Acceptance Speech, Faulkner affirms "the old verities and truths of the heart, the old universal truths," some of which are courage, honor, hope, pride, compassion, pity, and sacrifice. In short, though he recognizes that the world has changed, he still maintains that our basic values do not have to change.

In "Race at Morning," however, Mr. Ernest tells the young boy that the life he has been living "ain't enough any more." What does he mean by this and by the related statement that the boy has to belong to "the business of mankind"? Also, be prepared to discuss how these statements relate to Faulkner's basic philosophy, as expressed in "Man Will Prevail."

II
IMPLICATIONS

Discuss the following statements in the light of these selections and your own experience.

1. In life everyone has a job, which, when performed faithfully and honestly, not only brings self-satisfaction but also earns the esteem of mankind for a person.

2. A person who knows why something is right or wrong is more likely to do right and avoid wrong than a person who does not know the "whys."

3. School is the best place for a young boy to learn why some things are wrong and others are right.

4. Faulkner tremendously oversimplifies the matter of right and wrong.

5. Faulkner's optimism is sentimental and too easy.

6. Faulkner overrates the powers of the writer.

7. It is perfectly possible for a man to be completely happy in the modern world even though he is completely isolated from the rest of mankind.

III
TECHNIQUES

Structure

How does the "philosophical" discussion at the end of "Race at Morning" grow out of the earlier focus on the buck hunt? If you decide that they are not very closely related, would you conclude that the story is poorly structured, or what?

Symbolism

What—if anything—might the buck symbolize? If you decide that the animal is a symbol, try to relate its symbolic meaning to various facts in the story, especially to the fact that Mister Ernest purposely shoots at the buck with an empty rifle.

IV
WORDS

A. Using what you know about word parts and context clues, determine the meaning of the italicized words.

1. A little fire had been kindled that afternoon to *dissipate* the dampness.

2. His *singularity* impelled a closer *scrutiny*.

3. "For Heaven's sake," he cried with a strange mixture of alarm and *intimidation*.

4. Some of them knob the rod at the top . . . instead of *imperceptibly* carrying down the current into the earth. . . .

5. For one who would arm others with fearlessness, you seem unbeseeming *timorous* yourself.

6. Who has empowered you to peddle round your *indulgences* from divine ordinations.

7. A dedication for the money part of it *commensurate* with the purpose and significance of its origin.

8. . . . by using this *pinnacle* from which I might be listened to by young men and women.

9. . . . leaving no room in his workship for anything but the old *verities* and truths of the heart.

10. Harold's young college boy's assurance *piqued* him.

B. The same thing may be said in many different ways. The vocabulary of English, so rich in synonyms, gives many choices among words. We generally choose our words to fit the occasions, but our choices should reflect a consistency. Below is part of a paragraph from Faulkner's "Man Will Prevail." Discuss how the alternate choices change the tone as well as variety of standard English.

"It will not be (hard, difficult, arduous) to find a dedication for the (money, cash, legal tender) part of it (tantamount to, offsetting, commensurate with) the purpose and (significance, importance, meaning) of its (root, inception, origin). But I would like to do the same with the (acclaim, applause, hurrah) too, by using this moment as a (peak, apogee, pinnacle) from which I might be listened to by the young men and women already (devoted, dedicated, consecrated) to the same (heartache, agony, anguish) and (work, grind, travail), among whom is already that one who will some day stand here where I am standing."

C. It is no longer possible to draw precise lines about slang usage. We know that certain slang terms, such as *dig* (a curt remark), *put down* (deflate), *jittery* (nervous), *dirt* (gossip), may be appropriate to casual conversations and even to light, friendly writing. Much of the slang of yesterday has become part of our general vocabulary or at least appropriate to ordinary speech and writing.

Words, such as *rascal, varsity, hot dog, jazz* (particular kind of music), once considered slang are now generally accepted.

Slang has levels of its own. Which of the following expressions do you consider appropriate to general, informal conversation? to friendly, informal writing? Which do you consider inappropriate, in poor taste?

nuts (insane)	drag out
new lease on life	hang loose
hit the sack	fink
passion pit	dig (appreciate)
plastered	jalopy
cram	louses (people)
junkie	fin (five dollars)

FINAL REFLECTIONS

The Search for Values

VALUES AND LITERATURE

Literature relates to the search for values in many ways. Poems and stories like "The Hollow Men," "Richard Cory," and "In Another Country" may awaken in us a sense of the *need* for values in order to avoid living an empty life. Essays such as "Happiness" may persuade us to adopt specific values, or they may help us to understand better the reasons for living by a particular value or set of values.

A story like "Young Man Axelbrod" might serve to awaken our interest in art or music and thus broaden and enrich our lives. "The Traveler" shows us that we must look outside of ourselves in order to fully know ourselves.

It is important to note, however, that stories and poems are not simply devices for telling about someone else's experiences, they are experiences in themselves. Fully appreciated, they stir readers emotionally as well as intellectually. They may thereby have a deep and lasting effect on our own values—on how we live, on how we answer those persistent questions, "Why was I born? Why am I living?"

IMPLICATIONS

Discuss each of the following propositions. In your discussion you may call upon your experience, but be sure that you also make some reference to at least three of the selections in this unit for each of the propositions.

1. "The happiest person is the one who thinks the most interesting thoughts."

2. A man's values are determined by his emotions rather than by his intellect.

3. The search for values is a life-long search, for a person can never be sure he has the right or final answers.

4. Fear and inertia are far greater barriers to happiness than are lack of wealth and position.

5. The concentration upon one set of human needs to the exclusion of all the others is bound to cause unhappiness.

6. Skeptics and pessimists have little or nothing to contribute to the search for values.

7. Writers don't create values for a society; they merely reflect those that already exist.

8. Never before in history has it been more important to recognize "the brotherhood of man" as a major social value.

TECHNIQUES

Structure

Over two thousand years ago the famous Greek philosopher Plato wrote a dialogue in which he portrayed the writer as a divinely inspired madman. This image of the writer as a person full of passion but with little intellectual control has persisted down to the present day in the minds of some persons.

If this were a true picture of the writer, we would expect to find that his work would be structurally loose, that it would show little sign of careful control and planning. Analyze at least one prose selection and two poems in this unit and present the evidence (or lack of evidence) for thinking of the writer as a person who works chiefly from inspiration.

Symbolism

Select a poem and a prose selection that you think contain little or no symbolism and another poem and prose selection that you think are highly symbolic. Justify your choices by listing your reasons for thinking that one pair of selections is not symbolic and the other is.

William Lyon Phelps

Born in New Haven, Connecticut, William Lyon Phelps (1865–1933) took his bachelor's and doctor's degrees at Yale, and was a distinguished professor of English there for almost forty years. Known to countless Yale students as "Billy" Phelps, he was one of the outstanding teachers in the United States. His many books include early volumes on contemporary novelists, Russian novelists, the theater in the twentieth century. He also wrote widely for a popular audience: personal essays and literary criticism.

T. S. Eliot

Regarded by many as the outstanding poet of contemporary English letters, T. S. Eliot (1888–1965) was born in St. Louis in 1888, lived there for 18 years, and then went to Harvard to take both a bachelor's and a master's degree in four years. Work at the Sorbonne and more graduate work at Harvard were followed by a period at Oxford and then a series of jobs in England. His poem "The Wasteland" (1922) brought him international recognition. Though a controversial poem, it had major influence on other twentieth-century writers. In 1948 he was awarded the Nobel Prize in Literature. Much of his popularity in later life in both England and the United States came from his plays *Murder in the Cathedral* and *The Cocktail Party*. In 1927 he became a British subject in deed as he had been in spirit most of his life. However, he returned to the United States in the thirties to lecture at Harvard; and for the rest of his life he made periodic visits, usually lecture tours, to his native land.

Edwin Arlington Robinson

Plagued by poverty, illness, and poor eyesight, Edwin Arlington Robinson (1869–1935) worked against great odds in his determination to write poetry. During his two years at Harvard, a number of his poems, including "Richard Cory," were published by campus periodicals. His first books of poetry were privately underwritten and made little stir on the American literary scene. Theodore Roosevelt, however, was impressed by *The Children of the Night* and gave Robinson a post in the New York Customs House. Years passed without the sale of a single poem, but finally friends made it possible for Robinson to devote all his energies to writing. With the publication of *The Man Against the Sky* in 1915, critical success came to Robinson, and in the 1920's he became one of America's most widely read poets. During that decade, he won the Pulitzer Prize for Poetry three times.

Ernest Hemingway

Ernest Hemingway (1898–1962) was one of America's most widely read twentieth-century writers. During World War I, he served first with the French ambulance corps and then in the Italian army, where he was wounded and decorated. He stayed on in Europe as a correspondent, later joining the expatriates and coming under the influence of Gertrude Stein, Ezra Pound, and Sherwood Anderson. In the early 20's, his first work appeared in print: verse and short stories. His first novel, *The Sun Also Rises*, a story of the so-called lost generation, was published in 1926. His other major works include *Death in the Afternoon, A Farewell to Arms, For Whom the Bell Tolls*, and *The Old Man and the Sea*. Included in several collections are these significant short stories: "The Killers," "The Snows of Kilimanjaro," "The Big Two-Hearted River," and "The Short Happy Life of Francis Macomber." Several of Hemingway's works have appeared as motion pictures. In 1954 he was awarded the Nobel Prize in Literature. During his lifetime Hemingway became the prototype of the strong, virile outdoorsman—deep-sea fisherman, big-game hunter—hearty, tough, courageous. His stories reflect this strong, masculine approach to life.

Ray Bradbury

Probably America's best-known writer of science-fiction and fantasy, Ray Bradbury (1920–   ) has seen many of his stories appear in collections of "best stories" of the year. Though his work is high in entertainment value, much of it also illustrates his serious interest in using the short story as a weapon against those who attempt to control freedom of thought and expression. Since 1947 he has written almost two dozen books. Some of his most popular works are: *Martian Chronicles* (1950), *Fahrenheit 451* (1953), *Switch on the Night* (1955), *A Medicine for Melancholy* (1959), *Something Wicked This Way Comes* (1962).

Karl Shapiro

Karl Shapiro (1913–   ) served with the army in the South Pacific from 1942 to 1945, and it was while he was there that some of his first books appeared. *Person, Place and Thing* appeared in 1942 and won him immediate recognition; just two years later he published *V-Letter and Other Poems*, which won the Pulitzer Prize in Poetry in 1945. Shapiro has also been Consultant in Poetry at the Library of Congress, a teacher of English, and the editor of such well-established literary magazines as *The Prairie Schooner* and *Poetry*.

Richard Wilbur

Born in New York, Richard Wilbur (1921–   ) was educated at Amherst and Harvard. He served in the army during the Second World War. In addition to his writing, he has done a good deal of teaching. His books of poems include *Things of This World*, which won the Pulitzer Prize in Poetry in 1957.

Robinson Jeffers

Robinson Jeffers (1887–1962) spent part of his childhood in Europe and moved with his family to California in 1903. After taking his bachelor's degree at Occidental College, he studied at various colleges for many years, attempting to find a suitable profession. In 1914 he fell heir to his uncle's fortune and was able to settle down to a life of writing. On Point Sur, near Carmel, California, he found a solitary existence which he prized for the rest of his life. Jeffers wrote many volumes of poetry, many of which were powerful and heavily symbolic. His best-known longer work was *Medea*, his adaptation of Euripides' drama.

Sinclair Lewis

Born in small-town Sauk Centre, Minnesota, Sinclair Lewis (1885–1951) later portrayed that town in his novels, especially in *Main Street* (1920), a satire of American values and small-town life. While working for various publishing houses in New York, Lewis wrote articles and short stories. His first novel appeared in 1914. *Babbitt*, published in 1922, satirizes the American businessman, and *Arrowsmith* (1926) shows the contrast between men of science and men-of-science-turned-businessmen. This novel won a Pulitzer Prize, which he refused. In 1930 Lewis became the first American to win the Nobel Prize for Literature. Some of Lewis' later novels, *Elmer Gantry, Dodsworth, It Can't Happen Here,* and *Cass Timberlane,* found wide audience but failed to equal the sharp criticism of his satirical novels of the 20's.

Wallace Stegner

Growing up in a family that moved from place to place in the Western United States and Canada, Wallace Stegner (1909–   ) developed early an affinity for country life. He earned college degrees, including a Ph.D., and then settled down to a career of college teaching and writing. He has written many short stories and several novels. In 1945 he left a professorship at Harvard to become the director of the Creative Writing Center at Stanford University, where he since has inspired many writers, as well as continuing to write a succession of distinguished short stories. His writings have won a Little, Brown contest, a Houghton-Mifflin Award, and two O. Henry Memorial Awards. His best-received novel has been *The Big Rock Candy Mountain,* a story of the West during early decades of the twentieth century.

Herman Melville

The author of *Moby Dick,* which is often called one of the two greatest American novels, is Herman Melville (1819–1898), who went to sea as a seaman at the age of twenty. Eighteen months later he shipped aboard the *Acushnet,* bound for the southern waters of the Pacific. These voyages were to provide him the material and the locale for most of his novels. His experiences in the South Seas, especially during his captivity by cannibals, became the substance of *Typee* (1846) and *Omoo.* Other novels about the sea and seamen include *Mardi, Redburn,* and *White-Jacket.* His first two novels were especially successful with the reading public, and Melville became a popular writer. The reaction of the public and the critics to *Moby Dick,* however, was not only cool but in some instances hostile. His next novel, *Pierre,* was even

more unpopular. These reactions and a fire at his publisher's which destroyed the plates of his books led to oblivion for Melville. He later wrote a number of significant long stories and the short novel *Billy Budd,* but to the end of his life he was virtually overlooked by readers and critics. Not until three decades after his death did anyone give Melville the attention he deserved. Then, in a rising tide of literary scholarship and critical acclaim, he emerged as a significant figure in the literature of the United States.

Edna St. Vincent Millay

The first verses of Edna St. Vincent Millay (1892–1952) were published in the *St. Nicholas* magazine while she was still a young girl. She attended Vassar College and continued to write poetry. One of her most famous poems appeared as the title poem of *Renascence and Other Poems* (1917). A prototype of the Greenwich Village poet, Miss Millay wrote continuously and published a number of volumes in the twenties and thirties. *The Harp Weaver and Other Poems* won the Pulitzer Prize in 1923. Her style ranged from exuberance to great bitterness. With each succeeding generation, she has found receptive listeners.

William Faulkner

Born and reared in Mississippi, William Faulkner (1897–1962) spent most of his life writing, for years unrecognized and little read. Privately he published a book of poems and then, in 1926, his first novel, *Soldier's Pay. Sartoris* (1929), a novel about the degeneration of a family, paralleled in large measure Faulkner's own family, a story that was to emerge in several later stories and novels. Faulkner's prose demands a close reading and rereading. In some stories he uses a stream-of-consciousness technique. Gradually critics began to pay more attention to him, and eventually he moved, as a literary figure, from obscurity to international fame. In 1950 he won the Nobel Prize in Literature. His *A Fable* (1954) won both a National Book Award for fiction and a Pulitzer Prize.

ROBERT FROST

1874–1963

For Frost, poetry was very much a game he played with the world and his readers. The seriousness of the game did not detract from its fun nor from his joy in performance. He had, as he said, "a lover's quarrel with the world," and it was the peculiar nature of his genius that he could combine traditional forms, homely subjects, and serious insights with a perceptive sense of humor and wit.

When President Kennedy in 1961 decided to include a poet in his Inaugural Day ceremonies, it was natural for him to choose Robert Frost, a fellow-New Englander and the dean of American poets. Frost published his first volume, *A Boy's Will,* in 1913, his last, *In the Clearing,* in 1962. Four times he won the Pulitzer Prize. His verse was known wherever English poetry was read. Yet Robert Frost was never one to forget that he was forty years old before his genius was recognized, that his early life was filled with hardship and disappointment.

Although Frost will always be celebrated as a New England poet, he was actually born in San Francisco, in 1874. His father had left Maine and hastened to the West Coast because he hated New England. The poet and his younger sister, Jeanie, might have spent their whole lives on the Pacific Coast had their father not died early of tuberculosis, leaving the strange request that he be buried in the New England he had loathed. After the trip east, the widow and her children settled in Salem, New

Hampshire, and later in Lawrence, Massachusetts. Following graduation from Lawrence High School, Frost enrolled in Dartmouth College, but he stayed less than a year.

Until his marriage to Elinor White in 1895, Frost drifted from one job to another: mill work in Lawrence, school teaching, newspaper reporting. After marriage he spent two years teaching in his mother's small private school, then two years at Harvard College, hoping to prepare for a career as a college instructor. Although he enjoyed the classics and philosophy, he revolted against academic discipline. Because of his poor health, he had to live in the country; so he and his growing family tried farming and chicken raising in Derry, New Hampshire. Five years of near failure as a farmer sent him back to school teaching in Derry, and then in Plymouth; but he disliked teaching as much as tilling the stubborn New Hampshire soil. Since the day he sold his first poem, in 1894, he knew poetry should be his profession, indeed his whole life. In 1912, he took the gamble. Unable to find a publisher for his poetry, he sold his farm and packed off his wife and four children to Buckinghamshire, England, where living was cheaper and poetry had a larger audience. The decision was one of the wisest he ever made. *A Boy's Will* was issued by an English publisher in 1913 and was followed the next year by *North of Boston*. When Frost returned to the United States in 1915, his reputation was made; both books had been republished here. He bought a farm in Franconia, New Hampshire, with the hope of settling down to write the best poetry he could and to avoid the literary marketplace.

He succeeded in doing both. The National Institute of Arts and Letters elected him to membership in 1916. Amherst College offered him a professorship in English. Invitations to lecture and to give public readings came from all parts of the country. For the next forty-five years he was to become, almost against his will, a teacher-at-large. Though he was a splendid teacher and held audiences entranced by reading his own poetry, he also wished to remain close to the land. After his wife's death in 1938, he moved to the hills of Ripton, Vermont. To see Frost at home in Ripton was to see the poet next to his source, finally free from the enervating labor of cultivating the land for a living but still lovingly tied to the woodlands of Vermont where he could know "the line where man leaves off and nature starts."

There is a risk, of course, in thinking of Frost as only a New England poet and periodic visitor to college campuses. His friend and fellow-poet John Ciardi has warned us not to think of Frost as "a kindly, vague, white-haired great-grandfather" who just tells pleasant little stories in verse. Frost was a New Englander but not a mere recorder of regional folkways. He wrote of Vermont because he knew it best, but his subject was always man, the perils of the human condition. "It is the man we lose," Ciardi wrote after Frost's death, "a man salty and rough with the earth trace, and though towering above it, never removed from it, a man above all who could tower precisely because he was rooted in real earth." Naturally he put his characters in rural settings: small boys in deep woods, young married couples, transient farm workers, lumbermen, gum-gatherers, just as John Steinbeck chose to write of his native California and William Faulkner of Oxford, Mississippi. But like the good teacher he was, Frost was always intent on expanding his subject or, rather, on urging his reader to expand his subject along with him, to discover that essentially New England mirrored the world.

If on occasion Frost's poems seem to be about little things in simple words—a burned house, apple-picking, birch trees, ax handles, a west-running brook, stone walls, a drumlin woodchuck—it takes only a second reading to catch the hints Frost drops along the way that there is a deceptively simple surface poem here and a vital below-the-surface meaning. Frost quite clearly used the objects of the farm world as symbols of a deeper meaning, as a way of moving from the concrete world to abstract ideas.

For him a poem "begins in delight and ends in wisdom."

The delights of "Nothing Gold Can Stay" are obvious at first reading. Seven of its eight lines are clear and direct observation of nature:

> Nature's first green is gold,
> Her hardest hue to hold.
> Her earthly leaf's a flower;
> But only so an hour.
> Then leaf subsides to leaf.
> So Eden sank to grief.
> So dawn goes down to day.
> Nothing gold can stay.

The opening line may sound like a paradox, a self-contradictory statement, but our own memory of spring reinforces the poet's image: the yellow weeping willows, the first trees to bud. And he reminds us that as yellow turns to green, so flower turns to leaf, and leaves will fall. Growth and decay are natural. No one can hold that "ecstasy should be static and stand still in one place," as Frost says on another occasion. Even the golden sunrise must turn to the harsher light of day.

But the chief pleasure of poetry, as the careful reader will discover, is moving from the surface delight of local details to the wisdom of suggested meanings. Frost need plant only two words in this poem to suggest ulterior, or hidden, latent meanings: Eden and grief. With line six, the poem expands to include human nature. *Our* hardest hue to hold is innocence; our paradise, once golden, turned to grief. And as we reread the last line of the poem, our imagination seizes the word gold. In terms of the visual images—dawn's light and earth's first green—Frost is suggesting the abstract idea of loss. The verbs—subsides, sank, goes down—lead toward a double or triple meaning of gold,

but the poet stops short of equating. The art is the implication. He is not telling us; he is only suggesting. "Poems can be pressed too hard for meaning," he warns us, yet at the same time our imagination plays with the hints he has given. In human terms, does gold mean innocence, or love, or perhaps life? Or all three? Delight will lead to wisdom if we allow it.

One of the reasons for Frost's popularity as a poet was that he stayed close to traditional forms: the sonnet, blank verse, the dramatic monologue, the simple lyric. He was not afraid of rhyme; he found the couplet and the quatrain a challenge, not a confinement. And like Shakespeare, he knew how to contain natural speech rhythms in blank verse. Writing free verse—poetry with rhythm but without meter and regular rhyme scheme—he likened to playing tennis with the net down. "To the right person," he wrote, "it must seem naive to distort form as such. The very words of the dictionary are a restriction to make the best of or stay out of and be silent. Coining new words isn't encouraged. We play the words as we find them. We make them do."

For Frost, poetry was very much a game he played both with the world and with his readers. The seriousness of the game did not detract from its fun nor from his joy in performance. He had, as he said, "a lover's quarrel with the world," and it was the peculiar nature of his genius that he could combine traditional forms, homely subjects, and serious insights with a perceptive sense of humor and wit. He once offered this sly warning to those about to read his verse:

> It takes all kinds of in and outdoor schooling
> To get adapted to my kind of fooling.

Man and Nature

One of Frost's perennial subjects is rural New England,
the land he knew so well and loved. Although these three poems
are widely separated in time of composition ("Birches" appeared in 1916,
"Our Hold on the Planet" in 1942), they attest to the continuing attraction
nature's laws held for him. Frost always remains cautious,
or at least modest, in talking of man's relation to the natural forces
around him, but that does not keep him from being forever curious.

Dust of Snow

The way a crow
Shook down on me
The dust of snow
From a hemlock tree

Has given my heart
A change of mood
And saved some part
Of a day I had rued.

Our Hold on the Planet

We asked for rain. It didn't flash and roar.
It didn't lose its temper at our demand
And blow a gale. It didn't misunderstand
And give us more than our spokesman bargained for;
And just because we owned to a wish for rain,   5
Send us a flood and bid us be damned and drown.
It gently threw us a glittering shower down.
And when we had taken that into the roots of grain,
It threw us another and then another still
Till the spongy soil again was natal[1] wet.   10
We may doubt the just proportion of good to ill.
There is much in nature against us. But we forget:
Take nature altogether since time began,
Including human nature, in peace and war,
And it must be a little more in favor of man,   15
Say a fraction of one per cent at the very least,
Or our number living wouldn't be steadily more,
Our hold on the planet wouldn't have so increased.

1. natal\ˈnā·təl\ **wet,** as at birth; here, wet as on the
third day of Creation when the waters were gathered
together in one place and dry land appeared. Genesis
1:9.

Birches

When I see birches bend to left and right
Across the lines of straighter darker trees,
I like to think some boy's been swinging them.
But swinging doesn't bend them down to stay
As ice-storms do. Often you must have seen them   5
Loaded with ice a sunny winter morning
After a rain. They click upon themselves
As the breeze rises, and turn many-colored
As the stir cracks and crazes[1] their enamel.
Soon the sun's warmth makes them shed crystal shells   10
Shattering and avalanching on the snow-crust—
Such heaps of broken glass to sweep away
You'd think the inner dome of heaven had fallen.
They are dragged to the withered bracken[2] by the load,
And they seem not to break; though once they are bowed   15
So low for long, they never right themselves:
You may see their trunks arching in the woods
Years afterwards, trailing their leaves on the ground
Like girls on hands and knees that throw their hair
Before them over their heads to dry in the sun.   20
But I was going to say when Truth broke in
With all her matter-of-fact about the ice-storm
I should prefer to have some boy bend them
As he went out and in to fetch the cows—
Some boy too far from town to learn baseball,   25
Whose only play was what he found himself,
Summer or winter, and could play alone.
One by one he subdued his father's trees
By riding them down over and over again
Until he took the stiffness out of them,   30
And not one but hung limp, not one was left
For him to conquer. He learned all there was
To learn about not launching out too soon
And so not carrying the tree away
Clear to the ground. He always kept his poise   35
To the top branches, climbing carefully
With the same pains you use to fill a cup
Up to the brim, and even above the brim.
Then he flung outward, feet first, with a swish,
Kicking his way down through the air to the ground.   40
So was I once myself a swinger of birches.
And so I dream of going back to be.
It's when I'm weary of considerations,

1. **crazes**\ˈkrā·zəz\ makes small cracks in the surface of "enamel."
2. **bracken**\ˈbrä·kən\ large ferns.

717

And life is too much like a pathless wood
Where your face burns and tickles with the cobwebs   45
Broken across it, and one eye is weeping
From a twig's having lashed across it open.
I'd like to get away from earth awhile
And then come back to it and begin over.
May no fate willfully misunderstand me   50
And half grant what I wish and snatch me away
Not to return. Earth's the right place for love:
I don't know where it's likely to go better.
I'd like to go by climbing a birch tree,
And climb black branches up a snow-white trunk   55
Toward heaven, till the tree could bear no more,
But dipped its top and and set me down again.
That would be good both going and coming back.
One could do worse than be a swinger of birches.

I
NEW ENGLAND ROOTS

Though Frost's poetry is made up of materials and observations of his New England countryside—snow, birches, rain—his real subject is man. His poems talk of simple things in simple words, but these simple objects become symbols leading to deeper meanings. Neither a nature poet nor a lyricist, he sees in the birch trees and hemlocks of New England something that belongs to each man everywhere: joy, doubts, horror. Frost uses New England as a means of revealing what is universal, not merely local. He accomplishes this so well because he accepts the premise that human nature is purest and most understandable when closest to nature. Here, above all, he realizes how narrowly limited is his capacity for changing the world.

Dust of Snow

1. Frost originally titled this poem "A Favor." What relation between nature and man does this indicate?

2. This simple one-sentence poem leaves many things unsaid. The poet does not tell us what made him rue the day. He leads us to consider why he changed his mood. Why do you think he did?

Our Hold on the Planet

1. To whom is Frost referring by the pronoun "it" in the first line of this poem? How does this first line set up the basic contrast in the poem?

2. Granting that the poem deals with "our hold on the planet" and is rather philosophical in nature, how does the asking for rain which opens the poem relate to the broader, philosophical consideration?

Birches

1. How does the poet make the birch tree an appropriate symbol for one of man's dilemmas: the desire both to escape the earth and to return to it?

2. Why does Frost describe the digression (lines 5–16) by saying "when Truth broke in with all her matter-of-fact"? What is Truth opposed to here?

3. How is life a "pathless wood" as Frost suggests? What further meaning can you read into "cobwebs" and "twigs that lash the eye"?

II
IMPLICATIONS

Discuss the following statements.

1. Nature helps man to come to grips with ultimate problems of choice.

2. Man should not complacently accept only what nature is willing to give.

3. Every man must basically be an optimist or a pessimist.

Man and His Work

Because he lived so close to the soil, Frost understood early
in life that the farmer's code is not the city worker's code. Whether he is
splitting wood, picking apples, or sharpening knives, he speaks
"from within," from a deep understanding of how country living affects
man's behavior. But in each of these poems, Frost sees beyond the job
at hand. At the same time he is talking about tramps and grindstones,
he is enlarging his subject to a consideration of brotherhood,
independence, cooperation, and other universal, abstract ideas.

Two Tramps in Mud Time

Out of the mud two strangers came
And caught me splitting wood in the yard.
And one of them put me off my aim
By hailing cheerily "Hit them hard!"
I knew pretty well why he dropped behind   5
And let the other go on a way.
I knew pretty well what he had in mind:
He wanted to take my job for pay.

Good blocks of oak it was I split,
As large around as the chopping block;   10
And every piece I squarely hit
Fell splinterless as a cloven rock.
The blows that a life of self-control
Spares to strike for the common good
That day, giving a loose to my soul,   15
I spent on the unimportant wood.

The sun was warm but the wind was chill.
You know how it is with an April day
When the sun is out and the wind is still,
You're one month on in the middle of May.   20
But if you so much as dare to speak,
A cloud comes over the sunlit arch,
A wind comes off a frozen peak,
And you're two months back in the middle of March.

A bluebird comes tenderly up to alight   25
And turns to the wind to unruffle a plume
His song so pitched as not to excite
A single flower as yet to bloom.
It is snowing a flake: and he half knew
Winter was only playing possum.   30

Except in color he isn't blue,
But he wouldn't advise a thing to blossom.

The water for which we may have to look
In summertime with a witching-wand,[1]
In every wheelrut's now a brook,   35
In every print of a hoof a pond.
Be glad of water, but don't forget
The lurking frost in the earth beneath
That will steal forth after the sun is set
And show on the water its crystal teeth.   40

The time when most I loved my task
These two must make me love it more
By coming with what they came to ask.
You'd think I never had felt before
The weight of an ax-head poised aloft,   45
The grip on earth of outspread feet.
The life of muscles rocking soft
And smooth and moist in vernal[2] heat.

Out of the woods two hulking tramps
(From sleeping God knows where last night,   50
But not long since in the lumber camps).
They thought all chopping was theirs of right.
Men of the woods and lumberjacks,
They judged me by their appropriate tool.
Except as a fellow handled an ax,   55
They had no way of knowing a fool.

Nothing on either side was said.
They knew they had but to stay their stay
And all their logic would fill my head:
As that I had no right to play   60
With what was another man's work for gain.
My right might be love but theirs was need.
And where the two exist in twain
Theirs was the better right—agreed.

But yield who will to their separation,   65
My object in living is to unite
My avocation and my vocation
As my two eyes make one in sight.
Only where love and need are one,
And the work is play for mortal stakes,   70
Is the deed ever really done
For Heaven and the future's sakes.

After Apple-Picking

My long two-pointed ladder's sticking through a tree
Toward heaven still,
And there's a barrel that I didn't fill
Beside it, and there may be two or three
Apples I didn't pick upon some bough.   5
But I am done with apple-picking now.
Essence of winter sleep is on the night,
The scent of apples: I am drowsing off.
I cannot rub the strangeness from my sight
I got from looking through a pane of glass   10
I skimmed this morning from the drinking trough
And held against the world of hoary grass.
It melted, and I let it fall and break.
But I was well
Upon my way to sleep before it fell,   15
And I could tell
What form my dreaming was about to take.
Magnified apples appear and disappear,
Stem end and blossom end,
And every fleck of russet[1] showing clear.   20
My instep arch not only keeps the ache,
It keeps the pressure of a ladder-round.
I feel the ladder sway as the boughs bend.
And I keep hearing from the cellar bin
The rumbling sound   25
Of load on load of apples coming in.
For I have had too much
Of apple-picking: I am overtired
Of the great harvest I myself desired.
There were ten thousand thousand fruit to touch,   30
Cherish in hand, lift down, and not let fall.
For all
That struck the earth,
No matter if not bruised or spiked with stubble,
Went surely to the cider-apple heap   35
As of no worth.
One can see what will trouble
This sleep of mine, whatever sleep it is.
Were he not gone,
The woodchuck[2] could say whether it's like his   40
Long sleep, as I describe its coming on,
Or just some human sleep.

1. **russet**\ˈrə·sət\ reddish brown.
2. **woodchuck**\ˈwʊd·chək\ the ground hog, a marmot or rodent with a stout body. It burrows in the ground and hibernates in the winter.

The Grindstone

Having a wheel and four legs of its own
Has never availed the cumbersome grindstone
To get it anywhere that I can see.
These hands have helped it go, and even race;
Not all the motion, though, they ever lent,
Not all the miles it may have thought it went,
Have got it one step from the starting place.
It stands beside the same old apple tree.
The shadow of the apple tree is thin
Upon it now, its feet are fast in snow.
All other farm machinery's gone in,
And some of it on no more legs and wheel
Than the grindstone can boast to stand or go.
(I'm thinking chiefly of the wheelbarrow.)
For months it hasn't known the taste of steel,
Washed down with rusty water in a tin.
But standing outdoors hungry, in the cold,
Except in towns at night, is not a sin.
And, anyway, its standing in the yard
Under a ruinous live apple tree
Has nothing any more to do with me,
Except that I remember how of old
One summer day, all day I drove it hard,
And someone mounted on it rode it hard,
And he and I between us ground a blade.

I gave it the preliminary spin,
And poured on water (tears it might have been);
And when it almost gayly jumped and flowed,
A Father-Time-like man got on and rode,
Armed with a scythe and spectacles that glowed.
He turned on will-power to increase the load
And slow me down—and I abruptly slowed,
Like coming to a sudden railroad station.
I changed from hand to hand in desperation.
I wondered what machine of ages gone
This represented an improvement on.
For all I knew it may have sharpened spears
And arrowheads itself. Much use for years
Had gradually worn it an oblate

Spheroid[1] that kicked and struggled in its gait,   40
Appearing to return me hate for hate;
(But I forgive it now as easily
As any other boyhood enemy
Whose pride has failed to get him anywhere).
I wondered who it was the man thought ground—   45
The one who held the wheel back or the one
Who gave his life to keep it going round?
I wondered if he really thought it fair
For him to have the say when we were done.
Such were the bitter thoughts to which I turned.   50

Not for myself was I so much concerned.
Oh no!—although, of course, I could have found
A better way to pass the afternoon
Than grinding discord out of a grindstone,
And beating insects at their gritty tune.   55
Nor was I for the man so much concerned.
Once when the grindstone almost jumped its bearing
It looked as if he might be badly thrown
And wounded on his blade. So far from caring,
I laughed inside, and only cranked the faster,   60
(It ran as if it wasn't greased but glued);
I'd welcome any moderate disaster
That might be calculated to postpone
What evidently nothing could conclude.
The thing that made me more and more afraid   65
Was that we'd ground it sharp and hadn't known.
And now were only wasting precious blade.
And when he raised it dripping once and tried
The creepy edge of it with wary touch,
And viewed it over his glasses funny-eyed,   70
Only disinterestedly to decide
It needed a turn more, I could have cried
Wasn't there danger of a turn too much?
Mightn't we make it worse instead of better?
I was for leaving something to the whetter.[2]   75
What if it wasn't all it should be? I'd
Be satisfied if he'd be satisfied.

---

1. **oblate**\ˈŏb·lāt\ **spheroid**\ˈsfĭ·roid\ a sphere flattened
by rotation; here, a circle so flattened.
2. **whetter**\ˈhwĕ·tər\ the man who sharpened the
scythe by turning the wheel of the grindstone.

THE DIGNITY OF LABOR

One of Frost's major themes is the sheer joy of work. Man fulfills himself in his labor. Frost's preference for rural New England comes from a deep-rooted sense of the refreshment man gains from working close to the earth. The city shields man from nature and from the sense of creating with his own hands. Frost's poetry represents a return to a pastoral life, a revival of the dignity of manual labor. His rural viewpoint helps us to see all the virtues we have lost in a mechanized, "departmental" world. His poetry gives us experiences that renew our conviction that in the aching strain of labor, done with love, man fulfills his being.

Two Tramps in Mud Time

1. Is this poem about the two anonymous tramps or about the poet who is speaking?

2. Lines 9 to 40 deal with the experience of spring on an April day. How does this fit into the poem? Why is mud time the appropriate season?

3. Why are the tramps never given work? When is work "play for mortal stakes"?

4. Man must always make difficult choices. Why does the poet here make his choice?

After Apple-Picking

1. What are the most striking images or sensations that the poet uses to convey to us the dreamworld his drowsy laborer is entering?

2. How do lines 9 to 17, in which the "pane of glass" is a metaphor for ice, give the first impressions of drowsiness? Judging by your own experience, why are the strange and illogical details a precise and accurate description of the first entry into the world of dreams?

3. What can you tell about the character of the speaker? What is his present attitude toward his work? Does he have a sense of humor? Why would he like to discuss sleep with the woodchuck?

4. What different meanings does Frost use for the word "sleep" in this poem? If at times it means death, what are the virtues in not "speaking straight out," as Frost calls it?

5. "After Apple-Picking" is a poem about obligations unmet, tasks left unfinished, and duties forsaken. How is this meaning carried through the poem?

6. Why is the rhyme scheme of this poem irregular?

The Grindstone

1. Frost called "The Grindstone" one of his favorite poems and a symbol of the world. What kind of personality does Frost ascribe to the grindstone? Is it proud, indifferent, menacing? How does Frost make the grindstone a symbol of something ancient and evil?

2. What different aspects of creativity does each worker represent? What is Frost saying about the world of work through the relationship of these two men?

3. What do the last lines tell us of the speaker's fears of perfection? Why is he for "leaving something to the whetter"?

4. Could the blade be either an instrument of good or of evil, just like the act of creation? Why is this point left deliberately vague?

5. The speaker is a man of both good humor and scorn, resignation and protest. How does the poet show us this?

IMPLICATIONS

Discuss the following statements.

1. In Frost's poetry, the life of the imagination and the humble business of earning a living come together to the enrichment of both.

2. Each man must protect his right to choose his own work and his own play because they tie together his loves and his needs.

3. The dream world in "After Apple-Picking" carries over both the fatigue and the satisfactions of the day. It is not a nightmare world, but one in which man fulfills himself by his labor.

4. Reward and labor should not be separate, but the reward should come from labor well-performed.

5. "The Grindstone" gives us the historic sense of the aching strain man must exert to make nature subject to his own demands.

6. Man cannot create except in terms of some unattainable ideal.

Man and Society

The nature of man and how his behavior affects
his fellow men are two subjects Frost pursued all his life. In the first poem,
Frost's delightful sense of humor urges him to talk about man in relation
to the insect world. How do we compare to the lesser animals?
Are our codes of behavior naturally superior?
The second of these poems raises issues which touch every one of us:
private property and common property, rights and responsibilities.

Departmental, or My Ant Jerry

An ant on the tablecloth
Ran into a dormant[1] moth
Of many times his size.
He showed not the least surprise.
His business wasn't with such.   5
He gave it scarcely a touch,
And was off on his duty run.
Yet if he encountered one
Of the hive's enquiry squad
Whose work is to find out God   10
And the nature of time and space,
He would put him onto the case.
Ants are a curious race;
One crossing with hurried tread
The body of one of their dead   15
Isn't given a moment's arrest—
Seems not even impressed.
But he no doubt reports to any
With whom he crosses antennae,
And they no doubt report   20
To the higher up at court.
Then word goes forth in Formic:[2]
"Death's come to Jerry McCormic,
Our selfless forager[3] Jerry.
Will the special Janizary[4]   25
Whose office it is to bury
The dead of the commissary[5]
Go bring him home to his people.
Lay him in state on a sepal.[6]
Wrap him for shroud in a petal.   30

Embalm him with ichor[7] of nettle.
This is the word of your Queen,"
And presently on the scene
Appears a solemn mortician;
And taking formal position   35
With feelers calmly atwiddle,
Seizes the dead by the middle,
And heaving him high in air,
Carries him out of there.
No one stands round to stare.   40
It is nobody else's affair.

It couldn't be called ungentle.
But how thoroughly departmental.

---

1. **dormant**\ˈdȯr·mənt\ sleeping.
2. **Formic**\ˈfȯr·mĭk\ here, the language of ants. Ants
secrete formic acid used in dyeing and finishing textiles.
3. **selfless forager,** an unselfish seeker of provisions for
all.
4. **Janizary**\ˈjă·nə·zĕ·rē\ also spelled Janissary. Here,
the special service ant who buries the dead. The Janizary was an elite corps of Turkish troops organized in
the fourteenth century.
5. **commissary,** a store for equipment and provisions.
6. **sepal**\ˈsē·pəl\ one of the modified leaves of a flower
which surround the lower part of a blossom.
7. **ichor**\ˈī·kər\ in Greek myth, the fluid that flowed
through the veins of the gods.

Mending Wall

Something there is that doesn't love a wall,
That sends the frozen-ground-swell under it,
And spills the upper boulders in the sun;
And makes gaps even two can pass abreast.
The work of hunters is another thing: 5
I have come after them and made repair
Where they have left not one stone on a stone,
But they would have the rabbit out of hiding,
To please the yelping dogs. The gaps I mean,
No one has seen them made or heard them made,   10
But at spring mending-time we find them there.
I let my neighbor know beyond the hill;
And on a day we meet to walk the line
And set the wall between us once again.
We keep the wall between us as we go.   15
To each the boulders that have fallen to each.
And some are loaves and some so nearly balls
We have to use a spell to make them balance:
"Stay where you are until our backs are turned!"
We wear our fingers rough with handling them.   20
Oh, just another kind of outdoor game,
One on a side. It comes to little more:
There where it is we do not need the wall:
He is all pine and I am apple orchard.
My apple trees will never get across   25
And eat the cones under his pines, I tell him.
He only says, "Good fences make good neighbors."
Spring is the mischief in me, and I wonder
If I could put a notion in his head:
"*Why* do they make good neighbors? Isn't it   30
Where there are cows? But here there are no cows.
Before I built a wall I'd ask to know
What I was walling in or walling out,
And to whom I was like to give offense.
Something there is that doesn't love a wall,   35
That wants it down." I could say "Elves" to him,
But it's not elves exactly, and I'd rather
He said it for himself. I see him there
Bringing a stone grasped firmly by the top

In each hand, like an old-stone savage armed.   40
He moves in darkness as it seems to me,
Not of woods only and the shade of trees.
He will not go behind his father's saying,
And he likes having thought of it so well
He says again, "Good fences make good neighbors."   45

I
THE HUMAN COMMUNITY

Most of Frost's poetry centers on the family, the home, the individual. In these two poems, though, he looks at man in his relations with others: the human community. In each case, Frost's rich sense of humor enables him to strike gentle but well-aimed blows at the blind effects of custom and the indifference of man to man. Such indifference strikes at the roots of life, but the poet shows us, in his words, "a way of grappling with life." His poems, in fact, are strategies for overcoming that cold human indifference that comes from living in too much isolation.

Departmental, or My Ant Jerry

1. Like all good animal fables, this one is funny because it explores the resemblances between ants and men so thoroughly. Explain the resemblances you see in the poem. What rhymes and what images add to the humor of the poem?

2. If you read this poem as a satire on bureaucracy or specialization, just what defects are being ridiculed?

3. Apply these lines to our own lives: "No one stands round to stare./ It is nobody else's affair." What comment is Frost making on mankind? Is he saying that we should learn from the ants?

4. Why does the poet separate the last two lines from the rest of the poem? In what sense is this the moral of the fable? Is this the way the poet says: "Look out—I'm spoofing"?

Mending Wall

1. The meaning of this poem can be summed up in the problem it raises: Should man tear down the barriers which isolate one man from another, or are these boundaries and limits necessary to human life? What is the view of the speaker in the poem?

2. What is the "something" that doesn't love a wall?

3. Does the neighbor in this poem look on wall-mending as "just another kind of outdoor game"?

II
IMPLICATIONS

Discuss the following statements.

1. As human life becomes more specialized and mechanical, its cold efficiency comes closer to the blind instincts of the ant colony.

2. "Mending Wall" stands for all man-made barriers.

3. We change people's attitudes only by putting notions in their heads, by having them see things for themselves.

4. Those who unthinkingly inherit the opinions of their parents live forever in the mental darkness of childhood.

Life and Death

All poets, in time, face the major question: What is death?
Frost sees it not as an absolute, but as perpetually involved with life
and the living. These four poems will need several readings. The first is
intentionally simple but baffling, like a riddle; its meanings, however,
are multiple. The last two poems are narratives, unforgettable in their
local details but also universal in their contemplation of death.

Fire and Ice

Some say the world will end in fire,
Some say in ice.
From what I've tasted of desire
I hold with those who favor fire.
But if it had to perish twice,
I think I know enough of hate
To say that for destruction ice
Is also great
And would suffice.

Stopping by Woods on a Snowy Evening

Whose woods these are I think I know.
His house is in the village though;
He will not see me stopping here
To watch his woods fill up with snow.

My little horse must think it queer   5
To stop without a farmhouse near
Between the woods and frozen lake
The darkest evening of the year.

He gives his harness bells a shake
To ask if there is some mistake.   10
The only other sound's the sweep
Of easy wind and downy flake.

The woods are lovely, dark and deep,
But I have promises to keep,
And miles to go before I sleep,   15
And miles to go before I sleep.

"Out, Out—"

The buzz-saw snarled and rattled in the yard
And made dust and dropped stove-length sticks of wood,
Sweet-scented stuff when the breeze drew across it.
And from there those that lifted eyes could count
Five mountain ranges one behind the other   5
Under the sunset far into Vermont.
And the saw snarled and rattled, snarled and rattled,
As it ran light, or had to bear a load.
And nothing happened: day was all but done.
Call it a day, I wish they might have said   10
To please the boy by giving him the half hour
That a boy counts so much when saved from work.
His sister stood beside them in her apron
To tell them "Supper." At the word, the saw,
As if to prove saws knew what supper meant,   15
Leaped out at the boy's hand, or seemed to leap—
He must have given the hand. However it was,
Neither refused the meeting. But the hand!
The boy's first outcry was a rueful laugh,
As he swung toward them holding up the hand   20
Half in appeal, but half as if to keep
The life from spilling. Then the boy saw all—
Since he was old enough to know, big boy
Doing a man's work, though a child at heart—
He saw all spoiled. "Don't let them cut my hand off—   25
The doctor, when he comes. Don't let them, sister!"
So. But the hand was gone already.
The doctor put him in the dark of ether.
He lay and puffed his lips out with his breath.
And then—the watcher at his pulse took fright.   30
No one believed. They listened at his heart.
Little—less—nothing!—and that ended it.
No more to build on there. And they, since they
Were not the one dead, turned to their affairs.

The Death of the Hired Man

Mary sat musing on the lamp-flame at the table
Waiting for Warren. When she heard his step,
She ran on tip-toe down the darkened passage
To meet him in the doorway with the news
And put him on his guard. "Silas is back."   5
She pushed him outward with her through the door
And shut it after her. "Be kind," she said.
She took the market things from Warren's arms
And set them on the porch, then drew him down
To sit beside her on the wooden steps.   10

"When was I ever anything but kind to him?
But I'll not have the fellow back," he said.
"I told him so last haying, didn't I?
If he left then, I said, that ended it.
What good is he? Who else will harbor him   15
At his age for the little he can do?
What help he is there's no depending on.
Off he goes always when I need him most.
He thinks he ought to earn a little pay,
Enough at least to buy tobacco with,   20
So he won't have to beg and be beholden.[1]
'All right,' I say, 'I can't afford to pay
Any fixed wages, though I wish I could.'
'Someone else can.' 'Then someone else will have to.'
I shouldn't mind his bettering himself   25
If that was what it was. You can be certain,
When he begins like that, there's someone at him
Trying to coax him off with pocket-money,—
In haying time, when any help is scarce.
In winter he comes back to us. I'm done."   30

"Sh! not so loud: he'll hear you," Mary said.

"I want him to: he'll have to soon or late."

"He's worn out. He's asleep beside the stove.
When I came up from Rowe's I found him here,

---

1. **be beholden**\bē ˈhōl·dən\ be under obligation for a
favor or a gift.

Huddled against the barn-door fast asleep,   35
A miserable sight, and frightening, too—
You needn't smile—I didn't recognize him—
I wasn't looking for him—and he's changed.
Wait till you see."

          "Where did you say he'd been?"   40

"He didn't say. I dragged him to the house,
And gave him tea and tried to make him smoke.
I tried to make him talk about his travels.
Nothing would do: he just kept nodding off."

"What did he say? Did he say anything?"   45

"But little."

         "Anything? Mary, confess
He said he'd come to ditch the meadow[2] for me."

"Warren!"

       "But did he? I just want to know."   50

"Of course he did. What would you have him say?
Surely you wouldn't grudge the poor old man
Some humble way to save his self-respect.
He added, if you really care to know,
He meant to clear the upper pasture, too.   55
That sounds like something you have heard before?
Warren, I wish you could have heard the way
He jumbled everything. I stopped to look
Two or three times—he made me feel so queer—
To see if he was talking in his sleep.   60
He ran on[3] Harold Wilson—you remember—
The boy you had in haying four years since.
He's finished school, and teaching in his college.
Silas declares you'll have to get him back.
He says they two will make a team for work: 65
Between them they will lay this farm as smooth!
The way he mixed that in with other things.
He thinks young Wilson a likely lad, though daft
On education—you know how they fought
All through July under the blazing sun,   70
Silas up on the cart to build the load,
Harold along beside to pitch it on."

---

2. **to ditch the meadow,** to dig ditches to drain the meadow.
3. **He ran on,** he talked of.

"Yes, I took care to keep well out of earshot."

"Well, those days trouble Silas like a dream.
You wouldn't think they would. How some things linger!   75
Harold's young college boy's assurance piqued[4] him.
After so many years he still keeps finding
Good arguments he sees he might have used.
I sympathize. I know just how it feels
To think of the right thing to say too late.   80
Harold's associated in his mind with Latin.
He asked me what I thought of Harold's saying
He studied Latin like the violin
Because he liked it—that an argument!
He said he couldn't make the boy believe   85
He could find water with a hazel prong—
Which showed how much good school had ever done him.
He wanted to go over that. But most of all
He thinks if he could have another chance
To teach him how to build a load of hay—"   90

"I know, that's Silas' one accomplishment.
He bundles every forkful in its place,
And tags and numbers it for future reference,
So he can find and easily dislodge it
In the unloading. Silas does that well.   95
He takes it out in bunches like big birds' nests.
You never see him standing on the hay
He's trying to lift, straining to lift himself."

"He thinks if he could teach him that, he'd be
Some good perhaps to someone in the world.   100
He hates to see a boy the fool of books.
Poor Silas, so concerned for other folk,
And nothing to look backward to with pride,
And nothing to look forward to with hope,
So now and never any different."   105

Part of a moon was falling down the west,
Dragging the whole sky with it to the hills.
Its light poured softly in her lap. She saw it
And spread her apron to it. She put out her hand
Among the harp-like morning-glory strings,   110
Taut with the dew from garden bed to eaves,
As if she played unheard some tenderness

---

4. **piqued**\pēkd\ irritated, provoked.

That wrought on him beside her in the night.
"Warren," she said, "he has come home to die:
You needn't be afraid he'll leave you this time." 115

"Home," he mocked gently.

     "Yes, what else but home?
It all depends on what you mean by home.
Of course he's nothing to us, any more
Than was the hound that came a stranger to us 120
Out of the woods, worn out upon the trail."

"Home is the place where, when you have to go there,
They have to take you in."

     "I should have called it
Something you somehow haven't to deserve." 125

Warren leaned out and took a step or two,
Picked up a little stick, and brought it back
And broke it in his hand and tossed it by.
"Silas has better claim on us you think
Than on his brother? Thirteen little miles 130
As the road winds would bring him to his door.
Silas has walked that far no doubt today.
Why doesn't he go there? His brother's rich,
A somebody—director in the bank."

"He never told us that." 135

    "We know it though."

"I think his brother ought to help, of course.
I'll see to that if there is need. He ought of right
To take him in, and might be willing to—
He may be better than appearances. 140
But have some pity on Silas. Do you think
If he had any pride in claiming kin
Or anything he looked for from his brother,
He'd keep so still about him all this time?"

"I wonder what's between them." 145

     "I can tell you.
Silas is what he is—we wouldn't mind him—
But just the kind that kinsfolk can't abide.
He never did a thing so very bad.

He don't know why he isn't quite as good   150
As anybody. Worthless though he is,
He won't be made ashamed to please his brother."

"I can't think Si ever hurt anyone."

"No, but he hurt my heart the way he lay
And rolled his old head on that sharp-edged chair-back.   155
He wouldn't let me put him on the lounge.
You must go in and see what you can do.
I made the bed up for him there tonight.
You'll be surprised at him—how much he's broken.
His working days are done; I'm sure of it."   160

"I'd not be in a hurry to say that."

"I haven't been. Go, look, see for yourself.
But Warren, please remember how it is:
He's come to help you ditch the meadow.
He has a plan. You mustn't laugh at him.   165
He may not speak of it, and then he may.
I'll sit and see if that small sailing cloud
Will hit or miss the moon."

                              It hit the moon.
Then there were three there, making a dim row,   170
The moon, the little silver cloud, and she.

Warren returned—too soon, it seemed to her,
Slipped to her side, caught up her hand and waited.

"Warren?" she questioned.

                              "Dead," was all he answered.   175

I

THE ULTIMATE QUESTIONS

It is one of the jobs of the poet to ask the ultimate questions and to suggest some partial yet penetrating answers. They may not be the only answers or ours, but they are comments that reveal something about the nature of man. The poet extends our horizons and our experiences by allowing us to see and to judge human passions, obligations, and death through his eyes. Through the honesty and courage of his vision, he reminds us of the strength of human passions and creates a sympathy for human frailties. The poet is a great teacher because he identifies values that make us human.

Fire and Ice

1. Frost's Yankee manner is not just a way of speaking, but a mode of thought, a way of facing the world. Find in this poem evidence of these characteristics of the Yankee manner:

   a. a harsh, tight-lipped, yet humorous manner.

   b. a recurrent understatement.

   c. a homey, informal, and dryly factual speech.

d. a restraint of one's strongest feelings.

2. Why are fire and ice such appropriate symbols for desire and hatred?

Stopping by Woods on a Snowy Evening

1. Why does the traveler stop at the woods? Why should his horse think this queer?

2. What similarity does the rural traveler's journey have with that of anyone journeying through life? How does the poet make a personal experience the image of experiences common to us all?

3. Why does the traveler leave with reluctance?

4. Why does the poet repeat the last line?

"Out, Out—"

1. The title, "Out, Out—" comes from a famous soliloquy in Shakespeare's *Macbeth,* in which life "is a tale/Told by an idiot, full of sound and fury/Signifying nothing." How does the same meaningless view of life fit into this poem?

2. The contrast between man and machine is central to this poem. How does Frost suggest this contrast?

3. The hand is the symbol of power and creativity. Here it is not merely the symbol, but the instrument. In this rural world, for this "boy, doing a man's work," what does the loss of his hand mean?

4. Some critics feel Frost is heartless when he writes "and that ended it./No more to build on there." What is your opinion?

5. In the last two lines, do those who "turn to their affairs" do so out of shock, indifference, or a frank acceptance of realities?

The Death of the Hired Man

1. This poem is a dramatic narrative. Like all good drama, it is essentially psychological. What is the psychological conflict in the poem?

2. We never see or hear Silas. What does the poet gain by keeping Silas offstage?

3. Warren's gradual conversion to pity and mercy through his wife's deliberate and gentle persuasiveness is the real subject of this poem. Trace the stages in Warren's transformation and the strategies by which Mary achieves this.

4. Why is Warren's discovery of Silas' death an ironic but not surprising fulfillment and end of the dramatic conflict?

II
IMPLICATIONS

Discuss the following statements:

1. The intensity of man's deepest passions, love and hate, create the greatest forces for destruction.

2. Men wish to make permanent their moments of honest pleasure and discovery. Why?

3. In life, the shock of the truth and all its implications is often more fatal than mere physical loss or impairment.

4. It is not the death of Silas, but Mary's intuitive sympathy for Silas and Warren's slow searching for justice that are the subject of "The Death of the Hired Man."

III
TECHNIQUES

Blank Verse

Shakespeare and Milton first popularized *blank verse.* It is based on five stresses or beats to each line and it is unrhymed. "Mending Wall," "Birches," and "The Death of the Hired Man" are particularly fine examples of the ease with which Frost handles this traditional form. The first lines of "Birches" are built around a wholly regular beat: ten syllables, alternately unaccented and accented. We call this regular line *iambic pentameter.* But note that by line 5 Frost is ready to vary this beat, in order to avoid monotony. He still keeps five accents to each line, but their order varies. To suggest even greater naturalness, even closer approximation to ordinary speech, in "The Death of the Hired Man," Frost breaks the sentences in the middle of the line, lets sentences run on for three or four lines, splits a line between two speakers; yet the beat is always five to the line.

Frost on Poetry

Frost often discussed the art of poetry. The following quotations from Robert Frost should be studied and discussed in terms of the poems you have just read.

1. And were an epitaph to be my story
I'd have a short one ready for my own.
I would have written of me on my stone
I had a lover's quarrel with the world.

2. A poem is a reaching-out toward expression: an effort to find fulfillment. A complete poem is one where an emotion has found its thought, and the thought has found the words.

THORNTON WILDER

1897–

Thornton Wilder playing the Stage Manager in Our Town, *New York, 1938. He was convinced that the confining three walls, the curtain, and the proscenium arch of the modern theater "shut the play up into a museum showpiece."*
Instead of the universals he was witnessing only local happenings. "The novel," he argued, "is pre-eminently the vehicle of the unique occasion, the theatre of the generalized one. It is through the theatre's power to raise the exhibited individual action into the realm of idea and type and universal that it is able to evoke our belief."

Thornton Wilder can always be counted on to try new forms, to avoid the obvious, even though it is traditional. Since 1915, he has been experimenting in prose fiction and in the drama, but it was 1927 before he achieved critical approval and a national reputation. Born in Madison, Wisconsin, he moved to China at the age of nine when his father was appointed consul general at Hong Kong and Shanghai. He returned to California to finish high school and in 1915 entered Oberlin College. Two years later he left his classes to serve in the Coast Artillery and, when World War I was over, took his B.A. degree at Yale University. The following year he sailed for Europe to study archaeology at the American Academy in Rome, the first of several prolonged visits outside the United States. When he returned, he accepted a teaching job at The Lawrenceville School near Princeton, New Jersey, where he taught English and French for the next six years at the same time he worked on his novels. *The Cabala* appeared in 1926, *The Bridge of San Luis Rey* in 1927.

It is natural that a young scholar back from

Rome should want to gather his impressions of the Eternal City into a romantic story with himself at the center. *The Cabala* is that kind of novel but, as readers have come to expect from Wilder, it is fantasy with an ironic twist. The young American introduces us to the wealthy and eccentric aristocrats who make up a group known as the Cabala. He soon becomes intrigued with these people as people only to discover they are the pagan gods of Europe masquerading as citizens of Rome, 1920. Not all readers of the novel were as convinced as the narrator seemed to be, but Wilder was not deterred. He had had his first try at combining a realistic setting with a fantastic plot, and he had the satisfaction of shaping his novel from his own pattern. Originality was to play an important role in Wilder's development.

The Bridge of San Luis Rey not only won him a Pulitzer Prize, the first of three, but made him financially independent for several years following its publication. Like *The Cabala, The Bridge* is a philosophical novel, but it is set in eighteenth-century Peru, not Europe. Wilder was convinced that America had had enough stark realism in the novels of John Dos Passos (see page 87), enough critical examination of our own society in the work of Sinclair Lewis (see page 711). It was ready now for historical romance, and what he provided in *The Bridge* was made to the public's order: memorable characters, a remote and ornate setting, religious themes, a sense of mystery, and above all concise dialogue. The central incident is simple: on a Friday in July, 1714, a bridge collapses on the road between Lima and Cuzco, sending five people to their deaths. The plot is more complex: Brother Juniper, who was present at the accident, sets out to discover why *these* five people should have died. He tells us the story of a lonely old marquesa and her lovely daughter, then of an actor-manager and his mistress, finally of twin brothers and a secret passion. Wilder's purpose in letting Brother Juniper tell the stories is made clear in the epilogue, called "Perhaps an Intention." Here Wilder enters the book, as omniscient narrator, to underscore his theme: Love is a moral responsibility; the world we live in is purposeless without it. "There is a land of the living and a land of the dead," his last sentence reads, "and the bridge is love, the only survival, the only meaning."

Following his resignation from Lawrenceville, Wilder spent two years in Europe studying Continental drama. On his return he published his third novel, *The Woman of Andros,* a failure with both the public and the critics. Set in pre-Christian Greece, it tried to probe further into the hidden meanings in men's lives. With his next novel, however, Wilder recouped his reputation and if anything enlarged his audience. In *Heaven's My Destination* (1935) he shifted gears, adopted the conventional realistic method for this social satire, set the story of George Brush, a traveling salesman, in the Middle West Bible Belt about 1930, and concentrated on pitting this humanitarian hero against a materialistic society. In his travels about the country, Brush moves from comedy to pathos and back again. At one moment we laugh at his naïveté, at another we wince at the grim truths he demonstrates. The novel quite rightly has been compared to Mark Twain's *Huckleberry Finn.* Wilder commenced work on his fifth novel, *The Ides of March* (1948), after serving three years with the Intelligence Corps of the Air Force in World War II. Another best-seller, it tells the familiar story of the last months of Julius Caesar's life with such originality that again Wilder turned history into perceptive character study. Using only letters and documents, some seventy, all of them imaginary, to retell the events leading up to the assassination, for the first time in his fiction Wilder stood wholly outside the main action, not commenting as omniscient narrator on the moral of his story. The letters, however, are of such variety and fascination that the reader needs no guide to discover their implications.

Had Wilder published only novels, he would have had a satisfying if modest reputation among American literary artists. When *Our Town* opened on Broadway in 1938, the critics knew a genuine theatrical talent had blossomed. *The Skin of Our Teeth* (1942) and *The Matchmaker* (1954) are the full flowering. "Toward the end of the twenties," Wilder tells us, "I began to lose pleasure in going to the theatre. I ceased to believe in the stories I saw presented there." He feared that the playwrights of his day were afraid to disturb their middle-class patrons with biting comedy or social satire and consequently soothed them with comfortable, tidy plays of little consequence. But chief among his reasons for disbelief was the box set. He was convinced that the confining three walls, the curtain, and the proscenium arch of the modern theater "shut the play up into a museum showcase." Instead of the universals he was witnessing only local happenings. "The novel," he argued, "is pre-eminently the vehicle of the unique occasion, the theatre of the generalized one. It is through the theatre's power to raise the exhibited individual action into the realm of idea and type and universal that it is able to evoke our belief."

Our Town breaks down the confinements of a box set in order to speak of universals. It was not Wilder's first attempt. As early as 1931 he had published *The Long Christmas Dinner and Other Plays*. These one-act experiments tried "to capture not versimilitude but reality," as he put it. In other words, he did not wish to hamper his audience with elaborate sets that looked like reproductions of our own dining rooms or the interior of actual pullman cars; he avoided placing the action in a specific year or a certain town; his characters were dressed in ordinary clothes, not costumes. *The Long Christmas Dinner,* for example, spans ninety years, yet the basic set never changes. In *Pullman Car Hiawatha* plain chairs serve as berths. In *The Happy Journey to Trenton and Camden* four kitchen chairs and a low platform represent an automobile; Pa's hands hold an imaginary steering wheel; and the family travels seventy miles in twenty minutes. The Stage Manager acts as interpreter and scene changer as well as various characters in the play. In *Our Town,* Wilder experiments even further.

Though set in Grover's Corners, the play is not offered, Wilder insists, "as a picture of life in a New Hampshire village; or as a speculation about the conditions of life after death." He is attempting here "to find a value above all price for the smallest events in our daily life." He makes the claim "as preposterous as possible," for he has "set the village against the largest dimensions of time and place."

To bring belief back into the theater, in other words, Wilder strives to embody universal meaning in specific incidents, actions, and characters. His primary concern is not with the individual lives of the Gibbs family or the Webbs but with life itself, with all its vain strivings, its petty concerns, its joys and sorrows. Small wonder that this play has been performed in the best theaters of the world; it translates easily because the audience identification is almost immediate. Grover's Corners could be Denmark or Italy, Brazil or Japan. The need for love is a theme of much of Wilder's fiction; the need for awareness, for savoring every minute of our brief lives is at the heart of his tragic play. Failing to realize life's potential, no matter how modestly life is lived, leads only to frustration and waste. Emily Webb comes to know this truth too late. Have *we* made this discovery in time, Wilder seems to ask his audience. He does not wait for our answer, for he knows how man has trapped himself in his getting and spending, his overweening pride, his ignorance of the value of time. To Simon Stimson, the town drunk, Wilder gives his most biting lines, but Simon ironically speaks from the grave: "Now you know! That's what it was to be alive. To move about in a cloud of ignorance; to go up and down trampling on the feelings of those . . . of those about you. To spend and waste time as though you had a million years. To be always at the mercy of one self-centered passion, or another . . . that's the happy existence you wanted to go back to. Ignorance and blindness." *The Bridge of San Luis Rey* taught this moral to a legion of readers. *Our Town* continues to speak this truth on stages everywhere.

When this play opened in New York
in February, 1938, the first-night audience was not quite prepared
for the bare and dimly lit stage as it entered the theater, a stage
without curtain and without scenery. Since that time,
audiences have grown accustomed to the easy informality of the Stage Manager
as he introduces each scene, interrupts the action with commentary,
takes the part of several minor characters, improvises scenery, and speaks the epilogue.
Playwrights of another age would have called him the Chorus. What he adds to this play
is invaluable: an affectionate understanding of the simple, ordinary life that goes on
day after day in Grover's Corners and an earnest desire to make us share
that understanding. He wants us to see ourselves in these people,
to laugh and cry with them, to enjoy life as they do. Because so many audiences
willingly respond, *Our Town* is one of the most successful plays
in the modern American theater.

OUR TOWN

a play in three acts

CHARACTERS

*(in the order
of their appearance)*

STAGE MANAGER	MR. WEBB
DR. GIBBS	WOMAN IN THE BALCONY
JOE CROWELL	MAN IN THE AUDITORIUM
HOWIE NEWSOME	LADY IN THE BOX
MRS. GIBBS	SIMON STIMSON
MRS. WEBB	MRS. SOAMES
GEORGE GIBBS	CONSTABLE WARREN
REBECCA GIBBS	SI CROWELL
WALLY WEBB	THREE BASEBALL PLAYERS
EMILY WEBB	SAM CRAIG
PROFESSOR WILLARD	JOE STODDARD

*The entire play takes place
in Grover's Corners,
New Hampshire.*

Act I

No curtain.

No scenery.

The audience, arriving, sees an empty stage in half-light.

Presently the STAGE MANAGER, *hat on and pipe in mouth, enters and begins placing a table and three chairs downstage left, and a table and three chairs downstage right. He also places a low bench at the corner of what will be the Webb house, left.*

"Left" and "right" are from the point of view of the actor facing the audience. "Up" is toward the back wall.

As the house lights go down he has finished setting the stage and leaning against the right proscenium pillar watches the late arrivals in the audience.

When the auditorium is in complete darkness he speaks:

STAGE MANAGER. This play is called "Our Town." It was written by Thornton Wilder; produced and directed by A. . . . [or: produced by A. . . . ; directed by B. . . .]. In it you will see Miss C. . . . ; Miss D. . . . ; Miss E. . . . ; and Mr. F. . . . ; Mr. G. . . . ; Mr. H. . . . ; and many others. The name of the town is Grover's Corners, New Hampshire—just across the Massachusetts line: latitude 42 degrees 40 minutes; longitude 70 degrees 37 minutes. The First Act shows a day in our town. The day is May 7, 1901. The time is just before dawn. (*A rooster crows.*)

The sky is beginning to show some streaks of light over in the East there, behind our mount'in.

The morning star always gets wonderful bright the minute before it has to go,—doesn't it? (*He stares at it for a moment, then goes upstage.*)

Well, I'd better show you how our town lies.

Up here—(*That is: parallel with the back wall.*) is Main Street. Way back there is the railway station; tracks go that way. Polish Town's across the tracks, and some Canuck[1] families.

(*Toward the left.*) Over there is the Congregational Church; across the street's the Presbyterian.

Methodist and Unitarian are over there.

Baptist is down in the holla' by the river.

Catholic Church is over beyond the tracks.

Here's the Town Hall and Post Office combined; jail's in the basement.

Bryan once made a speech from these very steps here.

Along here's a row of stores. Hitching posts and horse blocks in front of them. First automobile's going to come along in about five years—belonged to Banker Cartwright, our richest citizen . . . lives in the big white house up on the hill.

Here's the grocery store and here's Mr. Morgan's drugstore. Most everybody in town manages to look into those two stores once a day.

Public School's over yonder. High School's still farther over. Quarter of nine mornings, noontimes, and three o'clock afternoons, the hull town can hear the yelling and screaming from those schoolyards.

He approaches the table and chairs downstage right.

This is our doctor's house,—Doc Gibbs'. This is the back door. (*Two arched trellises, covered with vines and flowers, are pushed out, one by each proscenium pillar.*) There's some scenery for those who think they have to have scenery.

This is Mrs. Gibbs' garden. Corn . . . peas . . .

---

1. **Canuck**\kə ˄nək\ slang for French Canadian, usually used disparagingly.

beans . . . hollyhocks . . . heliotrope[2] . . . and a lot of burdock.[3] (*Crosses the stage.*)

In those days our newspaper come out twice a week—the Grover's Corners *Sentinel*—and this is Editor Webb's house.

And this is Mrs. Webb's garden.

Just like Mrs. Gibbs', only it's got a lot of sunflowers, too.

He looks upward, center stage.

Right here . . . 's a big butternut tree. (*He returns to his place by the right proscenium[4] pillar and looks at the audience for a minute.*)

Nice town, y'know what I mean?

Nobody very remarkable ever come out of it, s'far as we know.

The earliest tombstones in the cemetery up there on the mountain say 1670–1680— they're Grovers and Cartwrights and Gibbses and Herseys—same names as are around here now.

Well, as I said: it's about dawn.

The only lights on in town are in a cottage over by the tracks where a Polish mother's just had twins. And in the Joe Crowell house, where Joe Junior's getting up so as to deliver the paper. And in the depot, where Shorty Hawkins is gettin' ready to flag the 5:45 for Boston. (*A train whistle is heard. The* STAGE MANAGER *takes out his watch and nods.*)

Naturally, out in the country—all around— there've been lights on for some time, what with milkin's and so on. But town people sleep late.

So—another day's begun.

There's Doc Gibbs comin' down Main Street now, comin' back from that baby case. And here's his wife comin' downstairs to get breakfast. (MRS. GIBBS, *a plump, pleasant woman in the middle thirties, comes "down-stairs" right. She pulls up an imaginary window shade in her kitchen and starts to make a fire in her stove.*)

Doc Gibbs died in 1930. The new hospital's named after him.

Mrs. Gibbs died first—long time ago, in fact. She went out to visit her daughter, Rebecca, who married an insurance man in Canton, Ohio, and died there—pneumonia—but her body was brought back here. She's up in the cemetery there now—in with a whole mess of Gibbses and Herseys—she was Julia Hersey 'fore she married Doc Gibbs in the Congregational Church over there.

In our town we like to know the facts about everybody.

There's Mrs. Webb, coming downstairs to get her breakfast, too.

—That's Doc Gibbs. Got that call at half past one this morning. And there comes Joe Crowell, Jr., delivering Mr. Webb's *Sentinel*.

DR. GIBBS *has been coming along Main Street from the left. At the point where he would turn to approach his house, he stops, sets down his—imaginary—black bag, takes off his hat, and rubs his face with fatigue, using an enormous handkerchief.*

MRS. WEBB, *a thin, serious, crisp woman, has entered her kitchen, left, tying on an apron. She goes through the motions of putting wood into a stove, lighting it, and preparing breakfast.*

Suddenly, JOE CROWELL, JR., *eleven, starts down Main Street from the right, hurling imaginary newspapers into doorways.*

JOE CROWELL, JR. Morning, Doc Gibbs.

DR. GIBBS. Morning, Joe.

JOE CROWELL, JR. Somebody been sick, Doc?

DR. GIBBS. No. Just some twins born over in Polish Town.

JOE CROWELL, JR. Do you want your paper now?

---

2. **heliotrope**\ˈhē·lē·ə·trōp\ plant that turns toward the sun and usually bears fragrant white or purplish flowers.

3. **burdock**, coarse weed with a bur; also called cocklebur.

4. **proscenium**\prō ˈsē·nē·əm\ the part of the stage in front of the curtain.

DR. GIBBS. Yes, I'll take it.—Anything serious goin' on in the world since Wednesday?

JOE CROWELL, JR. Yessir. My schoolteacher, Miss Foster, 's getting married to a fella over in Concord.

DR. GIBBS. I declare.—How do you boys feel about that?

JOE CROWELL, JR. Well, of course, it's none of my business—but I think if a person starts out to be a teacher, she ought to stay one.

DR. GIBBS. How's your knee, Joe?

JOE CROWELL, JR. Fine, Doc, I never think about it at all. Only like you said, it always tells me when it's going to rain.

DR. GIBBS. What's it telling you today? Goin' to rain?

JOE CROWELL, JR. No, sir.

DR. GIBBS. Sure?

JOE CROWELL, JR. Yessir.

DR. GIBBS. Knee ever make a mistake?

JOE CROWELL, JR. No, sir. (JOE *goes off.* DR. GIBBS *stands reading his paper.*)

STAGE MANAGER. Want to tell you something about that boy Joe Crowell there. Joe was awful bright—graduated from high school here, head of his class. So he got a scholarship to Massachusetts Tech. Graduated head of his class there, too. It was all wrote up in the Boston paper at the time. Goin' to be a great engineer, Joe was. But the war broke out and he died in France.—All that education for nothing.

HOWIE NEWSOME (*off left*). Giddap, Bessie! What's the matter with you today?

STAGE MANAGER. Here comes Howie Newsome, deliverin' the milk. (HOWIE NEWSOME, *about thirty, in overalls, comes along Main Street from the left, walking beside an invisible horse and wagon and carrying an imaginary rack with milk bottles. The sound of clinking milk bottles is heard. He leaves some bottles at* MRS. WEBB's *trellis, then, crossing the stage to* MRS. GIBBS', *he stops center to talk to* DR. GIBBS.)

HOWIE NEWSOME. Morning, Doc.

DR. GIBBS. Morning, Howie.

HOWIE NEWSOME. Somebody sick?

DR. GIBBS. Pair of twins over to Mrs. Goruslaw-ski's.

HOWIE NEWSOME. Twins, eh? This town's gettin' bigger every year.

DR. GIBBS. Goin' to rain, Howie?

HOWIE NEWSOME. No, no. Fine day—that'll burn through. Come on, Bessie.

DR. GIBBS. Hello, Bessie. (*He strokes the horse, which has remained up center.*) How old is she, Howie?

HOWIE NEWSOME. Going on seventeen. Bessie's all mixed up about the route ever since the Lockharts stopped takin' their quart of milk every day. She wants to leave 'em a quart just the same—keeps scolding me the hull trip. (*He reaches* MRS. GIBBS' *back door. She is waiting for him.*)

MRS. GIBBS. Good morning, Howie.

HOWIE NEWSOME. Morning, Mrs. Gibbs. Doc's just comin' down the street.

MRS. GIBBS. Is he? Seems like you're late today.

HOWIE NEWSOME. Yes. Somep'n went wrong with the separator. Don't know what 'twas. (*He passes* DR. GIBBS *up center.*) Doc!

DR. GIBBS. Howie!

MRS. GIBBS (*calling upstairs*). Children! Children! Time to get up.

HOWIE NEWSOME. Come on, Bessie! (*He goes off right.*)

MRS. GIBBS. George! Rebecca! (DR. GIBBS *arrives at his back door and passes through the trellis into his house.*)

MRS. GIBBS. Everything all right, Frank?

DR. GIBBS. Yes. I declare—easy as kittens.

MRS. GIBBS. Bacon'll be ready in a minute. Set down and drink your coffee. You can catch a couple hours' sleep this morning, can't you?

DR. GIBBS. Hm! . . . Mrs. Wentworth's coming at eleven. Guess I know what it's about, too. Her stummick ain't what it ought to be.

MRS. GIBBS. All told, you won't get more'n three hours' sleep. Frank Gibbs, I don't know what's goin' to become of you. I do wish I could get you to go away someplace and take a rest. I think it would do you good.

MRS. WEBB. Emileeee! Time to get up! Wally! Seven o'clock!

MRS. GIBBS. I declare, you got to speak to George. Seems like something's come over him lately. He's no help to me at all. I can't even get him to cut me some wood.

DR. GIBBS. (*Washing and drying his hands at the sink.* MRS. GIBBS *is busy at the stove.*) Is he sassy to you?

MRS. GIBBS. No. He just whines! All he thinks about is that baseball—George! Rebecca! You'll be late for school.

DR. GIBBS. M-m-m . . .

MRS. GIBBS. George!

DR. GIBBS. George, look sharp!

GEORGE'S VOICE. Yes, Pa!

DR. GIBBS (*as he goes off the stage*). Don't you hear your mother calling you? I guess I'll go upstairs and get forty winks.

MRS. WEBB. Walleee! Emileee! You'll be late for school! Walleee! You wash yourself good or I'll come up and do it myself.

REBECCA GIBBS' VOICE. Ma! What dress shall I wear?

MRS. GIBBS. Don't make a noise. Your father's been out all night and needs his sleep. I washed and ironed the blue gingham for you special.

REBECCA. Ma, I hate that dress.

MRS. GIBBS. Oh, hush-up-with-you.

REBECCA. Every day I go to school dressed like a sick turkey.

MRS. GIBBS. Now, Rebecca, you always look *very* nice.

REBECCA. Mama, George's throwing soap at me.

MRS. GIBBS. I'll come and slap the both of you,—that's what I'll do. (*A factory whistle sounds. The children dash in and take their places at the tables. Right,* GEORGE, *about sixteen, and* REBECCA, *eleven. Left,* EMILY *and* WALLY, *same ages. They carry strapped school-books.*)

STAGE MANAGER. We've got a factory in our town too—hear it? Makes blankets. Cartwrights own it and it brung 'em a fortune.

MRS. WEBB. Children! Now I won't have it. Breakfast is just as good as any other meal and I won't have you gobbling like wolves.

It'll stunt your growth,—that's a fact. Put away your book, Wally.

WALLY. Aw, Ma! By ten o'clock I got to know all about Canada.

MRS. WEBB. You know the rule's well as I do—no books at table. As for me, I'd rather have my children healthy than bright.

EMILY. I'm both, Mama: you know I am. I'm the brightest girl in school for my age. I have a wonderful memory.

MRS. WEBB. Eat your breakfast.

WALLY. I'm bright, too, when I'm looking at my stamp collection.

MRS. GIBBS. I'll speak to your father about it when he's rested. Seems to me twenty-five cents a week's enough for a boy your age. I declare I don't know how you spend it all.

GEORGE. Aw, Ma,—I gotta lotta things to buy.

MRS. GIBBS. Strawberry phosphates[5]—that's what you spend it on.

GEORGE. I don't see how Rebecca comes to have so much money. She has more'n a dollar.

REBECCA (*spoon in mouth, dreamily*). I've been saving it up gradual.

MRS. GIBBS. Well, dear, I think it's a good thing to spend some every now and then.

REBECCA. Mama, do you know what I love most in the world—do you?—Money.

MRS. GIBBS. Eat your breakfast.

THE CHILDREN. Mama, there's first bell.—I gotta hurry.—I don't want any more.—I gotta hurry. (*The children rise, seize their books and dash out through the trellises. They meet, down center, and chattering, walk to Main Street, then turn left. The* STAGE MANAGER *goes off, unobtrusively, right.*)

MRS. WEBB. Walk fast, but you don't have to run. Wally, pull up your pants at the knee. Stand up straight, Emily.

MRS. GIBBS. Tell Miss Foster I send her my best congratulations—can you remember that?

REBECCA. Yes, Ma.

MRS. GIBBS. You look real nice, Rebecca. Pick up your feet.

---

5. **strawberry phosphates,** beverage made of a mixture of soda water and strawberry flavoring.

ALL. Good-by. (MRS. GIBBS *fills her apron with food for the chickens and comes down to the footlights.*)

MRS. GIBBS. Here, chick, chick, chick.

No, go away, you. Go away.

Here, chick, chick, chick.

What's the matter with *you?* Fight, fight, fight,—that's all you do. Hm . . . *you* don't belong to me. Where'd you come from? (*She shakes her apron.*)

Oh, don't be so scared. Nobody's going to hurt you. (MRS. WEBB *is sitting on the bench by her trellis, stringing beans.*)

Good Morning, Myrtle. How's your cold?

MRS. WEBB. Well, I still get that tickling feeling in my throat. I told Charles I didn't know as I'd go to choir practice tonight. Wouldn't be any use.

MRS. GIBBS. Have you tried singing over your voice?

MRS. WEBB. Yes, but somehow I can't do that and stay on the key. While I'm resting myself I thought I'd string some of these beans.

MRS. GIBBS (*rolling up her sleeves as she crosses the stage for a chat*). Let me help you. Beans have been good this year.

MRS. WEBB. I've decided to put up forty quarts if it kills me. The children say they hate 'em, but I notice they're able to get 'em down all winter. (*Pause. Brief sound of chickens cackling.*)

MRS. GIBBS. Now, Myrtle. I've got to tell you something, because if I don't tell somebody I'll burst.

MRS. WEBB. Why, Julia Gibbs!

MRS. GIBBS. Here, give me some more of those beans. Myrtle, did one of those secondhand-furniture men from Boston come to see you last Friday?

MRS. WEBB. No-o.

MRS. GIBBS. Well, he called on me. First I thought he was a patient wantin' to see Dr. Gibbs. 'N he wormed his way into my parlor, and, Myrtle Webb, he offered me three hundred and fifty dollars for Grandmother Wentworth's highboy, as I'm sitting here!

MRS. WEBB. Why, Julia Gibbs!

MRS. GIBBS. He did! That old thing! Why, it was so big I didn't know where to put it and I almost give it to Cousin Hester Wilcox.

MRS. WEBB. Well, you're going to take it, aren't you?

MRS. GIBBS. I don't know.

MRS. WEBB. You don't know—three hundred and fifty dollars! What's come over you?

MRS. GIBBS. Well, if I could get the Doctor to take the money and go away someplace on a real trip, I'd sell it like that.—Y'know, Myrtle, it's been the dream of my life to see Paris, France.—Oh, I don't know. It sounds crazy, I suppose, but for years I've been promising myself that if we ever had the chance—

MRS. WEBB. How does the Doctor feel about it?

MRS. GIBBS. Well, I did beat about the bush a little and said that if I got a legacy—that's the way I put it—I'd make him take me somewhere.

MRS. WEBB. M-m-m . . . What did he say?

MRS. GIBBS. You know how he is. I haven't heard a serious word out of him since I've known him. No, he said, it might make him discontented with Grover's Corners to go traipsin' about Europe; better let well enough alone, he says. Every two years he makes a trip to the battlefields of the Civil War and that's enough treat for anybody, he says.

MRS. WEBB. Well, Mr. Webb just *admires* the way Dr. Gibbs knows everything about the Civil War. Mr. Webb's a good mind to give up Napoleon and move over to the Civil War, only Dr. Gibbs being one of the greatest experts in the country just makes him despair,

MRS. GIBBS. It's a fact! Dr. Gibbs is never so happy as when he's at Antietam or Gettysburg. The times I've walked over those hills, Myrtle, stopping at every bush and pacing it all out, like we were going to buy it.

MRS. WEBB. Well, if that secondhand man's really serious about buyin' it, Julia, you sell it. And then you'll get to see Paris, all right. Just keep droppin' hints from time to time—

that's how I got to see the Atlantic Ocean, y'know.

MRS. GIBBS. Oh, I'm sorry I mentioned it. Only it seems to me that once in your life before you die you ought to see a country where they don't talk in English and don't even want to. (*The* STAGE MANAGER *enters briskly from the right. He tips his hat to the ladies, who nod their heads.*)

STAGE MANAGER. Thank you, ladies. Thank you very much. (MRS. GIBBS *and* MRS. WEBB *gather up their things, return into their homes and disappear.*)

Now we're going to skip a few hours.

But first we want a little more information about the town, kind of a scientific account, you might say.

So I've asked Professor Willard of our State University to sketch in a few details of our past history here.

Is Professor Willard here? (PROFESSOR WIL-LARD, *a rural savant,*[6] *pince-nez*[7] *on a wide satin ribbon, enters from the right with some notes in his hand.*)

May I introduce Professor Willard of our State University. A few brief notes, thank you, Professor,—unfortunately our time is limited.

PROFESSOR WILLARD. Grover's Corners . . . let me see . . . Grover's Corners lies on the old Pleistocene[8] granite of the Appalachian range. I may say it's some of the oldest land in the world. We're very proud of that. A shelf of Devonian[9] basalt crosses it with vestiges of Mesozoic[10] shale, and some sandstone outcroppings; but that's all more recent: two hundred, three hundred million years old.

Some highly interesting fossils have been found . . . I may say: unique fossils . . . two miles out of town, in Silas Peckham's cow pasture. They can be seen at the museum in our University at any time—that is, at any reasonable time. Shall I read some of Professor Gruber's notes on the meteorological situation—mean precipitation, et cetera?

STAGE MANAGER. Afraid we won't have time for that, Professor. We might have a few words on the history of man here.

PROFESSOR WILLARD. Yes . . . anthropological data: Early Amerindian stock. Cotahatchee tribes . . . no evidence before the tenth century of this era . . . hm . . . now entirely disappeared . . . possible traces in three families. Migration toward the end of the seventeenth century of English brachiocephalic[11] blue-eyed stock . . . for the most part. Since then some Slav and Mediterranean—

STAGE MANAGER. And the population, Professor Willard?

PROFESSOR WILLARD. Within the town limits: 2,640.

STAGE MANAGER. Just a moment, Professor. (*He whispers into the* PROFESSOR'S *ear.*)

PROFESSOR WILLARD. Oh, yes, indeed?—The population, *at the moment,* is 2,642. The Postal District brings in 507 more, making a total of 3,149.—Mortality and birth rates: constant.—By MacPherson's gauge: 6.032.

STAGE MANAGER. Thank you very much, Professor. We're all very much obliged to you, I'm sure.

PROFESSOR WILLARD. Not at all, sir; not at all.

STAGE MANAGER. This way, Professor, and thank you again. (*Exit* PROFESSOR WILLARD.) Now the political and social report: Editor Webb. —Oh, Mr. Webb? (MRS. WEBB *appears at her back door.*)

---

6. **savant**\sa ᴧvant\ a learned man.
7. **pince-nez**\pĭns ᴧněz\ eyeglasses held on the nose by a spring.
8. **Pleistocene**\plaɪ·stə·sēn\ the great ice age.
9. **Devonian**\dĭ ᴧvō·nē·ən\ that period which began with the continents mainly dry. Later large areas were flooded and sediment forming old red sandstone was laid down. The sea was full of fish. Frogs and other amphibians appeared. The land was covered with great ferns and fern-like trees.
10. **Mesozoic**\mě·zə ᴧzō·ĭk\ the era when the Appalachian Mts. were elevated. Reptiles and dinosaurs were numerous, but became extinct when violent disturbances brought the era to an end.
11. **brachiocephalic**\bră·kē·ō·sə ᴧfa·lĭk\ (usually spelled brachycephalic) short-headed, with the breadth of the head at least four-fifths of its length.

MRS. WEBB. He'll be here in a minute. . . . He just cut his hand while he was eatin' an apple.

STAGE MANAGER. Thank you, Mrs. Webb.

MRS. WEBB. Charles! Everybody's waitin'. (*Exit* MRS. WEBB.)

STAGE MANAGER. Mr. Webb is Publisher and Editor of the Grover's Corners *Sentinel.* That's our local paper, y'know. (MR. WEBB *enters from his house, pulling on his coat. His finger is bound in a handkerchief.*)

MR. WEBB. Well . . . I don't have to tell you that we're run here by a Board of Selectmen.— All males vote at the age of twenty-one. Women vote indirect. We're lower middle class: sprinkling of professional men . . . ten per cent illiterate laborers. Politically, we're eighty-six per cent Republicans; six per cent Democrats; four per cent Socialists; rest, indifferent.

Religiously, we're eighty-five per cent Protestants; twelve per cent Catholics; rest, indifferent.

STAGE MANAGER. Have you any comments, Mr. Webb?

MR. WEBB. Very ordinary town, if you ask me. Little better behaved than most. Probably a lot duller.

But our young people here seem to like it well enough. Ninety per cent of 'em graduating from high school settle down right here to live—even when they've been away to college.

STAGE MANAGER. Now, is there anyone in the audience who would like to ask Editor Webb anything about the town?

WOMAN IN THE BALCONY. Is there much drinking in Grover's Corners?

MR. WEBB. Well, ma'am, I wouldn't know what you'd call *much.* Satiddy nights the farmhands meet down in Ellery Greenough's stable and holler some. We've got one or two town drunks, but they're always having remorses every time an evangelist comes to town. No, ma'am, I'd say likker ain't a regular thing in the home here, except in the medicine chest. Right good for snake bite, y'know—always was.

BELLIGERENT MAN AT BACK OF AUDITORIUM. Is there no one in town aware of—

STAGE MANAGER. Come forward, will you, where we can all hear you—What were you saying?

BELLIGERENT MAN. Is there no one in town aware of social injustice and industrial inequality?

MR. WEBB. Oh, yes, everybody is—somethin' terrible. Seems like they spend most of their time talking about who's rich and who's poor.

BELLIGERENT MAN. Then why don't they do something about it? (*He withdraws without waiting for an answer.*)

MR. WEBB. Well, I dunno. . . . I guess we're all hunting like everybody else for a way the diligent and sensible can rise to the top and the lazy and quarrelsome can sink to the bottom. But it ain't easy to find. Meanwhile, we do all we can to help those that can't help themselves and those that can we leave alone. —Are there any other questions?

LADY IN A BOX. Oh, Mr. Webb? Mr. Webb, is there any culture or love of beauty in Grover's Corners?

MR. WEBB. Well, ma'am, there ain't much—not in the sense you mean. Come to think of it, there's some girls that play the piano at High School Commencement; but they ain't happy about it. No, ma'am, there isn't much culture; but maybe this is the place to tell you that we've got a lot of pleasures of a kind here: we like the sun comin' up over the mountain in the morning, and we all notice a good deal about the birds. We pay a lot of attention to them. And we watch the change of the seasons; yes, everybody knows about them. But those other things—you're right, ma'am,— there ain't much.—*Robinson Crusoe* and the Bible; and Handel's "Largo," we all know that; and Whistler's "Mother"—those are just about as far as we go.

LADY IN A BOX. So I thought. Thank you, Mr. Webb.

STAGE MANAGER. Thank you, Mr. Webb. (MR. WEBB *retires.*) Now, we'll go back to the town.

It's early afternoon. All 2,642 have had their dinners and all the dishes have been washed. (MR. WEBB, *having removed his coat, returns and starts pushing a lawn mower to and fro beside his house.*) There's an early-afternoon calm in our town: a buzzin' and a hummin' from the school buildings; only a few buggies on Main Street—the horses dozing at the hitching posts; you all remember what it's like. Doc Gibbs is in his office, tapping people and making them say "ah." Mr. Webb's cuttin' his lawn over there; one man in ten thinks it's a privilege to push his own lawn mower.

No, sir. It's later than I thought. There are the children coming home from school already. (*Shrill girls' voices are heard, off left.* EMILY *comes along Main Street, carrying some books. There are some signs that she is imagining herself to be a lady of startling elegance.*)

EMILY. I *can't*, Lois. I've got to go home and help my mother. I *promised.*

MR. WEBB. Emily, walk simply. Who do you think you are today?

EMILY. Papa, you're terrible. One minute you tell me to stand up straight and the next minute you call me names. I just don't listen to you. (*She gives him an abrupt kiss.*)

MR. WEBB. Golly, I never got a kiss from such a great lady before. (*He goes out of sight.* EMILY *leans over and picks some flowers by the gate of her house.* GEORGE GIBBS *comes careening down Main Street. He is throwing a ball up to dizzying heights, and waiting to catch it again. This sometimes requires his taking six steps backward. He bumps into an old lady invisible to us.*)

GEORGE. Excuse me, Mrs. Forrest.

STAGE MANAGER (*as Mrs. Forrest*). Go out and play in the fields, young man. You got no business playing baseball on Main Street.

GEORGE. Awfully sorry, Mrs. Forrest.—Hello, Emily.

EMILY. H'lo.

GEORGE. You made a fine speech in class.

EMILY. Well . . . I was really ready to make a speech about the Monroe Doctrine, but at the last minute Miss Corcoran made me talk about the Louisiana Purchase instead. I worked an awful long time on both of them.

GEORGE. Gee, it's funny, Emily. From my window up there I can just see your head nights when you're doing your homework over in your room.

EMILY. Why, can you?

GEORGE. You certainly do stick to it, Emily. I don't see how you can sit still that long. I guess you like school.

EMILY. Well, I always feel it's something you have to go through.

GEORGE. Yeah.

EMILY. I don't mind it really. It passes the time.

GEORGE. Yeah.—Emily, what do you think? We might work out a kinda telegraph from your window to mine; and once in a while you could give me a kinda hint or two about one of those algebra problems. I don't mean the answers, Emily, of course not . . . just some little hint . . .

EMILY. Oh, I think *hints* are allowed.—So—ah—if you get stuck, George, you whistle to me; and I'll give you some hints.

GEORGE. Emily, you're just naturally bright, I guess.

EMILY. I figure that it's just the way a person's born.

GEORGE. Yeah. But, you see, I want to be a farmer, and my Uncle Luke says whenever I'm ready I can come over and work on his farm and if I'm any good I can just gradually have it.

EMILY. You mean the house and everything? (*Enter* MRS. WEBB *with a large bowl and sits on the bench by her trellis.*)

GEORGE. Yeah. Well, thanks . . . I better be getting out to the baseball field. Thanks for the talk, Emily.—Good afternoon, Mrs. Webb.

MRS. WEBB. Good afternoon, George.

GEORGE. So long, Emily.

EMILY. So long, George.

MRS. WEBB. Emily, come and help me string these beans for the winter. George Gibbs let himself have a real conversation, didn't he? Why, he's growing up. How old would George be?

EMILY. I don't know.

MRS. WEBB. Let's see. He must be almost sixteen.

EMILY. Mama, I made a speech in class today and I was very good.

MRS. WEBB. You must recite it to your father at supper. What was it about?

EMILY. The Louisiana Purchase. It was like silk off a spool. I'm going to make speeches all my life.—Mama, are these big enough?

MRS. WEBB. Try and get them a little bigger if you can.

EMILY. Mama, will you answer me a question, serious?

MRS. WEBB. Seriously, dear—not serious.

EMILY. Seriously,—will you?

MRS. WEBB. Of course, I will.

EMILY. Mama, am I good looking?

MRS. WEBB. Yes, of course you are. All my children have got good features; I'd be ashamed if they hadn't.

EMILY. Oh, Mama, that's not what I mean. What I mean is: am I *pretty*?

MRS. WEBB. I've already told you, yes. Now that's enough of that. You have a nice young pretty face. I never heard of such foolishness.

EMILY. Oh, Mama, you never tell us the truth about anything.

MRS. WEBB. I *am* telling you the truth.

EMILY. Mama, were *you* pretty?

MRS. WEBB. Yes, I was, if I do say it. I was the prettiest girl in town next to Mamie Cartwright.

EMILY. But, Mama, you've got to say *some*thing about me. Am I pretty enough . . . to get anybody . . . to get people interested in me?

MRS. WEBB. Emily, you make me tired. Now stop it. You're pretty enough for all normal purposes.—Come along now and bring that bowl with you.

EMILY. Oh, Mama, you're no help at all.

STAGE MANAGER. Thank you. Thank you! That'll do. We'll have to interrupt again here. Thank you, Mrs. Webb; thank you, Emily. (MRS. WEBB *and* EMILY *withdraw*.) There are some more things we want to explore about this town. (*He comes to the center of the stage. During the following speech the lights gradually dim to darkness, leaving only a spot on him.*) I think this is a good time to tell you that the Cartwright interests have just begun building a new bank in Grover's Corners— had to go to Vermont for the marble, sorry to say. And they've asked a friend of mine what they should put in the cornerstone for people to dig up . . . a thousand years from now. . . . Of course, they've put in a copy of the *New York Times* and a copy of Mr. Webb's *Sentinel*. . . . We're kind of interested in this because some scientific fellas have found a way of painting all that reading matter with a glue—a silicate glue—that'll make it keep a thousand—two thousand years.

We're putting in a Bible . . . and the Constitution of the United States—and a copy of William Shakespeare's plays. What do you say, folks? What do you think?

Y'know—Babylon once had two million people in it, and all we know about 'em is the names of the kings and some copies of wheat contracts . . . and contracts for the sale of slaves. Yet every night all those families sat down to supper, and the father came home from his work, and the smoke went up the chimney,—same as here. And even in Greece and Rome, all we know about the *real* life of the people is what we can piece together out of the joking poems and the comedies they wrote for the theatre back then.

So I'm going to have a copy of this play put in the cornerstone and the people a thousand years from now'll know a few simple facts about us—more than the Treaty of Versailles[12] and the Lindbergh flight.[13]

---

12. **Treaty of Versailles**\vĕr ▲sai\ the treaty between the Allies and Germany at the end of World War I.
13. **Lindbergh flight,** first nonstop transatlantic flight from west to east. Charles A. Lindbergh flew alone from New York to Paris, 1927, in his monoplane, *The Spirit of St. Louis.*

See what I mean?

So—people a thousand years from now—this is the way we were in the provinces north of New York at the beginning of the twentieth century.—This is the way we were: in our growing up and in our marrying and in our living and in our dying. (*A choir partially concealed in the orchestra pit has begun singing "Blessed Be the Tie That Binds."* SIMON STIMSON *stands directing them. Two ladders have been pushed onto the stage; they serve as indication of the second story in the Gibbs and Webb houses.* GEORGE *and* EMILY *mount them, and apply themselves to their schoolwork.* DR. GIBBS *has entered and is seated in his kitchen reading.*)

Well!—good deal of time's gone by. It's evening.

You can hear choir practice going on in the Congregational Church.

The children are at home doing their schoolwork.

The day's running down like a tired clock.

SIMON STIMSON. Now look here, everybody. Music come into the world to give pleasure. —Softer! Softer! Get it out of your heads that music's only good when it's loud. You leave loudness to the Methodists. You couldn't beat 'em, even if you wanted to. Now again. Tenors!

GEORGE. Hssst! Emily!

EMILY. Hello.

GEORGE. Hello!

EMILY. I can't work at all. The moonlight's so *terrible*.

GEORGE. Emily, did you get the third problem?

EMILY. Which?

GEORGE. The *third?*

EMILY. Why, yes, George—that's the easiest of them all.

GEORGE. I don't see it. Emily, can you give me a hint?

EMILY. I'll tell you one thing: the answer's in yards.

GEORGE. ! ! ! In yards? How do you mean?

Emily: "You're welcome. My, isn't the moonlight terrible?"

EMILY. In *square* yards.

GEORGE. Oh . . . in square yards.

EMILY. Yes, George, don't you see?

GEORGE. Yeah.

EMILY. In square yards of *wallpaper*.

GEORGE. Wallpaper,—oh, I see. Thanks a lot, Emily.

EMILY. You're welcome. My, isn't the moonlight *terrible?* And choir practice going on.—I think if you hold your breath you can hear the train all the way to Contoocook. Hear it?

GEORGE. M-m-m—What do you know!

EMILY. Well, I guess I better go back and try to work.

GEORGE. Good night, Emily. And thanks.

EMILY. Good night, George.

SIMON STIMSON. Before I forget it: how many of you will be able to come in Tuesday afternoon and sing at Fred Hersey's wedding?— show your hands. That'll be fine; that'll be right nice. We'll do the same music we did for Jane Trowbridge's last month.

—Now we'll do: "Art Thou Weary; Art Thou Languid?" It's a question, ladies and gentlemen, make it talk. Ready.

DR. GIBBS. Oh, George, can you come down a minute?

GEORGE. Yes, Pa. (*He descends the ladder.*)

DR. GIBBS. Make yourself comfortable, George; I'll only keep you a minute. George, how old are you?

GEORGE. I? I'm sixteen, almost seventeen.

DR. GIBBS. What do you want to do after school's over?

GEORGE. Why, you know, Pa. I want to be a farmer on Uncle Luke's farm.

DR. GIBBS. You'll be willing, will you, to get up early and milk and feed the stock . . . and you'll be able to hoe and hay all day?

GEORGE. Sure, I will. What are you . . . what do you mean, Pa?

DR. GIBBS. Well, George, while I was in my office today I heard a funny sound . . . and what do you think it was? It was your mother chopping wood. There you see your mother—getting up early; cooking meals all day long; washing and ironing;—and still she has to go out in the back yard and chop wood. I suppose she just got tired of asking you. She just gave up and decided it was easier to do it herself. And you eat her meals, and put on the clothes she keeps nice for you, and you run off and play baseball,—like she's some hired girl we keep around the house but that we don't like very much. Well, I knew all I had to do was call your attention to it. Here's a handkerchief, son. George, I've decided to raise your spending money twenty-five cents a week. Not, of course, for chopping wood for your mother, because that's a present you give her, but because you're getting older— and I imagine there are lots of things you must find to do with it.

GEORGE. Thanks, Pa.

DR. GIBBS. Let's see—tomorrow's your payday. You can count on it—Hmm. Probably Rebecca'll feel she ought to have some more too. Wonder what could have happened to your mother. Choir practice never was as late as this before.

GEORGE. It's only half past eight, Pa.

DR. GIBBS. I don't know why she's in that old choir. She hasn't any more voice than an old crow. . . . Traipsin' around the streets at this hour of the night . . . Just about time you retired, don't you think?

GEORGE. Yes, Pa. (GEORGE *mounts to his place on the ladder. Laughter and good nights can be heard on stage left and presently* MRS. GIBBS, MRS. SOAMES *and* MRS. WEBB *come down Main Street. When they arrive at the corner of the stage they stop.*)

MRS. SOAMES. Good night, Martha. Good night, Mr. Foster.

MRS. WEBB. I'll tell Mr. Webb; I *know* he'll want to put in in the paper.

MRS. GIBBS. My, it's late!

MRS. SOAMES. Good night, Irma.

MRS. GIBBS. Real nice choir practice, wa'n't it? Myrtle Webb! Look at that moon, will you? Tsk-tsk-tsk. Potato weather, for sure. (*They are silent a moment, gazing up at the moon.*)

MRS. SOAMES. Naturally, I didn't want to say a word about it in front of those others, but now we're alone—really, it's the worst scandal that ever was in this town!

MRS. GIBBS. What?

MRS. SOAMES. Simon Stimson!

MRS. GIBBS. Now, Louella!

MRS. SOAMES. But, Julia! To have the organist of a church *drink* and *drunk* year after year. You know he was drunk tonight.

MRS. GIBBS. Now, Louella! We all know about Mr. Stimson, and we all know about the troubles he's been through, and Dr. Ferguson knows too, and if Dr. Ferguson keeps him on there in his job the only thing the rest of us can do is just not to notice it.

MRS. SOAMES. *Not to notice it!* But it's getting worse.

MRS. WEBB. No, it isn't, Louella. It's getting better. I've been in that choir twice as long as you have. It doesn't happen anywhere near so often. . . . My, I hate to go to bed on a night like this.—I better hurry. Those children'll be sitting up till all hours. Good night, Louella. (*They all exchange good nights. She hurries downstage, enters her house and disappears.*)

MRS. GIBBS. Can you get home safe, Louella?

MRS. SOAMES. It's as bright as day. I can see Mr. Soames scowling at the window now. You'd think we'd been to a dance the way the menfolk carry on. (*More good nights.* MRS. GIBBS *arrives at her home and passes through the trellis into the kitchen.*)

MRS. GIBBS. Well, we had a real good time.

DR. GIBBS. You're late enough.

MRS. GIBBS. Why, Frank, it ain't any later 'n usual.

DR. GIBBS. And you stopping at the corner to gossip with a lot of hens.

MRS. GIBBS. Now, Frank, don't be grouchy. Come out and smell the heliotrope in the moonlight. (*They stroll out arm in arm along the footlights.*) Isn't that wonderful? What did you do all the time I was away?

DR. GIBBS. Oh, I read—as usual. What were the girls gossiping about tonight?

MRS. GIBBS. Well, believe me, Frank—there is something to gossip about.

DR. GIBBS. Hmm! Simon Stimson far gone, was he?

MRS. GIBBS. Worst I've ever seen him. How'll that end, Frank? Dr. Ferguson can't forgive him forever.

DR. GIBBS. I guess I know more about Simon Stimson's affairs than anybody in this town. Some people ain't made for small-town life. I don't know how that'll end; but there's nothing we can do but just leave it alone. Come, get in.

MRS. GIBBS. No, not yet . . . Frank, I'm worried about you.

DR. GIBBS. What are you worried about?

MRS. GIBBS. I think it's my duty to make plans for you to get a real rest and change. And if I get that legacy, well, I'm going to insist on it.

DR. GIBBS. Now, Julia, there's no sense in going over that again.

MRS. GIBBS. Frank, you're just *unreasonable!*

DR. GIBBS (*starting into the house*). Come on, Julia, it's getting late. First thing you know you'll catch cold. I gave George a piece of my mind tonight. I reckon you'll have your wood chopped for a while anyway. No, no, start getting upstairs.

MRS. GIBBS. Oh, dear. There's always so many things to pick up, seems like. You know, Frank, Mrs. Fairchild always locks her front door every night. All those people up that part of town do.

DR. GIBBS (*blowing out the lamp*). They're all getting citified, that's the trouble with them. They haven't got nothing fit to burgle and everybody knows it. (*They disappear.* REBECCA *climbs up the ladder beside* GEORGE.)

GEORGE. Get out, Rebecca. There's only room for one at this window. You're always spoiling everything.

REBECCA. Well, let me look just a minute.

GEORGE. Use your own window.

REBECCA. I did, but there's no moon there. . . . George, do you know what I think, do you? I think maybe the moon's getting nearer and nearer and there'll be a big 'splosion.

GEORGE. Rebecca, you don't know anything. If the moon were getting nearer, the guys that sit up all night with telescopes would see it first and they'd tell about it, and it'd be in all the newspapers.

REBECCA. George, is the moon shining on South America, Canada and half the whole world?

GEORGE. Well—prob'ly is. (*The* STAGE MANAGER *strolls on. Pause. The sound of crickets is heard.*)

STAGE MANAGER. Nine thirty. Most of the lights are out. No, there's Constable Warren trying a few doors on Main Street. And here comes Editor Webb, after putting his newspaper to bed. (MR. WARREN, *an elderly policeman, comes along Main Street from the right,* MR. WEBB *from the left.*)

MR. WEBB. Good evening, Bill.

CONSTABLE WARREN. Evenin', Mr. Webb.

MR. WEBB. Quite a moon!

CONSTABLE WARREN. Yepp.

MR. WEBB. All quiet tonight?

CONSTABLE WARREN. Simon Stimson is rollin' around a little. Just saw his wife movin' out to hunt for him so I looked the other way—there he is now. (SIMON STIMSON *comes down Main Street from the left, only a trace of unsteadiness in his walk.*)

MR. WEBB. Good evening, Simon . . . Town seems to have settled down for the night pretty well. . . . (SIMON STIMSON *comes up to him and pauses a moment and stares at him, swaying slightly.*) Good evening . . . Yes, most of the town's settled down for the night, Simon. . . . I guess we better do the same. Can I walk along a ways with you? (SIMON STIMSON *continues on his way without a word and disappears at the right.*) Good night.

CONSTABLE WARREN. I don't know how that's goin' to end, Mr. Webb.

MR. WEBB. Well, he's seen a peck of trouble, one thing after another. . . . Oh, Bill . . . if you see my boy smoking cigarettes, just give him a word, will you? He thinks a lot of you, Bill.

CONSTABLE WARREN. I don't think he smokes no cigarettes, Mr. Webb. Leastways, not more'n two or three a year.

MR. WEBB. Hm . . . I hope not.—Well, good night, Bill.

CONSTABLE WARREN. Good night, Mr. Webb. (*Exit.*)

MR. WEBB. Who's that up there? Is that you, Myrtle?

EMILY. No, it's me, Papa.

MR. WEBB. Why aren't you in bed?

EMILY. I don't know. I just can't sleep yet, Papa. The moonlight's so *won*-derful. And the smell of Mrs. Gibbs' heliotrope. Can you smell it?

MR. WEBB. Hm . . . Yes. Haven't any troubles on your mind, have you, Emily?

EMILY. *Troubles*, Papa? *No.*

MR. WEBB. Well, enjoy yourself, but don't let your mother catch you. Good night, Emily.

EMILY. Good night, Papa. (MR. WEBB *crosses into the house, whistling "Blessed Be the Tie That Binds" and disappears.*)

REBECCA. I never told you about that letter Jane Crofut got from her minister when she was sick. He wrote Jane a letter and on the envelope the address was like this: It said: Jane Crofut; The Crofut Farm; Grover's Corners; Sutton County; New Hampshire; United States of America.

GEORGE. What's funny about that?

REBECCA. But listen, it's not finished: the United States of America; Continent of North America; Western Hemisphere; the Earth; the Solar System; the Universe; the Mind of God—that's what it said on the envelope.

GEORGE. What do you know!

REBECCA. And the postman brought it just the same.

GEORGE. What do you know!

STAGE MANAGER. That's the end of the First Act, friends. You can go and smoke now, those that smoke.

I

DAILY LIFE IN "OUR TOWN"

The announced purpose of the first act is to give a picture of a day in "our town." Most of the details contribute to that picture, but there are others which may function to suggest the brevity and insignificance of human life. Professor Willard's speech, for example, serves that purpose, as does the long speech of the Stage Manager, the one in which he tells us how all Joe Crowell, Jr.'s, education went for nothing. Finally, Jane Crofut's letter shows human life to be the smallest element in a widening arena that ends in the mind of God. Ironically, however, that same life is given dignity and importance precisely because it lies at the center of God's mind.

And what can be said about the daily life itself and the people who live it? Are they cheerful and warm-hearted, good illustrations of the joys of simple living? Or are they dull and ordinary, good illustrations of the tragedies brought on by conformity? Is "the tie that binds" really "blessed," or does it make men "weary" and "languid"?

II
IMPLICATIONS

Discuss your own attitudes toward the following *pairs* of facts regarding Grover's Corners and its people.

1a. There is little culture or "love of beauty" in Grover's Corners.

b. The people in Grover's Corners appreciate sunrise and moonlight and the odor of flowers.

2a. Mrs. Gibbs' strong desire to visit Paris before she dies.

b. Dr. Gibbs' lack of interest in travel for fear that it might make him discontent with Grover's Corners.

3a. The unthinking acceptance of the ordinary, dull, and routine of life in Grover's Corners.

b. Editor Webb's straightforward admission that life in Grover's Corners *is* dull and ordinary.

4a. Mrs. Soames' gossip about Simon Stimson.

b. Dr. Gibbs' statement (near the end of the act) about Simon Stimson.

III
TECHNIQUES

Structure: Tension-Raising

A play is generally designed in such a manner that all of the major characters and all the major tensions (or conflicts) are introduced by the end of the first act. It is, therefore, a good practice to pause at the end of that act and ask yourself what the major tensions of the drama are. If you can identify them, you will be in a good position to follow the action in the ensuing acts more effectively.

We have already noted one of the chief tensions above (Section I); another important tension centers upon Emily. When we last see her, she is staring at the moonlight and her father asks her if she has any troubles on her mind. She answers, *"Troubles,* Papa. *No."* Her emphatic tone (conveyed in print by italics) suggests that it would be virtually impossible for her to have any serious troubles. Although we may take her at her word, we also know from our own experience that people's lives do not run as smoothly as Emily's for very long. Thus, ironically, the very fact that she is so emphatically untroubled creates a tension for the reader and suggests that we may find a change in her life in the near future.

Act II

The tables and chairs of the two kitchens are still on the stage.

The ladders and the small bench have been withdrawn.

The STAGE MANAGER *has been at his accustomed place watching the audience return to its seats.*

STAGE MANAGER. Three years have gone by.

Yes, the sun's come up over a thousand times.

Summers and winters have cracked the mountains a little bit more and the rains have brought down some of the dirt.

Some babies that weren't even born before have begun talking regular sentences already; and a number of people who thought they were right young and spry have noticed that they can't bound up a flight of stairs like they used to, without their heart fluttering a little.

All that can happen in a thousand days.

Nature's been pushing and contriving in other ways, too; a number of young people fell in love and got married.

Yes, the mountain got bit away a few fractions of an inch; millions of gallons of water went by the mill; and here and there a new home was set up under a roof.

Almost everybody in the world gets married, —you know what I mean? In our town there aren't hardly any exceptions. Most everybody in the world climbs into their graves married.

The First Act was called the Daily Life. This act is called Love and Marriage. There's another act coming after this: I reckon you can guess what that's about.

So:

It's three years later. It's 1904.

It's July 7th, just after High School Commencement.

That's the time most of our young people jump up and get married.

Soon as they've passed their last examinations in solid geometry and Cicero's Orations, looks like they suddenly feel themselves fit to be married.

It's early morning. Only this time it's been raining. It's been pouring and thundering.

Mrs. Gibbs' garden, and Mrs. Webb's here: drenched.

All those bean poles and pea vines: drenched.

All yesterday over there on Main Street, the rain looked like curtains being blown along.

Hm . . . it may begin again any minute.

There! You can hear the 5:45 for Boston. (MRS. GIBBS *and* MRS. WEBB *enter their kitchen and start the day as in the First Act.*)

And there's Mrs. Gibbs and Mrs. Webb come down to make breakfast, just as though it were an ordinary day. I don't have to point out to the women in my audience that those ladies they see before them, both of those ladies cooked three meals a day—one of 'em for twenty years, the other for forty—and no summer vacation. They brought up two children apiece, washed, cleaned the house,— and *never a nervous breakdown.*

It's like what one of those Middle West poets said: You've got to love life to have life, and you've got to have life to love life. . . .

It's what they call a vicious circle.

HOWIE NEWSOME (*off stage left*). Giddap, Bessie!

STAGE MANAGER. Here comes Howie Newsome delivering the milk. And there's Si Crowell delivering the papers like his brother before him. (SI CROWELL *has entered hurling imaginary newspapers into doorways;* HOWIE NEWSOME *has come along Main Street with Bessie.*)

SI CROWELL. Morning, Howie.

HOWIE NEWSOME. Morning, Si.—Anything in the papers I ought to know?

SI CROWELL. Nothing much, except we're losing

about the best baseball pitcher Grover's Corners ever had—George Gibbs.

HOWIE NEWSOME. Reckon he is.

SI CROWELL. He could hit and run bases, too.

HOWIE NEWSOME. Yep. Mighty fine ball player. —Whoa! Bessie! I guess I can stop and talk if I've a mind to!

SI CROWELL. I don't see how he could give up a thing like that just to get married. Would you, Howie?

HOWIE NEWSOME. Can't tell, Si. Never had no talent that way. (CONSTABLE WARREN *enters. They exchange good mornings.*) You're up early, Bill.

CONSTABLE WARREN. Seein' if there's anything I can do to prevent a flood. River's been risin' all night.

HOWIE NEWSOME. Si Crowell's all worked up here about George Gibbs' retiring from baseball.

CONSTABLE WARREN. Yes, sir; that's the way it goes. Back in '84 we had a player, Si—even George Gibbs couldn't touch him. Name of Hank Todd. Went down to Maine and became a parson. Wonderful ball player.— Howie, how does the weather look to you?

HOWIE NEWSOME. Oh, 'tain't bad. Think maybe it'll clear up for good. (CONSTABLE WARREN *and* SI CROWELL *continue on their way.* HOWIE NEWSOME *brings the milk first to* MRS. GIBBS' *house. She meets him by the trellis.*)

MRS. GIBBS. Good morning, Howie. Do you think it's going to rain again?

HOWIE NEWSOME. Morning, Mrs. Gibbs. It rained so heavy, I think maybe it'll clear up.

MRS. GIBBS. Certainly hope it will.

HOWIE NEWSOME. How much did you want today?

MRS. GIBBS. I'm going to have a houseful of relations, Howie. Looks to me like I'll need three-a-milk and two-a-cream.

HOWIE NEWSOME. My wife says to tell you we both hope they'll be very happy, Mrs. Gibbs. Know they *will.*

MRS. GIBBS. Thanks a lot, Howie. Tell your wife I hope she gits there to the wedding.

HOWIE NEWSOME. Yes, she'll be there; she'll be

there if she kin. (HOWIE NEWSOME *crosses to* MRS. WEBB's *house*.) Morning, Mrs. Webb.

MRS. WEBB. Oh, good morning, Mr. Newsome. I told you four quarts of milk, but I hope you can spare me another.

HOWIE NEWSOME. Yes'm . . . and the two of cream.

MRS. WEBB. Will it start raining again, Mr. Newsome?

HOWIE NEWSOME. Well. Just sayin' to Mrs. Gibbs as how it may lighten up. Mrs. Newsome told me to tell you as how we hope they'll both be very happy, Mrs. Webb. Know they *will*.

MRS. WEBB. Thank you, and thank Mrs. Newsome and we're counting on seeing you at the wedding.

IIOWIE NEWSOME. Yes, Mrs. Webb. We hope to git there. Couldn't miss that. Come on, Bessie. (*Exit* HOWIE NEWSOME. DR. GIBBS *descends in shirt sleeves, and sits down at his breakfast table.*)

DR. GIBBS. Well, Ma, the day has come. You're losin' one of your chicks.

MRS. GIBBS. Frank Gibbs, don't you say another word. I feel like crying every minute. Sit down and drink your coffee.

DR. GIBBS. The groom's up shaving himself— only there ain't an awful lot to shave. Whistling and singing, like he's glad to leave us.— Every now and then he says "I do" to the mirror, but it don't sound convincing to me.

MRS. GIBBS. I declare, Frank, I don't know how he'll get along. I've arranged his clothes and seen to it he's put warm things on,—Frank! they're too *young*. Emily won't think of such things. He'll catch his death of cold within a week.

DR. GIBBS. I was remembering my wedding morning, Julia.

MRS. GIBBS. Now don't start that, Frank Gibbs.

DR. GIBBS. I was the scaredest young fella in the State of New Hampshire. I thought I'd make a mistake for sure. And when I saw you comin' down that aisle I thought you were the prettiest girl I'd ever seen, but the only trouble was that I'd never seen you before.

There I was in the Congregational Church marryin' a total stranger.

MRS. GIBBS. And how do you think I felt!— Frank, weddings are perfectly awful things. Farces,—that's what they are! (*She puts a plate before him.*) Here, I've made something for you.

DR. GIBBS. Why, Julia Hersey—French toast!

MRS. GIBBS. 'Tain't hard to make and I had to do something. (*Pause.* DR. GIBBS *pours on the syrup.*)

DR. GIBBS. How'd you sleep last night, Julia?

MRS. GIBBS. Well, I heard a lot of the hours struck off.

DR. GIBBS. Ye-e-s! I get a shock every time I think of George setting out to be a family man— that great gangling thing!—I tell you, Julia, there's nothing so terrifying in the world as a *son*. The relation of father and son is the darndest, awkwardest—

MRS. GIBBS. Well, mother and daughter's no picnic, let me tell you.

DR. GIBBS. They'll have a lot of troubles, I suppose, but that's none of our business. Everybody has a right to their own troubles.

MRS. GIBBS. (*at the table, drinking her coffee, meditatively*). Yes . . . people are meant to go through life two by two. 'Tain't natural to be lonesome. (*Pause.* DR. GIBBS *starts laughing.*)

DR. GIBBS. Julia, do you know one of the things I was scared of when I married you?

MRS. GIBBS. Oh, go along with you!

DR. GIBBS. I was afraid we wouldn't have material for conversation more'n'd last us a few weeks. (*Both laugh.*) I was afraid we'd run out and eat our meals in silence, that's a fact.—Well, you and I been conversing for twenty years now without any noticeable barren spells.

MRS. GIBBS. Well,—good weather, bad weather —'tain't very choice, but I always find something to say. (*She goes to the foot of the stairs.*) Did you hear Rebecca stirring around upstairs?

DR. GIBBS. No. Only day of the year Rebecca hasn't been managing everybody's business up there. She's hiding in her room.—I got the impression she's crying.

MRS. GIBBS. Lord's sakes!—This has got to stop.—Rebecca! Rebecca! Come and get your breakfast. (GEORGE *comes rattling down the stairs, very brisk.*)

GEORGE. Good morning, everybody. Only five more hours to live. (*Makes the gesture of cutting his throat, and a loud "k-k-k," and starts through the trellis.*)

MRS. GIBBS. George Gibbs, where are you going?

GEORGE. Just stepping across the grass to see my girl.

MRS. GIBBS. Now, George! You put on your overshoes. It's raining torrents. You don't go out of this house without you're prepared for it.

GEORGE. Aw, Ma. It's just a *step!*

MRS. GIBBS. George! You'll catch your death of cold and cough all through the service.

DR. GIBBS. George, do as your mother tells you!

(DR. GIBBS *goes upstairs.* GEORGE *returns reluctantly to the kitchen and pantomimes putting on overshoes.*)

MRS. GIBBS. From tomorrow on you can kill yourself in all weathers, but while you're in my house you'll live wisely, thank you.—Maybe Mrs. Webb isn't used to callers at seven in the morning.—Here, take a cup of coffee first.

GEORGE. Be back in a minute. (*He crosses the stage, leaping over the puddles.*) Good morning, Mother Webb.

MRS. WEBB. Goodness! You frightened me!—Now, George, you can come in a minute out of the wet, but you know I can't ask you in.

GEORGE. Why not—?

MRS. WEBB. George, you know's well as I do: the groom can't see his bride on his wedding day, not until he sees her in church.

GEORGE. Aw!—that's just a superstition.—Good morning, Mr. Webb. (*Enter* MR. WEBB.)

MR. WEBB. Good morning, George.

GEORGE. Mr. Webb, you don't believe in that superstition, do you?

MR. WEBB. There's a lot of common sense in some superstitions, George. (*He. sits at the table, facing right.*)

MRS. WEBB. Millions have folla'd it, George, and you don't want to be the first to fly in the face of custom.

GEORGE. How is Emily?

MRS. WEBB. She hasn't waked up yet. I haven't heard a sound out of her.

GEORGE. Emily's *asleep! ! !*

MRS. WEBB. No wonder! We were up 'til all hours, sewing and packing. Now I'll tell you what I'll do; you set down here a minute with Mr. Webb and drink this cup of coffee; and I'll go upstairs and see she doesn't come down and surprise you. There's some bacon, too; but don't be long about it. (*Exit* MRS. WEBB. *Embarrassed silence.* MR. WEBB *dunks doughnuts in his coffee. More silence.*)

MR. WEBB (*suddenly and loudly*). Well, George, how are you?

GEORGE (*startled, choking over his coffee*). Oh, fine, I'm fine. (*Pause.*) Mr. Webb, what sense could there be in a superstition like that?

MR. WEBB. Well, you see,—on her wedding morning a girl's head's apt to be full of . . . clothes and one thing and another. Don't you think that's probably it?

GEORGE. Ye-e-s. I never thought of that.

MR. WEBB. A girl's apt to be a mite nervous on her wedding day. (*Pause.*)

GEORGE. I wish a fellow could get married without all that marching up and down.

MR. WEBB. Every man that's ever lived has felt that way about it, George; but it hasn't been any use. It's the womenfolk who've built up weddings, my boy. For a while now the women have it all their own. A man looks pretty small at a wedding, George. All those good women standing shoulder to shoulder making sure that the knot's tied in a mighty public way.

GEORGE. But . . . you *believe* in it, don't you, Mr. Webb?

MR. WEBB (*with alacrity*). Oh, yes; oh, *yes.* Don't you misunderstand me, my boy. Marriage is a wonderful thing,—wonderful thing. And don't you forget that, George.

GEORGE. No, sir.—Mr. Webb, how old were you when you got married?

MR. WEBB. Well, you see: I'd been to college and I'd taken a little time to get settled. But Mrs. Webb—she wasn't much older than what Emily is. Oh, age hasn't much to do with it, George,—not compared with . . . uh . . . other things.

GEORGE. What were you going to say, Mr. Webb?

MR. WEBB. Oh, I don't know.—Was I going to say something? (*Pause.*) George, I was thinking the other night of some advice my father gave me when I got married. Charles, he said, Charles, start out early showing who's boss, he said. Best thing to do is to give an order, even if it don't make sense; just so she'll learn to obey. And he said: if anything about your wife irritates you—her conversation, or anything—just get up and leave the house. That'll make it clear to her, he said. And, oh, yes! he said never, *never* let your wife know how much money you have, never.

GEORGE. Well, Mr. Webb . . . I don't think I could . . .

MR. WEBB. So I took the opposite of my father's advice and I've been happy ever since. And let that be a lesson to you, George, never to ask advice on personal matters.—George, are you going to raise chickens on your farm?

GEORGE. What?

MR. WEBB. Are you going to raise chickens on your farm?

GEORGE. Uncle Luke's never been much interested, but I thought—

MR. WEBB. A book came into my office the other day, George, on the Philo System of raising chickens. I want you to read it. I'm thinking of beginning in a small way in the back yard, and I'm going to put an incubator in the cellar—(*Enter* MRS. WEBB.)

MRS. WEBB. Charles, are you talking about that old incubator again? I thought you two'd be talking about things worth while.

MR. WEBB (*bitingly*). Well, Myrtle, if you want to give the boy some good advice, I'll go upstairs and leave you alone with him.

MRS. WEBB (*pulling* GEORGE *up*). George, Emily's got to come downstairs and eat her breakfast. She sends you her love but she doesn't want to lay eyes on you. Good-by.

GEORGE. Good-by. (GEORGE *cross the stage to his own home, bewildered and crestfallen. He slowly dodges a puddle and disappears into his house.*)

MR. WEBB. Myrtle, I guess you don't know about that older superstition.

MRS. WEBB. What do you mean, Charles?

MR. WEBB. Since the cave men: no bridegroom should see his father-in-law on the day of the wedding, or near it. Now remember that. (*Both leave the stage.*)

STAGE MANAGER. Thank you very much, Mr. and Mrs. Webb.—Now I have to interrupt again here. You see, we want to know how all this began—this wedding, this plan to spend a lifetime together. I'm awfully interested in how big things like that begin.

You know how it is: you're twenty-one or twenty-two and you make some decisions; then whisssh! you're seventy: you've been a lawyer for fifty years, and that white-haired lady at your side has eaten over fifty thousand meals with you.

How do such things begin?

George and Emily are going to show you now the conversation they had when they first knew that . . . that . . . as the saying goes . . . they were meant for one another.

But before they do it I want you to try and remember what it was like to have been very young.

And particularly the days when you were first in love; when you were like a person sleepwalking, and you didn't quite see the street you were in, and didn't quite hear everything that was said to you.

You're just a little bit crazy. Will you remember that, please?

Now they'll be coming out of high school at

three o'clock. George has just been elected President of the Junior Class, and as it's June, that means he'll be President of the Senior Class all next year. And Emily's just been elected Secretary and Treasurer. I don't have to tell you how important that is. (*He places a board across the backs of two chairs, which he takes from those at the Gibbs family's table. He brings two high stools from the wings and places them behind the board. Persons sitting on the stools will be facing the audience. This is the counter of Mr. Morgan's drugstore. The sounds of young people's voices are heard off left.*) Yepp,—there they are coming down Main Street now. (EMILY, *carrying an armful of—imaginary— schoolbooks, comes along Main Street from the left.*)

EMILY. I can't, Louise. I've got to go home. Good-by. Oh, Ernestine! Ernestine! Can you come over tonight and do Latin? Isn't that Cicero the worst thing—! Tell your mother you *have* to. G'by. G'by, Helen. G'by, Fred. (GEORGE, *also carrying books, catches up with her.*)

GEORGE. Can I carry your books home for you, Emily?

EMILY (*coolly*). Why . . . uh . . . Thank you. It isn't far. (*She gives them to him.*)

GEORGE. Excuse me a minute, Emily.—Say, Bob, if I'm a little late, start practice anyway. And give Herb some long high ones.

EMILY. Good-by, Lizzy.

GEORGE. Good-by, Lizzy.—I'm awfully glad you were elected, too, Emily.

EMILY. Thank you. (*They have been standing on Main Street, almost against the back wall. They take the first steps toward the audience when* GEORGE *stops and says:*)

GEORGE. Emily, why are you mad at me?

EMILY. I'm not mad at you.

GEORGE. You've been treating me so funny lately.

EMILY. Well, since you ask me, I might as well say it right out, George—(*She catches sight of a teacher passing.*) Good-by, Miss Corcoran.

GEORGE. Good-by, Miss Corcoran.—Wha— What is it?

EMILY (*not scoldingly; finding it difficult to say*). I· don't like the whole change that's come over you in the last year. I'm sorry if that hurts your feelings, but I've got to—tell the truth and shame the devil.

GEORGE. A *change?*—Wha—what do you mean?

EMILY. Well, up to a year ago I used to like you a lot. And I used to watch you as you did everything . . . because we'd been friends so long . . . and then you began spending all your time at baseball . . . and you never stopped to speak to anybody any more. Not even to your own family you didn't . . . and, George, it's a fact, you've got awful conceited and stuck-up, and all the girls say so. They may not say so to your face, but that's what they say about you behind your back, and it hurts me to hear them say it, but I've got to agree with them a little. I'm sorry if it hurts your feelings . . . but I can't be sorry I said it.

GEORGE. I . . . I'm glad you said it, Emily. I never thought that such a thing was happening to me. I guess it's hard for a fella not to have faults creep into his character. (*They take a step or two in silence, then stand still in misery.*)

EMILY. I always expect a man to be perfect and I think he should be.

GEORGE. Oh . . . I don't think it's possible to be perfect, Emily.

EMILY. Well, my *father* is, and as far as I can see *your* father is. There's no reason on earth why you shouldn't be, too.

GEORGE. Well, I feel it's the other way round. That men aren't naturally good; but girls are.

EMILY. Well, you might as well know right now that I'm not perfect. It's not as easy for a girl to be perfect as a man, because we girls are more—more—nervous.—Now I'm sorry I said all that about you. I don't know what made me say it.

GEORGE. Emily,—

EMILY. Now I can see it's not the truth at all. And suddenly I feel that it isn't important, anyway.

GEORGE. Emily . . . would you like an ice-cream soda, or something, before you go home?

EMILY. Well, thank you. . . . I would. (*They advance toward the audience and make an abrupt right turn, opening the door of Morgan's drugstore. Under strong emotion,* EMILY *keeps her face down.* GEORGE *speaks to some passers-by.*)

GEORGE. Hello, Stew,—how are you?—Good afternoon, Mrs. Slocum. (*The* STAGE MANAGER, *wearing spectacles and assuming the role of Mr. Morgan, enters abruptly from the right and stands between the audience and the counter of his soda fountain.*)

STAGE MANAGER. Hello, George. Hello, Emily.— What'll you have?—Why, Emily Webb,— what have you been crying about?

GEORGE (*he gropes for an explanation*). She . . . she just got an awful scare, Mr. Morgan. She almost got run over by that hardware-store wagon. Everybody says that Tom Huckins drives like a crazy man.

STAGE MANAGER (*drawing a drink of water*). Well, now! You take a drink of water, Emily. You look all shook up. I tell you, you've got to look both ways before you cross Main Street these days. Gets worse every year.— What'll you have?

EMILY. I'll have a strawberry phosphate, thank you, Mr. Morgan.

GEORGE. No, no, Emily. Have an ice-cream soda with me. Two strawberry ice-cream sodas, Mr. Morgan.

STAGE MANAGER (*working the faucets*). Two strawberry ice-cream sodas, yes sir. Yes, sir. There are a hundred and twenty-five horses in Grover's Corners this minute I'm talking to you. State Inspector was in here yesterday. And now they're bringing in these auto-mobiles, the best thing to do is to just stay home. Why, I can remember when a dog could go to sleep all day in the middle of Main Street and nothing come along to disturb him. (*He sets the imaginary glasses before them.*) There they are. Enjoy 'em. (*He sees a customer, right.*) Yes, Mrs. Ellis. What can I do for you? (*He goes out right.*)

EMILY. They're so expensive.

GEORGE. No, no,—don't you think of that. We're celebrating our election. And then do you know what else I'm celebrating?

EMILY. N-no.

GEORGE. I'm celebrating because I've got a friend who tells me all the things that ought to be told me.

EMILY. George, *please* don't think of that. I don't know why I said it. It's not true. You're—

GEORGE. No, Emily, you stick to it. I'm glad you spoke to me like you did. But you'll *see:* I'm going to change so quick—you bet I'm going to change. And, Emily, I want to ask you a favor.

EMILY. What?

GEORGE. Emily, if I go away to State Agriculture College next year, will you write me a letter once in a while?

EMILY. I certainly will. I certainly will, George . . . (*Pause. They start sipping the sodas through the straws.*) It certainly seems like being away three years you'd get out of touch with things. Maybe letters from Grover's Corners wouldn't be so interesting after a while. Grover's Corners isn't a very important place when you think of all—New Hampshire; but I think it's a very nice town.

GEORGE. The day wouldn't come when I wouldn't want to know everything that's happening here. I know *that's* true, Emily.

EMILY. Well, I'll try to make my letters interesting. (*Pause.*)

GEORGE. Y'know. Emily, whenever I meet a farmer I ask him if he thinks it's important to go to Agriculture School to be a good farmer.

EMILY. Why, George—

GEORGE. Yeah, and some of them say that it's even a waste of time. You can get all those things, anyway, out of the pamphlets the government sends out. And Uncle Luke's getting old,—he's about ready for me to start taking over his farm tomorrow, if I could.

EMILY. My!

GEORGE. And, like you say, being gone all that time . . . in other places and meeting other people . . . Gosh, if anything like that can happen I don't want to go away. I guess new people aren't any better than old ones. I'll bet they almost never are. Emily . . . I feel that you're as good a friend as I've got. I don't need to go and meet the people in other towns.

EMILY. But, George, maybe it's very important for you to go and learn all that about—cattle judging and soils and those things. . . . Of course, I don't know.

GEORGE (*after a pause, very seriously*). Emily, I'm going to make up my mind right now. I won't go. I'll tell Pa about it tonight.

EMILY. Why, George, I don't see why you have to decide right now. It's a whole year away.

GEORGE. Emily, I'm glad you spoke to me about that . . . that fault in my character. What you said was right; but there was *one* thing wrong in it, and that was when you said that for a year I wasn't noticing people, and . . . you, for instance. Why, you say you were watching me when I did everything . . . I was doing the same about you all the time. Why, sure, —I always thought about you as one of the chief people I thought about. I always made

sure where you were sitting on the bleachers, and who you were with, and for three days now I've been trying to walk home with you; but something's always got in the way. Yesterday I was standing over against the wall waiting for you, and you walked home with *Miss Corcoran.*

EMILY. George! . . . Life's awful funny! How could I have known that? Why, I thought—

GEORGE. Listen, Emily, I'm going to tell you why I'm not going to Agriculture School. I think that once you've found a person that you're very fond of . . . I mean a person who's fond of you, too, and likes you enough to be interested in your character . . . Well, I think that's just as important as college is, and even more so. That's what I think.

EMILY. I think it's awfully important, too.

GEORGE. Emily.

EMILY. Y-yes, George.

GEORGE. Emily, if I do improve and make a big change . . . would you be . . . I mean: *could* you be . . .

EMILY. I . . . I am now; I always have been.

GEORGE (*pause*). So I guess this is an important talk we've been having.

EMILY. Yes . . . yes.

GEORGE (*takes a deep breath and straightens his back*). Wait just a minute and I'll walk you home. (*With mounting alarm he digs into his pockets for the money. The* STAGE MANAGER *enters, right.* GEORGE, *deeply embarrassed, but direct, says to him:*) Mr. Morgan, I'll have to go home and get the money to pay you for this. It'll only take me a minute.

STAGE MANAGER (*pretending to be affronted*). What's that? George Gibbs, do you mean to tell me—!

GEORGE. Yes, but I had reasons, Mr. Morgan.— Look, here's my gold watch to keep until I come back with the money.

STAGE MANAGER. That's all right. Keep your watch. I'll trust you.

GEORGE. I'll be back in five minutes.

STAGE MANAGER. I'll trust you ten years, George,

—not a day over.—Got all over your shock, Emily?

EMILY. Yes, thank you, Mr. Morgan. It was nothing.

GEORGE (*taking up the books from the counter*). I'm ready. (*They walk in grave silence across the stage and pass through the trellis at the Webbs' back door and disappear. The* STAGE MANAGER *watches them go out, then turns to the audience, removing his spectacles.*)

STAGE MANAGER. Well,—(*He claps his hand as a signal.*) Now we're ready to go on with the wedding. (*He stands waiting while the set is prepared for the next scene. Stagehands remove the chairs, tables and trellises from the Gibbs and Webb houses. They arrange the pews for the church in the center of the stage. The congregation will sit facing the back wall. The aisle of the church starts at the center of the back wall and comes toward the audience. A small platform is placed against the back wall on which the* STAGE MANAGER *will stand later, playing the minister. The image of a stained-glass window is cast from a lantern slide upon the back wall. When all is ready the* STAGE MANAGER *strolls to the center of the stage, down front, and, musingly, addresses the audience.*) There are a lot of things to be said about a wedding; there are a lot of thoughts that go on during a wedding.

We can't get them all into one wedding, naturally, and especially not into a wedding at Grover's Corners, where they're awfully plain and short.

In this wedding I play the minister. That gives me the right to say a few things more about it.

For a while now, the play gets pretty serious. Y'see, some churches say that marriage is a sacrament. I don't quite know what that means, but I can guess. Like Mrs. Gibbs said a few minutes ago: People were made to live two-by-two.

This is a good wedding, but people are so put together that even at a good wedding there's a lot of confusion way down deep in people's minds and we thought that that ought to be in our play, too.

The real hero of this scene isn't on the stage at all, and you know who that is. It's like what one of those European fellas said: every child born into the world is nature's attempt to make a perfect human being. Well, we've seen nature pushing and contriving for some time now. We all know that nature's interested in quantity; but I think she's interested in quality, too—that's why I'm in the ministry.

And don't forget all the other witnesses at this wedding,—the ancestors. Millions of them. Most of them set out to live two-by-two, also. Millions of them.

Well, that's all my sermon. 'Twan't very long, anyway. (*The organ starts playing Handel's "Largo." The congregation streams into the church and sits in silence. Church bells are heard.* MRS. GIBBS *sits in the front row, the first seat on the aisle, the right section; next to her are* REBECCA *and* DR. GIBBS. *Across the aisle are* MRS. WEBB, WALLY *and* MR. WEBB. *A small choir takes its place, facing the audience under the stained-glass window.* MRS. WEBB, *on the way to her place, turns back and speaks to the audience.*)

MRS. WEBB. I don't know why on earth I should be crying. I suppose there's nothing to cry about. It came over me at breakfast this morning; there was Emily eating her breakfast as she's done for seventeen years and now she's going off to eat it in someone else's house, I suppose that's it.

And Emily! She suddenly said: I can't eat another mouthful, and she put her head down on the table and *she* cried. (*She starts toward her seat in the church, but turns back and adds:*) Oh, I've got to say it: you know, there's something downright cruel about sending our girls out into marriage this way.

I hope some of her girl friends have told her a thing or two. It's cruel, I know, but I couldn't bring myself to say anything. I went into it blind as a bat myself. (*In half-amused exasperation.*) The whole world's wrong, that's what's the matter.

There they come. (*She hurries to her place in the pew.* GEORGE *starts to come down the right aisle of the theatre, through the audience. Suddenly three members of his baseball team appear by the right proscenium pillar and start whistling and catcalling to him. They are dressed for the ball field.*)

THE BASEBALL PLAYERS. Eh, George, George! Hast—yaow! Look at him, fellas—he looks scared to death. Yaow! George, don't look so innocent, you old geezer. We know what you're thinking. Don't disgrace the team, big boy. Whoo-oo-oo.

STAGE MANAGER. All right! All right! That'll do. That's enough of that. (*Smiling, he pushes them off the stage. They lean back to shout a few more catcalls.*) There used to be an awful lot of that kind of thing at weddings in the old days,—Rome, and later. We're more civilized now,—so they say. (*The choir starts singing "Love Divine, All Love Excelling—."* GEORGE *has reached the stage. He stares at the congregation a moment, then takes a few steps of withdrawal, toward the right proscenium pillar. His mother, from the front row, seems to have felt his confusion. She leaves her seat and comes down the aisle quickly to him.*)

MRS. GIBBS. George! George! What's the matter?

GEORGE. Ma, I don't want to grow old. Why's everybody pushing me so?

MRS. GIBBS. Why, George . . . you wanted it.

GEORGE. No, Ma, listen to me—

MRS. GIBBS. No, no, George,—you're a man now.

GEORGE. Listen, Ma,—for the last time I ask you . . . All I want to do is to be a fella—

MRS. GIBBS. George! If anyone should hear you! Now stop. Why, I'm ashamed of you!

GEORGE (*he comes to himself and looks over the scene*). What's the matter? I've been dreaming. Where's Emily?

MRS. GIBBS (*relieved*). George! You gave me such a turn.

GEORGE. Cheer up, Ma. I'm getting married.

MRS. GIBBS. Let me catch my breath a minute.

GEORGE (*comforting her*). Now, Ma, you save Thursday nights. Emily and I are coming over to dinner every Thursday night . . . you'll see. Ma, what are you crying for? Come on; we've got to get ready for this. (MRS. GIBBS, *mastering her emotion, fixes his tie and whispers to him. In the meantime,* EMILY, *in white and wearing her wedding veil, has come through the audience and mounted onto the stage. She too draws back, frightened, when she sees the congregation in the church. The choir begins: "Blessed Be the Tie That Binds."*)

EMILY. I never felt so alone in my whole life. And George over there, looking so . . .! I *hate* him. I wish I were dead. Papa! Papa!

MR. WEBB (*leaves his seat in the pews and comes toward her anxiously*). Emily! Emily! Now don't get upset. . . .

EMILY. But, Papa,—I don't want to get married . . .

MR. WEBB. Sh—sh—Emily. Everything's all right.

EMILY. Why can't I stay for a while just as I am? Let's go away,—

MR. WEBB. No, no, Emily. Now stop and think a minute.

EMILY. Don't you remember that you used to say,—all the time you used to say—all the time: that I was *your* girl! There must be lots of places we can go to. I'll work for you. I could keep house."

MR. WEBB. Sh . . . you mustn't think of such things. You're just nervous, Emily. (*He turns and calls:*) George! George! Will you come here a minute? (*He leads her toward* GEORGE.) Why you're marrying the best young fellow in the world. George is a fine fellow.

EMILY. But Papa,—(MRS. GIBBS *returns unobtrusively to her seat.* MR. WEBB *has one arm around his daughter. He places his hand on* GEORGE'S *shoulder.*)

MR. WEBB. I'm giving away my daughter, George. Do you think you can take care of her?

GEORGE. Mr. Webb, I want to . . . I want to try. Emily, I'm going to do my best. I love you, Emily. I need you.

EMILY. Well, if you love me, help me. All I want is someone to love me.

GEORGE. I will, Emily. Emily, I'll try.

EMILY. And I mean for *ever*. Do you hear? For ever and ever. (*They fall into each other's arms. The March from* Lohengrin[1] *is heard. The* STAGE MANAGER, *as clergyman, stands on the box, up center.*)

MR. WEBB. Come, they're waiting for us. Now you know it'll be all right. Come, quick. (GEORGE *slips away and takes his place beside the* STAGE MANAGER-*clergyman.* EMILY *proceeds up the aisle on her father's arm.*)

STAGE MANAGER. Do you, George, take this woman, Emily, to be your wedded wife, to have . . . (MRS. SOAMES *has been sitting in the last row of the congregation. She now turns to her neighbors and speaks in a shrill voice. Her chatter drowns out the rest of the clergyman's words.*)

MRS. SOAMES. Perfectly lovely wedding! Loveliest wedding I ever saw. Oh, I do love a good wedding, don't you? Doesn't she make a lovely bride?

GEORGE. I do.

STAGE MANAGER. Do you, Emily, take this man, George, to be your wedded husband,— (*Again his further words are covered by those of* MRS. SOAMES.)

MRS. SOAMES. Don't know *when* I've seen such a lovely wedding. But I always cry. Don't know why it is, but I always cry. I just like to see young people happy, don't you? Oh, I think it's lovely. (*The ring. The kiss. The stage is suddenly arrested into silent tableau. The* STAGE MANAGER, *his eyes on the distance, as though to himself:*)

STAGE MANAGER. I've married over two hundred couples in my day.

Do I believe in it?

I don't know.

M. . . . marries N. . . . millions of them.

The cottage, the go-cart, the Sunday-afternoon drives in the Ford, the first rheumatism, the grandchildren, the second rheumatism, the deathbed, the reading of the will,—(*He now looks at the audience for the first time, with a warm smile that removes any sense of cynicism from the next line.*) Once in a thousand times it's interesting.

—Well, let's have Mendelssohn's "Wedding March!" (*The organ picks up the March. The bride and groom come down the aisle, radiant, but trying to be very dignified.*)

MRS. SOAMES. Aren't they a lovely couple? Oh, I've never been to such a nice wedding. I'm sure they'll be happy. I always say: *happiness, that's the great thing!* The important thing is to be happy. (*The bride and groom reach the steps leading into the audience. A bright light is thrown upon them. They descend into the auditorium and run up the aisle joyously.*)

STAGE MANAGER. That's all the Second Act, folks. Ten minutes' intermission.

I

MARRIAGE AND HAPPINESS

Just before the wedding, the Stage Manager says that even at a good wedding people are so put together that "there's a lot of confusion way down deep in people's minds." Judging from the action that follows his speech, it seems that the people of Grover's Corners are quite uncertain about marriage. The town minister (played by the Stage Manager) says flatly that he doesn't know whether he believes in marriage or not and that it is "interesting" only once in a thousand times. These statements are followed immediately by Mrs. Soames' last speech, in which she says, ". . . *happiness, that's the great thing! The important thing is to be happy.*"

By placing these speeches side by side, Wilder forces the reader to question the relationship between marriage and happiness; it strongly suggests

---

1. **Lohengrin**\ˈlō·ən·grĭn\ opera by Richard Wagner based on the legend of the Holy Grail.

that there are no grounds for assuming that marriage in itself (even a "good" marriage) is any guarantee of happiness. This is not to suggest, however, that marriage is an evil institution—the act ends with the bride and groom running up the aisle "joyously." But will they be happy "forever after"?

II
IMPLICATIONS

In his introductory speech to Act II, the Stage Manager remarks, "Most everybody in the world climbs into their graves married." Does this strike you as a strange way of expressing the simple thought that most persons get married? At any rate, after a brief street scene, we enter the Gibbs' home on George's wedding day. The following are some quotations from that scene:

1. DR. GIBBS. Well, Ma, the day has come. You're losin' one of your chicks.

2. MRS. GIBBS. He'll catch his death of cold within a week.

3. GEORGE. Only five more hours to live. (*Makes the gesture of cutting his throat. . . .*)

4. MRS. GIBBS. From tomorrow on you can kill yourself in all weathers. . . .

Is this clustering of death images with George's impending marriage of no special significance, or is it related to incidents and dialogue later in the act, like Mrs. Webb's speech before the wedding and George and Emily's drawing back from the altar?

III
TECHNIQUES

Structure

1. Act II takes place three years after Act I, yet the two are tied together quite intimately. Note, for example, that Mrs. Soames appears very close to the end of both acts. Compare the first scene (after the Stage Manager's introductory speech) of Act I with the first scene of Act II and note the similarities. In addition to the fact that these scenes help to tie the two acts together, what other reason or reasons might Wilder have had for using such similar openings?

2. The chances are that you thought at the end of Act I that Simon Stimson was going to play an important role in this play, yet he does not appear in Act II. Does this necessarily mean that he is not going to play an important role?

Act III

During the intermission the audience has seen the stagehands arranging the stage. On the right-hand side, a little right of the center, ten or twelve ordinary chairs have been placed in three openly spaced rows facing the audience.

These are graves in the cemetery.

Toward the end of the intermission the actors enter and take their places. The front row contains: toward the center of the stage, an empty chair; then MRS. GIBBS; SIMON STIMSON.

The second row contains, among others, MRS. SOAMES.

The third row has WALLY WEBB.

The dead do not turn their heads or their eyes to right or left, but they sit in a quiet without stiffness. When they speak their tone is matter-of-fact, without sentimentality and, above all, without lugubriousness.

The STAGE MANAGER *takes his accustomed place and waits for the house lights to go down.*

STAGE MANAGER. This time nine years have gone by, friends—summer, 1913.

Gradual changes in Grover's Corners. Horses are getting rarer.

Farmers coming into town in Fords.

Everybody locks their house doors now at night. Ain't been any burglars in town yet, but everybody's heard about 'em.

You'd be surprised, though—on the whole, things don't change much around here.

This is certainly an important part of Grover's Corners. It's on a hilltop—a windy hilltop—lots of sky, lots of clouds,—often lots of sun and moon and stars.

You come up here, on a fine afternoon and you can see range on range of hills—awful blue they are—up there by Lake Sunapee and Lake Winnipesaukee[1] . . . and way up, if you've got a glass, you can see the White Mountains and Mt. Washington—where North Conway and Conway is. And, of course, our favorite mountain, Mt. Monadnock, 's right here—and all these towns that lie around it: Jaffrey, 'n East Jaffrey, 'n Peterborough, 'n Dublin; and (*Then pointing down in the audience.*) there, quite a ways down, is Grover's Corners.

Yes, beautiful spot up here. Mountain laurel and li-lacks. I often wonder why people like to be buried in Woodlawn and Brooklyn when they might pass the same time up here in New Hampshire. Over there—(*Pointing to stage left.*) are the old stones,—1670, 1680. Strong-minded people that come a long way to be independent. Summer people walk around there laughing at the funny words on the tombstones . . . it don't do any harm. And genealogists come up from Boston—get paid by city people for looking up their ancestors. They want to make sure they're Daughters of the American Revolution and of the *Mayflower*. . . . Well, I guess that don't do any harm, either. Wherever you come near the human race, there's layers and layers of nonsense. . . .

Over there are some Civil War veterans. Iron flags on their graves . . . New Hampshire boys . . . had a notion that the Union ought to be kept together, though they'd never seen more than fifty miles of it themselves. All they knew was the name, friends—the United States of America. The United States of America. And they went and died about it.

This here is the new part of the cemetery. Here's your friend Mrs. Gibbs. 'N let me see—Here's Mr. Stimson, organist at the Congregational Church. And Mrs. Soames who enjoyed the wedding so—you remember? Oh, and a lot of others. And Editor Webb's boy, Wallace, whose appendix burst while he was on a Boy Scout trip to Crawford Notch.

Yes, an awful lot of sorrow has sort of quieted down up here.

People just wild with grief have brought their relatives up to this hill. We all know how it is . . . and then time . . . and sunny days . . . and rainy days . . . 'n snow . . . We're all glad they're in a beautiful place and we're coming up here ourselves when our fit's over.

Now there are some things we all know, but we don't take'm out and look at'm very often. We all know that *something* is eternal. And it ain't houses and it ain't names, and it ain't earth, and it ain't even the stars . . . everybody knows in their bones that *something* is eternal, and that something has to do with human beings. All the greatest people ever lived have been telling us that for five thousand years and yet you'd be surprised how people are always losing hold of it. There's something way down deep that's eternal about every human being. (*Pause.*)

You know as well as I do that the dead don't stay interested in us living people for very long. Gradually, gradually, they lose hold of the earth . . . and the ambitions they had . . . and the pleasures they had . . . and the things they suffered . . . and the people they loved.

They get weaned away from earth—that's the way I put it,—weaned away.

And they stay here while the earth part of 'em burns away, burns out; and all that time they slowly get indifferent to what's goin' on in Grover's Corners.

They're waitin'. They're waitin' for something that they feel is comin'. Something important, and great. Aren't they waitin' for the eternal part in them to come out clear?

Some of the things they're going to say maybe'll hurt your feelings—but that's the way it is: mother'n daughter . . . husband 'n

---

1. **Lake Sunapee**, boundary between Sullivan and Merrimack counties in New Hampshire; summer resort. **Lake Winnipesaukee**\'wĭ·nĭ·pĕ ▲sŏ·kē\ largest lake in New Hampshire.

wife . . . enemy 'n enemy . . . money 'n miser . . . all those terribly important things kind of grow pale around here. And what's left when memory's gone, and your identity, Mrs. Smith? (*He looks at the audience a minute, then turns to the stage.*)

Well! There are some *living* people. There's Joe Stoddard, our undertaker, supervising a new-made grave. And here comes a Grover's Corners boy, that left town to go out West. (JOE STODDARD *has hovered about in the background.* SAM CRAIG *enters left, wiping his forehead from the exertion. He carries an umbrella and strolls front.*)

SAM CRAIG. Good afternoon, Joe Stoddard.

JOE STODDARD. Good afternoon, good afternoon. Let me see now: do I know you?

SAM CRAIG. I'm Sam Craig.

JOE STODDARD. Gracious sakes' alive! Of all people! I should'a knowed you'd be back for the funeral. You've been away a long time, Sam.

SAM CRAIG. Yes, I've been away over twelve years. I'm in business out in Buffalo now, Joe. But I was in the East when I got news of my cousin's death, so I thought I'd combine things a little and come and see the old home. You look well.

JOE STODDARD. Yes, yes, can't complain. Very sad, our journey today, Samuel.

SAM CRAIG. Yes.

JOE STODDARD. Yes, yes. I always say I hate to supervise when a young person is taken. They'll be here in a few minutes now. I had to come here early today—my son's supervisin' at the home.

SAM CRAIG (*reading stones*). Old Farmer McCarty, I used to do chores for him—after school. He had the lumbago.

JOE STODDARD. Yes, we brought Farmer McCarty here a number of years ago now.

SAM CRAIG (*staring at* MRS. GIBBS' *knees*). Why, this is my Aunt Julia . . . I'd forgotten that she'd . . . of course, of course.

JOE STODDARD. Yes, Doc Gibbs lost his wife two-three years ago . . . about this time. And today's another pretty bad blow for him, too.

MRS. GIBBS (*to* SIMON STIMSON: *in an even voice*). That's my sister Carey's boy, Sam . . . Sam Craig.

SIMON STIMSON. I'm always uncomfortable when *they're* around.

MRS. GIBBS. Simon.

SAM CRAIG. Do they choose their own verses much, Joe?

JOE STODDARD. No . . . not usual. Mostly the bereaved pick a verse.

SAM CRAIG. Doesn't sound like Aunt Julia. There aren't many of those Hersey sisters left now. Let me see: where are . . . I wanted to look at my father's and mother's . . .

JOE STODDARD. Over there with the Craigs . . . Avenue F.

SAM CRAIG (*reading* SIMON STIMSON'S *epitaph*). He was organist at church, wasn't he?—Hm, drank a lot, we used to say.

JOE STODDARD. Nobody was supposed to know about it. He'd seen a peck of trouble. (*Behind his hand.*) Took his own life, y' know?

SAM CRAIG. Oh, did he?

JOE STODDARD. Hung himself in the attic. They tried to hush it up, but of course it got around. He chose his own epy-taph. You can see it there. It ain't a verse exactly.

SAM CRAIG. Why, it's just some notes of music—what is it?

JOE STODDARD. Oh, I wouldn't know. It was wrote up in the Boston papers at the time.

SAM CRAIG. Joe, what did she die of?

JOE STODDARD. Who?

SAM CRAIG. My cousin.

JOE STODDARD. Oh, didn't you know? Had some trouble bringing a baby into the world. 'Twas her second, though. There's a little boy 'bout four years old.

SAM CRAIG (*opening his umbrella*). The grave's going to be over there?

JOE STODDARD. Yes, there ain't much more room over here among the Gibbses, so they're opening up a whole new Gibbs section over by Avenue B. You'll excuse me now. I see they're comin'. (*From left to center, at the back of the stage, comes a procession. Four men carry a casket, invisible to us. All the rest are under umbrellas. One can vaguely see:* DR. GIBBS, GEORGE, *the* WEBBS, *etc. They gather about a grave in the back center of the stage, a little to the left of center.*)

MRS. SOAMES. Who is it, Julia?

MRS. GIBBS (*without raising her eyes*). My daughter-in-law, Emily Webb.

MRS. SOAMES (*a little surprised, but no emotion*). Well, I declare! The road up here must have been awful muddy. What did she die of, Julia?

MRS. GIBBS. In childbirth.

MRS. SOAMES. Childbirth. (*Almost with a laugh.*) I'd forgotten all about that. My, wasn't life awful—(*With a sigh.*) and wonderful.

SIMON STIMSON (*with a sideways glance*). Wonderful, was it?

MRS. GIBBS. Simon! Now, remember!

MRS. SOAMES. I remember Emily's wedding. Wasn't it a lovely wedding! And I remember her reading the class poem at Graduation Exercises. Emily was one of the brightest girls ever graduated from High School. I've heard Principal Wilkins say so time after time. I called on them at their new farm, just before I died. Perfectly beautiful farm.

A WOMAN FROM AMONG THE DEAD. It's on the same road we lived on.

A MAN AMONG THE DEAD. Yepp, right smart farm. (*They subside. The group by the grave starts singing "Blessed Be the Tie That Binds."*)

A WOMAN AMONG THE DEAD. I always liked that hymn. I was hopin' they'd sing a hymn. (*Pause. Suddenly* EMILY *appears from among the umbrellas. She is wearing a white dress. Her hair is down her back and tied by a white ribbon like a little girl. She comes slowly, gazing wonderingly at the dead, a little dazed. She stops halfway and smiles faintly. After looking at the mourners for a moment, she walks slowly to the vacant chair beside* MRS. GIBBS *and sits down.*)

EMILY (*to them all, quietly, smiling*). Hello.

MRS. SOAMES. Hello, Emily.

A MAN AMONG THE DEAD. Hello, M's Gibbs.

EMILY (*warmly*). Hello, Mother Gibbs.

MRS. GIBBS. Emily.

EMILY. Hello. (*With surprise.*) It's raining. (*Her eyes drift back to the funeral company.*)

MRS. GIBBS. Yes . . . They'll be gone soon, dear. Just rest yourself.

EMILY. It seems thousands and thousands of years since I . . . Papa remembered that that was my favorite hymn.

Oh, I wish I'd been here a long time. I don't like being new here.—How do you do, Mr. Stimson?

SIMON STIMSON. How do you do, Emily. (EMILY *continues to look about her with a wondering smile; as though to shut out from her mind the thought of the funeral company she starts speaking to* MRS. GIBBS *with a touch of nervousness.*)

EMILY. Mother Gibbs, George and I have made that farm into just the best place you ever saw. We thought of you all the time. We wanted to show you the new barn and a great long ce-ment drinking fountain for the stock. We bought that out of the money you left us.

MRS. GIBBS. I did?

EMILY. Don't you remember, Mother Gibbs— the legacy you left us? Why, it was over three hundred and fifty dollars.

MRS. GIBBS. Yes, yes, Emily.

EMILY. Well, there's a patent device on the drinking fountain so that it never overflows, Mother Gibbs, and it never sinks below a certain mark they have there. It's fine. (*Her voice trails off and her eyes return to the funeral group.*) It won't be the same to George without me, but it's a lovely farm. (*Suddenly she look directly at* MRS. GIBBS.) Live people don't understand, do they?

MRS. GIBBS. No, dear—not very much.

EMILY. They're sort of shut up in little boxes, aren't they? I feel as though I knew them last a thousand years ago . . . My boy is spending the day at Mrs. Carter's. (*She sees* MR. CARTER *among the dead.*) Oh, Mr.

Carter, my little boy is spending the day at your house.

MR. CARTER. Is he?

EMILY. Yes, he loves it there.—Mother Gibbs, we have a Ford, too. Never gives any trouble. I don't drive, though. Mother Gibbs, when does this feeling go away?—Of being . . . one of *them?* How long does it . . . ?

MRS. GIBBS. Sh! dear. Just wait and be patient.

EMILY (*with a sigh*). I know.—Look, they're finished. They're going.

MRS. GIBBS. Sh—. (*The umbrellas leave the stage.* DR. GIBBS *has come over to his wife's grave and stands before it a moment.* EMILY *looks up at his face.* MRS. GIBBS *does not raise her eyes.*)

EMILY. Look! Father Gibbs is bringing some of my flowers to you. He looks just like George, doesn't he? Oh, Mother Gibbs, I never realized before how troubled and how . . . how in the dark live persons are. Look at him. I loved him so. From morning till night, that's all they are—troubled. (DR. GIBBS *goes off.*)

THE DEAD. Little cooler than it was.—Yes, that rain's cooled it off a little. Those northeast winds always do the same thing, don't they? If it isn't a rain, it's a three-day blow.—(*A patient calm falls on the stage. The* STAGE MANAGER *appears at his proscenium pillar, smoking.* EMILY *sits up abruptly with an idea.*)

EMILY. But, Mother Gibbs, one can go back; one can go back there again . . . into the living. I feel it. I know it. Why just then for a moment I was thinking about . . . about the farm . . . and for a minute I *was* there, and my baby was on my lap as plain as day.

MRS. GIBBS. Yes, of course you can.

EMILY. I can go back there and live all those days over again . . . why not?

MRS. GIBBS. All I can say is, Emily, don't.

EMILY (*she appeals urgently to the* STAGE MANAGER). But it's true, isn't it? I can go and live . . . back there . . . again.

STAGE MANAGER. Yes, some have tried—but they soon come back here.

MRS. GIBBS. Don't do it, Emily.

MRS. SOAMES. Emily, don't. It's not what you think it'd be.

EMILY. But I won't live over a sad day. I'll choose a happy one—I'll choose the day I first knew that I loved George. Why should that be painful? (*They are silent. Her question turns to the* STAGE MANAGER.)

STAGE MANAGER. You not only live it; but you watch yourself living it.

EMILY. Yes?

STAGE MANAGER. And as you watch it, you see the thing that they—down there—never know. You see the future. You know what's going to happen afterwards.

EMILY. But is that—painful? Why?

MRS. GIBBS. That's not the only reason why you shouldn't do it, Emily. When you've been here longer you'll see that our life here is to forget all that, and think only of what's ahead, and be ready for what's ahead. When you've been here longer you'll understand.

EMILY (*softly*). But Mother Gibbs, how can I *ever* forget that life? It's all I know. It's all I had.

MRS. SOAMES. Oh, Emily. It isn't wise. Really, it isn't.

EMILY. But it's a thing I must know for myself. I'll choose a happy day, anyway.

MRS. GIBBS. *No!*—At least, choose an unimportant day. Choose the least important day in your life. It will be important enough.

EMILY (*to herself*). Then it can't be since I was married; or since the baby was born. (*To the* STAGE MANAGER, *eagerly.*) I can choose a birthday at least, can't I?—I choose my twelfth birthday.

STAGE MANAGER. All right. February 11th, 1899. A Tuesday.—Do you want any special time of day?

EMILY. Oh, I want the whole day.

STAGE MANAGER. We'll begin at dawn. You remember it had been snowing for several days; but it had stopped the night before, and they had begun clearing the roads. The sun's coming up.

EMILY (*with a cry; rising*). There's Main Street . . . why, that's Mr. Morgan's drugstore before he changed it! . . . And there's the livery stable. (*The stage at no time in this act has been very dark; but now the left half of the stage gradually becomes very bright—the brightness of a crisp winter morning.* EMILY *walks toward Main Street.*)

STAGE MANAGER. Yes, it's 1899. This is fourteen years ago.

EMILY. Oh, that's the town I knew as a little girl. And, *look*, there's the old white fence that used to be around our house. Oh, I'd forgotten that! Oh, I love it so! Are they inside?

STAGE MANAGER. Yes, your mother'll be coming downstairs in a minute to make breakfast.

EMILY (*softly*). Will she?

STAGE MANAGER. And you remember: your father had been away for several days; he came back on the early-morning train.

EMILY. No . . . ?

STAGE MANAGER. He'd been back to his college to make a speech—in western New York, at Clinton.

EMILY. Look! There's Howie Newsome. There's our policeman. But he's *dead; he died.* (*The voices of* HOWIE NEWSOME, CONSTABLE WARREN *and* JOE CROWELL, JR., *are heard at the left of the stage.* EMILY *listens in delight.*)

HOWIE NEWSOME. Whoa, Bessie!—Bessie! 'Morning, Bill.

CONSTABLE WARREN. Morning, Howie.

HOWIE NEWSOME. You're up early.

CONSTABLE WARREN. Been rescuin' a party; darn near froze to death, down by Polish Town thar. Got drunk and lay out in the snowdrifts. Thought he was in bed when I shook'm.

EMILY. Why, there's Joe Crowell. . . .

JOE CROWELL. Good morning, Mr. Warren. 'Morning, Howie. (MRS. WEBB *has appeared in her kitchen, but* EMILY *does not see her until she calls.*)

MRS. WEBB. Chil-*dren!* Wally! Emily! . . . Time to get up.

EMILY. Mama, I'm here! Oh! how young Mama looks! I didn't know Mama was ever that young.

MRS. WEBB. You can come and dress by the kitchen fire, if you like; but hurry. (HOWIE NEWSOME *has entered along Main Street and brings the milk to* MRS. WEBB's *door.*) Good morning, Mr. Newsome. Whhhh—it's cold.

HOWIE NEWSOME. Ten below by my barn, Mrs. Webb.

MRS. WEBB. Think of it! Keep yourself wrapped up. (*She takes her bottles in, shuddering.*)

EMILY (*with an effort*). Mama, I can't find my blue hair ribbon anywhere.

MRS. WEBB. Just open your eyes, dear, that's all. I laid it out for you special—on the dresser, there. If it were a snake it would bite you.

EMILY. Yes, yes . . . (*She puts her hand on her heart.* MR. WEBB *comes along Main Street, where he meets* CONSTABLE WARREN. *Their movements and voices are increasingly lively in the sharp air.*)

MR. WEBB. Good morning, Bill.

CONSTABLE WARREN. Good morning, Mr. Webb. You're up early.

MR. WEBB. Yes, just been back to my old college in New York State. Been any trouble here?

CONSTABLE WARREN. Well, I was called up this mornin' to rescue a Polish fella—darn near froze to death he was.

MR. WEBB. We must get it in the paper.

CONSTABLE WARREN. 'Twan't much.

EMILY (*whispers*). Papa. (MR. WEBB *shakes the snow off his feet and enters his house.* CONSTABLE WARREN *goes off, right.*)

MR. WEBB. Good morning, Mother.

MRS. WEBB. How did it go, Charles?

MR. WEBB. Oh, fine, I guess. I told'm a few things.—Everything all right here?

MRS. WEBB. Yes—can't think of anything that's happened, special. Been right cold. Howie Newsome says it's ten below over to his barn.

MR. WEBB. Yes, well, it's colder than that at Hamilton College.[2] Students' ears are falling off. It ain't Christian.—Paper have any mistakes in it?

MRS. WEBB. None that I noticed. Coffee's ready

---

2. **Hamilton College,** private men's college in Clinton, New York.

when you want it. (*He starts upstairs.*) Charles! Don't forget; it's Emily's birthday. Did you remember to get her something?

MR. WEBB (*patting his pocket*). Yes, I've got something here. (*Calling up the stairs.*) Where's my girl? Where's my birthday girl? (*He goes off left.*)

MRS. WEBB. Don't interrupt her now, Charles. You can see her at breakfast. She's slow enough as it is. Hurry up, children! It's seven o'clock. Now, I don't want to call you again.

EMILY (*softly, more in wonder than in grief*). I can't bear it. They're so young and beautiful. Why did they ever have to get old? Mama, I'm here. I'm grown up. I love you all, everything.—I can't look at everything hard enough. (*She looks questioningly at the* STAGE MANAGER, *saying or suggesting: "Can I go in?" He nods briefly. She crosses to the inner door to the kitchen, left of her mother, and as though entering the room, says, suggesting the voice of a girl of twelve:*) Good morning, Mama.

MRS. WEBB (*crossing to embrace and kiss her; in her characteristic matter-of-fact manner*). Well, now, dear, a very happy birthday to my girl and many happy returns. There are some surprises waiting for you on the kitchen table.

EMILY. Oh, Mama, you *shouldn't* have. (*She throws an anguished glance at the* STAGE MANAGER.) I can't—I can't.

MRS. WEBB (*facing the audience, over her stove*). But birthday or no birthday, I want you to eat your breakfast good and slow. I want you to grow up and be a good strong girl.

That in the blue paper is from your Aunt Carrie; and I reckon you can guess who brought the post-card album. I found it on the doorstep when I brought in the milk— George Gibbs . . . must have come over in the cold pretty early . . . right nice of him.

EMILY (*to herself*). Oh, George! I'd forgotten that. . . .

MRS. WEBB. Chew that bacon good and slow. It'll help keep you warm on a cold day.

EMILY (*with mounting urgency*). Oh, Mama, just look at me one minute as though you really saw me. Mama, fourteen years have gone by. I'm dead. You're a grandmother, Mama. I married George Gibbs, Mama. Wally's dead, too. Mama, his appendix burst on a camping trip to North Conway. We felt just terrible about it—don't you remember? But, just for a moment now we're all together. Mama, just for a moment we're happy. *Let's look at one another.*

MRS. GIBBS. That in the yellow paper is something I found in the attic among your grandmother's things. You're old enough to wear it now, and I thought you'd like it.

EMILY. And this is from you. Why, Mama, it's just lovely and it's just what I wanted. It's beautiful! (*She flings her arms around her mother's neck. Her mother goes on with her cooking, but is pleased.*)

MRS. WEBB. Well, I hoped you'd like it. Hunted all over. Your Aunt Norah couldn't find one in Concord, so I had to send all the way to Boston. (*Laughing.*)

Wally has something for you, too. He made it at manual-training class and he's very proud of it. Be sure you make a big fuss about it.—Your father has a surprise for you, too; don't know what it is myself. Sh—here he comes.

MR. WEBB (*off stage*). Where's my girl? Where's my birthday girl?

EMILY (*in a loud voice to the* STAGE MANAGER). I can't. I can't go on. It goes so fast. We don't have time to look at one another. (*She breaks down sobbing. The lights dim on the left half of the stage.* MRS. WEBB *disappears.*)

I didn't realize. So all that was going on and we never noticed. Take me back—up the hill—to my grave. But first: Wait! One more look.

Good-by, Good-by, world. Good-by, Grover's Corners . . . Mama and Papa. Good-by to clocks ticking . . . and Mama's sunflowers.

And food and coffee. And new-ironed dresses and hot baths . . . and sleeping and waking up. Oh, earth, you're too wonderful for anybody to realize you. (*She looks toward the* STAGE MANAGER *and asks abruptly, through her tears:*)

Do any human beings ever realize life while they live it?—every, every minute?

STAGE MANAGER. No. (*Pause.*) The saints and poets, maybe—they do some.

EMILY. I'm ready to go back. (*She returns to her chair beside* MRS. GIBBS. *Pause.*)

MRS. GIBBS. Were you happy?

EMILY. No . . . I should have listened to you. That's all human beings are! Just blind people.

MRS. GIBBS. Look, it's clearing up. The stars are coming out.

EMILY. Oh, Mr. Stimson, I should have listened to them.

SIMON STIMSON (*with mounting violence; bitingly*). Yes, now you know. Now you know! That's what it was to be alive. To move about in a cloud of ignorance; to go up and down trampling on the feelings of those . . . of those about you. To spend and waste time as though you had a million years. To be always at the mercy of one self-centered passion, or another. Now you know—that's the happy existence you wanted to go back to. Ignorance and blindness.

MRS. GIBBS (*spiritedly*). Simon Stimson, that ain't the whole truth and you know it. Emily, look at that star. I forget its name.

A MAN AMONG THE DEAD. My boy Joel was a sailor,—knew 'em all. He'd set on the porch evenings and tell 'em all by name. Yes, sir, wonderful!

ANOTHER MAN AMONG THE DEAD. A star's mighty good company.

A WOMAN AMONG THE DEAD. Yes. Yes, 'tis.

SIMON STIMSON. Here's one of them coming.

THE DEAD. That's funny. 'Tain't no time for one of them to be here.—Goodness sakes.

EMILY. Mother Gibbs, it's George.

MRS. GIBBS. Sh, dear. Just rest yourself.

EMILY. It's George. (GEORGE *enters from the left, and slowly comes toward them.*)

A MAN FROM AMONG THE DEAD. And my boy, Joel, who knew the stars—he used to say it took millions of years for that speck of light to git to the earth. Don't seem like a body could believe it, but that's what he used to say—millions of years. (GEORGE *sinks to his knees then falls full length at* EMILY's *feet.*)

A WOMAN AMONG THE DEAD. Goodness! That ain't no way to behave!

MRS. SOAMES. He ought to be home.

EMILY. Mother Gibbs?

MRS. GIBBS. Yes, Emily?

EMILY. They don't understand, do they?

MRS. GIBBS. No, dear. They don't understand. (*The* STAGE MANAGER *appears at the right, one hand on a dark curtain which he slowly draws across the scene. In the distance a clock is heard striking the hour very faintly.*)

STAGE MANAGER. Most everybody's asleep in Grover's Corners. There are a few lights on: Shorty Hawkins, down at the depot, has just watched the Albany train go by. And at the livery stable somebody's setting up late and talking.—Yes, it's clearing up. There are the stars—doing their old, old crisscross journeys in the sky. Scholars haven't settled the matter yet, but they seem to think there are no living beings up there. Just chalk . . . or fire. Only this one is straining away, straining away all the time to make something of itself. The strain's so bad that every sixteen hours everybody lies down and gets a rest. (*He winds his watch.*) Hm. . . . Eleven o'clock in Grover's Corners.—You get a good rest, too. Good night.

The End

I
"LIFE" AND "DEATH"

A title for the last act of *Our Town* might be "'Life' and 'Death'," with the terms in quotes to emphasize the ironic handling of the theme. The first "living" person the Stage Manager notices at the end of his introductory speech is, ironically, the undertaker. Again, during the funeral scene Emily, who has just left her coffin, says of the "living" people that "They're sort of shut up in little boxes. . . ." Later, as she relives her twelfth birthday, she proves to be more alive than the living. Her mother's statement that Emily could find her blue hair ribbon if she would just open her eyes is heavily charged with irony since it is Mrs. Webb and not her daughter whose eyes are not alive to the full potential of life.

II
IMPLICATIONS

Discuss the following statements in the light of this play and of your own experience.

1. Life in Grover's Corners is very much the same as life in any community, large or small.

2. All change is superficial; there is really no significant difference between life in the past and life in the present decade.

3. "Wherever you come near the human race, there's layers and layers of nonsense."

4. Marriage demands a great deal of conformity and severely limits an individual's freedom.

5. A person who tried to live every minute fully would probably suffer a mental breakdown in a very short time.

III
TECHNIQUES

Structure: Tension and Resolution

Structurally speaking, in a three-act play, we expect the first act to be a "tension-raising" act and the third to be a "tension-resolving" act. One of the basic tensions in this play concerns its attitude toward life in Grover's Corners. Is *Our Town* a celebration of the simple joys of small-town life, or is it a condemnation of the dullness, conformity, and lack of awareness in that life?

Does the final act serve to resolve this question, and if so, how? In your discussion pay special attention to the following parts of the third act:

1. The talk between Mrs. Soames, Mrs. Gibbs, and Simon Stimson, as they watch Emily's funeral.

2. The final argument between Mrs. Gibbs and Simon.

3. The last conversation between Emily and Mrs. Gibbs.

Glossary

This glossary contains those difficult words which are not found in the vocabularies of most students. Many specific and uncommon terms have been footnoted with the selections. The definitions apply to the uses of the words in this text. For more complete study of the range of meanings for these words, the student should consult his dictionary.

PRONUNCIATION GUIDE

A key to the pronunciation symbols is given at the bottom of every other (or odd numbered) page. The symbols used represent a series of compromises between current scholarly interpretations of sounds and less precise symbols which continue to have wide acceptance. A few minutes' study of the pronunciation key will make it possible to use the pronunciation transcriptions with ease and efficiency. Pronunciations given in the footnotes use the same key.

Generally, for simplicity's sake only one pronunciation is given. While it is one honored by wide and cultivated usage, other pronunciations are not necessarily wrong. Occasionally, a second pronunciation is sufficiently common to demand inclusion. In these cases either is satisfactory, and the first is not necessarily preferred.

While the entry syllabifications follow current dictionary practice, the syllabic divisions in the pronunciation transcriptions strive for consistency by following the principle that a consonant will accompany the vowel following it rather than that preceding it.

Accent marks precede the stressed syllables. The mark ▲ indicates the heaviest stress and the mark ' indicates an intermediate stress as needed.

Abbreviations indicate parts of speech and special spellings. The following are used:

n. noun	adj. adjective
v. verb	adv. adverb
irreg. v. irregular verb	pl. plural

abate\ə ▲bāt\ v. To make less.
abey·ance\ə ▲bā·əns\ n. Temporary inactivity.
ab·ject\▲ăb·jĕkt\ adj. Sunk to a low condition.
ab·jure\ăb ▲jūr\ v. To reject solemnly.
abort\ə ▲bȯrt\ v. To terminate or check development prematurely.

abrade\ə ▲brād\ v. 1. To rub or wear away by friction. 2. To wear down in spirit.

ab·ste·mi·ous\ăb ▲stē·mē·əs\ adj. Used sparingly esp. in eating and drinking.

ac·cli·mate\▲ăk·lə·māt\ v. To adapt to a new temperature, altitude, climate, environment, or situation.

ac·cliv·i·ty\ə ▲klĭ·və·tē\ n. An upward slope.

ac·cou·ter·ment\ə ▲kū·tər·mənt\ n. Equipment or accessories of a soldier other than arms and dress.

ac·qui·es·cent\▲ăk·wē ▲ĕs·ənt\ adj. Disposed to yield, accept, or comply passively.

acu·men\ə ▲kyū·mən\ n. Quickness, sharpness of perception esp. in practical matters.

ad·mo·ni·tion\▲ăd·mə ▲nĭ·shən\ n. 1. Gentle or friendly reproof. 2. A warning against error or misdeeds.

adren·a·line\ə ▲drĕ·nə·lən\ n. A secretion of the adrenal gland that acts as a stimulator.

ad·ven·ti·tious\▲ăd·vən ▲tish·əs\ adj. Accidentally acquired.

ad·vert\ăd ▲vərt\ v. To direct attention; to refer to.

aero·naut·id\▲ă·rə ▲nɔ·təd\ n. One belonging to the group of astronauts.

aes·thet·ic\ĕs ▲thĕ·tĭk\ adj. Relating to the beauty found in the fine arts.

af·front\ə ▲frənt\ v. To insult openly.

ague\▲ā·gyū\ n. A fever such as malaria marked by fits of shivering and sweating that recur at regular intervals.

alac·ri·ty\ə ▲lăk·rə·tē\ n. A cheerful promptness or readiness.

al·ter·ca·tion\▲al·tər ▲kā·shən\ n. A noisy or angry dispute often ending in blows.

al·ve·o·lar\ăl ▲vē·ə·lər\ adj. Relating to the part of jaws where the teeth arise.

amal·ga·ma·tor\ə ▲măl·gə'mā·tər\ n. One who unites or combines two things; one who causes two groups to mingle.

am·big·u·ous\ăm ▲bĭ·gū·əs\ adj. Having a double meaning.

anal·o·gy\ə ▲nă·lə·jē\ n. A resemblance in some particulars between things otherwise unlike.

anath·e·ma\ə ▲nă·thə·mə\ n. One who is cursed and denounced by the church.

an·i·mos·i·ty\▲ă·nə ▲mŏ·sə·tē\ n. Intense ill will that threatens to become hostility.

an·nu·i·ty\ə ▲nū·ə·tē\ n. An income paid yearly or at other regular intervals.

anom·a·lous\ə ▲nŏ·mə·ləs\ adj. Irregular, abnormal.

an·o·mym·i·ty\▲ă·nə ▲nĭ·mə·tē\ n. The quality of lacking individuality or personality.

an·ti·ma·cas·sar\▲ăn·tĭ·mə ▲kă·sər\ n. A cover to protect the back or arms of furniture.

apcx\▲ā·pĕks\ n. The highest point; the tip.

ap·pel·la·tion\▲ă·pə ▲lā·shən\ n. An identifying name or title.

ap·pend\ə ▲pĕnd\ v. To add as a supplement.

ap·prise\ə ▲praiz\ v. To give notice to.

ap·pro·ba·tion\▲ăp·rə ▲bā·shən\ n. Approval; praise.

ar·bi·trary\▲ŏr·bə 'trĕ·rē\ adj. Selected at random and without reason; subject to individual will or judgment.

ar·dor\▲ŏr·dər\ n. Great eagerness or energy.

arid·i·ty\ə ▲rĭ·də·tē\ n. Insufficient rainfall; dryness.

ar·rears\ə ▲rĭrz\ n. Unfinished duties; state of being behind in discharge of obligations.

ar·tic·u·late\ŏr ▲tĭk·yə·lĭt\ adj. 1. Marked by distinctness of parts. 2. Able to speak clearly and effectively.

ar·ti·fice\▲ŏr·tə·fəs\ n. Guile or clever trickery; ingenuity.

askance\ə ▲skăns\ adv. With disapproval or distrust.

as·sid·u·ous\ə ▲sĭj·wəs\ adj. Careful, diligent, with persistent application.

as·sim·i·late\ə ▲sĭ·mə·lāt\ v. To take into body or mind as nourishment; to absorb.

as·suage\ə ▲swāj\ v. To ease.

as·tral\▲ăs·trəl\ adj. Of or relating to the stars.

at·a·vism\▲ă·tə 'vĭ·zəm\ n. State of reversion to a primitive ancestral type; a throwback.

at·taint\ə ▲tānt\ v. To infect, corrupt, or disgrace.

au·ra\▲ɔ·rə\ n. A subjective sensation experienced before an attack of some nervous disorders.

au·re·o·la\ɔ ▲rē·ə·lə\ n. Bright light seen through mist.

au·ro·ral\a ▲rō·rəl\ adj. Pertaining to the dawn.

aus·tere\ɔ ▲stĭr\ adj. Stern and forbidding in appearance and manner.

au·to·crat·ic\▲ɔ·tə 'krăt·ĭk\ adj. Relating to a person who rules with unlimited authority.

av·a·rice\▲ăv·rəs\ n. Excessive desire for wealth or gain; greed.

avert\ə ▲vərt\ v. To turn away.

av·o·ca·tion\▲ă·və ▲kā·shən\ n. An occasional occupation or hobby.

bale·ful\▲bāl·fəl\ adj. Deadly, ominous, sinister.

bal·last\▲bă·ləst\ n. That which balances or gives stability.

bas·re·lief\'ba·rĭ ▲lēf\ n. A type of sculpture in which figures project slightly from the background.

be·foul\bĭ ▲faul\ v. To make foul with dirt or filth.

be·gird\bĭ ▲gərd\ v. To encompass with a band.

be·hold·en\bĭ ▲hōl·dən\ adj. Indebted; obligated.

bel·dame\▲bĕl·dəm\ n. An ugly old woman; a hag.

be·mused\bĭ ▲myūzd\ adj. 1. Confused; bewildered. 2. Deep in thought.

be·night·ed\bĭ ▲nai·təd\ adj. Overtaken by darkness.

be·nign\bĭ ▲nain\ adj. Showing gentleness or kindness.

be·reft\bĭ ▲rĕft\ v. Deprived of.

be·sot·ted\bĭ ▲sŏ·təd\ adj. Foolish, stupid, or muddled.

bes·tial\▲bĕs·chəl\ adj. Resembling a beast.

be·to·ken\bĭ ▲tō·kĕn\ v. To give evidence of; to foreshadow.

bi·be·lot\▲bĭb·lō\n. A small, decorative, and often rare trinket.

bib·u·lous\▲bĭ·byə·ləs\ adj. Inclined to drink.

bit·tern\▲bĭ·tərn\ n. A heron with a characteristic screaming cry.

ă bad, ā bake, a father, ĕ sell, ē equal, ai mile, ĭ sit, ŏ cot, ō note, ɔ law, ū boom, ʊ wood, yū you, yʊ fury, au cow, ɔi boy. The schwa is used for both stressed and unstressed sounds: ə mud, word, even. ch chase, itch; sh shell, wish; th path, thin, th the, either; ŋ wing; w wet, wheat; zh pleasure.

bi·zarre\bĭ ˄zar\ adj. Odd, fantastic, or out of the ordinary.

blanch\˄blănch\ v. To turn pale in the face.

blas·phe·my\˄blăs·fə·mē\ n. Vulgar speaking of God or of sacred persons or things.

bla·tant\˄blā·tənt\ adj. Offensively loud or noisy.

bo·he·mi·an\bō ˄hē·mē·ən\ adj. Living an unconventional life.

bought·en\˄bɔ·tən\ adj. Bought at a store.

brack·en\˄bră·kən\ n. A coarse, hardy fern; also called brake.

brake\˄brāk\ n. A clump of coarse, hardy fern. (see bracken)

brash\˄brăsh\ adj. Acting in haste without regard for consequences.

bra·va·do\brə ˄va·dō\ n. Pretense of bravery.

broach\˄brōch\ v. To open up a subject for discussion.

broil\˄broil\ n. An angry quarrel or struggle.

bruit\˄brūt\ v. To noise abroad.

buoy·ant\˄boi·ənt or ˄bū·ənt\ adj. Cheerful or gay.

bur·geon\˄bur·jən\ v. To flourish or expand.

bur·gher\˄bər·gər\ n. A citizen of a town.

bur·nish\˄bər·nĭsh\ v. To polish or make shiny.

bur·then\˄bər·thən\ n. Archaic form of **burden**.

ca·dav·er·ous\kə ˄dăv·rəs\ adj. Resembling a corpse.

cal·low\˄kă·lō\ adj. Inexperienced or immature.

can·ter\˄kăn·tər\ n. A moderate, easy gallop.

ca·pa·cious\kə ˄pā·shəs\ adj. Capable of holding much.

ca·price\kə ˄prēs\ n. A sudden, impulsive change of mind without evident motivation.

cap·tious\˄kăp·shəs\ adj. Marked by a tendency to confuse or entangle in argument.

car·a·van·sa·ry\˄kă·rə ˄văn·sə·rē\ n. A hotel or inn.

car·bun·cle\˄kər·buŋ·kəl\ n. A sore resembling a boil, only larger.

car·nage\˄kar·nĭj\ n. Extensive and bloody slaughter of men.

car·niv·o·rous\kar ˄nĭ·və·rəs\ adj. Eating or living on flesh of animals.

carp\˄karp\ v. To find fault or to complain unreasonably.

car·ri·on\˄kă·rē·ən\ n. Dead flesh.

cary·at·i·des\kă ˊrē ˄ăt·ə·dēz\ n. Supporting columns in the form of sculptured female figures.

cat·a·ract\˄kă·tə ˊrăkt\ n. 1. A clouding of the lens of the eye which obstructs passage of light. 2. Figuratively, a growth that obstructs light.

ca·vort\kə ˄vôrt\ v. To prance about.

cel·i·ba·cy\˄sĕ·lə·bə·sē\ n. Abstention by vow from marriage.

cen·taur\˄sĕn·tər\ n. In Greek mythology, one of a race fabled to be half man and half horse.

cen·trif·u·gal\sĕn ˄trĭ·fy·gəl\ adj. Directed away from a center or axis.

cen·tri·fuge\˄sĕn·trə·fyūj\ n. A rotary machine that separates substances of different densities or a machine which simulates gravitational effects.

ce·re·bral\sĕ ˄rē·bral or ˄sĕ·rə·bral\ adj. Of or relating to the brain or the intellect.

cer·ve·lat\˄sər·va ˊlăt\ n. Smoked sausage made of pork and beef.

chaf·fer\˄chă·fər\ v. To haggle or bargain about price.

chast·ened\˄chā·sənd\ adj. Softened or refined.

chat·tel\˄chăt·l\ n. An article of personal property; an item of movable property.

chit\˄chĭt\ n. A signed vouched of a small debt (as for food).

chiv·al·ric\shĭ ˄văl·rĭk\ adj. Pertaining to ideal qualities of knighthood.

cinch\˄sĭnch\ n. A strong girth for a pack or saddle.

ci·pher\˄sai·fər\ v. To write in code in order to conceal meaning.

clav·i·cle\˄klă·vĭ·kəl\ n. A bone of the vertebrate shoulder.

cleave\˄klēv\ v. To adhere, cling, or be faithful to.

cleft\˄klĕft\ n. A V-shaped indentation resembling a crack.

clem·en·cy\˄klĕ·mən·sē\ n. Act of showing mercy.

clew\˄klū\ v. To haul a sail up or down by ropes through a metal loop attached to the lower corner of a sail.

clois·tered\˄kloi·stərd\ adj. Secluded or separated from the world.

clo·ven\˄klō·vən\ adj. Parted or split. (alternative past participle of **cleave**, meaning to split)

cloy·ing\˄kloi·ĭŋ\ adj. Excess of something that is generally pleasing.

co·eval\kō ˄ē·vəl\ adj. Of the same age or time.

col·or·a·tu·ra\ˊkə·lə·rə ˄tyu·rə\ n. In vocal music, runs, trills, or decoration.

co·ma·tose\˄kō·mə ˊtōs\ adj. Resembling a coma.

come·ly\˄kəm·lē\ adj. Pleasing in person; handsome.

com·men·su·rate\kə ˄mĕn·sə·rət\ adj. Having the same measure.

com·mis·er·a·ting·ly\kə ˄mĭ·zə ˊrā·tĭŋ·lē\ adv. Sympathetically.

com·plai·sant\kəm ˄plā·sənt\ adj. Marked by desire to please or oblige.

con·cil·i·ate\kən ˄sĭ·lē·āt\ v. To gain goodwill by pleasing acts.

con·di·ment\˄kŏn·də·mənt\ n. Something used to enhance the flavor of food; a pungent seasoning.

con·fla·gra·tion\ˊkŏn·flə ˄grā·shən\ n. A large disastrous fire.

con·ge·nial·i·ty\kən ˊjē·nē ˄ă·lə·tē\ n. Quality of having similar character or tastes; harmony.

con·jure\˄kŏn·jər\ v. To call on or appeal to solemnly.

con·nings\˄kŏn·iŋs\ n. Periods of learning and committing to memory.

con·sign·ment\kən ˄sain·mənt\ n. Something transferred formally to another.

con·sort\kŏn ˄sort\ v. To keep company or associate with.

con·strict\kən ˄strĭkt\ v. To tighten, compress, or squeeze.

con·sum·mate\kən ˄su·mət or ˄kən·su·mət\ adj. Of the highest degree or of the greatest excellence.

con·sump·tion\kən ˄sump·shən\ n. A progressive wasting away of the body, esp. tuberculosis.

con·tem·pla·tion\ˊkŏn·təm ˄plā·shən\ n. Thoughtful consideration or study.

con·temp·tu·ous\kŏn ˄tĕmp·chə·wəs\ adj. Relating to a show of disobedience or disrespect.

774

con·tin·gent\kən ▲tĭn·jənt\ n. A quota or share of persons representative of a group.

con·tort\kən ▲tŏrt\ v. To twist violently.

con·tra·ri·ety\'kŏn·trə ▲rai·ə·tē\ n. The quality of being opposed in purpose; incompatibility.

con·trive\kən ▲traiv\ v. To plot, scheme, or devise.

con·ven·ti·cle\kən ▲vĕn·tĭ·kəl\ n. A meeting for religious worship, esp. a secret one not sanctioned by law.

con·verge\kən ▲vurj\ v. To move together gradually.

con·vo·lu·tion\'kŏn·və ▲lū·shən\ n. One of the irregular ridges upon the surface of the brain.

co·quet·ry\▲kō·kə·trē\ n. Act of flirting or showing trifling attention.

cor·dial\▲kor·jəl\ adj. Warm and hearty.

cork·er\▲kor·kər\ n. One that is excellent. (slang)

cor·nice\▲kor·nəs\ n. The molded projection at the top of a wall or building.

cor·po·re·al\kor ▲pō·rē·əl\ adj. Relating to a physical body.

cos·mog·ra·phy\kŏz ▲mŏg·rə·fē\ n. Science that describes the order of the universe.

coun·te·nance\▲kaun·tə·nəns\ n. Appearance, esp. the look or expression of the face.

coun·ter·poise\▲kaun·tər 'poiz\ n. A state of balance.

cov·ert\▲kə·vərt or ▲kō·vərt\ adj. Concealed or secret.

cow·er\▲kau·ər\ v. To display great fear of something that is domineering or threatening.

cox·comb\▲kŏk·skōm\ n. A conceited, foolish person.

coy·ly\▲koi·lē\ adv. Shyly or demurely.

cre·du·li·ty\krə ▲dyū·lə·tē\ n. Readiness to believe on slight evidence.

cre·tin\▲krē·tən\ n. a person with marked mental deficiency.

crux\▲kruks or ▲krəks\ n. A vital point; a baffling problem.

cul·mi·nate\▲kəl·mə 'nāt\ v. To reach a climactic or crucial point.

cult\▲kəlt\ n. A system of religious beliefs and ritual.

cu·po·la\▲kyū·pə·lə\ n. A rounded roof; dome.

cur·mudg·eon\kər ▲mə·jən\ n. A gruff, irritable old man.

cur·ry\▲kər·rē\ v. To arrange or dress the coat of a horse by combing and brushing.

cus·pid\▲kəs·pəd\ n. A canine tooth.

cyn·i·cism\▲sĭ·nə 'sĭ·zəm\ n. A deep disbelief or distrust of others.

cy·lin·dric\sə ▲lĭn·drĭk\ adj. Having the shape of a cylinder.

dal·li·ance\▲dă·lē·əns\ n. Romantic play or flirting.

daub\▲dŏb\ n. The act of applying something crudely.

de·bouch\dĭ ▲būsh\ v. To march out into open ground.

de·co·rum\dĭ ▲kō·rəm\ n. Good taste in conduct and appearance.

def·er·ence\▲def·rəns\ n. Respectful regard for another's wishes.

def·er·en·tial\'dĕ·fə ▲rĕn·chəl\ adj. Showing respectful regard for another.

de·file\dĭ ▲fail or dē ▲fail\ v. To make dirty; to corrupt the purity of.

deft\▲dĕft\ adj. Marked by skill and dexterity.

de·lin·ea·tion\dĭ 'lĭ·nē ▲ā·shən\ n. The act of describing or tracing out graphically.

de·lu·sive\dĭ ▲lū·sĭv\ adj. Misleading the mind or judgment.

dem·a·gog·ic\'dĕ·mə ▲gŏ·jĭk\ adj. Characteristic of a leader who makes false claims to gain power.

de·mean·or\dĭ ▲mē·nər\ n. The outward behavior of a person.

de·mo·ni·ac\dĭ ▲mō·nē 'ăk\ n. A person regarded as possessed by a demon.

demur\dĭ ▲mur\ v. To offer objections.

den·i·zen\▲dĕ·nə·zən\ n. An inhabitant.

de·ploy\dĭ ▲ploi\ v. To spread out or arrange strategically.

de·pose\dĭ ▲pōz\ v. To declare under oath.

dep·o·si·tion\'dĕ·pə ▲zĭ·shən\ n. Written testimony of someone under oath.

dep·re·cate\▲dĕp·rĭ 'kāt\ v. To express disapproval of.

dep·re·da·tion\'dĕp·rə ▲dā·shən\ n. A plundering or robbing.

de·ride\dĭ ▲raid\ v. To treat with scorn or ridicule.

des·e·crate\dĕ·sĭ 'krāt\ v. To treat irreverently or contemptuously.

des·pi·ca·ble\▲dĭs·pĭ·kə·bəl or dĕs ▲pĭ·kə·bəl\ adj. Deserving to be despised; contemptible.

des·po·tism\▲dĕs·pə 'tĭ·zəm\ n. A system of government in which the ruler has unlimited powers.

des·ti·tute\▲dĕs·tə 'tūt\ adj. Lacking something needed or desirable.

de·tes·ta·tion\'dē 'tĕs ▲tā·shən\ n. Extreme hatred or dislike.

dex·ter·i·ty\dĕk ▲stĕ·rə·tē\ n. Mental skill or quickness.

di·a·bol·i·cal\'dai·ə ▲bŏ·lĭ·kəl\ adj. Befitting the devil; fiendish.

di·a·dem\▲dai·ə·dĕm\ n. A headband or crown worn as a symbol of royalty.

di·a·pa·son\'dai·ə ▲pā·zən\ n. A full deep outburst of sound.

dif·fi·dence\▲dĭ·fə·dənts\ n. Quality of being reserved, timid, or unassertive.

dif·fuse\dĭ ▲fyūz\ v. To pour out and cause to spread freely.

di·lat·ed\dai ▲lā·təd or ▲dai·lā·təd\ adj. Expanded or made wider.

di·lem·ma\də ▲lĕ·mə\ n. A situation requiring a choice between two equally undesirable alternatives.

dil·et·tante\'dĭ·lə ▲tan·tē\ n. One who interests himself in a subject merely for amusement; an amateur.

di·min·u·tive\dĭ ▲mĭ·nyə·tĭv\ adj. Indicating small size.

dis·ar·tic·u·late\'dĭ·sər ▲tĭk·yə·lāt\ v. To separate the joints of.

dis·con·cert\dĭs·kən ▲sərt\ v. To throw into confusion or disturb.

ă bad, ā bake, a father, ĕ sell, ē equal, ai mile, ĭ sit, ŏ cot, ō note, ɔ law, ū boom, ᴜ wood, yū you, yᴜ fury, aᴜ cow, ɔi boy. The schwa is used for both stressed and unstressed sounds: ə mud, word, even. ch chase, itch; sh shell, wish; th path, thin, th̲ the, either; ŋ wing; w wet, wheat; zh pleasure.

dis·con·so·late·ly\dĭs ˄kŏn·sə·lət·lē\ adv. Hopelessly sad; cheerlessly.

dis·en·fran·chise\'dĭ·sən ˄frăn·chaiz\ v. To deprive of the right to vote.

dis·ha·bille\'dĭ·sə ˄bĕl\ n. State of being loosely or carelessly dressed.

di·shev·eled\dĭ ˄shĕ·vəld\ adj. Marked by disorder and loose arrangement, esp. with hair disarranged.

dis·port\dĭs ˄pōrt\ v. To frolic or amuse oneself.

dis·qui·etude\dĭs ˄kwai·ə·tūd\ n. State of uneasiness; anxiety.

dis·si·pa·tion\'dĭ·sə ˄pā·shən\ n. Excessive pursuit of pleasure and drink.

dis·so·lute\'dĭ·sə'lūt\ adj. Loose in morals or conduct.

dis·tend·ed\dĭs ˄tĕnd·əd\ adj. Swollen, expanded.

div·i·na·tion\'dĭ·və ˄nā·shən\ n. Unusual insight or art of discovering the unknown by means of supernatural powers.

doc·ile\˄da·səl\ adj. Easily taught or managed.

dog·ged\dɔ·gəd\ adj. Stubbornly determined.

dog·ma\˄dɔg·mə\ n. Doctrine maintained by a religious body.

do·lor·ous\˄dō·lə·rəs\ adj. Expressive of misery and grief.

dot·age\˄dō·tĭj\ n. A state of feeblemindedness, esp. in old age.

droll\˄drōl\ adj. Whimsical, humorous, or odd quality.

duc·tile\˄dək·təl\ adj. Easily fashioned into a new form; pliable.

dul·cet\˄dəl·sət\ adj. Pleasing to the ear.

du·ly\˄dū·lē\ adv. In due or proper manner.

ec·cen·tric·i·ty\'ĕk 'sĕn ˄trĭ·sə·tē\ n. A deviation from established pattern, rule, or norm.

ec·stat·ik\ĕk ˄stă·tĭk\ adj. Pertaining to intense delight.

ed·i·fice\˄ĕ·də·fəs\ n. A large structure or building.

ed·i·fy·ing\˄ed·ə'fai·ĭŋ\ adj. Instructional or enlightening.

ef·fem·i·nate\ə ˄fĕ·mə·nĭt\ adj. Having womanlike qualities.

ef·fete\ĕ ˄fēt\ adj. Worn out with age.

ef·fron·tery\ĭ ˄frən·tə·rē\ n. Shameless boldness.

egres·sion\ē ˄grĕ·shən\ n. Act of going out; emergence.

ejac·u·la·tion\ĭ 'jă·kyə ˄lā·shən\ n. A short sudden emotional utterance.

elic·it\ĭ ˄lĭ·sət\ v. To draw forth or bring out.

ema·ci·a·ted\ĭ ˄mă·shē 'ā·təd\ adj. Very lean, feeble; appearing to be wasted away physically.

en·fran·chised\ĭn ˄frăn 'chaizd\ adj. Admitted to political privileges or rights of a citizen.

en·gen·der\ĭn ˄jĕn·dər\ v. To give rise to; to produce.

enig·mat·ic\'ĕ·nĭg ˄mă·tĭk\ adj. Puzzling.

en·mi·ty\˄ĕn·mə·tē\ n. Positive hatred.

en·nui\˄ɔn 'wē\ n. A feeling of listless weariness or discontent resulting from lack of interest.

ep·i·taph\˄ĕ·pə·tăf\ n. Short piece of writing or an inscription honoring someone dead.

ep·i·thet\˄ĕ·pə·thĕt\ n. Descriptive word or phrase.

epit·o·mize\ĭ ˄pĭ·tə·maiz\ v. To represent whole class of.

ep·och\˄ĕ·pək *or* ˄ĕ·pŏk\ n. A period of time marked by memorable series of events.

equa·nim·i·ty\'ē·kwə ˄nĭ·mə·tē *or* 'ĕ·kwə ˄nĭ·mə·tē\ n. Evenness of mind or temper.

eques·tri·an\ĭ ˄kwĕs·trē·ən\ adj. Pertaining to horses and horsemanship.

er·rat·ic\ĕ ˄ră·tĭk\ adj. Marked by lack of consistency, regularity, or uniformity.

er·u·dite\˄ĕ·ryə 'dait\ adj. Learned.

es·cu·lent\˄ĕs·kyə·lənt\ adj. Edible.

eu·lo·gize\˄yū·lə·jaiz\ v. To speak or write in high praise of.

ev·a·nes·cent\'ĕ·və ˄nĕ·sənt\ adj. Passing away or liable to pass away like vapor.

evince\ĭ ˄vĭns\ v. To display clearly.

ev·i·ta·ble\˄ĕ·və·tə·bəl\ adj. Avoidable.

ex·cru·ci·a·ting\ĭks ˄krū·shē 'ā·tĭŋ\ adj. Causing intense pain; agonizing.

ex·em·pla·ry\ĭg ˄zĕm·plə·rē\ adj. Serving as an example worthy of imitation.

ex·ergue\˄ĕk 'sərg\ n. Space on a medal usually on the reverse below the central part of the design.

ex·hort·er\ĭg ˄zōr·tər\ n. One who urges by strong appeal or argument.

ex·pe·dite\˄ĕk·spə·dait\ v. To speed up a process.

ex·pe·di·tious\'ĕk·spə ˄dĭsh·əs\ adj. Acting with promptness and efficiency.

ex·ten·u·a·tion\ĭk 'stĕ·nyū ˄ā·shən\ n. That which partially excuses or makes something less serious.

ex·ult\ĭg ˄zəlt\ v. To rejoice greatly in triumph.

fa·çade\fə ˄sɔd\ n. The front of a building.

fac·to·tum\făk ˄tō·təm\ n. Someone with various duties.

fag end\˄făg ĕnd\ n. The last part.

fain\˄fān\ adj. Willing, content, or inclined.

fal·set·to\fɔl ˄sĕ·tō\ n. An artificially high voice, esp. one that extends beyond full voice range.

fash\˄făsh\ v. To worry or fret.

fas·tid·i·ous\făs ˄tĭ·dē·əs\ adj. Hard to please in matters of taste.

fat·u·ous·ly\˄fă·chū·əs·lē\ adv. Foolishly; in a silly way.

fawn\˄fɔn\ v. To court favor by excessive flattering.

fer·ret\˄fĕ·rət\ v. To search out by careful investigation.

fer·ule\˄fĕ·rəl\ n. A flat stick or ruler sometimes used for punishment.

fer·vid\˄fər·vəd\ adj. Ardent, zealous, or enthusiastic.

fes·toon\fĕs ˄tūn\ v. To shape into a decorative chain or strip hanging between two points.

fet·lock\˄fĕt 'lŏk\ n. A growth surrounded by a tuft of hair on the back of the leg above the hoof of a horse.

fil·i·al\˄fĭ·lē·əl\ adj. Befitting a son or daughter.

fire·brand\˄fair 'brănd\ n. One who stirs up trouble.

fir·ma·ment\˄fər·mə·mənt\ n. The expanse of the heavens.

flail\˄flāl\ v. To beat as if threshing grain by hand.

fledg·ling\˄flĕj·lĭŋ\ n. A young bird.

flor·id\˄flō·rĭd\ adj. Having a ruddy color; flushed with redness.

foal\˄fōl\ n. A young offspring of the horse family.

foi·ble\˄foi·bəl\ n. A personal weakness or failing in character.

fon·dle\˄fŏn·dəl\ v. To handle lovingly.

for·ay\˄fŏ·rā\ n. A raid for plunder.

foun·der\ˈfau̇n·dər\ v. To stumble and become lame.

fraught\ˈfrɔt\ adj. Filled or loaded down.

frit·ter\ˈfrĭ·tər\ v. To reduce or waste away a little at a time.

friv·o·lous\ˈfrĭ·və·ləs\ adj. Lacking seriousness or significance; playful.

froth\ˈfrŏth\ n. Any light, trivial thing.

frow·sy\ˈfrau̇·zē\ adj. Having unkempt or uncared-for appearance.

fru·gal·i·ty\frū ˈgă·lə·tē\ n. Thriftiness; wise and sparing use.

funk\ˈfəŋk\ n. A state of fear.

fur·row\ˈfər·rō\ v. To make a trench in the earth.

fur·tive\ˈfər·tĭv\ adj. Done secretly.

fu·sil·lad\ˈfyū·zə 'lad\ v. To fire shots in rapid succession.

gall\ˈgɔl\ v. To vex or irritate.

gal·va·nize\ˈgăl·və·naiz\ v. To rouse to action; to startle or excite.

gan·gling\ˈgăŋ·gliŋ\ adj. Awkwardly tall; lanky.

gan·gre·nous\ˈgăŋ·grə·nəs\ adj. Given to rotting of tissue as a result of a failure in blood circulation.

gant Dialect for **gaunt**\ˈgɔnt\ adj. Thin and hollow-eyed as from hunger or illness.

gar·goyle\ˈgar·gɔil\ n. A waterspout usually in the form of a grotesque human or animal figure.

gar·ru·lous\ˈgă·rə·ləs\ adj. Readiness to engage in talk that rambles or becomes tedious.

gas·con·ad·ing\ˈgăs·kə ˈnā·dĭŋ\ adj. Boasting.

gaunt·let\ˈgɔnt·lət\ n. A glove with a long extension over the wrist.

gibe\ˈjaib\ v. To reproach with mocking or insulting words.

glint\ˈglĭnt\ n. A gleam or reflection of light.

glut\ˈglʌt\ v. To feed or supply to an excess.

gnarled\ˈnarld\ adj. Full of knots and bulges.

gra·da·tion\grā ˈdā·shən\ n. A series forming successive stages by regular degrees.

grap·ple\ˈgră·pəl\ v. To struggle; to come to grips with.

green·horn\ˈgrēn·hɔrn\ n. An inexperienced person.

grid·iron\ˈgrĭd·airn\ n. Something covered with a network such as a football field.

gris·ly\ˈgrĭz·lē\ adj. Gruesome; inspiring horror.

grov·el·ing\ˈgru·və·liŋ\ adj. Hopelessly low condition; humble.

gull·ibil·i·ty\ˈgə·lə ˈbĭ·lə·tē\ n. The quality of being easily deceived.

gy·rat·ing\ˈjai·rā·tiŋ\ adj. Rotating, winding about, or oscillating.

ha·bil·i·ment\hə ˈbĭ·lə·mənt\ n. Clothing.

ham\ˈhăm\ n. The back part of the thigh and buttock.

ha·rangue\hə ˈrăŋ\ n. A lengthy, loud, and passionate speech.

harp·si·chord\ˈharp·sə·kɔrd\ n. A keyboard instrument similar to a piano but having strings plucked by quills or leather points.

har·row\ˈhă·rō\ v. To torment; to painfully distress.

heif·er\ˈhĕ·fər\ n. A young cow that has not produced a calf.

hei·nous\ˈhā·nəs\ adj. Extremely wicked; shockingly evil.

hel·i·cal\ˈhĕ·lĭ·kəl\ adj. Pertaining to or shaped like a spiral.

het·er·o·ge·neous\ˈhĕ·tə·rə ˈjē·nē·əs\ adj. A collection or group whose parts are not all alike.

hill·ock\ˈhĭ·lək\ n. A small hill or mound.

hoary\ˈhō·rē\ adj. Gray or white with age.

hock\ˈhŏk\ n. Joint of a hind leg of a horse; corresponds to the ankle of a man.

hom·i·ly\ˈhŏ·mə·lē\ n. A sermon or moral lecture.

hy·poth·e·sis\hai ˈpŏ·thə·sĭs\ n. An unproven conclusion drawn from known facts and used as basis for reasoning.

ig·ne·ous\ˈĭg·nē·əs\ adj. Formed by action of great heat within the earth.

im·med·i·ca·ble\ĭ ˈmĕ·dĭ·kə·bəl\ adj. Incurable.

im·pal·pa·ble\ĭm ˈpăl·pə·bəl\ adj. Incapable of being perceived by the senses.

im·pec·ca·ble\ĭm ˈpĕ·kə·bəl\ adj. Flawless.

im·per·a·tive·ness\ĭm ˈpĕ·rə·tĭv·nəs\ n. State of being urgently necessary.

im·pe·ri·ous ĭm ˈpĭ·rē·əs\ adj. Commanding or domineering attitude.

im·per·vi·ous\ĭm ˈpər·vē·əs\ adj. Incapable of being passed through; impenetrable.

im·pi·ous\ˈĭm·pē·əs or ĭm ˈpai·əs\ adj. Not showing loyal reverence for a person or thing.

im·por·tune\'ĭm·pōr ˈtūn\ v. To urge persistently or troublesomely.

im·po·tent\ˈĭm·pə·tənt\ adj. Powerless or helpless.

im·pre·ca·tion\'ĭm·prə ˈkā·shən\ n. A curse.

im·pu·ni·ty\ĭm ˈpyū·nə·tē\ n. Freedom from punishment.

in·aus·pi·cious\'ĭn·ɔ ˈspĭ·shəs\ adj. Unfavorable or ill-omened.

in·can·ta·tion\'ĭn ˈkăn ˈtā·shən\ n. The use of spells and words chanted as part of a ritual of magic.

in·con·gru·ous·ly\ĭn ˈkŏŋ·grū·əs·lē\ adv. On a manner inconsistent with what is reasonable or proper.

in·cor·ri·gi·ble\ĭn ˈkŏ·rə·jə·bəl\ n. Incapable of being changed or corrected.

in·cre·du·li·ty\'ĭn·krə ˈdū·lə·tē\ n. State of disbelief; unwillingness to believe.

in·dem·ni·ty\ĭn ˈdĕm·nə·tē\ n. That which is given as compensation for a loss or damage.

in·den·ture\ĭn ˈdĕn·chər\ v. To bind by contract to the services of another.

in·dig·e·nous\ĭn ˈdĭj·ə·nəs\ adj. Living naturally in a particular environment.

in·dom·i·ta·ble\ĭn ˈdŏ·mə·tə·bəl\ adj. Not easily defeated; unconquerable.

in·dul·gent\ĭn ˈdəl·jənt\ adj. Prone to humor or gratify whims; lenient.

ă bad, ā bake, a father, ĕ sell, ē equal, ai mile, ĭ sit, ŏ cot, ō note, ɔ law, ū boom, u̇ wood, yū you, yu̇ fury, au̇ cow, ɔi boy. The schwa is used for both stressed and unstressed sounds: ə mud, word, even. ch chase, itch; sh shell, wish; th path, thin, ṯẖ the, either; ŋ wing; w wet, wheat; zh pleasure.

in·eq·ui·ta·ble\ĭn ˈĕk·wə·tə·bəl\ adj. Unfair or unjust.

in·ex·pli·ca·bly\ĭn·ĕks ˈplĭ·kə·blē\ adv. Impossible to explain.

in·fal·li·bly\ĭn ˈfă·lə·blē\ adv. Unfailingly.

in·fa·mous\ˈĭn·fə·məs\ adj. Having a notoriously bad reputation.

in·fer·nal\ĭn ˈfərn·əl\adj. Of or relating to hell.

in·gen·ious\ĭn ˈjĕn·yəs\ adj. Having inventive ability; cleverly skillful.

in·gen·u·ous\ĭn ˈjĕn·yū·əs\ adj. Straightforward; simple.

in·gres·sion\ĭn ˈgrĕ·shən\ n. Act of going in.

in·her·ent\ĭn ˈhĭ·rənt\ adj. Forming an essential, inseparable element or quality of something.

in·im·i·ta·ble\ĭn ˈĭm·ə·tə·bəl\ adj. Defying imitation; matchless.

in·iq·ui·ty\ĭ ˈnĭk·wə·tē\ n. A wrong act; wickedness.

in·nate·ly\ĭ ˈnāt·lē\ adv. Within one's own nature.

in·noc·u·ous\ĭ ˈnŏ·kyə·wəs\ adj. Not likely to give offense.

in·sa·tiate\ĭn ˈsā·sh(ē)ət\ adj. Incapable of being satisfied.

in·scru·ta·ble\ĭn ˈskrū·tə·bəl\ adj. Cannot readily be understood or searched.

in·tan·gi·ble\ĭn ˈtăn·jə·bəl\ adj. Not touchable; realized by the mind in a vague and imprecise way.

in·ter·lard\'ĭn·tər ˈlärd\ v. To introduce something foreign or irrelevant.

in·tim·i·da·tion\ĭn 'tĭ·mə ˈdā·shən\ n. State of being made timid or fearful.

in·trin·sic\ĭn ˈtrĭn·zĭk\ adj. Belonging to the true nature of a thing.

in·tu·i·tive\ĭn ˈtū·ə·tĭv\ adj. Capable of being learned without conscious attention.

in·un·da·tion\'ĭn·ən ˈdā·shən\ n. State of being covered by overflowing; flood.

in·ure\ĭn ˈyŭr\ v. To accustom to accept something undesirable.

in·vet·er·ate\ĭn ˈvĕ·tə·rət\ adj. Firmly established; habitual.

iro·ny\ˈai·rə·nē\ n. An event or result which is the opposite of what was expected.

ir·ra·di·a·tion\ĭr 'ād·ē ˈā·shən\ n. Giving off radiant energy such as heat and light.

itin·er·ant\ai ˈtĭ·nə·rənt\ adj. Going from place to place.

jack\ˈjăk\ n. 1. A man employed to do odd jobs; a servant. 2. Slang for money.

jal·ap\ˈja·ləp\ n. Dried root of a plant used as a purgative.

jaun·dice\ˈjŏn·dĭs\ v. To affect with a diseased condition of the liver; marked by yellowness of skin and eyeballs.

jet·ti·son\ˈjĕ·tə·sən\ n. The act of dropping a cargo to lighten load in time of distress.

joc·u·lar\ˈjŏ·kyə·lər\ adj. Making jokes; given to joking; playful.

jo·cund\ˈjŏ·kənd\ adj. Marked by cheerfulness.

jos·tle\ˈjŏs·əl\ v. To make one's way by pushing and shoving.

jug·ger·naut\ˈjə·gər 'nŏt\ n. A massive, relentless force or object that crushes everything in its path.

ki·net·ic\kə ˈnĕ·tĭk\ adj. Related to the motion of material bodies and the energy associated therewith.

knav·ery\ˈnā·və·rē\ n. Trickery; deceitfulness.

knoll\ˈnōl\ n. A small round hill.

lab·y·rin·thine\lă·bə ˈrĭn·thĭn\ adj. Pertaining to a confusing and intricate state of affairs.

lac·er·a·tion\'lă·sə ˈrā·shən\ n. Act of wounding the flesh by tearing.

la·con·ic\lə ˈkŏ·nĭk\ adj. Using few words; being brief.

lac·te·al\ˈlăk·tē·əl\ adj. Pertaining to milk.

lam·en·ta·tion\'lă·mən ˈtā·shən\ n. The act of expressing sorrow or regret.

lan·guid\ˈlăŋ·gwəd\ adj. Condition marked by weariness or little interest in any activity.

lan·guor\ˈlăŋ·gər\ n. Lack of energy or enthusiasm.

leer·ing\ˈlĭ·rĭŋ\ adj. Having a knowing, malicious expression.

le·o·nine\ˈlē·ə·nain\ adj. Characteristic of a lion.

leth·ar·gy\ˈlĕ·thər·jē\ n. A state of sluggish inactivity; indifference.

le·vant\lə ˈvănt\ n. A kind of Morocco leather with an irregularly grained surface.

lev·i·ty\ˈlĕ·və·tē\ n. An act characterized by lack of seriousness; humor.

lewd\ˈlūd\ adj. Obscene; given to lust.

lex·i·con\ˈlĕk·sə·kən\ n. A book containing an alphabetical list of words together with their definitions; a dictionary.

lief\ˈlēf\ adv. Willingly; readily.

lim·pid\ˈlĭm·pəd\ adj. Clear and untroubled.

lin·ea·ment\ˈlĭ·nē·ə·mənt\ n. Facial contour or feature.

lin·tel\ˈlĭn·təl\ n. A horizontal part spanning the opening of a door or window.

lit·i·gant\ˈlĭ·tə·gənt\ n. A participant in a lawsuit.

liv·id\ˈlĭ·vĭd\ adj. 1. Black and blue as if bruised. 2. Pale, ashen.

lo·qua·cious\lō ˈkwā·shəs\ adj. Given to excessive talking.

lore\ˈlōr\ n. The body of traditional knowledge about a subject.

low\ˈlō\ v. To call; to summon; to moo.

lu·di·crous\ˈlū·də·krəs\ adj. Meriting laughter or scorn as being foolish.

lu·gu·bri·ous\lŭ ˈgū·brē·əs\ adj. Very mournful, esp. in an exaggerated manner exciting ridicule.

lum·ber\ˈlŭm·bər\ v. To move in a heavy or clumsy manner.

lu·mi·nes·cent\'lū·mə ˈnĕ·sənt\ adj. Characterized by the giving off of light.

lus·tral\ˈləs·trəl\ adj. Pertaining to something used in purification.

lus·trum\ˈləs·trəm\ n. A period of five years.

mag·na·nim·i·ty\'măg·nə ˈnĭ·mə·tē\ n. The quality of being generous in forgiving others.

ma·lef·ic\mə ˈlĕ·fĭk\ adj. Causing evil or disaster.

manèd\ˈmānd\ or poetical\ ˈmān·əd\ adj. Having long heavy hair about the neck.

man·i·fold\ˈmă·nə 'fōld\ adj. Having many and varied forms.

mar·i·tal\ˈmă·rə·təl\ adj. Pertaining to marriage.

mas·tiff\\ᵃmăs·təf\ n. A very large, powerful, deep-chested, smooth-coated dog used as a watchdog.

maud·lin\\ᵃmɔd·lən\ adj. Being emotionally silly.

mead\\ᵃmēd\ n. Meadow.

mea·gre or **mea·ger**\\ᵃmē·gər\ adj. Deficient in quantity or quality.

mer·ce·nar·y\\ᵃmər·sə 'nē·rē\ adj. Influenced by a desire for gain or reward; greedy.

meta·phys·i·cal\'mĕ·tə ᵃfĭ·zĭ·kəl\ adj. Marked by a highly complex subtlety of thought and expression.

me·tem·psy·cho·sis\mə 'tĕm·sĭ ᵃkō·səs\ n. The passing of the soul after death into another body, either human or animal.

me·tic·u·lous\mə ᵃtĭ·kyə·ləs\ adj. Showing extreme care with detail.

mim·ic·ry\\ᵃmĭ·mĭk·rē\ n. The act of imitating.

min·a·ret\'mĭ·nə ᵃrĕt\ n. A slender lofty tower with a balcony from which a summons to prayer is made.

min·is·cule\\ᵃmĭn·əs 'kyūl\ n. Variant of minuscule, meaning very small or having simplified and small forms.

mi·nu·tia\mə ᵃnyū·shə\ n. A minor detail.

mire\\ᵃmair\ n. Wet, soggy earth; mud.

mo·les·ta·tion\mō 'lĕs ᵃtā·shən\ n. An annoyance or state of being annoyed or disturbed.

mon·ger\\ᵃməŋ·gər\ n. One engaged in dealing or trading.

mo·ni·tion\mō ᵃnĭ·shən\ n. A warning, possibly of impending danger.

mon·o·lith\\ᵃmŏ·nə·lĭth\ n. A single block of stone, usually very large.

mo·no·po·ly\mə ᵃnŏ·pə·lē\ n. Exclusive ownership or possession of something by one person or one group.

mon·tage\mŏn ᵃtozh\ n. A rapid sequence of images to show a group of ideas.

mor·ti·fi·ca·tion\'mɔr·tə·fə ᵃkā·shən\ n. A feeling of humiliation or shame.

mor·tise\\ᵃmɔr·təs\ v. To fasten securely.

mo·tif\mō ᵃtēf\ n. The underlying theme or idea.

muck\\ᵃmək\ n. Moist dung mixed with decomposed vegetable matter.

mul·ti·far·i·ous\'məl·tə ᵃfä·rē·əs\ adj. Having a great variety.

na·ive·té\nɔ ᵃē·və ᵃlä\ n. The state or quality of having a simple nature; lacking worldly experience.

na·tal\nāt·l\ adj. Pertaining to time of birth.

ne·ces·si·tous\nə ᵃsĕ·sə·təs\ adj. Extremely needy.

ne·phri·tis\nĭ ᵃfrai·tĭs\ n. Inflammation of the kidneys.

neu·ri·tis\nu ᵃrai·tĭs\ n. Inflammation of a nerve.

nig·gling\\ᵃnĭg·liŋ\ adj. Spending too much effort on minor detail; finding fault in a petty way.

noc·turne\\ᵃnŏk·tərn\ n. A night scene in painting.

non·plus\'nŏn ᵃpləs\ v. To cause to be at a loss as to what to say, think, or do.

nov·ice\\ᵃnŏ·vəs\ n. A beginner.

nox·ious\\ᵃnŏk·shəs\ adj. Tending to cause injury to health or morals.

oblate\\ᵃōb ᵃlāt\ adj. The state of being flattened at the poles.

oblique·ly\ō ᵃblēk·lē or ə ᵃblēk·lē\ adv. Indirectly or without straightforwardness in meaning.

ob·lo·quy\\ᵃŏb·lə·kwē\ adj. Abusive language.

ob·trude\əb ᵃtrūd\ v. To force oneself upon another.

ob·tuse\əb ᵃtūs\ adj. Lacking acuteness of intellect or feeling.

oc·u·lar\\ᵃŏ·kyə·lər\ adj. Of or related to the eye or sight.

om·i·nous\\ᵃŏ·mə·nəs\ adj. Foreshadowed by an omen of coming evil; threatening.

om·nip·o·tent\ŏm ᵃnĭ·pə·tənt\ adj. Not limited in power or authority; almighty.

om·ni·pres·ence\'ŏm·nə ᵃprĕ·zəns\ n. The quality of being everywhere present at the same time.

oner·ous\\ᵃŏ·nə·rəs\ adj. Troublesome; distasteful.

or·a·cle\\ᵃɔ·rə·kəl\ n. A person who gives wise opinions or reveals hidden knowledge.

or·di·na·tion\'ɔr·də ᵃnā·shən\ n. The rite of being ordained into the ministry.

or·i·fice\\ᵃɔ·rə·fĭs\ n. An opening into a cavity; a mouth.

os·cil·late\\ᵃŏs·ə·lāt\ v. To swing back and forth between various courses of action or thought.

os·ten·si·ble\ŏs ᵃtĕn·sə·bəl\ adj. Offered as real or genuine.

os·ten·ta·tion\'ɔ·stən ᵃtā·shən\ n. Excessive display.

os·tra·cism\\ᵃŏs·trə 'sĭ·zəm\ n. Temporary banishment.

pa·lav·er\pə ᵃlă·vər\ v. To talk idly.

pal·li·ate\\ᵃpă·lē ᵃāt\ v. To cover by excuses.

pal·lid\\ᵃpă·ləd\ adj. Lacking color; pale.

pan·der·er\\ᵃpăn·də·rər\ n. Someone who exploits the weaknesses of others.

pan·o·ply\\ᵃpă·nə·plē\ n. The complete covering or armor of a warrior.

par·a·dox\\ᵃpă·rə·dŏks\ n. A statement seemingly absurd or self-contradictory.

par·a·gon\\ᵃpä·rə 'gŏn\ n. A clothing fabric of silk and wool.

par·o·dy\\ᵃpă·rə·dē\ n. A ridiculous imitation.

par·ox·ysm\\ᵃpă·rək 'sĭ·zəm\ n. A sudden, violent emotion or action.

patho·log·i·cal\'pă·thə ᵃlŏ·jĭ·kəl\ adj. Caused by disease.

pa·tron·age\\ᵃpă·trə·nĭj or ᵃpā·trə·nĭj\ n. Making a display of courtesy with an air of superiority toward inferiors.

peak·ed\\ᵃpē·kəd\ adj. Looking pale or sickly.

pelf\\ᵃpĕlf\ n. Money, esp. if dishonestly acquired.

pen·dent\\ᵃpĕn·dənt\ adj. Hanging downward.

per·ad·ven·ture\\ᵃpər·əd 'vĕn·chər\ adv. Perhaps or possibly.

per·am·bu·la·tion\pər ᵃăm·byə ᵃlā·shən\ n. The act of walking about.

pe·remp·to·ry\pə ᵃrĕm·tə·rē\ adj. Putting an end to.

per·fid·i·ous\'pər ᵃfĭ·dē·əs\ adj. Characterized by disloyalty or faithlessness.

ă bad, ā bake, a father, ĕ sell, ē equal, ai mile, ĭ sit, ŏ cot, ō note, ɔ law, ū boom, u wood, yū you, yu fury, au cow, ɔi boy. The schwa is used for both stressed and unstressed sounds: ə mud, word, even. ch chase, itch; sh shell, wish; th path, thin, th the, either; ŋ wing; w wet, wheat; zh pleasure.

per·func·to·ry\pər ˈfəŋ·tə·rē\ adj. Characterized by a routine or mechanical performance.

peri·he·lion\'pĕ·rə ˈhēl·yən\ n. The point in the path of a planet that is nearest the sun.

pe·riph·er·al\pə ˈrĭf·rəl\ adj. Relating to an area lying away from center.

per·spi·ca·cious\'pər·spə ˈkā·shəs\ adj. Especially keen mental vision.

per·ti·nac·i·ty\'pər·tə ˈnă·sə·tē\ n. The quality of adhering without yielding to a purpose.

pet·u·lant\ˈpĕ·chū·lənt\ adj. Displaying fretfulness, insolence, or peevishness.

phan·tas·mal\făn ˈtăz·məl\ adj. Relating to deceptive appearance or illusion of a thing.

phil·an·throp·ic\'fĭl·ən ˈthrŏ·pĭk\ adj. Related to effort to help human welfare.

phleg·mat·ic\flĕg ˈmă·tĭk\ adj. Having a slow, stolid temperament.

phos·pho·res·cence\'fŏs·fə ˈrĕ·səns\ n. Light that continues after possible source of energy has stopped.

phys·i·ol·o·gy\'fĭ·zē ˈŏl·ə·jē\ n. The branch of biology that treats processes of living matter.

pi·ca·resque\'pĭ·kə ˈrĕsk\ adj. Pertaining to a type of fiction that deals with rogues, rascals, and vagabonds.

pin·ion\ˈpĭn·yən\ v. To bind fast so as to render helpless.

pi·pet\paı ˈpĕt\ v. To draw liquid by suction through a glass tube and hold it by closing the upper end.

pique\ˈpēk\ n. Resentment, offense. v. To arouse anger or resentment in.

pith\ˈpĭth\ n. A central strand of spongy tissue in the stem of a plant.

plaque\ˈplăk\ n. A plate or tablet artistically ornamented.

ple·be·ian\plĭ ˈbē·ən\ adj. Pertaining to the common people; hence, something common.

plen·i·tude\ˈplĕ·nə·tūd\ n. Fullness in quantity, measure, or degree; abundance.

ply\ˈplaı\ v. To go or travel regularly.

poi·gnant\ˈpoı·nyənt\ adj. Painfully cutting or to the point; deeply affecting one's feelings.

pol·troon\pŏl ˈtrūn\ n. A mean, spiritless coward.

poly·chrome\'pŏ·lĭ ˈkrōm\ adj. Made with several colors.

pom·mel\ˈpə·məl\ n. The protruding portion at the front end and top of a saddle.

por·ten·tous\pōr ˈtĕn·təs\ adj. Having the nature of a sign indicating what is to happen; ominous.

prec·i·pice\ˈprĕ·sə·pĭs\ n. A very steep place; the brink of a cliff.

pre·cip·i·tate\prĭ ˈsĭ·pə·tāt\ v. To throw hastily and unexpectedly into something.

pre·co·cious\prĭ ˈkō·shəs\ adj. Marked by exceptional development at an unusually early age.

pre·des·ti·na·tion\prē 'dĕs·tə ˈnā·shən\ n. The belief that all things are decided beforehand by God.

pre·dis·pose\'prē·dĭs ˈpōz\ v. To influence an attitude toward something; to incline.

pre·mo·ni·tion\'prē·mə ˈnĭsh·ən or prē·mə ˈnish·ən\ n. A warning or feeling of something about to occur.

pre·mon·i·tory\prē ˈmɔ·nə 'tō·rē\ adj. Giving previous warning.

pre·sen·ti·ment\prĭ ˈzĕn·tə·mənt\ n. A feeling that something will happen or is about to take place.

pre·ten·sion\prĭ ˈtĕn·chən\ n. The act of making a claim of doubtful value to something.

pro·cre·ate\ˈprō·krē·āt\ v. To produce offspring.

pro·di·gious\prə ˈdĭ·jəs\ adj. Extraordinary amount of; enormous.

prod·i·gy\ˈprŏ·də·jē\ n. An extraordinary deed or event.

pro·fane\prō ˈfān\ v. To treat with abuse or vulgarity.

prof·li·ga·cy\ˈprŏf·lə·gə·cē\ n. The state of being insensible to principle, virtue, or decency.

pro·le·tar·i·an\'prō·lə ˈtĕ·rē·ən\ n. A member of the lowest social class; one who sells his labor to live.

pro·lif·ic\prə ˈlĭ·fĭk\ adj. Marked by ability to reproduce abundantly.

prom·on·to·ry\ˈprŏ·mən 'tō·rē\ n. A high point of land or rock projecting into a body of water.

pro·mul·ga·tion\'prō·məl ˈgā·shən\ n. A proposed law; state of being made public; proclamation.

pro·nun·ci·a·men·to\prə 'nən·sē·ə ˈmĕn·tō\ n. A public announcement; a proclamation.

pro·pen·si·ty\prə ˈpĕn·sə·tē\ n. A deeply rooted longing or natural inclination.

pro·pi·tia·to·ry\prō ˈpĭsh·ə 'tō·rē\ adj. Relating to making favorable, or appeasing.

pros·e·lyte\ˈprŏ·sə·lait\ n. One who has been brought over to any belief; a convert.

prov·en·der\ˈprŏ·vən·dər\ n. Dry food for domestic animals.

psy·cho·so·mat·ic\'sai·kō·sə ˈmă·tĭk or 'sai·kə·sə ˈmă·tĭk\ adj. Relating to the interrelationship of mind and body in causing disease.

pu·er·ile\ˈpyū·ə·rĭl\ adj. Childish, juvenile.

pun·cheon\ˈpən·chən\ n. A split or heavy log with a smoothed face.

pun·dit\ˈpən·dət\ n. A learned man.

pur·loin\pər ˈloin or ˈpər·loin\ v. To steal.

quad·ru·ped\ˈkwŏd·rə·pĕd\ n. An animal having four feet.

quaff\ˈkwŏf\ v. To drink deeply and with great relish.

quar·to\ˈkwɔr·tō\ n. A book or pamphlet having pages the size of a fourth of a sheet.

quell\ˈkwĕl\ v. To put down, subdue, or suppress.

qui·etude\ˈkwai·ə·tūd\ n. A state of calmness or quietness.

quin·tes·sen·tial\'kwĭn·tə ˈsĕn·chəl\ adj. Pertaining to the most essential part of anything.

rail·lery\ˈrā·lə·rē\ n. Mocking; imitating in order to make fun of; good-natured ridicule.

rai·ment\ˈrā·mənt\ n. Wearing apparel.

ran·cor\ˈrăŋ·kər\ n. Intense brooding over wrong; bitterness.

ra·pa·cious\rə ˈpā·shəs\ adj. Grasping, greedy.

ra·ti·o·ci·na·tion\'răsh·ē 'ŏs·ə ˈnā·shən\ n. The process of exact thinking.

ra·tion·ale\'ră·shən ˈăl\ n. Logical basis of something.

rav·en·ous\ˈră·və·nəs\ adj. Violently hungry; extremely eager for satisfaction.

re·cal·ci·trant\rĭ ˈkăl·sə·trənt\ adj. Stubbornly disobedient; rebellious.

780

rec·i·ta·tive\'rĕ·sə·tā ▴tĭv\ n. A narrative of facts and details; also, language in rhythm of ordinary speech, but set to music.

re·it·er·a·tion\'rē·ĭ·tə ▴rā·shən\ n. The act of repeating or doing something again.

re·ju·ve·nes·cent\rĭ 'ju·və ▴nĕ·sənt\ adj. Pertaining to the renewal of youth.

rem·i·nis·cence\'rĕ·mə ▴nĭ·sənts\ n. Recollection of some previous experience.

re·mon·strance\rĭ ▴mŏn·strəns\ n. The act of pleading in protest or opposition.

re·mu·ner·a·tion\rĭ 'myū·nə ▴rā·shən\ n. Equal payment for services rendered.

re·plete\rĭ ▴plēt\ adj. Abundantly supplied or provided for.

re·pug·nant\rĭ ▴pəg·nənt\ adj. Being against one's ideas; causing distaste and resistance.

req·ui·site\'rĕk·wə·zĭt\ adj. Required by the nature of things; necessary.

re·sil·ient\rĭ ▴zĭl·yənt\ adj. Capable of recovering from shock and adjusting to misfortune or change.

res·o·nance\▴rĕ·zə·nəns\ n. State or quality of sending back or prolonging sound.

re·spite\'rĕs·pĭt\ n. A temporary suspension of labor or effort; a time for rest.

ret·i·cent\'rĕ·tə·sənt\ adj. Inclined to keep silent; reserved or restrained in expression.

ret·i·nue\'rĕ·tə 'nyū\ n. Group of followers.

re·vamp\rē ▴vămp\ v. To make over, reorganize, or reconstruct.

re·ver·ber·ate\rĭ ▴vər·bə·rāt\ v. To resound or echo.

re·vile\rĭ ▴vaìl\ v. To use abusive language; to slander or curse someone.

roil\▴rɔil\ v. To make muddy or turbid.

ruck\▴rək\ n. A jumbled mass.

rue\▴rū\ v. To feel sorrow, regret, or remorse.

rue·ful·ly\▴rū·fə·lē\ adv. With expression of regret or pity.

sac·ri·le·gious\'săk·rə ▴lĭ·jəs\ adj. Gross irreverence toward a sacred person, place, or thing.

sa·dis·tic\sə ▴dĭs·tĭk\ adj. Delighting in excessive cruelty.

sa·gac·i·ty\sə ▴gă·sə·tē\ n. The quality of being shrewd and wise.

sa·lient\▴sā·lyənt\ adj. Standing out conspicuously from its surroundings.

sal·low\▴să 'lō\ adj. A grayish greenish yellow color.

sar·don·ic\sŏr ▴dŏ·nĭk\ adj. Marked by cynicism and bitterness.

scep·tic, skep·tic\▴skĕp·tĭk\ n. One who continually doubts or questions what is generally accepted in philosophy, science, or religion.

scup·per·nong\'skə·pər·nɔŋ\ n. A variety of grapes cultivated in the United States.

scut\▴skət\ n. A short erect tail, as of a rabbit.

seer\▴sĭ·ər\ n. One with extreme wisdom and the ability to predict events; a prophet.

sen·su·ous·ly\▴sĕnch·ə·əs·lē\ adv. In a manner delighting to the senses, esp. in beauty of color, sound, texture, etc.

se·pal\▴sē·pəl\ n. One of the leaves of the leafy part of a flower.

sere\▴sĭr\ adj. Withered or dried up.

ser·vi·tor\▴sər·və·tər\ n. A male servant.

sib·i·lant\▴sĭ·bə·lənt\ adj. Having or producing a hissing sound.

sil·i·cate\▴sĭ·lə·kāt or ▴sĭ·lə·kĭt\ n. A salt compound of silica and water.

si·mil·i·tude\sə ▴mĭ·lə·tūd\ n. Points of likeness and comparison.

skit·ter\▴skĭ·tər\ v. To glide lightly along, touching the surface at intervals.

sluice\▴slūs\ v. To wash in a trough through which water is run in order to separate gold ore.

smite\▴smait\ v. To attack or afflict suddenly and injuriously.

smut\▴smət\ v. To taint, blacken, or stain.

snaf·fle\▴snă·fəl\ n. A simple jointed bit for a bridle.

so·lace\▴sŏ·ləs or ▴sō·ləs\ n. A source of relief or comfort.

som·no·lence\▴sŏm·nə·ləns\ n. Overpowering drowsiness.

sor·did·ness\▴sor·dĭd·nəs\ n. 1. Filth, dirt, or squalor. 2. A low covetous desire for gain.

spas·mod·ic\spăz ▴ma·dĭk\ adj. Subject to outbursts of emotion occurring at irregular intervals.

spate\▴spāt\ n. A sudden or vigorous outpouring.

spec·trum\▴spĕk·trəm\ n. A series of images produced when a beam of light is dispersed.

spit\▴spĭt\ n. A slender pointed rod for holding meat over a fire.

stanch\▴stɔnch\ v. To stop the flow of blood from a wound.

stig·ma\▴stĭg·mə\ n. A blemish or blot indicating a defect.

sto·i·cal\▴stŏ·ĭk·əl\ adj. Indifferent to pleasure or pain; not affected by passion or feeling.

sto·lid·i·ty\stŏ ▴lĭ·də·tē\ n. The quality of having little or no sensibility.

strop\▴strŏp\ n. A strip of leather for sharpening a straight razor.

stub·ble\▴stə·bəl\ n. Grasses remaining growing after a harvest.

stul·ti·fy\▴stul·tə·faì\ v. To cause to appear absurd; to allege to be of unsound mind.

sua·vi·ty\▴swa·və·tē\ n. The state of being able to encourage easy dealing with others; smoothness.

sub·li·mate\▴səb·lə·māt\ v. To convert energy of something primitive in aim into something more socially and culturally acceptable.

sub·lu·na·ry\▴səb·lū·nə·rē\ adj. Situated beneath the moon.

suf·fu·sion\sə ▴fyū·zhən\ n. The act of overspreading as with color or light.

sul·len\▴sə·lən\ adj. Gloomily silent.

ă bad, ā bake, a father, ĕ sell, ē equal, ai mile, ĭ sit, ŏ cot, ō note, ɔ law, ū boom, ᴜ wood, yū you, yᴜ fury, aᴜ cow, ɔi boy. The schwa is used for both stressed and unstressed sounds: ə mud, word, even. c̶h̶ chase, itch; s̶h̶ shell, wish; t̶h̶ path, thin, t̶h̶ the, either; ŋ wing; w wet, wheat; z̶h̶ pleasure.

sul·ly\ˆsə·lē\ v. To soil or tarnish.

su·per·cil·i·ous\'sū·pər ˆsĭ·lē·əs\ adj. Haughty, proud, arrogant.

su·per·erog·a·to·ry\'sū·pə·rə ˆrŏ·gə·tō·rē\ adj. Pertaining to excess of demands or requirements.

su·per·nal\sʊ ˆpər·nəl\ adj. Being or coming from the heavens.

su·per·nu·mer·ar·y\'sū·pər ˆnū·mə·rĕ·rē\ n. A performer who appears in a scene, esp. a mob scene, without a speaking part. adj. Exceeding the needed amount.

sur·feit\ˆsər·fət\ v. To indulge in or partake of to an excess.

sur·plice\ˆsər·pləs\ n. A loose white garment worn by the clergy and choir.

sur·rep·ti·tious\'sə·rəp ˆtĭ·shəs\ adj. Accomplished by secret or improper means.

swarthy\ˆswɔr·thē\ adj. Being of dark color, complexion, or cast.

tab·leau\ˆtăb·lō\ n. A striking dramatic scene done as if it were a picture or drawing.

tac·i·turn\ˆtă·sə·tərn\ adj. Not inclined by temperament to talk.

taw·ny\ˆtɔ·nē\ adj. Brownish yellow.

tem·per·ance\ˆtĕm·pə·rəns\ n. The practice of not consuming alcohol.

te·na·cious\tə ˆnā·shəs\ adj. Tending to hold fast.

ten·on\ˆtĕ·nən\ v. To insert in a socket to form a joint.

te·o·cal·li\'tē·ə ˆkä·lē\ n. A mound upon which an ancient temple was built.

ter·ma·gant\ˆtər·mə·gənt\ n. A nagging, overbearing woman.

tes·ty\ˆtĕs·tē\ adj. Touchy, easily irritated.

the·oc·ra·cy\thē ˆŏk·rə·sē\ n. A government of a state which recognizes a god or God as their ruler.

the·o·logue\ˆthē·ə 'lŏg\ n. A student engaged in religious training.

throes\ˆthrōz\ n. Violent activity; hard and painful struggle.

tim·o·rous\ˆtĭ·mə·rəs\ adj. Afraid, timid.

toady\ˆtō·dē\ v. To flatter and act servile toward in hope of gaining favors.

to·pog·ra·phy\tə ˆpŏg·rə·fē\ n. The physical and natural features of a region.

tor·pid\ˆtɔr·pĭd\ adj. Inactive or sluggish.

tou·sle\ˆtaʊ·zəl\ v. To wrinkle, dishevel, or rumple.

trac·ta·ble\ˆträk·tə·bəl\ adj. Capable of being easily led or managed.

tra·jec·to·ry\trə ˆjĕk·tə·rē\ n. The curve that a rocket or other body follows in space after being fired.

tran·scen·dent\'trăn ˆsən·dənt\ adj. Extending beyond the limits of ordinary experience.

trans·lu·cent\trăns ˆlū·sənt\ adj. Allowing the passage of light, but not permitting a clear view of objects beyond.

trav·ail\tra ˆvāl\ n. Strenuous physical or mental labor.

trem·u·lous\ˆtrĕ·myə·ləs\ adj. Affected by trembling.

tur·pi·tude\ˆtər·pə 'tyūd\ n. By nature lacking moral values; a depraved condition.

tu·te·lage\ˆtū·tə·lĭj\ n. Instruction.

ubiq·ui·tous\yū ˆbĭk·wə·təs\ adj. Existing or seeming to exist everywhere at once.

um·bil·i·cal\'əm ˆbĭ·lĭ·kəl\ n. A servicing cable that is detached from a rocket at launching.

unc·tion\'əŋk·shən\ n. A state of being affected by deep religious or spiritual fervor.

un·du·la·tion\'ən·jə ˆlā·shən\ n. Wavelike motion of rising and falling.

un·ob·tru·sive\ən·əb ˆtrū·sĭv\ adj. Not forcing oneself or one's opinions upon another without a request; not aggressive.

un·or·tho·dox\ən ˆŏr·thə 'dŏks\ adj. Not conforming to established doctrine in religion.

un·wont·ed\ən ˆwɔn·tĭd\ adj. Pertaining to something unusual or out of the ordinary.

util·i·tar·i·an\yū 'tĭ·lə ˆtĕ·rē·ən\ adj. Pertaining to something useful or designed to be used.

va·ga·ry\ˆvā·gə·rē\ n. An eccentric, unpredictable action.

var·i·e·gat·ed\ˆvă·rē·ə 'gā·təd\ adj. Varied in colors.

ve·ra·cious\və ˆrā·shəs\ adj. Truthful; habitually speaking the truth.

ver·dant\ˆvər·dənt\ adj. Green in color.

ver·i·est\ˆvĕ·rē·əst\ adj. Absolute, actual.

ver·nal\ˆvər·nəl\ adj. Appearing in the spring.

ves·ti·gi·al\vĕs ˆtĭ·jē·əl\ adj. Of the nature of a visible trace of something gone.

vice·roy\ˆvais·rɔi\ n. A representative; a governor who represents a king or sovereign.

vict·ual\ˆvĭt·əl\ v. To supply with food.

vil·i·fy\ˆvĭ·lə·fai\ v. To abuse with language; to slander.

vir·ile\ˆvĭ·rəl\ adj. Characteristic of masculinity; manly.

vis·à·vis\'vē·zə ˆvē\ n. One who is face-to-face with another.

vit·ri·ol\ˆvĭ·trē·əl\ n. Sulfuric acid.

vol·u·ble\ˆvŏ·lyə·bəl\ adj. Having a fluency in speaking; glib, smooth talking.

vo·lup·tuous\və ˆlup·chō·əs\ adj. Relating to satisfaction of the physical desires and sensual pleasures.

vor·tex\ˆvɔr·tĕks\ n. State of affairs that is similar to a whirlwind or whirlpool.

vo·tive\ˆvō·tĭv\ adj. Offered in devotion or in fulfillment of a vow.

waft\ˆwaft\ v. To convey as if on air or water; to float.

waif\ˆwāf\ n. A homeless child.

wan\ˆwŏn\ adj. Pale, as from sickness.

wily\ˆwai·lē\ adj. Crafty or sly.

wont\ˆwŏnt\ adj. Doing habitually; accustomed to.

worthy\ˆwər·thē\ n. An important person.

wot\ˆwɔt\ v. To know.

wry\ˆrai\ adj. 1. Cleverly or grimly humorous. 2. Twisted.

yeo·man·ry\ˆyō·mən·rē\ n. A body of small, middle class landowners.

Index of Terms

Literary

alliteration, 494
assonance, 494
blank verse, 735
characterization, 14, 20, 31, 55, 69, 85, 100, 109, 122, 140
climax, 156, 171, 191, 200, 210, 220, 222, 235, 243, 254, 270, 680
comedy, 278, 283, 300, 310, 317, 327, 334, 342, 343, 344, 364, 376, 388, 396
complication, 680
conflict, 44, 122, 156, 171, 191, 200, 210, 220, 221, 222, 235, 243, 254, 270, 387, 388, 391, 680
denouement, 680
essay, 31, 61, 253, 543
exaggeration, 473, 474
exposition, 680
fable, 99
figurative language, 670
folk tale, 282
foreshadowing, 254
free verse, 494
humor, 272, 294
intention, 405, 414, 420, 425, 436, 472, 473, 504, 512
irony, 472
light verse, 310
local color, 413, 414
metaphor, 20, 670
moment of illumination, 156, 171, 191, 200, 210, 223, 235, 254, 270
multiple meanings, 243
nonsense comedy, 342
one-act play, 269
parallel construction, 494
plot, 156
poetry
    lyric, 215, 735
    narrative, 20
    romantic, 24
protagonist, 235
quatrain, 451
rhyme scheme, 451, 494
satire, 364, 396
setting, 13, 20, 24, 31, 44, 55, 85, 100, 103, 109, 122, 140, 253
short story, 44, 253
significant detail, selection of, 521, 537, 543, 558, 562, 579, 586, 593, 594, 632
simile, 670
structure
    in the drama, 753, 765, 772
    in the essay, 639, 710
    in the poem, 451, 651, 696, 710

in the short story, 663, 680, 687, 708, 710
style, 605
suspense, 663
symbolism, 171, 253, 334, 648, 652, 656, 680, 687, 692, 696, 708
sympathy and detachment, 278, 283, 294, 300, 317, 327, 334, 343, 344, 364, 376, 388, 396
theme, 253, 405, 414, 425, 437, 450, 474, 494, 504, 512
titles, significance of, 12
tone, 44, 79, 85, 521, 537, 543, 550, 558, 562, 571, 579, 586, 593, 594, 618
understatement, 473, 474
unity of effect, 44

Word Study

antonyms, 437, 512, 551, 572, 696
archaic words, 156
colloquialisms, 221
context clues, 31, 55, 69, 109, 201, 221, 254, 300, 327, 437, 512, 551, 572, 681, 708
denotation, 31
dialect words, 201, 221, 283, 437, 551, 586
economy of statement, 681
etymology, 84
homographs, 652
homonyms, 652
homophones, 652
idioms, 572
levels of usage, 31, 84, 414, 420, 512, 513, 652, 709
slang, 709
synonyms, 31, 55, 69, 109, 201, 283, 343, 414, 437, 551, 681, 696, 709

Index of Literary Types

Dramas

In the Zone, 259, Eugene O'Neill
Our Town, 739, Thornton Wilder
Thompson's Vacation, 335, Ring Lardner
Twelve Angry Men, 452, Reginald Rose

Fables

The Glass in the Field, 394, James Thurber
The Owl Who Was God, 395, James Thurber
The Shrike and the Chipmunks, 393, James Thurber
The Very Proper Gander, 392, James Thurber

Formal Essays

Happiness, 635, William Lyon Phelps
Man Will Prevail, 707, William Faulkner
The Unimagined America, 80, Archibald MacLeish
Walden, 600, Henry David Thoreau
The West Is Our Great Adventure of the Spirit, 56, A. B. Guthrie, Jr.

Biographical and Historical Essays

Benjamin Franklin: Multiple Genius, 538, Donald Culross Peattie
The Campers at Kitty Hawk, 76, John Dos Passos
Crisis in Chicago, 573, Elinor Richey
Don't Fence Me In: The Cowboy, 563, Marshall W. Fishwick
The Dying City, 587, Thomas A. Dooley, M.D.
Henry Ford, 62, Allan Nevins
"I looked down into my open grave . . . ," 202, John F. Kennedy
Lee in Battle, 552, Gamaliel Bradford, Jr.
Lincoln Becomes a Lawyer, 544, Paul Horgan
The Smart Ones Got Through, 25, George R. Stewart
Susan B. Anthony, 421, Louis Untermeyer
Trials at Salem, 399, Stephen Vincent Benét

Informal Essays

The Camp of the Wild Horse, 100, Washington Irving
The Creole Village, 104, Washington Irving
I Sell a Dog, 356, Mark Twain

Poetry

Short Stories

Index of Fine Art

General Index

Acknowledgments

Designer: William Nicoll, Edit, Inc., Chicago, Illinois.

Photo Consultant: Frances L. Orkin, New York, New York.

Fine Art: Richard Brunell, Washington University, St. Louis, Missouri.

Consultants who by suggestions and direction, time and material, have contributed generously to the development of the THEMES AND WRITERS series are acknowledged as follows: Dwight Burton, of the Curriculum Center in English, Florida State University; Stephen Dunning, Department of English and School of Education, University of Michigan; Julie Alm, Assistant Professor of Education, University of Hawaii, Honolulu, Hawaii; Ethel Barton, formerly Elizabeth High School, Elizabeth, New Jersey; John Baughman, Central High School, Fort Wayne, Indiana; Edith Bell, formerly Head of English Department, Polytechnic High School, San Francisco, California; Dr. Elizabeth Berry, Metropolitan Junior College, Kansas City, Missouri; Jeanette Bigge, Associate Professor of Education, Kansas State Teachers College Laboratory School, Emporia, Kansas; Janet M. Cotter, English Department, Chabot College, Hayward California; Margaret Ann Cummings, English Department, Mt. Vernon Township High School, Mt. Vernon, Illinois; Ted De

Vries, English Department, Burris Laboratory School, Ball State University, Muncie, Indiana; Maxine Delmare, Supervisor of English, Kirkwood High School, Kirkwood, Missouri; Frances Erickson, Ballard High School, Seattle, Washington; Dr. Phillip Ford, Board of Education, Chicago, Illinois; Dr. Mary Elizabeth Fowler, Central Connecticut State College, New Britain, Connecticut; Philip Fraser, Wayzata High School, Wayzata, Minnesota; Emilie L. Harris formerly Assistant Principal, West High School, Cleveland, Ohio; Mary Hopkins, Supervisor of Language Arts, Topeka High School, Topeka, Kansas; Sister M. Judine, I.H.M., Marian High School, Birmingham, Michigan; Gladys Mansir, formerly Head of English Department, Staples High School, Westport Connecticut; Marietta McCown, Anderson College, Anderson, South Carolina; Mae Belle Pelton Mc Kune, Thomas Jefferson High School, Port Arthur, Texas; Kenneth L. Meinke, Superintendent of Schools, Board of Education, Hartford, Connecticut; Agnes Murphy, Eastchester High School, Eastchester, New York; Joy L. Nevin, formerly Head of English Department, Quincy High School, Quincy, Massachusetts; Marjorie J. Nickel, Reading Center Director, Pulaski High School, Milwaukee, Wisconsin; Mary Ohm, Woodrow Wilson Junior High School, Terre Haute, Indiana; Gertrude H. Overton, Central High School, Pontiac, Michigan; James Pendleton, Curriculum Assistant, English, Berkeley Public Schools, Berkeley, California; Julie Phillips, Sunrise Park Junior High School, White Bear, Minnesota; Huberta Randolph, Director of Curriculum, Salt Lake City Public Schools, Salt Lake City, Utah; Ruth Reeves, Supervisor of English, Junior and Senior High Schools, Houston Independent School District, Houston, Texas; Anne Richmond, Bay Point Junior High School, English Department, St. Petersburgh, Florida; Dr. Edwin H. Sauer, Professor of English and Chairman of the English Department, Illinois Teachers College; Chicago-South, Chicago, Illinois; Lorietta Scheerer, Redondo Union High School, Redondo Beach, California; Bessie Stuart, Teacher, Dearborn, Michigan; Robert Taylor, Assistant Professor of Humanities and Social Studies, Montana College of Mineral Science and Technology, Butte, Montana; Dr. Darwin Turner, Chairman, Department of English, Agricultural and Technical College of North Carolina, Greensboro, North Carolina; Dr. Hazel Brown Williams, Professor of English Education, University of Missouri at Kansas City, Kansas City, Missouri.

Illustration Sources